THE CAMBRIDGE EDITION OF THE
COMPLETE FICTION OF
HENRY JAMES

THE CAMBRIDGE EDITION OF THE
COMPLETE FICTION OF
HENRY JAMES

GENERAL EDITORS
Michael Anesko, *Pennsylvania State University*
Tamara L. Follini, *University of Cambridge*
Philip Horne, *University College London*
Adrian Poole, *University of Cambridge*

ADVISORY BOARD
Martha Banta†, *University of California, Los Angeles*
Ian F. A. Bell, *Keele University*
Gert Buelens, *Universiteit Gent*
Susan M. Griffin, *University of Louisville*
Julie Rivkin, *Connecticut College*
John Carlos Rowe, *University of Southern California*
Ruth Bernard Yeazell, *Yale University*
Greg Zacharias, *Creighton University*

THE CAMBRIDGE EDITION OF THE
COMPLETE FICTION OF

HENRY JAMES

1 *Roderick Hudson*
2 *The American*
3 *Watch and Ward*
4 *The Europeans*
5 *Confidence*
6 *Washington Square*
7 *The Portrait of a Lady*
8 *The Bostonians*
9 *The Princess Casamassima*
10 *The Reverberator*
11 *The Tragic Muse*
12 *The Other House*
13 *The Spoils of Poynton*
14 *What Maisie Knew*
15 *The Awkward Age*
16 *The Sacred Fount*
17 *The Wings of the Dove*
18 *The Ambassadors*
19 *The Golden Bowl*
20 *The Outcry*
21 *The Sense of the Past*
22 *The Ivory Tower*
23 *A Landscape Painter and Other Tales, 1864–1869*
24 *A Passionate Pilgrim and Other Tales, 1869–1874*
25 *Daisy Miller and Other Tales, 1874–1879*
26 *The Siege of London and Other Tales, 1879–1884*
27 *The Aspern Papers and Other Tales, 1884–1888*
28 *The Lesson of the Master and Other Tales, 1888–1891*
29 *The Middle Years and Other Tales, 1892–1894*
30 *The Turn of the Screw and Other Tales, 1895–1898*
31 *The Beast in the Jungle and Other Tales, 1899–1903*
32 *The Jolly Corner and Other Tales, 1903–1910*
33 *The Prefaces*
34 *The Notebooks*

HENRY JAMES
The Prefaces

EDITED BY
OLIVER HERFORD

Shaftesbury Road, Cambridge CB2 8EA, United Kingdom

One Liberty Plaza, 20th Floor, New York, NY 10006, USA

477 Williamstown Road, Port Melbourne, VIC 3207, Australia

314–321, 3rd Floor, Plot 3, Splendor Forum, Jasola District Centre, New Delhi – 110025, India

103 Penang Road, #05–06/07, Visioncrest Commercial, Singapore 238467

Cambridge University Press is part of Cambridge University Press & Assessment, a department of the University of Cambridge.

We share the University's mission to contribute to society through the pursuit of education, learning and research at the highest international levels of excellence.

www.cambridge.org
Information on this title: www.cambridge.org/9781107002685

DOI: 10.1017/9780511756573

© Cambridge University Press & Assessment 2024

This publication is in copyright. Subject to statutory exception and to the provisions of relevant collective licensing agreements, no reproduction of any part may take place without the written permission of Cambridge University Press & Assessment.

First published 2024

A catalogue record for this publication is available from the British Library

Library of Congress Cataloging-in-Publication Data
NAMES: James, Henry, 1843–1916, author. | Herford, Oliver (Oliver Simon), editor.
TITLE: The prefaces / Henry James ; edited by Oliver Herford.
DESCRIPTION: Cambridge ; New York, NY : Cambridge University Press, 2024. | SERIES: The Cambridge edition of the complete fiction of Henry James 34 | Includes bibliographical references and index.
IDENTIFIERS: LCCN 2023054011 | ISBN 9781107002685 (hardback) | ISBN 9780511756573 (ebook)
SUBJECTS: LCSH: American literature – 20th century. | Prefaces. | James, Henry, 1843–1916 – Criticism and interpretation. | James, Henry, 1843–1916 – Criticism, Textual.
CLASSIFICATION: LCC PS2112 H47 2024 | DDC 810.8/005–dc23/eng/20231219
LC record available at https://lccn.loc.gov/2023054011

ISBN 978-1-107-00268-5 Hardback

Cambridge University Press & Assessment has no responsibility for the persistence or accuracy of URLs for external or third-party internet websites referred to in this publication and does not guarantee that any content on such websites is, or will remain, accurate or appropriate.

CONTENTS

List of Illustrations	*page* viii
Acknowledgements	ix
List of Abbreviations	xi
General Editors' Preface	xv
General Chronology of James's Life and Writings	xxii
Introduction	xxix
Textual Introduction	cxlix
Chronology of Composition and Production	clvi
Bibliography	clxix

The Prefaces 1

Glossary of Foreign Words and Phrases	278
Notes	280
Textual Variants	591
Emendations	597
Index	598

ILLUSTRATIONS

1. An example of Henry James's 1906–7 autograph revisions to *The American*, using pages of the two-volume *Collective Edition* text (London: Macmillan, 1883) pasted onto large sheets of paper. Houghton Library, Harvard University, GEN MS Am 1237. This sheet shows James's revisions to vol. I, p. 188 of the novel; one of these revisions is discussed in note 78 to the text in the present volume. *page* lxi
2. Alvin Langdon Coburn, 'The Curiosity Shop', photogravure frontispiece to the first volume of *The Golden Bowl* (*NYE* XXIII). Cambridge University Library, Syn.5.90.235. ciii
3. Title page of *Roderick Hudson* (*NYE* I, 'limited issue'). Cambridge University Library, Syn.5.90.213. cl
4. Typescript of the Preface to *The Portrait of a Lady* (1906) with James's autograph corrections, p. 33. Houghton Library, Harvard University, GEN MS Am 1237.17. clii
5. Detail of the *Portrait* Preface typescript, p. 21, showing James's autograph insertion to fill a gap in the typescript. Houghton Library, Harvard University. cliv

Figures 1, 4 and 5 reproduced by permission of the Houghton Library, Harvard University.

Figures 2 and 3 reproduced by permission of Cambridge University Library.

ACKNOWLEDGEMENTS

My first debt – registered in detail in the apparatus to this volume – is to previous editors and annotators of the Prefaces, and to the many other scholars whose work I have drawn on in preparing my edition. I am especially grateful to those volume editors in *The Complete Fiction of Henry James* who kindly shared their research and answered my questions about the Prefaces to novels or stories in their volumes: Michael Anesko, Tamara Follini, Simone Francescato, Philip Horne, Kathleen Lawrence, T. J. Lustig, Neil Reeve, Richard Salmon, Rebekah Scott, Pierre A. Walker, Merle Williams and Rosella Mamoli Zorzi. Philip Horne supplied me with transcriptions of passages from James's notebooks which will appear in his forthcoming edition of *The Notebooks* (*CFHJ* 34). Greg Zacharias, Co-General Editor of *The Complete Letters of Henry James* and Director of the Center for Henry James Studies at Creighton University, generously provided copies of unpublished letters. I have benefited greatly from the online collections of the Internet Archive and the Hathi Trust Digital Library, as well as from the assistance – in person and remotely – of the staff of various research libraries: the Beinecke Rare Book and Manuscript Library at Yale University, the Bodleian Library at the University of Oxford, the British Library, Cambridge University Library, the Clifton Waller Barrett Library of American Literature at the University of Virginia, the Houghton Library at Harvard University, the Library of Congress and Princeton University's Special Collections Department. Periods of leave granted me by Lincoln College, Oxford and by the University of Birmingham were essential for completing the research and writing for this edition, as were the patience and enthusiasm of my colleagues at both institutions. For specific assistance and good ideas on various occasions, I would like to thank Anthony Cummins, James Lello, Adelais Mills, Melanie Ross, David J. Supino and Ross Wilson; for their vital help and encouragement throughout, I cannot thank Miranda El-Rayess and Alicia Rix enough. My warm thanks as well to Linda Bree, Liz Davey and Bethany Thomas at Cambridge University Press, and to Leigh Mueller, who copy-edited the volume. I also record my deep gratitude to the General

ACKNOWLEDGEMENTS

Editors of *CFHJ* – Michael Anesko, Tamara Follini, Adrian Poole, and in particular Philip Horne, the General Editor with special responsibility for *The Prefaces* – for their steady support, expert advice and scrupulous attention to draft material.

I could not have done any of this without the love and forbearance of my family. I dedicate my part in this volume to the memory of my mother Lesley Herford, née Meade (1948–2016).

ABBREVIATIONS

Works by Henry James

AN	*The Art of the Novel: Critical Prefaces*, introduction by R. P. Blackmur (New York: Charles Scribner's Sons, 1934)
AS	*The American Scene* (London: Chapman and Hall, 1907)
Aut	*Autobiographies: A Small Boy and Others; Notes of a Son and Brother; The Middle Years; Other Writings*, ed. Philip Horne (New York: Library of America, 2016)
CE	*Collective Edition of 1883*, 14 vols. (London: Macmillan and Co., 1883)
CFHJ	The Cambridge Edition of the *Complete Fiction of Henry James*, general eds. Michael Anesko, Tamara L. Follini, Philip Horne and Adrian Poole, 34 vols. (Cambridge: Cambridge University Press, 2015–)
CLHJ	*The Complete Letters of Henry James*, ed. Pierre A. Walker and Greg W. Zacharias; Michael Anesko and Greg W. Zacharias (Lincoln, NE: University of Nebraska Press, 2006–). (NB: Quotations from this source will appear as clear text; i.e., evidence of HJ's cancellations and insertions will not appear unless warranted by their context.)
CN	*The Complete Notebooks of Henry James*, ed. Leon Edel and Lyall H. Powers (New York and Oxford: Oxford University Press, 1987)
CP	*The Complete Plays of Henry James*, ed. Leon Edel (London: Rupert Hart-Davis, 1949)
CTW1	*Collected Travel Writings: Great Britain and America: English Hours, The American Scene, Other Travels*, ed. Richard Howard (New York: Library of America, 1993)

LIST OF ABBREVIATIONS

CTW2	*Collected Travel Writings: The Continent: A Little Tour in France, Italian Hours, Other Travels*, ed. Richard Howard (New York: Library of America, 1993)
CWAD1	*The Complete Writings of Henry James on Art and Drama*, vol. 1: *Art*, ed. Peter Collister (Cambridge: Cambridge University Press, 2016)
CWAD2	*The Complete Writings of Henry James on Art and Drama*, vol. 2: *Drama*, ed. Peter Collister (Cambridge: Cambridge University Press, 2016)
CWJ	*The Correspondence of William James*, vols. I–III: *William and Henry*, ed. Ignas K. Skrupskelis and Elizabeth M. Berkeley (Charlottesville, VA: University Press of Virginia, 1992–4)
ELE	*Essays in London and Elsewhere* (London: James R. Osgood, McIlvaine & Co., 1893)
'EZ'	'Émile Zola', *Atlantic Monthly* 92 (August 1903), 193–210
'GDA'	'Gabriele D'Annunzio', *Quarterly Review* 199 (April 1904), 383–419
'GF'	'Gustave Flaubert', introduction to Flaubert, *Madame Bovary*, ed. Edmund Gosse (London: William Heinemann, 1902), pp. v–xliii
'HdB'	'Honoré de Balzac', introduction to Balzac, *The Two Young Brides* [*Mémoires de deux jeunes mariées*], ed. Edmund Gosse (London: William Heinemann, 1902), pp. v–xliii
HJC	*Henry James on Culture: Collected Essays on Politics and the American Social Scene*, ed. Pierre A. Walker (Lincoln, NE: University of Nebraska Press, 1999)
HJEW	*Henry James and Edith Wharton, Letters: 1900–1915*, ed. Lyall H. Powers (New York: Charles Scribner's Sons, 1990)
HJL	*Henry James Letters*, ed. Leon Edel, 4 vols. (Cambridge, MA: Belknap Press of Harvard University Press; London: Macmillan and Co., 1974–84)
LC1	*Literary Criticism: Essays on Literature, American Writers, English Writers*, ed. Leon Edel and Mark Wilson (New York: Library of America, 1984)

LIST OF ABBREVIATIONS

LC2	*Literary Criticism: French Writers, Other European Writers, The Prefaces to the New York Edition*, ed. Leon Edel and Mark Wilson (New York: Library of America, 1984)
LFL	*Letters, Fictions, Lives: Henry James and William Dean Howells*, ed. Michael Anesko (New York and Oxford: Oxford University Press, 1997)
LHJ	*The Letters of Henry James*, ed. Percy Lubbock, 2 vols. (London: Macmillan and Co., 1920)
LL	*Henry James: A Life in Letters*, ed. Philip Horne (Harmondsworth, Middx.: Allen Lane, The Penguin Press, 1999)
'LRLS'	'The Letters of Robert Louis Stevenson', *North American Review* 170 (January 1900), 61–77
LTF	*A Little Tour in France*, 2nd edn, with ninety-four illustrations by Joseph Pennell (London: William Heinemann, 1900)
NYE	*The New York Edition of the Novels and Tales of Henry James*, 24 vols. (New York: Charles Scribner's Sons, 1907–9)
PPL	*Portraits of Places* (London: Macmillan and Co., 1883)
SLHJEG	*Selected Letters of Henry James to Edmund Gosse 1882–1915: A Literary Friendship*, ed. Rayburn S. Moore (Baton Rouge, LA: Louisiana State University Press, 1988)
SP	*The Sense of the Past* (London: W. Collins Sons & Co., 1917)
TS	*Transatlantic Sketches* (Boston, MA: James R. Osgood and Company, 1875)
WF	W. D. Howells, Mary E. Wilkins Freeman, Mary Heaton Vorse, Mary Stewart Cutting, Elizabeth Jordan, John Kendrick Bangs, Henry James, Elizabeth Stuart Phelps, Edith Wyatt, Mary R. Shipman Andrews, Alice Brown and Henry Van Dyke, *The Whole Family: A Novel by Twelve Authors* (New York: Harper & Brothers, 1908)
WWS	*William Wetmore Story and His Friends: From Letters, Diaries, and Recollections*, 2 vols. (Edinburgh: William Blackwood and Sons, 1903)

LIST OF ABBREVIATIONS

Archival Resources

ODTB — Theodora Bosanquet Papers, Houghton Library, Harvard University. Original Diaries of Theodora Bosanquet. MS Eng 1213–1213.8, MS Eng 1213.1

Princeton — Archives of Charles Scribner's Sons, C0101, Manuscripts Division, Department of Special Collections, Princeton University Library. Series 3: Author Files, 1768–1989, Subseries 3A: Author Files I, 1768–1989, James, Henry, Box 104, Folders 2 (1900–1904, undated), 3 (1905–1907, undated) and 4 (1908–1910, undated)

Virginia — Papers of Henry James, 1855–1969, n.d., Accession #6251, etc., Special Collections, University of Virginia Library. Series II: Henry James Correspondence, Subseries A: Dated Correspondence, Boxes 5 and 6

Yale — Henry James Collection, Yale Collection of American Literature, Beinecke Rare Book and Manuscript Library, Yale University. Pinker, James B., two bound volumes of autograph letters, notes and typed letters, signed, from James (1898–1915). YCAL MSS 830, Box 2, Vols. 1 (7 May 1898–9 November 1905) and 2 (15 November 1905–24 April 1910)

GENERAL EDITORS' PREFACE

The Cambridge Edition of the *Complete Fiction of Henry James* (hereafter *CFHJ*) has been undertaken in the belief that there is a need for a full scholarly, informative, historical edition of his work, presenting the texts in carefully checked, accurate form, with detailed annotation and extensive introductions. James's texts exist in a number of forms, including manuscripts (though most are lost), serial texts and volumes of various sorts, often incorporating significant amounts of revision, most conspicuously the so-called *New York Edition* (hereafter *NYE*) published by Charles Scribner's Sons in New York and Macmillan & Co. in London (1907–9). Besides these there are also pirated editions, unfinished works published posthumously and other questionable forms. The *CFHJ* takes account of these complexities, within the framework of a textual policy which aims to be clear, orderly and consistent.

This edition aims to represent James's fictional career as it evolves, with a fresh and expanded sense of its changing contexts and an informed sense of his developing style, technique and concerns. Consequently it does not attempt to base its choices on the principle of the 'last lifetime edition', which in the case of Henry James is monumentally embodied in the twenty-four volumes of the *NYE*, the author's selection of nine longer novels (six of them in two volumes) and fifty-eight shorter novels and tales, and including eighteen specially composed Prefaces. The *CFHJ*, as a general rule, adopts rather the text of the first published book edition of a work, unless the intrinsic particularities and the publishing history of that work require an alternative choice, on the ground that emphasis on the first context in which it was written and read will permit an unprecedented fullness of attention to the transformations in James's writing over five decades, as well as the rich literary and social contexts of their original publication.

There are inevitably cases where determining 'the first published book edition' requires some care. If, for instance, James expresses a preference for the text of one particular early book edition over another, or if the first edition to be published is demonstrably inferior to a later impression or edition, or if authorial supervision of a particular early edition or impression can be established, then a case can be made for choosing a text other than the first published book edition. Volume Editors have exercised their judgment accordingly. They have made a full collation of authoritative versions including serial as well as volume publication in Britain and America, and specify which version serves as their copy text.

The *CFHJ*'s Introductions aim to be full and authoritative, detailing the histories of composition, publication (in magazine and book form), reception and authorial revision, and making economical reference to subsequent adaptation and transformation into other forms, including drama, film and opera. Editors have refrained from offering emphatic interpretations or mounting critical arguments of their own, though it is hoped the material they present will inform and stimulate new readings. Particular attention has been given to the social, political and cultural contexts of James's period, and especially those of the countries in which a specific work is set; details of James's personal exposure to relevant people and events, of the magazines and publishing houses where he published (editors, policies, politics, etc.), have provided valuable material. Introductions conclude with a Bibliography in support of the information supplied and the aspects of the text's production emphasized in the Introduction, including a list of contemporary reviews.

Each volume contains, in addition to a Chronology of James's life and literary career, a volume-specific Chronology, incorporating dates of composition, negotiation with publishers and editors, dispatch of instalments, stages of printing and initial reception history, as well as relevant comments by or to James appearing in letters or other forms.

Fullness and helpfulness of annotation is one of the main aims of the *CFHJ*. As James's world recedes into the past, more and more of its features need explanation to readers: both the physical, geographical and historical world of places and people, and the cultural world of beliefs, values, conventions, social practices and points of reference – to operas, plays, books, paintings – and indeed certain linguistic explanations have become increasingly necessary (especially regarding the presence of slang or linguistic innovation, both English and American). For such explanations, James's correspondence, criticism and other writings have been drawn on as a prime source of helpful comment, conveying his own experience and attitudes in a way that richly illuminates his fictional texts. Newspapers and magazines of the period, travel guides, the work of other writers, also contribute, filling out the picture of the implied worlds beyond the text. Furthermore, the *CFHJ* sets out to provide the fullest possible details of James's allusions to poetry, the Bible and the plays of Shakespeare, as well as other literary and culturally significant works – offering suggestive but concise plot summaries when appropriate or quotation of the passages drawn on, so that the act of allusion is brought to life and the reader can trace something of James's allusive processes. Editors have abstained, on the other hand, from purely interpretative notes, speculation and personal comments: the notes always concern a point of information, even if that point has a critical bearing.

Appendices include sources and relevant contextual documents, including correspondence, entries from the Prefaces to the *NYE* and from the Notebooks, where appropriate. For the novels revised and published in the *NYE*, the whole Preface is printed in an Appendix; for tales revised and published in the *NYE*, the relevant extract from the Preface is reproduced. The Prefaces and Notebooks have also been collected in newly edited volumes of their own.

*

Most of James's fiction exists in a number of different textual states, most notably in the difference between initial publication (in periodical and volume form) and the revised versions of the novels and tales prepared near the end of his career for the *NYE*. (In the case of three late tales – 'Fordham Castle', 'Julia Bride' and 'The Jolly Corner' – first book publication was in the *NYE*.) Works excluded by James from the *NYE* were incorporated in the edition posthumously published in thirty-five volumes by Macmillan in 1921–3, but these were of course published without authorial revision. The textual differences affecting those works that *are* included in the *NYE* are predictably most extensive in the case of early works such as *Roderick Hudson* (1875), *The American* (1877), 'Daisy Miller' (1879) and *The Portrait of a Lady* (1881).

Readers may see for themselves the full extent of James's revisions, along with all other variants, both preceding and succeeding the texts printed here, in the lists of Textual Variants. These are normally presented in the following form. Each volume includes a comprehensive list of all substantive variants

GENERAL EDITORS' PREFACE

in the line of textual transmission leading up to copy text ('Textual Variants I'), preceded by a brief commentary, in which editors address this stage of the textual history, drawing attention to the main features of the changes and dealing with questions such as house style. Variations in punctuation within a sentence (usually by the insertion or removal of commas, or changes in the use of colons and semi-colons) have not normally been considered substantive. Over end-of-sentence punctuation, however, particularly in the matter of changing full stops to exclamations or vice versa, Volume Editors have exercised their judgment. A second section ('Textual Variants II') offers a comprehensive list of all substantive variants subsequent to copy text, and a brief commentary which summarizes the main issues raised by the changes made. The length of lists of variants and commentary inevitably varies greatly from case to case. In certain cases, for reasons explained in the volume concerned, there is a single list of 'Textual Variants'.

*

The *Complete Fiction of Henry James* consists of 22 novels (vols. 1–22), 113 tales (vols. 23–32), and 2 supplementary volumes (vols. 33 and 34) devoted respectively to the Prefaces that James wrote for the *NYE* and to his Notebooks. They appear in this edition in the order in which they were first published. The distinction between 'novels' and 'tales' is sometimes a crude one: between long fictions such as *The Portrait of a Lady* and *The Golden Bowl* and short ones such as 'Benvolio' and 'The Beldonald Holbein', there lie many shorter novels and longer tales that it is hard to categorize with confidence, well-known works such as *Washington Square* and *The Sacred Fount*, 'The Aspern Papers' and 'The Turn of the Screw'. We have deemed to be 'novels' those fictions which when they first took volume form were published as independent entities (with the single exception of *In the Cage* which despite its relative brevity first appeared as a slim volume), and those to be 'tales' all which were not. The former include some of James's lesser-known works, such as *Watch and Ward, Confidence, The Other House, The Outcry* and the two unfinished at the time of his death, *The Sense of the Past* and *The Ivory Tower*.

The division of James's tales into ten volumes has been ordered chronologically on the basis of first publication, according to the following principles:

1) The determining date of a story's publication is that of the first appearance of any part of it (as some straddle three issues of a magazine). Thus, for example, 'A London Life' (June–September 1888, *Scribner's Magazine*) precedes 'The Lesson of the Master' (July–August 1888, *Universal Review*).
2) Where two tales have the same start date, the priority is determined by which completes its publication earlier. Thus, for example, 'The Modern Warning' (originally entitled 'Two Countries', June 1888, *Harper's New Monthly Magazine*) precedes 'A London Life' (June–September 1888, *Scribner's Magazine*).
3) Where two tales have the same start date and the same date of completion (often only taking one issue), the priority is determined by alphabetical order (of tale title). Thus, for example, 'De Grey: A Romance' (July 1868, *Atlantic Monthly*) precedes 'Osborne's Revenge' (July 1868, *Galaxy*).
4) Because it cannot usually be determined exactly *when* a magazine dated only 'June' actually appeared, 'June' is treated as preceding any particular date in June, including '1 June'. Thus 'The Private Life' (April 1892, *Atlantic Monthly*) precedes 'The Real Thing' (16 April 1892, *Black and White*); and principle 4 overrides principle 2, so that 'The Author of "Beltraffio"' (June–July 1884, *English Illustrated Magazine*) precedes 'Pandora' (1 and 8 June 1884, *New York Sun*).
5) Where tales have not been published in periodicals before being collected in book form, the precise date of book publication counts as first publication and determines their place in the order.
6) Where tales have not been published in periodicals before being collected in book form, and several tales appear in the same book, the order of tales in the book determines our ordering (even when their order of composition is known to have been different), as it is closer to the order in which original readers would preponderantly have read them.
7) In the single case where only a fragment of a tale survives and therefore was not published within James's lifetime, 'Hugh Merrow', the tale has been placed provisionally in accordance with the date of the only extant Notebooks entry, 11 September 1900.

*

Emendations have been made sparingly and only to clearly erroneous readings. Where there is only one version of a work and it requires emendation, the original (erroneous) reading has been recorded in the List of Emendations. Where a later or earlier text has a reading that shows the copy text to be in error, this reading has been incorporated and the copy text's reading recorded in the apparatus. The fact that a later or earlier text has a reading that seems preferable to that of the copy text has not in itself provided sufficient grounds for emendation, although like all other variants, it has been recorded in the list of Textual Variants. Unusual and inconsistent spellings have not been altered, and only annotated in exceptional cases. Misprints and slipped letters have been corrected, and the corrections noted. Contractions have not been expanded, superscript has not been converted, and spelling and punctuation have not normally been changed.

James's writings were of course published on both sides of the Atlantic, and there are corresponding differences in spelling between British and American texts, in volume and serial form: 'colour/color', 'recognise/recognize', 'marvellous/marvelous' and so on. These differences have been preserved when they occur in the textual variants, but they have not been systematically recorded, being deemed to be matters of accident rather than substance. The form taken by inverted commas (single or double) also varies between texts, as does their placement (before or after commas, full stops, etc.); being judged matters of accident, these have been regularized. Double quotation marks have been adopted for all the James texts published in this edition. When the text of the *NYE* is cited in the introduction, notes or textual apparatus, its distinctive typography has not been retained, and this also applies to the texts of the tales first published in the *NYE* and of the Prefaces: the contractions rendered there as, for example, 'is n't' and 'did n't' have here been normalized as single words, 'isn't' and 'didn't'. Editorial ellipses have been enclosed in square brackets but authorial ellipses have not.

The punctuation of the copy text adopted has also been preserved. There are considerable differences of punctuation between the different forms in which a particular work of James's appears. It is often hard to distinguish with certainty those which can be accounted for by differences in the house styles of particular publishers, British and American, and those which are matters of authorial choice. Whatever the agency behind such differences, there is a case for recognizing the difference of sense made by the presence or absence of a comma, by the change of an exclamation to a full stop, and so on. Nevertheless, the scale of such differences is too great to make a comprehensive record feasible within the limits of a print edition. Volume editors have therefore exercised their judgment over the most helpful way to inform readers of the nature of such differences.

References to money pose particular difficulties for modern readers, not only because the sums concerned have to be multiplied by an apparently ever-inflating figure to produce approximate modern equivalents, but because the quantity and quality of what could be bought and done with these sums (especially involving property or real estate) has also changed radically – and will very possibly continue to do so during the lifetime of this edition. We do however know that throughout James's own life the pound sterling was equal to $4.85, and certain other figures can be established, such as that in 1875 the US dollar was equivalent to 5.19 French francs. For the calculation of particular sums in James's writings, volume editors have supplied readers with as much reliable information as they can command at the date of publication for this edition, but as time goes on readers will inevitably have to make adjustments.

Translations have been provided for all foreign words and phrases that appear in the text. Those which are common and uncontroversial (such as 'piazza', 'table d'hôte') are collected in a glossary at the end; those judged to be less than obvious in meaning, or dependent for their meaning on the specific context, are explained in an endnote.

The General Editors warmly acknowledge the gracious permission of Bay James, custodian of the James Estate, for the publication of material still in copyright, and the generous cooperation of Greg Zacharias and his associates at the Center for Henry James Studies at Creighton University in Omaha, Nebraska, home of an indispensable parallel project, *The Complete Letters of Henry James*, published by the University of Nebraska Press. We thank David Supino for offering his sage advice whenever it was sought. Finally, we are deeply grateful for the guidance and support provided by our editors at Cambridge University Press, Linda Bree and Bethany Thomas, and Senior Content Managers, Victoria Parrin and Sharon McCann.

GENERAL CHRONOLOGY OF JAMES'S LIFE AND WRITINGS

Compiled by Philip Horne

1843   Henry James (HJ) is born on 15 April 1843 at 21 Washington Place in New York City, second of the five children of Henry James (1811–82), speculative theologian and social thinker, and his wife Mary Walsh Robertson James (1810–82). Siblings: William (1842–1910), psychologist, philosopher, Harvard professor; Garth Wilkinson ('Wilky', 1845–83); Robertson ('Bob', 1846–1910); Alice (1848–92), diarist.

1843–5   Taken to Paris and London by his parents; earliest memory (from age 2) is of the Place Vendôme in Paris.

1845–7   Returns to United States. Childhood in Albany.

1847–55   Family settles in New York City; taught by tutors and in private schools.

1855–8   Family travels in Europe: Geneva, London, Paris, Boulogne-sur-Mer.

1858   Jameses reside in Newport, Rhode Island.

1859–60   James family travels: HJ at scientific school, then the Academy (later the University) in Geneva. Summer 1860: HJ learns German in Bonn.

1860–2   James family returns to Newport in September 1860. HJ's friendships develop with future critic Thomas Sergeant Perry, and with artist John La Farge, fellow student at William Morris Hunt's art academy. From 1860, HJ 'was continually writing stories, mainly of a romantic kind' (Perry). In 1861 HJ injures his back helping extinguish a fire in Newport. Along with William James, is exempted from service in Civil War, in which younger brothers fight, and Wilky is seriously wounded.

1862   Enters Harvard Law School for two terms. Begins to send stories to magazines.

GENERAL CHRONOLOGY OF JAMES'S LIFE AND WRITINGS

1864   February: first short story of HJ's 113, 'A Tragedy of Error', published anonymously in *Continental Monthly*. May: Jameses move to 13 Ashburton Place, Boston. October: first of HJ's many reviews, of Nassau W. Senior's *Essays on Fiction*, published unsigned in *North American Review*.

1865   March: first signed tale, 'The Story of a Year', appears in *Atlantic Monthly*. July: HJ appears also as a critic in first number of the *Nation* (New York).

1866–8   Summer 1866: becomes friends with William Dean Howells, novelist, critic and influential editor. November 1866: James family move to 20 Quincy Street, beside Harvard Yard. November 1867: meets Charles Dickens at home of Charles Eliot and Susan Norton, and 'tremble[s] [. . .] in every limb' (*Notes of a Son and Brother*). HJ continues reviewing and writing stories in Cambridge.

1869–70   On 27 February 1869 lands at Liverpool. Travels in England, meeting John Ruskin, William Morris, Charles Darwin and George Eliot; also Switzerland and Italy. March 1870: death of his much-loved cousin 'Minny' Temple.

1870–2   May 1870: reluctantly returns to Cambridge. August–December 1871: publishes first novel, *Watch and Ward*, in the *Atlantic Monthly*; January–March 1872: publishes art reviews in *Atlantic*.

1872–4   May 1872: HJ accompanies invalid sister Alice and aunt Catharine Walsh, 'Aunt Kate', to Europe. Writes travel pieces for the *Nation*. October 1872–September 1874: periods (without family) in Paris, Rome, Switzerland, Homburg, Italy again. Spring 1874: begins first long novel, *Roderick Hudson*, in Florence. September 1874: returns to the USA.

1875   First three books published: *A Passionate Pilgrim, and Other Tales* (January); *Transatlantic Sketches* (April); *Roderick Hudson* (November). Six months in New York City (111 East 25th Street); then three in Cambridge.

1875–6   11 November 1875: arrives at 29 Rue de Luxembourg as Paris correspondent for *New York Tribune*. Begins *The American*.

GENERAL CHRONOLOGY OF JAMES'S LIFE AND WRITINGS

	Meets Gustave Flaubert, Ivan Turgenev, Edmond de Goncourt, Alphonse Daudet, Guy de Maupassant and Émile Zola.
1876–7	December 1876: moves to London, taking rooms at 3 Bolton Street, off Piccadilly. Visits to Paris, Florence, Rome. May 1877: *The American* published in Boston. Meets William Ewart Gladstone, Alfred Lord Tennyson and Robert Browning.
1878	February: *French Poets and Novelists* published, first collection of essays, first book published in London. May: revised version of *Watch and Ward* published in book form in Boston. June–July: 'Daisy Miller' appears in the *Cornhill Magazine* and is quickly pirated by two American periodicals, establishing reputation in Britain and America. September: *The Europeans* published.
1879	June: first English edition of *Roderick Hudson*, revised. October: *The Madonna of the Future and Other Tales*. December: *Confidence* (novel); *Hawthorne* (critical biography).
1880	April: *The Diary of a Man of Fifty and A Bundle of Letters*. Late winter 1880: travels to Italy; meets Constance Fenimore Woolson in Florence. December 1880: *Washington Square*.
1881–3	October 1881: returns to the USA; travels between Cambridge, New York and Washington DC. November 1881: *The Portrait of a Lady*. January 1882: death of mother. May: returns to England till father dies in December 1882. February 1883: *The Siege of London, The Pension Beaurepas, and The Point of View*. August 1883: returns to London; will not return to the USA for twenty-one years. September 1883: *Daisy Miller: A Comedy*. November 1883: Macmillan publish fourteen-volume collected edition of HJ's fiction; death of Wilky James. December 1883: *Portraits of Places* (travel essays).
1884	Sister Alice joins HJ in London, living nearby. September 1884: *A Little Tour in France* published; also HJ's important artistic statement 'The Art of Fiction'. October 1884: *Tales of Three Cities*. Becomes friends with Robert Louis Stevenson,

	Edmund Gosse. Writes to his friend Grace Norton: 'I shall never marry [...] I am both happy enough and miserable enough, as it is.'
1885–6	Writes two serial novels: *The Bostonians* (*Century*, February 1885–February 1886); *The Princess Casamassima* (*Atlantic*, September 1885–October 1886). February 1885: collection of tales, *The Author of Beltraffio [&c]*. May 1885: *Stories Revived*, in three vols.
1886–7	February 1886: *The Bostonians* published. 6 March 1886: moves into flat, 34 De Vere Gardens, in Kensington, West London. October 1886: *The Princess Casamassima* published. December 1886–July 1887: visits Florence and Venice. Continues friendship with American novelist Constance Fenimore Woolson.
1888	*The Reverberator*, *The Aspern Papers [&c]* and *Partial Portraits* all published.
1888–90	1889: Collection of tales, *A London Life [&c]*, published. June 1890: *The Tragic Muse*. Temporarily abandons the novel form in favour of playwriting.
1890–1	Dramatizes *The American*, which has a short run in 1891. December 1891: young friend and (informal) agent Wolcott Balestier dies of typhoid in Dresden.
1892	February: *The Lesson of the Master [&c]* (story collection) published. March: death of Alice James in London.
1893	Volumes of tales published – March: *The Real Thing and Other Tales*; June: *The Private Life [&c]*; September: *The Wheel of Time [&c]*; also, June: *Picture and Text* (essays on illustration) and *Essays in London and Elsewhere* (critical and memorial essays).
1894	Deaths of Constance Fenimore Woolson (January) and Robert Louis Stevenson (December).
1895	5 January: première of *Guy Domville*, greeted by boos and applause. James abandons playwriting for years. Visits Ireland.

GENERAL CHRONOLOGY OF JAMES'S LIFE AND WRITINGS

	Volumes of tales published – May: *Terminations*; June: *Embarrassments*. Takes up cycling.
1896–7	*The Other House* (1896), *The Spoils of Poynton* (1897), *What Maisie Knew* (1897). February 1897: starts dictating, due to wrist problems. September 1897: takes lease on Lamb House, Rye.
1898	May: by this time has signed up with literary agent James Brand Pinker, who will represent him for the rest of his life. June: moves into Lamb House. August: *In the Cage* published. October: 'The Turn of the Screw' published (in *The Two Magics*); proves his most popular work since 'Daisy Miller'. Kent and Sussex neighbours include Stephen Crane, Joseph Conrad, H. G. Wells and Ford Madox Hueffer (Ford).
1899	April: *The Awkward Age* published. August: buys the freehold of Lamb House.
1900	May: shaves off his beard. August: *The Soft Side* (tales). Friendship with Edith Wharton develops. Begins *The Sense of the Past*, but leaves it unfinished.
1901	February: *The Sacred Fount*.
1902–3	August 1902: *The Wings of the Dove* published. February 1903: *The Better Sort* (tales) published. September 1903: *The Ambassadors* published (completed mid-1901, before *The Wings of the Dove*, but delayed by serialization); also *William Wetmore Story and his Friends* (biography).
1904–5	August: James sails to the USA for first time in twenty-one years. November 1904: *The Golden Bowl* published. Visits New England, New York, Philadelphia, Washington DC, the South, St Louis, Chicago, Los Angeles and San Francisco. Lectures on 'The Lesson of Balzac' and 'The Question of Our Speech'. Meets President Theodore Roosevelt. Elected to American Academy of Arts and Letters.
1905	July: writes early chapters of *The American Scene*; simultaneously begins revising works for *New York Edition of the Novels*

and Tales of Henry James. October: *English Hours* (travel essays) published.

1906–8   Selects, arranges, prefaces and has illustrations made for the *NYE* (published 1907–9, twenty-four volumes). January 1907: *The American Scene* published. August 1907: hires new amanuensis, Theodora Bosanquet. 1908: *The High Bid* (play) produced in Edinburgh.

1909–11   October 1909: *Italian Hours* (travel essays) published. Health problems, aggravated by failure of the *NYE*. Death of Robertson ('Bob') James. Travels to the USA. William James dies 26 August 1910. October 1910: *The Finer Grain* (tales). Returns to England August 1911. October 1911: *The Outcry* (play converted into novel) published.

1911   In autumn, begins work on autobiography.

1912   June: honorary doctorate at Oxford. October: takes flat at 21 Carlyle Mansions, Cheyne Walk, Chelsea; suffers from shingles.

1913   March: *A Small Boy and Others* (first autobiographical book) published. Portrait painted by John Singer Sargent for seventieth birthday.

1914   March: *Notes of a Son and Brother* (second autobiographical book) published. (The fragment of a third, *The Middle Years*, appears posthumously in 1917.) When World War One breaks out, becomes passionately engaged with the British cause, working with Belgian refugees, and later wounded soldiers. October: *Notes on Novelists* published. Begins *The Ivory Tower*; resumes work on *The Sense of the Past*, but is unable to complete either novel.

1915   Honorary President of the American Volunteer Motor Ambulance Corps. July: quarrels with H. G. Wells about purpose of art, declaring 'It is art that *makes life*, makes interest, makes importance'; becomes a British citizen in protest against US neutrality, describing the decision to his nephew Harry (Henry James III) as 'a simple act and offering of allegiance and devotion' after his forty-year domicile. Writes essays about the War (collected in *Within the Rim*, 1919), and Preface to *Letters from America* (1916) by his dead friend Rupert Brooke. On 2 December suffers a stroke. First volumes of Uniform Edition of Tales by Martin Secker, published in fourteen vols. 1915–20.

1916   Awarded the Order of Merit. Dies on 28 February. Funeral in Chelsea Old Church; ashes smuggled back to America by sister-in-law and buried in the family plot in Cambridge, Massachusetts.

INTRODUCTION

1 Origins and Literary Contexts

The texts printed in this volume were first published as prefaces to a collected edition, the *New York Edition of The Novels and Tales of Henry James* (1907–9). While the Prefaces' later career would be significantly shaped by removal from that bibliographical frame and republication in various other formats, the *New York Edition* was the immediate context for their conception and composition. The first step in its long process of production was taken in August 1904, when James's literary agent James B. Pinker wrote to Edward L. Burlingame – a senior editor at the New York publishing house of Charles Scribner's Sons – to revive a proposal for a collected edition which the Scribners had put to him in 1900: 'I thought you would like to know that Mr. James thinks the time for that has come.'[1] James would have had several inducements to take up this offer. In the interval the Scribners had brought out three of his novels, *The Sacred Fount* (1901), *The Wings of the Dove* (1902) and *The Golden Bowl* (1904), and his story collection *The Better Sort* (1903); and their subscription list contained several notable collected editions of modern literary authors, including editions of George Meredith, Robert Louis Stevenson and Rudyard Kipling which contributed to James's understanding of the bibliographic and prefatory possibilities of the form. At this time, too, James was already engaged in various forms of personal and textual retrospect. After completing *The Golden Bowl*, he spent ten months touring the United States (August 1904–July 1905), and on this first return to his native country in twenty-one years he was struck by memories of his American childhood and youth almost as much as by new impressions of the modern nation. In 1903 he had written a Life-and-Letters biography of the expatriate American sculptor William Wetmore Story, which took him back to his own travels in Italy in the 1870s, and to the earlier transatlantic journeys of his parents' generation. And in 1905 and

---

[1] Pinker to Burlingame, 3 August 1904; Princeton.

1909 he would publish collections of his English and Italian travel essays which called for the same textual and imaginative operations as the *New York Edition* – renewing his old impressions of familiar places, in memory and in fact (he made his final trip to Italy in 1907), and revising the old texts in which they had been first recorded. The Prefaces grew out of all this work of recollection and renovation. In their critical and theoretical aspects also, they returned to questions James had pursued in essays and lectures over the whole course of his career.

In June 1905, Pinker crossed the Atlantic at James's request to discuss the proposed edition with the Scribners in New York. James was still in the United States at this point but was engaged to give the Commencement Day address at Bryn Mawr College in Pennsylvania. Despite problems caused by the Scribners' doubts about the profitability of a collected edition, negotiations for the Edition were opened and planning begun by the time James sailed for home the following month.[2] Authorial prefaces were integral to his thinking about a collected edition from the outset. As Pinker had noted to Burlingame the previous year, 'Mr. James' idea is to write for each volume a preface of a rather intimate, personal character, and there is no doubt that such a preface would add greatly to the interest of the books.'[3] On his return from America, James now dictated a memo to the Scribners outlining his plans for 'a handsome "definitive edition" of the greater number of my novels and tales'.[4] It would present a comprehensive selection of his works, with some strategic omissions.[5] The shorter fictions would be grouped in

---

[2] Philip Horne, *Henry James and Revision: The New York Edition* (Oxford: Clarendon Press, 1990), pp. 5–6. Michael Anesko, *'Friction with the Market': Henry James and the Profession of Authorship* (New York and Oxford: Oxford University Press, 1986), pp. 144–6.

[3] Pinker to Burlingame, 3 August 1904; Princeton.

[4] James to Scribners, 30 July 1905; *HJL* 4:366.

[5] James told Pinker on 6 June 1905 that he had decided 'not to let [the *New York Edition*] include absolutely *everything*. It is best I think, that it should be selective as well as collective; I want to quietly disown a few things by not thus supremely adopting them' (*LL* 412). The omissions included *Watch and Ward* (1871, 1878), *The Europeans* (1878), *Confidence* (1879), *Washington Square* (1880), *The Bostonians* (1886), *The Other House* (1896), *The Sacred Fount* (1901) and nearly half the short stories he had published by the end of 1908. As Anesko has shown, the scope and contents of the *New York Edition* were determined by complex publishing considerations as well as by James's preferences, and some of his omissions were reluctantly made (*'Friction with the Market'*, pp. 143–53).

thematic series, and the texts would be closely revised. And the volumes would have prefaces:

> Lastly, I desire to furnish each book, whether consisting of a single fiction, or of several minor ones, with a freely colloquial and even, perhaps, as I may say, confidential preface or introduction, representing, in a manner, the history of the work or the group, representing more particularly, perhaps, a frank critical talk about its subject, its origin, its place in the whole artistic chain, and embodying, in short, whatever of interest there may be to be said about it. I have never committed myself in print in any way, even so much as by three lines to a newspaper, on the subject of anything I have written, and I feel as if I should come to this part of the business with a certain freshness of appetite and effect. My hope would be, at any rate, that it might count as a feature of a certain importance in any such new and more honourable presentation of my writings. (*HJL* 4:367)

James was not quite accurate when he told the Scribners that he had never publicly commented on his own work 'in any way'. He had written no authorial introductions for the Macmillan *Collective Edition* of his works (1883), and only a brief Notice to the first volume of *Stories Revived* (1885) explaining the circumstances of the stories' first publication and stating that the texts of earlier pieces had been 'in every case minutely revised and corrected'.[6] The short notes and notices appended to his essay collections *Portraits of Places* (1883), *Partial Portraits* (1888), *Picture and Text* (1893) and *Essays in London and Elsewhere* (1893) similarly confined themselves to bibliographical information and questions of dating.[7] But his introductory paratexts to later volumes show signs of the rhetorical expansiveness and critical-theoretical curiosity that would so strongly characterize the *New York Edition* Prefaces. These qualities appear for the first time in a comparatively brief (two-page) Note prefixed to the volume entitled *Theatricals* (1894) and signed 'H.J.', in which James defended his decision to publish a pair of unperformed play-texts:

---

[6] *Stories Revived*, 3 vols. (London: Macmillan and Co., 1885), vol. I, p. [v].

[7] The Notice to *Partial Portraits* points out, for example, that 'The reminiscences of Turgénieff were written immediately after his death, the article on Anthony Trollope on the same occasion, before the publication of his interesting Autobiography, and the appreciation of Alphonse Daudet before that of his three latest novels' (*Partial Portraits* (London and New York: Macmillan, 1888), p. [vii]).

INTRODUCTION

If it be very naturally and somewhat sternly inquired [...] why, failing of their sole application, they appear in a form which is an humiliating confession of defeat, I am afraid the only answer is that the unacted dramatist has still the consolation—poor enough, alas!—of the performance imaginary. There are degrees of representation, and it breaks his fall and patches up his retreat a little to be correctly printed—which is after all a morsel of the opportunity of the real dramatist.

James staved off the humiliation of this circumstance – or performed that staving off – by addressing his readers theatrically, as though from the proscenium, and developing the conceit of book publication as 'the performance imaginary': 'The covers of the book may, in a seat that costs nothing, figure the friendly curtain, and the legible "lines" the various voices of the stage; so that if these things manage at all to disclose a picture or to drop a tone into the reader's ear the ghostly ordeal will in a manner have been passed and the dim foot-lights faced.'[8] In the much longer (ten-page) unsigned Note to a second series of *Theatricals* published the same year, he confessed to 'a lively general mistrust of the preface to a work of fiction and the explanation of a work of art', but maintained all the same 'that an unacted play stands in a certain need of introduction'; again, the author's prefatory discourse is imagined as 'a substitute for the [theatrical] representation originally aimed at', 'some argued equivalent of the merciful curtain that was never either to rise or to fall'.[9] By such substitutions and equivalences, James began to move from the bare introductory notes to his early collections of republished pieces towards the Prefaces' elaborate authorial performance.

In his Preface to the second edition of *A Little Tour in France* (1900), signed and dated 'H.J. / August 9, 1900' (*LTF* viii), he came a step further in that direction, again in response to a specific bibliographical circumstance. The essays in that volume, originally collected with 'an expectation [...] that they should accompany a series of drawings' but not in the event so accompanied, were now appearing for the first time with illustrations: 'The little book thus goes forth finally as the picture-book it was designed to

---

[8] *Theatricals. Two Comedies: Tenants, Disengaged* (London: Osgood, McIlvaine & Co., 1894), pp. [v]–vi.

[9] *Theatricals. Second Series: The Album, The Reprobate* (London: Osgood, McIlvaine, 1894), p. [v]–vi.

be' (*LTF* v, vi). James took the opportunity of reprinting in this enhanced format to reflect in general terms on 'the pictorial spirit' in travel writing: 'From the moment the principle of selection and expression, with a tourist, is not the delight of the eyes and the play of fancy, it should be an energy in every way much larger; there is no happy mean [...] between the sense and the quest of the picture, and the surrender to it, and the sense and the quest of the constitution, the inner springs of the subject—springs and connections social, economic, historic' (*LTF* v–vi). In presence of those alternatives, he preferred the pictorial to the sociohistorical, as he would do again in the Preface to his travelogue *The American Scene* (1907).[10] In the Note to the second series of *Theatricals*, he had likewise reflected upon the constraints of genre, in that case the strict time-limit imposed on a play's length by British theatrical conditions and the consistency of form and idea demanded of dramatic comedy. The Prefaces to the *New York Edition* would extend such critical-theoretical commentary to an array of prose genres – novel, *nouvelle*, short story – sometimes by explicit analogy with dramatic or scenic form. The Preface to the second edition of *A Little Tour in France* also anticipates the *New York Edition* Prefaces in its remarks on the complex adventure of authorial retrospect. As James observed there, 'Many things come back to me on reading my pages over—such a world of reflection and emotion as I can neither leave unmentioned nor yet, in this place, weigh them down with the full expression of' (*LTF* vi). Reissuing the volume gave him a prevision of the rueful discovery he would make in preparing the *New York Edition* – that the flood of his response to rereading his own early work overflowed all available channels, and could be fully expressed neither in the textual revisions to his novels and tales nor in the retrospective discourse of the Prefaces. The *Little Tour* Preface notably reflects, too, on the 'missed occasions' of James's relation to France: 'Not one of these small chapters but suggests to me a regret that I might not, first or last, have gone farther, penetrated deeper, spoken oftener—closed, in short, more intimately with the great general subject' (*LTF* vii). With more at stake in every

---

[10] In writing about his return to America, James resolved to 'take my stand on my gathered impressions' and accepted that 'There would be a thousand matters—matters already the theme of prodigious reports and statistics—as to which I should have no sense whatever' (*AS* [v]–vi).

way, this would be his experience again with the *New York Edition* – above all in rereading *The Wings of the Dove*, whose Preface is dominated by the recognition of all he had not been able to do in composing the novel.

The brief Note to another volume from this period, the revised collection of travel essays *English Hours* (1905), formulates an important crux of Jamesian revision. On the one hand, for James to reread his own early work is to re-encounter a 'fine freshness' which he can count himself unfortunate to have 'outlived'; and yet the 'curious interest' of that encounter is not incompatible with his desire to alter and improve early texts by revising them, 'to rewrite a sentence or a passage on judging it susceptible of a better turn' (*CTW1* 3). James appears to have done the textual work for *English Hours* immediately before he sailed for America in August 1904.[11] The volume was published in October 1905 as he was starting to revise his early novels, and he would quote these sentences on revision in the Preface to the Edition's opening volume, *Roderick Hudson*.

James had also dictated 'preliminary *statements*' or introductory synopses for two recent novels – *The Wings of the Dove* and *The Ambassadors* – to solicit the interest of editors. One of those documents survives, the 'Project of Novel' for *The Ambassadors* that James dictated in August–September 1900 for his prospective American publishers Harper and Brothers.[12] It is in effect a preface to the unwritten novel. James sketches the plot and touches on points of theme and technique which he would revisit in the *New York Edition* Preface. And he opens with a circumstantial account of the novel's anecdotal *donnée* which he would recapitulate at slightly reduced length in the Preface's opening paragraphs: as he observes in the first sentence of the 'Project of Novel', 'It occurs to me that it may conduce to interest to begin with a mention of the comparatively small matter that gave me, in this case, the germ of my subject' (*CFHJ* 18, 497). The bid for interest on the basis of recounted origins is a constant factor in the Prefaces' appeal to readers.

---

[11] On 23 June 1904 he wrote to Joseph Pennell, who was just starting work on the illustrations for 'the "English book"': 'but oh, I must absolutely *revise* & tidy up the *text*—as I did that of the L. T. in France, before it goes to the Printers!' (*LL* 401–2).

[12] The 'Project of Novel' is printed in Nicola Bradbury's edition of *The Ambassadors* (*CFHJ* 18, 497–540).

INTRODUCTION

Since the late 1880s James had often supplied critical introductions for volumes of other writers' work. His essay 'Guy de Maupassant' was reprinted from *Harper's Weekly* as the introduction to Jonathan Sturges's translation of thirteen stories by Maupassant, *The Odd Number* (1889); he wrote a preface for his own English translation of Alphonse Daudet's novel *Port-Tarascon* (1890) and an introduction for Rudyard Kipling's story collection *Mine Own People* (1891). He also introduced several reprints of English classics and translations of French novels and stories.[13] Of these pieces, the introductory essays on Honoré de Balzac and Gustave Flaubert have a special relevance to the *New York Edition* Prefaces by virtue of their autobiographical focus on the act of rereading. In the Balzac essay (1902), James remarks that books read and assimilated in youth will be found later to have 'passed into our lives' and 'become a part of our personal history, a part of ourselves, very often, so far as we may have succeeded in best expressing ourselves' ('HdB' vi). The essay on Flaubert (also 1902) illustrates that principle with an episode from James's early life that anticipates the Prefaces' detailed recall of the rooms he wrote in and the outside sounds and sights that reached him as he worked or paused from working. Thus, when he remembers reading a serial instalment of *Madame Bovary* as a child in Paris in 1856, his surroundings come back to him as they would do again in the Prefaces' scenes of remembered composition: 'the sunny little *salon*, the autumn day, the window ajar, and the cheerful clatter, outside, of the Rue Montaigne, are all now for me more or less in the story, and the story more or less in them' ('GF' xvii).

The prospectus for the *New York Edition* published in December 1907 in the Scribners' house journal *The Book Buyer* claimed that the 'Special Prefaces' which would accompany the volumes were 'A still more important [...] feature' of the Edition than James's textual revisions, 'and equally novel':

---

[13] The volumes in question are: Pierre Loti, *Impressions* (London: Archibald Constable and Co., 1898); Oliver Goldsmith, *The Vicar of Wakefield* (New York: The Century Co., 1900); Honoré de Balzac, *The Two Young Brides* [*Mémoires de deux jeunes mariées*], ed. Edmund Gosse (London: William Heinemann, 1902); Gustave Flaubert, *Madame Bovary*, ed. Edmund Gosse (London: William Heinemann, 1902); *The Tempest*, vol. XVII in *The Complete Works of William Shakespeare*, ed. Sidney Lee (New York: George D. Sproul, 1907).

Nothing of the kind has ever been attempted. The Prefaces are of a threefold nature. Each, in the first place, narrates the circumstances in which the book it introduces was originally conceived and executed, what the idea was, how, when, and where it occurred to the author, and the various incidents of its working out. In the next place it is a critical examination of the book itself, perfectly candid and, as may readily be seen, uniquely piquant and interesting—an author's detailed criticism of his own works being a complete novelty. Finally, taken together the Prefaces constitute indirectly a unique body of criticism of the art of the novelist—at once philosophic, technical and authoritative. The Prefaces unite the interest of personal 'Confessions' with that of a profession of faith.[14]

This large claim for the Prefaces' uniqueness was essentially accurate: the 'threefold' combination of writerly autobiography, critical analysis and literary theory had not been attempted before in the context of an English-language collected edition. And yet other authors, obviously, had used prefaces for one or more of these purposes: to tell the origins of their works and the circumstances in which they were composed, or to analyse their own writing or theorize the genres they worked in; other authors had treated their prefaces as autobiographical sketches, repositories of socio-historical information, moral or aesthetic manifestos, or stages for the performance of authorship. James's understanding of the authorial preface as a genre around 1905 is another essential literary context for the *New York Edition* Prefaces, and it can be reconstructed from a survey of the collected editions that were his bibliographical models for the Edition and from his comments on other authors' prefatory and introductory writings.[15]

On 6 June 1905, a couple of months before his memo to the Scribners, James wrote to Pinker about the format he had in mind for his collected edition: 'remember, please, that my idea is a Handsome Book, distinctly' (*LL* 412). The handsomeness of the *New York Edition* certainly mattered to him, and he thought of the Prefaces not only as texts but as book parts also, elements of a bibliographical ensemble that included paper, page design, typeface, frontispieces and bindings. As he remarked to his old friend

---

[14] 'The Novels and Tales of Henry James', *The Book Buyer* 32 (December 1907), 212–13; 212.
[15] For James's Prefaces in the broader Western tradition of literary paratexts, see Gérard Genette, *Seuils* (Paris: Éditions du Seuil, 1987); trans. Jane E. Lewin as *Paratexts: Thresholds of Interpretation* (Cambridge: Cambridge University Press, 1997).

and former editor W. D. Howells of the first three novels in the Edition (*Roderick Hudson*, *The American* and *The Portrait of a Lady*), textual revision in this context was partly a question of living up to the material conditions of republication: 'It was absolutely impossible to me to hand them over to new & high honours of type, paper, form, plates, prefaces (these latter very "important",) without retouching their original roughness.'[16] Early readers recognized the honourable cooperation of textual and bibliographical elements: the New York *Bookman*, for instance, while predicting that the Prefaces would 'constitute in their entirety one of the most interesting of personal documents', also noted that the Edition was putting some of James's 'most curious and entertaining' early writing back into circulation, and that the volumes themselves were 'admirable in typography and binding. It is not often that a uniform edition of the works of a living writer can be justified on so many valid counts.'[17]

James's idea of 'a Handsome book' meant, he told Pinker in June 1905, not *less* handsome 'than the definitive RLS, or the ditto GM' (*LL* 412). It is not clear which editions of Robert Louis Stevenson and George Meredith he had in mind: in each case, there was more than one candidate for 'the definitive' collected edition, including editions of both writers published by Charles Scribner's Sons. 'We are in a moment of definitive editions', James had observed almost a decade earlier, thinking then, too, primarily of Stevenson and Meredith.[18] But no collected edition of Meredith from this

---

[16] James to Howells, 1 November 1906; *LFL* 419.
[17] 'The New Edition of James', *Bookman* (New York) 28 (September 1908), 12–13; 13. For the *New York Edition* in the context of the contemporary culture of collected editions, see Michael Anesko, 'Collected Editions and the Consolidation of Cultural Authority: The Case of Henry James', *Book History* 12 (2009), 186–208; Eric Leuschner, '"Utterly, Insurmountably, Unsaleable": Collected Editions, Prefaces, and the "Failure" of Henry James's New York Edition', *Henry James Review* 22.1 (2001), 24–40; Anesko, 'Ambiguous Allegiances: Conflicts of Culture and Ideology in the Making of the New York Edition', in David McWhirter (ed.), *Henry James's New York Edition: The Construction of Authorship* (Stanford, CA: Stanford University Press, 1995), pp. 77–89; and Stuart Culver, 'Ozymandias and the Mastery of Ruins: The Design of the New York Edition', in McWhirter (ed.), *Henry James's New York Edition*, pp. 39–57.
[18] 'London. January 15, 1897', *Harper's Weekly* 41 (6 February 1897), 134–5; 135. See the essays by Simon Gatrell (on Hardy, James and Meredith) and Andrew Nash (on Stevenson) in Nash (ed.), *The Culture of Collected Editions* (Basingstoke: Palgrave Macmillan, 2003), pp. 80–94, 111–27.

period incorporated prefaces.[19] All contemporaneous collected editions of Stevenson on the other hand were introduced either by the author or by an editorially appointed substitute, and those introductions will afford a convenient starting-point for an examination of James's awareness of the genre around the turn of the century.

The 'Edinburgh Edition' of *The Works of Robert Louis Stevenson* (1894-8) reprinted Stevenson's dedications and prefaces to his early editions, but added no new authorial paratexts. Stevenson died in December 1894, just after the publication of the first volumes. Some fifteen years later, an American reviewer of the *New York Edition* – surveying the recent history of authors' prefaces and claiming Stevenson as the first anglophone novelist who had used them to analyse his own writing – would assume that the absence of prefaces from the Edinburgh Edition was a simple accident of mortality:

> Even Stevenson, thriftily as he cultivated every corner of his copy-bearing garden, did not do this work systematically or thoroughly. Doubtless he would have done so if he had attained to the honor of a 'definitive' edition in his own lifetime, and would have left other introductions to rank with the charming introduction to the reprint of 'Treasure Island'.[20]

The reference is to Stevenson's essay 'My First Book—"Treasure Island"' (1894), which the Scribners opportunistically reprinted as a de facto preface to the novel in their 'Thistle Edition' (1895-9).[21] Of course, Stevenson *had* been honoured with a collected edition in his lifetime, albeit only just, and the denial of the opportunity to review his own work 'systematically or thoroughly' was not in the first place a consequence of his early death but a matter of editorial veto. In January 1894, Stevenson had written to Charles Baxter – one of the two editors of the Edinburgh Edition – offering

---

[19] The relevant editions of Meredith are the 'Edition de Luxe' (London: Archibald Constable and Co., 1896-8), which James described as 'the beautiful, the stately "definitive" edition' ('London. January 15, 1897', 135); the 'Library Edition' (London: Archibald Constable and Co., 1897-9); and the 'Boxhill Edition' (New York: Charles Scribner's Sons, 1898).

[20] Montgomery Schuyler, 'Henry James Done Over', *New York Times Saturday Review of Books* 13 (11 January 1908), 13-15; 14.

[21] *The Novels and Tales of Robert Louis Stevenson*, 24 vols. (New York: Charles Scribner's Sons, 1895-9), vol. II, pp. ix-xx.

to write prefaces for the volumes 'if it were thought desirable', and pointing out that he had already 'written a paper on *Treasure Island*' and 'drafted' another on *The Master of Ballantrae*.[22] That offer was firmly rejected by Baxter's co-editor Sidney Colvin: 'As to the query about explanatory prefaces – for God's sake let there be none of them.' Colvin allowed that they might print 'Strictly historical notes' where the subject-matter required them, 'but the trick of picking the sawdust out of the puppets, before the eyes of the world, is a disastrous one, which (as I am glad to find you also think) we should all do our best to discourage.'[23] Stevenson's essays on *Treasure Island* (1883) and *The Master of Ballantrae* (1889) would make it into the Edinburgh Edition after his death, but as a consequence of this ruling by Baxter and Colvin they did not figure there as prefaces; instead they were gathered into a series of miscellanies.[24]

In many ways, those two essays do typically prefatory work, recounting the origins and development of Stevenson's novels, identifying sources, and reflecting on the conversion of real acquaintances into fictional characters. Stevenson was not new to this sort of writing, and had already published autobiographical sketches on places and circumstances connected with other fictions.[25] And yet all of these pieces might invite the puzzled comment James made in his review of Colvin's posthumous edition of *The Letters of Robert Louis Stevenson to his Family and Friends* (1899) on the author's loose, unanalytical way of talking about work in prospect and in progress. James detected a 'conscious [...] want of method' in Stevenson's

---

[22] Stevenson to Charles Baxter, 1 January 1894; *The Letters of Robert Louis Stevenson*, ed. Bradford A. Booth and Ernest Mehew, 8 vols. (New Haven, CT: Yale University Press, 1994–5), vol. VIII, p. 226.

[23] Sidney Colvin to Charles Baxter, 7 February 1894; *The Letters of Robert Louis Stevenson*, ed. Booth and Mehew, vol. VIII, pp. 226–7 n. 5.

[24] Stevenson, 'My First Book—"Treasure Island"' and 'The Genesis of "The Master of Ballantrae"', in *The Works of Robert Louis Stevenson*, 'Edinburgh Edition', 28 vols. (Edinburgh: printed by T. and A. Constable, 1894–8), vol. XXI, pp. 285–97, 297–302.

[25] See 'Memoirs of an Islet' (1887), about the Isle of Erraid in the Inner Hebrides, a setting in *Kidnapped* (1886) and 'The Merry Men' (1882), and 'A Chapter on Dreams' (1888), about unconscious factors in the conception of 'Olalla' (1885) and *Strange Case of Dr Jekyll and Mr Hyde* (1886); in *The Works of Robert Louis Stevenson*, 'Edinburgh Edition', vol. I, pp. 164–70, 317–34.

reports of his first ideas for stories, 'his flurries and fancies, imaginations, evocations, quick infatuations, as a teller of possible tales':

> He communicates, to his confidant, with the eagerness of a boy, in holidays, confabulating over a Christmas charade; but I remember no instance of his expressing a subject, as one may say, *as* a subject—hinting at what novelists mainly know, I imagine, as the determinant thing in it, the idea out of which it springs. The form, the envelope, is there with him, headforemost, *as* the idea; titles, names, that is, chapters, sequences, orders, while we are still asking ourselves how it was that he primarily put to his own mind what it was all to be about. ('LRLS' 70, 71)

That is especially true of the essay on *Treasure Island*, where Stevenson recalls that he began to write the novel with no thought of a plot but only a map of an imaginary island, a list of chapter titles and a working title for the book. It appeared to James at the turn of the century that Stevenson either could not or would not tell what his stories were 'to be about': this was 'always the one dumb sound, the only inarticulate thing, in all his contagious candor' ('LRLS' 71). James would voice a similar frustration with another novelist in an essay of the same period, 'Winchelsea, Rye and *Denis Duval*' (1901), which anticipates the mixed mode of the *New York Edition* Prefaces: it is ostensibly an account of rereading W. M. Thackeray's unfinished last novel *Denis Duval* (1863), but its relaxed, conversational form accommodates digressions on authorship, historical loss and the phenomenology and aesthetics of place. James complained that neither the text of *Denis Duval* nor the contextual evidence supplied by the modern collected edition he was reading it in – the 'Biographical Edition' of *The Works of William Makepeace Thackeray* (1898–9), assembled and introduced by the novelist's daughter Anne Thackeray Ritchie – was sufficient to show what the true subject of the novel was to have been. And there was no help in simply concluding that its subject was to have been 'the adventures of [the] hero; inasmuch as, turn the thing as we will, these "adventures" could at the best have constituted nothing more than its *form*. [...] The book was, obviously, to have been, as boys say, "about" them. But what were *they* to have been about? Thackeray carried the mystery to his grave' (*CTW1* 242). In the *New York Edition* Prefaces, by contrast, James would lay a particular emphasis on explaining what his own works were to have been about.

In 'Winchelsea, Rye, and *Denis Duval*' James praised Anne Thackeray Ritchie's 'charming series of introductions' to the Biographical Edition of Thackeray (*CTW1* 241). These introductions are cast in the same miscellaneous Victorian 'Life and Letters' format which he would adopt two years later for his own foray into commemorative biography, *William Wetmore Story and His Friends: From Letters, Diaries, and Recollections* (1903).[26] Ritchie's introductions are stuffed with material: passages reprinted from her already-published memoirs and fresh recollections of growing up in the Thackeray household, quotations from Thackeray's unpublished correspondence, diaries and essays, and designs for his own illustrations. Ritchie often points out the originals of fictional characters and settings, but her main concern is with her father's biography, and she attempts no sustained literary analysis.[27] This model for collected edition paratexts was used by later editions of Stevenson: the Scribners' 'Biographical Edition' (1905–12) featured prefaces by Stevenson's widow Fanny Van de Grift Osbourne Stevenson, and Cassell's 'Pentland Edition' (1906–7) included short 'Bibliographical Notes' by Edmund Gosse, one of a few surviving friends 'who had the happiness to share Stevenson's literary experiences and listen to his schemes, at the opening of his career', and who was thus able to 'bring forward such trifling recollections as shall help readers to put themselves more quickly and completely in relation with the author'.[28] James was also aware of a French variant on the biographical paratext, Gustave Flaubert's 'Préface' to a posthumous volume of poems by his friend and schoolfellow Louis Bouilhet, *Dernières chansons: poésies posthumes* (1872). Flaubert's impressionistic tribute combines an appreciation of Bouilhet's life with unsystematic comments on his verse and aesthetic principles. The 'Préface' finds an obvious echo in the brief obituary introductions James wrote for posthumous

---

[26] Anne Thackeray Ritchie was an old friend of James's and would write to him 'kindly and *seeingly*' about *William Wetmore Story* when it appeared (James to Anne Thackeray Ritchie, 19 November 1903; *HJL* 4:290).

[27] The texts of Ritchie's introductions are collected in *The Two Thackerays: Anne Thackeray Ritchie's Centenary Biographical Introductions to the Works of William Makepeace Thackeray*, critical introduction by Carol Hanbery MacKay, bibliographical introduction by Peter L. Shillingsburg and Julia Maxey, 2 vols. (New York: AMS Press, Inc., 1988).

[28] Gosse, 'Preface to the Pentland Edition', in *The Works of Robert Louis Stevenson*, 20 vols. (London: Cassell and Company, 1906–7), vol. I, pp. xi–xiv; xiii.

volumes by two young acquaintances, Wolcott Balestier's novel *The Average Woman* (1892) and Hubert Crackanthorpe's story collection *Last Studies* (1897),[29] but in its critical-theoretical aspect it would also inform James's comments on reading aloud in the Preface to *The Golden Bowl*.[30]

In his July 1905 memo, James had suggested one of the Scribners' own collected editions as a bibliographical 'model' for the *New York Edition*: the 'Outward Bound Edition' of Rudyard Kipling, which they had been publishing since 1897, 'offers to my mind the right type of form and appearance, the right type of print and size of page, for our undertaking' (*HJL* 4:368). Kipling wrote two authorial paratexts for this edition, which appear in the first volume, *Plain Tales from the Hills*. In a short '"Outward Bound" Edition Preface' he notes that 'For the convenience of the reader, an attempt has been made in this edition to group the stories by their subjects': separate volumes were devoted to 'military stories', 'tales of native life in India' and tales dealing 'with matters more or less between the two worlds'.[31] This was a common practice for collected editions of the period, modelled on the grouping of works by philosophical and sociological categories in Honoré de Balzac's *La Comédie humaine* (1829–48). Balzac's complex scheme of thematic series is outlined in his 'Avant-propos', or general preface, to the *Comédie* (1842): three series of 'Études' (Studies of Manners, Philosophical Studies and Analytical Studies), the first of those three subdivided into six 'Scènes' (Scenes of Private Life, Provincial Life, Parisian Life, Political Life, Military Life and Country Life).[32] On a greatly reduced scale, and without giving any formal indication of his categories, James too would follow this precedent in the *New York Edition* by gathering together tales of the literary life, tales on supernatural or uncanny subjects, tales on the international theme, and so on; he described this arrangement to the Scribners as 'a fresh grouping or classification, a placing together, from series to series, of those [stories] that will help each other, those that will conduce to something of

[29] For the texts of those introductions, see *Aut* 661–9 (Balestier) and *LC1* 839–44 (Crackanthorpe).
[30] See note 932 to the text.
[31] Kipling, '"Outward Bound" Edition Preface', in *The Writings in Prose and Verse of Rudyard Kipling*, 36 vols. (New York: Charles Scribner's Sons, 1897–1937), vol. I, pp. vii–viii; vi.
[32] Balzac, *La Comédie humaine*, ed. Pierre-Georges Castex et al., 12 vols. (Paris: Gallimard, 1976–81), vol. I, pp. 7–20; 18–19.

a common effect' (*HJL* 4:366). Kipling's second paratext to the Outward Bound Edition was an introductory letter from the author to his editor F. N. Doubleday, cast in the form of a 'BILL OF INSTRUCTION' from the owner of a merchant ship to 'THE NAKHODA OR SKIPPER OF THIS VENTURE' telling him how he should trade with various types of customer, or reader – a flourish of authorial fancy-dress that foregrounds but also disguises the commercial rationale of the enterprise.[33] In the *New York Edition* Prefaces, too, such matters of trade are displaced onto the level of literary style, but in a different manner: James speaks throughout in his own voice, and the mercantile dimension of authorship is refracted into extended metaphors of voyaging, dealing, bargaining, accounting and defrauding.

Another exemplar of the late nineteenth-century 'moment of definitive editions',[34] the revised 'Wessex Novels Edition' of *Thomas Hardy's Works* published by the London firm of Osgood, McIlvaine & Co. (1895–6), incorporated newly written authorial prefaces explaining the historical references of Hardy's fiction, identifying sources in local history and noting such manifestations of change as the restoration of old buildings and loss of rural customs.[35] James would touch on similar matters in his *New York Edition* Prefaces, but with reference to the places in which he wrote his works rather than to the settings of the fictions. The relation of real places to their fictional counterparts – another recurring topic of Hardy's prefaces – was also graphically embodied in the Wessex Novels volumes in ways that may have contributed to James's sense of the possibilities of illustrating a collected edition. Each volume contained a pictorial frontispiece, engraved from a drawing by Henry Macbeth-Raeburn of an actual place doubling as a fictional setting in Hardy's Wessex: the frontispiece to *A Pair of Blue Eyes*, for instance, is captioned 'THE "CASTLE BOTEREL" OF THE STORY | Drawn on the spot'.[36] Like Alvin Langdon Coburn's photogravure frontispieces to the *New York Edition*, which James would describe in the *Golden*

---

[33] Kipling, 'Introduction to Outward Bound Edition', in *The Writings in Prose and Verse of Rudyard Kipling*, vol. I, pp. ix–xiii.
[34] James, 'London. January 15, 1897', 135.
[35] The prefaces to the Wessex Novels Edition are collected in *Thomas Hardy's Personal Writings: Prefaces, Literary Opinions, Reminiscences*, ed. Harold Orel (London: Macmillan, 1967).
[36] Hardy, *The Works of Thomas Hardy*, 16 vols. (London: Osgood, McIlvaine and Co., 1895–6), vol. IV, p. [i].

Bowl Preface as 'pictures of our "set" stage with the actors left out' (p. 265), Macbeth-Raeburn's images were not visualizations of incidents from the stories but depopulated views of their key locations.

The great model for nineteenth-century collected editions of British novelists was the illustrated and revised 'Magnum Opus Edition' of Walter Scott's *Waverley Novels* (1829–33), with its massive apparatus of authorial introductions, notes and appendices. Scott has been comparatively neglected by scholars of the *New York Edition*, but he would have been an obvious point of reference for early twentieth-century anglophone authors, publishers and readers of collected editions.[37] Reviewing the first volumes of the *New York Edition* in the *New York Times*, Montgomery Schuyler directly compared the Prefaces with Scott's Magnum Opus Edition paratexts: 'The practice of providing prefaces for the several works of a collective edition is as old in English literature at least as Walter Scott', but until very recently 'a rather absurd pudicity has restrained English writers from making these prefaces mediums of anything but information and reminiscence'.[38] Scott's introductions were not merely historical and anecdotal, though they did indeed provide 'information' of various sorts about the fictions they accompany, recording – as the 'Advertisement' to the Magnum Opus Edition put it – 'the various legends, family traditions, or obscure historical facts, which have afforded the ground-work of these Novels', locating 'the places where the scenes are laid, when these are altogether, or in part, real' and identifying 'particular incidents founded on fact'.[39] Scott's 'General Preface' to the Magnum Opus Edition also contained substantial passages of autobiography, notably an account of the genesis and composition of his first novel *Waverley* (1814), and a playful discourse on the labour and ingenuity required to maintain his authorial incognito – an elaborate pretence

---

[37] In his study of nineteenth- and twentieth-century writers' efforts to control the posthumous presentation of their lives and works, Michael Millgate has argued that Scott offered 'the supreme model of career closure' in the period, and that the format of the Magnum Opus Edition 'established a pattern for collected editions'; he does not consider Scott's possible influence on James in this regard (*Testamentary Acts: Browning, Tennyson, James, Hardy* (Oxford: Clarendon Press, 1992), p. 1).

[38] Schuyler, 'Henry James Done Over', 14.

[39] *The Edinburgh Edition of the Waverley Novels*, editor-in-chief David Hewitt, 30 vols. (Edinburgh: Edinburgh University Press, 1993–), vol. XXVa, p. 7.

of anonymity which Scott abandoned only when the bankruptcy of his publisher and printer made the issuing of an authorized collective edition financially expedient. But while the Magnum Opus Edition paratexts attempted nothing that James would have recognized as literary analysis, Scott nevertheless understood their display of historical source-material as a demonstration of the mechanism of his fiction: as he drily noted in the General Preface, 'It remains to be tried whether the public (like a child to whom a watch is shown) will, after having been satiated with looking at the outside, acquire some new interest in the object when it is opened, and the internal machinery displayed to them.'[40]

Jane Millgate has argued that James 'accepted the Scott precedent not merely as a model but as a challenge' when he came to assemble the *New York Edition*. She sees James in the Prefaces as consciously outdoing Scott with regard to both authorial commentary and textual revision – flaunting 'open delight' at the potentially 'infinite amplitude' of circumstantial reminiscence, and elaborating on one of Scott's metaphors for textual revision to justify his own much more interventionist approach to reissuing his works.[41] Scott had announced in the Advertisement that his revisions for the Magnum Opus Edition would not 'alter the tenor of the stories, the character of the actors, or the spirit of the dialogue', nor involve 'such apparent deviations from the original stories as to disturb the reader's old associations'; rather, they were to be 'slight alterations [...] like the last touches of an Artist, which contribute to heighten and finish the picture, though an inexperienced eye can hardly detect in what they consist'.[42] As Millgate observes: 'Taking up Scott's metaphor of the "last touches of the artist", James makes of the act of revarnishing a transforming process completely different from anything Scott had envisaged.'[43] This painterly metaphor organizes the discussion of textual revision in the Preface to *Roderick Hudson*; in the *Golden Bowl* Preface, too, James appears to draw on other figures for revision in Scott's Magnum Opus Advertisement.[44]

---

[40] Ibid., p. 21.
[41] Jane Millgate, *Scott's Last Edition: A Study in Publishing History* (Edinburgh: Edinburgh University Press, 1987), p. 115.
[42] *The Edinburgh Edition of the Waverley Novels*, vol. XXVa, pp. 6–7.
[43] Millgate, *Scott's Last Edition*, p. 115.
[44] See notes 40, 41 and 902 to the text.

INTRODUCTION

The relevance to the *New York Edition* of Scott's French counterpart Honoré de Balzac is manifest, but the specific Balzacian influence has been in some ways too readily assumed: Leon Edel's speculative claim that James took *La Comédie humaine* as an exact bibliographical model for the *New York Edition* was accepted without question for several decades, and only conclusively dismissed in the 1980s.[45] Balzac's role as a writer of prefaces has been mostly overlooked in these reckonings, moreover. In an essay of 1875, James made a brief, sceptical comment on the 'Avant-propos' to the *Comédie humaine*, the 'general preface' in which Balzac 'explains the unity of his work and sets forth that each of his tales is a block in a single immense edifice and that this edifice aims to be a complete portrait of the civilization of his time' – a sociohistorical study of French manners and morals in the period of the Bourbon Restoration and the July Monarchy (1815–48), structured by analogy with the scientific classification of species and underpinned by religio-political principles of monarchism and Catholicism. James comments in passing on 'this remarkable manifesto': 'If we call it remarkable, it is not that we understand it [...]. From the moment that Balzac attempts to philosophize, readers in the least sensible of the difference between words and things must part company with him' (*LC2* 39). James's resistance to Balzac's philosophical abstraction is symptomatic of his impatience with a broad class of French literary prefaces that present themselves as manifestos or treatises. Thus he complained in 1896 that the moralizing 'prefaces and treatises' of Alexandre Dumas *fils* 'show a mistrust of disinterested art': 'Woe, in the æsthetic line, to any example that requires the escort of precept. It is like a guest arriving to dine accompanied by constables.'[46]

And yet James made a partial exception in this line for an essay by Guy de Maupassant, entitled 'Le Roman', which appeared in prefatory position in the first edition of Maupassant's short novel *Pierre et Jean* (1888). James's essay on Maupassant from the same year begins:

[45] Edel first made this claim in '"The Architecture of Henry James's "New York Edition"', *The New England Quarterly* 24.2 (1951), 169–78; it is restated in his *Henry James: The Master, 1901–1916* (London: Rupert Hart-Davis, 1972), pp. 329–32. For the disproof, see Anesko, 'Friction with the Market', pp. 141–62.

[46] 'On the Death of Dumas the Younger', *The New Review* 14 (March 1896), 288–302; *CWAD2* 432.

The first artists, in any line, are doubtless not those whose general ideas about their art are most often on their lips—those who most abound in precept, apology, and formula and can best tell us the reasons and the philosophy of things. We know the first usually by their energetic practice, the constancy with which they apply their principles, and the serenity with which they leave us to hunt for their secret in the illustration, the concrete example. None the less it often happens that a valid artist utters his mystery, flashes upon us for a moment the light by which he works, shows us the rule by which he holds it just that he should be measured. (*LC2* 521)

James describes 'Le Roman' in this essay as 'the preface to *Pierre et Jean*', but he also notes its indirect relation to the fiction it accompanies: it is a 'little disquisition on the novel in general, attached to that particular example of it which [Maupassant] has just put forth' (*LC2* 521, 522). In the opening sentences of 'Le Roman' Maupassant frames *Pierre et Jean* not as an object of analysis or apology, but as an occasion for general discussion: 'Je n'ai point l'intention de plaider ici pour le petit roman qui suit. Tout au contraire les idées que je vais essayer de faire comprendre entraîneraient plutôt la critique du genre d'étude psychologique que j'ai entrepris dans *Pierre et Jean*. | Je veux m'occuper du Roman en général.'[47] The bibliographical combination of a general essay with a novel it does not specifically refer to produces an odd effect, rather as though James had published his own literary-theoretical essay 'The Art of Fiction' (1884) as a preface to his novel *The Reverberator* (1888). Answering Walter Besant's 1884 lecture of the same title, 'The Art of Fiction' had joined a contemporary discussion of the professional and artistic status of fictional prose that also involved W. D. Howells, Andrew Lang, Robert Louis Stevenson and others.[48] In this essay James expressed two fundamental convictions which he shared with Maupassant, that to say in advance what a novel ought to be was to misunderstand the essential freedom of the form, and that this generic liberty had a correlative in the

---

[47] Maupassant, 'Le Roman', in *Pierre et Jean* (Paris: Paul Ollendorf, 1888), pp. [i]–xxxv; [i]. In a contemporary translation: 'I do not intend in these pages to put in a plea for this little novel. On the contrary, the ideas I shall try to set forth will rather involve a criticism of the class of psychological analysis which I have undertaken in *Pierre and Jean*. I propose to treat of novels in general' ('Of "The Novel"', in *Pierre and Jean*, trans. Clara Dell (New York: P. F. Collier & Son, 1902), pp. xli–lxiii; xli).

[48] See Mark Spilka, 'Henry James and Walter Besant: "The Art of Fiction" Controversy', *NOVEL: A Forum on Fiction* 6.2 (1973), 101–19.

individual author's freedom to represent things as she or he saw them; he would restate these principles in the Prefaces to the *New York Edition*. James and Maupassant both championed 'disinterested art' against the twinned dogmas of moralism and the market. James also valued the French writer for insisting on an author's right to set the terms on which his work should be read. In 'Le Roman', he observed, Maupassant had expressed 'his most general idea, his own sense of his direction', and critics who now came to make 'a sketch of him' would find that the author 'has arranged, as it were, the light in which he wishes to sit', 'chosen the spot' and 'made the chalk-mark on the floor' (*LC2* 521). James would certainly understand his own Prefaces as laying claim to that privilege.

Although the 'Avant-propos' to the *Comédie humaine* was the most prominent nineteenth-century example of the authorial preface as manifesto, Balzac's prefatory output was not limited to that general, abstract mode: he also wrote prefaces to the early editions of his novels, typically discarding them as each title took its place in the growing series of his works. In their specific reference to individual fictions and their close consideration of technical and circumstantial matters, Balzac's early prefaces are much closer to James's concerns as a commentator on his own writing than are the grandiose schematics of the 'Avant-propos'. They address central points of structure and technique (e.g., the systematic use of recurring characters) and expand on favourite subjects and themes (e.g., French provincial life) in ways that find obvious echoes in the *New York Edition* Prefaces. They also explicitly address a topic conspicuously absent from James's Prefaces, the material and economic contingencies of authorship. James found Balzac's ready communicativeness on such matters distasteful but compelling. He commented in 1875: '[Balzac] has against him that he lacks that slight but needful thing—charm. To feel how much he lacked it, you must read his prefaces, with their vanity, avidity, and garrulity, their gross revelation of his processes, of his squabbles with his publishers, their culinary atmosphere' (*LC2* 68). Balzac habitually used the prefaces to early editions of his works to complain about the conditions of the literary marketplace and the mechanisms of publishing, advertising and reviewing. But James may be referring specifically to Balzac's 'Historique du procès auquel a donné lieu "Le Lys dans la vallée"', a lengthy preface to the second edition of his novel *Le Lys dans la vallée* (1836), which describes a law-suit brought against Balzac by François Buloz, the editor of the *Revue de Paris*.[49] Balzac had ceased to supply copy for the novel in December 1835, thereby halting its serialization in the *Revue*, when he learned that Buloz was selling uncorrected proofs of the early instalments to a French-language journal in St Petersburg; Buloz unsuccessfully sued him for damages. As the record of a trial – the French word is *procès* – turning on the details of print production and compositional method, Balzac's preface to the second edition of *Le Lys* was very exactly a 'revelation of his processes'. With such contexts in mind, one is better able to appreciate how thoroughly the *New York Edition* Prefaces occlude James's own negotiations and occasional disputes with publishers.

James would find the 'charm' he missed in Balzac's prefaces in those of the novelist's contemporary George Sand. As he wrote in an essay of 1877:

To the cheap edition of her novels, published in 1852–'3, [Sand] prefixed a series of short prefaces, in which she relates the origin of each tale—the state of mind and the circumstances in which it was written. These prefaces are charming; they almost justify the publisher's declaration that they form the 'most beautiful examination that a great mind has ever made of itself'. (*LC2* 718)

James refers to the authorial prefaces to the *Œuvres illustrées de George Sand* (1852–6). These writings corroborated his view that Sand was a wholly intuitive, unanalytical artist. In the same essay, he pointed out that in the autobiography which she published while the volumes of the *Œuvres illustrées* were still coming out, Sand gave 'no account of how she learned to write, no record of effort or apprenticeship', and made no analysis of her own practice: 'she seems never to have felt the temptation to examine the pulse of the machine'. Likewise, while Sand's brief prefaces to the illustrated edition recounted instances of her 'extraordinary facility and spontaneity' in fictional composition with a beautiful 'limpidity of reminiscence', they had no critical ambitions (*LC2* 718, 719). James cites a few prefatory passages of this type: Sand's slight, glancing memories of writing *Gabriel* (1839) in a room in an inn at Marseilles while her two children played around her, or of sitting down to transcribe her surroundings – a sombre hotel room in Venice during a cold and miserable carnival season – as a way of starting

---

[49] Balzac, *La Comédie humaine*, ed. Castex et al, vol. IX, pp. 917–66.

work on *Leone Leoni* (1835) (*LC2* 718–19).⁵⁰ And he translates from memory almost the entirety of another preface:

In the few prefatory lines to 'Isidora' [1845] I remember she says something of this kind: 'It was a beautiful young woman who used to come and see me, and profess to relate her sorrows. I saw that she was attitudinizing before me, and not believing herself a word of what she said. So it is not her I described in "Isidora."' This is a happy way of saying how a hint—a mere starting point—was enough for her. (*LC2* 719)⁵¹

That would also be true of James's own starting points, with important qualifications: his preference for a 'casual hint', 'the minimum of valid suggestion', is theorized in the Prefaces to *The Spoils of Poynton* and *The Aspern Papers* (pp. 94, 128), but there is no parallel in Sand's prefaces for such moments of self-analysis, or for James's close attention to the working-out of fictional subjects.

The quality of 'charm' was for James also a keynote of the prefaces of a very different author, the American novelist Nathaniel Hawthorne: in his critical biography *Hawthorne* (1879), he had remarked, with reference to the preface to the second edition of *Twice-Told Tales* (1851), that 'there is always a charm in Hawthorne's prefaces which makes one grateful for a pretext to quote from them' (*LC1* 345). Hawthorne did not publish a collected edition in his lifetime: his prefaces were all written for early editions, though they would be retained in many posthumous editions of his complete works.⁵² His two most important prefaces, 'The Custom-House' and 'The Old Manse', are not so much introductions to the volumes they were written for as independent essays in literary autobiography. James valued them very highly: 'The Custom-House' in particular was, for him, 'as simple writing, one of the most perfect of Hawthorne's compositions, and one of the most gracefully and humorously autobiographic' (*LC1* 398). This roundabout introduction to Hawthorne's historical romance *The Scarlet Letter*

---

⁵⁰ *Préfaces de George Sand*, ed. Anna Szabó, 2 vols. (Debrecen: Kossuth Lajos Tudományegyetem, 1997), I:228–9, 199–200.
⁵¹ *Ibid.*, I:205.
⁵² The prefaces were included, for example, in James R. Osgood's 'Illustrated Library Edition' of *Nathaniel Hawthorne's Works* (1871–6), and in Houghton, Mifflin's 'Riverside Edition' of *The Works of Nathaniel Hawthorne*, 12 vols. (1883).

L

(1850) sets a fancifully supernatural account of the book's origin alongside a satirical group portrait of Hawthorne's co-workers in the Custom House at Salem, Massachusetts during his employment there as Surveyor in 1846-9. 'The Old Manse', the preface to Hawthorne's story collection *Mosses from an Old Manse* (1846), describes a three-year residence in 1842-5 in the former minister's house at Concord, Massachusetts. Subtitled 'The Author Makes the Reader Acquainted with His Abode', 'The Old Manse' is especially suggestive as an analogue for James's Prefaces by virtue of its dwelling upon the local circumstances of literary work: its subject is 'a moss-grown country parsonage, and [the author's] life within its walls, and on the river, and in the woods,—and the influences that wrought upon him, from all these sources'.[53] The Old Manse at Concord was for this time technically a workplace, a scene of literary production, but the labour and process of writing are barely mentioned here; instead, according to Hawthorne, the 'few tales and essays' which we are about to read in *Mosses* 'blossomed out like flowers in the calm summer of my heart and mind'.[54] Often in the *New York Edition* Prefaces, James similarly recalls the atmospheres and soundscapes of rooms in which he wrote, and seems to substitute an account of those circumstances for a representation of the work itself.

These examples from Balzac, Sand and Hawthorne all suggest that James thought of 'charm' in prefatory writing – or the lack of it – as a function of autobiographical reference. In an essay of 1883, his reading of the prefaces of Alphonse Daudet would move him to reflect sustainedly on the preface as an occasion for autobiography. The whole tenor of Daudet's output was, for James, autobiographical: 'Daudet expresses many things; but he most frequently expresses himself—his own temper in the presence of life, his own feeling on a thousand occasions.' This 'personal note' in his writing was 'very present in the series of prefaces which he has undertaken to supply to the octavo edition of his works' (*LC2* 231), the *Œuvres complètes de Alphonse Daudet* (1881–6). James continues:

In these prefaces he gives the history of each successive book—relates the circumstances under which it was written. These things are ingeniously told, but what we

---

[53] Hawthorne, *Tales and Sketches*, ed. Roy Harvey Pearce (New York: Library of America, 1982), p. 1147.
[54] Ibid., p. 1148.

are chiefly conscious of in regard to them, is that Alphonse Daudet must express himself. His brother informs us that he is writing his memoirs, and this will have been another opportunity for expression. (*LC2* 231–2)

What James describes here as two discrete projects – 'prefaces' and 'memoirs' – in fact significantly overlapped with each other. Daudet would redistribute the prefaces to the *Œuvres complètes* amongst two volumes of reminiscences, *Trente ans de Paris: à travers ma vie et mes livres* and *Souvenirs d'un homme de lettres* (both 1888), identifying the chapters which had formerly been prefaces by the collective title 'Histoire de mes livres'. They were explicitly conceived as instalments of literary autobiography: in the preface to *Numa Roumestan* (1881), Daudet speaks of 'cette histoire de mes livres, où l'on a pu voir de la fatuité d'auteur, mais qui me semblait à moi la vraie façon, originale et distinguée, d'écrire les mémoires d'un homme de lettres dans la marge de son oeuvre'.[55]

Daudet's histories of his books are most directly relevant to James's Prefaces for this idea of a literary autobiography written 'dans la marge de son oeuvre': the Preface to *The Golden Bowl* insistently figures James's textual and retrospective work on the *New York Edition* as a form of marginal writing.[56] Daudet also offers an important precedent for the Prefaces' rapt notation of the circumstances of literary composition, as for instance in the preface to *Numa Roumestan*, which recalls the sounds of the Parisian spring permeating Daudet's workroom on avenue de l'Observatoire, 'au-dessus de ces beaux marronniers du Luxembourg, bouquets géants tout pommés de grappes blanches et roses, traversés de cris d'enfants, de sonnettes de marchands de coco, de bouffées de cuivres militaires'.[57] The Preface to *The American*

---

[55] Daudet, *Souvenirs d'un homme de lettres* (Paris: C. Marpon et E. Flammarion, n.d. [1888]), pp. 41–2. In a contemporary translation: 'this history of my books, wherein some persons may have detected the self-conceit of an author, but which seemed to me the true method, original and distinctive, of writing the memoirs of a man of letters on the margin of his books' (*Memories of a Man of Letters, Artists' Wives, Etc.*, trans. George Burnham Ives (Boston, MA: Little, Brown, and Company, 1900), p. 31).

[56] See note 925 to the text.

[57] Daudet, *Souvenirs d'un homme de lettres*, pp. 52–3. In a contemporary translation: 'above the noble chestnuts in the Luxembourg gardens, giant nosegays of pink and white clusters, with the cries of children, the bells of cocoa-dealers, and blasts of military music ascending through the foliage' (*Memories of a Man of Letters, Artists' Wives, Etc.*, p. 38).

is comparably charmed by, and charming about, the remembered street-noises of springtime Paris as the auditory backdrop to James's writing of the novel (p. 21). And Daudet's 'fatuité d'auteur' finds an echo in the Prefaces' characterization of the composing author's state of mind as 'fond fatuity' or 'beautiful infatuation' (pp. 8, 29), as well as in the 'confirmed infatuation of retrospect' that grips James in the act of rereading (p. 66).

Hawthorne had been characteristically circumspect about the autobiographical reference of his introductions and prefaces, observing in the preface to *The Snow-Image* (1851) that readers had 'pronounced [him] egotistical, indiscreet, and even impertinent' for indulging in this mode of writing, and pointing out that, 'with whatever appearance of confidential intimacy, I have been especially careful to make no disclosures respecting myself which the most indifferent observer might not have been acquainted with'.[58] James, too, while in many ways newly intimate and confiding in his address to readers in the Prefaces, makes very few specific disclosures from his life, and does not fundamentally depart from the feeling that in 1883 had moved him to comment restrictively on Daudet's unreserve: 'To be *personnel* to that point, transparent, effusive, gushing, to give one's self away in one's books, has never been, and will never be, the ideal of us of English speech' (*LC2* 233). Daudet's prefaces repeatedly admitted their readers to the spaces and relations of his life, as a man and an author: the two dimensions of privacy coincide, for instance, in the preface to *Fromont jeune et Risler aîné* (1874), which describes a collaborative working method whereby Daudet passes the pages of his first draft to his wife for copying, editing and comment, and receives them back to revise. This preface affectionately restages a scene of domestic literary production in Daudet's study in the Marais district of Paris (also the setting of the novel), as the sounds of the neighbourhood drift into the room and pages of manuscript pass back and forth between the married co-workers in the hands of their small son.[59] James never approaches that degree of personal or professional exposure

---

[58] Hawthorne, *Tales and Sketches*, ed. Pearce, p. 1154.
[59] Daudet, *Trente ans de Paris: à travers ma vie et mes livres* (Paris: C. Marpon et E. Flammarion, 1888), pp. 313–15. For the same passage in a contemporary English translation, see *Thirty Years in Paris*, trans. George Burnham Ives (Boston, MA: Little, Brown, and Company, 1900), pp. 202–3.

in the Prefaces. He says little about his working routine at any period of his career, and, with the exception of a passage in the *Golden Bowl* Preface on his collaboration with the photographer Alvin Langdon Coburn, he makes no mention at all of the numerous others whose labour helped to produce the *New York Edition* – a group containing his literary agent, his publishers and editors, his regular amanuensis and various typists and typesetters. Their contributions to the writing of the Prefaces are described in the following section.

2 Composition

The *New York Edition* occupied James for the better part of four years, from July 1905 to March 1909, and proved to be a much more demanding job than he had anticipated. As he observed to Edith Wharton in March 1908, with a long way still to go, 'I cut out for myself a *colossal* task, really, in dealing with the mass of my productions as I undertook—all lucidly!—to do; & though I don't for a moment regret it the quantity & continuity of application required has been beyond what I had at all intimately measured.'[60] Assembling the Edition involved many distinct operations: selecting works for inclusion, deciding on the order of volumes and the thematic grouping of *nouvelles* and short stories, locating photographic subjects for the frontispieces and getting the photographs taken, revising the texts, correcting proofs. And, of course, writing the Prefaces. In his letters to friends and colleagues from this period, James complained about the Prefaces more than about any other aspect of the Edition, and he seems to have found them more difficult and less rewarding to write as he went on: his correspondence shows a steady decline in enthusiasm from the 'freshness of appetite' with which he imagined commencing the Prefaces in July 1905 (*HJL* 4:367) to a 'staleness of sensibility, in connection with them' that, as he confessed to Howells three years later, 'blocks out for the hour every aspect but of their being all done, and of their perhaps helping the Edition to sell two or three copies more!'[61]

---

[60] James to Edith Wharton, 7 March 1908; *HJEW* 89.
[61] James to Howells, 17 August 1908; *LFL* 425.

INTRODUCTION

At a comparatively early stage in the Edition's progress, James told Grace Norton that 'the real tussle is in writing the Prefaces (to each vol. or book,) which are to be long—very long!—and loquacious—and competent perhaps to *pousser à la vente* [boost sales]'; they were 'difficult to do—but I have found them of a jolly interest'.[62] When he wrote this letter in March 1907, he had composed only the first three Prefaces (to *Roderick Hudson*, *The Portrait of a Lady* and *The American*). In August of the same year, with the next Preface (to *The Princess Casamassima*) ready for dispatch, he told Owen Wister of the absorbing interest he found in 'decking out my Volumes with long—perhaps too long—Prefaces, in which it has much diverted me to air, once for all, my convictions, meditations, fantastications (whatever they may be abusively called,) on the great Craft & Mystery'.[63] The pace of composition was still fairly slow at this point, but soon picked up: in the twelve months from October 1907 to September 1908, James began a further twelve Prefaces and completed ten of them. That sustained intensity of work took a toll on him. In August 1908, he confessed to Howells that his 'actual attitude' about the Prefaces now was 'almost only, and quite inevitably, that they make, to me, for weariness; by reason of their number and extent'. He added: 'I've now but a couple more to write' (*LFL* 425). An unforeseen crisis at the end of the year would prolong that labour, as the call for an extra volume of tales to accommodate the overflow from his too generous lists of contents meant that he had to patch together one more Preface (to *The Author of Beltraffio*) from off-cuts of others.

The final phase of James's work on the Edition was overshadowed by his knowledge that the project was not succeeding commercially. The monetary motive had been an important factor in his decision to undertake the *New York Edition* at all; this represented a gamble, however, inasmuch as the labour of revision and preface-writing took up time which he could have given to more immediately remunerative projects. In September 1908, Pinker privately asked Charles Scribner for a remittance of any royalties owing from the Edition and reminded him that James's 'devotion to the preparation of the collected edition' had severely limited his income from

---

[62] James to Grace Norton, 5 March 1907; *LHJ* 2:72.
[63] James to Owen Wister, 28 August 1907; Owen Wister Papers, 1829–1966, Manuscript Division, Library of Congress, Washington, DC. General Correspondence, 1875–1936. Box 25.

other writing over the previous year.[64] He was told, with regret, that 'it has been possible as yet to place only a small sum to the credit of the author and [...] this did not on August 1st make good the payment made to The Macmillan Co. [for the use of titles to which they held the copyright].'[65] Pinker explained the situation to James and enclosed a statement of his account with the Scribners. James experienced this news as 'a greater disappointment than I have been prepared for; & after my long & devoted labour a great, I confess, & a bitter grief. I hadn't built *high* hopes—had done everything to keep them down; but feel as if comparatively I have been living in a fool's paradise. Is there *anything* for me at all? I don't quite make out or understand.'[66] There really was nothing. As he struggled at the close of the year to redistribute tales and adjust the corresponding Prefaces, James was still digesting the fact that the Edition had thus far brought him 'no reward whatever', 'no penny of profit'.[67] Amongst the conclusions he could have drawn was that the Prefaces had conspicuously failed as a selling-point, and indeed his attitude towards them appears to harden from this moment. In July 1909, he applauded Howells's decision not to write authorial prefaces for a projected 35-volume 'Library Edition' of his works: 'I can't but congratulate you on your wisdom in keeping out of so desperately arduous a job, which would have crowned your life with an intolerable fatigue. I found mine—of much scanter number—an almost insurmountable grind toward the end.' James worked up his resentment of that 'grind' into a mechanical figuration of preface-writing as alienated labour: 'What a monstrously & brutally stupid race is the avid & purblind one of Publishers, who seem never dimly to guess that authors can't to advantage be worked like ice-cream freezers or mowing-machines.'[68] He appeared to have forgot-

---

[64] Pinker to Charles Scribner, 16 September 1908; Princeton. According to the evidence collected by Michael Anesko, James's literary income in 1908 ($997) was lower than it had been for any year since 1872 (see *'Friction with the Market'*, pp. 175–8).
[65] Charles Scribner to Pinker, 6 October 1908; Princeton.
[66] James to Pinker, 20 October 1908; *LL* 468.
[67] James to Howells, 31 December 1908; *LFL* 430. That situation did not significantly improve with time. James wrote to Edith Wharton on 20 December 1911: 'A dismal document from the Scribners flanked by an appalling one from the Macmillans this a.m., tells me that the sales of my Edition, on which I counted for the bread of my vieux jours [old age], is rapidly & hopelessly falling to derisive figures' (*HJEW* 202–3).
[68] James to Howells, 23 July 1909; *LFL* 435.

ten already that the Prefaces had not in the first place been the Scribners' idea, but his own.

Though the *New York Edition* dominated James's horizon between 1905 and 1909, it was not the only thing he was working on during that period. The Prefaces shared his attention with a host of other projects – travel impressions, critical essays, short stories and other fictions, stage-plays, non-fictional revisions, note-taking for future works – as well as with all the other elements of the Edition. In correlating these activities with the writing of the Prefaces, I have drawn on existing research into the sequence of James's work on the Edition, wherever possible consulting copies of the documents that underpin the published chronologies.[69] The principal archival sources are the letters exchanged by James with the Scribners, Pinker and Coburn: his outgoing and incoming correspondence records when instalments of revised copy and completed Prefaces were delivered, and preserves much of his decision-making about the order and contents of volumes, as well as about the choice of subjects for frontispiece images and the taking of the photographs. I have also made use of a manuscript source not fully incorporated into any chronology of James's work in this period: the diary of his amanuensis Theodora Bosanquet, who started working with him at Lamb House in Rye, East Sussex in October 1907 and typed fourteen of the Prefaces from his dictation.[70] Bosanquet's diary supplies start- and end-dates for the dictation of many Prefaces, and records the daily progress of a few in detail; it also documents James's working routine, corroborating and adding texture to the account later given by Bosanquet in her memoir *Henry James at Work* (1924). As she recalled there, 'it was only between breakfast and luncheon that [James] undertook what he called "inventive" work', a category

---

[69] Hershel Parker, 'Henry James "In the Wood": Sequence and Significances of his Literary Labors, 1905–1907', *Nineteenth-Century Fiction* 38.4 (1984), 492–513; Ralph F. Bogardus, *Pictures and Texts: Henry James, A. L. Coburn, and New Ways of Seeing in Literary Culture* (Ann Arbor, MI: UMI Research Press, 1984), pp. 9–22; Anesko, 'Friction with the Market', pp. 141–62; Philip Horne, 'A Chronology: James during the Period of the New York Edition', in *Henry James and Revision*, pp. 325–57; and Ira B. Nadel, 'Henry James, Alvin Langdon Coburn, and the New York Edition: A Chronology', in McWhirter (ed.), *Henry James's New York Edition*, pp. 274–7.

[70] Priscilla Gibson Hicks draws attention to the significance of Bosanquet's diary in 'A Turn in the Formation of James's New York Edition: Criticism, the Historical Record, and the Siting of *The Awkward Age*', *Henry James Review* 16.2 (1995), 195–221.

that included the Prefaces: 'he gave the hours from half-past ten to half-past one to the composition of the prefaces which are so interesting a feature of the [New York] edition. In the evenings, he read over again the work of former years, treating the printed pages like so many proof-sheets of extremely corrupt text.'[71] That allocation of time meant that James was usually working on two different tasks concurrently, revising or reading proofs for the Edition in the evenings and in the mornings dictating either a Preface, some other original composition (a short story, play-text or essay) or letters. The diary further shows that James habitually worked with Bosanquet through weekends and Bank Holidays; it also records a few exceptional occasions – moments of crisis in the production of the Edition – when he kept her on beyond their regular hours and dictated into the evenings.

With a single exception (described in the Textual Introduction), the Jamesian archive contains no textual witnesses to the Prefaces prior to their publication in the *New York Edition* – no manuscripts, typescripts or proofs. Some compositional activities show up in the surviving sources more consistently than others. It is thus possible to determine with a fair degree of certainty such things as the sequence in which the Prefaces were composed, or the chronological relationship between the composition of a given Preface and the revision of the text or texts it refers to, or the alternation of Prefaces with other original compositions in this period; but *not* how – or, mostly, even when – James received, corrected and dispatched proofs for the Prefaces.[72] Enough survives to show that he *did* read proofs, and took care over them.[73] Indeed, it appears that significant textual work was sometimes done at this stage: in September 1908, for instance, worried that the Preface to *Daisy Miller* was too long, James asked the Scribners 'to

---

[71] Bosanquet, *Henry James at Work*, ed. Lyall H. Powers (Ann Arbor, MI: University of Michigan Press, 2006), p. 39.

[72] Questions about these specific aspects of the writing of the Prefaces have been raised by Hershel Parker: see *Flawed Texts and Verbal Icons: Literary Authority in American Fiction* (Evanston, IL: Northwestern University Press, 1984), pp. 107–9; 'Henry James "In the Wood"', 513; and 'Deconstructing *The Art of the Novel* and Liberating James's Prefaces', *Henry James Review* 14.3 (1993), 284–307; 289–90.

[73] For James's proof corrections to the Prefaces to *Roderick Hudson* and *The Portrait of a Lady*, see the Textual Introduction, pp. cliv–clv.

print it as it stands' and let him cut it in proof.[74] But the documentary record does not provide enough information to incorporate the handling of proofs consistently into a chronology of his work on the Edition.

The ordering of volumes in the *New York Edition* changed several times between 1905 and 1909, even after the first volumes had begun to appear. To minimize the potential for confusion in the chronological account that follows, I normally refer to volumes and their Prefaces *by title rather than by number* – and in the case of volumes of shorter fictions, by the italicized title of the tale that leads the volume. Thus, for example, the title *The Altar of the Dead* refers to the *New York Edition* volume which opens with the short story 'The Altar of the Dead'; this volume was originally planned by James as the sixteenth in a sequence of twenty-three, and published as the seventeenth of twenty-four (*NYE* XVII).

July 1905–August 1906: *Roderick Hudson, The Portrait of a Lady*

In his memorandum to the Scribners on 30 July 1905 James indicated that his 'preference would be to publish first, one after the other, four of the earlier novels, not absolutely in the order of their original appearance but with no detrimental departure from it; putting *The American*, that is, first, *Roderick Hudson* second, *The Portrait of a Lady* third, and *Princess Casamassima* fourth' (*HJL* 4:367). With what seems astonishing optimism, he undertook to deliver by 25 September 1905 – less than two months from the date of the memo – 'the two first books, completely revised [...] and with their respective Prefaces, of from 3000 to 5000 words' (*HJL* 4:368). Of course he could not meet that deadline, and in the event none of his initial specifications about the first two volumes of the Edition were adhered to: delivery dates, sequencing of titles and length of Prefaces would all change in due course.

James had begun textual work on the Edition in mid-Atlantic, as he returned from America in early July 1905 on board the Cunard liner SS *Ivernia*: according to his friend and fellow-passenger Elizabeth Robins he began to revise *Roderick Hudson* in a desultory way during the voyage.[75]

---

[74] James to Scribners, 25 September 1908; Princeton.
[75] Robins remembers James 'with "Roderick Hudson" lightly in hand lolling, yes, positively lolling, at length in a steamer chair on a sunlit deck at sea' (*Theatre and Friendship: Some Henry James Letters* (New York: G. P. Putnam's Sons, 1932), pp. 251, 274).

Once back in the UK he began to revise *The American* too, and found that the texts of both novels called for 'extreme (and very interesting) deliberation'.[76] The Prefaces testify to his fascination with the imaginative and material processes of textual revision: the relevant passages occur in the first and last Prefaces – to *Roderick Hudson* and *The Golden Bowl* – and were written respectively as James was revising his three earliest novels in the Edition and as he looked back over the collected series of his works (pp. 8–10, 263–77). For the first three novels, he revised longhand on specially prepared pages. Two or more copies of an early edition of each novel were cut up and the pages mounted on large sheets of paper, thus creating wide margins in which James wrote his emendations and insertions (see Figure 1); the 'pasting-up' was arranged by Pinker, and it put the texts 'into a form it is a joy to me to work upon'.[77]

James thought of this working method by analogy with Balzac's composition of his novels through multiple stages of elaborate proof correction.[78] As it had done for Balzac, here too it produced manuscripts which printers struggled to use as copy. The compositors at the Riverside Press would have great difficulty setting type from James's autograph revisions on the pasted-up pages of *Roderick Hudson*, and for the next two novels – *The American* and *The Portrait* – James employed a typist to create fair copies of the most heavily revised sheets before dispatching them to America, an

---

[76] James to Scribners, 30 July 1905; *HJL* 4:368.
[77] James to Pinker, 1 September 1905; Yale. A month before this James thanked Pinker 'for having the "Roderick Hudson" pages so beautifully put into condition for revision for me', 'a brilliant piece of work which will greatly help me' (7 August 1905; Yale). The revised sheets for *Roderick Hudson* no longer exist; those for *The American* and *The Portrait of a Lady* are held in the Houghton Library at Harvard University. James kept the 'original revised sheets' for *The American* and gave them to his agent 'as a curiosity of literature (at least of *my* literature)' (to Pinker, 27 June 1906; *LL* 436). They are published as *The American: The Version of 1877 Revised in Autograph and Typescript for the New York Edition of 1907, Reproduced in Facsimile from the Original in the Houghton Library, Harvard University*, introduction by Rodney G. Dennis (Ilkley: The Scolar Press, 1976).
[78] For James's comments on Balzac as a revising author in the Preface to *The Golden Bowl*, see p. 273, and notes 920 and 921 to the text.

INTRODUCTION

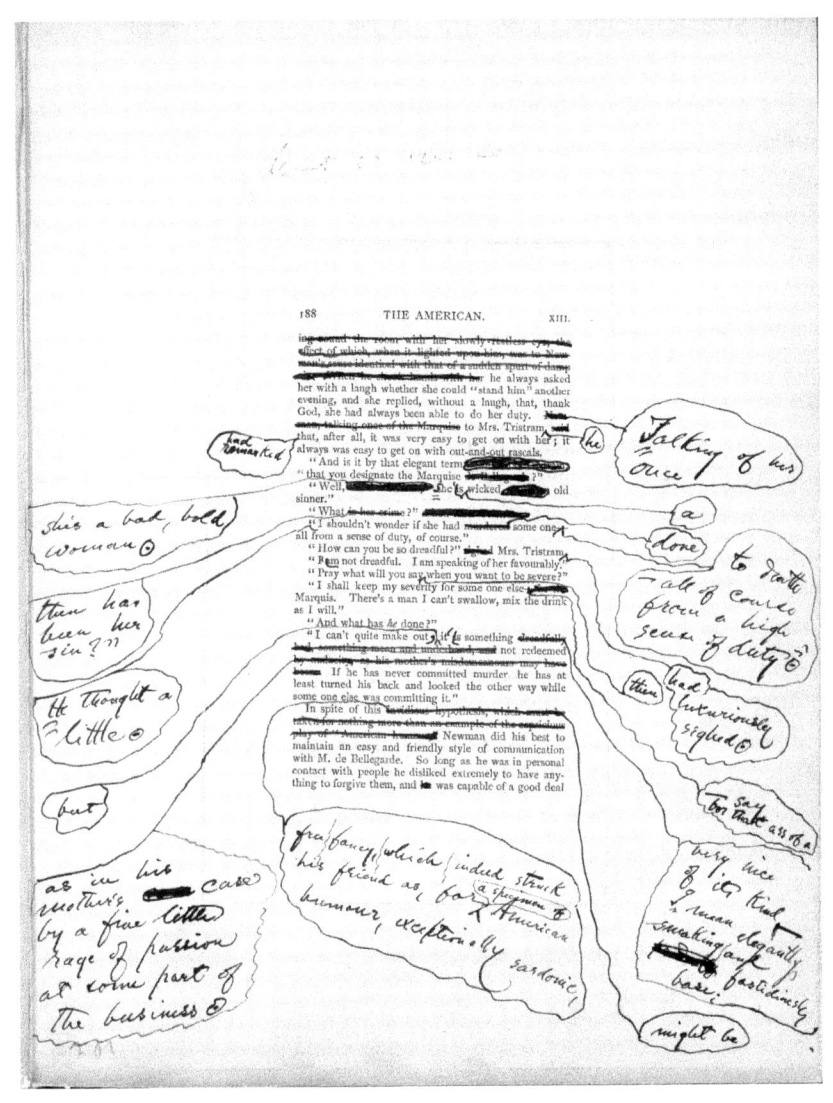

1 An example of Henry James's 1906–7 autograph revisions to *The American*, using pages of the two-volume *Collective Edition* text (London: Macmillan, 1883) pasted onto large sheets of paper. Houghton Library, Harvard University, GEN MS Am 1237. This sheet shows James's revisions to vol. I, p. 188 of the novel; one of these revisions in discussed in note 78 to the text in the present volume.

additional stage of textual work that caused significant delays in the early months of the Edition.[79]

The 25 September deadline passed amid tense negotiations – mostly handled by Pinker – with various publishers of James's works whose permission was needed to reprint titles planned for inclusion in the Edition.[80] Throughout the autumn and winter of 1905–6, James worked steadily at Lamb House, revising *Roderick Hudson* and *The American* and writing most of the travel essays that would become *The American Scene*.[81] He may also have begun to revise *The Portrait of a Lady*: he told his niece Peggy in November 1905 that since his return to the UK he had been 'revising with extreme minuteness three or four of my early works for the Edition Définitive'.[82] The revisions to *Roderick Hudson* were finished first, by early March 1906. According to the scheme set out in James's memo, textual work was now complete on what was to be the second novel in the Edition but not on the first, and James accordingly proposed a change to the order of volumes: *Roderick Hudson* was now to be 'the first book' in the *New York Edition*.[83] A version of the *Roderick* Preface evidently existed by this time, but it was on the point of being superseded. As James observed to Pinker on 9 March, sending him the final instalment of revised copy for the novel to mail to the Scribners: 'If you send R.H. now to New York I will follow it with its new Preface as soon as possible.'[84] It seems likely that James rejected the early version of the Preface because he had composed it on the assumption that *Roderick Hudson* was to be the second work in the Edition; as he would

---

[79] For the printing of the Edition at the Riverside Press of Houghton, Mifflin and Company, see below, pp. cv–cvi, cli–cliii.
[80] Anesko, '*Friction with the Market*', pp. 144–9; Horne, *Henry James and Revision*, pp. 3–11.
[81] James composed nine of these American essays between August 1905 and January 1906: 'New York Revisited', 'New York and the Hudson: A Spring Impression', 'New York: Social Notes', 'Boston', 'The Bowery and Thereabouts', 'Concord and Salem', 'The Sense of Newport', 'Philadelphia' and 'Washington' (see Horne, *Henry James and Revision*, pp. 330–2). 'New England: An Autumn Impression', which would become the first chapter of *The American Scene*, was written and serialized while James was in America (*North American Review*, April–June 1905).
[82] James to Margaret Mary ('Peggy') James, 3 November 1905; *LHJ* 2:37–8.
[83] Pinker to Scribners, 8 March 1906; Princeton.
[84] James to Pinker, 9 March 1906; Yale. The word 'new' in this sentence is an insertion above the line.

have realized now, the new order of volumes meant that the Preface to this novel had to launch the whole enterprise.

In March and early April 1906 James wrote two more American travel essays, 'Baltimore' and 'Richmond, Virginia'.[85] Towards the end of March, the Scribners complained to Pinker about the revised copy they had received for *Roderick Hudson*: the autograph 'interlineations and emendations' on James's pasted-up pages were 'so numerous and, from the point of view of "copy", so intricate' that asking the printers to set type from them was 'simply out of the question'.[86] James responded by offering to have the revised sheets of *Roderick* copied by 'a very good Typist whom I have employed for 20 years, & more, who is extremely expert & devoted & careful, & will, I think, be up to the job'; realizing that the revised sheets of *The American* would likewise need to be typed for clarity, he also proposed changing the order of volumes once more to open the Edition with *The Portrait of a Lady*, which he thought would need less revision.[87] In the event, the Scribners opted to continue setting up *Roderick* directly from James's copy and hoped 'that the future volumes will not be so difficult in this respect'.[88] On 9 May, therefore, James put *Roderick* back into first place in the Edition but changed the relative positions of his two other early novels: *The Portrait* would now come second and *The American* third. At the same time he promised to supply a new Preface to *Roderick* 'very quickly'; the Preface to *The Portrait* would follow 'with the copy' for that novel (*HJL* 4:402–3).

A new voice enters the transatlantic correspondence around this moment – the American literary critic and Scribner editor W. C. Brownell, who coordinated the production of the *New York Edition* and who would play a major role in determining its final form when at a late stage it became necessary to remake some of the volumes of short stories. James cannot have been unaware of an irony in this situation: the previous year, Brownell had published a long essay in the *Atlantic Monthly* which voiced serious reservations about the central principles of James's art and was severely

---

[85] James to Pinker, 7 April 1906; Yale.
[86] Scribners to Pinker, 27 March 1906; quoted in Michael Anesko, *Generous Mistakes: Incidents of Error in Henry James* (Oxford: Oxford University Press, 2017), p. 19.
[87] James to Pinker, 7 April 1906; Yale.
[88] Scribners to James, 27 April 1906; Princeton.

critical of his later work.[89] Scholars of the *New York Edition* have speculated about the effects of this circumstance on James's working relationship with his producing editor.[90] Responding to the Scribners' announcement that Brownell would be involved in the Edition, James gave nothing away: 'It gives me great pleasure to hear of Mr. Brownell's interest and attention, & I shall be grateful for any help he can give the enterprise.'[91] Whatever his feelings about the essay, he appears to have been able to make a mild joke of it when he encountered Brownell in America in 1905, as Brownell later told Edith Wharton: 'Did I ever write you how cunning H.J. was with me? After quite an allocution (very kindly as well as, of course, courtly) on my paper, he remarked as we separated: "Don't despair of me. I may do something yet!"'[92]

In the early summer of 1906, James was reading proofs for the revised text of *Roderick Hudson* and concurrently revising *The Portrait* and *The American*. He continued to write up the impressions of his American tour: by the end of June, he had finished another essay for *The American Scene* ('Charleston') and accepted a proposal from *Harper's Bazar* for a series of four short papers on 'The Speech of American Women', which he wrote during the second half of July.[93] The revisions of *The Portrait* were completed at the end of July. On 17 August, James returned the last corrected proofs for *Roderick Hudson*, and sent off the Preface to that novel (in its new version) and the Preface to *The Portrait*. No record survives of when exactly he composed those two Prefaces, but he certainly did so on the understanding that they were to accompany the first and second novels in the Edition;

---

[89] Brownell, 'Henry James', *Atlantic Monthly* 95 (April 1905), 496–519.
[90] See Hicks, 'A Turn in the Formation of James's New York Edition', 213–14; and Philip Horne, 'Henry James and the Cultural Frame of the New York Edition', in Nash ed., *The Culture of Collected Editions*, pp. 95–110; 103–7.
[91] Scribners to James, 27 April 1906; Princeton. James to Scribners, 9 May 1906; *HJL* 4:404.
[92] Brownell to Edith Wharton, 7 September 1905; Archives of Charles Scribner's Sons, C0101, Manuscripts Division, Department of Special Collections, Princeton University Library. Series 15: Letterbooks, 1854–1929 May 17, Subseries 15A: W. C. Brownell, 1904 October 26–1910 December 16, Box 884. I am grateful to Philip Horne for drawing my attention to this unpublished letter, not seen by him when he wrote the chapter cited in fn. 90.
[93] James to Pinker, 25 June 1906; Yale. James to Elizabeth Jordan, 27 June, 17, 20 and 27 July 1906; 'Henry James and the *Bazar* Letters', eds. Leon Edel and Lyall H. Powers, *Bulletin of the New York Public Library* 62.2 (February 1958), 75–103; 87–9.

in the event, *Roderick* and *The Portrait* would be separated by *The American* in the published sequence of volumes.

James remarked on the first two Prefaces:

They are a little long, you will see; but my whole idea of them was that they should be a 'feature', and I don't think they *would* be on much scanter terms. I find them very interesting to do, and promise you good ones for all the other books. [...] Of course you will select for them a type putting more on a page than in the rest of the text.[94]

The Prefaces to *Roderick Hudson* and *The Portrait* are approximately 5,800 and 6,600 words long respectively, a little under the eventual average length for the Prefaces (6,800 words) but still longer than James had proposed or the Scribners had expected – hence the choice of a smaller type.[95] James had approved a specimen page for the Edition several months before, writing that 'It seems to me handsome and charming, and abates nothing of the *dignity* of aspect which was, for this presentment of my books, my dream and desire.'[96] Realizing that the length of his Prefaces would compromise the Edition's dignity somewhat, he now urged the Scribners to 'Please put as pretty a type as possible for the Prefaces—though of course I recognise that their page must be fuller than that of the Text.'[97] When he received copies of the first published volumes at the end of the following year, James found them 'beautiful', and was able to be philosophical about the typographical subordination of the Prefaces to the main text: 'I am sorry the length of the Prefaces has demanded a type a little too small, but I "guess" they make up for that defect in other ways.'[98]

In August 1906 the Scribners wrote to express their 'absolute delight' with the 'charming' Prefaces to *Roderick Hudson* and *The Portrait of a Lady*, 'which seem to us not only to constitute a real feature of the edition but to

---

[94] James to Scribners, 17 August 1906; Princeton.
[95] By the following autumn James's sense of the length of the Prefaces had settled at 'some 7000 (seven thousand) words each' (James to William James, 17–18 October 1907; *CWJ* 3:349).
[96] James to Scribners, 9 May 1906; *HJL* 4:403.
[97] James to Scribners, 14 September 1906; Princeton. Anesko notes from the compositors' markings on the typescript of the *Portrait* Preface that the Scribners chose 'eleven-point Caslon type font' for the Prefaces (*Generous Mistakes*, p. vii).
[98] James to Pinker, 31 December 1907; *LL* 455.

furnish something very nearly, if not quite, unique in literature itself': 'we cannot imagine anything more enhancing to the interest of your readers and the attractiveness of the volumes'.[99] James plainly found these responses encouraging.[100] He thanked his publishers for their 'so cordial appreciation' of the first two Prefaces: 'In this I greatly rejoice, for I think I can promise you with confidence that the whole set will be at least up to that mark. I find it greatly interests me to do them, and that so far as material or "inspiration" for them goes, I have decidedly rather too inconveniently much than too little.'[101] He had registered the same sense of abundance at the close of the Preface to *The Portrait*: 'There is really too much to say' (p. 45).

April 1906–February 1907: *The American* and Alvin Langdon Coburn

In mid-August 1906, with the revisions to *Roderick Hudson* and *The Portrait of a Lady* complete and the Prefaces to those volumes dispatched, James assured the Scribners 'that a certain inevitable delay in getting off to you Copy for "The American" shall now imminently cease'.[102] In the event, the revised text of *The American* would not be ready for another six months. During this period, James worked on several projects unrelated to the *New York Edition*. In August and September, he sent two short stories to *Harper's Monthly Magazine*, 'The Jolly Corner' (under its original title 'The Second House') and 'Julia Bride'.[103] *The American Scene* was taking shape as a volume: the last chapter ('Florida') was written by the end of September, and James read book proofs the following month.[104] In October he began to negotiate with the editor of *Harper's Bazar*, Elizabeth Jordan, about contributing a chapter to her fictional project *The Whole Family: A Novel by Twelve Authors*.[105] While writing his *Harper's Bazar* papers on 'The Speech of American Women', in July he had also proposed to Jordan a matching

---

[99] Brownell to James, 28 August 1906; Princeton.
[100] The following year he told his brother William that the Scribners were 'pleased with [the Prefaces] to the extent quite—for publishers—of giving themselves away' and had 'pronounce[d] them "absolutely unique"!' (17–18 October 1907; *CWJ* 3:348–9).
[101] James to Scribners, 14 September 1906; Princeton.
[102] James to Scribners, 17 August 1906; Princeton.
[103] James to Frederick A. Duneka, 28 August 1906, 14 September 1906; *LL* 437, 438.
[104] James to Pinker, 27 September 1906, 4 and 12 October 1906; Yale.
[105] James to Elizabeth Jordan, 16 October 1906; 'Henry James and the *Bazar* Letters', 89.

series on 'The Manners of American Women', and he wrote those four papers between late October and mid-December.[106] As already noted, James ordinarily revised in the evenings and reserved his mornings for original composition, so these miscellaneous activities were not directly stealing time from the Edition: the slow pace of his revision of *The American* was the main cause of delay at this point. But that delay was compounded by the question of how the Edition should be illustrated, which had become a serious problem earlier in the year.

In his initial memo to the Scribners, James had requested 'a single very good plate in each volume, only one, but of thoroughly fine quality' (*HJL* 4:368). By the early summer of 1906, however, the only decision that had been made about these frontispieces was to use a photographic portrait of James in the first volume. This portrait was taken in London in April by the American photographer Alvin Langdon Coburn, who had met and photographed James in New York the year before. James was due to sit for Coburn again at Lamb House in early June. In the meantime, the Scribners noted that 'The question [...] of illustrations gives us some concern' and asked James for 'any information or suggestions' he could offer.[107] James's reply took for granted that they wanted photographic images rather than 'the common black-and-white drawing, of the magazine sort'; each frontispiece should represent 'some scene, object or locality [...] associated with some one or other of the tales in the volume, both consummately photographed and consummately reproduced'. But in the same breath he exclaimed at the apparently insuperable 'difficulty' of achieving those images: 'To *find* more than twenty such felicitous and characteristic bits, rather scattered about Europe as they really are, and then get them beautifully captured, represents more time [...] than I can now command for the purpose, so I merely stare at the prospect, as you see, in humiliated impotence' (*HJL* 4:408). James dictated this letter on 12 June, the day after his second portrait sitting with Coburn, but he appears not yet to have thought of the young photographer as a potential collaborator on the Edition. He wrote to Pinker on the same day: 'this preliminary *find* of the right, the representative or symbolic, scene

---

[106] James to Elizabeth Jordan, 31 October, 27 and 30 November, 18 December 1906; 'Henry James and the *Bazar* Letters', 89–91.
[107] Brownell to James, 1 June 1906; Princeton.

or object, really looms so monstrous, that I am hoping our friends [the Scribners] won't insist on it, or else take it into their own hands'.[108]

Pinker's response to this letter does not survive, but its drift can be inferred from the reply James sent him two days later:

> Your letter this morning received, on the question of illustrations, re-animates and inspires me. It isn't that I don't see what an ornament a thoroughly good one to each volume will be to the series, but only that I have been rather frightened and flustered at the thought of having to give time to the invention and preparation of them—in addition to providing (which, however, I *shall* enjoy!) some sixteen or seventeen perfect Introductions. The prospect clears beautifully if you will kindly write to our friends in New York that I will gladly aid and abet them with suggestion and sympathy on this ground, if they see their way to taking over, themselves, the *procuring* and, as it were, working out of the pictures. (14 June 1906; *HJL* 4:409)

The next day, Pinker told the Scribners that James understood 'that if he will only, as he goes through the books for revision, make a note of suitable subjects, no doubt you can secure photographs'.[109] With the exception of the first three novels, which by now were already revised in full or in part, James would in fact choose almost all the frontispiece subjects long before he made the corresponding revisions or wrote the Prefaces, and in doing so would start to make decisions about the allocation of his *nouvelles* and short stories into volumes of the Edition.

Coburn was brought on board as the Edition's photographer in July 1906, after another visit to Rye to photograph Lamb House. The lack of frontispiece images was now threatening to hold up production of the first volumes. As Brownell acknowledged receipt of the Prefaces to *Roderick Hudson* and *The Portrait* in late August, he reminded James that they still lacked the revised copy for *The American* and had 'but one photograph for the first group of three novels in four volumes, that is, your own portrait'.[110] *The American* was the sticking point in both connections: not only were the revisions not finished, its frontispiece required a Parisian subject and Coburn was unlikely to get to Paris until November.[111] Without

---

[108] James to Pinker, 12 June 1906; Yale.
[109] Pinker to Scribners, 15 June 1906; Princeton.
[110] Brownell to James, 28 August 1906; Princeton.
[111] James to Pinker, 7 September 1906; Yale.

INTRODUCTION

those materials, it would not be possible to begin publishing in the autumn of 1906 as the Scribners had hoped, since their plan involved issuing the Edition in regular two-volume instalments and thus required the copy for multiple volumes to be ready in advance of publication. Recognizing that they had been brought to an impasse, on 14 September James asked the Scribners 'to regard the beginning of publication as delayed to the earliest possible date after the New Year', and suggested February:

This will give me ample and valuable margin, and I can promise you that the Books would then begin appearing with the advantage and comfort of your having (I think even) half-a-dozen in your hands and quite ready. [...] I can assure you of four or five additional Books, finished as to revision, with their Prefaces and plate-subjects, for your definite Start.[112]

When February arrived, however, James had still not finished revising *The American*: as he mailed the last materials for the volume in the middle of the month he begged pardon for 'my long delay' and attributed it to 'the intrinsic difficulty of happy & right & *intimate* revision—which defied considerations of time: the process has had to be so extremely deliberate'.[113] The start date for publishing the Edition would be set back by another ten months in consequence. That second postponement got things back on schedule: by the time the first volumes appeared in December 1907, James was more or less where he had planned to be at the start of publication, having delivered revised copy and Prefaces for four more books (*The Princess Casamassima, The Tragic Muse, The Awkward Age* and *The Spoils of Poynton*) and nearly finished work on a fifth (*What Maisie Knew*).

The English and Continental frontispiece subjects were all found during the autumn and winter of 1906–7.[114] James sent Coburn to Paris and Venice with elaborate instructions for seeking out and photographing particular buildings and views, and eagerly accompanied him in search of most of the London subjects. Revisions to *The American* continued, slowly, throughout this period. After the printers' difficulties in setting type for *Roderick Hudson*, James decided to have his revised copy for *The American* 'all typed

---

[112] James to Scribners, 14 September 1906; Princeton.
[113] James to Scribners, 15 February 1907; Princeton.
[114] See the Chronology of Composition and Production.

LXIX

over' in London before mailing it to America; and revision of the second half of the novel was held up in December when his regular copyist fell ill and Pinker had to find him a replacement.[115] Once again, another task filled the gap: James composed his chapter ('The Married Son') for Elizabeth Jordan's multi-author novel *The Whole Family* in January.[116] Revised and fair-typed copy for the second half of *The American* was finally dispatched to the Scribners on 14 February, followed the next day by the novel's Preface. There is no record of when James composed the Preface relative to his revision of the novel.

Coburn sailed for New York the same month and took with him prints for the Scribners of the frontispiece images already selected by James; he also had instructions from James about a couple more photographs 'to be taken over there'.[117] With this, as they all supposed, the photographic work on the Edition would be complete; as it turned out, an additional American frontispiece would be needed later on, when the total number of volumes grew to twenty-four. After a busy working winter, James left England in mid-March and spent four months visiting friends in France and Italy. His absence would occasion a further delay later in the year, when proofs for the Prefaces to *Roderick Hudson* and *The Portrait* arrived at Lamb House and, 'through a stupid oversight', were not sent on after him; he found them on his return from the Continent in July and apologetically dispatched them to the Scribners, adding that 'The corrected Preface (Proof) to *The American* has also just gone to you.'[118] Around this time, a final change was made to the publication order of the first three novels in the Edition, though it is not

---

[115] James to Pinker, 17 December 1906; Yale.
[116] James to Elizabeth Jordan, 2, 11, 22 and 25 January 1907; 'Henry James and the *Bazar* Letters', 91–4.
[117] James to Scribners, 15 February 1907; Princeton. As Hicks points out, it can be inferred that by this moment 'James had selected eight short fictions that must come under *separate* covers, in each of the eight agreed volumes [of his *nouvelles* and short stories]', and may thus already have begun to think about the rationale for his groupings of shorter fictions ('A Turn in the Formation of James's New York Edition', 212). Contents lists for those volumes were not drawn up for the Scribners for another twelve months, and in them James explicitly associates the frontispiece subject for each volume with a particular story. Eight had been the maximum number of *NYE* volumes allocated to such works in the July 1905 memo, and James accepted it as the actual number on 6 May 1906 (*HJL* 4:367, 403).
[118] James to Scribners, 17 July 1907; Princeton.

clear when or why the decision was taken or whether it resulted in proof changes to any of the Prefaces. James confirmed the new volume order on 2 August 1907, replying to a letter of 22 July from the Scribners which does not appear to survive: *Roderick Hudson* would remain as the first volume, but *The American* would now occupy the second and *The Portrait* the third and fourth. *The Princess Casamassima* would follow as the fifth and sixth.[119]

March–December 1907: *The Princess Casamassima*, *The Tragic Muse* and Theodora Bosanquet, *The Awkward Age*, *The Spoils of Poynton*

As he mailed the *American* Preface to the Scribners on 15 February 1907, James had promised that work on the next volumes would 'go fast & straight' and that he would 'quickly' deliver revised copy for *The Princess Casamassima*, *The Tragic Muse* and *The Awkward Age*.[120] This letter is the first indication of a significant change in the structure of the *New York Edition*. The scheme originally set out by James in his memo of 30 July 1905 had specified an opening sequence of four 'earlier novels' (*The American*, *Roderick Hudson*, *The Portrait of a Lady* and *The Princess Casamassima*), followed by 'three or four volumes of the longer of my short stories', then *The Tragic Muse*, then 'three or four more volumes' of short stories, and then four 'later novels' (*The Awkward Age*, *The Wings of the Dove*, *The Ambassadors* and *The Golden Bowl*) (HJL 4:367–8). James would appear to have abandoned that disposition of volumes if he was now proposing to revise *The Tragic Muse* and *The Awkward Age* before assembling any volumes of shorter fictions; there is no extant record of when he did so, and no formal statement of the new scheme, but the new volume order can be inferred from the sequence of his subsequent work on the Edition and his numbering of volumes in letters to the Scribners.[121]

At the beginning of March 1907, James was halfway through *The Princess* and finding that, as he had predicted, the revision was going 'much faster now'.[122] He took the novel abroad with him in the spring and finished

---

[119] James to Scribners, 2 August 1907; Princeton.
[120] James to Scribners, 15 February 1907; Princeton.
[121] Hicks discusses this structural change in detail in 'A Turn in the Formation of James's New York Edition'.
[122] James to Pinker, 5 March 1907; Yale.

INTRODUCTION

revising it in Paris and Rome. On his return to Lamb House in July, he moved on to *The Tragic Muse*, which he had completely revised by 6 August. The revision of these novels appears to have gone so fast that it outstripped composition of the corresponding Prefaces. When James mailed the Preface to *The Princess* at the end of August, he had already begun to revise *The Awkward Age*, the next novel but one in the sequence of volumes; he told the Scribners that he would supply the Prefaces to *The Tragic Muse* and *The Awkward Age* with the balance of revised copy for the latter book.[123] It is not clear when exactly the *Princess* Preface was composed, but its opening recollections of walking in London may connect it to the three days James spent shortly before its dispatch (22–24 August 1907) making notes in the City of London for a non-fiction book he was contracted to write for Macmillan and Co.[124] Once again, the Scribners were delighted with the material he was sending them. As Brownell wrote, 'the preface to the "Princess Casamassima" [...] confirms, if anything were needed to do so, our already strong conviction of the advantage to the edition of these unique prefaces'; it made the firm 'look forward with real impatience' to the next one.[125]

James continued revising *The Awkward Age* and started on the title story for the first volume of shorter fictions, *The Spoils of Poynton*. At some point in September or early October, he composed a version of the *Tragic Muse* Preface. He would presently rewrite it, however, in the wake of an important change to his domestic working conditions. This was the arrival of a new amanuensis: Theodora Bosanquet, engaged via a London secretarial

---

[123] James to Scribners, 28 August 1907; Princeton.

[124] James gave another day to this research in the autumn (8 October 1907). He would postpone delivery of the book, provisionally entitled *London Town*, the following spring, pleading the overwhelming pressure of work on the New York Edition (James to Frederick Macmillan, 5 April 1908; *LL* 459–61), but he did not take it up again and it was never written. James's 'Notes for "London Town"' are printed in *CN* 273–8.

[125] Brownell to James, 27 September 1907; Princeton. The Scribners would find the next two Prefaces (to *The Tragic Muse* and *The Awkward Age*) 'as absorbing as their predecessors had foreshadowed', and told James that 'The receipt of each one of these prefaces renews our conviction of the extraordinary and unique interest which they will add to the New York Edition, not only directly, as expository of the works to which they relate, but for the indirect interpretation they contain of the art of the novelist' (Brownell to James, 25 November 1907; Princeton).

INTRODUCTION

agency in late August, who began work for him at Lamb House on 11 October.[126] James had been dictating to typists since the late 1890s. His most recent long-term amanuensis, Mary Weld, had held the post from April 1901 until his departure for America in August 1904, but she married while he was abroad and did not come back to work for him.[127] Very little evidence survives of James's arrangements for dictation in the interval between his return to the UK in July 1905 and Bosanquet's arrival in October 1907 – a period during which he composed the final versions of four Prefaces and drafted a fifth. Pinker told the Scribners that he had typed the 30 July 1905 memorandum himself from James's dictation.[128] James was just back in the UK at this point and presumably had not had time to engage a typist. That he eventually did so appears from a reference in a letter he wrote fourteen months later to Elizabeth Robins about a set of notes he wanted to make on a draft of the first act of her play *Votes for Women* (1907): 'What I want to do is to *dictate*, for you, in type, some groping ghost of a Scenario. But my amanuensis is away till *Tuesday*. But after Tuesday!'[129] This letter was dated from Lamb House on Friday 9 November 1906. James's amanuensis evidently returned as planned, and over four days from Tuesday 13 November he dictated a long letter to Robins comprising forty-nine pages of commentary on her draft.[130] I have found no other explicit account of James dictating to an amanuensis during this period, but Leon Edel is surely wrong to claim that he 'had required no typist during the revising of the New York Edition'.[131] James was doing more than just revising in this period, and it is hard to believe that without access to typists he could have produced so much original work after July 1905: twelve chapters of *The American Scene*, two series of papers for *Harper's Bazar*, two long stories ('The Jolly Corner' and 'Julia Bride') and his chapter of *The Whole Family*, plus the early Prefaces. His professional correspondence during these months contains numerous typed letters besides the commentary-letter to Elizabeth Robins.

[126] Edel, *Henry James: The Master 1901–1916*, pp. 367–9.
[127] Ibid., pp. 93–5, 238.
[128] Pinker to Scribners, 1 August 1905; Princeton.
[129] James to Elizabeth Robins, 9 November 1906; in Robins, *Theatre and Friendship*, p. 259.
[130] See Joanne E. Gates, 'Henry James's Dictation Letter to Elizabeth Robins: "The Suffragette Movement Hot from the Oven"', *Henry James Review* 31.3 (2010), 254–63.
[131] Edel, *Henry James: The Master 1901–1916*, p. 367.

On the evidence of Bosanquet's memoir, moreover, it seems unlikely that James could have done any of this typing for himself: as she recalls, he observed her initial 'struggles' with his unfamiliar Remington typewriter patiently but 'helplessly, for he was one of the few men without the smallest pretension to the understanding of a machine'.[132]

The Remington was a recent acquisition: James told Bosanquet shortly before she arrived in Rye that he had just bought 'a new & apparently admirable' model.[133] It seems to have marked a new beginning in his working routine – or, rather, a return to tried methods after a lengthy interruption. After a successful first week's dictation to his 'new excellent amanuensis', on 18 October 1907 James told his brother William that he had been working without a typist for the last 'eight months' (*CWJ* 3:348–9). If he was right about the amount of time, that would mean he had had no typist to dictate to since the middle of February. That was also when the Preface to *The American* was mailed to the Scribners, and it may be that the temporary unavailability of an amanuensis after that moment was part of the reason why his revision of *The Princess Casamassima*, *The Tragic Muse* and *The Awkward Age* could get so far ahead of the Prefaces to those novels. Other comments in this letter to William support the inference that, from late July or early August 1905 until the early spring of 1907, James had been dictating to temporary amanuenses – perhaps getting them from Mary Petherbridge's Secretarial Bureau, the same London agency that had found Mary Weld for him and would find Bosanquet also.[134] The 'young, boyish Miss Bosanquet', James wrote to his brother, 'is worth all the other (females) that I have had put together, & [...] confirms me in the perception, afresh—after eight months without such an agent—that for certain, for most, kinds of diligence & production, the intervention of the agent is, to *my* perverse

---

[132] Bosanquet, *Henry James at Work*, p. 34.

[133] James to Bosanquet, 9 October 1907; Theodora Bosanquet Papers, Houghton Library, Harvard University, MS Eng 1213 (04).

[134] For The Secretarial Bureau and its proprietor, the librarian and indexer Mary Petherbridge (1870–1940), see Margaret Anderson, 'Some Personalities', *The Indexer: The International Journal of Indexing* 7.1 (1970), 19–23; 22–3. H. Montgomery Hyde identifies The Secretarial Bureau as the agency through which James employed both Weld and Bosanquet (*Henry James at Home* (London: Methuen & Co., 1969), pp. 148–50, 156–7).

constitution, an intense aid & a true economy. There is no *comparison!*' (*CWJ* 3:348–9).

Scattered comments in Bosanquet's diary suggest that since his return from America James had employed a series of short-term typists at Lamb House, and had found them unsatisfactory. On her second day with him, he remarked 'that his former amanuenses had never at all fathomed what he wrote & made many "exceedingly fantastic mistakes"'; he referred again to '"the faults of my previous amanuenses"' at the end of her first week; and after five weeks he told her that she 'typed faster than any of his previous amanuenses—"Faster much than the snail-paced young ladies"'.[135] A Rye neighbour, Mrs Granville Bradley, informed Bosanquet early on that James 'had dismissed one or two amanuenses because they dared to suggest things!'[136] And her agency chief, Mary Petherbridge, offered to write to 'Mrs Kingdon—formerly Miss Weld, my pre-predecessor here & get her to ask folks to call' – that is, get her to encourage her friends in Rye to call on the person who was now doing her old job.[137] If Mary Weld was Bosanquet's 'pre-predecessor' in this role, then other typists – more recent predecessors – must have been employed at Lamb House since Weld's departure.

Taking all this evidence into account, it is reasonable to suppose that James dictated the Prefaces to *Roderick Hudson*, *The Portrait of a Lady* and *The American* to temporary amanuenses. The Preface to *The Princess Casamassima* and the first version of the *Tragic Muse* Preface, however, which were composed after the middle of February 1907, were probably written longhand – a method James would continue to use for certain types of material even after he had Bosanquet to dictate to.[138] A week before her arrival in October 1907, he told the Scribners that he was 'only waiting for the Copyist to send me home the Preface for The Tragic Muse to despatch it to you'.[139] As we have seen, James had employed London typists the year before to make clean copies of the revised sheets of *The American* and *The Portrait of a Lady*, and it would seem that he had sent an autograph text

---

[135] ODTB 12, 19 October, 18 November 1907.
[136] ODTB 14 October 1907.
[137] ODTB 21 November 1907.
[138] Bosanquet records that James 'was well aware that the manual labour of writing was his best aid to desired brevity' when composing short stories and plays (*Henry James at Work*, p. 35).
[139] James to Scribners, 5 October 1907; Princeton.

of the first *Tragic Muse* Preface to be copied in the same way. By the time Bosanquet took up her post, he had presumably received the typed copy and found that it needed reworking, or seen an irresistible opportunity to rework it in his preferred medium: a typescript of the Preface would thus have become the textual basis for his dictated revisions. Bosanquet noted on her first day at work that James was 'dictating prefaces to a revised edition of his earlier works—and this morning was devoted to one on "The Tragic Muse"—in the tone of a personal reminiscence'. He seems to have started again at the beginning: in the same diary entry, Bosanquet mentioned a reference to W. M. Thackeray's novel *The Newcomes* (1854-5) which occurs not quite a third of the way into the published text of the Preface.[140] They spent just three mornings on it. Later Prefaces would take much longer to dictate, but that would make sense if on this occasion James was working from an existing text; and indeed Bosanquet noticed that he began to dictate the next Preface, to *The Awkward Age*, 'not from previously written matter but straight away'.[141] Work on the *Tragic Muse* Preface was completed by half past twelve on the third morning of dictation (a Sunday), and James sent the copy to the Scribners three days later.

After this atypical beginning, dictation of the Preface to *The Awkward Age* established what would become for Bosanquet a familiar rhythm of work. James was in effect composing aloud, and Bosanquet noted that he went 'very slowly', sometimes painfully so: 'The nervous tension of the situation when he is "agonising" for a word is appalling.'[142] Work on this Preface took nine mornings at most, including two mornings going over what had been dictated so far, either to correct typos or make revisions, or both.[143] Perhaps on account of the novelty of her situation, Bosanquet appears to have taken a special interest in the composition of the *Awkward Age* Preface, and her diary entries track its progress in some detail. On the first day of dictation, she noted that James 'goes in, more than I had noticed for alliteration—& I didn't quite like "a fine purple peach" which occurred this morning. Peaches

---

[140] ODTB 11 October 1907.
[141] ODTB 14 October 1907.
[142] ODTB 14 October 1907.
[143] On 15 October, Bosanquet noted: 'We spent a lot of time correcting yesterday's work—didn't get on *very* much further'; and on 21 October, James 'spent the morning revising the past week's work' (ODTB).

have too *mellow* a colour to be called purple.'[144] That alliterative formula occurs in the second paragraph of the Preface. The next day, author and typist conferred about the feasibility of 'having accents put on the machine': the question may have arisen in the course of 'correcting yesterday's work', as the only word in the published text of the Preface that needs diacritical accents is the French '*idée-mère*', which occurs in the third paragraph.[145] At such moments, Bosanquet's diary can be usefully contrasted with the accounts of progress James gave to his publishers – although it must be remembered that we do not have the original typescript of this Preface, only the published text, so our judgements must remain speculative. On Tuesday 15 October, James told the Scribners that the *Awkward Age* Preface was 'two-thirds written & will be finished within this week'.[146] Was this optimistic or disingenuous of him? He had only begun dictating the Preface the day before and would complete it the following Tuesday (22 October), and judging from Bosanquet's record of verbal markers they were not yet halfway through the text.[147] James may have been misled by the rapidity of his dictated revision of the *Tragic Muse* Preface; or he may simply have found that he had more to say than he first thought, so that what looked like 'two-thirds written' after two days would turn out to have been not quite half-done a week later. If so, that would be entirely characteristic of his imaginative processes. He would overstate the progress of subsequent Prefaces more drastically than this.

The Preface to *The Awkward Age* was mailed to the Scribners on 25 October. James commented to his publishers: 'It is, alas, a little longer than that of *The Tragic Muse*—but not, I hope, fatally!'[148] He now transferred his attention to the dictation of a play, begun on 23 October in response to the renewal of an old request from the actor-manager Johnston Forbes-Robertson for a stage version of his story 'Covering End' (1898); this would become *The High Bid*, and James worked on it with Bosanquet until the

---

[144] ODTB 14 October 1907.
[145] ODTB 15 October 1907.
[146] James to Scribners, 15 October 1907; Princeton.
[147] The next marker noted by Bosanquet – the word 'typographically' – occurs in the seventh of the Preface's fifteen paragraphs (p. 84). Its dictation is an incident in her diary entry for 17 October 1907, two days after James wrote to the Scribners (ODTB).
[148] James to Scribners, 25 October 1907; Princeton.

second week in November.[149] At the same time he continued to revise stories for the next volume of the Edition, *The Spoils of Poynton*. The old excitement of writing for the theatre, lost to James since the mid-1890s, appears to have revived for him now, and in quick succession he began work on dramatic adaptations of two more of his stories: first a scenario for a play based on 'The Chaperon' (1891), a story which he had just finished revising for the Edition; and then a stage version of 'Owen Wingrave' (1892), entitled *The Saloon* and intended as 'a one-act curtain-raiser to go with *The High Bid*'.[150] This work occupied him until the start of December, when he appears to have come guiltily back to the neglected Edition: he remarked to Bosanquet that the Preface to *The Spoils of Poynton* was '"screaming to be written"'.[151] Dictation of that Preface began on 5 December and went slowly, at least to begin with: on the third day, Bosanquet noted that 'an arduous (for him) morning's work' had drawn from James the comment, '"Its [sic] so difficult not to do things 'cheaply'"'.[152] She does not record when the *Spoils* Preface was completed. James mailed it to the Scribners on 12 December, and announced that the next Preface, to *What Maisie Knew*, 'follows, with revised Copy, immediately'.[153] He did not immediately begin to dictate the *Maisie* Preface, however, but returned to his theatrical work and spent the remaining mornings of the old year dictating *The High Bid* and *The Saloon*.[154]

January–March 1908: *What Maisie Knew, The Wings of the Dove, The Ambassadors, The Aspern Papers*

The first two volumes of the *New York Edition* – *Roderick Hudson* and *The American* – were published in America on 14 December 1907. James's copies arrived at Lamb House towards the end of December, and on New Year's Eve he wrote to the Scribners that he was 'delighted with the appearance, beauty and dignity of the Book' and 'serenely content' with the progress of

---

[149] ODTB 23 October–12 November 1907.
[150] ODTB 14 November 1907. CP 607.
[151] ODTB 3 December 1907.
[152] ODTB 5, 7 December 1907.
[153] James to Scribners, 12 December 1907; Princeton.
[154] ODTB 12–31 December 1907.

the Edition: 'The whole is a perfect felicity, so let us go on rejoicing' (*HJL* 4:484). At this juncture, however, the course of his work was altered by a misunderstanding about the order of the remaining volumes. The confusion arose from the publicity materials which had accompanied James's copies of *NYE* I–II. As he pointed out to the Scribners on 31 December, they had just sent him an advertising circular for the *New York Edition* which announced 'the later Long Novels' – *The Wings of the Dove*, *The Ambassadors* and *The Golden Bowl* – 'as publishable directly after *The Awkward Age*' and without any intervening volumes of 'Shorter Things':

> This I hadn't quite understood to be your view; but, on consideration, I am entirely ready to make it my own […]. I shall send you next at once the Preface and Text of *What Maisie Knew* and so forth, because I have them all but ready; but after that I shall send you straight the revised *Wings of the Dove* and its two successors. (*HJL* 4:484–5)

James had evidently been expecting the volumes following *The Awkward Age* to contain a selection of his *nouvelles* and short stories; *The Spoils of Poynton* was the first of those volumes. It is not clear whether he was already revising the texts for *What Maisie Knew* by this time, but the Preface was certainly not 'all but ready' on 31 December: according to Bosanquet, James would not begin to dictate it until 2 January. *Maisie* must, nevertheless, have been sufficiently present to his imagination as the next volume of shorter fictions for him to hold his course and compose that Preface now instead of turning immediately to *The Wings of the Dove*. Work on the *Maisie* Preface was slow and considerably interrupted: James appears to have taken eight or nine mornings over it across seventeen days, with a six-day absence from Rye in the midst and shorter breaks for catching up with correspondence and reworking a draft of *The Saloon*. At one point he told Bosanquet that 'this preface […] was giving him more trouble than all the others'.[155] It was finished at last on 18 January; revised copy for the title story to the volume was dispatched that day, but James held on to the Preface for four days more, eventually mailing it with the revised copy for 'The Pupil' and *In the Cage*.[156]

---

[155] ODTB 8 January 1908.
[156] James to Scribners, 18, 22 January 1908; Princeton.

INTRODUCTION

James now restated to the Scribners what he understood to be the plan they were all following as regards the sequence of *New York Edition* volumes:

> I am aware that the publication of my three latest Novels will take precedence of this volume [*Maisie*], as well as of that of the *Spoils of Poynton &c* (already sent you, with Preface;) but I let the present batch of Copy go to you because I had prepared it before I had definitely embraced the fact in question (which I now see is much the best arrangement,) & it will be in your hands for later use.[157]

In accordance with that understanding, he now began to dictate the Preface to *The Wings of the Dove*, starting on 19 January (a Sunday) and continuing for a further seven mornings apparently without a break; Bosanquet noted that the Preface was finished on 26 January. On just the fourth day of dictation, confusingly, James wrote to the Scribners: 'The Preface to "The Wings of the Dove" has already gone to the copyist.'[158] It is not clear from the documentary record what occurred at this point. James may have been over-stating his progress to the Scribners and implying that he had finished a Preface which in fact he was still dictating. It is equally possible that after four mornings' dictation he believed that he had produced a complete draft of the *Wings* Preface, though this would have been quick work compared with the other Prefaces he had dictated to Bosanquet from scratch. Perhaps more likely, he may have dictated a portion of the Preface and immediately made autograph revisions on the typescript, so that he would now need a clean copy of that material to correct for dispatch or to revise further. Bosanquet herself would not begin to copy for James until the middle of February, so the dictated typescript was presumably sent from Rye to a copyist in London, and James pressed on with dictating the rest of the Preface while he waited for the copy to be sent back. In any case, Bosanquet definitely records a composite process of revision and new dictation on the final morning of work, four days later: 'Mʳ James sat reading over & revising the preface till about 12.30 & then dictated a page & a half to finish it!'[159]

---

[157] James to Scribners, 18 January 1908; Princeton.
[158] James to Scribners, 22 January 1908; Princeton.
[159] ODTB 26 January 1908.

LXXX

INTRODUCTION

James dictated the Preface to *The Wings of the Dove* concurrently with his revision of the novel, but the two processes were not quite in step. He was working from a copy of the two-volume Scribner first edition of *The Wings*, and on 27 January he dispatched revised copy for the first volume (containing Books First to Fifth), to be followed 'immediately' by the balance of copy and the Preface.[160] The completed Preface went to the Scribners three days later, followed the next day by revised copy for 'the First Half of the Second Volume' (the mid-point of that volume comes approximately two chapters into Book Eighth).[161] The remaining revised copy for the second volume would not be dispatched for another nine months, however. In February 1908, James's understanding of the structure of the *New York Edition* would shift once more, leaving the novel stranded in mid-revision. It would thus appear that he composed the Preface to *The Wings of the Dove* having only revised about three-quarters of the text.

On 27 January, immediately after he finished dictating the *Wings* Preface, James began the Preface to the next of his long novels, *The Ambassadors*. After three and a half mornings' work on that with Bosanquet, a letter arrived from Forbes-Robertson about cuts to *The High Bid*, which James 'attended to then and there', presumably setting the Preface aside to do so.[162] Bosanquet's diary breaks off here for nearly three weeks. James was away from Rye during the first two weeks of February, attending rehearsals of *The High Bid* in London (*CP* 550). I infer that the *Ambassadors* Preface was left unfinished at the end of January 1908.[163] This pause in Edition work coincided with another change of direction for James. At some point in early February, a letter arrived from Brownell explaining that the advertising circular sent with James's copies of *Roderick Hudson* and *The American*

---

[160] James to Scribners, 27 January 1908; Princeton.
[161] James to Scribners, 31 January 1908; Princeton.
[162] ODTB 30 January 1908.
[163] Michael Anesko assumes that it was 'completed' on 29 January 1908 after 'just three days' of dictation (*Generous Mistakes*, p. 89). This seems unlikely: apart from the Preface to *The Tragic Muse*, which James re-dictated from an existing typescript in three mornings, there is no record of a Preface being completed in so short a time. On the second day of dictation, Bosanquet noted that James was 'going ahead finely with "The Ambassadors" preface', but her diary entry for the following day does not sound as though it was close to completion: 'M' James remarked that there were *too* many things to say about "The Ambassadors" they got "congested"' (ODTB 28 and 29 January 1908).

contained an error 'for which we can hardly account', and that – as James had supposed to begin with – the Scribners still wished the Edition to proceed from a series of earlier novels concluding with *The Awkward Age* to eight volumes of *nouvelles* and stories, and then to the three late novels.[164] James acknowledged the correction on 12 February; acting accordingly, he undertook to 'send you next the 3ᵈ Volume (revised Copy & Preface for it) of the group of Shorter Novels & Tales [*The Aspern Papers*], leaving the last, the later (at least) Novels to come after this series has spent itself'.[165] In his letter of 29 January, Brownell appears to have been trying to steer James towards accepting a chronological order for his volumes of shorter fictions, as well as for the overall trajectory of the novels in the Edition. James quietly ignored whatever pressure he may have felt from his editor and held to his original plan of making 'a fresh grouping or classification' of his stories, 'a placing together, from series to series, of [...] those that will conduce to something of a common effect' (*HJL* 4:366); that intention was already embodied in the non-chronological arrangement of the *Spoils* and *Maisie* volumes, which were complete and delivered by this time.[166]

Back in Rye on 15 February, James started to dictate the Preface to *The Aspern Papers* but was 'seized with influenza that afternoon', and while he was ill Bosanquet 'put in two mornings copying the previous preface': presumably this was the Preface to *The Ambassadors*, or as much of it as he had dictated the previous month.[167] This was the first copying she had done for him. Work on the *Aspern Papers* Preface would encounter further interruptions. James resumed dictation on 22 February after a break of six days – three days of illness and convalescence, two mornings spent dictating an additional passage for *The High Bid* at Forbes-Robertson's request, and one morning drawing up lists of contents for the remaining volumes of shorter fictions; the following week he made a trip to London and did some more work on the insertion for *The High Bid*.[168] The Preface was finished at last on 4 March and given to Bosanquet to copy; it was dispatched to the Scribners

[164] Brownell to James, 29 January 1908; Princeton.
[165] James to Scribners, 12 February 1908; Princeton.
[166] See Hicks, 'A Turn in the Formation of Henry James's New York Edition', 209–11.
[167] ODTB 20 February 1908.
[168] ODTB 20–28 February 1908.

on 13 March. James had already sent the Scribners full revised copy for this volume: unusually for the volumes of shorter fictions, the *Aspern Papers* Preface was thus apparently dictated on the basis of a complete revision of the stories it referred to.

March–April 1908: *The Reverberator, Lady Barbarina*

At the end of January 1908, writing to correct the misapprehension caused by the Scribners' erroneous advertising circular, Brownell had also asked James for 'an accurate forecast of the contents of each of the remaining volumes of shorter works in its order'.[169] James replied on 12 February from London, where *The High Bid* was in rehearsal: his 'list of the intended Contents of the Eight volumes of shorter things' was 'all made out', but it was at Lamb House and he would have to wait 'till I have put my hand on that Document'.[170] He could not put his hand on it without reworking it: according to Bosanquet he spent a morning later in the month 'with lists of his shorter Tales arranging them as they are to be finally published'.[171] The contents for the five volumes in question – *The Reverberator, Lady Barbarina, The Lesson of the Master, The Altar of the Dead* and *Daisy Miller* – were set out for the first time in a long letter to the Scribners dated 21–26 February, and the Prefaces to those volumes were dictated between March and September 1908. The constitution of some volumes changed several times over that period; for the sake of clarity and relevance, in the following sections I shall focus mainly on the version or versions of each contents list that were valid *at the time the corresponding Preface was composed*, so far as they can be reconstructed from James's correspondence with the Scribners.

James began dictating the Preface to *The Reverberator* on 5 March 1908, immediately after completing the Preface to *The Aspern Papers*. On 11 March, after six days of apparently uninterrupted dictation, Bosanquet noted that James 'revised the first part of his preface by way of a little refreshment as he was feeling weary'.[172] It would presently need structural alteration too, as the contents of this volume changed several times before

---

[169] Brownell to James, 29 January 1908; Princeton.
[170] James to Scribners, 12 February 1908; Princeton.
[171] ODTB 21 February 1908.
[172] ODTB 11 March 1908.

the end of April. The first four items remained constant throughout this period:

> *The Reverberator*
> 'Madame de Mauves'
> 'A Passionate Pilgrim'
> 'The Madonna of the Future'

The initial list of contents for the volume had included two further stories, 'The Author of Beltraffio' and 'Louisa Pallant'.[173] On 13 March, James told the Scribners that he had found that 'Louisa Pallant' would make the volume too long and decided to replace it with the shorter story 'Europe'. At this point he was halfway through revising the first text in the contents list, the short novel *The Reverberator*; he promised to send revised copy for the second half, plus the Preface, 'by the next mail', and revised copy for the other stories in the volume 'by the next after that'.[174] To free up his mornings for revision, he now left off dictating the *Reverberator* Preface and asked Bosanquet to copy it.[175] It is not clear whether that meant he considered it to be complete. In the final paragraph of the published text, he refers to rereading the third and fourth stories in the volume, which he had almost certainly not yet revised by 13 March: 'As I read over "A Passionate Pilgrim" and "The Madonna of the Future" they become in the highest degree documentary for myself' (p. 155). Reading over need not imply revising, perhaps; the Preface mainly focuses on the personal memories these stories released for James, which a glance might have been enough to revive. In any case, he would dictate the Prefaces to other volumes of stories before he had fully revised their contents.

On 16 March, James went up to London again to watch the last rehearsals of *The High Bid*, and the following day Bosanquet finished copying the *Reverberator* Preface and posted it to him. On 18 March, he sent the Scribners the second half of the revised title story to the volume but kept back the Preface, 'as I find it will require some rewriting of last few pages in

---

[173] James to Scribners, 21–26 February 1908; Princeton.
[174] James to Scribners, 13 March 1908; Princeton.
[175] ODTB 13 March 1908.

LXXXIV

consequence of a table of Contents altered as to its last item (or 2 items)'.[176] He had miscalculated the amount of material he could fit into the volume, and now decided that it could accommodate 'The Author of Beltraffio' and 'Louisa Pallant' after all. The Preface's very brief comments on 'Louisa Pallant' are confined to its last four sentences, with a passing reference at the start of the final paragraph (pp. 156, 155): it is easy enough to imagine this material as a late addendum. It is also possible, however, that James made more substantial changes or additions to the text after 18 March, as his reference to 'rewriting of last few pages' seems to imply. Copy for this Preface was not sent to the Scribners until 23 April: by that time, James had revised 'Madame de Mauves' and 'the greater part' of 'A Passionate Pilgrim', and there are echoes of both stories in the published text of the Preface which may represent augmentations or adjustments in light of continuing revision.[177] 'The Author of Beltraffio' is not mentioned in the Preface to *The Reverberator* and was not in fact added to this volume; as James explained to the Scribners in June, he had decided to allocate it to the next volume but one, *The Lesson of the Master*, which 'consists practically *all* of "Tales of the literary life"' and would thus make a more congruous setting.[178]

Work on the *Reverberator* volume was briefly suspended in mid-March while James supervised the final rehearsals and first provincial performances of *The High Bid*. He was with Forbes-Robertson's company in Edinburgh for the first night on 26 March, and wrote to Bosanquet that it had been 'an unmistakeably complete and charming and rewarding success'.[179] Coming back to the *New York Edition* after this working holiday, he seems to have been seized with worry at how much remained to be done; he was about to take a longer absence from Lamb House, too, and may have felt that he needed to catch up on arrears before he left. Panicked figures of flight and pursuit recur in his letters from this period. To Edith Wharton on 29 March: 'My awful Monster of the Edition is close at my heels' (*HJEW* 97). To Violet Hunt on 1 April: 'I am ridden—and have been for months

---

[176] James to Scribners, 18 March 1908; Princeton; Princeton. James was evidently working from the 2-volume Macmillan first edition of *The Reverberator* (1888): in this letter, he says he has revised the 'first volume of original London issue'.

[177] James to Scribners, 23 April 1908; Princeton. See notes 535, 539 and 543 to the text.

[178] James to Scribners, 20 June 1908; Princeton.

[179] *CP* 550. James to Theodora Bosanquet, 30 March 1908; *HJL* 4:490.

and months—by the fearful nightmare of an Edition Definitive, or rather pursued there by a pack of hell-hounds; the hell-hounds being the volumes already out, revised, rewritten, copiously prefaced and seen through the Press, and crowding close on my heels as I pant and strain over the preparation of the awful bloated remainder.'[180] And to his nephew Harry on 3 April: 'The printers and publishers tread on my heels, and I feel their hot breath behind me—whereby I keep *at* it in order not to be overtaken' (*LHJ* 2:99). These extravagantly metaphorical fears would be confirmed in fact towards the end of the month, when Brownell announced that 'the printers are out of "copy" and clamorous for more.'[181]

On 6 April, James began to dictate the Preface for the next volume of shorter fictions, *Lady Barbarina*: it was completed on 15 April, but he set it aside and did not dispatch it for more than a month. At this point, he was still catching up with the revision of stories for the previous volume, *The Reverberator*, and he would thus seem to have dictated the Preface to *Lady Barbarina* before he had revised *any* of the stories in its volume. On 16 April, he began 'amplifying' his one-act play *The Saloon* in the hopes of getting Forbes-Robertson to stage it as a double bill with *The High Bid*; he spent the next five mornings with Bosanquet at this work.[182] He then appears to have taken up the *Reverberator* Preface again and made the rewrites he had mentioned to the Scribners the previous month; it was mailed at last on 23 April, and crossed in mid-Atlantic with an anxious letter from Brownell asking what had become of it.[183]

James now left Rye and was away for most of the spring and early summer. He stayed with Edith Wharton in Paris and then based himself at the Reform Club in London, making short visits to Stratford-upon-Avon and to Oxford, where William James was delivering the Hibbert Lectures in theology. At the end of June, James returned to Lamb House with his brother and sister-in-law, who stayed with him for several weeks over the summer and early autumn, joined at different times by their three youngest children. The Preface to *Lady Barbarina*, held back since the middle of April,

---

[180] Quoted in Hyde, *Henry James at Home*, p. 163.
[181] Brownell to James, 24 April 1908; Princeton.
[182] ODTB 16–20 April 1908.
[183] Brownell to James, 24 April 1908; Princeton.

was mailed to the Scribners on 20 May along with 'the greater part' of the revised copy for the volume's title story.[184] James appears to have confirmed the final list of contents when he dispatched a further batch of revised copy three days later, thus:

> 'Lady Barbarina'
> 'The Siege of London'
> 'An International Episode'
> 'A Bundle of Letters'
> 'The Point of View'
> 'The Pension Beaurepas'[185]

The published volume contains all those stories, but not quite in the same order: 'The Pension Beaurepas' comes fourth, after 'An International Episode'.[186] The Preface, however, follows the contents list as drawn up on 23 May and treats 'The Pension Beaurepas' as the last item in the volume.

July–September 1908: *The Lesson of the Master, The Altar of the Dead, Daisy Miller*

Back at work at Lamb House in July 1908 after James's early summer absence, Bosanquet noted: 'Began another preface & it really seemed as if I hadn't been gone a day.'[187] This was the Preface to *The Lesson of the Master*. Bosanquet did not describe its progress in detail, but twelve days later she recorded: 'Mʳ James very nearly finished his preface—he's been *ages* over this one.'[188] He must have actually finished it the day after that entry (23 July), as Bosanquet spent the next two days copying it.

An updated contents list for the *Lesson* volume had gone to the Scribners earlier that month:

> 'The Lesson of the Master'
> 'The Death of the Lion'

---

[184] James to Scribners, 20 May 1908; Princeton.
[185] 'Contents of Volume Fourteenth. (V of *Shorter Novels & Tales*)', apparently a half-sheet torn from James's letter to the Scribners, 23 May 1908; Princeton.
[186] The eventual published order of stories is set out in James's letter to the Scribners of 10 July 1908 (Princeton).
[187] ODTB 10 July 1908.
[188] ODTB 22 July 1908.

INTRODUCTION

> 'The Figure in the Carpet'
> 'The Next Time'
> 'The Coxon Fund'
> 'The Middle Years'
> 'Greville Fane'
> 'The Author of Beltraffio'
> 'Broken Wings'
> 'The Abasement of the Northmores'
> 'The Great Good Place'[189]

Instalments of revised copy for the volume were dispatched throughout the second half of July and into August. The Preface was dictated concurrently with the revisions to the first five stories, but James held it back and mailed it on 4 August with the final instalment of revised copy.

Almost immediately after completing the *Lesson* Preface, he went straight on to the next one. Bosanquet recorded on 26 July: 'Inspiration flowed so strong over the beginning of the new preface—part about "The Altar of the Dead" that Mʳ James quite forgot the time & went on gaily till 2!'[190] That was half an hour beyond their usual time for stopping, and on a Sunday. The *Altar* Preface evidently seized Bosanquet's imagination also, as she noted the topics it touched on as they went ('account of the origin of "The Private Life"'; 'interesting bit [...] dealing with Mʳ James' views on the treatment of the supernatural') and copied out a passage on friendship to show her Rye friend Nellie Bradley.[191] After five or six mornings of dictation, James spent three mornings 'correcting & emending' the text, and Bosanquet commented on the second of those days that he was 'much pleased with this preface'; he appears to have completed it on the third day, 6 August, after 'further emendations'.[192] Bosanquet spent the next two mornings copying it.

---

[189] James to Scribners, 14 July 1908; Princeton. 'The Tree of Knowledge' is missing from this list – probably by accident, as it appears in the list of contents for this volume in James's letter of 21–26 February 1908, and again in the list of tales transferred from *The Lesson of the Master* to *The Author of Beltraffio* (see Brownell to James, 2 December 1908; Princeton).
[190] ODTB 26 July 1908.
[191] ODTB 29 July, 1, 2 August 1908.
[192] ODTB 4–6 August 1908.

LXXXVIII

James dictated the *Altar* Preface concurrently with the revisions to the remaining stories for the previous volume (*The Lesson of the Master*) and at least the first three stories in this one, up to and including 'The Birthplace'. The contents of *The Altar of the Dead* at this stage can be reconstructed from his correspondence with the Scribners:

> 'The Altar of the Dead'
> 'The Beast in the Jungle'
> 'The Birthplace'
> 'The Private Life'
> 'Owen Wingrave'
> 'The Friends of the Friends'
> 'Sir Edmund Orme'
> 'The Real Right Thing'
> 'The Jolly Corner'
> 'Four Meetings'
> 'Mrs Medwin'[193]

On 11 August, James announced that he had completed the Preface but was holding it back to send with the 'final Copy for the volume'; he mailed it three days later, with a further – though not yet final – instalment of revised copy.[194] Towards the end of September, after returning corrected proofs, he would need to emend the Preface again in light of 'a very urgent application' from *The English Review* to publish 'The Jolly Corner'.[195] That story had been rejected by *Harper's Monthly Magazine* in 1906, and James had referred to its appearance in the *New York Edition* as its first publication; the turn of events had happily falsified that reference, and he made the correction accordingly.

Dictation of the Preface to *Daisy Miller* began on 14 August and continued intermittently for the next three weeks. It was at this juncture that James wrote to Howells of his 'staleness of sensibility' about the Prefaces and confessed to being 'sick of the mere doing of them' (*LFL* 425–6).[196] As he

---

[193] James to Scribners, 4, 11 August 1908; Princeton.
[194] James to Scribners, 11, 14 August 1908; Princeton.
[195] James to Scribners, 25 September 1908; Princeton. See note 700 to the text.
[196] This typed letter was presumably the 'long & most interesting one' described by Bosanquet on 13 August (ODTB). If so, James was not attempting to conceal his frustration with the continuing grind of the Prefaces from his amanuensis.

dictated the *Daisy Miller* Preface, he was still revising stories for *The Altar of the Dead*; he had been trying and failing to catch up with himself for most of the summer. He was also just beginning to revise his Italian travel essays for an illustrated volume, *Italian Hours* (1909), designed as a commercially attractive sequel to *English Hours* (1905). Textual revision had become an obstacle to the writing of new novels and tales: as James now told Howells, 'I could really shed salt tears of impatience and yearning to get back, after so prolonged a blocking of traffic, to too-dreadfully postponed and neglected "creative" work; an accumulated store of ideas and reachings-out for which even now clogs my brain' (*LFL* 427). He also appears to have been actually unwell at this time, and fell back on simpler tasks as a change from the Preface. On 25 August, Bosanquet noted: 'M' James feeling seedy—so confined himself to redictating "Four Meetings" [a story he had just revised for the *Altar* volume]—he nearly went to sleep over it many times.' Two days later: 'M' James better—began "inventive work" again', which sounds in context like a resumption of the *Daisy* Preface. On 2 September. he was making cuts – as Bosanquet put it, 'hacking at his preface which is too long'. That appears to have been depressing work, and the next day he changed tack again ('"to cheer me up morally"') and began to adapt his novel *The Other House* (1896) for the stage; he worked at this adaptation for the rest of the month.[197]

Bosanquet does not record when the *Daisy* Preface was finally completed. James mailed it on 25 September along with the revised copy for the volume's title story. He told the Scribners that he was 'a little anxious' about this Preface 'in regard to the question of its length; which is exceptionally great':

I have immensely struggled with it, but should be glad if you can get it in as it stands, in spite of its being, by some ten pages of Copy, the longest. This is because I think it, on the whole, the best and most important—as winding up the series of the Shorter Things and tucking in all I have to say about them. I don't seem to be able to get anything more out; the different parts and heads in it being, as it were, of equal importance. I beg you, at any rate, to print it as it stands and then allow me—if it does prove too monstrously big—to perform, at whatever cost, some mutilation on

---

[197] ODTB 3–27 September 1908.

the Proof; keeping a duplicate meanwhile for the uncurtailed whole. This service I shall much appreciate.[198]

James sent batches of revised copy for the *Daisy* volume over the next month, confirming the list of contents with the final instalment:

'Daisy Miller'
'Pandora'
'The Patagonia'
'The Marriages'
'The Real Thing'
'Brooksmith'
'Flickerbridge'
'The Beldonald Holbein'
'The Story in It'
'Paste'
'Europe'
'Miss Gunton of Poughkeepsie'
'Fordham Castle'
'Julia Bride'[199]

By the time he sent the final instalment of copy on 23 October, he would probably have received a letter from Brownell telling him that the Scribners did not consider the Preface to *Daisy Miller* so much longer than the other Prefaces as to be 'in any degree objectionable', but agreeing to 'have it put into type and [...] leave it entirely to your judgment to curtail or not as you may on the whole prefer'.[200]

October–November 1908: *The Ambassadors, The Golden Bowl*

With work now completed – as he thought – on the volumes of tales, James picked up the threads left dangling earlier in the year by his premature start on the revisions and Prefaces for his late novels. The Scribners had been asking after the outstanding revised copy for *The Wings of the Dove* (the final quarter of the novel) since April 1908, and James had assured them

---

[198] James to Scribners, 25 September 1908; Princeton.
[199] James to Scribners, 23 October 1908; Princeton.
[200] Brownell to James, 9 October 1908; Princeton.

in May that he had that 'last portion' of the text 'safe' and promised to send it, but did not do so; he sent it now at the end of October.[201] He now also told them that the complete revised copy and Preface for *The Ambassadors* would follow 'a very few days hence'.[202] He would not in fact dispatch those materials until the New Year. The sequence of his work at this time is impossible to reconstruct exactly, but it seems likely that he took up the *Ambassadors* Preface again after dispatching the Preface to *Daisy Miller* on 25 September, and made whatever changes and additions were necessary to complete the text he had laid aside in January 1908. There is no record of when the *Golden Bowl* Preface was begun: Bosanquet refers to it only once, on 28 October, noting that James had 'nearly finished' dictating it.[203] After that there are no entries at all in Bosanquet's diary until 14 November, when we find James getting back to work 'after a week's break' and starting to dictate 'a new fiction': this was 'The Top of the Tree', published in *The English Review* in March 1909 under the title 'The Velvet Glove'.[204] Their working mornings for the rest of November were spent dictating that story and a commemorative essay on James's old friend Charles Eliot Norton, who had died the month before at the age of 80.[205] It seems likely therefore that James completed a first version of the *Golden Bowl* Preface before the start of his 'week's break' on or around 7 November. In mid-December he would tell the Scribners that the Prefaces to both *The Ambassadors* and *The Golden Bowl* were 'already these many weeks done'.[206]

On 28 October, Bosanquet recorded that James was 'depressed': he had almost completed the *Golden Bowl* Preface but was 'bored by it—says he's "lost his spring" for it'.[207] It may be relevant to this account of his mood that just a week earlier he had learnt that no profits whatever had accrued to him from royalties on the *New York Edition* volumes so far published. As he

---

[201] Brownell to James, 24 April 1908; Princeton. James to Scribners, 20 May, 27 October 1908; Princeton.
[202] James to Scribners, 27 October 1908; Princeton.
[203] ODTB 28 October 1908.
[204] ODTB 14 November 1908.
[205] ODTB 19–21, 26 November 1908. 'An American Art-Scholar: Charles Eliot Norton', *Burlington Magazine* 14 (January 1909), 201–4.
[206] James to Scribners, 14–15 December 1908; Princeton.
[207] ODTB 28 October 1908.

told Pinker on 20 October, this unexpected news had 'knocked me rather flat' (*LL* 468). Three days later, he assured his agent that he had 'recovered the perspective and proportion of things' and was 'aching in every bone to get back to out-and-out "creative" work, the long interruption of which has fairly sickened and poisoned me' (*HJL* 4:498). 'The Top of the Tree' was the immediate result of this rebound towards new fiction. Before James could do much more in that direction, however, a crisis arose in regard to the volumes of tales that called him back imperatively to the Edition.

December 1908–January 1909: The Redistribution of Tales and *The Author of Beltraffio*

At the start of December 1908, Brownell wrote with news of 'a serious complication' for the Edition. As the last three volumes of short stories – *The Lesson of the Master*, *The Altar of the Dead* and *Daisy Miller* – had entered the production process, it had become apparent that they would be of a much greater extent than the Scribners had expected, so much so as to be 'destructive of almost all expectation of profitable publication'. James had significantly overestimated how many words could be accommodated in a single volume, and his piecemeal dispatch of revised copy had masked the problem until now.[208] Brownell acknowledged that any alteration to James's thematic groupings of the stories in these volumes 'would lose in both art and logic, as well as involve a disconcerting and nearly tragic recasting of the carefully considered and concatenated prefaces, which are such a vital feature of the edition': nevertheless, the volumes were too long to be printed in their present state. Approaching the problem 'on its purely mechanical side' and considering only how to achieve volumes of the right extent, Brownell suggested that they remove tales from the over-long volumes and create an extra volume to receive the displaced items. *The Lesson of the Master* (Volume XV) would be the simplest volume to rearrange as 'the first 320 pages, exclusive of the preface, are *already printed*', and Brownell proposed

---

[208] James had originally accepted a limit of 'as nearly as possible 120,000 words apiece' for the volumes of tales (James to Scribners, 12 June 1906; *HJL* 4:407). By the time he began to assemble the volumes two years later, he was thinking of 150,000 words as 'the usual number' (James to Scribners, 20 July 1908; Princeton); the copy he delivered considerably exceeded even that inflated limit.

simply cutting it down to its first five tales and leaving it in its place in the sequence of volumes. The additional volume would be made up of the tales taken from *Lesson* and some others taken from the end of *Daisy Miller*, and it would become the new Volume XVI. *The Altar of the Dead* (the old Volume XVI) was already 'cast' – Brownell meant presumably that the electrotype plates had been manufactured – and would therefore 'remain intact' but move along one place in the Edition to become the new Volume XVII. The reduced *Daisy Miller* (the old Volume XVII) would budge up in its turn and become the new Volume XVIII. The Prefaces would have to be rewritten accordingly, and a new Preface composed for the extra volume; another frontispiece would be needed also.[209]

The time-lag of transatlantic mail protected James from this news for almost a fortnight, during which time Bosanquet recorded that 'the tide of life flows smoothly on'; he was working 'steadily […] on a quite short story for Harper's', probably 'Crapy Cornelia'.[210] Brownell's letter arrived in due course, however, and James responded in a long letter dictated on 14 and 15 December. He began by accepting Brownell's proposals unreservedly, seeing 'no redistribution possible *but* the mere mechanical one' and dismissing 'any other style of attempt (at new juxtapositions)' as too difficult. James's work on the Edition had left him feeling 'pretty well finished and voided', he observed, and he would need 'every inch of the quite ghostly presence, I fear, of any surviving energy to face the question of what may now have to be done in respect to the two or three compromised Prefaces':

Alas, I can absolutely supply nothing *more* in the way of prefatory matter. What I will look into, as soon as I can turn round […] is the question of piecing together after some fashion such morsels of reference to the things contained in the extra volume as may make an adequate introduction to them. This will require some artful picking out; but I will get at it at the first possible moment—and in short will furbish up something! I only seem to see that the last of the 'Tales' Prefaces will have to be the shortest—at which, however, you will doubtless not repine. If my Remarks seem to drop or languish at that point, I trust them to pick up and carry themselves well again in connection with each of the three last novels.[211]

[209] Brownell to James, 2 December 1908; Princeton.
[210] ODTB 12 December 1908.
[211] James to Scribners, 14–15 December 1908; Princeton.

Even as he gave the Scribners 'a free hand' to rearrange the volumes, James could not resist 'making a suggestion or two, and noting two or three preferences, for your guidance'. And yet the instructions he gave in this letter were neither clear nor consistent: he repeatedly assigned the wrong numbers to volumes, confused old and new numberings (at one point conjuring into existence a phantom Volume XIX) and lost track of which volume was the additional one. The body of the letter was dictated to Bosanquet on 14 December. The following day James dictated an 'Important Postscript' and added a handwritten 'P.P.S.' to the top of the first page indicating that the postscript should be read '*first*!—before my letter, which has been thereby rather superseded!' In the postscript, he announced that he was enclosing 'Tables of Contents for the new [volumes] XVI, XVII, and XVIII'. The first of those tables appears to have been lost. Two pencilled lists of tales in James's hand, undated and filed elsewhere in the sequence of his correspondence with the Scribners, appear to refer to this rearrangement of volumes and do in fact correspond quite closely to the contents of the published *NYE* XVII and XVIII; but they are confusing documents, omitting a couple of tales and giving contradictory indications about the placement of two titles in particular, 'Daisy Miller' and 'Julia Bride'.[212] That intractable question is not cleared up by a further autograph fragment on a slip of paper which appears to have been pinned to the first sheet of the letter, in which James countermands the instructions given in the postscript and then once more grants the Scribners discretion to decide the matter for themselves.[213]

On 15 December – the day of the postscript – Bosanquet noted that James was 'wrestling with the problem of redistribution of contents of three volumes of short tales – to make up four. Also with the consequent alterations in prefaces. I went back for extra work after tea.' This was an unusual extension of their working hours, and it confirms the sense of a crisis; they worked from 6 till 8 o'clock the following evening too.[214] In his postscript, James told the Scribners that he believed he had managed to rearrange the volumes of tales 'with the practical minimum of misfortune':

---

[212] Undated contents lists for 'Vol. 17*th*' and 'Vol: 18*th*', filed between letters dated 27 and 28 February 1908; Princeton.
[213] Undated fragment filed after James to Scribners, 14–15 December 1908; Princeton.
[214] ODTB 15, 16 December 1908.

INTRODUCTION

The misfortune—though I have recuperated a little since yesterday!—still strikes me as attaching rather poignantly to the question of these three Prefaces; though, now that I *have* each new Series worried out I see my way a little better for making some corresponding redivision of the prefatory stuff. This business I will proceed to immediately and send you what is necessary for the issue of the Volumes. I'm afraid I can only redistribute the prefatory passages already existing, making them decently fit and match: heaven forbid I should attempt any new ones. The only thing is that each of the Prefaces will then be shorter—which for that matter they can afford.[215]

As we shall see, even getting the redistributed passages to 'fit and match' would turn out to be beyond James. As he dispatched copy for the adjusted Prefaces in the new year, he trusted that there would be 'no *bad* irregularities [...] by reason of these changes' but acknowledged 'two or three slight and venial ones. Some things are now alluded to not in their order in the Contents; two or three are scarcely alluded to at all—which couldn't anyway be helped; and in Vol. XVIII I have had to refer back to a previous Volume in my remarks about "Fordham Castle"; but on the whole I pull through!'[216]

It is impossible to reconstruct James's plan for the rearrangement of these volumes solely from his letter of 14–15 December 1908, which must be read alongside the Scribners' responses to his directions. Replying to that letter a month later, Brownell assured him that 'We have followed your rearrangement implicitly and have had no disposition to take advantage of your permission to vary it'; but the Scribners must have had to clarify James's scheme for themselves in order to put it into practice, and Brownell now set out their interpretation of his intentions, with lists of contents for the rearranged Volumes XV–XVIII, 'in order to be absolutely explicit and avoid all possible misunderstanding'.[217] James would accept those lists in turn as 'definitely the right ones'.[218]

The contents of the four volumes as listed by Brownell were as follows:

NYE XV: *The Lesson of the Master*

'The Lesson of the Master'

---

[215] James to Scribners, 14–15 December 1908; Princeton.
[216] James to Scribners, 5 January 1909; Princeton.
[217] Brownell to James, 12 January 1909; Princeton.
[218] James to Scribners, 22 January 1909; Princeton.

INTRODUCTION

'The Death of the Lion'
['The Next Time'][219]
'The Figure in the Carpet'
'The Coxon Fund'

The previous list of contents for *The Lesson of the Master* was thus reduced to its first five stories, but the volume was not otherwise altered. The Preface was presumably cut off after the passage discussing 'The Coxon Fund', the abrupt ending of the published text betraying the arbitrariness of that procedure.

NYE XVI: The Author of Beltraffio

'The Author of Beltraffio'
'The Middle Years'
'Greville Fane'
'Broken Wings'
'The Tree of Knowledge'
'The Abasement of the Northmores'
'The Great Good Place'
'Four Meetings'
'Paste'
'Europe'
'Miss Gunton of Poughkeepsie'
'Fordham Castle'

The Author of Beltraffio was the additional volume, and material was assigned to it from all the other volumes involved in the redistribution. The first seven tales in the list of contents were taken from *The Lesson of the Master*, and they presumably brought a solid block of Preface along with them (pp. 184–8). The last four tales were taken from *Daisy Miller*; of these four, only 'Paste' and 'Europe' are discussed at all in the *Beltraffio* Preface (pp. 188–9). James's remarks on 'Fordham Castle' stayed in the Preface to *Daisy Miller*, where they were closely interwoven with commentary on 'Daisy Miller' and 'Pandora' (pp. 219–20), and a couple of passing references to

---

[219] 'The Next Time' was inadvertently left off the list supplied by Brownell, but it had occupied this position in the *Lesson* volume since at least the previous summer (see James to Scribners, 14 July 1908; Princeton). Brownell apologized for the omission in his next letter to James on 18 January 1909 (Princeton).

INTRODUCTION

'Miss Gunton of Poughkeepsie' were left in that Preface also (pp. 217, 219). The story 'Four Meetings' was taken from *The Altar of the Dead*, and is not mentioned in any Preface. The Preface to *The Author of Beltraffio* is by far the shortest in the Edition – at just 2,800 words, less than half the average length – and its perfunctory character is obviously the result of this volume's construction. It may be relevant, too, that the volume has no natural leading tale: James consistently took the direction of his prefatory remarks from the first story or group of stories in a volume, and the contents of *The Author of Beltraffio* were mostly taken from the second half of *The Lesson of the Master* and the last third of *Daisy Miller*. James never intended any of those stories to lead off a volume of the Edition.

NYE XVII: *The Altar of the Dead*

'The Altar of the Dead'
'The Beast in the Jungle'
'The Birthplace'
'The Private Life'
'Owen Wingrave'
'The Friends of the Friends'
'Sir Edmund Orme'
'The Real Right Thing'
'The Jolly Corner'
'Julia Bride'

The Altar of the Dead lost only two tales in the redistribution: 'Four Meetings', which moved to *The Author of Beltraffio*; and 'Mrs Medwin', which moved to *Daisy Miller*. Those transfers caused very few knock-on effects to the corresponding Prefaces: as already noted, 'Four Meetings' is not mentioned in any Preface and 'Mrs Medwin' gets only a brief, functional reference in the *Daisy Miller* Preface (p. 227). At a late stage, this volume acquired 'Julia Bride' from *Daisy Miller* (as described below).

NYE XVIII: *Daisy Miller*

'Daisy Miller'
'Pandora'
'The Patagonia'
'The Marriages'
'The Real Thing'

XCVIII

INTRODUCTION

'Brooksmith'
'The Beldonald Holbein'
'The Story in It'
'Flickerbridge'
'Mrs Medwin'

Daisy Miller lost five tales in the redistribution, four of them to the newly created *The Author of Beltraffio*. The other tale, 'Julia Bride', was given to *The Altar of the Dead*. That last transfer was the single most complex manoeuvre involved in the reshaping of the volumes of shorter fictions, and it gave rise to James's only serious uncertainty in adjusting the Prefaces: the relative placement of 'Julia Bride' and 'Daisy Miller'.

The difficulty here was closely connected to the choice of frontispiece images. As Brownell had seen from the start, an additional frontispiece would be required if they were to add a volume to the Edition. He had presented this to James as a minor obstacle, 'a simple matter compared with the disintegration of your carefully composed unities, the difficulty of creating new ones and the labor of readjusting the prefaces'.[220] In practice, however, all those operations turned out to be interrelated. In his letter of 14–15 December 1908, James nominated the New York story 'Julia Bride' as the best option to supply a new photographic subject. By good luck Coburn happened to be in New York at the time and could be commissioned to photograph some local subject 'that will hook on, not too irrelevantly, to "Julia Bride"': a view of Central Park, 'or better still almost any aspect or vista or favourable view of the Metropolitan Museum, in which the scene of the first half of the tale is laid'.[221] And yet the same letter betrays some confusion about which volume 'Julia Bride' and its new frontispiece were to occupy. Prior to the redistribution of tales, James had placed 'Julia Bride' in the closing position in the *Daisy Miller* volume.[222] A frontispiece image for that volume already existed, however, in Coburn's photograph 'By St. Peter's' – a view of Piazza San Pietro in Rome with an obvious connection

---

[220] Brownell to James, 2 December 1908; Princeton.
[221] James to Scribners, 14–15 December 1908; Princeton.
[222] 'Julia Bride' is first listed in that position in James's letter to the Scribners of 23 October 1908 (Princeton).

to the story 'Daisy Miller'. The volume which now needed a frontispiece was *The Altar of the Dead*. At least as early as February 1908, the frontispiece image for this volume had been associated for James with the story 'Four Meetings'.[223] Brownell had not proposed any changes to the textual constitution of the *Altar* volume, but in the letter of 14–15 December James directed that 'Four Meetings' should move from this volume to the new Volume XVI, *The Author of Beltraffio*. He did not refer to the fact in his letter, but that move would have the knock-on effect of displacing the *Altar* volume's frontispiece image – and indeed Coburn's photograph 'The New England Street' would be used as the frontispiece to the published *NYE* XVI. As things stood, James thus had two frontispieces for the *Daisy Miller* volume and none for *The Altar of the Dead*. It is not easy to follow his line of thought through the letter of 14–15 December and its addenda, but it appears that he finally offered the Scribners two ways of resolving this problem. They could either move 'Julia Bride' to the end of the new Volume XVII (*The Altar of the Dead*) and use Coburn's New York photograph as the frontispiece to that volume, leaving 'Daisy Miller' to open the new Volume XVIII (*Daisy Miller*) accompanied by its existing frontispiece image; or they could move 'Daisy Miller' to the end of Volume XVII and use its frontispiece image for *that* volume, and place 'Julia Bride' somewhere in Volume XVIII with the New York photograph as frontispiece.

Brownell chose the first of these alternatives, which he understood to have been James's 'original arrangement': thus, 'Julia Bride' would close Volume XVII and 'Daisy Miller' would open Volume XVIII.[224] The delay intrinsic to their transatlantic correspondence complicated matters at this point. By the time Brownell wrote to convey this decision, James had already gone ahead and made his own adjustments, and had sent the Scribners what he called 'the proper *data* for the rearranged Prefaces to the Edition—or rather, in point of fact, the absolute Prefaces themselves, as they can only

---

[223] In James's letter to the Scribners of 21–26 February 1908, the final item in the list of contents for *The Altar of the Dead* is given as 'Four Meetings, (illustration.)' (Princeton). Quite possibly James had made the connection a year earlier, when he sent Coburn to America with plates of the existing frontispiece photographs and instructions for taking two more images, including 'The New England Street' (see Chronology of Composition and Production, entry for Late February 1907).

[224] Brownell to James, 12 January 1909; Princeton.

now stand'.²²⁵ Towards the end of January, James received and answered Brownell's letter, assented to the new lists of contents and thanked the Scribners for 'the restoration of "Daisy Miller" to the first place in XVIII': 'So be it! Everything seems thus provided for.' But he also voiced a caveat about the Prefaces, which had been 'inevitably somewhat rearranged—and inevitably also a trifle *awkwardly* re-arranged': 'all I ask of you is not to worry if here and there a reference [...] is to something in some other volume. I'm not sure, thus, that "Daisy Miller" is talked of in the Volume that belongs to her; but at any rate let matters stand as they are, please, in spite of any such small irregularity.'²²⁶

It is clear from subsequent correspondence that James had assumed Brownell would adopt his *other* proposed solution and elect to move 'Daisy Miller' to the *Altar* volume, and had rewritten the Prefaces accordingly. By 18 January, Brownell had received James's copy for the rewritten Prefaces and found the resulting discrepancies. He now asked James for 'a further consideration' of the Prefaces connected with these two tales, sending back the proofs for that purpose:

You will have some time since received our recent letter [12 January 1909], mentioning that in accordance with your permission and with what we understand to be your real wishes, as well as with our own preference, we restored 'Daisy Miller' to the head of Volume XVIII and placed 'Julia Bride' at the end of Volume XVII. If, now, you agree with this disposition, we shall have to reque[st] of course a corresponding change in the prefaces as finall[y] arranged by you, and for this purpose we are returning the prefaces to you once more [...]. We had begun, as you will see by the changes in pagination, to make this transposition ourselves, but found 'Julia Bride' too deeply imbedded in her surroundings for us to venture ourselves to extricate her.²²⁷

James duly supplied 'the right little facilities for relegating the part of the 18th: Vol. Preface referring to "Julia Bride" back to the end of the Preface of Vol. 17th': 'I do think this tucks in the last loose end.'²²⁸ He evidently found the alteration of the Prefaces a difficult job, and some visible holes

---

[225] James to Scribners, 5 January 1909; Princeton.
[226] James to Scribners, 22 January 1909; Princeton.
[227] Brownell to James, 18 January 1909; Princeton.
[228] James to Scribners, 2 February 1909; Princeton.

and joins remain in the published texts.[229] Reviewing his first attempts at remaking the Prefaces, he had ruefully noted that 'the majestic coherency, so to speak, of these introductions, has not a little, I fear, lost itself; though perhaps that, after all, won't be perceived of those who don't know how they *might* have unrolled'.[230] But exasperated irony about readers' failure to grasp his intentions had been a conspicuous feature of James's commentary in the Prefaces themselves,[231] and the thought that, with any luck, people might not realize what these writings *ought* to have been cannot have brought him much comfort now.

January–March 1909: *The Golden Bowl*

Towards the end of January 1909 James wrote to Coburn acknowledging receipt of his frontispiece photograph for 'Julia Bride' ('The Halls of Julia': a view of the Metropolitan Museum in New York), and answering his 'very touching and justified little appeals about the mention and specification of your authorship of the Frontispieces'.[232] The Scribners' prospectus for the *New York Edition* had credited Coburn with photographing the frontispiece images 'in the true spirit of the labor of love', and quoted George Bernard Shaw calling him '"one of the most accomplished and sensitive artist-photographers now living"'; but his name appeared nowhere in the volumes themselves.[233] Rather than 'attempting further to gouge out of the House any merely meagre and obscure reference to your labour', James now undertook to 'commemorate it myself, charmingly and appreciatively', in the Preface to *The Golden Bowl*, 'which deals with points general to the Edition and not with points special to the book itself. At any rate so far as it does this latter, I shall, by a happy inspiration, change those three or four pages into a little friendly and felicitous recital of our hunt about for illustrative

---

[229] See notes 718–20 and 722 to the *Altar* Preface, and 750, 753, 755 and 758 to the *Daisy Miller* Preface.
[230] James to Scribners, 5 January 1909; Princeton.
[231] See, e.g., the Preface to *The Lesson of the Master* on the 'odd numbness of the general sensibility, which seemed ever to condemn it, in presence of a work of art, to a view scarce of half the intentions embodied, and moreover but to the scantest measure of these' (p. 180).
[232] James to Coburn, 22 January 1909; Virginia.
[233] 'The Novels and Tales of Henry James', *The Book Buyer* 32 (December 1907), 213.

2 Alvin Langdon Coburn, 'The Curiosity Shop', photogravure frontispiece to the first volume of *The Golden Bowl* (*NYE* XXIII). Cambridge University Library, Syn.5.90.235.

subjects.'[234] James retained his comments on narrative point of view in that Preface, but added just over 1,500 words on his collaboration with Coburn, the finding of the two London frontispiece subjects for *The Golden Bowl* and the general relation of images to fictional texts (pp. 263–6). This presumably was the textual change James referred to when, on 8 March 1909, he sent the Scribners the final instalment of revised copy for the novel: 'The Preface goes to you by the next mail—or the next after that. It has been written these many weeks, but I am making an alteration in it' (*LL* 477).

That late 'alteration' was not quite the final incident in the Prefaces' compositional history. At some point in the spring of 1908, James corrected a proof of the Preface to *The Golden Bowl* but forgot to return it, and in late June the Scribners had to cable him to ask for it. The realization of his mistake prompted first a telegram ('Missing preface just mailed writing') and then a letter whose vexed, apologetic account of the mistake makes an ironic counterpoint to James's remarks on authorial responsibility, care, control and fallibility at the close of the *Golden Bowl* Preface itself. It will serve as a last word on the composition of the Prefaces:

Messrs. Charles Scribner's Sons.

Dear Sirs.

On receiving your cable about the missing Preface (corrected Proof) to Golden Bowl I immediately wrote to my servant in the country (for I am spending some weeks in London) to look up & send me the *Duplicate* of the Proofs. What has been found, & what I am just cabling you that I mail to-day, is the original, the corrected Proof, which I now see that through some deplorable inadvertance [sic] I put back in the file (after correction) instead of putting it into an envelope & returning it to *you*. I never dreamed but that the Duplicate *only* would be resting there. Great are my shame, consternation & regret. I am afraid I have not a little incommoded you—& my aberration—my wretched absent-mindedness (which, alas, *grows!*)—remains to me alike unaccountable & discreditable. But the Revise *does* go [to] you positively today—& I hope in a swift ship. Yours very truly

Henry James[235]

---

[234] James to Coburn, 22 January 1909; Virginia.
[235] James to Scribners, 22 June 1909 [telegram and ALS]; Princeton.

3 Publication and Private Responses

The serial publication of the *New York Edition* was a long, slow process. For more than a year after the volumes began to come out, James continued to revise novels and stories, compose Prefaces and determine the contents of volumes, and readers offered their verdicts – private and public – on the early instalments before the later ones were assembled (the public reception of the Edition is described in the next section of the Introduction). The Edition appeared first in America. It was published by Charles Scribner's Sons as a subscription edition: purchasers subscribed for the entire set and received the volumes in pairs at irregular intervals over the course of one and a half years. NYE I–II appeared on 14 December 1907 and NYE XXIII–XXIV on 31 July 1909. The standard bibliography of Henry James describes two distinct American issues: an ordinary issue ($2 per volume in a cloth binding or $4 in half-levant), and a limited issue (156 numbered sets, printed 'on Ruisdael handmade paper' and priced at $8 per volume).[236] All copies were printed at the Riverside Press in Cambridge, Massachusetts by H. O. Houghton & Company, the printing subsidiary of the Boston publishing firm Houghton, Mifflin.[237] The first impression consisted of 1,500 copies of NYE I–X and 1,000 copies of NYE XI–XXIV. Those numbers may indicate an early downward adjustment of expectations – already low – for the sale of the Edition. The Scribners' records show that approximately 1,000 sets of the Edition had been sold by 1913, when another 500 copies

---

[236] Leon Edel and Dan H. Laurence, *A Bibliography of Henry James*, 3rd edn, revised with the assistance of James Rambeau (Oxford: Clarendon Press, 1982), pp. 137–8.

[237] David J. Supino, *A Bibliographical Catalogue of a Collection of Editions to 1921*, 2nd edn, revised (Liverpool: Liverpool University Press, 2014), p. 511. According to the terms agreed with the Scribners on 10 April 1906, Houghton, Mifflin were granted the right to manufacture the electrotype plates and do the printing and binding for volumes of the Edition containing works to which they held the copyrights, for a period of three years from publication (the contract between the firms is printed in Supino, *A Bibliographical Catalogue*, Appendix G, pp. 629–30). It would seem that Houghton, Mifflin subsequently convinced the Scribners to let them print the whole Edition. At the start of their negotiations with the Scribners the previous year, they had been confident 'that we can quote prices that will make it worth your while to have all the volumes manufactured by us, instead of those only which we control' (Houghton, Mifflin and Co. to Charles Scribner's Sons, 19 September 1905; Princeton). Almost all volumes of the first impression contain the colophon of the Riverside Press (see the collations in Supino, *A Bibliographical Catalogue*, pp. 500–8, 514–21).

of the last fourteen volumes were printed to match the remaining copies of the first ten volumes and make up 500 new sets.[238]

James had at his disposal six author's copies per volume of the Scribners' ordinary issue, and one copy per volume of the limited issue. As publication began, he asked to receive one copy of the ordinary issue himself as the volumes came out, and directed that the remaining five copies should be regularly sent to William James, Edith Wharton, W. D. Howells, Rudyard Kipling and Paul Bourget.[239] Shortly afterwards, he emended his instructions. Howells was travelling in Europe and could wait for his copies until he was back in the country, and Wharton had already subscribed and did not need to be gifted a set of the Edition.[240] Wharton would presently write to James about the Preface to *The Portrait of a Lady* in terms that gave him, as he told her on 7 March 1908, 'pure joy & ravishment' (*HJEW* 89). Her letter does not survive, but a few days later she wrote to Sara ('Sally') Norton, the eldest daughter of Charles Eliot Norton: 'I can't agree with you about the James prefaces,—I think the one to "The Portrait of a Lady" the best definition of the novelist's art ever written—& there are masterly things in the Casamassima one. Read them with detachment & tell me if I am not right!'[241] Sara's contrary opinion of the first four Prefaces (to *Roderick*, *American*, *Portrait* and *Princess*) is disclosed in a letter addressed to Howells by her father:

I have not read them, but Sally has read them and finds them too self-occupied, and dislikes the disturbances of her old associations with the stories, and dislikes also the unreality which this criticism of the old characters gives to them. She does not like to have her puppets taken to pieces and the wires which moved them shown to her; nor does she think it a dignified proceeding to take for granted so largely

---

[238] Supino, *A Bibliographical Catalogue*, pp. 510–11.
[239] James to Scribners, 3 January 1908; Princeton.
[240] At this point, James relinquished his claim to receive the ordinary issue of the Edition, so that he now had three more sets to dispose of: he directed that those volumes be sent on publication to Owen Wister, Mary Cadwalader Jones and Evelyn Smalley (James to Scribners, 22 January 1908; Princeton).
[241] Wharton to Sara Norton, 16 March 1908; *The Letters of Edith Wharton*, ed. R. W. B. Lewis and Nancy Lewis (New York: Charles Scribner's Sons, 1988), p. 137.

the interest of the public in the conception and execution of the work of the living writer.[242]

Perhaps anticipating this sort of response from the Norton household, a year earlier James had asked Charles's sister Grace to 'kindly keep a little in the dark for the present my fond chatter about my poor Edition'; in the same letter, he told her that 'though I am not going to let you read one of the fictions themselves over I shall expect you to read all the said Introductions'.[243] No evidence survives for what she made of them.

Sara Norton seems to have reacted to the Prefaces merely as someone who had once read James's early novels, protective of 'her old associations with the stories' and uninterested to the point of disapproval in questions of 'conception and execution'. Howells, the recipient of the letter transmitting her relentlessly negative verdict, was likewise an old acquaintance but also a fellow author and critic, and on 2 August 1908 he wrote to James in a correspondingly different spirit. The first three Prefaces had given his whole family 'great satisfaction, as read aloud by me':

We especially enjoyed you where you rounded upon yourself, and as it were took yourself to pieces, in your self-censure. The analysis of The American seemd [sic] happiest, but all the analyses were good, most subtle, and wise, and just, and the biographies of the three novels—Roderick Hudson and The Portrait of a Lady were the other two which I have yet received—were full of instruction for me, who as their godfather had fancied I knew all about them, but had really known them only from their birth, and not from their conception through their gestation. I remember so well your telling me, on such a Sunday afternoon as this, when we were rowing on Fresh Pond, what R.H. was to be. You have done a lot of good work, but nothing better than the last half of each of those prefaces; and I think the public will understand from them what I tried to note to you, that miserable hot afternoon when we sat glued to our chairs here: the fact, namely, that you have imagined your fiction, as a whole, and better fulfilled a conscious intention in it than any of your contemporaries. It took courage to do those introductions, and a toil as great, but how you must have liked doing them—or having done them! (*LFL* 422–3)

---

[242] Charles Eliot Norton to Howells, 26 March 1908; quoted *LFL* 422 n. 1.
[243] James to Grace Norton, 5 March 1907; *LHJ* 2:72.

Even Howells, who had known James since the 1860s and had been his editor at the *Atlantic Monthly* for all three novels named here, could find new material in the Prefaces to supplement his own knowledge of these works' textual histories, and his domestic reading-aloud of the Prefaces satisfyingly extended a continuum of literary talk with James that already spanned decades of friendly conversation – from an autumn afternoon in 1874 at Cambridge, Massachusetts to their recent meeting at Howells's home in Kittery Point, Maine in June 1905, towards the end of James's American tour. Personal retrospect was a significant component of early readers' responses to the Prefaces, whether appreciative or resentful. At the same time, it was the analytical element of those writings which Howells most enjoyed, and for which he voiced an unqualified praise: 'You have done a lot of good work, but nothing better than the last half of each of those prefaces.'

On 29 September 1908, nine months after the first volumes appeared in America, the British publishers Macmillan and Co. began to publish a small issue of the Edition. According to David J. Supino, this British issue was made up of 'imported American sheets with new prelims'. 'Macmillan initially purchased 100 sets of sheets from Scribner's' – that is, enough to make 100 copies of each volume – 'and were given a further five sets of sheets "gratis"'; orders for additional sheets sufficient to make from 25 to 100 copies per volume were placed between August 1909 and March 1911, the variation in the number of sheets ordered for different volumes perhaps indicating that Macmillan sold individual volumes of this issue as well as complete sets.[244] In December 1908, James directed that copies of the Macmillan issue should be sent to four friends, three of them authors: Joseph Conrad, Edmund Gosse, Paul Bourget and Henrietta Reubell.[245] Conrad responded at once on receipt of the first six volumes: 'to celebrate the event I have given myself a holiday for the morning, not to read any one of them—I

---

[244] Supino, *A Bibliographical Catalogue*, pp. 499, 521, 512–13.
[245] James to Frederick Macmillan, 8 December 1908; *The Correspondence of Henry James and the House of Macmillan, 1877–1914: 'All the Links in the Chain'*, ed. Rayburn S. Moore (Baton Rouge, LA: Louisiana State University Press, 1993), p. 216 and notes. James may have forgotten that he had already named Bourget as a recipient of the Scribner issue, as noted above. Because Macmillan were buying their sheets from the Scribners, James had to pay his British publishers 3s 6d per volume for copies of this issue (5s less than the retail price as reported in Edel and Laurence, *A Bibliography of Henry James*, p. 138).

could not settle to that—but to commune with them all, and gloat over the promise of the prefaces'. Like Howells, Conrad read these texts in a compound light of personal reminiscence and professional appreciation. He told James that he had already read the Preface to *The American* before he received these copies of the Edition and that the novel itself was 'the first of your long novels I ever read'; that was in 1891, several years before he became an author and at a time when the nautical metaphors of the Preface's early pages were the literal facts of his working life (see pp. 16–17). Turning to it now again, he found it

quite a thrill to be taken thus into your confidence; a strong emotion it is a privilege to be made to feel—[à] cinquante ans! [at fifty years!] Afterward I could not resist the temptation of reading the beautiful and touching last ten pages of the story. There is in them a perfection of tone which calmed me; and I sat for a long while with the closed volume in my hand going over the preface in my mind and thinking—that's how it began, that's how it was done![246]

Conrad's meditation on the ending of a well-loved novel, encountered again in a revised text and reintroduced by a differently familiar Preface, comprehended more than one remembered beginning.

4 Contemporary Reviews

As he thanked Edith Wharton in March 1908 for her ravishing appreciation of the *Portrait* Preface, James alluded to an old anxiety about critical neglect:

My effusions & lucubrations always affect me as giving forth into such a soundless void, from which no repercussion as of the stone dropped into the deep well ever comes back to my ear (& the Edition & the Prefaces & everything else about it form no apparent exception) that the hint of recording intelligence anywhere brings tears to my eyes. (*HJEW* 89–90)

He would complain to Gosse some years later that, with regard to his revision of early works, the Edition 'has never had the least intelligent

---

[246] Conrad to James, 12 December 1908; *The Collected Letters of Joseph Conrad*, ed. Frederick R. Karl and Laurence Davies, 9 vols. (Cambridge: Cambridge University Press, 1983–2007), vol. IV, pp. 161–2.

critical justice done it—any sort of critical attention at all paid it'. James was still bitterly conscious that 'from the point of view of profit either to the publishers or to myself' the Edition had been 'practically a complete failure; vulgarly speaking, it doesn't sell': 'No more commercially thankless job of the literary order was (Prefaces & all—*they* of a thanklessness!) accordingly ever achieved.'[247] But while it is true that much contemporary public response was dismissive of James's revisions, the Edition got a good deal of 'critical attention' from reviewers and the Prefaces in particular did receive 'intelligent critical justice' in some quarters. James had been especially delighted by a long, laudatory review in the *Times Literary Supplement* (8 July 1909) that attended very closely indeed to the Prefaces. Gosse saw it when it came out and wrote to congratulate James: 'full of pleasure' at Gosse's liking the piece, James described it as 'really intelligent & superior; a difficult thing very ably done'.[248] He sent a copy to his brother William in America, calling it 'much the most intelligent series of remarks ever dedicated, I think, to H.J.'[249]

The circumstances of this review show the importance of coterie appreciation to the first phase of the Prefaces' public reception. As was standard practice at the *Times Literary Supplement* for much of the twentieth century, the piece was unsigned; but James knew the reviewer. The young essayist and literary biographer Percy Lubbock was at this time a friendly acquaintance and on the way to becoming a disciple. Lubbock had been taught at Eton College by James's close friend A. C. Benson, and now belonged to the circle of another friend, the American novelist Howard Overing Sturgis; after James's death, Lubbock would publish an extremely influential synthesis of the Prefaces' comments on literary theory and would edit James's correspondence and unfinished novels.[250] James wrote warmly to Sturgis on 11 July 1909 about 'Percy's admirable and exquisite article': 'It is a very superior and a charmingly distinguished thing, the lovely paper, and I intensely and gratefully and almost tearfully appreciate it' (*HJL* 4:525). James's wider

---

[247] James to Edmund Gosse, 25 August 1915; *SLHJEG* 313, 314.
[248] James to Gosse, 28 July 1909; *SLHJEG* 243.
[249] James to William James, 17 August 1909; *CWJ* 3:398.
[250] For Lubbock in this editorial role, see Michael Anesko, *Monopolizing the Master: Henry James and the Politics of Modern Literary Scholarship* (Stanford, CA: Stanford University Press, 2012), pp. 73–108.

acquaintance noticed and appreciated it too. As he remarked again to Sturgis on 16 July, a week after it had appeared in print, 'Percy's article is having a *succès-fou* [wild success] among my friends—and deeply deserves it' (*HJL* 4:527).²⁵¹ Two other highly significant contemporary reviews of the *New York Edition* were also written by friends of the author: those by the English civil servant, editor and translator Edward Marsh in the New York *Bookman* (October 1909), and the American journalist Morton Fullerton in the English *Quarterly Review* (April 1910). There might have been at least one more: the novelist Ford Madox Hueffer, as he then was (later Ford Madox Ford), meant 'to give the complete edition a long full-dress review in the second number' of *The English Review*, the journal he co-edited with Conrad, but was apparently prevented from doing so by the unavailability of copies.²⁵² The editorial to the first number of *The English Review* hailed the publication of the Edition as 'an event at least as important in the history of a civilisation as the recording of the will of a sovereign people with regard to some policy of exclusion, of admission, of humanitarianism, of pugnacity'; but no review ever appeared.²⁵³

The contemporary reviewing overall was inconsistent in scope and variable in quality. Reviews in American periodicals tended to follow the Edition sequentially, instalment by instalment. Thus, the *Nation* kept up with

---

[251] James replied to at least two letters from friends mentioning this review. To Mary Augusta Ward: 'Yes, the article in the Times Litt. Supp. on my long-drawn Edition (by Percy Lubbock,) is really a beautiful & intelligent thing—with no end of admirable *saying* as well as of excellent perception; & it gives the very greatest pleasure. It does that gentle & thoroughly literary & finely critical young man great honour, I think—but it does me no less; & I somehow feel as if it drove in with an audible tap a sort of shining silver nail & marked, in a manner, a date. It is soon for me to give way to elation, no doubt (at 66!) but it does seem to suggest that the more or less interpretative critic has after all his uses. Let us at least *hope* that may be verified' (11 July 1909; Virginia). And to Ariana Sargent Curtis: 'All thanks for your friendly allusion to Percy Lubbock's so intelligent article in the Times Litt. Supp.—which I found charming, & far & away the most appreciative & *fine* tribute I have ever received' (17 July 1909; Virginia).

[252] In October 1908, Hueffer asked Pinker – his literary agent as well as James's - to borrow a set of *New York Edition* volumes for him from Macmillan & Co., 'as I cannot at this moment afford to buy them' (Hueffer to Pinker, 16 October 1908; *Letters of Ford Madox Ford*, ed. Richard M. Ludwig (Princeton, NJ: Princeton University Press, 1965), p. 27). Macmillan had only begun issuing volumes the previous month, and probably only the first twelve volumes of the Edition had been published in America.

[253] 'Editorial', *English Review* 1 (December 1908), 157–60; 159.

the volumes as they appeared, though its short notices became increasingly perfunctory and many were mere collages of quotations. A few American newspapers doggedly reviewed every volume; others started with the apparent intention of tracking the Edition from start to finish but lost interest (the *New York Times* noticed the first ten volumes and then ignored the Edition for a year, then ran an isolated review of volumes XVII–XVIII, then finally gave up); others dropped out for a while and came back for the final volumes. Only Edward Marsh's essay in the New York *Bookman* surveyed the Edition as a whole, and in this regard it duplicated the retrospective, panoramic approach of the few English periodicals that noticed the Edition at all, as exemplified in the long essays by Lubbock and Fullerton. No English periodical undertook to review the successive instalments of the Edition. These divergent approaches led to broadly different types of commentary: the American explicitly conditioned by the Scribners' prospectus, often bothered by James's textual revisions, and sometimes entering into combative discussion with the Prefaces' critiques of particular novels and tales; the English more obviously understanding and accepting of James's methods and intentions, and tending to emphasize the Prefaces' unified theoretical ambitions rather than their readings of individual fictions. The American reviews seem altogether less sure of what James was trying to do in assembling the Edition, and American newspaper coverage in particular could take an irreverent, rough-housing tone: 'It is beyond our power to render in proper æsthetic terms the vulgar but expressive concepts of "bumptiousness" and "flapdoodle," yet the ideas may flit through the minds of the readers of these prefaces.'[254] But in their puzzlement or amusement or hostility, the American reviews are also attentive to aspects of the Prefaces which would not receive serious critical comment until the 1960s – to their wild variability of tone (confiding, vulnerable, boastful, playful, self-conscious, self-important), and to the emotional importance of their sustained act of personal retrospect.

On a superficial level, many American reviewers of the *New York Edition* found the Prefaces easy to like: notices of the early volumes called them 'bright and [...] amusing', 'piquant and entertaining', 'as noteworthy literary

---

[254] *New York Sun* (22 February 1908), 5.

criticism as any Mr. James has done', 'a delightful treat'.[255] Several reviewers concurred with the *Literary Digest* in judging the Prefaces 'the feature of highest value that the new edition presents'.[256] They were certainly the least controversial element of the Edition, as compared with the omission of specific titles or with James's textual revisions. As Richard Nicholas Foley observes, in general 'the prefaces were welcomed and applauded, but the revisions of the individual stories, particularly the early ones such as *Roderick Hudson* and *The American*, were resented and ridiculed'.[257] Montgomery Schuyler, reviewing *NYE* I–II in the *New York Times*, fairly represents this line of response, regretting the exclusion of *The Bostonians* (1886) from the Edition and confessing himself 'bewildered by the indirection and circuitousness of the additions' to passages of dialogue in the revised text, but finding the Prefaces 'thoroughly enjoyable, as well as highly instructive and exemplary'; 'Apparently the judicious reader will consult his interest and his pleasure if he reads the new prefaces very carefully, looks over the revised version for passages of exposition and comment, and then recurs to the original text.'[258]

Reviewers' enjoyment of the Prefaces was tempered by uncertainty as to whom exactly these writings were meant for. Their obvious but limited appeal to specialists was noted: the 'intricate' Prefaces to *The Portrait of a Lady* and *The Princess Casamassima* 'will provide material for discussion as to their meaning in H. James clubs wherever they exist'.[259] By analogy with a field of activity – sport – where technical analysis was an accepted part of popular discourse, Edward Marsh recommended the Prefaces to readers 'who regard fiction as one of the greatest of pastimes, and therefore worthy of as serious discussion and consideration as tennis or chess': 'Here is one of the great masters of the game making a complete, thoroughgoing analysis of his own "play" over a third of a century.'[260] There was disagreement, however,

---

[255] *New York Sun* (28 December 1907), 5; *Boston Evening Transcript* (8 January 1908), 16; *Chicago Evening Post* (29 January 1908), 4; *Chicago Record-Herald* (8 February 1908), 6.
[256] *Literary Digest* 36 (21 March 1908), 418.
[257] Richard Nicholas Foley, *Criticism in American Periodicals of the Works of Henry James from 1866 to 1916* (Washington, DC: The Catholic University of America Press, 1944), p. 123.
[258] *New York Times Saturday Review of Books* 13 (11 January 1908), 13–15.
[259] *New York Sun* (22 February 1908), 5.
[260] *Bookman* (New York) 30 (October 1909), 138–43; 140.

about their suitability for would-be novelists, the 'aspirants in our arduous profession' who made an important part of their target audience (*LFL* 426; and see below, pp. cxxiii–cxxiv). The *Chicago Record-Herald* thought that James's 'discussions of sundry questions of literary technic will be extremely interesting and helpful to young writers'.[261] The *New York Times*, on the other hand, reviewed the Prefaces to *The Awkward Age* and *The Spoils of Poynton* alongside a popular treatise on novel-writing, and found James by comparison 'too personal, too involved, generally too delightfully vague, in formulating his theory of fiction, to be of use to any but the most advanced student of the art, if there is such an art, and it has students'; 'matter more to our immediate purpose' was to be found in Charles F. Horne's *The Technique of the Novel* (1908), 'the latest practical attempt to reduce novel writing to a theory'.[262] Some casually optimistic reviewers predicted that the Prefaces would be of interest to all: to 'the ardent and avowed disciple' and 'the unregenerate' alike, to 'the literary expert and the student of fiction' but also 'the general reader'.[263] They would be 'a delight to all Jamesians', whom they would help to understand 'the novel as a literary form,—to put it in very academic language'; 'to be more practical', they would also assist 'the new, fresh, unsophisticated reader of James, if there are any such, [...] to see what the author is driving at'.[264] That claim about accessibility was given an ironic inflection by a notice in the *Louisville Courier-Journal* under the title 'Henry James Will Elucidate', which figured the Prefaces as a gloss or guide for 'the unintelligent reader', 'telling "what the idea was" in each book': 'Not to know James is to be benighted, and an opportunity to read him with a pony, as Caesar, Virgil and Livy are read by undergraduates, will be appreciated by the mere reader of tales who loses his interest when he loses his way in the labyrinth.'[265]

---

[261] *Chicago Record-Herald* (8 February 1908), 6.
[262] *New York Times Saturday Review of Books* 13 (30 May 1908), 306.
[263] *Bookman* (New York) 28 (September 1908), 12–13; *San Francisco Chronicle* (26 January 1908), 10.
[264] *Dial* 44 (16 March 1908), 174–6; 175.
[265] *Louisville Courier-Journal* (11 January 1908), 6. In American slang, a 'pony' is 'A literal translation or summary of a text used as a short cut or study aid; a crib' (*Oxford English Dictionary*, 'pony', n.¹, sense 4).

INTRODUCTION

Conscious of the notorious difficulty of James's late style, some reviews were openly derisive about the explanatory value of the Prefaces. In an article whose title called for 'More Plainness and Less Art', the *Minneapolis Tribune* thought it likely 'that to the average reader his elucidation will fail to elucidate, but will succeed only in making the darkness more visible'.[266] Two early reviews shared the punning title 'Henry James to Explain Himself', the first remarking 'that after his critical and explanatory work is completed there will be more need than ever before for a critic to explain his explanations'.[267] This quip was a nineteenth-century commonplace deriving from a comment by Lord Byron on S. T. Coleridge's *Biographia Literaria* (1817), a difficult, hybrid work of autobiography, philosophy, literary theory and close reading:

> And Coleridge, too, has lately taken wing,
>   But, like a hawk encumber'd with his hood,
> Explaining metaphysics to the nation—
> I wish he would explain his Explanation.[268]

The second 'Henry James to Explain Himself' notice made the same point with the bluntness of a proverb: 'One can imagine the halt teaching the lame to walk, or the blind leading the blind. But Henry James explaining Henry James is something to baffle the imagination.'[269] Where, on the other hand, the clarity of James's self-explanation was granted, the Prefaces raised the prospect of redundancy for all other critics. Elisabeth Luther Cary felt the paradoxical difficulty of analysing the work of an author 'acutely conscious of every step of his process. Such confidingness of self-revelation leaves the critic high and dry. There is nothing left for him to do but stand like a post on the street corner pointing the way to the legitimate halls of instruction, which are now in a double sense the books themselves.'[270] Nevertheless

---

[266] *Minneapolis Tribune* (26 July 1908), 4.
[267] *New York Times Saturday Review of Books* 12 (6 December 1907), 776.
[268] Byron, *Don Juan*, Dedication to Cantos I–II (1819), stanza 2, ll. 13–16; Byron, *The Complete Poetical Works*, ed. Jerome J. McGann, 7 vols. (Oxford: Clarendon Press, 1980–93), vol. V, p. 3. For an allusion to this passage in the Preface to *NYE* XIV, see note 547 to the text.
[269] *Chicago Inter Ocean* (8 January 1908), 6.
[270] *Book News Monthly* 27 (May 1909), 641–5; 645.

many other reviewers felt able to question James's particular critiques in one Preface or another, and Montgomery Schuyler predicted that readers in general would disagree with his diagnoses of faults in the early novels (the hurried time scheme of *Roderick Hudson*, the improbability of the Bellegardes' attitude to Christopher Newman in *The American*, the undue prominence of Henrietta Stackpole in *The Portrait*): on such points of detail, 'the reader will be apt to demur and to come to the defense of the artist against the auto-critic'.[271]

A great deal of attention was given to the Prefaces' staging of an encounter between James's inventive and critical selves, and many reviewers recognized this strange meeting as a source of pleasure for author and reader alike. The *New York Sun* thought that James was 'having the time of his life': 'The joy [he] feels in rereading his books of thirty years ago and the boyish delight he takes in making the older James pick out the faults of the younger James and pat him on the shoulder when he is good are contagious.'[272] In the *Chicago Daily Tribune*, Elia W. Peattie found an esoteric religious analogy for the same phenomenon, likening James's 'obvious delight and surprise' to the emotions of 'a Theosophist who, having progressed through many incarnations, should return to an early experience to find himself enchanted by a simpler and sweeter phase of his illimitable career'.[273] Reviewers saw the erotic potential of this intergenerational romance: thus, James was 'as pleased over what he finds of old forgotten qualities in himself as a woman is at coming unexpectedly upon a bunch of yellowed love letters'; another notice imagined him in a suggestively tactile relation with his early texts, at the 'unmistakably agreeable task of turning his old works of art about in his hands, caressingly examining their every curve or angle, and expressing as subtly as he can the emotions they inspire in him to-day'.[274] Such charmed rereading seemed to include not only James's early novels and stories but his old critical axioms and generalizations also: 'The same principles which

---

[271] *New York Times Saturday Review of Books* 13 (11 January 1908), 14.
[272] *New York Sun* (28 December 1907), 5.
[273] *Chicago Daily Tribune* (6 March 1908), 9.
[274] *Chicago Daily Tribune* (18 January 1908), 9. *New-York Daily Tribune* (18 July 1908), 5.

Mr. James has discust [sic] in his other critical writing now take on an unwonted intensity and intimacy.'[275]

For Peattie, the Prefaces' fostering of intimate relations with past selves, texts and ideas also brought James 'nearer to intimacy with his public than he ever has [come] before. He shows the inside of his mind, after all these years of almost appalling reticence, with something akin to joyous fellowship.' The reference is to an American public: Peattie thought that James's attitude to his native country had 'mellowed' with age, and he wrote now 'as if his barriers had been enchantingly broken down; as if, after all his irritation at us, his detached scrutiny of us, he had decided upon a brotherly heart confidence'. The long period of 'detached scrutiny' presumably dated from James's international stories of the 1870s–80s, and came as close to the present day as his critiques of American culture and society in 'The Question of Our Speech' (1905), his *Harper's Bazar* articles on the speech and manners of American women (1906–7) and *The American Scene* (1907). Peattie also recognized that James was taking a risk by thus confiding in his readers, and he saw the Prefaces' performance of intimacy as proof that James now felt secure enough 'to dare to be ridiculous':

Never in the history of literature [...] has there been anything comparable to Mr. James' unsophisticated delight in his own sophistication; Mr. James' subtle joy in his own subtlety; or Mr. James' incoherent exuberance over his own incoherency. At times he tries, almost touchingly, to restrain his pride and satisfaction in the elaborate products of his pen, but after a brief struggle he abandons himself to his delight, and laughs with glee at the emotions produced by his own inimitable methods.[276]

The quality of tone which Peattie refers to here provoked sharply differing responses in early readers of the Prefaces. It could be heard either as 'naive self-complacency'[277] or as 'a power of self-dissection absolutely free from vanity', 'frank' and 'searchingly true': 'In spite of the many critics to the contrary, these introductions in which [James] explains the motives, errors, delusions and enthusiasms which influenced the composition are among

---

[275] *Literary Digest* 36 (21 March 1908), 418. Later reviewers identified 'The Art of Fiction' (1884) as a specific source for the Prefaces' critical principles: *Contemporary Review* 101 (January 1912), 69–78; 69. *Bookman* (London) 43 (March 1913), 299–306; 302–3.
[276] *Chicago Daily Tribune* (6 March 1909), 9.
[277] *Chicago Record-Herald* (23 September 1909), 8.

the best things he has ever written.'²⁷⁸ Several reviewers found the Prefaces actually or potentially ridiculous on this account. As the *Nation* tersely put it, even when discussing 'mere short stories, Mr. James takes himself with portentous seriousness. He dwells at interminable length on the details of unimportant matters.'²⁷⁹ For George Hamlin Fitch in the *San Francisco Chronicle*, these characteristics made the Prefaces fair game for detractors: James 'takes himself far more seriously than even his admirers take him, and he discusses his early mistakes and limitations with a Jove-like solemnity and unction that will appeal to the caricaturists'.²⁸⁰ Peattie, too, found it 'easily imaginable that in those periodic revivals of James, which will stir the literary world from time to time in the years to come, this position of reverence before the altar on which James has laid many offerings will be regarded with satiric delight'.²⁸¹ Just six years later, H. G. Wells would find a cruelly satirical use for that same figure, likening the typical James novel to '"a church lit but without a congregation to distract you, with every light and line focused on the high altar. And on the altar, very reverently placed, intensely there, is a dead kitten, an egg-shell, a bit of string."'²⁸²

James's self-involvement was more tolerantly regarded by reviewers who read the Prefaces as primarily autobiographical, rather than critical, writings. Edwin Francis Edgett in the *Boston Evening Transcript* noted that, while the 'marvellously introspective and minutely reminiscent prefaces' had been 'regularly scoffed at and derided in some quarters', 'the chief objections to them—their egotism and their devotion to apparent trivialities—are exactly the reasons why other minds find them of the utmost appealing interest': they 'form a vividly intimate narrative of the course of Henry

---

[278] *Louisville Courier-Journal* (27 June 1908), 5.
[279] *Nation* 88 (22 April 1909), 410.
[280] *San Francisco Chronicle* (26 January 1908), 10.
[281] *Chicago Daily Tribune* (4 September 1909), 11.
[282] H. G. Wells, *Boon, The Mind of the Race, The Wild Asses of the Devil, and The Last Trump* (London: T. Fisher Unwin, 1915), pp. 106–7. Wells does not refer to the Prefaces in *Boon*, an omission that acquires significance in the context of other critics' neglect of the Prefaces in assessing James's career in the second decade of the twentieth century (see below, pp. cxxv–cxxvi). When, earlier in the same chapter, Boon's interlocutor Dodd says of James, '"Recently he's been explaining himself"' – a formula which we have seen used in a jocular spirit by two contemporary reviewers of the *New York Edition* – Boon assumes that the reference is to the essays in *Notes on Novelists* (1914) (*Boon*, p. 103).

James's life and art during a period of almost half a century'.[283] The critic of the *Outlook* similarly characterized the first two Prefaces as 'really chapters in autobiography'.[284] Reviewers consistently enjoyed their simpler autobiographical elements, the circumstantial accounts of inspiration and composition, and the occasional 'plums and spice' of literary anecdote.[285] The *New York Sun* found it 'pleasant to discover this human everyday side in Mr. James', and wished that 'he would expatiate more on the circumstances connected with his composition, the delightful glimpses of London and Paris and other places'.[286] But such passages also suggested something important about James's recall of past experience: as the reviewer of the *Boston Evening Transcript* remarked, 'if the prefaces [...] are to be accepted literally, there is nothing that lingers longer in his memory than the local associations' of the act of writing.[287] Coleridge, once more, served as a term of comparison for the autobiographical aspect of the Prefaces: the *Nation* predicted that they 'will form a *biographia literaria* of uncommon interest and significance'.[288] Under the title 'Henry James: Auto-Critic', Edward Marsh presented the Prefaces as the apotheosis of literary autobiography, 'a document, or series of documents, without parallel in literature': until James, 'no one has undertaken to tell from beginning to end the origin and growth of practically all the products of his creative effort'.[289] For Marsh, the Prefaces surpassed a list of distinguished but 'partial, incomplete registers of the artist's critical sense turned on his own works' in writings by Leo Tolstoy, Guy de Maupassant, Walter Besant, Anthony Trollope, George Moore, Robert Louis Stevenson and W. M. Thackeray.[290]

And yet reviewers also found the Prefaces to be a resolutely *literary* type of autobiography, unrevealing of private details. As Marsh noted, 'There is

---

[283] *Boston Evening Transcript* (1 May 1909), Part III, 5.
[284] *Outlook* (New York) 88 (18 January 1908), 145.
[285] *New York Times Saturday Review of Books* (1 May 1909), 275.
[286] *New York Sun* (4 April 1908), 7–8; 8.
[287] *Boston Evening Transcript* (18 March 1908), 19.
[288] *Nation*, 86 (2 January 1908), 11.
[289] *Bookman* (New York) 30 (October 1909), 140, 141.
[290] Marsh does not always give the titles of the works he refers to, but the unidentified works are mostly guessable: Tolstoy's *What Is Art?* (1897), Maupassant's 'Le Roman' (1888), Besant's *The Art of Fiction* (1884), Trollope's *An Autobiography* (1883), Moore's *Memoirs of My Dead Life* (1906), Stevenson's letters and Thackeray's 'De Finibus' (1862).

scarcely a living author of distinction whom one would not more readily associate with the literary confessional' than James, and in this regard the Prefaces remained 'true to the artistic practice of a lifetime. There is no vulgar personal revelation; there are records of places and dates, but the man himself, as separate from the artist, is to be discovered only obliquely as in his novels.'[291] Marsh had first met James through Edmund Gosse in the 1890s and knew him socially but not intimately; some years after the Edition, he would commission James to write a different sort of preface, to accompany the posthumous publication of Rupert Brooke's *Letters from America* (1915).[292] Gosse himself, an older and closer friend, wrote warmly to James about the Edition when it appeared; but nearly fifteen years later, he would publicly admit to finding the Prefaces 'highly disappointing' as instalments of autobiography, 'dry, remote, and impersonal to a strange degree'.[293] Gosse was thinking of what James had told him about the Prefaces before they were written: 'They were to be full and confidential, they were to throw to the winds all restraints of conventional reticence, they were to take us, with eyes unbandaged, into the inmost sanctum of his soul.'[294] James may have been exaggerating, or Gosse allowing disappointed curiosity to colour his recollection. Either way, this does not sound much like the cautious phrasing of James's memo to the Scribners: 'a freely colloquial and even, perhaps, as I may say, confidential preface or introduction' to each *New York Edition* volume (*HJL* 4:367). Gosse grants a Coleridgean intensity to the Prefaces' frustrated impulse to communicate, and casts James as a would-be Ancient Mariner: 'It is as though the author felt a burning desire to confide in the reader, whom he positively button-holes in the endeavour, but that the experience itself evades him, fails to find expression, and falls

---

[291] *Bookman* (New York) 30 (October 1909), 139.

[292] Marsh, *A Number of People: A Book of Reminiscences* (London: William Heinemann, 1939), pp. 114–15, 118–19.

[293] Gosse, *Aspects and Impressions* (London: Cassell and Company, 1922), p. 18. Gosse's letter about the Edition does not survive, but James told him at the time that it had given him 'extraordinary pleasure' and declared it '*the* most precious pearl [...] of my crown of recognition. None other, whatever, begins to approach it in lustre or loveliness. The Edition has been a weary grind (such a mass of obscure & unmeasurable labour,) but I feel all you say as the most delightful consequence of it' (29 December 1908; *SLHJEG* 239).

[294] Gosse, *Aspects and Impressions*, pp. 17–18.

stillborn, while other matters, less personal and less important, press in and take their place against the author's wish.'²⁹⁵ In the Prefaces themselves, it may be noted, autobiography is figured as a 'monstrous' mode of writing and confined to the subjunctive mood. James remarks in the Preface to *The Portrait of a Lady* that questions about the personal origins of a fictional idea *might* be answered 'beautifully, doubtless, if one could do so subtle, if not so monstrous, a thing as to write the history of the growth of one's imagination' (p. 37); in the event, that attempt would be put off for another five years, until he came to write his first volume of memoirs, *A Small Boy and Others* (1913).

The most perceptive contemporary responses to the Edition treated the Prefaces as foundational texts of novel theory. The key contribution was made by Percy Lubbock in the *Times Literary Supplement* review already referred to, which greeted the Prefaces as 'an event, indeed the first event, in the history of an art almost as confusedly apprehended as it is enormously practised'. Recapitulating a point from 'The Art of Fiction' about the theoretical unselfconsciousness of the Anglo-American novel tradition, Lubbock announced the opening of a new critical era: 'Mr. James's Prefaces sweep aside all such artless conceptions and place the novel at once in a completely new light.' Lubbock presented James as the first novelist 'who has seen his art as a deliberate process of which a complete account can be given'; his long review-essay was a digest of that 'account' as given in the Prefaces. James's 'summary achievement on behalf of the novel', Lubbock argued, was to clarify 'the question of form', which ought to be understood not as 'one [...] element of the many that might go to make up a novel' but as 'a condition uniformly laid upon' *all* those elements. 'This strict fusion of material with form is Mr. James's point of departure', and in the later novels it was most apparent in the focalizing of the action from 'a single point of view' – a formal concept which Lubbock would do much to popularize in his later critical work.²⁹⁶ In the *TLS* review, he also offered readings of *The Awkward Age*, *What Maisie Knew* and the three major-phase novels which highlighted the Prefaces' remarks on the 'scenic' principle of composition.²⁹⁷

---

[295] Ibid., p. 18.
[296] *Times Literary Supplement* (8 July 1909), 249–50; 249.
[297] Ibid., 250.

Another substantial contemporary essay on the *New York Edition* – in effect a review of the Prefaces – was written by Morton Fullerton. A friend of James's since the 1890s, at the time of the Edition Fullerton was conducting a love affair with Edith Wharton; his review was produced at her urging and with her assistance.[298] It explicitly positioned James as a successor and equal to Balzac, and attempted to formulate 'the lesson of Mr James' from a survey of his fiction in light of the Prefaces.[299] Like Lubbock, Fullerton framed the Prefaces as an inaugural discourse on 'the art of fiction in general. They represent, in fact, the first serious attempt ever made in English to call upon that bewildered art to pause and give a conscious account of itself; to present its credentials and justify its existence.'[300] Like Lubbock too, he read the Prefaces as a teleological narrative of technical development, and saw James's gradual advance from simpler to more complex modes of representation as proceeding by 'a series of syntheses now clearly traceable in the collected edition.'[301] Fullerton accepted the Prefaces' central aesthetic principles (e.g., the use of a central focalizing consciousness, 'the indivisibility of form and content', 'morality' in art as a function of the artist's sensibility); he used James's technical terms (e.g., 'foreshortening') as though their general currency were already established; and he validated choices of subject-matter which James had felt compelled to defend in the

---

[298] Fullerton lectured on James at Bryn Mawr College in the autumn of 1907, and on this trip to America he visited Wharton at her home in Massachusetts, their shared friendship with James and interest in his work making a ready occasion for sociability; a few months afterwards, they became lovers. Wharton encouraged Fullerton to rewrite his lecture as an article, and in March 1908 she offered it to *Scribner's Magazine* as a review of the *New York Edition*; it was apparently submitted to the Scribners and rejected by them that spring, and finally appeared in the *Quarterly Review* two years later. This information is drawn from the headnote printed with the text of the review – 'The Art of Henry James' – in *Edith Wharton: The Uncollected Critical Writings*, ed. Frederick Wegener (Princeton, NJ: Princeton University Press, 1996), pp. 299–304. James seems to have been ambivalent about the piece during its long gestation, but he gratefully acknowledged it to Wharton when it came out: 'the bounty of the article is a joy to me' (25 April 1910; *HJEW* 158).

[299] *Quarterly Review* 212 (April 1910), 393–408; 396, 407.

[300] Ibid., 393.

[301] Ibid., 394. Compare Lubbock: 'With the author himself [...] to point the way, we can see the whole process by which the easy finished lightness of "Roderick Hudson" and "The Portrait of a Lady" develops naturally and inevitably into the packed elaboration of "The Ambassadors" and "The Golden Bowl"' (*Times Literary Supplement* (8 July 1909), 249).

Prefaces – notably, the consciousness of girls and young women, and the international situation ('that vast epic—the modern Iliad, when its peripatetic and romantic elements do not make it more like an Odyssey—the clash between two societies, the mutual call of two sundered worlds').[302]

Lubbock was the first reviewer to suggest that the critical substance of the Prefaces could have a life apart from the *New York Edition*: 'It is greatly to be hoped that these penetrating criticisms, so far-reaching in their general application, may be made more accessible.' Could James not 'find time to gather together in a volume of their own at least the main results of his work as a theorist in his art?'[303] Edward Marsh would make the same point: if somebody could 'disengage' the Prefaces' 'general observations and range them in an orderly sequence [...] the result would be the most searching analysis of the novelist's art that has ever been put to paper'.[304] A similar thought had already occurred to James, but whereas Lubbock and Marsh seem to have envisaged something like a redaction of the Prefaces' principles or an anthology of key passages, he was plainly thinking of collecting and republishing the texts themselves. Writing to Howells on 17 August 1908, he made a now famous statement about the general applicability of the Prefaces that is too often detached from its context, a private confession of 'weariness' with 'the heavy lucubrations in question':

This staleness of sensibility, in connection with them blocks out for the hour every aspect but that of their being all done, and of their perhaps helping the Edition to sell two or three copies more! They will have represented much labour to this latter end—though in that they will have differed indeed from no other of their fellow-manifestations (in general) whatever; and the resemblance will be even increased if the two or three copies *don't*, in the form of an extra figure or two, mingle with my withered laurels. They are, in general, a sort of plea for Criticism, for Discrimination, for Appreciation on other than infantine lines—as against the so almost universal Anglo-Saxon absence of these things; which tends so, in our general trade, it seems to me, to break the heart. However, I am afraid I'm too sick of the mere doing of them, and of the general strain of the effort to avoid the deadly danger of repetition, to say much to the purpose about them. They ought, collected

---

[302] *Quarterly Review* 212 (April 1910), 394–400.
[303] *Times Literary Supplement* (8 July 1909), 249.
[304] *Bookman* (New York) 30 (October 1909), 141.

together, none the less, to form a sort of comprehensive manual or *vade-mecum* for aspirants in our arduous profession. Still, it will be long before I shall want to collect them together for that purpose and furnish *them* with a final Preface. I've done with prefaces for ever. (*LFL* 425–6)

The eighteen Prefaces which James eventually composed are haunted by two unwritten companions: as well as the 'final Preface' he mentions here, there was the Preface that would have gone with *The Bostonians* if that novel had been included in the *New York Edition*. As he remarked to Gosse on 25 August 1915, just over a year into the First World War: 'I should have liked to write that Preface to The Bostonians—which will never be written now. But think of noting now that *that* is a thing that has perished!' (*SLHJEG* 314). This sense of loss – loss both of opportunity and of desire – was the obverse to the pride that led James to conceive of the gathered Prefaces as a vade mecum for novelists of the future: from the Latin *vade mecum* ('go with me'), 'A book or manual suitable for carrying about with one for ready reference', 'a handbook or guidebook' (*OED*). Here in the August 1908 letter to Howells is the first recorded thought of *reprinting* the Prefaces, a bibliographical event that would have profound consequences for their later reception history. And yet that thought arose from James's anxiety about the Edition's commercial failure and from his fatigued distaste for 'the mere doing' of the Prefaces, such that he was content to defer repurposing them to an unimaginable future and could talk about the book they 'ought [...] to form' as though that were a project for someone else to undertake – as, in fact, it would become.

5 Early Critical Responses

In December 1915, Edward Marsh – now Assistant Private Secretary to the British Prime Minister, Herbert Asquith – cited the Prefaces in a private letter recommending James for the Order of Merit: 'Apart from fiction, his critical work is of the highest order; & his introductions to his own novels in the Library Edition are I think a uniquely illuminating account of an artist's creative processes.' Marsh had made the same point in his *Bookman* review six years before, and the terms in which he sought to exonerate James from criticism 'for dealing only with characters drawn from the hothouse life of the leisured classes' show as well that he had internalized one of the

Prefaces' most important aesthetic principles: 'an artist shd be judged not by his choice of material but by his treatment'.[305] James would receive the Order of Merit in the New Year's Honours of 1916. When he died in February of that year, the *New York Times* ran an obituary that read the Prefaces as his 'critical autobiography' and found in them evidence of discipline and devotion – 'His capacity for unremitting attention to his task and his definite attitude toward his art, his laborious reduction of multiplicity to order, his resolute rejection of any temptation to wander free of technical laws and boundaries' – that added up 'to a quite stupendous total of character'.[306]

Nevertheless, the Prefaces were not widely discussed in the years immediately before and after James's death, and some prominent surveys of his career by younger writers in this period either ignored them or pointedly downplayed their importance. In her posthumous study *Henry James* (1916), Rebecca West relegated them to a miscellaneous group of writings from James's final decade, oddly lumping them in with *The American Scene*, the story collection *The Finer Grain* (1910) and the novelized play *The Outcry* (1911): 'the crystal bowl of Mr. James' art' in this late phase 'was not, as one had feared, broken. He had but gilded its clear sides with the gold of his genius for phrase-making, and now, instead of lifting it with a priest-like gesture to exhibit a noble subject, held it on his knees as a treasured piece of bric-à-brac and tossed into it, with an increasing carelessness, any sort of subject—a jewel, a rose, a bit of string, a visiting card—confident that the surrounding golden glow would lend it beauty.'[307] West figured the Prefaces as the trivia of James's dotage, and made no direct reference to them in assessing his fiction.[308] In his *Henry James: A Critical Study* (1913), Ford

[305] Edward Howard Marsh Collection of Papers, The Henry W. and Albert A. Berg Collection of English and American Literature, The New York Public Library. Edward Marsh to Herbert Henry Asquith, 1st Earl of Oxford and Asquith, 18 December [1915]; partly quoted in Edel, *Henry James: The Master 1901–1916*, pp. 558–9. For judging the treatment and not the subject, see the Preface to *The Portrait of a Lady*, pp. 34–5.
[306] 'Henry James, Interpreter of American Types', *New York Times* (5 March 1916), Magazine Section, 7–8; 7.
[307] West, *Henry James* (London: Nisbet & Co., 1916), p. 115.
[308] Hazel Hutchison has argued that this passage shows West engaging indirectly with Jamesian 'metaphors for the act of writing', most importantly the Prefaces' complex figure of the *ficelle* – 'literally a bit of string' (see pp. 43, 256). Hutchison also notes the significant occurrence of 'a bit of string' in H. G. Wells's contemporaneous satire *Boon* (for which, see fn. 282); she

INTRODUCTION

Madox Hueffer complained that he had looked forward to writing a chapter on James's 'Methods', but had found when he came to do it that, 'alas, there is nothing to write!': 'Mr. James has done it himself. In the matchless—and certainly bewildering series of Prefaces to the collected edition, there is no single story that has not been annotated, critically written about and (again critically) sucked as dry as any orange. There is nothing left for the poor critic but the merest of quotations.' Hueffer accordingly padded out this chapter with long quotations from several Prefaces, focusing on passages about anecdotal origins and the ironic relation between source material and achieved fictions, but offering very little by way of his own commentary.[309] Ezra Pound, too, looking back over James's career in the August 1918 'Henry James Number' of his journal *The Little Review*, observed that 'James, in his prefaces, has written explanation to death (with sometimes a very pleasant necrography).' Rather than stitch together quotations, Pound chose to avoid the Prefaces altogether, offering instead a set of 'elliptical notes' on James's novels and tales – an annotated list of titles arranged 'as nearly as possible in their order of publication (as distinct from their order as rearranged and partially weeded out in the collected edition)'.[310] And while he allowed that 'it should come as no surprise that Henry James has left us some sort of treatise on novel-writing', he perversely located that 'treatise' not in the Prefaces but in the dictated Notes for James's unfinished American novel *The Ivory Tower*, which had come out the previous year in a posthumous edition by Percy Lubbock. Pound's final contribution to the 'Henry James Number' was an incomplete list of axioms derived from those Notes, the headings of a 'formula for building a novel'.[311]

When Lubbock reviewed Hueffer's *Henry James* in 1914, he rebuked the book for shirking a proper analysis of the Prefaces: 'the task of tracing the how and the why of Mr. James's steady advance from the simplicities of narrative to the complex adjustments of "drama" and "picture" (to use his own nomenclature) in his latest novel, is one, interesting and rewarding as

conjectures that West and Wells – who were lovers at this period and composed these works simultaneously – 'shared notes and ideas as they wrote' ('A Bit of String: Rebecca West on Henry James', *Henry James Review* 39.3 (2018), 247–55; 251–3).
[309] Hueffer, *Henry James: A Critical Study* (London: Martin Secker, 1913), pp. 152, 155–67.
[310] Pound, 'A Shake Down', *The Little Review* 5.4 (August 1918), 9–39; 22.
[311] Pound, 'The Notes to "The Ivory Tower"', *The Little Review* 5.4 (August 1918), 62–4; 62, 63.

it would be, which still remains to be accomplished'.[312] This was in effect a preview of the next phase of the Prefaces' reception, which would be concerned with ordering their contents, extracting general principles and a usable technical vocabulary from James's discussions of particular fictions, and working them into the chronology of his development as a novelist and critic. Over the next two decades, that work would be mainly done by American and Canadian academics.[313] Lubbock's contribution was *The Craft of Fiction* (1921), a general study of the novel which adopted the Jamesian terms he had isolated in his review of Hueffer – 'drama' and 'picture' – as labels for 'contrasted manners of treatment' discernible across a broad array of eighteenth- and nineteenth-century European and Russian works. Lubbock chose these terms, he explained, because 'they *have* been used technically in the criticism of fiction, with specific meaning'; at the same time, he admitted that he was using them 'in a rather more extended sense' than James did in the Prefaces. With reference to 'fiction generally', for Lubbock 'picture' denoted a mode of narration in which the action is reflected in the consciousness of a narrator or a focalizing character, and 'drama' a mode in which the action is presented as though objectively, without the interposition of another consciousness. By using this dichotomy to frame a general account of narrative construction, Lubbock installed a simplified Jamesian principle of focalization at the heart of his theory of the novel: 'The whole intricate question of method, in the craft of fiction, I take to be governed by the question of the point of view—the question of the relation in which the narrator stands to the story'.[314]

Lubbock's enormously influential account of 'point of view' in fiction, illustrated by set-piece analyses of *The Ambassadors*, *The Wings of the Dove* and *The Awkward Age* but designedly detachable from those examples, would be taken up over the course of the twentieth century by successive

---

[312] [Lubbock], 'The Quest of the Golden Bowl', *Times Literary Supplement* (22 January 1914), 38.
[313] See Stuart P. Sherman, 'The Aesthetic Idealism of Henry James', *Nation* 104 (5 April 1917), 393–9; Joseph Warren Beach, *The Method of Henry James* (New Haven, CT: Yale University Press, 1918); Pelham Edgar, *Henry James, Man and Author* (Boston, MA and New York: Houghton Mifflin Company, 1927); Morris Roberts, *Henry James's Criticism* (Cambridge, MA: Harvard University Press, 1929); and Leon Edel, *The Prefaces of Henry James* (Paris: Jouve et Cie, 1931).
[314] Lubbock, *The Craft of Fiction* (London: Jonathan Cape, 1921), pp. 110–12, 251.

schools of Anglo-American novel theory.³¹⁵ Its independent success, however, would come at a cost for the Prefaces themselves. Forty years on from *The Craft of Fiction*, Wayne C. Booth described a 'process of reduction' whereby James's 'flexible explorations' of narrative technique in the Prefaces were first 'schematized' by Lubbock and others, and then promulgated as 'dogma' by their successors, so that by the 1950s it had become 'easy' for critics 'to quote James's own precepts, codified and elevated a notch or two, against the master' and to convict him of inconsistency by appealing to rules he had never proposed as such. Booth viewed the whole episode, with a wry face, as a demonstration of 'what has happened to James in the hands of Jamesians'.³¹⁶

This summarizing, synthesizing phase of the Prefaces' critical reception came to an effectual end in 1934, when Charles Scribner's Sons reprinted the texts of the Prefaces themselves as a single volume entitled *The Art of the Novel*. The idea came from the American critic R. P. Blackmur, and it occurred to him in the course of writing the article that would become the introduction to the volume: 'The Prefaces of Henry James', which first appeared in the Henry James special issue of *Hound & Horn* (July–September 1934), alongside essays by Marianne Moore, Edmund Wilson and Stephen Spender. The Scribners were not at first persuaded of the project's commercial viability, and copyright considerations would be an important factor in their eventual decision to reprint. The US Copyright Act of 1909 had set the term of copyright at twenty-eight years from first publication, with the option of renewal for the same period; the *New York Edition* had been published between 1907 and 1909, so the Scribners would need to start renewing their copyrights in the Prefaces from 1935. They seem to

---

³¹⁵ See Norman Friedman, 'Point of View in Fiction: The Development of a Critical Concept', *PMLA* 70.5 (1955), 1160–84; 1160–8; reprinted with an updated literature review in Friedman, *Form and Meaning in Fiction* (Athens, GA: The University of Georgia Press, 1975), pp. 134–42. For the later dissemination of the concept, see Fredric Jameson, *The Political Unconscious: Narrative as a Socially Symbolic Act* (Ithaca, NY: Cornell University Press, 1981), pp. 154, 219–24; Dorothy J. Hale, 'Henry James and the Invention of Novel Theory', in Jonathan Freedman (ed.), *The Cambridge Companion to Henry James* (Cambridge: Cambridge University Press, 1998), pp. 79–101; and Julie Rivkin, *False Positions: The Representational Logics of Henry James's Fiction* (Stanford, CA: Stanford University Press, 1996), pp. 203–4 n. 2.

³¹⁶ Booth, *The Rhetoric of Fiction* (Chicago, IL: University of Chicago Press, 1961), pp. 24–5, 58–9.

INTRODUCTION

have felt that they might as well do so by accepting Blackmur's proposal.[317] The publication of *The Art of the Novel* effected an immediate revolution in the availability of the Prefaces. Previously they could only be read in the volumes of a collected edition, either the *New York Edition* itself or, later, Macmillan's *Novels and Stories of Henry James* (1921–3).[318] That made them expensive and inconvenient to acquire. *The Art of the Novel* now offered all eighteen Prefaces in a single volume, priced at $3 in America and 10s 6d in the UK – much less expensive for American readers than subscribing to the *New York Edition*, and for English readers comparable to the cost of two or three individual volumes of the cheapest available complete edition.[319] The opening move for most reviewers of *The Art of the Novel*, unsurprisingly, was to express gratitude. This was 'a book for which all admirers of Henry James have waited impatiently', and by publishing it Blackmur and the Scribners had 'performed a service to English letters which it is difficult to overstate'.[320] 'To those who have been put off from knowing [the Prefaces] by the fact that they have, until now, been so annoyingly scattered, they will come as a revelation and a joy.'[321]

The same reviewers nevertheless saw that collecting the Prefaces in a single volume raised difficult questions about their status and authority. Were they detachable from the *New York Edition* or embedded in it? Were they one thing or many things: a treatise in aesthetics and literary theory with a general application to fiction at large, as Blackmur argued in his introduction, or a series of particular analyses of individual novels and stories? In their often marked dissent from Blackmur's claims and working assumptions, contemporary reviewers of *The Art of the Novel* anticipated questions that would be forcefully put by revisionist criticism of the

---

[317] For the publishing of *The Art of the Novel*, see Anesko, *Monopolizing the Master*, pp. 127–33.
[318] For Lubbock's insistence that the Macmillan *Novels and Stories of Henry James* should use James's revised *New York Edition* texts and print the Prefaces, see Anesko, 'Collected Editions and the Consolidation of Cultural Authority', 200–2.
[319] The initial price of the Macmillan *Novels and Stories of Henry James* was 7s 6d per volume, subsequently reduced to 5s for the 'Crown Octavo' impression and 3s 6d for the 'Pocket' impression (Supino, *A Bibliographical Catalogue*, p. 600). The prices for *The Art of the Novel* are taken from contemporary reviews.
[320] *Times Literary Supplement* (9 May 1935), 299; *The Criterion* 14 (July 1935), 667–9; 667.
[321] *New York Times Book Review* (18 November 1934), 2.

INTRODUCTION

New York Edition in the 1990s, at another turning point in the Prefaces' reception history; although, in the event, those later scholars' critique of *The Art of the Novel* as James's de facto 'canonization' by the American New Critical establishment would be produced without reference to the early reviews of the volume.[322]

The introduction to *The Art of the Novel* opens:

> The Prefaces of Henry James were composed at the height of his age as a kind of epitaph or series of inscriptions for the major monument of his life, the sumptuous, plum-coloured, expensive New York Edition of his works. The labour was a torment, a care, and a delight, as his letters and the Prefaces themselves amply show. The thinking and the writing were hard and full and critical to the point of exasperation; the purpose was high, the reference wide, and the terms of discourse had to be conceived and defined as successive need for them arose. He had to elucidate and to appropriate for the critical intellect the substance and principle of his career as an artist, and he had to do this—such was the idiosyncrasy of his mind—specifically, example following lucid example, and with a consistency of part with part that amounted almost to the consistency of a mathematical equation, so that, as in the *Poetics,* if his premises were accepted his conclusions must be taken as inevitable.
>
> (*AN* vii)

While Blackmur plainly assumes the contents of *The Art of the Novel* to constitute a coherent, unified discourse on literary aesthetics, in these opening sentences he noticeably hesitates between general and particular understandings of the Prefaces. Even as he presides over their reissue, he acknowledges them as originally belonging to the *New York Edition*: he begins with their bibliographical context, the Scribners' ordinary issue in its 'smooth plum cloth' binding,[323] and continues to refer to them in volume-specific ways throughout the introduction. The Edition itself he figures as monumental and tomb-like, but he cannot decide whether the text on that monument is singular and conclusive ('a kind of epitaph') or plural and serial (a 'series of inscriptions'). The comparison with Aristotle's *Poetics*

---

[322] The term 'canonization' occurs in David McWhirter, '"The Whole Chain of Relation and Responsibility": Henry James and the New York Edition', and Ross Posnock, 'Breaking the Aura of Henry James', both in McWhirter (ed.), *Henry James's New York Edition*, pp. 2, 25. See also Hershel Parker, 'Deconstructing *The Art of the Novel* and Liberating James's Prefaces'.

[323] Supino, *A Bibliographical Catalogue*, p. 501.

frames the Prefaces as a general treatise, a work of philosophical literary theory whose value depends on its logico-mathematical 'consistency', yet here and elsewhere Blackmur insists on specificity as a fundamental quality of the Prefaces' argumentation: 'James unfailingly, unflaggingly reveals for his most general precept its specific living source. [...] That is his unique virtue as a critic, that the specific object is always in hand; as it was analogously his genius as a novelist that what he wrote about was always present in somebody's specific knowledge of it' (AN xi–xii).

The fact that James himself had thought of collecting and reprinting the Prefaces had been generally known since the appearance of Lubbock's edition of *The Letters of Henry James* (1920), which printed the letter to Howells in which James had imagined the gathered Prefaces as 'a sort of comprehensive manual or *vade-mecum*' (*LHJ* 2:101–7; 102). Blackmur quoted this passage early in his introduction, and cited it as evidence that James regarded the Prefaces as 'an essay in general criticism which had an interest and a being aside from any connection with his own work, and [...] a fairly exhaustive reference book on the technical aspects of the art of fiction' (AN viii). This was the most obvious justification for the existence of *The Art of the Novel*, yet some reviewers of the volume were unconvinced. G. W. Stonier in the *New Statesman and Nation* accepted the letter to Howells as a statement of James's intention ('the string of introductions was planned to be a single revelation of his artistic method') but found the Prefaces 'neither as conclusive nor as revealing [as a group] as one might have expected from reading them separately. To be properly understood each must be taken with the book to which it was originally attached.'[324] Stonier found it simply 'fantastic' of Blackmur to claim 'that *The Art of the Novel* "is the most sustained and [...] most eloquent and original piece of literary criticism in existence" [AN viii]'; on the contrary, the Prefaces were 'essentially a piece of private pleading' and would not stand comparison with 'a real masterpiece of criticism' – the letters of Flaubert, for instance: 'Flaubert of course, like James, is arguing a particular case (what artist does not?), but his criticism can be read apart from the context of his novels, and even the most incidental remarks on his method, scrawled at two o'clock in the

---

[324] *New Statesman and Nation Literary Supplement* (1 June 1935), 813–14; 813.

morning, reverberate in a way which few of James's sentences, penned for the occasion, are capable of doing.'[325]

Conrad Aiken in the *Criterion* likewise saw the general applicability of the Prefaces as strictly limited by James's focus on his own work: 'he is concerned entirely with that sort of pure fiction [...] of which he himself became the first practitioner and the consummate master', and his project consists of 'taking himself as a critical *corpus vile* [experimental subject] and making of his own practice a theory'.[326] For Aiken, James was 'not a "great" critic in the sense of being a wide one', but certainly 'a great *specialist* in criticism', and *The Art of the Novel* was 'in some respects the most important single book of English criticism—*practical* criticism—since the time of Arnold: even some might say, since the time of Coleridge and Hazlitt'.[327] To speak of a 'single book' might imply a claim for coherence, but two of the three English critics named by Aiken were primarily essayists, and their most important books of literary criticism not treatises but collections: Matthew Arnold's *Essays in Criticism* (1865, 1888), and William Hazlitt's *Characters of Shakespear's Plays* (1817) or the series of literary lectures he published between 1818 and 1820. Once again, Coleridge's 'most important single book' in this connection must surely be *Biographia Literaria*, an unstable compound work that persistently undoes its own aspirations to unity. Coleridge, too, was the coiner of the term isolated for emphasis and qualification in the sentence quoted above: 'English criticism' for Aiken means '*practical* criticism', an interpretive procedure that privileges the close analysis of particulars over general or theoretical argumentation.[328]

Blackmur's private sense of the Prefaces likewise oscillated between the models of the treatise and the essay collection, as exemplified by Aristotle

---

[325] *Ibid.*, 814.

[326] *The Criterion* 14 (July 1935), 668.

[327] *Ibid.*, 667.

[328] The phrase 'practical criticism' occurs in chapter 15 of *Biographia Literaria* (the chapter is titled '*The specific symptoms of poetic power elucidated in a critical analysis of Shakespeare's Venus and Adonis, and Lucrece*'): 'In the application of these principles to purposes of practical criticism [...], I have endeavoured to discover what the qualities in a poem are, which may be deemed promises and specific symptoms of poetic power' (S. T. Coleridge, *Biographia Literaria*, ed. J. Shawcross, 2 vols. (Oxford: Oxford University Press, 1907), vol. II, p. 13). Aiken's review was written just five years after the publication of I. A. Richards's *Practical Criticism: A Study of Literary Judgement* (1929).

and Arnold respectively. As he remarked to the Scribner editor John Hall Wheelock in January 1934: 'The things do make as much of a classic, and I think really a more substantial one, as Arnold's *Essays in Criticism*, and almost, I feel now (because of their greater eloquence), as much as the *Poetics*.'[329] In the public introduction to *The Art of the Novel*, Blackmur nevertheless championed the second model, taking for granted James's belief that the Prefaces constituted 'an essay in general criticism', and on that basis proposing 'to indicate by example and a little analysis, by a kind of provisional reasoned index, how the contents of his essay may be made more available' (*AN* viii). Blackmur's editorial attitude appears by turns grandiose and modestly utilitarian. The first section of the introduction offers an accurate general description of 'what kind of thing, as a type by itself, a James preface is': 'the story of a story', comprising James's memory of the point of origin of a given fiction, an account of the circumstances of writing and the development and working-out of the subject, and an analysis of the technical and moral problems of the case (*AN* ix). The third and last section is an exposition of a sample Preface (that to *The Ambassadors*), a cogent summary that falls some way short of Blackmur's wildly ambitious goal: by 'imitating his thought, step by step and image by image', to become 'as intimate as it is possible to be with the operation of an artist's mind' and so 'in the end be able to appropriate in a single act of imagination all he has to say' (*AN* xxxii). In between comes 'a kind of eclectic index or provisional glossary' to the Prefaces (*AN* xiv), an annotated and cross-referenced list of sixty major and minor 'themes', including topics relating to artistic attitude (e.g., '*The Relation of Art and the Artist*', '*The Relation of Art and Life*'), subject-matter ('*The International Theme*') and literary form and technique ('*The Nouvelle as a Form*', '*On Foreshortening*', etc.) (*AN* xiv–xxxi).

Blackmur closed his introduction by observing that there was, 'in any day of agonised doubt and exaggerated certainty as to the relation of the artist to society, an unusual attractive force in the image of a man whose doubts are conscientious and whose certainties are all serene'. The Prefaces showed James to be this kind of artist, 'relentlessly' scrupulous about 'the minor aspects of his art' but sure of 'its major purpose and essential

---

[329] Quoted in Anesko, *Monopolizing the Master*, p. 131.

character' (*AN* xxxvii). In the disastrous economic and geopolitical circumstances of the mid-1930s, reviewers of *The Art of the Novel* were more exercised than those of the *New York Edition* had been by the Prefaces' immovable confidence in the importance of art, and by the apparent disproportion between technique and substance in the works they referred to. Stonier approvingly cited a hostile reading of James's care for literary form: James, he argued, 'developed language as an instrument by which he could *avoid* telling a great deal, his subtlety is often evasion, and the judgment of Mr. Van Wyck Brooks—that "he makes the very substance of his art out of his own failure to grasp the materials of it"—appears to me essentially right'.[330] The quotation is from *The Pilgrimage of Henry James* (1925), in which the American critic Van Wyck Brooks had cited examples from the Prefaces as damning evidence that the later James – his grasp on objective reality loosened by long expatriation – had come to care more for the process of fictional representation than for his increasingly tenuous subject-matter. Brooks turned James's metaphors jeeringly back on him: 'He had emerged as an impassioned geometer—or, shall we say, some vast arachnid of art, pouncing upon the tiny air-blown particle and wrapping it round and round.'[331] On the other side of this argument, C. Hartley Grattan in the *New York Times* sought to defend James against Blackmur's misleadingly exclusive emphasis on aesthetics: 'large issues' of socio-economics were 'discoverable in the prefaces' in connection with such subjects as the international theme, 'and, to use a Jamesian construction, Mr. Blackmur's failure to touch on them is a triumph of limited reference'.[332] In the *Times Literary Supplement*, the English poet-critic, art historian and anarchist Herbert Read located the Prefaces' general validity and relevance for the modern moment in their feeling for 'the whole difference between the outlook of the artist and of all those who, in the name of dogmatic belief [...], would bend the artist to some purpose or propaganda'. Read associated

---

[330] *New Statesman and Nation Literary Supplement* (1 June 1935), 814.
[331] Brooks, *The Pilgrimage of Henry James* (New York: E. P. Dutton & Company, 1925), pp. 138, 130. Compare the writer in the Preface to *Roderick Hudson* who works 'by a geometry of his own' (p. 4), and the metaphor of experience as a 'spider-web [...] suspended in the chamber of consciousness, and catching every air-borne particle in its tissue' in 'The Art of Fiction' (*LC1* 52).
[332] *New York Times Book Review* (18 November 1934), 2.

Jamesian art with 'individual values' and with 'the sense of limitation, of partiality, of non-participation', and he offered those characteristics – which critics in the Van Wyck Brooks camp regarded as failings – as the essential conditions of artistic liberty. Read closed his review with a quotation from the passage at the close of the Preface to *The Princess Casamassima* (pp. 60–1) asserting James's competence to treat a revolutionary proletarian subject without direct experience of that class and its struggle: this passage, which James called 'a defence of *his* "artistic position"', 'might be quoted as a defence of *the* artistic position'.[333]

Artists themselves produced the most vital responses to the Prefaces in this period. As Michaela Bronstein has shown, from the early 1940s onward the American novelist Ralph Ellison's thinking about 'the potential for aesthetic theory to echo the ethical dilemmas of political action' was informed by an intensive reading of the Prefaces: Ellison's marginal annotations of the Preface to *The Princess Casamassima* in his copy of *The Art of the Novel* give evidence for his developing a conception of the aesthetic as a mode of political protest 'that does not map onto New Critical ideas of form'.[334] Ten years after Blackmur, F. W. Dupee's edited volume *The Question of Henry James* (1945) brought together twenty-five essays and a single poem: W. H. Auden's 'At the Grave of Henry James' (1943), which was appearing in print for the first time. Written in wartime exile in America, Auden's elegy appeals to James as a secular muse and exemplar of art's responsibilities in an age of political crisis. Auden hails the dead writer in his own words: 'O poet of the difficult, dear addicted artist'.[335] In the Preface to *The Portrait of a Lady*, James had characterized himself as 'the really addicted artist', thrilled and inspired 'to see deep difficulty braved' (p. 40).

---

[333] *Times Literary Supplement* (9 May 1935), 299.
[334] Bronstein, '*The Princess* among the Polemicists: Aesthetics and Protest at Midcentury', *American Literary History* 29.1 (2017), 26–49; 31, 33–5.
[335] Auden, 'At the Grave of Henry James', in F. W. Dupee (ed.), *The Question of Henry James: A Collection of Critical Essays* (New York: Henry Holt and Company, 1945), pp. 246–50; 247. Dupee also reprinted an essay by the American critic and editor Morton D. Zabel which recommended the Prefaces to 'the attention of contemporary poets', as 'a warning against license and [...] a guide through the deceptive privileges of a free age for authorship', with specific relevance to 'the contemporary poetic problem' ('The Poetics of Henry James' (1935), pp. 212–17; 212, 213).

INTRODUCTION

Perhaps not coincidentally, those phrases also occur in one of the two sentences from the *Portrait* Preface which Blackmur had quoted at the close of his introduction to *The Art of the Novel*, offering them there as the last word on James's aesthetic commitment: 'It is because such sentiments rose out of him like prayers that for James art was enough' (*AN* xxxix). Likewise, when Auden asks James for strength to resist the 'vague incitement' of 'the / Resentful muttering Mass', he does so with an ironic echo of the Prefaces' acknowledgement of constitutional unfitness for the literary marketplace:

> Yours be the disciplinary image that holds
>   Me back from agreeable wrong
> And the clutch of eddying muddle, lest Proportion shed
> The alpine chill of her shrugging editorial shoulder
>   On my loose impromptu song.
> [...]
>   Lightly, lightly, then, may I dance
> Over the frontier of the obvious and fumble no more
> In the old limp pocket of the minor exhibition,
>   Nor riot with irrelevance.[336]

Auden's lines remember 'the alpine chill [...] shed by the cold editorial shoulder' in the Preface to *The Wings of the Dove* (p. 234) and the rueful comment in the Preface to *NYE* XVIII on the limitations of American experience that had condemned James to a repetition of 'international' subjects: '[...] I was but to feel myself fumble again in the old limp pocket of the minor exhibition' (p. 219). In his contemporaneous poem on the same subject, the prose monologue 'Caliban to the Audience' in 'The Sea and the Mirror' (1944), Auden ventriloquizes James rather than addressing him. Auden's pastiche of late Jamesian prose style draws on multiple sources, but the rhetorical situation of Caliban's monologue – a public address by an authorial delegate or substitute – obviously recalls the Prefaces, and its final clauses follow the audibly conclusive syntactical contours of the last sentence of the *Golden Bowl* Preface: 'the working charm is the full bloom of the unbothered state; the sounded note is the restored relation'.[337] Auden

---

[336] Auden, 'At the Grave of Henry James', p. 249.
[337] Auden, 'The Sea and the Mirror: A Commentary on Shakespeare's *The Tempest*' (III: 'Caliban to the Audience'), in *The Collected Poetry of W. H. Auden* (New York: Random House, 1945),

would remark in 1946 that 'Henry James' *Prefaces* are the best stuff I know about the nature of the creative act'.[338] In these fond, questioning poems he re-enacted the gestures, rhythms and phrasings by which James had approached that subject, creatively mis-fitting them to his own context and its new problems.

The American 'James Revival' of the 1940s produced little sustained critical engagement with the Prefaces, though they were constantly referred to in passing as evidence of what James had said about such and such a fiction or point of technique. F. O. Matthiessen's *Henry James: The Major Phase* (1944) subordinated the Prefaces to James's recently discovered working notebooks as contexts for understanding the late novels; Matthiessen would presently redress the balance in his edition of *The Notebooks of Henry James* (1947), which cross-referred to the Prefaces 'wherever they amplified points raised by the notebooks themselves', and so allowed readers to compare James's preliminary views of fictional subjects with his retrospective analyses of the finished works.[339] As Philip Horne observes, 'Generations of critics and students' would use *The Art of the Novel* and the Matthiessen and Murdock *Notebooks* together as 'a pair of volumes which jointly provided a high-minded training in Jamesian aesthetic theory and practice'.[340] In the meantime, critics continued to use the Prefaces as a source of technical principles, but had to look further afield for material to apply them to. Francis Fergusson's essay in the 1943 'Henry James Number' of the *Kenyon Review*, for instance, sought to demonstrate their relevance to the form of James's plays, and to formal constants in European drama at large.

---

pp. 373–403; 403. Compare James: 'the proved error is the base apologetic deed, the helpless regret is the barren commentary' (p. 277). The 'attention articulately *sounded*' by reading aloud and the revising author's reconstitution of 'the whole chain of relation and responsibility' are subjects of the final pages of this Preface (pp. 275, 277). See also Anthony Curtis, 'Auden and Henry James', *London Magazine* 33 (1 August 1993), 49–55.

[338] Auden to Ursula and Reinhold Niebuhr, 19 June 1946; quoted in Ursula Niebuhr, 'Memories of the 1940s', in Stephen Spender (ed.), *W. H. Auden: A Tribute* (New York: Macmillan, 1975), pp. 104–18; 113.

[339] Matthiessen, *Henry James: The Major Phase* (New York: Oxford University Press, 1944). *The Notebooks of Henry James*, ed. Matthiessen and Kenneth B. Murdock (New York and Oxford: Oxford University Press, 1947), p. xx.

[340] Horne, 'Letters and Notebooks', in David McWhirter (ed.), *Henry James in Context* (Cambridge: Cambridge University Press, 2010), pp. 68–79; 72.

INTRODUCTION

The generalizing impulse that had dominated response to the Prefaces since Lubbock's *The Craft of Fiction* was still evident here, but with a wider gap between the derived concepts and their textual sources: Fergusson dealt with the Prefaces at second hand, referring to James's 'technical notions' as they had 'become generally available' through the work of Beach, Lubbock and Blackmur.[341]

A similar sense of detachment from the object of study hangs about the repetition of old dogmas and complaints in this period. F. R. Leavis opened his severely critical discussion of 'The Later James' in *The Great Tradition* (1948) by recording his disappointment with the Prefaces as collected in *The Art of the Novel*: Leavis offers a trenchant early example of resistance to that volume and to 'the contemporary cult of Henry James (if it can be called that)' centred on the 1934 Henry James issue of *Hound & Horn* where Blackmur's introduction had first appeared. The Prefaces, he announced, made 'not merely difficult but unrepaying reading', and he located the cause of the difficulty in what the Preface to *The Wings of the Dove* called 'the author's instinct everywhere for the *indirect* presentation of his main image' (p. 242), an instinct shared by the Prefaces and the late novels:

> This inveterate indirectness of the later James, this aim of presenting, of leaving presented, the essential thing by working round and behind so that it shapes itself in the space left amidst a context of hints and apprehensions, is undoubtedly a vice in the Prefaces; it accounts for their unsatisfactoriness. It appears there, in criticism, as an inability to state—an inability to tackle his theme, or to get anything out clearly and finally. [...] [T]he developed and done is exasperatingly disproportionate to the laboured doing and the labour of reading.[342]

Leavis objected on the same grounds to the oblique presentation of those characters and situations in the late novels which James associated with 'life'. The dying Milly Theale (an 'emptiness' at the centre of *The Wings* around which the other characters make a sentimental 'fuss'), or the glamorous vitality of Paris in *The Ambassadors* (not 'adequately realized'): these produced 'an effect of disproportionate "doing"—of a technique the

---

[341] Fergusson, 'James's Idea of Dramatic Form', *Kenyon Review* 5.4 (1943), 495–507; 498.
[342] Leavis, *The Great Tradition: George Eliot, Henry James, Joseph Conrad* (London: Chatto & Windus, 1948), pp. 155, 158.

subtleties and elaborations of which are not sufficiently controlled by a feeling for value and significance in living'. James's 'interest in his material' had become 'too specialized', and 'in the technical elaboration expressing this specialized interest he had lost his full sense of life and let his moral taste slip into abeyance'.[343] The Prefaces were not only the documents of that overspecialization, as they had been for Van Wyck Brooks; for Leavis, they were symptoms of it also.

Fifteen years later, once more arguing against the assumption 'that in the volume of the collected Prefaces [*The Art of the Novel*] we have a major critical classic', Leavis would go over exactly the same ground again.[344] James's self-analysis in the Prefaces 'serves a special technical preoccupation' and has no broader value, whereas in the critical essays by James which Leavis is prepared to recommend – those on Flaubert and Maupassant, for example – 'there is nothing technical or esoteric about the critique', and the central point is always a moral evaluation based on 'the human significance of the art in question' and its reference to '"life"'.[345] Originally delivered as a lecture for the undergraduate English Tripos at the University of Cambridge, in 1963 Leavis's 'James as Critic' was printed as an introduction to a selection of James's criticism 'intended for the general reader' – a volume that tellingly included no extracts from the Prefaces.[346] Leavis invited his general readers to remark 'an irony' in the fact that James now 'figures academically as prescribed reading for students of "English" who are to take papers on Literary Criticism'. Academic study – another kind of 'special technical preoccupation' – did not guarantee 'any just recognition of [James's] strengths and his limitations', and might even discourage students from making that kind of judgement:

Those academics who take seriously the suggestion that [*The Art of the Novel*] is the 'novelist's *vade-mecum*' will indeed be drawing from it a new academicism, for that

---

[343] *Ibid.*, pp. 158, 161.
[344] Leavis, 'James as Critic', in *Henry James: Selected Literary Criticism*, ed. Morris Shapira (London: Heinemann Educational Books, 1963), pp. xiii–xxiii; xiii.
[345] Leavis, 'James as Critic', pp. xiv–xvi.
[346] Shapira, 'Editor's Note', in *Henry James: Selected Literary Criticism*, pp. ix–xi; ix. The Prefaces were still in copyright at this point, which may have been a factor in excluding them, but they are not even mentioned amongst the recommendations 'for the reader who would like to explore further' (p. x).

is what the attempt to establish a general interest and validity in it must yield. And one can only deplore any offer to deaden the undergraduate reading English with such a misdirection and such a *corvée*.[347]

'James as Critic' is representative of a larger blockage in critical discourse at this moment. Leavis apparently could not imagine an academic use for the Prefaces other than the obviously unsatisfactory one of setting them as required reading for undergraduates (the literal meaning of the French word *corvée* is labour imposed by the state, or military fatigue-duty – figuratively, mere drudgery). The sudden flowering of new critical work in the years following Leavis's essay would escape from this stalemate by simply discarding the question of whether the Prefaces ought to be 'prescribed as a critical classic'.[348] Over the next decade, the established modes of exposition and synthesis would give way, rapidly and decisively, to interpretation and analysis; where the Prefaces had been viewed as a repository of Jamesian aesthetic theory and technical principles, they now became objects of study in their own right.[349]

At the same time, the texts themselves were more widely and variously disseminated. The *New York Edition* came out of renewal copyright in 1965, and paperback editions of individual novels and stories at once began to print the relevant Prefaces and gatherings of prefatory extracts.[350] In a last effort to exploit their copyright before it expired, the Scribners had reissued the entire Edition from 1961, a move welcomed by Allison Shumsky in the *Sewanee Review*: 'everything about it seems designed to restore

---

[347] Leavis, 'James as Critic', p. xiii.
[348] *Ibid.*, p. xiv.
[349] For early examples of this new approach, see D. W. Jefferson, *Henry James and the Modern Reader* (Edinburgh and London: Oliver & Boyd, 1964), pp. 3–21 (on the Prefaces as a comic portrait of the artist torn between an ideal of technical economy and the 'lavishness' of his own imaginative and expressive resources); and Laurence Bedwell Holland, *The Expense of Vision: Essays on the Craft of Henry James* (Princeton, NJ: Princeton University Press, 1964), pp. 3–16, 155–82 (on the continuities of metaphor between Prefaces and the fictions they accompany, and on the *Portrait* Preface as 'a conscience-stricken enquiry into the deepest implications of James's craft'). In both readings, literary qualities – tone, metaphor – control, complicate or contradict the Prefaces' expository discourse.
[350] See, e.g., the 1966 Penguin Classics reprints of *The Golden Bowl* and *The Awkward Age*, and the W. W. Norton Critical Editions of *The Turn of the Screw* (ed. Robert Kimbrough, 1966) and *The Portrait of a Lady* (ed. Robert D. Bamberg, 1975).

INTRODUCTION

James to the *reader*' – as distinct from the librarian or collector or scholar or student – and, amongst other happy consequences, 'The prefaces are back where they belong.'[351] That sounds like another swipe at *The Art of the Novel*, with the implication that the Prefaces ought to accompany the texts they were written for. But there could be no going back now, and no straightforward measure of where the Prefaces belonged as texts – only the lengthening list of actual contexts for their reappearance. Over the second half of the twentieth century, they were translated into French and Italian, at different stages of James's incorporation into those linguistic cultures: Agostino Lombardo's *Le prefazioni* (1956) preceded Italian translations of most of James's fiction and laid a foundation for modern James studies in Italy, whereas Marie-Françoise Cachin's *La Création littéraire: préfaces de l'édition de New York* (1980) arrived on a francophone critical scene that had already elaborated its own theoretical accounts of Jamesian narrative without reference to his commentary.[352] In 1984, the Prefaces entered the authoritative Library of America series in a two-volume set of James's *Literary Criticism*; two years later, a selection of nine Prefaces appeared in an annotated anthology of his critical writings.[353] *The Art of the Novel* remains in print.[354] Academic paperback editions of James's novels and stories routinely print the corresponding Prefaces as part of their apparatus: they are acknowledged as essential contexts for the fiction, although the question of their interpretative authority is energetically debated. As texts in themselves, they have become a frequent focus of critical attention, and over the past half-century have figured in seminal discussions of James's autobiographical writing; his literary and cultural criticism; his relations with the literary marketplace; his cultural authority and legacy; his theory and

---

[351] Shumsky, 'James Again: The New New York Edition', *Sewanee Review*, 70.3 (1962), 522–5; 522–3.

[352] For these translations, see the chapters by Sergio Perosa, Donatella Izzo, and Jean Bessière and Miceala Symington in Annick Duperray (ed.), *The Reception of Henry James in Europe* (London: Continuum, 2006), pp. 47–68, 69–92, 15–35. The Prefaces have also been translated into Spanish, German and (in extracts) Bulgarian (Duperray (ed.), *Reception*, pp. xxiv–xlviii).

[353] *The Art of Criticism: Henry James on the Theory and the Practice of Fiction*, ed. William Veeder and Susan M. Griffin (Chicago, IL: Chicago University Press, 1986).

[354] The most recent edition is published by the University of Chicago Press (2011) and has a new foreword by the novelist Colm Tóibín.

practice of textual revision; his imagination of race, gender and sexuality; and his style and rhetoric – as well as in broader studies of novel theory and literary paratexts. The voluminous academic literature on the Prefaces is beyond the scope of this Introduction – there is really too much to say – but its abundance is proof of the established centrality of these writings to modern Henry James studies.[355]

Contemporary Reception of the *New York Edition*

This is a selection of reviews and critical commentary on the Prefaces from the first announcements of the publication of the *New York Edition* in December 1907 up to the announcement of James's death in March 1916. Most of the items listed below are reviews of instalments of the Edition: the numbers of the volumes under review are given in square brackets at the end of each listing, unless that information is included in the title of the review. As indicated in the listings, some of these pieces are reprinted – in full or as excerpts – in Roger Gard (ed.), *Henry James: The Critical Heritage* (London: Routledge & Kegan Paul, 1968); Peter Rawlings (ed.), *Critical Essays on Henry James*, Critical Thought Series: 5 (Aldershot: Scolar Press, 1993); and *Edith Wharton: The Uncollected Critical Writings*, ed. Frederick Wegener (Princeton, NJ: Princeton University Press, 1996); hereafter, Gard, Rawlings and Wegener, respectively. Brief outlines of many of the American reviews can be found in Linda J. Taylor, *Henry James, 1866–1916: A Reference Guide* (Boston, MA: G. K. Hall & Co., 1982). All reviews and articles are unsigned unless otherwise indicated.

'The Novels and Tales of Henry James', *Book Buyer* 32 (December 1907), 212–13.
'Literary Notes', *New-York Daily Tribune* (1 December 1907), 7.
'Henry James to Explain Himself', *New York Times Saturday Review of Books* 12 (6 December 1907), 776.

---

[355] For orientation amid the mass of work on the Prefaces published since the 1960s, see *The Art of Criticism*, ed. Veeder and Griffin, p. 406; the 'Chronological List of Secondary Works on the New York Edition', in McWhirter (ed.), *Henry James's New York Edition*, pp. 266–73; and Linda Simon, *The Critical Reception of Henry James: Creating a Master* (Rochester, NY: Camden House, 2007), pp. 27–41.

'Notes', *Nation* 85 (12 December 1907), 540-3; 540.
'Literary Notes', *New-York Daily Tribune* (15 December 1907), 7.
'Mr. Henry James Collects Himself', *New York Sun* (28 December 1907), 5. [*NYE* I-II]
N., 'Views of Readers | Plea for the Protection and Preservation of the Early Work of Henry James' (28 December 1907, 863).
'Casual Comment', *Dial*, 44 (1 January 1908), 10.
'Notes', *Nation* 86 (2 January 1908), 11-14; 11. [*NYE* I-II]
'Henry James to Explain Himself', *Chicago Inter Ocean* (8 January 1908), 6.
E. F. E. [Edwin Francis Edgett], 'The New Henry James', *Boston Evening Transcript* (8 January 1908), 16. [*NYE* I-II]
Boston Daily Advertiser (10 January 1908), 8. [*NYE* II]
'Henry James Will Elucidate', *Louisville Courier-Journal* (11 January 1908), 6.
'Scribner's Edition of the Novels and Tales of Henry James', *Louisville Courier-Journal* (11 January 1908), 5. [*NYE* I-II]
Hackett, Francis, 'James on James', *Chicago Evening Post* (11 January 1908), 4. [*NYE* I-II]
Schuyler, Montgomery, 'Henry James Done Over', *New York Times Saturday Review of Books* 13 (11 January 1908), 13-15; in Rawlings 102-6. [*NYE* I-II]
'Henry James's Collected Works', *Outlook* (New York) 88 (18 January 1908), 145. [*NYE* I-II]
'On Revised Versions', *New York Times Saturday Review of Books* 13 (18 January 1908), 30.
Peattie, Elia W., 'Henry James Rewrites Earlier Novels into His Later Style', *Chicago Daily Tribune* (18 January 1908), 9. [*NYE* I-II]
Fitch, George Hamlin, 'New Edition of Henry James and Other Books', *San Francisco Chronicle* (26 January 1908), 10. [*NYE* I-II]
Hackett, Francis, 'News and Views of Books', *Chicago Evening Post* (29 January 1908), 4. [*NYE* I-II]
'The First Volume of the New Edition of Henry James', *Book Buyer* 33 (February 1908), 15.
Shuman, Edwin L., 'With Authors and Books', *Chicago Record-Herald* (8 February 1908), 6. [*NYE* I-II]
'The New York Henry James', *New York Sun* (22 February 1908), 5. [*NYE* III-VI]
'News and Views of Books', *Chicago Evening Post* (25 February 1908), 4. [*NYE* III-VI]

INTRODUCTION

'Mr. Henry James on His Own Art', *New York Times Saturday Review of Books* 13 (29 February 1908), 111. [*NYE* III–IV]

'Notes', *Nation* 86 (5 March 1908), 215–17; 215. [*NYE* III–VI]

Peattie, Elia W., 'Henry James Enjoying His Earlier Literary Incarnations', *Chicago Daily Tribune* (6 March 1908), 9. [*NYE* III–VI]

'Henry James on the "Casamassima"', *New York Times Saturday Review of Books* 13 (7 March 1908), 128.

'New Edition of Henry James', *Louisville Courier-Journal* (14 March 1908), 5. [*NYE* III–IV]

Hale, Edward E., Jr, 'The Rejuvenation of Henry James', *Dial* 44 (16 March 1908), 174–6; in Rawlings 99–101. [*NYE* I–VI]

E. F. E. [Edwin Francis Edgett], 'Writers and Books', *Boston Evening Transcript* (18 March 1908), 19. [*NYE* III–IV]

Boston Daily Advertiser (20 March 1908), 8. [*NYE* III–IV]

'A Guide to the New Books', *Literary Digest* 36 (21 March 1908), 418. [*NYE* I–VI]

'Princess Casamassima', *Louisville Courier-Journal* (21 March 1908), 5.

Fitch, George Hamlin, 'Modern Egypt and Other Books', *San Francisco Chronicle* (29 March 1908), 10. [*NYE* III–VI]

E. F. E. [Edwin Francis Edgett], 'Writers and Books', *Boston Evening Transcript* (1 April 1908), 21. [*NYE* V–VI]

'The Scribner Henry James', *New York Sun* (4 April 1908), 7–8. [*NYE* VII–VIII]

Shuman, Edwin L., 'With Authors and Books', *Chicago Record-Herald* (4 April 1908), 8. [*NYE* III–VI]

'Henry James. | The New Collected Edition of His Novels and Tales', *New-York Daily Tribune* (5 April 1908), Part II, 6–7. [*NYE* I–VIII]

'Scribner Edition of The Tragic Muse', *Louisville Courier-Journal* (11 April 1908), 5.

Dithmar, Edward A., '"The Tragic Muse" in New Edition', *New York Times Saturday Review of Books* 13 (11 April 1908), 198.

'Books of the Season', *Chicago Evening Post* (16 April 1908), 6. [*NYE* VII–VIII]

'Notes', *Nation* 86 (23 April 1908), 375–8; 376. [*NYE* VII–VIII]

'New Edition of "Tragic Muse"', *San Francisco Chronicle* (3 May 1908), 54.

'Books and Authors', *New-York Daily Tribune* (16 May 1908), 5. [*NYE* IX–X]

'Mr. H. James Again', *New York Sun* (23 May 1908), 7. [*NYE* IX–X]

'Analyzing the Novel', *New York Times Saturday Review of Books* 13 (30 May 1908), 306. [*NYE* IX–X]

'Notes', *Nation* 86 (4 June 1908), 510–14; 511. [*NYE* IX–X]
'The Works of Henry James', *Louisville Courier-Journal* (27 June 1908), 5. [*NYE* IX]
'News Notes', *Bookman* (London) 34 (July 1908), 127–32; 127.
Shuman, Edwin L., 'With Authors and Books', *Chicago Record-Herald* (1 July 1908), 10. [*NYE* VII–VIII]
'Novels and Tales of Henry James', *Louisville Courier-Journal* (4 July 1908), 5. [*NYE* X]
'Old Friends in New Dress', *Baltimore Sun* (5 July 1908), 19. [*NYE* III–VI]
'Books and Authors', *New-York Daily Tribune* (18 July 1908), 5. [*NYE* XI–XII]
'The Scribner Henry James', *New York Sun* (18 July 1908), 5. [*NYE* XI–XII]
'More Plainness and Less Art', *Minneapolis Tribune* (26 July 1908), 4. [*NYE* VII–VIII]
'Notes', *Nation* 87 (6 August 1908), 115–18; 115–16. [*NYE* XI–XII]
'Henry James', *Philadelphia Public Ledger and Philadelphia Times* (22 August 1908), 11. [*NYE* IX–XII]
Fitch, George Hamlin, 'Two Good Novels and Other Books', *San Francisco Chronicle* (23 August 1908), 10. [*NYE* IX–X]
'Writers and Books', *Boston Evening Transcript* (26 August 1908), 17. [*NYE* IX–XII]
'The New Edition of James', *Bookman* (New York) 28 (September 1908), 12–13.
'Henry James Will Break His Silence', *Cincinnati Commercial Tribune* (13 September 1908), 14.
Hackett, Francis, 'Mr. James's Art', *Chicago Evening Post* (16 September 1908), 7. [*NYE* IX–XII]
'Volume XI of Scribner's James', *Louisville Courier-Journal* (26 September 1908), 5.
'Volume XII. of the New James', *Louisville Courier-Journal* (3 October 1908), 5.
'Literary Notes', *New-York Daily Tribune* (4 October 1908), 7.
'Henry James' Works', *San Francisco Chronicle* (11 October 1908), 10. [*NYE* XI–XII]
[Ford Madox Hueffer], 'Editorial', *English Review* 1 (December 1908), 157–60.
'The Scribner Henry James', *New York Sun* (12 December 1908), 7–8. [*NYE* XIII–XIV]
'Mr. Henry James. | Some Further Autobiographical Fragments', *New-York Daily Tribune* (13 December 1908), 6. [*NYE* XIII–XIV]

'Notes', *Nation* 87 (17 December 1908), 600–3; 601. [*NYE* XIII–XIV]
'Novels and Tales | XIII. James Volume', *Louisville Courier-Journal* (19 December 1908), 5.
'James Edition, Volume XIV', *Louisville Courier-Journal* (9 January 1909), 5.
'Henry James' Novels and Tales', *San Francisco Chronicle* (7 February 1909), 10. [*NYE* XIII–XIV]
Shuman, Edwin L., 'In Realm [*sic*] of Books', *Chicago Record-Herald* (20 February 1909), 6. [*NYE* IX–XIV]
Peattie, Elia W., 'Two More Volumes of the New York Edition of Henry James' Novels', *Chicago Daily Tribune* (6 March 1909), 9. [*NYE* XIII–XIV]
'Henry James Complete', *New York Sun* (28 March 1909), Section III, 2. [*NYE* XV–XVI]
'Scribner-James Edition, XV. Volume', *Louisville Courier-Journal* (3 April 1909), 5.
'Notes', *Nation* 88 (8 April 1909), 359–62; 359. [*NYE* XV–XVI]
'Mr. Henry James. | New Volumes in the Collected Edition of His Works', *New-York Daily Tribune* (10 April 1909), 8. [*NYE* XV–XVI]
'Stories of Henry James', *Philadelphia Public Ledger and Philadelphia Times* (10 April 1909), 15. [*NYE* XV–XVI]
'XVI. Scribner-James Volume', *Louisville Courier-Journal* (17 April 1909), 5.
'Henry James Again', *New York Sun* (17 April 1909), 7. [*NYE* XVII–XVIII]
'Notes', *Nation* 88 (22 April 1909), 410–12; 410. [*NYE* XVII–XVIII]
'Books and Authors', *New-York Daily Tribune* (24 April 1909), 8. [*NYE* XVII–XX]
'More Henry James', *New York Sun* (24 April 1909), 7. [*NYE* XIX–XX]
'Scribner-James XVII. Volume', *Louisville Courier-Journal* (24 April 1909), 5.
Fitch, George Hamlin, 'Some New Novels and Other Books', *San Francisco Chronicle* (25 April 1909), 10. [*NYE* XV–XVI]
'Notes', *Nation* 88 (29 April 1909), 439–41; 439. [*NYE* XIX–XX]
Cary, Elisabeth Luther, 'Henry James: An Appreciation', *Book News Monthly* 27 (May 1909), 641–5.
'XVIII. Volume of the Scribner-James', *Louisville Courier-Journal* (1 May 1909), 5.
'Novels of Henry James', *New York Times Saturday Review of Books* 14 (1 May 1909), 275. [*NYE* XVII–XVIII]
E. F. E. [Edwin Francis Edgett], 'Writers and Books', *Boston Evening Transcript* (1 May 1909), Part III, 5. [*NYE* XVII–XX]
'Literary Notes', *Boston Daily Advertiser* (14 May 1909), 8. [*NYE* XVII–XX]

Fitch, George Hamlin, 'Joaquin Miller's Poems and Other Books', *San Francisco Chronicle* (23 May 1909), 10. [*NYE* XVII–XX]

Shuman, Edwin L., 'With Authors and Books', *Chicago Record-Herald* (11 June 1909), 8. [*NYE* XV–XX]

'Books and Authors', *New-York Daily Tribune* (26 June 1909), 8. [*NYE* XXI–XXII]

'More Volumes of the Scribner–James', *Louisville Courier-Journal* (26 June 1909), 5. [*NYE* XIX–XX]

S., 'Some Recent Books', *The Dublin Review* 145 (July 1909), 426–9.

'Notes', *Nation* 89 (1 July 1909), 11–14; 11–12. [*NYE* XXI–XXII]

[Percy Lubbock], 'The Novels of Mr Henry James', *Times Literary Supplement* (8 July 1909), 249–50. [*NYE* I–XXIV]

'Mr. James on His Art and the Revision of His Novels', *New-York Daily Tribune* (7 August 1909), 8. [*NYE* XXIII–XXIV]

'The Scribner Henry James Completed', *New York Sun* (7 August 1909), 5. [*NYE* XXIII–XXIV]

'Three Feet of Henry James', *Wilkes-Barre Record* (11 August 1909), 8.

'The Novels and Tales of Henry James', *Baltimore Sun* (15 August 1909), 21. [*NYE* XXI–XXIV]

E. F. E. [Edwin Francis Edgett], 'Writers and Books', *Boston Evening Transcript* (18 August 1909), 17. [*NYE* XXI–XXIV]

'Notes', *Nation* 89 (19 August 1909), 159–61; 159. [*NYE* XXIII–XXIV]

'The Novels and Tales of Henry James', *Chicago Evening Post Friday Literary Review* (20 August 1909), 6. [*NYE* XIII–XXIV]

'Portland Place', *Chicago Evening Post Friday Literary Review* (20 August 1909), 1. [*NYE* XXIII–XXIV]

'Why Mr. James "Revised"', *Literary Digest* 39 (21 August 1909), 275–6. [*NYE* XXIII–XXIV]

Peattie, Elia W., 'Among the New Books', *Chicago Daily Tribune* (4 September 1909), 11. [*NYE* XXI–XXIV]

Fitch, George Hamlin, '"The White Prophet" and Other Books', *San Francisco Chronicle* (12 September 1909), 6. [*NYE* XXI–XXIV]

Shuman, Edwin L., 'With Authors and Books', *Chicago Record-Herald* (23 September 1909), 8. [*NYE* XIX–XXIV]

'Volume Twenty-Third of the Scribner-James', *Louisville Courier-Journal* (25 September 1909), 5.

Marsh, Edward Clark, 'Henry James: Auto-Critic', *Bookman* (New York) 30 (October 1909), 138–43; in Rawlings 107–11. [*NYE* I–XXIV]

'Scribner-James | The Ambassadors', *Louisville Courier-Journal* (2 October 1909), 4.

Fullerton, Morton, 'The Art of Henry James', *Quarterly Review* 212 (April 1910), 393–408; in Wegener 299–304. [*NYE* I–XXIV]

Gretton, M. Sturge, 'Mr. Henry James and His Prefaces', *Contemporary Review* 101 (January 1912), 69–78; in Gard 503–12, Rawlings 119–28.

Scott, Dixon, 'Henry James', *Bookman* (London) 43 (March 1913), 299–306.

TEXTUAL INTRODUCTION

The Prefaces were published only once in James's lifetime, in the *New York Edition of The Novels and Tales of Henry James*. The *NYE* was published in America by Charles Scribner's Sons (December 1907–July 1909). A small British issue was published by Macmillan and Co. from September 1908, using sheets purchased from the Scribners and imported for binding and sale under the Macmillan imprint: the two issues are thus textually identical.

The present edition uses the *NYE* as copy text, and prints the Prefaces in the order in which they were first published in its volumes.[356] They appear in the copy text as follows:

Roderick Hudson: *NYE* I, v–[xx]
The American: *NYE* II, v–[xxiii]
The Portrait of a Lady, Volume I: *NYE* III, v–[xxi]
The Princess Casamassima, Volume I: *NYE* V, v–[xxiii]
The Tragic Muse, Volume I: *NYE* VII, v–[xxii]
The Awkward Age: *NYE* IX, v–[xxiv]
The Spoils of Poynton, A London Life, The Chaperon: *NYE* X, v–[xxiv]
What Maisie Knew, In the Cage, The Pupil: *NYE* XI, v–[xxii]
The Aspern Papers, The Turn of the Screw, The Liar, The Two Faces: *NYE* XII, v–[xxiv]

---

[356] As Hershel Parker first pointed out thirty years ago, the Prefaces were not written in that order, and the sequence of their composition presents some striking divergences from the sequence of their eventual publication; nevertheless, James assented to the published order of *NYE* volumes, and this was the order in which the Prefaces were encountered by their first readers. I have therefore not taken up the challenge issued by Parker to editors of the future to 'reorder the prefaces and their parts into something closely approximating the sequence of James's labors' and 'publish them' in that order ('Deconstructing *The Art of the Novel* and Liberating James's Prefaces', *Henry James Review* 14.3 (1993), 284–307; 290). A full account of the composition and production of the Prefaces can be found in the Introduction to the present edition, and inconsistencies caused by the redistribution of prefatory material between volumes of short stories (*NYE* XV–XVIII) are addressed in the relevant Notes.

TEXTUAL INTRODUCTION

Roderick Hudson

BY

HENRY JAMES

NEW YORK
CHARLES SCRIBNER'S SONS
1907

3 Title page of *Roderick Hudson* (*NYE* I, 'limited issue'). Cambridge University Library. Syn.5.90.213.

CL

The Reverberator, Madame de Mauves, A Passionate Pilgrim and Other Tales: NYE XIII, v–[xxi]
Lady Barbarina, The Siege of London, An International Episode and Other Tales: NYE XIV, v–[xxii]
The Lesson of the Master, The Death of the Lion, The Next Time and Other Tales: NYE XV, v–[xviii]
The Author of Beltraffio, The Middle Years, Greville Fane and Other Tales: NYE XVI, v–[xii]
The Altar of the Dead, The Beast in the Jungle, The Birthplace and Other Tales: NYE XVII, v–[xxix]
Daisy Miller, Pandora, The Patagonia and Other Tales: NYE XVIII, v–[xxiv]
The Wings of the Dove, Volume I: NYE XIX, v–[xxiii]
The Ambassadors, Volume I: NYE XXI, v–[xxiii]
The Golden Bowl, Volume I: NYE XXIII, v–[xxv]

In the respective volumes of the *NYE*, each Preface is titled simply 'PREFACE', and the author's name appears at the end of the text as a virtual signature, on a new line and justified to the right-hand margin: 'HENRY JAMES'. The present edition omits those signatures and gives each Preface the title of its volume: thus, 'PREFACE to *Roderick Hudson*', etc.

Only one prepublication textual witness is known to survive for any Preface: a complete typescript of the Preface to *The Portrait of a Lady* with James's autograph corrections, which is now held in the Houghton Library at Harvard University along with an incomplete set of the pasted-up pages on which James revised *The Portrait* (see Figure 4). These materials were used at the Riverside Press as printers' copy for NYE III–IV.[357] As Michael Anesko notes, the pages of the Preface typescript bear the smudges of the compositors' inky fingers, and 'blue-pencilled slashes' divide the text into numbered batches of galley proof, each marked with the name of the compositor it was allocated to.[358] James's corrections and alterations on the

---

[357] They were acquired by the Houghton Library from Charles Scribner's Sons in 1943 (see Michael Anesko, *Generous Mistakes: Incidents of Error in Henry James* (Oxford: Oxford University Press, 2017), p. vii). Digitized page images of the *Portrait* Preface typescript (Houghton GEN MS Am 1237.17, pp. 1–35) are available as part of Harvard University Library's online collection: nrs.harvard.edu/urn-3:FHCL.HOUGH:5332246.

[358] Anesko, *Generous Mistakes*, pp. vii–viii. The batches of galley proof are allocated to named compositors as follows: Galleys 1, 5 and 7 (pp. 1–6, 19–23, 30–5) to Bolton; Galley 2 and first

TEXTUAL INTRODUCTION

> *Paragraph.*   33
>
> minimum of strain. The interest was to be raised to its pitch and yet
> the elements to be kept in their key; so that, should the whole thing
> duly impress, I might show what an "exciting" inward life may do for
> the person leading it even while it remains perfectly normal. And I
> can not think of a more consistent application of that ideal unless
> it be in the long statement, just beyond the middle of the book, of my
> *on the occasion that was to become for her such a landmark* young woman's extraordinary meditative vigil. Reduced to its essence,
> it is but the vigil of searching criticism; but it throws the action
> further forward than twenty "incidents" might have done. It *was designed to have* all
> the viv- *acity* of incident and all the economy of picture. She sits
> up, by her dying fire, far into the night, under the spell of recogni-
> tions on which she finds the last sharpness suddenly wait. It is a
> representation simply of her motionlessly seeing, and an attempt with-
> al to make the mere still lucidity of her act as "interesting" as
> the surprise of a caravan or the identification of a pirate. It re-
> presents, for that matter, one of the identifications dear to the

4 Typescript of the Preface to *The Portrait of a Lady* (1906) with James's autograph corrections, p. 33. Houghton Library, Harvard University, GEN MS Am 1237.17.

typescript are not extensive, which would seem to suggest that the document was a fair copy which he subjected to last-minute revisions before dispatching it to the Scribners. He had been using freelance typists to make fair copies of his work since at least the 1880s, and he continued this practice into the period of the *NYE*, even though by this time he was dictating most of his public writing directly to an amanuensis at a typewriter. In the early months of the Edition, James appears to have employed temporary amanuenses in Rye to type Prefaces from his dictation, and then sent the resulting material to London to be type-copied; Theodora Bosanquet, his last and most satisfactory long-term amanuensis, arrived at Lamb House in October 1907 and was soon made responsible for both dictation-typing and type-copying in situ.[359] Whoever was actually doing the typing at each stage, this compositional routine would have afforded James at least two distinct chances to rework the dictated text of a Preface: he could make handwritten revisions on the dictated typescript, and could then have those revisions incorporated into a clean typed copy, which he could lightly revise once more before dispatch. This is what he appears to have done with the *Portrait* Preface (which was completed by August 1906, more than a year before Bosanquet's advent): from the Houghton typescript, we can see that he made a few verbal insertions and substitutions, repunctuated some sentences, confirmed existing paragraph breaks and introduced a new one (using red ink for this), put acute accents on two French words and corrected a small number of typos. A full record of his autograph revisions can be found in the list of Textual Variants.

One of the errors in the Houghton typescript looks like a phrase misheard by an amanuensis in dictation: where the published text of the Preface has 'the vain critic's quarrel [...] with one's subject', the typescript reads '[...] with one subject'.[360] Other traces of dictation are discernible in James's revisions, most strikingly on page 21 when the typing stops abruptly halfway through a line and resumes on a new line. Some text is obviously

---

portion of Galley 6 (pp. 6–10, 23–6) to Snell; Galley 3 (pp. 10–14) to Davis; and Galley 4 and second portion of Galley 6 (pp. 14–19, 26–30) to Hamilton.

[359] The evidence for James's dictation of *NYE* material to temporary amanuenses before he employed Bosanquet is considered in detail in the Introduction, pp. lxxii–lxxv.

[360] See Textual Variants. James did not correct this error on the typescript; it must have been spotted and altered by the typesetters or else corrected by James in proof.

> in these conditions, the greatest the case permits of. So I remember feeling here (in presence, always, that is, of the particular uncertainty of my ground,) that there would be one way better than another—oh, ever so much better than any other!—of making it fight out its battle. The frail

5 Detail of the *Portrait* Preface typescript, p. 21, showing James's autograph insertion to fill a gap in the typescript. Houghton Library, Harvard University.

missing here: James has just opened a parenthesis at this point in the Preface, and comparison of the typescript with the published text shows that the new line of typing picks up the same sentence on the far side of the parenthesis. James fills up the blank space and closes his parenthesis with a handwritten insertion: 'So I remember feeling here (in presence always, that is, of the particular uncertainty of my ground,) that there would be one way better than another [...]' (see Figure 5). Various conjectural scenarios could account for this gap in the typescript. The most likely explanation may be that James's amanuensis was unable to keep up with him and simply stopped typing and waited until she could latch onto his dictation again, losing a few words and leaving a blank space on the page which she assumed he would know how to fill later.[361] If James then sent the dictated typescript away to be copied without looking it over (or without making a decision about how to complete the passage), the blank would have been replicated in the typed copy.

Although the Houghton typescript is clearly the final copy for the *Portrait* Preface which James mailed to the Scribners in August 1906, it does not represent the last stage of the textual process. The following summer, James returned proofs for this Preface and the Preface to *Roderick Hudson* 'with 3 small corrections' and reminded his publishers that 'the 3 small corrections are, please, though small, important'.[362] No proofs survive for any of the Prefaces, so we cannot tell how or whether James altered the *Roderick*

---

[361] I am grateful to Michael Anesko for this suggestion.
[362] James to Scribners, 17 July 1907; Princeton.

Hudson Preface at this stage, but the nature of his proof corrections for the Preface to *The Portrait* can be inferred from a collation of the typescript with the published text in *NYE* III. On this evidence, it appears that his only changes were indeed small ones: adding and removing a few commas, and correcting grammatical and typographic errors which he had presumably missed in going over the typescript. And yet he had already emphasized the importance of these matters in May 1906, when he assumed that his publishers were 'taking for granted' that he would wish to read proof for the volumes of the *NYE* in order 'to ensure that absolutely supreme impeccability that such an Edition must have & that the Author's eye alone can finally contribute to'; on that occasion, too, he specifically begged 'the Compositors to *adhere irremoveably* to my punctuation & *never* to insert death-dealing commas'.[363] As he would assert again in the closing pages of the Preface to *The Golden Bowl*, for James 'the play of *representational* values' in literature comprehended such 'humblest' textual questions as 'the position of a comma' (pp. 274–5).

---

[363] James to Scribners, 12 May 1906; *LL* 432–3.

CHRONOLOGY OF COMPOSITION AND PRODUCTION

References to the diary of Theodora Bosanquet (cited as ODTB) list all the dates on which, according to this manuscript source, James either *was* or *could have been* dictating a given Preface. The symbol † indicates a date on which Bosanquet records that a Preface was started, and the symbol * indicates a date on which she records that a Preface was completed (she does not give start- and end-dates for all the Prefaces she typed). Within the period of dictation for a given Preface, square brackets enclose dates on which Bosanquet records that she worked with James, but does not mention what he was dictating on that day. Thus, e.g., the Chronology entry for the dictation of the Preface to *The Awkward Age* reads: 'ODTB 14†, 15, [16], 17, 18, [19], [20], 21, 22* October 1907'. Bosanquet records that dictation of this Preface was begun on 14 October and concluded on 22 October; she explicitly records work on the Preface on 15, 17, 18 and 21 October; on 16, 19 and 20 October she records that she worked with James but does not specify the material (e.g., on 20 October: 'Work as usual').

1904

3 August: J. B. Pinker writes to E. L. Burlingame – senior editor at Charles Scribner's Sons – signalling James's interest in a collected edition of his works (Princeton).

1905

April: Alvin Langdon Coburn photographs James in New York for *Century Magazine* (Coburn, *Alvin Langdon Coburn, Photographer*, ed. Helmut and Alison Gernsheim (New York: Dover Publications, Inc., 1978), p. 52).

Early June: Pinker meets the Scribners in New York to discuss collected edition (Philip Horne, *Henry James and Revision: The New York Edition* (Oxford: Clarendon Press, 1990), pp. 4–6).

30 July: James dictates memo on the *NYE* for the Scribners. Contents and sequence of volumes at this point are as follows: four early novels (*The American, Roderick Hudson, The Portrait of a Lady, The Princess Casamassima*); 'three or four volumes of the longer of my short stories'; *The Tragic Muse*; 'three or four more volumes' of short stories; four late novels (*The Awkward Age, The Wings of the Dove, The Ambassadors, The Golden Bowl*). Each novel or volume of stories is to have 'a freely colloquial and even, perhaps, as I may say, confidential preface or introduction'. James proposes to deliver revised copy and Prefaces for first two novels – *The American* and *Roderick Hudson* – by 25 September 1905 (HJL 4:367, 368).

1906

8 March: Pinker to Scribners: mails revised copy for first half of *Roderick Hudson* and announces that this novel is now to be 'the first book' in *NYE* (Princeton).

9 March: James to Pinker: mails last instalment of revised copy for *Roderick Hudson* to be sent to Scribners. Early version of *Roderick Hudson* Preface exists by this date (Yale).

12 March: Pinker to Scribners: mails remainder of revised copy for *Roderick Hudson*; 'the preface shall follow as soon as Mr. James can get it to his satisfaction' (Princeton).

27 March: Scribners complain to Pinker that James's revised pages of *Roderick Hudson* cannot be used as copy by the American printers (quoted in Michael Anesko, *Generous Mistakes: Incidents of Error in Henry James* (Oxford: Oxford University Press, 2017), p. 19).

6 April: Coburn photographs James in London for frontispiece to *Roderick Hudson* (Pinker to Scribners, 28 March 1906 [Princeton]).

7–9 April: Responding to Scribners' letter of 27 March, Pinker suggests that James ask for the revised sheets of *Roderick Hudson* to be returned so that they can be copied by a London typist. James agrees, and suggests changing *NYE* volume order again: revised copy for *The American* will also need to be copied by a typist, and, anticipating lighter revisions to *The Portrait*, he wonders whether that novel could move to the opening position in *NYE* (James to Pinker, 7 April 1906 [Yale]). Pinker transmits this information to the Scribners (9 April 1906 [Princeton]).

27 April: Scribners to James: decline his offer to have revised sheets of *Roderick Hudson* typed for legibility and will go on with the copy they have; announce that William Crary Brownell – editor and literary advisor at Charles Scribner's Sons – 'has taken a special interest' in the production of *NYE* (Princeton).

9 May: James to Scribners: accepts their decision of 27 April about revised sheets of *Roderick Hudson*; will have his copy for *The American* 'completely re-typed' before delivery, and will deliver revised copy for *The Portrait* 'with all the worst pages (I mean the most amended ones) re-copied'. Changes *NYE* volume order again: *Roderick Hudson* to appear first, *The Portrait* second and *The American* third. Will 'very quickly' deliver the Preface to *Roderick Hudson*, 'sending that of *The Portrait* with the [revised] Copy' (*HJL* 4:402–3).

11 June: Coburn photographs James at Lamb House (James to Scribners, 12 June 1906; *HJL* 4:407).

12 June: James to Scribners: worries that finding and photographing images for *NYE* volumes will demand 'more time […] than I can now command for the purpose' (*HJL* 4:408).

14–15 June: James has been reassured by Pinker about the frontispieces and 'will gladly aid and abet' the Scribners if they can 'see their way to taking over, themselves, the *procuring* and […] working out of the pictures' (James to Pinker, 14 June 1906; *HJL* 4:409). Pinker communicates this to the Scribners (15 June 1906 [Princeton]).

First week of July: Coburn photographs Lamb House for use as frontispiece image (James to Pinker, 27 June 1906; *LL* 436).

11 July: James to Coburn: the idea of using an existing photograph of St Paul's Cathedral as a frontispiece 'strikes me as a very happy thought' (first volume of *The Princess Casamassima*: 'The Dome of St. Paul's') (11 July 1906 [Virginia]).

13 July: Pinker to Scribners: mails the frontispiece photographs taken so far by Coburn. James wants Coburn to do 'as much more of the work as is possible' (Princeton).

31 July: James to Pinker: mails last instalment of revised copy for *The Portrait* to send to Scribners (Yale).

17 August: James to Scribners: returns final corrected proofs for *Roderick Hudson* (writes 'for "Portrait"' but this must be an error: he could not have received proof for the end of *The Portrait* by this date). Also mails Prefaces to *Roderick Hudson* (new version) and *The Portrait*; promises revised copy for *The American* plus Preface 'imminently' (Princeton).

28 August: Brownell to James: Scribners are delighted with Prefaces to *Roderick Hudson* and *The Portrait*. Doubtful that they will be able to publish first four *NYE* volumes in the autumn as intended, as *The American* is not yet revised and three frontispiece images still have to be found (Princeton).

14 September: James asks Scribners to postpone publication of first *NYE* volumes to 'the earliest possible date after the New Year'; promises to deliver revised copy, Prefaces and frontispieces for 'four or five additional Books' by that time (Princeton).

21 September: Coburn photographs Lamb House (James to Coburn, 14 and 18 September 1906 [Virginia]). James instructs him to photograph Hardwick House in Oxfordshire as a frontispiece for *The Portrait* (first volume: 'The English Home'); this subject was selected by James in June (James to Pinker, 14 June 1906; *HJL* 4:410).

25 September: James and Coburn photograph frontispiece subject in London for *The Tragic Muse* (first volume: 'St. John's Wood') (James to Pinker, 27 September 1906 [Yale]; *Alvin Langdon Coburn, Photographer*, pp. 56–8).

October: Coburn photographs frontispiece subjects in Paris for *The American* ('Faubourg St. Germain'), *The Princess Casamassima* (second volume: '"Splendid Paris, Charming Paris"'), *The Tragic Muse* (second volume: 'The Comédie Française'), *The Reverberator* (referring to the title story: 'The Court of the Hotel') and *The Ambassadors* (both volumes: 'By Notre Dame'

CHRONOLOGY OF COMPOSITION AND PRODUCTION

and 'The Luxembourg Gardens') (James to Pinker, 27 September 1906 [Yale]; James to Coburn, 2 October 1906; *HJL* 4:416–18; *Alvin Langdon Coburn, Photographer*, pp. 52–4).

November–December: James and Coburn photograph frontispiece subjects in London for *The Golden Bowl* (both volumes: 'The Curiosity Shop' and 'Portland Place'), *The Lesson of the Master* (referring to 'The Coxon Fund': 'Saltram's Seat') and *The Spoils of Poynton* (referring to the title story: 'Some of the Spoils'). They still need a subject for *What Maisie Knew* (referring to *In the Cage*: 'a London corner, if possible, with a grocer's shop containing a postal-telegraph office'). One of Coburn's photographs of Lamb House from July can be used as frontispiece for *The Awkward Age* ('Mr. Longdon's') (James to Coburn, 6, 7 and 9 December 1906; *HJL* 4:428–31).

16 November: Pinker to Scribners: mails revised copy for first half of *The American* (Princeton).

Mid-December: Coburn photographs frontispiece subjects in Rome for *The Portrait of a Lady* (second volume: 'The Roman Bridge') and *Daisy Miller* ('By St. Peter's'), and in Venice for *The Aspern Papers* ('Juliana's Court') and *The Wings of the Dove* (second volume: 'The Venetian Palace') (James to Coburn, 6 and 9 December 1906; *HJL* 4:426–8, 431; *Alvin Langdon Coburn, Photographer*, pp. 54–6).

1907

2 January: James asks Coburn to search for two more frontispiece subjects in London: 'a corner grocery' for *What Maisie Knew* (referring to *In the Cage*: 'The Cage'), 'a Harley St old, old, old Door' for *The Wings of the Dove* (first volume: 'The Doctor's Door') (Virginia).

14 February: Pinker to Scribners: mails revised copy for second half of *The American*; Preface to the novel will follow 'in a few days' (Princeton).

15 February: James to Scribners: mails Preface to *The American* (Princeton).

Late February: Coburn travels to New York carrying prints of 'photographs for *all* the illustrations' made so far and instructions about others 'to be taken over there' (James to Scribners, 15 February 1907 [Princeton]). Coburn photographs two more frontispiece subjects in America. One is for *Lady Barbarina* (referring to the title story: '"On Sundays, now, you might be at Home?"') (James to Coburn, 30 April 1907 [Virginia]). The other, referring to the story 'Europe', was intended for *The Altar of the Dead* but eventually used in *The Author of Beltraffio* ('The New England Street').

March–July: James visits France and Italy.

22 May: James to Scribners, from Rome: mails last instalment of revised copy for *The Princess Casamassima* (Princeton).

Early July: On his return to Rye from the Continent, James finds proofs of the Prefaces to *Roderick Hudson*, *The Portrait of a Lady* and *The American* waiting for him; corrects and returns them. He is halfway through revising *The Tragic Muse*, and will deliver the Prefaces to *The Princess Casamassima* and *The Tragic Muse* when he has finished those revisions (James to Scribners, 17 July 1907 [Princeton]).

2 August: James to Scribners: confirms the order of NYE I–VI, '"Roderick H." making the 1st vol.; "The American" the 2nd; "The Portrait" the 3^{d} & 4th "The Princess C." the 5th & 6th. "The American" thus *before* the [sic] "The Portrait"' (Princeton).

6 August: James to Scribners: mails last instalment of revised copy for *The Tragic Muse* (Princeton).

28 August: James to Scribners: mails Preface to *The Princess Casamassima* and revised copy for first half of *The Awkward Age*; will 'now immediately' deliver remaining copy for *The Awkward Age* plus Prefaces for *The Tragic Muse* and *The Awkward Age* (Princeton).

9 September: James to Scribners: mails revised copy for second half of *The Awkward Age* (Princeton).

5 October: James to Scribners: mails first instalment of revised copy for *The Spoils of Poynton* (first half of title story); will send Preface to *The Tragic Muse* when he gets it back from his copyist, and Prefaces for *The Awkward Age* and *The Spoils* will follow 'immediately thereafter'. He is 'expecting' a proof of the *Princess* Preface (Princeton).

CHRONOLOGY OF COMPOSITION AND PRODUCTION

7 October: James to Scribners: mails more revised copy for *The Spoils* (second half of title story) (Princeton).

11–13 October: James dictates Preface to *The Tragic Muse* to Theodora Bosanquet, apparently working from an existing text (ODTB 11†, 12, 13* October 1907).

14–22 October: James dictates Preface to *The Awkward Age*, 'not from previously written matter' (ODTB 14†, 15, [16], 17, 18, [19], [20], 21, 22* October 1907).

15 October: James to Scribners: will mail *Tragic Muse* Preface 'tomorrow'; Preface to *The Awkward Age* 'is two-thirds written & will be finished within this week' (Princeton).

16 October: James to Scribners: mails *Tragic Muse* Preface (Princeton).

25 October: James to Scribners: mails *Awkward Age* Preface (Princeton).

12 November: James to Scribners: mails last instalment of revised copy for *The Spoils of Poynton* ('A London Life' and 'The Chaperon'); Preface to this volume 'will go in a week or two' (Princeton).

5–9 December: Dictation of Preface to *The Spoils of Poynton* (ODTB 5†, 6, [7], [8], 9, [12] December 1907).

12 December: James to Scribners: mails *Spoils* Preface; Preface to *What Maisie Knew* 'follows, with revised Copy, immediately' (Princeton).

14 December: *Roderick Hudson* and *The American* (NYE I–II) published in US.

31 December: James thanks Scribners for his author's copies of *NYE* I–II. On the basis of an advertising circular enclosed with these volumes, he assumes that *NYE* volume order has been changed so as to make an unbroken series of all his novels, followed by eight volumes of shorter fictions; he has the revised copy and Preface for *What Maisie Knew* 'all but ready' so will deliver these next, but will then revise *The Wings of the Dove, The Ambassadors* and *The Golden Bowl* (HJL 4:484–5).

1908

2–18 January: Dictation of Preface to *What Maisie Knew* (ODTB 2†, [4], [5], [7], 8, [15], [17], 18* January 1908).

18 January: James to Scribners: mails first instalment of revised copy for *What Maisie Knew* (the title story); has already revised the other stories for the volume ('The Pupil' and *In the Cage*) but keeps them back until 'the next mail' to send with the Preface. After that will deliver revised copy and Preface for *The Wings of the Dove* (Princeton).

19–26 January: Dictation of Preface to *The Wings of the Dove* (ODTB 19†, 20, 21, 22, 23, 24, [25], 26* January 1908).

22 January: James to Scribners: mails remaining revised copy for *What Maisie Knew* ('The Pupil' and *In the Cage*) plus Preface. *Wings* Preface 'has already gone to the copyist' (Princeton).

27 January: James to Scribners: mails revised copy for first volume of *The Wings of the Dove* in the two-volume Scribner first edition (1902) (Princeton).

27–29 January: James begins to dictate Preface to *The Ambassadors* (ODTB 27†, 28, 29, [30] January 1908).

29 January: Brownell to James: corrects misunderstanding about order of *NYE* volumes (see 31 December 1907). Eight volumes of shorter fictions will come before the three late novels as originally planned. Asks for 'an accurate forecast of the contents' of the remaining volumes of short stories (Princeton).

30 January: James to Scribners: mails Preface to *The Wings of the Dove*; revised copy for second volume will follow 'a few days hence' (Princeton).

31 January: James to Scribners: mails 'Revised Copy of the First Half of the Second Volume of *The Wings of the Dove*'; copy for the remainder of the novel 'follows this immediately' (Princeton).

12 February: James to Scribners: accepts Brownell's explanation about order of *NYE* volumes (see 29 January) and agrees to revert to original order.

CLXIII

Has a list of contents for the volumes of shorter fictions 'all made out', but it is at Lamb House and he is in London; will mail it when he returns to Rye (Princeton).

15 February–4 March: Dictation of Preface to *The Aspern Papers* (ODTB 15†, 22, [23], 29 February, [1], [2], [3], 4* March 1908).

16–18 February: James is unwell; Bosanquet spends 'two mornings copying the previous preface [? to *The Ambassadors*]' (ODTB 20 February 1908).

21 February: James works on lists of contents for the remaining volumes of short stories (ODTB).

23 February: James mails first batch of revised copy for *Aspern Papers* volume ('The Aspern Papers' and 'The Turn of the Screw') (James to Scribners, 21–26 February 1908 [Princeton]).

26 February: James mails remainder of revised copy for *Aspern Papers* volume ('The Liar' and 'The Two Faces') plus contents lists for *The Reverberator, Lady Barbarina, The Lesson of the Master, The Altar of the Dead* and *Daisy Miller* (James to Scribners, 21–26 February 1908 [Princeton]).

4 March: Bosanquet is given *Aspern Papers* Preface to copy (ODTB).

5–11 March: Dictation of Preface to *The Reverberator* (ODTB 5†, 6, [7], 9, 11, [12] March 1908).

9 March: Bosanquet finishes copying *Aspern Papers* Preface (ODTB).

13 March: Bosanquet is to copy 'the next preface [to *The Reverberator*] during the mornings' since James 'wants the time for revision' (ODTB). James to Scribners: mails Preface to *The Aspern Papers*. Also mails revised copy for first half of title story in *Reverberator* volume; the second half of that story plus the Preface will follow 'by the next mail' and 'the rest of the Copy [for the volume] by the next after that' (Princeton).

16 March: James leaves Rye for London, Manchester and Edinburgh to attend final rehearsals and opening performances of his play *The High Bid* (*CP* 550). Returns to Lamb House at start of April.

17 March: Bosanquet finishes copying Preface to *The Reverberator* and sends typescript to James (ODTB).

18 March: James to Scribners: mails revised copy for second half of title story in *Reverberator* volume; keeps back Preface for rewrites 'in consequence of a table of contents altered as to its last item (or 2 items.)' (Princeton).

6–15 April: Dictation of Preface to *Lady Barbarina* (ODTB 6†, 7, 8, 12, 13, [14], 15* April 1908).

16 April: Bosanquet copies *Lady Barbarina* Preface (ODTB).

23 April: James to Scribners: mails *Reverberator* Preface plus instalment of revised copy for its volume ('Madame de Mauves' and 'the greater part' of 'A Passionate Pilgrim'); remainder of revised copy for the volume will follow 'immediately' (rest of 'A Passionate Pilgrim', 'The Madonna of the Future' and 'Louisa Pallant') (Princeton).

20 May: James to Scribners: mails Preface to *Lady Barbarina* plus revised copy for 'the greater part' of the title story. Preface and remainder of revised copy for *Reverberator* volume have already been dispatched (Princeton).

10–22 July: Dictation of Preface to *The Lesson of the Master* (ODTB 10†, 11, [12], [16], [17], [20], 22 July 1908).

14 July: James to Scribners: mails first instalment of revised copy for *Lesson* volume (part of 'The Lesson of the Master') and updated contents list for the volume (Princeton).

17 July: James to Scribners: mails more revised copy for *Lesson* volume (rest of 'The Lesson of the Master' and 'The Death of the Lion') (Princeton).

20 July: James to Scribners: mails more revised copy for *Lesson* volume ('The Next Time', 'The Figure in the Carpet' and part of 'The Coxon Fund') (Princeton).

24 July: James to Scribners: mails more revised copy for *Lesson* volume (rest of 'The Coxon Fund' and 'nearly the first half' of 'The Author of Beltraffio') (Princeton).

24–25 July: Bosanquet copies the *Lesson* Preface (ODTB).

26 July–6 August: Dictation of Preface to *The Altar of the Dead* (ODTB 26†, [27], 29 July, 1, 2, [3] 4, 5, 6 August 1908).

28 July: James to Scribners: mails more revised copy for *Lesson* volume (rest of 'The Author of Beltraffio') (Princeton).

4 August: James to Scribners: mails *Lesson* Preface with last instalment of revised copy for the volume ('The Middle Years', 'Greville Fane', 'Broken Wings', 'The Abasement of the Northmores' and 'The Great Good Place'). First instalment of revised copy for *The Altar of the Dead* will go 'by the next post' ('The Altar of the Dead', 'The Beast in the Jungle' and 'The Birthplace') (Princeton).

7–8 August: Bosanquet copies *Altar* Preface (ODTB).

11 August: James to Scribners: mails more revised copy for *Altar* volume ('The Private Life', 'Owen Wingrave' and 'The Friends of the Friends'); the Preface is ready but he keeps it back 'for posting with final Copy' (Princeton).

14 August: James to Scribners: mails *Altar* Preface with more revised copy for the volume ('Sir Edmund Orme', 'The Real Right Thing' and 'The Jolly Corner') (Princeton).

14–31 August: Dictation of Preface to *Daisy Miller* (ODTB 14†, 15, 17, 18, 19, [23], [27], 31 August 1908).

1 September: James to Scribners: mails last instalment of revised copy for *Altar* volume ('Four Meetings' and 'Mrs Medwin') (Princeton).

2 September: James makes cuts for length in Preface to *Daisy Miller* (ODTB).

25 September: James to Scribners: mails *Daisy Miller* Preface and first instalment of revised copy for the volume (title story); worries that the Preface is too long, but asks Scribners 'to print it as it stands' and let him cut it in proof. Will need to rewrite a passage in the *Altar* Preface – having already corrected and returned the proofs – to reflect unexpected publication of 'The Jolly Corner' in *The English Review*. Remainder of revised copy for the *Daisy Miller* volume 'now promptly follows' (Princeton).

9 October: Brownell to James: Scribners are not worried about length of the *Daisy Miller* Preface, but agree that James may make cuts in proof (Princeton).

20 October: James to Pinker: acknowledges receipt of Scribners' first financial statement for *NYE*. No royalty payment due on the volumes published so far (*LL* 468).

23 October: James to Scribners: mails last batch of revised copy for *Daisy Miller* plus updated list of contents for the volume (Princeton).

27 October: James to Scribners: mails outstanding revised copy for *The Wings of the Dove* (second half of second volume); complete revised copy for *The Ambassadors*, plus the Preface will follow 'a very few days hence' (Princeton).

28 October: James has 'nearly finished "Golden Bowl" preface' (ODTB).

2 December: Brownell to James: discovery of 'a serious complication in the issue of the New York Edition'. Final three volumes of short stories (*The Lesson of the Master*, *The Altar of the Dead* and *Daisy Miller*) have become impracticably large: Brownell asks James to redistribute contents of these volumes 'in such a way as to make an additional volume' and suggests plan for that redistribution (Princeton).

14–15 December: James to Scribners: accepts Brownell's proposal for an extra volume of short stories; will try and adjust Prefaces accordingly; suggests slightly different redistribution of titles from the one outlined by Brownell (Princeton).

15–16 December: James moves short stories between volumes and alters the corresponding Prefaces; asks Bosanquet to come back for 'extra work' in the evenings (ODTB).

1909

5 January: James to Scribners: mails 'rearranged Prefaces' to *The Lesson of the Master*, *The Author of Beltraffio* (the additional volume), *The Altar of the Dead* and *Daisy Miller*. Also mails Preface to *Ambassadors* with an instalment of revised copy for the novel (Books 8 and 9; 'Books One to Seven you will some time since have received') (Princeton).

12 January: Brownell to James: accepts rearrangement of volumes set out in James's letter of 14–15 December 1908 and writes out the new lists of contents 'in order to be absolutely explicit and avoid all possible misunderstanding'. Scribners will start printing the volumes when they receive the Prefaces (Princeton).

18 January: Brownell to James: acknowledges receipt of rewritten Prefaces sent by James on 5 January; asks for corrections to errors of reference in *Altar* and *Daisy Miller* Prefaces (Princeton).

22 January: James to Scribners: confirms that the lists of contents given by Brownell on 12 January are 'definitely the right ones'; alerts Scribners to possibility of minor discrepancies in the rewritten Prefaces (Princeton). James to Coburn: promises to commemorate his work on the frontispieces in the *Golden Bowl* Preface (Virginia).

26 January: James to Scribners: mails first instalment of revised copy for *The Golden Bowl* (Princeton).

2 February: James to Scribners: returns *Altar* and *Daisy Miller* Prefaces with corrections requested by Brownell on 18 January (Princeton).

8 March: James to Scribners: mails final instalment of revised copy for *NYE*, 'that for the End of The Golden Bowl. The Preface goes to you by the next mail—or the next after that. It has been written these many weeks, but I am making an alteration in it' (Princeton).

22 June: Alerted by telegram from Scribners, James discovers that he has failed to return corrected proof of *Golden Bowl* Preface: assures them that 'the Revise *does* go [to] you positively today' (Princeton).

BIBLIOGRAPHY

The Bibliography serves the editorial materials in the volume as a whole. It does not aim for comprehensive coverage of everything that has been written about the Prefaces. It is limited to works that are explicitly cited in the editorial matter or, if not cited, works that contribute information and evidence directly relevant to the history of the text's genesis, composition, reception and afterlife.

The Prefaces

Preface to *The Portrait of a Lady*, corrected typescript, Houghton Library, Harvard University, Cambridge, MA, MS Am 1237.17.

The New York Edition of the Novels and Tales of Henry James, 24 vols. (New York: Charles Scribner's Sons, 1907–9; London: Macmillan and Co., 1908–9).

The Art of the Novel: Critical Prefaces, introduction by R. P. Blackmur (New York: Charles Scribner's Sons, 1934).

Le prefazioni, trans. Agostino Lombardo (Venice: Neri Pozza Editore, 1956).

La Création littéraire: préfaces de l'édition de New York, trans. Marie-Françoise Cachin (Paris: Denoël-Gonthier, 1980).

Literary Criticism: French Writers, Other European Writers, The Prefaces to the New York Edition, ed. Leon Edel and Mark Wilson (New York: The Library of America, 1984), pp. 1035–341.

The Art of Criticism: Henry James on the Theory and the Practice of Fiction, ed. William Veeder and Susan M. Griffin (Chicago, IL: University of Chicago Press, 1986), pp. 257–422 (Prefaces to NYE I–III, IX, XI, XII and XIX–XXIII with annotations and commentary).

El arte de la novela: prefacios críticos, trans. Félix Rodríguez Rodríguez (Madrid: Langre, 2014).

BIBLIOGRAPHY

Archival Resources Consulted

Archives of Charles Scribner's Sons, C0101, Manuscripts Division, Department of Special Collections, Princeton University Library.

David J. Supino Collection of Henry James, Beinecke Rare Book and Manuscript Library, Yale University.

Edward Howard Marsh Collection of Papers, The Henry W. and Albert A. Berg Collection of English and American Literature, The New York Public Library.

Henry James Collection, Yale Collection of American Literature, Beinecke Rare Book and Manuscript Library, Yale University.

J. M. Barrie Collection, Beinecke Rare Book and Manuscript Library, Yale University.

Owen Wister Papers, 1829–1966, Manuscript Division, Library of Congress, Washington, DC.

Papers of Henry James, 1855–1969, n.d., Accession #6251, etc., Clifton Waller Barrett Library of American Literature, Albert and Shirley Small Special Collections Library, University of Virginia.

Theodora Bosanquet Papers, Houghton Library, Harvard University.

Other Works by Henry James

The American: The Version of 1877 Revised in Autograph and Typescript for the New York Edition of 1907, Reproduced in Facsimile from the Original in the Houghton Library, Harvard University, introduction by Rodney G. Dennis (Ilkley: The Scolar Press, 1976).

The American, ed. Adrian Poole (Oxford: Oxford University Press, 1999).

'An American Art-Scholar: Charles Eliot Norton', *Burlington Magazine* 14 (January 1909), 201–4.

The American Scene (London: Chapman and Hall, 1907).

'The Art of Fiction', *Longman's Magazine* 4 (September 1884), 502–21.

The Aspern Papers. Louisa Pallant. The Modern Warning, 2 vols. (London and New York: Macmillan and Co., 1888).

The Aspern Papers and Other Stories, ed. Adrian Poole (Oxford: Oxford University Press, 2013).

BIBLIOGRAPHY

Autobiographies: A Small Boy and Others; Notes of a Son and Brother; The Middle Years; Other Writings, ed. Philip Horne (New York: Library of America, 2016).
The Awkward Age (London: William Heinemann, 1899).
The Awkward Age (New York: Harper & Brothers, 1899).
The Better Sort (London: Methuen & Co., 1903).
'Browning in Venice. Being Recollections by the Late Katharine De Kay Bronson, with a Prefatory Note by Henry James', *Cornhill Magazine* 12 n.s. (February 1902), 145-71.
Collected Travel Writings: The Continent: A Little Tour in France, Italian Hours, Other Travels, ed. Richard Howard (New York: Library of America, 1993).
Collected Travel Writings: Great Britain and America: English Hours, The American Scene, Other Travels, ed. Richard Howard (New York: Library of America, 1993).
Collective Edition of 1883, 14 vols. (London: Macmillan and Co., 1883).
The Complete Fiction of Henry James, general eds. Michael Anesko, Tamara L. Follini, Philip Horne and Adrian Poole, 34 vols. (Cambridge: Cambridge University Press, 2015–).
The Complete Letters of Henry James 1855–1872, 2 vols., ed. Pierre A. Walker and Greg W. Zacharias, with an introduction by Alfred Habegger (Lincoln, NE: University of Nebraska Press, 2006).
The Complete Letters of Henry James 1872–1876, 3 vols., ed. Pierre A. Walker and Greg W. Zacharias, with an introduction by Millicent Bell (Lincoln, NE: University of Nebraska Press, 2008).
The Complete Letters of Henry James 1876–1878, 2 vols., ed. Pierrre A. Walker and Greg W. Zacharias, with an introduction by Martha Banta (Lincoln, NE: University of Nebraska Press, 2012, 2013).
The Complete Letters of Henry James 1878–1880, 2 vols., ed. Pierrre A. Walker and Greg W. Zacharias, with an introduction by Michael Anesko (Lincoln, NE: University of Nebraska Press, 2014, 2015).
The Complete Letters of Henry James 1880–1883, 2 vols., ed. Michael Anesko and Greg W. Zacharias, associate editor Katie Sommer, with an introduction by Susan M. Griffin (Lincoln, NE: University of Nebraska Press, 2016, 2017).

BIBLIOGRAPHY

The Complete Letters of Henry James 1883–1884, 2 vols., ed. Michael Anesko and Greg W. Zacharias, associate editor Katie Sommer, with an introduction by Kathleen Lawrence (Lincoln, NE: University of Nebraska Press, 2018, 2019).

The Complete Letters of Henry James 1884–1886, 2 vols., ed. Michael Anesko and Greg W. Zacharias, associate editor Katie Sommer, with an introduction by Adrian Poole (Lincoln, NE: University of Nebraska Press, 2020, 2021).

The Complete Letters of Henry James 1887–1888, 2 vols., ed. Michael Anesko and Greg W. Zacharias, associate editor Katie Sommer, with an introduction by Sarah Wadsworth (Lincoln, NE: University of Nebraska Press, 2022, 2023).

The Complete Notebooks of Henry James, ed. Leon Edel and Lyall H. Powers (New York and Oxford: Oxford University Press, 1987).

The Complete Plays of Henry James, ed. Leon Edel (London: Rupert Hart-Davis, 1949).

The Complete Writings of Henry James on Art and Drama, vol. 1: *Art*, ed. Peter Collister (Cambridge: Cambridge University Press, 2016).

The Complete Writings of Henry James on Art and Drama, vol. 2: *Drama*, ed. Peter Collister (Cambridge: Cambridge University Press, 2016).

The Correspondence of Henry James and the House of Macmillan, 1877–1914: 'All the Links in the Chain', ed. Rayburn S. Moore (Baton Rouge, LA: Louisiana State University Press, 1993).

The Correspondence of William James, vols. I–III: *William and Henry*, eds. Ignas K. Skrupskelis and Elizabeth M. Berkeley (Charlottesville, VA and London: University Press of Virginia, 1992–4).

Daisy Miller and *An International Episode*, ed. Adrian Poole (Oxford: Oxford University Press, 2013).

Dearly Beloved Friends: Henry James's Letters to Younger Men, ed. Susan E. Gunter and Steven H. Jobe (Ann Arbor, MI: University of Michigan Press, 2001).

'Émile Zola', *Atlantic Monthly* 92 (August 1903), 193–210.

English Hours (London: William Heinemann, 1905).

Essays in London and Elsewhere (London: James R. Osgood, McIlvaine & Co., 1893).

The Finer Grain (New York: Charles Scribner's Sons, 1910).

'Gabriele D'Annunzio', *Quarterly Review* 199 (April 1904), 383–419.
'George Sand: The New Life', *North American Review* 174 (April 1902), 536–54.
'The Grand Canal', in Richard Harding Davis, W. W. Story, Andrew Lang, Henry James, Francisque Sarcey, Paul Lindau and Isabel F. Hapgood, *Great Streets of the World* (New York: Charles Scribner's Sons, 1892), pp. 141–72.
'Gustave Flaubert', introduction to Flaubert, *Madame Bovary*, ed. Edmund Gosse (London: William Heinemann, 1902), pp. v–xliii.
Henry James: A Life in Letters, ed. Philip Horne (Harmondsworth, Middx.: Allen Lane, The Penguin Press, 1999).
Henry James: Selected Literary Criticism, ed. Morris Shapira (London: Heinemann Educational Books, 1963).
'Henry James and the *Bazar* Letters', ed. Leon Edel and Lyall H. Powers, *Bulletin of the New York Public Library* 62.2 (February 1958), 75–103.
Henry James and Edith Wharton, Letters: 1900–1915, ed. Lyall H. Powers (New York: Charles Scribner's Sons, 1990).
Henry James Letters, ed. Leon Edel, 4 vols. (Cambridge, MA: Belknap Press of Harvard University Press; London: Macmillan and Co., 1974–84).
Henry James on Culture: Collected Essays on Politics and the American Social Scene, ed. Pierre A. Walker (Lincoln, NE and London: University of Nebraska Press, 1999).
'Honoré de Balzac', introduction to Balzac, *The Two Young Brides* [*Mémoires de deux jeunes mariées*], ed. Edmund Gosse (London: William Heinemann, 1902), pp. v–xliii.
'Introduction' to Oliver Goldsmith, *The Vicar of Wakefield* (New York: The Century Co., 1900), pp. xi–xx; reprinted in G. S. Rousseau (ed.), *Oliver Goldsmith: The Critical Heritage* (London and New York: Routledge, 1974), pp. 65–9.
'Introduction' to William Shakespeare, *The Tempest*, ed. Sidney Lee (New York: George D. Sproul, 1907), pp. ix–xxxii.
Italian Hours (London: William Heinemann, 1909).
Letters, Fictions, Lives: Henry James and William Dean Howells, ed. Michael Anesko (New York and Oxford: Oxford University Press, 1997).
Letters from the Palazzo Barbaro, ed. Rosella Mamoli Zorzi (London: Pushkin Press, 1998).

The Letters of Henry James, ed. Percy Lubbock, 2 vols. (London: Macmillan and Co., 1920).

'The Letters of Robert Louis Stevenson', *North American Review* 170 (January 1900), 61–77.

Literary Criticism: Essays on Literature, American Writers, English Writers, eds. Leon Edel and Mark Wilson (New York: The Library of America, 1984).

Literary Criticism: French Writers, Other European Writers, The Prefaces to the New York Edition, ed. Leon Edel and Mark Wilson (New York: The Library of America, 1984).

A Little Tour in France, 2nd edn, with ninety-four illustrations by Joseph Pennell (London: William Heinemann, 1900).

'London. January 15, 1897', *Harper's Weekly* 41 (6 February 1897), 134–5.

'London. July 1, 1897', *Harper's Weekly* 41 (31 July 1897), 754.

'London. July 31, 1897', *Harper's Weekly* 41 (21 August 1897), 834.

'*A London Life*' and '*The Reverberator*', ed. Philip Horne (Oxford: Oxford University Press, 1989).

'The Married Son', in W. D. Howells, Mary E. Wilkins Freeman, Mary Heaton Vorse, Mary Stewart Cutting, Elizabeth Jordan, John Kendrick Bangs, Henry James, Elizabeth Stuart Phelps, Edith Wyatt, Mary R. Shipman Andrews, Alice Brown and Henry Van Dyke, *The Whole Family: A Novel by Twelve Authors* (New York and London: Harper & Brothers, 1908), pp. 144–84.

'Matilde Serao', *North American Review* 172 (March 1901), 367–80.

The Notebooks of Henry James, ed. F. O. Matthiessen and Kenneth B. Murdock (New York and Oxford: Oxford University Press, 1947).

Notes on Novelists (New York: Charles Scribner's Sons, 1914).

The Other House, 2 vols. (London: William Heinemann, 1896).

Parisian Sketches: Letters to the 'New York Tribune' 1875–1876, ed. Leon Edel and Ilse Dusoir Lind (London: Rupert Hart-Davis, 1958).

Partial Portraits (London and New York: Macmillan and Co., 1888).

'Pierre Loti', introduction to Pierre Loti, *Impressions* (London: Archibald Constable and Co., 1898), pp. [1]–21.

The Portrait of a Lady (Boston and New York: Houghton, Mifflin and Company, 1882).

The Portrait of a Lady, ed. Philip Horne (London: Penguin, 2011).

Portraits of Places (London: Macmillan and Co., 1883).
The Princess Casamassima, 3 vols. (London and New York: Macmillan, 1886).
The Real Thing (New York: Macmillan, 1893).
Selected Letters of Henry James to Edmund Gosse 1882-1915: A Literary Friendship, ed. Rayburn S. Moore (Baton Rouge, LA: Louisiana State University Press, 1988).
The Sense of the Past (London: W. Collins Sons & Co., 1917).
'She and He: Recent Documents', *The Yellow Book* 12 (January 1897), 15-38.
The Spoils of Poynton, ed. Bernard Richards (Oxford: Oxford University Press, 1982).
Stories Revived, 3 vols. (London: Macmillan and Co., 1885).
The Tales of Henry James. Volume Two: 1870-1874, ed. Maqbool Aziz (Oxford: Clarendon Press, 1978).
The Tales of Henry James. Volume Three: 1875-1879, ed. Maqbool Aziz (Oxford: Clarendon Press, 1984).
Theatricals. Second Series: The Album, The Reprobate (London: Osgood, McIlvaine & Co., 1894).
Theatricals. Two Comedies: Tenants, Disengaged (London: Osgood, McIlvaine & Co., 1894).
The Tragic Muse, 2 vols. (Boston and New York: Houghton, Mifflin and Company, 1890).
The Tragic Muse, ed. Philip Horne (London: Penguin, 1995).
Transatlantic Sketches (Boston, MA: James R. Osgood and Company, 1875).
The Turn of the Screw and Other Stories, ed. T. J. Lustig (Oxford: Oxford University Press, 1992).
What Maisie Knew, ed. Adrian Poole (Oxford: Oxford University Press, 1996).
William Wetmore Story and His Friends: From Letters, Diaries, and Recollections, 2 vols. (Edinburgh: William Blackwood and Sons, 1903).

Secondary and Related Works

Adams, Herbert B., *The Life and Writings of Jared Sparks*, 2 vols. (Boston, MA: Houghton, Mifflin and Company, 1893).
Aiken, Conrad, [review of *The Art of the Novel: Critical Prefaces*], *Criterion* 14 (July 1935), 667-9.

Anderson, Margaret, 'Some Personalities', *The Indexer: The International Journal of Indexing* 7.1 (1970), 19–23.

Anesko, Michael, 'Ambiguous Allegiances: Conflicts of Culture and Ideology in the Making of the New York Edition', in David McWhirter (ed.), *Henry James's New York Edition: The Construction of Authorship* (Stanford, CA: Stanford University Press, 1995), pp. 77–89.

'Collected Editions and the Consolidation of Cultural Authority: The Case of Henry James', *Book History* 12 (2009), 186–208.

'*Friction with the Market': Henry James and the Profession of Authorship* (New York and Oxford: Oxford University Press, 1986).

Generous Mistakes: Incidents of Error in Henry James (Oxford: Oxford University Press, 2017).

Monopolizing the Master: Henry James and the Politics of Modern Literary Scholarship (Stanford, CA: Stanford University Press, 2012).

Arnold, Matthew, *The Complete Prose Works of Matthew Arnold*, ed. R. H. Super, 11 vols. (Ann Arbor, MI: University of Michigan Press, 1960–77).

Auden, W. H., 'At the Grave of Henry James' (1943), in F. W. Dupee (ed.), *The Question of Henry James: A Collection of Critical Essays* (New York: Henry Holt and Company, 1945), pp. 246–50.

The Collected Poetry of W. H. Auden (New York: Random House, 1945).

Baedeker, Karl, *Paris and its Environs*, 6th edn (Leipzig: Karl Baedeker, 1878).

Paris and Environs, 9th edn (Leipzig: Karl Baedeker, 1888).

Paris and Northern France (Koblenz: Karl Baedeker, 1867).

Balzac, Honoré de, *La Comédie humaine*, ed. Pierre-Georges Castex et al., 12 vols. (Paris: Gallimard, 1976–81).

The Baptist Hymnal, for Use in the Church and Home (Philadelphia, PA: American Baptist Publication Society, 1883).

Baudelaire, Charles, *Œuvres complètes*, ed. Y.-G. le Dantec and Claude Pichois (Paris: Bibliothèque de la Pléiade, 1961).

Beach, Joseph Warren, *The Method of Henry James* (New Haven, CT: Yale University Press, 1918).

Besant, Walter, *The Art of Fiction: A Lecture* (London: Chatto & Windus, 1884).

Bessière, Jean, and Miceala Symington, 'The French Reception of Henry James', in Annick Duperray (ed.), *The Reception of Henry James in Europe* (London: Continuum, 2006), pp. 15–35.

Bilston, Sarah, *The Awkward Age in Women's Popular Fiction, 1850–1900: Girls and the Transition to Womanhood* (Oxford: Oxford University Press, 2004).

Blair, Sara, *Henry James and the Writing of Race and Nation* (Cambridge: Cambridge University Press, 1996).

Blomfield, Reginald, *Memoirs of an Architect* (London: Macmillan and Co., 1932).

Bogardus, Ralph F., *Pictures and Texts: Henry James, A. L. Coburn, and New Ways of Seeing in Literary Culture* (Ann Arbor, MI: University of Michigan Research Press, 1984).

Booth, Wayne C., *The Rhetoric of Fiction* (Chicago, IL: University of Chicago Press, 1961).

Bosanquet, Theodora, *Henry James at Work*, ed. Lyall H. Powers (Ann Arbor, MI: University of Michigan Press, 2006).

Bourget, Paul, *A Cruel Enigma*, trans. Julian Cray (London: Vizetelly & Co., 1887).

Brendon, Piers, *Thomas Cook: 150 Years of Popular Tourism* (London: Secker & Warburg, 1991).

Bronstein, Michaela, '*The Princess* among the Polemicists: Aesthetics and Protest at Midcentury', *American Literary History* 29.1 (2017), 26–49.

Brooks, Van Wyck, *The Pilgrimage of Henry James* (New York: E. P. Dutton & Company, 1925).

Brown, Bill, 'Jamesian Matter', in Greg W. Zacharias (ed.), *A Companion to Henry James* (Chichester: Wiley-Blackwell, 2008), pp. 292–308.

Brownell, W. C., 'Henry James', *Atlantic Monthly* 95 (April 1905), 496–519.

Butcher, S. H., *Aristotle's Theory of Poetry and Fine Art, with a Critical Text and Translation of The Poetics*, 3rd edn (London: Macmillan and Co., 1902).

Byron, George Gordon, Lord, *The Complete Poetical Works*, ed. Jerome J. McGann, 7 vols. (Oxford: Clarendon Press, 1980–93).

Carleton, William, *Traits and Stories of the Irish Peasantry*, ed. D. J. O'Donoghue, 4 vols. (London: J. M. Dent and Co.; New York: Macmillan and Co., 1896).

Carlyle, Thomas, *The French Revolution: A History*, ed. David R. Sorensen, Brent E. Kinser and Mark Engel (Oxford: Oxford University Press, 2019).

Carter, E. J., 'Breaking the Bank: Gambling Casinos, Finance Capitalism, and German Unification', *Central European History* 39.2 (2006), 185–213.

Champfleury, *Balzac: sa méthode de travail. Étude d'après ses Manuscrits* (Paris: Librairie A. Patay, 1879).

Chaucer, Geoffrey, *The Riverside Chaucer*, 3rd edn, general editor Larry D. Benson (Boston, MA: Houghton Mifflin Company, 1987).

'The Circus, Past and Present', *Yankee Notions* 8.3 (March 1859), 78.

Clark, C. E. Frazer, Jr, *Nathaniel Hawthorne: A Descriptive Bibliography* (Pittsburgh, PA: University of Pittsburgh Press, 1978).

Clarke, John M., *The Brookwood Necropolis Railway*, 4th revised and enlarged edn (Usk: The Oakwood Press, 2006).

Coburn, Alvin Langdon, *Alvin Langdon Coburn, Photographer*, ed. Helmut and Alison Gernsheim (New York: Dover Publications, 1978).

Coleridge, S. T., *Biographia Literaria*, ed. J. Shawcross, 2 vols. (Oxford: Oxford University Press, 1907).

The Complete Poetical Works of Samuel Taylor Coleridge, ed. Ernest Hartley Coleridge, 2 vols. (Oxford: Clarendon Press, 1912).

The Literary Remains of Samuel Taylor Coleridge, ed. Henry Nelson Coleridge, 4 vols. (London: William Pickering, 1836–9).

The Concise Oxford Dictionary of Art Terms, 2nd edn, ed. Michael Clarke (Oxford: Oxford University Press, 2010).

Conrad, Joseph, *The Collected Letters of Joseph Conrad*, ed. Frederick R. Karl and Laurence Davies, 9 vols. (Cambridge: Cambridge University Press, 1983–2007).

Cowper, William, *The Poetical Works of William Cowper*, 4th edn, ed. H. S. Milford (London: Geoffrey Cumberlege, Oxford University Press, 1934).

Culver, Stuart, 'Ozymandias and the Mastery of Ruins: The Design of the New York Edition', in David McWhirter (ed.), *Henry James's New York Edition: The Construction of Authorship* (Stanford, CA: Stanford University Press, 1995), pp. 39–57.

Curtis, Anthony, 'Auden and Henry James', *London Magazine* 33 (1 August 1993), 49–55.

Dargan, E. Preston, 'Introduction: Balzac's Method of Revision', in Dargan and Bernard Weinberg (eds.), *The Evolution of Balzac's 'Comédie humaine'* (Chicago: University of Chicago Press, 1942), pp. 1–21.

Dasent, Arthur Irwin, *Piccadilly in Three Centuries, with Some Account of Berkeley Square and the Haymarket* (London: Macmillan and Co., 1920).

Daudet, Alphonse, *Memories of a Man of Letters, Artists' Wives, Etc.*, trans. George Burnham Ives (Boston, MA: Little, Brown, and Company, 1900).

Souvenirs d'un homme de lettres (Paris: C. Marpon et E. Flammarion, n.d. [1888]).

Thirty Years in Paris, trans. George Burnham Ives (Boston, MA: Little, Brown, and Company, 1900).

Trente ans de Paris: à travers ma vie et mes livres (Paris: C. Marpon et E. Flammarion, 1888).

Dickens, Charles, *David Copperfield*, ed. Nina Burgis (Oxford: Clarendon Press, 1981).

Martin Chuzzlewit, ed. Margaret Cardwell (Oxford: Clarendon Press, 1982).

Dictionary of National Biography, ed. Leslie Stephen and Sidney Lee, 63 vols. (London: Smith, Elder, and Co., 1885–1900).

Diebel, Anne, '"The Dreary Duty": Henry James, *The Yellow Book*, and Literary Personality', *Henry James Review* 32.1 (2011), 45–59.

Disraeli, Isaac, *The Literary Character*, ed. B. Disraeli (New York: A. C. Armstrong, 1881).

Dryden, John, *The Works of John Dryden*, ed. Edward Niles Hooker, H. T. Swedenberg, V. A. Dearing et al., 20 vols. (Berkeley, CA: University of California Press, 1956–2000).

Dumas, Alexandre, *Histoire de mes bêtes*, 2nd edn (Paris: Michel Lévy Frères, 1868).

Dumas-Vorzet, Eduard, *Paris et Ses Environs* ([Paris]: Institut Geographique de Paris, 1878).

Duperray, Annick (ed.), *The Reception of Henry James in Europe* (London: Continuum, 2006).

Eagle, Dorothy, and Hilary Carnell, *The Oxford Illustrated Literary Guide to Great Britain and Ireland*, revised edn (Oxford: Oxford University Press, 1981).

Edel, Leon, 'The Architecture of Henry James's "New York Edition"', *The New England Quarterly* 24.2 (1951), 169–78.

Henry James: The Conquest of London, 1870–1883 (London: Rupert Hart-Davis, 1962).

Henry James: The Master, 1901–1916 (London: Rupert Hart-Davis, 1972).

Henry James: The Middle Years 1884–1894 (London: Rupert Hart-Davis, 1963).

Henry James: The Untried Years, 1843–1870 (London: Rupert Hart-Davis, 1953).

The Prefaces of Henry James (Paris: Jouve et Cie, 1931).

Edel, Leon, and Dan H. Laurence, *A Bibliography of Henry James*, 3rd edn, revised with the assistance of James Rambeau (Oxford: Clarendon Press, 1982).

Edel, Leon, and Adeline R. Tintner, *The Library of Henry James* (Ann Arbor, MA: UMI Research Press, 1987).

Edgar, Pelham, *Henry James, Man and Author* (Boston, MA and New York: Houghton Mifflin Company, 1927).

El-Rayess, Miranda, *Henry James and the Culture of Consumption* (Cambridge: Cambridge University Press, 2014).

Eliot, George, *Adam Bede*, ed. Carol A. Martin (Oxford: Clarendon Press, 2001).

Daniel Deronda, ed. Graham Handley (Oxford: Clarendon Press, 1984).

Eliot, T. S., 'The Hawthorne Aspect', *The Little Review* 5.4 (August 1918), 47–53.

Emerson, Ralph Waldo, *Collected Poems and Translations*, ed. Harold Bloom and Paul Kane (New York: Library of America, 1994).

Essays and Lectures, ed. Joel Porte (New York: Library of America, 1983).

The English and Scottish Popular Ballads, ed. Francis James Child, 10 vols. (Boston and New York: Houghton, Mifflin and Company, 1883–98).

English Fairy Tales, collected by Joseph Jacobs (London: David Nutt, 1890).

Faguet, Émile, *Flaubert* (Paris: Librairie Hachette et Cie, 1899).

Flaubert, trans. Mrs R. L. Devonshire (London: Constable and Company, 1914).

Farmer, John, and W. E. Henley, *Slang and Its Analogues, Past and Present*, 7 vols. ([London]: Printed for subscribers only, 1890–1904).

Fergusson, Francis, 'James's Idea of Dramatic Form', *Kenyon Review* 5.4 (1943), 495–507.

Flaubert, Gustave, *Lettres de Gustave Flaubert à George Sand* (Paris: G. Charpentier et Cie, 1884).

'Préface', in Louis Bouilhet, *Dernières chansons: poésies posthumes* (Paris: Michel Levy Frères, 1872), pp. 1–34.

Flower, Dean, *Henry James in Northampton: Visions and Revisions* (Northampton, MA: Friends of the Smith College Library, 1971).

Foley, Richard Nicholas, *Criticism in American Periodicals of the Works of Henry James from 1866 to 1916* (Washington, DC: The Catholic University of America Press, 1944).

Follini, Tamara, 'The Friendship of Fanny Kemble and Henry James', *Cambridge Quarterly* 19.3 (1990), 230–42.

Ford, Ford Madox, *Letters of Ford Madox Ford*, ed. Richard M. Ludwig (Princeton, NJ: Princeton University Press, 1965).

Forman, Maurice Buxton, *A Bibliography of the Writings in Prose and Verse of George Meredith* (Edinburgh: The Dunedin Press for The Bibliographical Society, 1922).

'The Fortunes of Quotations', *The Saturday Review of Politics, Literature, Science, and Art* 47 (7 June 1879), 700.

Friedman, Norman, *Form and Meaning in Fiction* (Athens, GA: University of Georgia Press, 1975).

'Point of View in Fiction: The Development of a Critical Concept', *PMLA* 70.5 (1955), 1160–84.

Gale, Robert L., 'Henry James and Italy', *Nineteenth-Century Fiction* 14.2 (1959), 157–70.

Gard, Roger (ed.), *Henry James: The Critical Heritage* (London: Routledge & Kegan Paul, 1968).

Gates, Joanne E., 'Henry James's Dictation Letter to Elizabeth Robins: "The Suffragette Movement Hot from the Oven"', *Henry James Review* 31.3 (2010), 254–63.

Gatrell, Simon, 'The Collected Editions of Hardy, James, and Meredith, with Some Concluding Thoughts on the Desirability of a Taxonomy of the Book', in Andrew Nash (ed.), *The Culture of Collected Editions* (Basingstoke: Palgrave Macmillan, 2003), pp. 80–94.

Gautier, Théophile, *Honoré de Balzac* (Paris: Poulet-Malassis et de Broise, 1859).

Genette, Gérard, *Paratexts: Thresholds of Interpretation*, trans. Jane E. Lewin (Cambridge: Cambridge University Press, 1997).

Gittings, Robert, and Jo Manton, *Claire Clairmont and the Shelleys 1789-1879* (Oxford: Oxford University Press, 1992).

Glanz, Rudolf, 'German-Jewish Names in America', *Jewish Social Studies* 23.3 (1961), 143–69.

Goldberg, Shari, 'Hanging Fire, or A New Ontology for *Poynton*', *Henry James Review* 37.1 (2016), 51–63.

Goldsmith, Oliver, *The Collected Works of Oliver Goldsmith*, ed. Arthur Friedman, 5 vols. (Oxford: Clarendon Press, 1966).

Goncourt, Edmond and Jules de, *Journal des Goncourt: Mémoires de la vie littéraire*, 9 vols. (Paris: G. Charpentier et E. Fasquelle, 1887–96).

Goode, John, 'The Art of Fiction: Walter Besant and Henry James', in David Howard et al. (eds.), *Tradition and Tolerance in Nineteenth-Century Fiction: Critical Essays on Some English and American Novels* (London: Routledge and Kegan Paul, 1966), pp. 243–81.

Gordon, Lyndall, *A Private Life of Henry James: Two Women and His Art* (London: Chatto & Windus, 1998).

Gosse, Edmund, *Aspects and Impressions* (London: Cassell and Company, 1922).

Grattan, C. Hartley, 'Henry James in the Critic's Role', *New York Times Book Review* (18 November 1934), 2.

Gray, Thomas, *The Complete Poems of Thomas Gray*, ed. H. W. Starr and J. R. Hendrickson (Oxford: Clarendon Press, 1966).

Habegger, Alfred, *Henry James and the 'Woman Business'* (Cambridge: Cambridge University Press, 1989).

—— 'New York Monumentalism and Hidden Family Corpses', in David McWhirter (ed.), *Henry James's New York Edition: The Construction of Authorship* (Stanford, CA: Stanford University Press, 1995), pp. 185–205.

Hale, Dorothy J., 'Henry James and the Invention of Novel Theory', in Jonathan Freedman (ed.), *The Cambridge Companion to Henry James* (Cambridge: Cambridge University Press, 1998), pp. 79–101.

Hardy, Thomas, *Thomas Hardy's Personal Writings: Prefaces, Literary Opinions, Reminiscences*, ed. Harold Orel (London: Macmillan, 1967).

The Works of Thomas Hardy, Wessex Novels Edition, 16 vols. (London: Osgood, McIlvaine and Co., 1895-6).

Harland, Henry, 'Concerning the Short Story', *The Academy* 51 (5 June 1897), Fiction Supplement, 6-7.

Harrison, Frederic, 'Rome Revisited', *Fortnightly Review* 53 n.s. (May 1893), 702-21.

Harte, Bret, 'The Rise of the "Short Story"', *Cornhill Magazine* 7 n.s. (July 1899), 1-8.

Hawthorne, Nathaniel, *Tales and Sketches*, ed. Roy Harvey Pearce (New York: Library of America, 1982).

Hayes, Kevin J. (ed.), *Henry James: The Contemporary Reviews* (Cambridge: Cambridge University Press, 1996).

'Henry James, Interpreter of American Types', *New York Times* (5 March 1916), Magazine Section, 7-8.

Herford, Oliver, *Henry James's Style of Retrospect: Late Personal Writings, 1890-1915* (Oxford: Oxford University Press, 2016).

'James and the Habit of Allusion', in Annick Duperray et al. (eds.), *Henry James's Europe: Heritage and Transfer* (Cambridge: Open Book Publishers, 2011), pp. 179-89.

'The Roman Lotus: Digestion and Retrospect', *Henry James Review* 31.1 (2010), 54-60.

Hicks, Priscilla Gibson, 'A Turn in the Formation of James's New York Edition: Criticism, the Historical Record, and the Siting of *The Awkward Age*', *Henry James Review* 16.2 (1995), 195-221.

Highways of Commerce: The Ocean Lines, Railways, Canals, and Other Trade Routes of Foreign Countries, Special Consular Reports, Vol. XII (Washington, DC: Government Printing Office, 1895).

Hill, Hamlin L., Jr, '"The Revolt of the Daughters": A Suggested Source for "The Awkward Age"', *Notes and Queries* n.s. 8.9 (1961), 347-9.

Hillairet, Jacques, *Dictionnaire historique des rues de Paris*, 7th edn, 2 vols. ([Paris]: Les Éditions de Minuit, 1979).

Holland, Laurence Bedwell, *The Expense of Vision: Essays on the Craft of Henry James* (Princeton, NJ: Princeton University Press, 1964).

Holt, J. C., *Magna Carta* (Cambridge: Cambridge University Press, 1965).

Horne, Philip, 'Henry James and the Cultural Frame of the New York Edition', in Andrew Nash (ed.), *The Culture of Collected Editions* (Basingstoke: Palgrave Macmillan, 2003), pp. 95–110.
   'Henry James and the Economy of the Short Story', in Ian Willison, Warwick Gould and Warren Chernaik (eds.), *Modernist Writers and the Marketplace* (Basingstoke: Macmillan, 1996), pp. 1–35.
   'Henry James and the *English Review*', *International Ford Madox Ford Studies* 9 (2010), 25–51.
   'Henry James and the Poetry of Association', essay awarded the Le Bas Essay Prize, Cambridge University, October 1982.
   Henry James and Revision: The New York Edition (Oxford: Clarendon Press, 1990).
   'Letters and Notebooks', in David McWhirter (ed.), *Henry James in Context* (Cambridge: Cambridge University Press, 2010), pp. 68–79.
   '"A Palpable Imaginable *Visitable* Past": Henry James and the Eighteenth Century', *Eighteenth-Century Life* 32.2 (2008), 14–28.
   'Revisitings and Revisions in the New York Edition of the Novels and Tales of Henry James', in Greg W. Zacharias (ed.), *A Companion to Henry James* (Chichester: Wiley-Blackwell, 2008), pp. 208–30.
   'Strings of Pearls: James, Maupassant, and "Paste"', *Literary Imagination* 21.2 (2019), 137–57.
Howells, W. D., 'Leo Tolstoï', introduction to Count Leo Tolstoï, *Sebastopol*, trans. Frank D. Millet (New York: Harper & Brothers, 1887), pp. 5–12.
   'Some Anomalies of the Short Story', *North American Review* 173 (September 1901), 422–32.
Hueffer, Ford Madox, *Henry James: A Critical Study* (London: Martin Secker, 1913).
Hunt, Violet, *I Have This to Say: The Story of My Flurried Years* (New York: Boni and Liveright, 1926).
Hutchison, Hazel, 'A Bit of String: Rebecca West on Henry James', *Henry James Review* 39.3 (2018), 247–55.
Hyde, H. Montgomery, *Henry James at Home* (London: Methuen & Co., 1969).
Ibsen, Henrik, *Hedda Gabler: A Drama in Four Acts*, trans. Edmund Gosse (London: William Heinemann, 1891).

Ibsen's Prose Dramas, ed. William Archer, 5 vols. (London: Walter Scott, 1890–1).

The Imperial Dictionary of the English Language, ed. John Ogilvie, new edn revised by Charles Annandale, 4 vols. (London: Blackie & Son, 1882).

Irving, Washington, *History, Tales and Sketches*, ed. James W. Tuttleton (New York: Library of America, 1983).

Izzo, Donatella, '"Appearing and Disappearing in Public": James Studies in Italy, from Local to Global', in Annick Duperray (ed.), *The Reception of Henry James in Europe* (London: Continuum, 2006), pp. 69–92.

James, Alice, *Alice James: Her Brothers—Her Journal*, ed. Anna Robeson Burr (New York: Dodd, Mead & Company, 1934).

James, Henry, Sr, *The Secret of Swedenborg: Being an Elucidation of His Doctrine of the Divine Natural Humanity* (Boston, MA: Fields, Osgood, 1869).

James, William, *Writings 1902–1910*, ed. Bruce Kuklick (New York: Library of America, 1987).

Jameson, Fredric, *The Political Unconscious: Narrative as a Socially Symbolic Act* (Ithaca, NY: Cornell University Press, 1981).

Jefferson, D. W., *Henry James and the Modern Reader* (Edinburgh and London: Oliver & Boyd, 1964).

Johnson, William Woolsey, and William E. Story, 'Notes on the "15" Puzzle', *American Journal of Mathematics* 2.4 (1879), 397–404.

Jolly, Roslyn, *Henry James: History, Narrative, Fiction* (Oxford: Clarendon Press, 1993).

Keats, John, *The Poems of John Keats*, ed. Miriam Allott (London: Longman, 1970).

Kennedy, Michael, *Portrait of Elgar*, 3rd edn (Oxford: Clarendon Press, 1987).

Kieve, J. L., *The Electric Telegraph: A Social and Economic History* (Newton Abbot: David and Charles, 1973).

Kipling, Rudyard, *The Writings in Prose and Verse of Rudyard Kipling*, 36 vols. (New York: Charles Scribner's Sons, 1897–1937).

Leavis, F. R., *The Great Tradition: George Eliot, Henry James, Joseph Conrad* (London: Chatto & Windus, 1948).

'James as Critic', in *Henry James: Selected Literary Criticism*, ed. Morris Shapira (London: Heinemann Educational Books, 1963), pp. xiii–xxiii.

Lee, Vernon, *Hauntings: Fantastic Stories*, 2nd edn (London: John Lane, The Bodley Head, 1906).

Le Gallienne, Richard, *Prose Fancies (Second Series)* (London: John Lane; Chicago: H. S. Stone and Co., 1896).

Lello, James, '"The Auditive Intelligence": Intonation in Henry James', PhD thesis, University of Cambridge (2019).

Leuschner, Eric, '"Utterly, Insurmountably, Unsaleable": Collected Editions, Prefaces, and the "Failure" of Henry James's New York Edition', *Henry James Review* 22.1 (2001), 24–40.

Littré, Émile, *Dictionnaire de la langue française*, 4 vols. (Paris: Librairie Hachette et Cie, 1873–5).

Longfellow, Henry Wadsworth, *The Complete Poetical Works of Henry Wadsworth Longfellow*, ed. Horace E. Scudder (Boston, MA, and New York: Houghton, Mifflin and Company, 1893).

Lubbock, Percy, *The Craft of Fiction* (London: Jonathan Cape, 1921).

'The Quest of the Golden Bowl', *Times Literary Supplement* (22 January 1914), 38.

Lustig, T. J., 'James, Arnold, "Culture", and "Modernity"; or, A Tale of Two Dachshunds', *Cambridge Quarterly* 37.1 (2008), 164–93.

Macaulay, Thomas Babington, *The History of England from the Accession of James II*, 5 vols. (London: printed for Longman, Brown, Green, and Longmans, 1849).

MacCarthy, Desmond, *Portraits I* (New York: The Macmillan Company, 1932).

Marlowe, Christopher, *Marlowe's 'Doctor Faustus' 1604–1616: Parallel Texts*, ed. W. W. Greg (Oxford: Clarendon Press, 1950).

Marsh, Edward, *A Number of People: A Book of Reminiscences* (London: William Heinemann, 1939).

Matthews, Brander, 'The Philosophy of the Short-Story', *Lippincott's Monthly Magazine* 36 (October 1885), 366–74.

Matthiessen, F. O., *Henry James: The Major Phase* (New York: Oxford University Press, 1944).

Maupassant, Guy de, *Pierre et Jean* (Paris: Paul Ollendorf, 1888).

Pierre and Jean, trans. Clara Dell (New York: P. F. Collier & Son, 1902).

McCauley, Elizabeth Anne, Alan Chong, Rosella Mamoli Zorzi and Richard Lingner (eds.), *Gondola Days: Isabella Stewart Gardner and the Palazzo Barbaro Circle* (Boston, MA: Isabella Stewart Gardner Museum, 2004).

McKay, George L., *A Stevenson Library: Catalogue of a Collection of Writings by and about Robert Louis Stevenson formed by Edwin J. Beinecke*, 6 vols. (New Haven, CT: Yale University Library, 1951–64).

McWhirter, David, '"The Whole Chain of Relation and Responsibility": Henry James and the New York Edition', in McWhirter (ed.), *Henry James's New York Edition: The Construction of Authorship* (Stanford, CA: Stanford University Press, 1995), pp. 1–19.

Menke, Richard, 'Telegraphic Realism: Henry James's *In the Cage*', *PMLA* 115.5 (2000), 975–90.

Mill, John Stuart, *Principles of Political Economy*, 2 vols. (London: John W. Parker, 1848).

The Spirit of the Age, introductory essay by Frederick A. von Hayek (Chicago, IL: University of Chicago Press, 1942).

Miller, J. Hillis, *Literature as Conduct: Speech Acts in Henry James* (New York: Fordham University Press, 2005).

Millgate, Jane, *Scott's Last Edition: A Study in Publishing History* (Edinburgh: Edinburgh University Press, 1987).

Millgate, Michael, *Testamentary Acts: Browning, Tennyson, James, Hardy* (Oxford: Clarendon Press, 1992).

Milton, John, *The Poems of John Milton*, ed. John Carey and Alastair Fowler (London and New York: Longman, 1968).

Mix, Katherine Lyon, *A Study in Yellow: The 'Yellow Book' and Its Contributors* (Lawrence, KS: University of Kansas Press, 1960).

Molière, *Oeuvres complètes*, ed. Georges Couton, 2 vols. (Paris: Gallimard, 1971).

Monteiro, George, 'The *Atlantic Monthly*'s Rejection of "The Pupil": An Exchange of Letters between Henry James and Horace Scudder', *American Literary Realism, 1870–1910* 23.1 (1990), 75–83.

Moore, Thomas, *The Poetical Works of Thomas Moore*, ed. Charles Kent (London: George Routledge and Sons, 1879).

Mounsey, Augustus H., *A Journey Through the Caucasus and the Interior of Persia* (London: Smith, Elder, & Co., 1872).

Nadel, Ira B., 'Henry James, Alvin Langdon Coburn, and the New York Edition: A Chronology', in David McWhirter (ed.), *Henry James's New York Edition: The Construction of Authorship* (Stanford, CA: Stanford University Press, 1995), pp. 274–7.

Nash, Andrew, '"The Dead Should Be Protected from Their Own Carelessness": The Collected Editions of Robert Louis Stevenson', in Nash (ed.), *The Culture of Collected Editions* (Basingstoke: Palgrave Macmillan, 2003), pp. 111–27.

Niebuhr, Ursula, 'Memories of the 1940s', in Stephen Spender (ed.), *W. H. Auden: A Tribute* (New York: Macmillan, 1975), pp. 104–18.

O'Gorman, Donal, 'Henry James's Reading of *The Turn of the Screw*: Parts II and III', *Henry James Review* 1.3 (1980), 231–40.

Ordnance Survey Maps of London, Five Feet to the Mile, 1893–1896, Sheets VI.88–9, National Library of Scotland [https://maps.nls.uk/os/town-plans-england/london-1056-1890s.html].

Ormond, Richard, *John Singer Sargent: Portraits in Charcoal* (New York and Washington, DC: The Morgan Library and National Portrait Gallery, Smithsonian Institution, 2019).

Ourliac, Édouard, 'Malheurs et aventures de *César Birotteau* avant sa naissance', reprinted from *Le Figaro* (15 December 1837), in Honoré de Balzac, *Histoire de la grandeur et de la décadence de César Birotteau*, 2 vols. (Paris: n.p., 1838), vol. II, pp. [341–4].

The Oxford Dictionary of Nursery Rhymes, ed. Iona and Peter Opie (Oxford: Oxford University Press, 1951).

Parker, Hershel, 'Deconstructing *The Art of the Novel* and Liberating James's Prefaces', *Henry James Review* 14.3 (1993), 284–307.

Flawed Texts and Verbal Icons: Literary Authority in American Fiction (Evanston, IL: Northwestern University Press, 1984).

'Henry James "In the Wood": Sequence and Significances of His Literary Labors, 1905–1907', *Nineteenth-Century Fiction* 38.4 (1984), 492–513.

Pater, Walter, *The Renaissance: Studies in Art and Poetry*, 4th edn (London and New York: Macmillan and Co., 1893).

Pedrocco, Filippo, *Tiepolo: The Complete Paintings* (New York: Rizzoli, 2002).

Perosa, Sergio, 'Italian Translations of Henry James', in Annick Duperray (ed.), *The Reception of Henry James in Europe* (London: Continuum, 2006), pp. 47–68.

Perrault, Claude, *Ordonnance for the Five Kinds of Columns after the Method of the Ancients*, trans. Indra Kagis McEwen (Santa Monica, CA: The Getty Center for the History of Art and the Humanities, 1993).

Pettinelli, Fabrizio, *Firenze in Tranvai: Breve cronistoria del trasporto pubblico* (Florence: AIDA, 2008).

Poe, Edgar Allan, *Poetry and Tales*, ed. Patrick F. Quinn (New York: Library of America, 1984).

Posnock, Ross, 'Breaking the Aura of Henry James', in David McWhirter (ed.), *Henry James's New York Edition: The Construction of Authorship* (Stanford, CA: Stanford University Press, 1995), pp. 23–38.

Pound, Ezra, 'The Notes to "The Ivory Tower"', *The Little Review* 5.4 (August 1918), 62–4.

'A Shake Down', *The Little Review* 5.4 (August 1918), 9–39.

Purdy, Richard Little, *Thomas Hardy: A Bibliographical Study* (London, New York and Toronto: Geoffrey Cumberlege for Oxford University Press, 1954).

Quintilian, *The Orator's Education: Books 1–2*, ed. and trans. Donald A. Russell (Cambridge, MA: Harvard University Press, 2001).

Rawlings, Peter (ed.), *Critical Essays on Henry James*, Critical Thought Series: 5 (Aldershot: Scolar Press, 1993).

Read, Herbert, 'The Art of Henry James', *Times Literary Supplement* (9 May 1935), 299.

Richards, Bernard, 'James and His Sources: *The Spoils of Poynton*', *Essays in Criticism* 29.4 (1979), 302–22.

'The Sources of Henry James's "The Marriages"', *Review of English Studies* 30.119 (1979), 316–22.

Ritchie, Anne Thackeray, *The Two Thackerays: Anne Thackeray Ritchie's Centenary Biographical Introductions to the Works of William Makepeace Thackeray*, critical introduction by Carol Hanbery MacKay, bibliographical introduction by Peter L. Shillingsburg and Julia Maxey, 2 vols. (New York: AMS Press, 1988).

Rivkin, Julie, *False Positions: The Representational Logics of Henry James's Fiction* (Stanford, CA: Stanford University Press, 1996).

Rix, Alicia, '"The Lives of Others": Motoring in Henry James's "The Velvet Glove"', *Journal of Modern Literature* 36.3 (2013), 31–49.

Roberts, Morris, *Henry James's Criticism* (Cambridge, MA: Harvard University Press, 1929).

Robertson, William, *The Works of Wm. Robertson, D.D.*, 8 vols. (London and Oxford: W. Pickering and Talboys and Wheeler, 1825).

Robins, Elizabeth, *Theatre and Friendship: Some Henry James Letters* (New York: G. P. Putnam's Sons, 1932).

Rossetti, William Michael, *Some Reminiscences of William Michael Rossetti*, 2 vols. (New York: Charles Scribner's Sons, 1906).

Rowe, John Carlos, *The Theoretical Dimensions of Henry James* (Madison, WI: The University of Wisconsin Press, 1984).

Ruskin, John, *The Works of John Ruskin*, ed. E. T. Cook and Alexander Wedderburn, 39 vols. (London: George Allen, 1903–12).

Saint-Beuve, Charles-Augustin, *Causeries du Lundi*, 3rd edn, 15 vols. (Paris: Garnier frères, 1857–70).

Saint Simon, Fernand de, *La Place Vendôme* (Paris: Éditions Vendôme, 1982).

Salmon, Richard, *Henry James and the Culture of Publicity* (Cambridge: Cambridge University Press, 1997).

Sand, George, *Préfaces de George Sand*, ed. Anna Szabó, 2 vols. (Debrecen: Kossuth Lajos Tudományegyetem, 1997).

Scott, Rebekah, '"The Dreadful Done": Henry James's Style of Abstraction', *Textual Practice* 35.6 (2021), 941–66.

'Henry James: "In the Minor Key"', in Leonardo Buonomo (ed.), *The Sound of James: The Aural Dimension in Henry James's Work* (Trieste: Edizioni Università di Trieste, 2021), pp. 17–34.

Scott, Walter, *The Edinburgh Edition of the Waverley Novels*, editor-in-chief David Hewitt, 30 vols. (Edinburgh: Edinburgh University Press, 1993–).

Poetical Works of Sir Walter Scott, Bart., ed. William Minto, 2 vols. (Edinburgh: Adam and Charles Black, 1887–8).

Sedgwick, Ellery, 'Henry James and the *Atlantic Monthly*: Editorial Perspectives on James' "Friction with the Market"', *Studies in Bibliography* 45 (1992), 311–32.

Segnitz, T. M., 'The Actual Genesis of Henry James's "Paste"', *American Literature* 36.2 (1964), 216–19.

Shelley, Percy Bysshe, *Poetical Works*, ed. Thomas Hutchinson, corrected by Geoffrey Matthews (London: Oxford University Press, 1970).

Sherman, Stuart P., 'The Aesthetic Idealism of Henry James', *Nation* 104 (5 April 1917), 393–9.

Short, R. W., 'Some Critical Terms of Henry James', *PMLA* 65.5 (1950), 667–80.

Shumsky, Allison, 'James Again: The New New York Edition', *Sewanee Review*, 70.3 (1962), 522–5.

Simon, Linda, *The Critical Reception of Henry James: Creating a Master* (Rochester, NY: Camden House, 2007).

Smiles, Samuel, *Self-Help; With Illustrations of Character and Conduct* (London: John Murray, 1859).

Smith, William George, *The Oxford Dictionary of English Proverbs* (Oxford: Clarendon Press, 1935).

Snyder, Lawrence D., *German Poetry in Song: An Index of Lieder* (Berkeley, CA: Fallen Leaf Press, 1995).

Southey, Caroline Bowles, *The Poetical Works of Caroline Bowles Southey* (Edinburgh and London: William Blackwood and Sons, 1867).

'Spain: her Manners and Amusements', *Cornhill Magazine* 25 (January 1872), 60–76.

Spilka, Mark, 'Henry James and Walter Besant: "The Art of Fiction" Controversy', *NOVEL: A Forum on Fiction* 6.2 (1973), 101–19.

Stevenson, Robert Louis, *The Letters of Robert Louis Stevenson*, ed. Bradford A. Booth and Ernest Mehew, 8 vols. (New Haven, CT: Yale University Press, 1994–5).

The Novels and Tales of Robert Louis Stevenson, 'Thistle Edition', 26 vols. (New York: Charles Scribner's Sons, 1895–1912).

The Works of Robert Louis Stevenson, 'Edinburgh Edition', 28 vols. (Edinburgh: printed by T. and A. Constable, 1894–8).

The Works of Robert Louis Stevenson, 'Pentland Edition', 20 vols. (London: Cassell and Company, 1906–7).

Stonier, G. W., 'The Henry James Prefaces', *New Statesman and Nation Literary Supplement* (1 June 1935), 813–14.

Supino, David J., *A Bibliographical Catalogue of a Collection of Editions to 1921*, 2nd edn, revised (Liverpool: Liverpool University Press, 2014).

Survey of London: Volume 42, Kensington Square to Earl's Court, ed. Hermione Hobhouse (London: London County Council, 1986), British History Online (www.british-history.ac.uk/survey-london/vol42).

Swearingen, Roger G., *The Prose Writings of Robert Louis Stevenson: A Guide* (London: Macmillan, 1980).

Swinburne, Algernon Charles, *The Poems of Algernon Charles Swinburne*, 6 vols. (London: Chatto & Windus, 1904).

Symonds, John Addington, *Renaissance in Italy. Italian Literature: Part II* (London: Smith, Elder, & Co., 1881).

Taylor, Archer, and Bartlett Jere Whiting, *A Dictionary of American Proverbs and Proverbial Phrases, 1820–1880* (Cambridge, MA: Belknap Press of Harvard University Press, 1958).

Taylor, Linda J., *Henry James, 1866–1916: A Reference Guide* (Boston, MA: G. K. Hall & Co., 1982).

Tennyson, Alfred, *The Poems of Tennyson*, 2nd edn, ed. Christopher Ricks, 3 vols. (London: Longman, 1987).

Thackeray, William Makepeace, *The Works of William Makepeace Thackeray*, 13 vols. (New York and London: Harper and Brothers, 1898–9).

Thomson, James, *The Seasons*, ed. James Sambrook (Oxford: Clarendon Press, 1981).

'Transformation Scenes: How They Are Made and Worked', *Strand Magazine* 6 (December 1893), 705–10.

Vincec, Sister Stephanie, '"Poor Flopping *Wings*": The Making of Henry James's *The Wings of the Dove*', *Harvard Library Bulletin* 24.1 (1976), 60–93.

Vivante, Paolo, 'On Homer's Winged Words', *Classical Quarterly* 25.1 (1975), 1–12.

Voltaire, *Candide and Other Stories*, trans. Roger Pearson (Oxford: Oxford University Press, 2006).

    Œuvres complètes de Voltaire, ed. Louis Moland, 52 vols. (Paris: Garnier frères, 1877–85).

Waller, Philip, *Writers, Readers, and Reputations: Literary Life in Britain 1870–1918* (Oxford: Oxford University Press, 2006).

Walmisley, Arthur T., 'The Port of Dover', *Journal of the Royal Society of Arts* 58 (15 April 1910), 526–38.

Watkinson, William L., *Studies in Christian Character* (New York: Fleming H. Revell Company, 1903).
Wells, H. G., *Boon, The Mind of the Race, The Wild Asses of the Devil, and The Last Trump* (London: T. Fisher Unwin, 1915).
  Experiment in Autobiography: Discoveries and Conclusions of a Very Ordinary Brain (since 1866) (New York: The Macmillan Company, 1934).
Werdet, Edmond, *Portrait intime de Balzac: sa vie, son humeur et son caractère* (Paris: A. Silvestre, 1859).
West, Rebecca, *Henry James* (London: Nisbet & Co., 1916).
Wharton, Edith, *A Backward Glance* (New York and London: D. Appleton-Century Company, 1934).
  Edith Wharton: The Uncollected Critical Writings, ed. Frederick Wegener (Princeton, NJ: Princeton University Press, 1996).
  The Letters of Edith Wharton, ed. R. W. B. Lewis and Nancy Lewis (New York: Charles Scribner's Sons, 1988).
Worden, Ward S., 'A Cut Version of *What Maisie Knew*', *American Literature* 24.4 (1953), 493–504.
Wordsworth, William, *The Poetical Works of William Wordsworth*, ed. Ernest de Selincourt and Helen Darbishire, 5 vols. (Oxford: Clarendon Press, 1940–9).
  The Prelude or Growth of a Poet's Mind, ed. Ernest de Selincourt, 2nd edn revised by Helen Darbishire (Oxford: Clarendon Press, 1959).
Wrenn, Angus, *Henry James and the Second Empire* (London: Legenda, 2009).
Yeats, W. B. (ed.), *Fairy and Folk Tales of the Irish Peasantry* (London: Walter Scott, 1888).
The Yellow Book Digital Edition, ed. Dennis Denisoff and Lorraine Janzen Kooistra, 2010. Yellow Nineties 2.0, Ryerson University Centre for Digital Humanities, 2019 [1890s.ca/yellow-book-volumes].
Young, Filson, *Christopher Columbus and the New World of His Discovery*, 2nd edn, 2 vols. (London: E. Grant Richards, 1906).
Zabel, Morton D. 'The Poetics of Henry James' (1935), in F. W. Dupee (ed.), *The Question of Henry James: A Collection of Critical Essays* (New York: Henry Holt, 1945), pp. 212–17.

Zorzi, Rosella Mamoli, '"Figures Reflected in the Clear Lagoon": Henry James, Daniel and Ariana Curtis, and Isabella Stewart Gardner', in Elizabeth Anne McCauley et al. (eds.), *Gondola Days: Isabella Stewart Gardner and the Palazzo Barbaro Circle* (Boston, MA: Isabella Stewart Gardner Museum, 2004), pp. 129–54.

Ralph W. Curtis. Un pittore americano a Venezia (Venice: Supernova, 2019).

THE PREFACES

PREFACE to *Roderick Hudson* (*NYE* I)

"Roderick Hudson" was begun in Florence in the spring of 1874, designed from the first for serial publication in "The Atlantic Monthly," where it opened in January 1875 and persisted through the year.[1] I yield to the pleasure of placing these circumstances on record, as I shall place others, and as I have yielded to the need of renewing acquaintance with the book after a quarter of a century. This revival of an all but extinct relation with an early work may often produce for an artist, I think, more kinds of interest and emotion than he shall find it easy to express, and yet will light not a little, to his eyes, that veiled face of his Muse which he is condemned for ever and all anxiously to study.[2] The art of representation bristles with questions[3] the very terms of which are difficult to apply and to appreciate; but whatever makes it arduous makes it, for our refreshment, infinite, causes the practice of it, with experience, to spread round us in a widening, not in a narrowing circle. Therefore it is that experience has to organise, for convenience and cheer, some system of observation—for fear, in the admirable immensity, of losing its way. We see it as pausing from time to time to consult its notes,[4] to measure, for guidance, as many aspects and distances as possible, as many steps taken and obstacles mastered and fruits gathered and beauties enjoyed. Everything counts, nothing is superfluous in such a survey; the explorer's note-book strikes me here as endlessly receptive. This accordingly is what I mean by the contributive value—or put it simply as, to one's own sense, the beguiling charm—of the *accessory* facts in a given artistic case. This is why, as one looks back, the private history of any sincere work, however modest its pretensions, looms with its own completeness in the rich, ambiguous æsthetic air, and seems at once to borrow a dignity and to mark, so to say, a station. This is why, reading over, for revision, correction and republication, the volumes here in hand, I find myself, all attentively, in presence of some such recording scroll or engraved commemorative table[5]—from which the "private" character, moreover, quite insists on dropping out. These notes represent, over a considerable course, the continuity of an artist's endeavour, the growth of his whole operative consciousness and, best of all, perhaps, their own tendency to multiply, with the implication, thereby, of a memory much enriched. Addicted to "stories"[6] and inclined to retrospect, he fondly takes, under this backward view, his whole unfolding, his process of production, for a thrilling tale, almost for a wondrous adventure,[7] only asking himself at what stage of remembrance the mark of the relevant will begin to fail. He frankly proposes to take this mark everywhere for granted.

"Roderick Hudson" was my first attempt at a novel,[8] a long fiction with a "complicated" subject, and I recall again the quite uplifted sense with which my idea, such as it was, permitted me at last to put quite out to sea. I had but hugged the shore on sundry previous small occasions; bumping about, to acquire skill, in the shallow waters and sandy coves of the "short story" and master as yet of no vessel constructed to carry a sail.[9] The subject of "Roderick" figured to me vividly this employment of canvas, and I have not forgotten, even after long years, how the blue southern sea seemed to spread immediately before me and the breath of the spice-islands[10] to be already in the breeze. Yet it must even then have begun for me too, the ache of fear, that was to become so familiar, of being unduly tempted and led on by "developments";[11] which is but the desperate discipline of the question involved in them. They are of the very essence of the novelist's process, and it is by their aid, fundamentally, that his idea takes form and lives; but they impose on him, through the principle of continuity that rides them, a proportionate anxiety. They are the very condition of interest, which languishes and drops without them; the painter's subject[12] consisting ever, obviously, of the related state, to each other, of certain figures and things. To exhibit these relations, once they have all been recognised, is to "treat" his idea,[13] which involves neglecting none of those that directly minister to interest; the degree of that directness remaining meanwhile a matter of highly difficult appreciation, and one on which felicity of form and composition, as a part of the total effect, mercilessly rests. Up to what point is such and such a development *indispensable* to the interest? What is the point beyond which it ceases to be rigorously so? Where, for the complete expression of one's subject, does a particular relation stop—giving way to some other not concerned in that expression?

Really, universally, relations stop nowhere, and the exquisite problem of the artist is eternally but to draw, by a geometry of his own, the circle within which they shall happily *appear* to do so.[14] He is in the perpetual predicament that the continuity of things is the whole matter, for him, of comedy and tragedy; that this continuity is never, by the space of an instant or an inch, broken, and that, to do anything at all, he has at once intensely to consult and intensely to ignore it. All of which will perhaps pass but for a supersubtle way of pointing the plain moral[15] that a young embroiderer of the canvas of life soon began to work in terror, fairly, of the vast expanse of that surface, of the boundless number of its distinct perforations for the needle, and of the tendency inherent in his many-coloured flowers and figures to cover and consume as many as possible of the little holes.[16] The development of the flower, of the figure, involved thus an immense counting of holes and a careful selection among them. That would have been, it seemed to him, a brave enough process, were it not the very nature of the holes so to invite, to solicit, to persuade, to practise positively a thousand lures and deceits. The prime effect of so sustained a system, so prepared a surface, is to lead on and on; while the fascination of following resides, by the same token, in the presumability *somewhere* of a convenient, of a visibly-appointed stopping-place. Art would be easy indeed if, by a fond power disposed to "patronise" it, such conveniences, such simplifications, had been provided. We have, as the case stands, to invent and establish them, to arrive at them by a difficult, dire process of selection and comparison, of surrender and sacrifice. The very meaning of expertness is acquired courage to brace one's self for the cruel crisis from the moment one sees it grimly loom.

"Roderick Hudson" was further, was earnestly pursued during a summer partly spent in the Black Forest and (as I had returned to America early in September) during three months passed near Boston.[17] It is one of the silver threads of the recoverable texture of that embarrassed phase, however, that the book was not finished when it had to begin appearing in monthly fragments:[18] a fact in the light of which I find myself live over again, and quite with wonderment and tenderness, so intimate an experience of difficulty and delay. To have "liked" so much writing it,[19] to have worked out with such conviction the pale embroidery, and yet not, at the end of so many months, to have come through, was clearly still to have fallen short of any facility and any confidence: though the long-drawn process now most appeals to memory, I confess, by this very quality of shy and groping duration. One fact about it indeed outlives all others; the fact that, as the loved Italy was the scene of my fiction—so much more loved than one has ever been able, even after fifty efforts, to say![20]—and as having had to leave it persisted as an inward ache, so there was soreness in still contriving, after a fashion, to hang about it and in prolonging, from month to month, the illusion of the golden air.[21] Little enough of that medium may the novel, read over to-day, seem to supply; yet half the actual interest lurks for me in the earnest, baffled intention of making it felt. A whole side of the old consciousness, under this mild pressure, flushes up and prevails again; a reminder, ever so penetrating, of the quantity of "evocation" involved in my plan, and of the quantity I must even have supposed myself to achieve. I take the lingering perception of all this, I may add—that is of the various admonitions of the whole reminiscence—for a signal instance of the way a work of art, however small, if but sufficiently sincere, may vivify and even dignify the accidents and incidents of its growth.

I must that winter (which I again like to put on record that I spent in New York) have brought up my last instalments in due time,[22] for I recall no haunting anxiety: what I do recall perfectly is the felt pleasure, during those months—and in East Twenty-fifth Street!—of trying, on the other side of the world, still to surround with the appropriate local glow the characters that had combined, to my vision, the previous year in Florence. A benediction, a great advantage, as seemed to me, had so from the first rested on them, and to nurse them along was really to sit again in the high, charming, shabby old room which had originally overarched them and which, in the hot May and June, had looked out, through the slits of cooling shutters, at the rather dusty but ever-romantic glare of Piazza Santa Maria Novella.[23] The house formed the corner (I delight to specify) of Via della Scala, and I fear that what the early chapters of the book most "render" to me to-day is not the umbrageous air of their New England town, but the view of the small cab-stand sleepily disposed—long before the days of strident electric cars—round the rococo obelisk of the Piazza, which is supported on its pedestal, if I remember rightly, by four delightful little elephants.[24] (That, at any rate, is how the object in question, deprecating verification, comes back to me with the clatter of the horse-pails, the discussions, in the intervals of repose under well-drawn hoods, of the unbuttoned *cocchieri*, sons of the most garrulous of races, and the occasional stillness as of the noonday desert.)

Pathetic, as we say,[25] on the other hand, no doubt, to re-perusal, the manner in which the evocation, so far as attempted, of the small New England town of my first two chapters, fails of intensity—if intensity, in such a connexion, had been indeed to be looked for. *Could* I verily, by the terms of my little plan, have "gone in" for it[26] at the best, and even though one of these terms was the projection, for my fable, at the outset, of some more or less vivid antithesis to a state of civilisation providing for "art"?[27] What I wanted, in essence, was the image of some perfectly humane community which was yet all incapable of providing for it, and I had to take what my scant experience furnished me. I remember feeling meanwhile no drawback in this scantness, but a complete, an exquisite little adequacy, so that the presentation arrived at would quite have served its purpose, I think, had I not misled myself into naming my place. To name a place, in fiction, is to pretend in some degree to represent it—and I speak here of course but of the use of existing names, the only ones that carry weight. I wanted one that carried weight—so at least I supposed; but obviously I was wrong, since my effect lay, so superficially, and could only lie, in the local *type*, as to which I had my handful of impressions.[28] The particular local case was another matter, and I was to see again, after long years, the case into which, all recklessly, the opening passages of "Roderick Hudson" put their foot.[29] I was to have nothing then, on the spot, to sustain me but the rather feeble plea that I had not *pretended* so very much to "do" Northampton Mass.[30] The plea was charmingly allowed, but nothing could have been more to the point than the way in which, in such a situation, the whole question of the novelist's "doing,"[31] with its eternal wealth, or in other words its eternal torment of interest, once more came up. He embarks, rash adventurer, under the star of "representation,"[32] and is pledged thereby to remember that the art of interesting us in things—once these things are the right ones for his case—can *only* be the art of representing them. This relation to them, for invoked interest, involves his accordingly "doing"; and it is for him to settle with his intelligence what that variable process shall commit him to.

Its fortune rests primarily, beyond doubt, on somebody's having, under suggestion, a *sense* for it—even the reader will do, on occasion, when the writer, as so often happens, completely falls out. The way in which this sense has been, or has not been, applied constitutes, at all events, in respect to any fiction, the very ground of critical appreciation. Such appreciation takes account, primarily, of the thing, in the case, to have *been* done, and I now see what, for the first and second chapters of "Roderick," that was. It was a peaceful, rural New England community *quelconque*[33]—it was not, it was under no necessity of being, Northampton Mass. But one nestled, technically, in those days, and with yearning, in the great shadow of Balzac; his august example, little as the secret might ever be guessed, towered for me over the scene;[34] so that what was clearer than anything else was how, if it was a question of Saumur, of Limoges, of Guérande, he "did" Saumur, did Limoges, did Guérande. I remember how, in my feebler fashion, I yearned over the preliminary presentation of my small square patch of the American scene, and yet was not sufficiently on my guard to see how easily his high practice might be delusive for my case. Balzac talked of Nemours and Provins:[35] therefore why shouldn't one, with fond fatuity, talk of almost the only small American *ville de province*[36] of which one had happened to lay up, long before, a pleased vision? The reason was plain: one was not in the least, in one's prudence, emulating his systematic closeness.[37] It didn't confuse the question either that he would verily, after all, addressed as he was to a due density in his material, have found little enough in Northampton Mass to tackle. He tackled no group of appearances, no presented face of the social organism (conspicuity thus attending it), *but* to make something of it. To name it simply and not in some degree tackle it would have seemed to him an act reflecting on his general course the deepest dishonour. Therefore it was that, as the moral of these many remarks, I "named," under his contagion, when I was really most conscious of not being held to it; and therefore it was, above all, that for all the effect of representation I was to achieve, I might have let the occasion pass. A "fancy" indication[38] would have served my turn—except that I should so have failed perhaps of a pretext for my present insistence.

Since I do insist, at all events, I find this ghostly interest perhaps even more reasserted for me by the questions begotten within the very covers of the book, those that wander and idle there as in some sweet old overtangled walled garden, a safe paradise of self-criticism.[39] Here it is that if there be air for it to breathe at all, the critical question swarms, and here it is, in particular, that one of the happy hours of the painter's long day may strike. I speak of the painter in general and of his relation to the old picture, the work of his hand, that has been lost to sight and that, when found again, is put back on the easel for measure of what time and the weather may, in the interval, have done to it. Has it too fatally faded, has it blackened or "sunk," or otherwise abdicated, or has it only, blest thought, strengthened, for its allotted duration, and taken up, in its degree, poor dear brave thing, some shade of the all appreciable, yet all indescribable grace that we know as pictorial "tone"?[40] The anxious artist has to wipe it over, in the first place, to see; he has to "clean it up," say, or to varnish it anew,[41] or at the least to place it in a light, for any right judgement of its aspect or its worth. But the very uncertainties themselves yield a thrill, and if subject and treatment, working together, have had their felicity, the artist, the prime creator, may find a strange charm in this stage of the connexion. It helps him to live back into a forgotten state, into convictions, credulities too early spent perhaps,[42] it breathes upon the dead reasons of things, buried as they are in the texture of the work, and makes them revive, so that the actual appearances and the old motives fall together once more, and a lesson and a moral and a consecrating final light are somehow disengaged.

All this, I mean of course, if the case will wonderfully take any such pressure, if the work doesn't break down under even such mild overhauling. The author knows well enough how easily that may happen—which he in fact frequently enough sees it do. The old reasons then are too dead to revive; they were not, it is plain, good enough reasons to live. The only possible relation of the present mind to the thing is to dismiss it altogether.[43] On the other hand, when it is not dismissed—as the only detachment is the detachment of aversion—the creative intimacy is reaffirmed, and appreciation, critical apprehension, insists on becoming as active as it can. Who shall say, granted this, where it shall not begin and where it shall consent to end? The painter who passes over his old sunk canvas the wet sponge that shows him what may still come out again makes his criticism essentially active. When having seen, while his momentary glaze remains, that the canvas *has* kept a few buried secrets, he proceeds to repeat the process with due care and with a bottle of varnish and a brush, he is "living back," as I say, to the top of his bent, is taking up the old relation, so workable apparently, yet,[44] and there is nothing logically to stay him from following it all the way. I have felt myself then, on looking over past productions, the painter making use again and again of the tentative wet sponge. The sunk surface has here and there, beyond doubt, refused to respond: the buried secrets, the intentions, are buried too deep to rise again, and were indeed, it would appear, not much worth the burying. Not so, however, when the moistened canvas does obscurely flush and when resort to the varnish-bottle is thereby immediately indicated. The simplest figure for my revision of this present array of earlier, later, larger, smaller, canvases, is to say that I have achieved it by the very aid of the varnish-bottle. It is true of them throughout that, in words I have had occasion to use in another connexion (where too I had revised with a view to "possible amendment of form and enhancement of meaning"), I have "nowhere scrupled to re-write a sentence or a passage on judging it susceptible of a better turn."[45]

To re-read "Roderick Hudson" was to find one remark so promptly and so urgently prescribed that I could at once only take it as pointing almost too stern a moral. It stared me in the face that the time-scheme of the story is quite inadequate, and positively to that degree that the fault but just fails to wreck it. The thing escapes, I conceive, with its life: the effect sought is fortunately more achieved than missed, since the interest of the subject bears down, auspiciously dissimulates, this particular flaw in the treatment. Everything occurs, none the less, too punctually and moves too fast: Roderick's disintegration, a gradual process, and of which the exhibitional interest is exactly that it *is* gradual and occasional, and thereby traceable and watchable, swallows two years in a mouthful, proceeds quite *not* by years, but by weeks and months, and thus renders the whole view the disservice of appearing to present him as a morbidly special case. The very claim of the fable is naturally that he *is* special, that his great gift makes and keeps him highly exceptional; but that is not for a moment supposed to preclude his appearing typical (of the general type) as well; for the fictive hero successfully appeals to us only as an eminent instance, as eminent as we like, of our own conscious kind. My mistake on Roderick's behalf—and not in the least of conception, but of composition and expression—is that, at the rate at which he falls to pieces, he seems to place himself beyond our understanding and our sympathy. These are not our rates, we say; we ourselves certainly, under like pressure,—for what is it after all?—would make more of a fight. We conceive going to pieces—nothing is easier, since we see people do it, one way or another, all round us; but this young man must either have had less of the principle of development to have had so much of the principle of collapse, or less of the principle of collapse to have had so much of the principle of development. "On the basis of so great a weakness," one hears the reader say, "where was your idea of the interest? On the basis of so great an interest, where is the provision for so much weakness?"[46] One feels indeed, in the light of this challenge, on how much too scantly projected and suggested a field poor Roderick and his large capacity for ruin are made to turn round. It has all begun too soon, as I say, and too simply, and the determinant function attributed to Christina Light, the character of well-nigh sole agent of his catastrophe that this unfortunate young woman has forced upon her, fails to commend itself to our sense of truth and proportion.

It was not, however, that I was at ease on this score even in the first fond good faith of composition; I felt too, all the while, how many more ups and downs, how many more adventures and complications my young man would have had to know, how much more experience it would have taken, in short, either to make him go under or to make him triumph. The greater complexity, the superior truth, was all more or less present to me; only the question was, too dreadfully, how make it present to the reader? How boil down so many facts in the alembic, so that the distilled result, the produced appearance, should have intensity, lucidity, brevity, beauty, all the merits required for my effect? How, when it was already so difficult, as I found, to proceed even as I *was* proceeding? It didn't help, alas, it only maddened, to remember that Balzac would have known how, and would have yet asked no additional credit for it. All the difficulty I could dodge still struck me, at any rate, as leaving more than enough; and yet I was already consciously in presence, here, of the most interesting question the artist has to consider. To give the image and the sense of certain things while still keeping them subordinate to his plan, keeping them in relation to matters more immediate and apparent, to give all the sense, in a word, without all the substance or all the surface, and so to summarise and foreshorten, so to make values both rich and sharp, that the mere procession of items and profiles is not only, for the occasion, superseded, but is, for essential quality, almost "compromised"[47]—such a case of delicacy proposes itself at every turn to the painter of life who wishes both to treat his chosen subject and to confine his necessary picture. It is only by doing such things that art becomes exquisite, and it is only by positively becoming exquisite that it keeps clear of becoming vulgar, repudiates the coarse industries that masquerade in its name.[48]

This eternal time-question is accordingly, for the novelist, always there and always formidable; always insisting on the *effect* of the great lapse and passage, of the "dark backward and abysm,"[49] by the terms of truth, and on the effect of compression, of composition and form, by the terms of literary arrangement. It is really a business to terrify all but stout hearts into abject omission and mutilation, though the terror would indeed be more general were the general consciousness of the difficulty greater. It is not by consciousness of difficulty, in truth, that the story-teller is mostly ridden; so prodigious a number of stories would otherwise scarce get themselves (shall it be called?) "told."[50] None was ever very well told, I think, under the law of mere elimination—inordinately as that device appears in many quarters to be depended on. I remember doing my best not to be reduced to it for "Roderick," at the same time that I did so helplessly and consciously beg a thousand questions. What I clung to as my principle of simplification was the precious truth that I was dealing, after all, essentially with an Action,[51] and that no action, further, was ever made historically vivid without a certain factitious compactness; though this logic indeed opened up horizons and abysses of its own. But into these we must plunge on some other occasion.[52]

It was at any rate under an admonition or two fished out of their depths that I must have tightened my hold of the remedy afforded, such as it was, for the absence of those more adequate illustrations of Roderick's character and history. Since one was dealing with an Action one might borrow a scrap of the Dramatist's all-in-all, his intensity[53]—which the novelist so often ruefully envies him as a fortune in itself. The amount of illustration I could allow to the grounds of my young man's disaster was unquestionably meagre, but I might perhaps make it lively; I might produce illusion if I should be able to achieve intensity. It was for that I must have tried, I now see, with such art as I could command; but I make out in another quarter above all what really saved me. My subject, all blissfully, in face of difficulties, had defined itself—and this in spite of the title of the book—as not directly, in the least, my young sculptor's adventure. This it had been but indirectly, being all the while in essence and in final effect another man's, his friend's and patron's, view and experience of him. One's luck was to have felt one's subject right—whether instinct or calculation, in those dim days, most served; and the circumstance even amounts perhaps to a little lesson that when this has happily occurred faults may show, faults may disfigure, and yet not upset the work. It remains in equilibrium by having found its centre, the point of command of all the rest.[54] From this centre the subject has been treated, from this centre the interest has spread, and so, whatever else it may do or may not do, the thing has acknowledged a principle of composition and contrives at least to hang together. We see in such a case why it should so hang; we escape that dreariest displeasure it is open to experiments in this general order to inflict, the sense of any hanging-together precluded as by the very terms of the case.

The centre of interest throughout "Roderick" is in Rowland Mallet's consciousness, and the drama is the very drama of that consciousness—which I had of course to make sufficiently acute in order to enable it, like a set and lighted scene, to hold the play. By making it acute, meanwhile, one made its own movement—or rather, strictly, its movement in the particular connexion—interesting; this movement really being quite the stuff of one's thesis. It had, naturally, Rowland's consciousness, not to be *too* acute—which would have disconnected it and made it superhuman:[55] the beautiful little problem was to keep it connected, connected intimately, with the general human exposure, and thereby bedimmed and befooled and bewildered, anxious, restless, fallible, and yet to endow it with such intelligence that the appearances reflected in it, and constituting together there the situation and the "story," should become by that fact intelligible. Discernible from the first the joy of such a "job"[56] as this making of his relation to everything involved a sufficiently limited, a sufficiently pathetic, tragic, comic, ironic, personal state to be thoroughly natural, and yet at the same time a sufficiently clear medium to represent a whole. This whole was to be the sum of what "happened" to him, or in other words his total adventure; but as what happened to him was above all to feel certain things happening to others,[57] to Roderick, to Christina, to Mary Garland, to Mrs. Hudson, to the Cavaliere, to the Prince, so the beauty of the constructional game was to preserve in everything its especial value for *him*. The ironic effect of his having fallen in love with the girl who is herself in love with Roderick, though he is unwitting, at the time, of that secret—the conception of this last irony, I must add, has remained happier than my execution of it; which should logically have involved the reader's being put into position to take more closely home the impression made by Mary Garland. The ground has not been laid for it, and when that is the case one builds all vainly in the air:[58] one patches up one's superstructure, one paints it in the prettiest colours, one hangs fine old tapestry and rare brocade over its window-sills, one flies emblazoned banners from its roof—the building none the less totters and refuses to stand square.

It is not really *worked-in* that Roderick himself could have pledged his faith in such a quarter, much more at such a crisis, before leaving America: and that weakness, clearly, produces a limp in the whole march of the fable. Just so, though there was no reason on earth (unless I except one, presently to be mentioned) why Rowland should *not*, at Northampton, have conceived a passion, or as near an approach to one as he was capable of, for a remarkable young woman there suddenly dawning on his sight, a particular fundamental care was required for the vivification of that possibility. The care, unfortunately, has not been skilfully enough taken, in spite of the later patching-up of the girl's figure. We fail to accept it, on the actual showing, as that of a young person irresistible at any moment, and above all irresistible at a moment of the liveliest *other* preoccupation, as that of the weaver of (even the highly conditioned) spell that the narrative imputes to her. The spell of attraction is cast upon young men by young women in all sorts of ways, and the novel has no more constant office than to remind us of that. But Mary Garland's way doesn't, indubitably, convince us; any more than we are truly convinced, I think, that Rowland's destiny, or say his nature, would have made him accessible at the same hour to two quite distinct commotions, each a very deep one, of his whole personal economy. Rigidly viewed, each of these upheavals of his sensibility must have been exclusive of other upheavals, yet the reader is asked to accept them as working together. They are different vibrations, but the whole sense of the situation depicted is that they should each have been of the strongest, too strong to walk hand in hand. Therefore it is that when, on the ship, under the stars,[59] Roderick suddenly takes his friend into the confidence of his engagement, we instinctively disallow the friend's title to discomfiture. The whole picture presents him as for the time on the mounting wave,[60] exposed highly enough, no doubt, to a hundred discomfitures, but least exposed to that one. The damage to verisimilitude is deep.

The difficulty had been from the first that I required my antithesis—my antithesis to Christina Light, one of the main terms of the subject. One is ridden by the law that antitheses, to be efficient, shall be both direct and complete. Directness seemed to fail unless Mary should be, so to speak, "plain," Christina being essentially so "coloured";[61] and completeness seemed to fail unless she too should have her potency. She could moreover, by which I mean the antithetic young woman could, perfectly have had it; only success would have been then in the narrator's art to attest it. Christina's own presence and action are, on the other hand, I think, all firm ground; the truth probably being that the ideal antithesis rarely does "come off," and that it has to content itself for the most part with a strong term and a weak term, and even then to feel itself lucky. If one of the terms *is* strong, that perhaps may pass, in the most difficult of the arts, for a triumph. I remember at all events feeling, toward the end of "Roderick," that the Princess Casamassima had been launched, that, wound-up with the right silver key, she would go on a certain time by the motion communicated;[62] thanks to which I knew the pity, the real pang of losing sight of her. I desired as in no other such case I can recall to preserve, to recover the vision; and I have seemed to myself in re-reading the book quite to understand why. The multiplication of touches had produced even more life than the subject required, and that life, in other conditions, in some other prime relation, would still have somehow to be spent. Thus one would watch for her and waylay her at some turn of the road to come—all that was to be needed was to give her time. This I did in fact, meeting her again and taking her up later on.[63]

PREFACE to *The American* (*NYE* II)

"The American," which I had begun in Paris early in the winter of 1875–76, made its first appearance in "The Atlantic Monthly"[64] in June of the latter year and continued there, from month to month, till May of the next. It started on its course while much was still unwritten,[65] and there again come back to me, with this remembrance, the frequent hauntings and alarms of that comparatively early time; the habit of wondering what would happen if anything *should* "happen," if one should break one's arm by an accident or make a long illness or suffer, in body, mind, fortune, any other visitation involving a loss of time. The habit of apprehension became of course in some degree the habit of confidence that one would pull through, that, with opportunity enough, grave interruption never yet *had* descended, and that a special Providence, in short, despite the sad warning of Thackeray's "Denis Duval" and of Mrs. Gaskell's "Wives and Daughters" (that of Stevenson's "Weir of Hermiston" was yet to come) watches over anxious novelists condemned to the economy of serialisation.[66] I make myself out in memory as having at least for many months and in many places given my Providence much to do: so great a variety of scenes of labour, implying all so much renewal of application, glimmer out of the book as I now read it over. And yet as the faded interest of the whole episode becomes again mildly vivid what I seem most to recover is, in its pale spectrality, a degree of joy, an eagerness on behalf of my recital, that must recklessly enough have overridden anxieties of every sort, including any view of inherent difficulties.

I seem to recall no other like connexion in which the case was met, to my measure, by so fond a complacency, in which my subject can have appeared so apt to take care of itself. I see now that I might all the while have taken much better care of it; yet, as I had at the time no sense of neglecting it, neither acute nor rueful solicitude, I can but speculate all vainly to-day on the oddity of my composure. I ask myself indeed if, possibly, recognising after I was launched the danger of an inordinate leak—since the ship has truly a hole in its side more than sufficient to have sunk it—I may not have managed, as a counsel of mere despair, to stop my ears against the noise of waters and *pretend* to myself I was afloat;[67] being indubitably, in any case, at sea, with no harbour of refuge till the end of my serial voyage. If I succeeded at all in that emulation (in another sphere) of the pursued ostrich[68] I must have succeeded altogether; must have buried my head in the sand and there found beatitude. The explanation of my enjoyment of it, no doubt, is that I was more than commonly enamoured of my idea, and that I believed it, so trusted, so imaginatively fostered, not less capable of limping to its goal on three feet than on one. The lameness might be what it would: I clearly, for myself, felt the thing *go*—which is the most a dramatist can ever ask of his drama;[69] and I shall here accordingly indulge myself in speaking first of how, superficially, it did so proceed; explaining then what I mean by its practical dependence on a miracle.[70]

It had come to me, this happy, halting view of an interesting case, abruptly enough, some years before: I recall sharply the felicity of the first glimpse, though I forget the accident of thought that produced it. I recall that I was seated in an American "horse-car"[71] when I found myself, of a sudden, considering with enthusiasm, as the theme of a "story," the situation, in another country and an aristocratic society, of some robust but insidiously beguiled and betrayed, some cruelly wronged, compatriot: the point being in especial that he should suffer at the hands of persons pretending to represent the highest possible civilisation and to be of an order in every way superior to his own. What would he "do" in that predicament, how would he right himself, or how, failing a remedy, would he conduct himself under his wrong? This would be the question involved, and I remember well how, having entered the horse-car without a dream of it, I was presently to leave that vehicle in full possession of my answer. He would behave in the most interesting manner—it would all depend on that: stricken, smarting, sore, he would arrive at his just vindication and then would fail of all triumphantly and all vulgarly enjoying it. He would hold his revenge and cherish it and feel its sweetness, and then in the very act of forcing it home would sacrifice it in disgust. He would let them go, in short, his haughty contemners, even while feeling them, with joy, in his power, and he would obey, in so doing, one of the large and easy impulses *generally* characteristic of his type. He wouldn't "forgive"[72]—that would have, in the case, no application; he would simply turn, at the supreme moment, away, the bitterness of his personal loss yielding to the very force of his aversion. All he would have at the end would be therefore just the moral convenience, indeed the moral necessity, of his practical, but quite unappreciated, magnanimity; and one's last view of him would be that of a strong man indifferent to his strength and too wrapped in fine, too wrapped above all in *other* and intenser, reflexions for the assertion of his "rights." This last point was of the essence and constituted in fact the subject: there would be no subject at all, obviously,—or simply the commonest of the common,—if my gentleman should enjoy his advantage. I was charmed with my idea, which would take, however, much working out; and precisely because it had so much to give, I think, must I have dropped it for the time into the deep well of unconscious cerebration: not without the hope, doubtless, that it might eventually emerge from that reservoir, as one had already known the buried treasure to come to light, with a firm iridescent surface and a notable increase of weight.[73]

This resurrection then took place in Paris, where I was at the moment living, and in December 1875; my good fortune being apparently that Paris had ever so promptly offered me, and with an immediate directness at which I now marvel (since I had come back there, after earlier visitations, but a few weeks before[74]), everything that was needed to make my conception concrete. I seem again at this distant day to see it become so quickly and easily, quite as if filling itself with life in that air. The objectivity it had wanted it promptly put on, and if the questions had been, with the usual intensity, for my hero and his crisis—the whole formidable list, the who? the what? the where? the when? the why? the how?—they gathered their answers in the cold shadow of the Arc de Triomphe,[75] for fine reasons, very much as if they had been plucking spring flowers for the weaving of a frolic garland. I saw from one day to another my particular cluster of circumstances, with the life of the splendid city playing up in it like a flashing fountain in a marble basin. The very splendour seemed somehow to witness and intervene; it was important for the effect of my friend's discomfiture that it should take place on a high and lighted stage, and that his original ambition, the project exposing him, should have sprung from beautiful and noble suggestions—those that, at certain hours and under certain impressions, we feel the many-tinted medium by the Seine irresistibly to communicate. It was all charmingly simple, this conception, and the current must have gushed, full and clear, to my imagination, from the moment Christopher

Newman rose before me, on a perfect day of the divine Paris spring, in the great gilded Salon Carré of the Louvre.[76] Under this strong contagion of the place he would, by the happiest of hazards, meet his old comrade, now initiated and domiciled; after which the rest would go of itself. If he was to be wronged he would be wronged with just that conspicuity, with his felicity at just that pitch and with the highest aggravation of the general effect of misery mocked at. Great and gilded the whole trap set, in fine, for his wary freshness and into which it would blunder upon its fate. I have, I confess, no memory of a disturbing doubt; once the man himself was imaged to me (and *that* germination is a process almost always untraceable) he must have walked into the situation as by taking a pass-key from his pocket.[77]

But what then meanwhile would be the affront one would see him as most feeling? The affront of course done him as a lover; and yet not that done by his mistress herself, since injuries of this order are the stalest stuff of romance. I was not to have him jilted, any more than I was to have him successfully vindictive: both his wrong and his right would have been in these cases of too vulgar a type. I doubtless even then felt that the conception of Paris as the consecrated scene of rash infatuations and bold bad treacheries[78] belongs, in the Anglo-Saxon imagination, to the infancy of art. The right renovation of any such theme as *that* would place it in Boston or at Cleveland, at Hartford or at Utica[79]—give it some local connexion in which we had not already had so much of it. No, I should make my heroine herself, if heroine there was to be, an equal victim—just as Romeo was not less the sport of fate[80] for not having been interestedly sacrificed by Juliet; and to this end I had but to imagine "great people" again, imagine my hero confronted and involved with them, and impute to them, with a fine free hand, the arrogance and cruelty, the tortuous behaviour, in given conditions, of which great people have been historically so often capable. But as this was the light in which they were to show, so the essence of the matter would be that he should at the right moment find them in his power, and so the situation would reach its highest interest with the question of his utilisation of that knowledge. It would be here, in the possession and application of his power, that he would come out strong and would so deeply appeal to our sympathy. Here above all it really was, however, that my conception unfurled, with the best conscience in the world, the emblazoned flag of romance; which venerable ensign it had, though quite unwittingly, from the first and at every point sported in perfect good faith. I had been plotting arch-romance without knowing it,[81] just as I began to write it that December day without recognising it and just as I all serenely and blissfully pursued the process from month to month and from place to place; just as I now, in short, reading the book over, find it yields me no interest and no reward comparable to the fond perception of this truth.

The thing is consistently, consummately—and I would fain really make bold to say charmingly—romantic; and all without intention, presumption, hesitation, contrition. The effect is equally undesigned and unabashed, and I lose myself, at this late hour, I am bound to add, in a certain sad envy of the free play of so much unchallenged instinct. One would like to woo back such hours of fine precipitation. They represent to the critical sense which the exercise of one's *whole* faculty has, with time, so inevitably and so thoroughly waked up, the happiest season of surrender to the invoked muse and the projected fable: the season of images so free and confident and ready that they brush questions aside and disport themselves, like the artless schoolboys of Gray's beautiful Ode,[82] in all the ecstasy of the ignorance attending them. The time doubtless comes soon enough when questions, as I call them, rule the roost and when the little victim, to adjust Gray's term again to the creature of frolic fancy, doesn't dare propose a gambol till they have all (like a board of trustees discussing a new outlay) sat on the possibly scandalous case. I somehow feel, accordingly, that it was lucky to have sacrificed on this particular altar while one still could; though it is perhaps droll—in a yet higher degree—to have done so not simply because one was guileless, but even quite under the conviction, in a general way, that, since no "rendering" of any object and no painting of any picture can take effect without some form of reference and control, so these guarantees could but reside in a high probity of observation. I must decidedly have supposed, all the while, that I was acutely observing—and with a blest absence of wonder at its being so easy. Let me certainly at present rejoice in that absence; for I ask myself how without it I could have written "The American."

Was it indeed meanwhile my excellent conscience that kept the charm as unbroken as it appears to me, in rich retrospect, to have remained?—or is it that I suffer the mere influence of remembered, of associated places and hours, all acute impressions, to palm itself off as the sign of a finer confidence than I could justly claim? It is a pleasure to perceive how again and

PREFACE TO *THE AMERICAN* (NYE II)

again the shrunken depths of old work yet permit themselves to be sounded or—even if rather terrible the image—"dragged": the long pole of memory stirs and rummages the bottom,[83] and we fish up such fragments and relics of the submerged life and the extinct consciousness as tempt us to piece them together. My windows looked into the Rue de Luxembourg—since then meagrely re-named Rue Cambon—and the particular light Parisian click of the small cab-horse on the clear asphalt, with its sharpness of detonation between the high houses, makes for the faded page to-day a sort of interlineation of sound.[84] This sound rises to a martial clatter at the moment a troop of cuirassiers charges down the narrow street, each morning, to file, directly opposite my house, through the plain portal of the barracks occupying part of the vast domain attached in a rearward manner to one of the Ministères that front on the Place Vendôme;[85] an expanse marked, along a considerable stretch of the street, by one of those high painted and administratively-placarded garden walls that form deep, vague, recurrent notes in the organic vastness of the city. I have but to re-read ten lines to recall my daily effort not to waste time in hanging over the window-bar for a sight of the cavalry the hard music of whose hoofs so directly and thrillingly appealed; an effort that inveterately failed—and a trivial circumstance now dignified, to my imagination, I may add, by the fact that the fruits of this weakness, the various items of the vivid picture, so constantly recaptured, must have been in themselves suggestive and inspiring, must have been rich strains, in their way, of the great Paris harmony. I have ever, in general, found it difficult to write of places under too immediate an impression—the impression that prevents standing off and allows neither space nor time for perspective. The image has had for the most part to be dim if the reflexion was to be, as is proper for a reflexion, both sharp and quiet: one has a horror, I think, artistically, of agitated reflexions.

Perhaps that is why the novel, after all, was to achieve, as it went on, no great—certainly no very direct—transfusion of the immense overhanging presence. It had to save as it could its own life, to keep tight hold of the tenuous silver thread, the one hope for which was that it shouldn't be tangled or clipped. This earnest grasp of the silver thread was doubtless an easier business in other places—though as I remount the stream of composition[86] I see it faintly coloured again: with the bright protection of the Normandy coast (I worked away a few weeks at Etretat); with the stronger glow of southernmost France, breaking in during a stay at Bayonne;[87] then with the fine historic and other "psychic" substance of Saint-Germain-en-Laye, a purple patch of terraced October before returning to Paris.[88] There comes after that the memory of a last brief intense invocation of the enclosing scene, of the pious effort to unwind my tangle, with a firm hand, in the very light (that light of high, narrowish French windows in old rooms, the light somehow, as one always feels, of "style" itself[89]) that had quickened my original vision. I was to pass over to London that autumn;[90] which was a reason the more for considering the matter—the matter of Newman's final predicament—with due intensity: to let a loose end dangle over into alien air would so fix upon the whole, I strenuously felt, the dishonour of piecemeal composition. Therefore I strove to finish—first in a small dusky hotel of the Rive Gauche, where, though the windows again were high, the days were dim and the crepuscular court, domestic, intimate, "quaint," testified to ancient manners almost as if it had been that of Balzac's Maison Vauquer in "Le Père Goriot":[91] and then once more in the Rue de Luxembourg, where a black-framed Empire portrait-medallion,[92] suspended in the centre of each white panel of my almost noble old salon, made the coolest, discreetest, most measured decoration, and where, through casements open to the last mildness of the year, a belated Saint Martin's summer,[93] the tale was taken up afresh by the charming light click and clatter, that sound as of the thin, quick, quite feminine surface-breathing of Paris, the shortest of rhythms for so huge an organism.

    I shall not tell whether I did there bring my book to a close—and indeed I shrink, for myself, from putting the question to the test of memory. I follow it so far, the old urgent ingenious business, and then I lose sight of it: from which I infer—all exact recovery of the matter failing—that I did not in the event drag over the Channel a lengthening chain;[94] which would have been detestable. I reduce to the absurd perhaps, however, by that small subjective issue, any undue measure of the interest of this insistent recovery of what I have called attendant facts. There always has been, for the valid work of art, a history—though mainly inviting, doubtless, but to the curious critic, for whom such things grow up and are formed very much in the manner of attaching young lives and characters, those conspicuous cases of happy development as to which evidence and anecdote are always in order. The development indeed must be certain to have been happy, the life sincere, the character fine: the work of art, to create or repay critical curiosity, must in short have been very "valid" indeed. Yet there is on the other hand no mathematical measure of that importance—it may be a matter of widely-varying appreciation; and I am willing to grant, assuredly, that this interest, in a given relation, will nowhere so effectually kindle as on the artist's own part. And I am afraid that after all even his best excuse for it must remain the highly personal plea—the joy of living over, as a chapter of experience, the particular intellectual adventure. Here lurks an immense homage to the general privilege of the artist,[95] to that constructive, that creative passion—portentous words, but they are convenient—the exercise of which finds so many an occasion for appearing to him the highest of human fortunes, the rarest boon of the gods. He values it, all sublimely and perhaps a little fatuously, for itself—as the great extension, great beyond all others, of experience and of consciousness; with the toil and trouble a mere sun-cast shadow[96] that falls, shifts and vanishes, the result of his living in so large a light. On the constant nameless felicity of this Robert Louis Stevenson has, in an admirable passage and as in so many other connexions, said the right word: that the partaker of the "life of art" who repines at the absence of the rewards, as they are called, of the pursuit might surely be better occupied. Much rather should he endlessly wonder at his not having to pay half his substance for his luxurious immersion.[97] He enjoys it, so to speak, without a tax; the effort of labour involved, the torment of expression,[98] of which we have heard in our time so much, being after all but the last refinement of his privilege. It may leave him weary and worn; but how, after his fashion, he will have lived![99] As if one were to expect at once freedom and ease! That silly safety is but the sign of bondage and forfeiture. Who can imagine free selection—which is the beautiful, terrible *whole* of art—without free difficulty? This is the very franchise of the city and high ambition of the citizen. The vision of the difficulty, as one looks back, bathes one's course in a golden glow by which the very objects along the road are transfigured and glorified; so that one exhibits them to other eyes with an elation possibly presumptuous.

Since I accuse myself at all events of these complacencies I take advantage of them to repeat that I value, in my retrospect, nothing so much as the lively light on the romantic property of my subject that I had not expected to encounter. If in "The American" I invoked the romantic association without malice prepense,[100] yet with a production of the romantic effect that is for myself unmistakeable, the occasion is of the best perhaps for penetrating a little the obscurity of that principle. By what art or mystery, what craft of selection, omission or commission,[101] does a given picture of life appear to us to surround its theme, its figures and images, with the air of romance while another picture close beside it may affect us as steeping the whole matter in the element of reality? It is a question, no doubt, on the painter's part, very much more of perceived effect, effect *after* the fact, than of conscious design—though indeed I have ever failed to see how a coherent picture of anything is producible save by a complex of fine measurements. The cause of the deflexion, in one pronounced sense or the other, must lie deep, however; so that for the most part we recognise the character of our interest only after the particular magic, as I say, has thoroughly operated—and then in truth but if we be a bit critically minded, if we find our pleasure, that is, in these intimate appreciations (for which, as I am well aware, ninety-nine readers in a hundred have no use whatever). The determining condition would at any rate seem so latent that one may well doubt if the full artistic consciousness ever reaches it; leaving the matter thus a case, ever, not of an author's plotting and planning and calculating, but just of his feeling and seeing, of his conceiving, in a word, and of his thereby inevitably expressing himself, under the influence of one value or the other. These values represent different sorts and degrees of the communicable thrill, and I doubt if any novelist, for instance, ever proposed to commit himself to one kind or the other with as little mitigation as we are sometimes able to find for him. The interest is greatest—the interest of his genius, I mean, and of his general wealth—when he commits himself in both directions; not quite at the same time or to the same effect, of course, but by some need of performing his whole possible revolution, by the law of some rich passion in him for extremes.

Of the men of largest responding imagination before the human scene, of Scott, of Balzac, even of the coarse, comprehensive, prodigious Zola, we feel, I think, that the deflexion toward either quarter has never taken place;[102] that neither the nature of the man's faculty nor the nature of his experience has ever quite determined it. His current remains therefore extraordinarily rich and mixed, washing us successively with the warm wave of the near and familiar and the tonic shock, as may be, of the far and strange. (In making which opposition I suggest not that the strange and the far are at all necessarily romantic:[103] they happen to be simply the unknown, which is quite a different matter. The real represents to my perception the things we cannot possibly *not* know, sooner or later, in one way or another; it being but one of the accidents of our hampered state, and one of the incidents of their quantity and number, that particular instances have not yet come our way. The romantic stands, on the other hand, for the things that, with all the facilities in the world, all the wealth and all the courage and all the wit and all the adventure, we never *can* directly know; the things that can reach us only through the beautiful circuit and subterfuge of our thought and our desire.) There have been, I gather, many definitions of romance, as a matter indispensably of boats, or of caravans, or of tigers, or of "historical characters," or of ghosts, or of forgers, or of detectives, or of beautiful wicked women, or of pistols and knives,[104] but they appear for the most part reducible to the idea of the facing of danger, the acceptance of great risks for the fascination, the very love, of their uncertainty, the joy of success if possible and of battle in any case. This would be a fine formula if it bore examination; but it strikes me as weak and inadequate, as by no means covering the true ground and yet as landing us in strange confusions.

The panting pursuit of danger is the pursuit of life itself, in which danger awaits us possibly at every step and faces us at every turn; so that the dream of an intenser experience easily becomes rather some vision of a sublime security like that enjoyed on the flowery plains of heaven,[105] where we may conceive ourselves proceeding in ecstasy from one prodigious phase and form of it to another. And if it be insisted that the measure of the type is then in the *appreciation* of danger—the sign of our projection of the real being the smallness of its dangers, and that of our projection of the romantic the hugeness, the mark of the distinction being in short, as they say of collars and gloves and shoes, the size and "number"[106] of the danger—this discrimination again surely fails, since it makes our difference not a difference of kind, which is what we want, but a difference only of degree, and subject by that condition to the indignity of a sliding scale and a shifting measure. There are immense and flagrant dangers that are but sordid and squalid ones, as we feel, tainting with their quality the very defiances they provoke; while there are common and covert ones, that "look like nothing" and that can be but inwardly and occultly dealt with, which involve the sharpest hazards to life and honour and the highest instant decisions and intrepidities of action. It is an arbitrary stamp that keeps these latter prosaic and makes the former heroic; and yet I should still less subscribe to a mere "subjective" division—I mean one that would place the difference wholly in the temper of the imperilled agent. It would be impossible to have a more romantic temper than Flaubert's Madame Bovary, and yet nothing less resembles a romance than the record of her adventures.[107] To classify it by that aspect—the definition of the spirit that happens to animate her—is like settling the question (as I have seen it witlessly settled) by the presence or absence of "costume." Where again then does costume begin or end?—save with the "run" of one or another sort of play?[108] We must reserve vague labels for artless mixtures.

The only *general* attribute of projected romance that I can see, the only one that fits all its cases, is the fact of the kind of experience with which it deals—experience liberated, so to speak; experience disengaged, disembroiled, disencumbered, exempt from the conditions that we usually know to attach to it and, if we wish so to put the matter, drag upon it, and operating in a medium which relieves it, in a particular interest, of the inconvenience of a *related*, a measurable state,[109] a state subject to all our vulgar communities. The greatest intensity may so be arrived at evidently—when the sacrifice of community, of the "related" sides of situations, has not been too rash. It must to this end not flagrantly betray itself; we must even be kept if possible, for our illusion, from suspecting any sacrifice at all. The balloon of experience is in fact of course tied to the earth, and under that necessity we swing, thanks to a rope of remarkable length, in the more or less commodious car of the imagination; but it is by the rope we know where we are, and from the moment that cable is cut we are at large and unrelated:[110] we only swing apart from the globe—though remaining as exhilarated, naturally, as we like, especially when all goes well. The art of the romancer is, "for the fun of it," insidiously to cut the cable, to cut it without our detecting him. What I have recognised then in "The American," much to my surprise and after long years, is that the experience here represented is the disconnected and uncontrolled experience—uncontrolled by our general sense of "the way things happen"—which romance alone more or less successfully palms off on us. It is a case of Newman's own intimate experience all, that being my subject, the thread of which, from beginning to end, is not once exchanged, however momentarily, for any other thread;[111] and the experience of others concerning us, and concerning him, only so far as it touches him and as he recognises, feels or divines it. There is our general sense of the way things happen—it abides with us indefeasibly, as readers of fiction, from the moment we demand that our fiction shall be intelligible; and there is our particular sense of the way they don't happen, which is liable to wake up unless reflexion and criticism, in us, have been skilfully and successfully drugged. There are drugs enough, clearly—it is all a question of applying them with tact; in which case the way things don't happen may be artfully made to pass for the way things do.

Amusing and even touching to me, I profess, at this time of day, the ingenuity (worthy, with whatever lapses, of a better cause) with which, on behalf of Newman's adventure, this hocus-pocus is attempted: the value of the instance not being diminished either, surely, by its having been attempted in such evident good faith. Yes, all is romantic to my actual vision here, and not least so, I hasten to add, the fabulous felicity of my candour. The way things happen is frankly not the way in which they are represented as having happened, in Paris, to my hero: the situation I had conceived only saddled me with that for want of my invention of something better. The great house of Bellegarde, in a word, would, I now feel, given the circumstances, given the *whole* of the ground, have comported itself in a manner as different as possible from the manner to which my narrative commits it; of which truth, moreover, I am by no means sure that, in spite of what I have called my serenity, I had not all the while an uneasy suspicion. I had dug in my path, alas, a hole into which I was destined to fall. I was so possessed of my idea that Newman should be ill-used—which was the essence of my subject—that I attached too scant an importance to its fashion of coming about. Almost any fashion would serve, I appear to have assumed, that would give me my main chance for him; a matter depending not so much on the particular trick played him as on the interesting face presented by him to *any* damnable trick. So where I part company with *terra-firma* is in making that projected, that performed outrage so much more showy, dramatically speaking, than sound. Had I patched it up to a greater apparent soundness my own trick, artistically speaking, would have been played; I should have cut the cable without my reader's suspecting it. I doubtless at the time, I repeat, believed I had taken my precautions; but truly they should have been greater, to impart the air of truth to the attitude—that is first to the pomp and circumstance,[112] and second to the queer falsity—of the Bellegardes.

They would positively have jumped then, the Bellegardes, at my rich and easy American, and not have "minded" in the least any drawback[113]—especially as, after all, given the pleasant palette from which I have painted him, there were few drawbacks to mind. My subject imposed on me a group of closely-allied persons animated by immense pretensions—which was all very well, which might be full of the promise of interest: only of interest felt most of all in the light of comedy and of irony. This, better understood, would have dwelt in the idea not in the least of their not finding Newman good enough for their alliance and thence being ready to sacrifice him, but in that of their taking with alacrity everything he could give them, only asking for more and more, and then adjusting their pretensions and their pride to it with all the comfort in life. Such accommodation of the theory of a noble indifference to the practice of a deep avidity is the real note of policy in forlorn aristocracies—and I meant of course that the Bellegardes should be virtually forlorn. The perversion of truth is by no means, I think, in the displayed acuteness of their remembrance of "who" and "what" they are, or at any rate take themselves for; since it is the misfortune of all insistence on "worldly" advantages—and the situation of such people bristles at the best (by which I mean under whatever invocation of a superficial simplicity) with emphasis, accent, assumption—to produce at times an effect of grossness. The picture of their tergiversation, at all events, however it may originally have seemed to me to hang together, has taken on this rococo appearance precisely because their preferred course, a thousand times preferred, would have been to haul him and his fortune into their boat[114] under cover of night perhaps, in any case as quietly and with as little bumping and splashing as possible, and there accommodate him with the very safest and most convenient seat. Given Newman, given the fact that the thing constitutes itself organically as *his* adventure, that too might very well be a situation and a subject: only it wouldn't have been the theme of "The American" as the book stands, the theme to which I was from so early pledged. Since I had wanted a "wrong" this other turn might even have been arranged to give me *that*, might even have been arranged to meet my requirement that somebody or something should be "in his power" so delightfully; and with the signal effect, after all, of "defining" everything. (It is as difficult, I said above, to trace the dividing-line between the real and the romantic[115] as to plant a milestone between north and south; but I am not sure an infallible sign of the latter is not this rank vegetation of the "power" of bad people that good get into, or *vice versa*. It is so rarely, alas, into *our* power that any one gets!)

It is difficult for me to-day to believe that I had not, as my work went on, *some* shade of the rueful sense of my affront to verisimilitude; yet I catch the memory at least of no great sharpness, no true critical anguish, of remorse: an anomaly the reason of which in fact now glimmers interestingly out. My concern, as I saw it, was to make and to keep Newman consistent; the picture of his consistency was all my undertaking, and the memory of *that* infatuation perfectly abides with me. He was to be the lighted figure, the others—even doubtless to an excessive degree the woman who is made the agent of his discomfiture—were to be the obscured; by which I should largely get the very effect most to be invoked, that of a generous nature engaged with forces, with difficulties and dangers, that it but half understands. If Newman was attaching enough, I must have argued, his tangle would be sensible enough; for the interest of everything is all that it is *his* vision, *his* conception, *his* interpretation: at the window of his wide, quite sufficiently wide, consciousness we are seated, from that admirable position we "assist."[116] He therefore supremely matters; all the rest matters only as he feels it, treats it, meets it. A beautiful infatuation this, always, I think, the intensity of the creative effort to get into the skin of the creature;[117] the act of personal possession of one being by another at its completest—and with the high enhancement, ever, that it is, by the same stroke, the effort of the artist to preserve for his subject that unity, and for his use of it (in other words for the interest he desires to excite) that effect of a *centre*, which most economise its value. Its value is most discussable when that economy has most operated; the content and the "importance" of a work of art are in fine wholly dependent on its *being* one: outside of which all prate of its representative character, its meaning and its bearing, its morality and humanity, are an impudent thing. Strong in that character, which is the condition of its really bearing witness at all, it is strong every way. So much remains true then on behalf of my instinct of multiplying the fine touches by which Newman should live and communicate life; and yet I still ask myself, I confess, what I can have made of "life," in my picture, at such a juncture as the interval offered as elapsing between my hero's first accepted state and the nuptial rites that are to crown it. Nothing here is in truth "offered"—everything is evaded, and the effect of this, I recognise, is of the oddest. His relation to Madame de Cintré takes a great stride, but the author appears to view that but as a signal for letting it severely alone.

I have been stupefied, in so thoroughly revising the book, to find, on turning a page, that the light in which he is presented immediately after Madame de Bellegarde has conspicuously introduced him to all her circle as her daughter's husband-to-be is that of an evening at the opera quite alone;[118] as if he wouldn't surely spend his leisure, and especially those hours of it, with his intended. Instinctively, from that moment, one would have seen them intimately and, for one's interest, beautifully together; with some illustration of the beauty incumbent on the author. The truth was that at this point the author, all gracelessly, could but hold his breath and pass; lingering was too difficult—he had made for himself a crushing complication. Since Madame de Cintré was after all to "back out"[119] every touch in the picture of her apparent loyalty would add to her eventual shame. She had acted in clear good faith, but how could I give the *detail* of an attitude, on her part, of which the foundation was yet so weak? I preferred, as the minor evil, to shirk the attempt—at the cost evidently of a signal loss of "charm"; and with this lady, altogether, I recognise, a light plank, too light a plank, is laid for the reader over a dark "psychological" abyss.[120] The delicate clue to her conduct is never definitely placed in his hand: I must have liked verily to think it *was* delicate and to flatter myself it was to be felt with finger-tips rather than heavily tugged at. Here then, at any rate, is the romantic *tout craché*—the fine flower of Newman's experience blooming in a medium "cut off" and shut up to itself. I don't for a moment pronounce any spell proceeding from it necessarily the less workable, to a rejoicing ingenuity, for that; beguile the reader's suspicion of *his* being shut up, transform it for *him* into a positive illusion of the largest liberty, and the success will ever be proportionate to the chance. Only all this gave me, I make out, a great deal to look to, and I was perhaps wrong in thinking that Newman by himself, and for any occasional extra inch or so I might smuggle into his measurements, would see me through my wood.[121] Anything more liberated and disconnected, to repeat my terms, than his prompt general profession, before the Tristrams, of aspiring to a "great" marriage,[122] for example, could surely not well be imagined. I had to take that over with the rest of him and fit it in—I had indeed to exclude the outer air. Still, I find on re-perusal that I have been able to breathe at least in my aching void;[123] so that, clinging to my hero as to a tall, protective, good-natured elder brother in a rough place, I leave the record to stand or fall by his more or less convincing image.

PREFACE to *The Portrait of a Lady*
(*NYE* III–IV)

"The Portrait of a Lady" was, like "Roderick Hudson," begun in Florence, during three months spent there in the spring of 1879.[124] Like "Roderick" and like "The American," it had been designed for publication in "The Atlantic Monthly,"[125] where it began to appear in 1880. It differed from its two predecessors, however, in finding a course also open to it, from month to month, in "Macmillan's Magazine"; which was to be for me one of the last occasions of simultaneous "serialisation" in the two countries that the changing conditions of literary intercourse between England and the United States had up to then left unaltered.[126] It is a long novel, and I was long in writing it; I remember being again much occupied with it, the following year, during a stay of several weeks made in Venice.[127] I had rooms on Riva Schiavoni, at the top of a house near the passage leading off to San Zaccaria;[128] the waterside life, the wondrous lagoon spread before me, and the ceaseless human chatter of Venice came in at my windows, to which I seem to myself to have been constantly driven, in the fruitless fidget of composition, as if to see whether, out in the blue channel, the ship of some right suggestion, of some better phrase, of the next happy twist of my subject, the next true touch for my canvas, mightn't come into sight. But I recall vividly enough that the response most elicited, in general, to these restless appeals was the rather grim admonition that romantic and historic sites, such as the land of Italy abounds in, offer the artist a questionable aid to concentration[129] when they themselves are not to be the subject of it. They are too rich in their own life and too charged with their own meanings merely to help him out with a lame phrase; they draw him away from his small question to their own greater ones; so that, after a little, he feels, while thus yearning toward them in his difficulty, as if he were asking an army of glorious veterans to help him to arrest a peddler who has given him the wrong change.[130]

There are pages of the book which, in the reading over, have seemed to make me see again the bristling curve of the wide Riva, the large colour-spots of the balconied houses and the repeated undulation of the little hunchbacked bridges, marked by the rise and drop again, with the wave, of foreshortened clicking pedestrians. The Venetian footfall and the Venetian cry—all talk there, wherever uttered, having the pitch of a call across the water—come in once more at the window,[131] renewing one's old impression of the delighted senses and the divided, frustrated mind. How can places that speak *in general* so to the imagination not give it, at the moment, the particular thing it wants? I recollect again and again, in beautiful places, dropping into that wonderment. The real truth is, I think, that they express, under this appeal, only too much—more than, in the given case, one has use for; so that one finds one's self working less congruously, after all, so far as the surrounding picture is concerned, than in presence of the moderate and the neutral, to which we may lend something of the light of our vision. Such a place as Venice is too proud for such charities; Venice doesn't borrow, she but all magnificently gives. We profit by that enormously, but to do so we must either be quite off duty or be on it in her service alone. Such, and so rueful, are these reminiscences; though on the whole, no doubt, one's book, and one's "literary effort" at large, were to be the better for them. Strangely fertilising, in the long run, does a wasted effort of attention often prove.[132] It all depends on *how* the attention has been cheated, has been squandered. There are high-handed insolent frauds, and there are insidious sneaking ones. And there is, I fear, even on the most designing artist's part, always witless enough good faith, always anxious enough desire, to fail to guard him against their deceits.

Trying to recover here, for recognition, the germ of my idea,[133] I see that it must have consisted not at all in any conceit of a "plot," nefarious name,[134] in any flash, upon the fancy, of a set of relations, or in any one of those situations that, by a logic of their own, immediately fall, for the fabulist, into movement, into a march or a rush, a patter of quick steps; but altogether in the sense of a single character, the character and aspect of a particular engaging young woman, to which all the usual elements of a "subject," certainly of a setting, were to need to be superadded. Quite as interesting as the young woman herself, at her best, do I find, I must again repeat, this projection of memory upon the whole matter of the growth, in one's imagination, of some such apology for a motive. These are the fascinations of the fabulist's art, these lurking forces of expansion, these necessities of upspringing in the seed, these beautiful determinations, on the part of the idea entertained, to grow as tall as possible, to push into the light and the air and thickly flower there; and, quite as much, these fine possibilities of recovering, from some good standpoint on the ground gained, the intimate history of the business—of retracing and reconstructing its steps and stages. I have always fondly remembered a remark that I heard fall years ago from the lips of Ivan Turgenieff in regard to his own experience of the usual origin of the fictive picture.[135] It began for him almost always with the vision of some person or persons, who hovered before him, soliciting him, as the active or passive figure, interesting him and appealing to him just as they were and by what they were.[136] He saw them, in that fashion, as *disponibles*, saw them subject to the chances, the complications of existence, and saw them vividly, but then had to find for them the right relations, those that would most bring them out; to imagine, to invent and select and piece together the situations most useful and favourable to the sense of the creatures themselves, the complications they would be most likely to produce and to feel.

"To arrive at these things is to arrive at my 'story,'" he said, "and that's the way I look for it. The result is that I'm often accused of not having 'story' enough.[137] I seem to myself to have as much as I need—to show my people, to exhibit their relations with each other; for that is all my measure. If I watch them long enough I see them come together, I see them *placed*, I see them engaged in this or that act and in this or that difficulty. How they look and move and speak and behave, always in the setting I have found for them, is my account of them—of which I dare say, alas, *que cela manque souvent d'architecture*.[138] But I would rather, I think, have too little architecture than too much—when there's danger of its interfering with my measure of the truth. The French of course like more of it than I give—having by their own genius such a hand for it; and indeed one must give all one can. As for the origin of one's wind-blown germs themselves, who shall say, as you ask, where *they* come from? We have to go too far back, too far behind, to say. Isn't it all we can say that they come from every quarter of heaven, that they are *there* at almost any turn of the road? They accumulate, and we are always picking them over, selecting among them. They are the breath of life[139]—by which I mean that life, in its own way, breathes them upon us. They are so, in a manner prescribed and imposed—floated into our minds by the current of life. That reduces to imbecility the vain critic's quarrel, so often, with one's subject, when he hasn't the wit to accept it.[140] Will he point out then which other it should properly have been?—his office being, essentially, *to* point out. *Il en serait bien embarrassé.* Ah, when he points out what I've done or failed to do with it, that's another matter: there he's on his ground. I give him up my 'architecture,'" my distinguished friend concluded, "as much as he will."

So this beautiful genius, and I recall with comfort the gratitude I drew from his reference to the intensity of suggestion that may reside in the stray figure, the unattached character, the image *en disponibilité*. It gave me higher warrant than I seemed then to have met for just that blest habit of one's own imagination, the trick of investing some conceived or encountered individual, some brace or group of individuals, with the germinal property and authority. I was myself so much more antecedently conscious of my figures than of their setting—a too preliminary, a preferential interest in which struck me as in general such a putting of the cart before the horse. I might envy, though I couldn't emulate, the imaginative writer so constituted as to see his fable first and to make out its agents afterwards: I could think so little of any fable that didn't need its agents positively to launch it; I could think so little of any situation that didn't depend for its interest on the nature of the persons situated, and thereby on their way of taking it. There are methods of so-called presentation, I believe—among novelists who have appeared to flourish—that offer the situation as indifferent to that support; but I have not lost the sense of the value for me, at the time, of the admirable Russian's testimony to my not needing, all superstitiously, to try and perform any such gymnastic. Other echoes from the same source linger with me, I confess, as unfadingly—if it be not all indeed one much-embracing echo.[141] It was impossible after that not to read, for one's uses, high lucidity into the tormented and disfigured and bemuddled question of the objective value, and even quite into that of the critical appreciation, of "subject" in the novel.[142]

One had had from an early time, for that matter, the instinct of the right estimate of such values and of its reducing to the inane the dull dispute over the "immoral" subject and the moral. Recognising so promptly the one measure of the worth of a given subject, the question about it that, rightly answered, disposes of all others—is it valid, in a word, is it genuine, is it sincere, the result of some direct impression or perception of life?[143]—I had found small edification, mostly, in a critical pretension that had neglected from the first all delimitation of ground and all definition of terms.[144] The air of my earlier time shows, to memory, as darkened, all round, with that vanity—unless the difference to-day be just in one's own final impatience, the lapse of one's attention. There is, I think, no more nutritive or suggestive truth in this connexion than that of the perfect dependence of the "moral" sense of a work of art on the amount of felt life concerned in producing it.[145] The question comes back thus, obviously, to the kind and the degree of the artist's prime sensibility, which is the soil out of which his subject springs. The quality and capacity of that soil, its ability to "grow" with due freshness and straightness any vision of life, represents, strongly or weakly, the projected morality.[146] That element is but another name for the more or less close connexion of the subject with some mark made on the intelligence, with some sincere experience. By which, at the same time, of course, one is far from contending that this enveloping air of the artist's humanity—which gives the last touch to the worth of the work—is not a widely and wondrously varying element; being on one occasion a rich and magnificent medium and on another a comparatively poor and ungenerous one. Here we get exactly the high price of the novel as a literary form—its power not only, while preserving that form with closeness, to range through all the differences of the individual relation to its general subject-matter, all the varieties of outlook on life, of disposition to reflect and project,[147] created by conditions that are never the same from man to man (or, so far as that goes, from man to woman), but positively to appear more true to its character in proportion as it strains, or tends to burst, with a latent extravagance, its mould.

The house of fiction has in short not one window, but a million—a number of possible windows not to be reckoned, rather; every one of which has been pierced, or is still pierceable, in its vast front, by the need of the individual vision and by the pressure of the individual will.[148] These apertures, of dissimilar shape and size, hang so, all together, over the human scene that we might have expected of them a greater sameness of report than we find. They are but windows at the best, mere holes in a dead wall,[149] disconnected, perched aloft; they are not hinged doors opening straight upon life. But they have this mark of their own that at each of them stands a figure with a pair of eyes, or at least with a field-glass, which forms, again and again, for observation, a unique instrument, insuring to the person making use of it an impression distinct from every other. He and his neighbours are watching the same show, but one seeing more where the other sees less, one seeing black where the other sees white, one seeing big where the other sees small, one seeing coarse where the other sees fine. And so on, and so on; there is fortunately no saying on what, for the particular pair of eyes, the window may *not* open; "fortunately" by reason, precisely, of this incalculability of range. The spreading field, the human scene, is the "choice of subject"; the pierced aperture, either broad or balconied or slit-like and low-browed, is the "literary form"; but they are, singly or together, as nothing without the posted presence of the watcher—without, in other words, the consciousness of the artist. Tell me what the artist is, and I will tell you of what he has *been* conscious. Thereby I shall express to you at once his boundless freedom[150] and his "moral" reference.

All this is a long way round, however, for my word about my dim first move toward "The Portrait," which was exactly my grasp of a single character[151]—an acquisition I had made, moreover, after a fashion not here to be retraced. Enough that I was, as seemed to me, in complete possession of it, that I had been so for a long time, that this had made it familiar and yet had not blurred its charm, and that, all urgently, all tormentingly, I saw it in motion and, so to speak, in transit. This amounts to saying that I saw it as bent upon its fate—some fate or other; *which*, among the possibilities, being precisely the question. Thus I had my vivid individual—vivid, so strangely, in spite of being still at large, not confined by the conditions, not engaged in the tangle, to which we look for much of the impress that constitutes an identity. If the apparition was still all to be placed how came it to be vivid?—since we puzzle such quantities out, mostly, just by the business of placing them. One could answer such a question beautifully, doubtless, if one could do so subtle, if not so monstrous, a thing as to write the history of the growth of one's imagination.[152] One would describe then what, at a given time, had extraordinarily happened to it, and one would so, for instance, be in a position to tell, with an approach to clearness, how, under favour of occasion, it had been able to take over (take over straight from life) such and such a constituted, animated figure or form.[153] The figure has to that extent, as you see, *been* placed—placed in the imagination that detains it, preserves, protects, enjoys it, conscious of its presence in the dusky, crowded, heterogeneous back-shop of the mind[154] very much as a wary dealer in precious odds and ends, competent to make an "advance" on rare objects confided to him, is conscious of the rare little "piece" left in deposit by the reduced, mysterious lady of title or the speculative amateur, and which is already there to disclose its merit afresh as soon as a key shall have clicked in a cupboard-door.

That may be, I recognise, a somewhat superfine analogy for the particular "value" I here speak of, the image of the young feminine nature that I had had for so considerable a time all curiously at my disposal; but it appears to fond memory quite to fit the fact—with the recall, in addition, of my pious desire but to place my treasure right.[155] I quite remind myself thus of the dealer resigned not to "realise,"[156] resigned to keeping the precious object locked up indefinitely rather than commit it, at no matter what price, to vulgar hands. For there *are* dealers in these forms and figures and treasures capable of that refinement. The point is, however, that this single small corner-stone, the conception of a certain young woman affronting her destiny,[157] had begun with being all my outfit for the large building of "The Portrait of a Lady." It came to be a square and spacious house—or has at least seemed so to me in this going over it again; but, such as it is, it had to be put up round my young woman while she stood there in perfect isolation. That is to me, artistically speaking, the circumstance of interest; for I have lost myself once more, I confess, in the curiosity of analysing the structure. By what process of logical accretion was this slight "personality," the mere slim shade of an intelligent but presumptuous girl, to find itself endowed with the high attributes of a Subject?[158]—and indeed by what thinness, at the best, would such a subject not be vitiated? Millions of presumptuous girls, intelligent or not intelligent, daily affront their destiny, and what is it open to their destiny to *be*, at the most, that we should make an ado about it? The novel is of its very nature an "ado," an ado about something,[159] and the larger the form it takes the greater of course the ado. Therefore, consciously, that was what one was in for—for positively organising an ado about Isabel Archer.

One looked it well in the face, I seem to remember, this extravagance; and with the effect precisely of recognising the charm of the problem. Challenge any such problem with any intelligence, and you immediately see how full it is of substance; the wonder being, all the while, as we look at the world, how absolutely, how inordinately, the Isabel Archers, and even much smaller female fry, insist on mattering. George Eliot has admirably noted it—"In these frail vessels is borne onward through the ages the treasure of human affection."[160] In "Romeo and Juliet" Juliet has to be important, just as, in "Adam Bede" and "The Mill on the Floss" and "Middlemarch" and "Daniel Deronda," Hetty Sorrel and Maggie Tulliver and Rosamond Vincy and Gwendolen Harleth[161] have to be; with that much of firm ground, that much of bracing air, at the disposal all the while of their feet and their lungs. They are typical, none the less, of a class difficult, in the individual case, to make a centre of interest; so difficult in fact that many an expert painter, as for instance Dickens and Walter Scott, as for instance even, in the main, so subtle a hand as that of R. L. Stevenson, has preferred to leave the task unattempted.[162] There are in fact writers as to whom we make out that their refuge from this is to assume it to be not worth their attempting; by which pusillanimity in truth their honour is scantly saved. It is never an attestation of a value, or even of our imperfect sense of one, it is never a tribute to any truth at all, that we shall represent that value badly. It never makes up, artistically, for an artist's dim feeling about a thing that he shall "do" the thing as ill as possible. There are better ways than that, the best of all of which is to begin with less stupidity.

It may be answered meanwhile, in regard to Shakespeare's and to George Eliot's testimony, that their concession to the "importance" of their Juliets and Cleopatras and Portias[163] (even with Portia as the very type and model of the young person intelligent and presumptuous) and to that of their Hettys and Maggies and Rosamonds and Gwendolens, suffers the abatement that these slimnesses are, when figuring as the main props of the theme, never suffered to be sole ministers of its appeal, but have their inadequacy eked out with comic relief and underplots, as the playwrights say, when not with murders and battles and the great mutations of the world.[164] If they are shown as "mattering" as much as they could possibly pretend to, the proof of it is in a hundred other persons, made of much stouter stuff, and each involved moreover in a hundred relations which matter to *them* concomitantly with that one. Cleopatra matters, beyond bounds, to Antony, but his colleagues, his antagonists, the state of Rome and the impending battle also prodigiously matter; Portia matters to Antonio, and to Shylock, and to the Prince of Morocco, to the fifty aspiring princes, but for these gentry there are other lively concerns; for Antonio, notably, there are Shylock and Bassanio and his lost ventures and the extremity of his predicament. This extremity indeed, by the same token, matters to Portia—though its doing so becomes of interest all by the fact that Portia matters to *us*. That she does so, at any rate, and that almost everything comes round to it again, supports my contention as to this fine example of the value recognised in the mere young thing. (I say "mere" young thing because I guess that even Shakespeare, preoccupied mainly though he may have been with the passions of princes, would scarce have pretended to found the best of his appeal for her on her high social position.) It is an example exactly of the deep difficulty braved—the difficulty of making George Eliot's "frail vessel," if not the all-in-all for our attention, at least the clearest of the call.

Now to see deep difficulty braved is at any time, for the really addicted artist, to feel almost even as a pang the beautiful incentive, and to feel it verily in such sort as to wish the danger intensified. The difficulty most worth tackling can only be for him, in these conditions, the greatest the case permits of. So I remember feeling here (in presence, always, that is, of the particular uncertainty of my ground), that there would be one way better than another—oh, ever so much better than any other!—of making it fight out its battle. The frail vessel, that charged with George Eliot's "treasure," and thereby of such importance to those who curiously approach it, has likewise possibilities of importance to itself, possibilities which permit of treatment and in fact peculiarly require it from the moment they are considered at all. There is always the escape from any close account of the weak agent of such spells by using as a bridge for evasion, for retreat and flight, the view of her relation to those surrounding her. Make it predominantly a view of *their* relation and the trick is played: you give the general sense of her effect, and you give it, so far as the raising on it of a superstructure goes, with the maximum of ease. Well, I recall perfectly how little, in my now quite established connexion, the maximum of ease appealed to me, and how I seemed to get rid of it by an honest transposition of the weights in the two scales. "Place the centre of the subject in the young woman's own consciousness,"[165] I said to myself, "and you get as interesting and as beautiful a difficulty as you could wish. Stick to *that*—for the centre; put the heaviest weight into *that* scale, which will be so largely the scale of her relation to herself. Make her only interested enough, at the same time, in the things that are not herself, and this relation needn't fear to be too limited. Place meanwhile in the other scale the lighter weight (which is usually the one that tips the balance of interest): press least hard, in short, on the consciousness of your heroine's satellites, especially the male; make it an interest contributive only to the greater one. See, at all events, what can be done in this way. What better field could there be for a due ingenuity? The girl hovers, inextinguishable, as a charming creature, and the job will be to translate her into the highest terms of that formula, and as nearly as possible moreover into *all* of them. To depend upon her and her little concerns wholly to see you through will necessitate, remember, your really 'doing' her."

So far I reasoned, and it took nothing less than that technical rigour, I now easily see, to inspire me with the right confidence for erecting on such a plot of ground the neat and careful and proportioned pile of bricks that arches over it and that was thus to form, constructionally speaking, a literary monument. Such is the aspect that to-day "The Portrait" wears for me: a structure reared with an "architectural" competence, as Turgenieff would have said, that makes it, to the author's own sense, the most proportioned of his productions after "The Ambassadors"—which was to follow it so many years later and which has, no doubt, a superior roundness. On one thing I was determined; that, though I should clearly have to pile brick upon brick for the creation of an interest, I would leave no pretext for saying that anything is out of line, scale or perspective. I would build large—in fine embossed vaults and painted arches, as who should say, and yet never let it appear that the chequered pavement, the ground under the reader's feet, fails to stretch at every point to the base of the walls. That precautionary spirit, on re-perusal of the book, is the old note that most touches me: it testifies so, for my own ear, to the anxiety of my provision for the reader's amusement. I felt, in view of the possible limitations of my subject, that no such provision could be excessive, and the development of the latter was simply the general form of that earnest quest. And I find indeed that this is the only account I can give myself of the evolution of the fable: it is all under the head thus named that I conceive the needful accretion as having taken place, the right complications as having started. It was naturally of the essence that the young woman should be herself complex; that was rudimentary—or was at any rate the light in which Isabel Archer had originally dawned. It went, however, but a certain way, and other lights, contending, conflicting lights, and of as many different colours, if possible, as the rockets, the Roman candles and Catherine-wheels of a "pyrotechnic display," would be employable to attest that she was. I had, no doubt, a groping instinct for the right complications, since I am quite unable to track the footsteps of those that constitute, as the case stands, the general situation exhibited. They are there, for what they are worth, and as numerous as might be; but my memory, I confess, is a blank as to how and whence they came.

I seem to myself to have waked up one morning in possession of them—of Ralph Touchett and his parents, of Madame Merle, of Gilbert Osmond and his daughter and his sister, of Lord Warburton, Caspar Goodwood and Miss Stackpole, the definite array of contributions to Isabel Archer's history. I recognised them, I knew them, they were the numbered pieces of my puzzle,[166] the concrete terms of my "plot." It was as if they had simply, by an impulse of their own, floated into my ken, and all in response to my primary question: "Well, what will she *do?*"[167] Their answer seemed to be that if I would trust them they would show me; on which, with an urgent appeal to them to make it at least as interesting as they could, I trusted them. They were like the group of attendants and entertainers who come down by train when people in the country give a party; they represented the contract for carrying the party on. That was an excellent relation with them—a possible one even with so broken a reed[168] (from her slightness of cohesion) as Henrietta Stackpole. It is a familiar truth to the novelist, at the strenuous hour, that, as certain elements in any work are of the essence, so others are only of the form; that as this or that character, this or that disposition of the material, belongs to the subject directly, so to speak, so this or that other belongs to it but indirectly—belongs intimately to the treatment. This is a truth, however, of which he rarely gets the benefit—since it could be assured to him, really, but by criticism based upon perception, criticism which is too little of this world. He must not think of benefits, moreover, I freely recognise, for that way dishonour lies:[169] he has, that is, but one to think of—the benefit, whatever it may be, involved in his having cast a spell upon the simpler, the very simplest, forms of attention. This is all he is entitled to; he is entitled to nothing, he is bound to admit, that can come to him, from the reader, as a result on the latter's part of any act of reflexion or discrimination. He may *enjoy* this finer tribute—that is another affair, but on condition only of taking it as a gratuity "thrown in," a mere miraculous windfall,[170] the fruit of a tree he may not pretend to have shaken. Against reflexion, against discrimination, in his interest, all earth and air conspire; wherefore it is that, as I say, he must in many a case have schooled himself, from the first, to work but for a "living wage." The living wage is the reader's grant of the least possible quantity of attention required for consciousness of a "spell." The occasional charming "tip" is an act of his intelligence over and beyond this, a golden apple, for the writer's lap, straight from the wind-stirred tree. The artist may of course, in wanton moods, dream of some Paradise (for art) where the direct appeal to the intelligence might be legalised; for to such extravagances as these his yearning mind can scarce hope ever completely to close itself. The most he can do is to remember they *are* extravagances.

All of which is perhaps but a gracefully devious way of saying that Henrietta Stackpole was a good example, in "The Portrait," of the truth to which I just adverted—as good an example as I could name were it not that Maria Gostrey, in "The Ambassadors," then in the bosom of time, may be mentioned as a better.[171] Each of these persons is but wheels to the coach; neither belongs to the body of that vehicle, or is for a moment accommodated with a seat inside. There the subject alone is ensconced, in the form of its "hero and heroine," and of the privileged high officials, say, who ride with the king and queen. There are reasons why one would have liked this to be felt, as in general one would like almost anything to be felt, in one's work, that one has one's self contributively felt. We have seen, however, how idle is that pretension, which I should be sorry to make too much of. Maria Gostrey and Miss Stackpole then are cases, each, of the light *ficelle*,[172] not of the true agent; they may run beside the coach "for all they are worth," they may cling to it till they are out of breath (as poor Miss Stackpole all so visibly does), but neither, all the while, so much as gets her foot on the step, neither ceases for a moment to tread the dusty road. Put it even that they are like the fishwives who helped to bring back to Paris from Versailles, on that most ominous day of the first half of the French Revolution, the carriage of the royal family.[173] The only thing is that I may well be asked, I acknowledge, why then, in the present fiction, I have suffered Henrietta (of whom we have indubitably too much) so officiously, so strangely, so almost inexplicably, to pervade. I will presently say what I can for that anomaly—and in the most conciliatory fashion.

A point I wish still more to make is that if my relation of confidence with the actors in my drama who *were*, unlike Miss Stackpole, true agents, was an excellent one to have arrived at, there still remained my relation with the reader, which was another affair altogether and as to which I felt no one to be trusted but myself. That solicitude was to be accordingly expressed in the artful patience with which, as I have said, I piled brick upon brick. The bricks, for the whole counting-over—putting for bricks little touches and inventions and enhancements by the way—affect me in truth as well-nigh innumerable and as ever so scrupulously fitted together and packed-in. It is an effect of detail, of the minutest; though, if one were in this connexion to say all, one would express the hope that the general, the ampler air of the modest monument still survives. I do at least seem to catch the key to a part of this abundance of small anxious, ingenious illustration as I recollect putting my finger, in my young woman's interest, on the most obvious of her predicates. "What will she 'do'? Why, the first thing she'll do will be to come to Europe; which in fact will form, and all inevitably, no small part of her principal adventure. Coming to Europe is even for the 'frail vessels,' in this wonderful age, a mild adventure; but what is truer than that on one side—the side of their independence of flood and field, of the moving accident,[174] of battle and murder and sudden death—her adventures are to be mild? Without her sense of them, her sense *for* them, as one may say, they are next to nothing at all; but isn't the beauty and the difficulty just in showing their mystic conversion by that sense, conversion into the stuff of drama or, even more delightful word still, of 'story'?" It was all as clear, my contention, as a silver bell. Two very good instances, I think, of this effect of conversion, two cases of the rare chemistry, are the pages in which Isabel, coming into the drawing-room at Gardencourt, coming in from a wet walk or whatever, that rainy afternoon, finds Madame Merle in possession of the place, Madame Merle seated, all absorbed but all serene, at the piano, and deeply recognises, in the striking of such an hour, in the presence there, among the gathering shades, of this personage, of whom a moment before she had never so much as heard, a turning-point in her life.[175] It is dreadful to have too much, for any artistic demonstration, to dot one's i's and insist on one's intentions, and I am not eager to do it now; but the question here was that of producing the maximum of intensity with the minimum of strain.

The interest was to be raised to its pitch and yet the elements to be kept in their key; so that, should the whole thing duly impress, I might show what an "exciting" inward life may do for the person leading it even while it remains perfectly normal. And I cannot think of a more consistent application of that ideal unless it be in the long statement, just beyond the middle of the book, of my young woman's extraordinary meditative vigil[176] on the occasion that was to become for her such a landmark. Reduced to its essence, it is but the vigil of searching criticism; but it throws the action further forward than twenty "incidents" might have done.[177] It was designed to have all the vivacity of incident and all the economy of picture. She sits up, by her dying fire, far into the night, under the spell of recognitions on which she finds the last sharpness suddenly wait. It is a representation simply of her motionlessly *seeing*, and an attempt withal to make the mere still lucidity of her act as "interesting" as the surprise of a caravan or the identification of a pirate.[178] It represents, for that matter, one of the identifications dear to the novelist, and even indispensable to him; but it all goes on without her being approached by another person and without her leaving her chair. It is obviously the best thing in the book, but it is only a supreme illustration of the general plan. As to Henrietta, my apology for whom I just left incomplete, she exemplifies, I fear, in her superabundance, not an element of my plan, but only an excess of my zeal. So early was to begin my tendency to *overtreat*, rather than undertreat (when there was choice or danger) my subject.[179] (Many members of my craft, I gather, are far from agreeing with me, but I have always held overtreating the minor disservice.) "Treating" that of "The Portrait" amounted to never forgetting, by any lapse, that the thing was under a special obligation to be amusing. There was the danger of the noted "thinness"—which was to be averted, tooth and nail, by cultivation of the lively. That is at least how I see it to-day. Henrietta must have been at that time a part of my wonderful notion of the lively. And then there was another matter. I had, within the few preceding years, come to live in London, and the "international" light lay, in those days, to my sense, thick and rich upon the scene.[180] It was the light in which so much of the picture hung. But that *is* another matter. There is really too much to say.

PREFACE to *The Princess Casamassima* (*NYE* V–VI)

THE simplest account of the origin of "The Princess Casamassima" is, I think, that this fiction proceeded quite directly, during the first year of a long residence in London, from the habit and the interest of walking the streets.[181] I walked a great deal—for exercise, for amusement, for acquisition, and above all I always walked home at the evening's end, when the evening had been spent elsewhere, as happened more often than not; and as to do this was to receive many impressions, so the impressions worked and sought an issue, so the book after a time was born. It is a fact that, as I look back, the attentive exploration of London, the assault directly made by the great city upon an imagination quick to react, fully explains a large part of it. There is a minor element that refers itself to another source, of which I shall presently speak; but the prime idea was unmistakeably the ripe round fruit of perambulation. One walked of course with one's eyes greatly open, and I hasten to declare that such a practice, carried on for a long time and over a considerable space, positively provokes, all round, a mystic solicitation, the urgent appeal, on the part of everything, to be interpreted and, so far as may be, reproduced. "Subjects" and situations, character and history, the tragedy and comedy of life, are things of which the common air, in such conditions, seems pungently to taste; and to a mind curious, before the human scene, of meanings and revelations the great grey Babylon[182] easily becomes, on its face, a garden bristling with an immense illustrative flora. Possible stories, presentable figures, rise from the thick jungle as the observer moves, fluttering up like startled game, and before he knows it indeed he has fairly to guard himself against the brush of importunate wings. He goes on as with his head in a cloud of humming presences—especially during the younger, the initiatory time, the fresh, the sharply-apprehensive months or years, more or less numerous. We use our material up, we use up even the thick tribute of the London streets—if perception and attention but sufficiently light our steps. But I think of them as lasting, for myself, quite sufficiently long; I think of them as even still—dreadfully changed for the worse in respect to any romantic idea as I find them—

breaking out on occasion into eloquence,[183] throwing out deep notes from their vast vague murmur.

There was a moment at any rate when they offered me no image more vivid than that of some individual sensitive nature or fine mind, some small obscure intelligent creature whose education should have been almost wholly derived from them, capable of profiting by all the civilisation, all the accumulations to which they testify, yet condemned to see these things only from outside—in mere quickened consideration, mere wistfulness and envy and despair.[184] It seemed to me I had only to imagine such a spirit intent enough and troubled enough, and to place it in presence of the comings and goings, the great gregarious company, of the more fortunate than himself—all on the scale on which London could show them—to get possession of an interesting theme. I arrived so at the history of little Hyacinth Robinson—he sprang up for me out of the London pavement. To find his possible adventure interesting I had only to conceive his watching the same public show, the same innumerable appearances, I had watched myself, and of his watching very much as I had watched; save indeed for one little difference. This difference would be that so far as all the swarming facts should speak of freedom and ease, knowledge and power, money, opportunity and satiety, he should be able to revolve round them but at the most respectful of distances and with every door of approach shut in his face. For one's self, all conveniently, there had been doors that opened—opened into light and warmth and cheer, into good and charming relations;[185] and if the place as a whole lay heavy on one's consciousness there was yet always for relief this implication of one's own lucky share of the freedom and ease, lucky acquaintance with the number of lurking springs at light pressure of which particular vistas would begin to recede, great lighted, furnished, peopled galleries, sending forth gusts of agreeable sound.

That main happy sense of the picture was always there and that retreat from the general grimness never forbidden; whereby one's own relation to the mere formidable mass and weight of things was eased off and adjusted. One learned from an early period what it might be to know London in such a way as that—an immense and interesting discipline, an education on terms mostly convenient and delightful. But what would be the effect of the other way, of having so many precious things perpetually in one's eyes, yet of missing them all for any closer knowledge, and of the confinement of closer knowledge entirely to matters with which a connexion, however intimate, couldn't possibly pass for a privilege? Truly, of course, there are London mysteries (dense categories of dark arcana) for every spectator, and it's in a degree an exclusion and a state of weakness to be without experience of the meaner conditions, the lower manners and types, the general sordid struggle, the weight of the burden of labour, the ignorance, the misery and the vice. With such matters as those my tormented young man would have had contact—they would have formed, fundamentally, from the first, his natural and immediate London. But the reward of a romantic curiosity would be the question of what the total assault, that of the world of his work-a-day life and the world of his divination and his envy together, would have made of him, and what in especial he would have made of them. As tormented, I say, I thought of him, and that would be the point—if one could only see him feel enough to be interesting without his feeling so much as not to be natural.

This in fact I have ever found rather terribly the point—that the figures in any picture, the agents in any drama, are interesting only in proportion as they feel their respective situations; since the consciousness, on their part, of the complication exhibited forms for us their link of connexion with it. But there are degrees of feeling—the muffled, the faint, the just sufficient, the barely intelligent, as we may say; and the acute, the intense, the complete, in a word—the power to be finely aware and richly responsible. It is those moved in this latter fashion who "get most" out of all that happens to them and who in so doing enable us, as readers of their record, as participators by a fond attention, also to get most. Their being finely aware—as Hamlet and Lear, say, are finely aware—*makes* absolutely the intensity of their adventure, gives the maximum of sense to what befalls them. We care, our curiosity and our sympathy care, comparatively little for what happens to the stupid, the coarse and the blind; care for it, and for the effects of it, at the most as helping to precipitate what happens to the more deeply wondering, to the really sentient. Hamlet and Lear are surrounded, amid their complications, by the stupid and the blind, who minister in all sorts of ways to their recorded fate. Persons of markedly limited sense would, on such a principle as that, play a part in the career of my tormented youth; but he wouldn't be of markedly limited sense himself—he would note as many things and vibrate to as many occasions as I might venture to make him.

There wouldn't moreover simply be the question of his suffering—of which we might soon get enough; there would be the question of what, all beset and all perceptive, he should thus adventurously do, thus dream and hazard and attempt. The interest of the attitude and the act would be the actor's imagination and vision of them, together with the nature and degree of their felt return upon him. So the intelligent creature would be required and so some picture of his intelligence involved. The picture of an intelligence appears for the most part, it is true, a dead weight for the reader of the English novel to carry, this reader having so often the wondrous property of caring for the displayed tangle of human relations without caring for its intelligibility. The teller of a story is primarily, none the less, the listener to it, the reader of it, too; and, having needed thus to make it out, distinctly, on the crabbed page of life, to disengage it from the rude human character and the more or less gothic text in which it has been packed away, the very essence of his affair has been the *imputing* of intelligence. The basis of his attention has been that such and such an imbroglio has got started—on the page of life—because of something that some one has felt and more or less understood.

I recognise at the same time, and in planning "The Princess Casamassima" felt it highly important to recognise, the danger of filling too full any supposed and above all any obviously limited vessel of consciousness. If persons either tragically or comically embroiled with life allow us the comic or tragic value of their embroilment in proportion as their struggle is a measured and directed one, it is strangely true, none the less, that beyond a certain point they are spoiled for us by this carrying of a due light. They may carry too much of it for our credence, for our compassion, for our derision. They may be shown as knowing too much and feeling too much—not certainly for their remaining remarkable, but for their remaining "natural" and typical, for their having the needful communities with our own precious liability to fall into traps and be bewildered. It seems probable that if we were never bewildered there would never be a story to tell about us; we should partake of the superior nature of the all-knowing immortals whose annals are dreadfully dull so long as flurried humans are not, for the positive relief of bored Olympians,[186] mixed up with them. Therefore it is that the wary reader for the most part warns the novelist against making his characters too *interpretative* of the muddle of fate, or in other words too divinely, too priggishly clever. "Give us plenty of bewilderment," this monitor seems to say, "so long as there is plenty of slashing out in the bewilderment too. But don't, we beseech you, give us too much intelligence; for intelligence—well, *endangers*; endangers not perhaps the slasher himself, but the very slashing, the subject-matter of any self-respecting story. It opens up too many considerations, possibilities, issues; it *may* lead the slasher into dreary realms where slashing somehow fails and falls to the ground."[187]

That is well reasoned on the part of the reader, who can in spite of it never have an idea—or his earnest discriminations would come to him less easily—of the extreme difficulty, for the painter of the human mixture, of reproducing that mixture aright. "Give us in the persons represented, the subjects of the bewilderment (that bewilderment without which there would be no question of an issue or of the fact of suspense, prime implications in any story) as much experience as possible, but keep down the terms in which you report that experience, because we only understand the very simplest": such in effect are the words in which the novelist constantly hears himself addressed, such the plea made him by the would-be victims of his spell on behalf of that sovereign principle the economy of interest, a principle as to which their instinct is justly strong. He listens anxiously to the charge—nothing can exceed his own solicitude for an economy of interest; but feels himself all in presence of an abyss of ambiguities, the mutual accommodations in which the reader wholly leaves to him. Experience, as I see it, is our apprehension and our measure of what happens to us as social creatures—any intelligent report of which has to be based on that apprehension. The picture of the exposed and entangled state is what is required, and there are certainly always plenty of grounds for keeping down the complexities of a picture. A picture it still has to be, however, and by that condition has to deal effectually with its subject, so that the simple device of more and more keeping down may well not see us quite to our end or even quite to our middle. One suggested way of keeping down, for instance, is not to attribute feeling, or feelings, to persons who wouldn't in all probability have had any to speak of. The less space, within the frame of the picture, their feelings take up the more space is left for their doings—a fact that may at first seem to make for a refinement of economy.

All of which is charming—yet would be infinitely more so if here at once ambiguity didn't yawn; the unreality of the sharp distinction, where the interest of observation is at stake, between doing and feeling. In the immediate field of life, for action, for application, for getting through a job, nothing may so much matter perhaps as the descent of a suspended weight on this, that or the other spot, with all its subjective concomitants quite secondary and irrelevant. But the affair of the painter is not the immediate, it is the reflected field of life, the realm not of application, but of *appreciation*—a truth that makes our measure of effect altogether different. My report of people's experience—my report as a "story-teller"—is essentially my appreciation of it, and there is no "interest" for me in what my hero, my heroine or any one else does save through that admirable process. As soon as I begin to appreciate simplification is imperilled: the sharply distinguished parts of any adventure, any case of endurance and performance, melt together as an appeal. I then see their "doing," that of the persons just mentioned, as, immensely, their feeling, their feeling as their doing; since I can have none of the conveyed sense and taste of their situation without becoming intimate with them. I can't be intimate without that sense and taste, and I can't appreciate save by intimacy, any more than I can report save by a projected light. Intimacy with a man's specific behaviour, with his given case, is desperately certain to make us see it as a whole—in which event arbitrary limitations of our vision lose whatever beauty they may on occasion have pretended to. What a man thinks and what he feels are the history and the character of what he does; on all of which things the logic of intensity rests. Without intensity where is vividness, and without vividness where is presentability? If I have called the most general state of one's most exposed and assaulted figures the state of bewilderment—the condition for instance on which Thackeray so much insists in the interest of *his* exhibited careers, the condition of a humble heart, a bowed head, a patient wonder, a suspended judgement, before the "awful will" and the mysterious decrees of Providence[188]—so it is rather witless to talk of merely getting rid of that displayed mode of reaction, one of the oft-encountered, one of the highly recommended, categories of feeling.

The whole thing comes to depend thus on the *quality* of bewilderment characteristic of one's creature, the quality involved in the given case or supplied by one's data. There are doubtless many such qualities, ranging from vague and crepuscular to sharpest and most critical; and we have but to imagine one of these latter to see how easily—from the moment it gets its head at all—it may insist on playing a part. There we have then at once a case of feeling, of ever so many possible feelings, stretched across the scene like an attached thread on which the pearls of interest are strung.[189] There are threads shorter and less tense, and I am far from implying that the minor, the coarser and less fruitful forms and degrees of moral reaction, as we may conveniently call it, may not yield lively results. They have their subordinate, comparative, illustrative human value—that appeal of the witless which is often so penetrating. Verily even, I think, no "story" is possible without its fools—as most of the fine painters of life, Shakespeare, Cervantes and Balzac, Fielding, Scott, Thackeray, Dickens, George Meredith, George Eliot, Jane Austen, have abundantly felt.[190] At the same time I confess I never see the *leading* interest of any human hazard but in a consciousness (on the part of the moved and moving creature) subject to fine intensification and wide enlargement. It is as mirrored in that consciousness that the gross fools, the headlong fools, the fatal fools play their part for us—they have much less to show us in themselves. The troubled life mostly at the centre of our subject—whatever our subject, for the artistic hour, happens to be—embraces them and deals with them for its amusement and its anguish: they are apt largely indeed, on a near view, to be all the cause of its trouble. This means, exactly, that the person capable of feeling in the given case more than another of what is to be felt for it, and so serving in the highest degree to *record* it dramatically and objectively, is the only sort of person on whom we can count not to betray, to cheapen or, as we say, give away,[191] the value and beauty of the thing. By so much as the affair matters *for* some such individual, by so much do we get the best there is of it, and by so much as it falls within the scope of a denser and duller, a more vulgar and more shallow capacity, do we get a picture dim and meagre.

The great chroniclers have clearly always been aware of this; they have at least always either placed a mind of some sort—in the sense of a reflecting and colouring medium—in possession of the general adventure (when the latter has not been purely epic, as with Scott, say, as with old Dumas and with Zola[192]); or else paid signally, as to the interest created, for their failure to do so. We may note moreover in passing that this failure is in almost no case intentional or part of a plan, but has sprung from their limited curiosity, their short conception of the particular sensibility projected. Edgar of Ravenswood for instance, visited by the tragic tempest of "The Bride of

Lammermoor," has a black cloak and hat and feathers more than he has a mind; just as Hamlet, while equally sabled and draped and plumed, while at least equally romantic, has yet a mind still more than he has a costume.[193] The situation represented is that Ravenswood loves Lucy Ashton through dire difficulty and danger, and that she in the same way loves him; but the relation so created between them is by this neglect of the "feeling" question never shown us as primarily taking place. It is shown only in its secondary, its confused and disfigured aspects—where, however, luckily, it is presented with great romantic good faith. The thing has nevertheless paid for its deviation, as I say, by a sacrifice of intensity; the centre of the subject is empty and the development pushed off, all round, toward the frame—which is, so to speak, beautifully rich and curious. But I mention that relation to each other of the appearances in a particular work only as a striking negative case; there are in the connexion I have glanced at plenty of striking positive ones. It is very true that Fielding's hero in "Tom Jones" is but as "finely," that is but as intimately, bewildered as a young man of great health and spirits may be when he hasn't a grain of imagination: the point to be made is, at all events, that his sense of bewilderment obtains altogether on the comic, never on the tragic plane. He has so much "life" that it amounts, for the effect of comedy and application of satire, almost to his having a mind, that is to his having reactions and a full consciousness; besides which his author—*he* handsomely possessed of a mind—has such an amplitude of reflexion for him and round him that we see him through the mellow air of Fielding's fine old moralism, fine old humour and fine old style,[194] which somehow really enlarge, make every one and every thing important.

All of which furthers my remarking how much I have been interested, on reading "The Princess Casamassima" over, to recognise my sense, sharp from far back, that clearness and concreteness constantly depend, for any pictorial whole, on some *concentrated* individual notation of them. That notation goes forward here in the mind of little Hyacinth, immensely quickened by the fact of its so mattering to his very life what he does make of things: which passion of intelligence is, as I have already hinted, precisely his highest value for our curiosity and our sympathy. Yet if his highest it is not at all his only one, since the truth for "a young man in a book" by no means entirely resides in his being either exquisitely sensitive or shiningly clever. It resides in some such measure of these things as may consort with the fine measure of other things too—with that of the other faces of his situation and character. If he's too sensitive and too clever for *them*, if he knows more than is likely or natural—for *him*—it's as if he weren't at all, as if he were false and impossible. Extreme and attaching always the difficulty of fixing at a hundred points the place where one's impelled *bonhomme* may feel enough and "know" enough—or be in the way of learning enough—for his maximum dramatic value without feeling and knowing too much for his minimum verisimilitude, his proper fusion with the fable. This is the charming, the tormenting, the eternal little matter *to be made right*, in all the weaving of silver threads and tapping on golden nails;[195] and I should take perhaps too fantastic a comfort—I mean were not the comforts of the artist just of the raw essence of fantasy—in any glimpse of such achieved rightnesses, whether in my own work or that of others. In no work whatever, doubtless, are they the felicities the most frequent; but they have so inherent a price that even the traceable attempt at them, wherever met, sheds, I think, a fine influence about.

I have for example a weakness of sympathy with that constant effort of George Eliot's which plays through Adam Bede and Felix Holt and Tito Melema, through Daniel Deronda and through Lydgate in "Middlemarch," through Maggie Tulliver, through Romola, through Dorothea Brooke and Gwendolen Harleth; the effort to show their adventures and their history—the author's subject-matter all—as determined by their feelings and the nature of their minds.[196] Their emotions, their stirred intelligence, their moral consciousness, become thus, by sufficiently charmed perusal, our own very adventure. The creator of Deronda and of Romola is charged, I know, with having on occasion—as in dealing with those very celebrities themselves—left the figure, the concrete man and woman, too abstract by reason of the quantity of soul employed;[197] but such mischances, where imagination and humour still keep them company, often have an interest that is wanting to agitations of the mere surface or to those that may be only taken for granted. I should even like to give myself the pleasure of retracing from one of my own productions to another the play of a like instinctive disposition, of catching in the fact, at one point after another, from "Roderick Hudson" to "The Golden Bowl," that provision for interest which consists in placing advantageously, placing right in the middle of the light, the most polished of possible mirrors of the subject.[198] Rowland Mallet, in "Roderick Hudson," is exactly such a mirror, not a bit autobiographic or formally "first person" though he be, and I might exemplify the case through a long list, through the nature of such a "mind" even as the all-objective Newman in "The American," through the thickly-peopled imagination of Isabel Archer in "The Portrait of a Lady" (her imagination positively the deepest depth of her imbroglio) down to such unmistakeable examples as that of Merton Densher in "The Wings of the Dove," that of Lambert Strether in "The Ambassadors" (*he* a mirror verily of miraculous silver and quite pre-eminent, I think, for the connexion) and that of the Prince in the first half and that of the Princess in the second half of "The Golden Bowl." I should note the extent to which these persons are, so far as their other passions permit, intense *perceivers*, all, of their respective predicaments, and I should go on from them to fifty other examples; even to the divided Vanderbank of "The Awkward Age," the extreme pinch of whose romance is the vivacity in him, to his positive sorrow and loss, of the state of being aware; even to scanted Fleda Vetch in "The Spoils of Poynton," through whose own delicate vision of everything so little of the human value of her situation is wasted for us; even to the small recording governess confronted with the horrors of "The Turn of the Screw" and to the innocent child patching together all ineffectually those of "What Maisie Knew"; even in short, since I may name so few cases, to the disaffected guardian of an overgrown legend in "The Birthplace," to the luckless fine artist of "The Next Time," trying to despoil himself, for a "hit" and bread and butter, of his fatal fineness, to blunt the tips of his intellectual fingers,[199] and to the hapless butler Brooksmith, ruined by good talk, disqualified for common domestic service by the beautiful growth of his habit of quiet attention, his faculty of appreciation. But though this demonstration of a rooted vice—since a vice it would appear mainly accounted—might yield amusement, the examples referred to must await their turn.

    I had had for a long time well before me, at any rate, my small obscure but ardent observer of the "London world," saw him roam and wonder and yearn, saw all the unanswered questions and baffled passions that might ferment in him—once he should be made both sufficiently thoughtful and sufficiently "disinherited";[200] but this image, however interesting, was of course not by itself a progression, an action, didn't by itself make a drama. I got my action however—failing which one has nothing—under the prompt sense that the state of feeling I was concerned with might develop and beget another state, might return at a given moment, and with the greatest vivacity, on itself. To see this was really to feel one's subject swim into one's ken,[201] especially after a certain other ingenious connexion had been made for it. I find myself again recalling, and with the possible "fun" of it reviving too, how I recognised, as revealed and prescribed, the particular complexion, profession and other conditions of my little presumptuous adventurer, with his combination of intrinsic fineness and fortuitous adversity, his small cluster of "dingy" London associations and the swelling spirit in him which was to be the field of his strange experience. Accessible through his imagination, as I have hinted, to a thousand provocations and intimations, he would become most acquainted with destiny in the form of a lively inward revolution. His being jealous of all the ease of life of which he tastes so little, and, bitten, under this exasperation, with an aggressive, vindictive, destructive social faith, his turning to "treasons, stratagems and spoils"[202] might be as vivid a picture as one chose, but would move to pity and terror[203] only by the aid of some deeper complication, some imposed and formidable issue.

The complication most interesting then would be that he should fall in love with the beauty of the world, actual order and all, at the moment of his most feeling and most hating the famous "iniquity of its social arrangements";[204] so that his position as an irreconcileable pledged enemy to it, thus rendered false by something more personal than his opinions and his vows, becomes the sharpest of his torments. To make it a torment that really matters, however, he must have got practically involved, specifically committed to the stand he has, under the pressure of more knowledge, found impossible; out of which has come for him the deep dilemma of the disillusioned and repentant conspirator. He has thrown himself into the more than "shady" underworld of militant socialism, he has undertaken to play a part—a part that with the drop of his exasperation and the growth, simply expressed, of his taste, is out of all tune with his passion, at any cost, for life itself, the life, whatever it be, that surrounds him. Dabbling deeply in revolutionary politics of a hole-and-corner sort, he would be "in" up to his neck, and with that precarious part of him particularly involved,[205] so that his tergiversation is the climax of his adventure. What was essential with this was that he should have a social—not less than a socialist—connexion, find a door somehow open to him into the appeased and civilised state, into that warmer glow of things he is precisely to help to undermine. To look for this necessary connexion was for me to meet it suddenly in the form of that extremely *disponible* figure of Christina Light whom I had ten years before found left on my hands at the conclusion of "Roderick Hudson."[206] She had for so long, in the vague limbo of those ghosts we have conjured but not exorcised, been looking for a situation, awaiting a niche and a function.

    I shall not pretend to trace the steps and stages by which the imputability of a future to that young woman—which was like the act of clothing her chilled and patient nakedness—had for its prime effect to plant her in my little bookbinder's path. Nothing would doubtless beckon us on further, with a large leisure, than such a chance to study the obscure law under which certain of a novelist's characters, more or less honourably buried, revive for him by a force or a whim of their own and "walk" round his house of art like haunting ghosts,[207] feeling for the old doors they knew, fumbling at stiff latches and pressing their pale faces, in the outer dark, to lighted windows. I mistrust them, I confess, in general; my sense of a really expressed character is that it shall have originally so tasted of the ordeal of service as to feel no disposition to yield again to the strain. Why should the Princess of the climax of "Roderick Hudson" still have made her desire felt, unless in fact to testify that she had not been—for what she was—completely recorded? To continue in evidence, that had struck me from far back as her natural passion; in evidence at any price, not consenting to be laid away with folded hands in the pasteboard tomb, the doll's box, to which we usually relegate the spent puppet[208] after the fashion of a recumbent worthy on the slab of a sepulchral monument. I was to see this, after all, in the event, as the fruit of a restless vanity: Christina had felt herself, known herself, striking, in the earlier connexion, and couldn't resign herself not to strike again.[209] Her pressure then was not to be resisted—sharply as the question might come up of why she should pretend to strike just *there*. I shall not attempt to answer it with reasons (one can never tell everything); it was enough that I could recognise her claim to have travelled far—far from where I had last left her: that, one felt, was in character—that was what she naturally *would* have done. Her prime note had been an aversion to the *banal*,[210] and nothing could be of an effect less *banal*, I judged, than her intervention in the life of a dingy little London bookbinder whose sensibility, whose flow of opinions on "public questions" in especial, should have been poisoned at the source.

She would be world-weary—that was another of her notes; and the extravagance of her attitude in these new relations would have its root and its apparent logic in her need to feel freshly about something or other—it might scarce matter what. She can, or she believes she can, feel freshly about the "people"[211] and their wrongs and their sorrows and their perpetual smothered ferment; for these things are furthest removed from those others among which she has hitherto tried to make her life. That was to a certainty where I was to have looked for her—quite *off* and away (once granted the wisdom of listening to her anew at all): therefore Hyacinth's encounter with her could pass for natural, and it was fortunately to be noted that she was to serve for his experience in quite another and a more "leading" sense than any in which he was to serve for hers. I confess I was not averse—such are the possible weaknesses of the artist in face of high difficulties—to feeling that if his appearance of consistency were obtained I might at least try to remain comparatively at my ease about hers. I may add moreover that the resuscitation of Christina (and, on the minor scale, of the Prince and of Madame Grandoni) put in a strong light for me the whole question, for the romancer, of "going on with a character": as Balzac first of all systematically went on, as Thackeray, as Trollope, as Zola all more or less ingeniously went on.[212] I was to find no small savour in the reflexions so precipitated; though I may treat myself here only to this remark about them—that the revivalist impulse on the fond writer's part strikes me as one thing, a charmingly conceivable thing, but the effect of a free indulgence in it (effect, that is, on the nerves of the reader) as, for twenty rather ineffable reasons, quite another.

I remember at any rate feeling myself all in possession of little Hyacinth's consistency, as I have called it, down at Dover during certain weeks that were none too remotely precedent to the autumn of 1885 and the appearance, in the "Atlantic Monthly" again, of the first chapters of the story.[213] There were certain sunny, breezy balconied rooms at the quieter end of the Esplanade of that cheerful castle-crested little town—now infinitely perturbed by gigantic "harbour works,"[214] but then only faded and over-soldiered and all pleasantly and humbly submissive to the law that snubs in due course the presumption of flourishing resorts—to which I had already more than once had recourse in hours of quickened industry and which, though much else has been swept away, still archaically exist. To have lately noted this again from the old benched and asphalted walk by the sea, the twinkling Channel beyond which on occasion the opposite coast of France used to gleam as an incident of the charming tendency of the whole prospect (immediate picture and fond design alike) amusingly to *shine*, was somehow to taste afresh, and with a certain surprise, the odd quality of that original confidence that the parts of my plan *would* somehow hang together.[215] I may wonder at my confidence now—given the extreme, the very particular truth and "authority" required at so many points; but to wonder is to live back gratefully into the finer reasons of things, with all the detail of harsh application and friction (that there must have been)[216] quite happily blurred and dim. The finest of reasons—I mean for the sublime confidence I speak of—was that I felt in full *personal* possession of my matter; this really seemed the fruit of direct experience.[217] My scheme called for the suggested nearness (to all our apparently ordered life) of some sinister anarchic underworld, heaving in its pain, its power and its hate; a presentation not of sharp particulars, but of loose appearances, vague motions and sounds and symptoms, just perceptible presences and general looming possibilities. To have adopted the scheme was to have had to meet the question of one's "notes," over the whole ground, the question of what, in such directions, one had "gone into" and how far one had gone;[218] and to have answered that question—to one's own satisfaction at least—was truly to see one's way.

My notes then, on the much-mixed world of my hero's both overt and covert consciousness, were exactly my gathered impressions and stirred perceptions, the deposit in my working imagination of all my visual and all my constructive sense of London. The very plan of my book had in fact directly confronted me with the rich principle of the Note,[219] and was to do much to clear up, once for all, my practical view of it. If one was to undertake to tell tales and to report with truth on the human scene, it could be but because "notes" had been from the cradle the ineluctable consequence of one's greatest inward energy: to take them was as natural as to look, to think, to feel, to recognise, to remember, as to perform any act of understanding. The play of the energy had been continuous and couldn't change;

what changed was only the objects and situations pressing the spring of it. Notes had been in other words the things one couldn't *not* take, and the prime result of all fresh experience was to remind one of that. I have endeavoured to characterise the peremptory fashion in which my fresh experience of London—the London of the habitual observer, the preoccupied painter, the pedestrian prowler[220]—reminded me; an admonition that represented, I think, the sum of my investigations. I recall pulling no wires, knocking at no closed doors, applying for no "authentic" information;[221] but I recall also on the other hand the practice of never missing an opportunity to add a drop, however small, to the bucket of my impressions or to renew my sense of being able to dip into it. To haunt the great city and by this habit to penetrate it, imaginatively, in as many places as possible—*that* was to be informed, *that* was to pull wires, *that* was to open doors, *that* positively was to groan at times under the weight of one's accumulations.

Face to face with the idea of Hyacinth's subterranean politics and occult affiliations, I recollect perfectly feeling, in short, that I might well be ashamed if, with my advantages—and there wasn't a street, a corner, an hour, of London that was not an advantage—I shouldn't be able to piece together a proper semblance of those things, as indeed a proper semblance of all the odd parts of his life. There was always of course the chance that the propriety might be challenged—challenged by readers of a knowledge greater than mine. Yet knowledge, after all, of what? My vision of the aspects I more or less fortunately rendered *was*, exactly, my knowledge. If I made my appearances live, what was this but the utmost one could do with them? Let me at the same time not deny that, in answer to probable ironic reflexions on the full licence for sketchiness and vagueness and dimness taken indeed by my picture, I had to bethink myself in advance of a defence of my "artistic position." Shouldn't I find it in the happy contention that the value I wished most to render and the effect I wished most to produce were precisely those of our not knowing, of society's not knowing, but only guessing and suspecting and trying to ignore, what "goes on" irreconcileably, subversively, beneath the vast smug surface? I couldn't deal with that positive quantity for itself—my subject had another too exacting side; but I might perhaps show the social ear as on occasion applied to the ground, or catch some gust of the hot breath that I had at many an hour seemed to see escape and hover.[222] What it all came back to was, no doubt, something like *this* wisdom—that if you haven't, for fiction, the root of the matter in you, haven't the sense of life and the penetrating imagination, you are a fool in the very presence of the revealed and assured; but that if you *are* so armed you are not really helpless, not without your resource, even before mysteries abysmal.

PREFACE to *The Tragic Muse*
(*NYE* VII–VIII)

I PROFESS a certain vagueness of remembrance in respect to the origin and growth of "The Tragic Muse," which appeared in the "Atlantic Monthly" again, beginning January 1889 and running on, inordinately, several months beyond its proper twelve.[223] If it be ever of interest and profit to put one's finger on the productive germ of a work of art, and if in fact a lucid account of any such work involves that prime identification, I can but look on the present fiction as a poor fatherless and motherless, a sort of unregistered and unacknowledged birth. I fail to recover my precious first moment of consciousness of the idea to which it was to give form;[224] to recognise in it—as I like to do in general—the effect of some particular sharp impression or concussion. I call such remembered glimmers always precious, because without them comes no clear vision of what one may have intended, and without that vision no straight measure of what one may have succeeded in doing. What I make out from furthest back is that I must have had from still further back, must in fact practically have always had, the happy thought of some dramatic picture of the "artist-life" and of the difficult terms on which it is at the best secured and enjoyed, the general question of its having to be not altogether easily paid for. To "do something about art"—art, that is, as a human complication and a social stumbling-block—must have been for me early a good deal of a nursed intention, the conflict between art and "the world" striking me thus betimes as one of the half-dozen great primary motives. I remember even having taken for granted with this fond inveteracy that no one of these pregnant themes was likely to prove under the test more full of matter. This being the case, meanwhile, what would all experience have done but enrich one's conviction?—since if on the one hand I had gained a more and more intimate view of the nature of art and the conditions therewith imposed, so the world was a conception that clearly required, and that would for ever continue to take, any amount of filling-in. The happy and fruitful truth, at all events, was that there was opposition—why there *should* be was another matter—and that the opposition would beget an infinity of situations. What had doubtless occurred in fact, moreover, was that just this question of the essence and the reasons of the opposition had shown itself to demand the light of experience; so that to the growth of experience, truly, the treatment of the subject had yielded. It had waited for that advantage.

Yet I continue to see experience giving me its jog mainly in the form of an invitation from the gentle editor of the "Atlantic," the late Thomas Bailey Aldrich, to contribute to his pages a serial that should run through the year.[225] That friendly appeal becomes thus the most definite statement I can make of the "genesis" of the book; though from the moment of its reaching me everything else in the matter seems to live again. What lives not least, to be quite candid, is the fact that I was to see this production make a virtual end, for the time, as by its sinister effect—though for reasons still obscure to me—of the pleasant old custom of the "running" of the novel.[226] Not for many years was I to feel the practice, for my benefit, confidingly revive. The influence of "The Tragic Muse" was thus exactly other than what I had all earnestly (if of course privately enough) invoked for it, and I remember well the particular chill, at last, of the sense of my having launched it in a great grey void from which no echo or message whatever would come back.[227] None, in the event, ever came, and as I now read the book over I find the circumstance make, in its name, for a special tenderness of charity; even for that finer consideration hanging in the parental breast about the maimed or slighted, the disfigured or defeated, the unlucky or unlikely child—with this hapless small mortal thought of further as somehow "compromising." I am thus able to take the thing as having quite wittingly and undisturbedly existed for itself alone, and to liken it to some aromatic bag of gathered herbs of which the string has never been loosed; or, better still, to some jar of potpourri, shaped and overfigured and polished, but of which the lid, never lifted, has provided for the intense accumulation of the fragrance within. The consistent, the sustained, preserved *tone* of "The Tragic Muse," its constant and doubtless rather fine-drawn truth to its particular sought pitch and accent, are, critically speaking, its principal merit—the inner harmony that I perhaps presumptuously permit myself to compare to an unevaporated scent.

After which indeed I may well be summoned to say what I mean, in such a business, by an appreciable "tone" and how I can justify my claim to it—a demonstration that will await us later. Suffice it just here that I find the latent historic clue in my hand again with the easy recall of my prompt grasp of such a chance to make a story about art. *There* was my subject this time—all mature with having long waited, and with the blest dignity that my original perception of its value was quite lost in the mists of youth. I must long have carried in my head the notion of a young man who should amid difficulty—the difficulties being the story—have abandoned "public life" for the zealous pursuit of some supposedly minor craft; just as, evidently, there had hovered before me some possible picture (but all comic and ironic) of one of the most salient London "social" passions, the unappeasable curiosity for the things of the theatre; for every one of them, that is, except the drama itself, and for the "personality" of the performer (almost any performer quite sufficiently serving) in particular.[228] This latter, verily, had struck me as an aspect appealing mainly to satiric treatment; the only adequate or effective treatment, I had again and again felt, for most of the distinctively social aspects of London: the general artlessly histrionised air of things caused so many examples to spring from behind any hedge. What came up, however, at once, for my own stretched canvas, was that it would have to be ample, give me really space to turn round, and that a single illustrative case might easily be meagre fare. The young man who should "chuck" admired politics,[229] and of course some other admired object with them, would be all very well; but he wouldn't be enough—therefore what should one say to some other young man who would chuck something and somebody else, admired in their way too?

There need never, at the worst, be any difficulty about the things advantageously chuckable for art; the question is all but of choosing them in the heap. Yet were I to represent a struggle—an interesting one, indispensably— with the passions of the theatre (as a profession, or at least as an absorption) I should have to place the theatre in another light than the satiric. This, however, would by good luck be perfectly possible too—without a sacrifice of truth; and I should doubtless even be able to make my theatric case as important as I might desire it. It seemed clear that I needed big cases— small ones would practically give my central idea away; and I make out now my still labouring under the illusion that the case of the sacrifice for art *can* ever be, with truth, with taste, with discretion involved, apparently and showily "big." I dare say it glimmered upon me even then that the very sharpest difficulty of the victim of the conflict I should seek to represent, and the very highest interest of his predicament, dwell deep in the fact that his repudiation of the great obvious, great moral or functional or useful character, shall just have to consent to resemble a surrender for absolutely nothing. Those characters are all large and expansive, seated and established and endowed; whereas the most charming truth about the preference for art is that to parade abroad so thoroughly inward and so naturally embarrassed a matter is to falsify and vulgarise it; that as a preference attended with the honours of publicity it is indeed nowhere; that in fact, under the rule of its sincerity, its only honours are those of contraction, concentration and a seemingly deplorable indifference to everything but itself. Nothing can well figure as less "big," in an honest thesis, than a marked instance of somebody's willingness to pass mainly for an ass. Of these things I must, I say, have been in strictness aware; what I perhaps failed of was to note that if a certain romantic glamour (even that of mere eccentricity or of a fine perversity) may be flung over the act of exchange of a "career" for the æsthetic life in general, the prose and the modesty of the matter[230] yet come in with any exhibition of the particular branch of æsthetics selected. Then it is that the attitude of hero or heroine may look too much—for the romantic effect—like a low crouching over proved trifles. Art indeed has in our day taken on so many honours and emoluments[231] that the recognition of its importance is more than a custom, has become on occasion almost a fury: the line is drawn—especially in the English world—only at the importance of heeding what it may mean.

The more I turn my pieces over, at any rate, the more I now see I must have found in them, and I remember how, once well in presence of my three typical examples, my fear of too ample a canvas quite dropped. The only question was that if I had marked my political case, from so far back, for "a story by itself," and then marked my theatrical case for another, the joining together of these interests, originally seen as separate,[232] might, all disgracefully, betray the seam, show for mechanical and superficial. A story was a story, a picture a picture, and I had a mortal horror of two stories, two pictures, in one. The reason of this was the clearest—my subject was immediately, under that disadvantage, so cheated of its indispensable centre as to become of no more use for expressing a main intention than a wheel without a hub is of use for moving a cart. It was a fact, apparently, that one *had* on occasion seen two pictures in one; were there not for instance certain sublime Tintorettos at Venice, a measureless Crucifixion in especial, which showed without loss of authority half a dozen actions separately taking place?[233] Yes, that might be, but there had surely been nevertheless a mighty pictorial fusion, so that the virtue of composition had somehow thereby come all mysteriously to its own. Of course the affair would be simple enough if composition could be kept out of the question; yet by what art or process, what bars and bolts, what unmuzzled dogs and pointed guns, perform that feat? I had to know myself utterly inapt for any such valour and recognise that, to make it possible, sundry things should have begun for me much further back than I had felt them even in their dawn. A picture without composition slights its most precious chance for beauty, and is moreover not composed at all unless the painter knows *how* that principle of health and safety, working as an absolutely premeditated art,[234] has prevailed. There may in its absence be life, incontestably, as "The Newcomes" has life, as "Les Trois Mousquetaires," as Tolstoi's "Peace and War," have it; but what do such large loose baggy monsters,[235] with their queer elements of the accidental and the arbitrary, artistically *mean*? We have heard it maintained, we well remember, that such things are "superior to art";[236] but we understand least of all what *that* may mean, and we look in vain for the artist, the divine explanatory genius, who will come to our aid and tell us. There is life and life, and as waste is only life sacrificed and thereby prevented from "counting," I delight in a deep-breathing economy and an organic form.[237] My business was accordingly to "go in" for complete pictorial fusion, some such common interest between my two first notions as would, in spite of their birth under quite different stars, do them no violence at all.

I recall with this confirmed infatuation of retrospect that through the mild perceptions I here glance at there struck for "The Tragic Muse" the first hour of a season of no small subjective felicity; lighted mainly, I seem to see, by a wide west window that, high aloft, looked over near and far London sunsets,[238] a half-grey, half-flushed expanse of London life. The production of the thing, which yet took a good many months, lives for me again all contemporaneously in that full projection, upon my very table, of the good fog-filtered Kensington mornings; which had a way indeed of seeing the sunset in and which at the very last are merged to memory in a different and a sharper pressure, that of an hotel bedroom in Paris during the autumn of 1889, with the Exposition du Centenaire[239] about to end—and my long story, through the usual difficulties, as well. The usual difficulties—and I fairly cherish the record as some adventurer in another line may hug the sense of his inveterate habit of just saving in time the neck he ever undiscourageably risks—were those bequeathed as a particular vice of the artistic spirit, against which vigilance had been destined from the first to exert itself in vain, and the effect of which was that again and again, perversely, incurably, the centre of my structure would insist on placing itself *not*, so to speak, in the middle.[240] It mattered little that the reader with the idea or the suspicion of a structural centre is the rarest of friends and of critics—a bird, it would seem, as merely fabled as the phœnix:[241] the terminational terror was none the less certain to break in and my work threaten to masquerade for me as an active figure condemned to the disgrace of legs too short, ever so much too short, for its body.[242] I urge myself to the candid confession that in very few of my productions, to my eye, *has* the organic centre succeeded in getting into proper position.

Time after time, then, has the precious waistband or girdle, studded and buckled and placed for brave outward show, practically worked itself, and in spite of desperate remonstrance, or in other words essential counterplotting, to a point perilously near the knees—perilously I mean for the freedom of these parts. In several of my compositions this displacement has so succeeded, at the crisis, in defying and resisting me, has appeared so fraught with probable dishonour, that I still turn upon them, in spite of the greater or less success of final dissimulation, a rueful and wondering eye. These productions have in fact, if I may be so bold about it, specious and spurious centres altogether, to make up for the failure of the true. As to which in my list they are, however, that is another business, not on any terms to be made known.[243] Such at least would seem my resolution so far as I have thus proceeded. Of any attention ever arrested by the pages forming the object of this reference that rigour of discrimination has wholly and consistently failed, I gather, to constitute a part. In which fact there is perhaps after all a rough justice—since the infirmity I speak of, for example, has been always but the direct and immediate fruit of a positive excess of foresight, the overdone desire to provide for future need and lay up heavenly treasure[244] against the demands of my climax. If the art of the drama, as a great French master of it has said, is above all the art of preparations,[245] that is true only to a less extent of the art of the novel, and true exactly in the degree in which the art of the particular novel comes near that of the drama. The first half of a fiction insists ever on figuring to me as the stage or theatre for the second half, and I have in general given so much space to making the theatre propitious that my halves have too often proved strangely unequal. Thereby has arisen with grim regularity the question of artfully, of consummately masking the fault and conferring on the false quantity the brave appearance of the true.

But I am far from pretending that these desperations of ingenuity have not—as through seeming *most* of the very essence of the problem—their exasperated charm; so far from it that my particular supreme predicament in the Paris hotel, after an undue primary leakage of time, no doubt, over at the great river-spanning museum of the Champ de Mars and the Trocadero,[246] fairly takes on to me now the tender grace of a day that is dead.[247] Re-reading the last chapters of "The Tragic Muse" I catch again the very odour of Paris, which comes up in the rich rumble of the Rue de la Paix—with which my room itself, for that matter, seems impregnated—and which hangs for reminiscence about the embarrassed effort to "finish," not ignobly, within my already exceeded limits;[248] an effort prolonged each day to those late afternoon hours during which the tone of the terrible city seemed to deepen about one to an effect strangely composed at once of the auspicious and the fatal. The "plot" of Paris thickened at such hours beyond any other plot in the world, I think; but there one sat meanwhile with another, on one's hands, absolutely requiring precedence. Not the least imperative of one's conditions was thus that one should have really, should have finely and (given one's scale) concisely treated one's subject, in spite of there being so much of the confounded irreducible quantity still to treat. If I spoke just now, however, of the "exasperated" charm of supreme difficulty, that is because the challenge of economic representation so easily becomes, in any of the arts, intensely interesting to meet. To put all that is possible of one's idea into a form and compass that will contain and express it only by delicate adjustments and an exquisite chemistry, so that there will at the end be neither a drop of one's liquor left nor a hair's breadth of the rim of one's glass to spare—every artist will remember how often that sort of necessity has carried with it its particular inspiration. Therein lies the secret of the appeal, to his mind, of the successfully *foreshortened* thing, where representation is arrived at, as I have already elsewhere had occasion to urge,[249] not by the addition of items (a light that has for its attendant shadow a possible dryness) but by the art of figuring synthetically, a compactness into which the imagination may cut thick, as into the rich density of wedding-cake. The moral of all which indeed, I fear, is, perhaps too trivially, but that the "thick," the false, the dissembling second half of the work before me, associated throughout with the effort to weight my dramatic values as heavily as might be, since they had to be so few, presents that effort as at the very last a quite convulsive, yet in its way highly agreeable, spasm. Of such mild prodigies is the "history" of any specific creative effort composed!

But I have got too much out of the "old" Kensington light of twenty years ago—a lingering oblique ray of which, to-day surely quite extinct, played for a benediction over my canvas. From the moment I made out, at my high-perched west window, my lucky title,[250] that is from the moment Miriam Rooth herself had given it me, so this young woman had given me with it her own position in the book, and so that in turn had given me my precious unity, to which no more than Miriam was either Nick Dormer or Peter Sherringham to be sacrificed. Much of the interest of the matter was immediately therefore in working out the detail of that unity and—always entrancing range of questions—the order, the reason, the relation, of presented aspects. With three *general* aspects, that of Miriam's case, that of Nick's and that of Sherringham's, there was work in plenty cut out; since happy as it might be to say "My several actions beautifully become one," the point of the affair would be in *showing* them beautifully become so—without which showing foul failure hovered and pounced. Well, the pleasure of handling an action (or, otherwise expressed, of a "story") is at the worst, for a storyteller, immense, and the interest of such a question as for example keeping Nick Dormer's story his and yet making it also and all effectively in a large part Peter Sherringham's, of keeping Sherringham's his and yet making it in its high degree his kinsman's too, and Miriam Rooth's into the bargain; just as Miriam Rooth's is by the same token quite operatively his and Nick's, and just as that of each of the young men, by an equal logic, very contributively hers—the interest of such a question, I say, is ever so considerably the interest of the system on which the whole thing is done. I see to-day that it was but half a system to say: "Oh Miriam, a case herself, is the *link* between the two other cases"; that device was to ask for as much help as it gave and to require a good deal more application than it announced on the surface. The sense of a system saves the painter from the baseness of the *arbitrary* stroke, the touch without its reason, but as payment for that service the process insists on being kept impeccably the right one.

These are intimate truths indeed, of which the charm mainly comes out but on experiment and in practice; yet I like to have it well before me here that, after all, "The Tragic Muse" makes it not easy to say which of the situations concerned in it predominates and rules. What has become in that imperfect order, accordingly, of the famous centre of one's subject? It is surely not in Nick's consciousness—since why, if it be, are we treated to such an intolerable dose of Sherringham's? It can't be in Sherringham's—we have for that altogether an excess of Nick's. How on the other hand can it be in Miriam's, given that we have no direct exhibition of hers whatever, that we get at it all inferentially and inductively, seeing it only through a more or less bewildered interpretation of it by others.[251] The emphasis is all on an absolutely objective Miriam, and, this affirmed, how—with such an amount of exposed subjectivity all round her—can so dense a medium be a centre? Such questions as those go straight—thanks to which they are, I profess, delightful; going straight they are of the sort that makes answers possible. Miriam *is* central then to analysis, in spite of being objective; central in virtue of the fact that the whole thing has visibly, from the first, to get itself done in dramatic, or at least in scenic conditions—though scenic conditions which are as near an approach to the dramatic as the novel may permit itself and which have this in common with the latter, that they move in the light of *alternation*.[252] This imposes a consistency other than that of the novel at its loosest, and, for one's subject, a different view and a different placing of the centre. The charm of the scenic consistency, the consistency of the multiplication of *aspects*, that of making them amusingly various, had haunted the author of "The Tragic Muse" from far back, and he was in due course to yield to it all luxuriously, too luxuriously perhaps, in "The Awkward Age," as will doubtless with the extension of these remarks be complacently shown.[253]

To put himself at any rate as much as possible under the protection of it had been ever his practice (he had notably done so in "The Princess Casamassima," so frankly panoramic and processional); and in what case could this protection have had more price than in the one before us? No character in a play (any play not a mere monologue) has, for the right expression of the thing, a *usurping* consciousness; the consciousness of others is exhibited exactly in the same way as that of the "hero"; the prodigious consciousness of Hamlet, the most capacious and most crowded, the moral presence the most asserted, in the whole range of fiction, only takes its turn with that of the other agents of the story,[254] no matter how occasional these may be. It is left in other words to answer for itself equally with theirs: wherefore (by a parity of reasoning if not of example) Miriam's might without inconsequence be placed on the same footing; and all in spite of the fact that the "moral presence" of each of the men most importantly concerned with her—or with the second of whom she at least is importantly concerned—*is* independently answered for. The idea of the book being, as I have said, a picture of some of the personal consequences of the art-appetite raised to intensity, swollen to voracity, the heavy emphasis falls where the symbol of some of the complications so begotten might be made (as I judged, heaven forgive me!) most "amusing": amusing I mean in the blest very modern sense.[255] I never "go behind" Miriam;[256] only poor Sherringham goes, a great deal, and Nick Dormer goes a little, and the author, while they so waste wonderment, goes behind *them:* but none the less she is as thoroughly symbolic, as functional, for illustration of the idea, as either of them, while her image had seemed susceptible of a livelier and "prettier" concretion. I had desired for her, I remember, all manageable vividness—so ineluctable had it long appeared to "do the actress," to touch the theatre, to meet that connexion somehow or other, in any free plunge of the speculative fork into the contemporary social salad.

The late R. L. Stevenson was to write to me,[257] I recall—and precisely on the occasion of "The Tragic Muse"—that he was at a loss to conceive how one could find an interest in anything so vulgar or pretend to gather fruit in so scrubby an orchard; but the view of a creature of the stage, the view of the "histrionic temperament,"[258] as suggestive much less, verily, in respect to the poor stage *per se* than in respect to "art" at large, affected me in spite of that as justly tenable. An objection of a more pointed order was forced upon me by an acute friend later on and in another connexion: the challenge of one's right, in any pretended show of social realities, to attach to the image of a "public character," a supposed particular celebrity, a range of interest, of intrinsic distinction, greater than any such display of importance on the part of eminent members of the class as we see them about us. There *was* a nice point if one would—yet only nice enough, after all, to be easily amusing. We shall deal with it later on, however, in a more urgent connexion.[259] What would have worried me much more had it dawned earlier is the light lately thrown by that admirable writer M. Anatole France on the question of any animated view of the histrionic temperament—a light that may well dazzle to distress any ingenuous worker in the same field. In those parts of his brief but inimitable *Histoire Comique* on which he is most to be congratulated—for there are some that prompt to reserves—he has "done the actress," as well as the actor, done above all the mountebank, the mummer and the *cabotin*,[260] and mixed them up with the queer theatric air, in a manner that practically warns all other hands off the material for ever. At the same time I think I saw Miriam, and without a sacrifice of truth, that is of the particular glow of verisimilitude I wished her most to benefit by, in a complexity of relations finer than any that appear possible for the gentry of M. Anatole France.

Her relation to Nick Dormer, for instance, was intended as a superior interest—that of being (while perfectly sincere, sincere for *her*, and therefore perfectly consonant with her impulse perpetually to perform and with her success in performing) the result of a touched imagination, a touched pride for "art," as well as of the charm cast on other sensibilities still. Dormer's relation to herself is a different matter, of which more presently; but the sympathy she, poor young woman, very generously and intelligently offers him where most people have so stinted it, is disclosed largely at the cost of her egotism and her personal pretensions, even though in fact determined by her sense of their together, Nick and she, postponing the "world" to their conception of other and finer decencies. Nick can't on the whole see—for I have represented him as in his day quite sufficiently troubled and anxious—why he should condemn to ugly feebleness his most prized faculty (most prized, at least, by himself) even in order to keep his seat in Parliament, to inherit Mr. Carteret's blessing and money, to gratify his mother and carry out the mission of his father, to marry Julia Dallow in fine, a beautiful imperative woman with a great many thousands a year. It all comes back in the last analysis to the individual vision of decency, the critical as well as the passionate judgement of it under sharp stress; and Nick's vision and judgement, all on the æsthetic ground, have beautifully coincided, to Miriam's imagination, with a now fully marked, an inspired and impenitent, choice of her own: so that, other considerations powerfully aiding indeed, she is ready to see their interest all splendidly as one. She is in the uplifted state to which sacrifices and submissions loom large, but loom so just because they must write sympathy, write passion, large. Her measure of what she would be capable of for him—capable, that is, of *not* asking of him—will depend on what he shall ask of *her*, but she has no fear of not being able to satisfy him, even to the point of "chucking" for him, if need be, that artistic identity of her own which she has begun to build up. It will all be to the glory therefore of their common infatuation with "art": she will doubtless be no less willing to serve his than she was eager to serve her own, purged now of the too great shrillness.

This puts her quite on a different level from that of the vivid monsters of M. France, whose artistic identity is the last thing *they* wish to chuck—their only dismissal is of all material and social overdraping. Nick Dormer in point of fact asks of Miriam nothing but that she shall remain "awfully interesting to paint"; but that is *his* relation, which, as I say, is quite a matter by itself. He at any rate, luckily for both of them it may be, doesn't put her to the test: he is so busy with his own case, busy with testing himself and feeling his reality. He has seen himself as giving up precious things for an object, and that object has somehow not been the young woman in question, nor anything very nearly like her. She on the other hand has asked everything of Peter Sherringham, who has asked everything of *her;* and it is in so doing that she has really most testified for art and invited him to testify. With his professed interest in the theatre—one of those deep subjections that, in men of "taste," the Comédie Française used in old days to conspire for[261] and some such odd and affecting examples of which were to be noted—he yet offers her his hand and an introduction to the very best society if she will leave the stage. The power—and her having the sense of the power—to "shine" in the world is his highest measure of her, the test applied by him to her beautiful human value; just as the manner in which she turns on him is the application of her own standard and touchstone. She is perfectly sure of her own; for—if there were nothing else, and there is much—she has tasted blood, so to speak, in the form of her so prompt and auspicious success with the public, leaving all probations behind (the whole of which, as the book gives it, is too rapid and sudden, though inevitably so: processes, periods, intervals, stages, degrees, connexions, may be easily enough and barely enough named, may be unconvincingly stated, in fiction, to the deep discredit of the writer, but it remains the very deuce[262] to *represent* them, especially represent them under strong compression and in brief and subordinate terms; and this even though the novelist who doesn't represent, and represent "all the time," is lost, exactly as much lost as the painter who, at his work and given his intention, doesn't paint "all the time").

Turn upon her friend at any rate Miriam does; and one of my main points is missed if it fails to appear that she does so with absolute sincerity and with the cold passion of the high critic who knows, on sight of them together, the more or less dazzling false from the comparatively grey-coloured true. Sherringham's whole profession has been that he rejoices in her as she is, and that the theatre, the organised theatre, will be, as Matthew Arnold was in those very days pronouncing it, irresistible;[263] and it is the promptness with which he sheds his pretended faith as soon as it feels in the air the breath of reality, as soon as it asks of him a proof or a sacrifice, it is this that excites her doubtless sufficiently arrogant scorn. Where is the virtue of his high interest if it has verily never *been* an interest to speak of and if all it has suddenly to suggest is that, in face of a serious call, it shall be unblushingly relinquished? If he and she together, and her great field and future, and the whole cause they had armed and declared for, have not been serious things they have been base make-believes and trivialities—which is what in fact the homage of society to art always turns out so soon as art presumes not to be vulgar and futile. It is immensely the fashion and immensely edifying to listen to, this homage, while it confines its attention to vanities and frauds; but it knows only terror, feels only horror, the moment that, instead of making all the concessions, art proceeds to ask for a few. Miriam is nothing if not strenuous, and evidently nothing if not "cheeky," where Sherringham is concerned at least: these, in the all-egotistical exhibition to which she is condemned, are the very elements of her figure and the very colours of her portrait. But she is mild and inconsequent for Nick Dormer (who demands of her so little); as if gravely and pityingly embracing the truth that *his* sacrifice, on the right side, is probably to have very little of her sort of recompense. I must have had it well before me that she was all aware of the small strain a great sacrifice to Nick would cost her—by reason of the strong effect on her of his own superior logic, in which the very intensity of concentration was so to find its account.

If the man, however, who holds her personally dear yet holds her extremely personal message to the world cheap, so the man capable of a consistency and, as she regards the matter, of an honesty so much higher than Sherringham's, virtually cares, "really" cares, no straw for his fellow struggler. If Nick Dormer attracts and all-indifferently holds her it is because, like herself and unlike Peter, he puts "art" first; but the most he thus does for her in the event is to let her see how she may enjoy, in intimacy, the rigour it has taught him and which he cultivates at her expense. This is the situation in which we leave her, though there would be more still to be said about the difference for her of the two relations—that to each of the men—could I fondly suppose as much of the interest of the book "left over" for the reader as for myself. Sherringham for instance offers Miriam marriage, ever so "handsomely"; but if nothing might lead me on further than the question of what it would have been open to us—us novelists, especially in the old days—to show, "serially," a young man in Nick Dormer's quite different position as offering or a young woman in Miriam's as taking, so for that very reason such an excursion is forbidden me. The trade of the stage-player, and above all of the actress, must have so many detestable sides for the person exercising it that we scarce imagine a full surrender to it without a full surrender, not less, to every immediate compensation, to every freedom and the largest ease within reach: which presentment of the possible case for Miriam would yet have been condemned—and on grounds both various and interesting to trace—to remain very imperfect.[264]

I feel moreover that I might still, with space, abound in remarks about Nick's character and Nick's crisis suggested to my present more reflective vision. It strikes me, alas, that he is not quite so interesting as he was fondly intended to be, and this in spite of the multiplication, within the picture, of his pains and penalties; so that while I turn this slight anomaly over I come upon a reason that affects me as singularly charming and touching and at which indeed I have already glanced. Any presentation of the artist *in triumph* must be flat in proportion as it really sticks to its subject—it can only smuggle in relief and variety. For, to put the matter in an image, all we then—in his triumph—see of the charm-compeller is the back he turns to us as he bends over his work.[265] "His" triumph, decently, is but the triumph of what he produces, and that is another affair. His romance is the romance he himself projects; he eats the cake of the very rarest privilege, the most luscious baked in the oven of the gods—therefore he mayn't "have" it, in the form of the privilege of the hero, at the same time.[266] The privilege of the hero—that is of the martyr or of the interesting and appealing and comparatively floundering *person*—places him in quite a different category, belongs to him only as to the artist deluded, diverted, frustrated or vanquished; when the "amateur" in him gains, for our admiration or compassion or whatever, all that the expert has to do without. Therefore I strove in vain, I feel, to embroil and adorn this young man on whom a hundred ingenious touches are thus lavished: he has insisted in the event on looking as simple and flat as some mere brass check or engraved number,[267] the symbol and guarantee of a stored treasure. The better part of him is locked too much away from us, and the part we see has to pass for—well, what it passes for, so lamentedly, among his friends and relatives. No, accordingly, Nick Dormer isn't "the best thing in the book,"[268] as I judge I imagined he would be, and it contains nothing better, I make out, than that preserved and achieved unity and quality of tone, a value in itself, which I referred to at the beginning of these remarks. What I mean by this is that the interest created, and the expression of that interest, are things kept, as to kind, genuine and true to themselves. The appeal, the fidelity to the prime motive, is, with no little art, strained clear (even as silver is polished) in a degree answering—at least by intention—to the air of beauty. There is an awkwardness again in having thus belatedly to point such features out; but in that wrought appearance of animation and harmony, that effect of free movement and yet of recurrent and insistent reference, "The Tragic Muse" has struck me again as conscious of a bright advantage.

PREFACE to *The Awkward Age* (*NYE* IX)

I RECALL with perfect ease the idea in which "The Awkward Age" had its origin, but re-perusal gives me pause in respect to naming it. This composition, as it stands, makes, to my vision—and will have made perhaps still more to that of its readers—so considerable a mass beside the germ sunk in it and still possibly distinguishable, that I am half-moved to leave my small secret undivulged. I shall encounter, I think, in the course of this copious commentary, no better example, and none on behalf of which I shall venture to invite more interest, of the quite incalculable tendency of a mere grain of subject-matter to expand and develop and cover the ground when conditions happen to favour it. I say all, surely, when I speak of the thing as planned, in perfect good faith, for brevity, for levity, for simplicity, for jocosity, in fine, and for an accommodating irony. I invoked, for my protection, the spirit of the lightest comedy, but "The Awkward Age" was to belong, in the event, to a group of productions, here re-introduced, which have in common, to their author's eyes, the endearing sign that they asserted in each case an unforeseen principle of growth.[269] They were projected as small things, yet had finally to be provided for as comparative monsters. That is my own title for them, though I should perhaps resent it if applied by another critic—above all in the case of the piece before us, the careful measure of which I have just freshly taken. The result of this consideration has been in the first place to render sharp for me again the interest of the whole process thus illustrated, and in the second quite to place me on unexpectedly good terms with the work itself. As I scan my list I encounter none the "history" of which embodies a greater number of curious truths—or of truths at least by which I find contemplation more enlivened. The thing done and dismissed has ever, at the best, for the ambitious workman, a trick of looking dead, if not buried,[270] so that he almost throbs with ecstasy when, on an anxious review, the flush of life reappears. It is verily on recognising that flush on a whole side of "The Awkward Age" that I brand it all, but ever so tenderly, as monstrous—which is but my way of noting the *quantity* of finish it stows away.[271] Since I speak so undauntedly, when need is, of the value of composition, I shall not beat about the bush to claim for these pages the maximum of that advantage. If such a feat be possible in this field as really taking a lesson from one's own adventure I feel I have now not failed of it—to so much more demonstration of my profit than I can hope to carry through do I find myself urged. Thus it is that, still with a remnant of self-respect, or at least of sanity, one may turn to complacency, one may linger with pride. Let my pride provoke a frown till I justify it; which—though with more matters to be noted here than I have room for—I shall accordingly proceed to do.

Yet I must first make a brave face, no doubt, and present in its native humility my scant but quite ponderable germ. The seed sprouted in that vast nursery of sharp appeals and concrete images which calls itself, for blest convenience, London; it fell even into the order of the minor "social phenomena" with which, as fruit for the observer, that mightiest of the trees of suggestion bristles. It was not, no doubt, a fine purple peach, but it might pass for a round ripe plum,[272] the note one had inevitably had to take of the difference made in certain friendly houses and for certain flourishing mothers by the sometimes dreaded, often delayed, but never fully arrested coming to the forefront of some vague slip of a daughter. For such mild revolutions as these not, to one's imagination, to remain mild one had had, I dare say, to be infinitely addicted to "noticing"; under the rule of that secret vice or that unfair advantage, at any rate, the "sitting downstairs," from a given date, of the merciless maiden previously perched aloft[273] could easily be felt as a crisis. This crisis, and the sense for it in those whom it most concerns, has to confess itself courageously the prime propulsive force of "The Awkward Age." Such a matter might well make a scant show for a "thick book,"[274] and no thick book, but just a quite charmingly thin one, was in fact originally dreamt of. For its proposed scale the little idea seemed happy—happy, that is, above all in having come very straight; but its proposed scale was the limit of a small square canvas. One had been present again and again at the exhibition I refer to—which is what I mean by the "coming straight" of this particular London impression; yet one was (and through fallibilities that after all had their sweetness, so that one would on the whole rather have kept them than parted with them) still capable of so false a measurement. When I think indeed of those of my many false measurements that have resulted, after much anguish, in decent symmetries,

I find the whole case, I profess, a theme for the philosopher. The little ideas one wouldn't have treated save for the design of keeping them small, the developed situations that one would never with malice prepense have undertaken, the long stories that had thoroughly meant to be short, the short subjects that had underhandedly plotted to be long, the hypocrisy of modest beginnings, the audacity of misplaced middles, the triumph of intentions never entertained—with these patches, as I look about, I see my experience paved: an experience to which nothing is wanting save, I confess, some grasp of its final lesson.

This lesson would, if operative, surely provide some law for the recognition, the determination in advance, of the just limits and the just extent of the situation, *any* situation, that appeals, and that yet, by the presumable, the helpful law of situations, must have its reserves as well as its promises. The storyteller considers it because it promises, and undertakes it, often, just because also making out, as he believes, where the promise conveniently drops. The promise, for instance, of the case I have just named, the case of the account to be taken, in a circle of free talk, of a new and innocent, a wholly unacclimatised presence, as to which such accommodations have never had to come up, might well have appeared as limited as it was lively; and if these pages were not before us to register my illusion I should never have made a braver claim for it. They themselves admonish me, however, in fifty interesting ways, and they especially emphasise that truth of the vanity of the *a priori* test of what an *idée-mère* may have to give.[275] The truth is that what a happy thought has to give depends immensely on the general turn of the mind capable of it, and on the fact that its loyal entertainer, cultivating fondly its possible relations and extensions, the bright efflorescence latent in it, but having to take other things in their order too, is terribly at the mercy of his mind. That organ has only to exhale, in its degree, a fostering tropic air in order to produce complications almost beyond reckoning. The trap laid for his superficial convenience resides in the fact that, though the relations of a human figure or a social occurrence are what make such objects interesting, they also make them, to the same tune, difficult to isolate, to surround with the sharp black line, to frame in the square, the circle,[276] the charming oval, that helps any arrangement of objects to become a picture. The storyteller has but to have been condemned by nature to a liberally amused and beguiled, a richly sophisticated, view of relations and a fine inquisitive speculative sense for them, to find himself at moments flounder in a deep warm jungle. These are the moments at which he recalls ruefully that the great merit of such and such a small case, the merit for his particular advised use, had been precisely in the smallness.

I may say at once that this had seemed to me, under the first flush of recognition, the good mark for the pretty notion of the "free circle" put about[277] by having, of a sudden, an ingenuous mind and a pair of limpid searching eyes to count with. Half the attraction was in the current actuality of the thing: repeatedly, right and left, as I have said, one had seen such a drama constituted, and always to the effect of proposing to the interested view one of those questions that are of the essence of drama: what will happen, who suffer, who not suffer, what turn be determined, what crisis created, what issue found? There had of course to be, as a basis, the free circle, but this was material of that admirable order with which the good London never leaves its true lover and believer long unprovided. One could count them on one's fingers (an abundant allowance), the liberal firesides beyond the wide glow of which, in a comparative dimness, female adolescence hovered and waited.[278] The wide glow was bright, was favourable to "real" talk, to play of mind,[279] to an explicit interest in life, a due demonstration of the interest by persons qualified to feel it: all of which meant frankness and ease, the perfection, almost, as it were, of intercourse, and a tone as far as possible removed from that of the nursery and the schoolroom—as far as possible removed even, no doubt, in its appealing "modernity,"[280] from that of supposedly privileged scenes of conversation twenty years ago. The charm was, with a hundred other things, in the freedom—the freedom menaced by the inevitable irruption of the ingenuous mind; whereby, if the freedom should be sacrificed, what would truly *become* of the charm? The charm might be figured as dear to members of the circle consciously contributing to it, but it was none the less true that some sacrifice in some quarter would have to be made,[281] and what meditator worth his salt could fail to hold his breath while waiting on the event? The ingenuous mind might, it was true, be suppressed altogether, the general disconcertment averted either by some master-stroke of diplomacy or some rude simplification; yet these were ugly matters, and in the examples before one's eyes nothing ugly, nothing harsh or crude, had flourished. A girl might be married off the day after her irruption, or better still the day before it, to remove her from the sphere of the play of mind; but these were exactly not crudities, and even then, at the worst, an interval had to be bridged. "The Awkward Age" is precisely a study of one of these curtailed or extended periods of tension and apprehension, an account of the manner in which the resented interference with ancient liberties[282] came to be in a particular instance dealt with.

I note once again that I had not escaped seeing it actually and traceably dealt with—after (I admit) a good deal of friendly suspense; also with the nature and degree of the "sacrifice" left very much to one's appreciation. In circles highly civilised the great things, the real things, the hard, the cruel and even the tender things, the true elements of any tension and true facts of any crisis, have ever, for the outsider's, for the critic's use, to be translated into terms—terms in the distinguished name of which, terms for the right employment of which, more than one situation of the type I glance at had struck me as all irresistibly appealing. There appeared in fact at moments no end to the things they said, the suggestions into which they flowered; one of these latter in especial arriving at the highest intensity. Putting vividly before one the perfect system on which the awkward age is handled in most other European societies, it threw again into relief the inveterate English trick of the so morally well-meant and so intellectually helpless compromise.[283] We live notoriously, as I suppose every age lives, in an "epoch of transition";[284] but it may still be said of the French for instance, I assume, that their social scheme absolutely provides against awkwardness. That is it would be, by this scheme, so infinitely awkward, so awkward beyond any patching-up, for the hovering female young to be conceived as present at "good" talk, that their presence is, theoretically at least, not permitted till their youth has been promptly corrected by marriage—in which case they have ceased to be merely young. The better the talk prevailing in any circle, accordingly, the more organised, the more complete, the element of precaution and exclusion. Talk—giving the term a wide application—is one thing, and a proper inexperience another; and it has never occurred to a logical people that the interest of the greater, the general, need be sacrificed to that of the less, the particular. Such sacrifices strike them as gratuitous and barbarous, as cruel above all to the social intelligence; also as perfectly preventable by wise arrangement. Nothing comes home more, on the other hand, to the observer of English manners than the very moderate degree in which wise arrangement, in the French sense of a scientific economy, has ever been invoked; a fact indeed largely explaining the great interest of their incoherence, their heterogeneity, their wild abundance. The French, all analytically, have conceived of fifty different proprieties, meeting fifty different cases, whereas the English mind, less intensely at work, has never conceived but of one—the grand propriety, for every case, it should in fairness be said, of just being English. As practice, however, has always to be a looser thing than theory, so no application of that rigour has been possible in the London world without a thousand departures from the grim ideal.

The American theory, if I may "drag it in," would be, I think, that talk should never become "better" than the female young, either actually or constructively present, are minded to allow it. *That* system involves as little compromise as the French; it has been absolutely simple, and the beauty of its success shines out in every record of our conditions of intercourse—premising always our "basic" assumption that the female young read the newspapers.[285] The English theory may be in itself almost as simple, but different and much more complex forces have ruled the application of it; so much does the goodness of talk depend on what there may be to talk about. There are more things in London, I think, than anywhere in the world; hence the charm of the dramatic struggle reflected in my book, the struggle somehow to fit propriety into a smooth general case which is really all the while bristling and crumbling into fierce particular ones. The circle surrounding Mrs. Brookenham, in my pages, is of course nothing if not a particular, even a "peculiar" one—and its rather vain effort (the vanity, the real inexpertness, being precisely part of my tale) is toward the courage of that condition. It has cropped up in a social order where individual appreciations of propriety have not been formally allowed for, in spite of their having very often quite rudely and violently and insolently, rather of course than insidiously, flourished; so that as the matter stands, rightly or wrongly, Nanda's retarded, but eventually none the less real, incorporation means virtually Nanda's exposure.[286] It means this, that is, and many things beside—means them for Nanda herself and, with a various intensity, for the other participants in the action; but what it particularly means, surely, is the failure of successful arrangement and the very moral, sharply pointed, of the fruits of compromise. It is compromise that has suffered her to be in question at all, and that has condemned the freedom of the circle to be self-conscious, compunctious, on the whole much more timid than brave—the consequent muddle, if the term be not too gross,[287] representing meanwhile a great inconvenience for life, but, as I found myself feeling, an immense promise, a much greater one than on the "foreign" showing, for the painted picture of life. Beyond which let me add that here immediately is a prime specimen of the way in which the obscurer, the lurking relations of a motive apparently simple, always in wait for their spring, may by seizing their chance for it send simplicity flying. Poor Nanda's little case, and her mother's, and Mr. Longdon's and Vanderbank's and Mitchy's, to say nothing of that of the others, has only to catch a reflected light from over the Channel in order to double at once its appeal to the imagination. (I am considering all these matters, I need scarce say, only as they are concerned with that faculty. With a relation *not* imaginative to his material the storyteller has nothing whatever to do.)

It exactly happened moreover that my own material here was to profit in a particular way by that extension of view. My idea was to be treated with light irony—it would be light and ironical or it would be nothing; so that I asked myself, naturally, what might be the least solemn form to give it, among recognised and familiar forms. The question thus at once arose: What form so familiar, so recognised among alert readers, as that in which the ingenious and inexhaustible, the charming philosophic "Gyp" casts most of her social studies?[288] Gyp had long struck me as mistress, in her levity, of one of the happiest of forms—the only objection to my use of which was a certain extraordinary benightedness on the part of the Anglo-Saxon reader. One had noted this reader as perverse and inconsequent in respect to the absorption of "dialogue"—observed the "public for fiction" consume it, in certain connexions, on the scale and with the smack of lips that mark the consumption of bread-and-jam by a children's school-feast, consume it even at the theatre, so far as our theatre ever vouchsafes it, and yet as flagrantly reject it when served, so to speak, *au naturel*. One had seen good solid slices of fiction, well endued, one might surely have thought, with this easiest of lubrications, deplored by editor and publisher as positively not, for the general gullet as known to *them*, made adequately "slick." "'Dialogue,' always 'dialogue'!"[289] I had seemed from far back to hear them mostly cry: "We can't have too much of it, we can't have enough of it, and no excess of it, in the form of no matter what savourless dilution, or what boneless dispersion, ever began to injure a book so much as even the very scantest claim put in for form and substance." This wisdom had always been in one's ears; but it had at the same time been equally in one's eyes that really constructive dialogue, dialogue organic and dramatic,[290] speaking for itself, representing and embodying substance and form, is among us an uncanny and abhorrent thing, not to be dealt with on any terms. A comedy or a tragedy may run for a thousand nights without prompting twenty persons in London or in New York to desire that view of its text which is so desired in Paris, as soon as a play begins to loom at all large, that the number of copies of the printed piece in circulation far exceeds at last the number of performances.[291] But as with the printed piece our own public, infatuated as it may be with the theatre, refuses all commerce—though indeed this can't but be, without cynicism, very much through the infirmity the piece, *if* printed, would reveal—so the same horror seems to attach to any typographic hint of the proscribed playbook or any insidious plea for it. The immense oddity resides in the almost exclusively typographic order of the offence. An English, an American Gyp would typographically offend, and that would be the end of her. *There* gloomed at me my warning, as well as shone at me my provocation, in respect to the example of this delightful writer. I might emulate her, since I presumptuously would, but dishonour would await me if, proposing to treat the different faces of my subject in the most completely instituted colloquial form, I should evoke the figure and affirm the presence of participants by the repeated and prefixed name rather than by the recurrent and *a*ffixed "said he" and "said she." All I have space to go into here—much as the funny fact I refer to might seem to invite us to dance hand in hand round it[292]—is that I was at any rate duly admonished, that I took my measures accordingly, and that the manner in which I took them has lived again for me ever so arrestingly, so amusingly, on re-examination of the book.

But that I did, positively and seriously—ah so seriously!—emulate the levity of Gyp and, by the same token, of that hardiest of flowers fostered in her school, M. Henri Lavedan,[293] is a contribution to the history of "The Awkward Age" that I shall obviously have had to brace myself in order to make. Vivid enough to me the expression of face of any kindest of critics, even, moved to declare that he would never in the least have suspected it.[294] Let me say at once, in extenuation of the too respectful distance at which I may thus have appeared to follow my model, that my first care *had* to be the covering of my tracks—lest I truly should be caught in the act of arranging, of organising dialogue to "speak for itself." What I now see to have happened is that I organised and arranged but too well—too well, I mean, for any betrayal of the Gyp taint, however faded and feeble. The trouble appears to have been that while I on the one hand exorcised the baleful association, I succeeded in rousing on nobody's part a sense of any other association whatever, or of my having cast myself into any conceivable or calculable form. My private inspiration had been in the Gyp plan (artfully dissimulated, for dear life, and applied with the very subtlest consistency, but none the less kept in secret view); yet I was to fail to make out in the event that the book succeeded in producing the impression of *any* plan on any person. No hint of that sort of success, or of any critical perception at all in relation to the business, has ever come my way;[295] in spite of which when I speak, as just above, of what was to "happen" under the law of my ingenious labour, I fairly lose myself in the vision of a hundred bright phenomena. Some of these incidents I must treat myself to naming, for they are among the best I shall have on any occasion to retail. But I must first give the measure of the degree in which they were mere matters of the study. This composition had originally appeared in "Harper's Weekly" during the autumn of 1898 and the first weeks of the winter, and the volume containing it was published that spring. I had meanwhile been absent from England,[296] and it was not till my return, some time later, that I had from my publisher any news of our venture. But the news then met at a stroke all my curiosity: "I'm sorry to say the book has done nothing to speak of; I've never in all my experience seen one treated with more general and complete disrespect." There was thus to be nothing left me for fond subsequent reference—of which I doubtless give even now so adequate an illustration—save the rich reward of the singular interest attaching to the very intimacies of the effort.

It comes back to me, the whole "job," as wonderfully amusing and delightfully difficult from the first; since amusement deeply abides, I think, in any artistic attempt the basis and groundwork of which are conscious of a particular firmness. On that hard fine floor the element of execution feels it may more or less confidently *dance*;[297] in which case puzzling questions, sharp obstacles, dangers of detail, may come up for it by the dozen without breaking its heart or shaking its nerve. It is the difficulty produced by the loose foundation or the vague scheme that breaks the heart—when a luckless fatuity has over-persuaded an author of the "saving" virtue of treatment.[298] Being "treated" is never, in a workable idea, a mere passive condition, and I hold no subject ever susceptible of help that isn't, like the embarrassed man of our proverbial wisdom, first of all able to help itself.[299] I was thus to have here an envious glimpse, in carrying my design through, of that artistic rage and that artistic felicity which I have ever supposed to be intensest and highest, the confidence of the dramatist strong in the sense of his postulate. The dramatist has verily to *build*, is committed to architecture, to construction at any cost; to driving in deep his vertical supports and laying across and firmly fixing his horizontal, his resting pieces—at the risk of no matter what vibration from the tap of his master-hammer.[300] This makes the active value of his basis immense, enabling him, with his flanks protected, to advance undistractedly, even if not at all carelessly, into the comparative fairy-land of the mere minor anxiety. In other words his scheme *holds*, and as he feels this in spite of noted strains and under repeated tests, so he keeps his face to the day. I rejoiced, by that same token, to feel *my* scheme hold, and even a little ruefully watched it give me much more than I had ventured to hope. For I promptly found my conceived arrangement of my material open the door wide to ingenuity.[301] I remember that in sketching my project for the conductors of the periodical I have named I drew on a sheet of paper—and possibly with an effect of the cabalistic, it now comes over me, that even anxious amplification may have but vainly attenuated—the neat figure of a circle consisting of a number of small rounds disposed at equal distance about a central object.[302] The central object was my situation, my subject in itself, to which the thing would owe its title, and the small rounds represented so many distinct lamps, as I liked to call them,[303] the function of each of which would be to light with all due intensity one of its aspects. I had divided it, didn't they see? into aspects—uncanny as the little term might sound (though not for a moment did I suggest we should use it for the public), and by that sign we would conquer.[304]

They "saw," all genially and generously—for I must add that I had made, to the best of my recollection, no morbid scruple of not blabbing about Gyp and her strange incitement. I the more boldly held my tongue over this that the more I, by my intelligence, lived in my arrangement and moved about in it, the more I sank into satisfaction. It was clearly to work to a charm and, during this process—by calling at every step for an exquisite management—"to haunt, to startle and waylay."[305] Each of my "lamps" would be the light of a single "social occasion" in the history and intercourse of the characters concerned, and would bring out to the full the latent colour of the scene in question and cause it to illustrate, to the last drop, its bearing on my theme. I revelled in this notion of the Occasion as a thing by itself, really and completely a scenic thing, and could scarce name it, while crouching amid the thick arcana of my plan, with a large enough O. The beauty of the conception was in this approximation of the respective divisions of my form to the successive Acts of a Play[306]—as to which it was more than ever a case for charmed capitals. The divine distinction of the act of a play—and a greater than any other it easily succeeds in arriving at—was, I reasoned, in its special, its guarded objectivity. This objectivity, in turn, when achieving its ideal, came from the imposed absence of that "going behind," to compass explanations and amplifications, to drag out odds and ends from the "mere" storyteller's great property-shop of aids to illusion: a resource under denial of which it was equally perplexing and delightful, for a change, to proceed. Everything, for that matter, becomes interesting from the moment it has closely to consider, for full effect positively to bestride, the law of its kind. "Kinds" are the very life of literature, and truth and strength come from the complete recognition of them, from abounding to the utmost in their respective senses and sinking deep into their consistency. I myself have scarcely to plead the cause of "going behind,"[307] which is right and beautiful and fruitful in its place and order; but as the confusion of kinds is the inelegance of letters and the stultification of values, so to renounce that line utterly and do something quite different instead may become in another connexion the true course and the vehicle of effect. Something in the very nature, in the fine rigour, of this special sacrifice (which is capable of affecting the form-lover, I think, as really more of a projected form than any other) lends it moreover a coercive charm; a charm that grows in proportion as the appeal to it tests and stretches and strains it, puts it powerfully to the touch. To make the presented occasion tell all its story itself, remain shut up in its own presence and yet on that patch of staked-out ground become thoroughly interesting and remain thoroughly clear, is a process not remarkable, no doubt, so long as a very light weight is laid on it, but difficult enough to challenge and inspire great adroitness so soon as the elements to be dealt with begin at all to "size up."[308]

The disdainers of the contemporary drama deny, obviously, with all promptness, that the matter to be expressed by its means—richly and successfully expressed that is—*can* loom with any largeness; since from the moment it does one of the conditions breaks down. The process simply collapses under pressure, they contend, proves its weakness as quickly as the office laid on it ceases to be simple. "Remember," they say to the dramatist, "that you have to be, supremely, three things: you have to be true to your form, you have to be interesting, you have to be clear. You have in other words to prove yourself adequate to taking a heavy weight. But we defy you really to conform to your conditions with any but a light one. Make the thing you have to convey, make the picture you have to paint, at all rich and complex, and you cease to be clear. Remain clear—and with the clearness required by the infantine intelligence of any public consenting to see a play—and what becomes of the 'importance' of your subject? If it's important by any other critical measure than the little foot-rule the 'produced' piece has to conform to,[309] it is predestined to be a muddle. When it has escaped being a muddle the note it has succeeded in striking at the furthest will be recognised as one of those that are called high but by the courtesy, by the intellectual provinciality, of theatrical criticism, which, as we can see for ourselves any morning, is—well, an abyss even deeper than the theatre itself. Don't attempt to crush us with Dumas and Ibsen, for such values are from any informed and enlightened point of view, that is measured by other high values, literary, critical, philosophic, of the most moderate order. Ibsen and Dumas are precisely cases of men, men in their degree, in their poor theatrical straight-jacket, speculative, who have *had* to renounce the finer thing for the coarser, the thick, in short, for the thin and the curious for the self-evident.[310] What earthly intellectual distinction, what 'prestige' of achievement, would have attached to the substance of such things as 'Denise,' as 'Monsieur Alphonse,' as 'Francillon'[311] (and we take the Dumas of the supposedly subtler period) in any other form? What virtues of the same order would have attached to 'The Pillars of Society,' to 'An Enemy of the People,' to 'Ghosts,' to 'Rosmersholm' (or taking also Ibsen's 'subtler period') to 'John Gabriel Borkmann,' to 'The Master-Builder'? Ibsen is in fact wonderfully a case in point, since from the moment he's clear, from the moment he's 'amusing,' it's on the footing of a thesis as simple and superficial as that of 'A Doll's House'—while from the moment he's by apparent intention comprehensive and searching it's on the footing of an effect as confused and obscure as 'The Wild Duck.'³¹² From which you easily see *all* the conditions can't be met. The dramatist has to choose but those he's most capable of, and by that choice he's known."

So the objector concludes, and never surely without great profit from his having been "drawn." His apparent triumph—if it be even apparent—still leaves, it will be noted, convenient cover for retort in the riddled face of the opposite stronghold. The last word in these cases is for nobody who can't pretend to an *absolute* test. The terms here used, obviously, are matters of appreciation, and there is no short cut to proof (luckily for us all round) either that "Monsieur Alphonse" develops itself on the highest plane of irony or that "Ghosts" simplifies almost to excruciation. If "John Gabriel Borkmann" is but a pennyworth of effect as to a character we can imagine much more amply presented, and if "Hedda Gabler" makes an appeal enfeebled by remarkable vagueness, there is by the nature of the case no catching the convinced, or call him the deluded, spectator or reader in the act of a mistake. He is to be caught at the worst in the act of attention, of the very greatest attention, and that is all, as a precious preliminary at least, that the playwright asks of him, besides being all the very divinest poet can get.³¹³ I remember rejoicing as much to remark this, after getting launched in "The Awkward Age," as if I were in fact constructing a play; just as I may doubtless appear now not less anxious to keep the philosophy of the dramatist's course before me than if I belonged to his order. I felt, certainly, the support he feels, I participated in his technical amusement, I tasted to the full the bitter-sweetness of his draught—the beauty and the difficulty (to harp again on that string)³¹⁴ of escaping poverty *even though* the references in one's action can only be, with intensity, to each other, to things exactly on the same plane of exhibition with themselves.³¹⁵ Exhibition may mean in a "story" twenty different ways, fifty excursions, alternatives, excrescences, and the novel, as largely practised in English, is the perfect paradise of the loose end. The play consents to the logic of but one way, mathematically right, and with the loose end as gross an impertinence on its surface, and as grave a dishonour, as the dangle of a snippet of silk or wool on the right side of a tapestry.³¹⁶ We are shut up wholly to cross-relations, relations all within the action itself; no part of which is related to anything but some other part—save of course by the relation of the total to life. And, after invoking the protection of Gyp, I saw the point of my game all in the problem of keeping these conditioned relations crystalline at the same time that I should, in emulation of life, consent to their being numerous and fine and characteristic of the London world (as the London world was in this quarter and that to be deciphered). All of which was to make in the event for complications.

I see now of course how far, with my complications, I got away from Gyp; but I see to-day so much else too that this particular deflexion from simplicity makes scarce a figure among the others; after having once served its purpose, I mean, of lighting my original imitative innocence. For I recognise in especial, with a waking vibration of that interest in which, as I say, the plan of the book is embalmed for me, that my subject was probably condemned in advance to appreciable, or more exactly perhaps to almost preposterously appreciative, over-treatment. It places itself for me thus in a group of small productions exhibiting this perversity, representations of conceived cases in which my process has been to pump the case gaspingly dry, dry not only of superfluous moisture, but absolutely (for I have encountered the charge) of breatheable air.[317] I may note, in fine, that coming back to the pages before us with a strong impression of their recording, to my shame, that disaster, even to the extent of its disqualifying them for decent reappearance, I have found the adventure taking, to my relief, quite another turn, and have lost myself in the wonder of what "over-treatment" may, in the detail of its desperate ingenuity, consist of. The revived interest I speak of has been therefore that of following critically, from page to page, even as the red Indian tracks in the forest the pale-face,[318] the footsteps of the systematic loyalty I was able to achieve. The amusement of this *constatation* is, as I have hinted, in the detail of the matter, and the detail is so dense, the texture of the figured and smoothed tapestry so close, that the genius of Gyp herself, muse of general looseness, would certainly, once warned, have uttered the first disavowal of my homage. But what has occurred meanwhile is that this high consistency has itself, so to speak, constituted an exhibition, and that an important artistic truth has seemed to me thereby lighted. We brushed against that truth just now in our glance at the denial of expansibility to any idea the mould of the "stage-play" may hope to express without cracking and bursting; and we bear in mind at the same time that the picture of Nanda Brookenham's situation, though perhaps seeming to a careless eye so to wander and sprawl, yet presents itself on absolutely scenic lines, and that each of these scenes in itself, and each as related to each and to all of its companions, abides without a moment's deflexion by the principle of the stage-play.[319]

In doing this then it does more—it helps us ever so happily to see the grave distinction between substance and form in a really wrought work of art signally break down.[320] I hold it impossible to say, before "The Awkward Age," where one of these elements ends and the other begins: I have been unable at least myself, on re-examination, to mark any such joint or seam, to see the two *discharged* offices as separate. They are separate before the fact, but the sacrament of execution indissolubly marries them, and the marriage, like any other marriage, has only to be a "true" one for the scandal of a breach not to show.[321] The thing "done," artistically, is a fusion, or it has not *been* done—in which case of course the artist may be, and all deservedly, pelted with any fragment of his botch the critic shall choose to pick up. But his ground once conquered, in this particular field, he knows nothing of fragments and may say in all security: "Detach one if you can. You can analyse in *your* way, oh yes—to relate, to report, to explain; but you can't disintegrate my synthesis; you can't resolve the elements of my whole into different responsible agents or find your way at all (for your own fell purpose). My mixture has only to be perfect literally to bewilder you—you are lost in the tangle of the forest. Prove this value, this effect, in the air of the whole result, to be of my subject, and that other value, other effect, to be of my treatment, prove that I haven't so shaken them together as the conjurer I profess to be *must* consummately shake, and I consent but to parade as before a booth at the fair." The exemplary closeness of "The Awkward Age" even affects me, on re-perusal, I confess, as treasure quite instinctively and foreseeingly laid up against my present opportunity for these remarks. I have been positively struck by the quantity of meaning and the number of intentions, the extent of *ground for interest*, as I may call it, that I have succeeded in working scenically, yet without loss of sharpness, clearness or "atmosphere," into each of my illuminating Occasions—where, at certain junctures, the due preservation of all these values took, in the familiar phrase, a good deal of doing.

I should have liked just here to re-examine with the reader some of the positively most artful passages I have in mind[322]—such as the hour of

Mr. Longdon's beautiful and, as it were, mystic attempt at a compact with Vanderbank, late at night, in the billiard-room of the country-house at which they are staying; such as the other nocturnal passage, under Mr. Longdon's roof, between Vanderbank and Mitchy, where the conduct of so much fine meaning, so many flares of the exhibitory torch through the labyrinth of mere immediate appearances, mere familiar allusions, is successfully and safely effected; such as the whole array of the terms of presentation that are made to serve, all systematically, yet without a gap anywhere, for the presentation, throughout, of a Mitchy "subtle" no less than concrete and concrete no less than deprived of that officious explanation which we know as "going behind"; such as, briefly, the general service of co-ordination and vivification rendered, on lines of ferocious, of really quite heroic compression, by the picture of the assembled group at Mrs. Grendon's, where the "cross-references" of the action are as thick as the green leaves of a garden, but none the less, as they have scenically to be, counted and disposed, weighted with responsibility. Were I minded to use in this connexion a "loud" word—and the critic in general hates loud words as a man of taste may hate loud colours[323]—I should speak of the composition of the chapters entitled "Tishy Grendon," with all the pieces of the game on the table together and each unconfusedly and contributively placed, as triumphantly scientific. I must properly remind myself, rather, that the better lesson of my retrospect would seem to be really a supreme revision of the question of what it may be for a subject to suffer, to call it suffering, by over-treatment. Bowed down so long by the inference that its product had in this case proved such a betrayal, my artistic conscience meets the relief of having to recognise truly here no traces of suffering. The thing carries itself to my maturer and gratified sense as with every symptom of soundness, an insolence of health and joy. And from this precisely I deduce my moral; which is to the effect that, since our only way, in general, of knowing that we have had too much of anything is by *feeling* that too much: so, by the same token, when we don't feel the excess (and I am contending, mind, that in "The Awkward Age" the multiplicity yields to the order) how do we know that the measure not recorded, the notch not reached, does represent adequacy or satiety? The mere feeling helps us for certain degrees of congestion, but for exact science, that is for the criticism of "fine" art, we want the notation. The notation, however, is what we lack, and the verdict of the mere feeling is liable to fluctuate. In other words an imputed defect is never, at the worst, disengageable, or other than matter for appreciation—to come back to my claim for that felicity of the dramatist's case that his synthetic "whole" *is* his form, the only one we have to do with. I like to profit in his company by the fact that if our art has certainly, for the impression it produces, to defer to the rise and fall, in the critical temperature, of the telltale mercury, it still hasn't to reckon with the engraved thermometer-face.

PREFACE to *The Spoils of Poynton, A London Life, The Chaperon* (NYE X)

It was years ago, I remember, one Christmas Eve when I was dining with friends:[324] a lady beside me made in the course of talk one of those allusions that I have always found myself recognising on the spot as "germs." The germ, wherever gathered, has ever been for me the germ of a "story," and most of the stories straining to shape under my hand have sprung from a single small seed, a seed as minute and wind-blown as that casual hint for "The Spoils of Poynton" dropped unwittingly by my neighbour, a mere floating particle in the stream of talk. What above all comes back to me with this reminiscence is the sense of the inveterate minuteness, on such happy occasions, of the precious particle—reduced, that is, to its mere fruitful essence. Such is the interesting truth about the stray suggestion, the wandering word, the vague echo, at touch of which the novelist's imagination winces as at the prick of some sharp point: its virtue is all in its needle-like quality, the power to penetrate as finely as possible. This fineness it is that communicates the virus of suggestion,[325] anything more than the minimum of which spoils the operation. If one is given a hint at all designedly one is sure to be given too much; one's subject is in the merest grain, the speck of truth, of beauty, of reality, scarce visible to the common eye—since, I firmly hold, a good eye for a subject is anything but usual. Strange and attaching, certainly, the consistency with which the first thing to be done for the communicated and seized idea is to reduce almost to nought the form, the air as of a mere disjoined and lacerated lump of life, in which we may have happened to meet it. Life being all inclusion and confusion, and art being all discrimination and selection,[326] the latter, in search of the hard latent *value* with which alone it is concerned, sniffs round the mass as instinctively and unerringly as a dog suspicious of some buried bone. The difference here, however, is that, while the dog desires his bone but to destroy it, the artist finds in *his* tiny nugget, washed free of awkward accretions and hammered into a sacred hardness, the very stuff for a clear affirmation, the happiest chance for the indestructible. It at the same time amuses him again and again to note how, beyond the first step of the actual case, the case that constitutes for him his germ, his vital particle, his grain of gold, life persistently blunders and deviates,[327] loses herself in the sand. The reason is of course that life has no direct sense whatever for the subject and is capable, luckily for us, of nothing but splendid waste. Hence the opportunity for the sublime economy of art, which rescues, which saves, and hoards and "banks," investing and reinvesting these fruits of toil in wondrous useful "works" and thus making up for us, desperate spendthrifts that we all naturally are, the most princely of incomes. It is the subtle secrets of that system, however, that are meanwhile the charming study, with an endless attraction, above all, in the question—endlessly baffling indeed—of the method at the heart of the madness;[328] the madness, I mean, of a zeal, among the reflective sort, so disinterested. If life, presenting us the germ, and left merely to herself in such a business, gives the case away, almost always, before we can stop her, what are the signs for our guidance, what the primary laws for a saving selection, how do we know when and where to intervene, where do we place the beginnings of the wrong or the right deviation? Such would be the elements of an enquiry upon which, I hasten to say, it is quite forbidden me here to embark: I but glance at them in evidence of the rich pasture that at every turn surrounds the ruminant critic. The answer may be after all that mysteries here elude us, that general considerations fail or mislead, and that even the fondest of artists need ask no wider range than the logic of the particular case. The particular case, or in other words his relation to a given subject, once the relation is established, forms in itself a little world of exercise and agitation. Let him hold himself perhaps supremely fortunate if he can meet half the questions with which that air alone may swarm.

So it was, at any rate, that when my amiable friend, on the Christmas Eve, before the table that glowed safe and fair through the brown London night, spoke of such an odd matter as that a good lady in the north, always well looked on, was at daggers drawn with her only son, ever hitherto exemplary, over the ownership of the valuable furniture of a fine old house just accruing to the young man by his father's death,[329] I instantly became aware, with my "sense for the subject," of the prick of inoculation; the *whole* of the virus, as I have called it, being infused by that single touch. There had been but ten words, yet I had recognised in them, as in a flash, all the possibilities of the little drama of my "Spoils," which glimmered then and there into life; so that when in the next breath I began to hear of action taken, on the beautiful ground, by our engaged adversaries, tipped each, from that instant, with the light of the highest distinction, I saw clumsy Life again at her stupid work.[330] For the action taken, and on which my friend, as I knew she would, had already begun all complacently and benightedly further to report, I had absolutely, and could have, no scrap of use; one had been so perfectly qualified to say in advance: "It's the perfect little workable thing, but she'll strangle it in the cradle, even while she pretends, all so cheeringly, to rock it;[331] wherefore I'll stay her hand while yet there's time." I didn't, of course, stay her hand—there never *is* in such cases "time";[332] and I had once more the full demonstration of the fatal futility of Fact. The turn taken by the excellent situation—excellent, for development, if arrested in the right place, that is in the germ—had the full measure of the classic ineptitude; to which with the full measure of the artistic irony one could once more, and for the thousandth time, but take off one's hat. It was not, however, that this in the least mattered, once the seed had been transplanted to richer soil; and I dwell on that almost inveterate redundancy of the wrong, as opposed to the ideal right, in any free flowering of the actual, by reason only of its approach to calculable regularity.

If there was nothing regular meanwhile, nothing more so than the habit of vigilance, in my quickly feeling where interest would really lie, so I could none the less acknowledge afresh that these small private cheers of recognition made the spirit easy and the temper bland for the confused whole. I "took" in fine, on the spot, to the rich bare little fact[333] of the two related figures, embroiled perhaps all so sordidly; and for reasons of which I could most probably have given at the moment no decent account. Had I been asked why they were, in that stark nudity, to say nothing of that ugliness of attitude, "interesting," I fear I could have said nothing more to the point, even to my own questioning spirit, than "Well, you'll see!" By which of course I should have meant "Well, *I* shall see"—confident meanwhile (as against the appearance or the imputation of poor taste) that interest would spring as soon as one should begin really to see *anything*. That points, I think, to a large part of the very source of interest for the artist: it resides in the strong consciousness of his seeing all for himself. He has to borrow his motive, which is certainly half the battle; and this motive is his ground, his site and his foundation. But after that he only lends and gives, only builds and piles high, lays together the blocks quarried in the deeps of his imagination and on his personal premises. He thus remains all the while in intimate commerce with his motive, and can say to himself—what really more than anything else inflames and sustains him—that he alone has the *secret* of the particular case, he alone can measure the truth of the direction to be taken by his developed data. There can be for him, evidently, only one logic for these things; there can be for him only one truth and one direction—the quarter in which his subject most completely expresses itself. The careful ascertainment of how it shall do so, and the art of guiding it with consequent authority—since this sense of "authority" is for the master-builder the treasure of treasures, or at least the joy of joys—renews in the modern alchemist something like the old dream of the secret of life.[334]

Extravagant as the mere statement sounds, one seemed accordingly to handle the secret of life in drawing the positive right truth out of the so easy muddle of wrong truths in which the interesting possibilities of that "row," so to call it, between mother and son over their household gods[335] might have been stifled. I find it odd to consider, as I thus revert, that I could have had none but the most general warrant for "seeing anything in it," as the phrase would have been; that I couldn't in the least, on the spot, as I have already hinted, have justified my faith. One thing was "in it," in the sordid situation, on the first blush,[336] and one thing only—though this, in its limited way, no doubt, a curious enough value: the sharp light it might project on that most modern of our current passions, the fierce appetite for the upholsterer's and joiner's and brazier's work, the chairs and tables, the cabinets and presses, the material odds and ends, of the more labouring ages. A lively mark of our manners indeed the diffusion of this curiosity and this avidity,[337] and full of suggestion, clearly, as to their possible influence on other passions and other relations. On the face of it the "things" themselves would form the very centre of such a crisis; these grouped objects, all conscious of their eminence and their price, would enjoy, in any picture of a conflict, the heroic importance. They would have to be presented, they would have to be painted—arduous and desperate thought; something would have to be done for them not too ignobly unlike the great array in which Balzac, say, would have marshalled them:[338] *that* amount of workable interest at least would evidently be "in it."

It would be wrapped in the silver tissue of some such conviction, at any rate, that I must have laid away my prime impression[339] for a rest not disturbed till long afterwards, till the year 1896, I make out, when there arose a question of my contributing three "short stories" to "The Atlantic Monthly";[340] or supplying rather perhaps a third to complete a trio two members of which had appeared. The echo of the situation mentioned to me at our Christmas Eve dinner awoke again, I recall, at that touch—I recall, no doubt, with true humility, in view of my renewed mismeasurement of my charge. Painfully associated for me had "The Spoils of Poynton" remained, until recent re-perusal, with the awkward consequence of that fond error. The subject had emerged from cool reclusion all suffused with a flush of meaning; thanks to which irresistible air, as I could but plead in the event, I found myself—as against a mere commercial austerity—beguiled and led on. The thing had "come," the flower of conception had bloomed— all in the happy dusk of indifference and neglect; yet, strongly and frankly as it might now appeal, my idea wouldn't surely overstrain a *natural* brevity. A story that couldn't possibly be long would have inevitably to be "short," and out of the depths of that delusion it accordingly began to struggle. To my own view, after the "first number," this composition (which in the magazine bore another title)[341] conformed but to its nature, which was not to transcend a modest amplitude; but, dispatched in instalments, it felt itself eyed, from month to month, I seem to remember, with an editorial ruefulness excellently well founded—from the moment such differences of sense could exist, that is, as to the short and the long.[342] The sole impression it made, I woefully gathered, was that of length, and it has till lately, as I say, been present to me but as the poor little "long" thing.

It began to appear in April 1896, and, as is apt blessedly to occur for me throughout this process of revision, the old, the shrunken concomitants muster again as I turn the pages. They lurk between the lines; these serve for them as the barred seraglio-windows behind which, to the outsider in the glare of the Eastern street,[343] forms indistinguishable seem to move and peer; "association" in fine bears upon them with its infinite magic. Peering through the lattice from without inward I recapture a cottage on a cliff-side,[344] to which, at the earliest approach of the summer-time, redoubtable in London through the luxuriance of still other than "natural" forces, I had betaken myself to finish a book in quiet and to begin another in fear. The cottage was, in its kind, perfection; mainly by reason of a small paved terrace which, curving forward from the cliff-edge like the prow of a ship, overhung a view[345] as level, as purple, as full of rich change, as the expanse of the sea. The horizon was in fact a band of sea; a small red-roofed town, of great antiquity, perched on its sea-rock,[346] clustered within the picture off to the right; while above one's head rustled a dense summer shade, that of a trained and arching ash, rising from the middle of the terrace, brushing the parapet with a heavy fringe and covering the place like a vast umbrella. Beneath this umbrella and really under exquisite protection "The Spoils of Poynton" managed more or less symmetrically to grow.

I recall that I was committed to begin, the day I finished it, short of dire penalties, "The Other House";[347] with which work, however, of whatever high profit the considerations springing from it might be too, we have nothing to do here—and to the felt jealousy of which, as that of a grudging neighbour, I allude only for sweet recovery of the fact, mainly interesting to myself I admit, that the rhythm of the earlier book shows no flurry of hand. I "liked" it—the earlier book: I venture now, after years, to welcome the sense of that amenity as well; so immensely refreshing is it to be moved, in any case, toward these retrospective simplicities. Painters and writers, I gather, are, when easily accessible to such appeals, frequently questioned as to those of their productions they may most have delighted in; but the profession of delight has always struck me as the last to consort, for the artist, with any candid account of his troubled effort—ever the sum, for the most part, of so many lapses and compromises, simplifications and surrenders. Which is the work in which he hasn't surrendered, under dire difficulty, the best thing he meant to have kept? In which indeed, before the dreadful *done*, doesn't he ask himself what has become of the thing all for the sweet sake of which it was to proceed to that extremity? Preference and complacency, on these terms, riot in general as they best may; not disputing, however, a grain of which weighty truth, I still make out, between my reconsidered lines, as it were, that I must—my opera-box of a terrace and my great green umbrella indeed aiding—have assisted at the growth and predominance of Fleda Vetch.

For something like Fleda Vetch had surely been latent in one's first apprehension of the theme; it wanted, for treatment, a centre, and, the most obvious centre being "barred," this image, while I still wondered, had, with all the assurance in the world, sprung up in its place. The real centre, as I say, the citadel of the interest, with the fight waged round it, would have been the felt beauty and value of the prize of battle, the Things, always the splendid Things, placed in the middle light, figured and constituted, with each identity made vivid, each character discriminated, and their common consciousness of their great dramatic part established. The rendered tribute of these honours, however, no vigilant editor, as I have intimated, could be conceived as allowing room for; since, by so much as the general glittering presence should spread, by so much as it should suggest the gleam of brazen idols and precious metals and inserted gems in the tempered light of some arching place of worship, by just so much would the muse of "dialogue," most usurping influence of all the romancingly invoked, be routed without ceremony, to lay her grievance at the feet of her gods. The spoils of Poynton were not directly articulate, and though they might have, and constantly did have, wondrous things to say, their message fostered about them a certain hush of cheaper sound—as a consequence of which, in fine, they would have been costly to keep up. In this manner Fleda Vetch, maintainable at less expense[348]—though even she, I make out, less expert in spreading chatter thin than the readers of romance mainly like their heroines to-day—marked her place in my foreground at one ingratiating stroke. She planted herself centrally, and the stroke, as I call it, the demonstration after which she couldn't be gainsaid, was the simple act of letting it be seen she had character.

For somehow—that was the way interest broke out, once the germ had been transferred to the sunny south window-sill of one's fonder attention—character, the question of what my agitated friends should individually, and all intimately and at the core, show themselves, would unmistakeably be the key to my modest drama, and would indeed alone make a drama of any sort possible. Yes, it is a story of cabinets and chairs and tables; they formed the bone of contention, but what would merely "become" of them, magnificently passive, seemed to represent a comparatively vulgar issue. The passions, the faculties, the forces their beauty would, like that of antique Helen of Troy, set in motion,[349] was what, as a painter, one had really wanted of them, was the power in them that one had from the first appreciated. Emphatically, by that truth, there would have to be moral developments—dreadful as such a prospect might loom for a poor interpreter committed to brevity. A character is interesting as it comes out, and by the process and duration of that emergence; just as a procession is effective by the way it unrolls, turning to a mere mob if all of it passes at once. My little procession, I foresaw then from an early stage, would refuse to pass at once; though I could keep it more or less down, of course, by reducing it to three or four persons. Practically, in "The Spoils," the reduction is to four, though indeed—and I clung to that as to my plea for simplicity—the main agents, with the others all dependent, are Mrs. Gereth and Fleda. Fleda's ingratiating stroke, for importance, on the threshold, had been that she would understand; and positively, from that moment, the progress and march of my tale became and remained that of her understanding.

Absolutely, with this, I committed myself to making the affirmation and the penetration of it my action and my "story"; once more, too, with the re-entertained perception that a subject so lighted, a subject residing in somebody's excited and concentrated feeling about something—both the something and the somebody being of course as important as possible—has more beauty to give out than under any other style of pressure. One is confronted obviously thus with the question of the importances; with that in particular, no doubt, of the weight of intelligent consciousness, consciousness of the whole, or of something ominously like it, that one may decently permit a represented figure to appear to throw. Some plea for this cause, that of the intelligence of the moved mannikin, I have already had occasion to make,[350] and can scarce hope too often to evade it. This intelligence, an honourable amount of it, on the part of the person to whom one most invites attention, has but to play with sufficient freedom and ease, or call it with the right grace, to guarantee us that quantum of the impression of beauty which is the most fixed of the possible advantages of our producible effect. It may fail, as a positive presence, on other sides and in other connexions; but more or less of the treasure is stored safe from the moment such a quality of inward life is distilled, or in other words from the moment so fine an interpretation and criticism as that of Fleda Vetch's—to cite the present case—is applied without waste to the surrounding tangle.

It is easy to object of course "Why the deuce then Fleda Vetch, why a mere little flurried bundle of petticoats, why not Hamlet or Milton's Satan at once, if you're going in for a superior display of 'mind'?"[351] To which I fear I can only reply that in pedestrian prose, and in the "short story," one is, for the best reasons, no less on one's guard than on the stretch; and also that I have ever recognised, even in the midst of the curiosity that such displays may quicken, the rule of an exquisite economy. The thing is to lodge somewhere at the heart of one's complexity an irrepressible *appreciation*, but where a light lamp will carry all the flame I incline to look askance at a heavy. From beginning to end, in "The Spoils of Poynton," appreciation, even to that of the very whole, lives in Fleda; which is precisely why, as a consequence rather grandly imposed, every one else shows for comparatively stupid; the tangle, the drama, the tragedy and comedy of those who appreciate consisting so much of their relation with those who don't. From the presented reflexion of this truth my story draws, I think, a certain assured appearance of roundness and felicity. The "things" are radiant, shedding afar, with a merciless monotony, all their light,[352] exerting their ravage without remorse; and Fleda almost demonically both sees and feels, while the others but feel without seeing. Thus we get perhaps a vivid enough little example, in the concrete, of the general truth, for the spectator of life, that the fixed constituents of almost any reproducible action are the fools who minister, at a particular crisis, to the intensity of the free spirit engaged with them. The fools are interesting by contrast, by the salience they acquire, and by a hundred other of their advantages; and the free spirit, always much tormented, and by no means always triumphant, is heroic, ironic, pathetic or whatever, and, as exemplified in the record of Fleda Vetch, for instance, "successful," only through having remained free.

   I recognise that the novelist with a weakness for that ground of appeal is foredoomed to a well-nigh extravagant insistence on the free spirit, seeing the possibility of one in every bush;[353] I may perhaps speak of it as noteworthy that this very volume happens to exhibit in two other cases my disposition to let the interest stand or fall by the tried spontaneity and vivacity of the freedom. It is in fact for that respectable reason that I enclose "A London Life" and "The Chaperon" between these covers; my purpose having been here to class my reprintable productions as far as possible according to their kinds.[354] The two tales I have just named are of the same "kind" as "The Spoils," to the extent of their each dealing with a human predicament in the light, for the charm of the thing, of the amount of "appreciation" to be plausibly imputed to the subject of it. They are each—and truly there are more of such to come—"stories about women," very young women, who, affected with a certain high lucidity, thereby become characters; in consequence of which their doings, their sufferings or whatever, take on, I assume, an importance. Laura Wing, in "A London Life," has, like Fleda Vetch, acuteness and intensity, reflexion and passion, has above all a contributive and participant view of her situation; just as Rose Tramore, in "The Chaperon," rejoices, almost to insolence, very much in the same cluster of attributes and advantages. They are thus of a family[355]—which shall have also for us, we seem forewarned, more members, and of each sex.

As to our young woman of "The Spoils," meanwhile, I briefly come back to my claim for a certain definiteness of beauty in the special effect wrought by her aid. My problem had decently to be met—that of establishing for the other persons the vividness of their appearance of comparative stupidity, that of exposing them to the full thick wash of the penumbra surrounding the central light, and yet keeping their motions, within it, distinct, coherent and "amusing." But these are exactly of course the most "amusing" things to do; nothing, for example, being of a higher reward artistically than the shade of success aimed at in such a figure as Mrs. Gereth. A character she too, absolutely, yet the very reverse of a free spirit. I have found myself so pleased with Mrs. Gereth, I confess, on resuming acquaintance with her, that, complete and all in equilibrium as she seems to me to stand and move there, I shrink from breathing upon her any breath of qualification; without which, however, I fail of my point that, thanks to the "value" represented by Fleda, and to the position to which the elder woman is confined by that irradiation, the latter is at the best a "false" character, floundering as she does in the dusk of disproportionate passion. She is a *figure*, oh definitely—which is a very different matter;[356] for you may be a figure with all the blinding, with all the hampering passion in life, and may have the grand air in what shall yet prove to the finer view (which Fleda again, *e.g.*, could at any time strike off) but a perfect rage of awkwardness. Mrs. Gereth was, obviously, with her pride and her pluck, of an admirable fine paste;[357] but she was not intelligent, was only clever, and therefore would have been no use to us at all as centre of our subject—compared with Fleda, who was only intelligent, not distinctively able. The little drama confirms at all events excellently, I think, the contention of the old wisdom that the question of the personal will has more than all else to say to the verisimilitude of these exhibitions. The will that rides the crisis quite most triumphantly is that of the awful Mona Brigstock, who is *all* will, without the smallest leak of force into taste or tenderness or vision, into any sense of shades or relations or proportions.

She loses no minute in that perception of incongruities in which half Fleda's passion is wasted and misled, and into which Mrs. Gereth, to her practical loss, that is by the fatal grace of a sense of comedy, occasionally and disinterestedly strays. Every one, every thing, in the story is accordingly sterile *but* the so thriftily constructed Mona, able at any moment to bear the whole of her dead weight at once on any given inch of a resisting surface.[358] Fleda, obliged to neglect inches, sees and feels but in acres and expanses and blue perspectives; Mrs. Gereth too, in comparison, while her imagination broods, drops half the stitches of the web she seeks to weave.

If I speak of classifying I hasten to recognise that there are other marks for the purpose still and that, failing other considerations, "A London Life" would properly consort, in this series, with a dozen of the tales by which I at one period sought to illustrate and enliven the supposed "international" conflict of manners; a general theme dealing for the most part with the bewilderment of the good American, of either sex and of almost any age, in presence of the "European" order. This group of data might possibly have shown, for the reverse of its medal, the more or less desperate contortions of the European under American social pressure. Three or four tried glances in that direction[359] seemed to suggest, however, no great harvest to be gathered; so that the pictorial value of the general opposition was practically confined to one phase. More reasons are here involved than I can begin to go into—as indeed I confess that the reflexions set in motion by the international fallacy at large, as I am now moved to regard it, quite crowd upon me; I simply note therefore, on one corner of the ground, the scant results, above all for interesting detail, promised by confronting the fruits of a constituted order with the fruits of no order at all. We may strike lights by opposing order to order, one sort to another sort; for in that case we get the correspondences and equivalents that make differences mean something; we get the interest and the tension of disparity where a certain parity may have been in question. Where it may *not* have been in question, where the dramatic encounter is but the poor concussion of positives on one side with negatives on the other, we get little beyond a consideration of the differences between fishes and fowls.[360]

By which I don't mean to say that the appeal of the fallacy, as I call it, was not at one time quite inevitably irresistible; had it nothing else to recommend it to the imagination it would always have had the advantage of its showy surface, of suggesting situations as to which assurance seemed easy, founded, as it felt itself, on constant observation. The attraction was thus not a little, I judge, the attraction of facility; the international was easy to do, because, as one's wayside bloomed with it, one had but to put forth one's hand and pluck the frequent flower. Add to this that the flower *was*, so often, quite positively a flower—that of the young American innocence transplanted to European air.[361] The general subject had, in fine, a charm while it lasted; but I shall have much more to say about it on another occasion.[362] What here concerns us is that "A London Life" breaks down altogether, I have had to recognise, as a contribution to my comprehensive picture of bewildered Americanism. I fail to make out to-day why I need have conceived my three principal persons as sharers in that particular bewilderment.[363] There was enough of the general human and social sort for them without it; poor young Wendover in especial, I think, fails on any such ground to attest himself[364]—I needn't, surely, have been at costs to bring him all the way from New York. Laura Wing, touching creature as she was designed to appear, strikes me as a rare little person who would have been a rare little person anywhere, and who, in that character, must have felt and judged and suffered and acted as she did, whatever her producing clime.

The great anomaly, however, is Mrs. Lionel;[365] a study of a type quite sufficiently to be accounted for on the very scene of her development, and with her signs and marks easily mistakeable, in London, for the notes of a native luxuriance. I recall the emphasis, quite the derision, with which a remarkably wise old friend,[366] not American, a trenchant judge who had observed manners in many countries and had done me the honour to read my tale, put to me: "What on earth possessed you to make of your Selina an American, or to make one of your two or three Americans a Selina?—resembling so to the life something quite else, something which hereabouts one needn't go far to seek, but failing of any felicity for a creature engendered *là-bas*." And I think my friend conveyed, or desired to convey, that the wicked woman of my story was falsified above all, as an imported product, by something distinctly other than so engendered in the superficial "form" of her perversity, a high stiff-backed angular action which is, or was then, beyond any American "faking."[367] The truth is, no doubt, that, though Mrs. Lionel, on my page, doesn't in the least achieve character, she yet passes before us as a sufficiently vivid image, which was to be the effect designed for her—an image the hard rustle of whose long steps and the sinister tinkle of whose multiplied trinkets[368] belie the association invoked for them and positively operate for another. Not perhaps, moreover, as I am moved to subjoin, that the point greatly matters. What matters, for one's appreciation of a work of art, however modest, is that the prime intention shall have been justified—for any judgement of which we must be clear as to what it was. It wasn't after all of the prime, the very most prime, intention of the tale in question that the persons concerned in it should have had this, that or the other land of birth;[369] but that the central situation should really be rendered—that of a charming and decent young thing, from wheresoever proceeding, who has her decision and her action to take, horribly and unexpectedly, in face of a squalid "scandal" the main agent of which is her nearest relative, and who, at the dreadful crisis, to guard against personal bespattering,[370] is moved, with a miserable want of effect, to a wild vague frantic gesture, an appeal for protection that virtually proves a precipitation of her disgrace.

Nobody concerned need, as I say, have come from New York for that; though, as I have likewise intimated, I must have seen the creation of my heroine, in 1888, and the representation of the differences I wished to establish between her own known world and the world from which she finds herself recoiling, facilitated in a high degree by assured reference to the simpler social order across the sea. I had my vision (as I recover the happy spell) of her having "come over" to find, to her dismay, what "London" had made of the person in the world hitherto most akin to her; in addition to which I was during those years infinitely interested in almost any demonstration of the effect of London.[371] This was a form of response to the incessant appeal of the great city, one's grateful, one's devoted recognition of which fairly broke out from day to day. It was material ever to one's hand; and the impression was always there that no one so much as the candid outsider, caught up and involved in the sweep of the machine, could measure the values revealed. Laura Wing must have figured for me thus as the necessary candid outsider—from the moment some received impression of the elements about me was to be projected and embodied. In fact as I remount the stream it is the particular freshness of that enjoyed relation I seem to taste again; the positive fond belief that I had my right oppositions. They seemed to ensure somehow the perfect march of my tolerably simple action; the straightness, the artful economy of which—save that of a particular point where my ingenuity shows to so small advantage that, to anticipate opprobrium, I can but hold it up to derision—hasn't ceased to be appreciable. The thing made its first appearance in "Scribner's Magazine" during the summer of 1888,[372] and I remember being not long before at work upon it, remember in fact beginning it, in one of the wonderful faded back rooms of an old Venetian palace, a room with a pompous Tiepolo ceiling[373] and walls of ancient pale-green damask, slightly shredded and patched, which, on the warm mornings, looked into the shade of a court where a high outer staircase, strikingly bold, yet strikingly relaxed, held together one scarce knew how; where Gothic windows broke out, on discoloured blanks of wall, at quite arbitrary levels, and where above all the strong Venetian voice, full of history and humanity and waking perpetual echoes, seemed to say more in ten warm words, of whatever tone, than any twenty pages of one's cold pale prose.

In spite of all of which, I may add, I do penance here only for the awkwardness of that departure from the adopted form of my recital which resides in the picture of the interview with young Wendover contrived by Lady Davenant[374] in the interest of some better provision for their poor young friend. Here indeed is a lapse from artistic dignity, a confession of want of resource, which I may not pretend to explain to-day, and on behalf of which I have nothing to urge save a consciousness of my dereliction presumably too vague at the time. I had seen my elements presented in a certain way, settled the little law under which my story was to be told, and with this consistency, as any reader of the tale may easily make out for himself, interviews to which my central figure was not a party, scenes revolving on an improvised pivot of their own, had nothing to do with the affair. I might of course have adopted another plan—the artist is free, surely, to adopt any he fancies, provided it *be* a plan and he adopt it intelligently; and to that scheme of composition the independent picture of a passage between Lady Davenant and young Wendover might perfectly have conformed. As the case stands it conforms to nothing; whereas the beauty of a thing of this order really done as a whole is ever, certainly, that its parts are in abject dependence, and that even any great charm they may individually and capriciously put forth is infirm so far as it doesn't measurably contribute to a harmony. My momentary helplessness sprang, no doubt, from my failure to devise in time some way of giving the value of Lady Davenant's appeal to the young man, of making it play its part in my heroine's history and consciousness, without so awkwardly thrusting the lump sum on the reader.

Circumventions of difficulty of this degree are precisely the finest privilege of the craftsman, who, to be worth his salt, and master of *any* contrived harmony, must take no tough technical problem for insoluble. These technical subterfuges and subtleties, these indirectly-expressed values, kept indirect in a higher interest, made subordinate to some general beauty, some artistic intention that can give an account of itself, what are they after all but one of the nobler parts of our amusement? Superficially, in "A London Life," it might well have seemed that the only way to picture the intervention on Laura Wing's behalf of the couple just named was to break the chain of the girl's own consciousness and report the matter quite straight and quite shamelessly; this course had indeed every merit but that of its playing the particular game to which I had addressed myself. My prime loyalty was to the interest of the game, and the honour to be won the more desirable by that fact. Any muddle-headed designer can beg the question of perspective, but science is required for making it rule the scene. If it be asked how then we were to have assisted at the copious passage I thus incriminate without our privilege of presence, I can only say that my discovery of the right way should—and would—have been the very flower of the performance. The real "fun" of the thing would have been exactly to sacrifice my comparative platitude of statement—a deplorable depth at any time, I have attempted elsewhere to signify, for any pretending master of representation to sink to[375]—without sacrificing a grain of what was to be conveyed. The real fun, in other words, would have been in not, by an exceptional collapse of other ingenuity, making my attack on the spectator's consciousness a call as immediate as a postman's knock.[376] This attack, at every other point, reaches that objective only through the medium of the interesting girl's own vision, own experience, with which all the facts are richly charged and coloured. That saturates our sense of them with the savour of Laura's sense—thanks to which enhancement we get intensity. But from the chapter to which I have called attention, so that it may serve perhaps as a lesson, intensity ruefully drops. I can't say worse for it—and have been the more concerned to say what I do that without this flaw the execution might have appeared from beginning to end close and exemplary.

It is with all that better confidence, I think, that the last of my three tales here carries itself. I recapture perfectly again, in respect to "The Chaperon," both the first jog of my imagination and the particular local influence that presided at its birth—the latter a ramshackle inn on the Irish coast,[377] where the table at which I wrote was of an equilibrium so vague that I wonder to-day how any object constructed on it should stand so firm. The strange sad charm of the tearful Irish light hangs about the memory of the labour of which this small fiction—first published in two numbers of "The Atlantic Monthly" of 1891[378]—was one of the fruits; but the subject had glimmered upon me, two or three years before, in an air of comedy comparatively free from sharp under-tastes. Once more, as in the case of its companions here, the single spoken word, in London, had said all—after the manner of that clear ring of the electric bell that the barest touch of the button may produce.[379] The talk being of a certain lady who, in consequence of early passages, had lived for years apart from her husband and in no affluence of good company, it was mentioned of her that her situation had improved, and the desert around her[380] been more or less brought under cultivation, by the fact of her having at last made acquaintance with her young unmarried daughter, a charming girl just introduced to the world and thereby qualified for "taking her out," floating her in spite of whatever past damage.[381] Here in truth, it seemed to me, *was* a morsel of queer comedy[382] to play with, and my tale embodies the neat experiment. Fortunately in this case the principle of composition adopted is loyally observed; the values gathered are, without exception, gathered by the light of the intense little personal consciousness, invoked from the first, that shines over my field and the predominance of which is usurped by none other. That is the main note to be made about "The Chaperon"; except this further, which I must reserve, however—as I shall find excellent occasion—for an ampler development. A short story, to my sense and as the term is used in magazines, has to choose between being either an anecdote or a picture[383] and can but play its part strictly according to its kind. I rejoice in the anecdote, but I revel in the picture; though having doubtless at times to note that a given attempt may place itself near the dividing-line. This is in some degree the case with "The Chaperon," in which, none the less, on the whole, picture ingeniously prevails; picture aiming at those richly summarised and foreshortened effects—the opposite pole again from expansion inorganic and thin—that refer their terms of production, for which the magician has ever to don his best cap and gown, to the inner compartment of our box of tricks. From *them* comes the true grave close consistency in which parts hang together even as the interweavings of a tapestry. "The Chaperon" has perhaps, so far as it goes, something of that texture. Yet I shall be able, I think, to cite examples with still more.

PREFACE to *What Maisie Knew, In the Cage, The Pupil* (*NYE* XI)

I RECOGNISE again, for the first of these three Tales, another instance of the growth of the "great oak" from the little acorn;[384] since "What Maisie Knew" is at least a tree that spreads beyond any provision its small germ might on a first handling have appeared likely to make for it. The accidental mention had been made to me of the manner in which the situation of some luckless child of a divorced couple was affected, under my informant's eyes, by the re-marriage of one of its parents—I forget which;[385] so that, thanks to the limited desire for its company expressed by the step-parent, the law of its little life, its being entertained in rotation by its father and its mother, wouldn't easily prevail. Whereas each of these persons had at first vindictively desired to keep it from the other, so at present the re-married relative sought now rather to be rid of it—that is to leave it as much as possible, and beyond the appointed times and seasons, on the hands of the adversary; which malpractice, resented by the latter as bad faith, would of course be repaid and avenged by an equal treachery. The wretched infant was thus to find itself practically disowned, rebounding from racquet to racquet like a tennis-ball or a shuttlecock.[386] This figure could but touch the fancy to the quick and strike one as the beginning of a story—a story commanding a great choice of developments. I recollect, however, promptly thinking that for a proper symmetry the second parent should marry too—which in the case named to me indeed would probably soon occur, and was in any case what the ideal of the situation required. The second step-parent would have but to be correspondingly incommoded by obligations to the offspring of a hated predecessor for the misfortune of the little victim to become altogether exemplary. The business would accordingly be sad enough, yet I am not sure its possibility of interest would so much have appealed to me had I not soon felt that the ugly facts, so stated or conceived, by no means constituted the whole appeal.

The light of an imagination touched by them couldn't help therefore projecting a further ray, thanks to which it became rather quaintly clear that, not less than the chance of misery and of a degraded state, the chance of happiness and of an improved state might be here involved for the child,[387] round about whom the complexity of life would thus turn to fineness, to richness—and indeed would have but so to turn for the small creature to be steeped in security and ease. Sketchily clustered even, these elements gave out that vague pictorial glow which forms the first appeal of a living "subject" to the painter's consciousness; but the glimmer became intense as I proceeded to a further analysis. The further analysis is for that matter almost always the torch of rapture and victory, as the artist's firm hand grasps and plays it—I mean, naturally, of the smothered rapture and the obscure victory, enjoyed and celebrated not in the street but before some innermost shrine; the odds being a hundred to one, in almost any connexion, that it doesn't arrive by any easy first process at the *best* residuum of truth. That was the charm, sensibly, of the picture thus at first confusedly showing; the elements so couldn't but flush, to their very surface, with some deeper depth of irony than the mere obvious. It lurked in the crude postulate like a buried scent; the more the attention hovered the more aware it became of the fragrance. To which I may add that the more I scratched the surface and penetrated, the more potent, to the intellectual nostril, became this virtue. At last, accordingly, the residuum, as I have called it, reached, I was in presence of the red dramatic spark that glowed at the core of my vision and that, as I gently blew upon it, burned higher and clearer. This precious particle was the *full* ironic truth[388]—the most interesting item to be read into the child's situation. For satisfaction of the mind, in other words, the small expanding consciousness would have to be saved, have to become presentable as a register of impressions; and saved by the experience of certain advantages, by some enjoyed profit and some achieved confidence, rather than coarsened, blurred, sterilised, by ignorance and pain. This better state, in the young life, would reside in the exercise of a function other than that of disconcerting the selfishness of its parents—which was all that had on the face of the matter seemed reserved to it in the way of criticism applied to their rupture. The early relation would be exchanged for a later; instead of simply submitting to the inherited tie and the imposed complication, of suffering from them, our little wonder-working agent would create, without design, quite fresh elements of this order—contribute, that is, to the formation of a fresh tie, from which it would then (and for all the world as if through a small demonic foresight) proceed to derive great profit.

This is but to say that the light in which the vision so readily grew to a wholeness was that of a second marriage on both sides; the father having, in the freedom of divorce, but to take another wife, as well as the mother, under a like licence, another husband, for the case to begin, at least, to stand beautifully on its feet. There would be thus a perfect logic for what might come—come even with the mere attribution of a certain sensibility (if but a mere relative fineness) to either of the new parties. Say the prime cause making for the ultimate attempt to shirk on one side or the other, and better still if on both, a due share of the decreed burden should have been, after all, in each progenitor, a constitutional inaptitude for *any* burden, and a base intolerance of it: we should thus get a motive not requiring, but happily dispensing with, too particular a perversity in the step-parents. The child seen as creating by the fact of its forlornness a relation between its step-parents, the more intimate the better, dramatically speaking; the child, by the mere appeal of neglectedness and the mere consciousness of relief, weaving about, with the best faith in the world, the close web of sophistication; the child becoming a centre and pretext for a fresh system of misbehaviour, a system moreover of a nature to spread and ramify: *there* would be the "full" irony, there the promising theme into which the hint I had originally picked up would logically flower. No themes are so human as those that reflect for us, out of the confusion of life, the close connexion of bliss and bale,[389] of the things that help with the things that hurt, so dangling before us for ever that bright hard medal, of so strange an alloy, one face of which is somebody's right and ease and the other somebody's pain and wrong. To live with all intensity and perplexity and felicity in its terribly mixed little world would thus be the part of my interesting small mortal; bringing people together[390] who would be at least more correctly separate; keeping people separate who would be at least more correctly together; flourishing, to a degree, at the cost of many conventions and proprieties, even decencies; really keeping the torch of virtue alive in an air tending infinitely to smother it; really in short making confusion worse confounded by drawing some stray fragrance of an ideal across the scent of selfishness,[391] by sowing on barren strands, through the mere fact of presence, the seed of the moral life.

All this would be to say, I at once recognised, that my light vessel of consciousness, swaying in such a draught, couldn't be with verisimilitude a rude little boy;[392] since, beyond the fact that little boys are never so "present," the sensibility of the female young is indubitably, for early youth, the greater, and my plan would call, on the part of my protagonist, for "no end" of sensibility. I might impute that amount of it without extravagance to a slip of a girl whose faculties should have been well shaken up; but I should have so to depend on its action to keep my story clear that I must be able to show it in all assurance as naturally intense. To this end I should have of course to suppose for my heroine dispositions originally promising, but above all I should have to invest her with perceptions easily and almost infinitely quickened. So handsomely fitted out, yet not in a manner too grossly to affront probability, she might well see me through the whole course of my design; which design, more and more attractive as I turned it over, and dignified by the most delightful difficulty, would be to make and to keep her so limited consciousness the very field of my picture[393] while at the same time guarding with care the integrity of the objects represented. With the charm of this possibility, therefore, the project for "Maisie" rounded itself and loomed large—any subject looming large, for that matter, I am bound to add, from the moment one is ridden by the law of entire expression. I have already elsewhere noted, I think, that the memory of my own work preserves for me no theme that, at some moment or other of its development, and always only waiting for the right connexion or chance, hasn't signally refused to remain humble,[394] even (or perhaps all the more resentfully) when fondly selected for its conscious and hopeless humility. Once "out," like a house-dog of a temper above confinement, it defies the mere whistle, it roams, it hunts, it seeks out and "sees" life; it can be brought back but by hand and then only to take its futile thrashing.[395] It wasn't at any rate for an idea seen in the light I here glance at not to have due warrant of its value—how could the value of a scheme so finely workable *not* be great? The one presented register of the whole complexity would be the play of the child's confused and obscure notation of it, and yet the whole, as I say, should be unmistakeably, should be honourably there, seen through the faint intelligence, or at the least attested by the imponderable presence, and still advertising its sense.

I recall that my first view of this neat possibility was as the attaching problem of the picture restricted (while yet achieving, as I say, completeness and coherency) to what the child might be conceived to have *understood*—to have been able to interpret and appreciate. Further reflexion and experiment showed me my subject strangled in that extreme of rigour. The infant mind would at the best leave great gaps and voids; so that with a systematic surface possibly beyond reproach we should nevertheless fail of clearness of sense. I should have to stretch the matter to what my wondering witness materially and inevitably *saw;* a great deal of which quantity she either wouldn't understand at all or would quite misunderstand—and on those lines, only on those, my task would be prettily cut out. To that then I settled—to the question of giving it *all,* the whole situation surrounding her, but of giving it only through the occasions and connexions of her proximity and her attention; only as it might pass before her and appeal to her, as it might touch her and affect her, for better or worse, for perceptive gain or perceptive loss: so that we fellow witnesses, we not more invited but only more expert critics, should feel in strong possession of it. This would be, to begin with, a plan of absolutely definite and measurable application—that in itself always a mark of beauty; and I have been interested to find on re-perusal of the work that some such controlling grace successfully rules it. Nothing could be more "done," I think, in the light of its happiest intention; and this in spite of an appearance that at moments obscures my consistency. Small children have many more perceptions than they have terms to translate them;[396] their vision is at any moment much richer, their apprehension even constantly stronger, than their prompt, their at all producible, vocabulary. Amusing therefore as it might at the first blush have seemed to restrict myself in this case to the terms as well as to the experience, it became at once plain that such an attempt would fail. Maisie's terms accordingly play their part—since her simpler conclusions quite depend on them; but our own commentary constantly attends and amplifies.[397] This it is that on occasion, doubtless, seems to represent us as going so "behind" the facts of her spectacle as to exaggerate the activity of her relation to them. The difference here is but of a shade: it is her relation, her activity of spirit, that determines all our own concern—we simply take advantage of these things better than she herself. Only, even though it is her interest that mainly makes matters interesting for us, we inevitably note this in figures that are not yet at her command and that are nevertheless required whenever those aspects about her and those parts of her experience that she understands darken off into others that she rather tormentedly misses. All of which gave me a high firm logic to observe; supplied the force for which the straightener of almost any tangle is grateful while he labours, the sense of pulling at threads intrinsically worth it—strong enough and fine enough and entire enough.

Of course, beyond this, was another and well-nigh equal charm—equal in spite of its being almost independent of the acute constructional, the endless expressional question. This was the quite different question of the particular kind of truth of resistance I might be able to impute to my central figure—*some* intensity, some continuity of resistance being naturally of the essence of the subject. Successfully to resist (to resist, that is, the strain of observation and the assault of experience) what would that be, on the part of so young a person, but to remain fresh, and still fresh, and to have even a freshness to communicate?—the case being with Maisie to the end that she treats her friends to the rich little spectacle of objects embalmed in her wonder. She wonders, in other words, to the end, to the death—the death of her childhood, properly speaking; after which (with the inevitable shift, sooner or later, of her point of view) her situation will change and become another affair,[398] subject to other measurements and with a new centre altogether. The particular reaction that will have led her to that point, and that it has been of an exquisite interest to study in her, will have spent itself; there will be another scale, another perspective, another horizon. Our business meanwhile therefore is to extract from her current reaction whatever it may be worth; and for that matter we recognise in it the highest exhibitional virtue. Truly, I reflect, if the theme had had no other beauty it would still have had this rare and distinguished one of its so expressing the variety of the child's values. She is not only the extraordinary "ironic centre" I have already noted; she has the wonderful importance of shedding a light far beyond any reach of her comprehension; of lending to poorer persons and things, by the mere fact of their being involved with her and by the special scale she creates for them, a precious element of dignity. I lose myself, truly, in appreciation of my theme on noting what she does by her "freshness" for appearances in themselves vulgar and empty enough. They become, as she deals with them, the stuff of poetry and tragedy and art; she has simply to wonder, as I say, about them, and they begin to have meanings, aspects, solidities, connexions—connexions with the "universal!"[399]—that they could scarce have hoped for. Ida Farange alone, so to speak, or Beale alone, that is either of them otherwise connected—what intensity, what "objectivity" (the most developed degree of *being* anyhow thinkable for them) would they have? How would they repay at all the favour of our attention?

Maisie makes them portentous all by the play of her good faith, makes her mother above all, to my vision—unless I have wholly failed to render it—concrete, immense and awful; so that we get, for our profit, and get by an economy of process interesting in itself, the thoroughly pictured creature, the striking figured symbol. At two points in particular,[400] I seem to recognise, we enjoy at its maximum this effect of associational magic. The passage in which her father's terms of intercourse with the insinuating but so strange and unattractive lady whom he has had the detestable levity to whisk her off to see late at night, is a signal example of the all but incalculable way in which interest may be constituted. The facts involved are that Beale Farange is ignoble, that the friend to whom he introduces his daughter is deplorable, and that from the commerce of the two, *as* the two merely, we would fain avert our heads. Yet the thing has but to become a part of the child's bewilderment for these small sterilities to drop from it and for the *scene* to emerge and prevail—vivid, special, wrought hard, to the hardness of the unforgettable; the scene that is exactly what Beale and Ida and Mrs. Cuddon, and even Sir Claude and Mrs. Beale, would never for a moment have succeeded in making their scant unredeemed importances—namely *appreciable*. I find another instance in the episode of Maisie's unprepared encounter, while walking in the Park with Sir Claude, of her mother and that beguiled attendant of her mother, the encouraging, the appealing "Captain," to whom this lady contrives to commit her for twenty minutes while she herself deals with the second husband. The human substance here would have seemed in advance well-nigh too poor for conversion, the three "mature" figures of too short a radiation, too stupid[401] (*so* stupid it was for Sir Claude to have married Ida!) too vain, too thin, for any clear application; but promptly, immediately, the child's own importance, spreading and contagiously acting, has determined the *total* value otherwise. Nothing of course, meanwhile, is an older story to the observer of manners and the painter of life than the grotesque finality with which such terms as "painful," "unpleasant" and "disgusting" are often applied to his results;[402] to that degree, in truth, that the free use of them as weightily conclusive again and again re-enforces his estimate of the critical sense of circles in which they artlessly flourish. Of course under that superstition I was punctually to have had read to me the lesson that the "mixing-up" of a child with anything unpleasant[403] confessed itself an aggravation of the unpleasantness, and that nothing could well be more disgusting than to attribute to Maisie so intimate an "acquaintance" with the gross immoralities surrounding her.

The only thing to say of such lucidities is that, however one may have "discounted" in advance, and as once for all, their general radiance, one is disappointed if the hour for them, in the particular connexion, doesn't strike—they so keep before us elements with which even the most sedate philosopher must always reckon. The painter of life has indeed work cut out for him when a considerable part of life offers itself in the guise of that sapience. The effort really to see and really to represent is no idle business in face of the *constant* force that makes for muddlement. The great thing is indeed that the muddled state too is one of the very sharpest of the realities, that it also has colour and form and character, has often in fact a broad and rich comicality, many of the signs and values of the appreciable. Thus it was to be, for example, I might gather, that the very principle of Maisie's appeal, her undestroyed freshness, in other words that vivacity of intelligence by which she indeed does vibrate in the infected air, indeed does flourish in her immoral world, may pass for a barren and senseless thing, or at best a negligible one. For nobody to whom life at large is *easily* interesting do the finer, the shyer, the more anxious small vibrations, fine and shy and anxious with the passion that precedes knowledge, succeed in being negligible: which is doubtless one of many reasons why the passage between the child and the kindly, friendly, ugly gentleman who, seated with her in Kensington Gardens[404] under a spreading tree, positively answers to her for her mother as no one has ever answered, and so stirs her, filially and morally, as she has never been stirred, throws into highest relief, to my sense at least, the side on which the subject is strong, and becomes the type-passage—other advantages certainly aiding, as I may say—for the expression of its beauty. The active, contributive close-circling wonder, as I have called it, in which the child's identity is guarded and preserved, and which makes her case remarkable exactly by the weight of the tax on it, provides distinction for her, provides vitality and variety, through the operation of the tax—which would have done comparatively little for us hadn't it been monstrous. A pity for us surely to have been deprived of this just reflexion. "Maisie" is of 1907.[405]

I pass by, for the moment, the second of these compositions, finding in the third, which again deals with the experience of a very young person, a connexion more immediate; and this even at the risk of seeming to undermine my remark of a few pages back as to the comparative sensibility of the sexes. My urchin of "The Pupil" (1891) has sensibility in abundance, it would seem—and yet preserves in spite of it, I judge, his strong little male quality. But there are fifty things to say here; which indeed rush upon me within my present close limits in such a cloud as to demand much clearance. This is perhaps indeed but the aftersense of the assault made on my mind, as I perfectly recall, by every aspect of the original vision, which struck me as abounding in aspects. It lives again for me, this vision, as it first alighted; though the inimitable prime flutter, the air as of an ineffable sign made by the immediate beat of the wings of the poised figure of fancy that has just settled, is one of those guarantees of value that can never be re-captured. The sign has been made to the seer only—it is *his* queer affair; of which any report to others, not as yet involved, has but the same effect of flatness as attends, amid a group gathered under the canopy of night, any stray allusion to a shooting star. The miracle, since miracle it seems, is all for the candid exclaimer. The miracle for the author of "The Pupil," at any rate, was when, years ago, one summer day, in a very hot Italian railway-carriage, which stopped and dawdled everywhere, favouring conversation, a friend with whom I shared it, a doctor of medicine who had come from a far country to settle in Florence,[406] happened to speak to me of a wonderful American family, an odd adventurous, extravagant band, of high but rather unauthenticated pretensions, the most interesting member of which was a small boy, acute and precocious, afflicted with a heart of weak action, but beautifully intelligent, who saw their prowling precarious life exactly as it was, and measured and judged it, and measured and judged *them*, all round, ever so quaintly;[407] presenting himself in short as an extraordinary little person. Here was more than enough for a summer's day even in old Italy—here was a thumping windfall. No process and no steps intervened: I *saw*, on the spot, little Morgan Moreen, I saw all the rest of the Moreens; I felt, to the last delicacy, the nature of my young friend's relation with them (he had become at once my young friend) and, by the same stroke, to its uttermost fine throb, the subjection to *him* of the beguiled, bewildered, defrauded, unremunerated, yet after all richly repaid youth who would to a certainty, under stress of compassion, embark with the tribe on tutorship, and whose edifying connexion with it would be my leading document.

This must serve as my account of the origin of "The Pupil": it will commend itself, I feel, to all imaginative and projective persons who have had—and what imaginative and projective person hasn't?—any like experience of the suddenly-determined *absolute* of perception. The whole cluster of items forming the image is on these occasions born at once; the parts are not pieced together, they conspire and interdepend; but what it really comes to, no doubt, is that at a simple touch an old latent and dormant impression, a buried germ, implanted by experience and then forgotten, flashes to the surface as a fish, with a single "squirm," rises to the baited hook, and there meets instantly the vivifying ray. I remember at all events having no doubt of anything or anyone here; the vision kept to the end its ease and its charm; it worked itself out with confidence. These are minor matters when the question is of minor results; yet almost any assured and downright imaginative act is—granted the sort of record in which I here indulge—worth fondly commemorating. One cherishes, after the fact, any proved case of the independent life of the imagination; above all if by that faculty one has been appointed mainly to live. We are then *never* detached from the question of what it may out of simple charity do for us. Besides which, in relation to the poor Moreens, innumerable notes, as I have intimated, all equally urging their relevance, press here to the front. The general adventure of the little composition itself—for singular things were to happen to it,[408] though among such importunities not the most worth noting now—would be, occasion favouring, a thing to live over; moving as one did, roundabout it, in I scarce know what thick and coloured air of slightly tarnished anecdote, of dim association, of casual confused romance; a compound defying analysis, but truly, for the social chronicler, any student in especial of the copious "cosmopolite" legend,[409] a boundless and tangled, but highly explorable, garden. Why, somehow—these were the intensifying questions—did one see the Moreens, whom I place at Nice, at Venice, in Paris, as of the special essence of the little old miscellaneous cosmopolite Florence, the Florence of other, of irrecoverable years, the restless yet withal so convenient scene of a society that has passed away for ever with all its faded ghosts and fragile relics;[410] immaterial presences that have quite ceased to revisit (trust an old romancer's, an old pious observer's fine sense to have made sure of it!) walks and prospects once sacred and shaded, but now laid bare, gaping wide, despoiled of their past and unfriendly to any appreciation of it?—through which the unconscious Barbarians troop with the regularity and passivity of "supplies," or other promiscuous goods, prepaid and forwarded.[411]

They had nothing to do, the dear Moreens, with this dreadful period, any more than I, as occupied and charmed with them, was humiliatingly subject to it; we were, all together, of a better romantic age and faith; we referred ourselves, with our highest complacency, to the classic years of the great Americano-European legend; the years of limited communication, of monstrous and unattenuated contrast, of prodigious and unrecorded adventure. The comparatively brief but infinitely rich "cycle" of romance[412] embedded in the earlier, the very early American reactions and returns (mediæval in the sense of being, at most, of the mid-century), what does it resemble to-day but a gold-mine overgrown and smothered, dislocated, and no longer workable?—all for want of the right indications for sounding, the right implements for digging, doubtless even of the right workmen, those with the right tradition and "feeling," for the job. The most extraordinary things appear to have happened, during that golden age, in the "old" countries—in Asia and Africa as well as in Europe—to the candid children of the West, things admirably incongruous and incredible; but no story of all the list was to find its just interpreter, and nothing is now more probable than that every key to interpretation has been lost. The modern reporter's big brushes, attached to broom-handles that match the height of his skyscrapers,[413] would sadly besmear the fine parchment of our missing record. We were to lose, clearly, at any rate, a vast body of precious anecdote, a long gallery of wonderful portraits, an array of the oddest possible figures in the oddest possible attitudes. The Moreens were of the family then of the great unstudied precursors—poor and shabby members, no doubt; dim and superseded types. I must add indeed that, such as they were, or as they may at present incoherently appear, I don't pretend really to have "done" them;[414] all I have given in "The Pupil" is little Morgan's troubled vision of them as reflected in the vision, also troubled enough, of his devoted friend. The manner of the thing may thus illustrate the author's incorrigible taste for gradations and superpositions of effect; his love, when it is a question of a picture, of anything that makes for proportion and perspective, that contributes to a view of *all* the dimensions. Addicted to seeing "through"—one thing through another, accordingly, and still other things through *that*—he takes, too greedily perhaps, on any errand, as many things as possible by the way. It is after this fashion that he incurs the stigma of labouring uncannily for a certain fulness of truth—truth diffused, distributed and, as it were, atmospheric.

 The second in order of these fictions speaks for itself, I think, so frankly as scarce to suffer further expatiation. Its origin is written upon it large, and the idea it puts into play so abides in one of the commonest and most taken-for-granted of London impressions[415] that some such experimentally-figured situation as that of "In the Cage" must again and again have flowered (granted the grain of observation) in generous minds. It had become for me, at any rate, an old story by the time (1898) I cast it into this particular form. The postal-telegraph office in general, and above all the small local office of one's immediate neighbourhood,[416] scene of the transaction of so much of one's daily business, haunt of one's needs and one's duties, of one's labours and one's patiences, almost of one's rewards and one's disappointments, one's joys and one's sorrows, had ever had, to my sense, so much of London to give out, so much of its huge perpetual story to tell, that any momentary wait there seemed to take place in a strong social draught, the stiffest possible breeze of the human comedy.[417] One had of course in these connexions one's especial resort, the office nearest one's own door, where one had come to enjoy in a manner the fruits of frequentation and the amenities of intercourse. So had grown up, for speculation—prone as one's mind had ever been to that form of waste—the question of what it might "mean," wherever the admirable service was installed, for confined and cramped and yet considerably tutored young officials of either sex to be made so free, intellectually, of a range of experience otherwise quite closed to them.[418] This wonderment, once the spark was kindled, became an amusement, or an obsession, like another; though falling indeed, at the best, no doubt, but into that deepest abyss of all the wonderments that break out for the student of great cities. From the moment that he *is* a student, this most beset of critics, his danger is inevitably of imputing to too many others, right and left, the critical impulse and the acuter vision—so very long may it take him to learn that the mass of mankind are banded, probably by the sanest of instincts, to defend themselves to the death against any such vitiation of their simplicity. To criticise is to appreciate, to appropriate, to take intellectual possession, to establish in fine a relation with the criticised thing and make it one's own. The large intellectual appetite projects itself thus on many things, while the small—not better advised, but unconscious of need for advice—projects itself on few.

Admirable thus its economic instinct; it is curious of nothing that it hasn't vital use for. You may starve in London, it is clear, without discovering a use for any theory of the more equal division of victuals—which is moreover exactly what it would appear that thousands of the non-speculative annually do. Their example is much to the point, in the light of all the barren trouble they are saved; but somehow, after all, it gives no pause to the "artist," to the morbid, imagination. That rash, that idle faculty continues to abound in questions, and to supply answers to as many of them as possible; all of which makes a great occupation for idleness. To the fantastic scale on which this last-named state may, in favouring conditions, organise itself, to the activities it may practise when the favouring conditions happen to crop up in Mayfair or in Kensington,[419] our portrayal of the caged telegraphist may well appear a proper little monument. The composition before us tells in fact clearly enough, it seems to me, the story of its growth; and relevance will probably be found in any moral it may pluck—by which I mean any moral the impulse to have framed it may pluck—from the vice of reading rank subtleties into simple souls and reckless expenditure into thrifty ones. The matter comes back again, I fear, but to the author's irrepressible and insatiable, his extravagant and immoral, interest in personal character and in the "nature" of a mind, of almost any mind the heaving little sea of his subject may cast up—as to which these remarks have already, in other connexions, recorded his apology: all without prejudice to such shrines and stations of penance[420] as still shall enliven our way. The range of wonderment attributed in our tale to the young woman employed at Cocker's differs little in essence from the speculative thread on which the pearls of Maisie's experience, in this same volume—pearls of so strange an iridescence—are mostly strung.[421] She wonders, putting it simply, very much as Morgan Moreen wonders; and they all wonder, for that matter, very much after the fashion of our portentous little Hyacinth of "The Princess Casamassima," tainted to the core, as we have seen him, with the trick of mental reaction on the things about him and fairly staggering under the appropriations, as I have called them, that he owes to the critical spirit. He collapses, poor Hyacinth, like a thief at night, overcharged with treasures of reflexion and spoils of passion of which he can give, in his poverty and obscurity, no honest account.

It is much in this manner, we see on analysis, that Morgan Moreen breaks down—his burden indeed not so heavy, but his strength so much less formed. The two little spirits of maidens, in the group, bear up, oddly enough, beyond those of their brothers; but the just remark for each of these small exhibited lives is of course that, in the longer or the shorter piece, they are actively, are luxuriously, lived. The luxury is that of the number of their moral vibrations, well-nigh unrestricted—not that of an account at the grocer's:[422] whatever it be, at any rate, it makes them, as examples and "cases,"[423] rare. My brooding telegraphist may be in fact, on her ground of ingenuity, scarcely more thinkable than desirable; yet if I have made her but a libel, up and down the city, on an estimable class,[424] I feel it still something to have admonished that class, even though obscurely enough, of neglected interests and undivined occasions. My central spirit, in the anecdote, is, for verisimilitude, I grant, too ardent a focus of divination; but without this excess the phenomena detailed would have lacked their principle of cohesion. The action of the drama is simply the girl's "subjective" adventure— that of her quite definitely winged intelligence; just as the catastrophe, just as the solution, depends on her winged wit. Why, however, should I explain further—for a case that, modestly as it would seem to present itself, has yet already whirled us so far?[425] A course of incident complicated by the intervention of winged wit—which is here, as I say, confessed to—would be generally expected, I judge, to commit me to the explanation of everything. But from that undertaking I shrink, and take refuge instead, for an instant, in a much looser privilege.

If I speak, as just above, of the *action* embodied, each time, in these so "quiet" recitals, it is under renewed recognition of the inveterate instinct with which they keep conforming to the "scenic" law.[426] They demean themselves for all the world—they quite insist on it, that is, whenever they have a chance—as little constituted dramas, little exhibitions founded on the logic of the "scene," the unit of the scene, the general scenic consistency, and knowing little more than that. To read them over has been to find them on this ground never at fault. The process repeats and renews itself, moving in the light it has once for all adopted. These finer idiosyncracies of a literary form seem to be regarded as outside the scope of criticism—small reference to them do I remember ever to have met; such surprises of re-perusal, such recoveries of old fundamental intention, such moments of almost ruefully independent discrimination, would doubtless in that case not have waylaid my steps. Going over the pages here placed together has been for me, at all events, quite to watch the scenic system at play. The treatment by "scene," regularly, quite rhythmically recurs; the intervals between, the massing of the elements to a different effect and by a quite other law, remain, in this fashion, all preparative, just as the scenic occasions in themselves become, at a given moment, illustrative, each of the agents, true to its function, taking up the theme from the other very much as the fiddles, in an orchestra, may take it up from the cornets and flutes, or the wind-instruments take it up from the violins. The point, however, is that the scenic passages are *wholly* and logically scenic, having for their rule of beauty the principle of the "conduct," the organic development, of a scene—the entire succession of values that flower and bear fruit on ground solidly laid for them. The great advantage for the total effect is that we feel, with the definite alternation, how the theme *is* being treated. That is we feel it when, in such tangled connexions, we happen to care. I shouldn't really go on as if this were the case with many readers.[427]

PREFACE to *The Aspern Papers, The Turn of the Screw, The Liar, The Two Faces* (NYE XII)

I NOT only recover with ease, but I delight to recall, the first impulse given to the idea of "The Aspern Papers." It is at the same time true that my present mention of it may perhaps too effectually dispose of any complacent claim to my having "found" the situation. Not that I quite know indeed what situations the seeking fabulist does "find"; he seeks them enough assuredly, but his discoveries are, like those of the navigator, the chemist, the biologist, scarce more than alert recognitions. He *comes upon* the interesting thing as Columbus came upon the isle of San Salvador, because he had moved in the right direction for it—also because he knew, with the encounter, what "making land" then and there represented.[428] Nature had so placed it, to profit—if as profit we may measure the matter!—by his fine unrest, just as history, "literary history" we in this connexion call it, had in an out-of-the-way corner of the great garden of life thrown off a curious flower that I was to feel worth gathering as soon as I saw it. I got wind of my positive fact, I followed the scent. It was in Florence years ago;[429] which is precisely, of the whole matter, what I like most to remember. The air of the old-time Italy invests it, a mixture that on the faintest invitation I rejoice again to inhale—and this in spite of the mere cold renewal, ever, of the infirm side of that felicity, the sense, in the whole element, of things too numerous, too deep, too obscure, too strange, or even simply too beautiful, for any ease of intellectual relation. One must pay one's self largely with words,[430] I think, one must induce almost any "Italian subject" to *make believe* it gives up its secret, in order to keep at all on working—or call them perhaps rather playing—terms with the general impression. We entertain it thus, the impression, by the aid of a merciful convention which resembles the fashion of our intercourse with Iberians or Orientals whose form of courtesy places everything they have at our disposal.[431] We thank them and call upon them, but without acting on their professions. The offer has been too large and our assurance is too small; we peep at most into two or three of the chambers of their hospitality, with the rest of the case stretching beyond our ken and escaping our penetration. The pious fiction[432] suffices;

we have entered, we have seen, we are charmed. So, right and left, in Italy—before the great historic complexity at least—penetration fails; we scratch at the extensive surface, we meet the perfunctory smile, we hang about in the golden air.[433] But we exaggerate our gathered values only if we are eminently witless. It is fortunately the exhibition in all the world before which, as admirers, we can most remain superficial without feeling silly.

All of which I note, however, perhaps with too scant relevance to the inexhaustible charm of Roman and Florentine memories. Off the ground, at a distance, our fond indifference to being "silly" grows fonder still; the working convention, as I have called it—the convention of the real revelations and surrenders on one side and the real immersions and appreciations on the other—has not only nothing to keep it down, but every glimpse of contrast, every pang of exile and every nostalgic twinge to keep it up. These latter haunting presences in fact, let me note, almost reduce at first to a mere blurred, sad, scarcely consolable vision this present revisiting, re-appropriating impulse. There are parts of one's past, evidently, that bask consentingly and serenely enough in the light of other days—which is but the intensity of thought; and there are other parts that take it as with agitation and pain, a troubled consciousness that heaves as with the disorder of drinking it deeply in. So it is at any rate, fairly in too thick and rich a retrospect, that I see my old Venice of "The Aspern Papers," that I see the still earlier one of Jeffrey Aspern himself,[434] and that I see even the comparatively recent Florence that was to drop into my ear the solicitation of these things. I would fain "lay it on" thick[435] for the very love of them—that at least I may profess; and, with the ground of this desire frankly admitted, something that somehow makes, in the whole story, for a romantic harmony. I have had occasion in the course of these remarks to define my sense of the romantic,[436] and am glad to encounter again here an instance of that virtue as I understand it. I shall presently say why this small case so ranges itself, but must first refer more exactly to the thrill of appreciation it was immediately to excite in me. I saw it somehow at the very first blush as romantic—for the use, of course I mean, I should certainly have had to make of it—that Jane Clairmont, the half-sister of Mary Godwin, Shelley's second wife and for a while the intimate friend of Byron and the mother of his daughter Allegra, should have been living on in Florence, where she had long lived, up to our own day, and that in fact, had I happened to hear of her but a little sooner, I might have seen her in the flesh.[437] The question of whether I should have wished to do so was another matter—the question of whether I shouldn't have preferred to keep her preciously unseen, to run no risk, in other words, by too rude a choice, of depreciating that romance-value which, as I say, it was instantly inevitable to attach (through association above all, with another signal circumstance) to her long survival.

I had luckily not had to deal with the difficult option; difficult in such a case by reason of that odd law which somehow always makes the minimum of valid suggestion serve the man of imagination better than the maximum. The historian, essentially, wants more documents than he can really use; the dramatist only wants more liberties than he can really take.[438] Nothing, fortunately, however, had, as the case stood, depended on my delicacy; I might have "looked up" Miss Clairmont in previous years had I been earlier informed—the silence about her seemed full of the "irony of fate";[439] but I felt myself more concerned with the mere strong fact of her having testified for the reality and the closeness of our relation to the past than with any question of the particular sort of person I might have flattered myself I "found." I had certainly at the very least been saved the undue simplicity of pretending to read meanings into things absolutely sealed and beyond test or proof—to tap a fount of waters that couldn't possibly not have run dry. The thrill of learning that she had "overlapped," and by so much, and the wonder of my having doubtless at several earlier seasons passed again and again, all unknowing, the door of her house, where she sat above, within call and in her habit as she lived,[440] these things gave me all I wanted; I seem to remember in fact my more or less immediately recognising that I positively oughtn't—"for anything to come of it"—to have wanted more. I saw, quickly, how something might come of it *thus;* whereas a fine instinct told me that the effect of a nearer view of the case (the case of the overlapping) would probably have had to be quite differently calculable. It was really with another item of knowledge,[441] however, that I measured the mistake I should have made in waking up sooner to the question of opportunity. That item consisted of the action taken on the premises by a person who *had* waked up in time, and the legend of whose consequent adventure, as a few spoken words put it before me, at once kindled a flame. This gentleman, an American of long ago, an ardent Shelleyite,[442] a singularly marked figure and himself in the highest degree a subject for a free sketch—I had known him a little, but there is not a reflected glint of him in "The Aspern Papers"—was named to me as having made interest with Miss Clairmont to be accepted as a lodger on the calculation that she would have Shelley documents for which, in the possibly not remote event of her death, he would thus enjoy priority of chance to treat with her representatives. He had at any rate, according to the legend, become, on earnest Shelley grounds, her yearning, though also her highly diplomatic, *pensionnaire*—but without gathering, as was to befall, the fruit of his design.

Legend here dropped to another key; it remained in a manner interesting, but became to my ear a trifle coarse, or at least rather vague and obscure. It mentioned a younger female relative of the ancient woman as a person who, for a queer climax, had had to be dealt with; it flickered so for a moment and then, as a light, to my great relief, quite went out. It had flickered indeed but at the best—yet had flickered enough to give me my "facts," bare facts of intimation; which, scant handful though they were, were more distinct and more numerous than I mostly *like* facts: like them, that is, as we say of an etcher's progressive subject, in an early "state."[443] Nine tenths of the artist's interest in them is that of what he shall add to them and how he shall turn them. Mine, however, in the connexion I speak of, had fortunately got away from me, and quite of their own movement, in time not to crush me. So it was, at all events, that my imagination preserved power to react under the mere essential charm—that, I mean, of a final scene of the rich dim Shelley drama played out in the very theatre of our own "modernity."[444] This was the beauty that appealed to me; there had been, so to speak, a forward continuity, from the actual man, the divine poet, on; and the curious, the ingenious, the admirable thing would be to throw it backward again, to compress—squeezing it hard!—the connexion that had drawn itself out, and convert so the stretched relation into a value of nearness on our own part.[445] In short I saw my chance as admirable, and one reason, when the direction is right, may serve as well as fifty; but if I "took over," as I say, everything that was of the essence, I stayed my hand for the rest. The Italian side of the legend closely clung; if only because the so possible terms of my Juliana's life in the Italy of other days could make conceivable for her the fortunate privacy, the long uninvaded and uninterviewed state on which I represent her situation as founded.[446] Yes, a surviving unexploited unparagraphed Juliana was up to a quarter of a century since still supposeable—as much so as any such buried treasure, any such grave unprofaned, would defy probability now. And then the case had the air of the past just in the degree in which that air, I confess, most appeals to me—when the region over which it hangs is far enough away without being too far.

    I delight in a palpable imaginable *visitable* past—in the nearer distances and the clearer mysteries, the marks and signs of a world we may reach over to as by making a long arm we grasp an object at the other end of our own table.[447] The table is the one, the common expanse, and where we lean, so stretching, we find it firm and continuous. That, to my imagination, is the past fragrant of all, or of almost all, the poetry of the thing outlived and lost and gone, and yet in which the precious element of closeness, telling so of connexions but tasting so of differences, remains appreciable. With more moves back the element of the appreciable shrinks—just as the charm of looking over a garden-wall into another garden[448] breaks down when successions of walls appear. The other gardens, those still beyond, may be there, but even by use of our longest ladder we are baffled and bewildered— the view is mainly a view of barriers. The one partition makes the place we have wondered about *other*, both richly and recogniseably so; but who shall pretend to impute an effect of composition to the twenty? We are divided of course between liking to feel the past strange and liking to feel it familiar; the difficulty is, for intensity, to catch it at the moment when the scales of the balance hang with the right evenness. I say for intensity, for we may profit by them in other aspects enough if we are content to measure or to feel loosely. It would take me too far, however, to tell why the particular afternoon light that I thus call intense rests clearer to my sense on the Byronic age, as I conveniently name it,[449] than on periods more protected by the "dignity" of history. With the times beyond, intrinsically more "strange," the tender grace, for the backward vision, has faded, the afternoon darkened; for any time nearer to us the special effect hasn't begun. So there, to put the matter crudely, is the appeal I fondly recognise, an appeal residing doubtless more in the "special effect," in some deep associational force, than in a virtue more intrinsic. I am afraid I must add, since I allow myself so much to fantasticate, that the impulse had more than once taken me to project the Byronic age and the afternoon light across the great sea, to see in short whether association would carry so far and what the young century might pass for on that side of the modern world where it was not only itself so irremediably youngest, but was bound up with youth in everything else. There was a refinement of curiosity in this imputation of a golden strangeness to American social facts—though I cannot pretend, I fear, that there was any greater wisdom.

Since what it had come to then was, harmlessly enough, cultivating a sense of the past[450] under that close protection, it was natural, it was fond and filial, to wonder if a few of the distilled drops mightn't be gathered from some vision of, say, "old" New York.[451] Would that human congeries, to aid obligingly in the production of a fable, be conceivable as "taking" the afternoon light with the right happy slant?—or could a recogniseable reflexion of the Byronic age, in other words, be picked up on the banks of the Hudson? (Only just there, beyond the great sea, if anywhere: in no other connexion would the question so much as raise its head. I admit that Jeffrey Aspern isn't even feebly localised, but I *thought* New York as I projected him.) It was "amusing," in any case, always, to try experiments; and the experiment for the right *transposition* of my Juliana would be to fit her out with an immortalising poet as transposed as herself. Delicacy had demanded, I felt, that my appropriation of the Florentine legend should purge it, first of all, of references too obvious; so that, to begin with, I shifted the scene of the adventure. Juliana, as I saw her, was thinkable only in Byronic and more or less immediately post-Byronic Italy; but there were conditions in which she was ideally arrangeable, as happened, especially in respect to the later time and the long undetected survival; there being absolutely no refinement of the mouldy rococo, in human or whatever other form, that you may not disembark at the dislocated water-steps[452] of almost any decayed monument of Venetian greatness in auspicious quest of. It was a question, in fine, of covering one's tracks—though with no great elaboration I am bound to admit; and I felt I couldn't cover mine more than in postulating a comparative American Byron to match an American Miss Clairmont—she as absolute as she would. I scarce know whether best to say for this device to-day that it cost me little or that it cost me much; it was "cheap" or expensive[453] according to the degree of verisimilitude artfully obtained. If that degree appears *nil* the "art," such as it was, is wasted, and my remembrance of the contention, on the part of a highly critical friend[454] who at that time and later on often had my ear, that it had been simply foredoomed to be wasted, puts before me the passage in the private history of "The Aspern Papers" that I now find, I confess, most interesting. I comfort myself for the needful brevity of a present glance at it by the sense that the general question involved, under criticism, can't but come up for us again at higher pressure.

My friend's argument bore then—at the time and afterward—on my vicious practice, as he maintained, of postulating for the purpose of my fable celebrities who not only *hadn't* existed in the conditions I imputed to them, but who for the most part (and in no case more markedly than in that of Jeffrey Aspern) couldn't possibly have done so. The stricture was to apply itself to a whole group of short fictions in which I had, with whatever ingenuity, assigned to several so-called eminent figures positions absolutely unthinkable in our actual encompassing air, an air definitely unfavourable to certain forms of eminence. It was vicious, my critic contended, to flourish forth on one's page "great people," public persons, who shouldn't more or less square with our quite definite and calculable array of such notabilities; and by this rule I was heavily incriminated. The rule demanded that the "public person" portrayed should be at least of the tradition, of the general complexion, of the face-value, exactly, of some past or present producible counterfoil.[455] Mere private figures, under one's hand, might correspond with nobody, it being of their essence to be but narrowly known; the represented state of being conspicuous, on the other hand, involved before anything else a recognition—and none of my eminent folk were recogniseable. It was all very well for instance to have put one's self at such pains for Miriam Rooth in "The Tragic Muse"; but *there* was misapplied zeal, there a case of pitiful waste, crying aloud to be denounced. Miriam is offered not as a young person passing unnoticed by her age—like the Biddy Dormers and Julia Dallows, say, of the same book, but as a high rarity, a time-figure of the scope inevitably attended by other commemorations. Where on earth would be then Miriam's inscribed "counterfoil," and in what conditions of the contemporary English theatre, in what conditions of criticism, of appreciation, under what conceivable Anglo-Saxon star, might we take an artistic value of this order either for produced or for recognised?[456] We are, as a "public," chalk-marked by nothing, more unmistakeably, than by the truth that we know nothing of such values—any more than, as my friend was to impress on me, we are susceptible of consciousness of such others (these in the sphere of literary eminence) as my Neil Paraday in "The Death of the Lion," as my Hugh Vereker in "The Figure in the Carpet," as my Ralph

Limbert, above all, in "The Next Time,"[457] as sundry unprecedented and unmatched heroes and martyrs of the artistic ideal, in short, elsewhere exemplified in my pages. We shall come to these objects of animadversion in another hour, when I shall have no difficulty in producing the defence I found for them—since, obviously, I hadn't cast them into the world *all naked and ashamed*;[458] and I deal for the moment but with the stigma in general as Jeffrey Aspern carries it.

The charge being that I foist upon our early American annals a distinguished presence for which they yield me absolutely no warrant—"Where, within them, gracious heaven, were we to look for so much as an approach to the social elements of habitat and climate of birds of that note and plumage?"—I find his link with reality then just in the tone of the picture wrought round him. What was that tone but exactly, but exquisitely, calculated, the harmless hocus-pocus[459] under cover of which we might suppose him to have existed? This tone is the tone, artistically speaking, of "amusement," the current floating that precious influence home quite as one of those high tides watched by the smugglers of old[460] might, in case of their boat's being boarded, be trusted to wash far up the strand the cask of foreign liquor expertly committed to it. If through our lean prime Western period no dim and charming ghost of an adventurous lyric genius might by a stretch of fancy flit, if the time was really too hard to "take," in the light form proposed, the elegant reflexion, then so much the worse for the time[461]—it was all one could say! The retort to that of course was that such a plea represented no "link" with reality—which was what was under discussion—but only a link, and flimsy enough too, with the deepest depths of the artificial: the restrictive truth exactly contended for, which may embody my critic's last word rather of course than my own. My own, so far as I shall pretend in that especial connexion to report it, was that one's warrant, in such a case, hangs essentially on the question of whether or no the false element imputed would have borne that test of further development which so exposes the wrong and so consecrates the right. My last word was, heaven forgive me, that, occasion favouring, I could have perfectly "worked out" Jeffrey Aspern. The boast remains indeed to be verified when we shall arrive at the other challenged cases.

That particular challenge at least "The Turn of the Screw" doesn't incur; and this perfectly independent and irresponsible little fiction rejoices, beyond any rival on a like ground, in a conscious provision of prompt retort to the sharpest question that may be addressed to it. For it has the small strength—if I shouldn't say rather the unattackable ease—of a perfect homogeneity, of being, to the very last grain of its virtue, all of a kind; the very kind, as happens, least apt to be baited by earnest criticism, the only sort of criticism of which account need be taken. To have handled again this so full-blown flower of high fancy is to be led back by it to easy and happy recognitions. Let the first of these be that of the starting-point itself—the sense, all charming again, of the circle, one winter afternoon, round the hall-fire of a grave old country-house[462] where (for all the world as if to resolve itself promptly and obligingly into convertible, into "literary" stuff) the talk turned, on I forget what homely pretext, to apparitions and night-fears, to the marked and sad drop in the general supply, and still more in the general quality, of such commodities. The good, the really effective and heart-shaking ghost-stories (roughly so to term them) appeared all to have been told, and neither new crop nor new type in any quarter awaited us. The new type indeed, the mere modern "psychical" case, washed clean of all queerness as by exposure to a flowing laboratory tap, and equipped with credentials vouching for this—the new type clearly promised little, for the more it was respectably certified the less it seemed of a nature to rouse the dear old sacred terror.[463] Thus it was, I remember, that amid our lament for a beautiful lost form, our distinguished host expressed the wish that he might but have recovered for us one of the scantest of fragments of this form at its best. He had never forgotten the impression made on him as a young man by the withheld glimpse, as it were, of a dreadful matter that had been reported years before, and with as few particulars, to a lady with whom he had youthfully talked. The story would have been thrilling could she but have found herself in better possession of it, dealing as it did with a couple of small children in an out-of-the-way place, to whom the spirits of certain "bad" servants, dead in the employ of the house, were believed to have appeared with the design of "getting hold" of them.[464] This was all, but there had been more, which my friend's old converser had lost the thread of: she could only assure him of the wonder of the allegations as she had anciently heard them made. He himself could give us but this shadow of a shadow—my own appreciation of which, I need scarcely say, was exactly wrapped up in that thinness.

On the surface there wasn't much, but another grain, none the less, would have spoiled the precious pinch addressed to its end as neatly as some modicum extracted from an old silver snuff-box and held between finger and thumb. I was to remember the haunted children and the prowling servile spirits as a "value," of the disquieting sort, in all conscience sufficient; so that when, after an interval, I was asked for something seasonable by the promoters of a periodical dealing in the time-honoured Christmas-tide toy,[465] I bethought myself at once of the vividest little note for sinister romance that I had ever jotted down.

Such was the private source of "The Turn of the Screw"; and I wondered, I confess, why so fine a germ, gleaming there in the wayside dust of life, had never been deftly picked up. The thing had for me the immense merit of allowing the imagination absolute freedom of hand, of inviting it to act on a perfectly clear field, with no "outside" control involved, no pattern of the usual or the true or the terrible "pleasant"[466] (save always of course the high pleasantry of one's very form) to consort with. This makes in fact the charm of my second reference, that I find here a perfect example of an exercise of the imagination unassisted, unassociated—playing the game, making the score, in the phrase of our sporting day, off its own bat.[467] To what degree the game was worth playing I needn't attempt to say: the exercise I have noted strikes me now, I confess, as the interesting thing, the imaginative faculty acting with the *whole* of the case on its hands. The exhibition involved is in other words a fairy-tale pure and simple—save indeed as to its springing not from an artless and measureless, but from a conscious and cultivated credulity. Yet the fairy-tale belongs mainly to either of two classes,[468] the short and sharp and single, charged more or less with the compactness of anecdote (as to which let the familiars of our childhood, Cinderella and Blue-Beard and Hop o' my Thumb and Little Red Riding Hood and many of the gems of the Brothers Grimm directly testify), or else the long and loose, the copious, the various, the endless, where, dramatically speaking, roundness is quite sacrificed—sacrificed to fulness, sacrificed to exuberance, if one will: witness at hazard almost any one of the Arabian Nights. The charm of all these things for the distracted modern mind is in the clear field of experience, as I call it, over which we are thus led to roam; an annexed but independent world in which nothing is right save as we rightly imagine it. We have to do *that*, and we do it happily for the short spurt and in the smaller piece, achieving so perhaps beauty and lucidity; we flounder, we lose breath, on the other hand—that is we fail, not of continuity, but of an agreeable unity, of the "roundness" in which beauty and lucidity largely reside—when we go in, as they say, for great lengths and breadths. And this, oddly enough, not because "keeping it up" isn't abundantly within the compass of the imagination appealed to in certain conditions, but because the finer interest depends just on *how* it is kept up.

Nothing is so easy as improvisation,[469] the running on and on of invention; it is sadly compromised, however, from the moment its stream breaks bounds and gets into flood. Then the waters may spread indeed, gathering houses and herds and crops and cities into their arms and wrenching off, for our amusement, the whole face of the land—only violating by the same stroke our sense of the course and the channel, which is our sense of the uses of a stream and the virtue of a story. Improvisation, as in the Arabian Nights, may keep on terms with encountered objects by sweeping them in and floating them on its breast; but the great effect it so loses—that of keeping on terms with itself. This is ever, I intimate, the hard thing for the fairy-tale; but by just so much as it struck me as hard did it in "The Turn of the Screw" affect me as irresistibly prescribed. To improvise with extreme freedom and yet at the same time without the possibility of ravage, without the hint of a flood; to keep the stream, in a word, on something like ideal terms with itself: that was here my definite business. The thing was to aim at absolute singleness, clearness and roundness, and yet to depend on an imagination working freely, working (call it) with extravagance; by which law it wouldn't be thinkable except as free and wouldn't be amusing except as controlled. The merit of the tale, as it stands, is accordingly, I judge, that it has struggled successfully with its dangers. It is an excursion into chaos while remaining, like Blue-Beard and Cinderella, but an anecdote—though an anecdote amplified and highly emphasised and returning upon itself; as, for that matter, Cinderella and Blue-Beard return. I need scarcely add after this that it is a piece of ingenuity pure and simple, of cold artistic calculation, an *amusette* to catch those not easily caught (the "fun" of the capture of the merely witless being ever but small), the jaded, the disillusioned, the fastidious. Otherwise expressed, the study is of a conceived "tone," the tone of suspected and felt trouble, of an inordinate and incalculable sort—the tone of tragic, yet of exquisite, mystification. To knead the subject of my young friend's, the supposititious narrator's, mystification thick, and yet strain the expression of it so clear and fine that beauty would result: no side of the matter so revives for me as that endeavour. Indeed if the artistic value of such an experiment be measured by the intellectual echoes it may again, long after, set in motion, the case would make in favour of this little firm fantasy—which I seem to see draw behind it to-day a train of associations. I ought doubtless to blush for thus confessing them so numerous that I can but pick among them for reference. I recall for instance a reproach made me by a reader capable evidently, for the time, of some attention, but not quite capable of enough, who complained that I hadn't sufficiently "characterised" my young woman[470] engaged in her labyrinth; hadn't endowed her with signs and marks, features and humours, hadn't in a word invited her to deal with her own mystery as well as with that of Peter Quint, Miss Jessel and the hapless children. I remember well, whatever the absurdity of its now coming back to me, my reply to that criticism—under which one's artistic, one's ironic heart shook for the instant almost to breaking. "You indulge in that stricture at your ease, and I don't mind confiding to you that—strange as it may appear!—one has to choose ever so delicately among one's difficulties, attaching one's self to the greatest, bearing hard on those and intelligently neglecting the others. If one attempts to tackle them all one is certain to deal completely with none; whereas the effectual dealing with a few casts a blest golden haze under cover of which, like wanton mocking goddesses in clouds, the others find prudent to retire.[471] It was 'déja très-joli,' in 'The Turn of the Screw,' please believe, the general proposition of our young woman's keeping crystalline her record of so many intense anomalies and obscurities—by which I don't of course mean her explanation of them, a different matter; and I saw no way, I feebly grant (fighting, at the best too, periodically, for every grudged inch of my space) to exhibit her in relations other than those; one of which, precisely, would have been her relation to her own nature. We have surely as much of her own nature as we can swallow in watching it reflect her anxieties and inductions. It constitutes no little of a character indeed, in such conditions, for a young person, as she says, 'privately bred,'[472] that she is able to make her particular credible statement of such strange matters. She has 'authority,'[473] which is a good deal to have given her, and I couldn't have arrived at so much had I clumsily tried for more."

For which truth I claim part of the charm latent on occasion in the extracted reasons of beautiful things—putting for the beautiful always, in a work of art, the close, the curious, the deep. Let me place above all, however, under the protection of that presence the side by which this fiction appeals most to consideration: its choice of its way of meeting its gravest difficulty. There were difficulties not so grave: I had for instance simply to renounce all attempt to keep the kind and degree of impression I wished to produce on terms with the to-day so copious psychical record of cases of apparitions.[474] Different signs and circumstances, in the reports, mark these cases; different things are done—though on the whole very little appears to be—by the persons appearing; the point is, however, that some things are never done at all: this negative quantity is large—certain reserves and proprieties and immobilities consistently impose themselves. Recorded and attested "ghosts" are in other words as little expressive, as little dramatic, above all as little continuous and conscious and responsive, as is consistent with their taking the trouble—and an immense trouble they find it, we gather—to appear at all.[475] Wonderful and interesting therefore at a given moment, they are inconceivable figures in an *action*—and "The Turn of the Screw" was an action, desperately, or it was nothing. I had to decide in fine between having my apparitions correct and having my story "good"—that is producing my impression of the dreadful, my designed horror. Good ghosts, speaking by book,[476] make poor subjects, and it was clear that from the first my hovering prowling blighting presences, my pair of abnormal agents, would have to depart altogether from the rules. They would be agents in fact; there would be laid on them the dire duty of causing the situation to reek with the air of Evil. Their desire and their ability to do so, visibly measuring meanwhile their effect, together with their observed and described success—this was exactly my central idea; so that, briefly, I cast my lot with pure romance, the appearances conforming to the true type being so little romantic.

This is to say, I recognise again, that Peter Quint and Miss Jessel are not "ghosts" at all, as we now know the ghost, but goblins, elves, imps, demons as loosely constructed as those of the old trials for witchcraft; if not, more pleasingly, fairies of the legendary order, wooing their victims forth to see them dance under the moon.[477] Not indeed that I suggest their reducibility to any form of the pleasing pure and simple; they please at the best but through having helped me to express my subject all directly and intensely.

Here it was—in the use made of them—that I felt a high degree of art really required; and here it is that, on reading the tale over, I find my precautions justified. The essence of the matter was the villainy of motive in the evoked predatory creatures; so that the result would be ignoble—by which I mean would be trivial—were this element of evil but feebly or inanely suggested. Thus arose on behalf of my idea the lively interest of a possible suggestion and process of *adumbration;* the question of how best to convey that sense of the depths of the sinister without which my fable would so woefully limp. Portentous evil—how was I to save that, as an intention on the part of my demon-spirits, from the drop, the comparative vulgarity, inevitably attending, throughout the whole range of possible brief illustration, the offered example, the imputed vice, the cited act, the limited deplorable presentable instance? To bring the bad dead back to life for a second round of badness is to warrant them as indeed prodigious, and to become hence as shy of specifications as of a waiting anti-climax. One had seen, in fiction, some grand form of wrong-doing, or better still of wrong-being, imputed, seen it promised and announced as by the hot breath of the Pit[478]—and then, all lamentably, shrink to the compass of some particular brutality, some particular immorality, some particular infamy portrayed: with the result, alas, of the demonstration's falling sadly short. If *my* bad things, for "The Turn of the Screw," I felt, should succumb to this danger, if they shouldn't seem sufficiently bad, there would be nothing for me but to hang my artistic head lower than I had ever known occasion to do.

The view of that discomfort and the fear of that dishonour, it accordingly must have been, that struck the proper light for my right, though by no means easy, short cut. What, in the last analysis, had I to give the sense of? Of their being, the haunting pair, capable, as the phrase is, of everything[479]—that is of exerting, in respect to the children, the very worst action small victims so conditioned might be conceived as subject to.[480] What would *be* then, on reflexion, this utmost conceivability?—a question to which the answer all admirably came. There is for such a case no eligible *absolute* of the wrong; it remains relative to fifty other elements, a matter of appreciation, speculation, imagination—these things moreover quite exactly in the light of the spectator's, the critic's, the reader's experience. Only make the reader's general vision of evil intense enough, I said to myself—and that already is a charming job—and his own experience, his own imagination, his own sympathy (with the children) and horror (of their false friends) will supply him quite sufficiently with all the particulars. Make him *think* the evil, make him think it for himself, and you are released from weak specifications. This ingenuity I took pains—as indeed great pains were required—to apply; and with a success apparently beyond my liveliest hope. Droll enough at the same time, I must add, some of the evidence—even when most convincing—of this success. How can I feel my calculation to have failed, my wrought suggestion not to have worked, that is, on my being assailed, as has befallen me, with the charge of a monstrous emphasis, the charge of all indecently expatiating?[481] There is not only from beginning to end of the matter not an inch of expatiation, but my values are positively all blanks save so far as an excited horror, a promoted pity, a created expertness—on which punctual effects of strong causes no writer can ever fail to plume himself—proceed to read into them more or less fantastic figures. Of high interest to the author meanwhile—and by the same stroke a theme for the moralist—the artless resentful reaction of the entertained person who has abounded in the sense of the situation. He visits his abundance, morally, on the artist—who has but clung to an ideal of faultlessness. Such indeed, for this latter, are some of the observations by which the prolonged strain of that clinging may be enlivened!

I arrive with "The Liar" (1888) and "The Two Faces" (1900) at the first members of the considerable group of shorter, of shortest tales here republished; though I should perhaps place quite in the forefront "The Chaperon" and "The Pupil," at which we have already glanced. I am conscious of much to say of these numerous small productions as a family—a family indeed quite organised as such, with its proper representatives, its "heads," its subdivisions and its branches, its poor relations perhaps not least: its unmistakeable train of poor relations in fact, the very poorer, the poorest of whom I am, in family parlance, for this formal appearance in society, "cutting" without a scruple.[482] These repudiated members, some of them, for that matter, well-nourished and substantial presences enough, with their compromising rustiness plausibly, almost touchingly dissimulated, I fondly figure as standing wistful but excluded, after the fashion of the outer fringe of the connected whom there are not carriages enough to convey from the church—whether (for we have our choice of similes) to the wedding-feast or to the interment! Great for me from far back had been the interest of the whole "question of the short story," roundabout which our age has, for lamentable reasons, heard so vain a babble;[483] but I foresee occasions yet to come when it will abundantly waylay me. Then it will insist on presenting itself but in too many lights. Little else perhaps meanwhile is more relevant as to "The Liar" than the small fact of its having, when its hour came, quite especially conformed to that custom of shooting straight from the planted seed,[484] of responding at once to the touched spring, of which my fond appeal here to "origins" and evolutions so depicts the sway. When it shall come to fitting, historically, anything like *all* my small children of fancy with their pair of progenitors, and all my reproductive unions with their inevitable fruit, I shall seem to offer my backward consciousness in the image of a shell charged and recharged by the Fates with some patent and infallible explosive. Never would there seem to have been a pretence to such economy of ammunition!

However this may be, I come back, for "The Liar," as for so many of its fellows, to holding my personal experience, poor thing though it may have been, immediately accountable. For by what else in the world but by fatal design had I been placed at dinner one autumn evening of old London days face to face with a gentleman, met for the first time, though favourably known to me by name and fame, in whom I recognised the most unbridled colloquial romancer the "joy of life"[485] had ever found occasion to envy? Under what other conceivable coercion had I been invited to reckon, through the evening, with the type, with the character, with the countenance, of this magnificent master's wife, who, veracious, serene and charming, yet not once meeting straight the eyes of one of us, did her duty by each, and by her husband most of all, without so much as, in the vulgar phrase, turning a hair?[486] It was long ago, but I have never, to this hour, forgotten the evening itself—embalmed for me now in an old-time sweetness beyond any aspect of my reproduction. I made but a fifth person, the other couple our host and hostess; between whom and one of the company, while we listened to the woven wonders of a summer holiday, the exploits of a salamander,[487] among Mediterranean isles, were exchanged, dimly and discreetly, ever so guardedly, but all expressively, imperceptible lingering looks. It was exquisite, it *could* but become, inevitably, some "short story" or other, which it clearly pre-fitted as the hand the glove. I must reserve "The Two Faces" till I come to speak of the thrilling question of the poor painter's tormented acceptance, in advance, of the scanted canvas; of the writer's rueful hopeful assent to the conditions known to him as "too little room to turn round."[488] Of the liveliest interest then—or so at least I could luckily always project the case—to see how he may nevertheless, in the event, effectively manœuvre. The value of "The Two Faces"—by reason of which I have not hesitated to gather it in—is thus peculiarly an economic one. It may conceal rather than exhale its intense little principle of calculation; but the neat evolution, as I call it, the example of the turn of the *whole* coach and pair in the contracted court,[489] without the "spill" of a single passenger or the derangement of a single parcel, is only in three or four cases (where the coach is fuller still) more appreciable.

PREFACE to *The Reverberator, Madame de Mauves, A Passionate Pilgrim and Other Tales* (*NYE* XIII)

I HAVE gathered into this volume some early brevities, the third in order of which dates from further back than any tale comprised in the Edition. The first in order appeared considerably later, but I have given it precedence in this group by reason of its greatest length.⁴⁹⁰ It is the most recent in the list, but, as having originally (in the good old days, though they are as yet none so remote, of "pleasant" publication) enjoyed the honour of two pretty little volumes "all to itself," it falls into the category of Shorter Novels—under an indulgence not extended to several of its compeers.⁴⁹¹ "The Reverberator," which figured at birth (1888) in half a dozen numbers of "Macmillan's Magazine" may be described, I suppose, beyond any fiction here reproduced, as a *jeu d'esprit:* I can think at least of none other on the brow of which I may presume to place that laurel.⁴⁹² And yet as I cast about me for the nameable grounds of the hospitality I thus give it I find myself think of it in other rich lights as well; quite in the light of an exemplary anecdote, and at the same time quite in that of a little rounded drama. This is to press hard, it might seem, on so slight a composition; but I brave the extravagance under the interest of recognising again how the weight of expatiation is ever met in such cases—that of the slender production equally with that of the stout—by a surface really much larger than the mere offered face of the work. The face of the work may be small in itself, and yet the surface, the whole thing, the associational margin and connexion, may spread, beneath the fond remembering eye, like nothing more noble than an insidious grease-spot.⁴⁹³ It is of the essence of the anecdote to get itself told as it can—which truth represented clearly the best chance of life for the matter involved in "The Reverberator"; but also it is of the essence of the drama to conform to logic, and the pages I here treat of may appear at moments not quite predominantly sure either of their luck or of their law. This, however, I think, but to a cursory glance, for I perhaps do them a wrong in emphasising their anecdotic cast. Might I not, certainly, have invoked for them in some degree the anecdotic grace I wouldn't have undertaken them at all; but I now see how they were still to have been provided for if this had failed them.

The anecdote consists, ever, of something that has oddly happened to some one, and the first of its duties is to point directly to the person whom it so distinguishes. He may be you or I or any one else, but a condition of our interest—perhaps the principal one—is that the anecdote shall know him, and shall accordingly speak of him, as its subject. Who is it then that by this rule the specimen before us adopts and sticks to? Something happens, and to a certain person, or, better, to a certain group of persons, in "The Reverberator," but of whom, when it comes to the point, is the fable narrated? The anecdote has always a question to answer—of whom necessarily is it told? Is it told here of the Proberts or of the Dossons? To whom in the instance before us does the principal thing, the thing worth the telling, happen? To the fatal Mr. Flack, to Francie Dosson and her father and sister, lumping them, on the ground of their "racial consciousness," all together?[494]—or to the cluster of scandalised Parisians in general, if not to the girl's distracted young lover in particular? It is easy, alas, to defy a clear statement on this head to be made ("No, I can't say whom or what or *which* I'm about: I seem so sometimes to be about one set and sometimes about another!" the little story is free to plead) whereby anecdotic grace does break down. Fortunately there remains another string, a second, to my bow: I should have been nowhere, in the event of a challenge, had I not concomitantly felt my subject, for all its slightness, as a small straight *action*, and so placed it in that blest drama-light which, really making for intelligibility as nothing else does, orders and regulates, even when but faintly turned on; squares things and keeps them in happy relation to each other. What "happens," by that felicity, happens thus to every one concerned, exactly as in much more prodigious recitals: it's a case—just as we have seen it before, in more portentous connexions and with the support of mightier comparisons—of the planned rotation of aspects and of that "scenic" determination of them about which I fear I may already have been a bore.[495]

After which perhaps too vertiginous explanatory flight I feel that I drop indeed to the very concrete and comparatively trivial origin of my story—short, that is, of some competent critical attribution of triviality all round. I am afraid, at any rate, that with this reminiscence I but watch my grease-spot (for I cling to the homely metaphor) engagingly extend its bounds. Who shall say thus—and I have put the vain question but too often before!—where the associational nimbus of the all but lost, of the miraculously recovered, chapter of experience shall absolutely fade and stop?[496] That would be possible only were experience a chessboard of sharp black-and-white squares. Taking one of these for a convenient plot, I have but to see my particle of suggestion lurk in its breast, and then but to repeat in this connexion the act of picking it up, for the whole of the *rest* of the connexion straightway to loom into life, its parts all clinging together and pleading with a collective friendly voice[497] that I can't pretend to resist: "Oh but we too, you know; what were *we* but of the experience?" Which comes to scarce more than saying indeed, no doubt, that nothing more complicates and overloads the act of retrospect than to let one's imagination itself work backward as part of the business. Some art of preventing this by keeping that interference out would be here of a useful application; and would include the question of providing conveniently for the officious faculty in the absence of its natural caretakers, the judgement, the memory, the conscience, occupied, as it were, elsewhere. These truants, the other faculties of the mind without exception, I surmise, would then be free to remount the stream of time (as an earnest and enquiring band) with the flower of the flock, the hope of the family, left at home or "boarded out,"[498] say, for the time of the excursion. I have been unable, I confess, to make such an arrangement; the consequence of which failure is that everything I "find," as I look back, lives for me again in the light of *all* the parts, such as they are, of my intelligence. Or to express the phenomenon otherwise, and perhaps with still more complacency for it, the effort to reconstitute the medium and the season that favoured the first stir of life, the first perceived gleam of the vital spark, in the trifle before us, fairly makes everything in the picture revive, fairly even extends the influence to matters remote and strange. The musing artist's imagination—thus *not* excluded and confined—supplies the link that is missing and makes the whole occasion (the occasion of the glorious birth to him of still another infant motive) comprehensively and richly *one*. And this if that addition to his flock—his effusive parental welcome to which seems immediately to cause so splendid and furnished and fitted a world to arch over it—happens to be even of so modest a promise as the tiny principle of "The Reverberator."

It was in a grand old city of the south of Europe (though neither in Rome nor yet in Florence) long years ago, and during a winter spent there[499] in the seeing of many people on the pleasantest terms in the world, as they now seem to me to have been, as well as in the hearing of infinite talk, talk mainly, inexhaustibly, about persons and the "personal equation"[500] and the personal mystery. This somehow *had* to be in an odd, easy, friendly, a miscellaneous, many-coloured little cosmopolis,[501] where the casual exotic society was a thing of heterogeneous vivid patches, but with a fine old native basis, the basis that held stoutly enough together while the patches dangled and fluttered, stitched on as with thread of silver, pinned on as with pearls, lasting their time above all and brightening the scene. To allude to the scene, alas! seems half an undertaking to reproduce it, any humoursome indulgence in which would lead us much too far. Nor am I strictly—as if I cultivated an ideal of strictness!—concerned with any fact but that of the appearance among us, that winter, of a charming free young person,[502] superlatively introduced and infinitely admired, who, taken to twenty social bosoms, figured "success" in a form, that of the acclaimed and confident pretty girl of our prosaic and temperate climes, for which the old-world salon, with its windows of iridescent view and its different conception of the range of charm, had never much provided. The old-world salon, in our community, still, when all was said, more or less imposed the type and prescribed the tone; yet to the charming stranger even these penetralia had not been closed,[503] and, over them, to be brief, she had shed her influence, just as among them, not less, she had gathered her harvest. She had come, in fine, she had seen and had conquered;[504] after which she had withdrawn with her spoil. Her spoil, to put it plainly, had been a treasure of impressions; her harvest, as I have said, a wealth of revelations. I made an absence of several weeks, I went to Florence and to Rome, but I came back in the spring[505]—and all to encounter the liveliest chatter of surprise that had perhaps ever spent itself under the elegant massive ceilings for which the old-world salons were famous. The ingenuous stranger[506]—it was awfully coming to light—had *written* about them, about these still consciously critical retreats, many of them temples harbouring the very altar of the exclusive; she had made free with them, pen in hand, with the best conscience in the world, no doubt, but to a high effect of confidence betrayed, and to the amazement and consternation of every one involved, though most of all, naturally, to the dismay of her primary backers.

The young lady, frankly, a graceful amateur journalist, had made use of her gathered material; she had addressed to a newspaper in her native city (which no power on earth would induce me to designate, so that as to this and to the larger issue, not less, of the glamour of its big State-name, I defy all guesses) a letter as long, as confidential, as "chatty," as full of headlong history and limping legend, of aberration and confusion, as she might have indited to the most trusted of friends.[507] The friend trusted had been, as happened, simply the biggest "reading public" in the world, and the performance, typographically bristling, had winged its way back to its dishonoured nest like some monstrous black bird or beetle, an embodiment of popping eyes, a whirl of brandished feathers and claws. Strange, it struck me, to tell the truth, the fact itself of "anybody's knowing,"[508] and still more of anybody's caring—the fact itself, that is, of such prompt repercussion and recognition: one would so little, in advance, have supposed the reverberation of the bomb, its heeded reverberation, conceivable. No such consequence, clearly, had been allowed for by its innocent maker, for whose imagination, one felt sure, the explosion had not been designed to be world-shaking. The recording, slobbering sheet, as an object thinkable or visible in a medium so non-conducting, made of actual recognition, made even of the barest allusion, the falsest of false notes. The scandal reigned, however, and the commotion lasted, a nine days' wonder;[509] the ingenuous stranger's name became anathema, and all to the high profit of an incorrigible collector of "cases." Him in his depth of perversity, I profess, the flurry of resentment could only, after a little, affect as scarce more charged with wisdom than the poor young lady's miscalculated overflow itself; so completely beside the question of the finer *comparative* interest remained that of the force of the libel and that of the degree of the injury. The finer interest was in the facts that made the incident a case, and the true note of that, I promptly made sure, was just in the extraordinary amount of native innocence that positively *had* to be read into the perpetrated act. The couple of columns in the vulgar newspaper constituted no document whatever on the manners and morals of the company of persons "betrayed," but on the other hand, in its indirect way, flooded "American society" with light,[510] became on *that* side in the highest degree documentary. So it was, I soon saw, that though the perpetrated act was in itself and immediately no "situation," it nevertheless pointed to one, and was for that value to be stored up.

It remained for a long time thus a mere sketched finger-post: the perpetrated act had, unmistakeably, *meant* something—one couldn't make out at first exactly what; till at last, after several years of oblivion,[511] its connexions, its illustrative worth, came quite naturally into view. It fell in short into the wider perspective, the very largest fund of impressions and appearances, perhaps, that the particular observer's and designer's mind was to have felt itself for so long queerly weighted with. I have already had occasion to say that the "international" light lay thick, from period to period, on the general scene of my observation[512]—a truth the reasons and bearings of which will require in due course to be intelligibly stated; everything that possibly could, at any rate, managed at that time (as it had done before and was undiscourageably to continue to do) to *be* international for me: which was an immense resource and a happy circumstance from many points of view.[513] Therefore I may say at once that if no particular element or feature of the view had struck me from far back as receiving so much of the illumination as the comparative *state of innocence* of the spirit of my countryfolk, by that same token everything had a price, was of immediate application and found itself closely interwoven, that could tend to emphasise or vivify the innocence. I had indeed early to recognise that I was in a manner shut up to the contemplation of it—really to the point, it has often seemed to me these pages must testify, of appearing to wander, as under some uncanny spell, amid the level sands and across the pathless desert[514] of a single and of a not especially rich or fruitful aspect. Here, for that matter, comes in one of the oddest and most interesting of facts—as I measure it; which again will take much stating, but to which I may provisionally give *this* importance, that, sketchily speaking, if I hadn't had, on behalf of the American character, the negative aspects to deal with, I should practically, and given the limits of my range, have had no aspects at all. I shall on a near pretext, as I say, develop the sense of this;[515] but let it now stand for the obvious truth that the negative sides were always *at* me, for illustration, for interpretation, and that though I looked yearningly, from time to time, over their collective head, though, after an experimental baffled sniff, I was apt to find myself languish for sharper air than any they exhaled, they constantly gave me enough, and more than enough, to "tackle," so that I might even well ask myself what more miscellaneous justice I should have been able to render.

Given, after this fashion, my condition of knowledge, the most general appearance of the American (of those days) in Europe, that of being almost incredibly *unaware of life*—as the European order expressed life—had to represent for me the *whole* exhibitional range; the particular initiation on my own part that would have helped me to other apprehensions being absolutely bolted and barred to me. What this alternative would have stood for we shall immediately see; but meanwhile—and nothing could have been at once more inevitable, more logical and more ridiculous—I was reduced to studying my New Yorkers and my Bostonians, since there were enough of these alone and to spare, under the queer rubric of their more or less stranded helplessness. If asked why I describe in such terms the appearances that most appealed to me, I can only wonder how the bewildered state of the persons principally figuring in the Americano-European prospect could have been otherwise expressed. They come back to me, in the lurid light of contrast, as irresistibly destitute of those elements of preparedness that my pages show even the most limited European adventure to call into play. This at least was, by my retrospect, the inveterate case for the men—it differed only for certain of the women, the younger, the youngest, those of whom least might at the best have been expected, and in the interest of whose "success" their share of the characteristic blankness underwent what one might call a sea-change.[516] Conscious of so few things in the world, these unprecedented creatures—since that is what it came to for them— were least of all conscious of deficiencies and dangers; so that, the grace of youth and innocence and freshness aiding, their negatives were converted and became in certain relations lively positives and values. I might give a considerable list of those of my fictions, longer and shorter, in which this curious conversion is noted. Suffice it, at all events, in respect to the show at large, that, even as testifying but to a suffered and suffering state, and working beauty and comedy and pathos but into that compass, my procession of figures—which kept passing, and indeed kept pausing, by no act of my own—left me with all I could manage on my hands.

This will have seemed doubtless a roundabout approach to my saying that I seized the right connexion for our roaring young lioness of the old-world salons[517] from the moment I qualified her as, in spite of the stimulating commerce enjoyed with them, signally "unaware of life." What had she lacked for interest? what had her case lacked for application? what in the world but just that perceived reference to something larger, something more widely significant? What was so large, what so widely significant in its general sphere, as that, "otherwise" so well endowed and appointed, as that, altogether so well constituted and introduced, she *could* have kept up to the end (the end of our concern with her) the state of unawareness? Immense at any rate the service she so rendered the brooding critic capable of taking a hint from her, for she became on the spot an inimitable link with the question of what it might distinguishably be in their own flourishing Order that could *keep* them, the passionless pilgrims,[518] so unaware? This was the point—one had caught them in the act of it; of a disposition, which had perhaps even most a comic side, to treat "Europe," collectively, as a vast painted and gilded holiday toy, serving its purpose on the spot and for the time, but to be relinquished, sacrificed, broken and cast away, at the dawn of any other convenience. It seemed to figure thus not only as a gorgeous dressed doll, the most expensive plaything, no doubt, in the world, but as a *living* doll, precisely, who would speak and act and perform, all for a "charge"—which was the reason both of the amusement and of the cost. Only there was no more *responsibility* to a living doll than to a dead—so that, in fine, what seemed most absent from the frolic intercourse was the note of anything like reciprocity: unless indeed the so prompt and frequent newspaperisation of any quaint confidence extracted by pressure on the poor doll's stomach, of any droll sight of powers set in motion by twitch of whatever string, might serve for a rendering of that ideal. It had reached one's ear again and again from beyond the sea, this inveteracy, as one might almost call it, of the artless ventilation, and mainly in the public prints, of European matter originally gathered in under the supposed law of privilege enjoyed on the one hand and security enjoyed on the other. A hundred good instances confirmed this tradition[519] that nothing in the new world was held accountable to anything in the old, that the hemispheres would have been as dissociated as different planets hadn't one of them, by a happy miracle, come in for the comparatively antique right of free fishing[520] in the other.

It was the so oft-attested American sense of the matter that was meanwhile the oddity—the sense on the part of remote adventurous islanders that no custom of give-and-take between their bustling archipelago and the far, the massed continent was thinkable. Strangely enough, none the less, the continent was anecdotically interesting to the islands—though as soon as these were reached all difference between the fruit of the private and the fruit of the public garden naturally dropped. More than all was it striking that the "naturalness" was all of American making—in spite, as had ever seemed to me, of the American tradition to the contrary; the tradition that Europe, much rather, had originally made social commerce unequal. Europe had had quite other matters on her hands; Europe had, into the bargain, on what mightn't be newspaperised or otherwise ventilated, quite her own religion and her own practice. This superstition held true of the fruits of curiosity *wherever* socially gathered, whether in bustling archipelagos or in neighbouring kingdoms. It didn't, one felt, immensely signify, all the while; small harm was done, and it was surely rare that any was intended; for supreme, more and more, is the blest truth—sole safety, as it mostly seems, of our distracting age—that a given thing has but to be newspaperised *enough* (which it may, at our present rate of perfection, in a few hours) to return, as a quick consequence, to the common, the abysmal air and become without form and void.[521] This life of scant seconds, as it were, by the sky-scraping clock, is as good for our sense and measure of the vulgar thing, for keeping apprehension down and keeping immunity up, as no life at all; since in the midst of such preposterous pretensions to recorded or reflected existence what particular vulgarity, what individual blatancy, can prevail? Still over and above all of which, too, we are made aware of a large new direct convenience or resource—the beautiful facility thus rendered the individual mind for what it shall denominate henceforth ignoring in the lump: than which nothing is more likely to work better, I suggest, toward a finer economy of consciousness. For the new beauty is that the lump, the vast concretion of the negligible, is, thanks to prodigious expensive machinery working all *ad hoc*, carefully wrought and prepared for our so dealing with it; to the great saving of our labour of selection, our own not always too beguiled or too sweetened picking-over of the heap.

Our ingenuous young friend of the shocked saloons—to finish *her* history—had just simply acted in the tradition; she had figured herself one of the islanders, irresponsible in their very degree, and with a mind as closed to the "coming back" of her disseminated prattle as if it would have had in fact to be wafted from another planet. Thus, as I say, the friendliest initiations offered her among ancient seats had still failed to make her what I have called "aware." Here it was that she became documentary, and that in the flash of some new and accessory light, the continued procession of figures equally fallible, yet as little criminal, her bedimmed precedent shone out for me once more; so that when I got my right and true reference, as I say, for the instance commemorated in "The Reverberator," and which dangled loosely from the peg supplied by the earlier case, this reference was much more directly to the pathetic than to anything else. The Dosson family, here before us, are sunk in their innocence, sunk in their irremediable unawareness almost beyond fishing out. This constituted for handling them, I quite felt, a serious difficulty; they could be too abandoned and pathetic, as the phrase is, to live, and yet be perfectly true; but on the other hand they could be perfectly true and yet too abandoned for vivification, too consentingly feeble to be worth saving. Even this, still, wouldn't materially limit in them the force of the characteristic—it was exactly in such formless terms that they would speak best for the majority of their congeners; and, in fine, moreover, there was *this* that I absolutely had to save for the love of my subject-matter at large—the special appeal attached to the mild figure of Francina. I need scarcely point out that "round" Francie Dosson the tale is systematically constructed; with which fact was involved for me the clear sense that if I didn't see the Francie Dossons (by whom I mean the general quaint sisterhood, perfectly distinguishable then, but displaced, disfeatured, "discounted" to-day, for all I know) as always and at any cost—at whatever cost of repetition, that is—worth saving, I might as well shut up my international department. For practically—as I have said already more than enough to convey—they were what the American branch of that equation constantly threw me back upon; by reason indeed of a brace of conditions only one of which strictly inhered in the show itself.

In the heavy light of "Europe" thirty or forty years ago, there were more of the Francie Dossons and the Daisy Millers and the Bessie Aldens and the Pandora Days[522] than of all the other attested American objects put together—more of them, of course I mean, from the moment the weird harvester was at all preoccupied with charm, or at all committed to "having to have" it.[523] But quite apart from that truth was always the stiff fact, against which I might have dashed myself in vain, that I hadn't the *data* for a right approach to the minor quantities, such as they might have been made out to be. The minor quantities appeared, consistently, but in a single light—that of promiscuous obscure attendance on the Daisies and Bessies and Francies; a generalised crepuscular state at best, even though yielding little by little a view of dim forms and vague differences. These adumbrations, sufficient tests once applied, claimed identities as fathers, mothers, even sometimes as satellites more directly "engaged";[524] but there was always, for the author of this record, a prompt and urgent remark to be made about them—which placed him, when all was said, quite at his ease. The men, the non-European, in these queer clusters, the fathers, brothers, playmates, male appendages of whatever presumption, were visible and thinkable only as the American "business-man";[525] and before the American business-man, as I have been prompt to declare, I was absolutely and irredeemably helpless, with no fibre of my intelligence responding to his mystery. No approach I could make to him on his "business side" really got near it.[526] That is where I was fatally incompetent, and this in turn—the case goes into a nutshell—is so obviously why, for any decent documentation, I was simply shut up to what was left me. It takes but a glance to see how the matter was in such a fashion simplified. With the men wiped out, at a stroke, so far as any grasp of the principle of their activity was concerned (what in the name of goodness did I, or could I, know, to call know, about the very alphabet of their activity?), it wasn't the *elder* woman I could take, on any reckoning, as compensatory: her inveterate blankness of surface had a manner all its own of defying the imagination to hover or to hope. There was really, as a rule, nothing whatever to be done with the elder woman; not only were reason and fancy alike forewarned not to waste their time, but any attempt upon her, one somehow felt, would have been indecorous and almost monstrous. She wasn't so much as in question; since if one could work it out for the men that the depreciated state with which *they* vaguely and, as it were, somnolently struggled, was perhaps but casual and temporary, might be regarded in fact as the mere state of the medal with its right face accidentally turned down, this redemption never glimmered for the wife and mother, in whom nothing was in eclipse, but everything rather (everything there was at all) straight in evidence, and to whom therefore any round and complete embodiment had simply been denied.

"A Passionate Pilgrim," written in the year 1870, the earliest date to which anything in the whole present series refers itself,[527] strikes me to-day, and by the same token indescribably touches me, with the two compositions that follow it, as sops instinctively thrown to the international Cerberus[528] formidably posted where I doubtless then didn't quite make him out, yet from whose capacity to loom larger and larger with the years there must already have sprung some chilling portent. Cerberus would have been, thus, to one's younger artistic conscience, the keeper of the international "books";[529] the hovering disembodied critical spirit with a disengaged eye upon sneaking attempts to substitute the American romantic for the American real. To that comparatively artless category the fiction I have just named, together with "Madame de Mauves" and "The Madonna of the Future," belong. As American as possible, and even to the pitch of fondly coaxing it, I then desired my ground-stuff[530] to remain; so that such situations as are thus offered must have represented my prime view of the telling effect with which the business-man would be dodged. He *is* dodged, here, doubtless, to a charm—he is made to wait as in the furthest and coldest of an infinite perspective of more or less quaint antechambers; where my ingenuous theory of the matter must have been that, artfully trifled with from room to room and from pretext to pretext, he might be kept indefinitely at bay.[531] Thus if a sufficient amount of golden dust were kicked up in the foreground[532]—and I began to kick it, under all these other possible pretexts, as hard as I knew how, he would probably never be able, to my confusion, to break through at all. I had in the spring of 1869, and again in that of 1870, spent several weeks in England, renewing and extending, with infinite zest, an acquaintance with the country that had previously been but an uneffaced little chapter of boyish, or—putting it again far enough back for the dimmest dawn of sensibility—of infantine experience; and had, perceptively and æsthetically speaking, taken the adventure of my twenty-sixth year "hard,"[533] as "A Passionate Pilgrim" quite sufficiently attests.

A part of that adventure had been the never-to-be-forgotten thrill of a first sight of Italy, from late in the summer of 1869 on; so that a return to America at the beginning of the following year was to drag with it, as a lengthening chain,[534] the torment of losses and regrets. The repatriated victim of that unrest was, beyond doubt, acutely conscious of his case: the fifteen months just spent in Europe had absolutely determined his situation. The nostalgic poison had been distilled for him, the future presented to him but as a single intense question: was he to spend it in brooding exile, or might he somehow come into his "own"?—as I liked betimes to put it for a romantic analogy with the state of dispossessed princes and wandering heirs.[535] The question was to answer itself promptly enough[536]—yet after a delay sufficient to give me the measure of a whole previous relation to it.

I had from as far back as I could remember carried in my side, buried and unextracted, the head of one of those well-directed shafts from the European quiver to which, of old, tender American flesh was more helplessly and bleedingly exposed, I think, than to-day:[537] the nostalgic cup had been applied to my lips even before I was conscious of it—I had been hurried off to London and to Paris immediately after my birth, and then and there, I was ever afterwards strangely to feel, that poison had entered my veins.[538] This was so much the case that when again, in my thirteenth year, re-exposure was decreed, and was made effective and prolonged, my inward sense of it was, in the oddest way, not of my finding myself in the vague and the uncharted, but much rather restored to air already breathed and to a harmony already disclosed.[539] The unnatural precocity with which I had in fine "taken" to Europe was to be revealed to me later on and during another quite languishing American interval; an interval during which I supposed my young life to have been made bitter, under whatever appearances of smug accommodation, by too prompt a mouthful—recklessly administered to one's helplessness by responsible hands—of the fruit of the tree of knowledge.[540] Why otherwise so queer a taste, always, in so juvenile, so *generally* gaping, a mouth? Well, the queer taste doubtless had been there, but the point of my anecdote, with my brace of infatuated "short stories" for its occasion, is in the infinitely greater queerness it was to take on between the summer of '70 and that of '72, when it set me again in motion.

As I read over "A Passionate Pilgrim" and "The Madonna of the Future" they become in the highest degree documentary for myself—from all measure of such interest as they may possibly have at this time of day for others I stand off; though I disengage from them but one thing, their betrayal of their consolatory use. The deep beguilement of the lost vision recovered, in comparative indigence, by a certain inexpert intensity of art—the service rendered by them at need, with whatever awkwardness and difficulty—sticks out of them for me to the exclusion of everything else and consecrates them, I freely admit, to memory. "Madame de Mauves" and "Louisa Pallant" are another matter; the latter, in especial, belongs to recent years. The former is of the small group of my productions yielding to present research no dimmest responsive ghost of a traceable origin. These remarks have constituted to excess perhaps the record of what may have put this, that and the other treated idea into my head; but I am quite unable to say what, in the summer of 1873, may have put "Madame de Mauves." Save for a single pleasant image, and for the fact that, dispatched to New York, the tale appeared, early in the following year, in "The Galaxy," a periodical to which I find, with this, twenty other remembrances gratefully attached,[541] not a glimmer of attendant reference survives. I recall the tolerably wide court of an old inn at Bad-Homburg in the Taunus hills—a dejected and forlorn little place (its *seconde jeunesse* not yet in sight) during the years immediately following the Franco-Prussian war, which had overturned, with that of Baden-Baden, its altar, the well-appointed worship of the great goddess Chance—a homely enclosure on the ground-level of which I occupied a dampish, dusky, unsunned room, cool, however, to the relief of the fevered muse, during some very hot weather.[542] The place was so dark that I could see my way to and from my inkstand, I remember, but by keeping the door to the court open—thanks to which also the muse, witness of many mild domestic incidents, was distracted and beguiled. In this retreat I was visited by the gentle Euphemia; I sat in crepuscular comfort pouring forth again, and, no doubt, artfully editing, the confidences with which she honoured me.[543] She again, after her fashion, was what I might have called experimentally international; she muffled her charming head in the lightest, finest, vaguest tissue of romance and put twenty questions by. "Louisa Pallant," with still subtler art, I find, completely covers her tracks[544]—her repudiation of every ray of legend being the more marked by the later date (1888) of her appearance. Charitably affected to her and thus disposed, if the term be not arrogant, to hand her down, I yet win from her no shadow of an intelligible account of herself. I had taken possession, at Florence, during the previous year, of a couple of sunny rooms on the Arno just at the point where the Borg' Ognissanti begins to bore duskily westward;[545] and in those cheerful chambers (where the pitch of brightness differed so from that of the others just commemorated) I seem to have found my subject seated in extreme assurance. I did my best for it one February while the light and the colour and the sound of old Italy played in again through my open windows and about my patient table after the bold loud fashion that I had had, from so much before, to teach myself to think directly auspicious when it might be, and indirectly when it mightn't.

PREFACE to *Lady Barbarina, The Siege of London, An International Episode and Other Tales* (NYE XIV)

I HAVE gathered into this volume several short fictions of the type I have already found it convenient to refer to as "international"[546]—though I freely recognise, before the array of my productions, of whatever length and whatever brevity, the general applicability of that term. On the interest of *contrasted* things any painter of life and manners inevitably much depends, and contrast, fortunately for him, is easy to seek and to recognise; the only difficulty is in presenting it again with effect, in extracting from it its sense and its lesson. The reader of these volumes will certainly see it offered in no form so frequent or so salient as that of the opposition of aspects from country to country. Their author, I am quite aware, would seem struck with no possibility of contrast in the human lot so great as that encountered as we turn back and forth between the distinctively American and the distinctively European outlook. He might even perhaps on such a showing be represented as scarce aware, before the human scene, of any other sharp antithesis at all. He is far from denying that this one has always been vivid for him; yet there are cases in which, however obvious and however contributive, its office for the particular demonstration has been quite secondary, and in which the work is by no means merely addressed to the illustration of it. These things have had in the latter case their proper subject: as, for instance, the subject of "The Wings of the Dove," or that of "The Golden Bowl," has not been the exhibited behaviour of certain Americans as Americans, of certain English persons as English, of certain Romans as Romans. Americans, Englishmen, Romans are, in the whole matter, agents or victims; but this is in virtue of an association nowadays so developed, so easily to be taken for granted, as to have created a new scale of relations altogether, a state of things from which *emphasised* internationalism has either quite dropped or is well on its way to drop. The dramatic side of human situations subsists of course on contrast; and when we come to the two novels I have just named we shall see, for example, just how they positively provide themselves with that source of interest. We shall see nevertheless at the same time that the subject could in each case have been perfectly expressed had *all* the persons concerned been only American or only English or only Roman or whatever.

If it be asked then, in this light, why they deviate from that natural harmony, why the author resorts to the greater extravagance when the less would serve, the answer is simply that the course taken has been, on reflexion, the course of the greater amusement. That is an explanation adequate, I admit, only when itself a little explained[547]—but I shall have due occasion to explain it. Let me for the moment merely note that the very condition I here glance at—that of the achieved social fusion, say, without the sense and experience of which neither "The Wings of the Dove," nor "The Golden Bowl," nor "The Portrait of a Lady," nor even, after all, I think, "The Ambassadors," would have been written—represents a series of facts of the highest interest and one that, at this time of day, the late-coming observer and painter, the novelist sometimes depressed by all the drawbacks of a literary form overworked and relaxed, can only rejoice to meet in his path and to measure more and more as a portent and an opportunity. In proportion as he intelligently meets it, and more especially in proportion as he may happen to have "assisted" from far back at so many of the odd and fresh phenomena involved, must he see a vast new province, infinitely peopled and infinitely elastic—by which I mean with incalculable power to grow—annexed to the kingdom of the dramatist. On this point, however, much more is to be said than I can touch on by the way—so that I return to my minor contention; which is that in a whole group of tales I here collect the principle of illustration has on the other hand quite definitely been that the idea could *not* have expressed itself without the narrower application of international terms. The contrast in "Lady Barbarina"[548] depends altogether on the immitigable Anglicism of this young woman and that equally marked projection of New York elements and objects which, surrounding and framing her figure, throws it into eminent relief. She has her personal qualities, but the very interest, the very curiosity of the matter is that her imbroglio is able to attest itself with scarce so much as a reference to them. It plays itself out quite consistently on the plane of her general, her instinctive, her exasperatedly conscious ones. The others, the more intimate, the subtler, the finer—so far as there may have been such—virtually become, while the story is enacted, not relevant, though their relevancy might have come up on some other basis.

But that this is true, always in its degree, of each of the other contributions to the class before us, we shall sufficiently make out, I think, as we take them in their order. I am only struck, I may indeed parenthesise, with the inveteracy of the general ground (not to say of the extension I give it) over which my present remarks play. It does thus in truth come home to me that, combining and comparing in whatever proportions and by whatever lights, my "America" and its products would doubtless, as a theme, have betrayed gaps and infirmities enough without such a kicking-up of the dramatic dust (mainly in the foreground) as I could set my "Europe" in motion for; just as my Europe would probably have limped across our stage to no great effect of processional state without an ingenuous young America (constantly seen as ingenuous and young) to hold up its legendary train. At the same time I pretend not at all to regret my having had from the very first to see my workable world all and only as an unnatural mixture. No mixture, for that matter, is quite unnatural unless quite sterile, and the particular range of associations that betimes, to my eyes, blocked out everything else, blocked out aspects and combinations more simply conditioned, was at least not open to the reproach of not giving me results. These were but what they could be, of course; but such as they were, at all events, here am I at this time of day quite earnestly grouping, distinguishing, discussing them. The great truth in the whole connexion, however, is, I think, that one never really chooses one's general range of vision—the experience from which ideas and themes and suggestions spring: this proves ever what it has *had* to be, this is one with the very turn one's life has taken; so that whatever it "gives," whatever it makes us feel and think of, we regard very much as imposed and inevitable. The subject thus pressed upon the artist is the necessity of his case and the fruit of his consciousness; which truth makes and has ever made of any quarrel with his subject, any stupid attempt to go behind *that*, the true stultification of criticism.[549] The author of these remarks has in any case felt it, from far back, quite his least stupid course to meet halfway, as it were, the turn taken and the perceptions engendered by the tenor of his days. Here it is that he has never pretended to "go behind"—which would have been for him a deplorable waste of time. The thing of profit is to *have* your experience—to recognise and understand it, and for this almost any will do;[550] there being surely no absolute ideal about it beyond getting from it all it has to give. The artist—for it is of this strange brood we speak—has but to have his honest sense of life to find it fed at every pore even as the birds of the air are fed;[551] with more and more to give, in turn, as a consequence, and, quite by the same law that governs the responsive affection of a kindly-used animal, in proportion as more and more is confidently asked.

All of which, however, doubtless wanders a little far from my mild argument—that of my so grateful and above all so well-advised primary acceptance of a *determined* array of appearances. What I was clearly to be treated to by fate—with the early-taken ply I have already elsewhere glanced at[552]—was (should I have the intelligence to embrace it) some considerable occasion to appreciate the mixture of manners. So, as I say, there would be a decent economy in cultivating the intelligence; through the sincerity of which process I have plucked, I hold, every little flower of a "subject" pressed between the leaves of these volumes. I am tempted indeed to make for my original lucidity the claim of something more than bare prudence—almost that of a happy instinctive foresight. This is what I mean by having been "well-advised." It was as if I had, vulgarly speaking, received quite at first the "straight tip"—to back the right horse or buy the right shares.[553] The mixture of manners was to become in other words not a less but a very much more appreciable and interesting subject of study. The mixture of manners was in fine to loom large and constantly larger all round; it was to be a matter, plainly, about which the future would have much to say. Nothing appeals to me more, I confess, as a "critic of life" in any sense worthy of the name, than the finer—if indeed thereby the less easily formulated—group of the conquests of civilisation, the multiplied symptoms among educated people, from wherever drawn, of a common intelligence and a social fusion tending to abridge old rigours of separation.[554] This too, I must admit, in spite of the many-coloured sanctity of such rigours in general, which have hitherto made countries smaller but kept the globe larger, and by which immediate strangeness, immediate beauty, immediate curiosity were so much fostered. Half our instincts work for the maintained differences; without them, for instance, what would have been the point of the history of poor Lady Barbarina? I have but to put that question, I must add, to feel it beautifully large; for there looms before me at its touch the vision of a Lady Barbarina reconciled, domesticated, developed, of possibly greater vividness than the quite other vision expressed in these pages. It is a question, however, of the tendency, perceptive as well as reflective too, of the braver imagination—which faculty, in our future, strikes me as likely to be appealed to much less by the fact, by the pity and the misery and the greater or less grotesqueness, of the courageous, or even of the timid, missing their lives beyond certain stiff barriers, than by the picture of their more and more steadily making out their opportunities and their possible communications. Behind all the small comedies and tragedies of the international, in a word, has exquisitely lurked for me the idea of some eventual sublime consensus of the educated;[555] the exquisite conceivabilities of which, intellectual, moral, emotional, sensual, social, political—all, I mean, in the face of felt difficulty and danger—constitute stuff for such "situations" as may easily make many of those of a more familiar type turn pale. *There*, if one will—in the dauntless fusions to come—is the personal drama of the future.

We are far from it certainly—as I have delayed much too long to remark—in the chronicle of Lady Barb.[556] I have placed this composition (1888) at the top of my list, in the present cluster, despite the earlier date of some of its companions; consistently giving it precedence by reason of its greatest length.[557] The idea at the root of it scarcely brooks indication, so inevitable had it surely become, in all the conditions, that a young Englishwoman in some such predicament should figure as the happy pictorial thought. The whole thing rests, I need scarce point out, on the most primitive logic.[558] The international relation had begun to present itself "socially," after the liveliest fashion, a quarter of a century ago and earlier, as a relation of intermarrying; but nothing was meanwhile so striking as that these manifestations took always the same turn.[559] The European of "position" married the young American woman, or the young American woman married the European of position—one scarce knew how best to express the regularity of it; but the social field was scanned in vain for a different pairing. No American citizen appeared to offer his hand to the "European" girl, or if he did so offered it in vain. The bridal migrations were eastward without exception—as rigidly as if settled by statute. Custom clearly had acquired the force of law; a fact remarkable, significant, interesting and even amusing. And yet, withal, it seemed scarce to demand explanations. So far as they appeared indeed they were confident on the American side. The representatives of that interest had no call in life to go "outside" for their wives—having obviously close at hand the largest and choicest assortment of such conveniences; as was sufficiently proved by the European "run" on the market. What American run on any foreign market had been noted?—save indeed always on the part of the women! It all redounded to the honour and glory of the young woman grown in American conditions—to cast discredit on whose general peerlessness by attested preference for other types could but strike the domestic aspirant as an act of disloyalty or treachery. It was just the observed rarity of the case therefore that prompted one to put it to the imaginative test. Any case so unlikely to happen—taking it for at all conceivable—could only be worth attention when it *should*, once in a blue moon, occur. There was nothing meanwhile, in truth, to "go by"; we had seen the American girl "of position" absorbed again and again into the European social system, but we had only seen young foreign candidates for places as cooks and housemaids absorbed into the American. The more one viewed the possible instance, accordingly, the more it appealed to speculative study; so that, failing all valid testimony, one had studiously, as it were, to forge the very documents.[560]

I have only to add that I found mine, once I had produced them, thoroughly convincing: the most one could do, in the conditions, was to make one's picture appear to hang together, and I should have broken down, no doubt, had my own, after a superficial question or two, not struck me as decently hanging. The essential, at the threshold, I seem to recall, was to get my young man right—I somehow quite took for granted the getting of my young woman. Was this because, for the portrait of Lady Barb, I felt appealed to so little in the name of *shades?*[561] Shades would be decidedly neither of her general world nor of her particular consciousness: the image I had in view was a maiden nature that, after a fashion all its own, should show as fine and complete, show as neither coarse nor poor, show above all as a resultant of many causes, quite without them. I felt in short sure of Lady Barb, and I think there is no question about her, or about the depth of root she might strike in American soil, that I shouldn't have been ready on the spot to answer. Such is the luck of the conception that imposes itself *en bloc*—or such at least the artist's luck in face of it; such certainly, to begin with and "subjectively" speaking, is the great advantage of a character all of a piece: immediacy of representation, the best omens for felicity, then so honourably await it. It was Jackson Lemon and *his* shades, comparatively, and his comparative sense for shades, that, in the tale, most interested me.

The one thing fine-drawn in his wife was that she had been able to care for him as he was: to almost every one and every thing else equally American, to almost every one and every thing else so sensibly stamped, toned and warranted, she was to find herself quite otherwise affected. With her husband the law was reversed—he had, much rather, imputed authority and dignity, imputed weight and charm, to the antecedents of which she was so fine and so direct a consequence; his estimate, his appreciation of her being founded thus on a vision of innumerable close correspondences. It is that vision in him that is racked, and at so many fine points, when he finds their experiment come so near failure; all of which—at least as I seem to see it again so late in the day—lights his inward drama as with the never-quenched lamp of a sacred place. His wife's, on the other hand, goes on in comparatively close darkness.

It is indeed late in the day that I thus project the ray of *my* critical lantern, however; for it comes over me even as I write that the general air in which most of these particular flowers of fancy bloom is an air we have pretty well ceased to breathe. "Lady Barbarina" is, as I have said, scarce a quarter of a century old; but so many of the perceived conditions in which it took birth have changed that the account of them embodied in that tale and its associates will already pass for ancient history. "Civilisation" and education move fast, after all, and too many things have happened; too many *sorts* of things, above all, seem more and more likely to happen. This multiplication of kinds of occurrences, I make no doubt, will promote the inspiration of observers and poets to come; but it may meanwhile well make for an effect of superannuation in any record of the leaner years. Jackson Lemon's has become a more frequent adventure, and Lady Barbarina is to-day as much at her ease in New York, in Washington, at Newport, as in London or in Rome.[562] If this is her case, moreover, it is still more that of little Mrs. Headway, of "The Siege of London" (1883), who suffers, I feel, by the sad circumstance that her type of complication, or, more exactly speaking perhaps, that of the gentlemen concerned with her, is no longer eminent, or at least salient. Both she and her friends have had too many companions and successors; so that to reinvest them with historic importance, with individual dignity, I have to think of them rather as brave precursors, as adventurous skirmishers and *éclaireurs*.[563] This doesn't diminish, I recognise, any interest that may reside in the form either of "The Siege" aforesaid or of its congeners "An International Episode," "A Bundle of Letters" and "The Pension Beaurepas." Or rather indeed perhaps I should distinguish among these things and, if presuming to claim for several some hint of the distinction we may see exemplified in any first-class art-museum, the distinction of the archaic subject treated by a "primitive" master of high finish,[564] yet notice duly that others are no more "quaint" than need be. What has really happened, I think, is that the *great* international cases, those that bristle with fifty sorts of social reference and overflow, and, by the same token, with a hundred illustrations of social incoherence, are now equally taken for granted on all sides of the sea, have simply become incidents and examples of the mixture of manners, as I call it, and the thicker fusion: which may mean nothing more, in truth, but that social incoherence (with the sense for its opposite practically extinct among the nations) has at last got itself accepted, right and left, as normal.

So much, as I put it, for the great cases; but a certain freshness, I make out, still hangs strangely enough about the smaller and the more numerous; those to which we owe it that such anecdotes—in my general array—as "Pandora," as "Fordham Castle," as "Flickerbridge," as "Miss Gunton of Poughkeepsie,"[565] are by no means false even to present appearances. "The Pension Beaurepas" is not alone, thanks to some of its associations,[566] in glowing for me with the tender grace of a day that is dead; and yet, though the accidents and accessories, in such a picture, may have been marked for change, why shall not the essence of the matter, the situation of Mr. and Mrs. Ruck and their daughter at old Geneva—for there is of course a new, a newer Geneva—freely recur? I am careful to put it as a question, and all for a particular reason—the reason that, to be frank, I find myself, before the vast diluvian occidental presence in Europe,[567] with its remorseless rising tide and its positive expression of almost nothing but quantity and number, deprived, on definite and ample grounds, of the precious faculty of confidence. This confidence was of old all instinctive, in face of the "common run" of appearances, the even then multitudinous, miscellaneous minor international phenomena, those of which the "short story," as contemporaneously practised, could effect a fairly prompt and easy notation; but it is now unmistakeable that to come forth, from whatever privacy, to almost any one of the great European highways, and more particularly perhaps to approach the ports of traffic for the lately-developed and so flourishing "southern route" from New York and Boston,[568] is to encounter one of those big general questions that sturdily brush away the multiplication of small answers. "Who are they, what are they, whence and whither and why," the "critic of life," international or other, still, or more and more, asks himself, as he of course always asked, but with the actual difference that the reply that used to come so conveniently straight, "Why, they're just the American vague variety of the dear old Anglo-Saxon race," not only hangs fire[569] and leaves him to wait and wonder, but really affects him as having for this act of deference (as to which he can't choose, I admit) little more than a conscious mocking, baffling, in fact a just all but sinister, grimace. "Don't you wish you knew, or even *could* know?" the inscrutable grin seems to convey; and with resources of cynicism behind it not in the least to be disturbed by any such cheap retort as "Don't you wish that, on your side, *you* could say—or even, for your own convenience, so much as guess?"

For there is no communicating to the diluvian presence, on such a scale, any suspicion that convenience shall anywhere fail it: all its consciousness, on that general head, is that of itself representing and actively *being* the biggest convenience of the world. Little need to insist on the guarantee of subjective ease involved in such an attitude—the immense noted growth of which casts its chill, as I intimate, on the enquirer proceeding from settled premises. He was aware formerly, when it came to an analysis, of all his presumptions; he had but to glance for an immemorial assurance at a dozen of the myriad "registers" disposed in the vestibules of bankers, the reading-rooms of hotels and "exchanges," open on the most conspicuous table of visited palace and castle,[570] to see them bristle with names of a more or less conceivable tradition. Queer enough often, whether in isolation or in association, were these gages of identity: but their queerness, not independent of some more or less traceable weird law, was exactly, after all, their most familiar note. They had their way of not breaking, through it all, the old sweet Anglo-Saxon spell; they had their way of not failing, when all was said, to suggest more communities and comprehensions than conundrums and "stunts."[571] He would be brave, however, who should say that any such ghost of a quiet conformity presides in the fulness of time over the interminable passenger-lists[572] that proclaim the prosperity of the great conveying companies. If little books have their fates,[573] little names—and long ones still more—have their eloquence; the emphasis of nominal reference in the general roll-call falls so strongly upon alien syllables and sounds, representative signs that fit into our "English" legend (as we were mainly conscious up to a few years since of having inherited that boon) scarcely more than if borrowed from the stony slabs of Nineveh.[574] I may not here attempt to weigh the question of what these exotic symbols positively represent[575]—a prodigious question, I cannot but think; I content myself with noting the difference made for fond fancy by the so rapidly established change, by the so considerable drop of old associations. The point is of one's having the heart to assume that the Ninevites, as I may momentarily call them for convenience, are to be constantly taken as feeling in the same way about fifty associational matters as we used, in all satisfaction, to observe our earlier generations feel. One can but speak for one's self, and my imagination, on the great highways, I find, doesn't rise to such people, who are obviously beyond my divination. They strike one, above all, as giving no account of themselves in any terms already consecrated by human use; to this inarticulate state they probably form, collectively, the most unprecedented of monuments; abysmal the mystery of what they think, what they feel, what they want, what they suppose themselves to be saying. There would appear to be to-day no slim scrap even of a Daisy Miller to bridge the chasm; no light-footed Francie Dosson or Pandora Day to dance before one across the wavering plank.[576]

I plead a blank of memory as to the origin of "The Siege of London"; I get no nearer to the birth of the idea than by recalling a certain agitation of the spirit, a lively irritation of the temper, under which, one evening early in the autumn of 1877, that is more than thirty years ago, I walked away from the close of a performance at the Théâtre Français. The play had been "Le Demi-Monde" of the younger Dumas, a masterpiece which I had not heard for the first time,[577] but a particular feature of which on this occasion more than ever yet filled up the measure of my impatience. I could less than ever swallow it, Olivier de Jalin's denunciation of Madame d'Ange;[578] the play, from the beginning, marches toward it—it is the main hinge of the action; but the very perfection with which the part was rendered in those years by Delaunay (just as Croizette was pure perfection as Suzanne)[579] seemed to have made me present at something inhuman and odious. It was the old story—that from the positive, the prodigious *morality* of such a painter of the sophisticated life as Dumas,[580] not from anything else or less edifying, one must pray to be delivered. There are doubtless many possible views of such a dilemma as Olivier's, the conflict of propriety for him between the man he likes and esteems and the woman he has loved but hasn't esteemed and doesn't, and as to whom he sees his friend blind, and, as he thinks, befooled; in consequence of which I am not re-judging his case. But I recover with a pensive pleasure that is almost all a pang the intensity with which I could then feel it; to the extent of wondering whether the general situation of the three persons concerned, or something like it, mightn't be shown as taking quite another turn. Was there not conceivable an Olivier of our race, a different Olivier altogether,[581] moved to ask himself how at such a juncture a "real gentleman," distressed and perplexed, would yet most naturally act? The question would be interesting, it was easy to judge, if only by the light it might throw on some of the other, the antecedent and concomitant, phases of a real gentleman's connexion "at all at all" with such a business[582] and such a world. It remained with me, at all events, and was to prove in time the germ of "The Siege of London"; of the conception of which the state of mind so reflected strikes me as making, I confess, very ancient history.

Far away and unspeakably regretted the days, alas, or, more exactly, the nights, on which one could walk away from the Français under the spell of such fond convictions and such deep and agitating problems. The emphasis of the international proposition has indeed had time, as I say, to place itself elsewhere—if, for that matter, there be any emphasis or any proposition left at all—since the age when that particular pleasure seemed the keenest in life. A few months ago, one evening, I found myself withdrawing from the very temple and the supposedly sacred rites before these latter were a third over:[583] beneath that haunted dome itself they seemed to have become at last so accessible, cynically making their bargain with them, to the profanations long kept at bay. Only, with that evolution of taste possible on the part of the old worshipper in question, what world-convulsions mightn't, in general, well have taken place? Let me continue to speak of the rest of the matter here before us as therefore of almost pre-historic reference. I was to make, in due course, at any rate, my limited application of that glimmering image of a M. de Jalin with whom we might have more fellow-feeling, and I sent "The Siege of London" accordingly to my admirable friend the late Leslie Stephen, then editor of *The Cornhill Magazine*,[584] where it appeared during the two first months of 1883. That is all I remember about it save always the particular London light in which at that period I invoked the muse and drove the pen[585] and with which the compositions resulting strike my fancy to-day as so closely interfused that in reading over those of them I here preserve every aspect and element of my scene of application lives again for me. This scene consisted of small chambers in a small street that opened, at a very near corner, into Piccadilly and a view of the Green Park;[586] I had dropped into them almost instantaneously, under the accepted heavy pressure of the autumnal London of 1876, and was to sit scribbling in them for nearly ten years. The big human rumble of Piccadilly (all human and equine then and long after) was close at hand; I liked to think that Thackeray's Curzon Street, in which Becky Sharp, or rather Mrs. Rawdon Crawley, had lived, was not much further off: I thought of it preponderantly, in my comings and goings, as Becky's and her creator's; just as I was to find fifty other London neighbourhoods speak to me almost only with the voice, the thousand voices, of Dickens.[587]

A "great house," forming the southwest corner of Piccadilly and with its long and practically featureless side, continued by the high wall of its ample court, opposite my open-eyed windows, gloomed, in dusky brick, as the extent of my view,[588] but with a vast convenient neutrality which I found, soon enough, protective and not inquisitive, so that whatever there was of my sedentary life and regular habits took a sort of local wealth of colour from the special greyish-brown tone of the surface always before me. This surface hung there like the most voluminous of curtains—it masked the very stage of the great theatre of the town. To sit for certain hours at one's desk before it was somehow to occupy in the most suitable way in the world the proportionately ample interacts of the mightiest of dramas.[589] When I went out it was as if the curtain rose; so that, to repeat, I think of my tolerably copious artistry of that time as all the fruit of the interacts, with the curtain more or less quietly down and with the tuning of fiddles and only the vague rumble of shifted scenery playing round it and through it. There were absences of course: "A Bundle of Letters," here reproduced took birth (1879) during certain autumn weeks spent in Paris, where a friend of those years, a young London journalist, the late Theodore Child (of Merton College Oxford, who was to die, prematurely and lamentedly, during a gallant professional tour of exploration in Persia) was fondly carrying on, under difficulties, an Anglo-American periodical called *The Parisian*.[590] He invited me to contribute to its pages, and, again, a small sharply-resonant street off the Rue de la Paix,[591] where all existence somehow went on as a repercussion from well-brushed asphalt, lives for me as the scene of my response. A snowstorm of a violence rare in Paris raged, I recollect, for many hours, for the greater part of a couple of days; muffling me noiselessly into the small, shiny, shabby salon of an *hôtel garni* with a droll combinational, almost cosmic sign, and promoting (it comes back to me) a deep concentration, an unusual straightness of labour. "A Bundle of Letters" was written in a single long session and, the temperature apart, at a "heat."[592] Its companion-piece, "The Point of View,"[593] marks not less for memory, I find, an excursion associated with diligence. I have no heart to "go into" these mere ingenious and more or less effective pleasantries to any tune beyond this of glancing at the *other*, the extinct, actualities they hold up the glimmering taper to. They are still faintly scented, doubtless, with something of that authenticity, and a living work of art, however limited, pretends always, as for part of its grace, to some good faith of community, however indirect, with its period and place.

To read over "The Point of View" has opened up for me, I confess, no contentious vista whatever, nothing but the faded iridescence of a far-away Washington spring. This, in 1881, had been my first glimpse of that interesting city, where I then spent a few weeks, a visit repeated the following year;[594] and I remember beginning on the first occasion a short imaginary correspondence after the pattern of the then already published "Bundle of Letters." After an absence from America of some five years I inevitably, on the spot again, had impressions; and not less inevitably and promptly, I remember, recognised the truth that if one really was subject to such, and to a good many, and they were at all worth entertaining or imparting, one was likely to bristle with a quite proportionately smaller number of neat and complacent conclusions.[595] Impressions could mutually conflict—which was exactly the interest of them; whereas in ninety-nine connexions out of a hundred, conclusions could but raise the wind for large groups of persons incapable, to all appearance, of intelligently opening their eyes, though much occupied, to make up for it, with opening, and all vociferously, their mouths. "The Point of View," in fine, I fear, was but to commemorate, punctually enough, its author's perverse and incurable disposition to interest himself less in his own (always so quickly stale) experience, under certain sorts of pressure, than in that of conceivable fellow mortals, which might be mysteriously and refreshingly different.[596] The thing indeed may also serve, in its degree, as a punctual small monument to a recognition that was never to fail; that of the nature of the burden bequeathed by such rash multiplications of the candid consciousness. They are splendid for experience, the multiplications, each in its way an intensifier; but expression, liking things above all to be made comfortable and easy for it, views them askance. The case remains, none the less—alas for this faculty!—that no representation of life worth speaking of can go forward without them. All of which will perhaps be judged to have but a strained relevance, however, to the fact that, though the design of the short imaginary correspondence I speak of was interrupted during those first weeks in Washington, a second visit, the following spring, served it better; I had kept the thread (through a return to London and a return again thence) and, if I remember rightly, I brought my small scheme to a climax on the spot.[597] The finished thing appeared in *The Century Magazine* of December 1882. I recently had the chance to "look up," for old sake's sake, that momentary seat of the good-humoured satiric muse[598]—the seats of the muses, even when the merest flutter of one of their robes has been involved, losing no scrap of sanctity for me, I profess, by the accident of my having myself had the honour to offer the visitant the chair. The chair I had anciently been able to push forward in Washington had not, I found, survived the ravage of nearly thirty years; its place knew it no more, infirm and precarious dependence as it had struck me even at the time as being. So, quite exquisitely, as whenever that lapse occurs, the lost presence, the obliterated scene, translated itself for me at last into terms of almost more than earthly beauty and poetry.[599] Fifty intimate figures and objects flushed with life in the other time had passed away since then; a great chapter of history had made itself, tremendous things had happened; the ghosts of old cherished names, of old tragedies, of old comedies, even of old mere mystifications, had marshalled their array. Only the little rounded composition remained; which glowed, ever so strangely, like a swinging, playing lantern, with a light that brought out the past. The past had been most concretely that vanished and slightly sordid tenement of the current housing of the muse. I had had "rooms" in it, and I could remember how the rooms, how the whole place, a nest of rickety tables and chairs, lame and disqualified utensils of every sort, and of smiling, shuffling, procrastinating persons of colour, had exhaled for me, to pungency, the domestic spirit of the "old South."[600] I had nursed the unmistakeable scent; I had read history by its aid; I had learned more than I could say of what had anciently been the matter under the reign of the great problem of persons of colour—so badly the matter, by my vision, that a deluge of blood and fire and tears had been needed to correct it. These complacencies of perception swarmed for me again—while yet no brick of the little old temple of the revelation stood on another.

    I could scarcely have said where the bricks *had* stood;[601] the other, the superseded Washington of the exquisite spring-time, of the earlier initiation, of the hovering plaintive ghosts, reduced itself to a great vague blur of warmth and colour and fragrance. It kept flushing through the present—very much as if I had had my small secret for making it. I could turn on my finger the magic ring[602]—it was strange how slight a thing, a mere handful of pages of light persistent prose, could act as that talisman. So, at all events, I like to date, and essentially to synchronise, these sincere little studies in general. Nothing perhaps can vouch better for their having applied to conditions that superficially at least have changed than the fact that to fond memory—I speak of my own—there hangs about the last item on this list, the picture of "The Pension Beaurepas," the unearthly poetry, as I call it, of the Paquis, and that I should yet have to plunge into gulfs of explanation as to where and what the Paquis may have been. An old-world nook of one's youth was so named, a scrap of the lakeside fringe of ancient Geneva,[603] now practically quite reformed and improved away. The Pension Beaurepas, across the years, looks to me prodigiously archaic and incredibly quaint; I ask myself why, at the time, I so wasted the precious treasure of a sense that absolutely primitive pre-revolutionary "Europe" had never really been swept out of its cupboards, shaken out of its curtains, thumped out of its mattresses.[604] The echoes of the eighteenth century, to go no further back, must have been thick on its rather greasy stone staircase, up and down which, unconscious of the character of the fine old wrought-iron *rampe*, as of most other things in the world besides, Mr. and Mrs. and Miss Ruck, to speak only of them, used mournfully to straggle. But I mustn't really so *much* as speak only, as even speak, of them. They would carry me too far back—which possibly outlived verisimilitude in them is what I wish to acknowledge.

PREFACE to *The Lesson of the Master, The Death of the Lion, The Next Time and Other Tales*
(NYE XV)

My clearest remembrance of any provoking cause connected with the matter of the present volume applies, not to the composition at the head of my list—which owes that precedence to its greatest length and earliest date[605]—but to the next in order, an effort embalmed, to fond memory, in a delightful association. I make the most of this passage of literary history—I like so, as I find, to recall it. It lives there for me in old Kensington days;[606] which, though I look back at them over no such great gulf of years—"The Death of the Lion" first appeared but in 1894—have already faded for me to the complexion of ever so long ago. It was of a Sunday afternoon early in the spring of that year: a young friend, a Kensington neighbour and an ardent man of letters, called on me to introduce a young friend of his own and to bespeak my interest for a periodical about to take birth, in his hands, on the most original "lines" and with the happiest omens.[607] What omen could be happier for instance than that this infant *recueil*, joyously christened even before reaching the cradle, should take the name of *The Yellow Book*?—which so certainly would command for it the liveliest attention.[608] What, further, should one rejoice more to hear than that this venture was, for all its constitutional gaiety, to brave the quarterly form, a thing hitherto of austere, of awful tradition,[609] and was indeed in still other ways to sound the note of bright young defiance? The project, modestly and a little vaguely but all communicatively set forth, amused me, charmed me, on the spot—or at least the touchingly convinced and inflamed projector did. It was the happy fortune of the late Henry Harland[610] to charge everything he touched, whether in life or in literature, with that influence—an effect by which he was always himself the first to profit. If he came to me, about *The Yellow Book*, amused, he pursued the enterprise under the same hilarious star; its difficulties no less than its felicities excited, in the event, his mirth; and he was never more amused (nor, I may certainly add, more amusing) than when, after no very prolonged career, it encountered suddenly and all distressfully its term.[611] The thing had then been to him, for the few years, a humorous uneasy care, a business attended both with other troubles and other pleasures; yet when, before the too prompt harshness of his final frustration, I reflect that he had adventurously lived, wrought and enjoyed, the small square lemon-coloured quarterly, "failure" and all, figures to me perhaps his most beguiling dream and most rewarding hours.

The bravest of the portents that Sunday afternoon—the intrinsic, of course I mean; the only ones to-day worth speaking of—I have yet to mention; for I recall my rather embarrassed inability to measure as yet the contributory value of Mr. Aubrey Beardsley, by whom my friend was accompanied and who, as his prime illustrator, his perhaps even quite independent picture-maker, was to be in charge of the "art department." This young man, slender, pale, delicate, unmistakeably intelligent, somehow invested the whole proposition with a detached, a slightly ironic and melancholy grace. I had met him before, on a single occasion, and had seen an example or two of his so curious and so disconcerting talent—my appreciation of which seems to me, however, as I look back, to have stopped quite short.[612] The young *recueil* was to have pictures, yes, and they were to be as often as possible from Beardsley's hand; but they were to wear this unprecedented distinction, and were to scatter it all about them, that they should have nothing to do with the text—which put the whole matter on an ideal basis. To those who remember the short string of numbers of *The Yellow Book* the spasmodic independence of these contributions will still be present. They were, as illustrations, related surely to nothing else in the same pages—save once or twice, as I imperfectly recall, to some literary effort of Beardsley's own[613] that matched them in perversity; and I might well be at peace as to any disposition on the part of the strange young artist ever to emulate *my* comparatively so incurious text. There would be more to say about him, but he must not draw me off from a greater relevance—my point being simply that he had associated himself with Harland that brave day to dangle before me the sweetest aid to inspiration ever snatched by a poor scribbler from editorial lips. I should sooner have come to this turn of the affair, which at once bathed the whole prospect in the rosiest glow.

I was invited, and all urgently, to contribute to the first number, and was regaled with the golden truth that my composition might absolutely assume, might shamelessly parade in, its own organic form. It was disclosed to me, wonderfully, that—so golden the air pervading the enterprise—any projected contribution might conform, not only unchallenged but by this circumstance itself the more esteemed, to its true intelligible nature. For any idea I might wish to express I might have space, in other words, elegantly to express it[614]—an offered licence that, on the spot, opened up the millennium to the "short story." One had so often known this product to struggle, in one's hands, under the rude prescription of brevity at any cost,[615] with the opposition so offered to its really becoming a story, that my friend's emphasised indifference to the arbitrary limit of length struck me, I remember, as the fruit of the finest artistic intelligence. We had been at one—that we already knew—on the truth that the forms of wrought things, in this order, *were*, all exquisitely and effectively, the things;[616] so that, for the delight of mankind, form might compete with form and might correspond to fitness; might, that is, in the given case, have an inevitability, a marked felicity. Among forms, moreover, we had had, on the dimensional ground—for length and breadth—our ideal, the beautiful and blest *nouvelle;* the generous, the enlightened hour for which appeared thus at last to shine. It was under the star of the *nouvelle* that, in other languages, a hundred interesting and charming results, such studies on the minor scale as the best of Turgenieff's, of Balzac's, of Maupassant's, of Bourget's, and just lately, in our own tongue, of Kipling's,[617] had been, all economically, arrived at—thanks to their authors', as "contributors," having been able to count, right and left, on a wise and liberal support. It had taken the blank misery of our Anglo-Saxon sense of such matters to organise, as might be said, the general indifference to this fine type of composition. In that dull view a "short story" was a "short story," and that was the end of it. Shades and differences, varieties and styles, the value above all of the idea happily *developed*, languished, to extinction, under the hard-and-fast rule of the "from six to eight thousand words"[618]—when, for one's benefit, the rigour was a little relaxed. For myself, I delighted in the shapely *nouvelle*—as, for that matter, I had from time to time and here and there been almost encouraged to show.

However, these are facts quite of the smaller significance and at which I glance only because I seem still to recognise in those of my three bantlings held by Harland at the baptismal font—"The Death of the Lion" (1894), "The Coxon Fund" (1894), "The Next Time" (1895), *plus* a paper not here to be reproduced[619]—something of the less troubled confidence with which they entered on their first state of being. These pieces have this in common that they deal all with the literary life, gathering their motive, in each case, from some noted adventure, some felt embarrassment, some extreme predicament, of the artist enamoured of perfection,[620] ridden by his idea or paying for his sincerity. They testify indeed, as they thus stand together, to no general intention—they minister only, I think, to an emphasised effect. The particular case, in respect to each situation depicted, appealed to me but on its merits; though I was to note with interest, as my sense more and more opened itself, that situations of the order I speak of might again and again be conceived. They rose before me, in fine, as numerous, and thus, here, even with everything not included, they have added themselves up. I must further mention that if they enjoy in common their reference to the troubled artistic consciousness, they make together, by the same stroke, this other rather blank profession, that few of them recall to me, however dimly, any scant pre-natal phase.

In putting them sundry such critical questions so much after the fact I find it interesting to make out—critically interesting of course, which is all our interest here pretends to be—that whereas any anecdote about life pure and simple, as it were, proceeds almost as a matter of course from some good jog of fond fancy's elbow, some pencilled note on somebody else's case, so the material for any picture of personal states so specifically complicated as those of my hapless friends in the present volume will have been drawn preponderantly from the depths of the designer's own mind. This, amusingly enough, is what, on the evidence before us, I seem critically, as I say, to gather—that the states represented, the embarrassments and predicaments studied, the tragedies and comedies recorded, can be intelligibly fathered but on his own intimate experience. I have already mentioned the particular rebuke once addressed me on all this ground, the question of where on earth, where roundabout us at this hour, I had "found" my Neil Paradays, my Ralph Limberts, my Hugh Verekers and other such supersubtle fry.[621] I was reminded then, as I have said, that these represented eminent cases fell to the ground, as by their foolish weight, unless I could give chapter and verse for the eminence. I was reduced to confessing I couldn't, and yet must repeat again here how little I was so abashed. On going over these things I see, to our critical edification, exactly why—which was because I was able to plead that my postulates, my animating presences, were all, to their great enrichment, their intensification of value, ironic; the strength of applied irony being surely in the sincerities, the lucidities, the utilities that stand behind it. When it's not a campaign, of a sort, on behalf of the something better (better than the obnoxious, the provoking object) that blessedly, as is assumed, *might* be, it's not worth speaking of. But this is exactly what we mean by operative irony. It implies and projects the possible other case, the case rich and edifying where the actuality is pretentious and vain. So it plays its lamp; so, essentially, it carries that smokeless flame, which makes clear, with all the rest, the good cause that guides it. My application of which remarks is that the studies here collected have their justification in the ironic spirit, the spirit expressed by my being able to reply promptly enough to my friend: "If the life about us for the last thirty years refuses warrant for these examples, then so much the worse for that life. The *constatation* would be so deplorable that instead of making it we must dodge it: there are decencies that in the name of the general self-respect we must take for granted, there's a kind of rudimentary intellectual honour to which we must, in the interest of civilisation, at least pretend." But I must really reproduce the whole passion of my retort.

"What does your contention of non-existent conscious *exposures*, in the midst of all the stupidity and vulgarity and hypocrisy, imply but that we have been, nationally, so to speak, graced with no instance of recorded sensibility fine enough to react against these things?—an admission too distressing. What one would accordingly fain do is to baffle any such calamity, to *create* the record, in default of any other enjoyment of it; to imagine, in a word, the honourable, the producible case. What better example than this of the high and helpful public and, as it were, civic use of the imagination?—a faculty for the possible fine employments of which in the interest of morality my esteem grows every hour I live. How can one consent to make a picture of the preponderant futilities and vulgarities and miseries of life without the impulse to exhibit as well from time to time, in its place, some fine example of the reaction, the opposition or the escape? One does, thank heaven, encounter here and there symptoms of immunity from the general infection; one recognises with rapture, on occasion, signs of a protest against the rule of the cheap and easy;[622] and one sees thus that the tradition of a high æsthetic temper needn't, after all, helplessly and ignobly perish. These reassurances are one's warrant, accordingly, for so many recognitions of the apparent doom and the exasperated temper—whether with the spirit and the career fatally bruised and finally broken in the fray, or privileged but to gain from it a finer and more militant edge. I have had, I admit, to project *signal* specimens—have had, naturally, to make and to keep my cases interesting; the only way to achieve which was to suppose and represent them eminent. In other words I was inevitably committed, always, to the superior case; so that if this is what you reprehensively mean, that I have been thus beguiled into citing celebrities without analogues and painting portraits without models, I plead guilty to the critical charge. Only what I myself mean is that I carry my guilt lightly and have really in face of each perpetrated licence scarce patience to defend myself." So I made my point and so I continued.

"I can't tell you, no, who it is I 'aimed at' in the story of Henry St. George;[623] and it wouldn't indeed do for me to name his exemplar publicly even were I able. But I none the less maintain his situation to have been in *essence* an observed reality—though I should be utterly ashamed, I equally declare, if I hadn't done quite my best for it. It was the fault of this notable truth, and not my own, that it too obscurely lurked—dim and disengaged; but where is the work of the intelligent painter of life if not precisely in some such aid given to true meanings to be born? He must bear up as he can if it be in consequence laid to him that the flat grows salient and the tangled clear, the common—worst of all!—even amusingly rare, by passing through his hands. Just so when you ask who in the world I had in mind for a victim, and what in the world for a treasure, so sacrificed to the advertisement not even of their own merits but of all sorts of independent, of really indifferent, exhibitory egotism, as the practically harried and hunted Neil Paraday and his borrowed, brandished and then fatally mislaid manuscript, I'm equally confident of having again and again closely noted in the social air all the elements of such a drama.[624] I've put these elements together—that was my business, and in doing this wished of course to give them their maximum sense, which depended, for irony, for comedy, for tragedy, in other words for beauty, on the 'importance' of the poor foredoomed monarch of the jungle.[625] And then, I'm not ashamed to allow, it was *amusing* to make these people 'great,' so far as one could do so without making them intrinsically false. (Yes—for the mere accidental and relative falsity I don't care.) It was amusing because it was more difficult—from the moment, of course I mean, that one worked out at all their greatness; from the moment one didn't simply give it to be taken on trust. Working out economically almost anything is the very life of the art of representation; just as the request to take on trust, tinged with the least extravagance, is the very death of the same. (There may be such a state of mind brought about on the reader's part, I think, as a positive desire to take on trust; but that is only the final fruit of insidious proceedings, operative to a sublime end, on the author's side; and is at any rate a different matter.) As for the all-ingenious 'Figure in the Carpet,' let me perhaps a little pusillanimously conclude, nothing would induce me to come into close quarters with you on the correspondences of this anecdote.[626] Here exactly is a good example for you of the virtue of your taking on trust—when I have artfully begotten in you a disposition. All I can at this point say is that if ever I was aware of ground and matter for a significant fable, I was aware of them in that connexion."

My plea for "correspondences" will perhaps, however, after all, but bring my reader back to my having, at the outset of these remarks, owned to full unconsciousness of seed dropped here by that quick hand of occasion that had elsewhere generally operated; which comes to saying, no doubt, that in the world of letters things don't at this time of day very strikingly happen. Suggestive and illuminating incident is indeed scarce frequent enough to be referred to as administering the shake that starts up afresh the stopped watch of attention. I shouldn't therefore probably have accumulated these illustrations without the sense of something interchangeable, or perhaps even almost indistinguishable, between my own general adventure and the more or less lively illustration into which I was to find this experiment so repeatedly flower. Let it pass that if I am so oddly unable to say here, at any point, "what gave me my idea," I must just a trifle freely have helped myself to it from hidden stores. But, burdened thus with the imputation of that irregularity, I shall give a poor account of my homogeneous group without the charity of a glance, however brief, at its successive components. However I might have been introduced in fact to Henry St. George, of "The Lesson of the Master," or however I might have been deprived of him, my complete possession of him, my active sympathy with him as a known and understood and admired and pitied, in fine as a fully measured, quantity, hangs about the pages still as a vague scent hangs about thick orchard trees. The great sign of a grasped warrant—for identification, arrest or whatever[627]—is, after all, in the confidence that dissipates vagueness; and the logic of such developed situations as those of the pair commemorated at the head of my list imposed itself all triumphantly. Hadn't one again and again caught "society" in the very fact of not caring in the least what might become of the subject, however essentially fine and fragile, of a patronage reflecting such credit on all concerned, so long as the social game might be played a little more intensely, and if possible more irrelevantly, by this unfortunate's aid? Given the Lion, his "death" was but too conceivably the issue[628] of the cruel exposure thus involved for him; and if it be claimed by what I can but feel rather a pedantic view that so precious an animal exactly *couldn't*, in our conditions, have been "given," I must reply that I yet had met him—though in a preserve not perhaps known in all its extent to geographers.

Of such a fantasy as "The Next Time" the principle would surely soon turn up among the consulted notes of any sincere man of letters[629]—taking literature, that is, on the side of the money to be earned by it. There are beautiful talents the exercise of which yet isn't lucrative, and there are pressing needs the satisfaction of which may well appear difficult under stress of that failure of felicity. Just so there are other talents that leave any fine appreciation mystified and gaping, and the active play of which may yet be observed to become on occasion a source of vast pecuniary profit. Nothing then is at moments more attaching, in the light of "comparative" science,[630] than the study of just where and when, just how and why recognition denies itself to the appeal at all artfully, and responds largely to the appeal coarsely enough, commingled. The critical spirit—with leisure indeed to spare—may well, in its restlessness, seek to fix a bit exactly the point at which a beautiful talent, as I have called it, ceases, when imperilled by an empty pocket, to be a "worldly" advantage. The case in which impunity, for the *malheureux* ridden by that questionable boon, insists on breaking down would seem thus to become susceptible of much fine measurement. I don't know, I confess, that it proveably is; but the critical spirit at all afraid of so slight a misadventure as a waste of curiosity is of course deplorably false to its nature. The difficulty here, in truth, is that, from the moment a straight dependence on the broad-backed public is a part of the issue, the explicative quantity to be sought is precisely the mood of that monster—which, consistently and consummately unable to give the smallest account of itself, naturally renders no grain of help to enquiry. Such a study as that of Ray Limbert's so prolonged, so intensified, but so vain continuance in hope (hope of successfully growing in his temperate garden some specimen of the rank exotic whose leaves are rustling cheques[631]) is in essence a "story about the public," only wearing a little the reduced face by reason of the too huge scale, for direct portrayal, of the monstrous countenance itself. Herein resides, as I have hinted, the anxious and easy interest of almost any sincere man of letters in the mere vicinage, even if that be all, of such strained situations as Ray Limbert's. They speak of the public, such situations, to whoever it may concern. They at all events had from far back insidiously beset the imagination of the author of "The Next Time," who can scarce remember the day when he wasn't all sympathetically, all tenderly occupied with some presumed literary watcher—and quite of a sublime constitution—for that postponed redress. Therefore in however developed a state the image in question was at last to hover before him, some form of it had at least never been far to seek.

 I to *this* extent recover the acute impression that may have given birth to "The Figure in the Carpet," that no truce, in English-speaking air, had ever seemed to me really struck, or even approximately strikeable, with our so marked collective mistrust of anything like close or analytic appreciation—appreciation, to *be* appreciation, implying of course some such rudimentary zeal; and this though that fine process be the Beautiful Gate itself of enjoyment.[632] To have become consistently aware of this odd numbness of the general sensibility, which seemed ever to condemn it, in presence of a work of art, to a view scarce of half the intentions embodied, and moreover but to the scantest measure of these, was to have been directed from an early day to some of the possible implications of the matter, and so to have been led on by seductive steps, albeit perhaps by devious ways, to such a congruous and, as I would fain call it, fascinating case as that of Hugh Vereker and his undiscovered, not to say undiscoverable, secret. That strikes me, when all is said, as an ample indication of the starting-point of this particular portrayal. There may be links missing between the chronic consciousness I have glanced at—that of Hugh Vereker's own analytic projector, speaking through the mouth of the anonymous scribe—and the poor man's attributive dependence, for the sense of being understood and enjoyed, on some responsive reach of critical perception that he is destined never to waylay with success; but even so they scarce signify, and I may not here attempt to catch them. This too in spite of the amusement almost always yielded by such recoveries and reminiscences, or to be gathered from the manipulation of any string of evolutionary pearls.[633] What I most remember of my proper process is the lively impulse, at the root of it, to reinstate analytic appreciation, by some ironic or fantastic stroke, so far as possible, in its virtually forfeited rights and dignities. Importunate to this end had I long found the charming idea of some artist whose most characteristic intention, or cluster of intentions, should have taken all vainly for granted the public, or at the worst the not unthinkable private, exercise of penetration.[634] I couldn't, I confess, be indifferent to those rare and beautiful, or at all events odd and attaching, elements that might be imagined to grow in the shade of so much spent intensity and so much baffled calculation. The mere quality and play of an ironic consciousness in the designer left wholly alone, amid a chattering unperceiving world, with the thing he has most wanted to do, with the design more or less realised—some effectual glimpse of that might by itself, for instance, reward one's experiment. I came to Hugh Vereker, in fine, by this travelled road of a generalisation; the habit of having noted for many years how strangely and helplessly, among us all, what we call criticism—its curiosity never emerging from the limp state—is apt to stand off from the intended sense of things, from such finely-attested matters, on the artist's part, as a spirit and a form, a bias and a logic, of his own. From my definite preliminary it was no far cry to the conception of an intent worker who should find himself to the very end in presence but of the limp curiosity. Vereker's drama indeed—or I should perhaps rather say that of the aspiring young analyst whose report we read and to whom, I ruefully grant, I have ventured to impute a developed wit—is that at a given moment the limpness begins vaguely to throb and heave, to become conscious of a comparative tension. As an effect of this mild convulsion acuteness, at several points, struggles to enter the field, and the question that accordingly comes up, the issue of the affair, can be but whether the very secret of perception hasn't been lost. That is the situation, and "The Figure in the Carpet" exhibits a small group of well-meaning persons engaged in a test. The reader is, on the evidence, left to conclude.

The subject of "The Coxon Fund," published in *The Yellow Book* in 1894, had long been with me, but was, beyond doubt, to have found its interest clinched by my perusal, shortly before the above date, of Mr. J. Dyke Campbell's admirable monograph on S. T. Coleridge.[635] The wondrous figure of that genius had long haunted me, and circumstances into which I needn't here enter had within a few years contributed much to making it vivid.⁶³⁶ Yet it's none the less true that the Frank Saltram of "The Coxon Fund" pretends to be of his great suggester no more than a dim reflexion and above all a free rearrangement. More interesting still than the man—for the dramatist at any rate—is the S. T. Coleridge *type;* so what I was to do was merely to recognise the type, to borrow it, to re-embody and freshly place it; an ideal under the law of which I could but cultivate a free hand. I proceeded to do so; I reconstructed the scene and the figures—I had my own idea, which required, to express itself, a new set of relations—though, when all this is said, it had assuredly taken the recorded, transmitted person, the image embalmed in literary history, to fertilise my fancy. What I should, for that matter, like most to go into here, space serving, is the so interesting question—for the most part, it strikes me, too confusedly treated—of the story-teller's "real person" or actual contemporary transplanted and exhibited.⁶³⁷ But this pursuit would take us far, such radical revision do the common laxities of the case, as generally handled, seem to call for. No such process is *effectively* possible, we must hold, as the imputed act of transplanting; an act essentially not mechanical, but thinkable rather—so far as thinkable at all—in chemical, almost in mystical terms. We can surely account for nothing in the novelist's work that hasn't passed through the crucible of his imagination, hasn't, in that perpetually simmering cauldron his intellectual *pot-au-feu,* been reduced to savoury fusion.⁶³⁸ We here figure the morsel, of course, not as boiled to nothing, but as exposed, in return for the taste it gives out, to a new and richer saturation. In this state it is in due course picked out and served, and a meagre esteem will await, a poor importance attend it, if it doesn't speak most of its late genial medium, the good, the wonderful company it has, as I hint, æsthetically kept. It has entered, in fine, into new relations, it emerges for new ones. Its final savour has been constituted, but its prime identity destroyed—which is what was to be demonstrated. Thus it has become a different and, thanks to a rare alchemy, a better thing. Therefore let us have here as little as possible about its "being" Mr. This or Mrs. That. If it adjusts itself with the least truth to its new life it can't possibly be either. If it gracelessly refers itself to either, if it persists as the impression not artistically dealt with, it shames the honour offered it and can only be spoken of as having ceased to be a thing of fact and yet not become a thing of truth. I am tempted to add that this recommemorative strain might easily woo me to another light step or two roundabout "The Coxon Fund." For I find myself look at it most interestedly to-day, after all, in the light of a significance quite other than that just noted. A marked example of the possible scope, at once, and the possible neatness of the *nouvelle*, it takes its place for me in a series of which the main merit and sign is the effort to do the complicated thing with a strong brevity and lucidity—to arrive, on behalf of the multiplicity, at a certain science of control. Infinitely attractive—though I risk here again doubtless an effect of reiteration—the question of how to exert this control in accepted conditions and how yet to sacrifice no real value; problem ever dearest to any economic soul desirous to keep renewing, and with a frugal splendour, its ideal of economy. Sacred altogether to memory, in short, such labours and such lights. Thus "The Coxon Fund" is such a complicated thing that if it still seems to carry itself—by which I mean if its clearness still rules here, or still serves—some pursued question of how the trick was played would probably not be thankless.

PREFACE to *The Author of Beltraffio, The Middle Years, Greville Fane and Other Tales* (NYE XVI)

WHAT I had lately and most particularly to say of "The Coxon Fund"[639] is no less true of "The Middle Years," first published in *Scribner's Magazine* (1893)—that recollection mainly and most promptly associates with it the number of times I had to do it over to make sure of it. To get it right was to squeeze my subject into the five or six thousand words I had been invited to make it consist of—it consists, in fact, should the curious care to know, of some 5550[640]—and I scarce perhaps recall another case, with the exception I shall presently name, in which my struggle to keep compression rich, if not, better still, to keep accretions compressed, betrayed for me such community with the anxious effort of some warden of the insane engaged at a critical moment in making fast a victim's straitjacket. The form of "The Middle Years" is not that of the *nouvelle*, but that of the concise anecdote; whereas the subject treated would perhaps seem one comparatively demanding "developments"—if indeed, amid these mysteries, distinctions were so absolute. (There is of course neither close nor fixed measure of the reach of a development, which in some connexions seems almost superfluous and then in others to represent the whole sense of the matter; and we should doubtless speak more thoroughly by book had we some secret for exactly tracing deflexions and returns.) However this may be, it was as an anecdote, an anecdote only, that I was determined my little situation here should figure; to which end my effort was of course to follow it as much as possible from its outer edge in, rather than from its centre outward. That fond formula, I had alas already discovered, may set as many traps in the garden as its opposite may set in the wood; so that after boilings and reboilings[641] of the contents of my small cauldron, after added pounds of salutary sugar, as numerous as those prescribed in the choicest recipe for the thickest jam, I well remember finding the whole process and act (which, to the exclusion of everything else, dragged itself out for a month) one of the most expensive of its sort in which I had ever engaged.

But I recall, by good luck, no less vividly how much finer a sweetness than any mere spooned-out saccharine dwelt in the fascination of the questions involved. Treating a theme that "gave" much in a form that, at the best, would give little, might indeed represent a peck of troubles;[642] yet who, none the less, beforehand, was to pronounce with authority such and such an idea anecdotic and such and such another developmental? One had, for the vanity of *a priori* wisdom here, only to be so constituted that to see any form of beauty, for a particular application, proscribed or even questioned, was forthwith to covet that form more than any other and to desire the benefit of it exactly there. One had only to be reminded that for the effect of quick roundness the small smooth situation, though as intense as one will, is prudently indicated, and that for a fine complicated entangled air nothing will serve that doesn't naturally swell and bristle— one had only, I say, to be so warned off or warned on, to see forthwith no beauty for the simple thing that shouldn't, and even to perversity, enrich it, and none for the other, the comparatively intricate, that shouldn't press it out as a mosaic. After which fashion the careful craftsman would have prepared himself the special inviting treat of scarce being able to say, at his highest infatuation, before any series, which might be the light thing weighted and which the dense thing clarified. The very attempt so to discriminate leaves him in fact at moments even a little ashamed; whereby let him shirk here frankly certain of the issues presented by the remainder of our company—there being, independently of these mystic matters, other remarks to make. Blankness overtakes me, I confess, in connexion with the brief but concentrated "Greville Fane"—*that* emerges, how concentrated I tried to make it—which must have appeared in a London weekly journal at the beginning of the "nineties";[643] but as to which I further retain only a dim warm pleasantness as of old Kensington summer hours. I re-read, ever so kindly, to the promotion of a mild aftertaste—that of a certain feverish pressure, in a cool north room[644] resorted to in heavy London Augusts, with stray, rare echoes of the town, beyond near roofs and chimneys, making harmless detonations, and with the perception, over my page, as I felt poor Greville grow, that her scant record, to be anything at all, would have to be a minor miracle of foreshortening. For here is exactly an illustrative case: the subject, in this little composition, is "developmental" enough, while the form has to make the anecdotic concession; and yet who shall say that for the right effect of a small harmony the fusion has failed? We desire doubtless a more detailed notation of the behaviour of the son and daughter, and yet had I believed the right effect missed "Greville Fane" wouldn't have figured here.

Nothing, by the same stroke, could well have been condemned to struggle more for that harmony than "The Abasement of the Northmores" and "The Tree of Knowledge": the idea in these examples (1900) being developmental with a vengeance and the need of an apparent ease and a general congruity having to enforce none the less—as on behalf of some victim of the income-tax who would minimise his "return"[645]—an almost heroic dissimulation of capital. These things, especially the former, are novels intensely compressed,[646] and with that character in them yet keeping at bay, under stress of their failing else to be good short stories, any air of mutilation. They had had to be good short stories in order to earn, however precariously, their possible wage and "appear"—so certain was it that there would be no appearance, and consequently no wage, for them as frank and brave *nouvelles*. They could but conceal the fact that they *were* "nouvelles"; they could but masquerade as little anecdotes. I include them here by reason of that successful, that achieved and consummate—as it strikes me—duplicity: which, however, I may add, was in the event to avail them little—since they were to find nowhere, the unfortunates, hospitality and the reward of their effort.[647] It is to "The Tree of Knowledge" I referred just above, I may further mention, as the production that had cost me, for keeping it "down," even a greater number of full revolutions of the merciless screw than "The Middle Years." On behalf also of this member of the group, as well as for "The Author of Beltraffio," I recover exceptionally the sense of the grain of suggestion, the tiny air-blown particle. In presence of a small interesting example of a young artist long dead, and whom I had yet briefly seen and was to remember with kindness, a friend had made, thanks to a still greater personal knowledge of him and of his quasi-conspicuous father, likewise an artist,[648] one of those brief remarks that the dramatist feels as fertilising. "And then," the lady I quote had said in allusion to certain troubled first steps of the young man's career, to complications of consciousness that had made his early death perhaps less strange and less lamentable, even though superficially more tragic; "and then he had found his father out, artistically: having grown up in so happy a personal relation with him only to feel, at last, quite awfully, that he didn't and couldn't believe in him." That fell on one's ear of course only to prompt the inward cry: "How can there possibly *not* be all sorts of good things in it?" Just so for "The Author of Beltraffio"— long before this and some time before the first appearance of the tale in *The English Illustrated Magazine* (1884): it had been said to me of an eminent author, these several years dead and on some of the embarrassments of whose life and character a common friend was enlarging: "Add to them all, moreover, that his wife objects intensely to what he writes.[649] She can't bear it (as you can for that matter rather easily conceive) and that naturally creates a tension—!" *There* had come the air-blown grain which, lodged in a handful of kindly earth,[650] was to produce the story of Mark Ambient.

Elliptic, I allow, and much of a skipping of stages, so bare an account of such performances; yet with the constitutive process for each idea quite sufficiently noted by my having had, always, only to say to myself sharply enough: "Dramatise it, dramatise it!" That answered, in the connexion, always, all my questions—that provided for all my "fun." The two tales I have named but represent therefore their respective grains of seed dramatically handled. In the case of "Broken Wings" (1900), however, I but see to-day the produced result—I fail to disinter again the buried germ.[651] Little matters it, no doubt, that I recall as operative here the brush of no winged word;[652] for when had I been, as a fellow scribbler, closed to the general admonition of such adventures as poor Mrs. Harvey's, the elegant representative of literature at Mundham?—to such predicaments as Stuart Straith's, gallant victim of the same hospitality and with the same confirmed ache beneath his white waistcoat? The appeal of mature purveyors obliged, in the very interest of their presumed, their marketable, freshness, to dissimulate the grim realities of shrunken "custom," the felt chill of a lower professional temperature—any old note-book would show *that* laid away as a tragic "value" not much less tenderly than some small plucked flower of association left between the leaves for pressing. What had happened here, visibly, was that the value had had to wait long to become active. "Dramatise, dramatise, dramatise!" had been just there more of an easy admonition than of a ready feat; the case for dramatisation was somehow not whole. Under some forgotten touch, however, at its right hour, it was to round itself. What the single situation lacked the *pair* of situations would supply— there was drama enough, with economy, from the moment sad companions, looking each other, with their identities of pluck and despair, a little hard in the face, should confess each to the other, relievingly, what they kept from every one else. With the right encounter and the right surprise, that is with the right persons, postulated, the relief, if in the right degree exquisite, might be the drama—and the right persons, in fine, to make it exquisite, were Stuart Straith and Mrs. Harvey. There remains "The Great Good Place" (1900)—to the spirit of which, however, it strikes me, any gloss or comment would be a tactless challenge. It embodies a calculated effect, and to plunge into it, I find, even for a beguiled glance—a course I indeed recommend—is to have left all else outside. There then my indications must wait.

The origin of "Paste" is rather more expressive, since it was to consist but of the ingenious thought of transposing the terms of one of Guy de Maupassant's admirable *contes*.[653] In "La Parure" a poor young woman, under "social" stress, the need of making an appearance on an important occasion, borrows from an old school friend, now much richer than herself, a pearl necklace[654] which she has the appalling misfortune to lose by some mischance never afterwards cleared up. Her life and her pride, as well as her husband's with them, become subject, from the hour of the awful accident, to the redemption of their debt; which, effort by effort, sacrifice by sacrifice, franc by franc, with specious pretexts, excuses, a rage of desperate explanation of their failure to restore the missing object, they finally obliterate—all to find that their whole consciousness and life have been convulsed and deformed in vain, that the pearls were but highly artful "imitation" and that their passionate penance has ruined them for nothing. It seemed harmless sport simply to turn that situation round—to shift, in other words, the ground of the horrid mistake, making this a matter not of a false treasure supposed to be true and precious, but of a real treasure supposed to be false and hollow: though a new little "drama," a new setting for *my* pearls—and as different as possible from the other—had of course withal to be found.

"Europe," which is of 1899, when it appeared in *Scribner's Magazine*,[655] conspicuously fails, on the other hand, to disown its parentage; so distinct has its "genesis" remained to me. I had preserved for long years an impression of an early time, a visit, in a sedate American city—for there *were* such cities then—to an ancient lady whose talk, whose allusions and relics and spoils and mementoes and credentials, so to call them, bore upon a triumphant sojourn in Europe, long years before, in the hey-day of the high scholarly reputation of her husband, a dim displaced superseded celebrity at the time of my own observation.[656] They had been "much made of,"[657] he and she, at various foreign centres of polite learning, and above all in the England of early Victorian days; and my hostess had lived ever since on the name and fame of it; a treasure of legend and anecdote laid up against the comparatively lean half-century, or whatever, that was to follow. For myself even, after this, a good slice of such a period had elapsed; yet with my continuing to believe that fond memory would still somehow be justified of this scrap too, along with so many others: the unextinguished sense of the temperature of the January morning on which the little Sunday breakfast-party, at half-past nine across the snow, had met to the music of a chilly ghostly kindly tinkle; that of the roomful of cherished echoes and of framed and glazed, presented and autographed and thumb-marked mementoes[658]—the wealth of which was somehow explained (this was part of the legend) by the ancient, the at last almost prehistoric, glory of like matutinal hours, type and model of the emulous shrunken actual.

The justification I awaited, however, only came much later, on my catching some tender mention of certain admirable ladies, sisters and spinsters under the maternal roof, for whom the century was ebbing without remedy brought to their eminent misfortune (such a ground of sympathy always in the "good old" American days when the touching case was still possible) of not having "been to Europe."[659] Exceptionally prepared by culture for going,[660] they yet couldn't leave their immemorial mother, the headspring, precisely, of that grace in them, who on the occasion of each proposed start announced her approaching end—only to postpone it again after the plan was dished[661] and the flight relinquished. So the century ebbed, and so Europe altered—for the worse[662]—and so perhaps even a little did the sisters who sat in bondage; only so didn't at all the immemorial, the inextinguishable, the eternal mother. Striking to the last degree, I thought, that obscure, or at least that muffled, tragedy, which had the further interest of giving me on the spot a setting for my own so long uninserted gem and of enabling me to bring out with maximum confidence my inveterate "Dramatise!" "Make this *one* with such projection as you are free to permit yourself of the brooding parent in the other case," I duly remarked, "and the whole thing falls together; the paradise the good sisters are apparently never to attain becoming by this conversion just the social cake on which they have always been fed and that has so notoriously opened their appetite."

Or something of that sort. I recognise that I so but express here the "plot" of my tale as it stands; except for so far as my formula, "something of that sort," was to make the case bristle with as many vivid values, with as thick and yet as clear a little complexity of interest, as possible. The merit of the thing is in the feat, once more, of the transfusion; the receptacle (of form) being so exiguous, the brevity imposed so great.[663] I undertook the brevity, so often undertaken on a like scale before, and again arrived at it by the innumerable repeated chemical reductions and condensations that tend to make of the very short story, as I risk again noting, one of the costliest, even if, like the hard, shining sonnet, one of the most indestructible, forms of composition in general use. I accepted the rigour of its having, all sternly, in this case, to treat so many of its most appealing values as waste; and I now seek my comfort perforce in the mere exhibited result, the union of whatever fulness with whatever clearness.

PREFACE to *The Altar of the Dead, The Beast in the Jungle, The Birthplace and Other Tales* (*NYE* XVII)

"The Altar of the Dead" forms part of a volume bearing the title of "Terminations," which appeared in 1895.[664] Figuring last in that collection of short pieces, it here stands at the head of my list, not as prevailing over its companions by length, but as being ample enough and of an earlier date than several. I have to add that with this fact of its temporal order, and the fact that, as I remember, it had vainly been "hawked about," knocking, in the world of magazines, at half a dozen editorial doors impenetrably closed to it,[665] I shall have exhausted my fund of allusion to the influences attending its birth. I consult memory further to no effect; so that if I should seem to have lost every trace of "how I came to think" of such a motive, didn't I, by a longer reach of reflexion, help myself back to the state of not having *had* to think of it? The idea embodied in this composition must in other words never have been so absent from my view as to call for an organised search. It was "there"—it had always, or from ever so far back, been there, not interfering with other conceits, yet at the same time not interfered with; and it naturally found expression at the first hour something more urgently undertaken happened not to stop the way. The way here, I recognise, would ever have been easy to stop, for the general patience, the inherent waiting faculty, of the principle of interest involved, was conscious of no strain, and above all of no loss, in amusedly biding its time. Other conceits might indeed come and go, born of light impressions and passing hours, for what sort of free intelligence would it be that, addressed to the human scene, should propose to itself, all vulgarly, never to be waylaid or arrested, never effectively inspired, by some imaged appeal of the lost Dead?[666] The subject of my story is obviously, and quite as usual, the exhibition of a case; the case being that of an accepted, a cultivated habit (the cultivation is really the point)[667] of regularly taking thought for them. Frankly, I can but gather, the desire, at last of the acutest, to give an example and represent an instance of some such practised communion, was a foredoomed consequence of life, year after year, amid the densest and most materialised aggregation of men upon earth, the society most wedded by all its conditions to the immediate and the finite. More exactly speaking, it was impossible for any critic or "creator" at all worth his wage not, as a matter of course, again and again to ask himself what may not become of individual sensibility, of the faculty and the fibre itself, when everything makes against the indulgence of it save as a conscious, and indeed highly emphasised, dead loss.[668]

The impression went back for its full intensity, no doubt, neither to a definite moment nor to a particular shock; but the author of the tale before us was long to cherish the memory of a pair of illuminating incidents that, happily for him—by which I mean happily for the generalisation he here makes—placed themselves, at no great distance apart, so late in a sustained experience of London as to find him profitably prepared for them, and yet early enough to let confirmatory matter gather in abundance round. Not to this day, in fine, has he forgotten the hard, handsome, gentlemanly face, as it was expressionally affected in a particular conjunction, of a personage occasionally met in other years at one of the friendliest, the most liberal of "entertaining" houses and then lost to sight till after a long interval. The end of all mortal things had, during this period, and in the fulness of time, overtaken our delightful hosts and the scene of their long hospitality, a scene of constant welcome to my personage, as I have called him (a police-magistrate then seated, by reason of his office, well in the eye of London, but as conspicuous for his private urbanity as for his high magisterial and penal mask[669]). He too has now passed away, but what could exactly better attest the power of prized survival in personal signs than my even yet felt chill as I saw the old penal glare rekindled in him by the form of my aid to his memory. "We used sometimes to meet, in the old days, at the dear So-and-So's, you may recall." "The So-and-So's?" said the awful gentleman, who appeared to recognise the name, across the table, only to be shocked at the allusion. "Why, they're Dead, sir—dead these many years." "Indeed they are, sir, alas," I could but reply with spirit; "and it's precisely why I like so to speak of them!—Il ne manquerait plus que cela, that because they're dead I shouldn't!" is what I came within an ace of adding; or rather *might* have come hadn't I felt my indecency too utterly put in its place. I was left with it in fact on my hands—where however I was quite everlastingly, as you see, to cherish it. My anecdote is mild and its companion perhaps milder; but impressions come as they can and stay as they will.

A distinguished old friend, a very eminent lady and highly marked character, though technically, as it were, a private person, unencompassed by literary luggage or other monumental matter, had dropped from the rank at a great age and, as I was to note after a sufficient interval, to my surprise, with a singularly uncommemorated and unchronicled effect: given, I mean, her social and historical value.⁶⁷⁰ One blushed, as the days passed, for the want of manners in it—there being twenty reasons in the case why manners should have been remembered. A friend of the interesting woman, thereupon, seeing his opportunity, asked leave of an acquaintance of his own, the conductor of a "high class" periodical, to intervene on behalf of her memory in the pages under the latter's control.⁶⁷¹ The amiable editor so far yielded to a first good impulse as to welcome the proposal; but the proposer was disconcerted to receive on the morrow a colder retraction. "I really don't see why I should publish an article about Mrs. X *because*— and because *only*, so far as I can make out—she's dead." Again I felt the inhibition, as the psychologists say,⁶⁷² that I had felt in the other case; the vanity, *in the conditions*, of any yearning plea that this was the most beautiful of reasons. Clearly the conditions were against its being for an effective moment felt as such; and the article in question never appeared—nor, to the best of my knowledge, anything else of the sort: which fact was to take its place among other grim values. These pointed, as they all too largely accumulated, to the general black truth that London was a terrible place to die in; doubtless not so much moreover by conscious cruelty or perversity as under the awful doom of general dishumanisation. It takes space to feel, it takes time to know, and great organisms as well as small have to pause, more or less, to possess themselves and to be aware. Monstrous masses are, by this truth, so impervious to vibration that the sharpest forces of feeling, locally applied, no more penetrate than a pin or a paper-cutter penetrates an elephant's hide. Thus the very tradition of sensibility would perish if left only to their care. It has here and there to be rescued, to be saved by independent, intelligent zeal; which type of effort however, to avail, has to fly in the face of the conditions.

These are easily, one is obliged to add, too many for it; nothing being more visible for instance than that the life of inordinately numerous companies is hostile to friendship and intimacy⁶⁷³—unless indeed it be the impropriety of such names applied to the actual terms of intercourse. The sense of the state of the dead is but part of the sense of the state of the living; and, congruously with that, life is cheated to almost the same degree of the finest homage (precisely this our possible friendships and intimacies) that we fain would render it. We clutch indeed at some shadow of these things, we stay our yearning with snatches and stop-gaps;[674] but our struggle yields to the other arrayed things that defeat the *cultivation*, in such an air, of the finer flowers—creatures of cultivation as the finer flowers essentially are. We perforce fall back, for the application of that process, on the coarser—which form together the rank and showy bloom of "success," of multiplied contact and multiplied motion; the bloom of a myriad many-coloured "relations"— amid which the precious plant that is rare at the best becomes rare indeed. "The Altar of the Dead" then commemorates a case of what I have called the individual independent effort to keep it none the less tended and watered, to cultivate it, as I say, with an exasperated piety. I am not however here reconstituting my more or less vivid fable, but simply glancing at the natural growth of its prime idea, that of an invoked, a restorative reaction against certain general brutalities. Brutal, more and more, to wondering eyes, the great fact that the poor dead, all about one, were nowhere so dead as there; where to be caught in any rueful glance at them was to be branded at once as "morbid."[675] "Mourir, à Londres, c'est être bien mort!"—I have not forgotten the ironic emphasis of a distinguished foreign friend, for some years officially resident in England, as we happened once to watch together a funeral-train, on its way to Kensal Green or wherever,[676] bound merrily by. That truth, to any man of memories, was too repeatedly and intolerably driven home, and the situation of my depicted George Stransom is that of the poor gentleman who simply at last couldn't "stand" it.

 To desire, amid these collocations, to place, so far as possible, like with like, was to invite "The Beast in the Jungle" to stand here next in order. As to the accidental determinant of which composition, once more—of comparatively recent date and destined, like its predecessor, first to see the light in a volume of miscellanies ("The Better Sort," 1903)[677]—I remount the stream of time, all enquiringly, but to come back empty-handed. The subject of this elaborated fantasy—which, I must add, I hold a successful thing only as its motive may seem to the reader to stand out sharp—can't quite have belonged to the immemorial company of such solicitations; though in spite of this I meet it, in ten lines of an old note-book,[678] but as a recorded conceit and an accomplished fact. Another poor sensitive gentleman, fit indeed to mate with Stransom of "The Altar"—my attested predilection for poor sensitive gentlemen almost embarrasses me as I march!—was to have been, after a strange fashion and from the threshold of his career, condemned to keep counting with the unreasoned prevision of some extraordinary fate; the conviction, lodged in his brain, part and parcel of his imagination from far back, that experience would be marked for him, and whether for good or for ill, by some rare distinction, some incalculable violence or unprecedented stroke. So I seemed to see him start in life—under the so mixed star of the extreme of apprehension and the extreme of confidence; all to the logical, the quite inevitable effect of the complication aforesaid: his having to wait and wait for the right recognition; none of the mere usual and normal human adventures, whether delights or disconcertments, appearing to conform to the great type of his fortune. So it is that he's depicted. No gathering appearance, no descried or interpreted promise or portent, affects his superstitious soul either as a damnation deep enough (if damnation be in question) for his appointed *quality* of consciousness, or as a translation into bliss sublime enough (on *that* hypothesis) to fill, in vulgar parlance, the bill.[679] Therefore as each item of experience comes, with its possibilities, into view, he can but dismiss it under this sterilising habit of the failure to find it good enough and thence to appropriate it.

His one desire remains of course to meet his fate, or at least to divine it, to see it as intelligible, to learn it, in a word; but none of its harbingers, pretended or supposed, speak his ear in the true voice; they wait their moment at his door only to pass on unheeded, and the years ebb while he holds his breath and stays his hand and—from the dread not less of imputed pride than of imputed pusillanimity—stifles his distinguished secret. He perforce lets everything go—leaving all the while his general presumption disguised and his general abstention unexplained; since he's ridden by the idea of what things may lead to, since they mostly always lead to human communities, wider or intenser, of experience, and since, above all, in his uncertainty, he mustn't compromise others. Like the blinded seeker in the old-fashioned game he "burns," on occasion, as with the sense of the hidden thing near[680]—only to deviate again however into the chill; the chill that indeed settles on him as the striking of his hour is deferred. His career thus resolves itself into a great negative adventure, my report of which presents, for its centre, the fine case that has caused him most tormentedly to "burn," and then most unprofitably to stray. He is afraid to recognise what he incidentally misses, since what his high belief amounts to is not that he shall have felt and vibrated less than any one else, but that he shall have felt and vibrated more; which no acknowledgement of the minor loss must conflict with. Such a course of existence naturally involves a climax—the final flash of the light under which he reads his lifelong riddle and sees his conviction proved. He has indeed been marked and indeed suffered his fortune—which is precisely to have been the man in the world to whom nothing whatever was to happen.[681] My picture leaves him overwhelmed—at last he has understood; though in thus disengaging my treated theme for the reader's benefit I seem to acknowledge that this more detached witness may not successfully have done so. I certainly grant that any felt merit in the thing must all depend on the clearness and charm with which the subject just noted expresses itself.

If "The Birthplace" deals with another poor gentleman—of interest as being yet again too fine for his rough fate—here at least I can claim to have gone by book, here once more I lay my hand, for my warrant, on the clue of actuality.[682] It was one of the cases in which I was to say at the first brush of the hint: "How can there possibly *not* be innumerable things in it?" "It" was the mentioned adventure of a good intelligent man rather recently appointed to the care of a great place of pilgrimage, a shrine sacred to the piety and curiosity of the whole English-speaking race,[683] and haunted by other persons as well; who, coming to his office with infinite zest, had after a while desperately thrown it up—as a climax to his struggle, some time prolonged, with "the awful nonsense he found himself expected and paid, and thence quite obliged, to talk."[684] It was in these simple terms his predicament was named to me—not that I would have had a word more, not indeed that I hadn't at once to turn my back for very joy of the suppressed details: so unmistakeably, on the spot, was a splendid case all there, so complete, in fine, as it stood, was the appeal to fond fancy; an appeal the more direct, I may add, by reason, as happened, of an acquaintance, lately much confirmed, on my own part, with the particular temple of our poor gentleman's priesthood.[685] It struck me, at any rate, that here, if ever, was the perfect theme of a *nouvelle*—and to some such composition I addressed myself with a confidence unchilled by the certainty that it would nowhere, at the best (a prevision not falsified) find "acceptance."[686] For the rest I must but leave "The Birthplace" to plead its own cause; only adding that here afresh and in the highest degree were the conditions reproduced for that mystic, that "chemical" change wrought in the impression of life by its dedication to an æsthetic use, that I lately spoke of in connexion with "The Coxon Fund."[687] Beautiful on all this ground exactly, to the projector's mind, the process by which the small cluster of actualities latent in the fact reported to him was to be reconstituted and, so far as they might need, altered; the felt fermentation, ever interesting, but flagrantly so in the example before us, that enables the sense originally communicated to make fresh and possibly quite different terms for the new employment there awaiting it. It has been liberated (to repeat, I believe, my figure) after the fashion of some sound young draught-horse who may, in the great meadow, have to be re-captured and re-broken for the saddle.[688]

I proceed almost eagerly, in any case, to "The Private Life"—and at the cost of reaching for a moment over "The Jolly Corner":[689] I find myself so fondly return to ground on which the history even of small experiments may be more or less written. This mild documentation fairly thickens for me, I confess, the air of the first-mentioned of these tales; the scraps of records flit through that medium, to memory, as with the incalculable brush of wings of the imprisoned bat at eventide. This piece of ingenuity rests for me on such a handful of acute impressions as I may not here tell over at once; so that, to be brief, I select two of the sharpest. Neither of these was, in old London days, I make out, to be resisted even under its single pressure; so that the hour struck with a vengeance for "Dramatise it, dramatise it!" (dramatise, that is, the combination) from the first glimpse of a good way to work together two cases that happened to have been given me.[690] They were those—as distinct as possible save for belonging alike to the "world," the London world of a time when Discrimination still a little lifted its head—of a highly distinguished man, constantly to be encountered, whose fortune and whose peculiarity it was to bear out personally as little as possible (at least to *my* wondering sense) the high denotements, the rich implications and rare associations, of the genius to which he owed his position and his renown.[691] One may go, naturally, in such a connexion, but by one's own applied measure; and I have never ceased to ask myself, in this particular loud, sound, normal, hearty presence, all so assertive and so whole, all bristling with prompt responses and expected opinions and usual views, radiating all a broad daylight equality of emphasis and impartiality of address (for most relations)—I never ceased, I say, to ask myself what lodgement, on such premises, the rich proud genius one adored could ever have contrived, what domestic commerce the subtlety that was its prime ornament and the world's wonder have enjoyed, under what shelter the obscurity that was its luckless drawback and the world's despair have flourished. The whole aspect and *allure* of the fresh sane man,[692] illustrious and undistinguished—no "sensitive poor gentleman" he!—was mystifying; they made the question of who then had written the immortal things such a puzzle.

So at least one could but take the case—though one's need for relief depended, no doubt, on what one (so to speak) suffered. The writer of these lines, at any rate, suffered so much—I mean of course but by the unanswered question—that light *had* at last to break under pressure of the whimsical theory of two distinct and alternate presences, the assertion of either of which on any occasion directly involved the entire extinction of the other. This explained to the imagination the mystery: our delightful inconceivable celebrity was *double*, constructed in two quite distinct and "water-tight" compartments[693]—one of these figured by the gentleman who sat at a table all alone, silent and unseen, and wrote admirably deep and brave and intricate things; while the gentleman who regularly came forth to sit at a quite different table and substantially and promiscuously and multitudinously dine stood for its companion. They had nothing to do, the so dissimilar twins, with each other; the diner could exist but by the cessation of the writer, whose emergence, on his side, depended on his—and our!—ignoring the diner. Thus it was amusing to think of the real great man as a presence known, in the late London days, all and only to himself—unseen of other human eye and converted into his perfectly positive, but quite secondary, *alter ego*[694] by any approach to a social contact. To the same tune was the social personage known all and only to society, was he conceivable but as "cut dead," on the return home and the threshold of the closed study, by the waiting spirit who would flash at that signal into form and possession. Once I had so seen the case I couldn't see it otherwise; and so to see it moreover was inevitably to feel in it a situation and a motive. The ever-importunate murmur, "Dramatise it, dramatise it!" haunted, as I say, one's perception; yet without giving the idea much support till, by the happiest turn, the whole possibility was made to glow.

For didn't there immensely flourish in those very days and exactly in that society the apparition the most qualified to balance with the odd character I have referred to and to supply to "drama," if "drama" there was to be, the precious element of contrast and antithesis?—that most accomplished of artists and most dazzling of men of the world[695] whose effect on the mind repeatedly invited to appraise him was to beget in it an image of representation and figuration so exclusive of any possible inner self that, so far from there being here a question of an *alter ego*, a double personality, there seemed scarce a question of a real and single one, scarce foothold or margin for any private and domestic *ego* at all. Immense in this case too, for any analytic witness, the solicitation of wonder—which struggled all the while, not less amusingly than in the other example, toward the explanatory secret; a clear view of the perpetual, essential performer, consummate, infallible, impeccable, and with his high shining elegance, his intensity of presence, on these lines, involving to the imagination an absolutely blank reverse or starved residuum, no *other* power of presence whatever.[696] One said it under one's breath, one really yearned to know: was he, such an embodiment of skill and taste and tone and composition, of every public gloss and grace, thinkable even as occasionally single?—since to be truly single is to be able, under stress, to be separate, to be *solus*, to know at need the interlunar swoon[697] of *some* independent consciousness. Yes, *had* our dazzling friend any such alternative, could he so unattestedly exist, and was the withdrawn, the sequestered, the unobserved and unhonoured condition so much as imputable to him? Wasn't his potentiality of existence public, in fine, to the last squeeze of the golden orange,[698] and when he passed from our admiring sight into the chamber of mystery what, the next minute, was on the other side of the door? It was irresistible to believe at last that there was at such junctures inveterately nothing; and the more so, once I had begun to dramatise, as this supplied the most natural opposition in the world to my fond companion-view—the other side of the door *only* cognisant of the true Robert Browning. One's harmless formula for the poetic employment of this pair of conceits couldn't go much further than "Play them against each other"[699]—the ingenuity of which small game "The Private Life" reflects as it can.

I fear I can defend such doings but under the plea of my amusement in them—an amusement I of course hoped others might succeed in sharing. But so comes in exactly the principle under the wide strong wing of which several such matters are here harvested; things of a type that might move me, had I space, to a pleading eloquence. Such compositions as "The Jolly Corner," printed here not for the first time, but printed elsewhere only as I write and after my quite ceasing to expect it;[700] "The Friends of the Friends," to which I here change the colourless title of "The Way It Came" (1896), "Owen Wingrave" (1893), "Sir Edmund Orme" (1891), "The Real Right Thing" (1900),[701] would obviously never have existed but for that love of "a story as a story" which had from far back beset and beguiled their author.[702] To this passion, the vital flame at the heart of any sincere attempt to lay a scene and launch a drama, he flatters himself he has never been false; and he will indeed have done his duty but little by it if he has failed to let it, whether robustly or quite insidiously, fire his fancy and rule his scheme. He has consistently felt it (the appeal to wonder and terror and curiosity and pity and to the delight of fine recognitions, as well as to the joy, perhaps sharper still, of the mystified state) the very source of wise counsel and the very law of charming effect. He has revelled in the creation of alarm and suspense and surprise and relief, in all the arts that practise, with a scruple for nothing but any lapse of application, on the credulous soul of the candid or, immeasurably better, on the seasoned spirit of the cunning, reader. He has built, rejoicingly, on that blest faculty of wonder just named, in the latent eagerness of which the novelist so finds, throughout, his best warrant that he can but pin his faith and attach his car to it, rest in fine his monstrous weight and his queer case on it, as on a strange passion planted in the heart of man for his benefit, a mysterious provision made for him in the scheme of nature. He has seen this particular sensibility, the need and the love of wondering and the quick response to any pretext for it, as the beginning and the end of his affair—thanks to the innumerable ways in which that chord may vibrate. His prime care has been to master those most congruous with his own faculty, to make it vibrate as finely as possible—or in other words to the production of the interest appealing most (by its kind) to himself. This last is of course the particular clear light by which the genius of representation ever best proceeds—with its beauty of adjustment to any strain of attention whatever. Essentially, meanwhile, excited wonder must have a subject, must face in a direction, must be, increasingly, *about* something. Here comes in then the artist's bias and his range—determined, these things, by his own fond inclination. About what, good man, does he himself most wonder?— for upon that, whatever it may be, he will naturally most abound. Under that star will he gather in what he shall most seek to represent; so that if you follow thus his range of representation you will know how, you will see where, again, good man, he for himself most aptly vibrates.

All of which makes a desired point for the little group of compositions here placed together; the point that, since the question has ever been for me but of wondering and, with all achievable adroitness, of causing to wonder, so the whole fairy-tale side of life has used, for its tug at my sensibility, a cord all its own. When we want to wonder there's no such good ground for it as the wonderful—premising indeed always, by an induction as prompt, that this element can but be at best, to fit its different cases, a thing of appreciation. What is wonderful in one set of conditions may quite fail of its spell in another set; and, for that matter, the peril of the unmeasured strange, in fiction, being the silly, just as its strength, when it saves itself, is the charming, the wind of interest blows where it lists,[703] the surrender of attention persists where it can. The ideal, obviously, on these lines, is the straight fairy-tale, the case that has purged in the crucible all its *bêtises* while keeping all its grace. It may seem odd, in a search for the amusing, to try to steer wide of the silly by hugging close the "supernatural"; but one man's amusement is at the best (we have surely long had to recognise) another's desolation;[704] and I am prepared with the confession that the "ghost-story," as we for convenience call it, has ever been for me the most possible form of the fairy-tale. It enjoys, to my eyes, this honour by being so much the neatest—neat with that neatness without which *representation*, and therewith beauty, drops. One's working of the spell is of course—decently and effectively—but by the represented thing, and the grace of the more or less closely represented state is the measure of any success; a truth by the general smug neglect of which it's difficult not to be struck. To begin to wonder, over a case, I must begin to believe—to begin to give out (that is to attend) I must begin to take in, and to enjoy *that* profit I must begin to see and hear and feel. This wouldn't seem, I allow, the general requirement—as appears from the fact that so many persons profess delight in the picture of marvels and prodigies which by any, even the easiest, critical measure *is* no picture;

in the recital of wonderful horrific or beatific things that are neither represented nor, so far as one makes out, seen as representable: a weakness not invalidating, round about us, the most resounding appeals to curiosity. The main condition of interest—that of some appreciable rendering of sought effects—is absent from them; so that when, as often happens, one is asked how one "likes" such and such a "story" one can but point responsively to the lack of material for a judgement.

The apprehension at work, we thus see, would be of certain projected conditions, and its first need therefore is that these appearances be constituted in some other and more colourable fashion than by the author's answering for them on his more or less gentlemanly honour.[705] This isn't enough; *give* me your elements, *treat* me your subject, one has to say—I must wait till then to tell you how I like them. I might "rave" about them all were they given and treated; but there is no basis of opinion in such matters without a basis of vision, and no ground for that, in turn, without some communicated closeness of truth. There are portentous situations, there are prodigies and marvels and miracles as to which this communication, whether by necessity or by chance, works comparatively straight—works, by our measure, to some convincing consequence; there are others as to which the report, the picture, the plea, answers no tithe of the questions we would put. Those questions *may* perhaps then, by the very nature of the case, be unanswerable—though often again, no doubt, the felt vice is but in the quality of the provision made for them: on any showing, my own instinct, even in the service of great adventures, is all for the best *terms* of things; all for ground on which touches and tricks may be multiplied, the greatest number of questions answered, the greatest appearance of truth conveyed. With the preference I have noted for the "neat" evocation—the image, of any sort, with fewest attendant vaguenesses and cheapnesses, fewest loose ends dangling and fewest features missing, the image kept in fine the most susceptible of intensity—with this predilection, I say, the safest arena for the play of moving accidents and mighty mutations and strange encounters, or whatever odd matters, is the field, as I may call it, rather of their second than of their first exhibition. By which, to avoid obscurity, I mean nothing more cryptic than I feel myself show them best by showing almost exclusively the way they are felt, by recognising as their main interest some impression strongly made by them and intensely received. We but too probably break down, I have ever reasoned, when we attempt the prodigy, the appeal to mystification, in itself; with its "objective" side too emphasised the report (it is ten to one) will practically run thin. We want it clear, goodness knows, but we also want it thick, and we get the thickness in the human consciousness that entertains and records, that amplifies and interprets it. That indeed, when the question is (to repeat) of the "supernatural," constitutes the only thickness we do get; here prodigies, when they come straight, come with an effect imperilled; they keep all their character, on the other hand, by looming through some other history—the indispensable history of somebody's *normal* relation to something. It's in such connexions as these that they most interest, for what we are then mainly concerned with is their imputed and borrowed dignity. Intrinsic values they have none—as we feel for instance in such a matter as the would-be portentous climax of Edgar Poe's "Arthur Gordon Pym,"[706] where the indispensable history is absent, where the phenomena evoked, the moving accidents, coming straight, as I say, are immediate and flat, and the attempt is all at the horrific in itself. The result is that, to my sense, the climax fails—fails because it stops short, and stops short for want of connexions. There *are* no connexions; not only, I mean, in the sense of further statement, but of our own further relation to the elements, which hang in the void:[707] whereby we see the effect lost, the imaginative effort wasted.

I dare say, to conclude, that whenever, in quest, as I have noted, of the amusing, I have invoked the horrific, I have invoked it, in such air as that of "The Turn of the Screw," that of "The Jolly Corner," that of "The Friends of the Friends," that of "Sir Edmund Orme," that of "The Real Right Thing," in earnest aversion to waste and from the sense that in art economy is always beauty. The apparitions of Peter Quint and Miss Jessel, in the first of the tales just named, the elusive presence nightly "stalked" through the New York house[708] by the poor gentleman in the second, are matters as to which in themselves, really, the critical challenge (essentially nothing ever but the spirit of fine attention) may take a hundred forms—and a hundred felt or possibly proved infirmities is too great a number. Our friends' respective minds about them, on the other hand, are a different matter—challengeable, and repeatedly, if you like, but never challengeable without some consequent further stiffening of the whole texture. Which proposition involves, I think, a moral. The moving accident, the rare conjunction, whatever it be, doesn't make the story—in the sense that the story is our excitement, our amusement, our thrill and our suspense; the human emotion and the human attestation, the clustering human conditions we expect presented, only make it. The extraordinary is most extraordinary in that it happens to you and me, and it's of value (of value for others) but so far as visibly brought home to us. At any rate, odd though it may sound to pretend that one feels on safer ground in tracing such an adventure as that of the hero of "The Jolly Corner" than in pursuing a bright career among pirates or detectives, I allow that composition to pass as the measure or limit, on my own part, of any achievable comfort in the "adventure-story"; and this not because I may "render"—well, what my poor gentleman attempted and suffered in the New York house—better than I may render detectives or pirates or other splendid desperadoes, though even here too there would be something to say; but because the spirit engaged with the forces of violence interests me most when I can think of it as engaged most deeply, most finely and most "subtly" (precious term!) For then it is that, as with the longest and firmest prongs of consciousness, I grasp and hold the throbbing subject; *there* it is above all that I find the steady light of the picture.

After which attempted demonstration I drop with scant grace perhaps to the admission here of a general vagueness on the article of my different little origins. I have spoken of these in three or four connexions, but ask myself to no purpose, I fear, what put such a matter as "Owen Wingrave" or as "The Friends of the Friends," such a fantasy as "Sir Edmund Orme," into my head. The habitual teller of tales finds these things in old note-books[709]—which however but shifts the burden a step; since how, and under what inspiration, did they first wake up in these rude cradles? One's notes, as all writers remember, sometimes explicitly mention, sometimes indirectly reveal, and sometimes wholly dissimulate, such clues and such obligations. The search for these last indeed, through faded or pencilled pages, is perhaps one of the sweetest of our more pensive pleasures. Then we chance on some idea we *have* afterwards treated; then, greeting it with tenderness, we wonder at the first form of a motive that was to lead us so far and to show, no doubt, to eyes not our own, for so other; then we heave the deep sigh of relief over all that is never, thank goodness, to be done again. Would we have embarked on *that* stream had we known?—and what mightn't we have made of this one *hadn't* we known! How, in a proportion of cases, could we have dreamed "there might be something"?—and why, in another proportion, didn't we *try* what there might be, since there are sorts of trials (ah indeed more than one sort!) for which the day will soon have passed? Most of all, of a certainty, is brought back, before these promiscuities, the old burden of the much life and the little art,[710] and of the portentous dose of the one it takes to make any show of the other. It isn't however that one "minds" not recovering lost hints; the special pride of any tinted flower of fable, however small, is to be able to opine with the celebrated Topsy that it can only have "growed."[711] Doesn't the fabulist himself indeed recall even as one of his best joys the particular pang (both quickening and, in a manner, profaning possession) of parting with some conceit of which he can give no account but that his sense—of beauty or truth or whatever—has been for ever so long saturated with it? Not, I hasten to add, that measurements of time mayn't here be agreeably fallacious, and that the "ever so long" of saturation shan't often have consisted but of ten minutes of perception. It comes back to me of "Owen Wingrave," for example, simply that one summer afternoon many years ago, on a penny chair and under a great tree in Kensington Gardens,[712] I must at the end of a few such visionary moments have been able to equip him even with details not involved or not mentioned in the story. Would that adequate intensity *all* have sprung from the fact that while I sat there in the immense mild summer rustle and the ever so softened London hum a young man should have taken his place on another chair within my limit of contemplation, a tall quiet slim studious young man, of admirable type, and have settled to a book with immediate gravity?[713] Did the young man then, on the spot, just *become* Owen Wingrave, establishing by the mere magic of type the situation, creating at a stroke all the implications and filling out all the picture? That he would have been capable of it is all I can say—unless it be, otherwise put, that I should have been capable of letting him; though there hovers the happy alternative that Owen Wingrave, nebulous and fluid, may only, at the touch, have found *himself* in this gentleman; found, that is, a figure and a habit, a form, a face, a fate, the interesting aspect presented and the dreadful doom recorded; together with the required and multiplied connexions, not least that presence of some self-conscious dangerous girl of lockets and amulets offered by the full-blown idea to my very first glance.[714] These questions are as answerless as they are, luckily, the reverse of pressing—since my poor point is only that at the beginning of my session in the penny chair the seedless fable hadn't a claim to make or an excuse to give, and that, the very next thing, the pennyworth still partly unconsumed, it was fairly bristling with pretexts. "Dramatise it, dramatise it!" would seem to have rung with sudden intensity in my ears. But dramatise what? The young man in the chair? Him perhaps indeed—however disproportionately to his mere inoffensive stillness; though no imaginative response *can* be disproportionate, after all, I think, to any right, any really penetrating, appeal. Only, where and whence and why and how sneaked in, during so few seconds, so much penetration, so very much rightness? However, these mysteries are really irrecoverable; besides being doubtless of interest, in general, at the best, but to the infatuated author.

Moved to say that of "Sir Edmund Orme" I remember absolutely nothing, I yet pull myself up ruefully to retrace the presumption that this morsel must first have appeared, with a large picture, in a weekly newspaper[715] and, as then struck me, in the very smallest of all possible print—at sight of which I felt sure that, in spite of the picture (a thing, in its way, to be thankful for) no one would ever read it. I was never to hear in fact that any one had done so—and I therefore surround it here with every advantage and give it without compunction a new chance. For as I meditate I do a little live it over, do a little remember in connexion with it the felt challenge of some experiment or two in one of the finer shades, the finest (*that* was the point) of the gruesome. The gruesome gross and obvious might be charmless enough; but why shouldn't one, with ingenuity, almost infinitely refine upon it?—as one was prone at any time to refine almost on anything? The study of certain of the situations that keep, as we say, the heart in the mouth might renew itself under this star; and in the recital in question, as in "The Friends of the Friends," "The Jolly Corner" and "The Real Right Thing," the pursuit of such verily leads us into rarefied air. Two sources of effect must have seemed to me happy for "Sir Edmund Orme"; one of these the bright thought of a state of *unconscious* obsession or, in romantic parlance, hauntedness, on the part of a given person; the consciousness of it on the part of some other, in anguish lest a wrong turn or forced betrayal shall determine a break in the blest ignorance,[716] becoming thus the subject of portrayal, with plenty of suspense for the occurrence or non-occurrence of the feared mischance. Not to be liable herself to a dark visitation, but to see such a danger play about her child as incessantly as forked lightning may play unheeded about the blind, this is the penalty suffered by the mother, in "Sir Edmund Orme," for some hardness or baseness of her own youth. There I must doubtless have found my escape from the obvious; there I avoided a low directness and achieved one of those redoubled twists or sportive—by which I don't at all mean wanton—gambols dear to the fastidious, the creative fancy and that make for the higher interest. The higher interest—and this is the second of the two flowers of evidence that I pluck from the faded cluster—must further have dwelt, to my appraisement, in my placing my scene at Brighton, the old, the mid-Victorian, the Thackerayan Brighton;[717] where the twinkling sea and the breezy air, the great friendly, fluttered, animated, many-coloured "front," would emphasise the note I wanted; that of the strange and sinister embroidered on the very type of the normal and easy.

This was to be again, after years, the idea entertained for "The Jolly Corner," about the composition of which there would be more to say than my space allows; almost more in fact than categorical clearness might see its way to. A very limited thing being on this occasion in question, I was moved to adopt as my motive an analysis of some one of the conceivably rarest and intensest grounds for an "unnatural" anxiety, a *malaise* so incongruous and discordant, in the given prosaic prosperous conditions, as almost to be compromising. Spencer Brydon's adventure however is one of those finished fantasies that, achieving success or not, speak best even to the critical sense for themselves—which I leave it to do, while I apply the remark as well to "The Friends of the Friends" (and all the more that this last piece allows probably for no other comment).

I have placed "Julia Bride," for material reasons, at the end of this Volume, quite out of her congruous company,[718] though not very much out of her temporal order; and mainly with this drawback alone that any play of criticism she may seem formed to provoke rather misses its link with the reflexions I have here been making. That link is with others to come,[719] and I must leave it to suggest itself on the occasion of these others; when I shall be inevitably saying, for instance, that if there are voluminous, gross and obvious ways of seeking that effect of the distinctively rich presentation for which it has been my possibly rather thankless fate to strive, so doubtless the application of patches and the multiplication of parts make up a system with a train of votaries; but that the achieved iridescence from within works, I feel sure, more kinds of magic; and our interest, our decency and our dignity can of course only be to work as many kinds as possible. Such value as may dwell in "Julia Bride," for example, seems to me, on re-perusal, to consist to a high degree in the strength of the flushing through on the part of the subject-matter, and in the mantle of iridescence naturally and logically so produced. Julia is "foreshortened," I admit, to within an inch of her life; but I judge her life still saved and yet at the same time the equal desideratum, its depicted full fusion with other lives that remain undepicted, not lost. The other lives, the rest of the quantity of life, press in, squeeze forward, to the best of their ability; but, restricted as the whole thing is to implications and involutions only, they prevail at best by indirectness; and the bid for amusement, the effect presumably sought, is by making us conceive and respond to them, making us feel, taste, smell and enjoy them, without our really knowing why or how. Full-fed statement here, to repeat my expression[720]— the imaged résumé of as many of the vivifying elements as may be coherently packed into an image at once—is the predominant artifice; thanks to which we catch by the very small reflector, which is of absolutely minimum size for its task, a quite "unlikely" amount, I surmise, of the movement of life. But, again and again, it would take me long to retail the refinements of ingenuity I felt poor re-invoked Julia all anxiously, all intelligently invite me to place, for this belated, for this positively final appearance, at her disposal. "Here we are again!" she seemed, with a chalked grimace, to call out to me, even as the clown at the circus launches the familiar greeting;[721] and it was quite as if, while she understood all I asked of her, I confessed to her the oddity of my predicament. This was but a way, no doubt, of confessing it to myself—except indeed that she might be able to bear it. Her plea was—well, anything she would; but mine, in return, was that I really didn't take her for particularly important in herself, and would in fact have had no heart for her without the note, attaching to her as not in the least to poor little dim and archaic Daisy Miller, say; the note, so to call it, of multitudinous reference. I had had, for any confidence, to make it out to myself that my little frisking haunter, under private stress, of the New York public scene, was related with a certain intensity to the world about her; so that her case

PREFACE TO *THE ALTAR OF THE DEAD* (NYE XVII)

might lose itself promptly enough in a complexus of larger and stranger cases—even in the very air, by what seemed to promise, of the largest possibilities of comedy. What if she were the silver key, tiny in itself, that would unlock a treasure?—the treasure of a whole view of manners and morals, a whole range of American social aspects?

To put that question was to see one's subject swell at its mere touch; but to do this, by the same stroke, was to ask one's self, alas, how such a majestic mass could be made to turn round in a *nouvelle*. For, all tainted with the up-town debility though it still might be—and this too, after all, comparative—didn't it yet strain the minor key, to re-employ my expression,[722] almost to breaking? How had the prime idea come to me, in the first place, but as possibly and perhaps even minutely illustrating, in respect of consequences and remoter bearings, that freedom repeatedly to contract for the fond preliminaries of marriage which has been immemorially cherished by the American female young? The freedoms of American life are, together with some of its queer restrictions and timidities, the suggestive matter for painter, poet or satirist; and who should say that one of the greatest of all such birthrights, the large juvenile licence as to getting "engaged," disengaged and re-engaged,[723] had received half the attention the charmed dramatist or moralist would appear consistently to owe it? Presumably of the greatest its bearing on the social tone at large, on the manners, habits and ideals of communities clinging to it—of generations wedded, that is, to the young *speculative* exchange of intimate vows—as to the palladium of their liberties.[724] What had struck me nevertheless was that, in common with a hundred other native traditions and practices, it had suffered from the attitude of poets and statisticians banded alike to display it as quite devoid of attendant signs or appreciable effects. From far back a more perverse student, doubtless, of the human scene in general had ventured to suspect in it some at least of the properties of presentable truth: so hard it appeared to believe that the number of a young lady's accepted lovers wouldn't in some degree determine the mixture of the elements in the young lady's consciousness and have much to "say," in one way and another, to the young lady's general case. *What* it might have to say (of most interest to poet and moralist) was certainly meanwhile no matter for *a priori* judgement—it might have to say but the most charming, the most thrilling things in the world; this, however, was exactly the field for dramatic analysis, no such fine quantities being ever determinable till they have with due intelligence been "gone into." "Dramatise, dramatise!" one had, in fine, before the so signal appearance, said to one's self: then, and not sooner, would one see.

By the same token and the same process would one arrive at a similar profit on the score of that other almost equally prized social provision—which has indeed received more critical attention—the unrestricted freedom of re-marriage in the lifetime of the parties,[725] the unhampered ease of rupture and repudiation for each. On this ground, as I say, the fond interpreter of life has had, wherever we observe him, the acute appeal apparently enough in his ears; and it was to reach me in the present connexion but as a source of sound re-enforcement to my possibly too exiguous other example. "Superadd some view of the so enjoyed and so typical freedoms of the mother to the element, however presented, of the daughter's inimitable career of licence; work in, as who should say, a tablespoonful of the due display of responsible consciousness, of roused and reflective taste, of delicacy spreading a tentative wing; season and stir according to judgement and then set the whole to simmer, to stew, or whatever, serving hot and with extreme neatness"; such, briefly stated, had been my careful formula or recipe—by which I of course had to abide in spite of suspecting the process to promise, from an early stage, a much stronger broth, smoking in a much bigger bowl, than I had engaged to prepare. The fumes exhaled by the mixture were the gage, somehow, of twenty more ingredients than I had consciously put in; and this means in short that, even with the actual liquid drained off, I make out a residuum of admirable rich "stock," which—in common deference to professional and technical thrift—must again certainly serve. Such are both the penalties and the profits of that obsession by the sense of an ampler comedy in human things—latent and a little lost, but all responsive to the interested squeeze, to the roused passion of pursuit—than even quite expert and anxious preliminaries of artistic relation to any theme may always be trusted to give the measure of. So what does this truth amount to, after all, but a sort of consecration of what I have called, for "Julia Bride," my predicament?—the consciousness, in that connexion, but of finding myself, after so many years astride the silver-shod, sober-paced, short-stepping, but oh so hugely nosing, so tenderly and yearningly and ruefully sniffing, grey mule of the "few thousand words," ridiculously back where I had started. I clutch at the claim in question indeed, since I feel that without it the shadow I may have cast mightn't bear comparison even with that of limping Don Quixote assisted through his castle-gate and showing but thankless bruises for laurels—might in fact resign itself rather to recalling Moses Primrose welcomed home from the Fair.[726]

PREFACE to *Daisy Miller, Pandora, The Patagonia and Other Tales* (NYE XVIII)

It was in Rome during the autumn of 1877; a friend then living there but settled now in a South less weighted with appeals and memories happened to mention—which she might perfectly not have done—some simple and uninformed American lady of the previous winter, whose young daughter, a child of nature and of freedom, accompanying her from hotel to hotel, had "picked up" by the wayside, with the best conscience in the world, a good-looking Roman,[727] of vague identity, astonished at his luck, yet (so far as might be, by the pair) all innocently, all serenely exhibited and introduced: this at least till the occurrence of some small social check, some interrupting incident, of no great gravity or dignity, and which I forget. I had never heard, save on this showing, of the amiable but not otherwise eminent ladies, who weren't in fact named, I think, and whose case had merely served to point a familiar moral; and it must have been just their want of salience that left a margin for the small pencil-mark inveterately signifying, in such connexions, "Dramatise, dramatise!" The result of my recognising a few months later the sense of my pencil-mark was the short chronicle of "Daisy Miller," which I indited in London the following spring and then addressed, with no conditions attached, as I remember, to the editor of a magazine that had its seat of publication at Philadelphia and had lately appeared to appreciate my contributions.[728] That gentleman however (an historian of some repute) promptly returned me my missive, and with an absence of comment that struck me at the time as rather grim—as, given the circumstances, requiring indeed some explanation: till a friend to whom I appealed for light,[729] giving him the thing to read, declared it could only have passed with the Philadelphian critic for "an outrage on American girlhood." This was verily a light, and of bewildering intensity; though I was presently to read into the matter a further helpful inference. To the fault of being outrageous this little composition added that of being essentially and pre-eminently a *nouvelle*; a signal example in fact of that type, foredoomed at the best, in more cases than not, to editorial disfavour. If accordingly I was afterwards to be cradled, almost blissfully, in the conception that "Daisy" at least, among my productions, might approach "success," such success for example, on her eventual appearance, as the state of being promptly pirated in Boston—a sweet tribute I hadn't yet received and was never again to know[730]—the irony of things yet claimed its rights, I couldn't but long continue to feel, in the circumstance that quite a special reprobation had waited on the first appearance in the world of the ultimately most prosperous child of my invention.[731] So doubly discredited, at all events, this bantling met indulgence, with no great delay, in the eyes of my admirable friend the late Leslie Stephen and was published in two numbers of *The Cornhill Magazine* (1878).[732]

It qualified itself in that publication and afterwards as "a Study"; for reasons which I confess I fail to recapture unless they may have taken account simply of a certain flatness in my poor little heroine's literal denomination.[733] Flatness indeed, one must have felt, was the very sum of her story; so that perhaps after all the attached epithet was meant but as a deprecation, addressed to the reader, of any great critical hope of stirring scenes. It provided for mere concentration, and on an object scant and superficially vulgar—from which, however, a sufficiently brooding tenderness might eventually extract a shy incongruous charm. I suppress at all events here the appended qualification—in view of the simple truth, which ought from the first to have been apparent to me, that my little exhibition is made to no degree whatever in critical but, quite inordinately and extravagantly, in poetical terms. It comes back to me that I was at a certain hour long afterwards to have reflected, in this connexion, on the characteristic free play of the whirligig of time.[734] It was in Italy again—in Venice and in the prized society of an interesting friend, now dead,[735] with whom I happened to wait, on the Grand Canal, at the animated water-steps of one of the hotels. The considerable little terrace there was so disposed as to make a salient stage for certain demonstrations on the part of two young girls, children *they*, if ever, of nature and of freedom, whose use of those resources, in the general public eye, and under our own as we sat in the gondola, drew from the lips of a second companion, sociably afloat with us, the remark that there before us, with no sign absent, were a couple of attesting Daisy Millers. Then it was that, in my charming hostess's prompt protest, the whirligig, as I have called it, at once betrayed itself. "How can you liken *those* creatures to a figure of which the only fault is touchingly to have transmuted so sorry a type and to have, by a poetic artifice, not only led our judgement of it astray, but made *any* judgement quite impossible?" With which this gentle lady and admirable critic turned on the author himself. "You *know* you quite falsified, by the turn you gave it, the thing you had begun with having in mind, the thing you had had, to satiety, the chance of 'observing': your pretty perversion of it, or your unprincipled mystification of our sense of it, does it really too much honour—in spite of which, none the less, as anything charming or touching always to that extent justifies itself, we after a fashion forgive and understand you. But why *waste* your romance? There are cases, too many, in which you've done it again; in which, provoked by a spirit of observation at first no doubt sufficiently sincere, and with the measured and felt truth fairly twitching your sleeve, you have yielded to your incurable prejudice in favour of grace—to whatever it is in you that makes so inordinately for form and prettiness and pathos; not to say sometimes for misplaced drolling. Is it that you've after all too much imagination? Those awful young women capering at the hotel-door, *they* are the real little Daisy Millers that were; whereas yours in the tale is such a one, more's the pity, as—for pitch of the ingenuous, for quality of the artless—couldn't possibly have been at all." My answer to all which bristled of course with more professions than I can or need report here; the chief of them inevitably to the effect that my supposedly typical little figure was of course pure poetry, and had never been anything else; since this is what helpful imagination, in however slight a dose, ever directly makes for. As for the original grossness of readers, I dare say I added, that was another matter—but one which at any rate had then quite ceased to signify.

A good deal of the same element has doubtless sneaked into "Pandora," which I also reprint here for congruity's sake, and even while the circumstances attending the birth of this anecdote, given to the light in a New York newspaper (1884),[736] pretty well lose themselves for me in the mists of time. I do nevertheless connect "Pandora" with one of the scantest of memoranda, twenty words jotted down in New York during a few weeks spent there a year or two before.[737] I had put a question to a friend about a young lady present at a certain pleasure-party, but present in rather perceptibly unsupported and unguaranteed fashion, as without other connexions, without more operative "backers," than a proposer possibly half-hearted and a slightly sceptical seconder;[738] and had been answered to the effect that she was an interesting representative of a new social and local variety, the "self-made," or at least self-making, girl, whose sign was that—given some measurably amusing appeal in her to more or less ironic curiosity or to a certain complacency of patronage—she was anywhere made welcome enough if she only came, like one of the dismembered charges of Little Bo-Peep, leaving her "tail" behind her.[739] Docked of all natural appendages and having enjoyed, as was supposed, no natural advantages; with the "line drawn," that is, at her father and her mother, her sisters and her brothers, at everything that was hers, and with the presumption crushing as against these adjuncts, she was yet held free to prove her case and sail her boat herself; even quite quaintly or quite touchingly free, as might be—working out thus on her own lines her social salvation.[740] This was but five-and-twenty years ago; yet what to-day most strikes me in the connexion, and quite with surprise, is that at a period so recent there should have been novelty for me in a situation so little formed by more contemporary lights to startle or waylay. The evolution of varieties moves fast;[741] the Pandora Days can no longer, I fear, pass for quaint or fresh or for exclusively native to any one tract of Anglo-Saxon soil. Little Bo-Peep's charges may, as manners have developed, leave their tails behind them for the season, but quite knowing what they have done with them and where they shall find them again—as is proved for the most part by the promptest disavowal of any apparent ground for ruefulness. To "dramatise" the hint thus gathered was of course, rudimentarily, to see the self-made girl apply her very first independent measure to the renovation of her house, founding its fortunes, introducing her parents, placing her brothers, marrying her sisters (this care on her own behalf being—a high note of superiority—quite secondary), in fine floating the heavy mass on the flood she had learned to breast. Something of that sort must have proposed itself to me at that time as the latent "drama" of the case; very little of which, however, I am obliged to recognise, was to struggle to the surface.[742] What is more to the point is the moral I at present find myself drawing from the fact that, then turning over my American impressions, those proceeding from a brief but profusely peopled stay in New York,[743] I should have fished up that none so very precious particle as one of the pearls of the collection. Such a circumstance comes back, for me, to that fact of my insuperably restricted experience and my various missing American clues—or rather at least to my felt lack of the most important of them all—on which the current of these remarks has already led me to dilate.[744] There had been indubitably and multitudinously, for me, in my native city, the world "down-town"—since how otherwise should the sense of "going" down, the sense of hovering at the narrow gates and skirting the so violently overscored outer face of the monstrous labyrinth that stretches from Canal Street to the Battery,[745] have taken on, to me, the intensity of a worrying, a tormenting impression? Yet it was an impression any attempt at the active cultivation of which, one had been almost violently admonished, could but find one in the last degree unprepared and uneducated. It was essentially New York, and New York was, for force and accent, nothing else worth speaking of; but without the special lights it remained impenetrable and inconceivable; so that one but mooned about superficially, circumferentially, taking in, through the pores of whatever wistfulness, no good material at all. I had had to retire, accordingly, with my yearning presumptions all unverified—presumptions, I mean, as to the privilege of the imaginative initiation, as to the hived stuff of drama,[746] at the service there of the literary adventurer really informed enough and bold enough; and with my one drop of comfort the observation already made—that at least I descried, for my own early humiliation and exposure, no semblance of such a competitor slipping in at any door or perched, for raking the scene, on any coign of vantage.[747] *That* invidious attestation of my own appointed and incurable deafness to the major key I frankly surmise I could scarce have borne. For there it was; not only that the major key was "down-town" but that down-town was, all itself, the major key—absolutely, exclusively; with the inevitable consequence that if the minor was "up-town," and (by a parity of reasoning) up-town the minor,[748] so the field was meagre and the inspiration thin for any unfortunate practically banished from the true pasture. Such an unfortunate, even at the time I speak of, had still to confess to the memory of a not inconsiderably earlier season when, seated for several months at the very moderate altitude of Twenty-Fifth Street,[749] he felt himself day by day alone in that scale of the balance; alone, I mean, with the music-masters and French pastry-cooks, the ladies and children—immensely present and immensely numerous these, but testifying with a collective voice to the extraordinary absence (save as pieced together through a thousand gaps and indirectnesses) of a serious male interest. One had heard and seen novels and plays appraised as lacking, detrimentally, a serious female; but the higher walks in that community might at the period I speak of have formed a picture bright and animated, no doubt, but marked with the very opposite defect.

Here it was accordingly that loomed into view more than ever the anomaly, in various ways dissimulated to a first impression, rendering one of the biggest and loudest of cities one of the very least of Capitals; together with the immediate reminder, on the scene, that an adequate muster of Capital characteristics would have remedied half my complaint. To have lived in capitals, even in some of the smaller, was to be sure of that and to know why—and all the more was this a consequence of having happened to live in some of the greater. Neither scale of the balance, in these, had ever struck one as so monstrously heaped-up at the expense of the other; there had been manners and customs enough, so to speak, there had been features and functions, elements, appearances, social material, enough to go round. The question was to have appeared, however, and the question was to remain, this interrogated mystery of what American town-life had left to entertain the observer withal when nineteen twentieths of it, or in other words the huge organised mystery of the consummately, the supremely applied money-passion, were inexorably closed to him. My own practical answer figures here perforce in the terms, and in them only, of such propositions as are constituted by the four or five longest tales comprised in this series. What it came to was that up-town would do for me simply what up-town could—and seemed in a manner apologetically conscious that this mightn't be described as much. The kind of appeal to interest embodied in these portrayals and in several of their like companions was the measure of the whole minor exhibition, which affected me as virtually saying: "Yes I'm either *that*—that range and order of things, or I'm nothing at all; therefore make the most of me!" Whether "Daisy Miller," "Pandora," "The Patagonia," "Miss Gunton," "Julia Bride"[750] and *tutti quanti* do in fact conform to any such admonition would be an issue by itself and which mustn't overcome my shyness; all the more that the point of interest is really but this—that I was on the basis of the loved *nouvelle* form, with the best will in the world and the best conscience, almost helplessly cornered. To ride the *nouvelle* down-town, to prance and curvet and caracole[751] with it there—that would have been the true ecstasy. But a single "spill"—such as I so easily might have had in Wall Street[752] or wherever—would have forbidden me, for very shame, in the eyes of the expert and the knowing, ever to mount again; so that in short it wasn't to be risked on any terms.

There were meanwhile the alternatives of course—that I might renounce the *nouvelle*, or else might abjure that "American life" the characteristic towniness of which was lighted for me, even though so imperfectly, by New York and Boston—by those centres only. Such extremities, however, I simply couldn't afford—artistically, sentimentally, financially, or by any other sacrifice—to face; and if the fact nevertheless remains that an adjustment, under both the heads in question, had eventually to take place, every inch of my doubtless meagre ground was yet first contested, every turn and twist of my scant material economically used. Add to this that if the other constituents of the volume, the intermediate ones,[753] serve to specify what I was then thrown back on, I needn't perhaps even at the worst have found within my limits a thinness of interest to resent: seeing that still after years the common appeal remained sharp enough to flower again into such a composition as "Julia Bride" (which independently of its appearance here has seen the light but in *Harper's Magazine*, 1908).[754] As I wind up with this companion-study to "Daisy Miller" the considerable assortment of my shorter tales[755] I seem to see it symbolise my sense of my having waited with something of a subtle patience, my having still hoped as against hope that the so ebbing and obliging seasons would somehow strike for me some small flash of what I have called the major light—would suffer, I mean, to glimmer out, through however odd a crevice or however vouchsafed a contact, just enough of a wandering air from the down-town penetralia[756] as might embolden, as might inform, as might, straining a point, even conceivably inspire (always where the *nouvelle*, and the *nouvelle* only, should be concerned); all to the advantage of my extension of view and my variation of theme. A whole passage of intellectual history, if the term be not too pompous, occupies in fact, to my present sense, the waiting, the so fondly speculative interval: in which I seem to see myself rather a high and dry, yet irrepressibly hopeful artistic Micawber, cocking an ostensibly confident hat and practising an almost passionate system of "bluff"; insisting, in fine, that something (out of the just-named penetralia) *would* turn up[757] if only the right imaginative hanging-about on the chance, if only the true intelligent attention, were piously persisted in.

I forget exactly what Micawber, who had hung about so on the chance, I forget exactly what *he*, at the climax of his exquisite consciousness, found himself in fact reverting to; but I feel that my analogy loses nothing from the circumstance that so recently as on the publication of "Fordham Castle" (1904), for which I refer my reader to Volume XVI,[758] the miracle, after all, alas, hadn't happened, the stray emitted gleam hadn't fallen across my page, the particular supreme "something" those who live by their wits finally and *most* yearningly look for hadn't, in fine, turned up. What better proof of this than that, with the call of the "four or five thousand words"[759] of "Fordham Castle" for instance to meet, or even with the easier allowance of space for its successor to rise to, I was but to feel myself fumble again in the old limp pocket of the minor exhibition, was but to know myself reduced to finger once more, not a little ruefully, a chord perhaps now at last too warped and rusty for complicated music at short order? I trace myself, for that matter, in "Fordham Castle" positively "squirming" with the ingenuity of my effort to create for my scrap of an up-town subject—*such* a scrap as I at the same time felt myself admonished to keep it down to!—a certain larger connexion; I may also add that of the exceedingly close complexus of intentions represented by the packed density of those few pages it would take some ampler glance here to give an account. My point is that my pair of little up-town identities, the respectively typical objects of parental and conjugal interest, the more or less mitigated, more or less embellished or disfigured, intensified or modernised Daisy Millers, Pandora Days, Julia Brides, Miss Guntons or whatever, of the anxious pair, the ignored husband and relegated mother, brought together in the Swiss lakeside pension—my point is that these irrepressible agents yet betrayed the conscious need of tricking-out their time-honoured case. To this we owe it that the elder couple bear the brunt of immediate appearance[760] and are charged with the function of adorning at least the foreground of the general scene; they convey, by implication, the moral of the tale, at least its æsthetic one, if there be such a thing: they fairly hint, and from the very centre of the familiar field, at positive deprecation (should an imagined critic care not to neglect such a shade) of too unbroken an eternity of mere international young ladies. It's as if the international young ladies, felt by me as once more, as verily once too much, my appointed thematic doom, had inspired me with the fond thought of attacking them at an angle and from a quarter by which the peril and discredit of their rash inveteracy might be a bit conjured away.

These in fact are the saving sanities of the dramatic poet's always rather mad undertaking—the rigour of his artistic need to cultivate almost at any price variety of appearance and experiment, to dissimulate likenesses, samenesses, stalenesses, by the infinite play of a form pretending to a life of its own. There are not so many quite distinct things in his field, I think, as there are sides by which the main masses may be approached; and he is after all but a nimble besieger or nocturnal sneaking adventurer who perpetually plans, watches, circles for penetrable places. I offer "Fordham Castle," positively for a rare little memento of that truth: once I had to be, for the light wind of it in my sails, "internationally" American, what amount of truth my subject mightn't aspire to was urgently enough indicated—which condition straightway placed it in the time-honoured category; but the range of choice as to treatment, by which I mean as to my pressing the clear liquor of amusement and refreshment from the golden apple of composition, *that* blest freedom, with its infinite power of renewal, was still my resource, and I felt myself invoke it not in vain. There was always the difficulty—I have in the course of these so numerous preliminary observations repeatedly referred to it, but the point is so interesting that it can scarce be made too often—that the simplest truth about a human entity, a situation, a relation, an aspect of life, however small, on behalf of which the claim to charmed attention is made, strains ever, under one's hand, more intensely, *most* intensely, to justify that claim; strains ever, as it were, toward the uttermost end or aim of one's meaning or of its own numerous connexions; struggles at each step, and in defiance of one's raised admonitory finger, fully and completely to express itself.[761] Any real art of representation is, I make out, a controlled and guarded acceptance, in fact a perfect economic mastery, of that conflict: the general sense of the expansive, the explosive principle in one's material thoroughly noted, adroitly allowed to flush and colour and animate the disputed value, but with its other appetites and treacheries, its characteristic space-hunger and space-cunning, kept down. The fair flower of this artful compromise is to my sense the secret of "foreshortening"—the particular economic device for which one must have a name and which has in its single blessedness[762] and its determined pitch, I think, a higher price than twenty other clustered loosenesses; and just because full-fed statement, just because the picture of as many of the conditions as possible made and kept proportionate, just because the surface iridescent, even in the short piece, by what is beneath it and what throbs and gleams through, are things all conducive to the only compactness that has a charm, to the only spareness that has a force, to the only simplicity that has a grace—those, in each order, that produce the *rich* effect.

Let me say, however, that such reflexions had never helped to close my eyes, at any moment, to all that had come and gone, over the rest of the field, in the fictive world of adventure more complacently so called—the American world, I particularly mean, that might have put me so completely out of countenance by having drawn its inspiration, that of thousands of celebrated works, neither from up-town nor from down-town nor from my lady's chamber,[763] but from the vast wild garden of "unconventional" life in no matter what part of our country. I grant in fact that this demonstration of how consummately my own meagrely-conceived sources were to be dispensed with by the more initiated minds would but for a single circumstance, grasped at in recovery of self-respect, have thrown me back in absolute dejection on the poverty of my own categories. Why hadn't so quickened a vision of the great neglected native quarry *at large* more troubled my dreams, instead of leaving my imagination on the whole so resigned? Well, with many reasons I could count over, there was one that all exhaustively covered the ground and all completely answered the question: the reflexion, namely, that the common sign of the productions "unconventionally" prompted (and this positively without exception) was nothing less than the birthmark of Dialect, general or special[764]—dialect with the literary rein loose on its agitated back and with its shambling power of traction, not to say, more analytically, of *at*traction, trusted for all such a magic might be worth. Distinctly that was the odd case: the key to the *whole* of the treasure of romance independently garnered was the riot of the vulgar tongue.[765] One might state it more freely still and the truth would be as evident: the plural number, the vulgar tongues, each with its intensest note, but pointed the moral more luridly. Grand generalised continental riot or particular pedantic, particular discriminated and "sectional" and self-conscious riot—to feel the thick breath, to catch the ugly snarl, of all or of either, was to be reminded afresh of the only conditions that guard the grace, the only origins that save the honour, or even the life, of dialect: those precedent to the invasion, to the sophistication, of schools and unconscious of the smartness of echoes and the taint of slang. The thousands of celebrated productions raised their monument but to the bastard vernacular of communities disinherited of the felt difference between the speech of the soil and the speech of the newspaper,[766] and capable thereby, accordingly, of taking slang for simplicity, the composite for the quaint and the vulgar for the natural. These were unutterable depths, and, as they yawned about one, *what* appreciable coherent sound did they seem most to give out? Well, to my ear surely, at the worst, none that determined even a tardy compunction. The monument was there, if one would, but was one to regret one's own failure to have contributed a stone? Perish, and all ignobly, the thought!

Each of the other pieces of which this volume is composed would have its small history; but they have above all in common that they mark my escape from the predicament, as I have called it, just glanced at; my at least partial way out of the dilemma formed by the respective discouragements of down-town, of up-town and of the great dialectic tracts. Various up-town figures flit, I allow, across these pages; but they too, as it were, have for the time dodged the dilemma; I meet them, I exhibit them, in an air of different and, I think, more numerous alternatives. Such is the case with the young American subject in "Flickerbridge" (1902) and with the old American subject, as my signally mature heroine may here be pronounced, in "The Beldonald Holbein" (1901). In these two cases the idea is but a stray spark of the old "international" flame; of course, however, it was quite internationally that I from far back sought my salvation. Let such matters as those I have named represent accordingly so many renewed, and perhaps at moments even rather desperate, clutches of that useful torch. We may put it in this way that the scale of variety had, by the facts of one's situation, been rather oddly predetermined—with Europe so constantly in requisition as the more salient American stage or more effective *repoussoir*,[767] and yet with any particular *action* on this great lighted and decorated scene depending for half its sense on one of my outland importations. Comparatively few those of my productions in which I appear to have felt, and with confidence, that source of credit freely negligible; "The Princess Casamassima," "The Tragic Muse," "The Spoils of Poynton," "The Other House," "What Maisie Knew," "The Sacred Fount," practically, among the more or less sustained things, exhausting the list—in which moreover I have set down two compositions not included in the present series.⁷⁶⁸ Against these longer and shorter novels stand many of the other category; though when it comes to the array of mere brevities—as in "The Marriages" (1891) and four of its companions here⁷⁶⁹—the balance is more evenly struck: a proof, doubtless, that confidence in what he may call the *indirect* initiation, in the comparatively hampered saturation, may even after long years often fail an earnest worker in these fields. Conclusive that, in turn, as to the innumerable parts of the huge machine, a thing of a myriad parts, about which the intending painter of even a few aspects of the life of a great old complex society must either be right or be ridiculous. He has to be, for authority—and on all such ground authority is everything—but continuously and confidently right; to which end, in many a case, if he happens to be but a civil alien, he had best be simply born again⁷⁷⁰—I mean born differently.

Only then, as he's quite liable to say to himself, what would perhaps become, under the dead collective weight of those knowledges that he may, as the case stands for him, often separately miss, what would become of the free intensity of the perceptions which serve him in their stead, in which he never hesitates to rejoice, and to which, in a hundred connexions, he just impudently trusts? The question is too beguiling, alas, now to be gone into; though the mere putting of it fairly *describes* the racked consciousness of the unfortunate who has incurred the dread heritage of easy comparisons. His wealth, in this possession, is supposed to be his freedom of choice, but there are too many days when he asks himself if the artist mayn't easily know an excess of that freedom. Those of the smaller sort never use all the freedom they have—which is the sign, exactly, by which we know them; but those of the greater have never had too much immediately to use—which is the sovereign mark of their felicity. From which range of speculation let me narrow down none the less a little ruefully; since I confess to no great provision of "history" on behalf of "The Marriages."⁷⁷¹ The embodied notion, for this matter, sufficiently tells its story; one has never to go far afield to speculate on the possible pangs of filial piety in face of the successor, in the given instance, to either lost parent, but perhaps more particularly to the lost mother, often inflicted on it by the parent surviving. As in the classic case of Mrs. Glasse's receipt, it's but a question of "first catching" the example of piety intense enough.⁷⁷² Granted that, the drama is all there—all in the consciousness, the fond imagination, the possibly poisoned and inflamed judgement, of the suffering subject; where, exactly, "The Marriages" was to find it.

As to the "The Real Thing" (1890)[773] and "Brooksmith" (1891) my recollection is sharp; the subject of each of these tales was suggested to me by a briefly-reported case. To begin with the second-named of them, the appreciative daughter of a friend some time dead had mentioned to me a visit received by her from a servant of the late distinguished lady,[774] a devoted maid whom I remembered well to have repeatedly seen at the latter's side and who had come to discharge herself so far as she might of a sorry burden. She had lived in her mistress's delightful society and in that of the many so interesting friends of the house; she had been formed by nature, as unluckily happened, to enjoy this privilege to the utmost, and the deprivation of everything was now bitterness in her cup. She had had her choice, and had made her trial, of common situations or of a return to her own people, and had found these ordeals alike too cruel. She had in her years of service tasted of conversation and been spoiled for life; she had, in recall of Stendhal's inveterate motto, caught a glimpse, all untimely, of "la beauté parfaite,"[775] and should never find again what she had lost—so that nothing was left her but to languish to her end. *There* was a touched spring, of course, to make "Dramatise, dramatise!" ring out; only my little derived drama, in the event, seemed to require, to be ample enough, a hero rather than a heroine. I desired for my poor lost spirit the measured maximum of the fatal experience: the thing became, in a word, to my imagination, the obscure tragedy of the "intelligent" butler present at rare table-talk, rather than that of the more effaced tirewoman; with which of course was involved a corresponding change from mistress to master.

In like manner my much-loved friend George du Maurier had spoken to me of a call from a strange and striking couple desirous to propose themselves as artist's models for his weekly "social" illustrations to *Punch*,[776] and the acceptance of whose services would have entailed the dismissal of an undistinguished but highly expert pair, also husband and wife, who had come to him from far back on the irregular day and whom, thanks to a happy, and to that extent lucrative, appearance of "type" on the part of each, he had reproduced, to the best effect, in a thousand drawing-room attitudes and combinations. Exceedingly modest members of society, they earned their bread by looking and, with the aid of supplied toggery, dressing, greater favourites of fortune to the life; or, otherwise expressed, by skilfully feigning a virtue not in the least native to them. Here meanwhile were their so handsome proposed, so anxious, so almost haggard competitors, originally, by every sign, of the best condition and estate, but overtaken by reverses even while conforming impeccably to the standard of superficial "smartness" and pleading with well-bred ease and the right light tone, not to say with feverish gaiety, that (as in the interest of art itself) *they* at least shouldn't have to "make believe." The question thus thrown up by the two friendly critics of the rather lurid little passage was of whether their not having to make believe *would* in fact serve them, and above all serve their interpreter as well as the borrowed graces of the comparatively sordid professionals who had had, for dear life, to *know how*[777] (which was to have learnt how) to do something. The question, I recall, struck me as exquisite, and out of a momentary fond consideration of it "The Real Thing" sprang at a bound.

"Flickerbridge" indeed I verily give up: so thoroughly does this highly-finished little anecdote cover its tracks;[778] looking at me, over the few years and out of its bland neatness, with the fine inscrutability, in fact the positive coquetry, of the refusal to answer free-and-easy questions, the mere cold smile for their impertinence, characteristic of any complete artistic thing. "Dramatise, dramatise!"—there had of course been that preliminary, there couldn't not have been; but how represent here clearly enough the small succession of steps by which such a case as the admonition is applied to in my picture of Frank Granger's visit to Miss Wenham came to issue from the whole thick-looming cloud of the noted appearances, the dark and dismal consequences, involved more and more to-day in our celebration, our commemoration, our unguardedly-uttered appreciation, of any charming impression? Living as we do under permanent visitation of the deadly epidemic of publicity, any rash word, any light thought that chances to escape us, may instantly, by that accident, find itself propagated and perverted, multiplied and diffused, after a fashion poisonous, practically, and speedily fatal, to its subject—that is to our idea, our sentiment, our figured interest, our too foolishly blabbed secret. Fine old leisure, in George Eliot's phrase,[779] was long ago extinct, but rarity, precious rarity, its twin-sister, lingered on a while only to begin, in like manner, to perish by inches—to learn, in other words, that to be so much as breathed about is to be handed over to the big drum and the brazen blare, with all the effects of the vulgarised, trampled, desecrated state after the cyclone of sound and fury[780] has spent itself. To have observed that, in turn, is to learn to dread reverberation, mere mechanical ventilation, more than the Black Death;[781] which lesson the hero of my little apologue is represented as, all by himself and with anguish at his heart, spelling out the rudiments of. Of course it was a far cry, over intervals of thought, artistically speaking, from the dire truth I here glance at to my small projected example, looking so all unconscious of any such portentous burden of sense; but through that wilderness I shall not attempt to guide my reader. Let the accomplishment of the march figure for him, on the author's part, the arduous sport, in such a waste, of "dramatising."

Intervals of thought and a desolation of missing links strike me, not less, as marking the approach to any simple expression of my "original hint" for "The Story In It." What I definitely recall of the history of this tolerably recent production is that, even after I had exerted a ferocious and far from fruitless ingenuity to keep it from becoming a *nouvelle*—for it is in fact one of the briefest of my compositions—it still haunted, a graceless beggar, for a couple of years, the cold avenues of publicity; till finally an old acquaintance, about to "start a magazine," begged it in turn of me and published it (1903) at no cost to himself but the cost of his confidence, in that first number which was in the event, if I mistake not, to prove only one of a pair.[782] I like perhaps "morbidly" to think that the Story in it may have been more than the magazine could carry. There at any rate—*for* the "story," that is for the pure pearl of my idea—I had to take, in the name of the particular instance, no less deep and straight a dive into the deep sea of a certain general truth than I had taken in quest of "Flickerbridge." The general truth had been positively phrased for me by a distinguished friend, a novelist not to *our* manner either born or bred,[783] on the occasion of his having made such answer as he could to an interlocutor (he, oh distinctly, indigenous and glib!) bent on learning from him why the adventures he imputed to his heroines were so perversely and persistently but of a type impossible to ladies respecting themselves. My friend's reply had been, not unnaturally, and above all not incongruously, that ladies who respected themselves took particular care never to *have* adventures; not the least little adventure that would be worth (worth any self-respecting novelist's) speaking of. There were certainly, it was to be hoped, ladies who practised that reserve—which, however beneficial to themselves, was yet fatally detrimental to literature, in the sense of promptly making any artistic harmony pitched in the same low key trivial and empty. A picture of life founded on the mere reserves and omissions and suppressions of life, what sort of a performance—for beauty, for interest, for tone—could *that* hope to be? The enquiry wasn't answered in any hearing of mine, and of course indeed, on all such ground, discussion, to be really luminous, would have to rest on some such perfect definition of terms as is not of this muddled world. It is, not surprisingly, one of the rudiments of criticism that a human, a personal "adventure" is no *a priori*, no positive and absolute and inelastic thing, but just a matter of relation and appreciation[784]—a name we conveniently give, after the fact, to any passage, to any situation, that has added the sharp taste of uncertainty to a quickened sense of life. Therefore the thing is, all beautifully, a matter of interpretation and of the particular conditions; without a view of which latter some of the most prodigious adventures, as one has often had occasion to say, may vulgarly show for nothing. However that may be, I hasten to add, the mere stir of the air round the question reflected in the brief but earnest interchange I have just reported was to cause a "subject," to my sense, immediately to bloom there. So it suddenly, on its small scale, seemed to stand erect—or at least quite intelligently to lift its head; just *a* subject, clearly, though I couldn't immediately tell which or what. To find out I had to get a little closer to it, and "The Story In It" precisely represents that undertaking.

As for "The Beldonald Holbein," about which I have said nothing, *that* story—by which I mean the story *of* it—would take us much too far.[785] "Mrs. Medwin," published in *Punch* (1902) and in "The Better Sort" (1903), I have also accommodated here for convenience.[786] There is a note or two I would fain add to this; but I check myself with the sense of having, as it is, to all probability, vindicated with a due zeal, not to say a due extravagance, the most general truth of many a story-teller's case: the truth, already more than once elsewhere glanced at, that what longest lives to his backward vision, in the whole business, is not the variable question of the "success," but the inveterate romance of the labour.

PREFACE to *The Wings of the Dove* (*NYE* XIX-XX)

"The Wings of the Dove," published in 1902, represents to my memory a very old—if I shouldn't perhaps rather say a very young—motive;[787] I can scarce remember the time when the situation on which this long-drawn fiction mainly rests was not vividly present to me. The idea, reduced to its essence, is that of a young person conscious of a great capacity for life, but early stricken and doomed, condemned to die under short respite, while also enamoured of the world; aware moreover of the condemnation and passionately desiring to "put in" before extinction as many of the finer vibrations as possible,[788] and so achieve, however briefly and brokenly, the sense of having lived. Long had I turned it over, standing off from it, yet coming back to it; convinced of what might be done with it, yet seeing the theme as formidable. The image so figured would be, at best, but half the matter; the rest would be all the picture of the struggle involved, the adventure brought about, the gain recorded or the loss incurred, the precious experience somehow compassed. These things, I had from the first felt, would require much working-out; that indeed was the case with most things worth working at all;[789] yet there are subjects and subjects, and this one seemed particularly to bristle. It was formed, I judged, to make the wary adventurer walk round and round it[790]—it had in fact a charm that invited and mystified alike that attention; not being somehow what one thought of as a "frank" subject, after the fashion of some, with its elements well in view and its whole character in its face. It stood there with secrets and compartments, with possible treacheries and traps; it might have a great deal to give, but would probably ask for equal services in return, and would collect this debt to the last shilling. It involved, to begin with, the placing in the strongest light a person infirm and ill—a case sure to prove difficult and to require much handling; though giving perhaps, with other matters, one of those chances for good taste, possibly even for the play of the very best in the world, that are not only always to be invoked and cultivated, but that are absolutely to be jumped at from the moment they make a sign.[791]

Yes then, the case prescribed for its central figure a sick young woman, at the whole course of whose disintegration and the whole ordeal of whose consciousness one would have quite honestly to assist. The expression of her state and that of one's intimate relation to it might therefore well need to be discreet and ingenious; a reflexion that fortunately grew and grew, however, in proportion as I focussed my image—roundabout which, as it persisted, I repeat, the interesting possibilities and the attaching wonderments, not to say the insoluble mysteries, thickened apace. Why had one to look so straight in the face and so closely to cross-question that idea of making one's protagonist "sick"?[792]—as if to be menaced with death or danger hadn't been from time immemorial, for heroine or hero, the very shortest of all cuts to the interesting state. Why should a figure be disqualified for a central position by the particular circumstance that might most quicken, that might crown with a fine intensity, its liability to many accidents, its consciousness of all relations? This circumstance, true enough, might disqualify it for many activities—even though we should have imputed to it the unsurpassable activity of passionate, of inspired resistance. This last fact was the real issue, for the way grew straight from the moment one recognised that the poet essentially *can't* be concerned with the act of dying. Let him deal with the sickest of the sick, it is still by the act of living that they appeal to him, and appeal the more as the conditions plot against them and prescribe the battle. The process of life gives way fighting, and often may so shine out on the lost ground as in no other connexion. One had had moreover, as a various chronicler, one's secondary physical weaklings and failures, one's accessory invalids—introduced with a complacency that made light of criticism. To Ralph Touchett in "The Portrait of a Lady," for instance, his deplorable state of health was not only no drawback; I had clearly been right in counting it, for any happy effect he should produce, a positive good mark, a direct aid to pleasantness and vividness.[793] The reason of this moreover could never in the world have been his fact of sex; since men, among the mortally afflicted, suffer on the whole more overtly and more grossly than women, and resist with a ruder, an inferior strategy. I had thus to take *that* anomaly for what it was worth, and I give it here but as one of the ambiguities amid which my subject ended by making itself at home and seating itself quite in confidence.

With the clearness I have just noted, accordingly, the last thing in the world it proposed to itself was to be the record predominantly of a collapse.[794] I don't mean to say that my offered victim was not present to my imagination, constantly, as dragged by a greater force than any she herself could exert; she had been given me from far back as contesting every inch of the road, as catching at every object the grasp of which might make for delay, as clutching these things to the last moment of her strength.[795] Such an attitude and such movements, the passion they expressed and the success they in fact represented, what were they in truth but the soul of drama?—which is the portrayal, as we know, of a catastrophe determined in spite of oppositions.[796] My young woman would *herself* be the opposition—to the catastrophe announced by the associated Fates,[797] powers conspiring to a sinister end and, with their command of means, finally achieving it, yet in such straits really to *stifle* the sacred spark that, obviously, a creature so animated, an adversary so subtle, couldn't but be felt worthy, under whatever weaknesses, of the foreground and the limelight. She would meanwhile wish, moreover, all along, to live for particular things, she would found her struggle on particular human interests, which would inevitably determine, in respect to her, the attitude of other persons, persons affected in such a manner as to make them part of the action. If her impulse to wrest from her shrinking hour still as much of the fruit of life as possible, if this longing can take effect only by the aid of others, their participation (appealed to, entangled and coerced as they find themselves) becomes their drama too—that of their promoting her illusion, under her importunity, for reasons, for interests and advantages, from motives and points of view, of their own. Some of these promptings, evidently, would be of the highest order—others doubtless mightn't; but they would make up together, for her, contributively, her sum of experience, represent to her somehow, in good faith or in bad, what she should have *known*. Somehow, too, at such a rate, one would see the persons subject to them drawn in as by some pool of a Lorelei[798]—see them terrified and tempted and charmed; bribed away, it may even be, from more prescribed and natural orbits, inheriting from their connexion with her strange difficulties and still stranger opportunities, confronted with rare questions and called upon for new discriminations. Thus the scheme of her situation would, in a comprehensive way, see itself constituted; the rest of the interest would be in the number and nature of the particulars. Strong among these, naturally, the need that life should, apart from her infirmity, present itself to our young woman as quite dazzlingly liveable, and that if the great pang for her is in what she must give up we shall appreciate it the more from the sight of all she has.

One would see her then as possessed of all things, all but the single most precious assurance; freedom and money and a mobile mind and personal charm, the power to interest and attach; attributes, each one, enhancing the value of a future. From the moment his imagination began to deal with her at close quarters, in fact, nothing could more engage her designer than to work out the detail of her perfect rightness for her part; nothing above all more solicit him than to recognise fifty reasons for her national and social status. She should be the last fine flower—blooming alone, for the fullest attestation of her freedom—of an "old" New York stem;[799] the happy congruities thus preserved for her being matters, however, that I may not now go into, and this even though the fine association that shall yet elsewhere await me is of a sort, at the best, rather to defy than to encourage exact expression. There goes with it, for the heroine of "The Wings of the Dove," a strong and special implication of liberty, liberty of action, of choice, of appreciation, of contact—proceeding from sources that provide better for large independence, I think, than any other conditions in the world—and this would be in particular what we should feel ourselves deeply concerned with. I had from far back mentally projected a certain sort of young American as more the "heir of all the ages"[800] than any other young person whatever (and precisely on those grounds I have just glanced at but to pass them by for the moment); so that here was a chance to confer on some such figure a supremely touching value. To be the heir of all the ages only to know yourself, as that consciousness should deepen, balked of your inheritance, would be to play the part, it struck me, or at least to arrive at the type, in the light on the whole the most becoming. Otherwise, truly, what a perilous part to play *out*—what a suspicion of "swagger" in positively attempting it! So at least I could reason—so I even think I *had* to—to keep my subject to a decent compactness. For already, from an early stage, it had begun richly to people itself: the difficulty was to see whom the situation I had primarily projected might, by this, that or the other turn, *not* draw in. My business was to watch its turns as the fond parent watches a child perched, for its first riding-lesson, in the saddle; yet its interest, I had all the while to recall, was just in its making, on such a scale, for developments.

What one had discerned, at all events, from an early stage, was that a young person so devoted and exposed, a creature with her security hanging so by a hair, couldn't but fall somehow into some abysmal trap—this being, dramatically speaking, what such a situation most naturally implied and imposed. Didn't the truth and a great part of the interest also reside in the appearance that she would constitute for others (given her passionate yearning to live while she might) a complication as great as any they might constitute for herself?—which is what I mean when I speak of such matters as "natural." They would be as natural, these tragic, pathetic, ironic, these indeed for the most part sinister, liabilities, to her living associates, as they could be to herself as prime subject. If her story was to consist, as it could so little help doing, of her being let in, as we say, for this, that and the other irreducible anxiety, how could she not have put a premium on the acquisition, by any close sharer of her life, of a consciousness similarly embarrassed? I have named the Rhine-maiden, but our young friend's existence would create rather, all round her, very much that whirlpool movement of the waters produced by the sinking of a big vessel[801] or the failure of a great business; when we figure to ourselves the strong narrowing eddies, the immense force of suction, the general engulfment that, for any neighbouring object, makes immersion inevitable. I need scarce say, however, that in spite of these communities of doom I saw the main dramatic complication much more prepared *for* my vessel of sensibility than by her—the work of other hands (though with her own imbrued too, after all, in the measure of their never not being, in some direction, generous and extravagant, and thereby provoking).

The great point was, at all events, that if in a predicament she was to be, accordingly, it would be of the essence to create the predicament promptly and build it up solidly, so that it should have for us as much as possible its ominous air of awaiting her. That reflexion I found, betimes, not less inspiring than urgent; one begins so, in such a business, by looking about for one's compositional key, unable as one can only be to move till one has found it. To start without it is to pretend to enter the train and, still more, to remain in one's seat, without a ticket.[802] Well—in the steady light and for the continued charm of these verifications—I had secured my ticket over the tolerably long line laid down for "The Wings of the Dove" from the moment I had noted that there could be no full presentation of Milly Theale as *engaged* with elements amid which she was to draw her breath in such pain,[803] should not the elements have been, with all solicitude, duly prefigured. If one had seen that her stricken state was but half her case, the correlative half being the state of others as affected by her (they too should have a "case," bless them, quite as much as she!) then I was free to choose, as it were, the half with which I should begin. If, as I had fondly noted, the little world determined for her was to "bristle"—I delighted in the term!—with meanings,[804] so, by the same token, could I but make my medal hang free, its obverse and its reverse, its face and its back, would beautifully become optional for the spectator. I somehow wanted them correspondingly embossed, wanted them inscribed and figured with an equal salience; yet it was none the less visibly my "key," as I have said, that though my regenerate young New Yorker, and what might depend on her, should form my centre, my circumference was every whit as treatable. Therefore I must trust myself to know when to proceed from the one and when from the other. Preparatively and, as it were, yearningly—given the whole ground—one began, in the event, with the outer ring, approaching the centre thus by narrowing circumvallations.[805] There, full-blown, accordingly, from one hour to the other, rose one's process—for which there remained all the while so many amusing formulae.

The medal *did* hang free—I felt this perfectly, I remember, from the moment I had comfortably laid the ground provided in my first Book, ground from which Milly is superficially so absent.[806] I scarce remember perhaps a case—I like even with this public grossness to insist on it—in which the curiosity of "beginning far back," as far back as possible,[807] and even of going, to the same tune, far "behind," that is behind the face of the subject, was to assert itself with less scruple. The free hand, in this connexion, was above all agreeable—the hand the freedom of which I owed to the fact that the work had ignominiously failed, in advance, of all power to see itself "serialised."[808] This failure had repeatedly waited, for me, upon shorter fictions; but the considerable production we here discuss was (as "The Golden Bowl" was to be, two or three years later) born, not otherwise than a little bewilderedly, into a world of periodicals and editors, of roaring "successes" in fine, amid which it was well-nigh unnotedly to lose itself. There is fortunately something bracing, ever, in the alpine chill, that of some high icy *arête*, shed by the cold editorial shoulder;[809] sour grapes may at moments fairly intoxicate and the story-teller worth his salt rejoice to feel again how many accommodations he can practise. Those addressed to "conditions of publication" have in a degree their interesting, or at least their provoking, side; but their charm is qualified by the fact that the prescriptions here spring from a soil often wholly alien to the ground of the work itself. They are almost always the fruit of another air altogether and conceived in a light liable to represent *within* the circle of the work itself little else than darkness. Still, when not too blighting, they often operate as a tax on ingenuity—that ingenuity of the expert craftsman which likes to be taxed very much to the same tune to which a well-bred horse likes to be saddled. The best and finest ingenuities, nevertheless, with all respect to that truth, are apt to be, not one's compromises, but one's fullest conformities, and I well remember, in the case before us, the pleasure of feeling my divisions, my proportions and general rhythm, rest all on permanent rather than in any degree on momentary proprieties. It was enough for my alternations, thus, that they were good in themselves; it was in fact so much for them that I really think any further account of the constitution of the book reduces itself to a just notation of the law they followed.

There was the "fun," to begin with, of establishing one's successive centres—of fixing them so exactly that the portions of the subject commanded by them as by happy points of view, and accordingly treated from them, would constitute, so to speak, sufficiently solid *blocks* of wrought material, squared to the sharp edge, as to have weight and mass and carrying power; to make for construction, that is, to conduce to effect and to provide for beauty. Such a block, obviously, is the whole preliminary presentation of Kate Croy,[810] which, from the first, I recall, absolutely declined to enact itself save in terms of amplitude. Terms of amplitude, terms of atmosphere, those terms, and those terms only, in which images assert their fulness and roundness, their power to revolve, so that they have sides and backs, parts in the shade as true as parts in the sun—these were plainly to be my conditions, right and left, and I was so far from overrating the amount of expression the whole thing, as I saw and felt it, would require, that to retrace the way at present is, alas, more than anything else, but to mark the gaps and the lapses, to miss, one by one, the intentions that, with the best will in the world, were not to fructify. I have just said that the process of the general attempt is described from the moment the "blocks" are numbered, and that would be a true enough picture of my plan. Yet one's plan, alas, is one thing and one's result another; so that I am perhaps nearer the point in saying that this last strikes me at present as most characterised by the happy features that *were*, under my first and most blest illusion, to have contributed to it. I meet them all, as I renew acquaintance, I mourn for them all as I remount the stream, the absent values, the palpable voids, the missing links, the mocking shadows,[811] that reflect, taken together, the early bloom of one's good faith. Such cases are of course far from abnormal—so far from it that some acute mind ought surely to have worked out by this time the "law" of the degree in which the artist's energy fairly depends on his fallibility. How much and how often, and in what connexions and with what almost infinite variety, must he be a dupe, that of his prime object, to be at all measurably a master, that of his actual substitute for it[812]—or in other words at all appreciably to exist? He places, after an earnest survey, the piers of his bridge[813]—he has at least sounded deep enough, heaven knows, for their brave position; yet the bridge spans the stream, after the fact, in apparently complete independence of these properties, the principal grace of the original design. *They* were an illusion, for their necessary hour; but the span itself, whether of a single arch or of many, seems by the oddest chance in the world to be a reality; since, actually, the rueful builder, passing under it, sees figures and hears sounds above: he makes out, with his heart in his throat, that it bears and is positively being "used."

The building-up of Kate Croy's consciousness to the capacity for the load little by little to be laid on it was, by way of example, to have been a matter of as many hundred close-packed bricks as there are actually poor dozens. The image of her so compromised and compromising father was all effectively to have pervaded her life, was in a certain particular way to have tampered with her spring; by which I mean that the shame and the irritation and the depression, the general poisonous influence of him, were to have been *shown*, with a truth beyond the compass even of one's most emphasised "word of honour" for it,[814] to do these things. But where do we find him, at this time of day, save in a beggarly scene or two[815] which scarce arrives at the dignity of functional reference? He but "looks in," poor beautiful dazzling, damning apparition that he was to have been; he sees his place so taken, his company so little missed, that, cocking again that fine form of hat which has yielded him for so long his one effective cover, he turns away with a whistle of indifference that nobly misrepresents the deepest disappointment of his life. One's poor word of honour has *had* to pass muster for the show. Every one, in short, was to have enjoyed so much better a chance that, like stars of the theatre condescending to oblige, they have had to take small parts, to content themselves with minor identities, in order to come on at all. I haven't the heart now, I confess, to adduce the detail of so many lapsed importances; the explanation of most of which, after all, I take to have been in the crudity of a truth beating full upon me through these reconsiderations, the odd inveteracy with which picture, at almost any turn, is jealous of drama, and drama (though on the whole with a greater patience, I think) suspicious of picture. Between them, no doubt, they do much for the theme; yet each baffles insidiously the other's ideal and eats round the edges of its position; each is too ready to say "I can take the thing for 'done' only when done in *my* way." The residuum of comfort for the witness of these broils is of course meanwhile in the convenient reflexion, invented for him in the twilight of time and the infancy of art by the Angel, not to say by the Demon, of Compromise,[816] that nothing is so easy to "do" as not to be thankful for almost any stray help in its getting done. It wasn't, after this fashion, by making good one's dream of Lionel Croy that my structure was to stand on its feet—any more than it was by letting him go that I was to be left irretrievably lamenting. The who and the what, the how and the why, the whence and the whither of Merton Densher, these, no less, were quantities and attributes that should have danced about him with the antique grace of nymphs and fauns circling round a bland Hermes and crowning him with flowers.[817] One's main anxiety, for each one's agents, is that the air of each shall be *given;* but what does the whole thing become, after all, as one goes, but a series of sad places at which the hand of generosity has been cautioned and stayed? The young man's situation, personal, professional, social, was to have been so decanted for us that we should get all the taste; we were to have been penetrated with Mrs. Lowder, by the same token, saturated with her presence, her "personality," and felt all her weight in the scale.[818] We were to have revelled in Mrs. Stringham, my heroine's attendant friend, her fairly choral Bostonian, a subject for innumerable touches, and in an extended and above all an *animated* reflexion of Milly

Theale's experience of English society; just as the strength and sense of the situation in Venice, for our gathered friends, was to have come to us in a deeper draught out of a larger cup, and just as the pattern of Densher's final position and fullest consciousness there was to have been marked in fine stitches, all silk and gold, all pink and silver, that have had to remain, alas, but entwined upon the reel.

It isn't, no doubt, however—to recover, after all, our critical balance—that the pattern didn't, for each compartment, get itself somehow wrought, and that we mightn't thus, piece by piece, opportunity offering, trace it over and study it. The thing has doubtless, as a whole, the advantage that each piece is true to its pattern, and that while it pretends to make no simple statement it yet never lets go its scheme of clearness. Applications of this scheme are continuous and exemplary enough, though I scarce leave myself room to glance at them. The clearness is obtained in Book First—or otherwise, as I have said, in the first "piece," each Book having its subordinate and contributive pattern—through the associated consciousness of my two prime young persons, for whom I early recognised that I should have to consent, under stress, to a practical *fusion* of consciousness.[819] It is into the young woman's "ken" that Merton Densher is represented as swimming; but her mind is not here, rigorously, the one reflector. There are occasions when it plays this part, just as there are others when his plays it, and an intelligible plan consists naturally not a little in fixing such occasions and making them, on one side and the other, sufficient to themselves. Do I sometimes in fact forfeit the advantage of that distinctness? Do I ever abandon one centre for another after the former has been postulated? From the moment we proceed by "centres"—and I have never, I confess, embraced the logic of any superior process—they must *be*, each, as a basis, selected and fixed; after which it is that, in the high interest of economy of treatment, they determine and rule. There is no economy of treatment without an adopted, a related point of view, and though I understand, under certain degrees of pressure, a represented community of vision between several parties to the action when it makes for concentration, I understand no breaking-up of the register, no sacrifice of the recording consistency, that doesn't rather scatter and weaken. In this truth resides the secret of the discriminated occasion—that aspect of the subject which we have our noted choice of treating either as picture or scenically, but which is apt, I think, to show its fullest worth in the Scene. Beautiful exceedingly,[820] for that matter, those occasions or parts of an occasion when the boundary line between picture and scene bears a little the weight of the double pressure.

Such would be the case, I can't but surmise, for the long passage that forms here before us the opening of Book Fourth, where all the offered life centres, to intensity, in the disclosure of Milly's single throbbing consciousness, but where, for a due rendering, everything has to be brought to a head. This passage, the view of her introduction to Mrs. Lowder's circle, has its mate, for illustration, later on in the book[821] and at a crisis for which the occasion submits to another rule. My registers or "reflectors,"[822] as I so conveniently name them (burnished indeed as they generally are by the intelligence, the curiosity, the passion, the force of the moment, whatever it be, directing them), work, as we have seen, in arranged alternation; so that in the second connexion I here glance at it is Kate Croy who is, "for all she is worth," turned on.[823] She is turned on largely at Venice, where the appearances, rich and obscure and portentous (another word I rejoice in) as they have by that time become and altogether exquisite as they remain, are treated almost wholly through her vision of them and Densher's (as to the lucid interplay of which conspiring and conflicting agents there would be a great deal to say). It is in Kate's consciousness that at the stage in question the drama is brought to a head, and the occasion on which, in the splendid saloon of poor Milly's hired palace, she takes the measure of her friend's festal evening, squares itself to the same synthetic firmness as the compact constructional block inserted by the scene at Lancaster Gate. Milly's situation ceases at a given moment to be "renderable" in terms closer than those supplied by Kate's intelligence, or, in a richer degree, by Densher's, or, for one fond hour, by poor Mrs. Stringham's[824] (since to that sole brief futility is this last participant, crowned by my original plan with the quaintest functions, in fact reduced); just as Kate's relation with Densher and Densher's with Kate have ceased previously, and are then to cease again, to be projected for us, so far as Milly is concerned with them, on any more responsible plate than that of the latter's admirable anxiety.[825] It is as if, for these aspects, the impersonal plate—in other words the poor author's comparatively cold affirmation or thin guarantee—had felt itself a figure of attestation at once too gross and too bloodless, likely to affect us as an abuse of privilege when not as an abuse of knowledge.

Heaven forbid, we say to ourselves during almost the whole Venetian climax, heaven forbid we should "know" anything more of our ravaged sister than what Densher darkly pieces together, or than what Kate Croy pays, heroically, it must be owned, at the hour of her visit alone to Densher's lodging,[826] for her superior handling and her dire profanation of. For we have time, while this passage lasts, to turn round critically;[827] we have time to recognise intentions and proprieties; we have time to catch glimpses of an economy of composition, as I put it, interesting in itself: all in spite of the author's scarce more than half-dissimulated despair at the inveterate displacement of his general centre. "The Wings of the Dove" happens to offer perhaps the most striking example I may cite (though with public penance for it already performed[828]) of my regular failure to keep the appointed halves of my whole equal. Here the makeshift middle—for which the best I can say is that it's always rueful and never impudent—reigns with even more than its customary contrition, though passing itself off perhaps too with more than its usual craft. Nowhere, I seem to recall, had the need of dissimulation been felt so as anguish; nowhere had I condemned a luckless theme to complete its revolution, burdened with the accumulation of its difficulties, the difficulties that grow with a theme's development, in quarters so cramped. Of course, as every novelist knows, it is difficulty that inspires; only, for that perfection of charm, it must have been difficulty inherent and congenital, and not difficulty "caught" by the wrong frequentations. The latter half, that is the false and deformed half, of "The Wings" would verily, I think, form a signal object-lesson for a literary critic bent on improving his occasion to the profit of the budding artist. This whole corner of the picture bristles with "dodges"[829]—such as he should feel himself all committed to recognise and denounce—for disguising the reduced scale of the exhibition, for foreshortening at any cost, for imparting to patches the value of presences, for dressing objects in an *air* as of the dimensions they can't possibly have. Thus he would have his free hand for pointing out what a tangled web we weave when—well, when, through our mislaying or otherwise trifling with our blest pair of compasses,[830] we have to produce the illusion of mass without the illusion of extent. *There* is a job quite to the measure of most of our monitors—and with the interest for them well enhanced by the preliminary cunning quest for the spot where deformity has begun.

I recognise meanwhile, throughout the long earlier reach of the book, not only no deformities but, I think, a positively close and felicitous application of method, the preserved consistencies of which, often illusive, but never really lapsing, it would be of a certain diversion, and might be of some profit, to follow. The author's accepted task at the outset has been to suggest with force the nature of the tie formed between the two young persons first introduced—to give the full impression of its peculiar worried and baffled, yet clinging and confident, ardour. The picture constituted, so far as may be, is that of a pair of natures well-nigh consumed by a sense of their intimate affinity and congruity, the reciprocity of their desire, and thus passionately impatient of barriers and delays, yet with qualities of intelligence and character that they are meanwhile extraordinarily able to draw upon for the enrichment of their relation, the extension of their prospect and the support of their "game."[831] They are far from a common couple, Merton Densher and Kate Croy, as befits the remarkable fashion in which fortune was to waylay and opportunity was to distinguish them—the whole strange truth of their response to which opening involves also, in its order, no vulgar art of exhibition; but what they have most to tell us is that, all unconsciously and with the best faith in the world, all by mere force of the terms of their superior passion combined with their superior diplomacy, they are laying a trap for the great innocence to come. If I like, as I have confessed, the "portentous" look, I was perhaps never to set so high a value on it as for all this prompt provision of forces unwittingly waiting to close round my eager heroine (to the eventual deep chill of her eagerness) as the result of her mere lifting of a latch. Infinitely interesting to have built up the relation of the others to the point at which its aching restlessness, its need to affirm itself otherwise than by an exasperated patience, meets as with instinctive relief and recognition the possibilities shining out of Milly Theale. Infinitely interesting to have prepared and organised, correspondingly, that young woman's precipitations and liabilities, to have constructed, for Drama essentially to take possession, the whole bright house of her exposure.

These references, however, reflect too little of the detail of the treatment imposed; such a detail as I for instance get hold of in the fact of Densher's interview with Mrs. Lowder before he goes to America.[832] It forms, in this preliminary picture, the one patch not strictly seen over Kate Croy's shoulder; though it's notable that immediately after, at the first possible moment, we surrender again to our major convenience, as it happens to be at the time, that of our drawing breath through the young woman's lungs. Once more, in other words, before we know it, Densher's direct vision of the scene at Lancaster Gate is replaced by her apprehension, her contributive assimilation, of his experience: it melts back into that accumulation, which we have been, as it were, saving up. Does my apparent deviation here count accordingly as a muddle?—one of the muddles ever blooming so thick in any soil that fails to grow reasons and determinants. No, distinctly not; for I had definitely opened the door, as attention of perusal of the first two Books will show, to the subjective community of my young pair. (Attention of perusal, I thus confess by the way, is what I at every point, as well as here, absolutely invoke and take for granted; a truth I avail myself of this occasion to note once for all—in the interest of that variety of ideal reigning, I gather, in the connexion. The enjoyment of a work of art, the acceptance of an irresistible illusion, constituting, to my sense, our highest experience of "luxury," the luxury is not greatest, by my consequent measure, when the work asks for as little attention as possible. It is greatest, it is delightfully, divinely great, when we feel the surface, like the thick ice of the skater's pond, bear without cracking the strongest pressure we throw on it. The sound of the crack one may recognise, but never surely to call it a luxury.) That I had scarce availed myself of the privilege of seeing with Densher's eyes is another matter; the point is that I had intelligently marked my possible, my occasional need of it. So, at all events, the constructional "block" of the first two Books compactly forms itself. A new block, all of the squarest and not a little of the smoothest, begins with the Third—by which I mean of course a new mass of interest governed from a new centre. Here again I make prudent *provision*—to be sure to keep my centre strong. It dwells mainly, we at once see, in the depths of Milly Theale's "case," where, close beside it, however, we meet a supplementary reflector, that of the lucid even though so quivering spirit of her dedicated friend.

The more or less associated consciousness of the two women deals thus, unequally, with the next presented face of the subject—deals with it to the exclusion of the dealing of others; and if, for a highly particular moment, I allot to Mrs. Stringham the responsibility of the direct appeal to us, it is again, charming to relate, on behalf of that play of the portentous which

I cherish so as a "value" and am accordingly for ever setting in motion. There is an hour of evening, on the alpine height,[833] at which it becomes of the last importance that our young woman should testify eminently in this direction. But as I was to find it long since of a blest wisdom that no expense should be incurred or met, in any corner of picture of mine, without some concrete image of the account kept of it, that is of its being organically re-economised, so under that dispensation Mrs. Stringham has to register the transaction. Book Fifth is a new block mainly in its provision of a new set of occasions,[834] which readopt, for their order, the previous centre, Milly's now almost full-blown consciousness. At my game, with renewed zest, of driving portents home, I have by this time all the choice of those that are to brush that surface with a dark wing. They are used, to our profit, on an elastic but a definite system; by which I mean that having to sound here and there a little deep, as a test, for my basis of method, I find it everywhere obstinately present. It draws the "occasion" into tune and keeps it so, to repeat my tiresome term; my nearest approach to muddlement is to have sometimes—but not too often—to break my occasions small. Some of them succeed in remaining ample and in really aspiring then to the higher, the sustained lucidity. The whole actual centre of the work, resting on a misplaced pivot and lodged in Book Fifth, pretends to a long reach, or at any rate to the larger foreshortening—though bringing home to me, on re-perusal, what I find striking, charming and curious, the author's instinct everywhere for the *indirect* presentation of his main image.[835] I note how, again and again, I go but a little way with the direct—that is with the straight exhibition of Milly; it resorts for relief, this process, whenever it can, to some kinder, some merciful indirection: all as if to approach her circuitously, deal with her at second hand, as an unspotted princess is ever dealt with;[836] the pressure all round her kept easy for her, the sounds, the movements regulated, the forms and ambiguities made charming. All of which proceeds, obviously, from her painter's tenderness of imagination about her, which reduces him to watching her, as it were, through the successive windows of other people's interest in her. So, if we talk of princesses, do the balconies opposite the palace gates, do the coigns of vantage and respect enjoyed for a fee, rake from afar the mystic figure in the gilded coach as it comes forth into the great *place*.[837] But my use of windows and balconies is doubtless at best an extravagance by itself, and as to what there may be to note, of this and other supersubtleties, other arch-refinements, of tact and taste, of design and instinct, in "The Wings of the Dove," I become conscious of overstepping my space without having brought the full quantity to light. The failure leaves me with a burden of residuary comment of which I yet boldly hope elsewhere to discharge myself.[838]

PREFACE to *The Ambassadors* (*NYE* XXI–XXII)

Nothing is more easy than to state the subject of "The Ambassadors," which first appeared in twelve numbers of *The North American Review* (1903) and was published as a whole the same year.[839] The situation involved is gathered up betimes, that is in the second chapter of Book Fifth, for the reader's benefit, into as few words as possible—planted or "sunk," stiffly and saliently, in the centre of the current, almost perhaps to the obstruction of traffic. Never can a composition of this sort have sprung straighter from a dropped grain of suggestion,[840] and never can that grain, developed, overgrown and smothered, have yet lurked more in the mass as an independent particle. The whole case, in fine, is in Lambert Strether's irrepressible outbreak to little Bilham on the Sunday afternoon in Gloriani's garden, the candour with which he yields, for his young friend's enlightenment, to the charming admonition of that crisis. The idea of the tale resides indeed in the very fact that an hour of such unprecedented ease should have been felt by him *as* a crisis, and he is at pains to express it for us as neatly as we could desire. The remarks to which he thus gives utterance contain the essence of "The Ambassadors," his fingers close, before he has done, round the stem of the full-blown flower; which, after that fashion, he continues officiously to present to us. "Live all you can; it's a mistake not to. It doesn't so much matter what you do in particular so long as you have your life. If you haven't had that what *have* you had? I'm too old—too old at any rate for what I see. What one loses one loses; make no mistake about that. Still, we have the illusion of freedom; therefore don't, like me to-day, be without the memory of that illusion. I was either, at the right time, too stupid or too intelligent to have it, and now I'm a case of reaction against the mistake. Do what you like so long as you don't make it. For it *was* a mistake. Live, live!"[841] Such is the gist of Strether's appeal to the impressed youth, whom he likes and whom he desires to befriend; the word "mistake" occurs several times, it will be seen, in the course of his remarks[842]—which gives the measure of the signal warning he feels attached to his case. He has accordingly missed too much, though perhaps after all constitutionally qualified for a better part, and he wakes up to it in conditions that press the spring of a terrible question. *Would* there yet perhaps be time for reparation?—reparation, that is, for the injury done his character; for the affront, he is quite ready to say, so stupidly put upon it and in which he has even himself had so clumsy a hand? The answer to which is that he now at all events *sees;* so that the business of my tale and the march of my action, not to say the precious moral of everything, is just my demonstration of this process of vision.

Nothing can exceed the closeness with which the whole fits again into its germ. That had been given me bodily, as usual, by the spoken word, for I was to take the image over exactly as I happened to have met it. A friend had repeated to me, with great appreciation, a thing or two said to him by a man of distinction, much his senior, and to which a sense akin to that of Strether's melancholy eloquence might be imputed—said as chance would have, and so easily might, in Paris, and in a charming old garden attached to a house of art,[843] and on a Sunday afternoon of summer, many persons of great interest being present. The observation there listened to and gathered up had contained part of the "note" that I was to recognise on the spot as to my purpose—had contained in fact the greater part; the rest was in the place and the time and the scene they sketched: these constituents clustered and combined to give me further support, to give me what I may call the note absolute. There it stands, accordingly, full in the tideway;[844] driven in, with hard taps, like some strong stake for the noose of a cable, the swirl of the current roundabout it. What amplified the hint to more than the bulk of hints in general was the gift with it of the old Paris garden, for in that token were sealed up values infinitely precious. There was of course the seal to break and each item of the packet to count over and handle and estimate; but somehow, in the light of the hint, all the elements of a situation of the sort most to my taste were there. I could even remember no occasion on which, so confronted, I had found it of a livelier interest to take stock, in this fashion, of suggested wealth. For I think, verily, that there are degrees of merit in subjects—in spite of the fact that to treat even one of the most ambiguous with due decency we must for the time, for the feverish and prejudiced hour, at least figure its merit and its dignity as *possibly* absolute. What it comes to, doubtless, is that even among the supremely good—since with such alone is it one's theory of one's honour to be concerned—there is an ideal *beauty* of goodness the invoked action of which is to raise the artistic faith to its maximum. Then truly, I hold, one's theme may be said to shine, and that of "The Ambassadors," I confess, wore this glow for me from beginning to end. Fortunately thus I am able to estimate this as, frankly, quite the best, "all round," of all my productions; any failure of that justification would have made such an extreme of complacency publicly fatuous.

I recall then in this connexion no moment of subjective intermittence, never one of those alarms as for a suspected hollow beneath one's feet, a felt ingratitude in the scheme adopted, under which confidence fails and opportunity seems but to mock. If the motive of "The Wings of the Dove," as I have noted, was to worry me at moments by a sealing-up of its face—though without prejudice to its again, of a sudden, fairly grimacing with expression—so in this other business I had absolute conviction and constant clearness to deal with; it had been a frank proposition, the whole bunch of data, installed on my premises like a monotony of fine weather.[845] (The order of composition, in these things, I may mention, was reversed by the order of publication;[846] the earlier written of the two books having appeared as the later.) Even under the weight of my hero's years I could feel my postulate firm; even under the strain of the difference between those of Madame de Vionnet and those of Chad Newsome, a difference liable to be denounced as shocking, I could still feel it serene. Nothing resisted, nothing betrayed, I seem to make out, in this full and sound sense of the matter; it shed from any side I could turn it to the same golden glow. I rejoiced in the promise of a hero so mature, who would give me thereby the more to bite into—since it's only into thickened motive and accumulated character, I think, that the painter of life bites more than a little. My poor friend should have accumulated character, certainly; or rather would be quite naturally and handsomely possessed of it, in the sense that he would have, and would always have felt he had, imagination galore, and that this yet wouldn't have wrecked him. It was immeasurable, the opportunity to "do" a man of imagination,[847] for if *there* mightn't be a chance to "bite," where in the world might it be? This personage of course, so enriched, wouldn't give me, for his type, imagination in *predominance* or as his prime faculty, nor should I, in view of other matters, have found that convenient. So particular a luxury—some occasion, that is, for study of the high gift in *supreme* command of a case or of a career—would still doubtless come on the day I should be ready to pay for it; and till then might, as from far back, remain hung up well in view and just out of reach. The comparative case meanwhile would serve—it was only on the minor scale that I had treated myself even to comparative cases.

I was to hasten to add however that, happy stopgaps as the minor scale had thus yielded, the instance in hand should enjoy the advantage of the full range of the major; since most immediately to the point was the question of that *supplement* of situation logically involved in our gentleman's impulse to deliver himself in the Paris garden on the Sunday afternoon—or if not involved by strict logic then all ideally and enchantingly implied in it. (I say "ideally," because I need scarce mention that for development, for expression of its maximum, my glimmering story was, at the earliest stage, to have nipped the thread of connexion with the possibilities of the actual reported speaker.[848] *He* remains but the happiest of accidents; his actualities, all too definite, precluded any range of possibilities; it had only been his charming office to project upon that wide field of the artist's vision—which hangs there ever in place like the white sheet suspended for the figures of a child's magic-lantern—a more fantastic and more moveable shadow.[849]) No privilege of the teller of tales and the handler of puppets is more delightful, or has more of the suspense and the thrill of a game of difficulty breathlessly played, than just this business of looking for the unseen and the occult, in a scheme half-grasped, by the light or, so to speak, by the clinging scent, of the gage already in hand. No dreadful old pursuit of the hidden slave with bloodhounds and the rag of association can ever, for "excitement," I judge, have bettered it at its best.[850] For the dramatist always, by the very law of his genius, believes not only in a possible right issue from the rightly-conceived tight place;[851] he does much more than this—he believes, irresistibly, in the necessary, the precious "tightness" of the place (whatever the issue) on the strength of any respectable hint. It being thus the respectable hint that I had with such avidity picked up, what would be the story to which it would most inevitably form the centre? It is part of the charm attendant on such questions that the "story," with the omens true, as I say, puts on from this stage the authenticity of concrete existence. It then *is*, essentially—it begins to be, though it may more or less obscurely lurk; so that the point is not in the least what to make of it, but only, very delightfully and very damnably, where to put one's hand on it.

In which truth resides surely much of the interest of that admirable mixture for salutary application which we know as art. Art deals with what we see, it must first contribute full-handed that ingredient; it plucks its material, otherwise expressed, in the garden of life—which material elsewhere grown is stale and uneatable. But it has no sooner done this than it has to take account of a *process*—from which only when it's the basest of the servants of man, incurring ignominious dismissal with no "character," does it, and whether under some muddled pretext of morality or on any other, pusillanimously edge away. The process, that of the expression, the literal squeezing-out, of value is another affair—with which the happy luck of mere finding has little to do. The joys of finding, at this stage, are pretty well over; that quest of the subject as a whole by "matching," as the ladies say at the shops, the big piece with the snippet, having ended, we assume, with a capture. The subject is found, and if the problem is then transferred to the ground of what to do with it the field opens out for any amount of doing. This is precisely the infusion that, as I submit, completes the strong mixture. It is on the other hand the part of the business that can least be likened to the chase with horn and hound.[852] It's all a sedentary part—involves as much ciphering, of sorts, as would merit the highest salary paid to a chief accountant.[853] Not, however, that the chief accountant hasn't *his* gleams of bliss; for the felicity, or at least the equilibrium, of the artist's state dwells less, surely, in the further delightful complications he can smuggle in than in those he succeeds in keeping out. He sows his seed at the risk of too thick a crop; wherefore yet again, like the gentlemen who audit ledgers, he must keep his head at any price. In consequence of all which, for the interest of the matter, I might seem here to have my choice of narrating my "hunt" for Lambert Strether, of describing the capture of the shadow projected by my friend's anecdote, or of reporting on the occurrences subsequent to that triumph. But I had probably best attempt a little to glance in each direction; since it comes to me again and again, over this licentious record, that one's bag of adventures, conceived or conceivable, has been only half-emptied by the mere telling of one's story. It depends so on what one means by that equivocal quantity. There is the story of one's hero, and then, thanks to the intimate connexion of things, the story of one's story itself.[854] I blush to confess it, but if one's a dramatist one's a dramatist, and the latter imbroglio is liable on occasion to strike me as really the more objective of the two.

The philosophy imputed to him in that beautiful outbreak, the hour there, amid such happy provision, striking for him, would have been then, on behalf of my man of imagination, to be logically and, as the artless craft of comedy has it, "led up" to; the probable course to such a goal, the goal of so conscious a predicament, would have in short to be finely calculated. Where has he come from and why has he come, what is he doing (as we Anglo-Saxons, and we only, say, in our foredoomed clutch of exotic aids to expression) in that *galère?*[855] To answer these questions plausibly, to answer them as under cross-examination in the witness-box by counsel for the prosecution, in other words satisfactorily to account for Strether and for his "peculiar tone," was to possess myself of the entire fabric. At the same time the clue to its whereabouts would lie in a certain *principle* of probability: he wouldn't have indulged in his peculiar tone without a reason; it would take a felt predicament or a false position to give him so ironic an accent. One hadn't been noting "tones" all one's life without recognising when one heard it the voice of the false position.[856] The dear man in the Paris garden was then admirably and unmistakeably *in* one—which was no small point gained; what next accordingly concerned us was the determination of *this* identity. One could only go by probabilities, but there was the advantage that the most general of the probabilities were virtual certainties. Possessed of our friend's nationality, to start with, there was a general probability in his narrower localism; which, for that matter, one had really but to keep under the lens for an hour to see it give up its secrets. He would have issued, our rueful worthy, from the very heart of New England[857]—at the heels of which matter of course a perfect train of secrets tumbled for me into the light. They had to be sifted and sorted, and I shall not reproduce the detail of that process; but unmistakeably they were all there, and it was but a question, auspiciously, of picking among them. What the "position" would infallibly be, and why, on his hands, it had turned "false"—these inductive steps could only be as rapid as they were distinct. I accounted for everything—and "everything" had by this time become the most promising quantity—by the view that he had come to Paris in some state of mind which was literally undergoing, as a result of new and unexpected assaults and infusions, a change almost from hour to hour. He had come with a view that might have been figured by a clear green liquid, say, in a neat glass phial; and the liquid, once poured into the open cup of *application*, once exposed to the action of another air, had begun to turn from green to red, or whatever, and might, for all he knew, be on its way to purple, to black, to yellow. At the still wilder extremes represented perhaps, for all he could say to the contrary, by a variability so violent, he would at first, naturally, but have gazed in surprise and alarm; whereby the *situation* clearly would spring from the play of wildness and the development of extremes. I saw in a moment that, should this development proceed both with force and logic, my "story" would leave nothing to be desired. There is always, of course, for the story-teller, the irresistible determinant and the incalculable advantage of his interest in the story *as such*; it is ever, obviously, overwhelmingly, the prime and precious thing (as other than this I have never been able to see it); as to which what makes for it, with whatever headlong energy, may be said to pale before the energy with which it simply makes for itself. It rejoices, none the less, at its best, to seem to offer itself in a light, to seem to know, and with the very last knowledge, what it's about—liable as it yet is at moments to be caught by us with its tongue in its cheek[858] and absolutely no warrant but its splendid impudence. Let us grant then that the impudence is always there—there, so to speak, for grace and effect and *allure;* there, above all, because the Story is just the spoiled child of art, and because, as we are always disappointed when the pampered don't "play up,"[859] we like it, to that extent, to look all its character. It probably does so, in truth, even when we most flatter ourselves that we negotiate with it by treaty.

All of which, again, is but to say that the *steps*, for my fable, placed themselves with a prompt and, as it were, functional assurance—an air quite as of readiness to have dispensed with logic had I been in fact too stupid for my clue. Never, positively, none the less, as the links multiplied, had I felt less stupid than for the determination of poor Strether's errand and for the apprehension of his issue. These things continued to fall together, as by the neat action of their own weight and form, even while their commentator scratched his head about them; he easily sees now that they were always well in advance of him. As the case completed itself he had in fact, from a good way behind, to catch up with them, breathless and a little flurried, as he best could. *The* false position, for our belated man of the world—belated because he had endeavoured so long to escape being one, and now at last had really to face his doom—the false position for him, I say, was obviously to have presented himself at the gate of that boundless menagerie primed with a moral scheme of the most approved pattern which was yet framed to break down on any approach to vivid facts; that is to any at all liberal appreciation of them. There would have been of course the case of the Strether prepared, wherever presenting himself, only to judge and to feel meanly; but *he* would have moved for me, I confess, enveloped in no legend whatever. The actual man's note, from the first of our seeing it struck, is the note of discrimination, just as his drama is to become, under stress, the drama of discrimination. It would have been his blest imagination, we have seen, that had already helped him to discriminate; the element that was for so much of the pleasure of my cutting thick, as I have intimated, into his intellectual, into his moral substance. Yet here it was, at the same time, just here, that a shade for a moment fell across the scene.

There was the dreadful little old tradition, one of the platitudes of the human comedy, that people's moral scheme *does* break down in Paris;[860] that nothing is more frequently observed; that hundreds of thousands of more or less hypocritical or more or less cynical persons annually visit the place for the sake of the probable catastrophe, and that I came late in the day to work myself up about it. There was in fine the *trivial* association, one of the vulgarest in the world; but which give me pause no longer, I think, simply because its vulgarity is so advertised. The revolution performed by Strether under the influence of the most interesting of great cities was to have nothing to do with any *bêtise* of the imputably "tempted" state; he was to be thrown forward, rather, thrown quite with violence, upon his lifelong trick of intense reflexion: which friendly test indeed was to bring him out, through winding passages, through alternations of darkness and light, very much *in* Paris, but with the surrounding scene itself a minor matter, a mere symbol for more things than had been dreamt of in the philosophy of Woollett.[861] Another surrounding scene would have done as well for our show could it have represented a place in which Strether's errand was likely to lie and his crisis to await him. The *likely* place had the great merit of sparing me preparations; there would have been too many involved—not at all impossibilities, only rather worrying and delaying difficulties—in positing elsewhere Chad Newsome's interesting relation, his so interesting complexity of relations. Strether's appointed stage, in fine, could be but Chad's most luckily selected one. The young man had gone in, as they say, for circumjacent charm; and where he would have found it, by the turn of his mind, most "authentic," was where his earnest friend's analysis would most find *him;* as well as where, for that matter, the former's whole analytic faculty would be led such a wonderful dance.

"The Ambassadors" had been, all conveniently, "arranged for"; its first appearance was from month to month, in the *North American Review* during 1903, and I had been open from far back to any pleasant provocation for ingenuity that might reside in one's actively adopting—so as to make it, in its way, a small compositional law—recurrent breaks and resumptions.[862] I had made up my mind here regularly to exploit and enjoy these often rather rude jolts—having found, as I believed, an admirable way to it; yet every question of form and pressure, I easily remember, paled in the light of the major propriety, recognised as soon as really weighed; that of employing but one centre and keeping it all within my hero's compass. The thing was to be so much this worthy's intimate adventure that even the projection of his consciousness upon it from beginning to end without intermission or deviation would probably still leave a part of its value for him, and *a fortiori* for ourselves, unexpressed. I might, however, express every grain of it that there would be room for—on condition of contriving a splendid particular economy. Other persons in no small number were to people the scene, and each with his or her axe to grind, his or her situation to treat, his or her coherency not to fail of, his or her relation to my leading motive, in a word, to establish and carry on. But Strether's sense of these things, and Strether's only, should avail me for showing them; I should know them but through his more or less groping knowledge of them, since his very gropings would figure among his most interesting motions, and a full observance of the rich rigour I speak of would give me more of the effect I should be most "after" than all other possible observances together. It would give me a large unity, and that in turn would crown me with the grace to which the enlightened story-teller will at any time, for his interest, sacrifice if need be all other graces whatever. I refer of course to the grace of intensity, which there are ways of signally achieving and ways of signally missing—as we see it, all round us, helplessly and woefully missed. Not that it isn't, on the other hand, a virtue eminently subject to appreciation—there being no strict, no absolute measure of it; so that one may hear it acclaimed where it has quite escaped one's perception, and see it unnoticed where one has gratefully hailed it. After all of which I am not sure, either, that the immense amusement of the whole cluster of difficulties so arrayed may not operate, for the fond fabulist, when judicious not less than fond, as his best of determinants. That charming principle is always there, at all events, to keep interest fresh: it is a principle, we remember, essentially ravenous, without scruple and without mercy, appeased with no cheap nor easy nourishment. It enjoys the costly sacrifice and rejoices thereby in the very odour of difficulty—even as ogres, with their "Fee-faw-fum!" rejoice in the smell of the blood of Englishmen.[863]

Thus it was, at all events, that the ultimate, though after all so speedy, definition of my gentleman's job—his coming out, all solemnly appointed and deputed, to "save" Chad, and his then finding the young man so disobligingly and, at first, so bewilderingly not lost that a new issue altogether, in the connexion, prodigiously faces them, which has to be dealt with in a new light—promised as many calls on ingenuity and on the higher branches of the compositional art as one could possibly desire. Again and yet again, as, from book to book, I proceed with my survey, I find no source of interest equal to this verification after the fact, as I may call it, and the more in detail the better, of the scheme of consistency "gone in" for. As always—since the charm never fails—the retracing of the process from point to point brings back the old illusion. The old intentions bloom again and flower—in spite of all the blossoms they were to have dropped by the way. This is the charm, as I say, of adventure *transposed*—the thrilling ups and downs, the intricate ins and outs of the compositional problem, made after such a fashion admirably objective, becoming the question at issue and keeping the author's heart in his mouth. Such an element, for instance, as his intention that Mrs. Newsome, away off with her finger on the pulse of Massachusetts, should yet be no less intensely than circuitously present through the whole thing, should be no less felt as to be reckoned with than the most direct exhibition, the finest portrayal at first hand could make her,[864] such a sign of artistic good faith, I say, once it's unmistakeably there, takes on again an actuality not too much impaired by the comparative dimness of the particular success. Cherished intention too inevitably acts and operates, in the book, about fifty times as little as I had fondly dreamt it might; but that scarce spoils for me the pleasure of recognising the fifty ways in which I had sought to provide for it. The mere charm of seeing such an idea constituent, in its degree; the fineness of the measures taken—a real extension, if successful, of the very terms and possibilities of representation and figuration—such things alone were, after this fashion, inspiring, such things alone were a gage of the probable success of that dissimulated calculation with which the whole effort was to square. But oh the cares begotten, none the less, of that same "judicious" sacrifice to a particular form of interest! One's work should have composition, because composition alone is positive beauty;[865] but all the while—apart from one's inevitable consciousness too of the dire paucity of readers ever recognising or ever missing positive beauty—how, as to the cheap and easy, at every turn, how, as to immediacy and facility, and even as to the commoner vivacity, positive beauty might have to be sweated for and paid for! Once achieved and installed it may always be trusted to make the poor seeker feel he would have blushed to the roots of his hair for failing of it; yet, how, as its virtue can be essentially but the virtue of the whole, the wayside traps set in the interest of muddlement and pleading but the cause of the moment, of the particular bit in itself, have to be kicked out of the path! All the sophistications in life, for example, might have appeared to muster on behalf of the menace—the menace to a bright variety—involved in Strether's having all the subjective "say," as it were, to himself.

Had I, meanwhile, made him at once hero and historian, endowed him with the romantic privilege of the "first person"—the darkest abyss of romance this, inveterately, when enjoyed on the grand scale—variety, and many other queer matters as well, might have been smuggled in by a back door. Suffice it, to be brief, that the first person, in the long piece, is a form foredoomed to looseness, and that looseness, never much my affair, had never been so little so as on this particular occasion. All of which reflexions flocked to the standard from the moment—a very early one—the question of how to keep my form amusing while sticking so close to my central figure and constantly taking its pattern from him had to be faced. He arrives (arrives at Chester)[866] as for the dreadful purpose of giving his creator "no end" to tell about him—before which rigorous mission the serenest of creators might well have quailed. I was far from the serenest; I was more than agitated enough to reflect that, grimly deprived of one alternative or one substitute for "telling," I must address myself tooth and nail to another. I couldn't, save by implication, make other persons tell *each other* about him—blest resource, blest necessity, of the drama, which reaches its effects of unity, all remarkably, by paths absolutely opposite to the paths of the novel: with other persons, save as they were primarily *his* persons (not he primarily but one of theirs), I had simply nothing to do. I had relations for him none the less, by the mercy of Providence, quite as much as if my exhibition *was* to be a muddle; if I could only by implication and a show of consequence make other persons tell each other about him, I could at least make him tell *them* whatever in the world he must; and could so, by the same token—which was a further luxury thrown in—see straight into the deep differences between what that could do for me, or at all events for *him*, and the large ease of "autobiography." It may be asked why, if one so keeps to one's hero, one shouldn't make a single mouthful of "method," shouldn't throw the reins on his neck and, letting them flap there as free as in "Gil Blas" or in "David Copperfield,"[867] equip him with the double privilege of subject and object—a course that has at least the merit of brushing away questions at a sweep. The answer to which is, I think, that one makes that surrender only if one is prepared *not* to make certain precious discriminations.

The "first person" then, so employed, is addressed by the author directly to ourselves, his possible readers, whom he has to reckon with, at the best, by our English tradition, so loosely and vaguely after all, so little respectfully, on so scant a presumption of exposure to criticism. Strether, on the other hand, encaged and provided for as "The Ambassadors" encages and provides, has to keep in view proprieties much stiffer and more salutary than any our straight and credulous gape are likely to bring home to him, has exhibitional conditions to meet, in a word, that forbid the terrible *fluidity* of self-revelation. I may seem not to better the case for my discrimination if I say that, for my first care, I had thus inevitably to set him up a confidant or two,[868] to wave away with energy the custom of the seated mass of explanation after the fact, the inserted block of merely referential narrative, which flourishes so, to the shame of the modern impatience, on the serried page of Balzac,[869] but which seems simply to appal our actual, our general weaker, digestion. "Harking back to make up"[870] took at any rate more doing, as the phrase is, not only than the reader of to-day demands, but than he will tolerate at any price any call upon him either to understand or remotely to measure; and for the beauty of the thing when done the current editorial mind in particular appears wholly without sense. It is not, however, primarily for either of these reasons, whatever their weight, that Strether's friend Waymarsh is so keenly clutched at, on the threshold of the book, or that no less a pounce is made on Maria Gostrey—without even the pretext, either, of *her* being, in essence, Strether's friend. She is the reader's friend much rather—in consequence of dispositions that make him so eminently require one; and she acts in that capacity, and *really* in that capacity alone, with exemplary devotion, from beginning to end of the book. She is an enrolled, a direct, aid to lucidity; she is in fine, to tear off her mask, the most unmitigated and abandoned of *ficelles*.[871] Half the dramatist's art, as we well know—since if we don't it's not the fault of the proofs that lie scattered about us—is in the use of *ficelles;* by which I mean in a deep dissimulation of his dependence on them. Waymarsh only to a slighter degree belongs, in the whole business, less to my subject than to my treatment of it; the interesting proof, in these connexions, being that one has but to take one's subject for the stuff of drama to interweave with enthusiasm as many Gostreys as need be.

The material of "The Ambassadors," conforming in this respect exactly to that of "The Wings of the Dove," published just before it, is taken absolutely for the stuff of drama; so that, availing myself of the opportunity given me by this edition for some prefatory remarks on the latter work, I had mainly to make on its behalf the point of its scenic consistency. It disguises that virtue, in the oddest way in the world, by just *looking*, as we turn its pages, as little scenic as possible; but it sharply divides itself, just as the composition before us does, into the parts that prepare, that tend in fact to over-prepare, for scenes, and the parts, or otherwise into the scenes, that justify and crown the preparation. It may definitely be said, I think, that everything in it that is not scene (not, I of course mean, complete and functional scene, treating *all* the submitted matter, as by logical start, logical turn, and logical finish) is discriminated preparation, is the fusion and synthesis of picture. These alternations propose themselves all recogniseably, I think, from an early stage, as the very form and figure of "The Ambassadors"; so that, to repeat, such an agent as Miss Gostrey, pre-engaged at a high salary, but waits in the draughty wing with her shawl and her smelling-salts.[872] Her function speaks at once for itself, and by the time she has dined with Strether in London and gone to a play with him her intervention as a *ficelle* is, I hold, expertly justified. Thanks to it we have treated scenically, and scenically alone, the whole lumpish question of Strether's "past,"[873] which has seen us more happily on the way than anything else could have done; we have strained to a high lucidity and vivacity (or at least we hope we have) certain indispensable facts; we have seen our two or three immediate friends all conveniently and profitably in "action"; to say nothing of our beginning to descry others, of a remoter intensity, getting into motion, even if a bit vaguely as yet, for our further enrichment. Let my first point be here that the scene in question, that in which the whole situation at Woollett and the complex forces that have propelled my hero to where this lively extractor of his value and distiller of his essence awaits him, is normal and entire, is really an excellent *standard* scene; copious, comprehensive, and accordingly never short, but with its office as definite as that of the hammer on the gong of the clock,[874] the office of expressing *all that is in* the hour.

The "*ficelle*" character of the subordinate party is as artfully dissimulated, throughout, as may be, and to that extent that, with the seams or joints of Maria Gostrey's ostensible connectedness taken particular care of, duly smoothed over, that is, and anxiously kept from showing as "pieced on," this figure doubtless achieves, after a fashion, something of the dignity of a prime idea: which circumstance but shows us afresh how many quite incalculable but none the less clear sources of enjoyment for the infatuated artist, how many copious springs of our never-to-be-slighted "fun" for the reader and critic susceptible of contagion, may sound their incidental plash as soon as an artistic process begins to enjoy free development. Exquisite—in illustration of this—the mere interest and amusement of such at once "creative" and critical questions as how and where and why to make Miss Gostrey's false connexion carry itself, under a due high polish, as a real one. Nowhere is it more of an artful expedient for mere consistency of form, to mention a case, than in the last "scene" of the book, where its function is to give or to add nothing whatever, but only to express as vividly as possible certain things quite other than itself and that are of the already fixed and appointed measure. Since, however, all art is *expression*, and is thereby vividness, one was to find the door open here to any amount of delightful dissimulation. These verily are the refinements and ecstasies of method—amid which, or certainly under the influence of any exhilarated demonstration of which, one must keep one's head and not lose one's way. To cultivate an adequate intelligence for them and to make that sense operative is positively to find a charm in any produced ambiguity of appearance that is not by the same stroke, and all helplessly, an ambiguity of sense. To project imaginatively, for my hero, a relation that has nothing to do with the matter (the matter of my subject) but has everything to do with the manner (the manner of my presentation of the same) and yet to treat it, at close quarters and for fully economic expression's possible sake, as if it were important and essential—to do that sort of thing and yet muddle nothing may easily become, as one goes, a signally attaching proposition; even though it all remains but part and parcel, I hasten to recognise, of the merely general and related question of expressional curiosity and expressional decency.

I am moved to add after so much insistence on the scenic side of my labour that I have found the steps of re-perusal almost as much waylaid here by quite another style of effort in the same signal interest—or have in other words not failed to note how, even so associated and so discriminated, the finest proprieties and charms of the non-scenic may, under the right hand for them, still keep their intelligibility and assert their office. Infinitely suggestive such an observation as this last on the whole delightful head, where representation is concerned, of possible variety, of effective expressional change and contrast. One would like, at such an hour as this, for critical licence, to go into the matter of the noted inevitable deviation (from too fond an original vision) that the exquisite treachery even of the straightest execution may ever be trusted to inflict even on the most mature plan—the case being that, though one's last reconsidered production always seems to bristle with that particular evidence, "The Ambassadors" would place a flood of such light at my service. I must attach to my final remark here a different import; noting in the other connexion I just glanced at that such passages as that of my hero's first encounter with Chad Newsome,[875] absolute attestations of the non-scenic form though they be, yet lay the firmest hand too—so far at least as intention goes—on representational effect. To report at all closely and completely of what "passes" on a given occasion is inevitably to become more or less scenic; and yet in the instance I allude to, *with* the conveyance, expressional curiosity and expressional decency are sought and arrived at under quite another law. The true inwardness of this may be at bottom but that one of the suffered treacheries has consisted precisely, for Chad's whole figure and presence, of a direct presentability diminished and compromised—despoiled, that is, of its *proportional* advantage; so that, in a word, the whole economy of his author's relation to him has at important points to be redetermined. The book, however, critically viewed, is touchingly full of these disguised and repaired losses, these insidious recoveries, these intensely redemptive consistencies. The pages in which Mamie

Pocock gives her appointed and, I can't but think, duly felt lift to the whole action by the so inscrutably-applied side-stroke or short-cut of our just watching, and as quite at an angle of vision as yet untried, her single hour of suspense in the hotel salon, in our partaking of her concentrated study of the sense of matters bearing on her own case, all the bright warm Paris afternoon, from the balcony that overlooks the Tuileries garden[876]—these are as marked an example of the representational virtue that insists here and there on being, for the charm of opposition and renewal, other than the scenic. It wouldn't take much to make me further argue that from an equal play of such oppositions the book gathers an intensity that fairly adds to the dramatic—though the latter is supposed to be the sum of all intensities; or that has at any rate nothing to fear from juxtaposition with it. I consciously fail to shrink in fact from that extravagance—I risk it, rather, for the sake of the moral involved; which is not that the particular production before us exhausts the interesting questions it raises, but that the Novel remains still, under the right persuasion, the most independent, most elastic, most prodigious of literary forms.[877]

PREFACE to *The Golden Bowl* (*NYE* XXIII–XXIV)

Among many matters thrown into relief by a refreshed acquaintance with "The Golden Bowl" what perhaps most stands out for me is the still marked inveteracy of a certain indirect and oblique view of my presented action;[878] unless indeed I make up my mind to call this mode of treatment, on the contrary, any superficial appearance notwithstanding, the very straightest and closest possible. I have already betrayed, as an accepted habit, and even to extravagance commented on, my preference for dealing with my subject-matter, for "seeing my story," through the opportunity and the sensibility of some more or less detached, some not strictly involved, though thoroughly interested and intelligent, witness or reporter, some person who contributes to the case mainly a certain amount of criticism and interpretation of it. Again and again, on review, the shorter things in especial that I have gathered into this Series have ranged themselves not as my own impersonal account of the affair in hand, but as my account of somebody's impression of it—the terms of this person's access to it and estimate of it contributing thus by some fine little law to intensification of interest. The somebody is often, among my shorter tales I recognise, but an unnamed, unintroduced and (save by right of intrinsic wit) unwarranted participant, the impersonal author's concrete deputy or delegate, a convenient substitute or apologist for the creative power otherwise so veiled and disembodied. My instinct appears repeatedly to have been that to arrive at the facts retailed and the figures introduced by the given help of some other conscious and confessed agent is essentially to find the whole business—that is, as I say, its effective interest—enriched *by the way*. I have in other words constantly inclined to the idea of the particular attaching case *plus* some near individual view of it; that nearness quite having thus to become an imagined observer's, a projected, charmed painter's or poet's—however avowed the "minor" quality in the latter—close and sensitive contact with it. Anything, in short, I now reflect, must always have seemed to me better—better for the process and the effect of representation, my irrepressible ideal—than the mere muffled majesty of irresponsible "authorship." Beset constantly with the sense that the painter of the picture or the chanter of the ballad (whatever we may call him) can never be responsible *enough*, and for every inch of his surface and note of his song, I track my uncontrollable footsteps, right and left, after the fact, while they take their quick turn, even on stealthiest tiptoe, toward the point of view that, within the compass, will give me most instead of least to answer for.

I am aware of having glanced a good deal already in the direction of this embarrassed truth[879]—which I give for what it is worth; but I feel it come home to me afresh on recognising that the manner in which it betrays itself may be one of the liveliest sources of amusement in "The Golden Bowl." It's not that the muffled majesty of authorship doesn't here *ostensibly* reign; but I catch myself again shaking it off and disavowing the pretence of it while I get down into the arena and do my best to live and breathe and rub shoulders and converse with the persons engaged in the struggle that provides for the others in the circling tiers the entertainment of the great game.[880] There is no other participant, of course, than each of the real, the deeply involved and immersed and more or less bleeding participants; but I nevertheless affect myself as having held my system fast and fondly, with one hand at least, by the manner in which the whole thing remains subject to the register, ever so closely kept, of the consciousness of but two of the characters. The Prince, in the first half of the book, virtually sees and knows and makes out, virtually represents to himself everything that concerns us— very nearly (though he doesn't speak in the first person) after the fashion of other reporters and critics of other situations. Having a consciousness highly susceptible of registration, he thus makes us see the things that may most interest us reflected in it as in the clean glass held up to so many of the "short stories" of our long list; and yet after all never a whit to the prejudice of his being just as consistently a foredoomed, entangled, embarrassed agent in the general imbroglio, actor in the offered play. The function of the Princess, in the remainder, matches exactly with his; the register of *her* consciousness is as closely kept—as closely, say, not only as his own, but as that (to cite examples) either of the intelligent but quite unindividualised witness of the destruction of "The Aspern Papers," or of the all-noting heroine of "The Spoils of Poynton," highly individualised *though* highly intelligent; the Princess, in fine, in addition to feeling everything she has to, and to playing her part just in that proportion, duplicates, as it were, her value and becomes a compositional resource, and of the finest order, as well as a value intrinsic. So it is that the admirably-endowed pair, between them, as I retrace their fortune and my own method, point again for me the moral of the endless interest, endless worth for "delight," of the compositional contribution. Their chronicle strikes me as quite of the stuff to keep us from forgetting that absolutely *no* refinement of ingenuity or of precaution need be dreamed of as wasted[881] in that most exquisite of all good causes the appeal to variety, the appeal to incalculability, the appeal to a high refinement and a handsome wholeness of effect.

There are other things I might remark here, despite its perhaps seeming a general connexion that I have elsewhere sufficiently shown as suggestive; but I have other matter in hand and I take a moment only to meet a possible objection—should any reader be so far solicitous or even attentive—to what I have just said. It may be noted, that is, that the Prince, in the volume over which he nominally presides, is represented as in comprehensive cognition only of those aspects as to which Mrs. Assingham doesn't functionally—perhaps all too officiously, as the reader may sometimes feel it—supersede him.[882] This disparity in my plan is, however, but superficial; the thing abides rigidly by its law of showing Maggie Verver at first through her suitor's and her husband's exhibitory vision of her, and of then showing the Prince, with at least an equal intensity, through his wife's; the advantage thus being that these attributions of experience display the sentient subjects themselves at the same time and by the same stroke with the nearest possible approach to a desirable vividness. It is the Prince who opens the door to half our light upon Maggie, just as it is she who opens it to half our light upon himself; the rest of our impression, in either case, coming straight from the very motion with which that act is performed. We see Charlotte also at first, and we see Adam Verver, let alone our seeing Mrs. Assingham, and every one and every thing else, but as they are visible in the Prince's interest, so to speak—by which I mean of course in the interest of his being himself handed over to us. With a like consistency we see the same persons and things again but as Maggie's interest, *her* exhibitional charm, determines the view. In making which remark, with its apparently so limited enumeration of my elements, I naturally am brought up against the fact of the fundamental fewness of these latter—of the fact that my large demand is made for a group of agents who may be counted on the fingers of one hand. We see very few persons in "The Golden Bowl," but the scheme of the book, to make up for that, is that we shall really see about as much of them as a coherent literary form permits. That was my problem, so to speak, and my *gageure*[883]—to play the small handful of values really for all they were worth—and to work my system, my particular propriety of appeal, particular degree of pressure on the spring of interest, for all that this specific ingenuity itself might be. To have a scheme and a view of its dignity is of course congruously to work it out, and the "amusement" of the chronicle in question—by which, once more, I always mean the gathered cluster of all the *kinds* of interest—was exactly to see what a consummate application of such sincerities would give.

So much for some only of the suggestions of re-perusal here—since, all the while, I feel myself awaited by a pair of appeals really more pressing than either of those just met; a minor and a major appeal, as I may call them: the former of which I take first. I have so thoroughly "gone into" things, in an expository way, on the ground covered by this collection of my writings, that I should still judge it superficial to have spoken no word for so salient a feature of our Edition as the couple of dozen decorative "illustrations."[884] This series of frontispieces contribute less to ornament, I recognise, than if Mr. Alvin Langdon Coburn's beautiful photographs, which they reproduce, had had to suffer less reduction; but of those that have suffered least the beauty, to my sense, remains great, and I indulge at any rate in this glance at our general intention for the sake of the small page of history thereby added to my already voluminous, yet on the whole so unabashed, memoranda. I should in fact be tempted here, but for lack of space, by the very question itself at large—that question of the general acceptability of illustration coming up sooner or later, in these days, for the author of any text putting forward illustrative claims (that is producing an effect of illustration) by its own intrinsic virtue and so finding itself elbowed, on that ground, by another and a competitive process.[885] The essence of any representational work is of course to bristle with immediate images; and I, for one, should have looked much askance at the proposal, on the part of my associates in the whole business, to graft or "grow," at whatever point, a picture by another hand on my own picture—this being always, to my sense, a lawless incident. Which remark reflects heavily, of course, on the "picture-book" quality that contemporary English and American prose appears more and more destined, by the conditions of publication, to consent, however grudgingly, to see imputed to it.[886] But a moment's thought points the moral of the danger.

Anything that relieves responsible prose of the duty of being, while placed before us, good enough, interesting enough and, if the question be of picture, pictorial enough, above all *in itself,* does it the worst of services, and may well inspire in the lover of literature certain lively questions as to the future of that institution. That one should, as an author, reduce one's reader, "artistically" inclined, to such a state of hallucination by the images one has evoked as doesn't permit him to rest till he has noted or recorded them, set up some semblance of them in his own other medium, by his own other art—nothing could better consort than *that,* I naturally allow, with the desire or the pretension to cast a literary spell. Charming, that is, for the projector and creator of figures and scenes that are as nought from the moment they fail to become more or less visible appearances, charming for this manipulator of aspects to see such power as he may possess approved and registered by the springing of such fruit from his seed. His own garden, however, remains one thing, and the garden he has prompted the cultivation of at other hands[887] becomes quite another; which means that the frame of one's own work no more provides place for such a plot than we expect flesh and fish to be served on the same platter. One welcomes illustration, in other words, with pride and joy; but also with the emphatic view that, might one's "literary jealousy"[888] be duly deferred to, it would quite stand off and on its own feet and thus, as a separate and independent subject of publication, carrying its text in its spirit, just as that text correspondingly carries the plastic possibility, become a still more glorious tribute. So far my invidious distinction between the writer's "frame" and the draughtsman's; and if in spite of it I could still make place for the idea of a contribution of value by Mr. A. L. Coburn to each of these volumes—and a contribution in as different a "medium" as possible—this was just because the proposed photographic studies were to seek the way, which they have happily found, I think, not to keep, or to pretend to keep, anything like dramatic step with their suggestive matter. This would quite have disqualified them, to my rigour; but they were "all right," in the so analytic modern critical phrase, through their discreetly disavowing emulation. Nothing in fact could more have amused the author than the opportunity of a hunt for a series of reproducible subjects—such moreover as might best consort with photography—the reference of which to Novel or Tale should exactly be *not* competitive and obvious,⁸⁸⁹ should on the contrary plead its case with some shyness, that of images always confessing themselves mere optical symbols or echoes, expressions of no particular thing in the text, but only of the type or idea of this or that thing.⁸⁹⁰ They were to remain at the most small pictures of our "set" stage with the actors left out; and what was above all interesting was that they were first to be constituted.

This involved an amusing search which I would fain more fully commemorate; since it took, to a great degree, and rather unexpectedly and incalculably, the vastly, though but incidentally, instructive form of an enquiry into the street-scenery of London;⁸⁹¹ a field yielding a ripe harvest of treasure from the moment I held up to it, in my fellow artist's company, the light of our fond idea—the idea, that is, of the aspect of things or the combination of objects that might, by a latent virtue in it, speak for its connexion with something in the book, and yet at the same time speak enough for its odd or interesting self. It will be noticed that our series of frontispieces, while doing all justice to our need, largely consists in a "rendering" of certain inanimate characteristics of London streets; the ability of which to suffice to this furnishing forth of my Volumes ministered alike to surprise and convenience. Even at the cost of inconsistency of attitude in the matter of the "grafted" image, I should have been tempted, I confess, by the mere pleasure of exploration, abounding as the business at once began to do in those prizes of curiosity for which the London-lover is at any time ready to "back" the prodigious city. It wasn't always that I straightway found, with my fellow searcher, what we were looking for, but that the looking itself so often flooded with light the question of what a "subject," what "character," what a saving sense in things, is and isn't; and that when our quest was rewarded, it was, I make bold to say, rewarded in perfection. On the question, for instance, of the proper preliminary compliment to the first volume of "The Golden Bowl" we easily felt that nothing would so serve as a view of the small shop in which the Bowl is first encountered.

The problem thus was thrilling, for though the small shop was but a shop of the mind, of the author's projected world, in which objects are primarily related to each other, and therefore not "taken from" a particular establishment anywhere, only an image distilled and intensified, as it were, from a drop of the essence of such establishments in general, our need (since the to have as little to say to it and about it as possible, had been for years one's only law,⁹⁰¹ so, during that flat interregnum, involving, as who should say, the very cultivation of unacquaintedness, creeping superstitions as to what it might really have been had time to grow up and flourish. Not least among these rioted doubtless the fond fear that any tidying-up of the uncanny brood, any removal of accumulated dust, any washing of wizened faces, or straightening of grizzled locks, or twitching, to a better effect, of superannuated garments, might let one in, as the phrase is, for expensive renovations. I make use here of the figure of age and infirmity, but in point of fact I had rather viewed the reappearance of the first-born of my progeny—a reappearance unimaginable save to some inheritance of brighter and more congruous material form, of stored-up braveries of type and margin and ample page, of general dignity and attitude, than had mostly waited on their respective casual cradles—as a descent of awkward infants from the nursery to the drawing-room⁹⁰² under the kind appeal of enquiring, of possibly interested, visitors. I had accordingly taken for granted the common decencies of such a case—the responsible glance of some power above from one nursling to another, the rapid flash of an anxious needle, the not imperceptible effect of a certain audible splash of soap-and-water; all in consideration of the searching radiance of drawing-room lamps as compared with nursery candles. But it had been all the while present to me that from the moment a stitch should be taken or a hair-brush applied the *principle* of my making my brood more presentable under the nobler illumination would be accepted and established, and it was there complications might await me. I am afraid I had at stray moments wasted time in wondering what discrimination against the freedom of the needle and the sponge would be able to describe itself as not arbitrary. For it to confess to that taint would be of course to write itself detestable.

"Hands off altogether on the nurse's part!" was, as a merely barbarous injunction, strictly conceivable; but only in the light of the truth that it had never taken effect in any fair and stately, in any not vulgarly irresponsible re-issue of anything.⁹⁰³ Therefore it was easy to see that any such apologetic suppression as that of the "altogether," any such admission as that of a single dab of the soap, left the door very much ajar. Any request that an indulgent objector to drawing-room discipline, to the purification, in other words, of innocent childhood, should kindly measure out then the appropriate amount of ablutional fluid for the whole case, would, on twenty grounds, indubitably leave that invoked judge gaping. I had none the less, I repeat, at muddled moments, seemed to see myself confusedly invoke him; thanks to my but too naturally not being able to forecast the perfect grace with which an answer to all my questions was meanwhile awaiting me. To expose the case frankly to a test—in other words to begin to re-read—was at once to get nearer all its elements and so, as by the next felicity, feel it purged of every doubt. It was the nervous postponement of that respectful approach that I spoke of just now as, in the connexion, my waste of time. This felt awkwardness sprang, as I was at a given moment to perceive, from my too abject acceptance of the grand air with which the term Revision had somehow, to my imagination, carried itself—and from my frivolous failure to analyse the content of the word. To revise is to see, or to look over, again—which means in the case of a written thing neither more nor less than to re-read it. I had attached to it, in a brooding spirit, the idea of re-writing—with which it was to have in the event, for my *conscious* play of mind, almost nothing in common. I had thought of re-writing as so difficult, and even so absurd, as to be impossible—having also indeed, for that matter, thought of re-reading in the same light. But the felicity under the test was that where I had thus ruefully prefigured two efforts there proved to be but one—and this an effort but at the first blush. What re-writing might be was to remain—it has remained for me to this hour—a mystery.[904] On the other hand the act of revision, the act of seeing it again, caused whatever I looked at on any page to flower before me as into the only terms that honourably expressed it;[905] and the "revised" element in the present Edition is accordingly these terms, these rigid conditions of re-perusal, registered; so many close notes, as who should say, on the particular vision of the matter itself that experience had at last made the only possible one.

What it would be really interesting, and I dare say admirably difficult, to go into would be the very history of this effect of experience; the history, in other words, of the growth of the immense array of terms, perceptional and expressional, that, after the fashion I have indicated, in sentence, passage and page, simply looked over the heads of the standing terms—or perhaps rather, like alert winged creatures, perched on those diminished summits and aspired to a clearer air. What it comes back to, for the maturer mind— granting of course, to begin with, a mind accessible to questions of such an order—is this attaching speculative interest of the matter, or in vulgar parlance the inordinate intellectual "sport" of it: the how and the whence and the why these intenser lights of experience come into being and insist on shining. The interest of the question is attaching, as I say, because really half the artist's life seems involved in it—or doubtless, to speak more justly, the whole of his life intellectual. The "old" matter is there, re-accepted, re-tasted, exquisitely re-assimilated and re-enjoyed—believed in, to be brief, with the same "old" grateful faith (since wherever the faith, in a particular case, has become aware of a twinge of doubt I have simply concluded against the matter itself and left it out); yet for due testimony, for re-assertion of value, perforating as by some strange and fine, some latent and gathered force, a myriad more adequate channels.[906] It is over the fact of such a phenomenon and its so possibly rich little history that I am moved just fondly to linger—and for the reason I glanced at above, that to do so is in a manner to retrace the whole growth of one's "taste," as our fathers used to say: a blessed comprehensive name for many of the things deepest in us.[907] The "taste" of the poet is, at bottom and so far as the poet in him prevails over everything else, his active sense of life: in accordance with which truth to keep one's hand on it is to hold the silver clue to the whole labyrinth of his consciousness.[908] He feels this himself, good man—he recognises an attached importance—whenever he feels that consciousness bristle with the notes, as I have called them, of consenting re-perusal; as has again and again publicly befallen him, to our no small edification, on occasions within recent view.[909] It has befallen him most frequently, I recognise, when the supersessive terms of his expression have happened to be verse; but that doesn't in the least isolate his case, since it is clear to the most limited intelligence that the title we give him is the only title of *general* application and convenience for those who passionately cultivate the image of life and the art, on the whole so beneficial, of projecting it. The seer and speaker under the descent of the god is the "poet," whatever his form,[910] and he ceases to be one only when his form, whatever else it may nominally or superficially or vulgarly be, is unworthy of the god: in which event, we promptly submit, he isn't worth talking of at all. He becomes so worth it, and the god so adopts him, and so confirms his charming office and name, in the degree in which his impulse and passion are general and comprehensive—a definitional provision for them that makes but a mouthful of so minor a distinction, in the fields of light,[911] as that between verse and prose.

The circumstance that the poets then, and the more charming ones, *have* in a number of instances, with existing matter in hand, "registered" their renewals of vision, attests quite enough the attraction deeply working whenever the mind is, as I have said, accessible—accessible, that is, to the finer appeal of accumulated "good stuff" and to the interest of taking it in hand at all. For myself, I am prompted to note, the "taking" has been to my consciousness, through the whole procession of this re-issue, the least part of the affair: under the first touch of the spring my hands were to feel themselves full; so much more did it become a question, on the part of the accumulated good stuff, of seeming insistently to give and give. I have alluded indeed to certain lapses of that munificence—or at least to certain connexions in which I found myself declining to receive again on *any* terms;[912] but for the rest the sense of receiving has borne me company without a break; a luxury making for its sole condition that I should intelligently attend. The blest good stuff, sitting up, in its myriad forms, so touchingly responsive to new care of any sort whatever, seemed to pass with me a delightful bargain, and in the fewest possible words. "Actively believe in us and then you'll see!"[913]—it wasn't more complicated than that, and yet was to become as thrilling as if conditioned on depth within depth. I saw therefore what I saw, and what these numerous pages record, I trust, with clearness; though one element of fascination tended all the while to rule the business—a fascination, at each stage of my journey, on the noted score of that so shifting and uneven character of the tracks of my original passage. This by itself introduced the charm of suspense: what would the operative terms, in the given case, prove, under criticism, to have been—a series of waiting satisfactions or an array of waiting misfits? The misfits had but to be positive and concordant, in the special intenser light, to represent together (as the two sides of a coin show different legends) just so many effective felicities and substitutes. But I couldn't at all, in general, forecast these chances and changes and proportions; they could but show for what they were as I went; criticism after the fact was to find in them arrests and surprises, emotions alike of disappointment and of elation: all of which means, obviously, that the whole thing was a *living* affair.[914]

The rate at which new readings, new conductors of sense interposed, to make any total sense at all right, became, to this wonderful tune, the very record and mirror of the general adventure of one's intelligence; so that one at all times quite marvelled at the fair reach, the very length of arm, of such a developed difference of measure as to what might and what mightn't constitute, all round, a due decency of "rendering." What I have been most aware of asking myself, however, is how writers, on such occasions of "revision," arrive at that successful resistance to the confident assault of the new reading which appears in the great majority of examples to have marked their course. The term that superlatively, that finally "renders," is a flower that blooms by a beautiful law of its own (the fiftieth part of a second often so sufficing it) in the very heart of the gathered sheaf; it is *there* already, at any moment, almost before one can either miss or suspect it—so that in short we shall never guess, I think, the working secret of the revisionist for whom its colour and scent stir the air but as immediately to be assimilated. Failing our divination, too, we shall apparently not otherwise learn, for the simple reason that no revisionist I can recall has ever been communicative. "People don't do such things,"[915] we remember to have heard it, in this connexion, declared; in other words they don't really re-read—no, not *really*; at least they do so to the effect either of seeing the buried, the latent life of a past composition vibrate, at renewal of touch, into no activity and break through its settled and "sunk" surface[916] at no point whatever—on which conclusion, I hasten to add, the situation remains simple and their responsibility may lie down beside their work even as the lion beside the lamb; or else they have in advance and on system stopped their ears, their eyes and even their very noses.[917] This latter heroic policy I find myself glancing at, however, to wonder in what particular cases—failing, as I say, all the really confessed—it can have been applied. The actual non-revisionists (on any terms) are of course numerous enough, and with plenty to say for themselves;[918] their faith, clearly, is great,[919] their lot serene and their peace, above all, equally protected and undisturbed. But the tantalising image of the revisionist who isn't one, the partial, the piecemeal revisionist, inconsequent and insincere, this obscure and decidedly *louche* personage hovers before me mainly, I think, but to challenge my belief. Where have we met him, when it comes to that, in the walks of interesting prose literature, and why assume that we *have* to believe in him before we are absolutely forced?

If I turn for relief and contrast to some image of his opposite I at once encounter it, and with a completeness that leaves nothing to be desired, on any "old" ground, in presence of any "old" life, in the vast example of Balzac.[920] He (and these things, as we know, grew behind him at an extraordinary rate) re-assaulted by supersessive terms, re-penetrated by finer channels,[921] never had on the one hand seen or said all or had on the other ceased to press forward. His case has equal mass and authority—and beneath its protecting shade, at any rate, I move for the brief remainder of these remarks. We owe to the never-extinct operation of his sensibility, we have but meanwhile to recall, our greatest exhibition of felt finalities, our richest and hugest inheritance of imaginative prose. That by itself might intensify for me the interest of this general question of the reviving and reacting vision—didn't my very own lucky experience, all so publicly incurred, give me, as my reader may easily make out, quite enough to think of. I almost lose myself, it may perhaps seem to him, in that obscure quantity; obscure doubtless because of its consisting of the manifold delicate things, the shy and illusive, the inscrutable, the indefinable, that minister to deep and quite confident processes of change. It is enough, in any event, to be both beguiled and mystified by evolutions so near home, without sounding strange and probably even more abysmal waters. Since, however, an agreeable flurry and an imperfect presence of mind might, on the former ground, still be such a source of refreshment, so the constant refrain humming through the agitation, "If only one *could* re-write, if only one *could* do better justice to the patches of crude surface, the poor morsels of consciously-decent matter that catch one's eye with their rueful reproach for old stupidities of touch!"—so that yearning reflexion, I say, was to have its superlative as well as its positive moments. It was to reach its maximum, no doubt, over many of the sorry businesses of "The American,"[922] for instance, where, given the elements and the essence, the long-stored grievance of the subject bristling with a sense of over-prolonged exposure in a garment misfitted, a garment cheaply embroidered and unworthy of it, thereby most proportionately sounded their plaint. This sharpness of appeal, the claim for exemplary damages, or at least for poetic justice,[923] was reduced to nothing, on the other hand, in presence of the altogether better literary manners of "The Ambassadors" and "The Golden Bowl"—a list I might much extend by the mention of several shorter pieces.

Inevitably, in such a case as that of "The American," and scarce less indeed in those of "The Portrait of a Lady" and "The Princess Casamassima," each of these efforts so redolent of good intentions baffled by a treacherous vehicle, an expertness too retarded, I could but dream the whole thing over as I went—as I read; and, bathing it, so to speak, in that medium, hope that, some still newer and shrewder critic's intelligence subtly operating, I shouldn't have breathed upon the old catastrophes and accidents, the old wounds and mutilations and disfigurements, wholly in vain.[924] The same is true of the possible effect of this process of re-dreaming on many of these gathered compositions, shorter and longer; I have prayed that the finer air of the better form may sufficiently seem to hang about them and gild them over—at least for readers, however few, at all *curious* of questions of air and form. Nothing even at this point, and in these quite final remarks, I confess, could strike me as more pertinent than—with a great wealth of margin[925]—to attempt to scatter here a few gleams of the light in which some of my visions have all sturdily and complacently repeated and others have, according to their kind and law, all joyously and blushingly renewed themselves. These have doubtless both been ways of remaining unshamed; though, for myself, on the whole, as I seem to make out, the interest of the watched renewal has been livelier than that of the accepted repetition. What has the affair been at the worst, I am most moved to ask, but an earnest invitation to the reader to dream again in my company and in the interest of his own larger absorption of my sense? The prime consequence on one's own part of re-perusal is a sense for ever so many more of the shining silver fish afloat in the deep sea of one's endeavour than the net of widest casting could pretend to gather in; an author's common courtesy dictating thus the best general course for making that sense contagious—so beautifully tangled a web, when not so glorious a crown, does he weave[926] by having at heart, and by cherishing there, the confidence he has invited or imagined. There is then absolutely no release to his pledged honour on the question of repaying that confidence.

The ideally handsome way is for him to multiply in any given connexion all the possible sources of entertainment—or, more grossly expressing it again, to intensify his whole chance of pleasure. (It all comes back to that, to my and your "fun"—if we but allow the term its full extension;[927] to the production of which no humblest question involved, even to that of the shade of a cadence or the position of a comma, is not richly pertinent.) We have but to think a moment of such a matter as the play of *representational* values, those that make it a part, and an important part, of our taking offered things in that we should take them as aspects and visibilities—take them to the utmost as appearances, images, figures, objects, so many important, so many contributive items of the furniture of the world—in order to feel immediately the effect of such a condition at every turn of our adventure and every point of the representative surface. One has but to open the door to any forces of exhibition at all worthy of the name in order to see the imaging and qualifying agency called at once into play and put on its mettle. We may traverse acres of pretended exhibitory prose from which the touch that directly evokes and finely presents, the touch that operates for closeness and for charm, for conviction and illusion, for communication, in a word, is unsurpassably absent. All of which but means of course that the reader is, in the common phrase, "sold"[928]—even when, poor passive spirit, systematically bewildered and bamboozled on the article of his dues, he may be but dimly aware of it. He has by the same token and for the most part, I fear, a scarce quicker sensibility on other heads, least of all perhaps on such a matter as his really quite swindled state when the pledge given for his true beguilement fails to ensure him that fullest experience of his pleasure which waits but on a direct reading *out* of the addressed appeal. It is scarce necessary to note that the highest test of any literary form conceived in the light of "poetry"—to apply that term in its largest literary sense—hangs back unpardonably from its office when it fails to lend itself to *vivâ-voce* treatment. We talk here, naturally, not of non-poetic forms, but of those whose highest bid is addressed to the imagination, to the spiritual and the æsthetic vision, the mind led captive by a charm and a spell,[929] an incalculable art. The essential property of such a form as that is to give out its finest and most numerous secrets, and to give them out most gratefully, under the closest pressure—which is of course the pressure of the attention articulately *sounded*. Let it reward as much as it will and can the soundless, the "quiet" reading, it still deplorably "muffs" its chance and its success,[930] still trifles with the roused appetite to which it can never honestly be indifferent, by not having so arranged itself as to owe the flower of its effect to the act and process of apprehension that so beautifully asks most from it. It then infallibly, and not less beautifully, most responds; for I have nowhere found vindicated the queer thesis that the right values of interesting prose depend all on withheld tests[931]—that is on its being, for very pity and shame, but skimmed and scanted, shuffled and mumbled. Gustave Flaubert has somewhere in this connexion an excellent word—to the effect that any imaged prose that fails to be richly rewarding in return for a competent utterance ranks itself as wrong through not being "in the conditions of life."[932] The more we remain in *them*, all round, the more pleasure we dispense; the moral of which is—and there would be fifty other pertinent things to say about this—that I have found revision intensify at every step my impulse intimately to answer, by my light, to those conditions.

All of which amounts doubtless but to saying that as the whole conduct of life consists of things done, which do other things in their turn, just so our behaviour and its fruits are essentially one and continuous and persistent and unquenchable, so the act has its way of abiding and showing and testifying, and so, among our innumerable acts, are no arbitrary, no senseless separations. The more we are capable of acting the less gropingly we plead such differences; whereby, with any capability, we recognise betimes that to "put" things is very exactly and responsibly and interminably to do them.[933] Our expression of them, and the terms on which we understand that, belong as nearly to our conduct and our life as every other feature of our freedom; these things yield in fact some of its most exquisite material to the religion of doing.[934] More than that, our literary deeds enjoy this marked advantage over many of our acts, that, though they go forth into the world and stray even in the desert, they don't to the same extent lose themselves; their attachment and reference to us, however strained, needn't necessarily lapse—while of the tie that binds us to *them*[935] we may make almost anything we like. We are condemned, in other words, whether we will or no, to abandon and outlive, to forget and disown and hand over to desolation, many vital or social performances—if only because the traces, records, connexions, the very memorials we would fain preserve, are practically impossible to rescue for that purpose from the general mixture. We give them up even when we wouldn't—it is not a question of choice. Not so on the other hand our really "done" things of this superior and more appreciable order—which leave us indeed all licence of disconnexion and disavowal, but positively impose on us no such necessity. Our relation to them is essentially traceable, and in that fact abides, we feel, the incomparable luxury of the artist. It rests altogether with himself not to break with his values, not to "give away" his importances. Not to *be* disconnected, for the tradition of behaviour, he has but to feel that he is not; by his lightest touch the whole chain of relation and responsibility is reconstituted.[936] Thus if he is always doing he can scarce, by his own measure, ever have done. All of which means for him conduct with a vengeance, since it is conduct minutely and publicly attested. Our noted behaviour at large may show for ragged, because it perpetually escapes our control; we have again and again to consent to its appearing in undress—that is in no state to brook criticism.[937] But on all the ground to which the pretension of performance by a series of exquisite laws may apply there reigns one sovereign truth—which decrees that, as art is nothing if not exemplary, care nothing if not active, finish nothing if not consistent, the proved error is the base apologetic deed, the helpless regret is the barren commentary, and "connexions" are employable for finer purposes than mere gaping contrition.

GLOSSARY OF FOREIGN WORDS AND PHRASES

All French unless otherwise indicated. The foreign word or phrase is (or is not) italicized based on how it occurs in the text. The translations offered here refer to the contexts in which these words and phrases are used in the Prefaces; where necessary, the notes to particular passages supply further contextual information and parallel citations in James and other authors.

a fortiori (Latin)	from the stronger (argument)
allure	personal manner, bearing
amusette	toy, plaything
arête	mountain ridge
au naturel	(of food) without cooking, seasoning or dressing; plain
bêtise, bêtises	stupidity, foolishnesses
bonhomme	man, good fellow; manikin, puppet
cabotin	strolling player; bad actor
cocchieri (Italian)	cab-drivers
constatation	observation
contes	tales, short stories
déja très-joli	already a pretty enough task
disponible, en disponibilité	available, at one's disposal; unoccupied
éclaireurs	military scouts
en bloc	as a whole, in the mass
ficelle	thread; trick, artifice, theatrical device
gageure	challenge, wager
hôtel garni	hotel without a restaurant (offering breakfast but no other meals)

GLOSSARY OF FOREIGN WORDS AND PHRASES

idée-mère	governing idea; musical or literary motif
Il en serait bien embarrassé	He will be at a loss to do so
Il ne manquerait plus que cela	That would be the last straw
jeu d'esprit	playful display of wit or cleverness, esp. in a work of literature; witty or humorous trifle (*OED*)
là-bas	over there
louche	suspicious, equivocal; dubious, shifty, disreputable
malaise	discomfort, uneasiness
malheureux	unfortunate man
Mourir, à Londres, c'est être bien mort!	To die in London is to be dead indeed!
nouvelle	long story, short novel, novella
pensionnaire	lodger, occupant of a boarding-house or *pension*
place	public square
pot-au-feu	stew of beef and vegetables
que cela manque souvent d'architecture	that it often lacks structure
quelconque	any (an individually unremarkable example of a type)
rampe	banister, hand-rail
recueil	journal
repoussoir	foil, contrast
solus (Latin)	alone
terra-firma (Latin)	solid ground
tout craché	the spitting image (an exact likeness)
tutti quanti (Italian)	everyone
ville de province	provincial town
vivâ-voce (Latin)	aloud (as distinct from silent reading or repetition)

NOTES

As the General Editors state in their Preface to the Cambridge Edition, 'Fullness and helpfulness of annotation is one of the main aims' of *The Complete Fiction of Henry James*. The unusual breadth and density of reference in James's Prefaces make full annotation in this case a larger undertaking than it would be for even the most contextually entangled of his fictions. There has never been a complete annotated edition of all eighteen Prefaces: the complete editions have not been annotated, or not adequately so, and the annotated editions have not been complete. Reprinting the Prefaces for the first time in *The Art of the Novel* (1934), R. P. Blackmur supplied an elementary subject index but no notes; the annotation offered by Leon Edel and Mark Wilson in the relevant Library of America volume of James's *Literary Criticism* (1984) is thin and almost exclusively concerned with biographical and bibliographical information. William Veeder and Susan M. Griffin added notes and a commentary to the selection of nine Prefaces they included in their volume *The Art of Criticism: Henry James on the Theory and the Practice of Fiction* (1986), focusing on the Prefaces' links to James's other critical writings; modern paperback editions of individual novels or groups of stories in the Penguin Classics, Oxford World's Classics and Norton Critical Editions series typically print the relevant Prefaces, with varying degrees of annotation. I have drawn gratefully on all these sources in preparing the present edition. The Notes that follow attempt a fuller annotation than any offered so far, and aim to provide readers with as comprehensive a guide as possible to the Prefaces' multiple contexts and relations. They gloss references to persons and places, to books and essays, plays, paintings and other cultural phenomena, and to events in James's life – including the origins, writing and publication of works included in the *NYE*, and the production of the *NYE* itself. They identify quotations and literary allusions, explain instances of slang and specialized language, and suggest sources for terms in James's often idiosyncratic critical vocabulary. They indicate precedents in James's work and the work of other writers for critical and theoretical topics discussed in the Prefaces. They point out verbal echoes between the Prefaces and the fictions they accompany in the *NYE*, and where relevant correlate the composition of the Prefaces with the many other literary tasks – including textual revision – which James was engaged in during the period 1905–9. They also clarify his cross-references from one Preface to another, and alert readers to occasional inconsistencies and significant divergences between the sequence of the Prefaces' composition and the order in which they were published in the *NYE*.

Quotations from James's notebooks use the text established by Philip Horne for his edition of *The Notebooks* (*CFHJ* 34), which is in preparation at the time of writing. For the reader's convenience in the meantime, these quotations are cited below by the corresponding page number in *The Complete Notebooks of Henry James*, ed. Leon Edel and Lyall H. Powers (New York and Oxford: Oxford University Press, 1987), abbreviated to *CN*.

References to the Bible are to the King James Version. References to Shakespeare are to *The Riverside Shakespeare: The Complete Works*, 2nd edn, general editor G. Blakemore Evans (Boston, MA: Houghton Mifflin Company, 1997). Translations are my own unless otherwise indicated.

The following abbreviations have been used for the Notes, in addition to those in the List of Abbreviations:

Gard	Roger Gard (ed.), *Henry James: The Critical Heritage* (London: Routledge & Kegan Paul, 1968)
Hayes	Kevin J. Hayes (ed.), *Henry James: The Contemporary Reviews* (Cambridge: Cambridge University Press, 1996)
OED	*Oxford English Dictionary Online* (Oxford: Oxford University Press, 2012) (www.oed.com)
Slang	John S. Farmer and W. E. Henley, *Slang and Its Analogues, Past and Present*, 7 vols. ([London]: Printed for subscribers only: 1890–1904)

The following initials refer to members of the James family:

AJ	Alice James (sister)
AGJ	Alice Gibbens James (sister-in-law)
CW	Catharine Walsh (aunt)
HJ Sr	Henry James, Sr (father)
MWJ	Mary Walsh James (mother)
WJ	William James (brother)

PREFACE to *Roderick Hudson* (*NYE* I)

1 **designed from the first for serial publication in "The Atlantic Monthly," [...] through the year**: *Roderick Hudson* was serialized in twelve issues of the *Atlantic Monthly* (January–December 1875), but it was not straightforwardly 'designed from the first' for publication there. In March 1874, James received a proposal from the editor of *Scribner's Monthly*, Josiah Holland, to write a year-long serial for that magazine beginning in November. As James explained to W. D. Howells, his friend and editor at the *Atlantic Monthly*, he was eager to write a novel but felt 'as if there was a definite understanding between us that if I do so, the Atlantic should have the offer of it' (10 March [1874]; *CLHJ 1872–1876* 2:137). Howells had published James's most important fiction to date in the *Atlantic*, including 'A Passionate Pilgrim' (1871), *Watch and Ward* (1871), 'The Madonna of the Future' (1873) and 'The Last of the Valerii' (1874), and yet the interest of another periodical now gave James an opportunity to negotiate terms. He would refuse Holland's offer, he told Howells, if the *Atlantic* would take the novel instead and give as much for it as he was asking from Scribners' ($1,200 for the twelve instalments): a serial in the *Atlantic* would be his preference, but he had 'no right to let it be anything but a pure money question' (*CLHJ 1872–1876* 2:137). The news that Howells had accepted this proposal reached James in Florence in the middle of April, and by the start of May he had 'fairly settled down to work' on *Roderick Hudson* (to WJ, 3 May [1874]; *CLHJ 1872–1876* 2:161).

2 **that veiled face of his Muse [...] all anxiously to study**: In ancient Greek mythology, the nine Muses were the daughters of Zeus and Mnemosyne, the goddess of memory; they were the presiding goddesses of knowledge and the arts, and were conventionally invoked by artists for inspiration. According to Lemprière's *Classical Dictionary* (1788), the Muse most often depicted as veiled is Polyhymnia; ancient commentators variously associate her with rhetoric, music, song, sacred verse and hymnody, lyric verse, mime and pantomime. In the second chapter of Honoré de Balzac's novel *Séraphîta* (1835), the androgynous title character – a Swedenborgian angel – is likened to Polyhymnia in terms that anticipate the Preface's 'study': 'les plis de son vêtement eurent cette grâce indéfinissable qui arrête l'artiste [...] devant les délicieuses lignes du voile de la Polymnie antique' ('the folds of her garment had the same indefinable grace that halts the artist [...] before the delicious lines of the veil of the Polyhymnia of antiquity') (Balzac, *La Comédie humaine*, ed. Pierre-Georges Castex et al., 12

vols. (Paris: Gallimard, 1976–81), vol. XI, p. 755). James had discussed *Séraphîta* in his first essay on Balzac, which appeared in the *Galaxy* in December 1875 as the serial run of *Roderick Hudson* was coming to an end (see *LC2* 48).

3   **The art of representation bristles with questions**: James habitually speaks of fictional situations and subjects as 'bristling' with questions, opportunities, challenges, etc. The word occurs more than twenty times in the Prefaces: for an instance in the Preface to *The Wings of the Dove* that echoes the text of the novel, see note 804. James had already applied the term to literary representation in 'The Art of Fiction' (1884): 'the moral timidity of the usual English novelist' is an 'aversion to face the difficulties with which on every side the treatment of reality bristles' (*LC1* 63). See also a comment in his 1888 review of the *Journal* of the French critics and novelists Edmond (1822–96) and Jules de Goncourt (1830–70), on the brothers' 'strenuous' attitude to the literary life: 'They bristled (the word is their own) with responsible professions' (*LC2* 405). James appears to refer to the Goncourts' journal entry for 16 October 1856: 'Ces désespérances, ces doutes, non de nous, ni de nos ambitions, mais du moment et des moyens, au lieu de nous abaisser vers les concessions, font en nous, plus entière, plus intraitable, plus hérissée, la conscience littéraire' ('These despairs, these doubts – not of ourselves or our ambitions, but of the moment and the medium – rather than reducing us to making allowances, create in us, more stubborn, more intractable, more bristling, the literary conscience') (*Journal des Goncourt: Mémoires de la vie littéraire*, 9 vols. (Paris: G. Charpentier et E. Fasquelle, 1887–96), vol. I, p. 147).

4   **to consult its notes**: In later Prefaces, James speaks of searching in old notebooks for records of the first ideas for his short stories (see notes 678 and 709). The first editors of the notebooks, F. O. Matthiessen and Kenneth B. Murdock, inferred 'that he composed the prefaces with his notes at his elbow, and that it was to them he alluded in his seemingly general references [to note-taking]' (*The Notebooks of Henry James*, ed. Matthiessen and Murdock (New York: Oxford University Press, 1947), p. xi). James reflects on 'the rich principle of the Note' in the Preface to *The Princess Casamassima*, p. 59.

5   **recording scroll or engraved commemorative table**: Compare James's recent comment in 'New York Revisited' (1906) on the demolition of his old family home at 21 Washington Place: 'whereas the inner sense had positively erected there for its private contemplation a commemorative

mural tablet, the very wall that should have borne this inscription had been smashed as for demonstration that tablets, in New York, are unthinkable' (*AS* 91). The rapid pace of urban development in New York City, he felt, had deprived its buildings of plaques to mark their association with eminent figures: 'Where [...] is the point of inserting a mural tablet, at any legible height, in a building certain to be destroyed to make room for a sky-scraper?' (*AS* 92). A scheme to mark such locations in London had been inaugurated in 1867 by the Society of Arts and was taken over by London County Council in 1901 (see Howard Spencer, 'The Commemoration of Historians under the Blue Plaque Scheme in London', Institute of Historical Research, 2008 (archives.history.ac.uk/makinghistory/resources/articles/blue_plaques.html)).

6   **Addicted to "stories"**: James refers here to anecdotes about the origins and compositional circumstances of his novels and tales; see also note 854. For 'story' as a fictional narrative, see note 137.

7   **his process of production [...] a wondrous adventure**: In 'The Art of Fiction', James had similarly posited a category of 'adventure' broad enough to accommodate the act of literary composition: 'And what *is* adventure, when it comes to that, and by what sign is the listening pupil to recognise it? It is an adventure—an immense one—for me to write this little article' (*LC1* 61).

8   **my first attempt at a novel**: James omits to mention his first novel *Watch and Ward*, serialized in the *Atlantic Monthly* from August to December 1871 and published as a volume in 1878.

9   **hugged the shore on sundry previous small occasions [...] master as yet of no vessel constructed to carry a sail**: When he began to write *Roderick Hudson*, James had published twenty-one short stories in American periodicals; his first volume, *A Passionate Pilgrim, and Other Tales*, contained six of these stories and appeared in January 1875 as *Roderick Hudson* began its serial run. Philip Horne points out that the Preface's metaphor of a sea-voyage also occurs in the novel, where it figures the perils of artistic endeavour for Roderick (*Henry James and Revision: The New York Edition* (Oxford: Clarendon Press, 1990), pp. 113–14).

10   **the breath of the spice-islands**: From the sixteenth century, the Moluccas (the Maluku Islands in modern Indonesia) were known to Europeans as the Spice Islands because of their abundance of nutmeg and other valuable spices. On arrival in New York City in 1904, James had been struck by how

little the neighbourhoods he had known in childhood had changed since that 'primitive age' (1847–55): 'Sixth Avenue [...] wanted only, to carry off the illusion, the warm smell of the bakery on the corner of Eighth Street [...] the slow passing by which, on returns from school, must have had much in common with the experience of the ship-men of old who came, in long voyages, while they tacked and hung back, upon those belts of ocean that are haunted with the balm and spice of tropic islands' ('New York Revisited'; *AS* 90–1).

11 **led on by "developments"**: Compare James to Howells on the fictional subject that would become *The Portrait of a Lady* (1881): 'It is ~~the~~ a portrait of the character & recital of the adventures of a woman—a great swell, psychologically; a <u>grande nature</u>—accompanied with many "developments"' (2 February [1877]; *CLHJ 1876–1878* 1:50).

12 **the painter's subject**: For the novelist as a 'painter', see 'The Art of Fiction': 'the analogy between the art of the painter and the art of the novelist is, so far as I am able to see, complete' (*LC1* 46). The same idea is present in James's earlier literary essays, and ultimately derives from modern French sources. In 1876, he had summarized the theory on which Gustave Flaubert wrote his novels: 'We will "render" things—anything, everything, from a chimney-pot to the shoulders of a duchess—as painters render them' (*LC2* 170). For the verb 'render' in this sense, see note 24.

13 **to "treat" his idea**: The relevant sense of the verb 'treat' was common during James's lifetime: 'To deal with in the way of art (literary, pictorial, musical, etc.); to handle or represent artistically' (*OED*). The inverted commas around the word here do not indicate a technical idiom, therefore, and James's literary essays from the 1870s onwards contain many unmarked uses of the word. For 'treating' as the fundamental criterion of critical judgement, see his 'American Letter' (28 May 1898) in the journal *Literature*: 'we never really get near a book save on the question of its being good or bad, of its really treating, that is, or not treating, its subject. That is a classification that covers everything' (*LC1* 677). For James's acknowledged liability to 'overtreat' subjects, see notes 179 and 317.

14 **relations stop nowhere, [...] the circle within which they shall happily *appear* to do so**: James would return to the terms of this sentence in the chapter he contributed to *The Whole Family: A Novel by Twelve Authors* (1908), a project coordinated by the editor of *Harper's Bazar*, Elizabeth Jordan. The Preface to *Roderick Hudson* was completed by mid-August

1906, and James wrote his chapter of *The Whole Family* ('The Married Son') in January 1907. In the relevant passage, the narrator – a visual artist – observes that 'one has only to look at any human thing very straight [...] to see it shine out in as many aspects as the hues of the prism; or place itself, in other words, in relations that positively stop nowhere. I've often thought I should like some day to write a novel; but what would become of me in that case—delivered over, I mean, before my subject, to my extravagant sense that everything is a part of something else? When you paint a picture with a brush and pigments, that is on a single plane, it can stop at your gilt frame; but when you paint one with a pen and words, that is in *all* the dimensions, how are you to stop? Of course, as Lorraine [his wife] says, "Stopping, that's art; and what are we artists like, my dear, but those drivers of trolley-cars, in New York, who, by some divine instinct, recognize in the forest of pillars and posts the white-striped columns at which they may pull up?"' (*WF* 167–8). This passage is also relevant to the 'visibly-appointed stopping-place' referred to later in this paragraph of the *Roderick Hudson* Preface (p. 5), and to the metaphors of framing and encircling in the Preface to *The Awkward Age* (see note 276).

15 **a supersubtle way of pointing the plain moral**: This sentence combines two of James's favourite literary allusions, both of which recur in the Prefaces. The first is to Iago's line in Shakespeare's *Othello* (1604) slightly describing Desdemona as a 'super-subtle Venetian' (1.3.356). The second is to Samuel Johnson's couplet in 'The Vanity of Human Wishes' (1749) on Charles XII of Sweden, who was disastrously defeated by the Russian army at Poltava in 1709 after early military successes against neighbouring states: 'He left a name, at which the world grew pale, / To point a moral, or adorn a tale' (ll. 221–2) (*Samuel Johnson*, The Oxford Authors, ed. Donald Greene (Oxford: Oxford University Press, 1984), p. 17 and n.).

16 **a young embroiderer of the canvas of life [...] his many-coloured flowers and figures [...] as many as possible of the little holes**: James figures himself as an embroiderer in other Prefaces, for instance that to *The Wings of the Dove*: 'the pattern of Densher's final position and fullest consciousness' in Venice 'was to have been marked in fine stitches, all silk and gold, all pink and silver' (p. 237). Compare his comment on Nathaniel Hawthorne's short stories in an essay of 1896: 'What Hawthorne encountered he instinctively embroidered, working it over with a fine, slow needle, and with flowers pale, rosy, or dusky' (*LC1* 460). In the present passage, James seems to refer to a style of embroidery such as cross-stitch,

which requires a fabric with an even mesh; when loosely woven (e.g., 'Java canvas' or 'Aida cloth') such fabrics have the appearance of a grid of small squares with holes between the warp and weft threads.

17 **a summer partly spent in the Black Forest [...] three months passed near Boston**: James spent six weeks in the summer of 1874 at the spa town of Baden-Baden on the fringes of the Black Forest in south-west Germany. Baden appealed to him as a known haunt of the Russian novelist Ivan Turgenev (for whom see note 135): as James observed to his father, 'Many of [Turgenev's] tales were probably written here—which proves that the place is favorable to literary labor' (23 June 1874; CLHJ 1872–1876 2:181). Turgenev was not in residence and James was unable to call on him as he had hoped, but he stayed on and found Baden congenial. On 6 July, he told his brother William that his life there was 'very tranquil & uneventful': 'I scribble in the morning, walk in the woods in the afternoon & sit listening to the music on the promenade & eating an ice in the evening' (CLHJ 1872–1876 2:184). In Chapter 4 of the novel, Roderick spends a dissolute summer at Baden, where he runs up gambling debts and has to be rescued by Rowland Mallet. James left in early August 1874, journeying up the Rhine to Rotterdam and crossing to England, whence he took passage for America on 25 August. He spent the autumn of 1874 at the family home in the Boston suburb of Cambridge, Massachusetts.

18 **not finished when it had to begin appearing in monthly fragments**: At the start of the summer, James was hoping 'to bring [*Roderick Hudson*] home finished or nearly so' (to WJ, 3 May [1874]; CLHJ 1872–1876 2:161). For his work on the final instalments of the novel, see note 22.

19 **To have "liked" so much writing it**: In other Prefaces, James similarly notes that he '"liked"' writing *The Spoils of Poynton* and 'like[s] [...] to recall' the composition of 'The Lesson of the Master' (pp. 99, 172). The inverted commas he places around the verb here and elsewhere mark it as a term of naive appreciation. In an essay of 1903, for example, dismayed by the contemporary boom in fiction publishing, he falls back on 'The lame conclusion [...] that "stories" are multiplied, circulated, paid for, on the scale of the present hour, simply because people "like" them' ('EZ' 193–4); and in the Preface to *NYE* XVII he describes being at a loss for an answer 'when, as often happens, one is asked how one "likes" such and such a "story"' (p. 202). James nevertheless retained a fondness for 'liking' as a mode of readerly response. In 'The Art of Fiction' he had insisted that 'Nothing, of course, will ever take the place of the good old fashion of

'liking" a work of art or not liking it: the most improved criticism will not abolish that primitive, that ultimate test' (*LC1* 57). Nearly two decades later, in 'Winchelsea, Rye, and *Denis Duval*' (1901), he remarked that the force of biographical 'association' makes readers indulge in middle age: 'You go on liking "David Copperfield"—I don't say you go on reading it, which is a very different matter—because it is Dickens' (*CTW1* 234, 235).

20   **the loved Italy […] so much more loved than one has ever been able, even after fifty efforts, to say!**: If one counts the many stories and novels by James set in Italy, from 'Travelling Companions' (1870) to *The Wings of the Dove* (1902), along with the majority of the essays collected in *Italian Hours* (1909) and the evocations of Rome and Tuscany in *William Wetmore Story and His Friends* (1903), 'fifty efforts' by 1906 is hardly an exaggeration. As Robert L. Gale notes, 'James was in Italy for [visits ranging] from weeks to months in 1869, 1872, 1873, 1874, 1877, 1879, 1880, 1881, 1884, 1887, 1888, 1890, 1892, 1894, 1899, and finally 1907. Venice, Florence, and Rome remained his favorite areas, and probably in that order' ('Henry James and Italy', *Nineteenth-Century Fiction* 14.2 (1959), 157–70; 160). James returns to 'the loved Italy' as a subject in the Preface to *NYE* XII, pp. 126–7.

21   **prolonging […] the illusion of the golden air**: In *William Wetmore Story*, James had recently used the figure of 'the golden air' to evoke a lost mid-nineteenth-century Italy of personal and cultural memory (see *WWS* I:328–36). For the imaginative atmosphere designated by this phrase – a product of James's distance from the times and objects recollected, and of the haze of associations through which he regards them – see Oliver Herford, *Henry James's Style of Retrospect: Late Personal Writings, 1890–1915* (Oxford: Oxford University Press, 2016), pp. 81–2. The formula occurs again in the Preface to *NYE* XII with reference to the difficulty of writing about 'almost any "Italian subject"' (see pp. 126, 127). It also appears as a revision in the *NYE* text of *Roderick Hudson*, in a context that echoes the Preface's concern with prolongation. Rowland and Roderick ride in the Roman Campagna: 'Their rides were always drawn out, and Roderick insisted on making them longer by dismounting in picturesque spots and stretching himself, in the golden air, on some mild mass of over-tangled stones' (Ch. 7; *NYE* I, 148). In the Macmillan *Collective Edition* (1883) – the text James most likely used to revise the novel – Roderick simply reclines 'in the sun among a heap of over-tangled stones' (*CE* IV, 111). As he worked on *Roderick Hudson* in 1874, James was already conscious

of contriving to linger imaginatively in the novel's Italian settings even before he had left Europe. He wrote to Sarah Butler Wister from Baden-Baden: 'I have torn myself away from Florence & am making the best of existence in this degenerate and melancholy spot'; writing the novel was helping him with that, as 'It all goes on in Rome (or most of it) & I have been hugging my Roman memories with extraordinary gusto' (29 July [1874]; *CLHJ 1872–1876* 2:192, 193).

22 **I must that winter […] have brought up my last instalments in due time**: In 1874–5, James spent 'a bright cold unremunerative, uninteresting winter' (*CN* 215) in lodgings at 111 East 25th Street, New York City. He continued to write *Roderick Hudson*, corrected the proofs of *Transatlantic Sketches* and produced more than two dozen reviews of books, plays and art exhibitions for the *Nation*, *Atlantic Monthly* and *North American Review*. In March 1875, with *Roderick Hudson* three months into its serial run, he told Howells that he would be in Cambridge, Massachusetts, early the next month and would 'bring with me the "balance" as they say here, of my novel or at least the greater part of it' ([19 or 26 March 1875]; *CLHJ 1872–1876* 2:215). It was evidently completed by the end of August, when James wrote to his publishers requesting advance payment for the final four monthly parts, September–December (to H. O. Houghton and Co., 24 August [1875]; *CLHJ 1872–1876* 2:232).

23 **looked out, through the slits of cooling shutters, at the rather dusty but ever-romantic glare of Piazza Santa Maria Novella**: In mid-April 1874, James moved into an apartment in Florence at 10 Piazza Santa Maria Novella, on the corner with Via della Scala. He had been staying in hotels in the city since the start of the year, but after making a short tour to Lucca, Pisa and Livorno he 'couldn't face the idea of returning to live in one small room at an inn' and took 'a little appartment [sic] all to myself on the piazza of all Florence in which it always seemed to me I should choose to live' (to AJ, 18, [19] April [1874]; *CLHJ 1872–1876* 2:151). He worked on *Roderick Hudson* here until the first week of June. The Preface's account of this period tallies closely with his reports in letters home. He told his mother on 17 May, for example, that the Piazza was 'lively (& alas dusty)': 'The centre of the square is not paved and the dust hovers over it in clouds which compel one to live with closed windows' (*CLHJ 1872–1876* 2:167). By 3 June, summer had 'begun in good earnest—you would think so if you could peep with me through the closed lattice of my sitting-room out into the wide, glaring Piazza. It shines so as to scorch the eyes—in the

shade on one side is huddled a cabstand with the drivers all asleep on their boxes, and a collection of loungers of low degree & no costume to speak of lying flat on their faces on the stones & courting the siesta' (to MWJ; *CLHJ 1872–1876* 2:173). James recalls the cab-stand and its sleepy drivers in the next sentence of the Preface.

24 **what the early chapters of the book most "render" to me to-day is not the umbrageous air of their New England town, [...] the rococo obelisk of the Piazza, [...] four delightful little elephants**: As T. S. Eliot points out, this sentence of the Preface contains a verbal echo of James's critical biography of Nathaniel Hawthorne ('The Hawthorne Aspect', *The Little Review* 5.4 (August 1918), 47–53; 52 n). In Chapter 5 of *Hawthorne* (1879), James had remarked that *The House of the Seven Gables* (1851) possesses 'more literal actuality' than Hawthorne's other novels, 'and if it were not too fanciful an account of it, I should say that it renders, to an initiated reader, the impression of a summer afternoon in an elm-shadowed New England town. It leaves upon the mind a vague correspondence to some such reminiscence, and in stirring up the association it renders it delightful' (*LC1* 412–13). Elsewhere in the Prefaces, to 'render' usually means 'To represent or reproduce, esp. artistically; to depict, portray' (*OED*) (e.g., 'no "rendering" of any object and no painting of any picture', p. 20); but in the present context of authorial reminiscence, and in conjunction with the passage from *Hawthorne*, another sense of the word comes into play: 'To restore, return, give back' (*OED*). James in fact misremembers 'the rococo obelisk of the Piazza': Piazza Santa Maria Novella has not one obelisk but two, each supported not by 'four delightful little elephants' but by four tortoises. A large elephant carries the single obelisk in the Piazza di Minerva in Rome, and it is possible that James was confusing these monuments. The 'strident electric cars' he deplores in this sentence of the Preface were a comparatively recent development: the first electric trams in Florence were introduced in the 1890s (Fabrizio Pettinelli, *Firenze in Tranvai: Breve cronistoria del trasporto pubblico* (Florence: AIDA, 2008), pp. 49–55).

25 **Pathetic, as we say**: James seems to use 'pathetic' here in a modern colloquial sense: 'Miserably inadequate; of such a low standard as to be ridiculous or contemptible' (*OED*, earliest instance 1900). Later in the same Preface, the word carries its older meanings of 'Arousing sadness, compassion, or sympathy'; 'Producing an effect upon the emotions; moving, stirring, affecting' (*OED*): 'a sufficiently pathetic, tragic, comic, ironic, personal state' (p. 13).

26 **"gone in" for it**: A contemporary dictionary of British slang defines the 'colloquial' phrase 'TO GO IN FOR' as 'To enter for; to apply oneself to (*e.g.*, TO GO IN FOR honours). Also to devote oneself to (*e.g.*, to pay court); to take up (as a pastime, pursuit, hobby, or principle)' (*Slang* III:162). James used the phrase habitually, and often applied it to the efforts and aims of artists: as in his essay 'On Some Pictures Lately Exhibited' (1875), where the American painter Winslow Homer 'goes in, as the phrase is, for perfect realism' (*CWAD1* 117). See also the final sentence of 'The Art of Fiction' in its periodical text of 1884, where this formula supplies the essay's last word of encouragement to aspiring novelists: '"Be generous and delicate, and then, in the vulgar phrase, go in!"' ('The Art of Fiction', *Longman's Magazine* 4 (September 1884), 502–21; 521); when James collected the essay in *Partial Portraits* (1888), he revised this sentence to 'Be generous and delicate and pursue the prize' (*LC1* 65). On several occasions, the same phrase occurs as a revision in the *NYE* text of *Roderick Hudson*. In Chapter 2, for example, Rowland tells Roderick: '"if it's in you really to go in for sculpture, you ought to get to Rome and study the antique"' (*NYE* I, 34); in the 1883 *Collective Edition* text, the conditional clause was '"if you are to be a sculptor"' (*CE* IV, 27).

27 **some [...] antithesis to a state of civilisation providing for "art"**: Compare the inverted commas placed around the same word in 'The Art of Fiction', again in the context of Anglo-American hostility to aesthetic values: '"Art," in our Protestant communities, [...] is supposed in certain circles to have some vaguely injurious effect upon those who make it an important consideration, who let it weigh in the balance. It is assumed to be opposed in some mysterious manner to morality, to amusement, to instruction' (*LC1* 47).

28 **the local *type*, as to which I had my handful of impressions**: James had known a few New England towns and villages when he came to write *Roderick Hudson*. The family lived at Newport, Rhode Island for two extended periods between 1858 and 1862: for James's impressions of the place, see his essays 'Newport' (1870) and 'The Sense of Newport' (1906), and Chapters 4 and 12 of his memoir *Notes of a Son and Brother* (1914). In the summer and autumn of 1864, he took a course of hydrotherapy at Northampton, Massachusetts, the setting of the opening chapters of *Roderick Hudson* (Leon Edel, *Henry James: The Untried Years, 1843–1870* (London: Rupert Hart-Davis, 1953), pp. 208–10). He spent a memorable summer holiday in 1865 at North Conway, New Hampshire with a group of young

people including his cousin Minny Temple, which he would faintly allude to in 'New England: An Autumn Impression' (1905) and recall explicitly in *Notes of a Son and Brother* (*AS* 27–8, *Aut* 533–7), and another the following year at Swampscott, Massachusetts (see his notebook entry of 29 March 1905; *CN* 238–9). In an early travel essay, 'From Lake George to Burlington' (1870), he calls Burlington, Vermont 'the most truly charming, I fancy, of New England country towns' (*CTW1* 749). For the 'local *type*' instantiated by such places, see his comments in 'New England: An Autumn Impression' on recent visits to villages and small towns in Connecticut and Massachusetts, which had given him 'a resumed, or rather [...] a greatly-enlarged, acquaintance with the New England village in its most exemplary state': 'These communities stray so little from the type, that you often ask yourself by what sign or difference you know one from the other' (*AS* 38, 39).

29 **to see again, after long years, the case into which [...] the opening passages of "Roderick Hudson" put their foot**: James had revisited Northampton, Massachusetts on 6–7 May 1905 to read his lecture 'The Lesson of Balzac' to an audience at Smith College; he was entertained by faculty members and writers including George Washington Cable (1844–1925) and Ida Tarbell (1857–1944), and was photographed by Katherine Elizabeth McClellan (1859–1934). See Dean Flower, *Henry James in Northampton: Visions and Revisions* (Northampton, MA: Friends of the Smith College Library, 1971). When he says in the next sentence but one of the Preface that his 'rather feeble plea' about the rendering of Northampton in *Roderick Hudson* 'was charmingly allowed', he may be referring to comments made on that occasion.

30 **I had not *pretended* so very much to "do" Northampton Mass.**: James uses the verb 'pretend' here to mean 'To aspire, presume; to venture; to try, attempt' (*OED*); for a later use with the more usual sense ('to allege or declare falsely or with intent to deceive') see note 67. For 'doing' as representing a subject in any artistic medium (one of a cluster of senses of 'do' grouped together by *OED*: 'To work at or out, solve, translate, review, depict, etc.'), compare Chapter 26 of *Roderick Hudson*, where the landscape artist Sam Singleton exclaims of an approaching alpine storm: '"I should like awfully to *do* it"' (*NYE* I, 515).

31 **the whole question of the novelist's "doing,"**: James had recently considered this question in essays on three French novelists: Honoré de Balzac (1902), Gustave Flaubert (1902) and Émile Zola (1903). Thus, for

example, he notes that Balzac suffered from 'the obsession of the thing to be done' and was 'condemned' to a life of labour 'by his inveterately seeing this "thing to be done" as part and parcel, as of the very essence, of his subject'; James imagines him mockingly addressed by 'Destiny': '"You want to 'do' France, presumptuous, magnificent, miserable man [...]?"' ('HdB' xx). Again, Flaubert's *Madame Bovary* (1857) 'is a classic because the thing, such as it is, is ideally *done*, and because it shows that in such doing eternal beauty may dwell' ('GF' xviii). And Zola's *L'Assommoir* (1877) makes James ask 'How, after all, does it so get itself *done*—the "done" being, admirably, the sign and crown of it?' ('EZ' 207). See also note 934.

32 **He embarks, rash adventurer, under the star of "representation,"**: James consistently uses 'representation' to mean 'The action or fact of portraying a person or thing, esp. in an artistic medium; depiction' (*OED*). He had defended this as the prime function of the novel across two and a half decades of critical writing before the Prefaces. Apropos of Alphonse Daudet in 1883, for example: 'the main object of the novel is to represent life' (*LC2* 242). The same idea is strongly affirmed in 'The Art of Fiction': 'The only reason for the existence of a novel is that it does attempt to represent life' (*LC1* 46). A later example, catching the Preface's sense of hazard and adventure, comes in 'The Lesson of Balzac' (1905): 'The most fundamental and general sign of the novel, from one desperate experiment to another, is its being everywhere an effort at *representation*—this is the beginning and the end of it' (*LC2* 130).

33 **a peaceful, rural New England community** *quelconque*: The French word denotes an ordinary instance of a given type of thing, without special characteristics; thus *any* 'peaceful, rural New England community'. Compare James's comment in 'New England: An Autumn Impression' on a river seen from a train window on his American tour: 'I had supposed it for a moment, in my innocence, the Connecticut—which it decidedly was not; it was only, as appeared, a stream *quelconque*, a stream without an identity' (*AS* 32).

34 **the great shadow of Balzac; his august example [...] towered for me over the scene**: Honoré de Balzac (1799–1850), French novelist and playwright; author of *La Comédie humaine* (1829–48), a series of linked novels and stories surveying French society from 1815 to 1848. James's first critical essay on Balzac (1875), published in the same year as *Roderick Hudson*, had registered serious reservations about his philosophical pretensions, faulty moral sense, implausibility of characterization, coarseness of style

and want of charm, whilst simultaneously acknowledging that the 'huge, all-compassing, all-desiring, all-devouring love of reality which was the source of so many of his fallacies and stains, of so much dead-weight in his work, was also the foundation of his extraordinary power' (*LC2* 66–7). James would come to value Balzac much less reservedly than this, and his later essays anticipate the Preface's awed figuration of Balzac's stature and influence. In an essay on Charles de Bernard and Gustave Flaubert (1876), for example, 'Balzac is a genius of all time; he towers and overshadows' (*LC2* 160); a quarter of a century later, in 1902, Balzac is the only 'really monumental' novelist and 'the sturdiest-seated mass that rises in our path' ('HdB' xviii). The opening paragraphs of 'The Lesson of Balzac' explore 'the great dusky and deserted avenue that leads up to the seated statue of Balzac' (*LC2* 119); the lecture affirms Balzac's totemic value for contemporary novelists – 'our towering idol', 'some great practitioner, some concrete instance of the art, some ample cloak under which we may gratefully crawl' (*LC2* 139, 121). Originally written for American audiences on James's tour of 1904–5, 'The Lesson of Balzac' was still at the front of his mind when he conceived the *Roderick Hudson* Preface. An early version of the Preface was in existence by the start of March 1906, at which time James had very recently delivered 'The Lesson of Balzac' in London – at a meeting of the Sesame Club on 12 February 1906 ('Sesame Club, 29 Dover Street, W., Programme of literary evenings and debates: February to May, 1906', David J. Supino Collection of Henry James, Beinecke Rare Book and Manuscript Library, Yale University, Supino James 425a). Balzac's shadow would fall over the Preface to *The Golden Bowl* also. James cites his 'vast example' there as a validating instance of career-long commitment to textual revision, and observes: 'His case has equal mass and authority—and beneath its protecting shade [...] I move for the brief remainder of these remarks' (p. 273; and see notes 920 and 921).

35 **Saumur, [...] Limoges, [...] Guérande, [...] Nemours and Provins**: French provincial towns and settings of novels by Balzac: *Eugénie Grandet* (1833) takes place in Saumur, *Le Curé de village* (1839) in Limoges, and *Béatrix* (1839) in Guérande. James had observed in 1875: 'we know not what the natives of Limoges, of Saumur, of Angoulême, of Alençon, of Issoudun, of Guérande, thought of [Balzac's] presentation of these localities; but if the picture is not veracious, it is at least always definite and masterly' (*LC2* 50). Writing again on Balzac in 1902, James referred to 'his towns, his streets, his houses, his Saumurs, Angoulêmes, Guérandes'

('HdB' xvi). Nemours and Provins are the settings, respectively, for Balzac's novels *Ursule Mirouët* (1841) and *Pierrette* (1840).

36 **ville de province**: The French provincial town (*ville de province*) is an extremely important Balzacien location, the great opposite to Paris in the 'social antithesis' that organizes and nourishes his imagination of contemporary French life – as he puts it in the 1842 'Avant-Propos', or general preface, to the *Comédie humaine*: 'Paris et la province, cette antithèse sociale' (*La Comédie humaine*, ed. Castex et al., vol. I, p. 18). In 1902, James remarked on Balzac's 'intensely differentiated sphere of *la province*, evoked in each sharpest or faintest note of its difference': 'He feels, in his vast comedy, many things, but there is nothing he feels with the communicable shocks and vibrations, the sustained fury of perception [...] that *la province* excites in him' ('HdB' xxiii).

37 **his systematic closeness**: In 'The Lesson of Balzac', James had told his audiences that 'it is in the name of closeness that I am inviting you to let Balzac once more appeal to you'. The lecture compares the 'wrought texture' of Balzac's writing to that of a 'figured tapestry, all over-scored with objects in fine perspective': 'Such a tapestry, [...] with its myriad ordered stitches, its harmonies of tone and felicities of taste, is a work, above all, of closeness' (*LC2* 138). The figure is consistent across James's critical engagements with Balzac: he writes in 1875, for example, of the 'extraordinary closeness of tissue' of Balzac's novels (*LC2* 32), and in 1902 of 'his bristling surface, his closeness of texture, so suggestive, yet at the same time so akin to the crowded air we have in mind when we speak of not being able to see the wood for the trees' ('HdB' x). See also note 869.

38 **A "fancy" indication**: In this context, 'fancy' means 'Based upon or drawn from conceptions of the fancy [...], as *fancy picture* [etc.]' (*OED*). In the preface to *The House of the Seven Gables*, Hawthorne had used the same word when anticipating literal-minded readers' attempts 'to assign an actual locality to the imaginary events of this narrative' and bring its 'fancy-pictures almost into positive contact with the realities of the moment': to do so would be to mistake his project, which he compares to 'laying out a street that infringes upon nobody's private rights, and appropriating a lot of land which had no visible owner, and building a house, of materials long in use for constructing castles in the air'. Hawthorne's novel opens 'Half-way down a by-street of one of our New England towns', but it does not name that town; the fictional locators offered on its first

page ('Pyncheon-street', 'the old Pyncheon-house', 'the Pyncheon-elm') are examples of what James calls a '"fancy" indication' (*The House of the Seven Gables, A Romance* (Boston: Ticknor & Fields, 1851), pp. v, 9). For James's recent disappointment on visiting the original of the House of the Seven Gables in Salem, Massachusetts, see his essay 'Concord and Salem' (1907) (*AS* 265–72). See also note 24.

39 **some sweet old overtangled walled garden, a safe paradise of self-criticism**: James echoes a passage in Chapter 18 of the revised text of *Roderick Hudson* that describes the Palatine Hill in Rome – another 'overtangled' garden, yet suggestive of a different experience of rereading, full of interest for the revisiting author but not unequivocally safe: 'that sunny chaos of rich decay and irrelevant renewal, of scattered and overtangled fragments, half excavated and half identified, known as the Palace of the Cæsars. Nothing in Rome is more interesting than this confused and crumbling garden, where you stumble at every step on the disinterred bones of the past' (*NYE* I, 349–50). The thought of 'renewal' occurs as a revision in the *NYE* text; in the 1883 *Collective Edition*, this passage begins 'that sunny desolation of crumbling overtangled fragments' (*CE* V, 58). For the literary text as a 'walled garden', compare James's 1904 essay on Gabriele D'Annunzio, which characterizes his novel *Le vergini delle rocce* (1895) as, 'in the largest sense, but a theme for style, style of substance as well as of form. Within this compass it blooms and quivers and shimmers with light, becomes a wonderful little walled garden of romance' ('GDA' 408–9).

40 **blackened or "sunk," [...] pictorial "tone"**: Oil paintings can darken over time depending on the paints and varnishes used. In *William Wetmore Story*, James notes an extreme case of such deterioration in the career of the American artist William Page (1811–85), whose oil paintings blackened as 'the result of a technical theory, some fallacy as to pigments, some perversity as to bases, too fondly, too blindly entertained' (*WWS* I:173). In a painterly context, the verb 'sink' means 'Of oil paints: to seep into the surface or ground to which they are applied. Hence of an oil painting: to develop dull spots on the surface where the pigments have seeped into the ground' (*OED*). In his very recent essay on 'Boston' (1906), James had used this liability of painted canvases as an extended metaphor for the failure of memory: 'Can one *have*, in the conditions, an impression of Boston, any that has not been for long years as inappreciable as a "sunk" picture?—that

dead state of surface which requires a fresh application of varnish. [...] My "sunk" sense of Boston found itself vigorously varnished by mere renewal of vision at the end of long years' (AS 226). James uses the same figure to refer to rereading and revising in the Preface to *The Golden Bowl*, where 'the term Revision' is similarly defined as 'mere renewal of vision': 'to see, or to look over, again' (p. 269), For the associated figure of varnishing, see note 41. The standard painterly definitions of 'tone' are 'The prevailing effect of the combination of light and shade, and of the general scheme of colouring, in a painting' or 'the degree of luminosity of a colour' (*OED*). For the Preface's sense of 'pictorial "tone"' as a 'grace' acquired with time, see James's story 'The Tone of Time' (1900), not included in the *NYE*, where an artist is commissioned to paint an imaginary portrait which must look like an old picture: 'The "tone"—that of such a past as it pretended to—was there almost to excess, a brown bloom into which the image seemed mysteriously to retreat' (*The Better Sort* (London: Methuen & Co., 1903), p. 57).

41 **to wipe it over, [...] to varnish it anew**: A dulled oil painting can be temporarily revived by an application of water and more lastingly renewed by re-varnishing. In Chapter 23 of *The Tragic Muse* (1890), the painter Nick Dormer shows Gabriel Nash examples of his 'young work', and cleans up the pictures as described in the Preface: 'He rubbed old panels with his sleeve and dabbed wet sponges on surfaces that had sunk' (*NYE* VIII, 24). That process is converted into a metaphor in the first chapter of 'The Real Thing' (1892) when the 'dim smile' of the would-be artist's model Mrs Monarch has 'the effect of a moist sponge passed over a "sunk" piece of painting' (*NYE* XVIII, 308).

42 **to live back into a forgotten state, [...] credulities too early spent perhaps**: To 'live back into' is a frequent Jamesian formula for any act of retrospect, not only textual revision. In 'New York Revisited', for example, standing outside a house 'on the south side of Waverly Place' James says that he 'lived again into the queer mediæval costume (preserved by the daguerreotypist's art) of the very little boy' – his young self – who had gone to school there (*AS* 90). Some years after the *NYE*, in *Notes of a Son and Brother*, he would allow himself to 'live back of a sudden [...] into the odd hours' of his year at Harvard Law School in 1862-3 (*Aut* 457); similarly, rereading and editing a sequence of his brother William's letters as part of the same biographical project meant 'living back imaginatively [...] into' the time covered by that correspondence (to Harry James, 13-15

November 1913; *HJL* 4:800). The revised *NYE* text of *Roderick Hudson* anticipates the Preface's sense that to look or read again is to encounter 'credulities': when Roderick shows Rowland his early sculptures for the first time, he does so 'silently, making no explanations and looking at them himself with a strange air of refreshed credulity' (Ch. 2; *NYE* I, 36); the 1883 *Collective Edition* reads '[...] with a strange air of quickened curiosity' (*CE* IV, 28).

43 **to dismiss it altogether**: Compare James's letter of 7 August 1905 to the American novelist Robert Herrick: the '*raison d'être*' of the *New York Edition* 'is in its being selective as well as collective, and by the mere fact of leaving out certain things (I have tried to read over *Washington Square* and I can't, and I fear it must go!) I exercise a control, a discrimination, I treat certain portions of my work as unhappy accidents' (*HJL* 4:371).

44 **taking up the old relation, so workable apparently, yet**: As Horne points out, this phrasing echoes the revised text of the novel (*Henry James and Revision*, pp. 141–2 n. 44). In Chapter 25, Rowland, feeling angry and impatient with Roderick, is greeted by him unexpectedly and 'ungraciously glare[s]' at him: 'Roderick's face, on the other hand, took up, even before he spoke, something that evidently figured to him as their old relation. It was as if he had come back to him' (*NYE* I, 498). In the 1883 *Collective Edition*, the same passage reads: 'Roderick stood looking at him with an expression of countenance which had of late become rare' (*CE* V, 170).

45 **words I have had occasion to use in another connexion [...] a better turn.**": James quotes from the introductory note to his collection of revised travel essays *English Hours* (1905), which had appeared as he was at work on the revisions to *Roderick Hudson*. He observes there that his earlier travel essays, some of which date back to the early 1870s, 'represent a good many wonderments and judgments and emotions, whether felicities or mistakes, the fine freshness of which the author has—to his misfortune, no doubt—sufficiently outlived. But they may perhaps on that account present something of a curious interest. I may add that I have again attentively looked them over, with a view to any possible amendment of their form or enhancement of their meaning, and that I have nowhere scrupled to rewrite a sentence or a passage on judging it susceptible of a better turn' (*CTW1* 3).

46 **"where was your idea of the interest? [...] where is the provision for so much weakness?"**: James's generalized projection of a critical response in

this passage ('one hears the reader say') may be based on an actual criticism of *Roderick Hudson*. Reviewing the novel for the *Spectator* in July 1879, the English journalist R. H. Hutton had doubted 'whether any man of genius so great as Roderick Hudson's, ever could be so long and so completely diverted from the natural themes of that genius by an unhappy passion'; he 'must be quite a new type of artist, if, with the power and originality attributed to him, his imagination was simply dried up by his unreturned passion for Christina Light. His selfishness and egotism are not, perhaps, over-done. But his artistic sterility under pain and disappointment surely is' (Gard 76).

47   **foreshorten […] values […] the mere procession of items and profiles is […], for essential quality, almost "compromised"**: James borrows the terms 'foreshorten' and 'values' from the vocabulary of the graphic arts. In painting and drawing, foreshortening is 'The correct depiction in perspective of a single figure or object or part thereof in relation to its distance from the eye of the viewer' (*The Concise Oxford Dictionary of Art Terms*, 2nd edn, ed. Michael Clarke (Oxford: Oxford University Press, 2010)). In 'The Lesson of Balzac', James had isolated 'two elements of the art of the novelist which, as they present […] the greatest difficulty, tend thereby most to fascinate us': the first is 'that mystery of the foreshortened procession of facts and figures, of appearances of whatever sort, which is in some lights but another name for the picture governed by the principle of composition' (*LC2* 136); for the second, see note 49. In painterly contexts, 'value' refers to 'Due or proper effect or emphasis; relative tone of colour in each distinct section of a picture; a particular tone or emphasis' (*OED*). James often uses this pictorial terminology in his literary criticism: in his dialogue-essay '*Daniel Deronda*: A Conversation' (1876), for example, the musician Klesmer in George Eliot's novel 'comes in with a sort of Shakespearean "value," as a painter would say, and so, in a different tone, does Hans Meyrick' (*LC1* 991). To be socially 'compromised' is to be 'Exposed to risk, danger, or discredit' or 'damaged in reputation' (*OED*), a concern for many of James's characters. The Preface to *The Wings of the Dove* strengthens the present passage's association between social and artistic compromise: James refers to Lionel Croy, who has ruined his family by incurring some unspecified disgrace, as Kate's 'so compromised and compromising father', and in the same passage describes the technical challenge of foreshortening as an aspect of the novelist's dealings with 'the Angel, not to say […] the Demon, of Compromise' (pp. 235, 236).

48 **the coarse industries that masquerade in its name**: The industrial character of the popular literary marketplace is a recurring topic in James's criticism in the decade preceding the *NYE*. In 'The Future of the Novel' (1899), for example, he enforces a distinction between literary production proper and mere book-making, observing that 'The literature, as it may be called for convenience, of children is an industry that occupies by itself a very considerable quarter of the scene'; again, 'It is certain that there is no real health for any art—I am not speaking, of course, of any mere industry—that does not move a step in advance of its farthest follower' (*LC1* 101, 109). In 'The Lesson of Balzac', the modern novel 'has become an object of easy manufacture, showing on every side the stamp of the machine; it has become the article of commerce, produced in quantity' (*LC2* 134).

49 **the *effect* of the great lapse and passage, of the "dark backward and abysm,"**: The second technical 'difficulty' for the novelist especially highlighted in 'The Lesson of Balzac' (see note 47 for the first) is 'that of representing [...] the lapse of time, the duration of the subject' (*LC2* 136). The quotation in this sentence of the Preface comes from one of James's favourite passages in Shakespeare, Prospero's question to Miranda in *The Tempest* (1611) about the reach of memory: 'What seest thou else / In the dark backward and abysm of time?' (1.2.49–50). James had addressed the same subject ten years before the Preface: 'that side of the novelist's effort—the side of most difficulty and thereby of most dignity—which consists in giving the sense of duration, of the lapse and accumulation of time'. On this occasion, he drew attention to a general over-reliance on dialogue, 'an expedient' which had the effect of 'absolutely minimizing, in regard to time, our impression of lapse and passage': 'Thanks to this perversity, everything dealt with in fiction appears at present to occur simply on the occasion of a few conversations about it; there is no other constitution of it. [...] The process, the "dark backward and abysm," is really so little reproduced' ('London. July 1, 1897', *Harper's Weekly* 41 (31 July 1897), 754). The Preface to *Roderick Hudson* was completed by mid-August 1906; early the following year, James wrote an introduction to *The Tempest* for Sidney Lee's Renaissance Edition of *The Complete Works of William Shakespeare* (*LC1* 1205–20).

50 **not by consciousness of difficulty [...] that the story-teller is mostly ridden; [...] scarce get themselves (shall it be called?) "told."**: In an

essay of 1902, James had acclaimed Flaubert's *Madame Bovary* – the masterpiece of a novelist who was obsessively conscious of difficulty – as 'the most elaborate, the most *told* of anecdotes' ('GF' xv). James's early literary essays use the phrase 'story-teller' straightforwardly to denote a writer of prose fiction: as, for example, in his review of W. D. Howells's *A Foregone Conclusion* (1875), enumerating 'Mr. Lowell and Mr. Longfellow among the poets, and Mr. Howells, Bret Harte, and Mr. Aldrich among the story-tellers' (*LC1* 497). By the time of 'The Art of Fiction' (1884), which welcomed the English critic Walter Besant's publication of 'certain of his ideas on the mystery of story-telling' and proceeded to critique the underlying naivety of Besant's principles (*LC1* 44), James typically handled the term with analytical irony. For his use of 'story' in the same ironic spirit, see note 137.

51 **an Action**: In literary criticism, 'action' refers to 'The event or series of events represented or described in a play, film, novel, or similar work' (*OED*). This sense of the word ultimately derives from the *Poetics* of Aristotle (384–322 BCE), which defines the plot of a tragic drama or epic poem as the imitation of an 'action'. Tragedy, according to Aristotle, is 'an imitation of an action that is complete, and whole, and of a certain magnitude': such an action must have 'a beginning, a middle, and an end' whose relations to each other are determined by 'causal necessity', and it must be of 'a length which can be easily embraced by the memory' so that a spectator may perceive 'the unity and sense of the whole'. Aristotle's concept implies selection: in plotting the *Odyssey*, for example, Homer omitted those episodes in Odysseus' history 'between which there was no necessary or probable connexion'. In the resulting plot, 'the structural union of the parts [is] such that, if any one of them is displaced or removed, the whole will be disjointed and disturbed' (S. H. Butcher, *Aristotle's Theory of Poetry and Fine Art, with a Critical Text and Translation of The Poetics*, 3rd edn (London: Macmillan and Co., 1902); *The Poetics*, chs. 7–8, pp. 31–5). See also R. W. Short, 'Some Critical Terms of Henry James', *PMLA* 65.5 (1950), 667–80; 668–70. James refers to fictional subjects as 'actions' throughout the Prefaces, but only in the present passage does he give the word a capital letter. A reference to the 'charmed capitals' similarly awarded to the words 'Occasion' and 'Acts of a Play' in the Preface to *The Awkward Age* (p. 87) may suggest that his capitalizing of technical terms in the Prefaces is an index of excitement about the particular phase of the compositional process he is recalling.

52 **on some other occasion**: James returns to the related questions of foreshortening, 'compactness' and the handling of an 'action' in the Preface to *The Tragic Muse*, pp. 68–70.

53 **the Dramatist's all-in-all, his intensity**: Writing on Ibsen's *John Gabriel Borkman* in a short piece for *Harper's Weekly* (6 February 1897), James had referred to 'intensity' as 'the dramatist's great goal' (*CWAD2* 455). An early essay on 'The Parisian Stage' (1873) anticipates the Preface's comparison of novels with plays in these terms: 'An acted play is a novel intensified; it realizes what the novel suggests, and, by paying a liberal tribute to the senses, anticipates your possible complaint that your entertainment is of the meagre sort styled "intellectual".' The intensification of staging is in part an effect of temporal compression: James unfavourably compares the 'eternity' it takes to read an eighteenth-century novel such as Samuel Richardson's *Clarissa* (1748) with the evening one spends at the theatre (*CWAD2* 4). This, too, is in accord with the broadly Aristotelian conceptual framework of the *Roderick Hudson* Preface: Aristotle prefers tragedy to epic because it 'attains its end within narrower limits; for the concentrated effect is more pleasurable than one which is spread over a long time and so diluted' (*The Poetics*, ch. 26; in Butcher, *Aristotle's Theory of Poetry and Fine Art*, p. 111). James returns to these questions in the Preface to *The Ambassadors*, suggesting that the alternation of 'scenic' and non-scenic presentation in that novel produces 'an intensity that fairly adds to the dramatic—though the latter is supposed to be the sum of all intensities' (p. 259).

54 **its centre, the point of command of all the rest**: An important concept in James's understanding of fictional form and structure, the 'centre' of a work is often located – as in the next paragraph of the Preface – in the consciousness of a character from whose point of view the narration is focalized: 'The centre of interest [...] is in Rowland Mallet's consciousness' (p. 13). In the Preface to *The American*, similarly, James posits the 'effect of a *centre*' as fundamental to composition (p. 29); he is referring there to his use of Christopher Newman as a focalizing character. He returns to this topic, 'the famous centre of one's subject' (p. 70), in all the early Prefaces up to and including that to *NYE* XI.

55 **not to be *too* acute—which would have disconnected it and made it superhuman**: James comes back to these questions – the intelligence of focalizing characters and the necessity of their remaining in some degree 'bewildered' and so connected to the common human lot – in the

Preface to *The Princess Casamassima*, pp. 48–55. The representatives of 'superhuman' consciousness in that Preface are the 'all-knowing immortals' of Greek mythology (see note 186). Most pre-twentieth-century examples of the adjective 'superhuman' cited in *OED* similarly refer to divine beings, usually the Christian God; the earliest example to show the direct influence of Friedrich Nietzsche's *Also Sprach Zarathustra* (1883–5) is dated to 1896 and uses the noun 'superhuman' to render the German *Übermensch*. The usual English translation of Nietzsche's term is 'superman'.

56 **the joy of such a "job"**: James uses 'job' here colloquially, in the sense of 'A difficult task' (*OED*, earliest instance 1832). Compare his 1902 essay on Balzac: 'One would really scarce have liked to see such a job as *La Comédie Humaine* tackled without swagger' ('HdB' xxxiii).

57 **the sum of what "happened" to him, [...] to feel certain things happening to others**: In 'New York: Social Notes' (1906), James had similarly distinguished between objective happenings and subjective experiences: 'history is never, in any rich sense, the immediate crudity of what "happens," but the much finer complexity of what we read into it and think of in connection with it' (*AS* 182).

58 **one builds all vainly in the air**: The structure James refers to is a 'castle in the air', a 'visionary project or scheme, day-dream, idle fancy'; 'to form castles in the air' is 'to form unsubstantial or visionary projects' (*OED*, 'castle'). Hawthorne defends the fictive imagination in these terms in the preface to *The House of the Seven Gables*, in the passage quoted in note 38.

59 **on the ship, under the stars**: This scene closes Chapter 4 of *Roderick Hudson*.

60 **the mounting wave**: An echo of the opening of Alfred Tennyson's 'The Lotos-Eaters' (1832): '"Courage!" he said, and pointed toward the land, / "This mounting wave will roll us shoreward soon"' (ll. 1–2; *The Poems of Tennyson*, 2nd edn, ed. Christopher Ricks, 3 vols. (London: Longman, 1987), vol. I, p. 468). This poem's desire to linger irresponsibly in a foreign place informs the characters' longings in *Roderick Hudson*. In the first chapter, before meeting Roderick, Rowland contemplates spending a winter of '"lotus-eating"' in Rome (*NYE* I, 7). At Lake Como in Chapter 23, as they prepare to leave Italy for Switzerland, Roderick declares: '"I could be happy here and forget everything. Why not stay here for ever?"' Rowland's response gains a Tennysonian echo in the revision: 'It seemed

to Rowland also a place of irresistible persuasion, with the very taste of the lotus in the air' (*NYE* I, 465); in the 1883 *Collective Edition*, Italy had seemed only 'a place to stay in for ever; a place for perfect oblivion of the disagreeable' (*CE* V, 145). In *William Wetmore Story* (1903) and other non-fictional writings of the same period, James borrows figures from 'The Lotos-Eaters' to think about the pains and attractions of his own youthful experiences of Italy, and about the processes of memory: see Oliver Herford, 'The Roman Lotus: Digestion and Retrospect', *Henry James Review* 31.1 (2010), 54–60.

61 **"plain," […] "coloured"**: For the terms of this antithesis, compare the title of Robert Louis Stevenson's essay 'A Penny Plain and Twopence Coloured' (1884), which James had referred to in his 1888 essay on Stevenson as 'a delightful rhapsody on the penny sheets of figures for the puppet-shows of infancy' (*LC1* 1242). Black-and-white ('plain') sheets of printed images were sold for a penny to be coloured in by the purchaser, whereas ready-coloured versions cost twopence. In the same essay, James quotes Stevenson's *Travels with a Donkey in the Cevennes* (1879): '"If landscapes were sold […] like the sheets of characters of my boyhood, one penny plain and twopence coloured, I should go the length of twopence every day of my life"' (*LC1* 1242).

62 **wound-up with the right silver key, she would go on a certain time by the motion communicated**: In 'The Lesson of Balzac', this motion is imparted by the novelist's 'love' for his characters: James notes Balzac's 'joy in their communicated and exhibited movement, in their standing on their feet and going of themselves and acting out their characters' (*LC2* 131–2). Other figurative keys in the Prefaces open locks rather than winding up mechanisms – including another 'silver' key (p. 209), the title character in 'Julia Bride' (1908).

63 **meeting her again and taking her up later on**: Christina Light figures again, ten years after *Roderick Hudson*, as the title character in *The Princess Casamassima* (1886). James discusses her reappearance and the general question of recurring characters in the Preface to that novel, pp. 57–8. To 'take up' can mean 'To take (a person) into one's protection, patronage, or company; to adopt as a protégé' or 'to become interested or engaged in (a study, profession, or pastime)' (*OED*, 'take'), and these senses have a particular relevance to the relationships between characters in *Roderick Hudson* and other early novels in the *NYE*. In the revised text of *Roderick Hudson*, Rowland refers to Roderick as '"the *bel enfant* [step-child] of my

adoption"' (Ch. 15; *NYE* I, 293), a formula replacing "'Master Hudson'" in the 1883 *Collective Edition* (*CE* V, 15). In *The Portrait of a Lady* (1881), the novel James began to revise for the *NYE* immediately after *Roderick Hudson*, Ralph Touchett suggests to Isabel that his mother has '"adopted"' her in bringing her to Europe. Isabel tells him that she is '"not a candidate for adoption"', but accepts his comment in another sense: '"You meant she has taken me up. Yes; she likes to take people up"' (Ch. 2; *NYE* III, 23–4). And in *The Princess Casamassima*, the young book-binder Hyacinth Robinson is 'taken up by a great lady' when he is co-opted socially and politically by the Princess (Ch. 14; *NYE* V, 227).

PREFACE to *The American* (*NYE* II)

64 **made its first appearance in "The Atlantic Monthly"**: James omits to mention the negotiations for serializing *The American* in *The Atlantic Monthly*, which – as in the case of *Roderick Hudson* – involved a second periodical. He had first offered the novel to the editors of the New York *Galaxy*, Francis and William Church, who had published a dozen of his early stories, from 'A Day of Days' (1866) to 'Benvolio' (1875). On 1 December 1875, James told Francis Church that he 'propose[d] to take for granted [...] that you will be ready to publish, on receipt of them, the opening chapters of a novel. I have got at work upon one sooner than I expected, & particularly desire it to come out without delay' (*CLHJ 1872–1876* 3:13). Church appears to have agreed to begin the serial the following March. When, in January 1876, W. D. Howells invited James to contribute another novel to the *Atlantic Monthly*, James replied that he had approached the *Galaxy* because it was 'a matter of prime necessity to get a novel on the stocks immediately': 'It did not even occur to me to write to you about [*The American*], as I took for granted that the Atlantic could begin nothing till June or July, & it was the money question solely that had to determine me' (3 February [1876]; *CLHJ 1872–1876* 3:57–8). By this time, he had completed the first monthly instalment and the *Galaxy* had delayed the promised start of the serial run to April 1876. When, at the end of February, they postponed once more, James stopped writing and issued an ultimatum: serialization must start with the May issue at the latest or they must give up the novel and return the manuscript (to Francis Pharcellus Church or William Conant Church, 3 March [1876]; *CLHJ 1872–1876* 3:77–8). Howells intervened at this point and took over the novel for the

Atlantic, and *The American* ran there – as the Preface states – from June 1876 to May 1877.

65 **It started on its course while much was still unwritten**: James had delivered copy for the first four of a planned nine monthly parts of *The American* by the start of its serial run. At that point, he acknowledged that the instalments of copy he had been sending to the *Atlantic* were too long, and accepted Howells's proposal to extend the serialization to twelve months (to W. D. Howells, 28 May [1876]; *CLHJ 1872–1876* 3:126–7).

66 **a special Providence [...] watches over anxious novelists condemned to the economy of serialisation**: This sentence refers to the final novels of William Makepeace Thackeray (1811–63), Elizabeth Gaskell (1810–65) and Robert Louis Stevenson (1850–94), all of which were left unfinished at their authors' deaths. *Denis Duval* and *Wives and Daughters* had both been running in the *Cornhill Magazine* when their authors died; *Weir of Hermiston* was not in fact serialized. James alludes to Hamlet's lines on the unforeseeable hour of death: 'we defy augury. There is special providence in the fall of a sparrow' (5.2.219–20). In a letter to Stevenson lamenting the postponement of a promised visit to Europe from the South Seas in 1890, James had anticipated the Preface's fantasy of providential supervision: 'Seriously, it was a real heartbreak to have September substituted for June; but I have a general faith in the fascinated providence who watches over you, to the neglect of all other human affairs—I believe that even *He* has an idea that you know what you are about' (28 April 1890; *HJL* 3:278).

67 **an inordinate leak [...] *pretend* to myself I was afloat**: In 'The Lesson of Balzac' (1905), James had recently figured faults in literary construction in the same terms. Over-reliance on dialogue in a novel carries the 'besetting and haunting penalty of springing, unless watched, a leak in the effect'; as in the Preface, this 'leak' imperils the novel – figured as a seagoing vessel – by letting water in. In Balzac's case, the danger is averted by 'the master of the ship [...] keeping his eye on the pump; the pump, I mean, of relief and alternation, the pump that keeps the vessel free of too much water' (*LC2* 138). The Preface also echoes Valentin de Bellegarde's fatalistic prediction of his future life in *The American*: '"I'm good for three or four years more perhaps, but I foresee that after that I shall spring a leak and begin to sink"' (Ch. 7; *NYE* II, 136). For the necessity of pretending to oneself in such situations, compare 'The Lesson of Balzac', where James quotes his own reply to a fellow-novelist who complained that the novel, as a literary form, was 'absolutely too difficult': '"Too difficult indeed; yet there is one

way to master it—which is to pretend consistently that it isn't." We are all of us, all the while, pretending—as consistently as we can—that it isn't, and Balzac's great glory is that he pretended hardest' (*LC2* 134).

68 **the pursued ostrich**: The commonplace that ostriches hide their heads when threatened derives from classical antiquity: see, for example, the *Natural History* (*CE* 77) of Pliny the Elder, Book X, Ch. 1, where the ostrich is said to hide its head in a bush and think that the rest of its body is hidden. James would use the same figure for his own conduct at a later stage of work on the *NYE*, apologizing to the publisher Frederick Macmillan for his repeated failures to get on with a promised book (*London Town*) and wondering 'that some thunderbolt of reprobation hasn't descended upon me long before this. I have expected it very often, and crouched and grovelled, burying my head in the sand, whenever I could fancy the faintest distant mutter' (5 April 1908; *LL* 460).

69 **felt the thing *go* [...] the most a dramatist can ever ask of his drama**: In theatrical contexts, 'to go' means 'to meet with applause, acclaim, or support; to succeed' (*OED*). In James's story 'Broken Wings' (1900), for example, one member of a theatre audience asks another on the first night of a play: '"Is—a—this thing going?"' (Ch. 3; *NYE* XVI, 149). James's own stage adaptation of *The American* had a moderate success in 1891–2, touring Scotland, Ireland and the English provinces and running for seventy performances in the West End. The London critics had reservations about both text and production, however, and James did not see the financial profits he had hoped for (see *CP* 179–91).

70 **its practical dependence on a miracle**: The Prefaces repeatedly figure literary inspiration and authorial memory as miraculous phenomena, and miracles occur in James's accounts of the composition and reception of several of his works – most emphatically 'The Pupil' (p. 119). On 13 September 1906, he wrote to Howells about the 'staleness' of his impressions from the American tour of 1904–5, which was causing insuperable problems for his work on a planned companion-volume to *The American Scene* (1907): 'Wooing *back* freshness is hard—but we live (or we write at least, I think,) from one vouchsafed miracle to another' (*LFL* 416).

71 **I was seated in an American "horse-car"**: In the 1870s, James could have ridden in American 'horse-cars' (horse-drawn trams) in New York City and in Boston and its suburbs. John Carlos Rowe points out that this account of the original idea for *The American* recalls the story Christopher Newman tells Tom Tristram in Chapter 2 of the novel about his life-changing

decision not to pursue the advantage in a business deal (Rowe, *The Theoretical Dimensions of Henry James* (Madison, WI: The University of Wisconsin Press, 1984), pp. 238–9). Newman is travelling in a different sort of horse-drawn vehicle, a New York 'hack' or hackney-carriage (*NYE* II, 30–2).

72 **He wouldn't "forgive"**: Newman explicitly rejects this option in the final chapter of *The American*, when he visits Mrs Tristram on learning that Claire de Cintré has given him up and entered a convent. In the *NYE* text, Mrs Tristram observes: '"You're not so good a man as I thought. You're more—you're more—" "More what?" "More unreconciled." "Good God!" he cried; "do you expect me to forgive?"' (*NYE* II, 532). In the Macmillan *Collective Edition* of 1883, the edition James worked from when revising the novel, Mrs Tristram tells him that he is '"More unforgiving"' (*CE* VII, 202); she thus supplies Newman with the word which he immediately echoes, and which James would echo in the Preface.

73 **the deep well of unconscious cerebration: […] as one had already known the buried treasure to come to light, with a firm iridescent surface and a notable increase of weight**: The term 'unconscious cerebration' was coined by the English physiologist William Benjamin Carpenter (1813–85) 'to express that action of the brain which, though unaccompanied by consciousness, produces results which might have been produced by thought' (*OED*, 'cerebration'). William James refers to 'unconscious cerebration' in *The Varieties of Religious Experience* (1902) while discussing the involuntary aspects of conversion experiences (Lecture 9, 'Conversion'); he mentions Carpenter's formula as 'a popular phrase of explanation' for 'subconsciously maturing processes eventuating in results of which we suddenly grow conscious', but notes that subsequent discoveries have rendered 'the adjective "unconscious" […] almost certainly a misnomer' for many cases and suggests that it 'is better replaced by the vaguer term "subconscious" or "subliminal"' (William James, *Writings 1902–1910*, ed. Bruce Kuklick (New York: Library of America, 1987), pp. 192–3). James had used the phrase before: in the first book edition of 'The Aspern Papers', for example, the narrator explains a crucial change of mind by noting that 'in the unconscious cerebration of sleep I had swung back to a passionate appreciation of Miss Bordereau's papers' (*The Aspern Papers. Louisa Pallant. The Modern Warning*, 2 vols. (London and New York: Macmillan and Co., 1888), vol. I, p. 135). For the return of such items to full consciousness in a richer state, compare the notebook entry James made on 29 March 1905 at Coronado Beach, California,

anticipating the value his impressions of America would have acquired by the time he got back home to Rye: 'These things are all packed away, now, thicker than I can penetrate, deeper than I can fathom, & there let them rest, for the present, in their sacred cool darkness, till I shall let in upon them the mild still light of dear old L[amb].H[ouse].—in which they will begin to gleam & glitter & take form like the gold & jewels of a mine' (*CN* 237). The 'sea-change' of Ariel's song in *The Tempest* (1611) – from 'bones' to 'coral', from 'eyes' to 'pearls' – is relevant to James's imagination of such transformations: for an allusion to those Shakespearean lines in the Preface to *NYE* XIII, see note 516.

74 **in Paris [...] in December 1875; [...] I had come back there, after earlier visitations, but a few weeks before**: James had visited Paris on a number of previous occasions, sometimes making extended stays: once as an infant in 1844 and several times in childhood between 1855 and 1857 (see *A Small Boy and Others* (1913), Chs. 4–5, 21–2, 24–8; and *Notes of a Son and Brother* (1914), Ch. 3), then on his first adult European trip in 1869–70 and again in 1872–4. By midsummer 1875, after a year in America, he had formulated 'a tolerably definite plan of going in the autumn to Europe & fixing myself for a considerable period in Paris' (to John Milton Hay, 21 July [1875]; *CLHJ 1872–1876* 2:225). He arrived in England on 31 October 1875 and spent ten days in London before crossing to France.

75 **in the cold shadow of the Arc de Triomphe**: This monumental arch stands at the western end of the Avenue des Champs-Élysées in the centre of the Place de l'Étoile; commissioned in 1806 but not completed until the 1830s, it commemorates the victories of the French Revolutionary and Napoleonic armies. The American expatriate colony in Paris was centred in this neighbourhood. James had several friends there, including Edward Lee Childe and his French wife Blanche de Triqueti, Edward Darley Boit and Mary Louisa Boit, and Henrietta Reubell; in *The American*, the Tristrams too live 'behind one of those chalk-coloured façades which decorate with their pompous sameness the broad avenues distributed by Baron Haussmann over the neighbourhood of the Arc de Triomphe' (Ch. 3; *NYE* II, 35). The shadow of the arch extends along certain of those avenues depending on the season and time of day, but it could not actually have fallen over the lodgings James occupied while he was writing *The American*, a mile and a half away in rue de Luxembourg (see note 84). In this passage and elsewhere, he appears to think of the area shaded by the arch in ways that exceed literal geography: for Peter Sherringham in *The Tragic Muse* (1890),

lingering on through the summer in an exaggeratedly empty Paris, 'the Arc de Triomphe threw its cool thick shadow for a mile' (Ch. 12; *NYE* VII, 221).

76 **rose before me, on a perfect day of the divine Paris spring, in the great gilded Salon Carré of the Louvre**: The first chapter of *The American* opens with Newman 'reclining at his ease on the great circular divan which at that period [1868] occupied the centre of the Salon Carré, in the Museum of the Louvre'; tired out with looking at paintings, he is watching the copyist Noémie Nioche at work: 'At last he rose abruptly and [...] approached the young lady' (*NYE* II, 1, 5). The Salon Carré is on the first floor of the Louvre at the east end of the Grande Galerie; according to the guidebook consulted by Newman in Chapter 1, at this period it contained 'the choicest gems of the entire gallery' (Karl Baedeker, *Paris and Northern France* (Koblenz: Karl Baedeker, 1867), p. 60). In specifying the season as spring James is following the time-scheme of the novel, which opens 'On a brilliant day in May' (*NYE* II, 1), and not the sequence of his work upon it, which began in late November or early December 1875 (see note 64).

77 **taking a pass-key from his pocket**: A 'pass-key' is 'A special key of a door or gate giving privileged access, esp. a key which operates any one of a number of locks, a master key' (*OED*). In his critical biography *Hawthorne* (1879), James had used the figure of a pocketed key to a suggest an author's familiar access to the spaces of imagination: Hawthorne 'has all the ease [...] of a regular dweller in the moral, psychological realm; he goes to and fro in it, as a man who knows his way', and 'he keeps the key in his pocket' (*LC1* 368).

78 **the conception of Paris as the consecrated scene of rash infatuations and bold bad treacheries**: James returns to this traditional Anglo-American idea of Paris in the Preface to *The Ambassadors* (see note 860). He was fond of the melodramatic adjectival pairing 'bold bad': compare his recent travel essay 'New York Revisited' (1906), which figures '"almost any odd stroll"' through the city as '"an adventure [...] with some strident, battered, questionable beauty, truly some 'bold bad' charmer"'; and again on the next page, reversing the two adjectives, a '"bad bold beauty"' (*AS* 108, 109). A commonplace formula of reprobation in nineteenth-century literature, it appears to derive from Shakespeare's *Henry VIII* (1612–13), where Cardinal Wolsey is referred to as 'This bold bad man' (2.2.43). The reversed form of the phrase occurs in *The American* itself. In the revised text, Newman says of the Marquise de Bellegarde, '"Well, she's a bad, bold woman. She's a wicked old sinner"' (Ch. 13; *NYE* II, 246); in the Macmillan *Collective*

Edition of 1883, this reads: '"Well," said Newman, "she is wicked, she is an old sinner"' (*CE* VI, 188). See Figure 1 on p. lxi of this volume.

79 **Boston [...] Cleveland [...] Hartford [...] Utica**: In James's lifetime Boston, Massachusetts was the intellectual, cultural and moral centre of New England; the city was strongly associated with abolitionism and other social reform movements, as it is in his novel *The Bostonians* (1886), and he probably cites it here for its un-Parisian seriousness. The other American cities named in this sentence were significant manufacturing centres in the late nineteenth century: Cleveland, Ohio; Hartford, Connecticut; and Utica, New York. James's old friend John Hay (1838–1905), US Secretary of State under Presidents William McKinley and Theodore Roosevelt, had set his novel about an industrial dispute, *The Bread-Winners: A Social Study* (1884), in 'Buffland', a fictionalized version of Cleveland. In James's story 'Pandora' (1884), the heroine's social rise requires relocating her family from Utica to New York City: as one character observes, '"You can't have a social position at Utica any more than you can have an opera-box"' (Ch. 1; *NYE* XVIII, 120).

80 **the sport of fate**: A commonplace formula in poetry and verse drama from the late 17th century onwards. James used it often, e.g. in his American essay 'Washington' (1906), commenting on the misfortune of 'The American Woman' who has been left to sustain the whole of social life without male assistance: in accepting a bad bargain 'so confidently, so gleefully, yet so unguardedly,' 'she was to have been after all but the sport of fate' (*AS* 348). For a later reference to the Fates of classical mythology see note 797.

81 **I had been plotting arch-romance without knowing it**: For James's original belief in the realism of *The American*, see his response to Howells's disappointment with the conclusion of the novel: allowing Claire to marry Newman would have made for 'a prettier ending, certainly; but I should have felt as if I were throwing a rather vulgar sop to readers who don't really know the world & who don't measure the merit of a novel by its correspondence to the same' (30 March [1877]; *CLHJ 1876–1878* 1:88). The Preface's discussion of 'romance' as a literary mode revisits and extends ideas already articulated by James in essays on writers including Balzac, Flaubert, Hawthorne, George Sand, Edmond Rostand and Gabriele D'Annunzio; specific echoes are glossed in the following notes. James returns to the subject in the Preface to *NYE* XII, pp. 127–33.

82 **the artless schoolboys of Gray's beautiful Ode**: James alludes to Thomas Gray's 'Ode on a Distant Prospect of Eton College' (1747): 'Alas, regardless of their doom, / The little victims play! / No sense have they of ills to come, / Nor care beyond to-day' (ll. 51–4; *The Complete Poems of Thomas Gray*, ed. H. W. Starr and J. R. Hendrickson (Oxford: Clarendon Press, 1966), p. 8). In the same letter in which he defended the ending of *The American* to Howells (see note 81), James reported that a London acquaintance was going 'to take me some day soon down to Eton & show me an inside-view of the school, where her rosy little British boys are' (30 March [1877]; *CLHJ 1876–1878* 1:90).

83 **the shrunken depths of old work yet permit themselves to be sounded or […] "dragged": the long pole of memory stirs and rummages the bottom**: To 'sound' in this sense is 'To investigate (water, etc.) by the use of the line and lead or other means, in order to ascertain the depth or the quality of the bottom', and thus figuratively 'To measure, or ascertain, as by sounding'; to 'drag' is 'to search by means of a drag or grapnel as for the body of a person drowned' (*OED*). The combination of terms here recalls the episode of the drowned man of Esthwaite in William Wordsworth's *The Prelude*: 'some looked / In passive expectation from the shore, / While from a boat others hung o'er the deep, / Sounding with grappling irons and long poles' (1850 text, Book 5, ll. 444–7; *The Prelude or Growth of a Poet's Mind*, 2nd edn, ed. Ernest de Selincourt, rev. Helen Darbishire (Oxford: Clarendon Press, 1959), p. 163). There are some notable episodes of dragging rivers and pools for drowned persons in nineteenth-century fiction (e.g., for Zenobia in Hawthorne's *The Blithedale Romance* (1852), Ch. 27), but *The Prelude* seems especially relevant to James's concerns in the present Preface. Wordsworth takes autobiographical memory as a main subject and often uses images of water to figure its processes, as in the extended simile in Book 4 that compares the act of recollection to gazing into the waters of a lake: 'Such pleasant office have we long pursued / Incumbent o'er the surface of past time' (Book 4, ll. 271–2; p. 123).

84 **the Rue de Luxembourg […] the clear asphalt […] a sort of interlineation of sound**: From mid-November 1875 until early December 1876, James lived in an apartment on what was then rue de Luxembourg, in the Ier arrondissement. The street runs roughly north–south between rue de Rivoli and boulevard de la Madeleine. Its original name referred to the nearby *hôtel* and gardens of a seventeenth-century noble, the maréchal de Luxembourg; in August 1879, it was renamed rue Cambon after

Pierre-Joseph Cambon (1754/6–1820), an influential member of the Legislative Assembly and National Convention during the French Revolution who made the first proposal to create the Grand Livre de la Dette Publique (1792) (see Jacques Hillairet, *Dictionnaire historique des rues de Paris*, 7th edn, 2 vols. ([Paris]: Les Éditions de Minuit, 1979), vol. I, p. 260). On 18 November 1875, James described rue de Luxembourg as 'both central & noiseless' and his third-floor apartment at number 29 as 'snug' (to HJ Sr; *CLHJ 1872–1876* 3:9). Since this was late autumn, he presumably had his windows closed; the sounds of traffic commemorated in the Preface would become audible in the warmth of the following spring. As he wrote to Howells on 4 April 1876, resuming work on the novel in the certainty that it would appear in the *Atlantic Monthly* (see note 64): 'My windows are open, the spring is becoming serious, & the soft hum of this good old Paris comes into my sunny room' (*CLHJ 1872–1876* 3:95). The use of asphalt as a road surface was a feature of the comprehensive remodelling of Paris begun by Georges-Eugène Haussmann during his tenure as Prefect of the Seine *département* under Napoléon III (1853–70); this work continued into the Third Republic. In an essay from this period, 'Occasional Paris' (first published as 'Paris Revisited', January 1878), James had deplored 'The deadly monotony of the Paris that M. Haussmann called into being—its huge, blank, pompous, featureless sameness', and remarked of the just-completed avenue de l'Opéra: 'it smells of the modern asphalt' (*CTW2* 724). For the remembered circumstances of literary composition as an 'interlineation' of the printed text, see also the Preface to *NYE* X, p. 98.

85 **the vast domain attached in a rearward manner to one of the Ministères that front on the Place Vendôme**: James refers to the French Ministry of Justice, which was (and still is) located at Nos. 11 and 13 place Vendôme, on the west side of the square, backing onto rue de Luxembourg. The 'barracks' mentioned in this passage may have been attached to no. 7 place Vendôme, at this period the headquarters of the Paris military district (l'État-major de la Place de Paris); or to no. 9, the headquarters of the First Military Division and residence of the Military Governor of Paris. These indications appear on a contemporary street-map (Eduard Dumas-Vorzet, *Paris et Ses Environs* ([Paris]: Institut Geographique de Paris, 1878) retrievable from the Library of Congress (www.loc.gov/item/2012586603). See also Fernand de Saint Simon, *La Place Vendôme* (Paris: Éditions Vendôme, 1982), pp. 213–57.

86 **as I remount the stream of composition**: This figure of speech is habitual to James – there are four more occurrences in the Prefaces alone – and corresponds to the sense of the French verb *remonter* meaning to go upstream or retrace the course of a river. In James's unfinished time-travel romance *The Sense of the Past* (begun in 1899–1900), the American historian Ralph Pendrel is possessed by 'desire to remount the stream of time, really to bathe in its upper and more natural waters, to risk even, as he might say, drinking of them' (*SP* 47). In two essays on George Sand from the same period, James had spoken in these terms about rereading and textual memory, noting in 1897 that the publication of Sand's love letters to Alfred de Musset would allow readers of her novel *Elle et lui* (1859) – a fictionalized account of the affair – to 'remount to the origin of the volume' ('She and He: Recent Documents', *The Yellow Book* 12 (January 1897), 15–38; 17). Again, nearly thirty years after Sand's death in 1876, he judged that the publication of a new biography could only interest readers who were old enough to have read her while she was alive: 'The whole thing, of course, […] concerns at the best only those of us who can remount a little the stream of time' ('George Sand: The New Life', *North American Review* 174 (April 1902), 536–54; 538).

87 **a few weeks at Etretat […] a stay at Bayonne**: James spent the summer of 1876 out of Paris. He stayed for four weeks in July and August at the seaside town of Étretat on the Channel coast, where his American friends Edward Darley Boit and Mary Louisa Boit were summering. He next stayed for a fortnight with Edward Lee Childe and Blanche de Triqueti Childe at the Chateau de Varennes near Montargis, and then for a few days with Francis and Elizabeth Boott at Villiers-le-Bel just north of Paris. In September, he travelled south: first to Biarritz on the Basque coast, then to Bayonne where he found the Childes again and went with them to a bull-fight across the Spanish border in San Sebastián (see Leon Edel, *Henry James: The Conquest of London, 1870–1883* (London: Rupert Hart-Davis, 1962), pp. 263–7). These summer travels supplied copy for two essays, 'Etretat' (first published as 'A French Watering Place', 1876) and 'From Normandy to the Pyrenees' (1877) (*CTWC* 691–6, 697–720). As Adrian Poole notes, 'a critical phase' of James's novel *Confidence* (1879), Chapters 19–21, is set at Étretat (*The American*, ed. Poole (Oxford: Oxford University Press, 1999), p. 385).

88 **the fine historic and other "psychic" substance of Saint-Germain-en-Laye, a purple patch of terraced October before returning to Paris**: James came back from the south of France on 15 September 1876 to find

that his old apartment in rue de Luxembourg had been let in his absence; he was offered another apartment in the same building, but it would not be available until later that month. He moved first into a hotel on the opposite side of the Seine (see note 91), then left Paris again for the town of Saint-Germain-en-Laye, 12 miles north-west of the city (Edel, *Henry James: The Conquest of London*, p. 268). Saint-Germain has obvious 'historic' associations. It was a French royal residence until 1682, when Louis XIV moved the court to Versailles, and James II of England and VII of Scotland established his court in exile at the Château de Saint-Germain-en-Laye after the 'Glorious Revolution' of 1688; the town supported a Jacobite colony until the French Revolution. It is less clear what James means by the 'other "psychic" substance' of Saint-Germain. In the eighteenth century, the town was the focus of an investigation by the Académie des Sciences when the ventriloquial performances of a local grocer, M. de Saint-Gille, were taken for spirit voices: this anecdote had a wide currency in the early nineteenth century and appears in David Brewster's *Letters on Natural Magic, Addressed to Sir Walter Scott, Bart.* (1832), Letter VII. It may also be relevant that the controversial Scottish spirit medium Daniel Dunglas Home (1833–86), whose international fame had begun in the United States in the 1850s, was buried at Saint-Germain. For James's acquaintance with the Society for Psychical Research and other contemporary efforts to explain paranormal phenomena in scientific terms, see note 463. Saint-Germain is also the setting of a story which James published shortly before the period referred to in the Preface: 'Madame de Mauves' (1874) opens on the stone terrace constructed for Louis XIV by André Le Nôtre, with a celebrated view toward Paris. At the end of September, James told his mother: 'I have enjoyed nothing all Summer more than these few days on this noble terrace & in this enchanting old forest; with autumn clouds tumbling over it all, & yet the warm sunshine sufficiently transpiercing them' (27 September 1876; *CLHJ 1872–1876* 3:187–8). A 'purple patch' is originally 'An elaborate or excessively ornate passage in a literary composition', and hence 'A notable or colourful period of time, a person's life, etc.' (*OED*). As in other passages of the Preface, James is not quite right about dates: in fact, he returned to Paris from Saint-Germain before the start of October.

89 **the light somehow, as one always feels, of "style" itself**: In *A Small Boy and Others*, James would similarly associate the abstract quality of 'style' with Parisian visual art and architecture. In Chapter 25, recalling walks

across Paris in childhood to look at the collection of modern art at the Palais du Luxembourg, he evokes a memory of rue Tournon: 'Style, dimly described, looked down there, as with conscious encouragement, from the high grey-headed, clear-faced, straight-standing old houses'; later in the same chapter, the 'wondrous Galerie d'Apollon' in the Louvre serves as a 'bridge over to Style […], drawn out for me as a long but assured initiation' (*Aut* 204, 208).

90   **I was to pass over to London that autumn**: As early as July 1876, James was writing to his brother William of yielding to 'a long-encroaching weariness & satiety with the French mind & its utterance': 'Easy & smooth-flowing as life is in Paris, I would throw it over to morrow for an even very small chance to plant myself for a while in England. If I had but a single good friend in London I would go thither' (29 July [1876]; *CLHJ 1872–1876* 3:161). By the end of October, he had 'about decided to remove to London on Dec. 1st' (to WJ, 23 October [1876]; *CLHJ 1872–1876* 3:206).

91   **a small dusky hotel of the Rive Gauche, […] Balzac's Maison Vauquer in "Le Père Goriot"**: Finding his old apartment unavailable in mid-September 1876 (see note 88), James decamped to 'a quiet inn on the dusky side of the river' in rue de Beaune, just off Quai Voltaire in the *VIIe arrondissement* (to HJ Sr, 16 September [1876]; *CLHJ 1872–1876* 3:183). Leon Edel identifies this 'inn' as the Hôtel Lorraine, where James had dined with James Russell Lowell on an earlier visit to Paris in November 1872 (*Henry James: The Conquest of London*, pp. 268, 76–8). Parisians distinguish between left and right banks of the Seine: the 'Rive Gauche' – the left-hand bank when facing downstream – is the southern side of the river. The Maison Vauquer, a shabby boarding-house on the southern edge of the *quartier Latin*, is the central setting of Balzac's novel *Le Père Goriot* (1835). In an 1875 essay, James had declared: 'The portrait of the Maison Vauquer and its inmates is one of the most portentous settings of the scene in all the literature of fiction'; the house itself is 'the stage of vast dramas, […] a sort of concentrated focus of human life, with sensitive nerves radiating out into the infinite' (*LC2* 52, 60).

92   **a black-framed Empire portrait-medallion**: James refers to oval- or round-framed profile portraits, reliefs typically cast in bronze or modelled in unglazed biscuit porcelain or stoneware. The neoclassical 'Empire' style of architecture and décor flourished under the First French Empire of Napoleon I (1804–14, 1815). In the scenario for *The Ambassadors* (1903) which he dictated on 1 September 1900, James envisaged this later

Parisian novel as a serial in ten or twelve parts, 'each very full, as it were, and charged—like a rounded medallion, in a series of a dozen, hung, with its effect of high relief, on a wall' (*CFHJ* 18, 540).

93 **a belated Saint Martin's summer**: A 'St Martin's summer' is 'a season of fine, mild weather occurring about Martinmas' (*OED*); the feast-day of St Martin falls on 11 November. In a notebook entry of 13 July 1891, at the age of 48, James had referred thus to the literary work he felt he was still capable of: 'Go on, my boy, & strike hard; have a rich & long St. Martin's Summer. Try everything, do everything, render everything—be an artist, be distinguished, to the last' (*CN* 58). The dating of the Preface's meteorological recollections is approximate. In early October 1876, James had noted that the Parisian autumn was 'turning out very mild & delightful—indeed almost too warm'; by the actual date of Martinmas a month later, winter had 'begun in earnest' (to HJ Sr, 11 October [1876], 11 November [1876]; *CLHJ 1872–1876* 3:198, 215).

94 **I infer […] that I did not in the event drag over the Channel a lengthening chain**: James's inference is wrong: he had not in fact completed *The American* when he crossed from France to England on 10 December 1876. On 18 December, he wrote to Howells from London enclosing the eleventh instalment of the novel, 'which I have been keeping to post in England, as I never feel that I can take precautions enough'; the twelfth and last instalment 'will soon follow' (*CLHJ 1876–1878* 1:9). The phrase 'a lengthening chain' occurs in the poem *The Traveller, Or A Prospect of Society* (1765) by the Irish poet and novelist Oliver Goldsmith: 'Where'er I roam, whatever realms to see, / My heart untravell'd fondly turns to thee; / Still to my brother turns, with ceaseless pain, / And drags at each remove a lengthening chain' (ll. 7–10; *The Collected Works of Oliver Goldsmith*, ed. Arthur Friedman, 5 vols. (Oxford: Clarendon Press, 1966), vol. IV, p. 249). James would have found this phrase quoted and significantly elaborated upon in the second essay of Washington Irving's *The Sketch Book of Geoffrey Crayon, Gent.* (1819–20), 'The Voyage', which refers to a transatlantic crossing from America to Europe; the same formula occurs in the Preface to *The Reverberator* with reference to a reluctant return passage (p. 154). Compare also James's essay 'The London Theatres' (1877), written shortly after his relocation in December 1876: 'Removing lately from Paris to the British metropolis, I received a great many impressions—a sort of unbroken chain, in which the reflections passing through my fancy as I tried the different orchestra-stalls were the concluding link' (*CWAD2* 210). For the

relevance of all these figures to the 'chain of relation and responsibility' which is reconstituted by textual revision in the *Golden Bowl* Preface, see note 936.

95 **the general privilege of the artist**: An exhibition of portraits by the English artist G. F. Watts (1817–1904) had suggested to James in 1897 that 'all this experience on the part of the painter, all this luxury of surrender to the claim, to the possibilities, of another personality, is in itself a high form of success': 'the privilege of an artist of this temperament is perhaps greater still than his work. It represents indeed an enviable happiness' (*CWAD1* 496). Four years earlier, he had been puzzled and dismayed by the evidence given in Gustave Flaubert's letters of a wholly different attitude towards the artist's privilege, one characterized mainly by dissatisfaction and disgust: 'Why was [Flaubert] so unhappy if he was so active; why was he so intolerant if he was so strong? […] Why feel, and feel genuinely, so much about "art," in order to feel so little about its privilege?' (*LC2* 312–13).

96 **the great extension […] of experience and of consciousness; with the toil and trouble a mere sun-cast shadow**: In his introduction to *The Tempest* – which must have been written close in time to the Preface to *The American*, in January or February 1907 – James had imagined Shakespeare as the superlative case of such an 'extension': 'the spirit in hungry quest of every possible experience and adventure of the spirit' (*LC1* 1218). The phrase he uses here for the artist's difficulties has a Shakespearean source in the witches' incantation in *Macbeth* (1606): 'Double, double, toil and trouble; / Fire burn, and cauldron bubble' (4.1.10–11, 20–1, 35–6); and the 'shadow' in this sentence of the Preface may echo Macbeth's soliloquy prompted by the death of his wife: 'Out, out, brief candle! / Life's but a walking shadow' (5.5.23–4).

97 **Robert Louis Stevenson […] not having to pay half his substance for his luxurious immersion**: The reference is to a passage in Stevenson's 'A Letter to a Young Gentleman Who Proposes to Embrace the Career of Art' (1888), an essay which James had described in 1900 as a 'little mine of felicities' ('LRLS' 73). As Stevenson puts it there, the artist 'has already, in the practice of his art, more than his share of the rewards of life': 'The direct returns—the wages of the trade—are small, but the indirect—the wages of the life—are incalculably great. […] Suppose it ill paid: the wonder is it should be paid at all. Other men pay, and pay dearly, for pleasures

less desirable' (*The Works of Robert Louis Stevenson*, 28 vols. (Edinburgh: printed by T. and A. Constable, 1894–8), vol. XI, pp. 309, 305–6).

98 **the torment of expression**: James appears to be translating a French formula frequently used by Gustave Flaubert to refer to the difficulty of literary composition: 'les affres du style'. As Flaubert wrote to George Sand on 5 March 1866, for example: 'Vous ne savez pas, vous, ce que c'est que de rester toute une journée la tête dans ses deux mains à pressurer sa malheureuse cervelle pour trouver un mot. […] Ah! je les aurai connues, les *Affres du style!*' ('You don't know what it is to spend a whole day with your head in your hands, squeezing your miserable brain to find a word. […] Ah! I shall have known the *Terrors of style!*') (*Lettres de Gustave Flaubert à George Sand* (Paris: G. Charpentier et Cie, 1884), p. 5). Reviewing Flaubert's letters in 1893, James noted that 'Literature and life were a single business to him, and the "torment of style," that might occasionally intermit in one place, was sufficiently sure to break out in another' (*LC2* 301). For the contemporary English currency of this phrase, see 'Greville Fane' (1892), where we are told that the popular novelist whose pen-name gives the story its title 'never recognised the "torment of form"; the furthest she went was to introduce into one of her books […] a young poet who was always talking about it' (*NYE* XVI, 115). Mark Ambient complains of '"the torment of execution!"' in 'The Author of Beltraffio' (Ch. 3; *NYE* XVI, 43).

99 **how, after his fashion, he will have lived!**: Compare James's review of *The Letters of Robert Louis Stevenson to His Family and Friends* (1900): 'The free life would have been all [Stevenson's] dream, if so large a part of it had not been that love of letters, of expression and form, which is but another name for the life of service. Almost the last word about him, by the same law, would be that he had at any rate supremely written, were it not that he seems still better characterized by his having at any rate supremely lived' ('LRLS' 65).

100 **malice prepense**: The legal phrase means 'malice aforethought; wrong or injury purposely done' (*OED*, 'prepense'). James uses it again in the Preface to *The Awkward Age*, again pleading an honest artistic misjudgement: 'the developed situations that one would never with malice prepense have undertaken' (p. 79).

101 **what craft of selection, omission or commission**: The last two paired words associate more readily with 'sin' than with 'craft': Christian doctrine

distinguishes between 'sins of omission', or failures to perform a duty or good action, and 'sins of commission', or positive transgressions.

102 **Scott, [...] Balzac, [...] Zola, [...] the deflexion toward either quarter has never taken place**: Sir Walter Scott (1771–1832), bestselling Scottish poet and novelist, anonymous author of two series of historical fictions, the Waverley Novels and the Tales of My Landlord; Émile Zola (1840–1902), French novelist, journalist and playwright, the author of 'Les Rougon-Maquart', a series of novels following two branches of a single family throughout the period of the Second Empire (1852–70). For Honoré de Balzac, see note 34. Balzac notably figures in James's earlier criticism as an example of the coexistence of opposed imaginative tendencies. Thus in 1875, for example: 'There are two writers in Balzac—the spontaneous one and the reflective one' (*LC2* 44); and in 1902: 'Of imagination, on one side, all compact, he was on the other an insatiable reporter of the immediate, the material, the current combination, perpetually moved by the historian's impulse to fix them, preserve them, explain them' ('HdB' x). In the 1902 essay, James had found himself unable to judge whether Balzac's portrayals of noble ladies were 'directly historic or only, quite misguidedly, romantic' ('HdB' xl).

103 **not that the strange and the far are at all necessarily romantic**: In a public letter written in 1904 for the centenary of Nathaniel Hawthorne's birth, James had praised Hawthorne's 'charming discrimination [...] of looking for romance near at hand, and where it grows thick and true, rather than on the other side of the globe and in the Dictionary of Dates. We see it, nowadays, more and more, inquired and bargained for in places and times that are strange and indigestible to us; and for the most part, I think, we see those who deal in it on these terms come back from their harvest with their hands smelling, under their brave leather gauntlets, or royal rings, or whatever, of the plain domestic blackberry, the homeliest growth of our actual dusty waysides' (*LC1* 470–1).

104 **many definitions of romance, [...] pistols and knives**: In his 1904 letter on Hawthorne, James dismisses 'the mechanical, at best the pedantic, view' that romance is definable by conformity to a 'list of romantic properties': 'this, that or the other particular set of complications, machinations, co-incidences or escapes, this, that or the other fashion of fire-arm or cutlass, cock of hat, frizzle of wig, violence of scuffle or sound of expletive: mere accidents and outward patches, all, of the engaging mystery' (*LC1* 471).

105 **the flowery plains of heaven**: James may be referring to the Elysian Fields of classical Greek mythology, the resting-place of the souls of heroes and the virtuous; or to depictions of the Christian Heaven like the nineteenth-century English artist John Martin's vast painting *The Plains of Heaven* (1851–3).

106 **the size and "number"**: For an example of this sense of 'number' from the period of *The American*, see a letter from James's stay in Paris that refers respectively to his sister Alice and sister-in-law Caroline: 'Tell Alice to send me (what she believes to be) Carrie's number in gloves. I want to send her a pair or two' (to WJ, 14 March [1876]; *CLHJ 1872–1876* 3:82).

107 **It would be impossible to have a more romantic temper than Flaubert's Madame Bovary, and yet nothing less resembles a romance than the record of her adventures**: James had made the same point in his 1902 introduction to *Madame Bovary*. Flaubert's heroine is 'an embodiment of helpless romanticism' ('GF' xv), but the novel's success lies in its unsparingly realistic portrayal of the contrast between her imagination and the limits of her life as 'a country doctor's wife in a petty Norman town': 'Emma Bovary's poor adventures are a tragedy for the very reason that, in a world unsuspecting, unassisting, unconsoling, she has herself to distil the rich and the rare' ('GF' xiv, xv).

108 **the "run" of one or another sort of play**: A 'run' in this sense is 'A continuous sequence of theatrical performances; a continuous period of being put on stage' (*OED*).

109 **experience disengaged, disembroiled, disencumbered, [...] the inconvenience of a *related*, a measurable state**: James had anticipated the terms of this definition in two essays written in 1904, yet had also discriminated *within* the category of 'romance' on the basis of a greater or lesser degree of relatedness to the real. On Hawthorne: 'he saw the quaintness or the weirdness, the interest *behind* the interest, of things [...] as something deeply within us, not as something infinitely disconnected from us', and this makes his romances 'singularly fruitful examples of the real as distinguished from the artificial romantic note' (*LC1* 471). And on Gabriele D'Annunzio, referring to his novel *Le vergini delle rocce*: 'if its tone is thoroughly romantic, the romance is yet of the happiest kind, the kind that consists in the imaginative development of observable things, things present, significant, related to us, and not in a weak false fumble for the remote and the disconnected' ('GDA' 408).

110 **The balloon of experience is in fact of course tied to the earth, [...] from the moment that cable is cut we are at large and unrelated**: James had used a comparable figure in 1897 to assess the hazards of George Sand's 'wonderful charm of expression', a quality that enabled her to 'set the subject, whatever it be, afloat in the upper air': 'This is no drawback when she is on the ground of her own life, to which she is tied, in truth, by a certain number of tangible threads; but to embark on one of her confessed fictions is to have [...] a little too much the feeling of going up in a balloon. We are borne by a fresh, cool current, and the car delightfully dangles; but as we peep over the sides we see things—as we usually know them—at a dreadful drop beneath' ('She and He: Recent Documents', 36). A hot-air balloon also occurs in the notes James dictated in 1914 for his romance of time-travel *The Sense of the Past*, a case of still greater disconnection from the ground of the real: 'Ralph, taking leave of the Ambassador, the depositary of his extraordinary truth and the (as he hopes) secured connection with the world he cuts himself loose from, dropping as from a balloon thousands of feet up in the air, and not really knowing what smash or what magically *soft* concussion awaits him—Ralph, as I say, in entering the house then walks at a step straight into 1820' (*SP* 296).

111 **the thread of which, from beginning to end, is not once exchanged, however momentarily, for any other thread**: In fact we are given direct access to other, minor characters' past or present experience on several occasions in the novel: e.g., to M. Nioche's in Chapters 1 and 4, to Mrs Tristram's in Chapters 3 and 10, and to Mr Babcock's in Chapter 5.

112 **the pomp and circumstance**: James alludes to lines spoken by Shakespeare's Othello in the first throes of sexual jealousy: 'Farewell the neighing steed and the shrill trump, / The spirit-stirring drum, th'ear-piercing fife, / The royal banner, and all quality, / Pride, pomp, and circumstance of glorious war!' (3.3. 351–4). A commonplace throughout the nineteenth century, this formula gained a further popular currency from its use by the English composer Edward Elgar (1857–1934), the first three of whose 'Pomp and Circumstance' military marches (op. 39) had been premiered by the time James wrote the Preface to *The American*: Nos. 1 and 2 in 1901, and No. 3 in 1905. No. 4 was first performed on 24 August 1907, between the composition of the Preface and the publication of the novel as *NYE* II (Michael Kennedy, *Portrait of Elgar*, 3rd edn (Oxford: Clarendon Press, 1987), pp. 345–8).

113 **not have "minded" in the least any drawback**: For the inverted commas around the verb here, compare a passage in James's recent essay 'Boston' (1906) that similarly emphasizes money as removing the sense of drawbacks: 'To make so much money that you won't, that you don't "mind," don't mind anything—that is absolutely, I think, the main American formula' (*AS* 237).

114 **to haul him and his fortune into their boat**: The Preface here echoes – and reverses – a violent simile in *The American*, in which the actual (not would-be) husband of a Bellegarde is pushed out of (not hauled into) a boat. This comes at the crisis of the back-story in Chapter 22, when Mrs Bread states her belief that old Madame de Bellegarde murdered her sick husband by pouring away his medicine, telling him that she wanted to kill him and fixing him with '"her dreadful eyes"': '"You know my lady's eyes, I think, sir; it was with that look of hers she killed him; it was with the terrible strong will and all the cruelty she put into it. It was as if she had pushed him out of her boat, fevered and sick, into the cold sea, and remained there to push him again should he try to scramble back"' (*NYE* II, 461). The nautical figure in the second sentence quoted here was added in revision: Mrs Bread had originally said of Madame de Bellegarde's look simply that '"It was like a frost on flowers"' (*CE* VII, 149).

115 **to trace the dividing-line between the real and the romantic**: Compare James's 1901 essay on the French dramatist Edmond Rostand (1868–1918): 'By what sign in advance do we know the romantic? by what sign do we know the real? and by what instrument do we, as they diverge, measure their divergence?' (*CWAD2* 483). In the case of another French author, James found the dividing line comparatively easy to trace: he noted in 1902 that Flaubert 'was formed, intellectually, of two quite distinct compartments, a sense of the real and a sense of the romantic', and that the 'divisions' thus produced in his work 'are as marked as the sections on the back of a scarab' ('GF' xii–xiii).

116 **from that admirable position we "assist."**: To 'assist' in this sense means 'To be present (at a ceremony, entertainment, etc.), whether simply as a spectator, or taking part in the proceedings'; the former sense is 'now treated as a French idiom', from *assister à* (*OED*). Newman occupies a comparable position in the first stages of his courtship. An extended simile in Chapter 7 shows him thinking about his visit to Madame de Cintré in theatrical terms ('He felt as if he were at the play and as if his own speaking would be an

interruption'), and in Chapter 9 she remarks: "'You've sat and watched my visitors as comfortably as from a box at the opera'" (*NYE* II, 144, 166).

117 **the intensity of the creative effort to get into the skin of the creature**: James associated this mode of fictional imagination with Balzac. In his 1902 introduction for an English translation of *Mémoires de deux jeunes mariées* (1841), he notes that Balzac 'gets, for further intensity, into the very skin' of his two heroines ('HdB' xlii). And in 'The Lesson of Balzac': 'what he liked was absolutely to get into the constituted consciousness, into all the clothes, gloves and whatever else, into the very skin and bones, of the habited, featured, colored, articulated form of life that he desired to present' (*LC2* 132).

118 **an evening at the opera quite alone**: This evening occurs in Chapter 17. As Poole notes, when James revised the novel for the *NYE* he made changes in the same chapter 'to reduce the implausibility [...] of Newman's failure to spend more time with [Claire]' after the announcement of their engagement (*The American*, ed. Poole, p. 378). In the revised text, Claire explains to Newman 'a little strangely' that 'it was convenient, important, in fact vital to her' that they should see each other only for a 'single daily hour of reinvoked and reasserted confidence' (*NYE* II, 356); in the 1883 Collective Edition, his visit to her at this juncture is 'brief' but there is no equivalent for her stipulation (*CE* VII, 68).

119 **to "back out"**: This 'colloquial' phrase means 'To retreat cautiously and tacitly; from stable phraseology; *e.g.*, the BACKING OUT of a horse' (*Slang* I:89). The idiom occurs in the novel, but it is not applied to Claire de Cintré. In Chapter 12, referring to her consent to his marriage, Newman asks old Madame de Bellegarde: "'You'll not back out, eh?" "I don't know what you mean by 'backing out,'" said the Marquise with no small majesty. "It suggests a movement of which I think no Bellegarde has ever been guilty'" (*NYE* II, 234).

120 **a light plank [...] over a dark "psychological" abyss**: As Poole notes, this figure in the Preface recalls the metaphorical 'bridge' which Newman imagines in Chapter 13 when thinking about his relation to Claire (*The American*, ed. Poole, p. 378): 'she saw, he made out, that he had built a bridge which would bear the very greatest weight she should throw on it, and it was for him often, all charmingly, as if she were admiring from this side and that the bold span of arch and the high line of the parapet—as if indeed on occasion she stood straight there at the spring, just watching him at *his* extremity and with nothing, when the hour should strike, to

prevent her crossing with a rush' (*NYE* II, 245). This whole passage was added in revision.

121 **any occasional extra inch or so […] see me through my wood**: Valentin refers to Newman's height in Chapter 7 as he thinks about what he envies in his new friend: '"It's not your superfluous stature, though I should have rather liked to be a couple of inches taller"' (*NYE* II, 137). The 'extra inch' that might make a character more impressive was not for James necessarily a matter of stature, either physical or moral. Writing on George Eliot in 1866, he had complained that the eponymous hero of *Adam Bede* was 'too good. He is meant, I conceive, to be every inch a man; but, to my mind, there are several inches wanting. He lacks spontaneity and sensibility, he is too stiff-backed. He lacks that supreme quality without which a man can never be interesting to men,—the capacity to be tempted' (*LC1* 923). According to *OED*, to be 'in a wood' is to be 'in a difficulty, trouble, or perplexity; at a loss'; and the phrase 'out of the wood' is defined with reference to a rare or obsolete sense of 'wood' as 'A collection or crowd of spears or the like (suggesting the trees of a wood); gen. a collection, crowd, "lot", "forest"' – thus, a figurative thicket of difficulties, obstructions, etc. In letters from the period of the *NYE*, James repeatedly used this phrase to announce – with indefeasible optimism – that he had just emerged, or was on the point of emerging, from a particularly difficult phase of work. Thus, he wrote to Charles Scribner's Sons on 17 February 1907, apologising for taking so long over the revision of *The American*: 'But it is, thank goodness, ended; the aspect of the book is essentially improved, its attraction augmented, &, above all, I am now "out of the wood"' (Princeton). And to Owen Wister on 28 August 1907: 'But I am at last out of the wood; as I go on—in the order of time—there are fewer t's to cross & i's to dot' (Owen Wister Papers, 1829–1966, Manuscript Division, Library of Congress, Washington, DC. General Correspondence, 1875–1936. Box 25). See also his letters to Col. George Harvey, 6 September 1907 (*LL* 448); to Edith Wharton, 7 March 1908 (*HJEW* 89); to his nephew Harry James, 3 April 1908 (*LHJ* 2:99); and to Ellen Emmet, 2 November 1908 (*HJL* 4:499). Writing to Howard Sturgis on 17 October 1907, James combined this figure of speech with an allusion to the opening lines of Dante's *Inferno*, promising to visit Sturgis 'at the very 1st slight clearing of my *selva oscura*, my just now exceptionally dark & thick wood, a perfect tangle of occupation' (*Dearly Beloved Friends: Henry James's Letters to Younger Men*, ed. Susan E. Gunter and Steven H. Jobe (Ann Arbor, MI: University of

Michigan Press, 2001), p. 149). The colloquial phrase *to hallo* (cry) *before one is out of the wood* means 'To reckon beforehand upon a successful issue' (*Slang* II:91).

122 **his prompt general profession […] of aspiring to a "great" marriage**: Newman tells the Tristrams in Chapter 3 that he wants to marry '"a great woman"' (*NYE* II, 49).

123 **my aching void**: An allusion to the first of Cowper's contributions to the volume *Olney Hymns* (1779), titled 'Walking with God': 'What peaceful Hours I then enjoy'd! / How sweet their Mem'ry still! / But they have left an Aching Void, / The World can never fill' (ll. 9–12; *The Poetical Works of William Cowper*, 4th edn, ed. H. S. Milford (London: Geoffrey Cumberlege, Oxford University Press, 1934), p. 433). James had recently used this phrase in his American travel essay 'New England: An Autumn Impression' (1905) to register the sense of 'something deficient, absent' amid the 'democratic intensity' of the modern Boston and Cambridge, Massachusetts: 'in which case it was for the aching void to be (as an aching void) striking and interesting' (*AS* 56).

PREFACE to *The Portrait of a Lady* (*NYE* III–IV)

124 **begun in Florence, during three months spent there in the spring of 1879**: As James records in a retrospective notebook entry made in Boston on 25 November 1881, it was in fact in the spring of 1880 that he properly started work on the novel, during 'a couple of months' (April and May) spent in Florence: 'At the Hotel de l'Arno, in a room in that deep recess, in the front, I began the *Portrait of a Lady*—that is I took up, and worked over, an old beginning, made long before' (*CN* 219).

125 **designed for publication in "The Atlantic Monthly,"**: As early as 24 October 1876, during the serial run of *The American*, James had written to W. D. Howells about his next book: 'My novel is to be an Americana— the adventures in Europe of a female [Christopher] Newman.' That is recognisably *The Portrait of a Lady*, but the novel was not unambiguously 'designed for' the *Atlantic Monthly* at this point. As James explained to Howells, the journal's editor, the 'financial necessity' of publishing more serial fiction than the *Atlantic* could carry meant he had to write for other periodicals too: 'When my novels (if they ever do) bring me enough money to carry me over the intervals I shall be very glad to stick to the

Atlantic' (*CLHJ 1872–1876* 3:210). An early plan to serialize *The Portrait* in *Scribner's Monthly* came to nothing. On 15 March 1878, James told his mother that the novel was 'still on my hands' and had been offered 'again' to another periodical, *Lippincott's Magazine* (to MWJ; *CLHJ 1876–1878* 2:63), apparently without success. The following summer, Howells asked him for 'a novel for next year' (James to Howells, [c.18 July 1879]; *CLHJ 1878–1880* 1:238). James, however, wanted to serialize *The Portrait* simultaneously in Britain and the US, and the *Atlantic Monthly* made a point of not publishing serials that would also appear in British periodicals. This brought yet another American journal, *Harper's New Monthly Magazine*, into the frame. As James observed, 'If I publish in Macmillan or the Cornhill I can double my profits by appearing also in Harper, & I shall have, to a certain extent, to remember this in arranging to appear in one periodical exclusively' (*CLHJ 1878–1880* 1:238).

126 **one of the last occasions of simultaneous "serialisation" in the two countries [...] up to then left unaltered**: The idea of simultaneous transatlantic serialisation was first put to James in December 1877 by the English publisher Frederick Macmillan, who had offered to run *The Europeans* (1878) – already accepted by Howells for the *Atlantic Monthly* – in *Macmillan's Magazine*. That proved impossible to arrange, but in 1880 *Washington Square* was published as a serial in *Harper's New Monthly Magazine* and the *Cornhill Magazine*, and James was eager to publish *The Portrait* in this way also. The *Atlantic* usually made a point of not sharing its serials with British periodicals. Howells, however, was seeking simultaneous serialisation for his own novels at this time, and James had recently approached the *Cornhill* and *Macmillan's* on Howells's behalf, which probably strengthened his own cause (see the introduction to Michael Anesko's edition of *The Portrait*, *CFHJ* 6, lviii–lx). In August 1879, at any rate, Howells agreed to take *The Portrait* on these terms (*CLHJ 1878–1880* 1:262), and the novel was eventually serialized in *Macmillan's* (October 1880–November 1881) and the *Atlantic* (November 1880–December 1881). James's experience of this mode of serial publication would be short-lived: apart from *What Maisie Knew*, which ran in the American *Chap-Book* (January–May 1897) and the British *New Review* (February–June 1897), no other novel of his was simultaneously serialized in both countries. That was probably due as much to his changing relationship with the *Atlantic Monthly* as to what this sentence of the Preface calls 'the changing conditions of literary intercourse between England and the United States'. As Ellery Sedgwick notes, *The Portrait of a Lady* 'had not helped circulation of

the *Atlantic*, which had paid $3500 to serialize it, partly because copies of *Macmillan's*, which had paid only $1580 to carry each installment a month earlier, were available in the United States before the corresponding *Atlantic* number was issued' (Sedgwick, 'Henry James and the *Atlantic Monthly*: Editorial Perspectives on James' "Friction with the Market"', *Studies in Bibliography* 45 (1992), 311–32; 317). Prior to the passing of the Chase Act in 1891 (see note 730), in order to protect an American author's copyright in both territories a transatlantic serial could not appear first in the US; and because copies of the *Atlantic* actually appeared two weeks ahead of the journal's cover date, if *The Portrait* had been serialized with nominal simultaneity – i.e., had begun in the October 1880 issues of both periodicals – James would have failed to secure the British and colonial copyrights to the novel. The American serialization thus began in the November 1880 number of the *Atlantic*, with the consequence that eager American readers could read instalments of the novel first in imported copies of the previous month's *Cornhill* (*CFHJ* 6, lx–lxi). This was not a satisfactory arrangement for Houghton, Mifflin – the publishers of the *Atlantic Monthly* – and they 'henceforward ruled out all simultaneous publication' for James's serials (Sedgwick, 'Henry James and the *Atlantic Monthly*', 317).

127 **a stay of several weeks made in Venice**: See James's notebook entry of 25 November 1881 for this Venetian stage of composition, which lasted from late March of the same year until 'the last of June—between three and four months': 'It was a charming time; one of those things that don't repeat themselves; I seemed to myself to grow young again' (*CN* 221).

128 **Riva Schiavoni, […] San Zaccaria**: Riva degli Schiavoni begins near the Doge's Palace and extends to the Arsenale, and has a southerly view over the Venetian lagoon past the island of San Giorgio Maggiore and its Palladian church. A few yards to the west of James's lodging, a small passage leads off to Campo San Zaccaria and its church. As James recalls in his notebook entry of 25 November 1881: 'I lodged on the Riva, 4161, 4° p° [*quarto piano*: fourth floor]. The view from my windows was "una bellezza;" [a thing of beauty] the far-shining lagoon, the pink walls of San Giorgio, the downward curve of the Riva, the distant islands, the movement of the quay, the gondolas in profile. Here I wrote, diligently every day & finished, or virtually finished, my novel' (*CN* 221). James's essay 'Venice' (1882) also describes his lodgings, the view and the church of San Zaccaria (*PPL* 14–18, 32).

129 **a questionable aid to concentration**: James had noted the 'dreadful lure' of 'Venetian windows and balconies' in his 1882 essay on the city, remarking that 'Venice is not, in fair weather, a place for concentration of mind. The effort required for sitting down to a writing-table is heroic, and the brightest page of MS. looks dull beside the brilliancy of your *milieu*' (*PPL* 17). He had experienced the same difficulty in Florence the previous spring: asking Howells to delay the serialization of *Portrait* by two months, he explained that he had come away 'from London & its uproar, its distractions & interruptions, in order to concentrate myself upon my work. But if London is uproarious, Italy is insidious, perfidious, fertile in pretexts for one's haunting its lovely sights & scenes rather than one's writing=table; so that, in respect to my novel, it has been a month lost rather than gained' (18 April [1880]; *CLHJ 1878–1880* 2:167).

130 **a peddler who has given him the wrong change**: Encounters with peddlers and other merchants are recurring features of James's imaginative response to Italy. In *William Wetmore Story and His Friends* (1903), he had recently dreamed of haggling over prices 'in the Florentine street' with an antique-dealer whose card he had found amongst the Storys' journals (*WWS* I:97–8). In his lecture 'The Novel in *The Ring and the Book*' (1912), he would figure reading Robert Browning's long poem about a historical Italian murder trial in comparable terms: 'picking over and over [...], like some lingering talking pedlar's client, his great unloosed pack' (*LC1* 803).

131 **the Venetian cry [...] come in once more at the window**: Compare James's remarks in the 1882 Venice essay on the cries of gondoliers ('a vocal race'): 'the voice of the gondolier is, in fact, the sound of Venice. [...] There is no noise there save distinctly human noise; no rumbling, no vague uproar, nor rattle of wheels and hoofs. It is all articulate, personal sound.' Local acoustics favour this impression: 'The still water carries the voice, and good Venetians exchange confidences at a distance of half a mile' (*PPL* 19–20). In 'The Grand Canal' (1892), James writes of Venetian ferrymen and gondoliers: 'their voices travel far; they enter your windows and mingle even with your dreams' (Richard Harding Davis, W. W. Story, Andrew Lang, Henry James, Francisque Sarcey, Paul Lindau and Isabel F. Hapgood, *Great Streets of the World* (New York: Charles Scribner's Sons, 1892), pp. 141–72; 161).

132 **Strangely fertilising [...] does a wasted effort of attention often prove**: In 'The Lesson of Balzac' (1905), James had proposed that 'it is in the

waste [...]—the waste of time, of passion, of curiosity, of contact—that true initiation resides' for the artist (*LC2* 130). Compare his early review of Hippolyte Taine's *Histoire de la littérature anglaise* (1866–9) in an English translation of 1872: Taine was both a foreigner and 'a man with a method, the apostle of a theory', and so 'in the nature of the case his treatment of the subject lacks that indefinable quality of spiritual initiation which is the tardy consummate fruit of a wasteful, purposeless, passionate sympathy' (*LC2* 843).

133 **the germ of my idea**: James habitually speaks of the original conception of a fiction as its 'germ': 'An initial stage or state from which something may develop; a source, a beginning' (*OED*). The term occurs in his criticism at least as early as 1884, in the essay on Turgenev quoted in note 136, and he consistently applies it to his own work in his notebooks and in documents such as the 1900 'Project of Novel' for *The Ambassadors*, as well as throughout the Prefaces. Later Prefaces play on biological senses of the word as 'A seed or spore' and 'the causative agent or source of a disease, esp. an infectious disease' (*OED*): see, for example, the account of the origin and growth of *The Spoils of Poynton* in the Preface to *NYE* X, pp. 94–6, 98, 99–100.

134 **not at all in any conceit of a "plot," nefarious name**: James plays on two meanings of the word 'plot': 'The plan or scheme of a literary or dramatic work' and 'A plan made in secret by a group of people, esp. to achieve an unlawful end; a conspiracy' (*OED*). Such a conspiracy *is* the central narrative mechanism of *The Portrait of a Lady*. In Chapter 40, Isabel, still unaware of the true nature of her husband's prior relationship with Madame Merle, believes that 'the sole source of her mistake [in marrying Osmond] had been within herself. There had been no plot, no snare; she had looked and considered and chosen' (*NYE* IV, 160).

135 **a remark that I heard fall years ago from the lips of Ivan Turgenieff** [...] **the usual origin of the fictive picture**: The Russian novelist, short-story writer and playwright Ivan Sergeyevich Turgenev (1818–83), whose acquaintance James made in Paris in the winter of 1875–6. James published several reviews and critical surveys of his work between 1874 and 1896 (see *LC2* 968–1034). In a letter from the early weeks of their friendship, James summarized a conversation that sounds like the original of the occasion recalled here: Turgenev 'said he had never <u>invented</u> anything or any one. Every thing in his stories comes from some figure he has seen—tho' often the figure from whom the story has started may turn

out to be a secondary figure. He said moreover that he never consciously puts anything into his people and things. To his sense all the interest, the beauty, the poetry, the strangeness &c, are there, in the people & things (the definite ones, whom he has seen) in much larger measure than he can get out' (to WJ, 8 February 1876; *CLHJ 1872–1876* 3:66).

136 **the vision of some person or persons, […] appealing to him just as they were and by what they were**: In his first essay on Turgenev in 1874 – written before he knew the Russian author personally – James had emphasized 'his preference for a theme which takes its starting-point in character' (*LC2* 977). James's later essay 'Ivan Turgénieff' (1884) anticipates an important collocation of terms in the *Portrait* Preface ('germ' and 'plot') in its development of this point: 'The germ of a story, with him, was never an affair of plot—that was the last thing he thought of: it was the representation of certain persons. The first form in which a tale appeared to him was as the figure of an individual, or a combination of individuals, whom he wished to see in action, being sure that such people must do something very special and interesting. They stood before him definite, vivid, and he wished to know, and to show, as much as possible of their nature' (*LC2* 1021–2).

137 **to arrive at my 'story,' […] not having 'story' enough**: Compare James's 1884 essay on Turgenev: 'Story, in the conventional sense of the word—a fable constructed, like Wordsworth's phantom, "to startle and waylay"—there is as little as possible. The thing consists of the motions of a group of selected creatures, which are not the result of a preconceived action, but a consequence of the qualities of the actors' (*LC2* 1022). For the Wordsworthian allusion in this passage, see note 305. 'Story' is a complex word for James. When he uses it to mean the plot of a fiction, he typically associates it with the preferences of naive readers: compare his early observation that the plot of Henry D. Sedley's *Marian Rooke* (1865) 'may readily suffice to the entertainment of those jolly barbarians of taste who read novels only for what they call the "story"' (*LC1* 583). In 1884, he praised Turgenev's work for 'its power to tell us the most about men and women', but imagined 'numerous readers' complaining: '"Hang it, we don't care a straw about men and women: we want a good story!"' (*LC2* 1023). The year before, he had noted that the novelist Anthony Trollope (1815–82), 'with his perpetual "story," which was the only thing he cared about, […] responds in perfection to a certain English ideal. According to that ideal it is rather dangerous to be explicitly or consciously an artist—to have a system, a doctrine, a form' (*LC1* 1332). Contention over

the meaning and status of 'the story' in modern fiction was central to the critical dialogue begun in W. D. Howells's essay 'Henry James, Jr.' (1882) and Walter Besant's lecture *The Art of Fiction* (1884), which James took up in his response to Besant under the same title (*LC1* 44–65), and carried on in the 1884 essay on Turgenev already quoted, and in an essay on Howells from 1886 (*LC2* 1006–27, *LC1* 497–506). In these and other writings of the 1880s, James sought to correct contemporary prejudice about the sorts of plot and subject-matter that would qualify a fiction *as* a story. In 1888, he recommended the novel *Une vie* (1883) by the French Naturalist writer Guy de Maupassant (1850–93) to readers 'who are interested in the question of what constitutes a "story," offering as it does the most definite sequences at the same time that it has nothing that corresponds to the usual idea of a plot' (*LC2* 545); a later story of his own, 'The Story in It' (1902), continues that line of thought and deploys the word in a literary-critical debate about modern French authors' reliance on plots involving illicit sexual relations. In 'The Art of Fiction', James had rejected outright the critical naivety of 'talking as if there were a part of the novel which is the story and part of it which for mystical reasons is not' (*LC1* 59); in some later essays, he recognizes 'story' as a distinct element but treats it as a mere pretext for the exercise of style. Thus, writing in 1904 on Gabriele D'Annunzio's *Il trionfo della morte* (1894): 'The "story" may be told in three words', but 'the wealth of his expression drapes the situation represented in a mantle of voluminous folds, stiff with elaborate embroidery ('GDA' 399). And on Shakespeare in 1907: 'The "story" in The Tempest is a thing of naught', and the real 'charm and magic and [...] ineffable delicacy' of the play consist of 'the style handed over to its last disciplined passion of curiosity' (*LC1* 1213). For James's sense of 'the marked difference between that which is in old-fashioned parlance a "story" and that which has the distinctive characteristics of what *I* call a Subject' (*LL* 299), see note 398. For a contrastingly indulgent attitude to the element of 'story' in later Prefaces, see notes 702 and 859.

138 **I dare say, alas, *que cela manque souvent d'architecture***: James had anticipated this acknowledgement in his 1884 essay on Turgenev: 'as he said, the defect of his manner and the reproach that was made him was his want of "architecture"—in other words, of composition' (*LC2* 1022).

139 **They are the breath of life**: An echo of the biblical account of the creation of Adam: 'And the LORD God formed man *of* the dust of the ground, and breathed into his nostrils the breath of life; and man became a living soul' (Genesis 2:7).

140 **the vain critic's quarrel [...] with one's subject, when he hasn't the wit to accept it**: As early as 'The Art of Fiction', James had maintained that 'We must grant the artist his subject, his idea, his *donnée*: our criticism is applied only to what he makes of it' (*LC1* 56). John Goode suggests a French influence on this position in the work of the literary critic Charles-Augustin Sainte-Beuve (Goode, 'The Art of Fiction: Walter Besant and Henry James', in David Howard et al. (eds.), *Tradition and Tolerance in Nineteenth-Century Fiction: Critical Essays on Some English and American Novels* (London: Routledge and Kegan Paul, 1966), pp. 243–81; 264). The specific source Goode cites is a letter from Sainte-Beuve to the managing director of the newspaper *Le Moniteur*, dated 20 February 1860, 'sur la morale et l'art' ('on morality and art'): 'Le grand Gœthe, le maître de la critique, a établi ce principe souverain qu'il faut surtout s'attacher à l'exécution dans les œuvres de l'artiste, et voir s'il a fait, et comment il a fait, ce qu'il a voulu' ('The great Goethe, the master of criticism, has established the sovereign principle that one must apply oneself above all to the execution in an artist's works and examine whether he has done what he wanted to do, and how he has done it') (Saint-Beuve, *Causeries du Lundi*, 3rd edn, 15 vols. (Paris: Garnier frères, 1857–70), vol. XV, p. 347). James would restate the point shortly after concluding work on the *NYE*, in an epistolary exchange with George Bernard Shaw about his own play *The Saloon* (1908): 'I inveterately hold any quarrel with the subject of an achievable or achieved thing the most futile and profitless of demonstrations. Criticism begins, surely, with one's seeing and judging what the work has made of it—to which end there is nothing we *can* do but accept it' (23 January 1909; *LL* 475–6). But see also note 142.

141 **Other echoes from the same source [...] one much-embracing echo**: In his 1884 essay on Turgenev, James recalls finding 'something extraordinarily vivifying and stimulating in his talk' (*LC2* 1020–1) and refers to several conversations with him, none of which correspond directly to the words attributed to him in the Preface. He observes in general: 'Nothing that Turgénieff had to say could be more interesting than his talk about his own work, his manner of writing' (*LC2* 1021).

142 **the objective value [...] of "subject" in the novel**: James had noted in 1874 that Turgenev 'believes in the intrinsic value of "subject" in art; he holds that there are trivial subjects and serious ones, that the latter are much the best, and that their superiority resides in their giving us absolutely a greater amount of information about the human mind' (*LC2* 973).

In 'The Art of Fiction', James allows that we are not 'bound to like [the artist's subject] or find it interesting', but stipulates that in that case we must simply 'let it alone' and not make it a ground of criticism: 'We may believe that of a certain idea even the most sincere novelist can make nothing at all, and the event may perfectly justify our belief; but the failure will have been a failure to execute, and it is in the execution that the fatal weakness is recorded' (*LC1* 56).

143 **is it sincere, the result of some direct impression or perception of life?**: Compare 'The Art of Fiction': 'A novel is in its broadest definition a personal, a direct impression of life: that, to begin with, constitutes its value, which is greater or less according to the intensity of the impression'; as a corollary of that principle, 'the only condition that I can think of attaching to the composition of the novel is [...] that it be sincere' (*LC1* 50, 64). See also James's 1889 letter to the Deerfield Summer School: 'Any point of view is interesting that is a direct impression of life' (*LC1* 93).

144 **a critical pretension that had neglected [...] all definition of terms**: In 'The Art of Fiction', James had pointed out an instance of such neglect in Walter Besant's 'very cursory allusion to the "conscious moral purpose" of the novel' (*LC1* 62). Besant had argued that 'the modern English novel, whatever form it takes, almost always starts with a conscious moral purpose. When it does not, so much are we accustomed to expect it, that one feels as if there has been a debasement of the Art' (*The Art of Fiction: A Lecture* (London: Chatto & Windus, 1884), p. 24). James responded: 'Vagueness, in such a discussion, is fatal, and what is the meaning of your morality and your conscious moral purpose? Will you not define your terms [...]? [...] We are discussing the Art of Fiction; questions of art are questions (in the widest sense) of execution; questions of morality are quite another affair, and will you not let us see how it is that you find it so easy to mix them up?' (*LC1* 62–3).

145 **the amount of felt life concerned in producing it**: Writing in 1883 on Alphonse Daudet, James had argued that 'The reader's quarrel with Sidone Chèbe [a character in Daudet's novel *Fromont jeune et Risler aîné* (1874)] is not that she is bad, but that she is not *felt*, as the æsthetic people say' (*LC2* 225). In a contemporaneous letter to Mary Augusta Ward about her novel *Miss Bretherton* (1884), he implies a French source for this aesthetic way of talking: the book is 'very refined and <u>senti</u> [felt] (on your part)' (9 December [1884]; *CLHJ 1884–1886* 1:40).

146 **The quality and capacity of that soil, [...] the projected morality**: In 'The Art of Fiction', James had similarly appealed to 'the very obvious truth that the deepest quality of a work of art will always be the quality of the mind of the producer. In proportion as that intelligence is fine will the novel, the picture, the statue partake of the substance of beauty and truth' (*LC1* 64). For the Preface's horticultural figure, compare James in 1888 on Guy de Maupassant, who 'cultivates his garden with admirable energy; and if there is a flower you miss from the rich parterre, you may be sure that it could not possibly have been raised, his mind not containing the soil for it' (*LC2* 525). The allusion to Voltaire in that passage – at 'cultivates his garden' – occurs also in the Preface to *The Golden Bowl* (see note 887).

147 **all the varieties of outlook on life, of disposition to reflect and project**: In 'The Lesson of Balzac', James had recently reflected on 'this question of the projected light of the individual strong temperament in fiction—the color of the air with which this, that or the other painter of life (as we call them all), more or less unconsciously suffuses his picture', and had asked how such atmospheric conditions can 'strike us as different in Fielding and in Richardson, in Scott and in Dumas, in Dickens and in Thackeray, in Hawthorne and in Meredith, in George Eliot and in George Sand, in Jane Austen and in Charlotte Brontë [*sic*]?' (*LC2* 125).

148 **a number of possible windows not to be reckoned, [...] pierced, or [...] pierceable [...] by the need of the individual vision and by the pressure of the individual will**: In 1888, James had written of Robert Louis Stevenson that 'Each of his books is an independent effort—a window opened to a different view' (*LC1* 1234), and had extrapolated from that comment to a generalization about novels and novel-writing: 'The breath of the novelist's being is his liberty, and the incomparable virtue of the form he uses is that it lends itself to views innumerable and diverse, to every variety of illustration' (*LC1* 1248). Three years later, he hailed the example of Rudyard Kipling for 'showing that there are just as many kinds, as many ways, as many forms and degrees of the "right," as there are personal points of view'. James figures Kipling's 'extreme youth' in this passage as 'his window-bar—the support on which he somewhat rowdily leans while he looks down at the human scene with his pipe in his teeth' (*LC1* 1124). The Preface's reference to the piercing of such apertures is anticipated in an 1888 essay on the Goncourt brothers, in which James had imagined them defending the 'memorandum of the artistic life' they had made in

their shared *Journal*: '"The question is how many windows are opened, how many little holes are pierced, into the consciousness of the artist. Our contention would be that we have pierced more little holes than any other gimlet has achieved"' (*LC2* 414).

149 **a dead wall**: 'A blank wall, without windows or openings' (*The Imperial Dictionary of the English Language*, ed. John Ogilvie, new edn revised by Charles Annandale, 4 vols. (London: Blackie & Son, 1882), vol. I, p. 671). James had observed in 1888 that if Maupassant tells us nothing about 'the moral nature of man, it is because he has no window looking in that direction, and not because artistic scruples have compelled him to close it up. The very compact mansion in which he dwells presents on that side a perfectly dead wall' (*LC2* 531). Compare Isabel in Chapter 42 of *The Portrait*, confronting the disappointment of her marriage: 'she had suddenly found the infinite vista of a multiplied life to be a dark, narrow alley with a dead wall at the end' (*NYE* IV, 189). In other respects too, James's 'house of fiction' echoes the architecture of Isabel's married life, as she imagines it in this chapter: 'It was the house of darkness, the house of dumbness, the house of suffocation. Osmond's beautiful mind gave it neither light nor air; Osmond's beautiful mind indeed seemed to peep down from a small high window and mock at her' (*NYE* IV, 196).

150 **his boundless freedom**: Compare 'The Art of Fiction': 'It appears to me that no one can ever have made a seriously artistic attempt without becoming conscious of an immense increase—a kind of revelation—of freedom. One perceives in that case—by the light of a heavenly ray— that the province of art is all life, all feeling, all observation, all vision' (*LC1* 59).

151 **my grasp of a single character**: It is generally accepted that James refers to his cousin Mary Temple (1845–70), called Minny in the family, whom he had become close to in Newport during the 1860s and who died of tuberculosis while he was making his first solo visit to Europe in 1869–70. On 28 December 1880, he wrote to Grace Norton, who was reading the serialization of *The Portrait* and had seen a resemblance: 'You are both right & wrong about Minny Temple. I had her in mind & there is in the heroine a considerable infusion of my impression of her remarkable nature. But the thing is not a portrait. Poor Minny was essentially <u>incomplete</u> & I have attempted to make my young woman more rounded, more finished' (*CLHJ 1880–1883* 1:135). For Minny as a model for Milly Theale in *The Wings of the Dove* (1902), see note 787.

152 **to write the history of the growth of one's imagination**: In Chapter 11 of *Notes of a Son and Brother* (1914), James would comment on his late turn to autobiography, noting that 'The personal history, as it were, of an imagination [...] had always struck me as a task that a teller of tales might rejoice in'; he eventually recognized that his own life 'would give me what, artistically speaking, I wanted' for this project (*Aut* 479–80). See also note 847.

153 **to take over (take over straight from life) such and such a [...] figure or form**: James comes back to the subject of transferring persons from life to fiction in Chapter 13 of *Notes of a Son and Brother*, thinking of his friends Francis and Elizabeth Boott as the originals of Gilbert and Pansy Osmond in *The Portrait*. He observes that he had used the '"form" of the Frank Bootts' as a model for this relationship: 'An Italianate bereft American with a little moulded daughter in the setting of a massive old Tuscan residence was at the end of years exactly what was required by a situation of my own [...]; and I *had* it there, in the authenticated way, with its essential fund of truth, at once all the more because my admirable old friend had given it to me and none the less because he had no single note of character or temper, not a grain of the non-essential, in common with my Gilbert Osmond' (*Aut* 548–9). See also note 637.

154 **the [...] back-shop of the mind**: A 'back-shop' is 'A small and usually private shop behind the main one; a secret place of business' (*OED*). As Laurence Holland notes, the *Portrait* Preface alludes to a particular sort of shop, one 'which combined a retail trade with the business of pawn'. Holland also points out a resemblance to the curiosity-shop in *The Golden Bowl* (1904) (*The Expense of Vision: Essays on the Craft of Henry James* (Princeton, NJ: Princeton University Press, 1964), p. 12; the relevant episodes in *The Golden Bowl* occur in Book First, Chapter 6, and Book Fourth, Chapter 9). James frequently refers to metaphorical back-shops, and associates them with other recessed and occluded spaces of work or worship. In 'The Lesson of Balzac', for example, questions of fictional technique and process are confined to 'the back shop, the laboratory, or, more nobly expressed, the inner shrine of the temple' (*LC2* 138). The acting lesson Peter Sheringham watches Miriam Rooth take from Madame Carré in Chapter 10 of *The Tragic Muse* (1890) is 'the oddest hour our young man had ever spent, even in the course of investigations which had often led him into the *cuisine* [kitchen], the distillery or back shop, of the admired

profession' (*NYE* VII, 195). For the space of artistic production as a 'sacred back kitchen', see note 638.

155 **to place my treasure right**: James had written of Turgenev in 1874: 'If we are not mistaken, he notes down an idiosyncrasy of character, a fragment of talk, an attitude, a feature, a gesture, and keeps it, if need be, for twenty years, till just the moment for using it comes, just the spot for placing it' (*LC2* 969).

156 **the dealer resigned not to "realise,"**: To 'realise' in this sense means 'To convert (an asset, as securities, property, etc.) into a more concrete or readily accessible form of wealth; *esp.* to sell off (investments, land, a business, etc.) in order to obtain the monetary value' (*OED*). A sentence added in revision to Chapter 24 of *The Portrait* introduces a metaphor which corresponds directly to this passage in the Preface; there is no counterpart in earlier texts of the novel. Isabel visits Osmond's villa for the first time, and he talks to her about living in Italy: 'It met the case soothingly for the human, for the social failure—by which he meant the people who couldn't "realise," as they said, on their sensibility: they could keep it about them there, in their poverty, without ridicule, as you might keep an heirloom or an inconvenient entailed place that brought you in nothing' (*NYE* III, 370–1).

157 **a certain young woman affronting her destiny**: James had used the verb 'affront' in the same rare sense ('To face in defiance; to confront. Later chiefly *figurative*: to face (death, one's destiny, etc.)' (*OED*)) in his commemorative essay on the actress Fanny Kemble (1893): 'A prouder nature never affronted the long humiliation of life' (*LC1* 1073).

158 **the mere slim shade of an intelligent but presumptuous girl, [...] the high attributes of a Subject?**: The speakers in James's critical dialogue 'Daniel Deronda: A Conversation' (1876) had already debated the virtues and drawbacks of such a character. Pulcheria asserts that Gwendolen Harleth in George Eliot's novel is 'too light, too flimsy' to sustain 'a deep tragic interest': 'tragedy has no hold on such a girl'. Constantius agrees that 'She is perhaps at the first a little childish for the weight of interest she has to carry'; but Theodora counters in terms that recur in the *Portrait* Preface: 'Since when is it forbidden to make one's heroine young? Gwendolen is a perfect picture of youthfulness—its eagerness, its presumption, its preoccupation with itself, its vanity and silliness, its sense of its own absoluteness. But she is extremely intelligent and clever, and therefore tragedy *can* have a hold upon her' (*LC1* 989).

159 **an ado about something**: James plays with the title of Shakespeare's play *Much Ado about Nothing* (1598–9) in its quasi-proverbial aspect: 'a great deal of fuss or trouble over nothing of any significance' (*OED*).

160 **George Eliot has admirably noted it—"In these frail vessels is borne onward through the ages the treasure of human affection."**: George Eliot (1819–80), English novelist, essayist and poet whose work James regularly reviewed in the 1860s and 1870s, and whose career he surveyed in an 1885 review of John Cross's *Life* (see *LC1* 907–1010). In this sentence of the Preface, James slightly but significantly misquotes from her novel *Daniel Deronda* (1876). At the close of Book II, Chapter 11, Eliot's narrator asks whether there could be 'a slenderer, more insignificant thread in human history than this consciousness of a girl, busy with her small inferences of the way in which she could make her life pleasant?—in a time, too, when ideas were with fresh vigour making armies of themselves, and the universal kinship was declaring itself fiercely [...]. What in the midst of that mighty drama are girls and their blind visions? They are the Yea or Nay of that good for which men are enduring and fighting. In these delicate vessels is borne onward through the ages the treasure of human affections' (*Daniel Deronda*, ed. Graham Handley (Oxford: Clarendon Press, 1984), p. 109).

161 **Juliet [...] Hetty Sorrel and Maggie Tulliver and Rosamond Vincy and Gwendolen Harleth**: Anticipating a point about Shakespeare's heroines in the next paragraph of the Preface, James adds the Juliet of *Romeo and Juliet* (1595–6) to a list of young women in George Eliot's novels: Hetty Sorrel in *Adam Bede* (1859), Maggie Tulliver in *The Mill on the Floss* (1860), Rosamond Vincy in *Middlemarch* (1872) and Gwendolen Harleth in *Daniel Deronda*.

162 **Dickens and Walter Scott [...] R. L. Stevenson [...] to leave the task unattempted**: In his 1899 essay 'The Future of the Novel', James had recently coupled Scott with Charles Dickens (1812–70) as examples of nineteenth-century anglophone novelists' avoidance of 'the great relation between men and women', i.e., the sexual relation: 'I cannot so much as imagine Dickens and Scott *without* the "love-making" left, as the phrase is, out' (*LC1* 107, 108). In 1888, he had remarked Stevenson's 'absence of care for things feminine. His books are for the most part books without women.' James attributed this to Stevenson's 'sympathy with the juvenile and that feeling about life which leads him to regard women as so many superfluous girls in a boy's game' (*LC1* 1233, 1238).

163 **their Juliets and Cleopatras and Portias**: As well as Juliet once again, James refers to the heroines of Shakespeare's *Antony and Cleopatra* (1606–7) and *The Merchant of Venice* (1596–7).

164 **underplots, as the playwrights say, [...] the great mutations of the world**: An 'underplot' is 'A (dramatic or literary) plot subordinate to the principal plot, but connected with it' (*OED*, citing Dryden's *Essay of Dramatick Poesie*, 1668). Compare James's early review of Anthony Trollope's novel *Can You Forgive Her?* (1865): 'there is a leading story, which, being foreseen at the outset to be insufficient to protract the book during the requisite number of months, is padded with a couple of under-plots, one of which comes almost near being pathetic, as the other falls very far short of being humorous. The main narrative, of course, contains the settlement in life [...] of a beautiful young lady' (*LC1* 1317). Philip Horne hears in this sentence of the Preface an allusion to Sir Thomas Browne's *Hydriotaphia, Urn Burial, or, a Discourse of the Sepulchral Urns lately found in Norfolk* (1658), Chapter 5: "Tis too late to be ambitious. The great mutations of the world are acted, or time may be too short for our designes' (*The Portrait of a Lady*, ed. Horne (London: Penguin, 2011), p. 717 n. 7).

165 **"Place the centre of the subject in the young woman's own consciousness,"**: Alfred Habegger cites an American journal article of 1885 as context for the Preface's discussion of representing the consciousness of young women (see *Henry James and the 'Woman Business'* (Cambridge: Cambridge University Press, 1989), p. 116). In this article, Charlotte Porter describes a recent 'change in the treatment of heroines' in British and American novels: 'The transfer of the author's attention from the story about his characters to the representation of the life within them has revealed the individuality of the heroine, and developed an altogether new estimate of woman's moral value.' Porter points to James's Isabel as an example of this new mode of writing female characters and contrasts it to an 'old-time' tradition represented by Samuel Richardson and Frances Burney, and more recently by Dickens and Thackeray. Her other examples of modern heroines are three characters from novels by George Eliot of the 1860s and 1870s – Romola de' Bardi in *Romola* (1863), alongside Dorothea Brooke and Maggie Tulliver – and three characters closer in time to *The Portrait* – the eponymous heroine of Constance Fenimore Woolson's *Anne* (1882), Bertha Amory in Frances Hodgson Burnett's *Through One Administration* (1883) and Marcia Hubbard in Howells's *A Modern*

Instance (1882) (Porter, 'The Serial Story', *Century Magazine* 30 (September 1885), 812-13).

166 **the numbered pieces of my puzzle**: James may be thinking of the '15 puzzle', which enjoyed a craze in America in 1879-80. It consisted of 'A ruled square of 16 compartments' numbered 1-15, 'the 16th square being left blank. Fifteen counters, numbered in like manner, are placed at random upon the squares so that one square is vacant. The counter occupying any adjacent square may now be moved into the vacant square [...], but no diagonal move is allowed. The puzzle is to bring all the counters into their proper squares by successive moves' (William Woolsey Johnson and William E. Story, 'Notes on the "15" Puzzle', *American Journal of Mathematics* 2.4 (1879), 397-404; 397).

167 **"Well, what will she *do?*"**: In his 1884 essay on Turgenev, James had noted that once the Russian novelist thoroughly knew his characters, 'the story all lay in the question, What shall I make them do?' (*LC2* 1022). Ten years earlier, he had remarked that Turgenev's young heroines 'puzzle us almost too much to charm, and we fully measure their beauty only when they are called upon to act. Then the author imagines them doing the most touching, the most inspiring things' (*LC2* 979). The same question and the same puzzlement accompany Isabel in the novel: as Ralph Touchett wonders in Chapter 7, for example, 'She was intelligent and generous; it was a fine free nature; but what was she going to do with herself?' (*NYE* III, 87).

168 **so broken a reed**: A biblical formula: 'Lo, thou trustest in the staff of this broken reed, on Egypt; whereon if a man lean, it will go into his hand, and pierce it: so *is* Pharaoh king of Egypt to all that trust in him' (Isaiah 36:6).

169 **that way dishonour lies**: An adaptation of a famous line in Shakespeare's *King Lear* (1605), the hero's admonition to himself not to think about his daughters' betrayal: 'O, that way madness lies, let me shun that! / No more of that' (3.4.21-2). In his 1888 essay on Robert Louis Stevenson, James had wryly noted the 'usual judgement' on 'the writer whose effort is perceptibly that of the artist': 'he may be artistic, but [...] he must not be too much so; that way, apparently, lies something worse than madness' (*LC1* 1234).

170 **a mere miraculous windfall**: A 'windfall' is a bough or fruit blown down from a tree by the wind, and thus figuratively 'A casual or unexpected acquisition or advantage' (*OED*). Elsewhere, James applies this figure to the happy discovery of a subject or resolution of an artistic problem. In Chapter

42 of *The Tragic Muse*, Nick Dormer considers his first portrait of Miriam Rooth 'a mere light wind-fall of the shaken tree' (*NYE* VIII, 263–4); this figure was added to *NYE* in revision and replaces 'a kind of pictorial *obiter dictum* [remark in passing]' in the first edition (*The Tragic Muse*, 2 vols. (Boston and New York: Houghton, Mifflin and Company, 1890), vol. II, p. 691). In the Preface to *NYE* XI, the anecdote that gives James the idea for 'The Pupil' comes as 'a thumping windfall' (p. 119). The 'golden apple' that falls into 'the writer's lap, straight from the wind-stirred tree' later in this paragraph of the Preface seems to have dropped from the opening pages of James's recent American essay 'New England: An Autumn Impression' (1905), which record his 'confidence in the objective reality of impressions, so that they could deliciously be left to ripen, like golden apples, on the tree'. The apples in this passage, his first impressions on revisiting America after an absence of twenty-one years, are *prospective* windfalls: 'thick-growing items of the characteristic that were surely going to drop into one's hand [...] as soon as one could begin to hold it out' (*AS* 6).

171 **were it not that Maria Gostrey [...] may be mentioned as a better**: James discusses the narrative function performed by Maria Gostrey in the Preface to *The Ambassadors*, pp. 255–8.

172 **the light *ficelle***: The French word literally means a thread or string; figuratively, as applied to the arts and in particular to the stage, it means a technical device. For this sense, see Littré's *Dictionnaire de la langue française*, 4 vols. (Paris: Librairie Hachette et Cie, 1873–5), vol. II, p. 1663: 'On voit la ficelle, c'est-à-dire on voit comment la chose s'est faite. || De là, les ficelles d'un art, les procédés dans ce qu'ils ont de matériel, de grossier. Les ficelles dramatiques. Cet auteur connaît les ficelles du métier' ('To see the *ficelle* means to see how the thing is done. Hence, the *ficelles* of an art, its coarse material processes. Stage tricks. That author knows the tricks of the trade'). James's comment in his essay 'The Parisian Stage' (1873) on the treatment of adultery in the modern French drama exemplifies this sense of the word: 'It has been used now for so many years as a mere pigment, a source of dramatic color, a *ficelle*, as they say, that it has ceased to have any apparent moral bearings' (*CWAD2* 9). See also his remarks on two nineteenth-century French playwrights, Victorien Sardou (1831–1908) and Eugène Scribe (1791–1861), both prolific and popular authors of well-made plays (*pièces bien faites*): 'Sardou is very clever, certainly; but he seems to me only a more modern Scribe— dealing mainly in ficelles & machinery, &, in sentiment, very arid &

vulgar. But he is phenomenally skilful' (to William Ernest Henley, [11, 18 or 25 October 1878]; *CLHJ 1878–1880* 1:13–14). The French term has other relevant figurative meanings. According to Littré, 'Tenir la ficelle ou les ficelles' ('to hold the string or strings') means 'faire mouvoir à son gré des personnes; locution tirée de la ficelle avec laquelle on fait mouvoir les pantins' ('to make people move according to one's will; an idiom taken from the string with which one moves puppets'). In a contemporary English slang dictionary, the French phrase '*être ficelle*' is offered as an equivalent for 'to be a dodger' in the sense of a 'trickster' (*Slang* II:300). Compare Littré: 'une ficelle, un escroc, un filou. Méfiez-vous de lui, c'est une vraie ficelle' ('a *ficelle*, a swindler, a cheat. Watch out for him, he's a real *ficelle*'). See also note 195.

173 **the fishwives who helped to bring back to Paris from Versailles [...] the carriage of the royal family**: James refers to the popular uprising of 5–6 October 1789, which began as a bread-riot by Parisian market-women and grew into a march of several thousand protesters to the royal palace at Versailles. The crowd attacked the palace and compelled Louis XVI and his family to return with them to Paris the next day, the royal party travelling by coach and the women accompanying them on foot (see Thomas Carlyle, *The French Revolution: A History* (1837), vol. I, Book 7).

174 **flood and field, [...] the moving accident**: Shakespeare's Othello describes wooing Desdemona by telling her stories of his military exploits, 'Wherein I spoke of most disastrous chances: / Of moving accidents by flood and field' (1.3.134–5).

175 **the pages in which Isabel, [...] coming in from a wet walk or whatever, [...] finds Madame Merle in possession of the place, [...] a turning-point in her life**: This scene occurs in Chapter 18. James slightly misremembers Isabel's movements. She does not come into the drawing-room at Gardencourt 'from a wet walk'; in fact, after arriving at Gardencourt with Ralph and going to her room for an hour she comes downstairs looking for Mrs Touchett and does not find her, but hears someone playing the piano in the drawing-room and follows the sound. The weather has been 'damp and chill' and is 'now altogether spoiled', but it is in the next chapter that Isabel and Madame Merle take walks together 'in spite of the rain' (*NYE* III, 243, 269). The narrator appears to ironize Isabel's conviction of the importance of this encounter: we are told that 'she had not yet divested herself of a young faith that each new acquaintance would exert some momentous influence on her life' (*NYE* III, 244–5).

176 **my young woman's extraordinary meditative vigil**: This scene occupies Chapter 42.

177 **it throws the action further forward than twenty "incidents" might have done**: The term placed in inverted commas here had a particular relevance to James's sense of *The Portrait*'s vulnerability to criticism. See an undated notebook entry (c.December 1880–January 1881) made while he was still composing the novel: 'The weakness of the whole story is that it is too exclusively psychological—that it depends to[o] little on incident; but the complete unfolding of the situation that is established by Isabel's marriage may nonetheless be quite sufficiently dramatic' (*CN* 13). As Philip Horne notes, the same word was duly deployed by hostile reviewers: 'the London *Quarterly Review* said in January 1883 that "The book is one of the longest of recent times [...] and there is not a single interesting incident in it from beginning to end"' (*The Portrait of a Lady*, ed. Horne, p. 718 n. 12). In 'The Art of Fiction' the following year, James would contest the 'old-fashioned distinction between the novel of character and the novel of incident', asking: 'What is character but the determination of incident? What is incident but the illustration of character? [...] It is an incident for a woman to stand up with her hand resting on a table and look out at you in a certain way; or if it be not an incident I think it will be hard to say what it is. At the same time it is an expression of character' (*LC1* 54, 55). James's 1877 essay 'The Théâtre Français' suggests a theatrical source for his faith in the significance of objectively minor actions: the French comedians' 'attention to detail' had shown 'that so trivial an act as taking a letter from a servant or placing one's hat on a chair may be made a suggestive and interesting incident' (*CWAD2* 188).

178 **the surprise of a caravan or the identification of a pirate**: The Preface's association of narrative surprise with piracy is anticipated by a passage in 'The Art of Fiction' comparing Stevenson's *Treasure Island* (1883) with the Goncourt brothers' *Chérie* (1884): 'The moral consciousness of a child is as much a part of life as the islands of the Spanish Main, and the one sort of geography seems to me to have those "surprises" of which Mr. Besant speaks quite as much as the other' (*LC1* 61–2). For an antecedent of the 'caravan' in this sentence, see *The Golden Bowl*, Book Fifth, Chapter 2: Maggie Verver imagines the jealousy and anger she is conscious of *not* feeling at her husband's infidelity as 'nothing nearer to experience than a wild eastern caravan, looming into view with crude colours in the sun, fierce pipes in the air, high spears against the sky' (*NYE* XXIV, 236–7).

179 **my tendency to *overtreat* [...] my subject**: At work on *The Golden Bowl* in May 1904, James remarked to Pinker on the compositional method he was apparently 'condemned to', 'which is to *overtreat* my subject by developments and amplifications that have, in large part, eventually to be greatly compressed, but to the prior operation of which the thing afterwards owes what is most durable in its quality' (*LL* 400).

180 **the "international" light lay [...] thick and rich upon the scene**: James returns to his preoccupation with 'international' subjects in the period of *The Portrait* in the Prefaces to *NYE* XIII and XIV.

PREFACE to *The Princess Casamassima* (*NYE* V–VI)

181 **the first year of a long residence in London, [...] walking the streets**: James moved to London from Paris in December 1876 and took lodgings at 3 Bolton Street, Piccadilly (see note 586). This was his London address for most of the time he was writing *The Princess Casamassima*: he would remain there until the spring of 1886. In a notebook entry of 25 November 1881, he looked back to his first winter in London: 'I had very few friends, the season was of the darkest & wettest; but I was in a state of deep delight. I had complete liberty, and the prospect of profitable work; I used to take long walks in the rain. I took possession of London; I felt it to be the right place' (*CN* 218). For Hyacinth Robinson's 'interminable, restless, melancholy, moody, yet all-observant strolls through London', see *The Princess Casamassima*, Chapter 5 (*NYE* V, 76).

182 **the great grey Babylon**: The original city of Babylon was the capital of an empire in ancient Mesopotamia. In post-Reformation Protestant culture, the name 'Babylon' was used in a derogatory sense to refer to 'The city of Rome as the seat of the Pope and the centre of authority of the Roman Catholic Church'; by extension, it also came to mean 'Any large and luxurious city; *esp.* one seen as decadent and corrupt' (*OED*). Paris was often so designated, but for Victorian writers the 'modern Babylon' was by default London – as in W. T. Stead's series of investigative articles on child prostitution for the *Pall Mall Gazette* (July 1885), 'The Maiden Tribute of Modern Babylon'. In the opening paragraph of his 1888 essay 'London', James calls the city 'the murky modern Babylon' (*ELE* 1); his essays from the period of his first move to London also use this term, e.g. 'The Picture Season in London' (1877) and 'The Suburbs of London' (1877). It occurs

frequently in his letters also: to his mother, for example, he professed 'to like this murky Babylon really all the better' on coming back to it from Paris (24 December 1876; *CLHJ 1876-1878* 1:13-14).

183 **even still [...] breaking out on occasion into eloquence**: During the period of the *NYE*, James took several walks through the West End and the City of London as research for *London Town*, a non-fiction book he had contracted to write for Frederick Macmillan in June 1903 but never produced: he made notes on the spot for this project in August and October 1907, and again in September and October 1909 (see *CN* 273-80). He also made several expeditions in London with Alvin Langdon Coburn in search of photographic subjects for the frontispieces of various *NYE* volumes, finding and photographing scenes in St John's Wood, Bloomsbury, Marylebone and Hampstead during the autumn of 1906 (see the Introduction and Chronology, pp. lxix, clix–clx). James discusses the hunt for London subjects in the Preface to *The Golden Bowl*. See also note 220.

184 **condemned to see these things only from outside—in [...] mere wistfulness and envy and despair**: The novel repeatedly positions Hyacinth outside the material and cultural wealth of civilization, looking in. Window-shopping in Great Portland Street with Millicent Henning in Chapter 11, for example, 'He was liable to moods in which the sense of exclusion from all he would have liked most to enjoy in life settled on him like a pall' (*NYE* V, 168). At Medley in Chapter 24, the Princess exclaims to him: '"Fancy the strange, the bitter fate: to be constituted as you're constituted, to be conscious of the capacity you must feel, and yet to look at the good things of life only through the glass of the pastry-cook's window!"' (*NYE* VI, 60-1).

185 **with every door of approach shut in his face. For one's self [...] there had been doors that opened [...] into good and charming relations**: The doors that opened for James in London were both domestic and institutional. On his arrival in England in December 1876, he brought with him letters of introduction from American friends including Henry Adams, Francis Boott and Sarah Butler Wister. Even before he had presented all of those letters, he found within a couple of months that he was 'getting quite into the current of London life' (to MWJ, 31 January [1877]; *CLHJ 1876-1878* 1:41); from this time onward, his letters home include extensive reports of his dining out and other social engagements. He was proposed by American acquaintances as a temporary member of the *Athenæum* Club early in 1877, and quickly came to find it 'indispensable' and to dread the expiry of his

membership: 'When that melancholy day comes I shall feel at 1st as if London had become impossible' (to WJ, 28 February [1877]; *CLHJ 1876-1878* 1:70). He attended his first country-house party at Whitsun 1877. By the same sort of contrast he refers to in this sentence of the Preface, his essay 'An English Easter' (1877) described the public funeral of the trade unionist George Odger (1813-77), 'an English Radical agitator of humble origin, who had distinguished himself by a perverse desire to get into Parliament' but 'knocked in vain at the door that opens but to the refined' (*PPL* 198).

186 **all-knowing immortals [...] bored Olympians**: The Olympians were the twelve major divinities of ancient Greek mythology, whose home was Mount Olympus: Zeus, Hera, Poseidon, Demeter, Athena, Apollo, Artemis, Ares, Aphrodite, Hephaestus, Hermes and Dionysus. A long literary tradition describes the existence of the Olympian gods as perfectly calm and carefree: e.g. Lucretius' *De rerum natura* (Book III, ll. 18-24), the source for the Homeric gods in Tennyson's 'The Lotos-Eaters' (1832), who are said to be 'careless of mankind' (l. 155; *The Poems of Tennyson*, vol. I, p. 476).

187 **falls to the ground.**": To 'fall to the ground' is 'to come to nothing; *esp*. (of an argument, theory, etc.) to be shown to be false or invalid; (of a plan or project) to be unsuccessful' (*OED*, 'fall'). James had used the same phrase in his 1902 essay on *Madame Bovary*, remarking that when the book appeared in 1857 'Flaubert was prosecuted as author of a work scandalous to indecency' but that, in the event, 'The prosecution fell to the ground' ('GF' xvii): Flaubert was acquitted.

188 **the condition [...] on which Thackeray so much insists [...], the condition of a humble heart, a bowed head, [...] before the "awful will" and the mysterious decrees of Providence**: James alludes to the verse 'Epilogue' to W. M. Thackeray's Christmas book *Dr. Birch and His Young Friends* (1848-9): 'Come wealth or want, come good or ill, / Let young and old accept their part, / And bow before the Awful Will, / And bear it with an honest heart' (*The Works of William Makepeace Thackeray*, 13 vols. (New York and London: Harper and Brothers, 1898-9), vol. IX p. 101). The humbling of false pride or vanity is a typically Thackerayan preoccupation.

189 **an attached thread on which the pearls of interest are strung**: James habitually figures literary form in these terms. In 1904, for example, he wrote of Gabriele D'Annunzio: 'Each of his volumes offers [...] its little gallery of episodes that stand out like the larger pearls occurring at intervals on a string of beads' ('GDA' 393). See also notes 421 and 633.

190 **no "story" is possible without its fools—as most of the fine painters of life [...] have abundantly felt**: After the playwright and poet William Shakespeare (1564–1616), 'the fine painters of life' listed by James in this sentence are major European novelists: Miguel de Cervantes (1547–1616), Balzac, Henry Fielding (1707–54), Scott, Thackeray, Dickens, George Meredith (1828–1909), George Eliot and Jane Austen (1775–1817). With the exception of Cervantes, these writers often served as examples in James's general criticism: they are all cited in 'The Lesson of Balzac', for example, as are Alexandre Dumas and Émile Zola (for whom, see note 192). For an allusion to Cervantes's *Don Quixote* in the Preface to *NYE* XVII, see note 726. James returns to the uses of 'fools' in the Preface to *NYE* X, p. 102.

191 **to betray, to cheapen or, as we say, give away**: To give something away in this idiomatic sense means either to treat the object given as valueless or 'of little value', as in the 'derisive' formula 'given away with a pound of tea' (*OED*, earliest instance 1890); or, in an American slang usage, 'To betray, expose (oneself, another person) to detection or ridicule; to let slip (a secret), esp. through carelessness or stupidity' (*OED*, earliest instance 1878). James's frequent uses of the phrase often hover between these meanings, as, for example, towards the close of the *Golden Bowl* Preface (p. 277); and in the Venetian essay 'Two Old Houses and Three Young Women' (1899), where he likewise encounters 'a problem [...] of *giving* the particular thing as much as possible without, at the same time, giving it, as we say, away' ('Two Old Houses and Three Young Women', *Independent* (New York) 51 (September 1899), 2406–12; 2406).

192 **as with Scott, [...] as with old Dumas and with Zola**: The common factor in James's critical references to these three authors is an emphasis on the improvisational, plot-driven quality of their writing. His first critical essay, a review of Nassau W. Senior's *Essays on Fiction* (1864), acclaimed Walter Scott as 'a born story-teller': 'we can liken him to nothing better than to a strong and kindly elder brother, who gathers his juvenile public about him at eventide, and pours out a stream of wondrous improvisation' (*LC1* 1203). In an essay of 1877, he compared George Sand's novels to the historical romances of Alexandre Dumas (1802–70) in their 'spontaneous inventiveness' and 'pleasure in a story for a story's sake' (*LC2* 730). And in 1903 he remarked that, for all Zola's historical, sociological and scientific research, 'in his way too he improvises in the grand manner, the manner of Walter Scott and of Dumas the elder' ('EZ' 198).

193 **Edgar of Ravenswood [...] has a black cloak and hat and feathers more than he has a mind; just as Hamlet [...] has yet a mind still more than he has a costume**: In Scott's novel *The Bride of Lammermoor* (1819), Edgar, Master of Ravenswood, is the son of a proscribed supporter of James VII whose family estates were confiscated after the 'Glorious Revolution' of 1688. As first seen by the novel's heroine Lucy Ashton, Ravenswood's gloomy demeanour and dark costume betray 'Some secret sorrow, or the brooding spirit of some moody passion': 'A Montero cap and a black feather drooped over the wearer's brow, and partly concealed his features, which, so far as seen, were dark, regular, and full of majestic, though somewhat sullen, expression' (Vol. I, Ch. 5; in *The Edinburgh Edition of the Waverley Novels*, editor-in-chief David Hewitt, 30 vols. (Edinburgh: Edinburgh University Press, 1993–), vol. VIIa, p. 41). In shaping the contrast with *Hamlet* (1600-1), James appears to be thinking of Hamlet's lines to Gertrude rejecting the assumption that his interiority can be inferred from his mourning dress (his 'inky cloak' and 'customary suits of solemn black'): 'But I have that within which passes show, / These but the trappings and the suits of woe' (1.2.77, 78, 85–6).

194 **Fielding's fine old moralism, fine old humour and fine old style**: The narrator of Henry Fielding's *The History of Tom Jones, A Foundling* (1749) is a strongly characterized presence throughout the novel, directly addressing the reader and commenting on the action. In his 1864 review of Nassau W. Senior's *Essays on Fiction*, James had likened *Tom Jones* to 'a vast episode in a sermon preached by a grandly humorous divine' (*LC1* 1201–2).

195 **weaving of silver threads and tapping on golden nails**: James's notebooks and other working documents show him using comparable figures when planning and developing subjects. In his notes for *What Maisie Knew* (1897), for example, he refers to the two essential conditions of the projected novel – the fact that 'EVERYTHING TAKES PLACE BEFORE MAISIE' and 'the tenderness she inspires' in other characters – as 'the golden threads of my *form*' (22 December 1895; *CN* 149). In the 'Project of Novel' for *The Ambassadors* (1903), the 'extraordinary fancy' Maria Gostrey takes to Strether 'is a secondary thread in the web, a little palpable gold thread that plays through all the pattern' (*CFHJ* 18, 503); in the Prefaces to *The Ambassadors* and *The Portrait of a Lady*, he characterizes Maria as a '*ficelle*', a French term literally meaning a thread (see notes 172 and 871). The notes for *The Sense of the Past* which James would dictate between

December 1914 and May 1915 establish a connection between the 'golden nails' of this sentence of the Preface and another term – the French *clou* or nail. He writes of a particularly important juncture in the plot: 'There must be sequences here of the strongest, I make out—the successive driving in of the successive silver-headed nails at the very points and under the very taps that I reserve for them. That's it, the silver nail, the recurrence of it in the right place, the perfection and salience of each, and the trick is played' (*SP* 307). These 'silver-headed nails' are incidents and recognitions that significantly advance the plot. In the next sentence of the notes, James translates 'silver nail' into French as 'clou d'argent': 'I seem to see it thus a silver nail that my young man recognises—well—what he does recognise [...], and it's another one, another clou d'argent, when [...]' (*SP* 307). In earlier passages of the notes, James uses the French *clou* as an equivalent for the English 'hinge': 'my essential hinges or, as I have called 'em, *clous*, that mark the turns or steps of the action' (*SP* 301); the word seems to carry for him associations of fixing, turning and articulating. And *clou* also occurs in notebook entries prior to the period of the *NYE*. On 11 November 1899, for example, trying out ideas for the story 'Mrs Medwin' (1901): 'Or perhaps the *clou* lies elsewhere' (*CN* 187).

196 **that constant effort of George Eliot's [...] to show their adventures and their history [...] as determined by their feelings and the nature of their minds**: The characters referred to in this sentence belong in the following novels by George Eliot: Adam in *Adam Bede* (1859), Felix in *Felix Holt, the Radical* (1866), Tito Melema and Romola de' Bardi in *Romola* (1863), Daniel and Gwendolen Harleth in *Daniel Deronda* (1876), Tertius Lydgate and Dorothea Brooke in *Middlemarch* (1871-2), and Maggie Tulliver in *The Mill on the Floss* (1860). James had reviewed several of Eliot's novels as they appeared, and consistently praised her 'rare psychological penetration' (*LC1* 963) in the portrayal of certain characters and relationships: especially Tito, Lydgate and his wife Rosamond, and Gwendolen and her husband Grandcourt.

197 **left the figure, the concrete man and woman, too abstract by reason of the quantity of soul employed**: James's critical dialogue '*Daniel Deronda*: A Conversation' (1876) contains a debate about the success of Deronda's characterization as a man inspired by 'a general idea', in this case Zionism; the three speakers respectively judge him an unsuccessful attempt to represent 'a faultless human being', 'a dreadful prig' and 'an ideal character [...] triumphantly married to reality' (*LC1* 980-3). In his 1885 review

of *George Eliot's Life* by John Cross, James refers to complaints that Eliot emphasized 'general truth' at the expense of 'the special case': 'Such critics assure us that Gwendolen and Grandcourt, Deronda and Myra [*sic*: Mirah Lapidoth], are not concrete images, but disembodied types, pale abstractions, signs and symbols of a "great lesson." I give up Deronda and Myra to the objector, but Grandcourt and Gwendolen seem to me to have a kind of superior reality; to be, in a high degree, what one demands of a figure in a novel, planted on their legs and complete' (*LC1* 1003–4).

198 **mirrors of the subject**: Compare James's notebook entry of 22 December 1895 for *What Maisie Knew*, which speaks of Maisie as 'the mirror, the plate, on which [Sir Claude's relation to Mrs Beale] is represented as reflected' (*CN* 150). In later Prefaces, James speaks of such characters not as 'mirrors' but as 'reflectors': for that term, see note 822. The characters listed in the following sentences of this Preface as 'intense *perceivers*' mostly either narrate the fictions they appear in or offer a point of view from which to focalize the narration: exceptions are the author Ray Limbert in 'The Next Time' (1895) and the eponymous butler in 'Brooksmith' (1891), who do neither. The quasi-theatrical narrative mode of *The Awkward Age* gives us no direct access to Vanderbank's consciousness, or any other character's.

199 **trying [...], for a "hit" and bread and butter, [...] to blunt the tips of his intellectual fingers**: A 'hit' in this sense is 'any popular success (a person, a play, a song, etc.) in public entertainment', and 'bread and butter' means 'Ordinary or everyday food or sustenance. Hence also: a person's means of earning this, a livelihood' (*OED*). In 1878–9, James's story 'Daisy Miller: A Study' had been 'a really quite extraordinary hit' (to MWJ, 18 January [1879]; *CLHJ 1878–1880* 1:93), but it did not bring him significant financial reward (see note 731). In his essay 'The Science of Criticism' (1891), he noted that literary criticism in France 'handles the subject in general with finer finger-tips' than in Britain or America: 'The bluntness of ours, as tactile implements addressed to an exquisite process, is still sometimes surprising, even after frequent exhibition' (*LC1* 97).

200 **sufficiently "disinherited"**: This account of James's first conception of Hyacinth echoes the published text of the novel. In *The Princess*, 'disinherited' is an ideological catch-word for the French Socialists Monsieur and Madame Poupin, 'the constant theme' of whose talk is 'what M. Poupin called the *avènement* [advent, accession] of the disinherited': 'For them the social question was always in order, the political question always abhorrent, the disinherited always present' (Ch. 7; *NYE* V, 106). The Poupins

view Hyacinth as 'one of the disinherited, one of the expropriated, one of the exceptionally interesting' (Ch. 6; *NYE* V, 102).

201 **swim into one's ken**: An allusion to John Keats's sonnet 'On First Looking into Chapman's Homer' (1816): 'Then felt I like some watcher of the skies / When a new planet swims into his ken' (ll. 9–10; *The Poems of John Keats*, ed. Miriam Allott (London: Longman, 1970), p. 62). James alludes to these lines in other Prefaces (on one occasion changing the verb: 'floated into my ken', p. 42) and often elsewhere in the period of the *NYE*: e.g., in *William Wetmore Story and His Friends* (1903), in his 1907 essay on *The Tempest*, in the story 'Crapy Cornelia' (1909) and in the memoirs *A Small Boy and Others* (1913) and *Notes of a Son and Brother* (1914) (see Philip Horne, 'Henry James and the Poetry of Association', essay awarded the Le Bas Essay Prize, Cambridge University, October 1982, pp. 24–6).

202 **"treasons, stratagems and spoils"**: James quotes from Lorenzo's lines on music in Shakespeare's *The Merchant of Venice* (1596–7): 'The man that hath no music in himself, / Nor is not moved with concord of sweet sounds, / Is fit for treasons, stratagems, and spoils' (5.1.78, 83–5). When he came to revise 'The Aspern Papers' in February 1908 – six months after composing the Preface to *The Princess* – James would incorporate an allusion to the same passage at an important juncture. Encountering Miss Tina again after fleeing from her offer of marriage, the narrator sees that her 'sense of her failure had produced a rare alteration in her, but I had been too full of stratagems and spoils to think of that' (Ch. 9; *NYE* XII, 141); the Shakespearean words replace 'my literary concupiscence' in the first book edition of the story (*The Aspern Papers. Louisa Pallant. The Modern Warning*, 2 vols. (London and New York: Macmillan and Co., 1888), vol. I, p. 136).

203 **would move to pity and terror**: In Aristotelian literary theory, tragedy operates 'through pity and fear [to effect] the proper purgation of these emotions' (Aristotle, *The Poetics*, Ch. 6; in Butcher, *Aristotle's Theory of Poetry and Fine Art*, p. 23). Compare Maggie Verver's gesture in the final sentence of *The Golden Bowl* (1904), responding to her husband's words '"See'? I see nothing but *you*"': 'And the truth of it had with this force after a minute so strangely lighted his eyes that as for pity and dread of them she buried her own in his breast' (*NYE* XXIV, 369).

204 **the famous "iniquity of its social arrangements"**: This was a foundational concept for nineteenth-century Socialism. A relevant discussion of 'social arrangements' in the context of economic inequality can be found

in Book 2, Chapter 1 of John Stuart Mill's *The Principles of Political Economy* (1848), a work broadly sympathetic to contemporary Socialist ideals. The terms of the Preface's formula occur close together in Chapter 17 of the novel, when the Princess speaks to Hyacinth of 'her disgust with a thousand social arrangements, her rebellion against the selfishness, the corruption, the iniquity, the cruelty, the imbecility of the people who all over Europe had the upper hand' (*NYE* V, 293).

205 **revolutionary politics of a hole-and-corner sort, [...] "in" up to his neck, and with that precarious part of him particularly involved**: The adjectival phrase 'hole-and-corner' means 'Done or happening in a "hole and corner", or place which is not public; secret, private, clandestine, underhand' (*OED*). The other figures of speech in this sentence are borrowed from *The Princess*, where it is a matter of curiosity and anxiety whether any given character is 'in' the anarchist conspiracy, and if so, how 'deep' they are in. In Chapter 39, for example, Paul Muniment tells the Princess that he cannot see her motive for '"getting in so uncommon deep"': 'The light in her face flashed on the instant into pure passion. "Do you consider that I'm in—really far?" "Up to your neck, ma'am." "And do you think that *il y va* of my neck—I mean that it's in danger?" she translated eagerly' (*NYE* VI, 294).

206 **that extremely *disponible* figure of Christina Light [...] left on my hands at the conclusion of "Roderick Hudson."**: James had used the French term *disponible* in the Preface to *The Portrait of a Lady* to describe a character or group of characters who serve for an author as the origin of a novel or story, noting there that Turgenev's fictions began in a vision of 'the stray figure, the unattached character, the image *en disponibilité*' (p. 35). He refers at the close of the Preface to *Roderick Hudson* to Christina Light's reappearance as the Princess Casamassima (see note 63).

207 **"walk" round his house of art like haunting ghosts**: A special sense of the verb 'walk': 'Of a ghost, spectre, or fiend: to be seen moving about; to appear. Also of a dead person: to return as a ghost' (*OED*). In James's story 'The Jolly Corner' (1908) – a first version of which he had completed in August 1906, a year before he dictated this Preface – Spencer Brydon uses the same term in reference to the figure that haunts his old family house: 'His *alter ego* "walked"—that was the note of his image of him' (Ch. 2; *NYE* XVII, 456).

208 **the doll's box, to which we usually relegate the spent puppet**: In 1888, James had figured Guy de Maupassant as 'the showman exhilarated by the

success with which he feels that he makes his mannikins (and especially his womankins) caper and squeak, and who after the performance tosses them into their box with the irreverence of a practised hand' (*LC2* 538). James uses the figure of the puppet in this and other literary essays to organize his thoughts about the virtual autonomy of fictional characters. In 1896, for example, he remarked that 'not one' of the characters of Alexandre Dumas *fils* 'has felt the little invisible push that, even when shyly and awkwardly administered, makes the puppet, in spite of the string, walk off by himself and quite "cut", if the mood take him, that distant relation his creator' ('On the Death of Dumas the Younger'; *CWAD2* 434); for 'cut' in this sense, see note 482. W. M. Thackeray's novel *Vanity Fair* (1848) may have given James a precedent for talking about characters in this way. The novel closes with a version of the Preface's scene of relegation: the last sentence reads 'Come children, let us shut up the box and the puppets, for our play is played out' (*The Works of William Makepeace Thackeray*, vol. I, p. 676). In the first edition, these words appear above a vignette illustration by the author of two children closing a box of puppets; the underside of the box lid is marked 'FINIS' (*Vanity Fair: A Novel Without a Hero* (London: Bradbury and Evans, 1848), p. 624). Like Thackeray, whose narrator informs us in the preface to the novel that 'The famous little Becky Puppet [the character Becky Sharp] has been pronounced to be uncommonly flexible in the joints, and lively on the wire' ('Before the Curtain'; *The Works of William Makepeace Thackeray*, vol. I, p. xliv), in the Maupassant and Dumas essays James refers to marionettes rather than glove-puppets. In 1875, however, he half-assentingly referred to the critical view that Balzac had 'turned the feminine puppet, as it were, completely inside out' (*LC2* 61); thirty years later, in 'The Lesson of Balzac', he affirmed that the French novelist 'robustly loved the sense of another explored, assumed, assimilated identity—enjoyed it as the hand enjoys the glove when the glove ideally fits' (*LC2* 132).

209 **couldn't resign herself not to strike again**: Towards the end of *Roderick Hudson*, Christina Light attempts to break off her engagement to the Prince Casamassima, but backs down and consents to marry him when her mother threatens to reveal Christina's illegitimacy. On her final appearance in the novel – now as the Princess Casamassima – she gives various signs of unspent force. She tells Rowland Mallet that she has been wholly claimed by the world and the devil: '"It was their choice; may they never repent!" "I shall hear of you," said Rowland. "You'll hear of me. And whatever you do hear, remember this: I *was* sincere!"' Rowland

interprets this statement as a 'mysterious menace' directed at the world she has married into, and reflects that her union with the Prince 'might be sufficiently prolific in incident' (Ch. 24; *NYE* I, 492–3). The future itinerary Christina outlines for herself in this scene takes in a series of European cities that might well bring her into contact with revolutionary Socialists: Paris, London, Vienna, St Petersburg (*NYE* I, 493); and in *The Princess Casamassima*, she tells Hyacinth that she was introduced to the anarchist Hoffendahl by 'a couple of friends of mine in Vienna' (Ch. 24; *NYE* VI, 52).

210 **an aversion to the *banal***: In Chapter 20 of the revised *Roderick Hudson*, Christina explains to Rowland one of the reasons for her '"great friendship"' with Roderick: '"*Il n'est ni banal ni bête*"' ('He is neither commonplace nor stupid') (*NYE* I, 408); at this point in the Macmillan *Collective Edition* (1883), she had just said '"There is something very fine about him"' (*CE* V, 102). Roderick correspondingly judges her to be '"as far from *banal* as it's possible to be"' (Ch. 9; *NYE* I, 187); this is an insertion in the *NYE* text. The same note persists into *The Princess Casamassima* when the Princess complains to Hyacinth that '"The upper classes are so deadly *banals*"' (Ch. 17; *NYE* V, 291); the *NYE* here revises the text of the first edition, which reads '"[…] so insipid!"' (*The Princess Casamassima*, 3 vols. (London and New York: Macmillan, 1886), vol. II, p. 24). Later in the same chapter, Hyacinth tells her '"You're so kind I don't know what to do"', and she responds: '"Don't be *banal*, please. That's what other people are. What's the use of my looking for something fresh in other walks of life if you're going to be *banal* too?"' (*NYE* V, 297).

211 **She can […] feel freshly about the "people"**: Another echo of the novel: the Princess tells Hyacinth that 'she wanted to know the *people*, and know them intimately—the toilers and strugglers and sufferers—because she was convinced they were the most interesting portion of society' (Ch. 17; *NYE* V, 290).

212 **the whole question […] of "going on with a character": as Balzac […], as Thackeray, as Trollope, as Zola all […] went on**: The recurrence of characters from novel to novel is a structural principle of Balzac's *Comédie humaine*; the same technique was also used by Zola in his Rougon-Macquart series. Writing on Balzac in 1877, James had cited Thackeray and Trollope as English novelists who had made 'a limited attempt to create a permanent stock, a standing fund, of characters', though their efforts were 'faint shadows of Balzac's extravagant thoroughness—his fantastic cohesiveness'

(*LC2* 41). Characters recur across Trollope's six-novel series 'Chronicles of Barsetshire' (1855–67). Thackeray's novels display various types of 'going on': the eponymous hero of *Pendennis* (1850) reappears as the narrator of *The Newcomes* (1854–5); *The Virginians* (1858–9) is a sequel to *The History of Henry Esmond* (1852) and follows the lives of Esmond's grandsons. In his 1883 essay on Trollope, James acknowledged Thackeray and Balzac as precedents but remarked that 'It would be a great mistake [...] to speak of [the recurrence of characters] as an artifice which would not naturally occur to a writer proposing to himself to make a general portrait of a society. He has to construct that society, and it adds to the illusion in any given case that certain other cases correspond with it' (*LC1* 1352). Besides Christina Light, Madame Grandoni and the Prince Casamassima, James himself 'went on with' a few notable minor characters over the span of his career: the sculptor Gloriani, for instance, who also figures in *Roderick Hudson*, presides over Parisian social occasions in Book Fifth, Chapter 1 of *The Ambassadors* (1903) and in 'The Velvet Glove' (1909); and the Millers' Italian courier Eugenio in 'Daisy Miller' (1878) apparently rises to become majordomo of Milly Theale's Venetian household in *The Wings of the Dove* (1902).

213 **Dover [...] the autumn of 1885 and the appearance, in the "Atlantic Monthly" again, of the first chapters of the story**: The town of Dover in Kent on the English Channel coast was a nineteenth-century tourist resort and a major port for commercial, naval and passenger shipping. James described it to Mary Augusta Ward as 'a favourite & very convenient resort of mine', useful for uninterrupted work on account of its 'obscurity & a silence—a social silence, in which I may hear the scratching of my pen' (31 July [1885]; *CLHJ 1884–1886* 1:255). He spent a 'delightfully quiet' six weeks there in August and September 1885, 'pegging away to finish the Princess' (to Grace Norton, 23 August [1885]; *CLHJ 1884–1886* 1:272, 273). The novel ran in the *Atlantic Monthly* from September 1885 to October 1886.

214 **the Esplanade of that cheerful castle-crested little town [...] gigantic "harbour works,"**: Dover is one of the historic Cinque Ports, and its castle dates to the foundation of that confederacy in the eleventh century; the castle was enlarged and fortified in later periods, notably during the late eighteenth and early nineteenth centuries when Dover became a garrison town guarding against invasion by the French. James's lodgings in 1885 were at 15 Esplanade, overlooking the beach and harbour. He described his

situation to Elizabeth Boott on 3 August: 'Dover looks very pretty, with its silver=white cliffs, surmounted with the fine old castle, & the cool green sea covered with vessels whose sails take all kinds of lights' (*CLHJ 1884–1886* 1:257). The Port of Dover was greatly expanded over two decades from the early 1890s to create new commercial and naval harbours; the final phase of this work – the construction of the Admiralty Harbour – was eventually completed in 1909 (see Arthur T. Walmisley, 'The Port of Dover', *Journal of the Royal Society of Arts* 58 (15 April 1910), 526–38; 531–6).

215 **To have lately noted this again [...] that original confidence that the parts of my plan *would* somehow hang together**: When James composed the Preface to *The Princess* in July or August 1907, he had very recently passed through Dover on the way back from a spring and early summer spent on the Continent. The main Channel crossings at this period were Dover–Calais and Folkestone–Boulogne; on 24 June 1907, he announced his imminent return from Venice via 'Milan and Lausanne (by the Simplon orifice) and then [...] Paris—Dover—Rye' (to Jessie Allen; *HJL* 4:453). In a notebook entry made during his earlier residence at Dover in 1885, James had attempted to summon the confidence to complete the novel by plotting out its 'future evolution', noting that he had 'never yet become engaged in a novel in which, after I had begun to write & send off my MS., the details had remained so vague': 'The subject of the *Princess* is magnificent, & if I can only give up my mind to it properly—generously and trustfully—the form will shape itself as successfully as the idea deserves. I have plunged in rather blindly, and got a good many characters on my hands; but these will fall into their places if I keep cool & think it out' (10 August 1885; *CN* 31).

216 **harsh application and friction (that there must have been)**: As Adrian Poole points out, 'the writing of *The Princess* was fraught with anxiety' for James: he began work in uncertainty after the bankruptcy of the book's American publisher James R. Osgood in May 1885, and for the next year was 'constantly falling behind' with the delivery of the monthly parts of the serial (see *CFHJ* 9, xxxi–xxxvii).

217 **this really seemed the fruit of direct experience**: The breadth James grants to the category of 'experience' in 'The Art of Fiction' (1884) is relevant to his claim here: 'The power to guess the unseen from the seen, to trace the implication of things, to judge the whole piece by the pattern, the condition of feeling life in general so completely that you are well on

your way to knowing any particular corner of it—this cluster of gifts may almost be said to constitute experience' (*LC1* 53).

218 **what [...] one had "gone into" and how far one had gone**: To 'go into' a subject denotes a process of enquiry that might well involve the taking of 'notes' (see note 219): 'To examine or discuss minutely; to investigate' (*OED*, 'go'). Uncertainty about how *far* a person has gone or will go, on the other hand, is a question of their commitment to a given cause and the risks they are willing to run for it. The latter form of words is ubiquitous in the novel and most often refers to the Princess: Hyacinth, for example, tells her that if she knows Hoffendahl she has '"gone very far indeed"' (Ch. 24; *NYE* VI, 47). In a later exchange with the Princess, he seconds Lady Aurora's opinion of her behaviour: '"You do go too far," he none the less said to her [...]. To which she answered: "Of course I do—that's exactly what I mean. How else does one know one has gone far enough?"' (Ch. 38; *NYE* VI, 276).

219 **the rich principle of the Note**: James had considered the role of note-taking in the compositional process in several literary essays from the period just before *The Princess*. In 'The Art of Fiction', for example, the only item of Walter Besant's advice to young writers which he could 'positively [...] assent to' was 'the injunction as to entering one's notes in a common-place book' (*LC1* 51). Doing so would help the writer to achieve 'the air of reality (solidity of specification)' which was for James 'the supreme virtue of a novel': 'It is in regard to this that Mr. Besant is well inspired when he bids [the young novelist] take notes. He cannot possibly take too many, he cannot possibly take enough' (*LC1* 53). He observed in 1883 that 'The new school of fiction in France is based very much on the taking of notes; the library of the great Flaubert, of the brothers de Goncourt, of Emile Zola, and of the writer of whom I speak [Alphonse Daudet], must have been in a large measure a library of memorandum-books' (*LC2* 230). Turgenev, too, he had approvingly remarked in 1874, was 'a story-teller who has taken notes'; and James supposed that this 'must have been a life-long habit. His tales are a magazine of small facts, of anecdotes, of descriptive traits, taken, as the phrase is, *sur le vif* [from the life]' (*LC2* 968–9). Nevertheless, when James writes later in this paragraph of the Preface that 'Notes had been [...] the things one couldn't *not* take' (p. 60), he may not mean it literally. Compare the self-accusing opening of his notebook entry of 25 November 1881, written in an 'as yet unspotted blank-book, bought in London six months ago, but hitherto unopened. It is so long since I have kept any notes, taken any memoranda, written

down my current reflections, taken a sheet of paper, as it were, into my confidence. [...] I have lost too much by losing, or rather by not having acquired, the note-taking habit' (*CN* 213). On 22 August 1885, he did make a brief list of 'Phrases, of the people' apparently for use in *The Princess* (*CN* 32). But the characters who take notes in the novel itself are either ridiculous or untrustworthy: the argumentative Delancey, who records the political discussion in the Sun and Moon (Ch. 21); or Captain Sholto, who cynically collects information for the Princess about the lives of the Muniments' neighbours (Ch. 15).

220 **the pedestrian prowler**: The publication of Alvin Langdon Coburn's photo-book *London* in 1909 would remind James of their walks through the city in search of images for *NYE* frontispieces: 'the only matter for regret is that I didn't go about with you to hunt still more cunningly for more subjects. However, the present lot will have such success that you'll do a Second Series & then we'll have some prowls' (to Coburn, 14 October 1909; Virginia). Three days before this letter, James had told Coburn that he was 'on the prowl again myself for another London undertaking [the volume *London Town*]—for which J. Pennell, however, alas, is making—or has already made—the drawings' (11 October 1909; Virginia).

221 **I recall pulling no wires, [...] applying for no "authentic" information**: James nevertheless arranged to visit two institutional locations as part of his research for the early chapters of the novel. As he told Thomas Sergeant Perry on 12 December 1884, 'I have been all the morning at Millbank prison (horrible place) collecting notes for a fictive scene. You see I am quite the Naturalist' (*CLHJ 1884–1886* 1:43); in Chapter 3, Hyacinth and Miss Pynsent visit Hyacinth's mother in an unnamed prison that occupies Millbank's Thames-side location. On 12 March 1885, too, James went with his friend Christina Stewart Rogerson 'to spend a morning at Newgate & the old Bailey' (to Marian 'Clover' Hooper Adams, 9 March [1885]; *CLHJ 1884–1886* 1:137); presumably this was research for Chapters 2–3 of *The Princess*, in which Miss Pynsent remembers visiting Hyacinth's mother in Newgate prison some years before. According to *OED* ('wire'), the idiom 'to pull the wires' means to manipulate people or organizations as though they were puppets. In the present case, James appears to mean something more like the phrase 'to pull strings': 'to exert influence privately' (*OED*, 'string'). In the clandestine political context of *The Princess*, it may also be relevant that the nineteenth-century slang term 'wire-puller' denoted 'A manipulator of party and other interests, working by means more or less

secret; a political intriguer. Hence TO PULL THE WIRES = to exercise a commanding secret political influence' (*Slang* VII:359). In Chapter 24 of the novel, Hyacinth tells the Princess that the '"invisible impalpable wires"' of the anarchist underground '"are everywhere, passing through everything, attaching themselves to objects in which one would never think of looking for them"' (*NYE* VI, 49).

222 **some gust of the hot breath that I had at many an hour seemed to see escape and hover**: James was not in London for the Trafalgar Square Riot of 8 February 1886, when protesting unemployed workers had smashed windows, looted shops and robbed and threatened passers-by. Referring to this violence a month later, he told his brother William that, despite 'immense destitution' among the urban poor, 'what took place the other day, is I feel pretty sure, the worst that, for a long time to come, the British populace is likely to attempt' (9 March [1886]; *CLHJ 1884–1886* 2:49). To Charles Eliot Norton, he was less sanguine: 'the English upper class' seemed to be in 'very much the same rotten and collapsable' condition as 'the French aristocracy before the revolution [...]. Or perhaps it's more like the heavy, congested & depraved Roman world upon which the barbarians came down. In England the Huns & Vandals will have to come up—from the black depths of the (in the people) enormous misery' (6 December [1886]; *CLHJ 1884–1886* 2:254).

PREFACE to *The Tragic Muse* (*NYE* VII–VIII)

223 **in the "Atlantic Monthly" again, [...] several months beyond its proper twelve**: *The Tragic Muse* ran as a serial in the *Atlantic Monthly* for seventeen months, from January 1889 to May 1890. James predicted its extension to Robert Louis Stevenson on 31 July 1888: 'I have just begun a novel which is to run through the *Atlantic* from January 1st and which I aspire to finish by the end of this year. In reality I suppose I shall not be fully delivered of it before the middle of next' (*HJL* 3:240).

224 **the idea to which it was to give form**: In a notebook entry dated 19 June 1884, James attributes the idea for the strand of the plot involving Miriam Rooth and Peter Sherringham to the English novelist Mary Augusta Ward, often referred to as Mrs Humphry Ward (1851–1920): 'Mrs. H. Ward mentioned the other day to me an idea of hers for a story which might be made interesting—as a study of the histrionic character. A young actress is an

object of much attention & a great deal of criticism from a man who loves the stage [...] and finally, though she doesn't satisfy him at all, artistically, loves the girl herself' (*CN* 28). This idea became Ward's novel *Miss Bretherton* (1884). James wrote to Ward later the same year, anticipating the next sentence but one of the Preface – which refers his own interest in the idea of the actress to an unspecified past moment, 'still further back': 'The private history of the public woman (so to speak,) the drama of her feelings, heart, soul, personal relations, & the shock, conflict, complication between those things & her publicity, her career, ambition, artistic life—this has always seemed to me a tempting, challenging subject' (9 December [1884]; *CLHJ 1884–1886* 1:40). Seven years before, in a review of William Black's novel *Macleod of Dare* (1877), he had noted the 'dramatic' potential of a similar subject: 'the artistic temperament, the histrionic genius and Bohemian stamp of the *femme de théâtre*' as contrasted with 'the literal mind and purely moral development of her stalwart Highland lover' (*LC1* 739–40).

225 **the late Thomas Bailey Aldrich, [...] a serial that should run through the year**: Aldrich (1836–1907) took over from W. D. Howells as editor of the *Atlantic Monthly* in 1881, during the serial run of *The Portrait of a Lady*; he died on 19 March 1907, six months before James composed the *Tragic Muse* Preface. James had told Grace Norton on 23 July 1887 that he was 'just beginning a novel about ½ as long (thank God!) as the Princess—& which will probably appear, at no very distant day, as a volume, without preliminary publication in a magazine. It will be called (probably) The Tragic Muse; but don't tell of it' (*CLHJ 1887–1888* 1:168). From his surviving correspondence with Aldrich, it appears that he proposed a comparatively short novel with this title to the *Atlantic Monthly* early in 1888, and received a counter-offer in the form of an invitation to write 'a longer rather than a shorter serial': as James wrote to Aldrich on 3 March 1888, 'I succumb to your arguments & will undertake to manage a serial for the full twelvemonth of 1889' (*LL* 201).

226 **a virtual end [...] of the pleasant old custom of the "running" of the novel**: All James's novels up to this point had been serialized prior to book publication. After *The Tragic Muse* he would not serialize another novel until *The Spoils of Poynton* – a much shorter work, which ran in the *Atlantic Monthly* from April to October 1896 under the title *The Old Things*. In the next sentence of the Preface, James perhaps exaggerates the gap between these two serials ('many years': in fact, it was just over six years). Even before he finished *The Tragic Muse*, he was announcing to

correspondents that he meant to take a break from writing long novels. As early as 31 July 1888, for example, he wrote to Stevenson that once this novel was completed 'I propose, for a longish period, to do nothing but short lengths' (*HJL* 3:240). And to his brother William on 16 May 1890: '*The Tragic Muse* is to be my last long novel. For the rest of my life I hope to do lots of short things with irresponsible spaces between. I see even a great future (10 years) of such' (*CWJ* 2:136). Between 1890 and 1895, James was also much occupied with writing for the theatre.

227 **a great grey void from which no echo or message whatever would come back**: James overstates the critical neglect of *The Tragic Muse*. The novel was unenthusiastically noticed in the British press, but it received appreciative reviews from American critics, notably Howells in *Harper's Monthly Magazine* and Horace Scudder in the *Atlantic*. James wrote to thank Scudder for his 'pages of charming sympathy': 'They have really brought tears to my eyes—giving me a luxurious sense of being understood, perceived, felt. [...] Have you not achieved the miracle of suspecting there may be a *meaning* in what one writes? I don't notice that any one else ever has!' (30 August 1890; *LL* 230). T. J. Lustig observes that a modern collection of James's contemporary reviews 'reprints 16 echoes [i.e., notices of *The Tragic Muse*] and lists a further 27: a void that most writers would envy' (review of Hayes, *Journal of American Studies* 32.1 (1998), 133–4; 133). As Lustig also points out, James had told his British publisher that he did not wish to see reviews of the novel. He wrote to Frederick Macmillan on 29 May 1890: 'Kindly instruct that no "notice" of any kind be sent me' (*The Correspondence of Henry James and the House of Macmillan, 1877–1914: 'All the Links in the Chain'*, ed. Rayburn S. Moore (Baton Rouge, LA: Louisiana State University Press, 1993), p. 162).

228 **unappeasable curiosity for the things of the theatre; [...] and for the "personality" of the performer [...] in particular**: Writing on 'The London Theatres' in 1879, James had described a contemporary 'fashion' for the stage approaching 'the proportions of a mania': 'Plays and actors are perpetually talked about, private theatricals are incessant, and members of the dramatic profession are "received" without restriction. They appear in society, and the people of society appear on the stage; it is as if the great gate which formerly divided the theatre from the world had been lifted off its hinges' (*CWAD2* 235, 236). A major cause of this enthusiasm was the 1879 London season of the visiting Comédie-Française company

(see notes 261 and 263). As James remarked in his essay 'The Comédie-Française in London' (*Nation*, 31 July 1879), 'a certain section of the London world may be said for the last five weeks to have talked of nothing else' (*CWAD2* 244). In the same essay, he described 'the extraordinary vogue' enjoyed by the company's star Sarah Bernhardt (1844–1923) as 'the success of a celebrity, pure and simple': 'Charming as are some of her gifts, peculiar and picturesque as is her whole artistic personality, it cannot in the least be said that she is a consummate actress' (*CWAD2* 245, 246).

229 **"chuck" admired politics**: Colloquially, to 'chuck' something is to 'abandon', 'dismiss' or give it up (*OED*). An American reviewer of *NYE* VII–VIII remarked James's use of this word in the Preface: 'It is noticeable that for once the English language fails him and that he turns to slang to express his meaning. Yet having once adopted the phrase "to chuck" something for art he plays with it manfully, so that it may find its way into literature' ('The Scribner Henry James', *New York Sun* (4 April 1908), 7–8).

230 **a certain romantic glamour [...] the prose and the modesty of the matter**: Nick Dormer has the same thought in Chapter 42 of *The Tragic Muse*, reflecting that, while his abandonment of politics for art has made his life 'decidedly thrilling, for the hour', this excitement cannot last: 'it was well enough till the thrill abated. When this occurred, as it inevitably would, the romance and the glow of the adventure were exchanged for the chill and the prose' (*NYE* VIII, 264).

231 **honours and emoluments**: In the decade before he wrote *The Tragic Muse*, James had privately remarked on the 'worldly prosperity & success' of painters in late nineteenth-century Britain: as he wrote to Grace Norton in 1884, 'I can't help contrasting the great rewards of the successful painter, here, & his glory & honour generally, with the so much more modest emoluments of the man of letters' (29–31 March 1884; *CLHJ 1883–1884* 2:83). James was referring in particular to two painters, John Everett Millais (1829–96) and Frederic Leighton (1830–96), whose financial success was matched by professional and public honours: Leighton was knighted and elected President of the Royal Academy of Arts in the same year (1878), and he would be raised to the peerage in 1896; Millais received a baronetcy in 1885. Walter Besant, in his lecture *The Art of Fiction* (1884), had similarly complained that 'while the leaders in every other branch of Art, in every department of Science, and in every kind of profession, receive their share of the ordinary national distinctions, no one ever hears of honours being bestowed upon novelists.

Neither Thackeray nor Dickens was ever, so far as I know, offered a Peerage; neither King, Queen, nor Prince in any country throughout the whole world takes the least notice of them. I do not say they would be any the better for this kind of recognition, but its absence clearly proves, to those who take their opinions from others, that they are not a class at all worthy of special honour' (*The Art of Fiction: A Lecture*, p. 5). The year before Besant delivered his lecture, the Poet Laureate Alfred Tennyson became 'the first author ennobled solely for services to literature' when he was raised to the peerage; thereafter, 'no more peerages went to literary men', but lesser honours – 'knighthoods or baronetcies' – were increasingly offered and awarded to British authors, editors and actors throughout the 1890s and 1900s (Philip Waller, *Writers, Readers, and Reputations: Literary Life in Britain 1870–1918* (Oxford: Oxford University Press, 2006), pp. 448, 451; and see pp. 448-56). The international Nobel Prize for Literature was first awarded in 1901, and in 1907 Rudyard Kipling became the first British author to win it. James himself would receive an honorary DLitt from Oxford University in 1912, and was awarded the Order of Merit on his deathbed in January 1916.

232 **the joining together of these interests, originally seen as separate**: On 3 March 1888, James told Aldrich that in order to supply the *Atlantic* with a year-long serial novel he would 'probably run two stories (i.e. two subjects I have had in my head) together, interweaving their threads'; the central character would be 'an actress' but the book would be set in the London '"Artistic"' world (*LL* 201).

233 **certain sublime Tintorettos at Venice, a measureless Crucifixion in especial, [...] half a dozen actions separately taking place?**: James refers to the Venetian painter Tintoretto (Jacopo Robusti, 1518–94), whose *Crucifixion* (1565) hangs with many of his other works in the Scuola Grande di San Rocco in Venice. James wrote of it in 1882: 'in looking at this huge composition you look at many pictures; it has not only a multitude of figures, but a wealth of episodes; and you pass from one of these to the other as if you were "doing" a gallery' (*PPL* 27).

234 **an absolutely premeditated art**: James alludes to P. B. Shelley's ode 'To a Skylark' (1820), but emphatically reverses Shelley's praise of a natural principle of spontaneous creation: 'Hail to thee, blithe Spirit! / Bird thou never wert, / That from Heaven, or near it, / Pourest thy full heart / In profuse strains of unpremeditated art' (ll. 1–5; Shelley, *Poetical Works*, ed. Thomas Hutchinson, corrected by Geoffrey Matthews (London: Oxford

University Press, 1970), p. 602). In 1877, James had referred to George Sand as 'the great *improvisatrice* of literature—the writer who best answers to Shelley's description of the skylark singing "in profuse strains of unpremeditated art." No writer has produced such great effects with an equal absence of premeditation' (*LC2* 712). For the faculty of 'improvisation' in Sand and other authors, see note 469.

235 **"The Newcomes" [...] "Les Trois Mousquetaires," [...] Tolstoï's "Peace and War," [...] large loose baggy monsters**: James refers to three massive historical novels of the previous generation: Thackeray's *The Newcomes: Memoirs of a Most Respectable Family* (1854–5), *Les trois mousquetaires* (*The Three Musketeers*) (1844) by Alexandre Dumas, and *Voyna i mir* (*War and Peace*) (1869) by Lev Nikolaevich Tolstoy (1828–1910). The reversal of nouns in Tolstoy's title was not uncommon in contemporary anglophone literary journalism. W. D. Howells, for example, had used the same form in an essay of 1887: '"Peace and War," that great assertion of the sufficiency of common men in all crises, and the insufficiency of heroes' (Howells, 'Leo Tolstoï', introduction to Count Leo Tolstoï, *Sebastopol*, translated from the French by Frank D. Millet (New York: Harper & Brothers, 1887), pp. 5–12; 11). Writing on Turgenev in 1896, James had figured Tolstoy as 'a monster harnessed to his great subject—all human life!—as an elephant might be harnessed, for purposes of traction, not to a carriage, but to a coach-house' (*LC2* 1030).

236 **We have heard it maintained [...] that such things are "superior to art"**: James could have heard this view maintained by Howells, who had written in 1877 that he could not think of Tolstoy's novels 'as literature in the artistic sense at all. Some people complain to me, when I praise them, that they are too long, too diffuse, too confused [...]. In the presence of these criticisms I can only say that I find them nothing of the kind, but that each history of Tolstoï's is as clear, as orderly, as brief, as something I have lived through myself'; his writing 'leaves all tricks of fancy, all effects of art, immeasurably behind' (Howells, 'Leo Tolstoï', pp. 8–9, 10). In a near-contemporaneous essay, Matthew Arnold too asserted that 'we are not to take *Anna Karénine* as a work of art; we are to take it as a piece of life. A piece of life it is. The author has not invented and combined it, he has seen it; it has all happened before his inward eye, and it was in this wise that it happened.' In Arnold's estimation, 'what [Tolstoy's] novel in this way loses in art it gains in reality' ('Count Leo Tolstoi' (1887); *The Complete Prose*

Works of Matthew Arnold, ed. R. H. Super, 11 vols. (Ann Arbor, MI: University of Michigan Press, 1960–77), vol. XI, p. 285).

237 **an organic form**: The aesthetic concept of 'organic form' derives from German Romanticism; it was given a general currency in English by Samuel Taylor Coleridge (1772–1834), closely following the critic August Wilhelm Schlegel (1767–1845). See, for example, Coleridge's note on 'Shakspeare [sic], A Poet Generally': 'The form is mechanic, when on any given material we impress a pre-determined form, not necessarily arising out of the properties of the material;—as when to a mass of wet clay we give whatever shape we wish it to retain when hardened. The organic form, on the other hand, is innate; it shapes, as it developes [sic], itself from within, and the fulness of its development is one and the same with the perfection of its outward form. Such as the life is, such is the form' (*The Literary Remains of Samuel Taylor Coleridge*, ed. Henry Nelson Coleridge, 4 vols. (London: William Pickering, 1836–9), vol. II, pp. 67–8). James had already stated his preference for 'an organic form' in 'The Art of Fiction' (1884): 'A novel is a living thing, all one and continuous, like any other organism, and in proportion as it lives will it be found, I think, that in each of the parts there is something of each of the other parts' (*LC1* 54).

238 **a wide west window that, high aloft, looked over near and far London sunsets**: In March 1886, James moved from the lodgings in Bolton Street, Piccadilly which he had occupied for the past ten years into a fourth-floor flat at 34 De Vere Gardens, Kensington, where he would remain for the next twelve years. He remarked on the flat's western aspect to correspondents: he told his aunt, for example, that it got 'a good deal of sun (owing to a long row of western windows,)' (to CW, 26 July [1887]; *CLHJ 1887–1888* 1:176). And to his brother William: 'The place is excellent in every respect [...] & is, in particular, flooded with light like a photographer's studio. I commune with the unobstructed sky & have an immense birdseye view of housetops & streets. [...] I shall do far better work here than I have ever done before' (9 March [1886]; *CLHJ 1884–1886* 2:47–8). It was here that James began to write *The Tragic Muse* in July 1888. In a notebook entry of 22 October 1891, he describes his working conditions in De Vere Gardens as an aid to recovery from 'all the *déboires* [vexations] & distresses' of adapting and producing *The American* for the stage: 'the soothing, the healing, the sacred & salutary refuge from all these vulgarities & pains is simply to lose myself—in this

quiet, this blessed & uninvaded workroom & in the inestimable effort of & refreshment of art, in resolute & beneficent production'. James figures this space as 'the luminous paradise of art. As soon as I really re-enter it—cross the loved threshold—stand in the high chambers, and the gardens divine—the whole realm widens out again before me and around me—the air of life fills my lungs—the light of achievement flushes over all the place, & I believe, I see, I *do*' (*CN* 61).

239 **an hotel bedroom in Paris [...] the Exposition du Centenaire**: James was in Paris from 24 October to 30 November 1889, staying at the Hôtel de Hollande in rue de la Paix: as Philip Horne notes, Julia Dallow stays in the same hotel in the early chapters of the novel (*The Tragic Muse*, ed. Horne (London: Penguin, 1995), p. 494 n. 7). The Exposition Universelle of 1889 – one of several world's fairs held in Paris during the second half of the nineteenth century – commemorated the centenary of the outbreak of the French Revolution. It ran from May to the end of October, and James visited in its final fortnight: as he reported to his brother William, 'It was despoiled of its freshness & invaded by hordes of furious Franks & fiery Huns—but it was a great impression & I'm glad I sacrificed to it' (28 November [1889]; *CWJ* 2:126).

240 **the centre of my structure would insist on placing itself *not* [...] in the middle**: James had privately diagnosed the same structural failure in *The Wings of the Dove*: 'The centre [...] isn't in the middle, or the middle, rather, isn't in the centre, but ever so much too near the end, so that what was to come after it is truncated' (to Mary Cadwalader Jones, 23 October 1902; *HJL* 4:247). See also his notebook entry of 13 February 1896, written as he was approaching the end of *The Spoils of Poynton*: 'As usual I am crowded—my first two-thirds are too developed: my third bursts my space or is well nigh squeezed and mutilated to death in it. But that is my problem' (*CN* 155).

241 **a bird [...] as merely fabled as the phœnix**: The phoenix of classical legend was an immortal bird supposed to live in the Arabian desert; its name also denotes 'A person or thing of unique excellence or matchless beauty; a paragon' (*OED*).

242 **legs too short [...] for its body**: James had used variant forms of this metaphor of bodily disproportion in private correspondence to describe the same fault of construction in other works. To Howells, for example, acknowledging that the final third of 'Lady Barberina' was 'squeezed together & écourté [shortened]': 'It is always the fault of my things that the

head and trunk are too big & the legs too short. [...] My tendency to this disproportion remains incorrigibl [sic]. I begin short tales as if they were to be long novels' (21 February 1884; *CLHJ 1883–1884* 2:29). And to Mary Cadwalader Jones on *The Wings of the Dove*: 'The book, in fine, has too big a head for its body' (23 October 1902; *HJL* 4:247).

243 **not on any terms to be made known**: Contrary to this resolution, James acknowledges his misplacement of the 'centre' in *The Wings of the Dove* in his Preface to that novel; and he refers again in general terms to 'the audacity of misplaced middles' in the Preface to *The Awkward Age* (pp. 239, 79).

244 **lay up heavenly treasure**: An allusion to Jesus' words in the Sermon on the Mount: 'Lay not up for yourselves treasures upon earth, where moth and rust doth corrupt, and where thieves break through and steal: But lay up for yourselves treasures in heaven' (Matthew 6:19–20). James often uses this biblical formula in connection with the management of artistic resources. In *Roderick Hudson*, for example, the American artist Sam Singleton, summoned home from Europe to his family in Buffalo, New York, 'would have been grateful for another year in Rome, but [...] submitted to fate the more patiently that he had laid up treasure which at Buffalo would seem infinite' (Ch. 21; *NYE* I, 414). Elsewhere in the Prefaces, James speaks of laying up fictional subject-matter and the future opportunity to analyse his own work (pp. 8, 91).

245 **the art of preparations**: James appears to refer to an axiom of the French novelist and playwright Alexandre Dumas (1802–70): 'en fait d'art dramatique, tout est dans la préparation' (*Histoire de mes bêtes*, 2nd edn (Paris: Michel Lévy Frères, 1868), Ch. 1, p. 3). A few years after the publication of the *NYE*, the English theatre critic William Archer would attribute this statement to Dumas's son and namesake Alexandre Dumas *fils* (1824–95): 'No technical maxim is more frequently cited than the remark of the younger Dumas: "The art of the theatre is the art of preparations"' (*Play-Making: A Manual of Craftsmanship* (London: Chapman & Hall, 1912), p. 154).

246 **the great river-spanning museum of the Champ de Mars and the Trocadero**: The site of the 1889 Exposition Universelle covered a square kilometre in the centre of Paris, including Champ de Mars on the left bank of the Seine – a large public open space, formerly a military parade ground, where the Tour Eiffel was constructed for the occasion – and the

Palais du Trocadéro and its gardens on the right bank opposite, with the Pont d'Iéna between.

247 **the tender grace of a day that is dead**: As often elsewhere when considering the past in his late non-fiction, James alludes to the closing lines of Tennyson's lyric 'Break, break, break' (1842): 'But the tender grace of a day that is dead / Will never come back to me' (ll. 15–16; *The Poems of Tennyson*, vol. II, p. 24). See, for example, *William Wetmore Story and His Friends* (1903), with reference to the documentary record of Story's visit to Washington, DC in 1882–3: 'The particular pleasantness of Washington still abides in these reminders, giving out, for any initiated sense, a faint fragrance as of old dried rose-leaves; so fast, as we feel in the American air the pulse of change, does even a comparatively recent antiquity take on, with faded flowers and ribbons, with superseded performers, "the tender grace of a day that is dead"' (*WWS* II:270). For James's habitual reference to these lines, see Herford, *Henry James's Style of Retrospect*, pp. 133–4.

248 **the embarrassed effort to "finish," […] within my already exceeded limits**: In October 1889, Aldrich had given James three additional monthly parts (January–March 1890) beyond the twelve originally agreed on for *The Tragic Muse*; but 'The book expanded in the writing', as Horne observes, and in the event James would require two further parts (April–May 1890) to bring it to a conclusion (*The Tragic Muse*, ed. Horne, p. xi).

249 **as I have already elsewhere had occasion to urge**: James discusses 'foreshortening' as a fictional technique in the Preface to *Roderick Hudson*, pp. 11–12.

250 **my lucky title**: James mentions the title in his earliest surviving reference to the novel, in a letter to Grace Norton on 23 July 1887 (see note 225). It may have seemed 'lucky' for its equal aptness to the novel's twin subjects, the theatre and the visual arts: Horne notes that the most famous British image of Melpomene – the classical Muse of tragedy – was also a portrait of an actress, Joshua Reynolds's *Mrs Siddons as the Tragic Muse* (1784) (*The Tragic Muse*, ed. Horne, p. 500 n. 6). As they watch Miriam reading for Madame Carré in Chapter 7, Peter Sherringham tells Nick Dormer, '"You must paint her just like that." "Like that?" "As the Tragic Muse"' (*NYE* VII, 127).

251 **no direct exhibition of hers whatever, […] seeing it only through a more or less bewildered interpretation of it by others**: Reviewing *The Tragic Muse* in the *Atlantic Monthly* in September 1890, Horace Scudder noted as

an example of James's 'power of handling his material' the fact 'that from first to last Miriam Rooth is always seen *en face*. That is to say, though their author indulges in analysis of his other characters, he gives the reader only a front view of his heroine. [...] We see her reflected occasionally in the faces of her audience, but we are not helped to a more intimate knowledge through the private advices of her creator' (Gard 216). The narrator refers to this representational choice in Chapter 25, pointing out that we might know what Miriam felt about sitting to Nick for her portrait 'only were it open to us to regard this young lady through some other medium than the mind of her friends. We have chosen, as it happens, for some of the great advantages it carries with it, the indirect vision' (*NYE* VIII, 42–3). As Horne points out, however, James does in fact give 'a short rendering of Miriam's consciousness' when she visits the Théâtre Français with Peter Sherringham in Chapter 21 (*The Tragic Muse*, ed. Horne, p. 494 n. 11): the effect is clearest in her encounter with the actress Mademoiselle Voisin (*NYE* VII, 364–9). The two sentences in Chapter 12 beginning 'Miriam liked the Paris of the summer mornings' (*NYE* VII, 222) likewise appear to adopt her point of view. See also note 256.

252 **they move in the light of *alternation***: In 'The Lesson of Balzac', James had recently commented on the importance of 'relief and alternation' in fictional construction, with specific reference to the handling of dialogue (*LC2* 138). In 1886, similarly, he had regretted that W. D. Howells in his novels 'should neglect the effect that comes from alternation, distribution, relief. He has an increasing tendency to tell his story altogether in conversations, so that a critical reader sometimes wishes, not that the dialogue might be suppressed [...] but that it might be distributed, interspaced with narrative and pictorial matter' (*LC1* 505).

253 **as will doubtless [...] be complacently shown**: James returns to the linked topics of 'scenic' composition and the multiple '*aspects*' of a fictional situation in the next Preface, to *The Awkward Age*, pp. 86–7.

254 **the prodigious consciousness of Hamlet [...] only takes its turn with that of the other agents of the story**: The title-role of *Hamlet* (1600–1) is the largest in the Shakespearean canon and includes several soliloquies; but Hamlet also spends long periods of the play offstage, including the whole of Act 4.

255 **amusing I mean in the blest very modern sense**: James had recently glossed the word 'amusing' in the fourth paper of his series on 'The Speech

of American Women' (*Harper's Bazar*, February 1907) in a passage of invented dialogue between himself and a young woman. He urges that the careful discrimination of spoken sounds '"ought to make our medium [speech] amusing"', and then clarifies: '"I use the term in that higher, that charmingly modern sense that represents the something more than merely 'answering,' merely sufficing to its ordinary function, that we ask of almost any implement we employ"' (*HJC* 77). In 1897, he had noted that 'amusement' was the term used by George Du Maurier 'for his own technical tricks or those of others' (*LC1* 889–90); and this is presumably what he himself meant when he wrote in 1902 of 'the little technical amusements of [Balzac's] penetrating power' ('HdB' xlii). In the Preface to *The Golden Bowl*, James refers in these terms to the technical 'problem' he had set himself in that novel by choosing to deploy a small number of characters but show 'about as much of them as a coherent literary form permits': 'the "amusement" of the chronicle in question—by which, once more, I always mean the gathered cluster of all the *kinds* of interest—was exactly to see what a consummate application of such sincerities would give' (p. 263). For an older, less critically ambitious sense of 'amusing' as meaning simply entertaining, compare James in 1883 on Alphonse Daudet, 'a story-teller who has the great peculiarity of being "amusing," as the old-fashioned critics say, even when he touches the sources of tears' (*LC2* 241–2).

256 **I never "go behind" Miriam**: In James's idiosyncratic technical vocabulary, to 'go behind' means (for an author) to grant the reader direct access to a character's consciousness, or (for a character or a literary critic) to wonder about the causes of a given action, decision or phenomenon. James comes back to this formula in the Preface to *The Awkward Age* (see note 307). In the context of *The Tragic Muse*, it may also be relevant that 'to go behind' is a theatrical idiom meaning to go backstage – 'behind the scenes' – during or after a performance (see the nineteenth-century instances cited in *OED*, 'behind', 7. d.). The phrase occurs with this sense in the novel. In Chapter 20, Peter Sherringham talks with Miriam Rooth, her mother and the actor Basil Dashwood during 'the first *entr'acte*' of a performance at the Théâtre Français, and we are told that 'they were waiting for the second [interval] to go behind', where Peter intends to call on the actress Mademoiselle Voisin (*NYE* VII, 351). Their doing so coincides with the only passage in the novel where – contrary to James's insistence in the Preface – the narrative unequivocally adopts Miriam's point of view and gives the reader direct access to her consciousness (see note 251). In this chapter

and the next, Peter leads Miriam through a series of backstage areas: first a 'lobby' with a view of the wings and stage, then 'a sort of parlour' where simple costume changes can be made, then the *'foyer d'artistes'* or green-room, then up to Mademoiselle Voisin's *'loge'* or dressing-room; this last and most private backstage space is represented entirely as Miriam experiences it (Chs. 20–1; *NYE* VII, 352–69). James thus 'goes behind' Miriam in his technical sense when she herself 'goes behind' in the theatrical sense.

257 **The late R. L. Stevenson was to write to me**: Stevenson's letter does not survive. James promised to send him a copy of *The Tragic Muse* on 28 April 1890, as 'the sole and single Anglo-Saxon capable of perceiving—though he may care for little else in it—how well it is written' (*HJL* 3:279). At this time Stevenson had recently decided to settle in the South Seas and bought a plot of land at Vailima in the Samoan Islands. Postal delivery over such distances was uncertain: as Stevenson wrote to James on 29 December 1890, '*The Tragic Muse* you announced to me as coming; I had already ordered it from a Sydney bookseller; about two months ago he advised me that his copy was in the post; and I am still tragically museless' (*The Letters of Robert Louis Stevenson*, ed. Bradford A. Booth and Ernest Mehew, 8 vols. (New Haven, CT: Yale University Press, 1994–5), vol. VII, p. 64).

258 **the view of the "histrionic temperament,"**: James's first note for the strand of the plot involving Miriam Rooth had envisaged her as 'a study of the histrionic character', 'a study of a certain particular *nature d'actrice*: a very curious sort of nature to reproduce' (19 June 1884; *CN* 28).

259 **We shall deal with it [...] in a more urgent connexion**: James returns to this objection to his portrayals of fictional celebrities in the Prefaces to *NYE* XII and XV, pp. 131–3, 175–8.

260 **M. Anatole France [...] his brief but inimitable *Histoire Comique* [...] the *cabotin***: The novella *Histoire comique* (1903) by the French poet and novelist Anatole France (1844–1924) shares a central situation with *The Tragic Muse*: an actress, Félicie Nanteuil, is loved by a diplomat. The 'reserves' James mentions in this sentence of the Preface may have been prompted by France's explicitly sexual depiction of their love affair. Philip Horne writes: 'The last scene, shortly before her debut at the Comédie-Française, has her strip naked—as James says, dismiss "all material and social overdraping" [p. 73]—for this lover and incongruously perform her entire part in the classic comedy of manners *L'École des femmes* by

Molière' (*The Tragic Muse*, ed. Horne, pp. 494-5 n. 12). The vulgar French word *cabotin* (feminine *cabotine*) means a strolling player or simply a bad actor: 'Comédien ambulant, et, par extension, mauvais comédien' (Littré, *Dictionnaire de la langue française*, vol. I, p. 447). James had complained to Mary Augusta Ward that in her own theatre-novel *Miss Bretherton* she had made too little of her heroine's professional ambition: 'one doesn't feel her, see her, enough, as the pushing actress, the cabotine' (9 December [1884]; *CLHJ 1884-1886* 1:41).

261 **those deep subjections that, in men of "taste," the Comédie Française used in old days to conspire for**: The Comédie-Française or Théâtre Français is the French national theatre company, founded by Louis XIV in 1680; its Parisian home was and still is the 'salle Richelieu' at 2 rue de Richelieu. In his 1873 essay 'The Parisian Stage', James had remarked on the 'old gentlemen, classic playgoers', who 'haunted' the stalls of the Théâtre Français: 'I caught an echo of my impressions from one of them the other evening, when, as the curtain fell on Bressant and Plessy, he murmured ecstatically to his neighbor, "*Quelle connaissance de la scène ... et de la vie!*"' ('What knowledge of the stage ... and of life!') (*CWAD2* 7). Reviewing the French critic Francisque Sarcey's *Comédiens et Comédiennes: la Comédie Française* in 1877, he recalled his own delight on first seeing the company perform: 'I shall never forget how at first I was under the charm' (*CWAD2* 189). Ten years later, in his essay on the French actor Benoît-Constant Coquelin (1841-1909), he called the Théâtre Français as he had first known it 'a school for the education of taste' (*CWAD2* 321).

262 **the very deuce**: 'The deuce' is a euphemism for the Devil, so this is a milder version of the idiomatic phrase 'the very devil', meaning in context a provoking difficulty: 'something as bad as the Devil, or as bad as can be conceived' (*OED*, 'deuce', 'devil').

263 **the organised theatre, [...] as Matthew Arnold was in those very days pronouncing it, irresistible**: James refers to 'The French Play in London' (1879), an essay by the poet and critic Matthew Arnold (1822-88) occasioned by the Comédie-Française's visit to London (see note 228). For Arnold, this state-subsidized French company demonstrated 'not only what is gained by organising the theatre, but what is meant by organising it', and he made it the basis of his own suggestions for 'a better plan of public organisation for the English theatre': a resident company of actors

based in the West End of London, with companies to follow in the East End and the provinces, funded by government grants and performing a repertoire of Shakespeare and modern classics as well as new plays, with an associated school of dramatic elocution and declamation (*The Complete Prose Works of Matthew Arnold*, vol. IX, pp. 82–3, 84). James specifically alludes to the rallying cry of Arnold's essay, which appears twice in the text: 'The theatre is irresistible; *organise the theatre*' (pp. 82, 85).

264 **The trade of the stage-player, and above all of the actress, must have so many detestable sides for the person exercising it […] very imperfect**: Reviewing the English actress Fanny Kemble's memoir *Record of a Girlhood* in 1878, James had remarked a 'singular anomaly' in her attitude to the theatre: 'during the years of her early histrionic triumphs' (c.1829–34), she 'took no pleasure in the exercise of her genius. She went upon the stage from extrinsic considerations, and she never overcame a strong aversion to it. The talent, and the sort of activity that the talent involved, remained mutually unsympathetic.' And yet Kemble had not sought the kind of 'compensation' referred to in this sentence of the Preface: James also noted 'the complete absence of any touch of Bohemianism in her personal situation' (*LC1* 1071, 1070). Projecting *The Tragic Muse* to Aldrich on 3 March 1888, James had reassured him about the potential dangers, for a serial novel, of his theatrical and aesthetic subject-matter: 'It won't be improper; strange to say, considering the elements' (*LL* 201).

265 **Any presentation of the artist *in triumph* must be flat in proportion as it really sticks to its subject […] the back he turns to us as he bends over his work**: As when James reflects on the prosaic character of artistic work earlier in this Preface (see note 230), here again his technical problem as an author is anticipated by the characters in *The Tragic Muse*. In Chapter 42, Nick's vision of a future of steady application to portrait-painting '"sounds a little flat"' to Peter Sherringham (*NYE* VIII, 278). And in Chapter 49, Nick imagines Gabriel Nash visiting his studio at some point in that future: '"Some day you'll peep in here languidly and find me in such an attitude of piety—presenting my bent back to you as I niggle over some interminable botch—that I shall give cruelly on your nerves and you'll just draw away, closing the door softly"' (*NYE* VIII, 408–9). The image of the artist's turned back also recalls the uncanny moment in 'The Private Life' (1892) when the narrator enters the hotel room of the writer Clare Vawdrey, expecting to find it empty, and encounters Vawdrey's hard-working

alter ego: 'His back was half-turned to me and he bent over the table in the attitude of writing' (Ch. 1; *NYE* XVII, 237).

266 **he eats the cake of the very rarest privilege [...]—therefore he mayn't "have" it [...] at the same time**: James elaborates on an English proverb: 'to have one's cake and eat it' means 'to enjoy two desirable but mutually exclusive alternatives. Chiefly in negative contexts, esp. in *you can't have your cake and eat it too*' (*OED*, 'cake'). For the artist's 'privilege', see the Preface to *The American*, p. 23.

267 **some mere brass check or engraved number**: A 'check' in this sense is 'A token, usually a memorandum of receipt, a ticket, or piece of metal duly stamped or numbered, used for the purpose of identification, or as evidence of ownership or title: given, e.g. to the owner of luggage on a railway (as in U.S.), or to one who temporarily leaves luggage, cloaks, portable articles, at the cloakroom of a railway station, place of entertainment, etc., to enable him to identify and reclaim the same' (*OED*, 'check', *int.* and *n.*¹ 14. b.).

268 **"the best thing in the book,"**: Compare James's judgement on Isabel Archer's 'extraordinary meditative vigil' in *The Portrait of a Lady*, in the Preface to that novel: 'It is obviously the best thing in the book' (p. 45).

PREFACE to *The Awkward Age* (*NYE* IX)

269 **a group of productions [...] which have in common [...] an unforeseen principle of growth**: *The Spoils of Poynton* (1897) and *What Maisie Knew* (1897) are the most important other members of this 'group': James comments on their growth in the Prefaces to *NYE* X and XI, pp. 97–8, 111, 114. He first envisaged *The Awkward Age* in May 1895 as one of three 'short stories' he had undertaken to write for the *Atlantic Monthly*; as Edel notes, the other two stories would become *The Spoils of Poynton* and 'Glasses' (1896) (*CN* 121 and n. 1). Writing to Howells on 11 December 1902, James mentions his novel *The Sacred Fount* (1901), which does not appear in *NYE*, as 'one of several things of mine, in these last years, that have paid the penalty of having been conceived only as the "short story" [...] & then *grew* by a rank force of its own into something of which the idea had, modestly, never been to be a book'; in this letter, he also names *The Spoils*, *Maisie* and 'The Turn of the Screw' (*LFL* 380).

270 **The thing done and dismissed [...] looking dead, if not buried**: Compare James's letter of 5 December 1887 to Robert Louis Stevenson, referring to

Roderick Hudson. James can take only 'the slenderest' interest in this early novel, 'as in all my past & shuffled off emanations & efforts': 'directly my productions are finished, or at least thrust out to earn their living, they seem to me dead' (*CLHJ 1887–1888* 1:302).

271 **the *quantity* of finish it stows away**: In artisanal and artistic contexts, 'finish' means 'The condition or quality of being finished or perfected': *OED*'s nineteenth-century examples refer to tanning leather, minting coins and making paper, and also to musical performance. James's sense of *The Awkward Age* as having displayed a 'monstrous' capacity for growth suggests an idiomatic meaning for the phrase 'stow away': '*jocularly*, to "put out of sight", "dispose of", eat up (quantities of food)' (*OED*, 'stow').

272 **a fine purple peach [...] a round ripe plum**: Compare Mr Longdon's impression of Aggie as the successful product of a methodical upbringing in *The Awkward Age*, Book Fifth, Chapter 3: 'Since to create a particular little rounded and tinted innocence had been aimed at, the fruit had been grown to the perfection of a peach on a sheltered wall' (*NYE* IX, 238). Colloquially, a 'peach' is 'A particularly fine or desirable person or thing, esp. an attractive young woman; an exceptionally good example of its kind'; in British slang, similarly, a 'plum' is 'any desirable thing, a coveted prize' (*OED*).

273 **the "sitting downstairs," from a given date, of the merciless maiden previously perched aloft**: For an upper- or middle-class London girl in the late nineteenth century, 'sitting downstairs' would mean joining adult company in the drawing-room on the ground floor or first floor of the family home, as against remaining with the younger children in the day-nursery on an upper floor. On 4 March 1895, James had noted the idea for *The Awkward Age*: 'The idea of the little London girl who grows up to "sit with" the free-talking modern young mother—reaches 17, 18 &c—comes out—&, not marrying, has to "be there"—&, though the conversation is supposed to be expurgated for her, inevitably hears, overhears, guesses, follows, takes in, becomes acquainted with horrors' (*CN* 117–18).

274 **a scant show for a "thick book,"**: *The Awkward Age* runs to 414 pages in the English first edition (London: William Heinemann, 1899) and 458 pages in the American first edition (New York: Harper & Brothers, 1899). The anonymous reviewer in *Literature* (May 1899) complained of the book's 'inordinate' length and 'the intolerable thinness to which the material is beaten out' (Gard 283, 284).

275 **the vanity of the *a priori* test of what an *idée-mère* may have to give**: Writing on Matilde Serao in 1901, James had pronounced the notion of 'an *a priori* rule [...] as to subjects themselves' to be 'suicidal, when reflected upon' ('Matilde Serao', *North American Review* 172 (March 1901), 367–80; 368). His critical essays consistently argue against 'the oppressive *a priori*' in this regard, 'the cramped posture of foregone conclusions and narrow rules' ('American Letter', *Literature* (26 March 1898); *LC1* 651, 653). In 'The Art of Fiction' (1884), for example, he warned against Walter Besant's attempt 'to say so definitely beforehand what sort of an affair the good novel will be' and argued 'that certain traditions on the subject, applied *a priori*, have already had much to answer for' (*LC1* 49). Again, in 'The Future of the Novel' (1899): 'The form of novel that is stupid on the general question of its freedom is the single form that may, *a priori*, be unhesitatingly pronounced wrong' (*LC1* 106–7). The French term 'idée-mère' means a principal or governing idea, literally a 'mother-idea'; in nineteenth-century musical analysis, it denotes a compositional theme or motif, as, for example, in Antonin Reicha's *Traité de haute composition musicale* (1824–6), Book 6.

276 **to surround with the sharp black line, to frame in the square, the circle**: Compare James's introduction to the posthumous *Last Studies* (1897) of the English essayist and short-story writer Hubert Crackanthorpe (1870–96): in 'the tiny collection of "Vignettes"', Crackanthorpe delights in 'working the impression down to a few square inches of water-colour, framed, as it were, with a narrow line and suspended on a quiet wall' (*LC1* 843). For the 'circle' of literary form as limiting or containing 'the relations of a human figure or a social occurrence' (p. 79), see also note 14.

277 **put about**: To be 'put about' is to be caused 'inconvenience or trouble' (*OED*, 'put'). In *What Maisie Knew*, for example, Maisie's nurse Moddle uses this idiom to express one of the consequences of the legal decision that custody of the child should be shared by her divorced parents: '"Your papa wishes you never to forget, you know, that he has been dreadfully put about"' (Ch. 1; *NYE* XI, 11).

278 **the liberal firesides beyond the wide glow of which [...] female adolescence hovered and waited**: Amongst James's close London acquaintance around 1895 were several families with teenage daughters: for example, the daughters of Lucy Clifford (Ethel and Margaret, b. 1876 and 1877), Edmund Gosse (Tessa and Laura, b. 1877 and 1881), Anne Thackeray Ritchie (Hester, b. 1878) and Mary Augusta Ward (Janet, b. 1879). James

also knew at least three of the contributors to the exchange of articles on this topic in English periodicals begun in January 1894 by Blanche Alethea Crackanthorpe's 'The Revolt of the Daughters': Crackanthorpe herself (d. 1928), Ethel Bertha Harrison (1851–1916), and May Jeune, Lady St Helier (1845–1931). Jeune had two teenage daughters (Madeline and Osma, b. 1876 and 1877). For the relevance to the novel of this contemporary public debate, see Hamlin L. Hill, Jr, '"The Revolt of the Daughters": A Suggested Source for "The Awkward Age"', *Notes and Queries* n.s. 8.9 (1961), 347–9.

279 **play of mind**: In Matthew Arnold's essay 'The Function of Criticism at the Present Time' (1864) the phrase 'a free play of the mind on all subjects' is a central component of Arnold's characterization of disinterested criticism (*The Complete Prose Works of Matthew Arnold*, vol. III, pp. 268–71).

280 **"modernity,"**: James had described Matthew Arnold in 1884 as 'the poet of his age, of the moment in which we live, of our "modernity," as the new school of criticism in France gives us perhaps license to say' (*LC1* 727). As T. J. Lustig notes, for James 'it was as a conduit for French ideas that Arnold's "modernity" was most evident' ('James, Arnold, "Culture", and "Modernity"; or, A Tale of Two Dachshunds', *Cambridge Quarterly* 37.1 (2008), 164–93; 180), and an emphasis on this word also runs through James's contemporaneous essays on French novelists. Writing on Alphonse Daudet in 1883, for example, he observed that 'the word *modernité* perpetually occurs' in the family memoir written by Daudet's brother: 'M. Ernest Daudet, in *Mon Frère et Moi*, insists upon [Alphonse's] possession of the qualities expressed by this barbarous substantive, which is so indispensable to the new school' (*LC2* 229). In 1897, the mere fact of Paul Bourget lecturing on Flaubert at the University of Oxford struck James as an instance of 'the quickened notation of our "modernity." I feel that I can pay this last-named lively influence no greater tribute than by candidly accepting, as an aid to expression, its convenient name' ('London. July 31, 1897', *Harper's Weekly* 41 (21 August 1897), 834). In *The Awkward Age*, Mrs Brookenham describes the French fiction Mitchy has lent her as possessing '"A kind of a morbid modernity"'; Mitchy later uses the same formula to describe Nanda herself (Book Second, Chs. 4 and 5; *NYE* IX, 79, 100).

281 **some sacrifice [...] would have to be made**: In Book Fifth, Chapter 4, the Duchess characterizes Mrs Brookenham's dilemma in these terms: '"She's in a prodigious fix—she must sacrifice either her daughter or what

she once called to me her intellectual habits"' (*NYE* IX, 255). In his 1901 essay on Matilde Serao, James had remarked on the type of sacrifice usually called for in literary contexts by Anglo-American concerns about the innocence of 'the "young"': 'I know not whether it has ever officially been stated for us that, given the young, given literature, and given, under stress, the need of sacrificing one or the other party, it is not, certainly, by our sense of "style" that our choice would be determined' ('Matilde Serao', 369).

282 **ancient liberties**: This phrase refers to the collective legal rights originally belonging to Anglo-Saxon towns and recognized by royal charter following the Norman Conquest. Clause 13 of Magna Carta (1215) guarantees that 'the city of London is to have all its ancient liberties [*antiquas libertates*] and free customs both by land and water' (J. C. Holt, *Magna Carta* (Cambridge: Cambridge University Press, 1965), pp. 382–3).

283 **the perfect system on which the awkward age is handled in most other European societies, [...] the inveterate English trick of [...] intellectually helpless compromise**: The Duchess compares '"our fine old foreign [French] way"' of managing girls' upbringing and entry into society with '"the more and more extraordinary development of English manners"' in a conversation with Mrs Brookenham (Book Second, Ch. 2; *NYE* IX, 55). James envisaged this scene in his notebook: 'There may be the contrasted clever, *avisée* [prudent] foreign or foreignized friend or sister, who [...] takes *my* little lady to task for her inferior system & inferior virtue' (4 March 1895; *CN* 118). The phrase 'the awkward age' is a translation of the French *l'âge ingrat*, 'the time of life when one is no longer a child and yet not properly grown up' (*OED*, 'awkward'). For the cultural and literary currency of this formula in the period, see Sarah Bilston, *The Awkward Age in Women's Popular Fiction, 1850–1900: Girls and the Transition to Womanhood* (Oxford: Oxford University Press, 2004).

284 **an "epoch of transition"**: For the widespread contemporary historical understanding of the nineteenth century as a transitional period, see, for example, the first essay in the series by J. S. Mill entitled 'The Spirit of the Age' (1831): 'The first of the leading peculiarities of the present age is, that it is an age of transition. Mankind have outgrown old institutions and old doctrines, and have not yet acquired new ones' (John Stuart Mill, *The Spirit of the Age*, introductory essay by Frederick A. von Hayek (Chicago, IL: University of Chicago Press, 1942), p. 6).

285 **our "basic" assumption that the female young read the newspapers**: James had recently made the same assumption about newspapers when addressing an audience of young women – the graduating class at Bryn Mawr College, Pennsylvania – in June 1905, referring to 'that contribution to the idea of expression which you must feel yourselves everywhere getting, wherever you turn, from the mere noisy vision of their ubiquitous page' (*HJC* 54). In his second paper for *Harper's Bazar* on 'The Manners of American Women' (May 1907), he was pessimistic about the probable effect of newspapers on their female readers: 'Where or how […] do these unmitigatedly ugly things fit into a feminine sensibility that has begun to confess, at any point, to cultivation? […] What would be the natural effect on articulation and utterance themselves […] of all the unashamed grossness and blatancy and illiteracy and impudence […]?' (*HJC* 94–5).

286 **Nanda's exposure**: Compare the conversation in Book Fourth, Chapter 3, in which Mrs Brookenham raises '"the whole question […] of bringing girls forward or not. The question of—well, what do you call it?—their exposure. […] Nanda of course is exposed," Mrs. Brook pursued—"fearfully"' (*NYE* IX, 195).

287 **muddle, if the term be not too gross**: The Preface's term is not too gross for the Duchess: '"It's all a muddle, a compromise, a monstrosity, like everything else you [the English] produce"' (Book Second, Ch. 2; *NYE* IX, 55).

288 **What form so familiar […] as that in which […] "Gyp" casts most of her social studies?**: The popular French novelist Sibylle-Gabrielle-Marie-Antoinette de Riquetti de Mirabeau, comtesse de Martel de Janville (1849–1932), who used the *nom de plume* 'Gyp'; she was particularly associated with the *roman dialogué*, a form of novel written in dialogue and laid out on the page like a play-text. Gyp's comedies of fashionable French society offer various parallels of plot and theme with *The Awkward Age*. *Le Mariage de Chiffon* (1894), for example, concerns a frank, unconventional 16-year-old girl, the daughter of minor aristocrats without a fortune, at odds with her mother about the moral tone of her social set. The daughter scorns her mother's attempts to make a lucrative marriage for her, rejects the advances of two suitors and offers instead to keep house for her bachelor step-uncle, then realizes that she is in love with him and proposes to him herself. At least five English translations of *Le Mariage de Chiffon* were published in 1895, and several other Gyp titles were translated into English during the decade. James owned copies of Gyp's dialogue-novels *Petit*

Bob (1882), *Autour du mariage* (1883), *Autour du divorce* (1886) and *Monsieur le duc* (1893), all in French; his copies of the first three titles listed here were all later printings dated between 1895 and 1897, the period in which he wrote his first notebook entries and scenario for *The Awkward Age* (Leon Edel and Adeline R. Tintner, *The Library of Henry James* (Ann Arbor, MA: UMI Research Press, 1987), p. 37).

289 **"'Dialogue,' always 'dialogue'!":** In several essays around the turn of the century, James had complained of the heavy reliance on dialogue in modern British and American fiction, remarking in 1897, for example, that George Gissing in his novels 'is guilty of an almost fatal abuse of colloquy; though I hasten to add that this abuse is so general a sign, in these days, of the English and the American novel as to deprive a challenge of every hope of credit' ('London. July 1, 1897', 754).

290 **constructive dialogue, dialogue organic and dramatic:** In 'The Lesson of Balzac' (1905), James had recently contrasted dialogue in novels with dialogue on the stage: in prose fiction, 'dialogue has its function perverted, and therewith its life destroyed, when forced, all clumsily, into the constructive office. It is in the drama, of course, that it is constructive; but the drama lives by a law so different, verily, that everything that is right for it seems wrong for the prose picture, and everything that is right for the prose picture addressed directly, in turn, to the betrayal of the "play"' (*LC2* 137).

291 **that view of its text which is so desired in Paris [...] that the number of copies of the printed piece in circulation far exceeds at last the number of performances:** In James's dialogue-essay 'After the Play' (1889), the critic Dorriforth complains that discussion of the contemporary English drama is hampered by the unavailability of the play-texts: 'One can't put one's hand upon it; one doesn't know what one is discussing. There is no "authority"—nothing is ever published' (*CWAD2* 356). Closer in time to *The Awkward Age*, in a note on London life for *Harper's Weekly* (6 February 1897), James had remarked: 'It is one of the odd things of our actual æsthetics that the more theatres multiply the less any one reads a play—the less any one cares, in a word, for the text of the adventure. That no one ever *does* read a play has long been a commonplace of the wisdom of booksellers'; the plays of Ibsen were lonely exceptions to this rule (*CWAD2* 453-4). For Dorriforth in 'After the Play', 'A play isn't fully produced until it is in a form in which you can refer to it' (*CWAD2* 357). In the introductory Note to the first series of his *Theatricals* (1894) – a

volume of unproduced play-texts – James consoled himself for their non-appearance on the stage with the thought that 'to be correctly printed [...] is after all a morsel of the opportunity of the real dramatist': 'As Labiche and Ibsen would only be partly real to us if we had not their indispensable text, so the baffled aspirant may in offering his text delude or amuse himself with a certain pretension to indispensability' (*Theatricals. Two Comedies: Tenants, Disengaged* (London: Osgood, McIlvaine & Co., 1894), pp. [v]–vi). In the revised 1915 text of his 1887 essay on the actor Coquelin, he would recall the 'delightful octavo editions' of the plays of Alexandre Dumas *fils* published in Paris by Calmann-Lévy, 'with their projection into literature of the dignity of the theater, unless indeed one says their projection upon the theater of the dignity of literature!' (*CWAD2* 539). A play by Dumas mentioned later in this Preface (see note 311) exemplifies James's point about the French attitude to play-texts. First performed in Paris on 19 January 1885, Dumas's *Denise* was published by Calmann-Lévy as an octavo volume and quickly went through multiple printings: a copy held in the Widener Library at Harvard and accessible online via HathiTrust has a publication date of 1888 and is marked 'TRENTE ET UNIÈME ÉDITION', i.e., a thirty-first impression (id.lib.harvard.edu/alma/990029896730203941/catalog).

292 **to dance hand in hand round it**: James had figured a welcome opportunity for criticism in these terms in 1894, noting that the novels of George Du Maurier were well suited to readers 'who don't enjoy enough till they know *why* they enjoy, and [to] critics so oddly constituted that their sensation amuses them still more even than the work that produces that sensation. These critics, so often reviled for being "subjective," ought to join hands around Mr. Du Maurier and dance in a ring, so beautiful a chance does he put before them for the exercise of their subjectivity' (*LC1* 871). See also note 817.

293 **M. Henri Lavedan**: The French journalist, novelist and dramatist Henri Lavedan (1859–1940). Some of his works exist in dual versions, as both satirical stage comedies and *romans dialogués*: for instance, *Le Nouveau jeu*, published as a novel in 1892 and then adapted and staged as a five-act play in 1898; and *Le Vieux marcheur*, published as a novel in 1895 and staged in 1899.

294 **any kindest of critics [...] moved to declare that he would never in the least have suspected it**: Desmond MacCarthy would later recollect talking with James about *The Awkward Age* just after its publication and

learning 'to my astonishment' that 'in writing that searching diagnosis of sophisticated relations' James had 'conceived himself to be following in the footsteps, "of course, with a difference," of the sprightly Gyp!' (MacCarthy, *Portraits I* (New York: The Macmillan Company, 1932), pp. 151–2).

295 **No hint [...] of any critical perception at all [...] has ever come my way**: On 19 May 1899, James wrote to Howard Sturgis, to whom he had sent a copy of *The Awkward Age*: 'I greatly applaud the tact with which you tell me that scarce a human being will understand a word, or an intention, or an artistic element or glimmer of any sort, of my book. I tell *myself*—and the "reviews" tell me—such truths in much cruder fashion' (*HJL* 4:106). It is not clear whether he had actually read those reviews: to Howells he referred to the novel as 'much-battered (I'm told)' (25 September 1899; *LFL* 351). Desmond MacCarthy remembered James saying that '"Flat" was [...] too mild an expression to describe its reception, "My books make no more sound or ripple now than if I dropped them one after the other into mud"' (*Portraits I*, p. 151). The contemporary response to *The Awkward Age* was largely unfavourable, but it did show some evidence of 'critical perception': the critic of the *Athenæum*, for example, grasped the novel's dramatic principle, observing that 'It is by talk alone that the book advances: talk or significant silence broken by meaning gestures, marked emphasis, ejaculations, pauses', with 'no such thing as explanation [...] ever vouchsafed either by [James] himself or his characters. You overhear and interpret as you can, but nothing is said for your benefit' (Gard 290).

296 **originally appeared in "Harper's Weekly" [...] I had meanwhile been absent from England**: *The Awkward Age* was serialized in fourteen numbers of *Harper's Weekly*, from 1 October 1898 to 7 January 1899. The first book editions were published in England by William Heinemann (25 April 1899) and in America by Harper and Brothers (12 May). James was on the Continent from mid-February until early July 1899.

297 **any artistic attempt the basis and groundwork of which are conscious of a particular firmness. On that hard fine floor the element of execution [...] may more or less confidently** *dance*: The Preface's figure of a dance-floor is anticipated by a passage in *The Tragic Muse*, which James had finished revising for the *NYE* just two months before he wrote the *Awkward Age* Preface. In Chapter 42, Nick Dormer reflects with annoyance on his own hesitation about giving up a political career for art: 'It made him curse, and cursing, as a finality, lacked firmness—one had to

drive in posts somewhere under.' He is encouraged by the thought that he has already made a successful sketch of Miriam Rooth, and takes this 'as a sign that she would be still more feasible' as a subject for portraiture: 'Art was *doing*—it came back to that—which politics in most cases weren't. He thus, to pursue our image, planted his supports in the dimness beneath all cursing, and on the platform so improvised was able, in his relief, to dance' (*NYE* VIII, 267–8). James's revision elaborates on metaphors that are present in the first edition: 'cursing, as a finality, was shaky; so he would throw out a platform beyond it'; 'He found his platform, as I have called it, and for a moment, in his relief, he danced upon it' (*The Tragic* Muse, 2 vols. (Boston, MA: Houghton, Mifflin, 1890), vol. II, pp. 694, 695).

298 **the "saving" virtue of treatment**: In Christian theology, a 'saving' doctrine, power or virtue is one 'That preserves a person or soul from damnation; that offers redemption from sin'; the term is applied by extension to anything 'That delivers, rescues, or preserves from danger; that protects or guards from anything undesirable' or 'That delivers a person from moral or intellectual error; (of a quality) serving to mitigate (unqualified) condemnation or censure; redeeming' (*OED*).

299 **like the embarrassed man of our proverbial wisdom, first of all able to help itself**: Proverbially, 'Heaven helps those who help themselves': the formula is quoted as 'a well-worn maxim' in the first chapter of the Scottish journalist Samuel Smiles's enormously influential book on education and social mobility (*Self-Help; With Illustrations of Character and Conduct* (London: John Murray, 1859), p. 1). Reviewing Smiles in 1868, James had referred to 'the very good little book on "Self-Help"' (*LC1* 1221). By 'embarrassed' in this sentence of the Preface, he means 'Having or characterized by financial difficulties' (*OED*).

300 **his master-hammer**: In the light of James's subsequent discussion of Henrik Ibsen in this Preface, the 'master-hammer' of this sentence belongs presumably to a master builder, echoing the title of Ibsen's play *Bygmester Solness* (1892) in its first English translation by Edmund Gosse and William Archer, *The Master Builder* (1893). In the Preface to *NYE* X, James will refer to the novelist as 'the master-builder' (p. 97).

301 **open the door wide to ingenuity**: To 'open a door to' means 'to render possible the admission of; to furnish opportunity or facility for' (*OED*, 'door'); the idiom occurs again with this meaning in later Prefaces. Compare James's letter of 26 January 1900 to the Canadian novelist Mrs Everard Cotes (Sara Jeannette Duncan): 'we are both very intelligent and

observant and conscious that a work of art must make some small effort to *be* one; must sacrifice somehow and somewhere to the exquisite, or be an asininity altogether. So we open the door to the Devil himself—who is nothing but the sense of beauty, of mystery, of relations, of appearances, of abysses of the whole—*and* of EXPRESSION! That's *all* he is' (*HJL* 4:131).

302 **the neat figure of a circle consisting of a number of small rounds disposed at equal distance about a central object**: This diagram does not survive. James told Howells that he had sent 'a detailed statement of subject' for *The Awkward Age* to Henry Loomis Nelson, the editor of *Harper's Weekly* (28 January 1898; *LFL* 305).

303 **so many distinct lamps, as I liked to call them**: Compare the introductory chapter of John Ruskin's *The Seven Lamps of Architecture* (1849), which speaks of the attempt 'to determine, as the guides of every effort, some constant, general, and irrefragable laws of right': 'Those peculiar aspects of them which belong to the first of the arts [architecture], I have endeavoured to trace in the following pages; and since, if truly stated, they must necessarily be, not only safeguards against every form of error, but sources of every measure of success, I do not think that I claim too much for them in calling them the Lamps of Architecture' (*The Works of John Ruskin*, ed. E. T. Cook and Alexander Wedderburn, 39 vols. (London: George Allen, 1903–12), vol. VIII, pp. 21–2). Seven chapters follow: 'The Lamp of Sacrifice', 'The Lamp of Truth', etc. James told Henrietta Reubell on 12 November 1899 that the 'form' of *The Awkward Age* consisted 'of presented episodes, architecturally combined and each making a piece of the building' (*LHJ* 1:341).

304 **aspects—uncanny as the little term might sound [...] by that sign we would conquer**: In disclaiming the suggestion that his publishers should use the term 'aspects' 'for the public' James refers presumably to the odd sound it would have in the title of a novel. The word 'aspects' was associated rather with analytical non-fiction: it occurs frequently in the titles of contemporary volumes on religion and theology, medicine and public health, law, education and sport – and also literary criticism, e.g. W. H. Helm's *Aspects of Balzac* (London: Eveleigh Nash, 1905). In the novel itself, the word gives the measure of the Brookenham set's exhaustively systematic gossip, as on the subject of 'the imperturbable grandeur of [Lady Fanny's] almost total absence of articulation. Every aspect of the phenomenon had been freely discussed' (Book Sixth, Ch. 1; *NYE* IX, 279). In this sentence of the Preface James also alludes to a Latin phrase associated with the Roman

emperor Constantine I (272–337 CE), the imperative 'In hoc signo vinces' ('By this sign conquer'). According to the fourth-century Greek historian Eusebius, Constantine was granted a vision of the Cross accompanied by the Greek form of this phrase and interpreted it as a divine command to adopt the Christian Chi-Rho symbol as his military standard (Eusebius, *Vita Constantini*, Book 1, Chs. 28–31).

305 **"to haunt, to startle and waylay.":** James quotes William Wordsworth's lyric 'She was a Phantom of delight' (1807): 'A dancing Shape, an Image gay, / To haunt, to startle, and way-lay' (ll. 9–10; *The Poetical Works of William Wordsworth*, ed. Ernest de Selincourt and Helen Darbishire, 5 vols. (Oxford: Clarendon Press, 1940–9), vol. II, p. 213). As Horne observes, this line of Wordsworth 'itself haunts and waylays James often in his later prose' ('Henry James and the Poetry of Association', p. 39). There is another instance in the Preface to *Daisy Miller* (p. 215), and the isolated word 'waylay' occurs several times in other Prefaces.

306 **the respective divisions of my form […] the successive Acts of a Play:** *The Awkward Age* is divided into ten Books, each approximately preserving the dramatic unities of time and place. This structural division was introduced for volume publication and is not present in the serial text.

307 **I myself have scarcely to plead the cause of "going behind,":** James discusses 'going behind' in the previous Preface, to *The Tragic Muse* (see note 256). Writing to Mary Augusta Ward just after the publication of *The Awkward Age*, he insisted that he was not opposed in principle to 'going behind' as a fictional technique: 'I "go behind" right and left in "The Prss. Casamassima," "The Bostonians," "The Tragic Muse," just as I do the same but singly in "The American" & "Maisie," & just as I do it consistently *never at all* (save for a false and limited *appearance*, here & there, of doing it a *little*, which I haven't time to explain,) in *The Awkward Age*' (26 July 1899; *LL* 319). *The Awkward Age* appears to offer a brief direct representation of Mr Longdon's consciousness at the start of Book Fifth, Chapter 4 (*NYE* IX, 245–6). This is an exceptional instance, however, and the novel self-consciously renounces 'going behind' in narratorial comments such as this in Book Fifth, Chapter 1, on Vanderbank's reaction to Nanda's protest '"Oh Mr. Van, I'm 'true'!"': 'As Mr. Van himself couldn't have expressed at any subsequent time to any interested friend the particular effect upon him of the tone of these words his chronicler takes advantage of the fact not to pretend to a greater intelligence—to limit himself on the contrary

to the simpler statement that they produced in Mr. Van's cheek a flush just discernible' (*NYE* IX, 211–12). See also note 315.

308 **to "size up."**: The American idiom 'to size up' means 'to develop or take shape; to amount (*to* something); to reach the necessary standard' (*OED*, 'size').

309 **the little foot-rule the 'produced' piece has to conform to**: A 'foot-rule' is 'a ruler capable of measuring lengths of up to one foot', and figuratively 'a standard against which something is compared' (*OED*, 'foot'). Compare James on Balzac in 1902: the *Comédie humaine* 'makes us fold up our yard-measure and put away our note-book quite as we do with some extraordinary character, some mysterious and various stranger who brings with him his own standards and his own air' ('HdB' xxvi). To 'produce' in this sense is 'To bring (a performance) before the public; to administer the staging of (a play, opera, etc.)' (*OED*).

310 **Ibsen and Dumas […] in their poor theatrical straight-jacket, […] who have *had* to renounce the finer thing for the coarser, […] the curious for the self-evident.**: The Norwegian playwright Henrik Ibsen (1828–1906), and the French playwright and novelist Alexandre Dumas *fils*. James's essays on these writers emphasize both their mastery of dramatic form and the practical and imaginative constraints of the theatre. In 'On the Occasion of *Hedda Gabler*' (1891), for example, James had noted that the 'conditions' of the stage 'strike us for the most part as small enough, so that the game played in them is often not more inspiring than a successful sack-race. But Ibsen reminds us that if they do not in themselves confer life they can at least receive it, when the infusion is artfully attempted.' Indeed, James feels that Ibsen *needs* to be performed in order to be properly appreciated, and argues that his plays give a new idea of what can be done in the theatre: 'the conditions seem essentially enlarged' (*CWAD2* 371–2). In his essay 'On the Death of Dumas the Younger' (1896), James had noted that the stage did not suit all subjects: 'It is the nature of the theatre to give its victims, in exchange for melancholy concessions, a vision of the immediate not to be enjoyed in any other way; and consequently when the material offered it to deal with is not the immediate, but the contingent, the roundabout, the derived, our melancholy concessions have been made in vain and the inadequacy of the form comes out' (*CWAD2* 432–3). In his 'Note' to the second series of *Theatricals* (1894), he had complained specifically of the time constraints of the theatre: 'To treat a "big" subject

in the intensely summarised fashion demanded by an evening's traffic of the stage when the evening [...] is reduced to two hours and a half, is a feat of which the difficulty looms large to a writer accustomed to tell his story in another form. The only writer who can regard, and can treat, such a difficulty as small is the writer whose early practice as well as his later has been in the theatrical strait-jacket' (*Theatricals. Second Series: The Album, The Reprobate* (London: Osgood, McIlvaine & Co., 1894), p. vii). The word 'strait-jacket' is correctly spelled there, and misspelled in this sentence of the Preface.

311 **'Denise,'** [...] **'Monsieur Alphonse,'** [...] **'Francillon'**: In 1896, James had referred to *Denise* (1885) and *Francillon* (1887) as the final works in Dumas's 'rich argumentative series' of plays, 'the series in which every theme is a proposition to be established, and every proposition a form of duty to be faced' (*CWAD2* 431). Comparing the two plays' handling of moral themes, he found *Francillon* the more successful: because there, in the first place, Dumas 'has had the intelligence to give us a solution which is only a scenic sequence and not a real, still less a "philosophic", one; and because, in the second, [the play] deals with emotions and impulses and not with reflections and aspirations' (*CWAD2* 433). Outside of this Preface, James makes no critical comment on Dumas's play *Monsieur Alphonse* (1873).

312 **'The Pillars of Society,'** [...] **'An Enemy of the People,'** [...] **'Ghosts,'** [...] **'Rosmersholm'** [...] **'John Gabriel Borkmann,'** [...] **'The Master-Builder'** [...] **'A Doll's House'** [...] **'The Wild Duck.'**: James comments on Ibsen's plays *Ghosts* (1881), *The Wild Duck* (1884) and *Rosmersholm* (1886) in letters to Edmund Gosse (28 April 1891) and William Archer (5 July 1891), two of Ibsen's first English translators; the letter to Archer compares Ibsen favourably with Dumas (see *HJL* 3:339–40, 343–5). James personally knew another champion of Ibsen's work in the American actress Elizabeth Robins (1862–1952), who played Hedda Gabler and Hilda Wangel respectively in the first London performances of *Hedda Gabler* in 1891 and *The Master Builder* in 1893. He wrote essays on the occasions of both those productions, as well as on the publication of Archer's translation of *John Gabriel Borkman* (1896) (see *CWAD2* 367–82, 383–7, 453–6). The *Hedda Gabler* essay surveys Ibsen's plays up to 1891 and contains comments on *The Pillars of Society* (1877), *A Doll's House* (1879) and *An Enemy of the People* (1882). The objections to Ibsen's work ventriloquized in this passage of the Preface have no counterpart in any of these writings.

313 **all [...] that the playwright asks of him, [...] all the very divinest poet can get**: James had made the same observation in 'Henrik Ibsen: On the Occasion of *Hedda Gabler*' (1891): 'To be absorbed, assuredly, [...] is the highest tribute we can pay to any picture of life, and a higher one than most pictures attempted succeed in making us pay' (*CWAD2* 375).

314 **(to harp again on that string)**: 'to harp upon [or] on [...], a one, the same (*etc.*) string' means 'to repeat a statement or dwell on a subject to a wearisome or tedious length' (*OED*, 'harp'). In his 1891 essay on *Hedda Gabler*, James counts it as one of Ibsen's 'limitations' that he 'harps on the string of conduct' (*CWAD2* 379).

315 **the references in one's action can only be [...] to things exactly on the same plane of exhibition with themselves**: Compare James's remark to Henrietta Reubell that *The Awkward Age* was constructed 'with no going behind, no *telling about* the figures save by their own appearance and action and with explanations reduced to the explanation of everything by all the other things *in* the picture' (12 November 1899; *LHJ* 1:341).

316 **a snippet of silk or wool on the right side of a tapestry**: James tends to compare literature to tapestry-work when he is praising a writer's thoroughness. In 'The Lesson of Balzac', for example, he describes Balzac's *oeuvre* as 'the figured tapestry, all over-scored with objects in fine perspective, which symbolizes to me [...] the last word of the achieved fable' (*LC2* 138). Gabriele D'Annunzio's exhaustive rendering of sexual desire, James noted in 1904, 'left no dropped stitches for any worker of like tapestries to pick up' ('GDA' 391).

317 **to pump the case gaspingly dry, [...] absolutely (for I have encountered the charge) of breatheable air**: James had recently spoken in these terms about *The Golden Bowl*, acknowledging the justice of a private remark made by a friendly reader: 'Never, [...] I believe, was a Subject, a Situation, pumped so dry as that one—striking you as so pumped & left so thirsty for any remaining shade of mystery—by the time the last page is reached. It is *over-treated*—but that is my ruinous way & why I have never made my fortune' (to Elinor Mead Howells, 14 August 1905; *LL* 417). The 'over-treatment' noted in the previous sentence of the Preface was a common charge in contemporary reviews of *The Awkward Age*: the New York *Bookman* concluded that James 'works a delicate thing to death' (Gard 293).

318 **as the red Indian tracks in the forest the pale-face**: A word in American English chiefly used in the nineteenth century 'in representations of North American Indian speech', 'paleface' denotes 'A white person' (*OED*).

James uses metaphors of tracking and following in a person's footsteps to represent the processes of recalling, rereading and revising his own work in other Prefaces (see notes 544 and 897). In 'A Letter to Mr. Howells', a birthday tribute written in 1912, he would describe Howells as having mastered 'a method so easy and so natural [...] that the critic kept coming on its secret connection with the grace of letters much as Fenimore Cooper's Leatherstocking—so knowing to be able to do it!—comes in the forest on the subtle tracks of Indian braves' (*LC1* 510).

319 **presents itself on absolutely scenic lines, [...] abides [...] by the principle of the stage-play**: In the letter to Henrietta Reubell quoted above in connection with architectural form (see note 303), James states that *The Awkward Age* has 'a form all dramatic and scenic' (*LHJ* 1:341). The novel also follows theatrical principles by positing a spectator of its action – as, for example, in Book Fifth, Chapter 1: 'It might in fact have appeared to a spectator that some climax had come, on the young man's part, to some state of irresolution about the utterance of something' (*NYE* IX, 215). This hypothetical audience-representative, 'the acute observer we are constantly taking for granted' (Book Sixth, Ch. 2; *NYE* IX, 310), is present throughout the novel.

320 **to see the grave distinction between substance and form [...] break down**: James had noted in 1896 that Turgenev's work exemplified 'the happy truth of the unity, in a generous talent, of material and form,—of their being inevitable faces of the same medal' (*LC2* 1030); for uses of the 'medal' figure in the Prefaces, see note 389. British Aestheticism supplies a precedent for James's belief that 'substance and form in a really wrought work of art' are indivisible. See Walter Pater's essay 'The School of Giorgione' (1877): '*All art constantly aspires towards the condition of music.* For while in all other works of art it is possible to distinguish the matter from the form, and the understanding can always make this distinction, yet it is the constant effort of art to obliterate it. That the mere matter of a poem, for instance, its subject, namely, its given incidents or situation— that the mere matter of a picture, the actual circumstances of an event, the actual topography of a landscape—should be nothing without the form, the spirit, of the handling; that this form, this mode of handling, should become an end in itself, should penetrate every part of the matter:—this is what all art constantly strives after, and achieves in different degrees.' 'It is the art of music which most completely realises this artistic ideal, this

perfect identification of form and matter' (*The Renaissance: Studies in Art and Poetry*, 4th edn (London and New York: Macmillan and Co., 1893), pp. 141, 145).

321 **the sacrament of execution indissolubly marries them, [...] for the scandal of a breach not to show**: Compare James's 1904 essay on Gabriele D'Annunzio: 'So close is the marriage between his power of "rendering," in the light of his imagination, [and whatever] he sees and feels, that we scarce escape a clumsy confusion in speaking of his form as a thing distinct from the matter submitted to it' ('GDA' 390; the words in square brackets are an emendation taken from the text printed in *Notes on Novelists* (New York: Charles Scribner's Sons, 1914), p. 255, to correct an obvious grammatical error in the periodical text). The constant threat of marital scandals in the plot of *The Awkward Age* gives an ironic tone to the Preface's sacramental metaphor. Compare also the exchange in Book Tenth, Chapter 3, where Mitchy and Nanda discuss their future relationship after her rejection of him as a lover and his marriage to Aggie. Mitchy tells Nanda that she will now never be able to '"get rid of [him] on the specious plea that he's only her husband or her lover or her father or her son or her brother or her uncle or her cousin. There, as none of these characters, he just stands." "Yes," Nanda kindly mused, "he's simply her Mitchy." "Precisely. And a Mitchy, you see, is—what do you call it?—simply indissoluble"' (*NYE* IX, 517).

322 **some of the positively most artful passages I have in mind**: In the remainder of the Preface, James discusses three passages in particular: Vanderbank's scene with Mr Longdon in the smoking-room at Mertle in Book Fifth, Chapter 5; his scene with Mitchy at Mr Longdon's house in Book Seventh, Chapter 3; and 'the picture of the assembled group at Mrs. Grendon's' in Book Eighth (p. 92).

323 **a "loud" word [...] loud colours**: The phrase 'a loud word' occurs in nineteenth-century representations of Irish speech and denotes an offensive, rowdy or exuberant utterance. See, for example, William Carleton's story 'Shane Fadh's Wedding' (1830) on the restoration of peace after a brawl: '"Come away to dinner—by the powers, we'll duck the first man that says a loud word for the remainder of the day"' (Carleton, *Traits and Stories of the Irish Peasantry*, ed. D. J. O'Donoghue, 4 vols. (London: J. M. Dent and Co.; New York: Macmillan and Co., 1896), vol. I, pp. 92–3). With reference to 'colours, patterns, dress, manners, etc.', 'loud' means 'Vulgarly obtrusive, flashy' (*OED*).

PREFACE to *The Spoils of Poynton, A London Life, The Chaperon* (NYE X)

324 **one Christmas Eve when I was dining with friends**: James slightly mistakes the date of this occasion. He made a note of the subject for *The Spoils of Poynton* on Christmas Eve 1893, but the conversation in which it had come up occurred the evening before, 'last night, at dinner at Lady Lindsay's' (*CN* 79). James's hostess on 23 December was Caroline Blanche Elizabeth Lindsay, née Fitzroy (1844–1912), estranged wife of the artist Sir Coutts Lindsay, with whom she had founded the Grosvenor Gallery in 1877. The anecdote was told to James by Isabel Anstruther-Thomson, née Bruce (d. 1918), second wife of the Scottish landowner John Anstruther-Thomson (1818–1904).

325 **the prick of some sharp point: [...] the virus of suggestion**: The extended metaphor – continued in the next paragraph of the Preface – refers to the medical procedure of vaccination, developed in the 1790s by the English physician Edward Jenner (1749–1823) as a technique for immunizing persons against smallpox by infecting them with the milder cowpox virus. The commonest method of doing this involved puncturing the skin with a needle or scalpel and introducing a vaccine derived from cowpox lesions into the wound.

326 **Life being all inclusion and confusion, and art being all discrimination and selection**: In earlier critical writings, James had offered a less straightforwardly oppositional account of the relation between 'life' and 'art', 'inclusion' and 'selection'. In 'The Art of Fiction' (1884), he had cautioned against Walter Besant's 'rather unguarded talk about "selection." Art is essentially selection, but it is a selection whose main care is to be typical, to be inclusive' (*LC1* 58). In the essay's closing exhortation to young novelists: '"There is no impression of life, no manner of seeing it and feeling it, to which the plan of the novelist may not offer a place"' (*LC1* 64). James's 1903 essay on Zola similarly presents the novel as an intrinsically inclusive form: the Rougon-Macquart series of novels proves 'that a scheme of fiction so conducted is in fact a capacious vessel. It can carry anything—with art, with force, in the stowage; nothing in this case will sink it. And it is the only form for which such a claim can be made. All others have to confess to a smaller scope—to selection, to exclusion, to the danger of distortion, explosion, combustion' ('EZ' 195). The Preface's emphasis on 'discrimination and selection' recalls Mrs Gereth's achievement in *The*

Spoils in assembling and arranging her collection: 'in such an art of the treasure-hunter, in selection and comparison refined to that point, there was an element of creation, of personality' (Ch. 3; *NYE* X, 21–2).

327 **life persistently blunders and deviates**: Life here imitates the Brigstocks, of whom we are told in Chapter 1 of *The Spoils* that in decorating their family home, Waterbath, 'They had gone wildly astray over carpets and curtains; they had an infallible instinct for gross deviation' (*NYE* X, 7); 'gross deviation' there revises 'disaster' in the first edition (*The Spoils of Poynton* (London: William Heinemann, 1897), p. 5).

328 **the method at the heart of the madness**: A commonplace Shakespearean formula deriving from Polonius's judgement on Hamlet's pretended insanity: 'Though this be madness, yet there is method in't' (*Hamlet*, 2.2.205–6).

329 **a good lady in the north, [...] her only son, [...] the valuable furniture of a fine old house just accruing to the young man by his father's death**: As Bernard Richards notes, the lady was 'Rebecca Ross, née Barnes, of Balnagown Castle near Inverness' and the son was 'Sir Charles Henry Augustus Frederick Lockhart Ross (1872–1942)'. Lady Ross's husband 'Sir Charles William Augustus Lockhart Ross died in 1883, leaving his estate in the hands of his widow until the son should come of age' (*The Spoils of Poynton*, ed. Richards (Oxford: Oxford University Press, 1982), p. 185).

330 **action taken [...] by our engaged adversaries, [...] clumsy Life again at her stupid work**: James seems to allude to 'action' in a legal sense: 'A legal process, a lawsuit' (*OED*). As he had noted on 24 December 1893: 'It appears that the circumstance is about to come out in a process-at-law' (*CN* 79). For the case of 'Ross v Ross' as detailed in the *Scottish Law Reporter* (1896–7) see the introduction to Bernard Richards's edition of the novel, pp. xxi–xxii; also Richards's essay 'James and His Sources: *The Spoils of Poynton*', *Essays in Criticism* 29.4 (1979), 302–22; 304–5. The novel goes no further in this direction than a vague threat about '"coercion"' from Owen Gereth reported by Fleda Vetch in Chapter 10: '"What sort of coercion?" said Mrs Gereth. "Why legal, don't you know?—what he calls setting the lawyers at you"' (*NYE* X, 111). Aesthetic stupidity is an oppressive force in the novel: on the first page, escaping from the interior décor of Waterbath for a walk in the grounds, Mrs Gereth feels 'a renewal of everything she could secretly suffer from ugliness and stupidity' (Ch. 1; *NYE* X, 3). James's notebook entries view Owen's choice of Mona Brigstock in the same light: 'The son [...] perversely and stupidly, from the mother's

point of view, takes to a girl infatuated with hideousness'; 'This infatuated density, this singleness and stupidity of perception, so often characteristic of the young Englishman in regard to the inferior woman' (24 December 1893, 11 August 1895; *CN* 80, 127).

331 **she'll strangle it in the cradle, even while she pretends [...] to rock it**: In *The Other House* (1896), the novel James began to write immediately after completing *The Spoils* (see note 347), Rose Armiger pretends to care for the small daughter of the widowed Tony Bream, before drowning her to release Tony from his promise to his dying wife not to marry again in the child's lifetime (see Chs. 22–5; the drowned Effie is discovered in Ch. 28). In what may be the most famous instance of a strangling in the cradle in European culture, the child is the strangler: in ancient Greek myth, the infant hero Heracles strangles two snakes sent to kill him by the goddess Hera, to revenge herself on her husband Zeus for fathering the child on the mortal woman Alcmene.

332 **I didn't, of course, stay her hand—there never *is* in such cases "time"**: The novelist Violet Hunt (1862–1942) testifies that James did sometimes manage to stay the hands of his informants: 'I used to suffer, like other people, from the truncated anecdote. I used to take little mice—accounts of incidents or things I fancied would interest him—and lay them at his feet. So they did, as raw material. But while one was trying to be accurate, massing every detail painstakingly, so as to be of use, he would unerringly extract the ore from the matrix of one's recital and would hold it up— extend a finger—"thank you ... thank you, I've got as much—all I want—" and leave you with the point of your anecdote on your hands. You consoled yourself with the reflection that he might have perhaps got another "Turn of the Screw" out of your relation of some childish aberration or some more "Spoils of Poynton" from your reminiscence of your old North Country aunt' (Hunt, *I Have This to Say: The Story of My Flurried Years* (New York: Boni and Liveright, 1926), p. 45); this passage is quoted in the slightly different text of the British edition in John Attridge, '"Human Expertness": Professionalism, Training, and the Prefaces to the New York Edition', *Henry James Review* 32.1 (2011), 29–44; 35).

333 **I "took" in fine [...] to the rich bare little fact**: To 'take to' someone in this sense is 'To form a liking for [them], esp. within a short space of time; to conceive an affection for [them]' (*OED*, 'take'). Compare also a 'rare' sense of the phrase: 'To take in hand, to take charge of; *esp.* to undertake

the care of (a child)' (*OED*, citing Charles Kingsley's *The Water-Babies* (1863): 'All the little children whom the good fairies take to, because their cruel mothers and fathers will not').

334 **the modern alchemist [...] the old dream of the secret of life**: James appears to refer to the 'elixir of life' sought by medieval and early modern alchemy: 'A supposed drug or essence with the property of indefinitely prolonging life' (*OED*, 'elixir').

335 **that "row," so to call it, [...] over their household gods**: This is what Owen calls it to Fleda in Chapter 4: '"I must tell you I've been having an awful row with my mother"' (*NYE* X, 41). The word occurs also in James's first notebook entry for the novel: on the son's learning that his mother had removed 'pictures and other treasures' from the house, 'He inquired, protested, made a row' (24 December 1893; *CN* 79). The phrase 'household gods' literally denotes the *Lares* and *Penates* of ancient Roman religion, 'The tutelary deities of a house', and, by extension, 'household belongings regarded as defining or embodying a person's home; prized possessions' (*OED*).

336 **One thing was "in it," in the sordid situation, on the first blush**: In his first notebook entry for *The Spoils*, James similarly assesses the anecdotal germ of the novel: 'It is all rather sordid and fearfully ugly, but there is surely a story in it' (24 December 1893; *CN* 79). 'On the first blush' means 'at the first glance'; the phrase preserves an obsolete sense of 'blush' as 'A glance, glimpse, blink, look' (*OED*).

337 **the diffusion of this curiosity and this avidity**: The growth in the last decades of the nineteenth century of Anglo-American enthusiasm for collecting, interior decoration and the fine arts led to a proliferation of specialist periodicals. Bernard Richards mentions two British journals addressed to this market, *The Studio: An Illustrated Magazine of Fine and Applied Art* and *The Connoisseur*, launched in 1893 and 1901 respectively (*The Spoils of Poynton*, ed. Richards, p. 185). *The Burlington Magazine for Connoisseurs* was first published in 1903. Bill Brown cites examples of a contemporaneous American discourse of home decoration: Clarence Cook's *The House Beautiful: Essays on Beds and Tables, Stools and Candlesticks* (1878); the magazine *House Beautiful*, launched in 1896; and Edith Wharton and Ogden Codman's book *The Decoration of Houses* (1897) (Brown, 'Jamesian Matter', in Greg W. Zacharias (ed.), *A Companion to Henry James* (Chichester: Wiley-Blackwell, 2008), pp. 292–308; 297).

Oscar Wilde, too, had given a lecture entitled 'The House Beautiful' on his American tour of 1882. This would be James's working title for *The Spoils* (see note 341).

338 **the "things" themselves [...] the great array in which Balzac [...] would have marshalled them**: James's essays on Balzac consistently emphasize what he called in 1875 the French novelist's 'mighty passion for *things*—for material objects, for furniture, upholstery, bricks and mortar. The world that contained these things filled his consciousness, and *being*, at its intensest, meant simply being thoroughly at home among them' (*LC2* 48). James had recently returned to this topic, noting in 1902 the 'importunity' of Balzac's 'consciousness of the machinery of life, of its furniture and fittings, of all that, right and left, he causes to assail us, sometimes almost to suffocation, under the general rubric of *things*'; 'I am not sure that he does not see character too, see passion, motive, personality, as quite in the order of the "things" we have spoken of' ('HdB' xvi, xviii). In Chapter 3 of *The Spoils*, Fleda considers Mrs Gereth's 'strange, almost maniacal disposition to thrust in everywhere the question of "things", to read all behaviour in the light of some fancied relation to them' (*NYE* X, 24). The serial title of the novel was *The Old Things* (see note 341).

339 **wrapped in the silver tissue of some such conviction [...] I must have laid away my prime impression**: This figure recalls a moment in the previous novel in the *NYE*, *The Awkward Age*. In Book Fifth, Chapter 1, Nanda tells Vanderbank that she has kept all his old gifts, '"Laid away in a drawer of their own—done up in pink paper."' He counters that he has not forgotten the things she has given him: '"Where my heart's concerned I'm a walking reliquary. Pink paper? *I* use gold paper—and the finest of all, the gold paper of the mind"' (*NYE* IX, 209).

340 **long afterwards, [...] when there arose a question of my contributing three "short stories" to "The Atlantic Monthly"**: In fact it was less than eighteen months after hearing the story of Lady Ross and her son that James revisited the germ of *The Spoils of Poynton*. A notebook entry of 13 May 1895 records that he had 'just promised [Horace] Scudder 3 short stories for the *Atlantic*' (*CN* 121); they eventually became two novels, *The Spoils of Poynton* and *The Awkward Age*, and a long story, 'Glasses' (1896).

341 **this composition (which in the magazine bore another title)**: *The Spoils of Poynton* underwent several changes of title between conception and volume publication. James announced it to Horace Scudder on 8 June

1895 as 'The House Beautiful' (*LL* 280), but abandoned that title when he realized that it had already been used for a book on interior decoration. He wrote to Scudder on 18 December 1895: 'I think the title of Clarence Cook's book *is* an objection to the retention of the "H.B."' (quoted *LL* 289). Cook's *The House Beautiful* was first published in 1878 (see note 337), but Charles Scribner's Sons reprinted it in 1895, and this may have been what brought its title to James's attention. The letter to Scudder continues: 'Therefore I will re-christen the thing on sending you the next copy. I *may* call it "The Great House"—or something better' (quoted *LL* 289). The novel was eventually serialized as *The Old Things* (*Atlantic Monthly*, April–October 1896) and retitled *The Spoils of Poynton* for volume publication in February 1897.

342 **such differences of sense [...] as to the short and the long**: Horace Scudder set a limit of 10,000 words each for the three stories he commissioned from James in May 1895 (*LL* 280). *The Spoils* threatened to exceed those dimensions from the start, and it continued to grow as James worked. On 3 September 1895, James told Scudder that he had been 'trying for' 15,000 words but found that the subject 'will make nearer 25,000 and after a mortal struggle I have to give up the effort to keep it down. It must go elsewhere, as of the major length, and I must try again for you on a tinier subject—though I thought this *was* tiny. It is, probably; but what I put into it isn't' (*HJL* 4:18). On 15 October, he noted to himself: 'My little story has grown upon my hands [...] & will make a thing of 30 000 words' (*CN* 131). By November he had placed it with Heinemann as a novel, which the *Atlantic* agreed to serialize. Writing to Scudder about the serial on 3 March 1896, and apologizing for its length ('You catch me, as you have done before, in the act of finding my problem irreducible to *all* the brevity that my optimism has originally deluded itself into a belief in'), James predicted that it would run to eighteen or nineteen chapters 'if I don't throw in a 20*th* to make the round number'; in the event, it required twenty-two (*LL* 289 and n. 1). In the Heinemann first edition, *The Spoils* is just over 70,000 words long.

343 **barred seraglio-windows [...] the outsider in the glare of the Eastern street**: As Alicia Rix points out, James would revisit the orientalist figure of the 'seraglio' or harem in 'The Velvet Glove' (1909) (Rix, '"The Lives of Others": Motoring in Henry James's "The Velvet Glove"', *Journal of Modern Literature* 36.3 (2013), 31–49; 43–4). In that story, the author John

Berridge climbs into the Princess's motor-car – as he supposes, for a tryst, but in reality so that she can ask him to write a preface for her newest novel; through the car-window he sees the 'the rigid liveried backs' of the two servants sitting 'on the box' and fancies that they are 'like a protecting wall; such a guarantee of privacy as might come [...] from a vision of tall guards erect round Eastern seraglios' (*The Finer Grain* (New York: Charles Scribner's Sons, 1910), p. 34).

344 **a cottage on a cliff-side**: The cottage was Point Hill in the East Sussex village of Playden. James rented it from its owner, the architect and architectural historian Reginald Blomfield (1856–1942), for three months (May–July) in the summer of 1896. For the coincidental chime of James's Poynton with the name of Point Hill, and its audible influence on the Preface's sustained play with the word 'point', see Herford, *Henry James's Style of Retrospect*, pp. 198–200.

345 **a small paved terrace which [...] overhung a view**: To his architect friend Edward Prioleau Warren (1856–1937), who had arranged the lease of Point Hill for him, James wrote: 'The little terrace is as amiable as a *person*—as some *persons*' (quoted in H. Montgomery Hyde, *Henry James at Home* (London: Methuen & Co., 1969), p. 72). As Bernard Richards notes (*The Spoils of Poynton*, ed. Richards, p. 185), a contemporary photograph of the terrace appears in Dorothy Eagle and Hilary Carnell's *Oxford Illustrated Literary Guide to Great Britain and Ireland* (Oxford: Oxford University Press, 1981), p. 230. Reginald Blomfield later described the view from his terrace: 'Below to the right is the compact little town [of Rye], suggesting one of Durer's woodcuts, with the road passing through the Land-gate and reappearing on the further side. Immediately in front is the Rother, a tidal river, now brimming over, like an estuary, now shrinking to a mere channel, with wide mud flats on either side, as the tides come up and down. Then there is the wide expanse of Romney Marsh, green fields and innumerable sheep, with Lydd Tower in the middle distance and beyond, Hythe, Folkstone and the white cliffs beyond Eastwear Bay, to the south the English Channel, and over all the infinite sky. There are few views like it anywhere' (Blomfield, *Memoirs of an Architect* (London: Macmillan and Co., 1932), p. 91).

346 **a small red-roofed town, of great antiquity, perched on its sea-rock**: Along with its neighbour Winchelsea, the small fortified hilltop town of Rye was one of the Confederation of Cinque Ports from the twelfth century; both were originally coastal towns, but violent storms in the thirteenth

century and the gradual silting up of the River Rother changed the coastline and left them stranded inland. At the end of July 1896, James vacated Point Hill and moved into the Vicarage at Rye, where he remained for the next two months. Two years later, he would move to Rye on a permanent basis, to a substantial red-brick Georgian house – Lamb House – which he initially rented on a 21-year lease and then purchased in August 1899. His 1901 essay 'Winchelsea, Rye, and *Denis Duval*' traces some picturesque phases of the town's history and closes with a view of Rye looking back across Romney Marsh from Winchelsea: 'The best hour is that at which the compact little pyramid of Rye, crowned with its big but stunted church and quite covered by the westering sun, gives out the full measure of its old browns that turn to red and its old reds that turn to purple' (*CTW1* 251).

347 **committed to begin, the day I finished it, [...] "The Other House"**: On 30 March 1896, James estimated that he would need another '10 days of real application' to complete *The Old Things*, as *The Spoils* was then titled (*CN* 160). In the event, the final instalment of copy was not dispatched until 20 May (*LL* 289 n. 1), three weeks into his stay at Point Hill. The serialization of *The Other House* in the *Illustrated London News* was due to begin on 4 July, but on 20 May the book was 'à peine [barely] started in MS' and James was in 'a fearful funk' about it (to WJ and AGJ; *CWJ* 2:399). He later described this crisis to Edmund Gossse: 'in an evil hour I began to pay the penalty of having arranged to let a current serial begin when I was too little ahead of it, & when it proved a much slower & more difficult job than I expected. The printers & illustrators overtook & denounced me, the fear of breaking down paralysed me, the combination of rheumatism & fatigue rendered my hand & arm a torture—& the total situation made my existence a nightmare' (28 August [1896]; *SLHJEG* 145). James did not collect *The Other House* in the *NYE*.

348 **costly to keep up. [...] Fleda Vetch, maintainable at less expense**: This metaphor echoes a central economic fact of the novel: for much of the narrative Fleda is living at Mrs Gereth's expense, as her house-guest. The question of Fleda's maintenance comes up in Chapter 6 when she imagines Mona Brigstock regarding her as 'an underhand "companion," an inmate all but paid in shillings' (*NYE* X, 60).

349 **the forces their beauty would, like that of antique Helen of Troy, set in motion**: In ancient Greek myth, Helen was the daughter of Zeus and the Spartan queen Leda. Her beauty made her the indirect cause of the Trojan War: married to Menelaus, king of Sparta, she was abducted by the Trojan

prince Paris and pursued to Troy by the Achaean fleet, who besieged the city for ten years to recapture her. The most famous literary expression of Helen's capacity to set forces in motion is Christopher Marlowe's *Doctor Faustus*: granted a sight of her by the devil Mephostophilis, Faustus exclaims: 'Was this the face that Launcht a thousand ships, / And burnt the toplesse Towers of *Ilium*?' (B text, Act 5, Scene 1, ll. 1874–5; *Marlowe's 'Doctor Faustus' 1604–1616: Parallel Texts*, ed. W. W. Greg (Oxford: Clarendon Press, 1950), p. 279).

350 **Some plea for [...] the intelligence of the moved mannikin, I have already had occasion to make**: The argument that intelligence is a necessary quality for a principal character is a major topic of the Preface to *The Princess Casamassima* (see pp. 48–55). A 'manikin' is 'A small representation or statue of a human figure', e.g. the mechanical figures ('quarter jacks') whose movements mark intervals of time on a clock-face; or a 'lay figure', a 'jointed wooden figure of the human body, used by artists as a model for the arrangement of draperies, posing, etc.' (*OED*).

351 **why not Hamlet or Milton's Satan [...] a superior display of 'mind'?**: In this context, 'mind' means 'Intellectual quality, keenness of intellect, mental power' (*OED*). James had cited Hamlet as an example of intelligent awareness in two recently composed Prefaces, those to *The Princess Casamassima* and *The Tragic Muse*. Satan is the most intellectually dynamic character in John Milton's epic poem *Paradise Lost* (1674).

352 **The "things" are radiant, shedding afar [...] all their light**: The spoils are twice described in the novel as a source of metaphorical light. In Chapter 6, as Mrs Gereth selects objects to take with her from Poynton to Ricks: 'the old golds and brasses, old ivories and bronzes, the fresh old tapestries and deep old damasks threw out a radiance in which the poor woman saw in solution all her loves and patiences, all her old tricks and triumphs' (*NYE* X, 58). And in Chapter 19, as Fleda and Mrs Gereth imagine them restored to the old house: 'the replenishment of Poynton made a shining steady light' (*NYE* X, 231).

353 **seeing the possibility of one in every bush**: James alludes to the American proverb, 'To expect a Thief in every bush': see Bartlett Jere Whiting, *Early American Proverbs and Proverbial Phrases* (Cambridge, MA: Belknap Press of Harvard University Press, 1977), T46, p. 434.

354 **to class my reprintable productions as far as possible according to their kinds**: It had always been James's intention to group the novellas

and short stories in *NYE* in this way. As he put it in his memorandum to the Scribners on 30 July 1905: 'My impression is that my shorter things will gain in significance and importance, very considerably, by a fresh grouping or classification, a placing together, from series to series, of those that will help each other, those that will conduce to something of a common effect'; 'the interest and value of the edition will, I think, rest not a little on the proper association and collocation' of these items (*HJL* 4:366, 367). He likewise told Grace Norton on 5 March 1907 that he was implementing an 'illuminatory classification, collocation, juxtaposition and separation [of fictions] through the whole series' (*LHJ* 2:71). In practice, he found the distribution of stories across volumes 'very difficult to arrive at neatly and rightly': 'congruity of subject and tone' had to compete as an organizing principle with the several claims of chronological sequence, word-limits for individual volumes, the granting of precedence in the list of contents for each volume to a longer story and the choice of photographic subjects for the frontispieces (to Scribners, 21–26 February 1908; Princeton). And yet while James acknowledged the impossibility of achieving 'an *ideally* systematic sequence' of his short fictions, he repeated to his publishers that 'One of my great reasons for desiring an Edition was, from the first, that I might in a measure *classify* and (more or less illuminatingly) juxtapose; and this I have tried for' (to Scribners, 10 March 1908; Princeton).

355 **They are thus of a family**: James elaborates on this idea of his shorter fictions as comprising 'a family' in the Preface to *NYE* XII, p. 140.

356 **at the best a "false" character, [...] a *figure*, oh definitely—which is a very different matter**: In his earliest literary criticism, James had drawn a distinction between 'character' and 'figure' on other grounds than free intelligence. Reviewing *Our Mutual Friend* in 1865, he contrasts Dickens's many 'figures' – his eccentrics and grotesques, 'creatures of pure fancy' – with what he apparently cannot or will not write, probable or typical characters animated by the common principles of humanity: Dickens 'has created nothing but figure. He has added nothing to our understanding of human character' (*LC1* 854, 856). In an earlier review of Harriet Elizabeth Prescott's novel *Azarian* (1864), James complained that her 'inordinate fondness for the picturesque' had filled the book with elaborate, idealized descriptions of people whom we cannot know or care about as characters: 'an author's paramount charge is the cure of souls, to the subjection, and if need be to the exclusion, of the picturesque. Let him look to his

characters: his *figures* will take care of themselves' (*LC1* 605). The people in *The House of the Seven Gables* are likewise for James 'all figures rather than characters', 'all pictures rather than persons' (*LC1* 413).

357 **of an admirable fine paste**: In nineteenth-century usage, 'paste' can mean, figuratively, 'The material of which a person is regarded as made, seen as an indication of character or personality' (*OED*). In *William Wetmore Story*, James had observed that his proud, difficult friend Anne Procter, whom he had known as a very old woman, was 'such a character, such a figure, as the generations appear pretty well to have ceased to produce, quite as if the technical secret of the "paste," like that of some old fabric or mixture, had been lost to them' (*WWS* I:224–5). This passage draws on the literal sense of 'paste' as 'The mixture of clay, water, etc., from which porcelain and other ceramics are made' (*OED*).

358 **able [...] to bear the whole of her dead weight at once on any given inch of a resisting surface**: Mona is described in Chapter 17 as 'an image of successful immobility': 'She was a magnificent dead weight; there was something positive and portentous in her quietude' (*NYE* X, 199–200). The transitive use of the verb 'to bear' with the preposition 'on' in this sentence of the Preface sounds odd, and may represent a slip on James's part or an error somewhere in the textual process: the verbal phrase 'to bring to bear' would be more usual: 'To bring (something) into effective operation (*against*, *on*, or *upon* something else); to cause to act; to employ, exert' (*OED*, 'bear'). But compare a phrasing from an earlier passage of the same Preface, referring to the remembered circumstances of composition: '"association" in fine bears upon them with its infinite magic' (p. 98).

359 **Three or four tried glances in that direction**: Stories by James featuring Europeans in America from the period before 'A London Life' (1888) include 'Four Meetings' (1877), 'An International Episode' (1878–9), 'Lady Barberina' (1884) and 'Pandora' (1884), all of which are collected in the *NYE*; and 'The Modern Warning' (1888, periodical title 'Two Countries'), which is not. *The Europeans* (1878), also excluded from the *NYE*, has two Europeanized Americans returning to America.

360 **the differences between fishes and fowls**: James appears to echo an English proverb: 'To make fish of one and flesh (*or* fowl) of another' means 'to make an invidious distinction; to show partiality' (William George Smith, *The Oxford Dictionary of English Proverbs* (Oxford: Clarendon Press, 1935), p. 530).

361 **quite positively a flower—that of the young American innocence transplanted to European air**: This general characterization of James's international stories suggests, in particular, 'Daisy Miller' (1878).

362 **I shall have much more to say about it on another occasion**: James next returns to the subject of international fiction in the Preface to *NYE* XIII apropos of *The Reverberator* (1888), pp. 148–54.

363 **why I need have conceived my three principal persons as sharers in that particular bewilderment**: At its point of origin for James, the subject of 'A London Life' did not concern Americans in Europe. The idea for the story was given him by Paul Bourget on 20 June 1887 in the form of an anecdote about the suicide of a young French woman in Rome: 'Bourget had a theory about her—which was that she had perceived that her mother had lovers, that this weighed upon her horribly & that she wanted to escape from the house, to get away & cease to be the witness of the maternal *dérèglements* [irregularities]. The only way for her to do this was to marry' (*CN* 36). In the anecdote, she had humiliatingly failed to get a young male acquaintance to propose to her, and afterwards killed herself in despair. James noted: 'to make something of it I must modify it essentially—as I can't, & besides, don't particularly want to, depict in an American magazine, a woman carrying on adulteries under her daughter's eyes. That case, I imagine, is in America so rare as to be almost abnormal' (*CN* 37). The mother of Bourget's anecdote became a sister, and the situation became a transatlantic one. The London setting and the American nationality of Laura Wing and her sister Selina seem to have been determined by the contemporary fashion for American women marrying into English society (noted in the Preface to *NYE* XIV apropos of 'Lady Barbarina', pp. 161–2) and also by the opportunities for marital infidelity offered by 'the smart, dissipated set' of the Prince of Wales (*CN* 37).

364 **poor young Wendover […] fails on any such ground to attest himself**: James had first envisaged Wendover as 'an Englishman, a clerk in the foreign office', 'one of those competent, colourless, gentlemanly mediocrities of whom one sees so many in London & who have a career' (20 June 1887; *CN* 39).

365 **Mrs. Lionel**: As Philip Horne points out, in the revised *NYE* text 'Selina comes to be called by her husband's Christian name, "Mrs. Lionel" rather than "Mrs. Berrington"'; the 'slangy familiarity' of this name is apt for 'the loose Berringtons' and characteristic of other stories by James set in the same

London milieu, for example *What Maisie Knew* ('A London Life' and 'The Reverberator', ed. Horne (Oxford: Oxford University Press, 1989), p. 369).

366 **a remarkably wise old friend**: Horne suggests that this was the actress and author Frances Anne Kemble (1809–93), whom James had known since the early 1870s ('A London Life' and 'The Reverberator', ed. Horne, p. 348). Fanny Kemble was English but had married an American and lived for long periods in America and Continental Europe. She was also a forthright private critic of James's writing. As James told his mother, for example, Kemble agreed 'strongly' with R. H. Hutton's disappointed review of *Washington Square* (1880) (Gard 88–90): 'She takes much interest in my productions, but thinks they fail of justice to—I don't know exactly what! She is, however, a delightful woman to discuss with—she is so deeply in earnest, so perfectly honest, & so admirably intelligent' (to MWJ, 7 February [1881]; *CLHJ 1880–1883* 1:162). James commemorated her in an obituary essay, 'Frances Anne Kemble' (1893) (*LC1* 1071–97).

367 **a high stiff-backed angular action […] beyond any American "faking."**: In keeping with the horsey tone of the aristocratic English society Selina has married into – riding in the London parks, hunting on country estates, racing at Ascot and Newmarket – James uses 'action' here in a sense that implies 'reference to an animal, esp. a horse': 'the management of the body or limbs in movement' (*OED*). Early in 'A London Life' we are told that 'There were an immense number of horses, in one way and another, in Mrs. Lionel's life', and when she finally runs off with her lover her act is described in equine terms: 'this time Selina had really "bolted"' (Chs. 2 and 11; *NYE* X, 298, 395). For a horse to 'bolt' is 'To break away from the rider's control; to make a violent dash out of his course' (*OED*). As defined in a British slang dictionary of the 1890s, the term 'BOLTER' refers 'figuratively to persons in the sense of one given to throwing off restraint'; the examples cited, including a reference to Lady Dedlock in Dickens's *Bleak House* (1853), make clear the word's application to wives who leave their husbands (*Slang* I:278). 'A London Life' emphasizes the specifically English character of this word and the behaviour it describes. In Chapter 12, Lady Davenant tells Wendover, '"Selina has bolted, as they say"', and when he seems not to recognize the word, remarks: '"I don't know what you call it in America." "In America we don't do it," he made bold to say' (*NYE* X, 412). In the context referred to in this sentence of the Preface, the verb 'fake' means 'To engage in deception, fraudulent fabrication, pretence, simulation' (*OED*, 'Originally *U.S.*', earliest instance 1884).

368 **the hard rustle of whose long steps and the sinister tinkle of whose multiplied trinkets**: This description of Selina Berrington makes her sound strikingly like the English society lady Ida Farange in *What Maisie Knew* (1897), a novel collected in the next volume of the *NYE*; Adrian Poole notes Selina's influence on James's later characterization of Ida (*What Maisie Knew*, ed. Poole (Oxford: Oxford University Press, 1996), pp. xiii–xiv). Ida's small daughter Maisie experiences her mother's jewels as manifestations of her violent, abrasive character, noticing 'the rattle of her trinkets and the scratch of her endearments'; briefly embraced by Ida, 'The next moment [Maisie] was on her mother's breast, where, amid a wilderness of trinkets, she felt as if she had suddenly been thrust, with a smash of glass, into a jeweller's shop-front' (Chs. 9 and 15; *NYE* XI, 69, 145). The approaching 'rustle' of Ida's skirts is noted by the narrator, though not by a preoccupied Maisie, at the start of their final scene in Chapter 20 (*NYE* XI, 208). Selina is given none of these attributes in 'A London Life'.

369 **the prime [...] intention of the tale in question that the persons concerned in it should have had this, that or the other land of birth**: Despite James's protestation here, in the notebook entry that records the germ of 'A London Life' he had envisaged the story 'as an episode in that "international" series which, really, without forcing the matter or riding the horse to death, strikes me as an inexhaustible mine' (20 June 1887; *CN* 37). Compare his claim, in the Preface to *NYE* XIV, that *The Wings of the Dove* and *The Golden Bowl* were not primarily concerned with 'the exhibited behaviour of certain Americans as Americans, of certain English persons as English, of certain Romans as Romans', and that 'the subject could in each case have been perfectly expressed had *all* the persons concerned been only American or only English or only Roman or whatever' (pp. 157–8).

370 **to guard against personal bespattering**: An echo of the story: Selina Berrington leaves Laura compromisingly alone with Wendover in an opera-box in Chapter 11 while she makes her escape from her husband, and Laura feels that in doing so Selina has 'tried to splash her sister with the mud into which she herself had jumped' (*NYE* X, 395). In Chapter 12, Lady Davenant uses the same figure when she tries to explain to Wendover why Laura responded to this situation by offering herself to him: '"It seemed to her [...] that an honest man might save her from it, might give her his name and his faith and help her to pick her steps in the mud. She exaggerates the force of the splash"' (*NYE* X, 415).

371 **almost any demonstration of the effect of London**: During this period, James also wrote his essay 'London' (1888) and several novels and stories largely or wholly set in London and concerned with aspects of London life: e.g. *The Princess Casamassima* (1886), 'The Liar' (1888), 'The Lesson of the Master' (1888), *The Tragic Muse* (1890), 'Brooksmith' (1891), 'The Marriages' (1891) and 'The Chaperon' (1891).

372 **in "Scribner's Magazine" during the summer of 1888**: 'A London Life' was published in three issues of *Scribner's Magazine*, June–September 1888.

373 **an old Venetian palace [...] a pompous Tiepolo ceiling**: The palace was the fifteenth-century Palazzo Barbaro, near the Ponte dell'Accademia on the Grand Canal in Venice. The Preface recalls James's first stay there in May–June 1887 as the guest of his American friends Daniel and Ariana Curtis, who had purchased the palazzo in 1885; the notebook entry that contains the germ of 'A London Life' is dated 'Venice, June 20th 1887. (Palazzo Barbaro.)' (*CN* 36). Giovanni Battista Tiepolo (1696–1770) was the leading Venetian painter of the rococo period. Around 1750, he executed a large (254 × 467 cm) allegorical ceiling canvas for the Palazzo Barbaro, commonly referred to as *The Apotheosis of the Barbaro Family*. It was removed and sold in 1866, and was eventually donated to the Metropolitan Museum in New York in 1934 (Filippo Pedrocco, *Tiepolo: The Complete Paintings* (New York: Rizzoli, 2002), p. 281); the painting James saw in the late 1880s was thus presumably a copy. The Palazzo Barbaro is also the model for the Palazzo Leporelli in *The Wings of the Dove*; Alvin Langdon Coburn's photograph of its Gothic frontage (captioned 'The Venetian Palace') is the frontispiece for the second volume of that novel in the *NYE*.

374 **the interview with young Wendover contrived by Lady Davenant**: This scene occurs in Chapter 12, while Laura rests upstairs in bed at Lady Davenant's house: it is the only scene in the story not conducted in Laura's presence.

375 **platitude of statement—a deplorable depth [...], I have attempted elsewhere to signify, for any pretending master of representation to sink to**: James refers to a passage in the Preface to *The Tragic Muse*: 'processes, periods, intervals, stages, degrees, connexions [...] may be unconvincingly stated, in fiction, to the deep discredit of the writer, but it remains the very deuce to *represent* them' (pp. 73–4).

376 **a postman's knock**: A 'sharp rap or blow similar to that typically made by a postman' (*OED*). As Horne notes, 'James here recalls the mockable directness of the "postman's rap" given by the unsophisticated Mr. Wendover to Lady Davenant's front door' in Chapter 7 (*'A London Life' and 'The Reverberator'*, ed. Horne, p. 348). Encountering Wendover on her way to Lady Davenant's, Laura brings him to the door and suggests that he come in with her: 'They stepped into the porch and the young man, forestalling her hint, lifted the knocker and gave a postman's rap. She laughed at him for this and he looked bewildered' (*NYE* X, 346).

377 **a ramshackle inn on the Irish coast**: James stayed at the Marine Hotel at Kingstown (now Dún Laoghaire) on the eastern coast of Ireland from 7 July to 7 August 1891; he was recuperating from a bout of influenza and had come to the seaside on medical advice. As he told J. R. Lowell, 'It is a very charming coast, in this lovely weather, with great blueness of sea and greenness of shore, and all kinds of graceful Wicklow mountains and hills of Howth and Killiny [*sic*: Killiney]. The very waves have a brogue as they break' (20 July [1891]; *HJL* 3:346). To his brother William, he wrote that he had 'found [...] a command of my time which has enabled me to do a London month's work in a fortnight' (31 July [1891]; *CWJ* 2:180).

378 **two numbers of "The Atlantic Monthly" of 1891**: 'The Chaperon' appeared in the *Atlantic Monthly*, November–December 1891.

379 **the single spoken word [...] that clear ring of the electric bell that the barest touch of the button may produce**: In a notebook entry made on 13 July 1891, James recalled that he had 'some time ago' noted an idea for a story 'suggested by a word of Mrs. Earle's on the situation of Mrs. M. & one of her daughter's [*sic*]' (*CN* 58); the original note does not survive. According to Edel (*CN* 58 n. 2), James's informant was the horticulturalist Maria Theresa Earle (1836–1925), author of *Pot-Pourri from a Surrey Garden* (1897) and several sequels. For the electric bell as an emblem of clear and direct impressions, compare 'New England: An Autumn Impression' (1905): 'the shrill effect of the New England meeting-house, [...] the single straight breath with which it seems to blow the ground clear of the seated solidity of religion, is an impression that responds to the renewed sight of one of these structures as promptly as the sharp ring to the pressure of the electric button' (*AS* 24). Electric bells installed in the home for summoning servants are a sign of technological modernity in Chapter 4 of *The Other House* (1896), as well as a signal of the first crisis of the plot: 'the near vibration, from Mrs. Bream's room, of one of the smart, loud

electric bells which were for Mrs. Beever the very accent of the newness of Bounds' (*The Other House*, 2 vols. (London: William Heinemann, 1896), vol. I, p. 33).

380 **the desert around her**: The Preface echoes a repeated figure added to the NYE text of 'The Chaperon' in revision. In Chapter 2, Rose Tramore recalls her first meeting with her mother: 'Already on that first day she had talked about dressmakers. Of course, poor thing, it was to be remembered that in her desert-life there were not many things she *could* talk about' (*NYE* X, 448); the first book edition reads 'in her circumstances there were not many things' (*The Real Thing* (New York: Macmillan, 1893), p. 192). In Chapter 5, Rose 'had set herself a task [to rehabilitate her mother socially] and clung to it, but had now the sense of wading through desert sands' (*NYE* X, 482); the first edition reads 'but she appeared to herself despicably idle' (*The Real Thing*, p. 227).

381 **"taking her out," floating her in spite of whatever past damage**: Rose takes her mother out in the sense of chaperoning her in society, as a mother would ordinarily do for an unmarried daughter. James puts the central conceit of the story thus in his notebook: 'Her mother can do nothing for her in society, can't "take her out" &c; so she makes it her plan to bestow these services instead of receiving them. She will take her mother out—she will be *her* chaperon & protectress' (13 July 1891; *CN* 58). When they accept Mrs Vesey's lunch invitation in Chapter 5, Rose 'could feel for the first time that she was taking her mother out' (*NYE* X, 496). As a transitive verb, to 'float' means 'To set afloat' and, figuratively, 'to buoy up, support'; also 'To get (a company, scheme, etc.) afloat or fully started', 'to procure public support or acceptance for' (*OED*). The Preface's reference to 'past damage' likens Mrs Tramore to a ship that has run aground or collided with something, and the last chapter of the story tracks her re-acceptance into society via images of buoyancy. Captain Jay asks Rose to introduce him to her mother in the Piazza del Duomo in Milan: 'They were so close to [Mrs Tramore] that she probably heard, but she floated away with a single stroke of her paddle and an inattentive poise of her head' (Ch. 5; *NYE* X, 485). Later, in Venice, Mrs Tramore is significantly bowed to from a gondola and invited to lunch on a yacht (*NYE* X, 494–5). In the final sentence of the story, Captain Jay, now Rose's husband, 'commends her […] for the way she launched her mother' (*NYE* X, 500).

382 **a morsel of queer comedy**: The situation is recognized as such in the story: in Chapter 5, Mrs Vesey is 'capable of seeing what a "draw" there

would be in the comedy, if properly brought out, of the reversed positions of [mother and daughter]' (*NYE* X, 496–7).

383 **A short story [...] either an anecdote or a picture**: In a review of the American writer Henry Harland's story collection *Comedies and Errors* (1898), James had characterized the 'two quite distinct effects' a short story might produce: 'that of the detached incident, single and sharp, as clear as a pistol-shot'; or 'that of the impression, comparatively generalised—simplified, foreshortened, reduced to a particular perspective—of a complexity or a continuity'. Harland's stories belong to the second type: 'the picture of a particular figure—eccentric, comic, pathetic, tragic—disengaged from old remembrances, encounters, accidents, exhibitions and exposures, and resolving these glimpses and patches into the unity of air and feeling that makes up a character' (*LC1* 285–6). James's 1897 introduction to a posthumous collection of stories by Hubert Crackanthorpe made a similar distinction between 'two sorts': on the one hand, 'the chain of items, figures in a kind of sum [...] of movement, added up as on a schoolboy's slate and with the correct total and its little flourish constituting the finish and accounting for the effect'; on the other, 'an effort preferably pictorial, a portrait of conditions, an attempt to summarize and compress for purposes of presentation, to "render" even, if possible, for purposes of expression' (*LC1* 842). Later Prefaces propose variants of this antithesis between types of short fiction. Retaining 'anecdote' but changing the contrasting term, the Preface to *NYE* XII opposes a 'short and sharp and single' type of 'fairy-tale' that is 'charged more or less with the compactness of anecdote' to another type, 'the long and loose, the copious, the various, the endless' (p. 135); the Preface to *NYE* XIII discusses *The Reverberator* as simultaneously 'an exemplary anecdote' and 'a little rounded drama' (p. 143). For contemporary critical discussion of the short story as a form, see also note 483. James's promised 'ampler development' of his own commentary comes in the Prefaces to *NYE* XV and XVI and includes yet another antithesis, between 'the concise anecdote' and the *nouvelle* or long story (p. 184).

PREFACE to *What Maisie Knew, In the Cage, The Pupil* (*NYE* XI)

384 **the growth of the "great oak" from the little acorn**: Proverbially, '*great oaks from little acorns grow* [...]: a modest beginning may lead to a significant outcome' (*OED*, 'acorn'). James originally projected *What Maisie*

Knew as a story of 10,000 words for *The Yellow Book* (see his notebook entry on 22 December 1895; *CN* 147). In the event it was serialized in the fortnightly Chicago journal *The Chap-Book* (15 January–1 August 1897), whose publisher Herbert S. Stone advertised it in December 1896 – just a month before it was due to start appearing – as 'a novelette of about 25,000 words'. The completed text of *Maisie* would run to more than 90,000 words. Ward S. Worden cites 'unreliable' anecdotal evidence of 'Stone's astonishment and pique over the unexpected length of the serial' ('A Cut Version of *What Maisie Knew*', *American Literature* 24.4 (1953), 493–504; 496). As Worden shows, the parallel British serialization in William Heinemann's monthly journal the *New Review* (February–September 1897) presented a radically abridged text of the novel; the cuts were restored for the Heinemann first edition.

385 **the situation of some luckless child of a divorced couple [...] the re-marriage of one of its parents—I forget which**: James recorded this anecdote on 12 November 1892: 'Two days ago, at dinner at James Bryce's, Mrs. Ashton, Mrs. Bryce's sister, mentioned to me a situation that she had known of, of which it immediately struck me that something might be made in a tale' (*CN* 71). James's host was the jurist, historian and politician James Bryce, Viscount Bryce (1838–1922); he had married Elizabeth Marion Ashton in 1889. In this initial notebook entry, James recorded that 'Each parent married again', as they do in the novel (*CN* 71).

386 **rebounding from racquet to racquet like a tennis-ball or a shuttlecock**: In Chapter 2, the very small Maisie is 'the little feathered shuttlecock [her parents] could fiercely keep flying between them' (*NYE* XI, 14).

387 **the chance of happiness and of an improved state might be here involved for the child**: This possibility occurred to James in his first notebook entry for *What Maisie Knew*: 'The basis of almost any story, any development would be, that the child should prefer the new husband & the new wife to the old; that is that these latter should [...] become indifferent to it, whereas the others have become interested & attached, finally passionately so' (*CN* 71).

388 **the *full* ironic truth**: The truth elaborated in this and the next paragraph of the Preface is present in outline in James's first notebook entry, which entertains 'the idea of an odd & particular relation springing up / 1st between the child & each of these new parents. / 2^{d} between one of the new parents and the other—through the child—over and on account of &

by means of the child' (*CN* 71). In his second notebook entry for the novel (26 August 1893), James explicitly characterizes this reading of the situation *as* an irony: 'The little *donnée* will yield most, I think—most *ironic* effect, & this is the sort of thing mainly to try for in it, if I make the old parents—the original parents *live*— not die and transmit the little girl to the persons they each have married *en secondes noces* [the second time]' (*CN* 77).

389 **bliss and bale**: 'Bale' in this sense is 'Mental suffering; misery, sorrow, grief'; the word is often paired with its alliterative opposite, 'bliss' (*OED*). Compare Book Twelfth, Chapter 2 of *The Ambassadors*, where Madame de Vionnet's collapse into tears shows Strether 'a fine free range of bliss and bale' (*NYE* XXII, 286). The metaphor of the double-faced medal in this sentence of the Preface recurs in other Prefaces and figures other sorts of antithesis: with reference to fictional subjects and themes (Americans bewildered by Europe and Europeans bewildered by America, American business-men who travel abroad with their families and those who stay home and do business, pp. 104, 153); and to narrative form (Milly Theale's situation as seen by others and as experienced by herself, p. 233). For 'material and form' as the two faces of the medal, see the example cited in note 320.

390 **bringing people together**: The Preface echoes a recurring phrase in the novel. As Mrs Beale puts it to Sir Claude in Chapter 8: '"What seems to have happened is that she has brought you and me together"' (*NYE* XI, 64). He and Maisie take up the formula enthusiastically, and it becomes a shared joke between them.

391 **confusion worse confounded [...] across the scent of selfishness**: James alludes to the flight of the defeated rebel angels from Heaven in Milton's *Paradise Lost*: 'With ruin upon ruin, rout on rout, / Confusion worse confounded' (Book II, ll. 995–6; *The Poems of John Milton*, ed. John Carey and Alastair Fowler (London and New York: Longman, 1968), p. 555). Just over three months after dictating the Preface to *What Maisie Knew*, he apologized to Frederick Macmillan for his delay in starting a book he had agreed to write on London and referred in Miltonic terms to the immediate obstacle to his progress, the recent production of his play *The High Bid* (1907): 'It only needed a fresh plunge into the theatre—absolutely necessary at a time of long and laborious Editions with their fruit all in the future—to make my confusion worse confounded!' (5 April 1908; *LL*

461). The 'scent' in this sentence of the Preface is 'The characteristic odour of a person or animal by which hunting dogs or other animals are able to detect and track their quarry; (hence) a track or trail formed by this odour' (*OED*); James's extended metaphor refers to dragging something strongly scented *across* this trail, thus making it impossible to follow.

392 **my light vessel of consciousness [...] couldn't be with verisimilitude a rude little boy**: Compare James's initial note for *Maisie*: 'boy or girl would do, but I see a girl, which would make it different from *The Pupil*' (*CN* 71). 'The Pupil' (1891) is also collected in *NYE* XI. If little British boys of the upper and middle classes were 'never so "present"' as girls, as James goes on to observe, that is presumably because they were away from the family home at boarding-school for most of the year. Compare 'light vessel' here with the phrase James misquotes from George Eliot in the Preface to *The Portrait of a Lady*, 'frail vessels' (see note 160).

393 **to make and to keep her so limited consciousness the very field of my picture**: James arrives at this central principle of the novel's form in his third notebook entry (22 December 1895): 'Make my point of view, my *line*, the consciousness, the dim, sweet, scared, wondering, clinging perception of the child'; 'It takes place before Maisie—EVERYTHING TAKES PLACE BEFORE MAISIE. That is a part of the essence of the thing' (*CN* 148, 149).

394 **refused to remain humble**: James had commented on this behaviour in the Preface to *The Awkward Age*, p. 77.

395 **a house-dog of a temper above confinement, [...] its futile thrashing**: Philip Horne connects this figure to James's dog Nick, whose tendency to run off 'chasing sheep or chickens' on walks around Rye was reported by his 14-year-old niece Peggy in a letter home on 26 April 1901: 'It is too funny for words sometimes when this happens and it nearly drives Uncle Henry to distraction and he yells in a terribly loud voice "Oh! oh! oh! oh! oh! you little brute! you little brute! you beast! oh! oh! oh!" Then he hurries home with the unfortunate wretch and leaves Mama and me to follow on at our own sweet pace' (quoted in *Henry James and Revision*, p. 69).

396 **many more perceptions than they have terms to translate them**: As the narrator notes in Chapter 20, Maisie 'had ever of course in her mind fewer names than conceptions' (*NYE* XI, 204). The expansion of her vocabulary – in English and French – and her growing command of it are noted at intervals throughout the novel.

397 **our own commentary constantly attends and amplifies**: As Adrian Poole notes, the narrator 'attends' Maisie in this way 'up to a clearly marked point in Chapter XX' when she leaves London with Sir Claude (*What Maisie Knew*, ed. Poole, p. xxiv). After this point he signals the change in his relation to Maisie by drawing our attention to how much she can comprehend unaided: e.g., 'It was singular, but from this time she understood and she followed'; 'It sounds, no doubt, too penetrating'; 'Oh decidedly I shall never get you to believe the number of things she saw and the number of secrets she discovered!' (Ch. 20; *NYE* XI, 202, 204, 205).

398 **She wonders [...] to the end, to the death—the death of her childhood, properly speaking; after which [...] her situation will change and become another affair**: The novel repeatedly characterizes Maisie's cognitive processes in terms of 'wonder': the word is attributed to her some sixty times. Questioned by an early reader about what happened to Maisie after the end of the book, James answered: 'the case seems to me to illustrate the marked difference between that which is in old-fashioned parlance a "story" and that which has the distinctive characteristics of what *I* call a Subject. The story, in the old-fashioned sense, isn't, I dare say, told—told to the end that is,—in the book. But what the end—*where* the end, in that sort of thing, ever is, I feel that I can never say: the place, the point, the limit seem to me so arbitrary. Whereas, as regards the Subject of the poor little wretch, somehow—isn't it so?—*that* is treated. There would doubtless be another Subject later—but my mind, as yet, refuses to tackle it; for the reason, after all, I think, that it can only be essentially less interesting. The situation certainly didn't stay where I left it—the edifying step-parents didn't probably, for very long, make a very good thing of it together. Sir Claude and the lone infant bumped again against each other—and heaven only knows what *may* have occurred. Only, whatever it was, the best of it, for Art—forgive the vulgar expression—was over. The best of it was in other words all the *worst* of it—it must have been, though still doubtless curious and queer, less interesting afterwards. The subject was girl's childhood—it was the fact of that that was the whole note of the situation; and my climax, arrived at, was marked *by*, and consisted *of*, the stroke of the hour of the end of that childhood. Voilà' (to Mrs John Chandler Bancroft, 21 March 1898; *LL* 299–300).

399 **connexions with the "universal!"**: James had remarked of the first instalment of George Eliot's *Daniel Deronda* (1876): 'The "sense of the universal" is constant, omnipresent' (*LC1* 974). The phrase he quotes there is spoken

in the novel by the German musician Klesmer, voicing his contempt for the operatic aria by Bellini which Gwendolen sings in Book 1, Chapter 5: '"It is a form of melody which expresses a puerile state of culture [...]. There is a sort of self-satisfied folly about every phrase of such melody: no cries of deep, mysterious passion—no conflict—no sense of the universal"' (*Daniel Deronda*, ed. Handley, p. 43). This quality of Eliot's novel struck James 'sometimes perhaps as rather conscious and over-cultivated; but it gives us the feeling that the threads of the narrative, as we gather them into our hands, are not of the usual commercial measurement, but long electric wires capable of transmitting messages from mysterious regions' (*LC1* 974). Compare the previous paragraph of the Preface: 'the sense of pulling at threads intrinsically worth it—strong enough and fine enough and entire enough' (p. 116).

400 **At two points in particular**: The two scenes referred to in this paragraph occupy Chapter 16 (Maisie with the Captain) and Chapters 18–19 (Maisie with Beale and Mrs Cuddon). James conceived of them as a pair: a notebook entry of 26 October 1896 refers to the second scene as 'the pendant-scene' to the first (*CN* 163).

401 **too stupid**: This judgement echoes a rare direct intervention by the narrator – as Poole notes, stepping 'sharply outside the child's own vision' (*What Maisie Knew*, ed. Poole, p. xxiii) – but on that occasion it is Beale Farange who is described as 'stupid'. At the end of Chapter 18, Maisie sits on her father's knee, eager to help him to pretend 'that their relations were easy and graceful' and only waiting for 'the cue' from him to do so: 'She waited for it while, between his big teeth, he breathed the sighs she didn't know to be stupid. And as if, though he was so stupid all through, he had let the friendly suffusion of her eyes yet tell him she was ready for anything, he floundered about, wondering what the devil he could lay hold of' (*NYE* XI, 181).

402 **such terms as "painful," "unpleasant" and "disgusting" [...] applied to his results**: Such terms occur frequently in reviews of James's fiction from the late 1890s. Thus, for example, an otherwise appreciative notice of *What Maisie Knew* is sure of the novel's 'importance, if not its pleasantness', and remarks that 'this constant approximation of a child-mind [...] to the doings of the horrid quartet of persons who principally dominate her fate, is to the reader oppressive and painful'; and 'The Turn of the Screw' is described as 'another study of the same unpleasant kind of fact' as that represented in *Maisie* (Hayes 287–8, 304). In *The Awkward Age*, James 'seems to have reached the point of confusing an artist's gusto in

triumphing over difficulties with a gusto in an unpleasant subject for its own sake' (A. T. Q. C. [Arthur Thomas Quiller-Couch], 'A Literary Causerie', *The Speaker: The Liberal Review*, 15 July 1899, 44–5; 45). In February 1907, James had privately complained about an objection raised in these terms by Elizabeth Jordan to the chapter he contributed to *The Whole Family* (1908); the passage in question describes an Upper East Side boarding house or manicure parlour and its louche proprietress Mrs Chataway, with whom an eloping member of the family is supposed to have taken refuge (*WF* 177–84). As James wrote to Pinker, referring presumably to Jordan's 'reserves' about this material as typical of American editors in general: 'one can never sufficiently reckon with their strange prudery & pusillanimity [...]. What she calls "unpleasant,"—imbecile word!—seemed to me an indispensable Accent, or Note of Interest, in the damnable thing—which, otherwise, so vitally needed it' (18 February 1907; Yale).

403 **the "mixing-up" of a child with anything unpleasant**: To 'mix up' in this sense is 'to connect *with* or involve *in* (a compromising or discreditable affair, activity, etc.)' (*OED*, 'mix'). The Preface attributes this term to moralizing readers, but it occurs both in the novel itself and in James's notebook. In Chapter 17, Mrs Beale tells Maisie why Sir Claude is reluctant to see them in public: '"He says he doesn't want you mixed up." "Mixed up with what?" "That's exactly what *I* want to know: mixed up with what, and how you are any more mixed—?"' (*NYE* XI, 167). In the corresponding notebook entry, James describes Sir Claude and Mrs Beale's 'rather perplexed & slightly ashamed consciousness that [...] if they keep [Maisie] they keep her mixed up with their *malpropreté* [indecency], their illegitimate tie' (26 October 1896; *CN* 166).

404 **Kensington Gardens**: For this London park, see note 712.

405 **"Maisie" is of 1907**: As Poole notes, 'this seems to be a slip': *What Maisie Knew* was first published in 1897. 'It is true that James revised the novel in 1907, but when he assigns dates elsewhere in the Prefaces, it is always the year of initial publication of which he thinks, describing the tale "Europe", e.g., as "of 1899"' (*What Maisie Knew*, ed. Poole, p. 276).

406 **a very hot Italian railway-carriage, [...] a doctor of medicine who had come from a far country to settle in Florence**: In early July 1890, James stayed for a week in Florence with Dr William W. Baldwin, who had been a friend since 1887 and whom he described to Grace Norton as 'a dear little American physician of genius', 'a charming and glowing little man,

who, coming here eight or ten years ago, has made himself a first place, and who seems to consider it a blessing to him that I should abide a few days in his house (30 June [1890]; *HJL* 3:295, 296). During that visit, the two men made 'a little a tour of the most romantic and untrodden corners of Tuscany', accompanied by 'a very pleasant and wily Italian friend of Baldwin's, who is connected with the Ferrovie [railways] and very *pratico* of [well versed in] out of the way places, and [...] engages to give us impressions which the herd of tourists never have' (to Henrietta Reubell, 7 July [1890]; *HJL* 3:298). Edel identifies the friend as 'a stout Italian named Taccini' (*HJL* 3:298 n. 1).

407 **an odd adventurous, extravagant band, [...] measured and judged them, all round, ever so quaintly**: This account of the germ of 'The Pupil' echoes phrasings from the story. The young tutor Pemberton likens the Moreens to 'a band of gipsies', 'pickpockets or strolling players', 'a band of adventurers' (Chs. 2 and 4; *NYE* XI, 519, 520, 533). In Chapter 5, Pemberton sees that Mr and Mrs Moreen have guessed '"that the child [...] has judged us and how he regards us"' for taking advantage of his tutor (*NYE* XI, 539). And in their first interview, when Morgan tells Pemberton that he can ask for whatever salary he wants ('"We don't mind what anything costs—we live awfully well"'), his mother exclaims: '"My darling, you're too quaint!"' (Ch. 1; *NYE* XI, 514).

408 **singular things were to happen to it**: James may be referring to the difficult publication history of 'The Pupil'. He first offered the story to Horace Scudder, who had just taken over the editorship of the *Atlantic Monthly*, in October 1890. Scudder unexpectedly turned it down, and the fallout from his rejection caused a temporary breach in James's relationship with a journal he had been writing for since the 1860s. 'The Pupil' eventually appeared in two issues of *Longman's Magazine*, March–April 1891. George Monteiro prints the surviving correspondence between James and Scudder, and speculates that James may have found 'enough merit in what Scudder said to compel him to rewrite or at least revise the story before placing it with *Longman's*' (Monteiro, 'The *Atlantic Monthly*'s Rejection of "The Pupil": An Exchange of Letters between Henry James and Horace Scudder', *American Literary Realism, 1870–1910* 23.1 (1990), 75–83; 82).

409 **the copious "cosmopolite" legend**: The noun 'cosmopolite' designates 'A "citizen of the world"; one who regards or treats the whole world as his country; one who has no national attachments or prejudices' (*OED*).

James's biography of the American sculptor William Wetmore Story (1819–95), published shortly before the period of the *NYE*, is centrally concerned with the 'legend' of a mid-nineteenth-century generation of American and British cosmopolites: the Preface's word is used several times in *William Wetmore Story and His Friends* (1903) to refer to the chronicle of their experiences, a compound of family traditions, drawing-room anecdotes, printed letters and reminiscences and literary history. When, in Chapter 8, for example, James recalls talking with an elderly Isa Blagden (1816?–73), the close friend of Robert Browning and Elizabeth Barrett Browning, in her garden at Bellosguardo near Florence, the 'kindly little legend' of her own life in Italy overlaps with the larger 'Florentine legend' of British and American expatriates which James himself was just then entering on (see *WWS* II:94–5). James describes Story and his friends as 'our vanished cosmopolites'; and on the first page of the book he reminds his readers that, 'so far as we are contentedly cosmopolite to-day and move about in a world that has been made for us both larger and more amusing, we owe much of our extension and diversion to those comparatively few who, amid difficulties and dangers, set the example and made out the road' (*WWS* II:186, I:3). In 'The Pupil', Pemberton comes to find this formula inadequate to describe the Moreens: 'He had thought himself very sharp that first day in hitting them all off in his mind with the "cosmopolite" label. Later it seemed feeble and colourless—confessedly helplessly provisional' (Ch. 2; *NYE* XI, 519).

410 **whom I place at Nice, at Venice, in Paris, [...] the little old miscellaneous cosmopolite Florence, [...] a society that has passed away for ever with all its faded ghosts and fragile relics**: The action of 'The Pupil' opens in Nice on the French Riviera and moves, with the Moreens, first to Paris and then to Venice, where Pemberton finally leaves the family; in the last chapter, he finds them 'on the rebound, once more in Paris' (*NYE* XI, 564). The Moreens do visit Florence once, albeit very briefly: in Chapter 4, we learn that they 'all ran down to Florence' from Nice 'and then, at the end of ten days, liking it much less than they had intended, straggled back in mysterious depression' (*NYE* XI, 528). In *William Wetmore Story and His Friends*, James describes Florence as a centre of mid-nineteenth-century cosmopolitan society (see *WWS* II:93–6). The Story biography opens with him examining 'A boxful of old papers, personal records and relics all', and the access to the past that is afforded by such materials is figured throughout as a form of haunting: 'Boxfuls of old letters and relics

are, in fine, boxfuls of ghosts and echoes', and for James to sift through them is to meet 'the appeal, the ghostly claim as we may almost call it, of a dislodged, a vanished society' (*WWS* I:7, 14).

411 **the unconscious Barbarians [...] prepaid and forwarded**: Widely used from late antiquity to refer to the Germanic and Central Asian peoples who invaded the Roman Empire in the fourth and fifth centuries CE, the term 'Barbarians' also has a specific reference in nineteenth-century cultural criticism and sociology. Matthew Arnold had used the word in Chapter 3 of *Culture and Anarchy* (1869) to designate the British aristocracy, in a tripartite social schema that also included the 'Philistines' or middle classes (for whom, see note 895) and the 'Populace' or working classes. Thorstein Veblen would later treat 'barbarians' as a synonym for the American 'leisure class' in *The Theory of the Leisure Class* (1899). In his travel writing, James applies the word to British, American and German tourists encountered in Italy and Switzerland: in 'Other Tuscan Cities' (1909), for example, a late essay written after his final trip to Italy in 1907, a visit to Bagni di Lucca – in the mid nineteenth century a quiet summer resort for British and American expatriates – would prompt him to imagine what the place must have been like in 'that easier and not so inordinately remote past' before roads and railways opened up Italy to 'the contingent of beguiled barbarians' (*CTW*2 582, 583). If the Preface's 'prepaid and forwarded' travellers are seen as passive freight or cargo, they also reflect an important economic condition of mass tourism: from the late 1860s, the British travel agency Thomas Cook & Son began to introduce prepaid products including coupons exchangeable for meals and accommodation at hotels on the agency's list, an early form of traveller's cheques, and rail tickets valid on predetermined routes (see Piers Brendon, *Thomas Cook: 150 Years of Popular Tourism* (London: Secker & Warburg, 1991), pp. 110, 114–15, 163, 168–9). In his early essay 'The St. Gothard. Leaves from a Note-Book' (1873), James had described making a late September stay in Switzerland on the mistaken supposition that 'the last Cook's tourist would have paid out his last coupon and departed' (*TS* 230). He also noted the 'passivity' of modern tourists in his 1882 essay 'Venice', figuring them as 'helpless captives' guided by *valets de place* 'through churches and galleries in dense irresponsible groups' (*PPL* 8–9).

412 **"cycle" of romance**: James appears to use 'cycle' here in the sense of 'A series of poems or prose romances, collected round or relating to a central event or epoch of mythic history and forming a continuous narrative'

(*OED*) – an *unwritten* cycle, presumably, in light of his subsequent comments in this paragraph. But the word also resonated for him specifically with the American experience of Europe via an allusion to Alfred Tennyson's 'Locksley Hall' (1842): 'Better fifty years of Europe than a cycle of Cathay' (l. 184; *The Poems of Tennyson*, vol. II p. 130). A 'cycle' in this sense is 'A long indefinite period of time; an age' (*OED*). In *The Wings of the Dove*, the narrator observes that 'the five years in Switzerland and Germany' which Susan Stringham and her sister had enjoyed in their youth 'were to leave them ever afterwards a standard of comparison for all cycles of Cathay' (Book Third, Ch. 1; *NYE* XIX, 119).

413 **The modern reporter's big brushes, [...] sky-scrapers**: In 'New York Revisited' (1906), James had recently figured sky-scrapers as the architectural epitomes of the modern city, their rapid construction and dedication to the profit motive making them 'simply the most piercing notes in that concert of the expensively provisional into which your supreme sense of New York resolves itself' (*AS* 77). Another essay from the same American tour, 'Richmond, Virginia' (1906), associates the high-rise architecture of modern finance with the publicity of print media: 'the sky-scrapers, the newspaper-offices, the highly-rented pews and the billionaires' (*AS* 390).

414 **the great unstudied precursors [...] I don't pretend really to have "done" them**: The first chapter of *William Wetmore Story and His Friends* is titled 'The Precursors': James uses the word to refer to American and British travellers in Europe of the generation before his own. For the Preface's disclaimer about not having really represented the Moreens in 'The Pupil', compare another passage in the opening chapter of *William Wetmore Story*: 'The old relation, social, personal, æsthetic, of the American world to the European [...] is as charming a subject as the student of manners, morals, personal adventures, the history of taste, the development of a society, need wish to take up'; but it has 'never been "done," to call done, from any point of view' (*WWS* I:5–6).

415 **one of the commonest and most taken-for-granted of London impressions**: The electric telegraph was patented in Britain in 1837; the technology was adopted by railway companies in the 1840s, but its widespread use as a means of personal communication dates from 1870, when the telegraph network was nationalized and placed under the control of the Post Office (J. L. Kieve, *The Electric Telegraph: A Social and Economic History* (Newton Abbot: David and Charles, 1973)). For nineteenth-century literary responses to this new technology, including Anthony Trollope's

story 'The Telegraph Girl' (1877), see Richard Menke, 'Telegraphic Realism: Henry James's *In the Cage*', *PMLA* 115.5 (2000), 975–90.

416 **the small local office of one's immediate neighbourhood**: During the period of *In the Cage* (1898), James was living at 34 De Vere Gardens, Kensington; his local post office was less than half a mile away at 15–17 Young Street (see *Ordnance Survey Maps of London, Five Feet to the Mile, 1893–1896*, Sheets VI.88–9, accessible via the National Library of Scotland (https://maps.nls.uk/os/townplans-england/london-1056-1890s.html); and 'Kensington Square and Environs: Young Street, Thackeray Street and South End', in *Survey of London: Volume 42, Kensington Square To Earl's Court*, ed. Hermione Hobhouse (London: London County Council, 1986), pp. 46–54; accessible via British History Online (www.british-history.ac.uk/survey-london/vol42)).

417 **a strong social draught, the stiffest possible breeze of the human comedy**: The Preface's figures of moving air are borrowed from *In the Cage*. Information and personal influences reach the caged telegraphist 'in the waft that [Lady Bradeen] blew through and left behind her' (*NYE* XI, 379); the frenetic life of London society is a 'blast' and a 'wild wind' (*NYE* XI, 373, 419); commerce is a 'stir' of the air raised by 'flying' money, 'the very wind of the swift banknotes' (*NYE* XI, 409); the vicissitudes of fortune are 'a strange whirligig', and the 'door of the great world' makes an uncertain draught for those who depend on its patronage (*NYE* XI, 397, 486). James's phrase 'the human comedy' translates the title of Balzac's novel-series *La Comédie humaine*.

418 **for confined […] young officials of either sex to be made so free […] of a range of experience otherwise quite closed to them**: For this paradox of the telegraphist's situation, compare the first sentence of the story: 'It had occurred to her early that in her position—that of a young person spending, in framed and wired confinement, the life of a guinea-pig or a magpie—she should know a great many persons without their recognising the acquaintance' (*NYE* XI, 367). The Preface's phrasing also echoes the circumstances of Mrs Jordan, who arranges flowers for the wealthy and claims to be thereby 'made free of the greatest houses' (*NYE* XI, 372).

419 **Mayfair […] Kensington**: In the late nineteenth and early twentieth centuries, these were (as they still are) fashionable residential districts of London. Mayfair lies to the north of Piccadilly and the Green Park; Kensington extends westward and southward from Kensington Gardens. James

lived in both areas between 1876 and 1898, first in Bolton Street, just off Piccadilly, and then in De Vere Gardens, South Kensington. In his essay 'London' (1888), he associates Mayfair with divorce scandals and Kensington with the social 'Season', topics relevant to the affluent yet precarious lives of Lady Bradeen and Captain Everard (see *CTW1* 19, 43).

420 **shrines and stations of penance**: James refers to Roman Catholic devotional practices of pentitential prayer and meditation. Prayers may be offered at the shrines of Christian saints and martyrs; the fourteen Stations of the Cross are visual representations of events on the day of Christ's crucifixion, often arranged around the nave of a church and designed to be contemplated in sequence on occasions of penance in the church calendar, e.g. during Lent and especially on Good Friday. The 'interest in personal character and in the "nature" of a mind' (p. 123) which James mentions in this sentence of the Preface is particularly evident in his apologies for Isabel Archer and Fleda Vetch in the Prefaces to *The Portrait of a Lady* and *The Spoils of Poynton*, as well as in his comments on the other characters he names in this paragraph.

421 **the speculative thread on which the pearls of Maisie's experience [...] are mostly strung**: The same figure occurs in *What Maisie Knew* when Maisie reflects that she is learning 'more and more', and that if she goes on in this way she will soon know 'Most' and eventually 'Everything', 'All'. She wonders how her governess feels about this: 'it was as if this inevitability had become for Mrs. Wix a long, tense cord, twitched by a nervous hand, on which the valued pearls of intelligence were to be neatly strung' (Ch. 26; *NYE* XI, 281–2).

422 **an account at the grocer's**: The telegraph office of *In the Cage* is located in a grocery, and the telegraphist's fiancé Mr Mudge – the guarantor of her future financial security – is a grocer.

423 **examples and "cases,"**: James habitually uses the word 'case' to refer to a human situation that is in some way generally representative, and that lends itself to fictional development or critical investigation. As he had recently noted at the start of his 1904 essay on Gabriele D'Annunzio: 'The great feast-days of all, for the restless critic, are those much interspaced occasions of his really meeting a "case," as he soon enough learns to call, for his convenience and assistance, any supremely contributive or determinant party to the critical question' ('GDA' 383). James often draws on the word's late nineteenth-century associations with legal and medical

discourse, as, for example, in Robert Louis Stevenson's *Strange Case of Dr Jekyll and Mr Hyde* (1886); a later Preface, speaking of the terminally ill heroine of *The Wings of the Dove*, refers to 'the depths of Milly Theale's "case,"' (p. 241).

424 **a libel [...] on an estimable class**: At least one reviewer of *In the Cage* questioned the plausibility of an actual telegraphist acting as James's character does: 'which of us credits the automaton behind the wire with either power or inclination to read our history in [a telegram], weave a romance for us, know our face and watch for it again?' The story is 'drawn with such a subtle air of inevitability that we finish the book before discovering that it is all preposterous, and that we may go into the nearest telegraph office and flash off a message without fearing the innocent eyes of a caged maiden "à la Henry James"' ('Fiction', *Saturday Review*, 3 September 1898, 319–20).

425 **a case that, modestly as it would seem to present itself, has yet already whirled us so far?**: The collocation of 'whirled' in this sentence of the Preface and 'winged' in the sentences immediately preceding and following it suggests a verbal echo of *In the Cage* at a moment in the story when the telegraphist's desire to speak to Captain Everard briefly overcomes her modesty. In Chapter 12, she enters the apartment building where she believes he lives and sees his name on 'the gilded and lettered board' listing the residents: 'It was as if, in the immense intimacy of this, they were, for the instant and the first time, face to face outside the cage. Alas! they were face to face but a second or two: she was whirled out on the wings of a panic fear that he might just then be entering or issuing' (*NYE* XI, 420–1).

426 **conforming to the "scenic" law**: No notebook entries survive for 'The Pupil' or *In the Cage*, but James's notes for *What Maisie Knew* show that he planned and worked out that novel in scenic terms. On 26 October 1896: 'Ah, this *divine* conception of one's little masses & periods in the scenic light—as rounded ACTS; this patient pious, nobly "vindictive" application of the scenic philosophy & method' (*CN* 162). In this notebook entry, James writes 'Acts' with a capital A and double-underlines the word, and glosses '"vindictive"' at the top of the page as '*vindicating*'. And on 21 December 1896: 'I realise—none too soon—that the *scenic* method is my absolute, my imperative, my *only* salvation.' James connected that realization with the work of Ibsen: 'How reading Ibsen's splendid *John Gabriel* [*Borkman*] a day or two ago (in proof,) brought that, FINALLY & FOREVER,

home to me!' (*CN* 167); the words 'finally & forever' there are underlined four times. For the 'scenic' composition of *The Awkward Age*, see note 319.

427 **as if this were the case with many readers**: Compare James's hopeful speculation in the final paragraph of 'The Lesson of Balzac' about his audience's likely interest in technical matters: 'It will strike you perhaps that I speak as if we all, as if you all, without exception were novelists, haunting the back shop, the laboratory, or, more nobly expressed, the inner shrine of the temple; but such assumptions, in this age of print [...] are perhaps never too wide of the mark' (*LC2* 138). James had closed his 1902 introduction to *Madame Bovary* on the same note: 'Are we not [...] pretty well all novelists now?' ('GF' xliii).

PREFACE to *The Aspern Papers, The Turn of the Screw, The Liar, The Two Faces* (*NYE* XII)

428 **as Columbus came upon the isle of San Salvador, [...] what "making land" then and there represented**: The island of San Salvador in the Bahamas archipelago was widely accepted in James's lifetime as the site of the first landing made in the Americas by the Italian explorer Christopher Columbus (1451–1506) on 12 October 1492: see, for example, Filson Young, *Christopher Columbus and the New World of His Discovery*, 2nd edn, 2 vols. (London: E. Grant Richards, 1906), vol. I, pp. 159–64. Columbus was notoriously mistaken about the significance of this landfall, believing that he had circumnavigated the globe and arrived at the East Indies by a new route. In *The Wings of the Dove*, Susan Stringham draws the same analogy with reference to her 'brave Vermont mother', who in determining to take her daughters to Europe in their youth had 'apparently, almost like Columbus, worked out, all unassisted, a conception of the other side of the globe' (Book Third, Ch. 1; *NYE* XIX, 119). When James wrote the Preface to *The Aspern Papers* (15 February–4 March 1908), he had very recently revised at least the first half of *The Wings of the Dove* and composed the novel's Preface.

429 **in Florence years ago**: 'The Aspern Papers' grew from an anecdote told to James in Florence in January 1887 by the diplomat and poet Eugene Lee-Hamilton (1845–1907), the half-brother of the writer Violet Paget ('Vernon Lee', 1856–1935). See also note 441.

430 **pay one's self [...] with words**: Reviewing Ehrmann Syme Nadal's *Impressions of London Social Life* in 1875, James had noted that Nadal was 'rather

inclined [...] to be too susceptible to the charm of words' and 'sometimes pays himself, as the French say, with mere conceits' (*LC1* 555): the French idiom *se payer de mots* means to content oneself with words alone and neglect their correspondence with reality. Closer in time to the *NYE*, the narrator of the chapter James wrote for *The Whole Family* (1908) reflects on 'our inordinate habit of living by words. I have sometimes flattered myself that I live less exclusively by them than the people about me; paying with them, paying with them only, as the phrase is (there I am at it, exactly, again!) rather less than my companions' (*WF* 144).

431 **Iberians or Orientals whose form of courtesy places everything they have at our disposal**: Nineteenth-century British journalists and travel writers were sceptical about these celebrated forms of courtesy, noting, for example, a 'strange want of hospitality among the Spaniards' that belied their national reputation: 'The pretence in this matter is perhaps the queerest of all pretences. The foreigner is told that a house is "at his disposition," and the quantity of house-property he acquires of this very peculiar kind is respectable. But he is not expected to call at his house, and he is never invited specially to it' ('Spain: her Manners and Amusements', *Cornhill Magazine* 25 (January 1872), 60–76; 65). Augustus H. Mounsey makes the same observation about the Middle East: 'One hears a great deal about Oriental hospitality. [...] As far as Persians are concerned, this idea is certainly erroneous; if they receive at all, they do so, it is true, with admirable courtesy of manner, great professions of friendship, and much apparent cordiality: as in Spain, everything is *á la disposicion de usted*. But behind all this there is little, if anything, genuine and solid' (*A Journey Through the Caucasus and the Interior of Persia* (London: Smith, Elder, & Co., 1872), p. 90).

432 **pious fiction**: The phrase refers to a known and sanctioned untruth, originally in the field of religious belief; as in the commoner formula 'legal fiction', 'fiction' here means 'A supposition known to be at variance with fact, but conventionally accepted for some reason of practical convenience, conformity with traditional usage, decorum, or the like' (*OED*). See, for example, a late nineteenth-century British historian contemplating the entanglement of historical fact with 'tradition', 'superstition' and 'imposture' in the story of Christian Rome: 'What parts of this mighty and pathetic pageantry of Christian legend are real, and what parts are pious fiction or unholy fraud, we cannot tell' (Frederic Harrison, 'Rome

Revisited', *Fortnightly Review* 53 n.s. (May 1893), 702–21; 719–20). Compare James on London society at the end of the 1870s: 'I confess I find ~~the world~~ ₍ₐ₎people₍ₐ₎ in general very vulgar minded & superficial—& it is only by a pious fiction, to keep myself going, & to keep on the social harness, that I succeed in postulating them as anything else or better' (to MWJ, 18 January [1879]; *CLHJ 1878–1880* 1:92).

433 **we scratch at the extensive surface, [...] we hang about in the golden air**: Compare James's remarks to Grace Norton on American travellers' 'factitious & artificial relation' towards Europe, in a letter written from Florence in 1874: 'I feel forever how Europe keeps holding one at arms length & condemning one to a meagre scraping of the surface. I have been nearly a year in Italy & have hardly spoken to an Italian creature save washerwomen & waiters. This you'll say is my own stupidity; but granting this gladly, it proves that even a creature addicted as much to sentimentalizing as I am over the whole mise en scène of Italian life, doesn't find an easy initiation into what lies behind it. Some times I am overwhelmed with the pitifulness of this absurd want of reciprocity between Italy itself and all my rhapsodies about it' (14 January 1874; *CLHJ 1872–1876* 2:114–15). For 'the golden air' of Italy, see note 21.

434 **my old Venice of "The Aspern Papers," [...] the still earlier one of Jeffrey Aspern himself**: James had visited and written about Venice on many prior occasions: see his essays 'Venice: An Early Impression' (1873), 'Venice' (1882), 'The Grand Canal' (1892), 'Two Old Houses and Three Young Women' (1899) and 'Casa Alvisi' (1902), all of which he would reprint in revised texts in *Italian Hours* (1909). James's Venice indirectly touched the early nineteenth-century milieu he associates with Jeffrey Aspern via encounters like the one he recorded just six weeks after receiving the germ of 'The Aspern Papers' – with Countess Evelina van Millingen Pisani (1831–1900), the daughter of the English doctor Julius Millingen 'who bled Byron to death' at Missolonghi: 'She made an impression on me as of one not formed of the usual social stuff of today—but the sort of woman one might have found—receiving on a balcony, here, at 2 o'clock on a June morning—in the early years of the century' (to Sarah Butler Wister, 27, 28 February, 1 March [1887]; *CLHJ 1887–1888* 1:68).

435 **"lay it on" thick**: To 'lay it on thick' is 'to be excessive in flattery, eulogy, etc.' (*OED*, 'lay'). In 1901, James observed that the French dramatist Edmond Rostand had managed 'to regild [the] scutcheon' of romance as no other

recent writer had done, and admired his 'free use of that restorative gold-leaf of which our store seems to have run short. He lays it on thick, and gives it a splendid polish' (*CWAD2* 470).

436 **I have had occasion […] to define my sense of the romantic**: For that definition, see the Preface to *The American*, pp. 23–7.

437 **that Jane Clairmont […] should have been living on in Florence, where she had long lived, up to our own day, […] I might have seen her in the flesh**: Clara Mary Jane Clairmont (1798–1879) was the step-sister – not, as James says, 'the half-sister' – of Mary Wollstonecraft Godwin Shelley (1797–1851); she was known as Jane in the Godwin family but began to call herself Claire at 16. She was an intimate member of the Shelley–Byron circle in her youth, accompanying Mary Godwin and Percy Shelley on their elopement to the Continent in 1814, beginning an affair with Byron in the spring of 1816 and becoming pregnant by him, and joining the Shelleys, Byron and the physician John Polidori on their Alpine tour that summer. Her daughter Clara Allegra was born in Bath in January 1817 and died in 1822 at a convent school near Ravenna. Clairmont spent most of her later life on the Continent and settled in Florence in 1860, where James would have had several opportunities to encounter her. He made two short stays in Florence on his first visit to Italy (in October 1869 and January 1870), at which period Clairmont was occupying an apartment in Palazzo Orsini, Via Valfonda. He was in Florence again in May–June 1873, for six weeks in October–November 1873, and then from January to June 1874, by which time Clairmont was living in an apartment in Palazzo Cruciato, Via Romana (Robert Gittings and Jo Manton, *Claire Clairmont and the Shelleys 1789–1879* (Oxford: Oxford University Press, 1992), pp. 225, 232). James would spend another week in Florence in October 1877; by the time he next returned for a long stay in March–May 1880, Clairmont was dead.

438 **The historian […] wants more documents than he can really use; the dramatist only wants more liberties than he can really take**: An analogy between the novelist and the 'historian' is present in James's earliest critical essays: in a review of 1867, for example, he had described Balzac as 'the historian of contemporary manners' and claimed that he was 'as averse from taking liberties with' his 'incidents and character[s]' as John Lothrop Motley, American author of *The Rise of the Dutch Republic* (1856), would be 'from taking liberties with the history of Holland' (*LC1* 1155). That position would change over time: by 1902 James could imagine Balzac

taking the fundamental liberty of fabricating the 'documents' which the novel-as-history relied on (see note 560). The sustained defence of the novel in James's critical essays of the 1880s is founded on the same analogy. 'The Art of Fiction' (1884), for example, asserts that 'the novel is history' and points to a common basis in documentary evidence: 'The subject-matter of fiction is stored up likewise in documents and records' (*LC1* 46). For the nineteenth-century historiographical developments that shaped James's early understanding of the novelist as a 'historian', and his later departures from this model, see Roslyn Jolly, *Henry James: History, Narrative, Fiction* (Oxford: Clarendon Press, 1993), pp. 19–35, 195–223. For the actual historian wanting 'more documents than he can really use', compare *Hawthorne* (1879), where James had noted that prospective biographers would be grateful for the posthumous publication of Hawthorne's notebooks: 'the attitude of the biographer is to desire as many documents as possible' (*LC1* 349). And yet the editor-narrator of 'The Aspern Papers' comes 'to wish I had never heard of Aspern's relics': 'We had more than enough material without them' (Ch. 9; *NYE* XII, 137). Shortly before the period of the *NYE*, James had felt doubly hampered in writing the Life-and-Letters biography *William Wetmore Story and His Friends: From Letters, Diaries, and Recollections* (1903), by a paucity of documentary material and also by his awareness that here he was working not as a novelist – 'the prose painter of life, character, manners, licensed to render his experience in his own terms' – but as 'the mere enumerator, to whom liberties, as they are called, are forbidden' (*WWS* II:197). For the categorical difference between the 'liberties' of non-fictional reference and those taken by the Jamesian 'dramatist', see Herford, *Henry James's Style of Retrospect*, pp. 61–4. James's critical writings before the Prefaces typically use the term 'dramatist' in its literal sense to designate a playwright, but in 1874 he had observed that Turgenev in his novels and stories was 'constantly careful to be a dramatist. Everything, with him, takes the dramatic form; he is apparently unable to conceive anything independently of it, he has no recognition of unembodied ideas; an idea, with him, is such and such an individual […]. Abstract possibilities immediately become, to his vision, concrete situations' (*LC2* 977). A comparable process of working out the potential of a fictional subject seems to be indicated in later Prefaces by James's 'ever-importunate murmur, "Dramatise it, dramatise it!"' (p. 198).

439 **the "irony of fate"**: Irony in this sense is 'A state of affairs or an event that seems deliberately contrary to what was or might be expected; an outcome

cruelly, humorously, or strangely at odds with assumptions or expectations' (*OED*). For the specific resonance of the formula 'the irony of fate' in connection with James's family memoirs after the period of the *NYE*, see Herford, *Henry James's Style of Retrospect*, pp. 94–8.

440 **in her habit as she lived**: A commonplace formula in nineteenth-century life-writing, this was also one of James's favourite Shakespearean allusions – to Hamlet's line to Gertrude describing the ghost of Old Hamlet: 'My father, in his habit as he lived!' (3.4.135). I have argued elsewhere that James's frequent recourse to this line in his late non-fiction exemplifies 'the habitual dimension of his allusive practice': see Oliver Herford, 'James and the Habit of Allusion', in Annick Duperray et al. (eds.), *Henry James's Europe: Heritage and Transfer* (Cambridge: Open Book Publishers, 2011), pp. 179–89; 179.

441 **another item of knowledge**: In fact, James acquired these two 'item[s] of knowledge' – Clairmont's long survival and the pursuit of her papers by a literary enthusiast – at the same time and from the same informant, Eugene Lee-Hamilton (see note 429). James noted on 12 January 1887: 'Hamilton [...] told me a curious thing of Capt. [Edward] Silsbee—the Boston art-critic & Shelley-worshipper; that is of a curious adventure of his. Miss Claremont [*sic*], Byron's ci-devant [former] mistress (the mother of Allegra) was living, until lately, here in Florence, at a great age, 80 or thereabouts, & with her lived her niece, a younger Miss Claremont—of about 50. Silsbee knew that they had interesting papers—letters of Shelley's & Byron's—he had known it for a long time & cherished the idea of getting hold of them' (*CN* 33).

442 **an American of long ago, an ardent Shelleyite**: Edward Augustus Silsbee (1826–1900), a retired American merchant sea-captain from Salem, Massachusetts. The Preface echoes a phrase applied to Silsbee by William Michael Rossetti in a memoir published as James began work on the *NYE*: 'He was an ardent Shelleyite, and said from time to time some of the most penetrative and impressive things about Shelley that I have heard from the lips of any one' (*Some Reminiscences of William Michael Rossetti*, 2 vols. (New York: Charles Scribner's Sons, 1906), vol. II, pp. 511–12). Clairmont's modern biographers note that Silsbee first approached her with a view to acquiring literary manuscripts in October 1872, when she was trying to raise money by selling the Shelley letters in her possession. Silsbee could not meet her price for these documents, but he stayed on as a lodger

in her household in Florence until at least the summer of 1875, during which time he also became the lover of her niece Paula. After Clairmont's death in 1879, he returned from America and tried again to purchase the letters: 'Paula put her own price on the Shelley papers, but Silsbee would not give it; gossip said that it was marriage' (Gittings and Manton, *Claire Clairmont and the Shelleys 1789-1879*, pp. 232-4, 235-6). According to Eugene Lee-Hamilton, Paula told Silsbee: '"I will give you all the letters if you marry me!"' (*CN* 33). James speaks in this sentence of the Preface of having 'known [Silsbee] a little': that acquaintance may have come about through shared American friends in Venice, Daniel and Ariana Curtis and their son Ralph. As Rosella Mamoli Zorzi notes, Silsbee visited Venice in July 1879 and was taken by Ralph Curtis to view a picture by Tiepolo in the church of Sant'Alvise (see Zorzi, *Ralph W. Curtis. Un pittore americano a Venezia* (Venice: Supernova, 2019), p. 47 and n. 132). Silsbee was also connected to James's American expatriate circles through the artist John Singer Sargent (1856-1925), a close friend of James's since 1884. Sargent had first met Silsbee in Florence in the 1870s, and he made a portrait sketch of him in 1899 (see Richard Ormond, *John Singer Sargent: Portraits in Charcoal* (New York and Washington, DC: The Morgan Library and National Portrait Gallery, Smithsonian Institution, 2019), pp. 80-1, 131).

443 **as we say of an etcher's progressive subject, in an early "state."**: In the terminology of engraving and other printmaking techniques, a 'state' is 'Any of a number of differing versions of a plate from which a print or prints are made before or following alteration; a print made from such a version' (*OED*).

444 **our own "modernity."**: In an essay of 1884, James had called Matthew Arnold 'the poet [...] of our "modernity"', and glossed that remark with reference to the historical consciousness of the late nineteenth century: 'When [Arnold] speaks of the past, it is with the knowledge which only our own time has of it' (*LC1* 727). See also note 280.

445 **a forward continuity, [...] to throw it backward again, [...] a value of nearness on our own part**: In Chapter 4 of 'The Aspern Papers', the narrator feels that the assumed presence of Aspern's letters 'under my hand' in the Bordereaus' palazzo 'made my life continuous, in a fashion, with the illustrious life they had touched at the other end' (*NYE* XII, 43). Compare, too, James's 1893 essay on the death of the actress Frances Anne Kemble (1809-93), which attributes the 'impressiveness' of her personal presence

to 'its long backward reach into time. Even if Mrs. Kemble had been a less remarkable person she would have owed a distinction to the far-away past to which she gave continuity' (*LC1* 1073–4).

446 **the long uninvaded and uninterviewed state on which I represent her situation as founded**: In Chapter 1 of the story, the narrator is surprised to learn 'that self-effacement on such a scale had been possible [for Juliana Bordereau] in the latter half of the nineteenth century—the age of newspapers and telegrams and photographs and interviewers' (*NYE* XII, 8). In Chapter 6, asking Miss Tina to let him see the letters, he feels 'almost as base as the reporter of a newspaper who forces his way into a house of mourning' (*NYE* XII, 82).

447 **a palpable imaginable *visitable* past [...] a world we may reach over to as by making a long arm we grasp an object at the other end of our own table**: James's attraction to the idea of a past that may be touched and visited is most literally manifested in his late romance *The Sense of the Past*, when the American historian Ralph Pendrel's 'love of old things, of the scrutable, palpable past' (*SP* 41) makes him the time-travelling visitor and suitor of his early nineteenth-century ancestor's English fiancée. Ralph's direct participation in the life of the past is the fantastical outcome of his desire for historical 'evidence of a sort for which there had never been documents enough, or for which documents mainly, however multiplied, would never *be* enough' (*SP* 48) (compare note 438). James elsewhere refers to present subject-matter as 'palpable', by contrast with the historical past: writing to Sarah Orne Jewett, for example, about the 'fatal *cheapness*' of the historical novel as a genre, he urges her to give up the experiment that had produced her most recent book *The Tory Lover* (1901), a novel of the American Revolution, and return to present-day subjects: 'come back to the palpable present *intimate* that throbs responsive' (5 October 1901; *LL* 360). As Philip Horne points out, the Preface's word '*visitable*' 'has a real social meaning' and refers to the past as 'embodied in the form of an old person who can be visited and talked to, usually an old lady': Horne points to James's friendships with informants of this sort, including Mary Elizabeth Mohl (1793–1883), Anne Benson Procter (1799–1888) and Frances Anne Kemble (for whom, see note 445) ('"A Palpable Imaginable *Visitable* Past": Henry James and the Eighteenth Century', *Eighteenth-Century Life* 32.2 (2008), 14–28; 15–16). James prized Kemble for 'the curious contacts she was able [...] to transmit' from the eighteenth and early nineteenth centuries: 'She made us touch her aunt

Mrs. Siddons [the actress Sarah Siddons (1755–1831)], and whom does Mrs. Siddons not make us touch?' (*LC1* 1074). Referring to the Preface's figure of a 'table' for 'the common expanse' of time between past and present, Tamara Follini observes: 'For James, Kemble sat at the other end of the table' ('The Friendship of Fanny Kemble and Henry James', *Cambridge Quarterly* 19.3 (1990), 230–42; 239). In James's ghostly story 'The Real Right Thing' (1899), the biographer Withermore seems to sit tête-à-tête with his subject Ashton Doyne as he works on Doyne's papers in the dead man's study: 'There were moments when, had he been able to look up, the other side of the table would have shown him this companion as vividly as the shaded lamplight showed him his page' (Ch. 2; *NYE* XVII, 421). The table here figures the uncanny closeness of the past: 'Was it a matter of '67?—or but of the other side of the table?' (*NYE* XVII, 420). Figuratively, the phrase 'a long arm' denotes 'Far-reaching power or influence'; 'to make a long arm' is 'to stretch out one's arm; to extend one's reach' (*OED*).

448 **looking over a garden-wall into another garden**: Compare Ralph Pendrel's desire in Book Second of *The Sense of the Past* 'to scale the high wall into which the successive years, each a squared block, pile themselves in our rear and look over as nearly as possible with the eye of sense into, unless it should rather be called out of, the vast prison yard' (*SP* 47). The Preface's image has been linked to an anecdote about William James visiting Henry at Lamb House in the summer of 1908 and 'embarrass[ing] his brother by climbing the gardener's ladder to take a peek over the wall at G. K. Chesterton' who was staying next door (*The Aspern Papers and Other Stories*, ed. Adrian Poole (Oxford: Oxford University Press, 2013), p. 251). The ultimate source of this story is H. G. Wells's *Experiment in Autobiography: Discoveries and Conclusions of a Very Ordinary Brain (Since 1866)* (New York: The Macmillan Company, 1934), Ch. 8, pp. 453–4. The Preface to *NYE* XII was dispatched to the Scribners on 13 March 1908, however, some months before William's visit to Rye. James uses the same figure to represent Kate Croy's first encounter with Merton Densher in *The Wings of the Dove*, a novel he had been revising very shortly before composing the Preface to *NYE* XII in January 1908: 'She had observed a ladder against a garden-wall and had trusted herself so to climb it as to be able to see over into the probable garden on the other side. On reaching the top she had found herself face to face with a gentleman engaged in a like calculation at the same moment' (Book Second, Ch. 1; *NYE* XIX, 53).

449 **the Byronic age, as I conveniently name it**: The literary-historical period defined by the living fame of George Gordon, Lord Byron (1788-1824) might be said to begin with the publication of the first two Cantos of *Childe Harold's Pilgrimage* in March 1812, which brought him instant celebrity. Byron died at Missolonghi in Greece on 19 April 1824, participating in the armed struggle for Greek independence from the Ottoman Empire. James's convenient label 'the Byronic age' was a commonplace in the second half of the nineteenth century: in 1899, the first edition of the *Dictionary of National Biography*, for example, referred to Edward John Trelawny (1792-1881) as 'the sole distinguished survivor of the Byronic age' (*Dictionary of National Biography*, ed. Leslie Stephen and Sidney Lee, 63 vols. (London: Smith, Elder, and Co., 1885-1900), vol. LVII, p. 178). For James's attraction to this period of history, compare the civil servant Edward Hamilton's account of a conversation at Mentmore, the Buckinghamshire home of the Liberal politician and future Prime Minister the Earl of Rosebery, in October 1886, shortly before James received the germ of 'The Aspern Papers': 'We all agreed that the most interesting time to have lived in would have been from about 1760 to 1830. In that period one might have seen by far the most remarkable agglomeration of notabilities.' They asked each other 'Who was the personage during that era whom we should most liked [*sic*] to have seen', and James's answer was 'Byron' (quoted in Hyde, *Henry James at Home*, p. 43). In the same notebook entry containing the anecdote about Claire Clairmont, James also recorded Eugene Lee-Hamilton's story about the family of Byron's Italian lover Teresa, Contessa Guiccioli (1800-73), who had 'a lot of Byron's letters of which they are rather illiberal & dangerous guardians'. They refused to 'show them or publish any of them'; according to the Contessa Gamba, a representative of this family, 'the letters—addressed in Italian to the Guiccioli—are discreditable to Byron; & H. elicited from her that she had *burned* one of them!' (12 January 1887; *CN* 34).

450 **cultivating a sense of the past**: The formula 'a sense of the past' echoes the title of James's unfinished fiction of time-travel *The Sense of the Past*, which he began to write in the autumn of 1899 but set aside in January 1900, finding it 'diabolically, tormentingly *difficult*' (to Pinker, 17 January 1900; *LL* 335). He had arrived at a working title by that time: 'It wd. possibly be called "The Sense of the Past"' (to Pinker, 2 January 1900; quoted *LL* 335 n. 3). The book was unknown to the reading public at the time of the *NYE*. See also notes 447, 448 and 459.

451 **fond and filial, [...] "old" New York**: A comparably 'filial' impulse had informed James's titling of the *NYE*. He told the Scribners on 30 July 1905: 'If a *name* be wanted for the edition, for convenience and distinction, I should particularly like to call it the New York Edition [...]. My feeling about the matter is that it refers the whole enterprise explicitly to my native city—to which I have had no great opportunity of rendering that sort of homage' (*HJL* 4:368). Nevertheless, as Alfred Habegger points out, 'the two most openly autobiographical passages in [James's] entire output of fiction, both of which refer to his life in New York, do not appear in the New York Edition': the descriptions of Washington Square in Chapter 3 of *Washington Square* (1880) and of Upper Second Avenue in Chapter 21 of *The Bostonians* (1886) (Habegger, 'New York Monumentalism and Hidden Family Corpses', in David McWhirter (ed.), *Henry James's New York Edition: The Construction of Authorship* (Stanford, CA: Stanford University Press, 1995), pp. 185–205; 186–8). James also refers to '"old" New York' as Milly Theale's social milieu in the Preface to *The Wings of the Dove* (see note 799).

452 **the mouldy rococo, [...] water-steps**: The 'rococo' is 'an elaborately ornamental late baroque style of decoration prevalent in 18th-cent. Europe, with asymmetrical patterns involving intricate motifs and scrollwork' (*OED*). Venice was an important centre of the Italian rococo in visual art, architecture and interior décor, as embodied, for example, in the paintings of Giovanni Battista Tiepolo (1696–1770). In broader nineteenth- and early twentieth-century usage, the adjective 'rococo' means simply 'Old-fashioned, outmoded' (*OED*). James had written thus in 1902 of Balzac's 'ancient, superseded, comparatively *rococo* and quite patriarchal France' ('HdB' xxiii). Venetian houses and public buildings that abut directly onto a canal often have a set of 'water-steps' for the convenience of visitors arriving by boat.

453 **"cheap" or expensive**: James habitually uses monetary terms for the expenditure of time, labour and invention to produce fiction. In 1905, for example, he had drawn from Balzac 'the lesson that there is no convincing art that is not ruinously expensive': 'Many of those who have followed him affect us as doing it, in the vulgar phrase, "on the cheap;" by reason mainly, no doubt, of their having been, all helplessly, foredoomed to cheapness' (*LC2* 133). See also note 622.

454 **a highly critical friend**: I have not been able to identify this person. James anticipates the present passage in his reference to a complaint made by 'an acute friend' in the Preface to *The Tragic Muse*, p. 71.

455 **some past or present producible counterfoil**: A counterfoil is 'A complementary part of a bank cheque, official receipt, or the like, which registers the particulars of the principal part, and is retained by the person who gives out that part' (*OED*). In Chapter 4 of 'The Aspern Papers', the narrator notes that Juliana had 'never [...] sent me a receipt for my three months' rent' and is struck by her neglect of 'so indispensable and familiar a form': 'She had given me part of her house, but she wouldn't add to that so much as a morsel of paper with her name on it' (*NYE* XII, 41, 42).

456 **in what conditions of the contemporary English theatre [...] might we take an artistic value of this order either for produced or for recognised?**: Miriam Rooth, the actress-heroine of *The Tragic Muse* (1890), rises from obscurity to enjoy a triumph on the London stage as Shakespeare's Juliet, and becomes a theatrical celebrity. The narrator knowingly passes over the first night of that production, declining 'to describe again so famous an occasion—it has been described repeatedly by other reporters', but assures us that 'these great hours marked an era in contemporary art' (Ch. 51; *NYE* VIII, 430). As Adrian Poole points out, 'the absence of adequate English models means Miriam has to learn her art in Paris from the tradition that produced the legendary Rachel' (*The Aspern Papers and Other Stories*, ed. Poole, p. 251).

457 **Neil Paraday in "The Death of the Lion," [...] Hugh Vereker in "The Figure in the Carpet," [...] Ralph Limbert, above all, in "The Next Time,"**: These characters are all fictional authors dedicated to what this sentence of the Preface calls 'the artistic ideal'; the stories they appear in were published between 1894 and 1896 and are collected in *NYE* XV. James returns to the question of the verisimilitude of his 'public' characters in the Preface to that volume, pp. 175–81.

458 **cast them into the world *all* naked and ashamed**: Before the Fall, Adam and Eve 'were both naked, the man and his wife, and were not ashamed' (Genesis 2:25). Once they become conscious of their nakedness after eating the fruit of the tree of knowledge, they are cast out of Eden.

459 **harmless hocus-pocus**: From its use 'as a formula of conjuring or magical incantation', the phrase 'hocus-pocus' denotes 'A juggler's trick; conjuring, jugglery; sleight of hand; a method of bringing something about as if by magic; trickery, deception' (*OED*). The term and its associations recur in James's late writings on literary romance. In the Preface to *The American* he speaks of his attempt to pass off romance as realism in that novel as 'hocus-pocus' (p. 27), and in the notes for *The Sense of the Past* which he

would dictate in November 1914 he refers to a crucial (unwritten) scene as 'the climax of the romantic hocuspocus' (*SP* 329).

460 **the smugglers of old**: James had written on eighteenth-century smuggling in the coastal towns of East Sussex in his essay 'Winchelsea, Rye, and "Denis Duval"' (1901): 'It is to this hour a part of the small romance of Rye that you may fondly fancy such scant opulence as rears its head to have had its roots in the malpractice of forefathers not too rude for much cunning—in nightly plots and snares and flurries, a hurrying, shuffling, hiding, that might at any time have put a noose about most necks' (*CTW1* 238).

461 **so much the worse for the time**: James uses the same formula to dismiss the criterion of verisimilitude in other critical essays. On the town that is the setting for Alphonse Daudet's *Port-Tarascon* (1890): 'what most readers will say is that if the Tarascon of fact is not like the Tarascon of art, so much the worse for the former' (*LC2* 250). And on Balzac in 1902, referring to an episode in *Illusions perdues* (1837-43): 'If the great ladies in question *didn't* behave, wouldn't, couldn't have behaved, like a pair of frightened snobs, why, so much the worse, we say to ourselves, for the great ladies in question' ('HdB' xli). The formula 'so much the worse' also recurs in James's continuation of these remarks in the Preface to *NYE* XV, p. 176.

462 **the circle, one winter afternoon, round the hall-fire of a grave old country-house**: On 12 January 1895, James made a note of 'the ghost-story told me at Addington (evening of Thursday 10th,) by the Archbishop of Canterbury: the mere vague, undetailed, faint sketch of it—being all he had been told' (*CN* 109). In the nineteenth century, Addington Palace near Croydon was an official residence of the Archbishop of Canterbury. The Archbishop in 1895 was Edward White Benson (1829-96); James was a friend of his son Arthur Christopher Benson, who was at this time a schoolmaster at Eton College and in 1904 would become a fellow of Magdalene College, Cambridge. The Benson family had strong associations with the ghostly. As a Cambridge undergraduate in 1851, Edward White Benson had founded 'a "Ghost" Society, the forerunner of the Psychical Society, for the investigation of the supernatural' (A. C. Benson, *The Life of Edward White Benson, Sometime Archbishop of Canterbury*, 2 vols. (London: Macmillan and Co., 1899), vol. I, p. 98); three of his sons – Arthur Christopher Benson (1862-1925), Edward Frederic Benson (1867-1940) and Robert Hugh Benson (1871-1914) – wrote ghost-stories. The Preface's

recollection of the evening at Addington also echoes the prologue to 'The Turn of the Screw', which opens with a tale told 'round the fire, [...] on Christmas Eve in an old house' (*NYE* XII, 147).

463 **the mere modern "psychical" case, [...] the dear old sacred terror**: In late nineteenth-century usage, 'psychical' refers to 'faculties or phenomena, such as telepathy and clairvoyance, that are apparently inexplicable by natural laws and are attributed by some to spiritual or supernatural agency; involving paranormal phenomena of the mind, parapsychological' (*OED*). James alludes to accounts published by the Society for Psychical Research (SPR), a British organization formed in 1882 to apply scientific methods to the study of paranormal phenomena. James was acquainted with three of the SPR's founders: Frederick Myers, Edmund Gurney and Henry Sidgwick. In 1884, William James became a founder member of the American Society of Psychical Research, which was assimilated with the SPR, as a branch organization, between 1889 and 1905; as T. J. Lustig notes, William served as president of this American branch from 1894 to 1896 (*The Turn of the Screw and Other Stories*, ed. Lustig (Oxford: Oxford University Press, 1992), p. 246). For the published *Proceedings* of the SPR, see note 474. The poetical formula 'sacred terror' occurs in various canonical seventeenth- and eighteenth-century works: e.g. James Thomson's *The Seasons* (1730), where it refers to the awed exhilaration of poetic vision: 'Deep-rous'd, I feel / A sacred Terror, a severe Delight, / Creep thro' my mortal Frame' ('Summer', ll. 540–2; *The Seasons*, ed. James Sambrook (Oxford: Clarendon Press, 1981), p. 86). The phrase also occurs in a stage direction to *The Saloon*, James's adaptation of his own ghostly story 'Owen Wingrave', as Kate Julian begs Owen not to defy the evil of his family history just before the apparition of the ancestral ghost: 'KATE. (*Hovering, pressing, imploring; yet as kept off too, with her clasped hands, by a sort of sacred terror.*) Owen, Owen, I *love* you—but *silence!*' (*CP* 673). James dictated *The Saloon* to Theodora Bosanquet in December 1907, and reworked and amplified it in April 1908; the Preface to *NYE* XII was dictated between those two stints of work on the play, from 15 February to 4 March 1908. In his essay 'Concord and Salem' (written in 1905 and first published in *The American Scene* in 1907), James had noted that it was *not* 'a sacred terror' but instead 'an almost sacred tenderness' for the American past 'that stayed me from crossing the threshold of the Witch House' at Salem, Massachusetts (*AS* 268), the home of one of the judges involved in the Salem Witch Trials of 1692–3.

464 **the spirits of certain "bad" servants, [...] "getting hold" of them**: The inverted commas in this sentence isolate words that significantly occur in both the story and its germ. In James's notebook entry of 12 January 1895, it is the children – corrupted by the servants – who are said to be 'bad, full of evil, to a sinister degree' (*CN* 109). In the story, the word 'bad' is repeatedly applied to Miles: questioningly in Chapter 2, when the governess-narrator discusses the headmaster's letter with Mrs Grose ('"Is he really *bad?*"'); and exultantly, but perhaps also innocently, in Chapter 11, when Miles tells the governess that he went outside at night in order that she should '"Think me—for a change—*bad!*"' (*NYE* XII, 166, 234). The ghosts in E. W. Benson's anecdote 'try & try & try [...] to get hold of [the children]' (*CN* 109); just so, in Chapter 7, the governess tells Mrs Grose that Miss Jessel looked at Flora as though she wanted to '"get hold of her"' (*NYE* XII, 206). But in the final scene in Chapter 24, it is the governess herself who literally gets hold of Miles: Quint's apparition outside the room 'reduced me to the mere blind movement of getting hold of him, drawing him close and [...] instinctively keeping him with his back to the window'; she does not let go until she realizes that he is dead (*NYE* XII, 303).

465 **a periodical dealing in the time-honoured Christmas-tide toy**: 'The Turn of the Screw' was written in time for Christmas 1897 but did not appear until early the following year, in twelve instalments of the New York magazine *Collier's Weekly*, 26 January–16 April 1898. On 22 December 1897, James told George P. Brett, the manager of the New York office of Macmillan and Company, that 'the *Collier* people appear[ed] to think the little work in question—for *their* purposes at any rate—much of a hit' (*HJL* 4:66).

466 **the terrible "pleasant"**: James's 1888 essay on Guy de Maupassant had connected British and American writers' 'perpetual quest of pleasantness' with various tendencies in contemporary anglophone culture: 'The love of sport, the sense of decorum, the necessity for action, the habit of respect, the absence of irony, the pervasiveness of childhood', and 'the expansive tendencies of the race'. As James parenthetically observes, these characteristics were united in British imperial adventure fiction: '(does not Mr. Rider Haggard make even his African carnage pleasant?)' (*LC2* 539–40). For reviewers finding James's 1890s fiction 'unpleasant', see note 402.

467 **making the score [...] off its own bat**: In cricket, the phrase 'off his (*also her, etc.*) own bat' refers literally to 'the score made by a player's own hits' and hence figuratively to anything done 'solely by his or her own exertions,

by himself or herself' (*OED*). James was fond of this idiom 'of our sporting day'. In 1888, he wrote of Pierre Loti: 'He plays from his own bat, imitating no one' (*LC2* 505). So too does the young writer Paul Overt in 'The Lesson of the Master': as Henry St George approvingly remarks of Overt's novel *Ginistrella*, '"I said to myself, 'I see it's off his own bat'"' (Ch. 3; *NYE* XV, 40).

468 **the fairy-tale belongs mainly to either of two classes**: The European fairy-tales which exemplify the first of James's 'two classes' – 'the short and sharp and single, charged [...] with the compactness of anecdote' – were originally published in literary versions derived from old folk-tales by the French author Charles Perrault in his *Histoires ou contes du temps passé*, also known as *Les Contes de ma Mère l'Oye* (1697); German versions of many of Perrault's fairy-tales also appear in the *Kinder- und Hausmärchen* of the brothers Jacob and Wilhelm Grimm (1812–15). James's example of the second class of fairy-tale– 'the long and loose, the copious, the various, the endless' – is *The Arabian Nights' Entertainments*, sometimes abbreviated to *The Arabian Nights*: these are common English titles for *The One Thousand and One Nights*, a medieval Arabic compilation of folk-tales which circulated widely in English translations from the mid nineteenth century. On 3 May 1907, James answered an invitation from the *Harper's Bazar* editor Elizabeth Jordan to name his 'favourite fairy-tale': he nominated 'Hop o' my Thumb' (Perrault's 'Le Petit Poucet'), which he remembered reading 'by the nursery fire' in 'a fat little Boys'—or perhaps Children's Own Book which contained all the "regular" fairy-tales, dear to that generation' (*HJL* 4:446). As Leon Edel notes, Jordan quoted from this letter in her unsigned introduction to *Favorite Fairy Tales: The Childhood Choice of Representative Men and Women* (New York and London: Harper & Brothers, 1907) (*HJL* 4:447 n. 3). James alluded to the same tale in January 1907 in the chapter he wrote for *The Whole Family* (1908), a multi-author novel coordinated by Jordan: his narrator, noting down something he wants to remember, likens his memo to 'one of the white pebbles, or whatever they were, that Hop o' my Thumb, carried off to the forest, dropped, as he went, to know his way back' (*WF* 173). In Chapter 1 of 'The Turn of the Screw', as the governess-narrator is shown around Bly by the little girl she is to teach, she has 'the view of a castle of romance inhabited by a rosy sprite, such a place as would somehow [...] take all colour out of story-books and fairy-tales' (*NYE* XII, 163). By Chapter 12, however, she assumes that the children, who seem to be reading together, are really talking about Quint and Miss Jessel: '"even while they pretend to

be lost in their fairy-tale they're steeped in their vision of the dead restored to them"' (*NYE* XII, 236).

469 **Nothing is so easy as improvisation**: In an essay of 1874, James had cited Walter Scott, Charles Dickens and George Sand as possessors of 'the faculty of rapid, passionate, almost reckless improvisation' (*LC2* 968). In 'The Lesson of Balzac' (1905), he had recently contrasted Balzac with those 'great resounding improvisatori' of the nineteenth-century novel, the 'loose and easy producers': 'Balzac stands almost alone as an extemporizer achieving closeness and weight' (*LC2* 120, 121). The reference there is to 'the Italian tradition of improvisational poetry which was at its height in the late 17th to mid 19th centuries' (*OED*, 'improvisatore').

470 **a reader [...] who complained that I hadn't sufficiently "characterised" my young woman**: T. J. Lustig suggests that this reader was H. G. Wells (*The Turn of the Screw and Other Stories*, ed. Lustig, p. 247), to whom James wrote about the governess's narrative function in 'The Turn of the Screw': 'Of course I had, about my young woman, to take a very sharp line. The grotesque business I had to make her picture & the childish psychology I had to make her trace & present, were, for me at least, a very difficult job, in which absolute lucidity & logic, & singleness of effect were imperative. Therefore I had to rule out subjective complications of her own—play of tone &c.; and keep her impersonal save for the most obvious & indispensable little note of neatness, firmness & courage—without which she wouldn't have had her data' (9 December 1898; *LL* 312).

471 **under cover of which, like wanton mocking goddesses in clouds, the others find prudent to retire**: In Homeric and Virgilian epic, the Olympian gods conceal themselves in clouds when they visit the earth, and often wrap humans and heroes in clouds to remove them from the battlefield or otherwise protect them. Compare James's description in *The Wings of the Dove* of an act of improvisation by Kate Croy to conceal her true relation with Densher from her aunt: 'She invented the awkwardness under Densher's eyes, and he marvelled on his side at the instant creation. It served her as the fine cloud that hangs about a goddess in an epic, and the young man was but vaguely to know at what point of the rest of his visit she had, for consideration, melted into it and out of sight' (Book Tenth, Ch. 2; *NYE* XX, 335).

472 **a young person, as she says, 'privately bred,'**: The governess says this in Chapter 3, describing her first sighting of Quint: 'An unknown man in a

lonely place is a permitted object of fear to a young woman privately bred' (*NYE* XII, 176).

473 **She has 'authority,'**: Another echo of the story, this time from the prologue: 'There were plenty of people to help, but of course the young lady who should go down as governess would be in supreme authority' (*NYE* XII, 154).

474 **I had [...] simply to renounce all attempt to keep [...] on terms with the to-day so copious psychical record of cases of apparitions**: Nevertheless, as Lustig observes, twentieth-century scholarship has found 'numerous parallels' between 'The Turn of the Screw' and accounts of hauntings published in the *Proceedings of the Society for Psychical Research* (*The Turn of the Screw and Other Stories*, ed. Lustig, p. 246; citing Francis X. Roellinger, Jr, 'Psychical Research and "The Turn of the Screw"', *American Literature* 20.3 (1948), 401–12, and E. A. Sheppard, *Henry James and 'The Turn of the Screw'* (Auckland: Auckland University Press, 1974)). For other nineteenth-century reports of haunting and spirit-possession as contexts for the story, see Peter G. Beidler, *Ghosts, Demons, and Henry James: 'The Turn of the Screw' at the Turn of the Century* (Columbia, MO: University of Missouri Press, 1989).

475 **Recorded and attested "ghosts" are [...] as little expressive, as little dramatic, [...] as is consistent with their taking the trouble [...] to appear at all**: Other late nineteenth-century writers of ghost-stories had complained of the dullness of scientifically documented ghosts. See, for example, the Preface to Vernon Lee's *Hauntings* (1890): 'Altogether one quite agrees, having duly perused the collection of evidence on the subject, with the wisdom of these modern ghost-experts, when they affirm that you can always tell a genuine ghost-story by the circumstance of its being about a nobody, its having no point or picturesqueness, and being, generally speaking, flat, stale, and unprofitable' (Lee, *Hauntings: Fantastic Stories*, 2nd edn (London: John Lane, The Bodley Head, 1906), pp. viii–ix).

476 **speaking by book**: To do something '*by book*' or '*by the book*' is to do it 'in a set manner, by rote; formally' or 'conventionally, in accordance with the rules' (*OED*, 'book').

477 **the old trials for witchcraft; [...] fairies of the legendary order, wooing their victims forth to see them dance under the moon**: Trials for witchcraft were common in the British Isles and Europe during the sixteenth and seventeenth centuries; they declined in the first decades of the eighteenth century, and the Witchcraft Act of 1736 decriminalized witchcraft in

Britain. The Salem Witch Trials of 1692-3 in the Province of Massachusetts Bay were a notorious North American instance in the same period (see note 463). Donal O'Gorman considers potential references to witchcraft trials in the story in 'Henry James's Reading of *The Turn of the Screw*: Parts II and III', *Henry James Review* 1.3 (1980), 231-40. In European folklore, fairies are commonly encountered dancing outdoors by moonlight; they may steal children and replace them with changelings, or seduce adults and compel them to remain in fairy-land for a time. A version of the scenario referred to in the Preface is found in W. B. Yeats's poem 'The Stolen Child', in which Irish fairies woo a boy away from his home to dance with them by moonlight on the sea-shore (Yeats (ed.), *Fairy and Folk Tales of the Irish Peasantry* (London: Walter Scott, 1888), pp. 59-60).

478 **the hot breath of the Pit**: The *American Monthly Review of Reviews* had used this formula to praise James's portrayal of evil in 'The Turn of the Screw': 'the foul breath of the bottomless pit itself [...] strikes the reader full in the face' (Hayes 308).

479 **capable, as the phrase is, of everything**: This appears to be a literal translation of the French phrase *capable de tout*, which nineteenth-century anglophone commentators commonly attributed to Voltaire (1694-1778). A possible source of that attribution is the British statesman George Cornewall Lewis (1806-63), according to whom Voltaire 'had been convicted of misrepresenting facts in the prophet [Habbakuk]'s history, and replied, "C'est égal, Habacuc était capable de tout"' (G. G. L. and V. R., 'Notes on "King." IX', *Notes and Queries* 181.4 (26 July 1941), 46-7; this note is one in a series of annotations to William Francis Henry King's *Classical and Foreign Quotations*, 1887). James himself wrote in 1891 of Rudyard Kipling's fictional soldier Mulvaney: 'the inimitable Irishman is, like Voltaire's Habbakuk, *capable de tout*' (*LC1* 1126).

480 **the very worst action small victims [...] might be conceived as subject to**: As James told the SPR founder member Frederick Myers, 'The thing that, as I recall it, I most wanted not to fail of doing, under penalty of extreme platitude, was to give the impression of the communication to the children of the most infernal imaginable evil & danger—the condition, on their part, of being as *exposed* as we can humanly conceive children to be' (19 December 1898; *LL* 314).

481 **the charge of all indecently expatiating?**: As Lustig notes, 'the charge was most forcefully made in the *Independent* (5 Jan. 1899). The reviewer felt

that the children's souls had been defiled "in a way ... by no means darkly and subtly hinted", saw the tale as a study of "infernal human debauchery" and concluded that "human imagination can go no further into infamy"' (*The Turn of the Screw and Other Stories*, ed. Lustig, p. 247).

482 **much to say of these numerous small productions as a family—[...] its "heads," its subdivisions and its branches, its poor relations [...] "cutting" without a scruple**: James plays on two meanings of 'head': 'A person to whom others are subordinate', e.g. the senior or authoritative member of a family, and 'A chief or principal point or division of a discourse, subject, etc.; each of a set or succession of such points or divisions' (*OED*). The phrase 'poor relations' – in French 'Les Parents pauvres' – is the title of a thematic grouping of fictions in Balzac's *Comédie humaine*, containing the novels *La Cousine Bette* (1846) and *Le Cousin Pons* (1847). This sentence of the Preface exploits a colloquial sense of the verb 'cut' – 'To break off acquaintance or connection with (a person)' or 'to affect not to see or know (a person) on meeting or passing him' (*OED*) – and juxtaposes it with the literary sense of 'cutting' as eliminating material: in this context, omitting stories from the *NYE*.

483 **the whole "question of the short story," [...] so vain a babble**: In his 1898 review of Henry Harland's story-collection *Comedies and Errors*, James had noted that 'the "short story" [...] has of late become an object of [...] almost extravagant dissertation'. He contrasted that symptom of 'an age of organized talk' with the habits of an earlier, 'comparatively silent' period in which the short story 'took itself [...] less seriously, and there was perhaps a more general feeling that you both wrote and read your short story best when you did so in peace and patience'. Nowadays, 'each of us already knows what every other of us thinks of the short story [...]. Anything we may say about it is at best but a compendium of the current wisdom' (*LC1* 284–5). As William Veeder and Susan M. Griffin note, 'The short story was first treated seriously as a genre in the 1880s by, among others, Brander Matthews' (*The Art of Criticism: Henry James on the Theory and the Practice of Fiction* (Chicago, IL: University of Chicago Press, 1986), p. 416); they cite Matthews's essay 'Philosophy of the Short-Story' *Lippincott's Monthly Magazine* 36 (October 1885), 366–74. When James wrote the Preface to *NYE* XII, such discussion had been going on in English and American periodicals for more than two decades: see also, for example, Henry Harland, 'Concerning the Short Story', *The Academy* 51 (5 June 1897), Fiction Supplement, 6–7; Bret Harte, 'The Rise of the "Short Story"', *Cornhill Magazine* 7 n.s. (July 1899), 1–8; and W. D. Howells, 'Some

Anomalies of the Short Story', *North American Review* 173 (September 1901), 422–32. James discusses the short story as a form and its differences from the longer story or *nouvelle* in the Prefaces to *NYE* XV and XVI.

484 **shooting straight from the planted seed**: James uses the same metaphor in 'The Liar' itself to describe the mendacious invention of the title character. In Chapter 3, Colonel Capadose improvises a false account of being followed by an artist's model to cast suspicion on her as the slasher of his portrait; the artist-narrator Oliver Lyon – who knows this is a lie – reflects that 'The story had shot up and bloomed, from the dropped seed, on the spot' (*NYE* XII, 368).

485 **at dinner one autumn evening of old London days [...] the "joy of life"**: James recorded the idea for 'The Liar' in a notebook entry of 19 June 1884: 'One might write a tale (very short) about a woman married to a man of the most amiable character who is a tremendous, though harmless, liar' (*CN* 28). That note makes no mention of a London dinner-party or an original for the liar in James's acquaintance, though it does end with a reference to Alphonse Daudet's novel *Numa Roumestan* (1881), which contains a satirical portrayal of 'the Provençal turn of mind, the temperament of the man of the South', whose 'weak points [...] are the desire to please at any cost, and, as a natural result of this, a brilliant indifference to the truth' (*LC2* 217). In late nineteenth-century usage, the English phrase 'the joy of life' translates two influential foreign formulas. At the start of the 1890s, William Archer used it in his translation of Ibsen's play *Ghosts* to render the Norwegian term *livsglede*. See Archer's footnote to Pastor Manders's line in Act I (referring to Oswald Alving's debauched father), 'In his youth he overflowed with the joy of life ——*': '*"Var en særdeles livsglad mand"— literally, "was a man who took the greatest pleasure in life," *la joie de vivre*— an expression which frequently recurs in this play' (*Ibsen's Prose Dramas*, ed. William Archer, 5 vols. (London: Walter Scott, 1890–1), vol. II, p. 32). The French phrase 'la joie de vivre' was used by Émile Zola as the title of a novel (1884) about an orphan's life with her immiserated provincial relatives. James recommended the book to Howells: 'The title of course has a desperate irony; but the ~~thing~~ ₐwork₍ₐ₎ is admirably solid & serious' (21 February 1884; *CLHJ 1883–1884* 2:30). *La Joie de vivre* was first translated into English as *How Jolly Life Is!* (London: Vizetelly & Co., 1886); this translation was later retitled *The Joy of Life* (London: Chatto & Windus, 1901).

486 **without so much as [...] turning a hair?**: The 'vulgar phrase' James uses here has an equestrian origin: 'not to turn a hair' means, literally, 'of a

horse, not to show sweat by the roughening of his hair'; figuratively, the meaning is 'not to show any sign of being discomposed, ruffled, or affected by exertion' (*OED*, 'hair').

487 **the exploits of a salamander**: A salamander, in legend, was 'A lizard-like animal supposed to live in, or to be able to endure, fire'; the word is used figuratively to denote 'A soldier who exposes himself to fire in battle' (*OED*). The sense in the Preface seems to be that the gentleman was exaggerating his anecdotes of travel as a soldier might exaggerate his bravery in combat.

488 **"The Two Faces" [...] the writer's rueful hopeful assent to the conditions known to him as "too little room to turn round."**: There is no reference to the story 'The Two Faces' (first published in 1900 as 'The Faces') in any other Preface; for later discussion of the word-limits imposed by magazine editors on James's short stories, see the Preface to *NYE* XV, pp. 173–4. James repeatedly complains of the difficulty of making a fictional subject 'turn round' in the space available, even when writing novels: in other Prefaces, he speaks thus of *Roderick Hudson*, *The Tragic Muse*, 'Julia Bride' and *The Wings of the Dove*. On 4 October 1895, he wrote to Horace Scudder, his editor at the *Atlantic Monthly*: 'I find, in my old age, that I have too much manner & style, too great & invincible an instinct of completeness & of seeing things in all their relations, so that *development*, however squeezed down, becomes inevitable—too much of all this to be able to turn round in the small corners I used to' (*LL* 284).

489 **the turn of the *whole* coach and pair in the contracted court**: James refers to the manoeuvring of a horse-drawn coach in the courtyard of an inn. In Britain, stage-coaches had carried passengers along routes punctuated by coaching inns, where fresh horses could be obtained and travellers could rest and eat, since the end of the seventeenth century; the heyday of this mode of transport came in the late eighteenth and early nineteenth centuries, after the nationalization of postal delivery by mail-coaches in the 1780s and before the railway boom of the 1840s. See Sally Davis, *John Palmer and the Mailcoach Era* (Bath: Bath Postal Museum, 1984). The American narrator of 'A Passionate Pilgrim' (1871), a story collected in the next volume of the *NYE*, thinks back to this historical moment as he leaves his inn in the City of London: 'I lingered a moment beside the old inn-yard in which, upon a time, the coaches and post-chaises found space to turn and disgorge' (Ch. 1; *NYE* XIII, 347). For the Preface's comparison of the 'neat evolution' of a short story to the turning of a coach (p. 142),

compare James in 1888 on the very short stories of Guy de Maupassant: 'The little story is but scantily relished in England, where readers take their fiction rather by the volume than by the page, and the novelist's idea is apt to resemble one of those old-fashioned carriages which require a wide court to turn round' (*LC2* 534).

PREFACE to *The Reverberator, Madame de Mauves, A Passionate Pilgrim and Other Tales* (NYE XIII)

490 **precedence [...] by reason of its greatest length**: The first of five tales collected in *NYE* XIII, *The Reverberator* (1888) is much the longest, occupying nearly half the volume. What James described as 'precedence by *length*' (to the Scribners, 21–26 February 1908; Princeton) – the principle of granting first place in the list of contents to the longest item – was one of several competing factors that determined his allocation of stories to *NYE* volumes. See also notes 354 and 491.

491 **"pleasant" publication [...] the honour of two pretty little volumes "all to itself," [...] the category of Shorter Novels [...] an indulgence not extended to several of its compeers**: James's nostalgia for the '"pleasant" publication' of *The Reverberator* echoes his earlier comments on 'the pleasant old custom of the "running" of the novel' in the Preface to *The Tragic Muse* (p. 63). It may be relevant to both those cases that his relations with his long-time British publisher Frederick Macmillan had begun to be put under strain a couple of years before by the disappointing sales of *The Bostonians* and *The Princess Casamassima* (both 1886). That situation was brought to a crisis in 1890 when James's failure to negotiate a satisfactory contract for *The Tragic Muse* led to him breaking with Macmillan and engaging the services of the literary agent A. P. Watt (see Michael Anesko, *'Friction with the Market': Henry James and the Profession of Authorship* (New York and Oxford: Oxford University Press, 1986), pp. 119–30). *The Reverberator* appeared before things had come to that unpleasant pass: the first edition of the novella was published by Macmillan in June 1888, in two octavo volumes (7 in. by 4⅝ in.) of c. 200 pages each. Richard Salmon points out that James 'saw the two-volume *Reverberator* as a model for collecting his longer tales and *nouvelles* into library edition format' and proposed to Macmillan 'three further two-volume publications [...] based on "The Aspern Papers", "A London Life" and "The Lesson of the Master"' (*CFHJ* 10, xxxix). In this series, published between 1888 and 1892, only

The Reverberator was accorded 'the honour' of sole occupancy of its two volumes, probably as a function of its length: at 53,000 words in the first edition, it is approximately 9,000 words longer than the longest story in those other collections, 'A London Life', and more than twice the length of the shortest title story, 'The Lesson of The Master'. The Preface's reference to 'the category of Shorter Novels' seems to indicate a later moment of volume publication and to denote a grouping of tales within the *NYE*. In his initial memorandum to Charles Scribner's Sons, James had planned to gather his 'short stories' into a separate series of volumes from his 'distinctively *short* novels' (30 July 1905; *HJL* 4:366). Still thinking along these lines the following year, he debated whether to allow 'Four Volumes for the Shorter Novels and Four for the Tales', or whether 'to make the Tales Five and the Shorter Novels Three' (to Scribners, 9 May 1906; *HJL* 4:403). Those categorical distinctions would blur as the *NYE* proceeded. In late February 1908 – just before he began to dictate the Preface to *NYE* XIII – James wrote to his publishers of an undifferentiated eight-volume group of 'Shorter Novels & Tales', and explained that in distributing works amongst those volumes he was generally opening each volume with a long story and 'giving precedence, for consistency of method, in general, to the "shorter novels" that originally had the honours of a small volume to themselves— or more or less; as was the case with "The Reverberator"' (to Scribners, 21–26 February 1908; Princeton). That was also the case with the lead tales in *NYE* X (*The Spoils of Poynton*) and *NYE* XI (*What Maisie Knew*); the lead tale in *NYE* XII, 'The Aspern Papers', was the exception that called for James's 'more or less'.

492 **half a dozen numbers of "Macmillan's Magazine" [...] a *jeu d'esprit*: [...] none other on the brow of which I may presume to place that laurel**: *The Reverberator* was serialized in *Macmillan's Magazine* from February to July 1888. Richard Salmon notes that James had originally offered the story to *Macmillan's* as a serial of just 'three instalments of approximately eighteen pages each'; in the event, it grew to fill 'six parts of between twelve to fourteen pages (an overall expansion from fifty-four to seventy-seven pages)' (*CFHJ* 10, xxxv–xxxvi). The naturalized French formula 'jeu d'esprit' means 'A playful display of wit or cleverness, esp. in a work of literature; a witty or humorous trifle' (*OED*). The term does not appear elsewhere in the Prefaces. To H. G. Wells on 9 December 1898, James had called 'The Turn of the Screw' 'essentially a pot-boiler & a *jeu d'esprit*' (*LL* 312); writing to Mary Augusta Ward on 15 March 1901, he described his novel *The*

Sacred Fount (1901) – not collected in the *NYE* – as 'the merest of *jeux d'esprit*' (*HJL* 4:185–6). The foliage of the laurel or bay-tree (*Laurus nobilis*) was used from classical antiquity as 'an emblem of victory or of distinction in poetry, etc.' (*OED*, 'laurel'), typically in the form of a crown or chaplet.

493 **an insidious grease-spot**: James would return to this simile in the last chapter of *A Small Boy and Others* (1913), recalling an attack of typhoid fever which he suffered at the age of 13 at Boulogne-sur-Mer and which produced for him the sense of 'a great blur, well-nigh after the fashion of some mild domestic but quite considerably spreading grease-spot, in respect to the world of action, such as it was, more or less immediately about me' (*Aut* 237). In both the Preface and the memoir, James repeats the grease-spot figure and describes it on repetition as 'homely': in the next paragraph but one, 'I but watch my grease-spot (for I cling to the homely metaphor) engagingly extend its bounds' (p. 144); in *A Small Boy*, 'the expansive blur for which I found just above a homely image' (*Aut* 238).

494 **lumping them, on the ground of their "racial consciousness," all together?**: As Sara Blair notes, James's use of 'race' reflects the instability of the concept and its terminology in the late nineteenth and early twentieth centuries, when 'categories of descent—"blood," "stock," "tribe"—are increasingly overlaid with, and radically confused by, general terms of classification—"species" or "kind"—as well as assignments of nation' (Blair, *Henry James and the Writing of Race and Nation* (Cambridge: Cambridge University Press, 1996), p. 7). George Flack and the Dossons are white Americans and conscious in various ways of their cultural differences from the Parisian characters in the story. In the next Preface, American nationality is treated as a sub-division of a larger, 'racial' category when James refers to international travellers who represent '"just the American vague variety of the dear old Anglo-Saxon race"' (p. 165).

495 **about which I fear I may already have been a bore**: James discusses fictional construction in terms of 'aspects' and 'scenes' in the Prefaces to *The Tragic Muse* and *The Awkward Age*, pp. 70, 86–7.

496 **Who shall say thus—and I have put the vain question but too often before!—where the associational nimbus […] shall absolutely fade and stop?**: James puts this question most directly at the start of the Preface to *Roderick Hudson*, noting that the practice of literature 'spread[s] round' the retrospective author 'in a widening, not in a narrowing circle' and

'only asking himself at what stage of remembrance the mark of the relevant will begin to fail' in an account of the circumstances of writing (pp. 3, 4). He likewise figures textual revision as an unstoppable process: once the writer's 'creative intimacy' with a work is reaffirmed in this way, 'Who shall say [...] where it shall not begin and where it shall consent to end?' (p. 9).

497 **clinging together and pleading with a collective friendly voice**: Compare the behaviour of the 'ghosts' whom James had encountered in writing *William Wetmore Story and His Friends* (1903), a biography based upon an archive of family documents – Story's dimly remembered contemporaries, who cling to each other as representatives of their historical period and social group and plead for posthumous acknowledgement. As James writes in the opening chapter, 'our boxful of ghosts "compose," hang together, consent to a mutual relation, confess, in fact, to a mutual dependence. If it is a question of living again, they can live but by each other's help, so that they close in, join hands, press together for warmth and contact' (*WWS* I:16). Collectively, they present him with 'the appeal, the ghostly claim as we may almost call it, of a dislodged, a vanished society' (*WWS* I:14).

498 **the flower of the flock, the hope of the family, [...] "boarded out,"**: The poetic formula 'the flower of the flock' derives from the Scottish ballad tradition. It occurs, for example, in a version of the ballad 'Lamkin' collected by the nineteenth-century American scholar Francis James Child. A mason builds a castle for his lord but is not paid for his labour, and so murders the lord's wife and infant son in revenge; in Child's version, the lord's wife offers the murderer her daughter in exchange for her own life: '"O spare me my life / until one o'clock, / And I'll give you Queen Betsie, / the flower of the flock"' ('Lamkin', version T, stanza 15, in *The English and Scottish Popular Ballads*, ed. Francis James Child, 10 vols. (Boston and New York: Houghton, Mifflin and Company, 1883-98), vol. IV, p. 339). A commonplace of nineteenth-century literature, song and visual culture, this phrase was often associated with the untimely death of young people, as in Caroline Bowles Southey's poem 'To the Memory of Isabel Southey': "'Tis ever thus—'tis ever thus, with all that's best below; / The dearest, noblest, loveliest, are always first to go— / The bird that sings the sweetest, the pine that crowns the rock, / The glory of the garden, the flower of the flock' (*The Poetical Works of Caroline Bowles Southey* (Edinburgh and London: William Blackwood and Sons, 1867), p. 164). James had called on that association in *The Wings of the Dove*, describing the younger of Kate

Croy's two dead brothers as 'the flower of the flock, a middy [midshipman] on the *Britannia*, dreadfully drowned' (Book Second, Ch. 1; *NYE* XIX, 65). For 'the hope of the family' as a term for its youngest member, compare the final chapter of *The Reverberator*, where Gaston Probert – the youngest child and only surviving son – is ironically referred to as 'the hope of the Proberts' at the crisis of his disaffiliation from his family (*NYE* XIII, 202); the phrase is a revision for the *NYE* and replaces 'the poor fellow' in the two-volume British first edition (*The Reverberator*, 2 vols. (London: Macmillan, 1888), vol. II, p. 192) (for James's revision of the novel from this edition in 1908, see *CFHJ* 10, lxxx). 'Boarding-out' is 'the obtaining of stated meals at another person's house; the placing of destitute children in families where they are treated as members' (*OED*).

499 **in a grand old city of the south of Europe (though neither in Rome nor yet in Florence) […] during a winter spent there**: The city was Venice, where the events that gave James the idea for *The Reverberator* had taken place in the winter of 1885–6. He heard about those events the following year, however, and while staying in another Italian city, as he would record in a notebook entry made some months later still: 'Last winter [1886–7], in Florence, I was struck with the queer incident of Miss M^{c}C.'s writing to the New York World that inconceivable letter about the Venetian society whose hospitality she had just been enjoying' (17 November 1887; *CN* 40). The Preface persistently confuses these two cities and winters: see notes 501, 502 and 505.

500 **the "personal equation"** A scientific term derived from astronomy and denoting 'the correction required in scientific observations […] to compensate for the habitual inaccuracy of an individual observer'; more generally, it refers to 'the component of a situation which relates to or arises from an individual's personal qualities' (*OED*, 'personal'). The term had been applied to James's own work during the period of the New York Edition. Reviewing *The American Scene* in the *North American Review*, Frederic Taber Cooper remarked that it was one of those works 'in which the personal equation so frankly and agreeably obtrudes itself that they ought in fairness to be reviewed, not as separate and complete productions, but as links in the chain of an author's self-revelations, significant factors in the rounded sum of a lifetime's accomplishment' (Hayes 465).

501 **a miscellaneous, many-coloured little cosmopolis**: James's travel essays on Venice refer obliquely to the cosmopolitan social circles that centred on the homes of his American friends Ariana and Daniel Curtis and

Katharine De Kay Bronson. In 'The Grand Canal' (1892), he cites the Curtises' Palazzo Barbaro as an example of 'the success with which [...] the cosmopolitan habit, the modern sympathy, the intelligent, flexible attitude, the latest fruit of time, adjust themselves to the great, gilded, relinquished shell, and try to fill it out' (*Great Streets of the World*, pp. 153–4). Ten years later, in a commemorative essay on Katharine De Kay Bronson, he would describe Venice as 'the real, or certainly the finer, the more sifted Cosmopolis' and a long-standing place of resort for international 'seekers of poetry and dispensers of romance. It is a fact that almost every one interesting, appealing, melancholy, memorable, odd, seems at one time or another [...] to have gravitated to Venice by a happy instinct' ('Browning in Venice. Being Recollections by the Late Katharine De Kay Bronson, with a Prefatory Note by Henry James', *Cornhill Magazine* 12 n.s. (February 1902), 145–71; 149). Bronson had a personal connection to an earlier phase of nineteenth-century Venetian cosmopolitanism through her friendship with Robert Browning; in 'The Grand Canal', James had described Palazzo Rezzonico, the home of Browning's son Pen, as 'a wonderful cosmopolitan "document"' (*Great Streets of the World*, pp. 158–9). For James's cosmopolitan society in Venice, see also the essays collected in Elizabeth Anne McCauley et al. (eds.), *Gondola Days: Isabella Stewart Gardner and the Palazzo Barbaro Circle* (Boston, MA: Isabella Stewart Gardner Museum, 2004). In light of the Preface's conflation of Venice and Florence (see note 499) it may be noted that Florence was no less significant a cosmopolitan centre for Americans of James's and earlier generations: see his comments on 'the little old miscellaneous cosmopolite Florence' in the Preface to *NYE* XI, p. 120.

502 **the appearance among us, that winter, of a charming free young person**: The 'young person' was May McClellan, daughter of the US Army General George B. McClellan (1826–85), who was travelling on the Continent with her widowed mother and had received introductions to Venetian society, and who would subsequently publish an article in the American press exposing details of the domestic lives of the aristocratic Italian families who had entertained her: see Richard Salmon's edition of *The Reverberator* (*CFHJ* 10, xxvii–xxx). James's references to time and place in the Preface are unclear. By speaking of May McClellan as appearing 'among us, that winter', he implies that he was present in Venice when she arrived there in the winter of 1885–6, whereas in fact he was in London and Paris at that time; he did not meet the McClellans until the following winter, in

Florence, by which time May's article had been published and the news of it had reached Italy.

503 **even these penetralia had not been closed**: The Latin borrowing 'penetralia' refers to 'The innermost parts or recesses of a building; *spec.* the sanctuary or inner sanctum of a temple' (*OED*). James uses the word again in the Preface to *NYE* XVIII with ironic reference to the 'down-town' world of American business and finance: for that passage and parallel instances in *The American Scene*, see note 756.

504 **She had come, [...] she had seen and had conquered**: James alludes to a saying attributed to Julius Caesar by ancient Greek and Roman historians, referring to the rapidity of his victory over Pharnaces II of Pontus at the Battle of Zela in 47 BCE: 'Veni, vidi, vici' ('I came, I saw, I conquered').

505 **I made an absence of several weeks, I went to Florence and to Rome, but I came back in the spring**: Again James is unclear about the sequence of his own movements in relation to the May McClellan scandal. Earlier in this paragraph, he appears to place himself in Venice at the time of McClellan's entry into Venetian society in the winter of 1885–6 (see note 502). Now he seems to say that he *subsequently* left Venice for 'several weeks' and returned 'in the spring': for the Preface's chronology to be consistent, he would have in that case to be referring to the spring of 1886. In fact, James did not arrive in Venice until the early spring of the following year, in late February 1887; and he was not returning to the city after a short absence, but had travelled from London to Florence in December 1886 and remained there for two months before moving on to Venice. From this point, the Preface's chronology does approximately fit James's actual movements, albeit just over a year later than he implies. He stayed in Venice until 9 April 1887 as the guest of Katharine De Kay Bronson; then 'made an absence of several weeks' and 'went to Florence', spending a month at Bellosguardo overlooking the city; then 'came back' to Venice on 25 May and stayed with Ariana and Daniel Curtis until 1 July, when he left for London via the Italian Lakes and Switzerland.

506 **The ingenuous stranger**: In the copy text, this phrase reads 'The ingenious stranger' (*NYE* XIII, ix). I have followed Philip Horne's Oxford World's Classics edition of *The Reverberator* in emending 'ingenious' to 'ingenuous' twice in this Preface's discussion of May McClellan, here and in the later phrase 'Our ingenuous young friend of the shocked saloons' (*NYE* XIII, xv; see p. 151). As Horne points out, James calls McClellan

'ingenuous' in the next paragraph of the Preface ('the ingenuous stranger's name became anathema' (p. 147)), and this reading 'seems more fitting in all three contexts' (*'A London Life' and 'The Reverberator'*, ed. Horne, p. 348). James repeatedly observes that McClellan did not know what she was doing in publicizing her experiences in Venice, and he generalizes from this episode to the observation that travelling Americans, and young American women especially, were 'almost incredibly *unaware of life*—as the European order expressed life' (p. 148); 'ingenuous' accords better than 'ingenious' with both those emphases. In the Preface to *NYE* XIV, moreover, James applies the word collectively to the young American heroines of his international stories ('an ingenuous young America (constantly seen as ingenuous and young)' (p. 159)); and in the Preface to *NYE* XVIII, he quotes a friend describing his character Daisy Miller as straining plausibility by an excess of the same quality ('"such a one, more's the pity, as—for pitch of the ingenuous, for quality of the artless—couldn't possibly have been at all"' (p. 214)).

507 **a newspaper in her native city [...] a letter as long, as confidential, as "chatty," [...] as she might have indited to the most trusted of friends**: McClellan's letter was published in the New York *World* on 14 November 1886. 'Chatty' means 'Given to chat or light easy talk' (*OED*, citing a journalistic instance from 1882: 'A chatty and readable column'). In the story, this is how Francie's article strikes her family, who cannot understand the offence it has caused: 'The letter [...] appeared lively, "chatty," highly calculated to please' (Ch. 12; *NYE* XIII, 164). James uses the same word of May McClellan in his notebook: 'it seemed to her pleasant & natural & "chatty" to describe, in a horribly vulgar newspaper, the people she had been living with & their personal domestic arrangements & secrets' (17 November 1887; *CN* 40). He was also aware of the controversy surrounding the publication of Julian Hawthorne's interview with the American poet and diplomat James Russell Lowell, entitled 'Lowell in a Chatty Mood', in the same newspaper in October 1886 (see *CFHJ* 10, xxx–xxxiv).

508 **Strange, it struck me, [...] the fact itself of "anybody's knowing,"**: James's reaction at the time had been exactly the opposite of what he describes here. As he wrote to Katharine De Kay Bronson from Florence in January 1887, after talking with May McClellan's mother about the incident he was convinced that 'it was done in perfect good faith as regards their utterly failing to realize that Venice would ever hear of it. As if everyone didn't hear of everything to-day!' ([22 January 1887]; *CLHJ 1887–1888* 1:15).

509 **a nine days' wonder**: Proverbially, 'an event or phenomenon that attracts enthusiastic interest for a short while, but is then ignored or forgotten' (*OED*, 'nine'). The formula occurs twice in a novel of the same period, *The Princess Casamassima* (1886): in Chapter 33, Christina sells her collection of curios privately in an attempt 'to avoid the nine days' wonder of a public sale'; and in Chapter 38, she and Hyacinth discuss the likelihood of Lady Aurora 'making herself a scandal, a fable and a nine days' wonder' for the sake of marrying Paul Muniment (*NYE* VI, 183, 277).

510 **flooded "American society" with light**: James remarked to Katharine De Kay Bronson on the typically American quality of May McClellan's behaviour: 'what a superfluous product is the smart, forward, over-encouraged, thinking-she-can-write-and-that-her-writing-has-any-business-to-exist-American girl!'; 'she is Americanissimo [*sic*]—in the sense of being launched as a young person before the Lord' ([22 January 1887], 26 January [1887]; *CLHJ 1887–1888* 1:16, 22). For the Preface's figure of illumination, compare James's notebook entry of 17 November 1887: 'That she *should* have acted in good faith seemed to me to throw much light upon that mania for publicity which is one of the most striking signs of our time' (*CN* 40). As Richard Salmon points out, in the Preface 'James adopts a strategy of revelation similar to that of the journalist, but inverts it, so that the "light of the press" (to use a familiar trope, employed by Flack himself), is directed against the agents of publicity' (Salmon, *Henry James and the Culture of Publicity* (Cambridge: Cambridge University Press, 1997), p. 124). George Flack employs that trope in Chapter 4: '"it ain't going to continue to be possible to keep out anywhere the light of the Press. Now what I'm going to do is to set up the biggest lamp yet made and make it shine all over the place"' (*NYE* XIII, 63).

511 **several years of oblivion**: James exaggerates the lapse of time between first hearing about McClellan's letter in Florence (in December 1886 or January 1887) and making the notebook entry for 'The Reverberator' (in November 1887): a matter of months, not years. He had written to Katharine De Kay Bronson on 27 January 1887: 'I should like to write a story about the business, as a pendant to Daisy Miller, but I won't, to deepen the complication' (*CLHJ 1887–1888* 1:22).

512 **I have already had occasion to say that the "international" light lay thick […] on the general scene of my observation**: James had said so at the close of the Preface to *The Portrait of a Lady*.

513 **a happy circumstance from many points of view**: Compare a comment in James's notebook on the story that became 'Louisa Pallant' (1888): the characters 'may all be Americans—in Europe: since Howells writes to me that I do the "international" far better than anything else' (12 January 1887; *CN* 34).

514 **amid the level sands and across the pathless desert**: An echo of P. B. Shelley's sonnet 'Ozymandias' (1818), which describes a ruined statue of the pharaoh Rameses II (1303–1213 BCE) 'in the desert' of Egypt: 'Round the decay / Of that colossal wreck, boundless and bare / The lone and level sands stretch far away' (ll. 12–14; *Poetical Works*, p. 550). Several years later James would allude to another line in this poem (from its quotation of the statue's vainglorious inscription: '"My name is Ozymandias, king of kings: / Look on my works, ye Mighty, and despair!"', ll. 10–11) when he wrote to Edmund Gosse about the commercial failure of the *NYE*: 'my poor old rather truncated edition, in fact entirely frustrated one—which has the grotesque likeness for me of a sort of miniature Ozymandias of Egypt ("look on my *works* ye mighty & despair!")—round which the lone & level sands stretch further away than ever' (25 August 1915; *SLHJEG* 313). A few years before writing *The Reverberator*, he had noted the danger of exhausting the international theme in a note on the subject for a story not collected in the *NYE*, 'The Modern Warning' (1888): 'Of course internationalism &c, may be found overdone, threadbare' (9 July 1884; *CN* 30). Three years later, he wrote in the same spirit to the British author and translator Linda Villari, thanking her for the loan of a magazine containing an 'Anglo-Italian article' by her: 'Theoretically I have given up international comparisons & rapprochements as a vain job—but practically I am forever making them' (22 May [1887]; *CLHJ 1887–1888* 1:134).

515 **I shall on a near pretext [...] develop the sense of this**: James returns to the question of his limited knowledge of 'the American character' in his comments on American businessmen later in this Preface and in his discussion of 'down-town' and 'up-town' subjects in the Preface to *NYE* XVIII, pp. 152–3, 215–20.

516 **a sea-change**: An allusion to Ariel's song in *The Tempest* (1611), 'Full fadom five thy father lies', substituting a transatlantic crossing for the drowning in Shakespeare's original: 'Of his bones are coral made: / Those are pearls that were his eyes: / Nothing of him that doth fade, / But doth suffer a sea-change / Into something rich and strange' (1.2.397–402). Philip Horne discusses other allusions to these lines in the context of James's feeling for

the 'deep transformations' of textual revision (*Henry James and Revision*, pp. 87–9).

517 **our roaring young lioness of the old-world salons**: The metaphor refers to Francie Dosson's journalistic activity in *The Reverberator*. In the Preface to *Essays in Criticism* (1865), Matthew Arnold had ironically predicted an 'earnest, prosaic, practical, austerely literal future' in which 'the world will soon be the Philistines'! [...] and the whole earth [will be] filled and ennobled every morning by the magnificent roaring of the young lions of the *Daily Telegraph*' (*The Complete Prose Works of Matthew Arnold*, vol. III, p. 287); for Arnold's 'Philistines', see note 895. The formula has a biblical origin: 'The young lions roar after their prey, and seek their meat from God' (Psalm 104:21). As Horne points out, the American journalist George Flack '"roars" in the course of the story' ('*A London Life*' and '*The Reverberator*', ed. Horne, p. 349). He does so while arguing that the Proberts' outrage at Francie's letter is merely '"a pretext"' to cover their disapproval of her as a match for Gaston; the phrase 'her visitor roared' is an insertion in the revised text with no counterpart in earlier editions (Ch. 13; *NYE* XIII, 182).

518 **their own flourishing Order [...] the passionless pilgrims**: James refers to the American social 'Order' as distinct from the European. In the Preface to *NYE* X, he had recently spoken of 'the bewilderment of the good American, of either sex and of almost any age, in presence of the "European" order', and had asked whether America actually constituted a social 'order', or 'no order at all' (p. 104). The collective characterization of young American women in Europe as 'the passionless pilgrims' echoes the title of James's story 'A Passionate Pilgrim' (1871), which is also collected in *NYE* XIII.

519 **A hundred good instances confirmed this tradition**: When James repeated the story of the McClellan scandal to his aunt Catharine Walsh on 16 June 1887, he offered another instance of the same phenomenon: 'The strange things of that sort that the American female does!—as witness the terrible Mrs. Sherwood, poor "Posy" Emmet's mother-in-law. She invited me (& some others) to dine with her in London last summer, & then wrote a fearful letter about it [...] to the American journals, which she afterwards sent me as if I should be delighted to see it' (*CLHJ 1887–1888* 1:148).

520 **the comparatively antique right of free fishing**: English law discriminates between four types of 'fishery', or 'The right of fishing in certain

waters': '*free fishery*, an exclusive right of fishing in public water, derived from royal grant; *several fishery*, an exclusive right to fish derived from ownership of the soil; *common of fishery*, the right of fishing in another man's water; *common fishery*, the right of all to fish in public waters' (*OED*).

521 **without form and void**: In the biblical account of the Creation, 'the earth was without form, and void' until God's decree that there be light (Genesis 1:2).

522 **the Francie Dossons and the Daisy Millers and the Bessie Aldens and the Pandora Days**: James groups Francie Dosson in *The Reverberator* with the young American women at the centre of his international stories 'Daisy Miller' (1878), 'An International Episode' (1878–9) and 'Pandora' (1884). 'An International Episode' is collected in *NYE* XIV, the other two stories in *NYE* XVIII.

523 **at all committed to "having to have" it**: In James's story 'Mrs Medwin' (1901), the recognition by an English society hostess of an amusing American's value as a house-guest is phrased in these acquisitive terms: '"It's before her that he's the thing she'll have to have." "Have to?" "For Sundays in the country. A feature—*the* feature"' (Ch. 4; *NYE* XVIII, 504).

524 **satellites more directly "engaged"**: James refers to the fiancés of his young American women. In 'Pandora', Mrs Bonnycastle notes that it is characteristic of the social type she refers to as '"the self-made girl"' to have a fiancé: '"she's always engaged to some young man who belongs to her earlier phase"' (Ch. 2; *NYE* XVIII, 162). For 'the "self-made," or at least self-making, girl', see note 739.

525 **visible and thinkable only as the American "business-man"**: At the period of the international stories James is discussing in this Preface, he had observed in his biography *Hawthorne* (1879) 'that even to the present day it is a considerable discomfort in the United States not to be "in business." The young man who attempts to launch himself in a career that does not belong to the so-called practical order; the young man who has not, in a word, an office in the business-quarter of the town, with his name painted on the door, has but a limited place in the social system' (*LC1* 342). The Preface's characterization of the male companions of young American women largely tallies with the stories James refers to. George Flack in *The Reverberator* is a journalist but looks like a businessman: he 'would have been quite adequately marked as "young commercial American"' (Ch. 1; *NYE* XIII, 14). Francie Dosson's father in the same story is an

American businessman travelling with his daughters; Daisy Miller's father is left behind to manage his business in Schenectady, New York, while his wife and children make the European tour. In 'An International Episode', Mr Westgate remains in his office in New York City while his wife entertains their English visitors in Newport, Rhode Island, and Mrs Westgate laments 'the universal passionate surrender of the men [in America] to business-questions and business-questions only' (Ch. 1; *NYE* XIV, 327). Mr Westgate does not accompany his wife and sister-in-law to London in the second half of the story; the young American who follows them there, Willie Woodley, appears to be an Anglophile socialite and thus an exception to the rule James formulates here – as is the Europeanized student Winterbourne in 'Daisy Miller'. In 'Pandora', the heroine's fiancé Mr D. F. Bellamy is in '"some kind of business in Utica"' (Ch. 2; *NYE* XVIII, 164) until Pandora gets the US President to appoint him American Minister to Holland.

526 **No approach I could make to him on his "business side" really got near it**: The closest approach to the '"business side"' of a character in James's early fiction is perhaps his portrayal of Mr Ruck in 'The Pension Beaurepas' (1879), 'a jaded faded absolutely voided man of business' (*NYE* XIV, 400) who has been advised to travel for his health and learns that he is facing bankruptcy at home as he tours Europe with his wife and daughter. In his 'American Letter' of 26 March 1898 in the journal *Literature*, James had reflected that 'the typical American figure is above all that "business man" whom the novelist and the dramatist have scarce yet seriously touched': to represent him would involve considerable 'difficulty', inasmuch as the business world 'is as special and occult a one to the outsider as the world, say, of Arctic exploration—as impenetrable save as a result of special training'. Nevertheless, 'the American "business man" remains, thanks to the length and strength of the wires that move him, *the* magnificent theme *en disponibilité*' (*LC1* 655, 656). For the French phrase in that last quotation, see note 206.

527 **the earliest date to which anything in the whole present series refers itself**: 'A Passionate Pilgrim', published in the *Atlantic Monthly* in March and April 1871, is the earliest fiction included in the *NYE*; two other stories in *NYE* XIII, 'The Madonna of the Future' (1873) and 'Madame de Mauves' (1874), are the next earliest in order of publication. There is no record in James's letters of when exactly he wrote 'A Passionate Pilgrim'. The story draws on his travels in England in 1869 and 1870 (see note 533); as Edel points out, a passage from a letter he wrote to his brother

William from Oxford in April 1869 was incorporated into the story (*HJL* 1:110-11, 114 n. 3). Maqbool Aziz judges that James 'did no literary work during these months of travel' and wrote up his European experiences on his return to Cambridge, Massachusetts. Aziz accordingly places the composition of 'A Passionate Pilgrim' in summer 1870 (*The Tales of Henry James. Volume Two: 1870-1874*, ed. Aziz (Oxford: Clarendon Press, 1978), pp. xxvii, xxxi-xxxiii).

528 **sops instinctively thrown to the international Cerberus**: In ancient Greek mythology, Cerberus was a monstrous dog who guarded the gates of Hades, preventing the souls of the dead from leaving the underworld and barring entry to the living. Cerberus is commonly represented as a composite of dog and serpent, with multiple canine heads (usually three). In Book VI of Virgil's *Aeneid*, the Trojan hero Aeneas descends to the underworld guided by the Cumæan Sibyl, who throws Cerberus a drugged honey cake, a sleep-inducing 'sop' – 'A piece of bread or the like dipped or steeped in water, wine, etc., before being eaten or cooked' (*OED*) – that enables them to pass by safely. In Dryden's translation (1697): 'The prudent Sibyl had before prepar'd / A Sop, in Honey steep'd, to charm the Guard' (Book VI, ll. 566-7; *The Works of John Dryden*, ed. Edward Niles Hooker, H. T. Swedenberg, V. A. Dearing et al., 20 vols. (Berkeley, CA: University of California Press, 1956-2000), vol. V, pp. 545-7).

529 **the keeper of the international "books"**: The figure of an accountant or 'book-keeper' also occurs in the Preface to *The Ambassadors*, which James had composed – at least in part – immediately before the Preface to *NYE* XIII (see note p. 248).

530 **ground-stuff**: In the visual arts, a 'ground' is 'Any material surface, natural or prepared, which is taken as a basis for working upon: *esp.* in painting or decorative art, a main surface or first coating of colour, serving as a support for other colours or a background for designs'; the term also denotes the fabric upon which embroidery is worked, and the acid-resistant material that covers a metal plate in etching (*OED*).

531 **the business-man would be dodged. [...] an infinite perspective of more or less quaint antechambers; [...] kept indefinitely at bay**: This sentence of the Preface recalls James's story 'The Jolly Corner' (1908), in which the returning American expatriate Spencer Brydon stalks his spectral alter ego – the ravaged businessman he might have become had he stayed in America – through the New York family home. Brydon feels that

this other self has been '"dodging, retreating, hiding"' but that he must be confronted as '"the fanged or the antlered animal brought at last to bay"' (Ch. 2; *NYE* XVII, 461); the layout of rooms and 'multiplication of doors' on the upper stories of the old house produce in Brydon a hallucination of 'the presence encountered telescopically, [...] focussed and studied in diminishing perspective' (*NYE* XVII, 466). William James would joke with his brother about 'The Jolly Corner': '*what* an insult to the type of the N.Y. business man—the country's pride! I don't see how your good name can recover' (WJ to James, 24 January 1909; *CWJ* 3:376).

532 **golden dust [...] kicked up in the foreground**: James often uses the figure of kicking up dust to describe writers' attempts at concealing intractable problems or weaknesses in their work, as for example in the next Preface: 'my "America" and its products would doubtless, as a theme, have betrayed gaps and infirmities enough without such a kicking-up of the dramatic dust (mainly in the foreground) as I could set my "Europe" in motion for' (p. 159). He had recently asserted that Balzac 'never throws dust in our eyes, save only the fine gold-dust through the haze of which his own romantic vision operates' ('The Lesson of Balzac', 1905; *LC2* 124).

533 **several weeks in England, [...] an uneffaced little chapter of boyish, or [...] of infantine experience; [...] taken the adventure of my twenty-sixth year "hard,"**: James's first independent European tour (February 1869–April 1870) began and ended in England. He disembarked at Liverpool and came directly to London; memories of this arrival are recorded in the opening section of his essay 'London' (1888) (*ELE* 1–7) and in Chapters 1–5 of his unfinished memoir *The Middle Years* (1917). In April 1869, he took a course of hydrotherapy at the Worcestershire spa town of Great Malvern; he then made a three-week tour of England and Wales, visiting castles and cathedrals and spending a few days in Oxford, before passing through London again in May en route to the Continent. Still in poor health the following spring, he spent another two months at Great Malvern from February to April 1870 (see Edel, *Henry James: The Untried Years*, pp. 287–99, 325–6, 338). He would write about his childhood experiences of England in the mid-1850s in *A Small Boy and Others* (1913), Chs. 20, 22 and 23; for his earlier 'infantine' impressions of Europe, see note 538. James's sense of what it is 'to take something hard' differs slightly from the definition given in the *OED* ('to be very upset by something; to react to something with anguish, anger, or distress'; in

'hard', *adv.*). His 1874 essay on Turgenev supplies a relevant gloss: 'The foremost impression of M. Turgeniéff's reader is that he is morbidly serious, that he takes life terribly hard' (*LC2* 992). In 'The Madonna of the Future', the failed artist Theobald, realizing that he has '"wasted [his] life in preparation"', says: '"I've taken the whole business too hard"' (Ch. 3; *NYE* XIII, 486).

534 **a first sight of Italy, [...] a return to America [...] to drag with it, as a lengthening chain**: James entered Italy in August 1869, crossing the Simplon Pass on foot from Switzerland. He wrote at the time of 'the sense of going down into Italy—the delight of seeing the north slowly melt into the south—of seeing Italy gradually crop up in bits & vaguely latently betray itself—until finally, at the little frontier Village of Isella where I spent the night, it lay before me warm & living & palpable (warm, especially)—all these fine things bestowed upon the journey a delightful flavor of romance' (to AJ, 31 August [1869]; *CLHJ 1855–1872* 2:83). James spent the rest of the year in Italy, mostly in Florence and Rome; he returned via Menton, Nice and Paris, and reached London again in early February 1870 (see Edel, *Henry James: The Untried Years*, pp. 301–16, 324–5). After a second therapeutic stay at Great Malvern, he embarked for America at the end of April (see note 533); for the next two years, he would be based at the family home in Cambridge, Massachusetts. For dragging 'a lengthening chain', see note 94.

535 **might he somehow come into his "own"? [...] dispossessed princes and wandering heirs**: To 'come into one's own' is 'to receive what is due to one; to come into one's inheritance'; figuratively, 'to achieve due recognition, be properly esteemed; to fulfil one's potential' (*OED*, 'own'). The earliest example cited in *OED* comes from *The Cloister and the Hearth* (1861) by the English novelist and playwright Charles Reade; he was also the author of a historical novel whose title James alludes to in this sentence of the Preface. Reade's *The Wandering Heir* (1872) was a fictional version of the 'Annesley case', an eighteenth-century legal dispute over the inheritance of the earldom of Anglesey. In 1728, the orphaned James Annesley, the rightful heir to the earldom, was kidnapped in childhood and sold into indentured labour in the North American colonies at the command of his uncle to remove him from the line of succession; he returned to England in 1741 and mounted a successful lawsuit to claim his inheritance. The plot of 'A Passionate Pilgrim' turns on the rejection of the American Clement Searle by the English branch of his family. As they approach the family

seat in rural 'Middleshire', the narrator remarks to Searle: '"Here you can wander all day [...] like an exiled prince who has come back on tiptoe and hovers about the dominion of the usurper"' (Ch. 2; *NYE* XIII, 367).

536 **The question was to answer itself promptly enough**: On 22 May 1870, James wrote from Cambridge, Massachusetts to Grace Norton at Siena: 'I may safely assume—mayn't I?—that you are to be abroad two or three years yet. Largely within that time we shall meet again. When I next go to Italy it will be not for months but years' (*CLHJ 1855–1872* 2:360). He returned to the Continent in May 1872, travelling with his sister and aunt and then staying on alone until September 1874; it was not until November 1875 that he took up permanent residence in Europe.

537 **the head of one of those well-directed shafts from the European quiver to which, of old, tender American flesh was more helplessly and bleedingly exposed [...] than to-day**: On 26 September 1870, James wrote to Grace Norton from Cambridge, Massachusetts: 'The continuity of life & routine & sensation has long since so effectually re-established itself here, that I feel my European gains sinking gradually out of sight and sound & American experience closing bunchily together over them, as flesh over a bullet—the simile is àpropos! But I have only to probe a little to hear the golden ring of that precious projectile' (*CLHJ 1855–1872* 2:376). During the period of the *NYE*, he would use a comparable figure in his travel essay 'The Sense of Newport' (1906) to describe the cosmopolitan American society of Newport, Rhode Island, where the James family had settled on their first return from Europe in 1858: those reluctantly repatriated inhabitants exemplified 'the great—or perhaps I have a right only to say [...] the small—American complication; the state of one's having been so pierced, betimes, by the sharp outland dart as to be able ever afterwards but to move about, vaguely and helplessly, with the shaft still in one's side' (*AS* 223).

538 **hurried off to London and to Paris immediately after my birth, [...] that poison had entered my veins**: James's parents had first taken him and his brother William to Europe as infants in 1843–4. In Chapter 5 of *A Small Boy and Others*, he would record a precocious memory of Paris from that visit: 'Conveyed along the Rue St.-Honoré while I waggled my small feet, as I definitely remember doing, under my flowing robe, I had crossed the Rue de Castiglione and taken in, for all my time, the admirable aspect of the Place and the Colonne Vendôme' (*Aut* 37). James was 1 year old at the time. In Chapter 7 of *A Small Boy*, he states that he was

'prematurely poisoned' in later childhood by listening to his parents and aunt indulging their nostalgia for that visit: 'I had taken the twist, had sipped the poison' (*Aut* 53, 55). Shortly before the period of the *NYE*, in *William Wetmore Story* (1903), he had written in similar terms about the noted failure of visiting American and Northern European artists to work productively under the local influence of Rome: life in such agreeable conditions produced 'a sense of the sterner realities as sweetened and drugged as if, at the perpetual banquet, it had been some Borgia cup concocted for the strenuous mind' (*WWS* I:329, under the page heading 'THE BORGIA CUP'). The reference is to the rumoured poisoning of political enemies by the Borgia family in fifteenth- and sixteenth-century Rome.

539 **restored to air already breathed and to a harmony already disclosed**: James's second exposure to Europe occurred in June 1855, when Henry James Sr took his family to the Continent in pursuit of educational opportunities for his five children; they remained abroad until the summer of 1858, living at different times in London, Paris, Geneva and Boulogne. In Chapter 20 of *A Small Boy*, James notes that his first impressions of Paris confirmed his 'stores of preconception' about the city: he recalls standing on a hotel balcony overlooking rue de la Paix and responding to the 'appeal [...] of the whole perfect Parisianism I seemed to myself always to have possessed mentally—even if I had just turned twelve!—and that now filled out its frame or case for me from every lighted window, up and down, as if each of these had been [...] a word in some immortal quotation, the very breath of civilised lips' (*Aut* 170). The narrator of 'A Passionate Pilgrim' likewise notes 'The latent preparedness of the American mind even for the most characteristic features of English life': 'I had seen the coffee-room of the Red Lion [his London inn] years ago, at home—at Saragossa Illinois—in books, in visions, in dreams, in Dickens, in Smollett, in Boswell' (Ch. 1; *NYE* XIII, 335, 336).

540 **another quite languishing American interval; [...] the fruit of the tree of knowledge**: James refers to the period between September 1860, when his family returned to America from a final educational trip to Europe, and February 1869, when he embarked on his first independent tour of the Continent. In the biblical story of the Fall, 'the tree of the knowledge of good and evil' is the only tree in the garden of Eden whose fruit Adam and Eve are forbidden to eat (Genesis 2:17). James's story 'The Tree of Knowledge' (1900) makes European experience the ironic catalyst for a

son's enlightenment: Lancelot Mallow, the child of a pretentious English sculptor, gives up studying art in Paris when he realizes not only that he has no talent, but that his father has none either.

541 **"The Galaxy," a periodical to which I find [...] twenty other remembrances gratefully attached**: 'Madame de Mauves' was first published in two numbers of the *Galaxy*, February–March 1874. James's gratitude to this New York magazine may simply reflect the fact that it had provided him with an alternative publication venue for stories, reviews and travel essays during the 1860s and 1870s. The Preface, however, omits to mention the occasional inconvenience and annoyance of his dealings with the *Galaxy*'s editors William and Francis Church. Writing to his parents on 4 August 1873, for example, in the context of some 'bother' about Henry Sr receiving payment from the Churches on his behalf, James remarked: 'They are certainly shabby people; but with such, I suppose, is the lot of authors cast' (*CLHJ 1872–1876* 2:23). And to his father on 22 December 1873, reluctantly offering the travel essay 'An Autumn Journey' to the *Galaxy* because it had been rejected by *Scribner's Monthly*: 'I don't like the Galaxy's manners & customs, but one can't afford to be too fastidious' (*CLHJ 1872–1876* 2:81). A year after publishing 'Madame de Mauves', the *Galaxy* would disappoint James over the serialization of *The American* (see note 64). He continued to send material to the magazine after this date, nevertheless: most of the essays collected in *French Poets and Novelists* (1878) and several of those in *Portraits of Places* (1883) appeared there first.

542 **an old inn at Bad-Homburg [...] the Franco-Prussian war, [...] a dampish, dusky, unsunned room, cool [...] during some very hot weather**: James spent most of the summer of 1873 at the German spa town of Bad Homburg vor der Höhe, located in the Taunus mountains in the state of Hesse. Bad Homburg had grown into a major gambling centre during the mid nineteenth century, but in 1872 its casino was forced to close – along with those of two other Rhineland spa towns, Baden-Baden and Wiesbaden – when a ban on gambling was enacted in the newly unified Germany. James shares a common contemporary misconception in attributing this development to the Franco-Prussian War: as E. J. Carter points out, the casinos of the Rhineland had been 'scheduled to close at the end of 1872' in any case, in compliance with a policy made after the defeat of Austria by Prussia and its allies in 1866. 'Yet the fact that the final abolition of the casinos coincided so closely with the Prussian defeat

of France in 1870–1871 led most observers to connect the two events, interpreting the downfall of gambling as a consequence of the eviction of French cultural influences from the southern Rhineland'; the German casinos had been operated by French businessmen (Carter, 'Breaking the Bank: Gambling Casinos, Finance Capitalism, and German Unification', *Central European History* 39.2 (2006), 185–213; 189). See also James's travel essay 'Homburg Reformed' (1873) (*CTW2* 635–43). Bad Homburg would experience a revival – what the Preface calls its '*seconde jeunesse*' – when Kaiser Wilhelm II of Germany adopted it as a summer residence in 1888. The Preface's memory of 'very hot weather' in the summer of 1873 tallies with James's correspondence at the time. As he wrote on 1 August, the summer was 'fiercely hot', but Homburg was airy and shaded, and he was living 'very comfortably' at the Hôtel des Quatre Saisons 'in a little ground-floor room in a dépendance [annex], looking on the garden, with a window smothered in Virginia creeper' (to CW; *CLHJ 1872–1876* 2:18). The Preface recalls only the first six weeks of James's stay. By the middle of August he had moved to a lodging house because 'a change in the weather—toward cold—had made my room uncomfortable' (to HJ Sr and MWJ, 14 August [1873]; *CLHJ 1872–1876* 2:32). The final story in this volume of the *NYE*, 'Louisa Pallant' (1888), opens 'on the terrace of the Kursaal at Homburg, nearly ten years ago, one beautiful night toward the end of July' (*NYE* XIII, 495).

543 **visited by the gentle Euphemia; [...] the confidences with which she honoured me**: James's recollection of writing 'Madame de Mauves' reverses the conditions of communication in the story: the young American Longmore must himself either visit or waylay Euphemia de Mauves in order to talk with her at all, and she pointedly declines to confide her marital unhappiness either to him or to her friend Mrs Draper.

544 **"Louisa Pallant," with still subtler art, [...] completely covers her tracks**: The germ of 'Louisa Pallant' is recorded in James's notebook entry of 12 January 1887: 'The idea of a worldly mother & a worldly daughter—the latter of whom has been trained up so perfectly by the former that she excels & surpasses her, & the mother, who has some principle of goodness still left in her composition, is appalled at her own work' (*CN* 34). James often used a metaphor of covering tracks when writing about authors as the subjects of biographical enquiry. In 'The Birthplace' (1903), the custodian Morris Gedge says of the unnamed but unmistakably Shakespearean author whose scantly documented life he has to narrate to

visitors: '"He covered His tracks as no other human being has ever done"' (Ch. 4; *NYE* XVII, 165). Reviewing the letters of Robert Louis Stevenson in 1900, James observed 'that people—that artists perhaps in particular— are well advised to cover their tracks', but cited Stevenson as an exception: he 'never covered his tracks, and the tracks prove, perhaps, to be what most attaches us. We follow them here, from year to year and from stage to stage, with the same charmed sense with which he has made us follow one of his hunted heroes in the heather' ('LRLS' 63) – e.g., David Balfour or Alan Breck Stewart, the fugitive heroes of Stevenson's Jacobite adventure story *Kidnapped* (1886).

545 **a couple of sunny rooms on the Arno […] where the Borg' Ognissanti begins to bore duskily westward**: James recalls his rooms at the Hôtel du Sud on Piazza Carlo Goldoni, at the easternmost end of Borgo Ognissanti on the north bank of the river Arno, where he stayed for January and the first half of February 1887. In a letter dated from the Hôtel du Sud, he told Louisa Erskine, Lady Wolseley that he was finding Florence 'excellent for work—in the sunny mornings. My rooms are flooded with that element, & my windows overhang the shining Arno' (20 January [1887]; *CLHJ 1887–1888* 1:8). James's use of the verb 'bore' to describe narrow Florentine streets between high buildings is anticipated in another story in this volume of the *NYE*, 'The Madonna of the Future': leaving his hotel after dinner to walk about the city in the opening chapter, the narrator selects 'A narrow passage [that] wandered darkly away out of the little square before my hotel and looked as if it bored into the heart of Florence' (*NYE* XIII, 438). It leads him to the Piazza della Signoria where he encounters the painter Theobald.

PREFACE to *Lady Barbarina, The Siege of London, An International Episode and Other Tales* (*NYE* XIV)

546 **the type I have already found it convenient to refer to as "international"**: For James's earlier discussions of stories on '"international"' subjects, see the Prefaces to *NYE* X and XIII, pp. 104–7, 148–54.

547 **an explanation adequate […] only when itself a little explained**: An echo of Byron's mocking lines in the Dedication to the first two Cantos of *Don Juan* (1819) on S. T. Coleridge's philosophical memoir *Biographia Literaria* (1817): 'And Coleridge, too, has lately taken wing, / But, like a

hawk encumber'd with his hood, / Explaining metaphysics to the nation— / I wish he would explain his Explanation' (stanza 2, ll. 13-16; George Gordon, Lord Byron, *The Complete Poetical Works*, ed. Jerome J. McGann, 7 vols. (Oxford: Clarendon Press, 1980-93), vol. V, p. 3). James alludes to the same lines in *The Ambassadors* (1903) when Strether reflects on his obscurity as editor of the Woollett 'Review': 'His name on the green cover, where he had put it for Mrs. Newsome, expressed him doubtless just enough to make the world […] ask who he was. He had incurred the ridicule of having to have his explanation explained. He was Lambert Strether because he was on the cover, whereas it should have been, for anything like glory, that he was on the cover because he was Lambert Strether' (Book Second, Ch. 2; *NYE* XXI, 84). For a reviewer of the *NYE* applying the same formula to James's explanations in the Prefaces, see the Introduction, p. cxv.

548 **"Lady Barbarina"**: The title of this story is 'Lady Barberina' in all texts prior to *NYE*.

549 **makes […] of any quarrel with his subject, any stupid attempt to go behind *that*, the true stultification of criticism**: James here uses one of his idiosyncratic technical terms – 'going behind', which in earlier Prefaces denotes the direct representation of a fictional character's consciousness (see notes 256 and 307) – to refer to critical or biographical enquiry into the origins of fictional subjects. He had made the same point about the critic's 'quarrel' with the writer's subject in the Preface to *The Portrait of a Lady* (see note 140).

550 **The thing of profit is to *have* your experience […] and for this almost any will do**: Compare Strether's famous outburst to Little Bilham in *The Ambassadors*, as recalled and summarized in the first paragraph of the Preface to that novel: '"It doesn't so much matter what you do in particular so long as you have your life"' (see note 841). James had begun to write the *Ambassadors* Preface shortly before composing the Preface to *NYE* XIV.

551 **as the birds of the air are fed**: An allusion to the Sermon on the Mount: 'Behold the fowls of the air: for they sow not, neither do they reap, nor gather into barns; yet your heavenly Father feedeth them' (Matthew 6:26).

552 **the early-taken ply I have already elsewhere glanced at**: James discusses his precocious responsiveness to Europe in childhood and youth in the Preface to *NYE* XIII, pp. 154-5.

553 **the "straight tip"—to back the right horse or buy the right shares**: The word 'tip' in this sense means 'Special information; private knowledge. Specifically an advice concerning betting or a Stock-Exchange speculation intended to benefit the recipient: THE STRAIGHT TIP = an absolute CERT [a certainty, a tip offered with great confidence]; in racing = direct advice from owner or trainer' (*Slang* VII:131).

554 **a "critic of life" [...] a social fusion tending to abridge old rigours of separation**: As T. J. Lustig points out ('James, Arnold, "Culture", and "Modernity"', 183 n. 93), James alludes here to Matthew Arnold's description of literature as '*a criticism of life*', a formula first aired in his 1864 essay 'Joubert' (*The Complete Prose Works of Matthew Arnold*, vol. III, p. 209). Lustig also connects this passage of the *Lady Barbarina* Preface to the early letter to T. S. Perry in which James had stated his belief that 'to be an American is an excellent preparation for culture': 'To have no national stamp has hitherto been a defect & a drawback; but I think it not unlikely that American writers may yet indicate that a vast intellectual fusion and synthesis of the various national tendencies of the world is the condition of more important achievements than any we have seen' (20 September [1867]; *CLHJ 1855–1872* 1:179–80). The Preface shares its faith in cosmopolitan 'social fusion' with a character in 'Lady Barbarina': Lady Marmaduke, an American who has married into the English aristocracy, believes 'that an ultimate fusion [of British and American social life] was inevitable' (Ch. 2; *NYE* XIV, 30).

555 **some eventual sublime consensus of the educated**: James translates a phrase of the first-century CE Roman rhetorician Quintilian, whose work on rhetoric *Institutio oratoria* defines usage in speech ('consuetudinem sermonisas') as the consensus of the educated ('consensus eruditorum') (1.6.45; see Quintilian, *The Orator's Education: Books 1–2*, ed. and trans. Donald A. Russell (Cambridge, MA: Harvard University Press, 2001), p. 185). In 'The Question of Our Speech', a Commencement address delivered to the graduating class at Bryn Mawr College, Pennsylvania, in June 1905, James had recently used Quintilian's formula in his own discussion of the same subject: 'A virtual consensus of the educated, of any gathered group, in regard to the *speech* that, among the idioms and articulations of the globe, they profess to make use of, may well strike us, in a given case, as a natural, an inevitable assumption'; such a consensus is an 'indispensable preliminary' to 'any process of training', and without it 'the educative process cannot be thought of as at all even beginning' (*HJC* 43).

556 **Lady Barb**: This familiarly abbreviated form of the title character's name is much more frequent in the revised *NYE* text than in the first edition.

557 **I have placed this composition (1888) at the top of my list, [...] consistently giving it precedence by reason of its greatest length**: James misdates 'Lady Barbarina', which in fact first appeared (as 'Lady Barberina') in two numbers of the *Century Magazine*, May–July 1884, and was collected in *Tales of Three Cities* (1884). He was mostly consistent in placing longer stories first in the contents lists of *NYE* volumes (see note 490).

558 **the most primitive logic**: As James proceeds to explain, the 'logic' is that of inversion. He sketched the idea for 'Lady Barbarina' on 8 April 1883 in a letter to his publisher James R. Osgood, describing it as 'another "international episode"; i.e. a story of the same length & character as "Daisy Miller", the "Internat. Episode" & the "Siege of London." [...] The name to be "Lady Barberina." I have treated (more or less) in these other things the subject of the American girl who marries (or concerning whom it is a question whether she w̲i̲l̲l̲ marry) a British aristocrat. This one reverses the situation & presents a young m̲a̲l̲e̲ American who conceives the design of marrying a daughter of the aristocracy' (*CLHJ 1883–1884* 1:83). James transcribed passages from this letter into his notebook, and developed the subject in a further entry dated 17 May 1883 (*CN* 20, 21–2).

559 **a relation of intermarrying; [...] took always the same turn**: Three decades before the Preface, James had noted that, in Laurence Oliphant's satirical novel *The Tender Recollections of Irene Macgillicuddy* (1878), 'the eagerness and energy displayed by marriageable maidens in what is vulgarly called "hooking" a member of the English aristocracy' was presented as 'the great feature of New York fashion': 'The desire to connect itself by matrimony with the British nobility would seem to be, in the author's eyes, the leading characteristic of the New York "great world"' (*LC1* 1192). For the unidirectional character of this trend, see James's notebook entry of 26 November 1892 on the 'endless spectacle [...] of the Anglo-American marriage. The singular—the intensely significant circumstance of its being all on one side—or rather in one form; always the union of the male Briton to the female American—*never* the other way round' (*CN* 73).

560 **to forge the very documents**: In 1902, James had used the same figure to account for Balzac's acquisition of more 'multifarious knowledge' than direct experience could account for: 'Since history proceeds by documents,

he constructed, as he needed them, the documents too—fictive sources that imitated the actual to the life' ('HdB' xxxvii).

561 **appealed to so little in the name of *shades?***: Characters in several stories collected in *NYE* XIV are noted as lacking 'a perception of shades' – as the narrator of 'Lady Barbarina' says of the heroine's sister Agatha, who makes no objection to the strong American accent of the westerner Herman Longstraw. Longstraw himself resembles Lady Agatha in not being 'given to noticing shades of manner' (Ch. 5; *NYE* XIV, 112, 111). In the second half of 'An International Episode', the visiting American Mrs Westgate tells Percy Beaumont that it must be '"a great advantage"' for the English to be naively accepting of differences of social rank: '"I suppose that if I myself had a little more naïveté—of your blessed national lack of any approach to a sense for shades—I should enjoy it more. I should be content to sit on a chair in the Park and see the people pass, to be told that this is the Duchess of Suffolk and that the Lord Chamberlain, and that I must be thankful for the privilege of beholding them"' (Ch. 5; *NYE* XIV, 356); the parenthesis in the first sentence quoted here is an insertion in the *NYE* text and does not appear in earlier editions. In the eighth letter of 'A Bundle of Letters' (1879), the German academic Dr Rudolph Staub writes from his Parisian lodgings about 'two young Englanders [...] who hate all the Americans in a lump, making between them none of the distinctions and favourable comparisons which they insist upon, and for which, as involving the recognition of shades and a certain play of the critical sense, the still quite primitive insular understanding is wholly inapt' (*NYE* XIV, 530–1); everything quoted here after 'which they insist upon' is an insertion in the *NYE* text.

562 **in New York, in Washington, at Newport, [...] in London or in Rome**: These places – all international centres of commerce, government, tourism and leisured cosmopolitanism – are settings for several of James's stories of the late 1870s and early 1880s: 'An International Episode' is set in New York City, at Newport, Rhode Island and in London; 'Pandora' partly in Washington, DC; 'Daisy Miller' partly in Rome. In Chapter 5 of 'Lady Barbarina', there is a debate about which places Lady Barbarina ought to see in America. Jackson Lemon's proposal to show her Washington and Albany encounters 'cries of horror' from his friends, who suggest instead New York City, Boston, Niagara Falls and Newport. Barbarina is unenthusiastic: 'She was tired of their eternal Newport; she had heard of it a thousand times and felt already as if she had lived there half her life; she was sure moreover that she should hate the awful little place' (*NYE* XIV, 109).

563 **brave precursors, [...] adventurous skirmishers and *éclaireurs*:** A 'skirmisher' is 'One of a number of soldiers taking part in a skirmish or acting in loose order apart from the main body of an army or battalion' (*OED*); the French word *éclaireur* means a military scout. These terms occur together in the first chapter of *William Wetmore Story and His Friends* (1903), titled 'The Precursors', which figures the previous generation of American travellers in Europe as the advance guard of an exploratory force: 'the light skirmishers, the *éclaireurs*, who have gone before' (*WWS* I:3). See also note 414.

564 **a "primitive" master of high finish**: In art history, the label 'primitive' is applied to painters of the late medieval and early Renaissance periods, e.g. the Italian Giotto di Bondone (c. 1267–1337). In his early travel essay 'A Chain of Cities' (1874), James wrote on the frescoes attributed to Giotto and his contemporaries in the Basilica of Saint Francis in Assisi: 'the terribly distinct little faces which these artists loved to draw stare at you with a solemn formalism'. In this piece he praises Giotto's unsurpassed 'art of making an attitude unmistakable': 'Meagre, primitive, undeveloped as he is, he seems immeasurably strong' (*TS* 215–16). For artistic 'finish', see note 271.

565 **such anecdotes [...] as "Pandora," as "Fordham Castle," as "Flickerbridge," as "Miss Gunton of Poughkeepsie,"**: James discusses 'Pandora' (1884), 'Fordham Castle' (1904) and 'Flickerbridge' (1902) in the Preface to *NYE* XVIII. 'Miss Gunton of Poughkeepsie' (1900) is collected in *NYE* XVI; it is not discussed in any Preface.

566 **thanks to some of its associations**: James probably refers to the local 'associations' of 'The Pension Beaurepas': the story is set in the French-speaking Swiss city of Geneva, where he had spent several months with his family in 1859–60. He was enrolled first as a pupil at the Institution Rochette, a preparatory school for undergraduate study in scientific and technical disciplines; then at the Académie, which later became the University of Geneva. The narrator of the story, though a good deal older than the 16-year-old James, is likewise a young American attending lectures at the Académie. James recalls this period in the first chapter of *Notes of a Son and Brother* (1914); see also the pages on Geneva in his travel essay 'Swiss Notes' (1872) (*CTW*2 626–8). In 1886, he wrote to Henrietta Reubell about an earlier period of residence in the city in the summer of 1855 – subsequently recorded in Chapter 21 of *A Small Boy and Others* (1913) – during which he had been seriously unwell with malaria. Reubell herself

had lately been 'ill at Geneva', and James commented: 'I like the place—it is an old friend—a childhood's friend of mine—& ages ago I too was on my back there—tucked up with chills & fever in a certaine [*sic*] out of the way Campagne Gerebsoff, which seems very dim & romantic to me as I look back upon it' (12 November [1886]; *CLHJ 1884-1886* 2:225). For the Tennysonian allusion in this sentence of the Preface ('the tender grace of a day that is dead'), see note 247.

567 **the vast diluvian occidental presence in Europe**: James's periphrasis refers to American tourists in Europe as a flood ('diluvian': 'Of or pertaining to a deluge' (*OED*)) proceeding from the western world (or Occident). Many of his European travel essays resentfully notice the presence of other Americans: in 'Lichfield and Warwick' (1872), for example, Haddon Hall in Derbyshire is said to lie 'in a region infested, I was about to write, by Americans' (*TS* 25). In 'The Autumn in Florence' (1874), James enjoys the lull before the tourist season proper: 'Meanwhile, it is pleasant enough, for persons fond of the Florentine flavor, that the opera is indifferent, that the Americans have not all arrived, and that the weather has a monotonous, overcast softness' (*TS* 269-70); this sentence was substantially revised for *Italian Hours* (1909), shortly after James finished work on the *NYE*, and amongst other changes he added a clause ominously suggestive of an increase in traffic: 'that the Americans haven't all arrived, however many may be on their way' (*CTW2* 533).

568 **the lately-developed and so flourishing "southern route" from New York and Boston**: James appears to refer to the transatlantic steamship route from North America to Gibraltar and the Mediterranean ports of Genoa and Naples, as distinct from the routes that ran via Queenstown (Cobh) to Liverpool or via Southampton to the North Sea and the Baltic. According to a Special Consular Report of the American Department of State's Bureau of Statistics, this southern route ('now popularly known as the Mediterranean service') was introduced in the winter of 1891-2 by the North German Lloyd Steamship Company, which began to operate steamships between New York, Gibraltar and Genoa. The instant success of the venture led a commercial rival, the Hamburg-American Packet Company, first to put its own steamers on the same route, and then to strike a deal with North German Lloyd to manage the route jointly; they advertised '"the Genoa-New York line"' as offering '"the best opportunity for returning home to American travelers staying in Italy, the south of France, Switzerland, and on the Riviera"'. As of July 1894, the British

Cunard Steamship Company, which had hitherto operated between Liverpool, Boston and New York, was reported as proposing 'to employ its two largest steamers in the Mediterranean service the coming autumn and winter' (*Highways of Commerce: The Ocean Lines, Railways, Canals, and Other Trade Routes of Foreign Countries*, Special Consular Reports, Vol. XII (Washington, DC: Government Printing Office, 1895), pp. 368–9). On a recent trip to Italy in May–June 1907, James had attributed a marked increase in American tourism to this cause: 'The famous "Southern Route"—dire invention—now disgorges there its hundreds of thousands, from January to August (or rather *to* January again;) all other elements yield to the flood, & the effect, the impression, beggars description' (to Owen Wister, 28 August 1907; Owen Wister Papers, 1829–1966, Manuscript Division, Library of Congress, Washington, DC. General Correspondence, 1875–1936. Box 25). He wrote to Edith Wharton after the same journey of 'the compatriot-poisoned Italy (of early summer, drenched by the "Southern route")' (11 [and 12] August 1907; HJEW 70).

569 **hangs fire**: To 'hang fire' means '(of a firearm) to be slow in communicating the fire through the vent to the charge; (hence) *figurative* to hesitate or be slow in acting' (*OED*, 'hang'). James frequently used this idiom to describe the significant delay between a question or challenge and its answer. In 'The Jolly Corner' (composed in August 1906 but not published until two years later), Spencer Brydon asks himself whether he had not in fact closed a particular door in his old New York townhouse, which he now sees to be open – and which in that case must have been opened by his spectral alter ego: 'It was as sharp, the question, as a knife in his side, but the answer hung fire still and seemed to lose itself in the vague darkness' (Ch. 2; *NYE* XVII, 474). Shari Goldberg analyses the metaphorical implications of this figure of speech and cites instances in James and contemporary writers in 'Hanging Fire, or A New Ontology for *Poynton*', *Henry James Review* 37.1 (2016), 51–63.

570 **"registers" disposed in the vestibules of bankers, the reading-rooms of hotels and "exchanges," open on the most conspicuous table of visited palace and castle**: American travellers on the Continent inscribed their names publicly on various occasions – when registering with a local banker to draw money or collect mail, checking in and out of their hotels, or signing the visitors' books of historic houses. Such records constituted sources of information for other visitors as to which compatriots were currently present in a given place. Thus, for example, in Chapter 2 of

The Reverberator (1888) the Dossons consult 'the lists of Americans who "registered" at the bankers' and at Galignani's' (*NYE* XIII, 26). Galignani's Library was a popular Parisian reading room and circulating library where visitors could obtain English-language books and newspapers; it also published *Galignani's Messenger*, a newspaper carrying 'a daily list of English and American visitors in Paris, and another on Fridays of English and American visitors to the chief cities of Europe' (Karl Baedeker, *Paris and Environs*, 9th edn (Leipzig: Karl Baedeker, 1888), p. 40). Anticipating the Preface's focus on the ethnicity of American travellers' names (see note 574), *The Reverberator* draws attention to the register entries of a family whose surname suggests a German-Jewish heritage: 'Mr. and Mrs. D. S. Rosenheim and Miss Cora Rosenheim and Master Samuel Rosenheim' (*NYE* XIII, 27) (see Rudolf Glanz, 'German-Jewish Names in America', *Jewish Social Studies* 23.3 (1961), 143–69).

571 **conundrums and "stunts."**: In the present context, the most relevant senses of the colloquial word 'stunt' are 'A prescribed item in an athletic competition or display, an "event"; a feat undertaken as a defiance in response to a challenge' and 'A stint, a task, an exercise. Originally *U.S.*' (*OED*). For the latter sense, *OED* cites an instance from 1880 referring to a classroom copying exercise: 'used as a "stunt" for our childhood in the copy books'.

572 **passenger-lists**: Souvenir lists of the names of passengers travelling on ocean liners were commonly distributed on board. James had most recently made the transatlantic crossing on the SS *Kaiser Wilhelm* (North German Lloyd line) from Southampton to New York in August 1904, returning on the SS *Ivernia* (Cunard line) from Boston to Liverpool in July 1905.

573 **little books have their fates**: This formula derives from a line of the second-century CE Roman poet Terence (Terentianus Maurus): 'Pro captu lectoris habent sua fata libelli' ('Books have their destiny according to the capabilities of the reader'). James follows a common practice in abbreviating Terence's line to its last four words and treating them as an independent statement. As a British journal article of 1879 observes, 'it might be safely wagered that nine people out of ten [...] do not know who was the author of Habent sua fata libelli, nor could repeat the first half of the line' ('The Fortunes of Quotations', *The Saturday Review of Politics, Literature, Science, and Art* 47 (7 June 1879), 700).

574 **alien syllables and sounds, [...] the stony slabs of Nineveh**: The city of Nineveh on the Tigris River in Upper Mesopotamia was the capital of the ancient Assyrian Empire. Its ruins were first excavated in the 1840s and 1850s by the British archaeologist Austen Henry Layard (1817–94) and others, to great public interest. James knew Layard and his wife from the cosmopolitan social circles he frequented in Venice in the 1880s and 1890s (see Rosella Mamoli Zorzi, '"Figures Reflected in the Clear Lagoon": Henry James, Daniel and Ariana Curtis, and Isabella Stewart Gardner', in McCauley et al. (eds.), *Gondola Days*, pp. 129–54; 136). In the present passage he seems to refer to Assyrian inscriptions in the cuneiform writing system, whose wedge-shaped marks were cut into stone or impressed on clay; archaeologists discovered thousands of such inscriptions at Nineveh on sculptures, bas reliefs and clay tablets. The Preface's comments on the American passengers' names recall anxieties about mass immigration to America and its possible effects on national identity which James had recently voiced in 'New England: An Autumn Impression' (1905): 'a haunting wonder as to what might be becoming of us all, "typically," ethnically, and thereby physiognomically, linguistically, *personally*, was always in order' (*AS* 64). He consistently describes immigrants as 'aliens' in *The American Scene* (1907).

575 **I may not here attempt to weigh the question of what these exotic symbols positively represent**: James had offered a comparable disclaimer in 'New York and the Hudson: A Spring Impression' (1906), remarking that the 'facts' of American immigration 'loom, before the understanding, in too large a mass for a mere mouthful: it is as if the syllables were too numerous to make a legible word. The *il*legible word, accordingly, the great inscrutable answer to questions, hangs in the vast American sky [...] as something fantastic and *abracadabrant*, belonging to no known language' (*AS* 121–2).

576 **no [...] Daisy Miller to bridge the chasm; no [...] Francie Dosson or Pandora Day to dance before one across the wavering plank**: As in the Preface to *NYE* XIII (p. 152), James here groups together the heroines of his international stories 'Daisy Miller' (1878), *The Reverberator* (1888) and 'Pandora' (1884). In 'Lady Barbarina', we are told that Lady Marmaduke, an American who has married into English society and an enthusiastic promoter of other transatlantic unions, 'wished to add an arch or two to the bridge on which she had effected her transit from America [...]. This bridge, as yet a somewhat sketchy and rickety structure, she

saw—in the future—boldly stretch from one solid pier to another' (Ch. 2; *NYE* XIV, 30) (see also note 554). In 'The Siege of London', a similar figure expresses disapproval of such attempted transits: appealed to by the American divorcee Mrs Headway to help her enter respectable European society, Littlemore resists out of a belief that 'it was much better for society that the divisions, the categories, the differing values, should be kept clear. He didn't believe in bridging the chasms, in muddling the kinds' (Ch. 2; *NYE* XIV, 176). The phrase echoed by this sentence of the Preface – 'bridging the chasms' – is part of a revision in the *NYE* text of the story; in the first book edition, Littlemore believes that women with questionable pasts 'should not endeavor, as the French say, to *mêler les genres* [mix or confound the categories]' (*CE* XI, 36). The 'wavering plank' of the Preface recalls the gang-way used by transatlantic passengers to cross between an ocean liner and the dock: see the opening scene of 'Pandora', for example, where the German diplomat Vogelstein waits for his ship to sail from Southampton and watches 'as the American passengers crossed the plank' (*NYE* XVIII, 97).

577 **one evening early in the autumn of 1877, […] a performance at the Théâtre Français. […] "Le Demi-Monde" of the younger Dumas, a masterpiece which I had not heard for the first time**: James spent just over three months in Paris in the autumn of 1877 (9 September–18 December), and Leon Edel places the performance referred to in this sentence of the Preface in September (*Henry James: The Conquest of London*, pp. 295–6). *Le Demi-monde* (1855) is a prose comedy in five acts by Alexandre Dumas *fils*; for the Théâtre Français and its resident company, see note 261. 'The Siege of London' opens in the same theatre during a September performance of another modern French play, the verse comedy *L'Aventurière* by Émile Augier (1820–89), and the narrator observes at the end of the first chapter that Rupert Waterville, who is in the audience on this occasion, 'had seen "Le Demi-Monde" a few nights before' (*NYE* XIV, 166). In 'Occasional Paris' (1883), a travel essay first published in January 1878 as 'Paris Revisited', James says that he has seen Dumas's play 'several times' (*CTW*2 732–3).

578 **I could less than ever swallow it, Olivier de Jalin's denunciation of Madame d'Ange**: The plot of *Le Demi-monde* concerns the efforts of the Baronne Suzanne d'Ange, a kept woman who passes for a widow, to repair her social position by marrying the naive young army officer Raymond de Nanjac; to do this she must conceal her past affairs from her fiancé, who

happens to be the friend of one of her former lovers, Olivier de Jalin. Olivier determines to save Raymond from this marriage but is unwilling to denounce Suzanne directly by revealing his own affair with her. After two thwarted attempts to expose her compromised past, in the final act Olivier tricks her by pretending that he has killed Raymond in a duel, declaring his love for her and proposing that they run away together. Suzanne accepts; Raymond at once enters, having overheard the conversation as Olivier intended, and rejects her. James notes in 'Occasional Paris': 'In seeing the *Demi-Monde* again I was more than ever struck with the oddity of its morality and with the way that the ideal of fine conduct differs in different nations.' Olivier 'tells a thumping lie' to achieve his goal and has already given Suzanne 'a push along the downward path' by taking her as a lover in the past: 'But it is curious how little this is held by the author to disqualify him from fighting the battle in which she is so much the weaker combatant. An English-speaking audience is more "moral" than a French, more easily scandalised; and yet it is a singular fact that if the *Demi-Monde* were represented before an English-speaking audience, its sympathies would certainly not go with M. de Jalin. It would pronounce him rather a coward' (*CTW*2 733, 734).

579 **the very perfection with which the part was rendered in those years by Delaunay (just as Croizette was pure perfection as Suzanne)**: *Le Demi-monde* entered the repertoire of the Comédie-Française in 1874, with Louis-Arsène Delaunay (1826–1903) and Sophie Alexandrine Croizette (1847–1901) in the roles of Olivier de Jalin and Suzanne d'Ange. Delaunay and Croizette were both *sociétaires*, or permanent company members of the Comédie-Français; they were performing these roles when James saw *Le Demi-monde* 'admirably well played' in 1877 ('Occasional Paris'; *CTW*2 733).

580 **the prodigious *morality* of [...] Dumas**: James wrote to W. E. Henley in October 1878: 'I'm sorry you dislike Dumas fils so much—or rather so exclusively. In one way—as a "moralist"—he is detestable & a childish charlatan; but as a dramatist, I think he understands the business like none of the others' ([11, 18 or 25 October 1878]; *CLHJ 1878–1880* 1:13). In his 1896 essay 'On the Death of Dumas the Younger', James observed that although Dumas had inherited 'the passions' as a dramatic subject from the romantic generation of Victor Hugo, 'he was to study them not for the pleasure, the picture, the poetry they offer' but 'from the point of view of the idea of duty and conduct': 'He was, in short, to become, on the basis

of a determined observation of the manners of his time and country, a professional moralist' (*CWAD2* 428).

581 **an Olivier of our race, a different Olivier altogether**: The American characters in 'The Siege of London' are aware of Dumas's play as a precedent for their own situation. As Waterville points out in Chapter 9, with regard to his friend Littlemore's knowledge of Mrs Headway's compromising past: '"You're in the position of Olivier de Jalin in 'Le Demi-Monde'."' Neither man wants to be in that position, and Waterville resists Littlemore's suggestion that it is he who should inform Lord Demesne about Mrs Headway: '"Play the part of Olivier de Jalin? Oh I can't. I'm not Olivier"' (*NYE* XIV, 259). In a retrospective notebook entry dated 24 November 1893, James refers to 'my little tale of *The Siege of London*; with [...] its vague rappel [recall] of the "situation" in Dumas's *Demi-Monde*—the situation of a man of honour who has to testify about the antecedents of a woman he has known in the past' (*CN* 72).

582 **a real gentleman's connexion "at all at all" with such a business**: The reduplication of 'at all' for emphasis is characteristic of Irish English speech; 'In negative or conditional use', as here, it means 'in any way; to any degree; in the least; whatsoever' (*OED*).

583 **A few months ago, one evening, I found myself withdrawing from the very temple and the supposedly sacred rites before these latter were a third over**: James refers to time spent in Paris in the spring or summer of 1907. He was Edith Wharton's guest there from 7 March to 11 May 1907 (with an absence of three weeks in March–April for a motor-tour through the south of France), and he stopped again in Paris on his way back from Italy in early July (see *HJEW* 67–72). The Preface does not identify the play that was being performed when James walked out of the Théatre Française, but it could have been *Le Demi-monde*: there was only one performance of Dumas's play during the spring and early summer of that year, on the evening of 19 April 1907, and James was in Paris on that date (see the daily register of performances in Alexandre Joannidès, *La Comédie-française 1907* (Paris: Plon-Nourrit et Cie, 1908), p. 94).

584 **my admirable friend the late Leslie Stephen, then editor of *The Cornhill Magazine***: As James recalled in 1915 while making notes for a commemorative essay on the Boston publisher James T. Fields and his wife Annie Adams Fields, he had been introduced to the English editor and literary critic Leslie Stephen (1832–1904) at the Fieldses' home in 1863: 'first

477

moment of what was to be such a relation' (*CN* 537). The two men were reintroduced by Charles Eliot Norton when James came to London in 1869, and James would become a friend of the Stephen family. As editor of the *Cornhill Magazine*, Stephen published three stories which James would collect in the *NYE* ('Daisy Miller', 'An International Episode' and 'The Siege of London') and one novel which he would not (*Washington Square*). Stephen left the *Cornhill* in 1882 to become the founding editor of the *Dictionary of National Biography*.

585 **drove the pen**: For this idiom, which likens a professional writer's work to that of a ploughman or a drover of livestock, compare James's 1883 essay 'Anthony Trollope': 'He drove his pen as steadily on the tumbling ocean as in Montague Square' (*LC1* 1332).

586 **a small street that opened [...] into Piccadilly and a view of the Green Park**: Bolton Street runs northwards off Piccadilly in the West End of London. The Green Park is one of the Royal Parks of London, spaces owned by the Crown but open to the public since the mid nineteenth century; it is bounded by Piccadilly on its north side and by St James's Park to the south and east. James rented rooms in Bolton Street when he moved to London from Paris in December 1876, and he stayed there for nearly ten years, until March 1886. In a retrospective notebook entry made on 25 November 1881 during a visit to America, he wrote of his 'ferocious homesickness' for the London life that centred on those rooms: 'I took a lodging at 3 Bolton St., Piccadilly; and there I have remained till today—there I have left my few earthly possessions, to await my return. I have *lived* much there, felt much, thought much, learned much, produced much; the little shabby furnished apartment ought to be sacred to me' (*CN* 217).

587 **Thackeray's Curzon Street, [...] Becky Sharp, or rather Mrs. Rawdon Crawley, [...] the voice, the thousand voices, of Dickens**: Curzon Street in Mayfair runs roughly parallel to Piccadilly and intersects with the northern end of Bolton Street. In Chapter 36 of William Makepeace Thackeray's novel *Vanity Fair* (1848), Becky Sharp and her husband Rawdon Crawley set up home in 'a very small comfortable house in Curzon Street' (*The Works of William Makepeace Thackeray*, p. 348). In his essay 'London' (1888), James had noted that it was 'during the strictly social desolation of Christmas week, when the country-houses are filled at the expense of the metropolis [...] that I am most haunted with the London of Dickens, feel most as if it were still recoverable, still exhaling its queerness in patches perceptible to the appreciative' (*ELE* 32). He would identify one

such Dickensian patch of the city in his unfinished memoir *The Middle Years* (1917), recalling that Craven Street on the south side of the Strand, as he had experienced it in 1869, 'absolutely reeked, to my fond fancy, with associations born of the particular ancient piety embodied in one's private altar to Dickens'; 'the whole Dickens procession marched up and down, the whole Dickens world looked out of its queer, quite sinister windows' (*Auto* 604–5).

588 **A "great house," forming the southwest corner of Piccadilly […] gloomed, in dusky brick, as the extent of my view**: This was Bath House at 82 Piccadilly, built in 1821 by the banker and art collector Alexander Baring, 1st Baron Ashburton (1773–1848), on the site of a mansion acquired from the Pulteney family (see Arthur Irwin Dasent, *Piccadilly in Three Centuries, with Some Account of Berkeley Square and the Haymarket* (London: Macmillan and Co., 1920), pp. 71–3); it was demolished in the twentieth century. While James was living in Bolton Street, Bath House was occupied by Alexander Baring, 4th Baron Ashburton (1835–89). James wrote to his mother on 21 December 1877, just returned from a stay in Paris and glad to get 'back to regular work. Here I am then in my foggy little sitting room again, with my smutty fire on one side & Lord Ashburton's black bricks, seen through the window & muffled in a sort of livid sleet, on the other. Strange as it may seem, however, I enjoy these things, & am in very comfortable spirits' (*CLHJ 1876–1878* 2:6).

589 **the most voluminous of curtains […] the proportionately ample interacts of the mightiest of dramas**: James's figuration of writing in his Bolton Street lodging repeats the theatrical setting and rhythms of the first chapter of 'The Siege of London'. The story opens in the first interval of a performance at the Théâtre Français; the Preface's word 'interact' – from the French *entr'acte* – means 'The interval between two acts of a play' (*OED*). The immediate focus is on the curtain of the stage: 'That solemn piece of upholstery the curtain of the Comédie Française had fallen upon the first act of the piece'; Waterville scans the boxes with an opera-glass from his seat in the stalls, while his friend Littlemore 'star[es] with a bored expression at the new-looking curtain' (*NYE* XIV, 145, 146). They catch sight of Mrs Headway in the audience and discuss her questionable respectability. Littlemore is hesitant about meeting her again: 'By this time the *entr'acte* was at an end and the curtain going up' (*NYE* XIV, 148). In the next interval, the two men move to the public foyer, where they can hear the street noise which the next sentence of the Preface will figure as back-stage

noise, 'the vague rumble of shifted scenery': 'The windows were open [...]; a murmur of voices seemed to come up, and even in the foyer one heard the slow click of the horses and the rumble of the crookedly-driven fiacres on the hard smooth street-surface' (*NYE* XIV, 150–1). Here they encounter Mrs Headway, and their conversation with her and subsequent discussion of her case occupy the second interval, ending 'as the curtain rose' (*NYE* XIV, 161).

590 **the late Theodore Child [...] an Anglo-American periodical called *The Parisian***: Theodore E. Child (1846–92) was probably the 'very pleasant young Englishman' whom James encountered at Étretat in Normandy in the summer of 1876 and met again in Paris later that year (to MWJ, [24 December 1876]; *CLHJ 1876–1878* 1:14). Child was then a journalist for the *Pall Mall Gazette*; in 1877, he became Paris correspondent of the London *Telegraph*, and later worked as the Paris agent for the American publishers Harper and Brothers. He maintained a friendly literary correspondence with James for the rest of his life. 'A Bundle of Letters' appeared on 18 December 1879 in *The Parisian*, the bi-weekly English-language newspaper which Child edited from 1879 to 1884. Child died of cholera on 2 November 1892 at Isfahan in Persia (modern Iran) while travelling on a journalistic assignment for the Harpers.

591 **a small sharply-resonant street off the Rue de la Paix**: James refers to the former rue Neuve-Saint-Augustin (renamed rue Boffrand in 1864 and rue Daunou in 1881), which runs between rue Louis-le-Grand and boulevard de Capucines in the IIe arrondissement (Hillairet, *Dictionnaire historique des rues de Paris*, vol. I, p. 415); it is intersected at its mid-point by rue de la Paix. James was staying at the Hôtel de Choiseul et d'Égypte, which a contemporary travel guide describes as 'comparatively moderate' in its rates (Karl Baedeker, *Paris and its Environs*, 6th edn (Leipzig: Karl Baedeker, 1878), p. 7). In the next sentence of the Preface, James refers to the hotel's 'droll combinational, almost cosmic sign': the fun of the combination was presumably its yoking of large and small places, all of Egypt and the French village of Choiseul in the Haute-Marne *département*. The same effect is properly 'cosmic' in *The Reverberator* (1888), where the Dossons are staying at the fictional 'Hôtel de l'Univers et de Cheltenham' – just around the corner on rue de la Paix.

592 **A snowstorm of a violence rare in Paris [...] written in a single long session and, the temperature apart, at a "heat."**: An exceptionally heavy snowstorm swept France in early December 1879, hitting Paris during the

night of 4 December and paralysing the city. On 6 December, the local correspondent of the London *Standard* reported: 'The aspect of Paris at the present moment is more like a Siberian town than the gay capital of France. Such a sudden and copious fall of snow is not within the memory of those born in the present century' ('Paris Under the Snow', *Standard*, 6 December 1879, 5). A temperature of −20°C was recorded on 10 December ('Events in France', *Standard*, 10 December 1879, 3). The idiom 'at a heat' occurs with a helpful gloss in 'The Tone of Time' (1900), where a portrait-painter completes an especially compelling commission 'at a heat; rapidly, directly, at all events, for the sort of thing it proved to be' (*The Better Sort*, p. 55).

593 **Its companion-piece, "The Point of View,"**: 'A Bundle of Letters' and 'The Point of View' (1882) are companions in various ways: both stories are cast in epistolary form, and both register impressions of foreign travel; they also share a character, the American aesthete Louis Leverett.

594 **a far-away Washington spring. [...] my first glimpse of that interesting city, [...] a visit repeated the following year**: In fact, James first visited Washington, DC not in the spring of 1881, as he says here, but in January 1882, having arrived in America the previous November. He intended to remain in Washington 'till the middle of February' (to Isabella Stewart Gardner, 23 January [1882]; *CLHJ 1880–1883* 2:90), but his stay was cut short by news that his mother was seriously ill: a telegram summoned him back to Cambridge, Massachusetts on 29 January. Mary Walsh James died the same day, before he could get home. James returned to London in May 1882, but he would embark for America again in December 1882 on learning that his father was dying; once again he missed the death, and on this occasion the funeral also. He remained in America until August 1883, and during that long stay he spent an April week in Washington – the repeat visit referred to in the Preface.

595 **impressions; [...] a quite proportionately smaller number of neat and complacent conclusions**: James wrote from Washington to Isabella Stewart Gardner: 'I have been nearly three weeks & I ought to have a good many impressions. I have indeed a certain number, but when I write to you these generalities somehow grow vague & pointless. Everything sifts itself down to <u>one</u> impression—which I leave to your delicate imagination' (23 January [1882]; *CLHJ 1880–1883* 2:89). Earlier in the same visit, James wrote to the British diplomat Sir John Forbes Clark (1821–1910): 'I should like to put America into a nutshell for you; but like Carlyle's Mirabeau,

it has "swallowed all formulas"' (8 January [1882]; *CLHJ 1880–1883* 2:66). The reference is to *The French Revolution: A History* (1837), Volume I, Book 4, Chapter 4, where Carlyle quotes the claim of Honoré-Gabriel Riqueti, comte de Mirabeau (1749–91), an influential member of the National Assembly in the early phases of the French Revolution, that he had '"made away with (*humé*, swallowed, snuffed-up) all *Formulas*"'; Carlyle notes that this made Mirabeau an apt 'spokesman' for 'a Nation bent to do the same. For is it not precisely the struggle of France also to cast off despotism; to make away with *her* old formulas,—having found them naught, worn out, far from the reality? She will make away with *such* formulas;—and even go *bare*, if need be, till she have found new ones' (*The French Revolution: A History*, ed. David R. Sorensen, Brent E. Kinser and Mark Engel (Oxford: Oxford University Press, 2019), p. 119).

596 **his own (always so quickly stale) experience, […] that of conceivable fellow mortals, which might be mysteriously and refreshingly different**: James would later remark in Chapter 13 of *A Small Boy* that as a child he was 'constantly eager to exchange my lot for that of somebody else, on the assumed certainty of gaining by the bargain', supposing other people to possess 'a certain sort of richer consciousness' than his own: 'They were so *other*—that was what I felt; and to *be* other, other almost anyhow, seemed as good as the probable taste of the bright compound wistfully watched in the confectioner's window' (*Aut* 109–10).

597 **I had kept the thread (through a return to London and a return again thence) and […] brought my small scheme to a climax on the spot**: For the actual chronology of James's two visits to Washington in 1882 and 1883, see note 594. He cannot have finished 'The Point of View' 'on the spot' during his second visit, in April 1883, since – as he correctly notes in the next sentence of the Preface – the story had already been published by then.

598 **I recently had the chance to "look up," for old sake's sake, that momentary seat of the good-humoured satiric muse**: James made two visits to Washington during his American tour of 1904–5, in January and April–May 1905; his essay 'Washington' (1906), composed during the early stages of work on the *NYE*, records his latest impressions of the city. The colloquial phrase 'look up' means 'To visit or contact (a person), esp. for the first time or after loss of contact'; to do something 'for old sake's sake' is to do it 'for the sake of old friendship' (*OED*, 'look', 'sake'). In classical mythology and literary theory, there is no Muse of satire; the genre is presided over instead by the god Momus.

599 **the lost presence, the obliterated scene, translated itself for me at last into terms of almost more than earthly beauty and poetry**: James had recently experienced a comparable translation on visits to the old family home at Ashburton Place, Boston – first finding the house 'rather exposed and undermined' by demolition and new development in the vicinity of the Massachusetts State House, and then returning just 'a month later' to find that it too had been knocked down ('Boston' (1906); *AS* 228, 229). He wrote of 'the vanished objects' he had missed on his first visit, 'a scant but adequate cluster of "nooks," of such odds and ends as parochial schemes of improvement sweep away, positively overgrown, within one's own spirit, by a wealth of legend. There was at least the gain, at any rate, that one was now going to be free to picture them, to embroider them, at one's ease—to tangle them up in retrospect and make the real romantic claim for them' (*AS* 228).

600 **smiling, shuffling, procrastinating persons of colour, [...] the "old South."**: James had written to the New York journalist Edwin Laurence Godkin (1831–1902), founding editor of the *Nation*, on 22 January 1882: 'Washington is too much of a village—though the absence of trade & stockbroking is delightful. It is too niggerish, & that has rubbed off on some of the whites' (*CLHJ 1880–1883* 2:82). He had recently noted the historical persistence of 'the "old South"' in his American travel essays 'Richmond, Virginia' (1906) and 'Charleston' (1907), commenting there on the legacies of slavery and the American Civil War – the 'deluge of blood and fire and tears' referred to in the next sentence of the Preface – and on the social presence of Black people (*AS* 365–421). See also the passage under the page-heading 'The Negro as Servant' in the 'Florida' chapter of *The American Scene* (*AS* 422–4).

601 **I could scarcely have said where the bricks *had* stood**: James told Godkin on 1 January 1882 that Henry Adams had taken rooms for him at 720 Fifteenth Street, Washington (*CLHJ 1880–1883* 2:59). His letters from this trip are consistently dated from a nearby address, 723 Fifteenth Street – possibly the premises at that date of the Metropolitan Club, whose letter-paper he often uses and which according to Edel was 'in the same street' as his lodging (*Henry James: The Conquest of London*, p. 458).

602 **I could turn on my finger the magic ring**: Magic rings that grant the wearer a wish are common in German folk-tales: e.g. in 'The Drummer' ('Der Trommler'), one of the *Kinder- und Hausmärchen* of the Brothers Grimm, a princess has a wishing-ring that works when she turns it on her finger.

603 **An old-world nook of one's youth [...] a scrap of the lakeside fringe of ancient Geneva**: The Pâquis district of Geneva lies between the railway station and the shore of Lac Leman. For James's residence in the city 1859-60, see note 566.

604 **swept out of its cupboards, shaken out of its curtains, thumped out of its mattresses**: James's appreciation of the historical residue of 'pre-revolutionary "Europe"' picks up a figure from the first letter of 'A Bundle of Letters', where the young American traveller Miranda Hope tells her mother that she has encountered in Europe 'a great many people—and a great many things too' that have made her 'want to give them a good shaking': 'I should like to shake the starch out of some of them and the dust out of the others' (*NYE* XIV, 480).

PREFACE to *The Lesson of the Master, The Death of the Lion, The Next Time and Other Tales* (NYE XV)

605 **the composition at the head of my list—which owes that precedence to its greatest length and earliest date**: 'The Lesson of the Master' is the longest of the five stories in *NYE* XV (occupying more than a quarter of the volume), as well as the earliest. It first appeared in the July and August 1888 issues of the *Universal Review*.

606 **old Kensington days**: The stories collected in *NYE* XV were written in the late 1880s and early-mid 1890s, while James was living at 34 De Vere Gardens, Kensington (see note 238).

607 **a Sunday afternoon early in the spring of that year: a young friend, [...] a young friend of his own [...] a periodical about to take birth, [...] the happiest omens**: The 'young friend' was Henry Harland, *his* young friend was Aubrey Beardsley, and the periodical was *The Yellow Book* (see notes 608, 610 and 612). According to Harland, it was '"At exactly half-past one"' on 2 January 1894 – a Tuesday – that he, Beardsley and their publisher John Lane '"arranged over the telephone with Mr. Henry James for the publication of our first piece of fiction"' (quoted in Anne Diebel, '"The Dreary Duty": Henry James, *The Yellow Book*, and Literary Personality', *Henry James Review* 32.1 (2011), 45–59; 48). James would return to the Preface's figuration of the launch of a periodical as the auspicious birth of a child in his essay for the fiftieth anniversary of *The Nation*, 'The Founding of the "Nation": Recollections of the "Fairies" that Attended Its Birth' (1915) (*LC1* 177–81).

608 **the name of *The Yellow Book* [...] the liveliest attention**: *The Yellow Book: An Illustrated Quarterly* (1894–7) was an avant-garde literary magazine edited by Henry Harland and published by John Lane and Elkin Mathews of the Bodley Head Press. Richard Le Gallienne noted the contemporary fashion for the colour yellow in advertising, interior decoration and book-binding, remarking that '*The Yellow Book* with any other colour would hardly have sold as well' ('The Boom in Yellow', in *Prose Fancies (Second Series)* (London: John Lane; Chicago: H. S. Stone and Co., 1896), pp. 79–89; 81). The colour yellow was also associated with Decadence and had a particular link with Oscar Wilde's *The Picture of Dorian Gray* (1890, 1891) via the dangerously influential 'yellow book' – an unnamed French Symbolist novel suggestive of Joris-Karl Huysmans' *À rebours* (1884) – sent to Dorian by Lord Henry Wotton. James was uneasy about his connection with *The Yellow Book*. He did not send his brother and sister-in-law a copy of the first number (April 1894) 'because although my little tale which ushers it in ("The Death of the Lion") appears to have had, for a thing of mine, an unusual success, I hate too much the horrid aspect & company of the whole publication. And yet I am again to be intimately—conspicuously—associated with the 2^d number. It is for gold & to oblige the worshipful Harland' (to WJ and AGJ, 28 May 1894; *CWJ* 2:312).

609 **the quarterly form, [...] of austere, of awful tradition**: By the end of the nineteenth century, the quarterly periodical format – four instalments per year, appearing at three-monthly intervals – was associated with serious, long-running British journals of literature, culture, politics and religion, wholly unlike *The Yellow Book* in tone, format and contents: e.g., *The Edinburgh Review* (est. 1802), *The Quarterly Review* (est. 1809) and *The Westminster Review* (est. 1823, published quarterly until 1886).

610 **the late Henry Harland**: James met the American novelist, short-story writer and editor Henry Harland (1861–1905) in London in 1890. They had friends in common, including Edmund Gosse and W. D. Howells: James reported to Howells on 17 May 1890 that he had encountered 'your [...] young friend H. Harland, whom I had to fish out of a heaped-up social basket *as* your friend. I shall be glad to make him mine if he'll be so—he seems a very clever fellow' (*LFL* 278). James would review Harland's short-story collection *Comedies and Errors* in 1898 (see *LC1* 282–8).

611 **after no very prolonged career, it encountered [...] its term**: *The Yellow Book* survived for just over three years, April 1894–April 1897;

thirteen quarterly issues were published. As Katherine Lyon Mix notes, from the very start of its run observers had been wondering 'whether the *Yellow Book* would last'; the main reasons for its eventual termination were most likely financial (Mix, *A Study in Yellow: The 'Yellow Book' and Its Contributors* (Lawrence, KS: University of Kansas Press, 1960), pp. 271–6).

612 **Mr. Aubrey Beardsley, [...] his so curious and so disconcerting talent—my appreciation of which [...] stopped quite short.**: The British artist, illustrator and writer Aubrey Beardsley (1872–98) served as art editor of *The Yellow Book* for the first five volumes (April 1894–April 1895). No record survives of the prior meeting with him which James refers to in this passage of the Preface. After the period of the *NYE*, James wrote to André Raffalovich thanking him for a copy of *Last Letters of Aubrey Beardsley* (1904), for which Raffalovich's partner John Gray had written an introduction: 'I knew [Beardsley] a little, and he was himself to my vision touching, and extremely individual; but I hated his productions and thought them extraordinarily base—and couldn't find (perhaps didn't try enough to find!) the formula that reconciled this baseness, aesthetically, with his being so perfect a case of the artistic spirit' (7 November 1913; *HJL* 4:691–2). In the period of *The Yellow Book* and *The Savoy* (1896), the Decadent magazine which he went on to co-edit, Beardsley was notorious for his grotesque and often erotic monochrome illustrations to works of modern and classic literature, including Oscar Wilde's *Salome: A Tragedy in One Act* (1894), Aristophanes' *Lysistrata* (1896) and Alexander Pope's *The Rape of the Lock* (1896).

613 **as illustrations, related surely to nothing else in the same pages—save once or twice [...] to some literary effort of Beardsley's own**: The publishers' prospectus for *The Yellow Book* announced that 'The pictures will in no case serve as illustrations to the letter-press, but each will stand by itself as an independent contribution' (Prospectus for *The Yellow Book* 1 (April 1894). Digitized copy online at *The Yellow Book Digital Edition*, ed. Dennis Denisoff and Lorraine Janzen Kooistra, 2010. *Yellow Nineties 2.0*, Ryerson University Centre for Digital Humanities, 2019 (1890s.ca/wp-content/uploads/YB1-prospectus.pdf)). In fact, none of Beardsley's writing appeared in *The Yellow Book*. Beardsley would, however, publish – and illustrate – his own prose and verse in *The Savoy*: 'Under the Hill: A Romantic Story' (January and April 1896), 'The Ballad of a Barber' (July 1896) and 'Catullus: Carmen CI' (November 1896).

614 **For any idea I might wish to express I might have space […] to express it**: *The Yellow Book* imposed no word-limits on the short stories it published. As the prospectus stated, 'In many ways its contributors will employ a freer hand than the limitations of the old-fashioned periodical can permit. It will publish no serials; but its complete stories will sometimes run to a considerable length in themselves. Thus the tiresome "choppy" effect of so many magazines will be avoided' (Prospectus for *The Yellow Book* 1 (April 1894)).

615 **to struggle […] under the rude prescription of brevity at any cost**: Throughout the 1890s and 1900s, James experienced constant difficulty in meeting periodicals' word-limits for short fiction, and he took full advantage of what this sentence of the Preface calls Harland's 'emphasised indifference to the arbitrary limit of length': his *Yellow Book* stories are amongst his longest. According to Philip Horne's estimates 'based on average page-lengths', the serial text of 'The Death of the Lion' is 13,530 words in extent, 'The Coxon Fund' (1894) 21,450 words and 'The Next Time' (1895) 14,520 words (Horne, 'Henry James and the Economy of the Short Story', in Ian Willison, Warwick Gould and Warren Chernaik (eds.), *Modernist Writers and the Marketplace* (Basingstoke: Macmillan, 1996), pp. 1–35; 23, 26).

616 **the truth that the forms of wrought things, in this order,** *were* **[…] the things**: Compare James's 1907 essay on Shakespeare's *The Tempest* (1611) for 'the relation of style to meaning and of manner to motive': 'Unless it be true that these things, on either hand, are inseparable; unless it be true that the phrase, the cluster and order of terms, *is* the object and the sense […]: unless we recognise this reality the author of The Tempest has no lesson for us' (*LC1* 1211–12). See also note 320.

617 **the beautiful and blest** *nouvelle;* **[…] such studies on the minor scale as the best of Turgenieff's, of Balzac's, of Maupassant's, of Bourget's, […] of Kipling's**: The French word *nouvelle*, naturalized in English literary usage by the late nineteenth century, denotes 'A short fictional narrative, a short novel, a novella; *spec.* one dealing with a single situation, or with one aspect of a character or characters' (*OED*). Later Prefaces associate the *nouvelle* form with 'the minor scale' in other senses than that of extent (see note 748). James had praised many of the authors he names here for their short fiction, although with no consistency as regards length; in the examples cited below he sometimes refers to stories that are too short to be considered *nouvelles*. He had observed in 1874, for example, that Turgenev was 'remarkable for concision; few of his novels occupy the whole

of a moderate volume, and some of his best performances are tales of thirty pages' (*LC2* 974). He repeated this assessment in 1896: Turgenev 'has masterpieces of a few pages; his perfect things are sometimes his least prolonged' (*LC2* 1030). In 1875, he noted that the list of Balzac's 'shorter tales' contained some 'masterpieces': '"Le Curé de Tours," for all its brevity, will be read when "Le Député d'Arcis" lies unopened; and more than one literary adventurer will turn, out-wearied, from "La Peau de Chagrin" and find consolation in "Un Début dans la Vie"' (*LC2* 39). In 1888, he declared that Maupassant's 'short tales' 'deserve the first place in any candid appreciation of his talent': 'they represent him best in his originality, and their brevity, extreme in some cases, does not prevent them from being a collection of masterpieces' (*LC2* 534). Introducing a collection of stories by Rudyard Kipling published in America as *Mine Own People* (1891), James remarked that Kipling's 'talent' was 'eminently in harmony with the short story, and the short story is, on our side of the Channel and of the Atlantic, a mine which will take a great deal of working': Kipling 'appreciates the episode' and finds 'the detachable, compressible "case" an admirable, flexible form' (*LC1* 1130). In an 1898 review, he had cited Henry Harland's story collection *Comedies and Errors* as 'an excellent specimen of what can be done on the minor scale when art comes in' (*LC1* 286). For Paul Bourget, see note 783; I have found no specific comment by James on Bourget's short fiction.

618 **the hard-and-fast rule of the "from six to eight thousand words"**: James had complained to Howells on 10 August 1901 about the word-limits imposed by British periodicals: 'It is sternly enjoined upon one here […] that everything—every hundred—above 6 or 7 thousand words is fatal to "placing"' (*LFL* 366).

619 **my three bantlings held by Harland at the baptismal font […] *plus* a paper not here to be reproduced**: A 'bantling' is 'A young or small child, a brat. (Often used depreciatively, and formerly as a synonym of *bastard*.)' (*OED*). James uses the word of 'Daisy Miller' in the Preface to *NYE* XVIII, again in the context of editorial 'indulgence' shown towards a long story (p. 213). The 'paper not here to be reproduced' may be 'John Delavoy', first published in *Cosmopolis* (January–February 1898), a story of the literary life not included in the *NYE*. James wrote one other piece for *The Yellow Book*, the literary essay 'She and He: Recent Documents' (January 1897), on George Sand's affair with Alfred de Musset.

620 **some felt embarrassment [...] of the artist enamoured of perfection**: James had collected one of his *Yellow Book* stories, 'The Next Time', in a volume entitled *Embarrassments* (1896). The 'high theme of perfection' is at the centre of 'The Lesson of the Master', a story not published in *The Yellow Book* (Ch. 4; *NYE* XV, 53). In the starkest formulation of this predicament, the literary 'master' Henry St George tells the aspiring author Paul Overt that if he wishes '"to go in for some sort of decent perfection"' he ought not to marry: '"one's children interfere with perfection. One's wife interferes. Marriage interferes"' (Ch. 5; *NYE* XV, 66, 70).

621 **I have already mentioned the particular rebuke once addressed me [...] where on earth [...] I had "found" my Neil Paradays, my Ralph Limberts, my Hugh Verekers and other such supersubtle fry**: James refers to this 'rebuke' in the Preface to *NYE* XII, where the objection is to his positing Jeffrey Aspern and Miriam Rooth as literary and theatrical 'celebrities' who could not actually have existed in the societies they are supposed to belong to (see pp. 131–3). The characters named in this sentence, all fictitious authors, feature respectively in 'The Death of the Lion', 'The Next Time' and 'The Figure in the Carpet'.

622 **the rule of the cheap and easy**: James expressed dismay at various literary and cultural manifestations of 'the cheap and easy' in the years immediately preceding the *NYE*. In 'The Lesson of Balzac' (1905), the present moment is characterized as 'this age of superlative study of the cheap and easy' (*LC2* 121). In 'The Question of Our Speech' (1905), he hears in American pronunciation the proof of 'an immense body of limpness and slackness and cheapness. This note of cheapness—of the cheap and easy— is especially fatal to any effect of security of intention in the speech of a society—for it is scarce necessary to remind you that there are two very different kinds of ease: the ease that comes from the facing, the conquest of a difficulty, and the ease that comes from the vague dodging of it' (*HJC* 50–1).

623 **who it is I 'aimed at' in the story of Henry St. George**: On 5 January 1888, James noted a conversation with Theodore Child 'about the effect of marriage on the artist, the man of letters, etc.' that contained the germ of 'The Lesson of the Master': 'He mentioned the cases he had seen in Paris in which this effect had been fatal to the quality of the work &c—through over-production, need to meet expenses, make a figure &c. And I mentioned certain cases here. Child spoke of Daudet—his "30 Ans de Paris,"

as an example in point. "He would never have written that IF he hadn't married"' (*CN* 43).

624 **having again and again closely noted in the social air all the elements of such a drama**: James's first note for 'The Death of the Lion' asks: 'Could not something be done with the idea of the great (the distinguished, the celebrated) artist [...] who is tremendously made up to, *fêted*, written to for his autograph, portrait &c, and yet with whose work [...] not one of the persons concerned has the smallest acquaintance? It would have the merit, at least, of corresponding to an immense reality—a reality that strikes me every day of my life' (3 February 1894; *CN* 86).

625 **monarch of the jungle**: In nineteenth-century writing, this title is given more often to tigers or elephants, but its reference to lions is nonetheless common. See, for example, Florence Marryat on her disappointed first impression of Niagara Falls: 'It was like expecting to see a ramping, roaring lion, the monarch of the jungle, and being introduced to some subdued beast that crouched in the corner of his den' (*Tom Tiddler's Ground* (London: Swan Sonnenschein, Lowrey & Co., 1886), p. 97). The title of James's story plays on 'lion' in the sense of 'A person of note or celebrity who is much sought after', from the plural as 'Things of note, celebrity, or curiosity [...]; sights worth seeing' – originally, actual lions in the menagerie of the Tower of London (*OED*).

626 **the correspondences of this anecdote**: James noted the idea for 'The Figure in the Carpet' on 24 October 1895: 'that of the author of certain books who is known to hold [...] that his writings contain a very beautiful & valuable, very interesting & remunerative *secret*, or latent intention for those who read them with a right intelligence [...]. No reviewer, no "critic," has dreamed of it' (*CN* 136–7).

627 **a grasped warrant—for identification, arrest or whatever**: In 'The Death of the Lion', the newspaper editor Mr Morrow's intrusion on Neil Paraday's privacy is figured as an arrest: 'When [Paraday] came out it was exactly as if he had been in custody, for beside him walked a stout man with a big black beard, who, save that he wore spectacles, might have been a policeman' (Ch. 4; *NYE* XV, 112).

628 **Given the Lion, his "death" was but too conceivably the issue**: Compare James's prevision of the end of the story in his first notebook entry, referring to 'the crowd of lionisers' who take up Neil Paraday: 'They must *kill*

him, hein [what]?—kill him with the very fury of their selfish exploitation, and then not really have an idea of what they killed him *for*' (*CN* 86–7).

629 **among the consulted notes of any sincere man of letters**: On 26 January 1895, James noted the germ of 'The Next Time': 'The idea of the poor man, the artist, the man of letters, who all his life is trying—if only to get a living—to do something *vulgar*'; it would make 'a little story that might perhaps be a mate to the Death of the Lion?' (*CN* 109). The idea was 'suggested to me really by all the little backward memories of one's own frustrated ambition'; James connects it with two episodes in his own career, his stint as a Paris correspondent for the *New-York Daily Tribune* in 1876, and the shock and disappointment of the opening night of *Guy Domville* on 5 January 1895 (*CN* 109–10).

630 **"comparative" science**: A technical term: a 'comparative' approach to any intellectual discipline – e.g., comparative anatomy, mythology, philology – is one that involves 'comparison of different branches of a science or subject of study' (*OED*).

631 **the rank exotic whose leaves are rustling cheques**: According to proverbial wisdom, money does *not* grow on trees, bushes, etc. ('Money, 8,' in Archer Taylor and Bartlett Jere Whiting, *A Dictionary of American Proverbs and Proverbial Phrases, 1820–1880* (Cambridge, MA: Belknap Press of Harvard University Press, 1958), p. 248). In 'The Next Time', Ralph Limbert's plan of living cheaply in the country while he tries to write a successful novel is figured in horticultural terms: 'it was a forcing-house for the three or four other fine miscarriages to which his scheme was evidently condemned' (Ch. 5; *NYE* XV, 208).

632 **collective mistrust of anything like close or analytic appreciation [...] the Beautiful Gate itself of enjoyment**: One of the gates of the Second Temple of the Jews at Jerusalem is referred to in the Bible as 'the gate of the temple which is called Beautiful' (Acts 3:2). In an essay of 1897, James had recalled disagreeing with George Du Maurier – who 'was, frankly, not critical' – about what criticism might contribute to the 'enjoyment' of art: 'I regarding it as the very gate or gustatory mouth of pleasure, and he willing enough indeed to take it for a door, but a door closed in one's face' (*LC1* 877). James had recently opened his lecture 'The Lesson of Balzac' with the proposition 'that criticism is the only gate of appreciation, just

as appreciation is, in regard to a work of art, the only gate of enjoyment' (*LC2* 115).

633 **any string of evolutionary pearls**: In 'The Figure in the Carpet', Hugh Vereker uses this metaphor to represent the secret principle of his work, as an alternative to the figure suggested by the narrator ('something like a complex figure in a Persian carpet'): '"It's the very string," he said, "that my pearls are strung on!"' (Ch. 4; *NYE* XV, 240–1).

634 **some artist whose most characteristic intention […] should have taken all vainly for granted the […] exercise of penetration**: When the narrator of 'The Figure in the Carpet' asks Vereker if he doesn't think he '"ought—just a trifle—to assist the critic"' to understand his work, the author replies: '"Assist him? What else have I done with every stroke of my pen? I've shouted my intention in his great blank face!"' (Ch. 3; *NYE* XV, 231). See also 'The Middle Years', which likewise turns on the relation between an author and a well-meaning but imperceptive reader: 'Dencombe had told him what he "tried for"; with all his intelligence, on a first perusal, Doctor Hugh had failed to guess it. The baffled celebrity wondered then who in the world *would* guess it: he was amused once more at the diffused massive weight that could be thrown into the missing of an intention' (*NYE* XVI, 97).

635 **Mr. J. Dyke Campbell's admirable monograph on S. T. Coleridge**: James Dykes Campbell (whose name is misspelled in this sentence of the Preface) was the author of *Samuel Taylor Coleridge: A Narrative of the Events of His Life* (1894). On 17 April 1894, James noted that he had read the book and been 'infinitely struck with the suggestiveness of S.T.C.'s figure—wonderful, admirable figure—for pictorial treatment. What a subject some particular cluster of its relations would make for a little story, a small vivid picture' (*CN* 89).

636 **circumstances into which I needn't here enter had within a few years contributed much to making it vivid**: It is not clear exactly what circumstances James is referring to. A few years before reading Dykes Campbell's biography of Coleridge, however, he had stayed for three days with the poet's great-nephew John Duke Coleridge, first Baron Coleridge (1820–94) at the family seat in Ottery St Mary (see James's letter to Edwin L. Godkin, 20 September [1889]; *HJL* 3:258). James Russell Lowell was also a house-guest on that occasion, as James recalled in his commemorative essay on Lowell in 1892 (*LC1* 539); and four years earlier, Lowell had

delivered 'a charming address' at the ceremony to unveil a bust of Coleridge in Westminster Abbey, to which James had been invited but which he had not been able to attend (to Grace Norton, 9 May [1885]; *CLHJ 1884–1886* 1:179). Some combination of these circumstances may have contributed to making the image of S. T. Coleridge 'vivid' to James in 1894.

637 **the story-teller's "real person" or actual contemporary transplanted and exhibited**: James had been most directly confronted with this question by public and private responses to the serialization of *The Bostonians* in 1885–6, above all by readers' indignant identification of the reformer Elizabeth Palmer Peabody (1804–94) as the original of his character Miss Birdseye: for this controversy, see the introduction to Daniel Karlin's edition of *The Bostonians* (*CFHJ* 8, xcvii–ci). In *Notes of a Son and Brother* (1914), James would revisit 'that whole question of the "putting of people into books" as to which any ineptitude of judgment appears always in order' (*Aut* 548), with reference to Frank and Lizzie Boott's contributions to the characterization of Gilbert and Pansy Osmond in *The Portrait of a Lady* (see also note 153).

638 **in chemical, almost in mystical terms. [...] the crucible of his imagination, [...] that perpetually simmering cauldron his intellectual *pot-au-feu*, [...] reduced to savoury fusion**: Pointing out what seemed to him a weakness in Gabriele D'Annunzio's novel *Il fuoco* (1900), James had written in 1904: 'We get the impression of a direct transfer, a "lift," bodily, of something seen and known, something not really produced by the chemical process of art, the crucible or retort from which things emerge for a new function' ('GDA' 406). In 'The Lesson of Balzac', the same figure governs his comparison of Balzac and Zola: 'The mystic process of the crucible, the transformation of the material under æsthetic heat, is, in the "Comédie Humaine," thanks to an intenser and more submissive fusion, completer, and also finer' (*LC2* 130). A *pot-au-feu* is a traditional French stew of beef and vegetables. As early as his 1888 essay on Guy de Maupassant, James had spoken of 'that closed chamber of an artist's meditations, that sacred back kitchen' (*LC2* 532), and culinary metaphors for the 'fusion' of subject and form occur in several later essays, for example that on D'Annunzio quoted above: 'The fusion is complete and admirable [...]; we swallow our successive morsels with as little question as we swallow food that has, by proper preparation, been reduced to singleness of savour' ('GDA' 390).

PREFACE to *The Author of Beltraffio, The Middle Years, Greville Fane and Other Tales* (NYE XVI)

639 **What I had lately […] to say of "The Coxon Fund"**: The immediate reference back to the close of the previous Preface reflects the fact that James had meant *NYE* XV to contain other stories of the literary life. A number of stories were moved from that volume into the present one in December 1908 as part of a complex redistribution of the contents of *NYE* XV–XVIII, and the Prefaces were adjusted accordingly. See the Introduction, pp. xciii–cii.

640 **it consists, in fact, […] of some 5550**: By Philip Horne's estimate, the serial text of 'The Middle Years' is much longer than this, at 7,260 words ('Henry James and the Economy of the Short Story', p. 26).

641 **boilings and reboilings**: James had already used this culinary figure of reduction by boiling in letters about his short stories. He writes to Horace Scudder, for example, about 'The Pupil' (1891): 'I regarded it as a little masterpiece of compression (I so boiled and re-boiled it down)' (10 November [1890]; *HJL* 3:307).

642 **a peck of troubles**: Originally 'A unit of capacity for dry goods equal to a quarter of a bushel', a 'peck' is commonly used as a rough measurement: 'A considerable quantity or number; a great deal, a heap, a lot. Chiefly in *a peck of trouble(s)*' (*OED*).

643 **Blankness overtakes me […] in connexion with […] "Greville Fane" […] which must have appeared in a London weekly journal at the beginning of the "nineties"**: The subject of 'Greville Fane' is preserved in two notebook entries, ten years apart, the latest written over three years before the publication of the story – all of which may have made it harder for James to recollect the origin of the story when composing the Preface. On 22 January 1879, he remembered hearing 'that Anthony Trollope had a theory that a boy might be brought up to be a novelist, as to any other trade' and noted: 'The other day Miss [Anne] Thackeray, (Mrs. Ritchie) said to me that she and her husband meant to bring up their little daughter in that way. It hereupon occurred to me (as it had occurred before) that one might make a little story upon this' (*CN* 9). The idea came back to him 'with a certain vividness of solicitation' ten years later (27 February 1889; *CN* 48). 'Greville Fane' was published in two issues of the weekly *Illustrated London News* on 17 and 24 September 1892.

644 **a cool north room**: At this period James was living in a fourth-floor flat at 34 De Vere Gardens, Kensington. De Vere Gardens is a street of terraced buildings and runs roughly north–south; the houses on James's side front eastwards, so none of his rooms would have had a north-facing aspect. See note 238.

645 **some victim of the income-tax who would minimise his "return"**: In this context, a 'return' is 'A statement of wealth in terms of income or property [...] used by tax authorities to assess liability for tax' (*OED*).

646 **novels intensely compressed**: In his notebook entry for 'The Abasement of the Northmores', James envisaged the story as a 'Tiny fantasy', but after sketching an outline of the plot could not resist the thought of developments: '*Or is there anything ELSE in it?—in connection with the letters she eventually publishes????—???—???*' (12 November 1899; *CN* 188). He had described the subject of 'The Tree of Knowledge' as 'Practicable on the rigid Maupassant (at extremest brevity) system' (5 October 1899; *CN* 184).

647 **they were to find nowhere [...] the reward of their effort**: Neither 'The Abasement of the Northmores' nor 'The Tree of Knowledge' had periodical publication prior to their appearance in *The Soft Side* (1900), a collection which James brought out partly in order to achieve a financial return from recent stories which he had been unable to place with magazines. He described the volume to Mary Augusta Ward as 'but a little bundle of sordid potboilers' (22 November 1900; *LL* 349).

648 **a young artist long dead [...] his quasi-conspicuous father, likewise an artist**: The origin of 'The Tree of Knowledge' is recorded in a notebook entry of 1 May 1899 made while James was staying in Venice with Ariana and Daniel Curtis: 'Note the "Gordon Greenough" story told me by Mrs. C.—the young modern artist-son opening the eyes of his mother (his sculptor-father's *one* believer) to the misery & grotesqueness of the Father's work' (*CN* 182). Gordon Greenough (1850–80) belonged to an eminent Bostonian artistic family: his uncle Horatio Greenough (1805–52) had been the first professional American sculptor in marble; his father Richard Saltonstall Greenough (1819–1904) was also a sculptor, and was still living when James wrote and published 'The Tree of Knowledge'. The two elder Greenoughs are mentioned in *William Wetmore Story and His Friends* (1903) (see *WWS* I:114–15). For James's social links to the Greenough family via the Curtises, Francis Boott and others, see Nathalia

Wright, 'Henry James and the Greenough Data', *American Quarterly* 10.3 (1958), 338–43.

649 **some time before the first appearance of the tale [...] an eminent author, these several years dead and on some of the embarrassments of whose life and character a common friend was enlarging: [...] his wife objects intensely to what he writes**: The interval between James's receipt of the germ of 'The Author of Beltraffio' and the composition of the story was shorter than he implies here: he made a note of the subject on 26 March 1884, as something that had been reported to him 'the other day' (*CN* 25), and the story was published the same year in the June and July numbers of the *English Illustrated Magazine*. This notebook entry identifies the 'eminent author' as the poet, critic and cultural historian John Addington Symonds (1840–93), author of *Renaissance in Italy* (1875–86) and two privately printed works on homosexuality, *A Problem in Greek Ethics* (1883) and *A Problem in Modern Ethics* (1891); the 'common friend' was the critic and autobiographer Edmund Gosse (1849–1928), who later that year took up the post of Clark Lecturer in English literature at Trinity College, Cambridge. Gosse had told James that 'poor S.'s wife was in no sort of sympathy with what he wrote; disapproving of its tone, thinking his books immoral, pagan, hyper-aesthetic, &c. [...] It seemed to me qu'il y avait là un drame—un drame intime [that there was a drama there – an intimate drama]' (*CN* 25).

650 **a handful of kindly earth**: The poetic phrase 'kindly earth' would have been most likely familiar to James from Alfred Tennyson's 'Locksley Hall' (1842), a source of poetic allusions for him throughout his career (see also notes 412 and 800). Tennyson's speaker imagines a utopian future of peaceful governance by 'the Parliament of man, the Federation of the world': 'There the common sense of most shall hold a fretful realm in awe, / And the kindly earth shall slumber, lapt in universal law' (ll. 128–30; *The Poems of Tennyson*, vol. II, p. 126). With greater relevance to the Preface's figure of sowing and germination, the phrase also occurs in Georgic verse by nineteenth-century American poets whom James could have read in childhood and youth: for example, Alfred Billings Street's 'The Pioneer' (1844) and William Cullen Bryant's 'The Song of the Sower' (1864). In the specific context of John Addington Symonds's association with the germ of 'The Author of Beltraffio', it may be relevant that 'kindly earth' appears in Symonds's translation of a sestina by Jacopo Sannazaro: 'O universal mother, kindly earth, / Shall't ever be that, stretched on verdant fields,

/ In slumber deep, upon that latest eve, / I ne'er shall wake again [...]?' (Symonds, *Renaissance in Italy. Italian Literature: Part II* (London: Smith, Elder, & Co., 1881), p. 212).

651 **I fail to disinter again the buried germ**: James noted the subject of 'Broken Wings' on 16 February 1899: 'the idea of the 2 artists of some sort [...] who keep a stiff upper lip of secrecy & pride to each other as to how they're "doing," getting on, working off their wares, &c, till something sweeps them off their feet & breaks them down in confessions, AVEUX [avowals], tragic surrenders to the truth, which have at least the effect of bringing them, for some consolatory purpose, *together*' (CN 179).

652 **the brush of no winged word**: Literally, no anecdote or other spoken hint. In poetic contexts, the English phrase 'winged words' is a literal translation of a common Homeric formula for speech: see Paolo Vivante, 'On Homer's Winged Words', *Classical Quarterly* 25.1 (1975), 1–12.

653 **transposing the terms of one of Guy de Maupassant's admirable *contes***: James cites Maupassant's short story 'La Parure' (1884) as his source for 'Paste' (1899), but, as T. M. Segnitz notes, there is also 'a resemblance between "Paste" and Maupassant's story "Les Bijoux" (1883), from which James could have taken the same idea without transposing it. It was Maupassant himself who had transposed the terms of "Les Bijoux" only a year later to "La Parure"' (Segnitz, 'The Actual Genesis of Henry James's "Paste"', *American Literature* 36.2 (1964), 216–19; 217). For a detailed account of James's use of these and other sources in Maupassant, see Philip Horne, 'Strings of Pearls: James, Maupassant, and "Paste"', *Literary Imagination* 21.2 (2019), 137–57.

654 **a pearl necklace**: The lost piece of jewellery in 'La Parure' is a diamond necklace.

655 **"Europe," which is of 1899 [...] *Scribner's Magazine***: This story was published in the June 1899 issue of *Scribner's Magazine*. On that occasion, and again when James collected it in *The Soft Side*, its title was '"Europe"': the inverted commas were dropped for the *NYE*.

656 **an ancient lady [...] a triumphant sojourn in Europe, long years before, [...] her husband, a dim displaced superseded celebrity at the time of my own observation**: James appears to refer to Mary Crowninshield Silsbee Sparks (1809–87), who was the second wife of Jared Sparks (1789–1866), scholar of American history and president of Harvard College 1849–53. The Preface conflates two or more sojourns in Europe by

members of the Sparks family. Jared Sparks made two solo research trips to England and the Continent in the late 1820s and early 1840s (the latter exactly fitting the Preface's reference to 'early Victorian days') and was warmly welcomed by eminent political, literary and academic figures and given access to the British and French state archives; he returned to Europe in 1857-8 with his wife and young children, and spent a year travelling and renewing the social and professional contacts he had made on those earlier visits (see Herbert B. Adams, *The Life and Writings of Jared Sparks*, 2 vols. (Boston, MA: Houghton, Mifflin and Company, 1893), vol. II, pp. 52-131, 378-92, 548-53). The 'sedate American city' of the Preface is Boston – or rather its suburb Cambridge, where Sparks settled with his wife in 1847. After his death in March 1866, Mary Crowninshield Sparks 'continued to reside in the Quincy Street home, which she and Mr. Sparks had chosen together', and lived there 'to a serene old age' (*ibid.*, vol. II, p. 574). She would become a neighbour of the Jameses in November 1866 when Henry Sr moved his family out from Boston to a house at 20 Quincy Street. The 'little Sunday breakfast-party' which James recalls in the Preface could have taken place in the January of various years after that date, when he was either actually living at home in Cambridge or was elsewhere in the US but conceivably within range and available: 1867-9, 1871-2, 1875 or 1883. This is the first of two germs recorded for 'Europe' in this Preface, and it corresponds to no surviving notebook entry: for the second germ, see note 659.

657 **"much made of,"**: The commoner form of this idiom is 'made much of', meaning to be treated 'with marked courtesy and show of affection'; but *OED* records several sixteenth- and seventeenth-century instances with the reversed form as in the Preface, and also cites a nineteenth-century instance in Edward Bulwer-Lytton's novel *Alice, or The Mysteries* (1838): 'No queen could be more made of' (Book First, Ch. 2) (*OED*, 'make').

658 **framed and glazed [...] mementoes**: In the story, the Rimmles' parlour-walls are hung with 'pictorial and other reminders' of the parents' European tour; there are 'framed letters—tributes to their eminent father—suspended among the mementoes' (*NYE* XVI, 343). According to a contemporary source, in her home in Cambridge, Massachusetts the widowed Mary Crowninshield Sparks was likewise 'surrounded on every hand by memorials of [her husband]' (Adams, *The Life and Writings of Jared Sparks*, vol. II, p. 574).

659 **much later, [...] some tender mention of certain admirable ladies, sisters and spinsters under the maternal roof, [...] not having "been to Europe."**: This is the second germ for 'Europe', recorded by James in a notebook entry of 27 February 1895: 'I was greatly struck, the other day, with something that Lady Playfair told me of the prolongation—& the effects of it—of her aunt, old Mrs. Palfrey, of Cambridge, Mass. She is, or was, 95, or some such extraordinary age; & the little idea that struck me as a small *motif* in it was that of the consequences of this fact on [*sic*] the existence of her 2 or 3 poor old maid daughters, who have themselves grown old (old enough to die) while sitting there waiting, waiting endlessly for her to depart' (*CN* 117). Lady Playfair, née Edith Russell (1855-1932), was the American third wife of the Scottish scientist and Liberal politician Lyon Playfair (1819-98), 1st Baron Playfair. The subject of the anecdote was her great-aunt Mary Ann Hammond Palfrey (1800-97), the widow of the Bostonian minister, theologian and historian John Gorham Palfrey (1796-1881). The Palfreys had three daughters, none of whom married: Sara Hammond Palfrey (1823-1914), who published poetry and fiction as 'E. Foxton'; Anna (or Hannah) Russell Palfrey (1825-1905); and Mary Gorham Palfrey (1838-1917). Leon Edel conflates this 'much later' anecdote with the first germ for the story (for which, see note 656) and thus misidentifies Mary Ann Hammond Palfrey as the 'ancient lady' of the previous paragraph of the Preface (*LC2* 1379).

660 **Exceptionally prepared by culture for going**: In 'Europe', it is Becky, 'the most literary' of the three Rimmle daughters, who has been prepared for Europe by second-hand knowledge acquired as her father's editor and biographer: the narrator concurs with her sisters that 'Becky's wonderful preparation would be wasted if she were the one to stay with their mother' (Ch. 1; *NYE* XVI, 343, 344). This volume of the *NYE* contains another New England story about longing for Europe, 'Four Meetings' (1877): as the schoolteacher Caroline Spencer tells the narrator on their first meeting, '"I guess I've prepared my mind [for European travel] about as much as you *can*—in advance. I've not only read Byron—I've read histories and guide-books and articles and lots of things"' (Ch. 1; *NYE* XVI, 274).

661 **after the plan was dished**: The slang term 'dish' means 'To "do for", defeat completely, ruin; to cheat, circumvent' (*OED*).

662 **so Europe altered—for the worse**: In the first chapter of 'Four Meetings', the narrator looks at photographs of the Château de Chillon with

Caroline Spencer and observes 'that if she wished to recognise Byron's descriptions she must go abroad speedily—Europe was getting sadly dis-Byronised'; he allows her 'ten years' to make her visit (*NYE* XVI, 271). In 'Europe', the Rimmle daughters, faced with their mother's silent resistance, are reduced to the polite commonplace that 'Europe would keep' (Ch. 2; *NYE* XVI, 351).

663 **the brevity imposed so great**: By Philip Horne's estimate, the serial text of '"Europe"' is 6,930 words long ('Henry James and the Economy of the Short Story', p. 27).

PREFACE to *The Altar of the Dead, The Beast in the Jungle, The Birthplace and Other Tales* (NYE XVII)

664 **a volume bearing the title of "Terminations," which appeared in 1895**: James's collection *Terminations* was published in England by William Heinemann in May 1895, and the following month in America by Harper and Brothers. It contained 'The Death of the Lion', 'The Coxon Fund', 'The Middle Years' and 'The Altar of the Dead'.

665 **vainly been "hawked about," knocking [...] at half a dozen editorial doors impenetrably closed to it**: To 'hawk' in this sense, from the activity of a 'hawker' or itinerant vendor, means 'To carry *about* from place to place and offer for sale; to cry in the street' (*OED*). 'The Altar of the Dead' had no periodical publication. James found it difficult to place stories in magazines at this period, as he complained to W. D. Howells on 22 January 1895: 'what is clear is that periodical publication is practically closed to me—I'm the last hand that the magazines, in this country or in the U.S., seem to want' (*LFL* 298).

666 **never to be waylaid or arrested [...] by some imaged appeal of the lost Dead?**: James noted the subject of the story on 29 September 1894: 'I imagine a man whose noble and beautiful religion is the worship of the Dead. [...] He is struck with the way they are forgotten, are unhallowed—unhonoured, neglected, shoved out of sight; allowed to become so much more dead, even, than the fate that has overtaken them has made them. He is struck with the rudeness, the coldness, that surrounds their memory—the want of place made for them in the life of the survivors' (*CN* 98). When James made this note, he was lodging at 15 Beaumont Street, Oxford, in rooms that had been occupied by the American writer Constance Fenimore Woolson (1840-94) from

October 1891 to May 1893, and where James had visited her in 1892. For the possible influence on 'The Altar of the Dead' of Woolson's death in January 1894, either falling or jumping from a window in Venice, see Lyndall Gordon, *A Private Life of Henry James: Two Women and His Art* (London: Chatto & Windus, 1998), pp. 291-8.

667 **a cultivated habit (the cultivation is really the point)**: In Chapter 1 of 'The Altar of the Dead', we are told that Stransom 'had formed little by little the habit of numbering his Dead' (*NYE* XVII, 4-5). The horticultural metaphor implicit in 'cultivated' is developed in the Preface's subsequent comments on the story, p. 194. It also recalls a passage in 'The Marriages' (1891), a near-contemporaneous story also about stubborn devotion to the dead, which describes the solace Adela Chart finds in tending her late mother's garden: 'She loved the place as, had she been a good Catholic, she would have loved the smell of her parish church; and indeed there was in her passion for flowers something of the respect of a religion' (Ch. 4; *NYE* XVIII, 291).

668 **a conscious, and indeed highly emphasised, dead loss**: A 'dead loss' is 'a complete loss; frequently *colloquial*, a person or thing that is totally worthless, inefficient, or unsuccessful; a complete failure; an utter waste of time' (*OED*).

669 **a police-magistrate then seated [...] well in the eye of London, [...] his high magisterial and penal mask**: This sounds like Sir James Taylor Ingham (1805-90), Chief Magistrate of London from 1876 until his death, who presided over the central Metropolitan Police Court at Bow Street in the West End. Ingham's entry in the first edition of the *Dictionary of National Biography* (1891) calls him 'a man of dignified appearance' (vol. XXVIII, p. 435). A caricature by the *Punch* cartoonist Edward Linley Sambourne depicts him as an eagle clutching a perch labelled 'THE [BE]NCH' (the lettering is partly obscured by his talons); the accompanying caption 'The Eagle Beak of BOW STREET' plays on 'beak' as a slang term for a magistrate and also refers to Ingham's striking aquiline nose ('Punch's Fancy Portraits.—No. 135', *Punch, or the London Charivari*, 12 May 1883, p. 226).

670 **A distinguished old friend, [...] a singularly uncommemorated and unchronicled effect: [...] her social and historical value**: Edel suggests (*LC2* 1379) that this lady was Harriet Everilda Gore Stewart (1808-84), often referred to as Mrs Duncan Stewart, the mother of James's friend

Christina Stewart Rogerson. James had used her as a model for Lady Davenant in 'A London Life' (1888) (see *CN* 38), and the social displacement experienced by her lady's maid after her death was the inspiration for the eponymous butler's predicament in 'Brooksmith' (1891) (see note 774). Early in their acquaintance, James privately described Mrs Duncan Stewart as 'a rather picturesque & agreeable old lady, who has lived always in good London Society, wears voluminous capotes & capes of old white lace, talks of Lady Morgan & Mrs. Norton &c' (to AJ, 8 April [1877]; *CLHJ 1876-1878* 1:95); Sydney, Lady Morgan (bap. 1781–d. 1859) and Caroline Norton (1808–77) were authors and London society figures of the first half of the nineteenth century. See also James's remark in *William Wetmore Story and His Friends* (1903) about another elderly lady of his London acquaintance, Anne Benson Procter, widow of the Romantic-period poet Bryan Waller Procter (Barry Cornwall), who struck James after her death in 1888 'as having been—for what she personally and socially was—singularly uncommemorated' (*WWS* I:223). Unlike Mrs Duncan Stewart, however, Anne Procter had been a public person with significant 'literary luggage', as James says in this sentence of the Preface, and she was the subject of at least three obituary essays in the weeks following her death: *The Athenæum* (10 March 1888), 309; *The Saturday Review* (10 March 1888), 278–9; *The Academy* (17 March 1888), 187–8).

671 **A friend of the interesting woman, [...] asked leave of [...] the conductor of a "high class" periodical, to intervene on behalf of her memory in the pages under the latter's control**: It is not clear what periodical James refers to here, or who the friend or the editor was. A few sentences later, he says that 'the article in question never appeared—nor, to the best of my knowledge, anything else of the sort': a two-part commemorative essay on Mrs Duncan Stewart by Augustus J. C. Hare *did* appear in the British magazine *Good Words* in January 1892 (661–6, 764–71), but that was eight years after her death and thus well after the period presumably referred to in the Preface.

672 **the inhibition, as the psychologists say**: In psychological terminology, an 'inhibition' is 'A voluntary or involuntary restraint or check that prevents the direct expression of an instinctive impulse; also *colloq.*, in looser use, an inner hindrance to conduct or activity' (*OED*, citing an essay of 1876 by WJ as its earliest instance).

673 **too many for it; [...] hostile to friendship and intimacy**: To be 'too many for' something or someone is 'to be more than a match for' it or them

(*OED*, 'many'). James had recently made a similar complaint about modern social life in the first chapter of *William Wetmore Story*, in comparison with the easier conditions enjoyed by Story's generation in the mid nineteenth century: 'Friendships live on the possibility of contact, that contact which requires in some degree margin and space. We are planted at present so close that selection is smothered; contact we have indeed, but only in the general form which is cruel to the particular' (*WWS* I:18).

674 **we stay our yearning with snatches and stop-gaps**: Compare James's 'envy' of the American expatriates commemorated in *William Wetmore Story* for having had the necessary leisure for friendship: 'The particular contact [...] could flourish with them and give what it had; they were not always on the way to some other, snatching a mouthful between trains' (*WWS* I:18).

675 **the poor dead [...] were nowhere so dead as there; [...] branded at once as "morbid."**: James's attitude here echoes that of Adela Chart in 'The Marriages': 'she had already made up her mind that London was no treasure-house of delicacies. [...] The patient dead were sacrificed; they had no shrines, for people were literally ashamed of mourning' (Ch. 2; *NYE* XVIII, 269). The relevant sense of 'morbid' dates from the late eighteenth century: 'Of a person, mental state, etc.: characterized by excessive gloom or apprehension, or (in later use) by an unhealthy preoccupation with disease, death, or other disturbing subject; given to unwholesome brooding' (*OED*).

676 **a distinguished foreign friend, for some years officially resident in England, [...] a funeral-train, on its way to Kensal Green or wherever**: The 'foreign friend', Edel suggests (*LC2* 1379), was the French diplomat and author Jean Jules Jusserand (1855–1932), whom James had met in 1888 when Jusserand was attached to the French Embassy in London. Founded in 1832, Kensal Green Cemetery in suburban north-west London was the first of seven large private cemeteries to be established on the outskirts of the city during the 1830s and 1840s in response to concerns about public health from the overcrowding of inner-city burial sites. See Hugh Meller, *London Cemeteries: An Illustrated Guide and Gazetteer*, 3rd edn (Aldershot: Ashgate, 1999), pp. 6–12, 187–91. By the time James wrote 'The Altar of the Dead' he was familiar with Kensal Green Cemetery. He had attended Anne Procter's funeral there on 9 March 1888 and found 'the whole long pilgrimage [...] less lugubrious and dreary than I have sometimes seen it', perhaps on account of his

travelling companion: 'I went in a carriage with [Robert] Browning' (to Lady Constance Leslie, 10 March [1888]; *HJL* 3:224). Five years later he would make the same journey to 'dreary Kensal Green' for the funeral of Fanny Kemble (to WJ, 20 January [1893]; *CWJ* 2:251). The funeral trains of the London Necropolis Railway (LNR) conveyed corpses and mourners *not* in fact to Kensal Green, but to Brookwood Cemetery near Woking in Surrey. The LNR used the tracks of the London and South Western Railway; it had opened in 1854 and ran first from a dedicated terminus at York Street near Waterloo Station, moving to a new terminus at Westminster Bridge Road in 1902. The only other cemetery railway service in London had run from a private station near King's Cross to the Great Northern Cemetery at Colney Hatch, but James could not have known it, as it was only operational during the early–mid 1860s. See John M. Clarke, *The Brookwood Necropolis Railway*, 4th revised and enlarged edn (Usk: The Oakwood Press, 2006), pp. 9–44, 180.

677 **a volume of miscellanies ("The Better Sort," 1903)**: Of the eleven stories collected in this volume, three had no prior periodical publication: 'The Beast in the Jungle', 'The Birthplace' and 'The Papers'. Writing to Mary Augusta Ward in 1900, James described *The Better Sort* as 'another volume of similar snippets' to those he had just collected in *The Soft Side* (22 November 1900; *LL* 349). See note 647.

678 **in ten lines of an old note-book**: James had noted the subject of 'The Beast in the Jungle', which this sentence of the Preface calls an 'elaborated fantasy', on 27 August 1901: 'there is something else—a very tiny *fantaisie* probably—in small notion that comes to me of a man haunted by the fear, more & more, throughout life, that *something will happen to him*' (*CN* 199).

679 **to fill, in vulgar parlance, the bill**: To 'fill the bill' is a theatrical idiom, originally American: 'to fulfil the necessary requirements; to come up to the requisite standard', deriving from 'bill' as 'A list of the items on a (theatre) programme' (*OED*). But compare the definition offered by a contemporary slang dictionary: 'FILL THE BILL [...] (theatrical).—To excel in conspicuousness: as a star actor whose name is "billed" to the exclusion of the rest of the company' (*Slang* II:396).

680 **Like the blinded seeker in the old-fashioned game he "burns," [...] as with the sense of the hidden thing near**: This sense of 'burn' is used in games where an object is hidden and the seeker, who is usually blindfolded,

must find it by following the directions of the other players: 'of a person approaching so near to a concealed object sought, that he would feel it very warm or hot, if it were fire' (*OED*). The idiom occurs in another story collected in this volume of the *NYE*, 'The Friends of the Friends', where it is used of two people whom the narrator is trying to prevent from meeting: 'It was more and more impressed on me that they were approaching, converging. They were like the seekers for the hidden object in the game of blindfold; they had one and the other begun to "burn"' (Ch. 3; *NYE* XVII, 338). The second sentence quoted here is an addition to the *NYE* text with no counterpart in earlier versions.

681 **He has indeed been marked and indeed suffered his fortune […] to have been the man in the world to whom nothing whatever was to happen**: The Preface's phrasings are carried over from the climax of the story: 'The fate he had been marked for he had met with a vengeance […]; he had been the man of his time, *the* man, to whom nothing on earth was to have happened' (Ch. 6; *NYE* XVII, 125).

682 **the clue of actuality**: James noted the subject of 'The Birthplace' on 12 June 1901 in the form of an anecdote told him by Caroline, Lady Trevelyan, wife of the statesman and historian Sir George Otto Trevelyan (1838–1928), when he visited them the previous month at their country house Welcombe, near Stratford-upon-Avon in Warwickshire: 'the odd case of the couple who had formerly […] been for a couple of years—or a few—the people in charge of the Shakspeare [sic] house—the Birthplace—which struck me as possibly a little *donnée*' (*CN* 195). The couple referred to were the poet Joseph Skipsey (1832–1903) and his wife Sara, who were employed as custodians of William Shakespeare's birthplace in Stratford from June 1889 until their resignation in October 1891. See the Introduction to Neil Reeve's edition of *The Jolly Corner and Other Tales, 1903–1910* (*CFHJ* 32, xxxvii).

683 **a great place of pilgrimage, a shrine sacred to […] the whole English-speaking race**: The Preface follows the story in declining to name the poet whose birthplace this was; the custodian Morris Gedge thinks of the house as a 'shrine', 'the most sacred known to the steps of men, the early home of the supreme poet, the Mecca of the English-speaking race' (Ch. 1; *NYE* XVII, 134).

684 **who, coming to his office with infinite zest, had after a while desperately thrown it up […] "the awful nonsense he found himself expected**

[…] **to talk.":** This outline tallies with James's notebook entry. The Skipseys were 'rather strenuous & superior people from Newcastle, who had embraced the situation with joy' but 'at the end of 6 months […] grew sick and desperate from finding it—finding their office—the sort of thing that I suppose it is: full of humbug, full of lies & superstition *imposed* upon them by the great body of visitors' (*CN* 195).

685 **an acquaintance, lately much confirmed, on my own part, with the particular temple of our poor gentleman's priesthood:** It is not clear what timeframe 'lately' refers to here, but it may be relevant that James was the Trevelyans' guest again from 10 to 13 June 1908, shortly before he composed the material for this Preface. On 12 June, he wrote to Pinker from Welcombe, excited that Macmillan had agreed to publish the British issue of the *NYE* and 'grudging even this little absence from the scene of action' (Yale).

686 **the certainty that it would nowhere […] find "acceptance.":** In fact James did not even try to get 'The Birthplace' accepted by a periodical: as Neil Reeve has shown, it was one of three stories – along with 'The Beast in the Jungle' and 'The Papers' – which James wrote 'directly for volume publication alone [in *The Better Sort*], thus bypassing entirely the length-demands of magazine editors' (*CFHJ* 32, xxxii).

687 **that mystic, that "chemical" change […] that I lately spoke of in connexion with "The Coxon Fund.":** For this discussion of transforming actual persons into fictional characters, see the Preface to *NYE* XV, pp. 181–2.

688 **(to repeat, I believe, my figure) […] some sound young draught-horse […] re-captured and re-broken for the saddle:** There is no metaphor remotely like this in James's commentary on 'The Coxon Fund'. The closest equivalent elsewhere in the Prefaces comes in the Preface to *The Wings of the Dove*, in a reference to 'that ingenuity of the expert craftsman which likes to be taxed very much to the same tune to which a well-bred horse likes to be saddled' (p. 234). The Preface to *Wings* was composed before the Preface to *The Altar of the Dead* (see the Chronology, pp. clxiii, clxv), so in the present passage James may be half-recalling an equine figure he had set down some seven months earlier.

689 **I proceed […] to "The Private Life" […] at the cost of reaching for a moment over "The Jolly Corner":** In the published table of contents for *NYE* XVII, 'The Jolly Corner' does not come between 'The Birthplace' and 'The Private Life': it is the penultimate story in the volume, followed

only by 'Julia Bride'. James may be confusing the order of stories as published with a memory of an earlier arrangement. In the projected contents list for this volume which he drew up in February 1908, 'The Jolly Corner' occupies something like the position implied by the Preface's parenthetical comment: 'The Altar of the Dead. / The Beast in the Jungle. / The Birthplace. / The Jolly Corner, (never before published.) / The Way It Came. / The Real Right Thing. / The Private Life. / Owen Wingrave. / The Beldonald Holbein. / Flickerbridge. / Four Meetings, (illustration.)' (to the Scribners, 21–26 February 1908; Princeton). Both the distribution of short stories between *NYE* volumes and the order of stories within volumes changed several times between the date of this letter and the end of 1908.

690 **to work together two cases that happened to have been given me**: Two notebook entries survive for 'The Private Life', both predicated on the combination of two distinct 'cases'. On 27 July 1891, James refers to 'the little tale founded on the idea of F.L. and R.B.'; and on 3 August of the same year, 'the idea of rolling into one story the little conceit of the private identity of a personage suggested by F.L., and that of a personage suggested by R.B.' (*CN* 60). The initials in these entries refer to Frederic Leighton and Robert Browning (see notes 691 and 695).

691 **a highly distinguished man, […] to bear out personally as little as possible […] the genius to which he owed his position and his renown**: As James reveals later in the Preface, this was the English poet Robert Browning (1812–89). James had noticed a discrepancy between Browning's social persona and the character of his poetry during the course of his first London winter (1876–7). An encounter at a dinner party given by the American journalist George Washburn Smalley left a strong impression: 'I had a long talk with Browning, who, personally, is no more like to <u>Paracelsus</u> than I to Hercules, but is a great gossip & a very "sympathetic" easy creature' (to MWJ, 31 January [1877]; *CLHJ 1876–1878* 1:43). To Howells, of the same occasion: 'Browning is a great chatterer but no <u>Sordello</u> at all' (30 March [1877]; *CLHJ 1876–1878* 1:90). To his sister, James offered an early formulation of the idea of 'The Private Life': 'evidently there are 2 Brownings—an esoteric & an exoteric. The former never peeps out in society, & the latter has n't a ray of suggestion of <u>Men</u> & <u>Women</u>' (8 April [1877]; *CLHJ 1876–1878* 1:94). James refers in these letters to three of Browning's early volumes, *Paracelsus* (1835), *Sordello* (1840) and *Men and Women* (1855).

692 **The whole aspect and *allure* of the fresh sane man**: The use of italics here may indicate that '*allure*' is to be understood as a word not in English but in French, where it means a person's look, manner or demeanour. Compare James's description of New York City pedestrians in 'New York Revisited' (1906): 'the look, the tramp, the whole quality and *allure*, the consummate monotonous commonness, of the pushing male crowd' (*AS* 83).

693 **"water-tight" compartments**: James refers to the internal division of a ship's hull into sealed compartments by partitions or 'bulkheads', chiefly for reasons of safety: 'a leak or fire in any compartment can in most cases be prevented from affecting the other compartments' (E. J. Reed, *Shipbuilding in Iron and Steel* (London: John Murray, 1869), Ch. 11, p. 213). In the opening chapter of *The Golden Bowl* (1904), Maggie Verver tells her husband: '"I believe things enough about you, my dear, to have a few left if most of them even go to smash. [...] I've divided my faith into water-tight compartments. We must manage not to sink"' (*NYE* XXIII, 14).

694 **his [...] *alter ego***: The earliest instances in *OED* for the modern sense of the naturalized Latin formula 'alter ego' – 'A person's secondary or alternative personality; a persona' – date from the 1830s. This is how Spencer Brydon describes the spectral presence that haunts his old New York family home in 'The Jolly Corner': '"a strange *alter ego* deep down somewhere within me"' (Ch. 1; *NYE* XVII, 449).

695 **that most accomplished of artists and most dazzling of men of the world**: Sir Frederic Leighton (1830–96), English neoclassical painter and sculptor, President of the Royal Academy of Arts from 1878 until his death. James described him to Grace Norton as 'urbane' and 'agreeably artificial' ([c. 4 January 1888]; *HJL* 3:211).

696 **the perpetual, essential performer, [...] an absolutely blank reverse or starved residuum, no *other* power of presence whatever**: James noted on 3 August 1891: 'Lord Mellifont is the public *performer*—the man whose whole personality goes forth so in representation and aspect & sonority & phraseology & accomplishment & frontage that there is absolutely—but I *see* it: begin it—begin it!' (*CN* 60-1). In Chapter 2 of 'The Private Life', the narrator wonders 'what really became of [Lord Mellifont] when no eye could see': 'He relaxed and rested presumably; but how utter a blank mustn't it take to repair such a plenitude of presence!—how intense an *entr'acte* to make possible more such performances!' (*NYE* XVII, 248).

697 **interlunar swoon**: An allusion to P. B. Shelley's lyric 'With a Guitar, to Jane' (1822): 'When you die, the silent Moon, / In her interlunar swoon, / Is not sadder in her cell / Than deserted Ariel' (ll. 23–6; *Poetical Works*, p. 672). See James's uncollected essay 'London in the Dead Season', dated 7 September 1878: 'there is something about London in its interlunar swoon, as Shelley says, which an occasional survivor of the fashionable period finds decidedly agreeable' (*CTW1* 293). In the *NYE* text of *Roderick Hudson*, a phase of 'apathy' on Roderick's part strikes Rowland Mallet as one of 'the interlunar swoons of the true as distinguished from the false artist' (Ch. 23; *NYE* I, 472); the Shelleyan phrase revises 'only a lugubrious interlude' in the text of the 1883 *Collective Edition* (*CE* V, 150).

698 **to the last squeeze of the golden orange**: James often uses this figure to speak of exhausting a given resource or opportunity. In an early review of a posthumous selection of *Passages from the French and Italian Notebooks of Nathaniel Hawthorne* (1872), for example, he acknowledges that readers' respect for 'the proper limits of curiosity' about authors' literary remains will always yield to 'the general fondness for squeezing an orange dry' (*LC1* 307). Again, writing to his brother William from Florence in the spring of 1874: 'Four or five years hence I shall feel like you, about Italy, probably & be sorry that I didn't squeeze the orange tighter before the sensibilities of youth were quite extinct' ([28 February 1874]; *CLHJ 1872–1876* 2:129).

699 **"Play them against each other"**: In 'The Death of the Lion', another story about the private and public lives of artists, this formula refers to the society hostess Mrs Weeks Wimbush getting the artists and writers she is interested in to publicize each other. Neil Paraday is thus made to sit for his portrait to a promising young artist and also 'to write something somewhere' about him: 'She played her victims against each other with admirable ingenuity' (Ch. 8; *NYE* XV, 136).

700 **"The Jolly Corner," […] printed elsewhere only as I write and after my quite ceasing to expect it**: On 28 August 1906, James sent 'The Jolly Corner' – then titled 'The Second House' – to *Harper's Monthly Magazine*. He had been asked for a story of 5,000 words, but explained to the editor Frederick A. Duneka that after 'a big and desperate struggle' with the word-limit, he had finally been 'worsted' (*LL* 437): the story he delivered was over 14,000 words long (*CFHJ* 32, liii). Duneka rejected it, along with the slightly longer 'Julia Bride' (see note 754). James allocated 'The Jolly

Corner' to the *NYE* volume led by 'The Altar of the Dead' as early as 26 February 1908 (see the list of contents with that date quoted in note 689), and he evidently expected that this would be its first appearance in print. Shortly before that volume went to press, however, in December 1908, the story was published in the first issue of Ford Madox Hueffer's magazine *The English Review*. James had told Pinker in mid-September: 'Hueffer is grossly persistent in spite of a categorical refusal a month ago—but *like* the grossly persistent he seems to succeed' (to Pinker, 16 September 1908; quoted in Philip Horne, 'Henry James and the *English Review*', *International Ford Madox Ford Studies* 9 (2010), 25–51; 32). James evidently gave in and let Hueffer have 'The Jolly Corner', and he altered this passage of the Preface in proof in September or October 1908 to acknowledge the story's imminent periodical publication.

701 **"The Friends of the Friends," to which I here change the colourless title of "The Way It Came" (1896), "Owen Wingrave" (1893), [...] "The Real Right Thing" (1900)**: 'The Friends of the Friends' was titled 'The Way It Came' in all texts before the *NYE*: *The Chap-Book* (1 May 1896), *Chapman's Magazine of Fiction* (May 1896) and the volume *Embarrassments* (London: William Heinemann, 1896). The alteration of its title caused some confusion during the production of the *NYE*. As James mailed the revised copy for 'The Friends of the Friends' to his publishers in August 1908 he referred to the story as 'the thing already named to you as "The Way It Came," with its title, always unsatisfactory to me, altered for the better'. An asterisk at this point corresponds to a note at the bottom of the page: '*As I of course explain in Preface' (to the Scribners, 11 August 1908; Princeton). After James had rewritten the Prefaces to *NYE* XV–XVIII to accommodate a last-minute redistribution of tales between these volumes, his editor W. C. Brownell pointed out that he had referred to the story by its old title 'in what we take to be the last sentence of the preface' to *NYE* XVII (Brownell to James, 18 January 1909; Princeton). James corrected the discrepancy but did not admit to having made a mistake: 'I seem to recall that I had some reason for this, and that it was consciously done; but let us restore here, or rather let us establish, "The Friends of the Friends" as elsewhere for absolute smoothness' (to the Scribners, 2 February 1909; Princeton). He mistakes the publication dates of two other stories mentioned in this sentence: 'Owen Wingrave' was first published in 1892 (*The Graphic*, 28 November) and 'The Real Right Thing' in 1899 (*Collier's Weekly*, 16 December).

702 **that love of "a story as a story" which had from far back beset and beguiled their author**: An unexpected statement, in light of James's many prior observations about the naivety of this attitude to fiction (see note 137). Compare W. D. Howells's 'Editor's Study' column in the September 1890 number of *Harper's Monthly Magazine*: 'The fatuity of the story as a story is something that must early impress the story-teller who does not live in the stone age of fiction and criticism. To spin a yarn for the yarn's sake, that is an ideal worthy of a nineteenth-century Englishman, doting in forgetfulness of the English masters and grovelling in ignorance of the Continental masters; but wholly impossible to an American of Mr. Henry James's modernity' (*LFL* 279).

703 **the wind of interest blows where it lists**: An allusion to Jesus' words to Nicodemus in John's gospel: 'The wind bloweth where it listeth, and thou hearest the sound thereof, but canst not tell whence it cometh, and whither it goeth: so is every one that is born of the Spirit' (John 3:8).

704 **one man's amusement is at the best [...] another's desolation**: A variation on the proverb 'One man's meat is another man's poison' (Smith, *The Oxford Dictionary of English Proverbs*, p. 344).

705 **some other and more colourable fashion [...] answering for them on his more or less gentlemanly honour**: After the early nineteenth century, the word 'colourable' occurs most frequently in a legal sense: 'Capable of being presented as true or valid; having at least a *prima facie* appearance of justice or legality'. In earlier usage the word also means 'Having an appearance of truth or trustworthiness; plausible; reasonable' (*OED*). For the author's word of honour, see also the Preface to *The Wings of the Dove*, pp. 235–6.

706 **the would-be portentous climax of Edgar Poe's "Arthur Gordon Pym,"**: *The Narrative of Arthur Gordon Pym* (1838) breaks off as Edgar Allan Poe's first-person narrator, approaching the South Pole in a canoe on a warm, luminous, milk-white ocean, passes through a 'cataract' or 'curtain' of white vapour and has a vision of 'a shrouded human figure, very far larger in its proportions than any dweller among men. And the hue of the skin of the figure was of the perfect whiteness of the snow' (Edgar Allan Poe, *Poetry and Tales*, ed. Patrick F. Quinn (New York: Library of America, 1984), p. 1179). No explanation is offered; a concluding 'Note' by an unnamed authorial persona declares the *Narrative* incomplete. In the opening chapter of *The Golden Bowl*, Amerigo likens his situation with regard to the Ververs and their circle to Pym's situation at this climactic

moment: 'There were moments when he felt his own boat move upon some such mystery. The state of mind of his new friends [...] had resemblances to a great white curtain' (*NYE* XXIII, 22).

707 **hang in the void**: The Preface appears to echo a question which Edith Wharton in 1934 would remember putting to James about *The Golden Bowl*: '"What was your idea in suspending the four principal characters [...] in the void? [...] Why have you stripped them of all the *human fringes* we necessarily trail after us through life?"' As she recalls, 'He looked at me in surprise' and 'after a pause of reflection [...] answered in a disturbed voice: "My dear—I didn't know I had!"' (Wharton, *A Backward Glance* (New York and London: D. Appleton-Century Company, 1934), p. 191).

708 **the elusive presence nightly "stalked" through the New York house**: In Chapter 2 of 'The Jolly Corner', we are told of Spencer Brydon's pursuit of his alter ego that he 'had been introduced to no sport that demanded at once the patience and the nerve of this stalking of a creature more subtle, yet at bay perhaps more formidable, than any beast of the forest' (*NYE* XVII, 456–7).

709 **in old note-books**: Notebook entries survive for all three stories referred to in the previous sentence of the Preface: 'Owen Wingrave' (26 March and 8 May 1892; *CN* 66–8), 'The Friends of the Friends' (5 February and 21 December 1895, 10 January 1896; *CN* 112, 144, 151–4) and 'Sir Edmund Orme' (22 January 1879; *CN* 10).

710 **the old burden of the much life and the little art**: In an essay of 1877 on the French poet Alfred de Musset, James had similarly reflected on the number of incidents in Musset's life – 'his exaltations and weaknesses, his pangs and tears, his passions and debaucheries', etc. – that were 'necessary in order that we should have the two or three little volumes into which his *best* could be compressed. It takes certainly a great deal of life to make a little art!' (*LC2* 618). He appears to be recalling, and purposefully inverting, the classical Latin formula 'ars longa, vita brevis', a translation of an aphorism by the ancient Greek physician Hippocrates contrasting the shortness of a human life with the time it takes to master any art or craft – as rendered, for example, by Geoffrey Chaucer in the late fourteenth-century poem *The Parliament of Fowls*: 'The lyf so short, the craft so long to lerne' (l. 1; *The Riverside Chaucer*, 3rd edn, general editor Larry D. Benson (Boston, MA: Houghton Mifflin Company, 1987), p. 385).

711 **to opine with the celebrated Topsy that it can only have "growed.":** James refers to a famous scene in Harriet Beecher Stowe's abolitionist novel *Uncle Tom's Cabin* (1852), in which the Black slave girl Topsy is questioned about God by her new mistress. In Chapter 20, Miss Ophelia asks Topsy: '"Do you know who made you?" "Nobody, as I knows on," said the child, with a short laugh. The idea appeared to amuse her considerably; for her eyes twinkled, and she added, "I spect I grow'd. Don't think nobody never made me"' (Stowe, *Three Novels: Uncle Tom's Cabin, or Life Among the Lowly; The Minister's Wooing; Oldtown Folks* (New York: Library of America, 1982), p. 282). The saying became a nineteenth-century commonplace. James had appealed to its general currency in an article for *The Nation* on 'The Early Meeting of Parliament' (1878), with reference to the 'circumstances' that had given rise to the Second Anglo-Afghan War: 'If one is not pledged to look at the matter through partisan spectacles one may perhaps be free to conjecture that, like many other disagreeable things, they came about very naturally. Like Topsy in the novel, they "growed"' (*HJC* 26).

712 **on a penny chair and under a great tree in Kensington Gardens:** Kensington Gardens is one of London's Royal Parks; originally the formal garden of Kensington Palace, it lies immediately to the west of the larger Hyde Park and is bounded by the districts of Bayswater to the north, Notting Hill and Holland Park to the west and Kensington to the south. It was James's local park while he lived at 34 De Vere Gardens (1886–98): as he observed to Henrietta Reubell on 19 May 1886, 'Since I have come to live close to Kensington Gardens I see more of that paradise, which, especially at this season, is a wondrous thing to find in the heart of a great city' (*CLHJ 1884–1886* 2:99). In his uncollected essay 'The Suburbs of London' (1877), James had contrasted the 'rural scenery' of Kensington Gardens with the fashionable crowds of Hyde Park: 'In Hyde park [sic] you see fine people; in Kensington Gardens you see only fine trees' (*CTW1* 277, 278). Chairs were available for hire in Kensington Gardens for the relatively small sum of 1 penny, and James's characters often take advantage of them: Hyacinth and Millicent Henning in Chapter 41 of *The Princess Casamassima*, Paul Overt in Chapter 4 of 'The Lesson of the Master', Maisie and the Captain in Chapter 16 of *What Maisie Knew*, and Kate and Densher in Book Second, Chapter 3 of *The Wings of the Dove*.

713 **that while I sat there in [...] the ever so softened London hum a young man should have taken his place on another chair [...] and have settled to a book with immediate gravity?:** As John Carlos Rowe points out, the

Preface's recollected scene of inspiration in Kensington Gardens reappears in the first chapter of 'Owen Wingrave' (*The Theoretical Dimensions of Henry James*, pp. 241-2): 'The spring day was warm to [Owen's] young blood, and he had a book in his pocket which, when he had passed into the Gardens and, after a short stroll, dropped into a chair, he took out with the slow soft sigh that finally ushers in a pleasure postponed. He stretched his long legs and began to read it' (*NYE* XVII, 272). For T. J. Lustig, the 'ever so softened London hum' of the park in this sentence of the Preface 'recalls Matthew Arnold on "the girdling city's hum" in "Lines Written in Kensington Gardens [1852]"', an association strengthened by the connection James consistently drew between Arnold and Johann Wolfgang von Goethe (1749-1832), whose poems Owen is reading at the start of the story (*The Turn of the Screw and Other Stories*, ed. Lustig, p. 245). The Preface does not mention James's recent encounter with a relevant historical source for 'Owen Wingrave', the *Mémoires du général baron de Marbot* (1891): see his first notebook entry for the story (26 March 1892), which refers to 'The idea of the *Soldier*—produced a little by the fascinated perusal of Marbot's magnificent memoirs' (*CN* 66). Lustig observes that this notebook entry was made in spring, but the Preface refers to 'summer': 'Possibly the figure of the young man [in Kensington Gardens] combined with the Marbot germ later in the same year' (*The Turn of the Screw and Other Stories*, ed. Lustig, p. 245).

714 **that presence of some self-conscious dangerous girl of lockets and amulets offered by the full-blown idea to my very first glance**: A locket is Kate Julian's pretext for coming downstairs to continue arguing with Owen in Chapter 4, with the result that he determines to spend the night in the haunted room: '"I'm going down to look for something. I've lost a jewel. [...] A rather good turquoise, out of my locket"' (*NYE* XVII, 313). Kate entered James's scheme in his second notebook entry for the story (8 May 1892), as 'some woman, some girl, whom [the hero] loves but who has taken the line of despising him for his renunciation' (*CN* 68).

715 **with a large picture, in a weekly newspaper**: 'Sir Edmund Orme' was first published on 25 November 1891 in the Christmas issue of the magazine *Black and White: A Weekly Illustrated Record and Review*, with an illustration by John H. Bacon.

716 **a state of *unconscious* obsession or [...] hauntedness, [...] a break in the blest ignorance**: This idea occurs in a notebook entry made long before the composition of 'Sir Edmund Orme' on 22 January 1879: 'A young girl,

unknown to herself, is followed, constantly, by a figure which other persons see. She is perfectly unconscious of it—but there is a dread that she may cease to be so' (*CN* 10).

717 **the old, the mid-Victorian, the Thackerayan Brighton**: The English seaside town of Brighton in East Sussex was established as a fashionable health-resort in the eighteenth century, and was notably patronized by George, Prince of Wales (1762–1830), later George IV. In 1841, the town was linked to London by railway and became a popular destination for middle-class tourists and day-trippers. James spent the Christmas of 1906 at Brighton as the guest of the retired American journalist Manton Marble (1834–1917), and on 26 December he wrote to his old friend Thomas Sergeant Perry 'in presence of a shining silvery shimmery sea, on one of the prettiest possible south-coast mornings. It's like the old Brighton that you may read about (Miss Honeyman's) in the early chapters of the "Newcomes"' (*LHJ* 2:62–3). In W. M. Thackeray's novel *The Newcomes* (1854–5), the young hero Clive has an aunt, Miss Honeyman, who keeps a lodging-house in Brighton; Chapter 9 opens with a mock-heroic description of the town's sea-front. The Brighton of Thackeray's novels was not strictly 'mid-Victorian', though the novels themselves were: the action of *The Newcomes* is mostly set in the 1830s, and in Chapter 22 of *Vanity Fair* (1848) George and Amelia Osborne begin their honeymoon at Brighton in April 1815.

718 **I have placed "Julia Bride," for material reasons, at the end of this Volume, quite out of her congruous company**: In his original plan for the *NYE* volumes of short stories, James meant 'Julia Bride' to be the last item in a volume that would open with two other tales about young American women, 'Daisy Miller' and 'Pandora'. The 'material reasons' he refers to in this sentence of the Preface occasioned a general redistribution of tales in December 1908, in the course of which 'Julia Bride' moved to the closing position in *NYE* XVII (see the Introduction, pp. xciii–cii).

719 **That link is with others to come**: The remainder of James's commentary on 'Julia Bride' comes in the Preface to *NYE* XVIII, alongside his remarks on 'Daisy Miller', 'Pandora' and 'Fordham Castle' (pp. 218–20).

720 **Full-fed statement here, to repeat my expression**: For a reader who encounters the Prefaces in the order of publication, this will not seem to be a repetition: the only other instance of the expression 'full-fed statement' in the Prefaces occurs *after* this passage in the published sequence of *NYE* volumes, in a discussion of foreshortening in the Preface to *NYE*

XVIII (see pp. 220–1). This slip probably represents uncorrected fallout from James's redistribution of tales and consequent rewriting of the affected Prefaces in December 1908 and January 1909.

721 **"Here we are again!" [...] even as the clown at the circus launches the familiar greeting**: 'Here we are again!' is one of the Clown's catch-phrases in early nineteenth-century British pantomime, whence it migrated to the British and North American circus over the course of the century: it marks the reappearance of the Clown and Harlequin after the transformation scene that initiates the harlequinade, the slapstick section of a pantomime involving characters from the Italian *commedia dell'arte*. In *A Small Boy and Others* (1913), James would recall going as a child in the 1840s and 1850s to variety performances at the Niblo's Garden theatre in New York that incorporated elements of classic pantomime, and comparing them with 'the pantomimes in London' which he had read so much about 'in English story-books': 'We hadn't the transformation-scene, it was true, though what this really seemed to come to was clown and harlequin taking liberties with policemen [...]; but we had at Niblo's harlequin and columbine, albeit of less pure a tradition, and we knew moreover all about clowns, for we went to circuses too, [...] the good old orthodox circuses under tents set up in vacant lots, with which New York appears at that time to have bristled' (Ch. 12; *Aut* 105–6). At the end of the period described in *A Small Boy*, an American journalist recalled the delight of earlier child-audiences at the circus at the moment 'when Clown [...] burst upon our enraptured gaze. Jolly old Clown! how we did love him! How were we convulsed with laughter at his invariable "Here we are again!"' ('The Circus, Past and Present', *Yankee Notions* 8.3 (March 1859), 78). The nineteenth-century Clown's appearance, comic routines, songs and sayings derived from the innovations of the actor Joseph Grimaldi (1778–1837). An illustrated article in the English *Strand Magazine* in the 1890s describes the pantomime Clown – 'the irrepressible disciple of Joey Grimaldi', pictured in his traditional costume and white and red facial make-up – bursting onto the stage from a trap-door 'to thrust his hands in his capacious pockets, screw his highly coloured mouth into position, and shout out at the top of his voice: "Here we are again! A Muddy Christmas and a Sloppy New Year!"' ('Transformation Scenes: How They are Made and Worked', *Strand Magazine* 6 (December 1893), 705–10; 710).

722 **the up-town debility [...] the minor key, to re-employ my expression**: The expression 'the minor key' will not register here as a repetition for a

reader following the published order of the Prefaces; as with 'full-fed statement' in the previous paragraph (see note 720), here again James probably fails to adjust for changes made in the Prefaces to *NYE* XVII and XVIII on account of the last-minute transfer of tales between these volumes. The association between 'up-town' New York and 'the minor key' is explained in the Preface to *NYE* XVIII, pp. 216–17.

723 **the large juvenile licence as to getting "engaged," disengaged and re-engaged**: In an essay of 1886, James had praised W. D. Howells's depiction of American girls' freedom to engage themselves in marriage: in *The Rise of Silas Lapham* (1885), nothing is better than 'the whole picture of casual female youth and contemporaneous "engaging" one's self' (*LC1* 504).

724 **the palladium of their liberties**: A palladium is 'a thing on which the safety of a nation, institution, privilege, etc., is believed to depend; a source of protection, a safeguard'; it was originally 'An image of the goddess Pallas (Athene) in the citadel of Troy, whose presence was believed to guarantee the safety of the city' (*OED*).

725 **the unrestricted freedom of re-marriage in the lifetime of the parties**: James had recently written on 'cheap and easy divorce' as a factor in modern American life in his third *Harper's Bazar* paper on 'The Manners of American Women' (June 1907), speculating on its relevance to the forms of feminine behaviour he had encountered on his tour of 1904–5, 'especially in the hotels and trains': 'Fresh from the frequent statistic and accessible, all round, to the voices of the air, I couldn't, as a restless analyst, rid myself of the conviction that the majority of the mothers and wives thus met and noted were of divorced and divorcing condition and intention' (*HJC* 103–4).

726 **Don Quixote assisted through his castle-gate […] Moses Primrose welcomed home from the Fair**: In Part I, Chapter V of Miguel de Cervantes's *The Ingenious Gentleman Don Quixote of La Mancha* (1605), a bruised Don Quixote is brought home on the back of a peasant's ass at the close of his first series of chivalric adventures, having gone out to fight giants, fallen from his horse and been beaten by a muleteer. James also refers to a favourite episode in Oliver Goldsmith's sentimental novel *The Vicar of Wakefield* (1766): in Chapter 12, the vicar's son Moses Primrose is entrusted with selling the family's horse at a local fair, and returns having sold the horse but spent the money on '"a groce [gross] of green spectacles"' which he has been duped into buying as an investment (*The Collected Works of Oliver Goldsmith*, vol. IV, p. 67). In his introduction to a

1900 reprint of *The Vicar of Wakefield*, James had listed 'Moses and his spectacles' amongst Goldsmith's 'happiest strokes', 'the felicities that have become familiar and famous' (G. S. Rousseau (ed.), *Oliver Goldsmith: The Critical Heritage* (London and New York: Routledge, 1974), p. 67).

PREFACE to *Daisy Miller, Pandora, The Patagonia and Other Tales* (NYE XVIII)

727 **in Rome during the autumn of 1877; a friend then living there [...] a child of nature and of freedom, [...] "picked up" by the wayside [...] a good-looking Roman**: James was in Rome from late October to early December 1877. Leon Edel identifies the 'friend' mentioned in this passage of the Preface as Alice Bartlett, whom James had first met in Rome in the winter of 1873–4 (*LC2* 1380), and whom he encountered there again four years later, 'as excellent as ever' (*CLHJ 1876–1878* 1:222). She married a Texan banker in 1878 and settled in South Carolina. Maqbool Aziz suggests that the young American woman in Bartlett's anecdote was Julia Newberry, who had died in Rome in April 1876 at the age of 22 while making a tour of the Continent with her family and was buried in the Protestant Cemetery (*The Tales of Henry James. Volume Three: 1875–1879*, ed. Aziz (Oxford: Clarendon Press, 1984), pp. 15–16). In referring to her as 'a child of nature and of freedom', James alludes to Chapter 34 of Charles Dickens's novel *The Life and Adventures of Martin Chuzzlewit* (1844), where the American patriot Elias Pogram describes his '"fellow-countryman"' Mr Chollop as '"a child of Natur', and a child of Freedom"' (*Martin Chuzzlewit*, ed. Margaret Cardwell (Oxford: Clarendon Press, 1982), p. 533). On 31 March 1880, James had written thus to Charles Eliot Norton about the American painter Frank Duveneck: 'He is "a child of nature & a child of freedom," as Martin Chuzzlewit says [*sic*]; but he also struck me as much the most highly-developed phenomenon in the way of a painter that the U.S.A. have given birth to' (*CLHJ 1878–1880* 2:149). The phrase also occurs in *Daisy Miller: A Comedy* (1883), James's dramatic adaptation of his own story: Charles Reverdy – a new character invented for the stage version – describes Daisy's little brother Randolph as 'a dauntless American infant; a child of nature and of freedom' (*CP* 126). The inverted commas around '"picked up"' in this sentence of the Preface quote a discriminatory idiom from the story. In Chapter 1, the courier Eugenio's reaction on discovering Daisy talking with Winterbourne conveys 'an insinuation that she

"picked up" acquaintances'; in Chapter 3, Mrs Costello claims that Daisy '"has picked up half a dozen of the regular Roman fortune-hunters of the inferior sort"', and Mrs Walker complains of her '"[f]lirting with any man she can pick up"' (*NYE* XVIII, 20, 46, 64).

728 **the editor of a magazine that had its seat of publication at Philadelphia and had lately appeared to appreciate my contributions**: The magazine was *Lippincott's Magazine*, which was published in Philadelphia by J. B. Lippincott & Co.; the editor at this period was the American historian John Foster Kirk (1824–1904). *Lippincott's* had recently published three English travel essays by James ('An English Easter', 'Abbeys and Castles' and 'London at Midsummer', all 1877); in 1878, the magazine would publish his short story 'Théodolinde' (retitled 'Rose-Agathe' in 1885) and his travel essay 'The British Soldier'.

729 **a friend to whom I appealed for light**: Edel suggests that this was Leslie Stephen, who would publish 'Daisy Miller' in the *Cornhill Magazine* (*Henry James: The Conquest of London*, p. 304). See also notes 730 and 732.

730 **being promptly pirated in Boston—a sweet tribute I hadn't yet received and was never again to know**: Until the US government passed the International Copyright Act (commonly referred to as the 'Chase Act') in 1891, no reciprocal copyright agreement existed between Britain and America. British writers could not copyright their works in the US; American citizens were effectually protected under British copyright law if they were resident in England and either published simultaneously on both sides of the Atlantic, or published first in England and secured the American copyright by registering a pre-publication copy with the Library of Congress (see Anesko, '*Friction with the Market*', pp. 36, 163–6). 'Daisy Miller' appeared in the English *Cornhill Magazine* before James could secure copyright in the US. As Anesko notes, 'James intended to sell the advance sheets for simultaneous publication in America—probably to *Harper's*—but [Leslie] Stephen rushed the first half of the story into the June [1878] number, without leaving James sufficient margin to arrange for an authorized magazine appearance in America' ('*Friction with the Market*', p. 43). 'Daisy Miller' was duly 'pirated' – published without authorization – by two American magazines, *Littell's Living Age* in Boston (6 and 27 July 1878) and the *Home Journal* in New York (31 July, 7 and 14 August 1878). This was not in fact the last time that James would be so treated in Boston. He allowed 'A Bundle of Letters' to be published in a French newspaper in December 1879 without first securing the American copyright (see note

590), and in January 1880 the story was issued by the Boston publisher Frank Loring as an unauthorized 25-cent pamphlet. James wrote to his father on that occasion: 'The thing will be a lesson for me, & I shall never in future publish ten lines in an European journal without copyrighting it in advance in the U.S., as I can easily do' (15 February [1880]; *CLHJ 1878–1880* 2:123).

731 **the ultimately most prosperous child of my invention**: In financial terms, James prospered much less than he might have done from the phenomenal success of 'Daisy Miller'. The contract he signed with the Harpers for the cheap book edition (1878) brought him royalties at 10 per cent, but the low price of the volumes – 20 cents in paper wrappers and 35 cents in cloth – meant that he earned only $200 on initial sales of 20,000 copies. The two-volume English first edition (1879) published by Macmillan and Co., which also contained 'An International Episode' and 'Four Meetings', was an expensive book (21 shillings) and sold much more modestly. As Anesko points out, however, 'the catalytic effect of sudden publicity' was in itself valuable to James at this point in his career: 'Daisy Miller' introduced him to the British reading public and allowed him to operate 'as a professional man of letters' on a transatlantic basis (see *'Friction with the Market'*, pp. 43–4). The story sold steadily: new editions were published by the Harpers in 1883 and 1892, and by Macmillan in 1880, 1883 (in the *Collective Edition* of James's fiction) and 1888.

732 **my admirable friend the late Leslie Stephen [...] two numbers of** *The Cornhill Magazine* **(1878)**: James told his father that Stephen had accepted 'Daisy Miller' 'with effusion' (19 April [1878]; *CLHJ 1876–1878* 2:104); the story appeared in the *Cornhill* in June and July 1878. For James's friendship with Stephen, see note 584.

733 **"a Study"; [...] a certain flatness in my poor little heroine's literal denomination**: The title of the story in all texts before *NYE* is 'Daisy Miller: A Study'. In the visual arts, a 'study' is 'A preliminary drawing, painting, sculpture, etc., produced as an exercise in a particular skill or technique, or as preparation for subsequent work'; also 'a painting, drawing, photograph, etc., presenting a detailed treatment of a particular subject and aiming to capture its characteristics as they are revealed by especially careful observation' (*OED*). Philip Horne (*Henry James and Revision*, p. 229) quotes James using the word in this sense about his short novel of the same period, *The Europeans* (1878): 'It is only a sketch—very brief

& with no space for much action; in fact it is a "study," like Daisy Miller' (to WJ, 23 July [1878]; *CLHJ 1876–1878* 2:178). Horne also draws a connection between 'flatness' in this and the next sentence of the Preface and a vocal quality which Daisy Miller shares with the American heroine of another of James's international stories, Francie Dosson in *The Reverberator* (1888): Daisy speaks in a 'small flat monotone' (Ch. 2; *NYE* XVIII, 31), and Francie has a 'small flat patient voice', a 'little harmonising flatness' of tone (Chs. 4 and 10; *NYE* XIII, 52, 135) (see *Henry James and Revision*, pp. 255–6 n. 20). The last example quoted above is an addition to the revised *NYE* text of *The Reverberator* without any counterpart in earlier editions.

734 **the characteristic free play of the whirligig of time**: James's sentence combines two literary allusions: to Matthew Arnold's 'free play of the mind' (see note 279) and to Feste's remark to Malvolio at the close of Shakespeare's *Twelfth Night* (1601–2), 'And thus the whirligig of time brings in his revenges' (5.1.376–7). The term 'whirligig' is used for 'various toys that are whirled, twirled, or spun round', including tops and miniature windmills, and thus figuratively means the 'Plaything' or 'sport' of an external force; the line in *Twelfth Night* is cited as an instance of another figurative meaning of the word: 'circling course, revolution (of time or events)' (*OED*). In 'The Sense of Newport' (1906), James had recently noted this mechanism at work at Newport, Rhode Island, viewing the abandoned villas of Ocean Drive which he had first seen being built in the 1860s: 'I seemed to take full in my face [...] the cold stir of air produced when the whirligig of time has made one of its liveliest turns' (*AS* 213).

735 **in Venice and in the prized society of an interesting friend, now dead**: As Adrian Poole notes, 'interesting friends of James's associated with Venice, now dead, included the wealthy American hostess Katherine [or Katharine] de Kay Bronson (1834–1901)' (*Daisy Miller and An International Episode*, ed. Poole (Oxford: Oxford University Press, 2013), p. 203). James had recently commemorated Bronson in an essay first published as a prefatory note to her own reminiscences of Robert Browning ('Browning in Venice'; *Cornhill Magazine*, February 1902); when James revised this piece for *Italian Hours* (1909), he would change its title to 'Casa Alvisi', the name of Bronson's house on the Grand Canal. The next sentence but one of the Preface refers to this friend as 'my charming hostess': James was a frequent visitor to Bronson's salon at Casa Alvisi and had been her houseguest for several weeks in the spring of 1887 (see note 505).

736 **in a New York newspaper (1884)**: 'Pandora' was published in two issues of the New York *Sun*, 1 and 8 June 1884.

737 **twenty words jotted down in New York [...] a year or two before**: James refers to a brief notebook entry made between 17 and 30 May 1883 (quoted here in its entirety): '"The self-made girl"—a very good subject for a short-story [*sic*]. Very modern, very local; much might be done' (*CN* 22).

738 **I had put a question to a friend [...] "backers," [...] a proposer possibly half-hearted and a slightly sceptical seconder**: Edel suggests that the 'friend' was Marion 'Clover' Hooper Adams (1843–85), the wife of the American historian Henry Adams (1838–1918) (*LC2* 1380). James had met the Adamses socially in Washington, DC on the two visits he made to the city in January 1882 and April 1883 (described in the Preface to *NYE* XIV, pp. 169–71). When he began to work out the subject of 'Pandora' in January 1884, he thought that he 'might even *do* Henry Adams & his wife' (*CN* 24); in the event, he would use Clover Adams as a model for the political hostess Mrs Bonnycastle, who fulfils the same explanatory function in the story as the 'friend' does in this passage of the Preface. James here combines the language of finance ('backers' as investors) with that of politics or gentlemen's clubs (a parliamentary motion and a would-be member of a club would similarly require to be both proposed and seconded).

739 **a new social and local variety, the "self-made," or at least self-making, girl, [...] like one of the dismembered charges of Little Bo-Peep, leaving her "tail" behind her**: Compare James's note for 'Pandora' of 29 January 1884: 'I don't see why I shouldn't do the "self-made girl," whom I noted here last winter, in a way to make her a rival to D[aisy] M[iller]' (*CN* 24). Pandora Day is repeatedly described by other American characters in the story as an instance of a '"new type"'; the Bonnycastles identify this type – '"She's the self-made girl!"' – and define it for the German diplomat Vogelstein in Chapter 2 (*NYE* XVIII, 148–51). James rings a change on an English nursery rhyme: 'Little Bo-peep has lost her sheep, / And can't tell where to find them; / Leave them alone, and they'll come home, / And bring their tails behind them' (*The Oxford Dictionary of Nursery Rhymes*, ed. Iona and Peter Opie (Oxford: Oxford University Press, 1951), p. 93).

740 **working out [...] her social salvation**: To 'work out (one's own) salvation', figuratively, is 'to be independent or self-reliant in striving towards one's goal' (*OED*, 'salvation'). The source of the phrase is biblical: St Paul urges

the Philippians to 'work out your own salvation with fear and trembling' (Philippians 2:12).

741 **The evolution of varieties moves fast**: James takes his evolutionary metaphor from the text of 'Pandora'. In Chapter 2, for example, Alfred Bonnycastle observes that the self-made girl is '"the latest freshest fruit of our great American evolution"'; in the Bonnycastles' analysis, 'The natural history of this interesting creature was at last completely laid bare to the earnest stranger' (*NYE* XVIII, 148, 150).

742 **very little of which [...] was to struggle to the surface**: In the published story, Pandora has only one brother and one sister, and no detail is given of her successful provision for her family: she only tells Vogelstein that they are '"very happy"' and '"getting quite used to New York"' (Ch. 2; *NYE* XVIII, 160).

743 **a brief but profusely peopled stay in New York**: James refers to a phase of the long visit he made to America from November 1881 to May 1882. He spent most of December 1881 in New York as the guest of his old friend the editor Edwin Laurence Godkin: as he told Isabella Stewart Gardner, he had 'stepped into a network of engagements made for me by my genial host (Godkin,)' and had 'rarely been able to lay my hand upon the fleeting hour & say "This is my own"' (7 December [1881]; *CLHJ 1880–1883* 2:37–8).

744 **that fact of my insuperably restricted experience [...] on which the current of these remarks has already led me to dilate**: James here refers back to comments on his ignorance of the business side of American life in the Preface to *NYE* XIII, pp. 152–3.

745 **the world "down-town" [...] the monstrous labyrinth that stretches from Canal Street to the Battery**: James refers to the financial district of New York City at the southern end of Manhattan Island. In general American usage, the adjective 'downtown' means 'Of, situated in, or belonging to the central part or main business and commercial area of a town or city' (*OED*).

746 **the hived stuff of drama**: To 'hive' in this sense is 'To hoard or store *up*, as honey, in the hive'. The *OED* cites a poetical example from Byron's *Childe Harold's Pilgrimage*, Canto III (1816): the English historian Edward Gibbon (1737–94) is described as 'deep and slow, exhausting thought, / And hiving wisdom with each studious year' (stanza 107, ll. 995–6; Byron, *The Complete Poetical Works*, vol. II, p. 116). James had recently written to

Morton Fullerton about his American tour of 1904–5: 'I shall have uncannily hived enough acrid honey to make, probably, a couple of books (of social notes, &c) – instead of the *one* I had very timidly planned [*The American Scene*]' (2 December 1905; quoted *LL* 427 n. 2).

747 **perched, for raking the scene, on any coign of vantage**: To 'rake' in this sense is 'To sweep with the eyes; to look up and down' (*OED*). James had recently figured his observation of the American scene in comparable terms, taking in at a single glance the present topography of a familiar city and 'the whole backward vista' of his personal connection with it: 'The top of Beacon Hill quite rakes, with a but slightly shifting range, the old more definite Boston' ('Boston' (1906), *AS* 230). To 'rake' here – used of the viewpoint rather than the observer – is 'To command, dominate, *esp.* to command or afford a view of, overlook' (*OED*). See also the passage on the Capitol in 'Washington' (1906), which is printed in *The American Scene* under the page headline 'The Raking Terraces' (*AS* 362–3). The phrase 'coign of vantage', one of James's favourite Shakespearean allusions, refers to King Duncan's lines on the house-martins nesting on the walls of Macbeth's castle: 'no jutty, frieze, / Buttress, nor coign of vantage, but this bird / Hath made his pendant bed and procreant cradle' (1.6.6–8). The same allusion to *Macbeth* occurs again in combination with the verb 'rake' in the Preface to *The Wings of the Dove*, p. 242.

748 **not only that the major key was "down-town" but that down-town was, all itself, the major key […] the minor was "up-town," and […] up-town the minor**: The terms of this antithesis are drawn from the terminology of western tonal music: a 'key' in this sense is 'A system of notes comprising a scale, regarded as forming the tonal basis of a piece or passage of music'. According to the *OED*, the phrase 'the minor key' is often used figuratively to denote 'the sombre, plaintive, or subdued effect associated with minor chords and keys' in music; there is no entry in the *OED* for equivalent figurative uses of 'the major key' (*OED*, 'key', 'minor', 'major'). In other Prefaces, James uses 'major' and 'minor' in a different sense, to denote the greater or lesser extent of a literary form: in the Preface to *NYE* XV, for example, where *nouvelles* or long stories are described as 'studies on the minor scale' (p. 174), with 'scale' now meaning not a series of musical notes but 'Relative or proportionate size or extent' (*OED*, 'scale' *n.*³). The sense of restricted size or scope is present too in the Preface to *NYE* XVII when James connects 'the minor key' with the *nouvelle* as a form, and also with intrinsically slight 'up-town' subject-matter (p. 209): that passage seems

to have been detached from the present discussion by James's rewriting of the Prefaces to *NYE* XV–XVIII in December 1908 and January 1909. For the 'metaphorical drift' in James's work between these and other associations of the phrase 'the minor key', see Rebekah Scott, 'Henry James: "In the Minor Key"', in Leonardo Buonomo (ed.), *The Sound of James: The Aural Dimension in Henry James's Work* (Trieste: Edizioni Università di Trieste, 2021), pp. 17–34; 18. For 'down-town', see note 745; 'up-town' contrastingly refers to 'The higher or upper part of a town or city, *spec.* the residential or more prosperous area' (*OED*).

749 **a not inconsiderably earlier season [...] the very moderate altitude of Twenty-Fifth Street**: James refers to the winter and early spring of 1874–5, which he spent in lodgings at 111 East 25th Street (see note 22). The figure of 'altitude' refers to the fact that the numbering of cross streets in New York City starts at 1st Street in Lower Manhattan and rises as one moves northwards, or goes 'up-town'.

750 **"Daisy Miller," "Pandora," "The Patagonia," "Miss Gunton," "Julia Bride"**: The last two stories listed here do not appear in *NYE* XVIII, having been moved by James to other volumes in December 1908: 'Miss Gunton of Poughkeepsie' (1900) was transferred to *NYE* XVI and 'Julia Bride' to *NYE* XVII. There is no discussion of 'Miss Gunton of Poughkeepsie' or of 'The Patagonia' in any Preface; James's comments on 'Julia Bride' are divided between the Prefaces to *NYE* XVII and XVIII.

751 **curvet and caracole**: These two verbs correspond to technical terms originating in the French *haute école* of equestrianism: a 'curvet' is 'a leap in which a trained horse rears up and jumps forward on its hind legs without its forelegs touching the ground', and a 'caracole' is 'A half-turn or wheel to the right or left executed by a horseman' or '"a succession of such wheels to right and left alternately, movement in a zigzag course"'; both verbs are often used loosely to mean 'to caper, prance, leap' (*OED*). James employs a related image in 'The Lesson of Balzac' (1905) to characterize his English contemporary George Meredith as a novelist who – unlike Balzac – possesses 'The lyrical element', a poetic quality: 'that bright particular genius of our own day, George Meredith, who so strikes us as hitching winged horses to the chariot of his prose—steeds who prance and dance and caracole, who strain the traces, attempt to quit the ground, and yearn for the upper air' (*LC2* 122). Meredith was a writer of verse as well as a novelist.

752 **a single "spill" […] in Wall Street**: A 'spill' in this sense is 'A throw from a horse or vehicle; a fall or tumble; an upset' (*OED*, 'spill' *n.*⁴); the figure refers to James's sense of the risk of committing some solecism in his ignorance of business affairs. The New York Stock Exchange has been located at 11 Wall Street since 1865; for James's and subsequent generations, the street name was a metonym for 'the American financial world or money-market' (*OED*).

753 **the other constituents of the volume, the intermediate ones**: The earliest surviving list of contents for the *NYE* volume headed by 'Daisy Miller' was set out by James in a letter to the Scribners on 23 October 1908: 'Daisy Miller (illustration.) / Pandora / The Patagonia / The Marriages / The Real Thing / Brooksmith / Flickerbridge / The Beldonald Holbein / The Story in It / Paste / "Europe" / Miss Gunton of Poughkeepsie / Fordham Castle / Julia Bride' (Princeton). The Preface's reference to 'intermediate' stories makes more sense in relation to this list than to the published contents of *NYE* XVIII: James would thus be referring to the stories from 'The Marriages' through to 'Paste', which have British rather than American subjects.

754 **"Julia Bride" (which independently of its appearance here has seen the light but in *Harper's Magazine*, 1908)**: Like 'The Jolly Corner' (see note 700), 'Julia Bride' was planned as a very short story for *Harper's Monthly Magazine*, but grew to three times the desired length in the writing and was rejected in the autumn of 1906. At this point it appears that the president of Harper and Brothers, Colonel George Harvey, overrode the decision of his editor Frederick A. Duneka and secured the story's acceptance: 'Julia Bride' eventually appeared in two issues of *Harper's Monthly Magazine*, March–April 1908 (*CFHJ* 32, lii–lvi).

755 **As I wind up with this companion-study to "Daisy Miller" the considerable assortment of my shorter tales**: James originally intended 'Julia Bride' to close the final *NYE* volume of short stories, a volume headed by 'Daisy Miller'; for its eventual move to the volume headed by 'The Altar of the Dead', see the Introduction, pp. xcviii–ci. James had described 'Julia Bride' to Duneka on 14 September 1906 as a successor to his most famous early tale, telling him that it 'ought to knock "Daisy Miller" into a cocked hat!' (*LL* 438).

756 **the down-town penetralia**: For 'penetralia' as the closed social spaces of European salons in the Preface to *NYE* XIII, see note 503. In 'New York Revisited' (1906), James had recently used the same word to note

the unexpected ease of public access to American municipal buildings. He remarked of New York City Hall, a few blocks north of Wall Street in Lower Manhattan: 'The only drawback to such freedom is that penetralia it is so easy to penetrate fail a little of a due impressiveness' (*AS* 97–8). The Boston Public Library likewise struck him as 'practically without *penetralia*' ('Boston' (1906); *AS* 249).

757 **Micawber [...] practising an almost passionate system of "bluff"; insisting, in fine, that something [...]** *would* **turn up**: In Dickens's novel *David Copperfield* (1850), the comic character Wilkins Micawber alternates between suicidal despair at his financial difficulties and groundless confidence that 'something' will 'turn up': as David recalls in Chapter 11, 'I have known him come home to supper with a flood of tears, and a declaration that nothing was now left but a jail; and go to bed making a calculation of the expense of putting bow-windows to the house, "in case anything turned up," which was his favourite expression' (*David Copperfield*, ed. Nina Burgis (Oxford: Clarendon Press, 1981), p. 140). Dickens makes that expression Micawber's catch-phrase. The relevant sense of 'bluff' is 'The action of bluffing at cards, in the game of *poker* [...]. Hence, challenging or boastful language or demeanour, not intended to be carried out, but merely "tried on" with the design of frightening or influencing an opponent who allows himself to be imposed upon by it. (First used in U.S.)' (*OED*, citing American instances from the 1840s onward, and a first British instance in 1883).

758 **"Fordham Castle," (1904), for which I refer my reader to Volume XVI**: 'Fordham Castle' was published in *Harper's Monthly Magazine* in December 1904 and was collected for the first time in the *NYE*. Originally intended to occupy the volume of short stories headed by 'Daisy Miller', the story was moved to *NYE* XVI in December 1908. This cross-reference is one of the 'two or three slight and venial' inconsistencies in the texts of the rearranged Prefaces which James acknowledged to the Scribners on 5 January 1909: 'in Vol. XVIII I have had to refer back to a previous Volume in my remarks about "Fordham Castle"' (Princeton).

759 **the call of the "four or five thousand words"**: While there is no extant correspondence to suggest that *Harper's Monthly* had specifically asked for 'four or five thousand words' in the case of 'Fordham Castle', these were the word-lengths preferred by contemporary magazines, as James knew. He had noted in general on 21 December 1895: 'I can *place* 5000

words—that is the coercive fact, and I require, obviously, to be able to do this' (*CN* 145). An early notebook entry for 'Fordham Castle' fixes on this extent as an absolute upper limit: 'Would the little idea of the "suppressed (American) mother" be feasible in 5000 words? It wd. be worth trying— for I seem to see I shall never do it in any other way. [...] DO THESE IN 5000 AT WHATEVER COST. IT IS ONLY THE MUTILATED, *the indicated thing that* IS *feasible*' (15 February 1899; *CN* 175). James hardly ever succeeded in keeping within these bounds, even so: 'Fordham Castle' grew to nearly 9,000 words (*CFHJ* 32, l).

760 **the elder couple bear the brunt of immediate appearance**: For the form of 'Fordham Castle' as 'a series of confidences' between 'the shunted mother (of "presented" &c, daughters,) & the relegated husband (of presented &c wife,) who meet somewhere (in the absence of their launched correlatives[])]', see James's notebook entry of 5 October 1899 (*CN* 185).

761 **I have [...] repeatedly referred to it, [...] struggles at each step [...] fully and completely to express itself**: For important references to this phenomenon in earlier Prefaces, see James's comments on the expansive subjects of *The Portrait of a Lady*, *The Awkward Age* and *What Maisie Knew* (pp. 33–4, 77, 114).

762 **single blessedness**: This Shakespearean phrase comes from Theseus' lines to his daughter Hermia in *A Midsummer Night's Dream* (1595–6) on the choice she must make between marrying Demetrius or living out her life as a nun: 'Thrice blessed they that master so their blood / To undergo such maiden pilgrimage; / But earthlier happy is the rose distill'd, / Than that which withering on the virgin thorn / Grows, lives, and dies in single blessedness' (1.1.74–8). By the early nineteenth century, the formula was used 'more or less jocularly' to refer to 'the unmarried state' (*OED*, citing Charles Lamb's *Essays of Elia* (1823) and Dickens's *Sketches by Boz* (1836)).

763 **neither from up-town nor from down-town nor from my lady's chamber**: Another allusion to an English nursery rhyme: 'Goosey, goosey gander, / Whither shall I wander? / Upstairs and downstairs / And in my lady's chamber' (*The Oxford Dictionary of Nursery Rhymes*, pp. 191–2). See also note 739.

764 **Dialect, general or special**: In his 'American Letter' of 9 July 1898 in the journal *Literature*, James had used the publication of two novels about Appalachian mountain communities in Tennessee – *The Juggler* (1897)

by Charles Egbert Craddock (Mary Noailles Murfree) and Sarah Barnwell Elliott's *The Durket Sperret* (1898) – as an occasion to reflect on 'the invasive part played by the element of dialect in the subject-matter of the American fiction of the day': 'I am struck, right and left, with the fact that most of the "cleverness" goes to the study of the conditions—conditions primitive often to the limit of extreme barbarism—in which colloquial speech arrives at complete debasement' (*LC1* 699). As early as 1876 he had praised Charles Henry Doe for 'bravely attempt[ing] to write a characteristic American novel [*Buffets: A Story*, 1875], which should be a tale of civilization—be void of big-hearted backwoodsmen and of every form of "dialect"' (*LC1* 36).

765 **the riot of the vulgar tongue**: Compare again James's 'American Letter' for 9 July 1898: in Edward Waterman Townsend's '*Chimmie Fadden*', *Major Max, and Other Stories* (1895), 'the very riot of the abnormal—the dialect of the New York newsboy and bootblack—is itself the text of the volume of two hundred pages' (*LC1* 700).

766 **the felt difference between the speech of the soil and the speech of the newspaper**: In the 'American Letter' referred to in the previous two notes, James had remarked in Mary Noailles Murfree's *The Juggler* a disjunction between the 'simplicities' of rural dialect and a narrating voice strongly marked by the style of journalism: 'The author sits down by herself, as it were, whenever she can, to a perfect treat of "modernity," of contemporary newspaperese. The flower of an English often stranger still than the mountain variety blooms bright in this soil' (*LC1* 698). In 'The Question of Our Speech' (1905), he had recently lamented the combined influence of 'the common school and the newspaper' on the standard of spoken English in America (*HJC* 53).

767 **more effective *repoussoir***: The French word means a foil or contrast. In his 1872 review of *Middlemarch*, James had praised the character of Mr Causaubon as 'a dusky *repoussoir* to the luminous figure of his wife [Dorothea Brooke]' (*LC1* 964).

768 **those of my productions in which I appear to have felt [...] that source of credit freely negligible; [...] two compositions not included in the present series**: In James's list of novels supposedly without a transatlantic dimension, *What Maisie Knew* is perhaps an anomaly. While the major characters are all English, *Maisie* contains a minor yet far from 'negligible' American character in Beale's mistress Mrs Cuddon, and America is

where Beale claims to be going with her in his final scene with Maisie – a scene singled out for comment by James in the Preface to *NYE* XI (p. 117). The two novels listed here but not included in *NYE* are *The Other House* (1896) and *The Sacred Fount* (1901).

769 **"The Marriages" (1891) and four of its companions here**: Besides 'The Marriages', the non-transatlantic stories collected in *NYE* XVIII are 'The Real Thing' (1892), 'Brooksmith' (1891) and 'The Story in It' (1902). That makes only three 'companions'; the fourth is perhaps 'Paste' (1899), present in James's original list of contents for this volume (see note 753) but eventually published in *NYE* XVI.

770 **he had best be simply born again**: An echo of Jesus' words to Nicodemus in John's gospel: 'Verily, verily, I say unto thee, Except a man be born again, he cannot see the kingdom of God' (John 3:3).

771 **I confess to no great provision of "history" on behalf of "The Marriages."**: The germ of 'The Marriages' is preserved in a notebook entry of 12 January 1887 recording something James's sister Alice had told him about the remarriage of Sir John Rose (1820–88) – at the age of 67 – after the death of his first wife Charlotte Temple, an aunt of the James children's Temple cousins (*CN* 32–3). For this and another possible source, also noted by Alice James, in Lady Alexandra Leveson-Gower's sorrow over the remarriage of her father the 3rd Duke of Sutherland (1828–92), see Bernard Richards, 'The Sources of Henry James's "The Marriages"', *Review of English Studies* 30.119 (1979), 316–22.

772 **the classic case of Mrs. Glasse's receipt, [...] a question of "first catching" the example of piety intense enough**: According to the *OED*, the phrase '*first catch your hare* (i.e. as the first step to cooking him)' is 'a direction jestingly ascribed to Mrs. Glasse's Cookery Book [Hannah Glasse, *The Art of Cookery, made plain and easy* (1747)], but of much more recent origin'; the dictionary's earliest instances are mid-Victorian and come from W. M. Thackeray's *The Rose and the Ring* (1855) and the *Times* newspaper for 25 August 1858 ('Bitter experience has taught us not to cook our hare before we have caught it'). As pointed out in a later instance (*Daily News*, 20 July 1896), 'The familiar words, "First catch your hare", were never to be found in Mrs. Glasse's famous volume. What she really said was, "Take your hare when it is cased" [skinned]' (*OED*, 'hare').

773 **"The Real Thing" (1890)**: 'The Real Thing' was in fact first published on 16 April 1892, in the magazine *Black and White*.

774 **the appreciative daughter of a friend some time dead [...] a visit received by her from a servant of the late distinguished lady**: For the idea of 'Brooksmith', see James's notebook entry of 9 June 1884, recording an anecdote told him by Christina Rogerson about the lady's maid of her late mother Mrs Duncan Stewart, who had grown used to her mistress's company and suffered when she had to 'relapse into ordinary service' after her death: 'Her sorrow, the way she felt the change, & the way she expressed it to Mrs. R. "Ah yes ma'am, you have lost your mother, & it's a great grief, but what is your loss to mine? [...] Common, vulgar people now: that's my lot for the future!"' (*CN* 29).

775 **spoiled for life; [...] Stendhal's inveterate motto, [...] "la beauté parfaite,"**: When the narrator appeals to the friends of the late Mr Offord to find a suitable position for his butler Brooksmith, he finds them 'disposed [...] to entertain a suspicion that [Brooksmith] was "spoiled," with which I then would have nothing to do' (*NYE* XVIII, 365). But he eventually says the same thing of the demoralized Brooksmith in the last sentence of the story: 'He had indeed been spoiled' (*NYE* XVIII, 372). What James calls the 'motto' of the French novelist Stendhal (Marie-Henri Beyle, 1783–1842) is quoted from the epigraph to his travelogue *Promenades dans Rome*: 'ESCALUS.—Mon ami, vous m'avez l'air d'être un peu misanthrope et envieux?—MERCUTIO.—J'ai vu de trop bonne heure la beauté parfaite. *Shakspeare* [*sic*]' ('—My friend, you seem to me to be a little misanthropic and envious?—I saw perfect beauty too early') (Stendhal, *Promenades dans Rome*, 2 vols. (Paris: Delaunay, 1829), vol. I, title page). James alludes to the same tag in Chapter 13 of *Roderick Hudson*: as Roderick observes to Rowland, '"Your friend Stendhal writes on his book-covers (I never got further) that he has seen too early in life *la beauté parfaite*. I don't know how early he saw it; I saw it before I was born—in another state of being!"' (*NYE* I, 273). At work on *Roderick Hudson* in Florence in the spring of 1874, James had written to Sarah Butler Wister, with whom he had spent time in Rome the previous winter: 'I feel as if we had had a glimpse of the beauté parfaite (or something very like it) together' (10 May [1874]; *CLHJ 1872–1876* 2:164).

776 **my much-loved friend George du Maurier [...] artist's models for his weekly "social" illustrations to *Punch***: George Louis Palmella Busson Du Maurier (1834–96), Anglo-French illustrator and author of novels including the bestselling *Trilby* (1894). As a staff-artist for the humorous weekly magazine *Punch, or the London Charivari* (est. 1841), he became famous for his satirical cartoons on the manners and fashions of contemporary

upper-class London society and middle-class English family life. James and Du Maurier met in London literary circles in the late 1870s, and in 1880 Du Maurier illustrated *Washington Square* for its serialization in the *Cornhill Magazine*. Over the next decade, James became a close family friend and a frequent visitor to the Du Mauriers' home in Hampstead. He wrote on Du Maurier's graphic and literary work on several occasions: see 'Du Maurier and London Society' (1883), reprinted as 'George du Maurier [sic]' in *Partial Portraits* (1888); a review of an early number of *Trilby* (*LC1* 870–6); and the commemorative essay 'George du Maurier [sic]' (1897) (*LC1* 876–906). The first mention of 'The Real Thing' in James's notebooks comes in an entry made in Paris on 22 February 1891: 'I began yesterday the little story that was suggested to me some time ago by an incident related to me by George du Maurier [sic]—the lady & gentleman who called upon him with a word from [the painter William Powell] Frith, an oldish, faded, ruined pair [...] who unable to turn a penny in any other way, were trying to find employment as models' (*CN* 55).

777 **the standard of superficial "smartness" [...] to "make believe." [...] to know how**: The emphasized terms in these sentences of the Preface are all echoed from 'The Real Thing'. In Chapter 1, Mr Monarch tells his wife: '"Get up, my dear, and show how smart you are"'; the artist-narrator remarks that 'Her husband had used the word that described her: she was in the London current jargon essentially and typically "smart"' (*NYE* XVIII, 313). In Chapter 3, 'the real thing' as embodied by the Monarchs is confronted with 'the make-believe' of the professional model Miss Churm: 'they must have felt—in the air—that she was amused at them, secretly derisive of their ever knowing how' (*NYE* XVIII, 329).

778 **so thoroughly does this highly-finished little anecdote cover its tracks**: See, however, James's notebook entry of 19 February 1899, which is recognizably the source of 'Flickerbridge' (1902): 'Struck an hour ago by pretty little germ of small thing given out in 4 or 5 lines of charming volume of Miss Jewett—Tales of N.E.' The passage occurs in 'A Lost Lover', one of Sarah Orne Jewett's *Tales of New England* (1879), about 'A girl on a visit to new-found old-fashioned (spinster-gentlewoman) relation' (*CN* 181).

779 **Fine old leisure, in George Eliot's phrase**: James refers to a passage in Chapter 52 of Eliot's *Adam Bede* (1859), a novel set at the turn of the nineteenth century, where the narrator laments the lost 'Leisure' of earlier ages from the point of view of industrial modernity: 'Ingenious philosophers tell you, perhaps, that the great work of the steam-engine is to create

leisure for mankind. Do not believe them: it only creates a vacuum for eager thought to rush in. Even idleness is eager now—eager for amusement: prone to excursion-trains, art-museums, periodical literature, and exciting novels: prone even to scientific theorizing, and cursory peeps through microscopes. Old Leisure was quite a different personage: he only read one newspaper, innocent of leaders, and was free from that periodicity of sensations which we call post-time. [...] Fine old Leisure! Do not be severe upon him, and judge him by our modern standard' (*Adam Bede*, ed. Carol A. Martin (Oxford: Clarendon Press, 2001), pp. 476–7).

780 **sound and fury**: An allusion to Macbeth's blankly disillusioned lines on 'Life': 'It is a tale / Told by an idiot, full of sound and fury, / Signifying nothing' (5.5.24, 26–8).

781 **to dread reverberation [...] more than the Black Death**: The Black Death is the name commonly given to a pandemic of bubonic plague that spread across Europe from Central Asia in the mid-fourteenth century. The term 'reverberation' in this sentence of the Preface recalls the title of James's novella *The Reverberator* (1888), collected in *NYE* XIII – like 'Flickerbridge', a story about journalism and the violation of privacy.

782 **haunted [...] the cold avenues of publicity; [...] an old acquaintance, about to "start a magazine," [...] that first number which was in the event [...] to prove only one of a pair**: James sent 'The Story in It' to Pinker on 27 February 1900 (*LL* 336). Eighteen months later, he attributed his agent's continuing failure to place the story with a periodical to 'the amiable freedom of the *subject*, & the extremely unamiable & otherwise abject prudery of the usual Anglo-Saxon Editor' (to Pinker, 6 November 1901; *LL* 362). At that moment, the Belgian journalist Fernand Ortmans, who as editor of *Cosmopolis: An International Review* (1896–8) had previously published 'The Figure in the Carpet' (1896) and 'John Delavoy' (1898), had just approached James with a request for material for a new periodical, *The Anglo-American Magazine*. In the absence of other takers, and judging Ortmans sufficiently 'brave (!!)' to publish a story about adultery, James gave him 'The Story in It' without payment (*LL* 362). He underestimates the lifespan of *The Anglo-American Magazine*: it had already been going for a couple of years when Ortmans made his approach, and it ran for seven volumes (1899–1902). 'The Story in It' was published not in 1903 – as James states here – but in January 1902, in the first monthly number of the magazine's final volume; it was collected in *The Better Sort* (1903).

783 **a distinguished friend, a novelist not to *our* manner either born or bred**: Leon Edel suggests (*LC2* 1380) that this friend was the French novelist Paul Bourget (1852–1935). James had been introduced to Bourget in 1884 by John Singer Sargent; the two men spent time together that summer in London and Dover, and Bourget gratefully recalled their conversations on literature when he dedicated his novel *Cruelle énigme* to James the following year (see Edel, *Henry James: The Middle Years 1884–1894* (London: Rupert Hart-Davis, 1963), pp. 50–2). James complained to Theodore Child on 13 May 1885 that he was 'greatly compromised here by the dedication of Bourget's novel—the story being so malpropre [indecent]'; he was staying in the 'decidedly dull' seaside town of Bournemouth and addressed this letter to Child out of its 'depths of anti-literary British Philistinism' (*CLHJ 1884–1886* 1:194, 193). When *Cruelle énigme* appeared in English translation two years later, it carried – as well as the dedication to James – an introduction by the translator describing Bourget's subject here and elsewhere as love reduced to 'a single and simple fact: the physical, fleshly desire of man for woman and woman for man' (*A Cruel Enigma*, trans. Julian Cray (London: Vizetelly & Co., 1887), p. vi). James apparently sent Bourget a copy of *The Better Sort* in 1903 and marked it so as to indicate a story in the volume which Bourget had inspired: the copy is lost, but 'The Two Faces' and 'The Story in It' are likely candidates for the story in question (I. D. Macfarlane, 'A Literary Friendship: Henry James and Paul Bourget', *The Cambridge Journal* 4 (December 1950), 144–61; 157, cited in Angus Wrenn, *Henry James and the Second Empire* (London: Legenda, 2009), p. 150). This sentence of the Preface alludes to Hamlet's disapproving lines on the Danish court's heavy drinking under the new king Claudius: 'But to my mind, though I am native here / And to the manner born, it is a custom / More honor'd in the breach than the observance' (1.4.14–16).

784 **definition of terms […] a human, a personal "adventure" […] a matter of relation and appreciation**: The characters' conversations in 'The Story in It' are largely concerned with defining the 'terms' for personal relations, including the term set in inverted commas in this sentence of the Preface: '"The adventures of the honest lady? The honest lady hasn't, can't possibly have, adventures." Mrs. Blessingbourne only met his eyes at first, smiling with some intensity. "Doesn't it depend a little on what you call adventures?"' (Ch. 2; *NYE* XVIII, 425).

785 **"Mrs. Medwin," published in *Punch* (1902) […], I have also accommodated here for convenience**: James mistakes the year of publication: 'Mrs. Medwin' in fact appeared in four numbers of *Punch* from 28 August to 18 September 1901. The story does not appear in the original list of contents for the present volume of *NYE* (see note 753); James intended it for the volume headed by 'The Altar of the Dead' and transferred it to *NYE* XVIII in December 1908.

786 **"The Beldonald Holbein," […] *that* story—by which I mean the story *of* it—would take us much too far**: James noted the idea for 'The Beldonald Holbein' in Rome on 16 May 1899, on hearing from Maud Howe Elliott (1854–1948), the daughter of the American poet Julia Ward Howe (1819–1910), of 'what struck me as such a pretty little subject—her mother's (Julia W. H.'s) *success de beauté*, in Rome, while staying with her, the previous winter' (*CN* 183). The story was published in the October 1901 issue of *Harper's New Monthly Magazine*.

PREFACE to *The Wings of the Dove* (NYE XIX–XX)

787 **"The Wings of the Dove," published in 1902 […] a very old—if I shouldn't perhaps rather say a very young—motive**: *The Wings of the Dove* was published in book form in August 1902, without prior serialization; the first editions were issued by Charles Scribner's Sons in America (21 August) and Archibald Constable in England (30 August). James's earliest memo of the novel's 'motive' appears in a notebook entry of 3 November 1894: 'Isn't perhaps something to be made of the idea that came to me some time ago and that I have not hitherto made any note of—the little idea of the situation of some young creature (it seems to me preferably a woman, but of this I'm not sure), who, at 20, on the threshold of a life that has seemed boundless, is suddenly condemned to death (by consumption, heart-disease, or whatever) by the voice of the physician?' (*CN* 102). James's cousin Mary (Minny) Temple is generally acknowledged to be the source of this 'motive'. In the last chapter of *Notes of a Son and Brother* (1914), he would narrate her terminal illness and eventual death from pulmonary tuberculosis at the age of 24, remarking that the 'image' of her situation 'was long to remain with me' and 'appeared so of the essence of tragedy that I was in the far-off aftertime to seek to lay the ghost by wrapping it, a particular occasion aiding, in the beauty and dignity of

art' (*Aut* 569). For Minny Temple's influence on the characterization of Isabel Archer in *The Portrait of a Lady*, see note 151. In his late personal writings, James often remarks the paradox whereby the persons and places he revisits in memory are at once 'old' (long familiar to him) and 'young' (originally encountered in his and/or their youth). See, for example, his recollection of Newport, Rhode Island in the 1860s in Chapter 12 of *Notes of a Son and Brother*: 'Particular hours and old (that is young!) ineffable reactions come back to me' (*Aut* 507).

788 **aware […] of the condemnation and passionately desiring to "put in" before extinction as many of the finer vibrations as possible**: A contemporary journalist noted the 'curious resemblance' of James's phrasing at this point in the Preface 'to that famous "pulsation" passage of Pater's' (Dixon Scott, 'Henry James', *Bookman* (London) 43 (March 1913), 299–306; 302 n.). In his Conclusion to *The Renaissance: Studies in Art and Poetry* (first published in 1873 as *Studies in the History of the Renaissance*, and quoted here in the 1893 fourth edition), Water Pater had observed that 'A counted number of pulses only is given to us of a variegated, dramatic life. How may we see in them all that is to be seen in them by the finest senses?' The relevant passage comes later in the Conclusion: 'we are all *condamnés*, as Victor Hugo says: we are all under sentence of death but with a sort of indefinite reprieve—*les hommes sont tous condamnés à mort avec des sursis indéfinis*: we have an interval, and then our place knows us no more. Some spend this interval in listlessness, some in high passions, the wisest, at least among "the children of this world," in art and song. For our one chance lies in expanding that interval, in getting as many pulsations as possible into the given time' (Pater, *The Renaissance: Studies in Art and Poetry*, pp. 250–1, 252–3).

789 **These things […] would require much working-out; […] the case with most things worth working at all**: James began to work out the subject for *Wings* in two long notebook entries dated 3 and 7 November 1894 (*CN* 102–7). In 1899, he prepared a synopsis for magazine editors who might be interested in serializing the novel; writing to H. G. Wells on 15 November 1902, he compared that document with the 20,000-word 'Project of Novel' he had dictated two years before for *The Ambassadors*, describing the latter as 'the statement, full & vivid, I think, as a statement could be, of a subject as worked out' (*LL* 376). This sentence of the Preface uses a transitive sense of the verb 'work' that occurs frequently in *Wings*. In Book

Fourth, Chapter 2, for example, Lord Mark tells Milly that he is 'working Lancaster Gate for all it was worth: just as it was, no doubt, working *him*, and just as the working and the worked were in London [...] the parties to every relation' (*NYE* XIX, 178).

790 **formed [...] to make the wary adventurer walk round and round it**: James's description of the subject of *The Wings of the Dove* borrows figures from the characters' actions and relations in the novel. In Book Second, Chapter 2, Densher imagines Maud Lowder inviting him to consider her '"plan"' for marrying Kate to somebody other than him: '"Come [...] as near it as you like, walk all round it—don't be afraid you'll hurt it!—and live on with it before you"' (*NYE* XIX, 84). Again, in Book Fifth, Chapter 6, Milly and Kate agree that 'the American mind' is unable 'to understand English society without a separate confrontation with *all* the cases': 'it had to be led up and introduced to each aspect of the monster, enabled to walk all round it' (*NYE* XIX, 277). Veeder and Griffin point out parallel instances of the Preface's metaphor of warily walking 'round and round' a building in *The Golden Bowl* (1904) (Maggie's pagoda: Book Fourth, Ch. 1) and in James's lecture 'The Novel in *The Ring and the Book*' (1912) (Browning's long poem figured as a Gothic cathedral: *LC1* 791) (*The Art of Criticism*, p. 417).

791 **a case sure to prove difficult and to require much handling; [...] to be jumped at from the moment they make a sign**: Again the Preface borrows its terms from the novel's figurative vocabulary, implicitly comparing James's authorial activity to the behaviour of various characters towards Milly. Encountering Kate and Densher in the National Gallery in Book Fifth, Chapter 7, Milly 'knew herself handled and again, as she had been the night before, dealt with—absolutely even dealt with for her greater pleasure' (*NYE* XIX, 293). In Book Fourth, Chapter 1, Lord Mark assures Milly that Maud Lowder has '"jumped at"' her: '"To be seen, you must recognise, *is*, for you, to be jumped at [...]. Look round the table, and you'll make out, I think, that you're being, from top to bottom, jumped at"' (*NYE* XIX, 154–5). James's notebook entries of November 1894 assess the subject's several intrinsic difficulties: the terminal illness of the young heroine, the quasi-adulterous situation, the possible resemblance to the subject of a novel by Edmond About, and the question of how to resolve the plot in a way that will not be 'ugly & vulgar: I mean vulgarly ugly' (see *CN* 103–5; 105).

792 **so closely to cross-question that idea of making one's protagonist "sick"?**: For evidence of such questioning, see James's first notebook entry for the novel, which rejects his first thought that Densher should offer Milly a sexual relationship: 'It has bothered me in thinking of the little picture—this idea of the physical possession, the brief physical, passional rapture which at first appeared essential to it; bothered me on account of the ugliness, the incongruity, the nastiness, *en somme*, of the man's "having" a sick girl' (3 November 1894; CN 103).

793 **one's accessory invalids […] Ralph Touchett […] his deplorable state of health […] a direct aid to pleasantness and vividness**: In Chapter 33 of *The Portrait*, Isabel considers the grounds of her affection for Ralph as she realizes for the first time that he is seriously unwell: 'He was so charming that her sense of his being ill had hitherto had a sort of comfort in it; the state of his health had seemed not a limitation, but a kind of intellectual advantage; it absolved him from all professional and official emotions and left him the luxury of being exclusively personal. The personality so resulting was delightful; he had remained proof against the staleness of disease; he had had to consent to be deplorably ill, yet had somehow escaped from being formally sick' (*NYE* IV, 59–60). Other notable invalids in James's work include Rose Muniment in *The Princess Casamassima*, Morgan Moreen in 'The Pupil', and Dencombe in 'The Middle Years'.

794 **the last thing in the world it proposed to itself was to be the record predominantly of a collapse**: James would issue a similar disclaimer in Chapter 13 of *Notes of a Son and Brother* as he began to write about Minny Temple's last months: 'I should have little heart, I confess, for what is essentially the record of a rapid illness if it were not at the same time the image of an admirable soul' (*Aut* 538).

795 **dragged by a greater force than any she herself could exert; […] clutching these things to the last moment of her strength**: These figures are anticipated in James's notebook entry of 3 November 1894, which compares Milly to 'a creature dragged shrieking to the guillotine—to the shambles' (CN 103). The novel likewise uses the violence of the French Revolution to represent the inevitability of her early death: in Book Tenth, Chapter 2, Densher reflects that she 'had held with passion to her dream of a future, and she was separated from it, not shrieking indeed, but grimly, awfully silent, as one might imagine some noble young victim of the scaffold, in the French Revolution, separated at the prison-door from some object clutched for resistance' (*NYE* XX, 341–2).

796 **a catastrophe determined in spite of oppositions**: In early modern and neoclassical literary theory, the 'catastrophe' is '"The change or revolution which produces the conclusion or final event of a dramatic piece" [...]; the dénouement' (*OED*, quoting Samuel Johnson's *Dictionary*). John Dryden's *An Essay of Dramatick Poesie* (1668), for example, outlines a four-part model of tragic structure elaborated from Aristotle's *Poetics*, of which the final stage is 'the *Catastrophe*, which the *Grecians* call'd λύσις [*lusis*], the *French le dénouement*, and we the discovery or unravelling of the Plot' (*The Works of John Dryden*, vol. XVII, p. 23).

797 **the associated Fates**: In ancient Greek mythology, the three Fates (Moirai) are sister goddesses who have power over all human destinies, from birth to death: Clotho is commonly represented spinning the thread of life, Lachesis measuring it, and Atropos cutting it.

798 **drawn in as by some pool of a Lorelei**: The Lorelei is a legendary creature in German Romantic poetry and song, appearing in the form of 'a beautiful woman with long blonde hair who sat on the Lorelei rock [in the river Rhine] and with her fine singing distracted boatmen, so that they drowned when their ships foundered on the rock' (*OED*). Ostensibly derived from German folklore, she was in fact an early nineteenth-century literary invention. Her most famous manifestation is a poem first published in Heinrich Heine's collection *Die Heimkehr* (1826), 'Ich weiß nicht, was soll es bedeuten', which was set to music (as 'Die Lorelei' or 'Die Loreley') by several Romantic composers including Friedrich Silcher, Johanna Kinkel, Franz Liszt, Clara Schumann and Joachim Raff (Lawrence D. Snyder, *German Poetry in Song: An Index of Lieder* (Berkeley, CA: Fallen Leaf Press, 1995), p. 185). Harking back to this passage later on in the Preface, James refers to 'the Rhine-maiden' (p. 232), a term more usually associated with the three *Rheintöchter* (Rhine-daughters) of Richard Wagner's opera-cycle *Der Ring des Niebelungen* (1869–76). An allusion to the Lorelei in James's correspondence suggests an imaginative link between Milly Theale and Isabella Stewart Gardner, another fabulously wealthy American woman temporarily residing in a Venetian palazzo. On 30 June 1890, James wrote to Grace Norton that he was on the point of leaving Venice for Florence but had been 'solicited back there by a local (or would be) Lorelei in the shape of Mrs. Jack Gardner, whom the absent Curtises have lent Palazzo Barbaro to for the month of August and who requests the favour of my company (she seems to think I am "thrown in")' (*Letters from the Palazzo Barbaro*, ed. Rosella Mamoli Zorzi (London: Pushkin Press, 1998), p. 114).

799 **the last fine flower—blooming alone [...]—of an "old" New York stem**: James alludes to the song "'Tis the Last Rose of Summer' by the Irish poet Thomas Moore (1779–1852), first published in the fifth number of his *A Selection of Irish Melodies* (1813) and lastingly popular throughout the nineteenth and early twentieth centuries: "'Tis the last rose of summer / Left blooming alone; / All her lovely companions / Are faded and gone; / No flower of her kindred, / No rosebud is nigh, / To reflect back her blushes, / To give sigh for sigh' (ll. 1–8; *The Poetical Works of Thomas Moore*, ed. Charles Kent (London: George Routledge and Sons, 1879), p. 149). James uses the same figure for Milly in the novel, speaking in Book Third, Chapter 1, of 'the luxuriant tribe of which the rare creature was the final flower, the immense extravagant unregulated cluster, with free-living ancestors, handsome dead cousins, lurid uncles, beautiful vanished aunts [...], to say nothing of [...] closer growths of the stem' (*NYE* XIX, 111). In his essay 'Mr. Henry James's Later Work' (1903), W. D. Howells had praised this aspect of Milly's characterization: 'She is as convincingly imagined [...] as the daughter of an old New York family, as she is in her inherited riches. It is not the old New York family of the unfounded Knickerbocker tradition, but something as fully patrician, with a nimbus of social importance as unquestioned as its money. Milly is not so much the flower of this local root as something finer yet: the perfume of it, the distilled and wandering fragrance' (*LFL* 385–6). James had recently written about 'The Old New York' of the 1840s and 1850s in his travel essays 'New England: An Autumn Impression' (1905) and 'New York Revisited' (1906); when he reprinted the latter piece as the second chapter of *The American Scene*, he used this phrase as a page headline (*AS* 1–5, 79–80). An older '"old" New York' is referred to in the Preface to *NYE* XII: that of the fictional poet Jeffrey Aspern in 'The Aspern Papers' (see p. 131). The Preface to *NYE* XII was written after the Preface to *The Wings of the Dove*, and when James refers in this sentence to 'the fine association that shall yet elsewhere await me', he may be anticipating the reference to Aspern's early nineteenth-century New York. He would dwell at length upon his own '"old New York"' childhood in *A Small Boy and Others* (1913) (*Aut* 32).

800 **the "heir of all the ages"**: James quotes from Tennyson's 'Locksley Hall' (1842): 'I the heir of all the ages, in the foremost files of time' (l. 178; *The Poems of Tennyson*, vol. II, p. 129). The same line is alluded to in the novel: in Book Third, Chapter 1, Susan Stringham thinks of Milly as 'the potential heiress of all the ages' (*NYE* XIX, 109).

801 **the sinking of a big vessel**: Metaphors of ocean-going vessels and shipwreck are applied to Milly throughout the novel. In Book Third, Chapter 1, she makes Susan think of 'the term always used in the newspapers about the great new steamers, the inordinate number of "feet of water" they drew; so that if, in your little boat, you had chosen to hover and approach, you had but yourself to thank, when once motion was started, for the way the draught pulled you. Milly drew the feet of water, and […] her companion floated off with the sense of rocking violently at her side' (*NYE* XIX, 113). When in Book Fifth, Chapter 3, Milly tells Sir Luke Strett that all her immediate family are dead, she says, '"I'm a survivor—a survivor of a general wreck"' (*NYE* XIX, 241); for Densher too, in Book Sixth, Chapter 4, Milly '"affects one […] as a creature saved from a shipwreck"' (*NYE* XX, 53).

802 **to enter the train […] without a ticket**: The metaphor of train travel is another borrowing from the novel: as Milly talks with Lord Mark in Book Fourth, Chapter 1, 'she was more and more sharply conscious of having—as with the door sharply slammed upon her and the guard's hand raised in signal to the train—been popped into the compartment in which she was to travel for him' (*NYE* XIX, 157). Earlier in the same chapter, Milly has become aware of the 'lines' on which their conversation is going to proceed, both those 'immediately laid down' and those on which 'they would move later' (*NYE* XIX, 153): compare, from the next sentence of the Preface, 'I had secured my ticket over the tolerably long line laid down for "The Wings of the Dove"[…]'.

803 **to draw her breath in such pain**: An echo of Hamlet's dying injunction to Horatio: 'If thou didst ever hold me in thy heart, / Absent thee from felicity a while, / And in this harsh world draw thy breath in pain / To tell my story' (5.2.346–9). As Philip Horne points out ('Henry James and the Poetry of Association', p. 78 n. 89), James had recently introduced this allusion into the revised text of *The American* at the moment in the final chapter when Newman gives up his project of revenge against the Bellegardes, throwing into Mrs Tristram's fire the document in which old M. de Bellegarde had testified to his wife's attempt to murder him. Mrs Tristram asks Newman what the paper was, and he does not immediately reply: 'Leaning against the chimney-piece he seemed to grasp its ledge with force and to draw his breath a while in pain' (*NYE* II, 537). In the Macmillan *Collective Edition* of 1883, the edition James used to revise the novel, this reads: 'Newman, leaning against the fireplace, stretched his arms and drew a longer breath than usual' (*CE* VII, 206).

804 **to "bristle"—I delighted in the term!—with meanings**: In Book Fourth, Chapter 2 of *The Wings of the Dove*, Milly feels on entering London society that 'Mrs. Lowder's life bristled for her with elements that she was really having to look at for the first time' (*NYE* XIX, 170). And in Book Seventh, Chapter 4, she explains to Lord Mark why she has secluded herself in Venice: '"England bristles with questions. This is more, as you say there, my form"' (*NYE* XX, 152). For James's habitual use of this term, see note 3.

805 **approaching the centre thus by narrowing circumvallations**: A 'circumvallation' is 'A rampart or entrenchment constructed round any place by way of investment or defence'; the word also refers to the act of constructing such an earthwork, '*esp.* in besieging' (*OED*).

806 **my first Book, ground from which Milly is superficially so absent**: Milly does not appear in the novel until Book Third, and her social connections with the London world of the first two Books – her prior acquaintance with Merton Densher in America and Susan Stringham's old friendship with Maud Lowder – do not become apparent until the end of Book Third, Chapter 2.

807 **"beginning far back," as far back as possible**: In an earlier sentence of the Preface, James observes that the germ of *The Wings of the Dove*, as embodied in the idea of a dying young woman, 'had been given me from far back' (p. 230). In the novel itself, similarly, thoughts and relations and arrangements are thus represented as having begun long before the narrative present. In Book First, Chapter 2, for example, Kate 'knew herself now [...] as having been marked from far back' by Aunt Maud as a candidate for patronage (*NYE* XIX, 29); and in Book Second, Chapter 1, Densher 'had repeatedly said to himself—and from far back—that he should be a fool not to marry a woman whose value would be in her differences' (*NYE* XIX, 50). When Milly arrives in England in Book Fourth, Chapter 1, she plunges 'into the obscure depths of a society constituted from far back' (*NYE* XIX, 154).

808 **failed, in advance, of all power to see itself "serialised."**: At least three American magazines declined the serialization of *Wings* in 1899–1900: the *Atlantic Monthly*, *Scribner's Magazine* and a periodical provisionally identified by Sister Stephanie Vincec as the New York *Home Journal* (see Vincec, '"Poor Flopping *Wings*": The Making of Henry James's *The Wings of the Dove*', *Harvard Library Bulletin* 24.1 (1976), 60-93; 67-9, 71). As James observes in the next sentence of the Preface, *The Golden Bowl* too

was unserialized prior to book publication: he told W. D. Howells on 8 January 1904 that it had been 'contracted for, with Methuen here and the Scribners in New York, as a volume only, and on no brilliant terms' (*LL* 395).

809 **the alpine chill, that of some high icy *arête*, shed by the cold editorial shoulder**: The French word 'arête' means 'A sharp ascending ridge or "edge" of a mountain. The local name in French Switzerland, whence it has become a technical term with mountain-climbers'; to '*give* the cold shoulder' to someone is 'to display intentional and marked coldness, or studied indifference' (*OED*). The figure in this sentence of the Preface recalls the scene 'on the alpine height' in Book Third, Chapter 1 of *The Wings of the Dove*, which James will later single out for comment (see note 833). It also echoes Densher's feeling in Venice, at only a few inches above sea-level, that he is 'walking [...] on a high ridge, steep down on either side, where the proprieties—once he could face at all remaining there—reduced themselves to his keeping his head' (Book Eighth, Ch. 1, *NYE* XX, 175). The novel is sensitive to chills of dislike and disapproval: in Book First, Chapter 2, Aunt Maud's attitude to her sister's family is remembered by Kate as 'the chill breath of *ultima Thule*' (*NYE* XIX, 27); in Book Fourth, Chapter 2, Susan and Milly reflect that Maud's London society represents 'the world that, as a consequence of the cold shoulder turned to it by the Pilgrim Fathers, had never yet boldly crossed to Boston' (*NYE* XIX, 170).

810 **Such a block [...] is the whole preliminary presentation of Kate Croy**: This first 'block' of the novel's structure corresponds to Book First. The division into Books is present in the Scribner and Constable first editions of 1902, though in those editions the numbering of chapters continues throughout the novel rather than starting afresh with each Book, as it does in *NYE*.

811 **the absent values, [...] the mocking shadows**: James wrote to Ford Madox Hueffer (later Ford Madox Ford) on 9 September 1902: 'I thank you ever so kindly for your letter, which gives me extreme pleasure & almost for the moment makes me see the *Wings*, myself, not as a mass of mistakes, with everything I had intended absent & everything present botched!' (*LL* 370).

812 **a dupe, that of his prime object, [...] a master, that of his actual substitute for it**: In 1875 James had remarked that Balzac, with regard to his miscellaneous political, philosophical, sociological and physiological convictions, was himself 'his most perfect dupe; he believed in his own

magnificent rubbish, and if he made it up, as the phrase is, as he went along, his credulity kept pace with his invention': indeed, he was 'simply the greatest of dupes' (*LC2* 47, 67). James makes the same objection to the grandiose scope of the *Comédie humaine,* and yet acknowledges that 'it was in the convenient faculty of persuading himself that he could do everything that Balzac found the inspiration to do so much' (*LC2* 42).

813 **He places […] the piers of his bridge**: James had used comparable constructional figures when working out other subjects in his notebooks. On 'The Coxon Fund', for example: 'I see that my leaps and elisions, my flying bridges and great comprehensive loops (in a vivid, admirable sentence or two,) must be absolutely bold and masterly' (29 April 1894; *CN* 96). The surviving notes for the Cambridge and Boston sections of *The American Scene* deploy a figurative 'bridge' and also a 'flying leap' at a juncture where getting from one part of the subject to another involves crossing the Charles River (11 December 1904; see *CN* 235–7).

814 **were to have been *shown*, with a truth beyond […] one's most emphasised "word of honour" for it**: In *What Maisie Knew,* the novel James had revised and prefaced immediately before *The Wings of the Dove* in the sequence of his work on the *NYE,* the narrator admits that his 'rough method' does not allow him to *show* Maisie's 'vision' of how she must have appeared to Mrs Wix: 'I so despair of courting her noiseless mental footsteps here that I must crudely give you my word for its being from this time forward a picture literally present to her' (Ch. 26; *NYE* XI, 280–1).

815 **a beggarly scene or two**: Lionel Croy's only direct appearance in the novel is Kate's interview with him in his lodgings, which occupies Book First, Chapter 1. Kate tells Densher the story of her father's obscure disgrace in Book Second, Chapter 1, and his offstage presence is acutely felt in Mrs Condrip's house when Kate meets Densher there in Book Tenth, Chapter 5.

816 **the Angel, not to say […] the Demon, of Compromise**: In 'The Lesson of Balzac', James had recently observed that 'there is no art at all […] that is not on too many sides an abject compromise. The element of compromise is always there; it is of the essence; we live with it, and it may serve to keep us humble' (*LC2* 134). He would restate this conviction in a letter to Lady Victoria Welby written perhaps in August 1911: 'one somehow feels (at least I in my feebleness do) that expression is, at the most insurmountably, a compromise. Has it not, in the interest of finite form, to *keep* compromising, ever […]?' (*LL* 502).

817 **nymphs and fauns circling round a bland Hermes and crowning him with flowers**: In ancient Greek mythology, the god Hermes is the herald and messenger of the Olympian deities. A protector of travellers and shepherds and a guide of souls into the underworld, he is also associated with oratory, commerce, theft and trickery. James's figure of an encircled, crowned Hermes recalls the god's sculptural manifestation as a 'Herma' or 'herm': 'A statue composed of a head, usually that of the god Hermes, placed on the top of a quadrangular pillar, of the proportions of the human body', often used as a mile-stone or boundary-marker and in form and function resembling the ancient Roman 'Term', a statue depicting the god Terminus (*OED*). Pictorial representations of bacchanalia sometimes incorporate such sculptures: for example Nicolas Poussin's painting *A Bacchanalian Revel before a Term* (1632-3) in the National Gallery in London, or his ink drawing 'A dance before a herm of Pan' (c. 1631-2) in the British Royal Collection. James had imagined a comparable scene in *The American*: at Newman and Claire de Cintré's engagement party, the elder Madame de Bellegarde carries 'a fine old painted fan of the last century' depicting 'a *fête champêtre*—a lady singing to a guitar and a group of dancers round a garlanded Hermes' (Ch. 14; *NYE* II, 284).

818 **we were to have been penetrated with Mrs. Lowder, [...] saturated with her presence, her "personality," and felt all her weight in the scale**: These terms are applied to Maud Lowder in Book First, Chapter 2. As Kate sits upstairs at Lancaster Gate, she senses 'Aunt Maud's looming "personality." It was by her personality that Aunt Maud was prodigious' (*NYE* XIX, 30). 'Sitting far down-stairs Aunt Maud was yet a presence from which a sensitive niece could feel herself extremely under pressure'; 'her weight was in the scale of certain dangers—those dangers that, by our showing, made the younger woman linger and lurk above, while the elder, below, [...] covered as much of the ground as possible' (*NYE* XIX, 29, 31).

819 **a practical *fusion* of consciousness**: This effect of a narrative point of view jointly governed by the perspectives of Kate and Densher is not in fact obtained until Book Second; Densher is not directly portrayed in Book First, only referred to briefly.

820 **Beautiful exceedingly**: An echo of Coleridge's 'Christabel' (1816), describing the first appearance of the uncanny Geraldine: 'I guess, 'twas frightful there to see / A lady so richly clad as she— / Beautiful exceedingly!' (Part I, ll. 66-8; *The Complete Poetical Works of Samuel Taylor Coleridge*, ed.

Ernest Hartley Coleridge, 2 vols. (Oxford: Clarendon Press, 1912), vol. I, p. 218). James had recently alluded to the same passage in his American travel essay 'Concord and Salem' (1907): 'Beautiful exceedingly the local Emerson and Thoreau and Hawthorne and (in a fainter way) *tutti quanti* [all the rest]' (*AS* 260).

821 **This passage [...] has its mate, for illustration, later on in the book**: The two passages James refers to in this paragraph occur respectively in Book Fourth, Chapter 1 (Milly's first dinner at Lancaster Gate) and Book Eighth, Chapter 3 (Milly's party at the Palazzo Leporelli).

822 **"reflectors,"**: James had privately used this term for the character whose point of view organizes the narration in a notebook entry for 'The Death of the Lion': 'my narrator, my critical *reflector* of the whole thing' (9 February 1894; *CN* 87). Compare a passage in the Preface to *NYE* XVII, written after the *Wings* Preface but published before it in the sequence of *NYE* volumes: in 'Julia Bride', 'we catch by the very small reflector, which is of absolutely minimum size for its task, a quite "unlikely" amount [...] of the movement of life' (p. 208).

823 **it is Kate Croy who is, "for all she is worth," turned on**: Book Eighth, Chapter 3 is technically shown from Densher's point of view, not from Kate's, but the passage James refers to takes the form of a conversation between them and is obviously informed by Kate's assessment of the situation. To do something 'for all one is worth' is to do it 'with all one's energy or resources': according to *OED* the idiom was comparatively new for James's generation – the earliest cited instance dates from 1864 – and was originally American (*OED*, 'worth', *adj.*). James uses 'turn on' in a British colloquial sense meaning 'To set (a person) *to do* something, or *to* an activity; to employ (a person)' (*OED*, earliest instance 1894). In Book Fourth, Chapter 1, Lord Mark cites his present occupation of talking with Milly at dinner as an example of '"what [Maud Lowder] does with me"': '"This for instance—turning me straight on for *you*"' (*NYE* XIX, 156).

824 **Milly's situation ceases at a given moment to be "renderable" in terms closer than those supplied by Kate's intelligence, or [...] by Densher's, or [...] by poor Mrs. Stringham's**: There is no direct representation of Milly's consciousness after her interview with Lord Mark in Book Seventh, Chapter 4. On her first appearance in the novel in Book Third, Chapter 1, the narrator announces a principle of indirect treatment in noting 'the sort of interest she could inspire' in those around her: 'She worked—and

seemingly quite without design—upon the sympathy, the curiosity, the fancy of her associates, and we shall really ourselves scarce otherwise come closer to her than by feeling their impression and sharing, if need be, their confusion' (*NYE* XIX, 116).

825 **projected for us [...] on any more responsible plate than that of the latter's admirable anxiety**: James appears to refer to a photographic 'plate': 'A thin sheet of metal, glass, or other substance, coated with a light-sensitive film, on which single photographs are taken in larger or older types of camera' (*OED*). He had already used the photographic metaphor for a character's focalizing consciousness in *The Reverberator* (1888), where Gaston Probert gives thanks 'for the sensitive plate that nature had lodged in his brain and that culture had brought to so high a polish'; later in the book we are told that Mr Dosson 'hadn't, like his so differently-appointed young friend [Gaston], a sensitive plate for a brain, and the important events of his life had never been personal impressions' (Chs. 3 and 7; *NYE* XIII, 46, 101). Alvin Langdon Coburn, who took the photographs for the *NYE* frontispieces under James's direction, commented of their collaboration: 'Although not literally a photographer, I believe Henry James must have had sensitive plates in his brain on which to record his impressions! He always knew exactly what he wanted, although many of the pictures were but images in his mind and imagination' (*Alvin Langdon Coburn, Photographer*, ed. Helmut and Alison Gernsheim (New York: Dover Publications Inc., 1978), p. 58). See too James's 1888 essay on Guy de Maupassant: 'if a picture, a tale, or a novel be a direct impression of life [...], the impression will vary according to the plate that takes it, the particular structure and mixture of the recipient' (*LC2* 522–3).

826 **the whole Venetian climax, [...] her visit alone to Densher's lodging**: The novel moves to Venice in the final chapter of Book Seventh and remains there for the whole of Books Eighth and Ninth. Kate visits Densher in the interval *between* those two latter Books, keeping her promise to have sex with him if he agrees to stay on in Venice with Milly.

827 **we have time [...] to turn round critically**: To have 'time to turn round' is to have sufficient time 'to get into the proper position or condition for doing something required; time to get ready' (*OED*, 'turn').

828 **with public penance for it already performed**: James acknowledges and analyses the same kind of structural failure in the Preface to *The Tragic Muse*, pp. 67–9.

829 **bristles with "dodges"**: James's use of 'dodge' seems to hover between the nineteenth-century slang or colloquial meaning of 'A clever or adroit expedient or contrivance' and an older, related sense: 'A shifty trick, an artifice to elude or cheat' (*OED*). When Densher demands that Kate come to him in his Venetian lodgings, her momentary 'rigour' of resistance strikes him as 'a mask, a stop-gap and a "dodge"' (Book Eighth, Ch. 3, *NYE* XX, 230).

830 **what a tangled web we weave [...] our blest pair of compasses**: An allusion to a famous couplet in Walter Scott's poem *Marmion; A Tale of Flodden Field* (1808): '"O, what a tangled web we weave, / When first we practise to deceive!"' (Canto VI, section 17; *Poetical Works of Sir Walter Scott, Bart.*, ed. William Minto, 2 vols. (Edinburgh: Adam & Charles Black, 1887–8), vol. I, p. 314). See also note 926. The phrase 'blest pair' suggests an echo of John Milton's ode 'At a Solemn Music' (1645), set to music in 1887 by the English composer Hubert Parry as the anthem 'Blest Pair of Sirens'; the pair in question are the 'Sphere-borne harmonious sisters, Voice, and Verse' (l. 2; *The Poems of John Milton*, p. 162).

831 **their "game."**: 'Game' here means 'A policy or plan of action adopted by a person. Also: the course best suited to one's interests' (*OED*). The word occurs several times in this sense in an early notebook entry for *Wings*, where the 'game' is Kate Croy's: Densher's character '"reads her game" at last—she doesn't formally communicate it to him'; '"Play a certain game—and you'll have money from [Milly]"'; 'Lord X. goes [...] to the dying girl and tells her the other woman's "game"'; 'the "game" [Densher] consented in a manner to become the instrument of' (7 November 1894; *CN* 105–6).

832 **Densher's interview with Mrs. Lowder before he goes to America**: This scene occurs in Book Second, Chapter 2.

833 **an hour of evening, on the alpine height**: This scene, in which Susan Stringham follows Milly up a mountain path in Switzerland and finds her sitting on a ledge of rock 'looking down on the kingdoms of the earth' (*NYE* XIX, 124), occurs in Book Third, Chapter 1.

834 **Book Fifth is a new block mainly in its provision of a new set of occasions**: These 'occasions' are the house-party at Matcham (Book Fifth, Chapters 1–2), Milly's two appointments with Sir Luke (Chapter 3), Milly's walk through London after the second of these and Kate's visit to her to learn the news of the consultation (Chapter 4), Maud and Kate's dinner with Milly and Susan (Chapters 5–6), and Milly's visit to the National Gallery (Chapter 7).

835 **The whole actual centre of the work, resting on a misplaced pivot and lodged in Book Fifth, [...] the author's instinct everywhere for the *indirect* presentation of his main image**: This is a confusing sentence in various ways. It is not clear what James means by the novel's 'actual centre' or its 'pivot', nor how exactly he considers the latter to be 'misplaced'. By 'centre' he appears to refer to the structural centre or mid-point of the entire book (compare his reference to 'misplaced middles' in the Preface to *The Awkward Age*, p. 79), and not to a local effect of narrative centring or focalization produced by adopting a particular character's viewpoint. And yet the question of *who* focalizes any given episode is highly relevant to this section of the Preface, and James has already used 'centre' in that other sense a couple of sentences earlier when he observes that the 'occasions' of Book Fifth 'readopt [...] the previous centre' – i.e., the same narrative centre that was used in Book Fourth, 'Milly's now almost full-blown consciousness'. It is strangely contradictory, too, for James to draw from a re-perusal of Book Fifth the lesson of his own 'instinct [...] for the *indirect* presentation of his main image', since in this Book – as he has just acknowledged – Milly's consciousness is directly presented. Book Sixth on the other hand *does* display the 'merciful indirection' referred to in the next sentence of the Preface, in that it shows Milly only from the points of view of other characters. It may simply be that 'Book Fifth' in this sentence was a slip of the tongue in dictation or an error of memory on James's part, and that he meant to refer to Book Sixth.

836 **to [...] deal with her at second hand, as an unspotted princess is ever dealt with**: This is how Susan Stringham, who thinks of Milly as 'a princess', feels that she must deal with her: 'to leave her untouched because no touch one could apply, however light, however just, however earnest and anxious, would be half good enough, would be anything but an ugly smutch upon perfection' (Book Third, Ch. 1; *NYE* XIX, 120, 111–12).

837 **the balconies opposite the palace gates, [...] the coigns of vantage [...] as it comes forth into the great *place***: For the same allusion to *Macbeth* in the Preface to *NYE* XVIII ('coigns of vantage', in a passage describing a castle), see note 747. The italics in this sentence may be a cue to read '*place*' as a word in French, which in the context of James's metaphor would denote a public square.

838 **a burden of residuary comment of which I [...] hope elsewhere to discharge myself**: James returns to this topic in the opening paragraphs of the Preface to *The Golden Bowl*, pp. 260–3.

PREFACE to *The Ambassadors* (*NYE* XXI–XXII)

839 **first appeared in twelve numbers of *The North American Review* (1903) [...] published as a whole the same year**: *The Ambassadors* was serialized in the *North American Review*, which was owned at this period by Harper and Brothers, January–December 1903; the first book editions were published by Methuen in Britain (24 September 1903) and the Harpers in the US (6 November 1903).

840 **sprung [...] from a dropped grain of suggestion**: The scenario or 'Project of Novel' for *The Ambassadors* which James dictated for the Harpers in late summer 1900 begins by recounting the anecdote that had given him 'the germ of my subject' and then moves on to summarize 'the results' of his working-out of that idea: 'But I thought it might amuse you to take in also the dropped seed from which they were to spring' (*CFHJ* 18, 497, 499).

841 **"Live all you can; it's a mistake not to. [...] Live, live!"**: This is an abbreviated transcription of Lambert Strether's address to Little Bilham as it appears in *The Ambassadors*, Book Fifth, Chapter 2 (*NYE* XXI, 217–18): the Preface reproduces roughly a quarter of what Strether says in the novel, with a few minor rephrasings. Versions of the same speech occur also in James's notebook entry of 31 October 1895 (*CN* 140–2) and at the start of the 'Project of Novel' (*CFHJ* 18, 498).

842 **the word "mistake" occurs several times [...] in the course of his remarks**: The Preface's version of Strether's speech retains four of the novel's five uses of 'mistake', eliding the fourth: '"Do what you like so long as you don't make *my* mistake"' (*NYE* XXI, 218) becomes '"Do what you like so long as you don't make it."' The italics in the Preface at '"For it *was* a mistake"' are not present in the novel.

843 **A friend had repeated to me [...] a thing or two said to him by a man of distinction [...] in Paris, and in a charming old garden attached to a house of art**: The 'friend' was the American writer Jonathan Sturges (1864–1911) and the 'man of distinction' was W. D. Howells. See James's notebook entry of 31 October 1895: 'I was struck last evening with something that Jonathan Sturges, who has been staying here [Torquay] 10 days, mentioned to me: it was only 10 words, but I seemed, as usual, to catch a glimpse of a *sujet de nouvelle* in it. We were talking of W. D. H.' (*CN* 140). This notebook entry mentions Paris but does not specify the location further. In the 1900 'Project of Novel' James located the

incident 'in the charming old garden attached to the house of a friend [of Sturges's] (also a friend of mine) in a particularly old-fashioned and pleasantly quiet part of the town' (*CFHJ* 18, 497); the house and garden belonged to the American painter James McNeill Whistler (1834–1903), who lived at 110 rue du Bac in the *VIIe arrondissement*. In the 'Project of Novel' James allowed himself a lengthy digression on the personal and historical associations of the place: 'The old houses of the Faubourg St.-Germain close round their gardens and shut them in, so that you don't see them from the street—only overlook them from all sorts of picturesque excrescences in the rear. I had a marked recollection of one of these wondrous concealed corners in especial, which was contiguous to the one mentioned by my friend: I used to know, many years ago, an ancient lady, long since dead, who lived in the house to which it belonged and whom, also on Sunday afternoons, I used to go to see': this was the English writer and *salonnière* Mary Elizabeth Mohl (1793–1883), who lived near Whistler on rue du Bac and whom James commemorates in *William Wetmore Story and His Friends* (1903) (*WWS* I:364–6). 'It endeared to me, I recall, the house in question—the one where I used to call—that Madame Récamier had finally lived and died in an apartment of the *rez-de-chaussée* [ground floor]; that my ancient friend had known her and waited on her last days; and that the latter gave me a strange and touching image of her as she lay there dying, blind, and bereft of Chateaubriand, who was already dead. But I mention these slightly irrelevant things only to show that I *saw* the scene of my young friend's anecdote' (*CFHJ* 18, 497–8).

844 **full in the tideway**: A 'tideway' is 'A channel in which a tidal current runs; also the tidal part of a river' or 'a strong current running in such a channel' (*OED*). 'The Tideway' is the name given to the tidal part of the River Thames in London, extending as far upstream as Teddington Lock.

845 **a frank proposition, [...] installed on my premises like a monotony of fine weather**: Compare James's comments on the difficult 'motive' of *The Wings of the Dove* in the novel's Preface: 'not [...] somehow what one thought of as a "frank" subject' (p. 228). The arrival of 'fine weather' in the Paris of *The Ambassadors* coincides with the scene in Book Fifth, Chapter 1 that embodies its germ: 'The Sunday of the next week was a wonderful day'; 'the celebrated sculptor [Gloriani] had a queer old garden, for which the weather—spring at last frank and fair—was propitious' (*NYE* XXI, 193).

846 **The order of composition […] was reversed by the order of publication**: The Preface's implication that *The Wings of the Dove* – published before *The Ambassadors* – was written after it simplifies the intertwined compositional histories of the two novels. *The Wings of the Dove* was in fact begun first: in autumn 1899, James produced a synopsis for Pinker to send to magazine editors and began to compose the novel, but set it aside in April or May 1900 having failed find a publisher willing to serialize it (see his letter to Howells of 9 and 14 August 1900; *LFL* 360–1 and n. 3). At this point, in response to an invitation from the Harpers to run another serial novel, he started work on *The Ambassadors*, first producing the 'Project of Novel' (dated 1 September 1900) and then dictating the novel from September 1900 to early July 1901; he then came back to the interrupted *Wings*, dictating the remaining chapters from 9 July 1901 to 21 May 1902 (*LL* 356, citing the diary of James's then amanuensis Mary Weld). *The Ambassadors* was thus the first completed of the two novels, but a long delay before its serialization could begin meant that *The Wings of the Dove* appeared first – in August 1902, with no prior serial run. The volume order of the *NYE* preserves the novels' original publication order.

847 **the opportunity to "do" a man of imagination**: James's comment here anticipates his memoir *Notes of a Son and Brother* (1914), a work whose autobiographical reference would give him 'a long-sought occasion' to portray 'the imaginative faculty under cultivation': 'the man of imagination, and of an "awfully good" one, showed, as the creature of that force or the sport of that fate or the wielder of that arm, for the hero of a hundred possible fields—if one could but first "catch" him, after the fashion of the hare in the famous receipt'. James says that he eventually realized that this hero 'had been with me all the while, and only too obscurely and intimately': 'What was *I*, thus, within and essentially, what had I ever been and could I ever be but a man of imagination at the active pitch?' (Ch. 11; *Aut* 479, 480). For 'the hare in the famous receipt', see note 772.

848 **nipped the thread of connexion with […] the actual reported speaker**: As he began to work out the idea of *The Ambassadors* on 31 October 1895, James immediately separated the character inspired by W. D. Howells from his original: 'I can't make him a novelist—too like W.D.H., & too generally invraisemblable [improbable]' (*CN* 141). On 10 August 1901, James wrote to Howells about his role in the genesis of the novel, referring to Sturges's anecdote as 'the faint vague germ' and emphasizing that 'in the very act of striking me as a germ' it had 'got away from *you* or from anything like

you! had become impersonal & independent. Nevertheless your initials figure in my little note; & if you hadn't said the 5 words to Jonathan he wouldn't have had them (most sympathetically & interestingly) to relate, & I shouldn't have had them to work in my imagination. The moral is that you are responsible for the whole business' (*LFL* 367).

849 **the white sheet suspended for the figures of a child's magic-lantern—a more fantastic and more moveable shadow**: This figure recalls the very young Maisie's impressions of her parents' divorce in Chapter 1 of *What Maisie Knew*, a novel which James had recently finished revising when he wrote the *Ambassadors* Preface: 'She was taken into the confidence of passions on which she fixed just the stare she might have had for images bounding across the wall in the slide of a magic-lantern. Her little world was phantasmagoric—strange shadows dancing on a sheet' (*NYE* XI, 9).

850 **the gage already in hand. No dreadful old pursuit of the hidden slave with bloodhounds and the rag of association can ever, for "excitement," [...] have bettered it at its best**: A 'gage' is 'Something of value deposited to ensure the performance of some action, and liable to forfeiture in case of non-performance; a pawn, pledge, security', and specifically 'A pledge (usually a glove thrown on the ground) of a person's appearance to do battle in support of his assertions' (*OED*). The reference to its 'clinging scent' suggests that James is already thinking of the gage or glove as equivalent to 'the rag of association' in the next sentence: a piece of cloth belonging to the hunted person and used to give tracking dogs a scent to follow. He returned to the figure of the fugitive Black slave at intervals throughout his career. At work on *Roderick Hudson* in the summer of 1874, he had written to Sarah Butler Wister from Baden-Baden in the German Rhineland, complaining of the dullness of the town: 'I have taken to the woods, like the hunted negro of romance & amused myself with long solitary strolls in the Black Forest' (29 July [1874]; *CLHJ 1872–1876* 2:192). It is hard to guess how Wister received this fanciful comparison. Her father Pearce Butler (1807–67) had been a wealthy American slave-owner; her mother, the English actress Frances Anne Kemble – strongly opposed to slavery but apparently ignorant of Butler's connections with it during their courtship – had lived on one of his plantations early in their marriage and kept an outraged diary of her experiences there, which Butler forbade her to publish on pain of denying her access to their young daughters. Kemble eventually published it as *Journal of a Residence on a Georgian Plantation in 1838–1839* (1863). Shortly after the period of the *NYE*, in *A Small Boy*

and Others (1913), James would recall being taken as a child in New York City to see stage adaptations of *Uncle Tom's Cabin* (1852) and comparing different stagings of the scene in which Eliza and her 5-year-old son escape from slave-hunters across the frozen Ohio River (Ch. 12; *Aut* 99–103). Later in *A Small Boy*, he narrates the actual escape of two domestic slaves who had been brought to New York from Kentucky by their owners, a Southern family whose children were friends with the James boys: there was no 'hue and cry' and no pursuit in this case, but James observes that the fugitive Davy and his mother 'An'silvy' (Aunt Sylvia) 'had never been for us so beautifully slaves as in this achievement of their freedom' (Ch. 18; *Aut* 152–4). And in Chapter 4 of *The Bostonians* (1886), he had imagined the elderly abolitionist Miss Birdseye deriving a different sort of excitement from the same situation of flight and pursuit: 'Since the Civil War much of her occupation was gone; for before that her best hours had been spent in fancying that she was helping some Southern slave to escape. It would have been a nice question whether, in her heart of hearts, for the sake of this excitement, she did not sometimes wish the blacks back in bondage' (*CFHJ* 8, 26).

851 **a possible right issue from the rightly-conceived tight place**: A 'tight place', colloquially, is 'a position of difficulty' (*OED*, 'tight'). A comparable figure occurs twice in Book Tenth of the novel with reference to the characters' predicaments: in Chapter 1, Strether imagines the Pococks, invited to Chad's apartment to meet 'the whole circle of his society', to have been led into 'a brave blind alley, where to pass was impossible and where, unless they stuck fast, they would have—which was always awkward—publicly to back out' (*NYE* XXII, 160). And in Chapter 2, Waymarsh is forced to lie to Strether about being in Sarah Pocock's confidence, and just about manages to carry this off: 'He ended by squeezing through a passage in which three months before he would certainly have stuck fast' (*NYE* XXII, 192).

852 **the chase with horn and hound**: For the Preface's comparison of writing to fox-hunting, compare 'Winchelsea, Rye, and *Denis Duval*' (1901): 'The production of a novel finds perhaps its nearest analogy in the ride across country; the competent novelist—that is, the novelist with the real seat—presses his subject, in spite of hedges and ditches, as hard as the keen fox-hunter presses the game that has been started for his day with the hounds. The fox is the novelist's idea, and when he rides straight he rides, regardless of danger, in whatever direction that animal takes' (*CTW1* 241–2).

853 **ciphering [...] a chief accountant**: To 'cipher' in this sense is 'To work out arithmetically' and 'To calculate, cast in the mind, think *out*. (*U.S. colloquial*)' (*OED*). In notebook entries of the later 1890s, James uses the word to refer to the preliminary process of stating and developing fictional subjects. On 21 December 1895, for example, *The Awkward Age* is listed in his notebook as a subject 'to be completely ciphered out'; the following day, the idea for *What Maisie Knew* 'requires some more ciphering out, more extraction of the subject, of the drama' (*CN* 146, 147). On 13 February 1896, recording the germ of 'John Delavoy': 'The whole thing must of course reside in some little objective, concrete DRAMA—which I must cipher out'; and on the same date, trying to work out the conclusion of *The Spoils of Poynton*: 'I must cipher out here, to the last fraction, my last chapters & pages' (*CN* 155). On 9 August 1900, struggling with his historical romance *The Sense of the Past*, James falls back on the familiar process: 'I take up [...] this little blessed, this sacred small, "ciphering" pen that has stood me in such stead often already' (*CN* 190).

854 **the story of one's hero, [...] the story of one's story itself**: James anticipates this play on 'story' in 'The Lesson of Balzac' (1905), attributing popular enthusiasm for the works of the Brontë sisters to 'a sentimentalized vision' of 'the accidents and circumstances originally surrounding the manifestation of the genius': 'the attendant image of their dreary, their tragic history, their loneliness and poverty of life [...] has been made to hang before us as insistently as the vividest page of "Jane Eyre" or of "Wuthering Heights." If these things were "stories," as we say, and stories of a lively interest, the medium from which they sprang was above all in itself a story, such a story as has fairly elbowed out the rights of appreciation' (*LC2* 118).

855 **what is he doing [...] in that *galère?***: The French word 'galère' denotes a slave-galley. James alludes to a famous line in a comedy by Molière (1622–73), *Les Fourberies de Scapin* (1671): 'Que diable allait-il faire dans cette galère?' ('What the devil was he going to do in that galley?') (Act 2, Scene 7; Molière, *Oeuvres complètes*, ed. Georges Couton, 2 vols. (Paris: Gallimard, 1971), p. 926). This question is repeated seven times in this scene by the confused and irate father Géronte on learning that his son has been kidnapped by Turkish slave-traders. It is one of James's favourite allusions, and he typically uses it to refer to someone placed in a tricky or incongruous situation. See, for example, his letter of 24 April 1887 to Edmund

Gosse, about the same collocation of person and place that would produce the germ of *The Ambassadors*: 'I hear from Howells that he is coming this summer to Paris; but (once he has put his boy at the Beaux arts) que fera-t-il [what will he do] dans cette galère?' (*CLHJ 1887–1888* 1:114). Howells's son John Mead Howells was a student of architecture at the École des Beaux-Arts in Paris, and it was on a later visit to him in 1894 that Howells would tell Jonathan Sturges to live all he could. James had used the same allusion in *The Europeans* (1878) to register the oddness of the Baroness Silberstadt-Shreckenstein – an American brought up in Europe and unhappily married to a German prince – choosing to settle in rural New England: as her French maid Augustine wonders, 'What, indeed, was the Baroness doing *dans cette galère*?' (Chapter 4; *CFHJ* 4, 43). Géronte's line is listed in contemporary anglophone dictionaries of quotations: for example, translated as 'What the devil was he doing in that galley?' in Thomas Benfield Harbottle and Colonel Philip Hugh Dalbiac, *Dictionary of Quotations (French and Italian)* (London: Swan Sonnenschein & Co., 1901), p. 189; translated as 'What the devil did he go to do in that galley?' and described as a 'familiar saying' in *A New Dictionary of Foreign Phrases and Classical Quotations*, ed. Hugh Percy Jones, BA (London: Charles William Deacon and Co., 1901), p. 322.

856 **the false position**: From the French *fausse position*, 'a position which compels a person to act or appear in a manner inconsistent with his real character or aims' (*OED*, 'false'). As early as 1877, James had observed of Turgenev's novels: 'His central figure is usually a person in a false position, generally not of his own making, which, according to the peculiar perversity of fate, is only aggravated by his effort to right himself' (*LC2* 1003). In *The Ambassadors*, it is not only Strether who finds himself in such a position: Waymarsh, too, in Europe, 'was having a good time […] under the very protection of circumstances of which he didn't in the least approve; all of which placed him in a false position, with no issue possible—none at least by the grand manner' (Book Tenth, Ch. 2; *NYE* XXII, 190).

857 **from the very heart of New England**: In the 'Project of Novel', Strether is 'of sufficiently typical New England origin' and 'has always, in all relations and connections, been ridden by his "New England conscience"'; his fictional home town is 'a New England "important local centre" like Providence, R.I., like Worcester, Mass., or like Hartford, Conn.' (*CFHJ* 18, 499, 500, 503). 'The Heart of New England' is a page headline in *The American*

Scene (1907), in a section of the chapter 'New England: An Autumn 'Impression' that deals with 'the Berkshire country of Massachusetts' (*AS* 47-50).

858 **with its tongue in its cheek**: The idiom means 'with sly irony or humorous insincerity' (*OED*, 'tongue').

859 **the Story is just the spoiled child of art [...] "play up,"**: Compare Thomas Babington Macaulay's comments on Lord Byron in his review of Thomas Moore's 1830 biography: 'the world treated him as his mother treated him—sometimes with kindness, sometimes with severity, never with justice. It indulged him without discrimination, and punished him without discrimination. He was truly a spoiled child,—not merely the spoiled child of his parent, but the spoiled child of nature, the spoiled child of fortune, the spoiled child of fame, the spoiled child of society' (*Edinburgh Review* 53 (June 1831), 544-72; 546). In his 1900 introduction to *The Vicar of Wakefield*, James had called Goldsmith's novel 'the spoiled child of our literature. We cling to it as to our most precious example that we, too, in prose, have achieved the last amiability' (quoted in *Oliver Goldsmith: The Critical Heritage*, p. 68). To 'play up' in this sense – originally an English regional usage – is 'To behave in a boisterous, unruly, or troublesome manner; to misbehave; *spec.* (of a horse) to jump or frisk about' (*OED*, earliest instance 1849).

860 **the dreadful little old tradition [...] that people's moral scheme *does* break down in Paris**: This 'tradition' had troubled James in his first notebook entry for *The Ambassadors*: 'I don't altogether like the *banal* side of the revelation of Paris—it's so obvious, so usual to make Paris the vision that opens his eyes, makes him feel his mistake' (31 October 1895; *CN* 141). In Book Second, Chapter 2, Strether likewise reflects on 'the element of the usual, the immemorial' in the Parisian neighbourhood where Chad had first taken lodgings: 'Old imaginations of the Latin Quarter had played their part for him, and he had duly recalled its having been with this scene of rather ominous legend that, like so many young men in fiction as well as in fact, Chad had begun' (*NYE* XXI, 90). Strether may be thinking of the Latin Quarter – on the left bank of the Seine in the V^e and VIe *arrondissements* – as the setting of Henry Murger's episodic novel of the lives and loves of young Bohemians, *Scènes de la vie de bohème* (1851). Other French literary examples of a young man's moral scheme breaking down in Paris include *La Dame aux camélias* (1848) by Alexandre Dumas *fils*, and Balzac's *Le Père Goriot* (1835) and *Illusions perdues* (1837-43).

James had noted the particular sensual attractions of Paris to American tourists in his first letter as occasional Paris correspondent of the *New-York Daily Tribune* (dated 22 November 1875, published 11 December 1875): 'The ladies, week after week, are treading the devious ways of the great shops—the Bon Marché, the Louvre, the Compagnie Lyonnaise; the gentlemen are treading other ways, sometimes also, doubtless, a trifle devious' (see Henry James, *Parisian Sketches: Letters to the 'New York Tribune' 1875–1876*, ed. Leon Edel and Ilse Dusoir Lind (London: Rupert Hart-Davis, 1958), p. 6). The vulgar American tourist's view of Paris is represented in *The Ambassadors* by Jim Pocock asking Strether 'if there were anything new at the Varieties' – the Théâtre des Variétés, a boulevard theatre which presented popular farces, vaudevilles, operettas and burlesques – with 'a play of innuendo as vague as a nursery-rhyme, yet as aggressive as an elbow in his side' (*NYE* XXII, 88).

861 **more things than had been dreamt of in the philosophy of Woollett**: An allusion to Hamlet's lines on meeting the ghost of his father: 'There are more things in heaven and earth, Horatio, / Than are dreamt of in your philosophy' (1.5.166–7). In Chapter 2 of *The American* (1876), Christopher Newman comes to the same realization under the local influence of the Palais Royal: 'A vague sense that more answers were possible than his philosophy had hitherto dreamt of had already taken possession of him, and it seemed softly and agreeably to deepen as he lounged in this rich corner of Paris' (*NYE* II, 27–8).

862 **"The Ambassadors" had been, all conveniently, "arranged for"; [...] recurrent breaks and resumptions**: The Preface's account of the arrangements to serialize *The Ambassadors* occludes considerable difficulty and delay. In May 1900, James had been invited by a representative of the London office of Harper and Brothers, William D. Fitts, to write a serial novel for *Harper's Monthly Magazine*. Fitts enthusiastically approved the 'Project of Novel' which James delivered on 1 September 1900, and James must have begun to write *The Ambassadors* shortly afterwards, as he told his sister-in-law on 1 October that he was at work on it (*LL* 345). The American editor of *Harper's Monthly*, Henry Mills Alden, took a different view of the 'Project': 'I do not advise acceptance. We ought to do better' (undated memo, September or October 1900; quoted *CFHJ* 18, xliii). In January 1901, accordingly, the New York office instructed their London colleagues to back out of whatever unofficial agreement Fitts had made with James to

serialize the novel. Pinker intervened on James's behalf at this stage, and after some wrangling over the length of the serial a contract was issued on 1 May 1901. But it did not commit the Harpers to a firm start-date, and in the event the monthly parts of *The Ambassadors* would not begin to appear until January 1903 – and then not in *Harper's Monthly* but in another of the firm's journals, the *North American Review*. Howells may have used his influence with the president of Harper and Brothers, Colonel George Harvey, to achieve this outcome. As Nicola Bradbury observes, James 'had shaped [*The Ambassadors*] in twelve "Parts" to come out monthly over a year, making small adjustments to achieve equal length, including keeping back three and a half chapters' from the serial text (Chs. 19, 28 and 35 and part of Ch. 5) (*CFHJ* 18, xlix). This material was restored when the novel was published in book form, albeit erratically: confusion over the complex arrangements for correcting, revising and returning separate serial and book proofs to the Harpers, and for supplying copy to the English publishers (Methuen), led to serious textual discrepancies between the American and English first editions which were not identified in James's lifetime. See the introduction to Bradbury's edition of *The Ambassadors*, *CFHJ* 18, xlix–lvi; and Michael Anesko, *Generous Mistakes: Incidents of Error in Henry James* (Oxford: Oxford University Press, 2017), pp. 55–89.

863 **as ogres, with their "Fee-faw-fum!" rejoice in the smell of the blood of Englishmen**: James alludes to the ogre's refrain in the fairy-tale 'Jack and the Beanstalk': 'Fee-fi-fo-fum, / I smell the blood of an Englishman, / Be he alive, or be he dead / I'll have his bones to grind my bread' (*English Fairy Tales*, collected by Joseph Jacobs (London: David Nutt, 1890), p. 63). In 1902, he had noted that Balzac possessed 'an appetite, the appetite of an ogre, for *all* the kinds of facts' ('HdB' x).

864 **his intention that Mrs. Newsome [...] should be no less felt as to be reckoned with than the most direct exhibition [...] could make her**: James makes this point in the 'Project of Novel': 'We see Mrs. Newsome [...] altogether in this reflected manner, as she figures in our hero's relation to her and in his virtual projection, for us, *of* her. I may as well say at once, that, lively element as she is in the action, we deal with her presence and personality only as an affirmed influence, only in their deputed, represented form; and nothing, of course, can be more artistically interesting than such a little problem as to make her always out of it, yet always *of* it, always absent, yet always felt' (*CFHJ* 18, 505–6).

865 **composition alone is positive beauty**: The seventeenth-century French architectural theorist Claude Perrault proposed an influential distinction between 'positive beauty' (*beauté positive*), which is judged by criteria such as 'the richness of the materials, the size and magnificence of the building, the precision and cleanness of the execution' and the 'symmetry' or 'proportion' of parts, and 'arbitrary beauty' (*beauté arbitraire*), which depends on 'custom', 'association' and 'prejudice': see Perrault's Préface to his *Ordonnance des cinq espèces de colonnes selon la méthode des anciens* (1683) (trans. Indra Kagis McEwen as *Ordonnance for the Five Kinds of Columns after the Method of the Ancients* (Santa Monica, CA: The Getty Center for the History of Art and the Humanities, 1993), pp. 50–1). For the reference in the second half of this sentence of the Preface to 'the dire paucity of readers' who could be counted on to recognise the beauty arising from composition, compare James's 1902 introduction to *Madame Bovary*: 'a critic betrayed at artless moments into advocating the claims of composition is apt to find himself as blankly met as if he were advocating the claims of trigonometry' ('GF' xxvii). And again in 'The Lesson of Balzac': 'when one makes a plea for [composition], the plea might seemingly (for all it is understood!) be for trigonometry or osteology. "Composition?—what may that happen to *be*, and, whatever it is, what has it to do with the matter?"' (*LC2* 136).

866 **He arrives (arrives at Chester)**: Strether's ship docks at Liverpool, at that period the principal transatlantic port on the west coast of England, but the novel begins with his arrival at a hotel in the nearby 'picturesque old town of Chester' where he has 'pre-arranged' to meet his friend Waymarsh ('Project of Novel'; *CFHJ* 18, 500).

867 **throw the reins on his neck [...], letting them flap there as free as in "Gil Blas" or in "David Copperfield,"**: For a rider to throw the reins on a horse's neck is to let them fall slack or drop them altogether, not attempting to guide or check the animal, but allowing it to take its own course. The Preface to *NYE* XVIII similarly speaks of 'dialect with the literary rein loose on its agitated back' (p. 221). The novels *L'Histoire de Gil Blas de Santillane* (1715–35) by Alain-René Lesage (1668–1747) and Dickens's *David Copperfield* (1850) are fictional autobiographies, life-stories narrated in the first person. In Chapters 4 and 7 of *David Copperfield*, *Gil Blas* is among the books which David reads at home as a child and re-tells to his schoolfellows.

868 **a confidant or two**: In the 'Project of Novel' for *The Ambassadors*, James points out that 'we become *dramatically*, so to speak, acquainted' with the background to Strether's presence in Europe via his conversations with 'two persons' in the early chapters of the novel: Waymarsh and Maria Gostrey (*CFHJ* 18, 500).

869 **the serried page of Balzac**: In *A Small Boy and Others* (1913), James would recall passing a similar judgement on an essay which he supposed to be by Balzac, and which he had first read as a child in Paris in 1856. The essay – in fact the work of another French writer, Jacques Arago – was 'L'Habituée des Tuileries et L'Habituée du Luxembourg'; James encountered it in the illustrated sociological encyclopedia *Les Français peints par eux-mêmes* (1840–2) and found it 'very *serré*, in fact what I didn't then know enough to call very stodgy' (Ch. 25; *Aut* 204). The French adjective *serré* typically refers to objects or persons set close together – for example, ranks of soldiers – and the primary sense of English 'serried' probably derives from that military reference: 'Of files or ranks of armed men: Pressed close together, shoulder to shoulder, in close order'; as applied to 'argument, etc.', the English word also means 'Closely reasoned, compact in expression' (*OED*). James figures Balzac's process of revision as a military assault in the Preface to *The Golden Bowl*, and in the Preface to *Roderick Hudson* he refers to the 'systematic closeness' of Balzac's style (see notes 37 and 921).

870 **"Harking back to make up"**: This formula appears to be James's own, despite the quotation marks. To 'hark back' means 'Of hounds: To return along the course taken, when the scent has been lost, till it is found again; hence *figurative* to retrace one's course or steps; to return, revert; to return to some earlier point in a narrative, discussion, or argument' (*OED*, 'hark').

871 **the most unmitigated and abandoned of *ficelles***: James discusses the use of '*ficelles*' – characters who only exist to carry out a narrative function – in the Preface to *The Portrait of a Lady* (see note 172). For Maria Gostrey in that role, see also his letter to Violet Hunt of 16 January 1904: 'Maria G. is, dissimulatedly, but a *ficelle*, with a purely functional value, to help me to expose Strether's situation, constantly, in the dramatic & scenic way, without elementary explanations & the horrid novelists' "Now you must know that—" She is not *of the subject*. M*me* de V. *is*, of course, "of" the subject. But Strether *is* the subject, the subject itself' (*LL* 398).

872 **but waits in the draughty wing with her shawl and her smelling-salts**: This figuration of Maria Gostrey suggests an actress's companion or chaperone, who waits back-stage while the actress performs. In *The Tragic Muse* (1890), Peter Sherringham refuses to give up his diplomatic career in order to fulfil this function as Miriam Rooth's husband: '"But simply to stand in the wing and hold your shawl and your smelling-bottle—!" he concluded mournfully, as if he had ceased to debate' (Ch. 46; *NYE* VIII, 351). And yet a performer too may 'wait in the wings', in the sense of being 'ready to act or make an appearance' but '(for the moment) taking no part in the action' (*OED*, 'wing'). Compare a comment on the plot function of Daniel Deronda's mother – a Jewish actress – in James's essay on George Eliot's novel, '*Daniel Deronda*: A Conversation' (1876): 'To make [his] reversion to his native faith more dramatic and profound, the author has given him a mother who [...] has separated herself from this same faith and who has been kept waiting in the wing, as it were, for many acts, to come on and make her speech and say so' (*LC1* 987).

873 **we have treated scenically [...] the whole lumpish question of Strether's "past,"**: In Book Second, Chapter 1, Strether goes to the theatre with Maria Gostrey and dines with her at his London hotel, and in the course of this scene he tells her much of his personal history. At the close of the previous chapter, he remarks to her: '"You've cost me already—!" [...] "Cost you what?" "Well, my past—in one great lump"' (*NYE* XXI, 45).

874 **the hammer on the gong of the clock**: Many events in *The Ambassadors* occur at specified hours of the day, and horological metaphors abound in the novel. Strether is aware throughout of 'the tick of the great Paris clock' (Book Second, Ch. 2; *NYE* XXI, 79); he identifies this to Little Bilham as '"the clock of their freedom ticking as loud as it seems to do here"' (Book Fifth, Ch. 2; *NYE* XXI, 217). At the end of the novel, comparing his situation to the mechanism of a public clock, he reflects that 'he was out, in truth, as far as it was possible to be' and ought to think about 'getting in again': 'he was like one of the figures of the old clock at Berne. *They* came out, on one side, at their hour, jigged along their little course in the public eye, and went in on the other side' (Book Twelfth, Ch. 5; *NYE* XXII, 321–2). In the 'Project of Novel', too, after the Pococks leave Paris, Strether 'recognises that his hour has sounded. The sound is like the bell of the steamer calling him, from its place at the dock, aboard again, and by the same act ringing down the curtain on the play' (*CFHJ* 18, 537).

875 **my hero's first encounter with Chad Newsome**: Strether encounters Chad in Maria's box at the Théâtre Français in Book Third, Chapter 2; his first impression of Chad is rendered not scenically but in retrospect, as he 'was to go over it afterwards again and again' during the next few days (*NYE* XXI, 135).

876 **Mamie Pocock [...] her single hour of suspense in the hotel salon, [...] the balcony that overlooks the Tuileries garden**: James refers to Book Ninth, Chapter 3. Strether is shown into Sarah Pocock's empty salon and catches sight of Mamie outside on the balcony, leaning over the balustrade and looking down to the street. Watching her for a while unseen, he wonders about 'the possibility between them of some communication baffled by accident and delay—the possibility even of some relation as yet unacknowledged' (*NYE* XXII, 147); their scene together when she comes in from the balcony confirms his sense of those possibilities. James's references in this sentence of the Preface to adopting 'an angle of vision as yet untried' and 'partaking of [Mamie's] concentrated study' might seem to imply that we adopt her point of view in this scene, but in fact we only access her consciousness of the situation via Strether's surmises. The Pococks' hotel is on rue de Rivoli in the Ier *arrondissement*; the street runs along the north side of the Jardin des Tuileries, a public park which lies between the Louvre and the Place de la Concorde. It was originally laid out in the sixteenth century as the garden of the royal Palais des Tuileries; the palace was destroyed in the Paris Commune of 1871.

877 **the Novel remains still [...] the most independent, most elastic, most prodigious of literary forms**: Compare James's words to 'the ingenuous student' of the novel in the last paragraph of 'The Art of Fiction' (1884): 'I should remind him first of the magnificence of the form that is open to him, which offers to sight so few restrictions and such innumerable opportunities' (*LC1* 64).

PREFACE to *The Golden Bowl* (*NYE* XXIII–XXIV)

878 **the still marked inveteracy of a certain indirect and oblique view of my presented action**: James's remarks in the first three sentences of this Preface represent the 'burden of residuary comment' left unexpressed at the end of the Preface to *The Wings of the Dove* (p. 243).

879 **having glanced a good deal already in the direction of this embarrassed truth**: While James comments on the technique of focalizing narration from a particular character's perspective in numerous Prefaces, he notably refers to *his own habit of doing so* in the Preface to *The Princess Casamassima*, describing it there as 'a rooted vice' (pp. 54–5); and in the Prefaces to *NYE* X, XI and XVII, pp. 101, 121–2, 202–4.

880 **the arena [...] the struggle that provides for the others in the circling tiers the entertainment of the great game**: James had used the arena of the Roman Colosseum as a setting at the climax of 'Daisy Miller' (1878), lightly alluding to its violent past of gladiatorial contests, executions and battle re-enactments. When Winterbourne discovers Daisy there with Giovanelli, she remarks: '"Well, he looks at us as one of the old lions or tigers may have looked at the Christian martyrs!"' (*NYE* XVIII, 85). In the context of nineteenth-century international relations, the phrase 'the Great Game' refers to Britain's long-running conflict with Russia over the balance of power in Central Asia, which lasted from 1830 until 1895. Rudyard Kipling had recently made the Great Game central to his novel of British India, *Kim* (1901).

881 **quite of the stuff [...] dreamed of as wasted**: Two Shakespearean echoes, both frequent in James's work, seem to be compounded here: Prospero's speech on evanescence in *The Tempest* ('We are such stuff / As dreams are made on; and our little life / Is rounded with a sleep' (4.1.156–8)), and the lines in *Hamlet* already noted in the Preface to *The Ambassadors* (see note 861). James had alluded to the same two passages together on 26 December 1893 in a notebook entry for the subject that became his novel *The Other House* (1896): 'I seem to feel in it the stuff of a play of the particular limited style and category that can only be dreamed of for E.C. [the actor-manager Edward Compton]' (*CN* 82). Philip Horne notes another instance of this combination of allusions in '*Daniel Deronda*: A Conversation' (1876) ('Henry James and the Poetry of Association', p. 23).

882 **the Prince, in the volume over which he nominally presides, is represented as in comprehensive cognition only of those aspects as to which Mrs. Assingham doesn't functionally [...] supersede him**: In both the American and British first editions of *The Golden Bowl* (Charles Scribner's Sons, 2 vols., 1904; Methuen, 1 vol., 1905), the novel is divided into two 'Books' (each subdivided into three 'Parts'): Book First is titled 'The Prince' and Book Second 'The Princess'. James asked his American

publishers to use the Book-titles as running heads on the right-hand pages of the respective volumes: 'This is very important—that the reader should have the latter before him at each turn of the leaf' (to Charles Scribner's Sons, 17 September 1904; *LL* 404). In the *NYE*, these structural divisions and running heads are retained, but the two 'Books' are referred to as 'Volumes' (and the six 'Parts' become 'Books'). In fact, Prince Amerigo is either absent altogether or is supplanted as a focalizing consciousness in several sections of Volume First, and it is not always Fanny Assingham who supersedes him in this role: see Book First, Chapter 4 (Fanny and Bob Assingham); Book Second, Chapters 1–4 (Adam and Maggie Verver) and Chapters 5–7 (Adam with Charlotte Stant); and Book Third, Chapter 1 (Fanny with Charlotte), Chapter 2 (Fanny with Amerigo) and Chapters 3 and 10–11 (the Assinghams). Maggie's consciousness governs Volume Second much more consistently: she is only absent from Book Fourth, Ch. 7 (the Assinghams).

883 **That was my problem [...] and my *gageure*:** The French word means a wager. Its use, as here, with reference to a limitation deliberately imposed on a novel by its author was notably associated with Flaubert's *Madame Bovary* (1857). In an article first published in October 1857, Charles Baudelaire imagined Flaubert selecting for this novel a banal provincial setting, a cast of stupid self-important characters, an unheroic heroine and a thoroughly hackneyed theme (adultery), so as to prove '"que tous les sujets sont indifféremment bons ou mauvais, selon la manière dont ils sont traités, et que les plus vulgaires peuvent devenir les meilleurs"' ('that all subjects are indifferently good or bad, according to the manner in which they are treated, and that the most vulgar ones can become the best'). Baudelaire comments: 'Dès lors, *Madame Bovary*,—une gageure, une vraie gageure, un pari, comme toutes les œuvres d'art,—était créée' ('From that moment, *Madame Bovary* – a wager, a true wager, a bet, like all works of art – was created') ('*Madame Bovary* par Gustave Flaubert' (1857), in Charles Baudelaire, *Œuvres complètes*, ed. Y.-G. le Dantec and Claude Pichois (Paris: Bibliothèque de la Pléiade, 1961), pp. 647–57; 652). The word occurs again in Émile Faguet's 1899 study of Flaubert, when Faguet praises a description of Emma Bovary – 'astonishing by reason of its difficulty and amazingly successful' – in which the author's apparent intention is 'to show by the exterior the modifications brought by intimate sensations and impressions and to show nothing else; the soul is described through the body, the body being in our eyes the reflection and the very portrait of the soul. It seems to me that

Flaubert won his mad wager [a gagné la folle gageure]' (Faguet, *Flaubert*, trans. Mrs R. L. Devonshire (London: Constable and Company, 1914), p. 195; cf. Faguet, *Flaubert* (Paris: Librairie Hachette et Cie, 1899), p. 161).

884 **so salient a feature of our Edition as the couple of dozen decorative "illustrations."**: Each *NYE* volume has a captioned frontispiece reproduced in photogravure from a photograph taken by Alvin Langdon Coburn (1882–1966), a young American who at this time was a member of both the New York Photo-Secession and the English art-photographers' group The Linked Ring. The passage discussing the frontispieces was added to the Preface by James in response to two 'very touching and justified little appeals' from the photographer about the Scribners' limited public acknowledgement of his work on the *NYE* (to Coburn, 22 January 1909; Virginia). See the Introduction, pp. cii–civ.

885 **the general acceptability of illustration [...] a competitive process**: James's own work had often been illustrated – in magazines in the case of his stories, essays and serialized novels, and in book form in the case of his collected travel writing: the 1900 second edition of *A Little Tour in France* and the matching volumes *English Hours* (1905) and *Italian Hours* (1909) all had illustrations by Joseph Pennell (1857–1926). James had collected his own essays on contemporary artists, illustrators and caricaturists as *Picture and Text* (1893). He discussed American magazine illustration in an 'American Letter' for the periodical *Literature* (11 June 1898; *LC1* 681–5). And over the course of the 1890s he wrote twice on the literary and graphic work of his friend George Du Maurier, who illustrated the serial of *Washington Square* (1880) and provided the germ of 'The Real Thing' (1892), a tale about the models who pose for magazine illustrations (see note 776). James's essays on Du Maurier worry about the encroachment of illustrations upon the literary text, even when those illustrations are the author's own. In 1894, for example, James pronounced the effect of Du Maurier's 'admirable, lovable little pictorial notes to his text' in *Peter Ibbetson* (1891) 'insidious and corrupting': 'with such a perpetual nudging of the critical elbow', it is impossible to 'judge the text with adequate presence of mind', and the writing 'borrows from the illustrations illicit advantages and learns impertinent short-cuts' (*LC1* 873). The most comprehensive scholarly treatment of this topic is Amy Tucker, *The Illustration of the Master: Henry James and the Magazine Revolution* (Stanford, CA: Stanford University Press, 2010).

886 **the "picture-book" quality that contemporary English and American prose appears more and more destined […] to see imputed to it**: On 22 January 1895 James wrote grudgingly to Howells: 'I have always hated the magazine form, magazine conditions & manners, & much of the magazine company. I hate the horrid little subordinate part that one plays in the catchpenny picture book—& the negation of all literature that the insolence of the picture book imposes' (*LFL* 298).

887 **His own garden, […] the garden he has prompted the cultivation of at other hands**: James echoes the last line of Voltaire's novel *Candide, ou l'Optimisme* (1759), the hero's pragmatic riposte to the philosophizing of his tutor Pangloss: 'Cela est bien dit, répondit Candide, mais il faut cultiver notre jardin' (*Œuvres complètes de Voltaire*, ed. Louis Moland, 52 vols. (Paris: Garnier frères, 1877–85), vol. XXI, p. 218); '"That is well put," replied Candide, "but we must cultivate our garden"' (*Candide and Other Stories*, trans. Roger Pearson (Oxford: Oxford University Press, 2006), p. 88). In a notebook entry made during a short break from theatrical writing in May 1893, James had adopted the Voltairean formula as a motto: he was longing to return to fiction and 'add another little block to the small literary monument that it has been given me to erect. The dimensions don't matter—one must cultivate one's garden' (7 May 1893; *CN* 77).

888 **"literary jealousy"**: 'Literary Jealousy' is a chapter title in Isaac D'Israeli's sociological study *The Literary Character, Illustrated by the History of Men of Genius* (1818). The work was revised by D'Israeli and much reprinted throughout the nineteenth century; later editions dropped the title of this chapter but retained the formula 'literary jealousy' in the text: for example, 'Literary jealousy seems often proportioned to the degree of genius' (Isaac Disraeli [*sic*], *The Literary Character*, ed. Benjamin Disraeli (New York: A. C. Armstrong, 1881), Ch. 13, p. 207). D'Israeli refers to jealousy between authors. James's topic in this passage of the Preface is a writer's jealousy of illustration: compare his 1897 essay on George Du Maurier, which records a preference for the 'pictureless' English first edition of *Trilby* (1894) and confesses to 'general jealousy of any pictorial aid rendered to fiction from outside; jealousy on behalf of a form prized precisely because, so much more than any other, it can get on by itself' (*LC1* 898).

889 **Nothing […] could more have amused the author than the opportunity of a hunt for a series of reproducible subjects […] the reference of which to Novel or Tale should exactly *not* be competitive and obvious**: James

wrote to Coburn on 7 December 1906 about the photographic subject he had in mind for the *NYE* volume containing *In the Cage*: 'a London corner, if possible, with a grocer's shop containing a postal-telegraph office. This will be very good, and rather amusing to hunt for, if the right one be findable. It will all depend upon that, but a good deal of hunting may do it' (*HJL* 4:429). Miranda El-Rayess observes that the Preface's account of James and Coburn's hunt for another London frontispiece image, for the first volume of *The Golden Bowl*, 'is reminiscent of the two shopping excursions in this novel which lead to the Bloomsbury antique shop that the picture represents', and she points out verbal echoes of the conversation in Volume 1, Book First, Chapter 5, in which Charlotte asks the Prince to help her shop for a wedding gift for Maggie, which suggest 'resemblances between the intentions with which James and his characters set about their quests' (El-Rayess, *Henry James and the Culture of Consumption* (Cambridge: Cambridge University Press, 2014), p. 17). As Charlotte acknowledges, Maggie is already '"so gorged with treasure"' that '"it isn't a question of competing or outshining"'; she is only looking for '"some little thing with a charm. But absolutely *right*, in its comparative cheapness"' (*NYE* XXIII, 92). Compare, from this sentence of the Preface, 'subjects [...] the reference of which to Novel or Tale should exactly *not* be competitive and obvious'; and from the next paragraph but one, James's characterization of the antique shop he and Coburn were seeking as 'the instance that should oblige us by the marvel of an accidental rightness' (p. 266). Charlotte also remarks in this scene: '"Hunting in London, besides, is amusing in itself"' (*NYE* XXIII, 92).

890 **mere optical symbols or echoes, expressions [...] only of the type or idea of this or that thing**: At an early stage in the search for photographic subjects, James told Pinker that he wanted in each case 'the right, the representative or symbolic, scene or object' (12 June 1906; Yale). He later advised Coburn to look at the *porte cochère* of the British Embassy in Paris in rue du Faubourg St-Honoré 'for a grand specimen of the *type*' of such carriage-gates: 'once you get the Type into your head, you will easily recognise specimens' ([2 October 1906]; *HJL* 4:416, 417).

891 **an enquiry into the street-scenery of London**: In the autumn and winter of 1906, James supplied Coburn with detailed instructions for locating photographic subjects in other cities, notably Paris and Venice (see *HJL* 4:416–18, 426–31). But on at least three occasions, they went out together

in search of London subjects. James recalled their expeditions in a letter of 14 October 1909: 'I think ever so kindly of those we had for the Edition—of the hour of the find of the Antiquity Shop—of the day of St. John's Wood & the Buns—& even of that dismal wet one of the Sought Bench & Scotch Firs at Hampstead—which *should* have been at Wimbledon!' (Virginia). He refers in this sentence to the frontispieces for *NYE* XXIII ('The Curiosity Shop'), *NYE* VIII ('St. John's Wood') and *NYE* XV ('Saltram's Seat'). For the buns, see Coburn, *Alvin Langdon Coburn, Photographer*, p. 58.

892 **as London ends by giving one absolutely everything one asks**: Compare James's essay 'London' (1888): 'London is indeed an epitome of the round world, and just as it is a commonplace to say that there is nothing one can't "get" there, so it is equally true that there is nothing one can't study at first hand' (*ELE* 10).

893 **nothing [...] would induce me to say where**: Edel remarks: 'Following James's lead, Coburn himself always refused to reveal the location of the actual shop he had photographed, though he did note that he and the novelist had found it in almost the same spot where it was located in the novel' (*LC2* 1381). Maggie happens upon the shop somewhere in Bloomsbury while walking home to Portland Place from a visit to the British Museum (Volume 2, Book Fourth, Ch. 9). Edel's note seems to be based on private communication with the photographer, as Coburn says nothing of the making of this image in the relevant chapter of his autobiography (*Alvin Langdon Coburn, Photographer*, pp. 52–60). See also Edel, *Henry James: The Master, 1901–1916*, pp. 345, 576. 'The Curiosity Shop' is reproduced in the present edition as Figure 2, p. ciii.

894 **some generalised vision of Portland Place**: A grand residential street in Marylebone running north–south between Regent's Park and the northern end of Regent Street, Portland Place is the location of Maggie and Amerigo's London home; Coburn's photograph 'Portland Place' is the frontispiece image for *NYE* XXIV. James repeatedly urged Coburn to take 'generalised' or 'generalising' images: in Paris, for example, 'one or two big generalising glimpses or fragments (even of the Arc de Triomphe say)'; and in Venice, as well as the Palazzo Barbaro, 'do any other odd and interesting bit you can, that may serve for a sort of symbolised and generalised Venice in case everything else fails' ([2 October 1906], 6 December 1906; *HJL* 4:418, 428).

895 **the great featureless Philistine vista**: The original Philistines were an ancient people occupying lands in the southern Levant in the twelfth and eleventh centuries BCE; they appear in the Old Testament as enemies of the Israelites – for example, in the stories of Samson and Delilah and of David and Goliath. The term 'Philistine' was used in a derogatory sense by nineteenth-century German university students to mean 'a townsperson, a non-student'; more generally, from this period on, it also denotes 'An uneducated or unenlightened person; one perceived to be indifferent or hostile to art or culture, or whose interests and tastes are commonplace or material' (*OED*). This sense of the word was adopted by Matthew Arnold in his lecture 'Heinrich Heine' (1863) and given wider currency in his *Culture and Anarchy* (1869). Arnold's Philistines are the prosperous, respectable English middle class, 'of all people the most inaccessible to ideas and the most impatient of them' ('Heinrich Heine', in *The Complete Prose Works of Matthew Arnold*, vol. III, p. 113). James had discussed Arnold's use of 'the German term' in his review of *Essays in Criticism*, noting that 'An English review briefly defines it by saying that "it applies to the fat-headed respectable public in general." This definition must satisfy us here' (*LC1* 716). Returning to England in December 1877, after three months in France and Italy, he exclaimed at 'the foggy Philistinism, the grimy ugliness, of London!' (to MWJ, 21 December [1877]; *CLHJ 1876–1878* 2:6).

896 **putting the process through**: In this sense, which is originally American, to 'put through' means 'To help or cause to pass through a process; to bring to a conclusion; to carry through (successfully)' (*OED*, 'put', earliest instance 1847). In his story 'Pandora' (1884), James applies the phrase to the processes of transatlantic travel. Pandora Day, returning to America with her family after making the tour of Europe, tells the German diplomat Vogelstein that she anticipates trouble when their ship docks at New York: '"I'm afraid I shall have such a time putting my people through." "Putting them through?" "Through the Custom-House. We've made so many purchases"' (Ch. 1; *NYE* XVIII, 117). In a more general sense, the unofficial courier Maria Gostrey in *The Ambassadors* (1903) counts this among her services to Americans abroad: '"I'm a general guide—to 'Europe,' don't you know? I wait for people—I put them through"' (Book First, Ch.1; *NYE* XXI, 18).

897 **Into his very footprints the responsive, the imaginative steps of the docile reader […] all comfortably sink**: James often uses a figure of treading in another's footsteps to register the difficulty of working in an established

literary tradition or following a dominant predecessor. He wrote thus to Thomas Bailey Aldrich from Paris on 13 February 1884: 'Daudet spoke of his envy and admiration of the "serenity of production" of Turgénieff—working in a field and a language where the white snow had as yet so few foot-prints. In French, he said, it is all one trampled slosh—one has to look, forever, to see where one can put down one's step' (*CLHJ 1883–1884* 2:23). He repeats the image in his 1888 essay on Maupassant, noting that 'the simple man of taste and talent' – as distinct from the 'man of genius' – trying to write literature in French 'can only go step by step over ground where every step is already a footprint' (*LC2* 533). Again, writing in 1904 on Gabriele D'Annunzio: 'to handle any subject successfully handled by Zola [...] is quite inevitably to walk more or less in his footsteps, in prints so wide and deep as to leave little margin for passing round them' ('GDA' 405).

898 **as an image in cut paper [...] applied to a sharp shadow on a wall, matches [...] without excess or deficiency**: James refers to a 'silhouette', a portrait made by tracing the shadow of the sitter's profile and either filling in the outline in black or cutting it out of black paper; the process took its name 'from Étienne de Silhouette, the parsimonious French finance minister under Louis XV, who cut shadow portraits as a hobby', and it was 'extremely popular c. 1750–1850 as the quickest and cheapest method of portraiture' (*Concise Oxford Dictionary of Art Terms*). Here and elsewhere, James reverses the process and imagines comparing a person's shadow to an existing silhouette of their profile. In 'An International Episode', for example, the American heroine has 'an ideal of conduct' for a young English nobleman which she tries to 'adapt' to the actual behaviour of her admirer Lord Lambeth 'as you might attempt to fit a silhouette in cut paper over a shadow projected on a wall. Bessie Alden's silhouette, however, refused to coincide at all points with his lordship's figure' (*NYE* XIV, 368).

899 **almost any instance of my work previous to some dozen years ago**: The Preface to *The Golden Bowl* was composed between October 1908 and March 1909, so a dozen years before that would correspond to the period immediately following the end of James's theatrical experiments of the early–mid 1890s: works from that period collected in the *NYE* include *The Spoils of Poynton* (1896) and *What Maisie Knew* (1897). Theodora Bosanquet observed in 1924 that James 'had cultivated the habit of forgetting past achievements almost to the pitch of a sincere conviction that

nothing he had written before about 1890 could come with any shred of credit through the ordeal of critical inspection' (*Henry James at Work*, ed. Lyall H. Powers (Ann Arbor, MI: University of Michigan Press, 2006), p. 39).

900 **to a philosophic mind, a sudden large apprehension of the Absolute**: James's 'philosophic mind' seems to echo William Wordsworth's 'Ode: Intimations of Immortality From Recollections of Early Childhood' (1807), a poem about the *loss* of early apprehensions of the absolute: 'We will grieve not, rather find / Strength in what remains behind, / [...] In the faith that looks through death, / In years that bring the philosophic mind' (ll. 180–1, 186–7; *The Poetical Works of William Wordsworth*, vol. IV, p. 284). In the Preface to *NYE* XI, James had described his recognition of the subject of 'The Pupil'(1891) as 'the suddenly-determined *absolute* of perception' (p. 120). The philosophical background to his use of this term may lie partly in the American idealism of Ralph Waldo Emerson, who describes a similar experience in his essay 'Nature' (1836): 'Whilst we behold unveiled the nature of Justice and Truth, we learn the difference between the absolute and the conditional or relative. We apprehend the absolute' (Ch. 6; Emerson, *Essays and Lectures*, ed. Joel Porte (New York: Library of America, 1983), p. 37). Emerson's faith that material nature 'suggests the absolute' ('Nature', Ch. 7; *ibid.*, p. 40) is found also in the Swedenborgian mysticism embraced by James's father: 'philosophy never sees in the finite anything but a most specious mask or cloak of the infinite, in the relative anything but a most subtle revelation of the absolute' (Henry James [Sr], *The Secret of Swedenborg: Being an Elucidation of His Doctrine of the Divine Natural Humanity* (Boston, MA: Fields, Osgood, 1869), Ch. 26, p. 202). By contrast, the other American philosophical tradition James was personally close to – Pragmatism – rejects 'the Absolute' as a ground of meaning. In *Pragmatism: A New Name for Some Old Ways of Thinking* (1907), William James thus describes a turn 'away from abstraction and insufficiency, from verbal solutions, from bad *a priori* reasons, from fixed principles, closed systems, and pretended absolutes and origins' and 'towards concreteness and adequacy, towards facts, towards action and towards power' (Lecture 2, 'What Pragmatism Means'; William James, *Writings 1902–1910*, pp. 508–9). James read *Pragmatism* during the summer of 1907 and told William that he was 'lost in the wonder of the extent to which all my life I have [...] unconsciously pragmatized. You are immensely & universally right' (17–18 October 1907; *CWJ* 3:347). The Prefaces are most obviously

aligned with Pragmatism when James emphasizes the relativity of aesthetic judgements – as, for example, the Preface to *NYE* XII on the nature of the threat offered to Miles and Flora by the ghosts in 'The Turn of the Screw': 'There is for such a case no eligible *absolute* of the wrong; it remains relative to fifty other elements, a matter of appreciation, speculation, imagination' (p. 139). For James's resistance to *a priori* rules about fictional subjects, see note 275.

901 **to get and to keep finished and dismissed work well behind one [...] had been for years one's only law**: As James wrote on the date of the final performance of his play *Guy Domville* (1895): 'when a thing, for me (a piece of work,) is done, it's done: I get quickly detached & away from it, and am wholly given up to the better or fresher life of the next thing to come' (to WJ and AGJ, 2 February 1895; *CWJ* 2:343). Horne cites other instances of this attitude to 'finished and dismissed work' (*Henry James and Revision*, pp. 76–9). See also note 270.

902 **the reappearance of the first-born of my progeny [...] to some inheritance of brighter and more congruous material form, [...] a descent of awkward infants from the nursery to the drawing-room**: The metaphor of paternity for a male author's relation to his works is common in the English literary tradition. For an important instance in the history of collective editions of fiction, see the 1829 Advertisement to Walter Scott's Magnum Opus Edition, in which Scott speaks of reclaiming authority over his works by issuing them for the first time under his own name: 'the course of events which occasioned the disclosure of the Author's name [the bankruptcy of his publisher and printer], having, in a great measure, restored to him a sort of parental control over these Works, he is naturally induced to give them to the press in a corrected, and, he hopes, an improved form'. In light of the metaphors of washing, dressing and mending in this and the next paragraph of the Preface, it may be relevant that Scott's Advertisement also figures the textual and material enhancement of his works as a change of clothing, expressing the hope 'that the Waverley Novels, in their new dress, will not be found to have lost any part of their attractions in consequence of receiving illustrations [annotations] by the Author, and undergoing his careful revision' (*The Edinburgh Edition of the Waverley Novels*, editor-in-chief David Hewitt, 30 vols. (Edinburgh: Edinburgh University Press, 1993–), vol. XXVa, pp. 6, 7). The Preface locates these issues in the nursery of the middle-class English household, an important space for James's novels of the late 1890s. Nanda Brooken-

ham in *The Awkward Age* (1899) has just made the move downstairs to the drawing-room on a permanent basis, but the adult characters still remember her as a child: protesting against Mitchy's assertion that her daughter is in love with Vanderbank, Mrs Brookenham exclaims in Book Second, Chapter 4, '"Why he's twice her age—he has seen her in her pinafore with a dirty face and well slapped for it: he has never thought of her in the world"' (*NYE* IX, 88). Maisie's periodical moves from one parental household to the other in *What Maisie Knew* (1897) are occasions for anxious reviews of her appearance – as, for example, in Chapter 8, when Mrs Beale remarks to Sir Claude: '"She's not turned out as I should like—her mother will pull her to pieces"' (*NYE* XI, 65). In Chapter 29, Mrs Wix superintends a methodical scene of washing and dressing ('a thorough use of soap', 'an almost invidious tug [to make] a strained undergarment "meet"', fastening of 'posterior hooks', forceful brushing of hair and a final check 'before the glass') before Maisie can go out for breakfast in Boulogne with Sir Claude (*NYE* XI, 311–17). See also notes 913 and 937.

903 **any fair and stately [...] re-issue of anything**: The poetic phrase 'fair and stately' is common in nineteenth-century verse, and some notable instances fall within the likely range of James's reading. At the opening of Poe's 'The Haunted Palace' (1845): 'In the greenest of our valleys / By good angels tenanted, / Once a fair and stately palace— / Radiant palace— reared its head' (Edgar Allan Poe, *Poetry and Tales*, p. 76; ll. 1–4). Likewise at the opening of Emerson's 'To Eva' (1847): 'O fair and stately maid' (Ralph Waldo Emerson, *Collected Poems and Translations*, ed. Harold Bloom and Paul Kane (New York: Library of America, 1994), p. 75; l. 1). And in Longfellow's 'The Secret of the Sea' (1848): 'Telling how the Count Arnaldos, / With his hawk upon his hand, / Saw a fair and stately galley, / Steering onward to the land;—' (*The Complete Poetical Works of Henry Wadsworth Longfellow*, ed. Horace E. Scudder (Boston, MA, and New York: Houghton, Mifflin and Company, 1893), p. 104). These mid-century American instances may be looking back to the formula's occurrence in an English poem with an American subject – Wordsworth's 'Ruth' (1800), where the reference is to the moral influence of nature: 'For passions linked to forms so fair / And stately, needs must have their share / Of noble sentiment' (ll. 142–4; *The Poetical Works of William Wordsworth*, vol. II, p. 231). James often seems to have this formula in mind when thinking about bibliographical beauty and distinction. A decade before the first volumes of the *New York Edition* appeared, he had referred to the Constable 'Edi-

tion de Luxe' of George Meredith's collected works as 'the beautiful, the stately "definitive" edition' ('London. January 15, 1897', *Harper's Weekly* 41 (6 February 1897), 134–5; 135). What appears to be a variant of 'fair and stately' occurs in his July 1905 dictated memo to the Scribners, with reference to the 'dignity and beauty of outward aspect' which a collected edition will confer on his works: 'Their being thus presented [...] as fair and shapely will contribute, to my mind, to their coming legitimately into a "chance" that has been hitherto rather withheld from them' (30 July 1905; *HJL* 4:367). And on 11 April 1913, he would write to Hugh Walpole about the English first edition of *A Small Boy and Others* (1913): 'It was a pleasure to me to despatch you so handsome and goodly a volume—so fair and stately a page' (*HJL* 4:663).

904 **What re-writing might be was to remain—it has remained for me to this hour—a mystery**: In a letter to W. D. Howells on 3 May 1909, shortly after completing the *Golden Bowl* Preface, James would nevertheless describe the recent revision of his travel essays for publication in *Italian Hours* as rewriting: 're-touching and re-titivating them as much as possible, in fact not a little re-writing them' (*LFL* 433). And compare his Note to the first volume of *Stories Revived*, 3 vols. (London: Macmillan and Co., 1885): 'it is proper to add that [the] earlier stories have been in every case minutely revised and corrected—many passages being wholly rewritten' (vol. I, p. [v]).

905 **caused whatever I looked at on any page to flower before me as into the only terms that honourably expressed it**: Philip Horne connects this metaphor and others in the *Golden Bowl* Preface with 'the format of James's procedure of revision', arguing that such figures 'meditate on the physical relation on the page of earlier words to those of the *NYE*': in the present metaphor of flowering, for example, the printed words of the early text 'serve as the seed, which gives rise to a stem [a line running to the margin of the page], on the end of which comes the revision as a flower [a balloon containing the new wording]' (*Henry James and Revision*, pp. 152, 153). See Figure 1 on p. lxi of the present edition for an example of the revised sheets of *The American*.

906 **perforating [...] a myriad more adequate channels**: For textual revision as perforation, compare Dencombe's marginal revisions to his own novel in 'The Middle Years' (1893): 'This morning, in "The Middle Years," his pencil had pricked a dozen lights' (*NYE* XVI, 90). James had recently used the verb 'riddle' – 'To fill with holes, like those in a riddle [a sieve]; to

make holes throughout, esp. by means of bullets or other ammunition' (*OED*) – to describe his revision of early novels for the *NYE*. To Pinker, 8 January 1906: 'I am sending you instanter those revision-riddled pages of The American' (Yale). And to the Scribners, 9 May 1906: 'I shall send you the *American* completely re-typed, as I am here also obliged to riddle the margins practically as much as in the case of R.H. [*Roderick Hudson*]' (*HJL* 4:402).

907 **the whole growth of one's "taste," as our fathers used to say: a blessed comprehensive name for many of the things deepest in us**: James had made the same generational attribution of the term 'taste' in his 'American Letter' for the periodical *Literature* on 26 March 1898: 'The public taste, as our fathers used to say' (*LC1* 656). An important Victorian instance is John Ruskin's 1864 lecture 'Traffic', which addresses 'the deep significance of this word "taste"' and insists 'that good taste is essentially a moral quality': 'Taste is not only a part and an index of morality;—it is the ONLY morality. The first, and last, and closest trial question to any living creature is, "What do you like?" Tell me what you like, and I'll tell you what you are. Go out into the street, and ask the first man or woman you meet, what their "taste" is; and if they answer candidly, you know them, body and soul.' For Ruskin, 'it is not an indifferent nor optional thing whether we love this or that; but it is just the vital function of all our being' (*The Works of John Ruskin*, vol. XVIII, pp. 434–5, 436). James had taken a similar position when reviewing Zola's *Nana* in 1880: 'Go as far as we will, so long as we abide in literature, the thing remains always a question of taste, and we can never leave taste behind without leaving behind, by the same stroke, the very grounds on which we appeal, the whole human side of the business. Taste, in its intellectual applications, is the most human faculty we possess' (*LC2* 868). For the 'growth' of a critical taste, see James's essay of the same year on Charles-Augustin Sainte-Beuve (1804–69), which notes that the French critic 'never repudiated the charge of having strong "bents" of taste. This indeed would have been most absurd; for one's taste is an effect, more than a cause, of one's preferences; it is indeed the result of a series of particular tastes' (*LC2* 692).

908 **the silver clue to the whole labyrinth of his consciousness**: In ancient Greek myth, the Athenian hero Theseus enters the labyrinth of the Cretan king Minos and kills the Minotaur, its monstrous inhabitant, finding his way out again using a ball of thread – a clew or 'clue' – given to him by Minos' daughter Ariadne. The metaphor of the thread reappears in other

Prefaces, with reference to the principles of orientation and continuity that are operative both in reading or rereading a novel and in reviewing a literary career: thus James speaks of the 'delicate clue' to Claire de Cintré's 'conduct' in *The American* (1876) and the 'latent historic clue' to the theatrical plot of *The Tragic Muse* (1890) (pp. 30, 64) as threads that the reader or revising author might hold, figuratively, in their hand; again, he refers to his work on the serial text of *The American* as a matter of keeping 'tight hold of the tenuous silver thread' through his various changes of place, and fondly speaks of his failure to finish writing *Roderick Hudson* (1875) by the time its serialization began as 'one of the silver threads of the recoverable texture of that embarrassed phase' (pp. 21, 5).

909 **as has again and again publicly befallen him [...] on occasions within recent view**: As Horne points out (*Henry James and Revision*, p. 35), important revised editions of several British poets had appeared in the two decades before the NYE: *The Poetical Works of Robert Browning* (1888–9) and *The Works of Alfred Lord Tennyson* (1894), as well as the editions of George Meredith, Robert Louis Stevenson and Rudyard Kipling – all containing both prose and verse – which are discussed in the Introduction to the present edition, pp. xxxvii–xl, xlii–xliii. Reviewing the NYE in October 1909, Edward Marsh cited Meredith's prose revisions as a precedent for James: 'Meredith revised his *Richard Feverel* [1859] after nearly forty years, deleting passages which his admirers mourned [...]. In making his comparatively slight verbal changes Mr. James has followed at a conservative distance more than one respectable model and exemplar' (Edward Clark Marsh, 'Henry James: Auto-Critic', *The Bookman* [New York] 30 (October 1909), 138–43; 139). Meredith's publishers used his revisions as a selling point: as the prospectus for the Library Edition stated, 'For some time Mr. George Meredith has been carefully revising his works, and the text of Constable's Edition is the one which Mr. George Meredith wishes to be considered as final' (Maurice Buxton Forman, *A Bibliography of the Writings in Prose and Verse of George Meredith* (Edinburgh: The Dunedin Press for The Bibliographical Society, 1922), p. 289). In the same period, Thomas Hardy's Wessex Novels Edition (London: Osgood, McIlvaine & Co., 1895–6) was also announced as incorporating 'the author's revisions' ('The Wessex Novels', *The Bookman* (London) 8 (May 1895), 50).

910 **The seer and speaker under the descent of the god is the "poet," whatever his form**: For the admiring Dr Hugh in 'The Middle Years', the novelist Dencombe is 'more essentially a poet than many of those who went

in for verse' (*NYE* XVI, 89). James's criticism tends to draw a more conventional distinction between the qualities of 'the Novelist' and 'the Poet': in 'The Lesson of Balzac' (1905), for example, 'the Poet is most the Poet when he is preponderantly lyrical, when he speaks, laughing or crying, most directly from his individual heart, which throbs under the impressions of life. It is not the *image* of life that he thus expresses, so much as life itself, in its sources—so much as his own intimate, essential states and feelings. By the time he has begun to collect anecdotes, to tell stories, to represent scenes, to concern himself, that is, with the states and feelings of others, he is well on the way not to be the Poet pure and simple' (*LC2* 121–2). And while certain prose-writers may possess 'the lyrical element', Balzac is for James 'essentially' a novelist, a lover of 'the image of life', 'the very type and model of the projector and creator; so that when I think, either with envy or with terror, of the nature and the effort of the Novelist, I think of something that reaches its highest expression in him' (*LC2* 122). Reviewing Balzac's letters in 1877, James had similarly declared him to be 'as little as possible of a poet'; rather, 'the hardest and deepest of *prosateurs* [prose writers]' (*LC2* 82). The theoretical question had come up for James in two very early reviews of George Eliot's poem *The Spanish Gypsy* (1868), in the second of which (*North American Review*, October 1868) he was 'irresistibly tempted to fancy "The Spanish Gypsy" in prose,—a compact, regular drama' (*LC1* 951); half a century later, he would indulge that fancy in his lecture 'The Novel in *The Ring and the Book*' (1912), recasting Robert Browning's long poem of 1868–9 as a novel and reflecting on the categorical difference between novelists and poets (see *LC1* 791–811). For George Meredith as a contemporary novelist with poetic qualities, as well as literally a poet, see note 751.

911 **the fields of light**: A common periphrasis for 'heaven' in eighteenth- and nineteenth-century poetry, apparently deriving from the work of John Dryden. The phrase occurs twice with this sense in his *The State of Innocence, and Fall of Man: An Opera* (1677): for example, Lucifer is hailed as 'Prince of the Thrones, who, in the Fields of Light, / Led'st forth th'imbattel'd Seraphim to fight' (Act 1, Scene 1, ll. 17–18; *The Works of John Dryden*, vol. XII, p. 99). The same formula also occurs in Dryden's translation of Virgil's *Georgics* in senses modified by the poem's classical context: in the poet's invocation of the Muses in pursuit of knowledge of the cosmos, 'aspiring to the Height / Of Nature, and unclouded Fields of Light'; and in a mock-heroic description of the airborne combat of bees: 'in the Fields of

Light, / The shocking Squadrons meet in mortal Fight' (Book 2, ll. 686–7; Book 4, ll. 114–15; *The Works of John Dryden*, vol. V, pp. 203, 243). In Chapter 9 of 'The Altar of the Dead' (1895), Stransom loses himself in 'the large lustre' of the candle-lit altar he maintains, which is 'as dazzling as the vision of heaven in the mind of a child. He wandered in the fields of light' (*NYE* XVII, 52).

912 **I have alluded indeed […] to certain connexions in which I found myself declining to receive again on *any* terms**: See the Preface to *Roderick Hudson*, p. 9 and note 43.

913 **sitting up […] so touchingly responsive to new care of any sort whatever […] "Actively believe in us and then you'll see!"**: Philip Horne hears an echo of the famous moment in J. M. Barrie's play *Peter Pan* (1904) where the fairy Tinkerbell's recovery from deadly poison depends on the active belief of the child audience ('Revisitings and Revisions in the New York Edition of the Novels and Tales of Henry James', in Zacharias (ed.), *A Companion to Henry James*, pp. 208–30; 225, 228–9 n. 20). *Peter Pan* was first performed in London in December 1904. The playtext was not published until 1928 (Horne quotes Barrie's 1911 novelization *Peter and Wendy*), but this bit of audience interaction was part of the first production and immediately entered the popular discourse around the play via reviews and press commentary (see, e.g., J. W., 'The Stage from the Stalls: Christmas at the Theatres', *The Sketch* 48 (4 January 1905), 420; Oscar Parker, 'The London Stage', *The English Illustrated Magazine* 24 n.s. (March 1905), 608–17; and E. A. B., 'A Literary Causerie', *The Academy* (1 April 1905), 364–5). In the script of *Peter Pan* used for the 1904–5 London production, the moment reads as follows: '[PETER] She says she thinks she could get well again if children believed in fairies. Do you believe? Say quick that you believe! If you believe, clap your hands, clap clap. *Don't let Tink die*' (Typescript, 'Anon,' Acts I–III; Act 2, [84r]. J. M. Barrie Collection, Beinecke Rare Book and Manuscript Library, Yale University. GEN MSS 1400). The whole first act of *Peter Pan*, with its night-nursery setting, the Darling children being got ready for bed and Wendy sewing Peter's shadow back on, may be relevant to the Preface's figuration of textual revision as child-care. James knew Barrie socially in London literary and theatrical circles; friends in common included the writers Robert Louis Stevenson and Sidney Colvin and the actor Gerald Du Maurier, who played Mr Darling and Captain Hook in the first production of *Peter Pan*.

914 **the whole thing was a *living* affair**: Compare James's later description of his memoir *Notes of a Son and Brother* (1914) as 'an act of life': 'It's, I suppose, because I am that queer monster the artist, an obstinate finality, and inexhaustible sensibility. Hence the reactions—appearances, memories, many things go on playing upon it with consequences that I note & "enjoy" (grim word!) noting. It all takes doing—& I *do*. I believe I shall do yet again—it is still an act of life' (to Henry Adams, 21 March 1914; *LL* 533). See also note 42.

915 **"People don't do such things,"**: An echo of Judge Brack's shocked reaction to Hedda's suicide in the last line of Ibsen's *Hedda Gabler* (1891). As translated into English first by Edmund Gosse: 'But, may God take pity on us—people don't *do* such things as that!' (*Hedda Gabler: A Drama in Four Acts* (London: William Heinemann, 1891), p. 235). And then by Gosse and William Archer: 'Good God!—people don't do such things' (*The Collected Works of Henrik Ibsen*, 11 vols. (London: William Heinemann, 1906–7), vol. X, p. 185). On 30 May 1894, James had borrowed the same line in writing to Gosse about an unspecified request from the American photographer Fred Holland Day (1864–1933), which Gosse appears to have brokered and James declared to be 'utterly impossible': 'like somebody or other in *Hedda Gabler*, I "don't do such things." Ask me, my dear Gosse, for your "pleasure," to do one of those I do do. Then you'll see' (*SLHJEG* 110, 111).

916 **its settled and "sunk" surface**: For the painterly metaphor of revision keyed to this sense of '"sunk,"' see the Preface to *Roderick Hudson*, pp. 8–10.

917 **lie down [...] even as the lion beside the lamb; [...] stopped their ears, their eyes and even their very noses**: James here combines allusions to several biblical passages. The idea of apparently incompatible creatures lying down beside one another echoes a benign Old Testament prophecy: 'The wolf also shall dwell with the lamb, and the leopard shall lie down with the kid; and the calf and the young lion and the fatling together; and a little child shall lead them' (Isaiah 11:6). The stopping of ears, eyes and noses gathers together instances from the Psalms about incapacity or stubborn insensibility: for example, 'the heathen' 'have mouths, but they speak not: eyes have they, but they see not: They have ears, but they hear not: noses have they, but they smell not' (Psalm 115:5–6); 'The wicked' are 'like the deaf adder *that* stoppeth her ear' (Psalm 58: 3, 4).

918 **The actual non-revisionists [...] plenty to say for themselves**: For a recent instance of professed non-revisionism in an English poet, see Swinburne's 'Dedicatory Epistle' to Theodore Watts-Dunton in the first volume of *The Poems of Algernon Charles Swinburne* (1904): 'when [a writer] has nothing to regret and nothing to recant, when he finds nothing that he could wish to cancel, to alter, or to unsay, in any page he has ever laid before his reader, he need not be seriously troubled by the inevitable consciousness that the work of his early youth is not and cannot be unnaturally like the work of a very young man'. Swinburne remarks of his collection *Poems and Ballads* (1866) that 'all I have to say about this book was said once for all in the year of its publication: I have nothing to add to my notes then taken, and I have nothing to retract from them' (*The Poems of Algernon Charles Swinburne*, 6 vols. (London: Chatto & Windus, 1904), vol. I, pp. vi, vii). A contemporary reviewer of this collected edition connected Swinburne's 'consistency' of poetic aim with 'the unique finality of the Swinburnian printed text': 'Unlike Tennyson, Mr. Swinburne never revises his poetry after it appears in print. What he has written he has written: what he has printed he has printed' ('Literature', *The Athenæum*, 18 June 1904, p. 775). Early press commentary on the *NYE* included several statements of principled objection to James's textual revisions: see, for example, a letter in the 'Views of Readers' section of the *New York Times* headed 'Plea for the Protection and Preservation of the Early Work of Henry James' (28 December 1907, 863); also 'Casual Comment', *Dial*, 44 (1 January 1908), 10; and 'On Revised Versions', *New York Times Saturday Review of Books*, 13 (18 January 1908), 30.

919 **their faith, clearly, is great**: An allusion to the story in Matthew's gospel of the Canaanite woman who begs Jesus to heal her daughter: 'But he answered and said, It is not meet to take the children's bread, and to cast *it* to dogs. And she said, Truth, Lord: yet the dogs eat of the crumbs which fall from their masters' table. Then Jesus answered and said unto her, O woman, great *is* thy faith: be it unto thee even as thou wilt. And her daughter was made whole from that very hour' (Matthew 15:26–8).

920 **the vast example of Balzac**: Balzac was exemplary for James with regard to the *NYE* partly inasmuch as his compositional process involved the repeated revision and correction of successive sets of proofs. E. Preston Dargan describes several distinct stages of textual work starting from the first typesetting of Balzac's manuscript: 'Frequently we have *placards* or galleys arranged in columns which were often printed at his own expense.

These *placards* would be pasted on sheets of paper whose margin would receive the corrections. Later, *feuilles* of page proof (twelve or sixteen pages arranged end to end) would follow. Balzac would use either kind of proof, as we do typewritten material, for corrections and additions'; he typically made substantial insertions in proof, often amounting to 'whole paragraphs of manuscript' (Dargan, 'Introduction: Balzac's Method of Revision', in E. Preston Dargan and Bernard Weinberg (eds.), *The Evolution of Balzac's 'Comédie humaine'* (Chicago: University of Chicago Press, 1942), pp. 1–21; 4, 5). This method was notorious in Balzac's lifetime. A bravura journalistic account of the press-work involved in the composition of *César Birotteau* (1838) appended to the first edition of the novel claimed that Balzac corrected fifteen sets of proofs in twenty days, reworking the text at each stage (Édouard Ourliac, 'Malheurs et aventures de *César Birotteau* avant sa naissance', reprinted from *Le Figaro* (15 December 1837), in Balzac, *Histoire de la grandeur et de la décadence de César Birotteau*, 2 vols. (Paris: n.p., 1838), vol. II, pp. [314–4]; [344]). Accounts were published at mid-century by Balzac's publisher Edmond Werdet and by the poet and critic Théophile Gautier, each emphasizing the voluminous additions Balzac made to each set of proofs and the creative transformation undergone by the original text (Werdet, *Portrait intime de Balzac: sa vie, son humeur et son caractère* (Paris: A. Silvestre, 1859), pp. 96–101; Gautier, *Honoré de Balzac* (Paris: Poulet-Malassis et de Broise, 1859), pp. 71–7). (James owned a copy of Gautier's volume: Edel and Tintner, *The Library of Henry James*, p. 34.) James had commented on the relentless nature of Balzac's compositional process in an essay of 1877: 'The close texture of his work never relaxed; he went on doggedly and insistently, pressing it down and packing it together, multiplying erasures, alterations, repetitions, transforming proof-sheets, quarrelling with editors, enclosing subject within subject, accumulating notes upon notes' (*LC2* 73). None of James's own corrected proofs for the *NYE* have survived. Theodora Bosanquet, however, describes his process of revision as itself analogous to proof-correction: 'In the evenings, he read over again the work of former years, treating the printed pages like so many proof-sheets of extremely corrupt text' (Bosanquet, *Henry James at Work*, ed. Powers, p. 39). The format of James's revision manuscripts for at least the first three novels in the *NYE* – pages of early editions mounted like Balzac's *placards* on large sheets of blank paper, with longhand revisions entered in the margins – gives material substance to this analogy (see also note 925 and the Introduction, pp. lx–lxii).

921 **re-assaulted by supersessive terms, re-penetrated by finer channels**: In 1879, the French art critic Champfleury (Jules François Felix Fleury-Husson) had compared Balzac's demands for repeated proofs of his novels to the orders of a commander on the battlefield: 'Quel général, mais quelles fatigues il fit supporter à ses soldats, les compositeurs! Il fallait toujours être sur la brèche, toujours vaincre' ('What a general, but what labours he made his soldiers, the type-setters, endure! One had always to be on duty, one had always to overcome') (Champfleury, *Balzac: sa méthode de travail. Etude d'après ses Manuscrits* (Paris: Librairie A. Patay, 1879), p. 30). Developing this conceit of literary composition as a military assault, Champfleury remarked that the page-proofs of Balzac's *Un Début dans la vie* (1842, 1845) gave a better idea of the Siege of Sevastopol than some French history paintings of that subject: 'Sur un tel champ de bataille, ce qui tombe de phrases noyées dans l'encre est incalculable. De côté et d'autre, se pressent des troupes de pensées pour remplacer les pelotons décimés par les biffures; il en vient par bandes serrées, par petits groupes résolus: le *recto* ne suffit plus; derrière, au *verso*, s'avancent de gros bataillons' ('On such a battle-field the number of phrases that fall drowned in ink is incalculable. On one side and the other, troops of thoughts press in to replace the platoons decimated by crossings-out; they come in close-set companies, in small determined groups: the recto is no longer sufficient; overleaf, on the verso, the big battalions advance') (*Balzac: sa méthode de travail*, pp. 28, 29). In 'The Lesson of Balzac', James had anticipated the Preface's figure of penetration: if the work of the novelist's imagination is to open up 'a series of dusky passages' into its subject-matter, then 'Balzac's luxury [...] was in the extraordinary number and length of his radiating and ramifying corridors—the labyrinth in which he finally lost himself. [...] It is a question, you see, of *penetrating* into a subject; his corridors always went further and further and further' (*LC2* 127).

922 **was to reach its maximum [...] over many of the sorry businesses of "The American,"**: For the delays to the publishing schedule of the *NYE* caused by James's intensive revision of *The American*, see the Introduction, pp. lxvi–lxix.

923 **exemplary damages, [...] poetic justice**: In English and American law, 'exemplary damages' are 'damages exceeding simple compensation and awarded to punish the defendant'; 'poetical justice' is 'the ideal justice in distribution of rewards and punishments supposed to be appropriate in a poem or other work of imagination' (*OED*, 'exemplary', 'poetical'). In

1897, James had described the publication of George Meredith's novel *Evan Harrington* (1861) in his Edition de Luxe as 'A case of postponed, a case of poetic justice [...] to my mind quite august' ('London. January 15, 1897', *Harper's Weekly* 41 (6 February 1897), 135).

924 **shouldn't have breathed upon the old catastrophes and accidents, the old wounds and mutilations and disfigurements, wholly in vain**: These violent figures link the Preface with James's personal writings on family subjects immediately before and after the period of the *NYE*. Compare, for example, a notebook entry he had recently made at Coronado Beach, California, on 29 March 1905, thinking about his visit in November 1904 to the graves of his parents and sister in Cambridge, Massachusetts, and facing again 'the infinite pity & tragedy of all the past' that had confronted him on that occasion: 'But I can't go over this—I can only, oh, so gently, so tenderly, brush it & breathe upon it—breathe upon it & brush it' (*CN* 240). In these notes, James is sketching sections of *The American Scene* on Cambridge and Boston and wondering whether he can bring in his memories of those places from the years just following the Civil War, when he was 'miserably stricken' (*CN* 239) by back pain exacerbated by an accidental injury he had suffered some years earlier – in the spring of 1861, by his own account, while helping to fight a fire at Newport, Rhode Island. For this 'physical mishap', 'a private catastrophe or difficulty' which he closely associated with 'the great public convulsion' of the Civil War, see Chapter 9 of *Notes of a Son and Brother*, where he recalls 'the sense [...] of a huge comprehensive ache' uniting his own injured body with 'the enclosing social body, a body rent with a thousand wounds' (*Aut* 437–8). In Chapter 7 of *Notes*, he also writes about the 'grave wounds' suffered by his younger brother Garth Wilkinson (Wilky) in the Fifty-fourth Massachusetts Regiment's assault on Fort Wagner in July 1863 (see *Aut* 402–7). Extracts from Wilky's letters home from the Civil War are quoted in Chapter 11 of *Notes*. An undated letter of thanks from James to his brother's widow Caroline, who had sent him some of Wilky's early letters, echoes the Preface's sense of retrospect as a review of 'old catastrophes and accidents': 'I have had to wait indeed to read them over—so trying, so upsetting indeed to nerves and spirits do I sometimes find it to plunge into this far-away and yet so intimate ghostly past where everything and everyone lives again but to become lost over again, and what seems most to come forth are the old pains and sufferings and mistakes' (quoted in *Alice James: Her Brothers—Her Journal*, ed. Anna Robeson Burr (New York: Dodd, Mead & Company, 1934), p. 64).

925 **a great wealth of margin**: James thought of his work on the *NYE* as occupying a 'margin' in several ways. In literal terms, his revisions of the early novels were mostly written longhand in the wide margins of specially pasted-up sheets. Even with this allowance of space, the resulting manuscripts could be hard for compositors to read: as James observed to Pinker of the annotated pages of *The American*, which he was having to have typed before they could be sent to the printers, 'my marginally revised & interpolated sheets require care' (17 December 1906; Yale); for these revised sheets, see also notes 905 and 906. The *NYE* increasingly occupied James's time to the exclusion of other activities: as he observed to Edith Wharton on 7 March 1908, the 'quantity & continuity of application' he had to devote to it had produced 'a state of tension in which my correspondence, my freedom of movement, my *margin*, have gone utterly to the wall' (*HJEW* 89). In his chapter on 'Charleston' in *The American Scene* (1907), he had recently figured the unguessable societal and material potential of the United States as 'the Margin by which the total of American life, huge as it already appears, is still so surrounded': this page carries the headline 'The Sense of the Margin' (*AS* 401).

926 **so beautifully tangled a web, when not so glorious a crown, does he weave**: James here returns to – and significantly elaborates on – an allusion to Walter Scott he had recently made in the Preface to *The Wings of the Dove* (see note 830).

927 **my and your "fun"—if we but allow the term its full extension**: James's extension of the term 'fun' starts from its dictionary senses of 'Lighthearted pleasure, enjoyment, or amusement', 'entertainment' (a usage classed as 'somewhat familiar' by the *New English Dictionary* in 1898), and 'Noteworthy or exciting activity, esp. when providing entertainment for onlookers; action. Sometimes used with ironic force' (*OED*). Other Prefaces emphasize the entertainment of composition from the author's point of view, sometimes figuring it as a game played at the reader's expense: in the Preface to *The American*, for example, 'the romancer' practises his insidious art '"for the fun of it"' (p. 26). But such technical exhilaration ideally comes back for James to a shared enjoyment for author and reader. In 'The Lesson of Balzac', he had recently deplored Anglo-American readers' readiness to pay lip-service to Balzac as a great author but not to discuss his work, an 'empty form' of acknowledgement that excludes us 'so to speak, from the fun' of critical reading (*LC2* 119). The Prefaces can be seen as attempts to include readers in that fun. In James's discussion

of '*ficelles*' in the Preface to *The Ambassadors*, the same 'artistic process' produces 'quite incalculable but none the less clear sources of enjoyment for the infatuated artist' and 'copious springs of our never-to-be-slighted "fun" for the reader and critic susceptible of contagion' (p. 257). Jamesian 'fun' is a complex, self-conscious state, requiring effort to produce and sustain. James had commented in these terms in 1900 on Robert Louis Stevenson's awareness of the anomalies in his own character: 'Perpetually and exquisitely amusing as he was, his ambiguities and compatibilities yielded, for all the wear and tear of them, endless "fun" even to himself' ('LRLS' 65). Both Nanda Brookenham in *The Awkward Age*, repairing the damage to her mother's social circle caused by her own forced exit from it (Book Tenth, Ch. 2; *NYE* IX, 504), and Lambert Strether in *The Ambassadors*, embracing the false position created for him in Paris by everybody else (Book Seventh, Ch. 2; *NYE* XXII, 35), accept other characters' descriptions of what they are doing as 'fun'. For James's handling of the comparable terms 'amusing' and 'amusement', see note 255.

928 **in the common phrase, "sold"**: In British slang, a 'sell' is 'A successful hoax; a swindle' (*Slang* VI:140). To be 'sold' is thus to be tricked or practised upon. James plays on this sense of the word when he writes of the commercial prospects of the *NYE*: 'it *may* make a little money for me—the consummation sordidly aimed at. If it doesn't I shall be the most "sold" (or unsold) of men' (to W. E. Norris, 30 January 1908; *LL* 456).

929 **led captive by a charm and a spell**: The common poetic formula 'led captive' has a biblical antecedent: Christ is said to have 'led captivity captive' on his ascension into Heaven (Ephesians 4:8). Writing on Rudyard Kipling in 1891, James had observed that the Irish soldier Mulvaney, who recurs in Kipling's story-collections *Plain Tales from the Hills* and *Soldiers Three* (both 1888), 'has probably led captive those of Mr. Kipling's readers who have most given up resistance'; earlier in the same essay, he describes himself as 'most consentingly under the spell' of Kipling's work (*LC1* 1126, 1125). The phrase had come up for James in his textual work on the *NYE* – albeit as an early reading discarded in revision – in the description of Isabel's reaction to Lord Warburton's proposal of marriage in Chapter 12 of *The Portrait of a Lady*. In the 1882 second edition (the text James revised from in 1905–6), the relevant passage reads: 'her imagination was charmed, but it was not led captive' (*The Portrait of a Lady* (Boston and New York: Houghton, Mifflin and Company, 1882), p. 93). In *NYE*, this

becomes 'The "splendid" security so offered her was *not* the greatest she could conceive' (*NYE* III, 153).

930 **"muffs" its chance and its success**: 'To muff (something)' is originally a nineteenth-century sporting idiom meaning 'To miss (a catch, a ball), esp. in cricket; to play (a shot, a game, etc.) badly'; thence in general usage, 'To make a mess of, to bungle (something)' (*OED*, 'muff' *v.³*). Compare James closing a letter to Robert Louis Stevenson by reminding him of a hoped-for visit: 'Don't, oh *don't*, simply ruin our nerves and our tempers for the rest of life by *not* throwing the rope in September, to him who will, for once in his life, not muff his catch: / H.J.' (28 April 1890; *LHJ* 1:163).

931 **the queer thesis that the right values of interesting prose depend all on withheld tests**: James Lello suggests a source for this 'thesis' in Théophile Gautier's dismissive comments on Gustave Flaubert's concern for the sound of his prose, as reported in the *Journal* of the Goncourt brothers on 3 March 1862 and summarized by James in a review of 1888: 'Gautier makes the distinction that [Flaubert's] rhythms were addressed above all to the ear [...]; whereas those that he himself sought were ocular, not intended to be read aloud' (*LC2* 423). In the original French text, Gautier takes a stronger line: 'Moi, je crois qu'il faut surtout dans le phrase un *rhythme oculaire*. [...] Puis très souvent, son rhythme, à Flaubert, n'est que pour lui seul et nous échappe. Un livre n'est pas fait pour être lu à haute voix, et lui se gueule les siens à lui-meme' ('I believe that above all there must be an *ocular rhythm* in a phrase. [...] Besides, very often Flaubert's rhythm is only for himself and escapes us. A book is not made to be read out loud, and he mouths his to himself') (*Journal des Goncourt*, vol. II, p. 14). See Lello, '"The Auditive Intelligence": Intonation in Henry James', PhD thesis, University of Cambridge (2019), pp. 33–4.

932 **Gustave Flaubert has somewhere in this connexion an excellent word [...] not being "in the conditions of life."**: James refers to a passage in Flaubert's preface to the *Dernières chansons* of Louis Bouilhet (1872). Flaubert insists that both prose and verse 'doit [...] pouvoir être lue tout haut' ('must be capable of being read aloud'): 'Les phrases mal écrites ne résistent pas à cette épreuve; elles oppressent la poitrine, gênent les battements du cœur, et se trouvent ainsi en dehors des conditions de la vie' ('Badly written phrases do not stand up to this test; they lie heavy on the chest, constrain the beating of the heart, and thus find themselves outside the conditions of life') ('Préface', in Bouilhet, *Dernières chansons: poésies posthumes* (Paris: Michel Levy Frères, 1872), pp. 1–34; 30). In his 1888

review of the Goncourt brothers' *Journal*, James had noted that 'There was no style worth speaking of for Flaubert but the style that required reading aloud to give out its value' (*LC2* 423); writing on Flaubert in 1893, he recorded the novelist's conviction that 'style was made for the ear, the last court of appeal, the supreme touchstone of perfection' (*LC2* 311). Compare the critic-narrator of 'The Death of the Lion' (1894) inviting the reporter Mr Morrow to read Neil Paraday's latest novel aloud with him: '"You'll of course have perceived for yourself that one scarcely does read Neil Paraday till one reads him aloud; he gives out to the ear an extraordinarily full tone, and it's only when you expose it confidently to that test that you really get near his style"' (Ch. 5; *NYE* XV, 120).

933 **the whole conduct of life consists of things done, [...] to "put" things is very exactly and responsibly and interminably to do them**: J. Hillis Miller hears an echo of the title of Ralph Waldo Emerson's collection of moral essays *The Conduct of Life* (1860) (Miller, *Literature as Conduct: Speech Acts in Henry James* (New York: Fordham University Press, 2005), p. 1). The verb 'put' means here 'To express (something) *in* spoken or written words' (*OED*). James makes the same point in 'The Question of Our Speech' (1905), insisting that 'the way we say a thing, or fail to say it, [...] has an importance in life that it is impossible to overstate—a far-reaching importance, as the very hinge of the relation of man to man'; 'it is very largely by saying, all the while, that we live and play our parts' (*HJC* 47). But compare his earlier response to his brother William's disappointment with *The Europeans* (1878), which he had found '"thin," & empty': 'I think you take these things too rigidly & unimaginatively—too much as if an artistic experiment were a piece of conduct, to which one's life were somehow committed' (to WJ, 14 November [1878]; *CLHJ 1878–1880* 1:37).

934 **the religion of doing**: In nineteenth- and early twentieth-century Anglo-American popular theology, Christianity is often spoken of as a 'religion of doing' – as, for example, by the Wesleyan Methodist minister William L. Watkinson: 'The religion of Jesus Christ is a religion of doing; not a religion of mere feeling or contemplation, doctrine or worship, but one of character and conduct' (*Studies in Christian Character* (New York: Fleming H. Revell Company, 1903), p. 103). Various popular American ethical discourses of the period championed 'doing' in the sense of a commitment to practical action: see, for example, the closing exhortation of Longfellow's poem 'A Psalm of Life' (1838), 'Let us, then, be up and doing' (*The Complete Poetical Works of Henry Wadsworth Longfellow*, p. 3).

Rebekah Scott identifies philosophical Pragmatism and the masculinist nationalism voiced by Theodore Roosevelt in works such as *American Ideals* (1897) as 'contemporary "religions" of *doing* to which James may be offering a (wounded) challenge' in this passage of the Preface, and argues that James specifically associates 'writerly "doing"' with 'the Flaubertian "done" or "finished" thing' (Scott, '"The Dreadful Done": Henry James's Style of Abstraction', *Textual Practice* 35.6 (2021), 941–66; 949). For such 'doing', see also note 31. In a figurative sense, 'to make a religion of [something]' means 'To make a point of [doing that thing]; to be scrupulously careful to [do it]' (*OED*, 'religion'); for 'the religion of [something]' as a quasi-religious scrupulousness about that thing, compare James in 1888 on Flaubert's attitude to the sound of his own prose: 'Flaubert had the religion of rhythm' (*LC2* 423).

935 **the tie that binds us to *them***: An echo of the eighteenth-century English hymn by John Fawcett (1739–1817), first published in 1782 and widely reprinted in nineteenth-century Baptist hymnals, whose first verse is: 'Blest be the tie that binds / Our hearts in Christian love; / The fellowship of kindred minds / Is like to that above' (ll. 1–4; as, e.g., in *The Baptist Hymnal, for Use in the Church and Home* (Philadelphia, PA: American Baptist Publication Society, 1883), p. 146).

936 **the whole chain of relation and responsibility is reconstituted**: In his initial memo on the *New York Edition* (dated 30 July 1905), James had told Charles Scribner's Sons that the Prefaces would discuss, for each of his novels or groups of shorter fictions, 'its subject, its origin, its place in the whole artistic chain' (*HJL* 4:367). For the figure of the 'chain' and a cluster of associated terms in this and the previous four sentences of the *Golden Bowl* Preface ('traces', 'connexions', 'disconnexion', 'traceable', 'not to break with', 'Not to *be* disconnected'), compare Washington Irving's essay 'The Voyage' in *The Sketch-Book of Geoffrey Crayon, Gent.* (1819–20): 'In travelling by land there is a continuity of scene and a connected succession of persons and incidents, that carry on the story of life, and lessen the effect of absence and separation. We drag, it is true, "a lengthening chain" at each remove of our pilgrimage; but the chain is unbroken—we can trace it back link by link; and we feel that the last still grapples us to home. But a wide sea voyage severs us at once' (Irving, *History, Tales and Sketches*, ed. James W. Tuttleton (New York: Library of America, 1983), p. 746). The quotation in this passage is from Oliver Goldsmith's poem *The Traveller* (see note 94). In a retrospective notebook entry made in America on 29 March 1905,

James had exclaimed in comparable terms at the revival of memory in the act of rereading, thinking back to the summer of 1866 and his first 'thrilled' reading of George Eliot's novel *Felix Holt, the Radical*, which he was due to review for the *Nation*: 'To read over the opening pages of *Felix Holt* makes, even now, the whole time softly & shyly live again. Oh, strange little intensities of history, of ineffaceability; oh delicate little odd links in the long chain, kept unbroken for the fingers of one's tenderest touch!' (*CN* 239).

937 **appearing in undress—that is in no state to brook criticism**: 'Undress' means not nakedness but 'Partial or incomplete dress; dress of a kind not ordinarily worn in public; dishabille' (*OED*). In 1874, James had commented on the habitual care Sainte-Beuve took in 'revising his published writings, amending them, minutely annotating, and generally re-editing them': 'He had a passion for exactitude, and he wished, as it were, to make a certain toilet for his productions, on their appearance before posterity' (*LC2* 669). The posthumous work James was reviewing in this essay, Sainte-Beuve's *Premiers Lundis* (1874–5), consists of early material which the author did not have the chance to revise, and James found it 'a strange and uncomfortable thing' to read Sainte-Beuve 'uncommented by himself; the absence of the familiar footnotes, generally more characteristic and pointed than the text itself, has something melancholy and almost cruel; it reminds one afresh of his departure, and is like seeing a person thrust half-dressed into company' (*LC2* 670).

TEXTUAL VARIANTS

The following section presents all significant variants from the published text of the *New York Edition* (*NYE*) in the only prepublication textual witness to survive for any of the Prefaces, a corrected typescript (*TS*) of the Preface to *The Portrait of a Lady*. That document is described in the Textual Introduction.

In the list of variants, the first entry is keyed to the page and line number in the present edition; it is followed by the corresponding text in *TS*.

The following conventions of transcription have been employed:

Cancellation of a legible word or words is indicated by a ~~strikethrough~~.
The probable but not certain identity of a cancelled word is indicated by ? immediately preceding that word (as in 'the most ?~~felicitous~~'), or by ? if the word is contained within a larger cancellation, some of which is legible (as in 'It was impossible after that~~, ?in ?any ?case,~~ not to read').
An insertion is indicated, at its beginning and end, by ^ ^.
A substitution is indicated, at its beginning and end, by / /. A substitution is the introduction of a new word or words for a cancelled word or words.
Underlinings for emphasis have been retained as such and not converted into italic. A broken line beneath a word indicates a typed underlining which has been scratched out (as in 'what can be done in this way').
A new paragraph is indicated by §.

The majority of the variants recorded in the following list are autograph emendations made directly by James on the pages of the typescript; a few others appear to represent later corrections made either in the process of typesetting or by James himself in proof. Approximately one third of the total number of variants concern punctuation, and most of these involve adding or removing commas. James's notorious insistence on active care for the punctuation of *NYE* poses a challenge to the textual critic's conventional distinction between substantive and accidental variants. With a few exceptions (outlined below), all changes to the punctuation of *TS* are recorded in the list of Textual Variants: since the material available for collation in this case is limited to a single Preface, the number of variants is not prohibitive, and the survival of the corrected *Portrait* Preface typescript presents an unusual opportunity to study James's compositional practice during the period of the *NYE* in detail.

On 12 May 1906, at an early stage of work on the *NYE*, James wrote to his American publishers, Charles Scribner's Sons: 'I beg the Compositors to *adhere irremoveably* to my punctuation & *never* to insert death-dealing commas' (*LL* 433). In fact, the evidence of *TS* shows that the changes he made to the punctuation of the *Portrait* Preface – first in going over the typescript and then again in reading proof – involved adding commas as often as removing them; no consistent pattern is observable in this regard – rather, a general impression of restless minor adjustment. *TS* shows several instances where a typed punctuation mark mid-sentence appears to have been altered by overwriting (e.g., a colon converted to a semicolon). James's overwriting of punctuation can be hard to decipher, however, and he sometimes overwrites typed punctuation marks *not* to alter them but to reinforce or enlarge them, so that it is not always possible to tell which category a given example belongs to. Dubious variants of this sort are not recorded. It is easier to be sure of James's changes to punctuation at the end of a sentence. In correcting the Preface typescript, he introduced two sentence breaks and removed another, and on a single occasion he introduced a paragraph break; those interventions are recorded here. Corrections of obvious typos and grammatical errors are not recorded, nor are changes arising from the imposition of Scribner house style (e.g., spellings like 'connexion' and spaced-out contractions like 'one's self').

32.7	in "Macmillan's Magazine"; which was to be for me one of the last occasions of simultaneous "serialisation"]
TS	in "Macmillan's Magazine;" ~~to me so~~ /which was to be for me/ one of the last occasions ~~for~~ /of/ simultaneous "serialisation"
32.11	occupied with it, the following year,]
TS	occupied with it^,^ ~~in~~ the following year,
32.12	in Venice. I had rooms on Riva Schiavoni, at the top of a house]
TS	in Venice~~:~~/./ I had rooms on Riva Schiavoni, ~~on~~ /at/ the top ~~floor~~ of a house
32.15	I seem to myself]
TS	I seem~~ed~~ to myself
32.18	the next happy twist of my subject, the next true touch for my canvas,]
TS	the next happy twist of ~~one's~~ /my/ subject, the next true touch for ~~one's~~ /my/ canvas,

592

32.26	he feels, while thus yearning toward them]
TS	he feels, ~~in~~ /while/ thus yearning toward them
33.6	to the imagination not give it,]
TS	to the imagination~~,~~ not give it,
33.15	either be quite off duty or]
TS	either be quite off duty, or
33.28	a patter of quick steps;]
TS	a patter~~, in either case,~~ of quick steps;
34.5	I have always fondly remembered a remark]
TS	I have always ^fondly^ remembered ~~with interest~~ a remark
34.14	and piece together the situations]
TS	and piece together~~, in fine,~~ the situations
35.1	with one's subject,]
TS	with one subject,
35.3	his office being, essentially *to* point out.]¹
TS	his office being, essentially, <u>to</u> point out.
35.16	I might envy, though I couldn't emulate, the]
TS	I might envy, though I couldn't emulate the
35.19	to launch it; I]
TS	to launch it. I
35.28	It was impossible after that not to read, for one's uses, high lucidity]
TS	It was impossible after that~~, ?in ?any ?case,~~ not to read^,^ for one's uses^,^ high lucidity
36.6	truth in this connexion than]
TS	truth, in this connexion, than
36.14	with some mark made on the intelligence, with some sincere experience.]
TS	with some ^mark made on the intelligence, with some^ sincere experience.

---

¹ There is no comma after 'essentially' in the copy text (*NYE* III, viii). The text printed in this edition has been emended to follow the reading of *MS*.

36.36	a field-glass, which forms,]
TS	a field-glass, that forms,
37.32	to tell, with an approach to clearness, how,]
TS	to tell, with an approach to clearness how,
38.2	competent to make an "advance"]
TS	~~apt~~ /competent/ to make an "advance"
38.4	the reduced, mysterious lady of title or]
TS	the reduced, mysterious~~,~~ lady of title~~,~~ or
38.11	to place my treasure right.]
TS	to place my treasure <u>right</u>.
38.33	I seem to remember,]
TS	I seem~~ed~~ to remember,
40.11	"frail vessel," if not]
TS	"frail vessel" if not
40.18	(in presence, always, that is, of the particular uncertainty of my ground), that]
TS	(in presence, always, that is, of ^the particular uncertainty of my ground,)^ that
41.2	(which is usually the one]
TS	(which is <u>usually</u> the one
41.5	what can be done in this way.]
TS	what <u>can</u> be done in this way.
41.9	To depend upon her and her little concerns wholly]
TS	To depend upon her ^and ~~upon~~ her little concerns^ wholly
41.14	to form, constructionally speaking,]
TS	to form, ~~technically~~ /constructionally/ speaking,
41.18	the most proportioned of his productions]
TS	the most ~~felicitous~~ /proportioned/ of his productions
41.22	out of line, scale or perspective.]
TS	out of ~~proportion.~~ /line, scale or perspective./
41.36	but a certain way, and other lights,]
TS	but a certain way^,^—^and^ other lights,

594

TEXTUAL VARIANTS

42.6	there, for what they are worth, and]
TS	there, for what they are worth and
42.7	my memory, I confess, is a blank]
TS	my memory, I confess is a blank
43.6	of a "spell." The occasional]
TS	of a "spell~;~/./" ~t~/T/he occasional
44.8	touches and inventions and enhancements by the way—affect me]
TS	touches and inventions ^and enhancements^ by the way, ~as who should say~—affect me
44.16	which in fact will
TS	which~,~ in fact~,~ will
44.20	of battle and murder and sudden death]
TS	of ~shipwreck~ /battle and murder/ and sudden death
44.25	as a silver bell.]
TS	as a ^silver^ bell.]
44.31	this personage, of whom]
TS	this personage^,^ of whom
44.34	insist on one's intentions, and I am not eager to do it now; but]
TS	insist on one's intention~;~/,/ ^and I am not eager to do it now;^ but
45.1	with the minimum of strain. § The interest]
TS	with the minimum of strain. ^<u>Paragraph.</u>^ The interest
45.7	meditative vigil on the occasion that was to become for her such a landmark.]
TS	meditative vigil~.~ ^on the occasion that was to become for her such a landmark.^
45.10	It was designed to have all the vivacity of incident]
TS	It ~has~ /was designed to have/ all the viv~idness~/acity/ of incident
45.24	my subject. (Many […] I have always held overtreating the minor disservice.)]
TS	my subject. Many […] I have always held ~it~ /overtreating/ the minor disservice.

595

45.25	amounted to never forgetting,]
TS	~~was~~ /amounted to/ never forgetting,
45.30	I had, within the few preceding years, come]
TS	I had, within the few preceding years come

EMENDATIONS

Emendations have been based on comparison with another version of the text (the corrected typescript of the Preface to *The Portrait of a Lady* described in the Textual Introduction and the headnote to the list of Textual Variants), or on conformity with other passages in the copy text or clear typographical or punctuational error.

35.3	comma inserted after 'essentially'
106.9	'concerned in them' emended to 'concerned in it'
123.15	'in favoring conditions' emended to 'in favouring conditions'
128.25	'to remember in fact that my more or less immediately recognising' emended to 'to remember in fact my more or less immediately recognising'
134.30	'out-of-the way' emended to 'out-of-the-way'
146.28	'ingenious stranger' emended to 'ingenuous stranger'
151.28	'ingenious young friend' emended to 'ingenuous young friend'
157.17	comma removed after 'particular demonstration'
178.7	double inverted commas replaced with single inverted commas around 'Figure in the Carpet'
228.5	'that a of young person' emended to 'that of a young person'

INDEX

The Index lists names, places, events and titles of literary works and other artworks, and covers the editorial apparatus as well as the text of the Prefaces; it does not include entries for topics discussed in the Prefaces or for critical and technical terms used by James. Subject indexes to the Prefaces can be found in the following places: R. P. Blackmur's introduction to Henry James, *The Art of the Novel: Critical Prefaces* (New York: Charles Scribner's Sons, 1934), pp. xiii–xxxi; Rosemary F. Franklin, *An Index to Henry James's Prefaces to the New York Edition* (Charlottesville, VA: Bibliographical Society of America, 1966); and Jean Kimball, 'A Classified Subject Index to Henry James's Critical Prefaces to the *New York Edition* (Collected in *The Art of the Novel*)', *Henry James Review* 6.2 (1985), 89–133. Page numbers referring to the text of the Prefaces are given in **bold** type. Alternate titles of literary works by James are listed if the work in question was published under both titles (e.g., 'The Friends of the Friends' / 'The Way It Came'); in such cases, the superseded early title is listed second. In entries for *NYE* volumes, the subheading 'assembly' refers to information about the making of a given volume (its contents and placement in the sequence of *NYE* volumes, the selection and making of frontispiece photographs, and James's textual revision and composition of the Preface); the subheading 'Preface' refers to the text of that Preface, as distinct from the process of composing it. Similarly, in entries for works by James, the subheading 'revised text' refers to variants between *NYE* and earlier texts of a given work, as distinct from the process of revising that work.

About, Edmond 537n791
Adams, Henry 346n185, 483n601, 522n738; letter to 580n914
Adams, Marian Hooper (Clover) 522n738; letter to 359n221
Africa **121**, 437n466

Aiken, Conrad, review of *The Art of the Novel* cxxxii
Alden, Henry Mills 558n862
Aldrich, Thomas Bailey **63**, 301n50, 361n225, 369n248; letters to 361n225, 364n232, 374n264, 571n897

America, HJ revisits in 1904-5 xxix, xxxiii, xxxiv, lxii, lxiv, lxxiii, lxxv, cviii
American Civil War 483n600, 554n850, 584n924
Anesko, Michael xxx, xxxvii, xlvi, lvi, lvii, lxii, lxiii, lxv, lxxxi, cx, cxxix, cxxxiii, cli, cliv, clvii, 327n126, 445n491, 519n730, 520n731, 559n862
Anglo-American Magazine, The 533n782
Anstruther-Thomson, Isabel Bruce 392n324
Arabian Nights, The **135**, **136**, 438n468
Arago, Jacques, 'L'Habituée des Tuileries et L'Habituée du Luxembourg' 561n869
Archer, William 368n245; letter to 388n312; translations of Ibsen 384n300, 388n312, 443n485, 580n915
Archibald Constable & Co. 535n787, 543n810, 574-5n903, 577n909
Aristotle *Poetics* cxxx-cxxxi, cxxxii-cxxxiii, 301n51, 302n53, 352n203, 539n796
Arnold, Matthew 378nn279-80, 429n444; 'Count Leo Tolstoi' 365n236; *Culture and Anarchy* 418n411, 570n895; *Essays in Criticism* cxxxii-cxxxiii, 455n517, 570n895; 'The French Play in London' 373-4n263; 'The Function of Criticism at the Present Time' 378n279, 521n734; 'Heinrich Heine' 570n895; 'Joubert' 467n554; 'Lines Written in Kensington Gardens' 514n713
Asia **121**, 418n411, 533n781, 564n880
Asquith, Herbert, 1st Earl of Oxford and Asquith cxxiv-cxxv
Athenæum, The 383n295, 502n670, 581n918
Atlantic Monthly, The lxiii, cviii, **3**, **16**, **32**, **58**, **62**, **63**, **98**, **109**, 282n1, 284n8, 289n22, 305-6n64, 306n65, 313n84, 326-7n125, 327-8n126, 356n213, 360n223, 361nn225-6, 362n227, 364n232, 369-70n251, 375n269, 396n340, 396-7n341, 397n342, 407n378, 416n408, 444n488, 457n527, 542n808
Atlantic Ocean 488n617; transatlantic correspondence lxiii-lxiv, lxxxvi, xciv, c-ci; transatlantic crossings xxx, lix, lxx, c, 317n94, 454n516, 471-2n568, 473n572, 560n866, 570n896; transatlantic publication 327-8n126, 519-20n730; transatlantic subjects 403n363, 474-5n576, 529-30n768
Attridge, John 394n332
Auden, W. H. cxxxvi-cxxxvii; 'At the Grave of Henry James' cxxxv-cxxxvi; 'Caliban to the Audience' cxxxvi
Augier, Émile *L'Aventurière* 475n577
Austen, Jane **52**, 335n147, 348n190
Aziz, Maqbool 458n527, 518n727

Bad Homburg, Germany **156**, 463-4n542
Baden-Baden, Germany **156**, 287n17, 289n21, 463n542, 553n850
Bagni di Lucca, Italy 418n411

599

Baldwin, William W. 415–16n406
Balestier, Wolcott, *The Average Woman* xlii
Balzac, Honoré de lx, cxxii, **8**, **11**, **24**, **52**, **58**, **97**, **174**, **255**, **273**, 292–3n31, 293–4n34, 294–5n35, 295nn36–7, 304n62, 306–7n67, 311n81, 320n102, 324n117, 348n190, 354n208, 371n255, 385n304, 389n316, 396n338, 426–7n438, 433nn452–3, 439n469, 442n482, 459n532, 468–9n560, 488n617, 493n638, 525n751, 543–4n812, 559n863, 561n869, 578n910, 581–2n920, 583n921, 585n927; 'Avant-Propos' xlii, xlvi, xlviii, 295n36; *Béatrix* 294n35; *La Comédie humaine* xlii, xlvi, xlviii, 293n34, 295n36, 303n56, 355–6n212, 387n309, 420n417, 442n482, 493n638, 544n812; *Le Curé de Tours* 488n617; *Le Curé de village* 294n35; *Un Début dans la vie* 488n617, 583n921; *Le Député d'Arcis* 488n617; *Eugénie Grandet* 294n35; *Histoire de la grandeur et de la décadence de César Birotteau* 582n920; *Illusions perdues* 435n461, 557n860; *Le Lys dans la vallée* xlviii–xlix; *Mémoires de deux jeunes mariées* xxxv, 324n117; 'Les Parents pauvres' (*Le Cousin Pons*, *La Cousine Bette*) 442n482; *La Peau de chagrin* 488n617; *Le Père Goriot* **22**, 316n91, 557n860; *Pierrette* 295n35; prefaces xlviii–xlix, li; *Séraphîta* 282–3n2; *Ursule Mirouët* 295n35

Bancroft, Mrs John Chandler, letter to 413n398
Baring, Alexander, 4th Baron Ashburton 479n588
Barrie, J. M., *Peter Pan* 579n913
Bartlett, Alice 518n727
Baudelaire, Charles, 'Madame Bovary par Gustave Flaubert' 565n883
Baxter, Charles xxxviii–xxxix
Bayonne, France **22**, 314n87
Beach, Joseph Warren, *The Method of Henry James* cxxvii
Beardsley, Aubrey **173**, 484n607, 486nn612–13
Beidler, Peter G. 440n474
Benson, Arthur Christopher cx, 435n462
Benson, Edward Frederic 435n462
Benson, Edward White 435n462, 437n464
Benson, Robert Hugh 435n462
Bernhardt, Sarah 363n228
Besant, Walter, *The Art of Fiction: A Lecture* xlvii, cxix, 301n50, 332n137, 334n144, 344n178, 358n219, 363–4n231, 377n275, 392n326
Bessière, Jean cxli
Bible Acts 491n632; Ephesians 586n929; Genesis 332n139, 434n458, 456n521, 462n540; Isaiah 341n168, 580n917; John 511n703, 530n770; Matthew 368n244, 466n551, 581n919; Philippians 522–3n740; Psalms 455n517, 580n917
Bilston, Sarah 379n283

Black, William, *Macleod of Dare* 361n225
Black and White 514n715, 530n773
Black Forest, Germany **5**, 287n17, 553n850
Blackmur, R. P., *The Art of the Novel* cxxviii–cxxxvi, cxxxviii, cxli, 280
Blagden, Isa 417n409
Blair, Sara 447n494
Blomfield, Reginald 398nn344–5
Bogardus, Ralph F. lvii
Boit, Edward Darley and Mary Louisa 309n75, 314n87
Book Buyer, The xxxv–xxxvi, cii
Book News Monthly cxv
Bookman, The (London) cxvii, 536n788
Bookman, The (New York) xxxvii, cxi–cxiv, cxix–cxx, cxxiii, cxxiv, 389n317, 577n909
Booth, Wayne C. cxxviii
Boott, Elizabeth 314n87, 337n153, 493n637; letter to 356–7n214
Boott, Francis 314n87, 337n153, 346n185, 493n637, 495n648
Borgia family 462n538
Bosanquet, Theodora liv, lvii–lviii, lxxii–lxxviii, lxxix–lxxxiv, lxxxvi, lxxxvii, lxxxviii, lxxxix–xc, xcii, xciv–xcv, cliii, clvi–clxvii, 436n463; *Henry James at Work* lvii–lviii, lxxiii–lxxiv, lxxv, 571–2n899, 582n920; letter to lxxxv
Boston, MA **5**, **19**, **165**, **213**, **218**, 287n17, 296–7n40, 307n71, 311n79, 326nn123–4, 469n562, 471–2n568, 473n572, 483n599, 498n656, 519–20n730, 524n747, 527n756, 543n809, 544n813, 584n924; Bostonian characters and people **149**, **236**, 428n441, 477n584, 493n637, 495n648, 499n659
Boston Evening Transcript, The cxiii, cxviii–cxix
Boswell, James 462n539
Bouilhet, Louis *Dernières chansons* xli, 587n932
Boulogne-sur-Mer, France 357n215, 447n493, 462n539, 574n902
Bourget, Paul cvi, cviii, **174**, 378n280, 403n363, 488n617, 534n783; *Cruelle énigme* 534n783
Bournemouth, Dorset 534n783
Bradbury, Nicola xxxiv, 559n862
Bradley, Mrs Granville lxxv
Bradley, Nellie lxxxviii
Brett, George P., letter to 437n465
Brewster, David, *Letters on Natural Magic* 315n88
Brighton, East Sussex **207**, 515n717
Bronson, Katharine De Kay 450n501, 451n505, 521n735; letters to 452n508, 453nn510–11
Bronstein, Michaela cxxxv
Brontë, Charlotte 335n147; *Jane Eyre* 555n854
Brontë, Emily, *Wuthering Heights* 555n854
Brooke, Rupert, *Letters from America* cxx
Brooks, Van Wyck, *The Pilgrimage of Henry James* cxxxiv, cxxxv, cxxxix
Brown, Bill 395n337
Browne, Sir Thomas, *Hydriotaphia* 340n164

Brownell, William C. correspondence about *NYE* lxv–lxvi, lxvii, lxviii, lxxii, lxxxi–lxxxii, lxxxiii, lxxxvi, lxxxviii, xci–xcii, xciii–xciv, xcvi–cii, clviii, clix, clxiii–clxiv, clxvi, clxvii–clxviii, 510n701; 'Henry James' (critical essay) lxiii–lxiv
Browning, Elizabeth Barrett 417n409
Browning, Robert **199**, 417n409, 450n501, 503–4n676, 507nn690–1, 521n735; *Men and Women* 507n691; *Paracelsus* 507n691; *The Poetical Works of Robert Browning* 577n909; *The Ring and the Book* 329n130, 537n790, 578n910; *Sordello* 507n691
Browning, Robert Barrett (Pen) 450n501
Bryant, William Cullen, 'The Song of the Sower' 496n650
Bryce, James, Viscount Bryce and Elizabeth Marion Ashton 410n385
Bryn Mawr College, PA xxx, cxxii, 380n285, 467n555
Buffalo, NY 368n244
Burlingame, Edward L. xxix, xxx, clvi
Burlington, VT 292n28
Burlington Magazine, The xcii, 395n337
Burnett, Frances Hodgson, *Through One Administration* 340n165
Burney, Frances 340n165
Butler, Pearce 553n850
Byron, Clara Allegra **127**, 426n437, 428n441
Byron, George Gordon, Lord **127**, **131**, 425n434, 426n437, 428n441, 432n449, 499n660, 499–500n662,
557n859; 'the Byronic age' **130–1**, 432n449; *Childe Harold's Pilgrimage* 432n449, 523n746; *Don Juan* cxv, 465–6n547

Cable, George Washington 292n29
Cachin, Marie-Françoise cxli
Caesar, Julius cxiv, 451n504
Cambon, Pierre-Joseph 312–13n84
Cambridge, Cambridgeshire cxxxix, 435n462, 496n649
Cambridge, MA cvii–cviii, 287n17, 289n22, 326n123, 458n527, 460n534, 461nn536–7, 481n594, 498n656, 498n658, 499n659, 544n813, 584n924; Harvard University cli, 297n42, 497n656
Carleton, William, 'Shane Fadh's Wedding' 391n323
Carlyle, Thomas, *The French Revolution: A History* 343n173, 481–2n595
Carpenter, William Benjamin 308n73
Cary, Elisabeth Luther cxv
Century Magazine, The clvi, **170**, 340–1n165, 468n557
Cerberus **153–4**, 458n528
Cervantes, Miguel de **52**, 348n190; *Don Quixote* **211**, 517n726
Champfleury, *Balzac: sa méthode de travail* 583n921
Chap-Book, The 327n126, 410n384, 510n701
Chapman's Magazine of Fiction 510n701
Charles Scribner's Sons xxix, xxx, xxxvii–xxxviii, xli, xlii, liv, lvi–lvii, cv–cvi, cviii, cxxx, cxlix–cli, cliii,

397n341, 535n787, 543n808, 543n810, 564–5n882, 566n884; correspondence about *NYE* xxx–xxxi, xxxvi, xlii–xliii, lvii–lix, lix–civ, cvi, cxx, cliv–clv, clvi–clxviii, 325n121, 401n354, 431n448, 433n451, 445n490, 446n491, 507n689, 510n701, 526n753, 527n758, 575n903, 576n906, 589n936, 592; publicity for *NYE* xxxv–xxxvi, lxxix, lxxxi–lxxxii, cii, cxii; reprinting the Prefaces cxxviii–cxxix, cxxxiii, cxl–cxli; *see also* Brownell, William C.; Burlingame, Edward L.; Scribner, Charles; Wheelock, John Hall

Chaucer, Geoffrey, *The Parliament of Fowls* 512n710

Chester, Cheshire **254**, 560n866

Chesterton, G. K. 431n448

Chicago Daily Tribune, The cxvi, cxvii, cxviii

Chicago Evening Post, The cxiii

Chicago Inter Ocean, The cxv

Chicago Record-Herald, The cxiii, cxiv, cxvii

Child, Francis James, *The English and Scottish Popular Ballads* 448n498

Child, Theodore E. **168–9**, 480n590, 489–90n623; letter to 534n783

Childe, Edward Lee and Blanche de Triqueti 309n75, 314n87

Church, Francis and William 305n64, 463n541

Clairmont, Claire **127–9**, **131**, 426n437, 428n441, 428–9n442, 432n449

Clairmont, Paula 429n442

Clark, Sir John Forbes, letter to 481–2n595

Cleveland, OH **19**, 311n79

Clifford, Lucy 377n278

Coburn, Alvin Langdon xliii–xliv, liv, lvii, lxvii, lxviii, lxix, lxx, xcix–c, cii–civ, clvi, clvii, clviii, clix–clxi, **263**, **264–6**, 346n183, 406n373, 547n825, 566n884, 567–8n889, 568n890, 568–9n891, 569nn893–4; letters to cii, clviii, clix, clx, clxi, clxviii, 359n220, 566n884, 567–8n889, 568n890, 568–9n891, 569n894; *London* 359n220

Codman, Ogden, *The Decoration of Houses* 395n337

Coleridge, John Duke, 1st Baron Coleridge 492n636

Coleridge, Samuel Taylor cxx–cxxi, **181–2**, 492n635, 492–3n636; *Biographia Literaria* cxv, cxix, cxxxii, 465–6n547; 'Christabel' 545–6n820; 'Shakspeare [*sic*], A Poet Generally' 366n237

Collier's Weekly 437n465, 510n701

Columbus, Christopher **126**, 423n428

Colvin, Sidney xxxix, 579n913

La Comédie-Française **73**, 362–3n228, 372n260, 373n261, 373n263, 476n579; *see also* Paris: Théâtre Français

Connoisseur, The 395n337

Conrad, Joseph cviii–cix, cxi

Constantine I 385–6n304

Contemporary Review, The cxvii

Cook, Clarence, *The House Beautiful* 395n337, 397n341

Cooper, Frederic Taber 449n500

Cooper, James Fenimore, 'Leatherstocking Tales' 390n318
Coquelin, Benoît-Constant 373n261, 382n291
Cornhill Magazine, The **167–8, 213**, 306n66, 327n125, 327–8n126, 424n431, 442n483, 450n501, 478n584, 519nn729–30, 520n732, 521n735, 532n776
Coronado Beach, CA 308–9n73, 584n924
Cosmopolis 488n619, 533n782
Cotes, Mrs Everard, letter to 384–5n301
Cowper, William, 'Walking with God' 326n123
Crackanthorpe, Blanche Alethea, 'The Revolt of the Daughters' 378n278
Crackanthorpe, Hubert, *Last Studies* xlii, 377n276, 409n383
Criterion, The cxxix, cxxxii
Croizette, Sophie Alexandrine **166**, 476n579
Cross, John, *George Eliot's Life* 339n160, 350–1n197
Culver, Stuart xxxvii
Cunard Steamship Company lix, 471–2n568, 473n572
Curtis, Ariana Sargent 406n373, 429n442, 449–50n501, 451n505, 495–6n648, 539n798; letter to cxi
Curtis, Daniel 406n373, 429n442, 449–50n510, 451n505, 495–6n648, 539n798
Curtis, Ralph 429n442

D'Annunzio, Gabriele 311n81, 347n189, 389n316, 391n321, 421n423, 493n638, 571n897; *Il fuoco* 493n638; *Il trionfo della morte* 332n137; *Le vergini delle rocce* 296n39, 321n109
D'Israeli, Isaac, *The Literary Character* 567n888
Dante Alighieri, *Inferno* 325n121
Dargan, E. Preston 581–2n920
Daudet, Alphonse xxxi, 293n32, 358n219, 371n255, 378n280, 571n897; *Fromont jeune et Risler aîné* liii, 334n145; *Numa Roumestan* lii, 443n485; *Port-Tarascon* xxxv, 435n461; prefaces / *Trente ans de Paris, Souvenirs d'un homme de lettres* li–liii, 489–90n623
Daudet, Ernest, *Mon Frère et moi* lii, 378n280
Day, Fred Holland 580n915
Delaunay, Louis-Arsène **166**, 476n579
Dial, The cxiv, 581n918
Dickens, Charles **39, 52, 168**, 335n147, 339n162, 340n165, 348n190, 364n231, 439n469, 462n539, 478–9n587; *Bleak House* 404n367; *David Copperfield* **255**, 288n19, 527n757, 560n867; *Martin Chuzzlewit* 518n727; *Our Mutual Friend* 401n356; *Sketches by Boz* 528n762
Diebel, Anne 484n607
Doe, Charles Henry, *Buffets* 529n764
Dover, Kent **58–9**, 356n213, 356–7n214, 357n215, 534n783
Dryden, John *Essay of Dramatick Poesy* 340n164, 539n796; *The State of Innocence, and Fall of Man* 578n911; translations of Virgil 458n528, 578–9n911

Du Maurier, George **224-5**, 371n255, 382n292, 491n632, 531-2n776; *Peter Ibbetson* 566n885; *Trilby* 531-2n776, 567n888
Du Maurier, Gerald 579n913
Dumas, Alexandre **52**, 335n147, 348n190, 348n192; *Histoire de mes bêtes* 368n245; *Les trois mousquetaires* **66**, 365n235
Dumas, Alexandre, *fils* **88-9**, 354n208, 368n245, 382n291, 387n310, 388n312, 476-7n580; *La Dame aux camélias* 557n860; *Le Demi-monde* **166-7**, 475n577, 475-6n578, 476n578, 477n581, 477n583; *Denise* **88**, 382n291, 388n311; *Francillon* **88**, 388n311; *Monsieur Alphonse* **88, 89**, 388n311; prefaces xlvi
Dún Laoghaire, Ireland 407n377
Duneka, Frederick A. 526n754; letters to lxvi, 509n700, 526n755
Dupee, F. W., *The Question of Henry James* cxxxv
Duveneck, Frank 518n727
Dykes Campbell, James, *Samuel Taylor Coleridge: A Narrative of the Events of His Life* **181**, 492nn635-6

Earle, Maria Theresa 407n379
Edel, Leon xlvi, lxxiii, cv, cviii, cxxv, cxxvii, 280, 281, 291n28, 314n87, 315n88, 316n91, 375n269, 381n288, 407n379, 416n406, 438n468, 457-8n527, 459n533, 460n534, 475n577, 483n601, 499n659, 501-2n670, 503n676, 518n727, 519n729, 522n738, 534n783, 569n893, 582n920

Edgar, Pelham, *Henry James, Man and Author* cxxvii
Edgett, Edwin Francis cxviii-cxix
Edinburgh Review, The 485n609, 557n859
Elgar, Edward, 'Pomp and Circumstance' marches 322n112
Eliot, George **39, 40, 52**, 335n147, 348n190, 412n392; *Adam Bede* **39, 54, 225**, 325n121, 339n161, 350n196, 532-3n779; *Daniel Deronda* **39, 54**, 299n47, 338n158, 339nn160-1, 350n196, 350-1n197, 413-14n399, 562n872; *Felix Holt, the Radical* **54**, 350n196, 590n936; *Middlemarch* **39, 54**, 339n161, 340n165, 350n196; *The Mill on the Floss* **39, 54**, 339n161, 340n165, 350n197; *Romola* **54**, 340n165, 350n196; *The Spanish Gypsy* 578n910
Eliot, T. S., 'The Hawthorne Aspect' 290n24
Elliott, Maud Howe 535n785
Elliott, Sarah Barnwell, *The Durket Sperret* 529n764
Ellison, Ralph cxxxv
El-Rayess, Miranda 568n889
Emerson, Ralph Waldo 546n820; *The Conduct of Life* 588n933; 'Nature' 572n900; 'To Eva' 574n903
Emmet, Ellen, letter to 325n121
Emmet, Rosina (Posy) 455n519
English Channel **59, 83**, 314n87, 356n213, 398n345, 488n617; crossings **22**, 317-18n94, 357n215
English Illustrated Magazine, The **187**, 496n649, 579n913

English Review, The lxxxix, xcii, cxi, clxvi, 510n700
Erskine, Louisa, Lady Wolseley, letter to 465n545
Eton College, Berkshire cx, 312n82, 435n462
Étretat, France **21**, 314n87, 480n590
Europe Americans in **44**, **104-5**, **121**, **148-53**, **157-9**, **164-6**, **171**, **188-9**, **222**, 305n63, 309n74, 326n125, 336n151, 368n244, 402n359, 403n361, 403n363, 411n389, 419n412, 419n414, 423n428, 425n433, 451-2n506, 454n513, 455n518, 456-7n525, 457n526, 457-8n527, 459nn532-3, 461nn536-7, 461-2n538, 462n539, 462-3n540, 466n552, 470n563, 471n567, 472-3n570, 474-5n576, 484n604, 497-8n656, 498n658, 499n660, 499-500n662, 555-6n855, 556n856, 570n896; Americans marrying Europeans **161-2**, 468nn558-9; Europeans in America **104**, 402n359, 556n855

Faguet, Émile, *Flaubert* 565-6n883
fairy tales **135-6**, **201**, 409n383, 438-9n468, 441n477; see also *The Arabian Nights*; Grimm, Jacob and Wilhelm; 'Jack and the Beanstalk'; Perrault, Charles
Fates (Moirai) 539n797
Fawcett, John, 'Blest be the tie that binds' 589n935
Fergusson, Francis cxxxvii-cxxxviii
Fielding, Henry **52**, 335n147, 348n190; *Tom Jones* **53**, 349n194

Fields, James T. and Annie Adams 477n584
First French Empire **22**, 316n92
Fitch, George Hamlin cxviii
Fitts, William D. 558-9n862
Flaubert, Gustave cxxxix, 285n12, 311n81, 323n115, 358n219, 378n280, 587n931, 587-8n932, 589n934; letters cxxxi-cxxxii, 318n95, 319n98; *Madame Bovary* xxxv, **26**, 292-3n31, 300-1n50, 321n107, 347n187, 565-6n883; 'Préface' to Louis Bouilhet xli-xlii, **276**, 587n932
Florence, Italy **127**, 288n20, 289n21, 329n130, 425n433, 460n534, 471n567, 509n698, 539n798; Arno **156**, 465n545; Bellosguardo 417n409, 451n505; Borgo Ognissanti **156**, 465n545; and germs of fictions **119**, **120-1**, **126-8**, **131**, **145-6**, 415-16n406, 417n410, 423n429, 426n437, 428n441, 428-9n442, 449n499, 450n500, 450-1n502, 451n505, 452n508, 453n511; HJ writing in **3**, **6**, **32**, **156**, 282n1, 289-90n23, 326n124, 329n129, 465n545, 531n775; Piazza Santa Maria Novella **6**, 289-90n23, 290n24; Via della Scala **6**, 289n23
Flower, Dean 292n29
Foley, Richard Nicholas cxiii
Follini, Tamara 431n447
Forbes-Robertson, Johnston lxxvii, lxxxi, lxxxii, lxxxv, lxxxvi
Ford, Ford Madox, *see* Hueffer, Ford Madox

France, Anatole, *Histoire comique* **72**, 372–3n260
French Revolution **43**, 309n75, 312–13n84, 315n88, 343n173, 360n222, 367n239, 481–2n595, 538n795
Friedman, Norman cxxviii
Fullerton, Morton letter to 523–4n746; review of *NYE* cxi, cxii, cxxii–cxxiii

Galaxy, The **156**, 283n2, 305–6n64, 463n541
Gale, Robert L. 288n20
Gamba, Contessa 432n449
Gardner, Isabella Stewart 539n798; letters to 481n594, 523n743
Gaskell, E. C., *Wives and Daughters* **16**, 306n66
Gates, Joanne E. lxxiii
Gatrell, Simon xxxvii
Gautier, Théophile 587n931; *Honoré de Balzac* 582n920
Genette, Gérard xxxvi
Geneva **164**, **171**, 462n539, 470–1n566, 484n603
Genoa, Italy 471n568
Giotto di Bondone 470n564
Gissing, George 381n289
Gittings, Robert 426n437, 428–9n442
Glasse, Hannah, *The Art of Cookery* 530n772, 552n847
Godkin, Edwin Laurence 523n743; letters to 483nn600–1, 492n636
Goethe, Johann Wolfgang von 333n140, 514n713
Goldberg, Shari 472n569
Goldsmith, Oliver *The Traveller* 317n94, 589n936; *The Vicar of Wakefield* xxv, 517–18n726, 557n859

Goncourt, Edmond and Jules de 358n219; *Chérie* 344n178; *Journal* 283n3, 335–6n148, 587n931, 588n932
Good Words 502n671
Goode, John 333n140
Gordon, Lyndall 501n666
Gosse, Edmund xli, cviii, cxx–cxxi, 377n278, 485n610, 496n649; letters to cix–cx, cxx, cxxiv, 388n312, 454n514, 555–6n855, 580n915; translations of Ibsen 384n300, 388n312, 580n915
Graphic, The 510n701
Grattan, C. Hartley cxxxiv
Gray, Thomas, 'Ode on a Distant Prospect of Eton College' 312n82
Great Malvern, Worcestershire 459n533, 460n534
Greenough, Gordon 495–6n648
Greenough, Horatio 495–6n648
Greenough, Richard Saltonstall 495–6n648
Griffin, Susan M. cxli, cxlii, 280, 442n483, 537n790
Grimaldi, Joseph 516n721
Grimm, Jacob and Wilhelm **135**, 438n468; 'Blue-Beard' **135**, **136**; 'Cinderella' **135**, **136**; 'The Drummer' 483n602
Guérande, France **8**, 294n35
Guiccioli, Teresa 432n449
Gurney, Edmund 436n463
Gyp **83–5**, **86**, **90**, 380–1n288, 382–3n294; *Autour du divorce* 381n288; *Autour du mariage* 381n288; *Le Mariage de Chiffon* 380n288; *Monsieur le duc* 381n288; *Petit Bob* 380–1n288

Habegger, Alfred 340n165, 433n451
Haggard, Henry Rider 437n466
Hale, Dorothy J. cxxviii
Hamilton, Edward 432n449
Hardy, Thomas, 'Wessex Novels Edition' xxxvii, xliii–xliv, 577n909
Hare, Augustus J. C., 'Mrs. Duncan Stewart' 502n671
Harland, Henry *Comedies and Errors* 409n383, 442n483, 485n610, 488n617; 'Concerning the Short Story' 442n483; and *The Yellow Book* **172-4**, 484n607, 485n608, 487n615
Harper and Brothers xxxiv, 376n274, 383n296, 480n590, 500n664, 520n731, 526n754, 550nn839–40, 552n846, 558-9n862
Harper's Bazar lxiv, lxvi–lxvii, lxxiii, cxvii, 285n14, 370-1n255, 380n285, 438n468, 517n725
Harper's Monthly Magazine lxvi, lxxxix, xciv, **218**, 327nn125-6, 362n227, 509n700, 511n702, 519n730, 526n754, 527nn758-9, 535n785, 558-9n862
Harper's Weekly xxxv, xxxvii, **85**, **86**, 300n49, 302n53, 378n280, 381n291, 383n296, 385n302, 574-5n903, 584n923
Harrison, Ethel Bertha 378n278
Harrison, Frederic, 'Rome Revisited' 424-5n432
Harte, Bret 301n50; 'The Rise of the "Short Story"' 442n483
Hartford, CT **19**, 311n79, 556n857
Harvey, Col. George 526n754, 559n862; letter to 325n121

Haussmann, Georges-Eugène 309n75, 313n84
Hawthorne, Julian, 'Lowell in a Chatty Mood' 452n507
Hawthorne, Nathaniel 286n16, 310n77, 311n81, 320nn103-4, 321n109, 335n147, 546n820; *The Blithedale Romance* 312n83; 'The Custom-House' l–li; *The House of the Seven Gables* 290n24, 295-6n38, 303n58, 402n356; *Mosses from an Old Manse* li; notebooks 427n438, 509n698; 'The Old Manse' l–li; prefaces l–li, liii, 295n38, 303n58; *The Scarlet Letter* l–li; *The Snow-Image* liii; *Twice-Told Tales* l
Hay, John, *The Bread-Winners* 311n79
Hazlitt, William, *Characters of Shakespear's [sic] Plays* cxxxii
Heine, Heinrich, 'Ich weiß nicht, was soll es bedeuten' 539n798
Helen of Troy **100**, 399-400n349
Henley, William Ernest, letter to 342-3n172, 476n580
Heracles 394n331
Herford, Oliver 288n21, 304n60, 369n247, 398n344, 427n438, 428n439
Hermes **236**, 347n186, 545n817
Herrick, Robert, letter to 298n43
Hicks, Priscilla Gibson lvii, lxiv, lxx, lxxi, lxxxii
Hill, Hamlin L., Jr 378n278
Hippocrates 512n710
Holland, Josiah 282n1
Holland, Laurence Bedwell cxl, 337n154
Home, Daniel Dunglas 315n88

Home Journal, The 519n730, 542n808
Homer cxxiii, 301n51, 347n187, 352n201, 439n471, 497n652
Homer, Winslow 291n26
Horne, Charles F., *The Technique of the Novel* cxiv
Horne, Philip xxx, lvii, lxii, lxiv, cxxxvii, clvi, 281, 284n9, 298n44, 340n164, 344n177, 352n201, 367n239, 369n248, 369n250 370n251, 372-3n260, 386n305, 403-4n365, 404n366, 407n376, 412n395, 430n447, 451-2n506, 454-5n516, 455n517, 487n615, 494n640, 497n653, 500n663, 510n700, 520-1n733, 541n803, 564n881, 573n901, 575n905, 577n909, 579n913
Houghton, Mifflin and Company l, lxii, cv, 328n126
Hound & Horn cxxviii, cxxxviii
House Beautiful 395n337
Howe, Julia Ward 535n785
Howells, Elinor Mead, letter to 389n317
Howells, John Mead 556n855
Howells, William Dean 370n252, 390n318, 454n513, 550n843, 556n855, 559n862; as critic of HJ xlvii, 332n137, 362n227, 511n702, 540n799; as editor of *Atlantic Monthly* cviii, 282n1, 285n11, 289n22, 305-6n64, 306n65, 311n81, 312n82, 313n84, 317n94, 326-7n125, 327n126, 329n129, 361n225; *A Foregone Conclusion* 301n50; 'Leo Tolstoï' 365nn235-6; letters to xxxvi-xxxvii, liv, lv, lvi, lxxxix-xc, cxxiii-cxxiv, cxxxi, 307n70, 367-8n242, 375n269, 383n295, 385n302, 443n485, 485n610, 488n618, 500n665, 507n691, 543n808, 552n846, 552-3n848, 567n886, 575n904; 'Library Edition' vli; *A Modern Instance* 340-1n165; response to NYE Prefaces cvi-cviii, cix; *The Rise of Silas Lapham* 517n723; 'Some Anomalies of the Short Story' 442-3n483
Hueffer, Ford Madox cxi, 510n700; *Henry James: A Critical Study* cxxv-cxxvi, cxxvii; letter to 543n811
Hunt, Violet 394n332; letters to lxxxv-lxxxvi, 561n871
Hutchison, Hazel cxxv-cxxvi
Hutton, R. H. 299n46, 404n366
Huysmans, Joris-Karl, *À rebours* 485n608
Hyde, H. Montgomery lxxiv, lxxxvi, 398n345, 432n449

'Iberians' **126**, 424n431
Ibsen, Henrik **88-9**, 381-2n291, 387n310, 389nn313-14; *A Doll's House* **88**, 388n312; *An Enemy of the People* **88**, 388n312; *Ghosts* **88**, **89**, 388n312, 443n485; *Hedda Gabler* **89**, 387n310, 388n312, 389nn313-14, 580n915; *John Gabriel Borkmann* **88**, **89**, 302n53, 388n312, 422-3n426; *The Master Builder* **88**, 384n300, 388n312; *The Pillars of Society* **88**, 388n312; *Rosmersholm* **88**, 388n312; *The Wild Duck* **89**, 388n312

Illustrated London News, The 399n347, 494n643
Ingham, Sir James Taylor 501n669
Irving, Washington, 'The Voyage' 317n94, 589n936
Italy and fictional subjects **119**, **126-7**, 415–16n406, 425n433; HJ visits xxix–xxx, lxx, clxi, **5–6**, **154**, 288n20, 288–9n21, 303–4n60, 418n411, 460n534, 461n536, 471–2n568, 509n698; and the past **129**, **131**; as a site of fictional composition **32**, **156**, 329n129–30
Izzo, Donatella cxli

'Jack and the Beanstalk' 559n863
James, Alice 321n106, 461n536, 530n771; letters to 289n23, 460n534, 502n670
James, Alice Gibbens lxxxvi; letters to 399n347, 485n608, 558n862, 573n901
James, Caroline 321n106; letter to 584n924
James, Garth Wilkinson (Wilky) 584n924
James, Harry, letters to lxxxvi, 297–8n42, 325n121
James, Henry
  Homes
    Bolton Street, Piccadilly 345n181, 366n238, 421n419, 478nn586-7, 479n588, 479–80n589
    De Vere Gardens, Kensington 366–7n238, 420n416, 421n419, 484n606, 495n644, 513n712
    Lamb House, Rye lvii, lxii, lxvii, lxx, lxxii, lxxiii, lxxv, lxxviii, lxxxiii, lxxxv, lxxxvi, lxxxvii, cliii, clviii, clxiv, 309n73, 399n346, 431n448; as an *NYE* frontispiece subject lxviii, clviii, clix, clx
  Works
    'The Abasement of the Northmores' lxxxviii, xcvii, cxlvi, **186**, 495n646
    'Abbeys and Castles' 519n728
    'After the Play' 381n291
    'The Altar of the Dead' lix, lxxxix, xcviii, clxvi, **191-4**, **195**, 500nn664-6, 500–1n666, 501n667, 503n676, 505n681, 507n689, 579n911
    The Altar of the Dead (*NYE* XVII) assembly lix, lxxxiii, lxxxviii–lxxxix, xc, xciii–cii, clxi, clxiv, clxv, clxvi, clxvii–clxviii, **194**, **207**, 506–7n689, 509–10n700, 510n701, 515n718, 517n722, 524–5n748, 525n750, 526n755, 535n786; Preface 287n19, 348n190, 506n688, 516–17n722, 524n748, 564n879; publication cli
    The Ambassadors xxxiv, **41**, **43**, **55**, **158**, **244-59**, 316–17n92, 330n133, 349n195, 356n212, 411n389, 466n547, 466n550, 536n789, 550nn839-42, 550–1n843, 551n845, 552n846, 552–3n848, 556n855-7, 557–8n860, 558–9n862, 559n864, 561n868, 562n874, 563nn875-6, 570n896, 586n927

The Ambassadors (*NYE* XXI-XXII) assembly lxxi, lxxix, lxxxi, lxxxii, xcii, clvii, clix–clx, clxii, clxiii, clxiv, clxvii, **273**, 466n550, 552n846, 553n849; Preface xxxiv, 302n53, 310n78, 342n171, 349n195, 458n529, 564n881, 586n927; publication cli; reception cxxii, cxxvii, cxxxiii, cxxxviii–cxxxix

The American **16–24, 26–31, 32, 55**, 305–6n64, 306n65, 306n67, 307–8n71, 309n75, 310n76, 311n81, 312n82, 317n94, 323–4n116, 324n119, 325n121, 326n125, 386n307, 463n543, 545n817, 558n861; revised text 308n72, 310–11n78, 323n114, 324n118, 324–5n120, 541n803

The American (*NYE* II) assembly xxxvii, lv, lix, lx–lxii, lxiii, lxiv–lxv, lxvi–lxvii, lxviii–lxx, lxx–lxxi, lxxiv, lxxv, clvii– clxi, **273–4**, 318n96, 322n112, 325n121, 575n905, 575–6n906, 583n922, 585n925; Preface lii–liii, 302n54, 375n266, 426n436, 434n459, 576–7n908, 585n927; publication lxxviii–lxxix, lxxxi–lxxxii, cxlix, clxii; reception cvi–cviii, cix, cxiii, cxvi

The American (play) 307n69, 366–7n238

'An American Art-Scholar: Charles Eliot Norton' xcii

'American Letters', *Literature* (1898) 285n13, 377n275, 457n526, 528–9n674, 529nn765–6, 566n885, 576n907

The American Scene lxii, lxvi, lxxiii, cxvii, cxxv, 307n70, 449n500, 451n503, 474n574, 524n746; 'Baltimore' lxiii; 'Boston' lxii, 296–7n40, 323n113, 483n599, 524n747, 527n756; 'The Bowery and Thereabouts' lxii; 'Charleston' lxiv, 483n600, 585n925; 'Concord and Salem' lxii, 296n38, 436n463, 546n820; 'Florida' lxvi, 483n600; 'New England: An Autumn Impression' lxii, 292n28, 293n33, 326n123, 342n170, 407n379, 474n574, 540n799, 556–7n857; 'New York: Social Notes' lxii, 303n57; 'New York and the Hudson: A Spring Impression' lxii, 474n575; 'New York Revisited' lxii, 283–4n5, 284–5n10, 297n42, 310n78, 419n413, 508n692, 526–7n756, 540n799; notes for 292n28, 544n813, 584n924, 589–90n936; 'Philadelphia' lxii; Preface xxxiii; 'Richmond' / 'Richmond, Virginia' lxiii, 419n413, 483n600; 'The Sense of Newport' lxii, 291n28, 461n537, 521n734; 'Washington' lxii, 311n80, 482n598, 524n747

'Anthony Trollope' (1883) xxxi, 331n137, 356n212, 478n585

INDEX

James, Henry (Cont.)
    'The Art of Fiction' xlvii–xlviii, cxvii, cxxi, cxxxiv, 283n3, 284n7, 285n12, 287–8n19, 291nn26–7, 293n32, 301n50, 332n137, 333n140, 334nn142–4, 335n146, 336n150, 344nn177–8, 357–8n216, 358n219, 366n237, 377n275, 392n326, 427n438, 563n877
    The Art of the Novel cxxviii–cxxxvii, cxxxviii, cxxxix–cxl, cxli, 280
    'The Aspern Papers' **126–33**, **261**, 308n73, 423n429, 425n434, 427n438, 429n445, 430n446, 432n449, 434n455, 445n491; revised text 352n202
    The Aspern Papers (NYE XII) assembly lxxxii–lxxxiii, clx, clxiv, 352n202, 423n428, 431n448, 436n463, 446n491, 540n799; Preface l, 288n21, 311n81, 372n259, 401n355, 409n383, 489n621, 540n799; publication cxlix
    'The Author of Beltraffio' lxxxiv, lxxxv, lxxxviii, xcvii, clxv, clxvi, **186**, **187**, 319n98, 496n649, 496–7n650
    The Author of Beltraffio (NYE XVI) assembly lv, lxxxviii, xciii–c, clxi, clxvii, 470n565, 525n750, 527n758, 530n769; Preface 409n383, 443n483; publication cli
    'The Autumn in Florence' 471n567
    'An Autumn Journey' 463n541

    The Awkward Age **55**, **70**, **77–87**, **89–93**, 351n198, 375n268, 376nn271–4, 378n280, 378–9n281, 379n283, 382–3n294, 383nn295–6, 385n302–4, 386n306, 386–7n307, 389n315, 390n319, 391nn321–2, 396n339–40, 414–15n402, 423n426, 555n853, 573–4n902, 586n927
    The Awkward Age (NYE IX) assembly lxix, lxxi–lxxii, lxxiv, lxxvi–lxxvii, lxxix, lxxxii, clvi, clvii, clx, clxi, clxii, 383n297; Preface cxl, 286n14, 301n51, 302n54, 319n100, 368n243, 370n253, 371n256, 412n394, 447n495, 528n761, 549n835; publication cxlix; reception cxiv, cxxi, cxxvii
    'The Beast in the Jungle' lxxxix, xcviii, clxvi, **194–6**, 504n677–8, 506n686, 507n689
    'The Beldonald Holbein' xci, xcix, **222**, **227**, 507n689, 526n753, 535n785
    'Benvolio' 305n64
    The Better Sort xxix, **194**, **227**, 504n677, 506n686, 533n782, 534n783
    'The Birthplace' lxxxix, xcviii, clxvi, **55**, **196–7**, 464–5n544, 504n677, 505nn682–3, 505–6n684, 506n686, 506–7n689
    The Bostonians xxx, cxiii, cxxiv, 311n79, 386n307, 433n451, 455n491, 493n637, 554n850
    'The British Soldier' 519n728

INDEX

'Broken Wings' lxxxviii, xcvii, clxvi, **187–8**, 307n69, 497n651

'Brooksmith' xci, xcix, **55, 224**, 351n198, 406n371, 502n670, 526n753, 530n769, 531n774–5

'Browning in Venice' / 'Casa Alvisi' 425n434, 450n501, 521n735

'A Bundle of Letters' lxxxvii, **164, 168–9**, 480n590, 481n593, 484n604, 519–20n730; revised text 469n561

'A Chain of Cities' 470n564

'The Chaperon' lxxviii, clxii, **102–3, 109–10, 140**, 406n371, 407nn378–9, 408nn380–1, 408–9n382; revised text 408n380

'Charles de Bernard and Gustave Flaubert' / 'The Minor French Novelists' 285n12, 294n34

Collective Edition of 1883 xxxi, lxi, 288n21, 291n26, 296n39, 298n42, 298n44, 303–4n60, 304–5n63, 308n72, 324n118, 355n210, 509n697, 520n731, 541n803

'The Comédie-Française in London' 363n228

Confidence xxx, 314n87

'Coquelin' 373n261, 382n291

'Covering End' lxxvii

'The Coxon Fund' lxxxviii, xcvii, clx, clxv, **174–5, 181–3, 184, 197**, 487n615, 494n639, 500n664, 506nn687–8, 544n813

'Crapy Cornelia' xciv, 352n201

'Daisy Miller' xci, xcv, xcvii, xcviii–ci, cii, clxvi, **152, 166**, 208, 212–14, 217, 218, 219, 351n199, 356n212, 403n361, 453n511, 456n522, 457n525, 468n558, 469n562, 474n576, 478n584, 518–19n727, 519nn729–30, 520nn731–2, 520–1n733, 522n739, 526n753, 526n755, 564n880

Daisy Miller (*NYE* XVIII) assembly lviii–lix, lxxxiii, lxxxix–xci, xcii, xciii–cii, clx, clxiv, clxvi, clxvii–clxviii, **218, 222**, 456n522, 515n718, 516n720, 516–17n722, 524–5n748, 525n750, 526n753, 526n755, 527n758, 527n758, 530n769, 535n786; Preface 386n305, 451n503, 452n506, 454n515, 470n565, 488n619, 515n719, 515–16n720, 516–17n722, 525n750, 549n837, 560n867; publication cli

Daisy Miller: A Comedy 518n727

'*Daniel Deronda*: A Conversation' 299n47, 338n158, 350n197, 562n872, 564n881

'A Day of Days' 305n64

'On the Death of Dumas the Younger' xlvi, 354n208, 387n310, 388n311, 476–7n580

'The Death of the Lion' lxxxvii, xcvii, clxv, **132, 172–5, 177, 179**, 434n457, 485n608, 487n615, 489n621, 490n624, 490n627, 490–1n628, 491n629, 500n664, 509n699, 546n822, 588n932

James, Henry (Cont.)
   'The Early Meeting of
      Parliament' 513n711
   Embarrassments 489n620, 510n701
   'Émile Zola' 292-3n31, 348n192,
      392n326
   'An English Easter' 347n185, 519n728
   English Hours xxix-xxx, xxxiv, xc,
      298n45, 566n885
   Essays in London and
      Elsewhere xxxi
   'Etretat' / 'A French Watering
      Place' 314n87
   'Europe' lxxxiv, xci, xcvii, clxi,
      188-90, 415n405, 497n655,
      498n656, 498n658, 499nn659-
      60, 500n662, 526n753
   The Europeans xxx, 327n126,
      402n359, 520-1n733, 556n855,
      588n933
   'The Figure in the Carpet' lxxxviii,
      xcvii, clxv, **132**, **175**, **178**, **180-
      1**, 434n457, 489n621, 490n626,
      492nn633-4, 533n782
   The Finer Grain cxxv
   'Flickerbridge' xci, xcix, **164**, **222**,
      225-6, 470n565, 507n689,
      526n753, 532n778, 533n781
   'Fordham Castle' xci, xcvi, xcvii,
      164, **219-20**, 470n565,
      515n719, 526n753, 527n758,
      527-8n759, 528n760
   'The Founding of the
      "Nation"' 484n607
   'Four Meetings' lxxxix, xc, xcvii,
      xcviii, c, clxvi, 402n359,
      499n660, 499-500n662,
      507n689, 520n731

   'Frances Anne Kemble' 338n157,
      404n366, 429-30n445, 430-
      1n447
   French Poets and Novelists 463n541
   'The Friends of the Friends' / 'The
      Way It Came' lxxxix, xcviii,
      clxvi, **200**, **203**, **204**, **206**, **207**,
      507n689, 510n701, 512n709;
      revised text 505n680
   'From Lake George to
      Burlington' 292n28
   'From Normandy to the
      Pyrenees' 314n87
   'The Future of the Novel' 300n48,
      339n162, 377n275
   'Gabriele D'Annunzio' 296n39,
      321n109, 332n137, 347n189,
      389n316, 391n321, 421n423,
      493n638, 571n897
   'George du Maurier'
      (1897) 371n255, 491n632,
      532n776, 567n888
   'George du Maurier' / 'Du
      Maurier and London Society'
      (1883) 532n776
   'George Sand' (1877) xlix-l,
      348n192, 365n234
   'George Sand: The New
      Life' 314n86
   'Glasses' 375n269, 396n340
   The Golden Bowl xxix, **54-5**,
      157-8, **233**, **260**, **261-3**,
      337n154, 344n178, 345n179,
      352n203, 389n317, 405n369,
      508n693, 511-12n706,
      512n707, 537n790, 542-
      3n808, 564-5n882, 568n889,
      569nn893-4

The Golden Bowl (*NYE* XXIII–XXIV) assembly lxxi, lxxix, xcii, cii–civ, clvii, clx, clxii, clxvii, clxviii, **265–6, 273**, 569n891, 569n894, 571n899, 575n904; Preface xlii, xlv, lii, liv, lx, cxl, clv, 294n34, 297n40, 318n94, 335n146, 346n183, 348n191, 371n255, 549n838, 561n869; publication cv, cli; reception cxxii, cxxxvi

'The Grand Canal' 329n131, 425n434, 450n501

'The Great Good Place' lxxxviii, xcvii, clxvi, **188**

'Greville Fane' lxxxviii, xcvii, clxvi, **185–6**, 319n98, 494n643

'Gustave Flaubert' (1893) 318n95, 319n98, 588n932

'Gustave Flaubert' (1902) xxxv, 292–3n31, 300–1n50, 321n107, 323n115, 347n187, 423n427, 560n865

'Guy de Maupassant' (1888) xlvi–xlviii, 332n137, 335n146, 336n149, 353–4n208, 437n466, 445n489, 488n617, 493n638, 547n825, 571n897

Guy Domville 491n629, 573n901

Hawthorne l, 290n24, 310n77, 427n438, 456n525

The High Bid lxxvii–lxxviii, lxxxi–lxxxvi, clxiv, 411n391

'Homburg Reformed' 464n542

'Honoré de Balzac' (1875) xlvi, xlviii, 283n2, 293–4n34, 294n35, 295n37, 316n91, 320n102, 354n208, 396n338, 488n617, 543–4n812

'Honoré de Balzac' (1902) xxxv, 292–3n31, 294n34, 294n35, 295nn36–7, 303n56, 320n102, 324n117, 371n255, 387n309, 396n338, 426–7n438, 433n452, 435n461, 468–9n560, 559n863

In the Cage lxxix, clx, clxiii, **119**, **122–4**, 420nn417–18, 421n422, 422nn424–6, 568nn889

'An International Episode' lxxxvii, **164**, 402n359, 456n522, 457n525, 468n558, 469n562, 478n584, 520n731, 571n897; revised text 469n561

Introductions Balestier, *The Average Woman* xlii; Crackanthorpe, *Last Studies* xlii, 377, 409; Goldsmith, *The Vicar of Wakefield* xxxv, 517–18, 557; Kipling, *Mine Own People* xxxv, 335, 441, 488, 586; Loti, *Impressions* xxxv; Maupassant trans. Sturges, *The Odd Number* xxxv; Shakespeare, *The Tempest* xxxv, 300, 318, 332, 352, 487; *see also* James, Henry: Works – 'Émile Zola'; 'Gustave Flaubert' (1902); 'Honoré de Balzac' (1902); Prefaces

Italian Hours xxix–xxx, xc, 288n20, 425n434, 471n567, 521n735, 566n885, 575n904

'Ivan Turgenev (1818–1883)' (1896) 365n235, 390n320, 488n617

'Ivan Turgénieff' (1874) 331n136, 333n142, 338n155, 341n167, 358n219, 427n438, 439n469, 460n533, 487–8n617

INDEX

James, Henry (Cont.)
   'Ivan Turgénieff' (1884) xxxi, 330n133, 331n136, 331–2n137, 332n138, 333n141, 341n167
   The Ivory Tower cxxvi
   'James Russell Lowell' 492n636
   'John Delavoy' 488n619, 533n782, 555n853
   'The Jolly Corner' lxvi, lxxiii, lxxxix, xcviii, clxvi, **197**, **200**, **203–4**, **206**, **207**, 353n207, 458–9n531, 472n569, 506–7n689, 508n694, 509–10n700, 512n708, 526n754
   'The Journal of the Brothers de Goncourt' 589n934
   'Julia Bride' lxvi, lxxiii, xci, xcv, xcviii–ci, cii, **207–11**, **217**, **218**, **219**, 304n62, 444n488, 507n689, 509n700, 515nn718–19, 525n750, 526nn753–5, 546n822
   'Lady Barbarina' / 'Lady Barberina' lxxxvii, **158**, **160–3**, 367–8n242, 402n359, 403n363, 466n548, 467n554, 468nn557–8, 469nn561–2, 474–5n576; revised text 468n556
   Lady Barbarina (NYE XIV) assembly lxxxiii, lxxxvi–lxxxvii, clxi, clxiv, clxv, **157**, **158**, **160**, 456, 466; Preface cxv, 345n180, 403n363, 405n369, 447n494, 522n738; publication cli
   'The Last of the Valerii' 282n1
   'The Lesson of Balzac' 292n29, 293n32, 294n34, 295n37, 299n47, 300n48–9, 304n62, 306–7n67, 324n117, 329–30n132, 335n147, 337n154, 348n190, 354n208, 370n252, 381n290, 389n316, 423n427, 433n453, 439n469, 459n532, 489n622, 491–2n632, 493n638, 525n751, 544n816, 555n854, 560n865, 578n910, 583n921, 585n927
   'The Lesson of the Master' lxxxvii, xcvi, **177**, **178–9**, 287n19, 406n371, 438n467, 445–6n491, 484n605, 489n620, 513n712
   The Lesson of the Master (NYE XV) assembly lxxxiii, lxxxv, lxxxvii–lxxxviii, lxxxix, xciii–xciv, xcvi–xcviii, clx, clxiv–clxvii, **175**, 434n457, 484n605, 494n639, 569n891; Preface cii, 287n19, 372n259, 409n383, 434n457, 435n461, 443n483, 444n488, 494n639, 506n687, 524n748; publication cli
   'A Letter to Mr. Howells' 390n318
   'Letter to the Hon. Robert Rantoul' 320n103–4, 321n109
   The Letters of Henry James, ed. Lubbock cxxxi
   'The Letters of Honoré de Balzac' 355n212, 578n910, 582n920
   'The Letters of Robert Louis Stevenson' xxxix–xl, 318n97, 319n99, 465n544, 586n927
   'The Liar' clxiv, **140–1**, 406n371, 443nn484–5
   'Lichfield and Warwick' 471n567
   'The Life of George Eliot' 339n160, 350–1n197

INDEX

A Little Tour in France xxxii–xxxiii,
  xxxiv, 566n885
'London' (1888) 345n182,
  406n371, 421n419, 459n533,
  478n587, 569n892
'London at Midsummer' 519n728
'London in the Dead
  Season' 509n697
'A London Life' clxii, **102–3**,
  104–9, 402n359, 403nn363–4,
  404n367, 405nn368–70,
  406nn372–4, 407n376,
  445–6n491, 502n670; revised
  text 403–4n365,
'London Notes' xxxvii, 300n49,
  302n53, 378n280, 381n291,
  574–5n903, 584n923
'The London
  Theatres' (1877) 317n94
'The London Theatres'
  (1879) 362n228
London Town lxxii, 307n68,
  359n220, 411n391; notes for
  lxxii, 346n183
'Louisa Pallant' lxxxiv, lxxxv, clxv,
  155, **156**, 454n513, 464n542
'Madame de Mauves' lxxxiv, lxxxv,
  clxv, **154**, **155–6**, 315n88,
  457n527, 463n541, 464n543
'The Madonna of the
  Future' lxxxiv, clxv, **154**, **155**,
  282n1, 457n527, 460n533,
  465n545
'The Manners of American
  Women' lxvi–lxvii, cxvii,
  380n285, 517n725
'The Marriages' xci, xcviii, **223–4**,
  406n371, 501n667, 503n675,
  526n753, 530n769, 530n771

'The Married Son' lxvi, lxx, lxxiii,
  285–6n14, 415n402, 424n430,
  438n468
'Matilde Serao' 377n275, 379n281
'Matthew Arnold' 378n280,
  429n444
'The Middle Years' lxxxviii, xcvii,
  clxvi, **184–5**, **186**, 492n634,
  494n640, 500n664, 538n793,
  575n906, 577–8n910
The Middle Years 459n533,
  478–9n587
'Miss Gunton of Poughkeepsie' xci,
  xcvii–xcviii, **164**, **217**, **219**,
  470n565, 525n750, 526n753
'The Modern Novel'/ 'Letter
  to the Deerfield Summer
  School' 334n142
'The Modern Warning' / 'Two
  Countries' 402n359, 454n514
'Mr and Mrs James T.
  Fields' 477n584
'Mrs Medwin' lxxxix, xcviii, xcix,
  clxvi, **227**, 350n195, 456n523,
  535n786
'Nathaniel Hawthorne'
  (1896) 286n16
The New York Edition xxix–cxxiv,
  cxxviii–cxxxi, cxlii–clxviii, **3–4**,
  8–10, **263–77**, 298n43, 433n451,
  566n884, 568n890, 575n905,
  575–76n906, 581n918, 582n920,
  585n925, 586n928, 589n936
'Newport' 291n28
'The Next Time' lxxxviii, xcvii,
  clxv, **55**, **132–3**, **174**, **175**,
  179–80, 351n198, 434n457,
  487n615, 489n620–1, 491n629,
  491n631

617

James, Henry (Cont.)
    Notebooks and working
        notes lxxii, lxxiii, cxxvi,
        cxxxvii, **3–4**, **59–60**, **179**,
        187, **195**, **204–5**, 281, 283n4,
        289n22, 292n28, 308–9n73,
        317n93, 326n124, 328nn127–8,
        330n133, 344n177, 345n181,
        346n183, 349–50n195,
        351n198, 357n215, 358–9n219,
        360–1n224, 366–7n238,
        367n240, 372n258, 375n269,
        376n273, 379n283, 381n287,
        387n309, 392n324, 393–4n330,
        395nn335–6, 396n340,
        397n342, 399n347, 403n363,
        405n369, 406n373, 407n379,
        408n381, 409–10n384,
        410n385, 410n387, 410–
        11n388, 412n392–3, 414n400,
        415n403, 422–3n426, 428n441,
        429n442, 432n449, 435n462,
        437n464, 443n485, 449n499,
        452n507, 453nn510–11,
        454n513, 464n544, 468nn558–
        9, 477n581, 477–8n584,
        478n586, 489–90n623,
        490n624, 490n626, 490–1n628,
        491n629, 492n635, 494n643,
        495n646, 495n648, 496n649,
        497n651, 498n656, 499n659,
        500–1n666, 502n670, 504n678,
        505n682, 505–6n684, 507n690,
        508n696, 512n709, 514nn713–
        14, 514–5n716, 522nn737–9,
        527–8n759, 530n771, 531n774,
        532n776, 532n778, 535n785,
        535n787, 536n789, 537n791,
        538n792, 538n795, 544n813,
        546n822, 548n831, 550n841,
        550n843, 552n848, 555n853,
        557n860, 564n881, 567n887,
        584n924, 589–90n936
    Notes of a Son and Brother 291–
        2n28, 297n42, 309n74,
        337nn152–3, 352n201, 470n566,
        493n637, 535–6n787, 538n794,
        552n847, 580n914, 584n924
    Notes on Novelists cxviii, 391n321
    'The Novel in *The Ring and the
        Book*' 329n130, 537n790,
        578n910
    *The Novels and Stories of Henry
        James* cxxix
    'Occasional Paris' / 'Paris
        Revisited' 313n84, 475n577,
        476nn578–9
    'On the Occasion of *Hedda
        Gabler*' 387n310, 388n312,
        389nn313–14
    The Other House xxx, xc, **99**, **222**,
        394n331, 399n347, 407–8n379,
        530n768, 564n881
    'Other Tuscan Cities' 418n411
    The Outcry cxxv
    'Owen Wingrave' lxxviii, lxxxix,
        xcviii, clxvi, **200**, **204**, **205–6**,
        436n463, 507n689, 510n701,
        512n709, 513–14n713
    'Pandora' xci, xcvii, xcviii, **152**,
        164, **166**, **214–15**, **217**, **219**,
        311n79, 402n359, 456n522,
        456n524, 457n525, 469n562,
        470n565, 474–5n576, 515n718,
        522nn736–9, 523nn741–2,
        526n753, 570n896

618

'The Papers' 504n677, 506n686
Parisian Sketches: Letters to the 'New York Tribune' 558n860
'The Parisian Stage' 302n53, 342n172, 373n261
Partial Portraits xxxi, 291n26, 532n776
'A Passionate Pilgrim' lxxxiv, lxxxv, clxv, **153-5**, 282n1, 444n489, 455n518, 457-8n527, 460-1n535, 462n539
A Passionate Pilgrim, and Other Tales 284n9
'Paste' xci, xcvii, **188**, 497n653, 526n753, 530n769
'The Patagonia' xci, xcviii, **217**, 525n750, 526n753
'The Pension Beaurepas' lxxxvii, **164**, **171**, 457n526, 470n566
Picture and Text xxxi, 566n885
'The Picture Season in London' 345n182
'Pierre Loti' (1888) 438n467
'The Point of View' lxxxvii, **169-71**, 481n593, 482n597
The Portrait of a Lady **32-3**, **37-45, 55**, **158**, **229**, 285n11, 305n63, 326n124, 326-7n125, 327-8n126, 328nn127-8, 329n129, 330n134, 336n149, 336n151, 337nn153-4, 340n165, 341n167, 343n175, 344nn176-7, 361n225, 493n637, 536n787, 538n793; revised text 338n156, 586-7n929
The Portrait of a Lady (*NYE* III–IV) assembly xxxvii, lv, lviii, lix, lx–lxvi, lxviii, lxx–lxxi, lxxv, cli–clv, clvii–clviii, clix, clx, clxi, **274**, 305n63, 591-6; Preface lxvi, cxxi, cxxv, cxl, 302n54, 331n136, 349n195, 353n206, 375n268, 412n392, 421n420, 453n512, 466n459, 528n761, 561n871; publication cxlix; reception cvi–cviii, cix, cxiii, cxvi, cxxii, cxxv–cxxvi, cxxxv–cxxxvi, cxl
Portraits of Places xxxi, 463n541
Prefaces Brooke, *Letters from America* cxx; Daudet, *Port Tarascon* xxxv, 435; *see also* James, Henry: Works – Introductions
The Princess Casamassima **15**, **46-9, 53-4, 55-61, 70**, **123-4**, **222**, 304-5n63, 345n181, 346n184, 351-2n200, 353nn204-5, 355nn209-11, 356n213, 357n215-16, 358n218-19, 359-60n221, 361n225, 386n307, 406n371, 445n491, 453n509, 513n712, 538n793; revised text 355n210
The Princess Casamassima (*NYE* V–VI) assembly lv, lix, lxix, lxxi–lxxii, lxxiv, lxxv, clvii, clviii, clix, clxi, **274**, 352, 357; Preface 283n4, 302-3n55, 304n63, 358n219, 400n350, 564n879; publication cxlix; reception cvi–cvii, cxiii, cxxxv
'The Private Life' lxxxviii, lxxxix, xcviii, clxvi, **197-9**, 374-5n265, 506-7n689, 507nn690-1, 508n696

James, Henry (Cont.)
'The Pupil' lxxix, clxiii, **119–22**, **123–4**, **140**, 307n70, 342n170, 412n392, 416nn407–8, 417nn409–10, 419n414, 422n426, 494n641, 538n793, 572n900

'The Question of Our Speech' cxvii, 380n285, 467n5555, 489n622, 529n766, 588n933

'The Real Right Thing' lxxxix, xcviii, clxvi, **200**, **203**, **206**, 431n447, 507n689, 510n701

'The Real Thing' xci, xcviii, **224–5**, 297n41, 526n753, 530n769, 530n773, 532nn776–7, 566n885

The Reverberator xlvii, lxxxiv, clxiv, clxv, **143–4**, **145–8**, **149–53**, **166**, 403n362, 409n383, 445–6n491, 446n492, 447n494, 449n499, 452n507, 453nn510–11, 454n514, 456n522, 456–7n525, 472–3n570, 474n576, 480n591, 533n781, 547n825; revised text 449n498, 455n517, 521n733

The Reverberator (*NYE* XIII) assembly lxxxiii–lxxxv, lxxxvi, clix, clxiv–clxv, **143**, 445n490, 445–6n491, 455n518, 457n527, 458n529, 533n781; Preface lxxxv, 309n73, 317n94, 345n180, 403n362, 409n383, 447n493, 449n499, 450nn501–2, 451n505, 451–2n506, 454n515, 465n546, 466n552, 474n576, 523n744, 526n756; publication cli

Roderick Hudson 3, 4, **5–8**, **10–15**, **32**, **54–5**, **57**, 282n1, 283n2, 284n9, 287nn17–18, 288–9n21, 289nn22–3, 291n28, 292n30, 293n34, 298–9n46, 303n59, 304n63, 305n64, 354–5n209, 356n212, 368n244, 375–6n270, 531n775, 553n850; revised text 288n21, 291n26, 296n39, 298n42, 298n44, 303–4n60, 304–5n63, 355n210, 509n697

Roderick Hudson (*NYE* I) assembly xxxvii, lv, lviii, lix–lxvi, lxviii, lxix, lxx–lxxi, lxxv, cliv–clv, clvii–clviii, clix, clxi, 285–6n14, 298n45, 300n49, 305n63, 576n906; Preface xxxiv, xlv, 286n14, 292n29, 294n34, 302nn53–4, 353n206, 369n249, 444n488, 447–8n496, 561n869, 577n908, 579n912, 580n916; publication lxxviii, lxxxi, cv, cxlix–cli, clxii; reception cvi–cviii, cxiii, cxvi, cxxii, cxxxiv

'Rose-Agathe' / 'Théodolinde' 519n728

The Sacred Fount xxix, xxx, **222**, 375n269, 446–7n492, 530n768

The Saloon lxxviii, lxxix, lxxxvi, 333n140, 436n463

'The Science of Criticism' 351n199

The Sense of the Past 314n86, 322n110, 430n447, 431n448, 432n450, 555n853; notes for 349–50n195, 434–5n459

'She and He: Recent Documents' 314n86, 322n110, 488n619

INDEX

'The Siege of London' lxxxvii, **163–4, 166–8,** 468n558, 475n577, 477n581, 478n584, 479–80n589; revised text 475n576

'Sir Edmund Orme' lxxxix, xcviii, clxvi, **200, 203, 204, 206–7,** 512n709, 514n715, 514–15n716

A Small Boy and Others cxxi, 309n74, 315–16n89, 352n201, 447n493, 459n533, 461–2n538, 470n566, 482n596, 516n721, 540n799, 553–4, 561n869, 575n903

The Soft Side 495n647, 497n655, 504n677

'The Speech of American Women' lxiv, lxvi, cxvii, 370–1n255

The Spoils of Poynton (*NYE* X) assembly lxix, lxxii, lxxviii, lxxix, lxxx, lxxxii, clx, clxi–clxii, **102–3, 104,** 571; Preface l, 287n19, 302n54, 313n84, 330n133, 348n190, 375n269, 384n300, 398n344, 402n358, 421n420, 446n491, 455n518, 465n546, 564n879; publication cxlix; reception cxiv

The Spoils of Poynton / The Old Things **55, 94, 95–104, 222,** **261,** 361n226, 367n240, 375n269, 392n324, 392–3n326, 393–4n330, 395n336, 396nn337–8, 396n340, 396–7n341, 397n342, 399nn347–8, 400n352, 402n358, 446n491, 555n853; revised text 393n327

'The St. Gothard' 418n413

Stories Revived xxxi, 575n904

'The Story in It' xci, xcix, **226–7,** 332n137, 526n753, 530n769, 533n782, 534nn783–4

'The Suburbs of London' 345n182, 513n712

'Swiss Notes' 470n566

Terminations **191,** 500n664

'The Théâtre Français' 344n177

Theatricals xxxi–xxxii, 381–2n291

Theatricals. Second Series xxxii, xxxiii, 387–8n310

'The Tone of Time' 297n40, 481n592

The Tragic Muse **62–76, 132, 222,** 297n41, 309–10n75, 337–8n154, 360nn223–4, 361n225, 361–2n226, 362n227, 363n230, 364n232, 366n238, 367n239, 369n248, 369n250, 369–70n251, 371–2n256, 372nn257–8, 372n260, 374n265, 386n307, 406n371, 434n456, 445n491, 562n872; revised text 341–2n170, 383–4n297

The Tragic Muse (*NYE* VII–VIII) assembly lxix, lxxi–lxxii, lxxiv, lxxv–lxxvi, lxxvii, lxxxi, clvii, clix, clxi, clxii, 361n225, 383n297, 569n891; Preface 302n52, 372n260, 374n265, 386n307, 400n351, 406n375, 433n454, 444n488, 445n491, 447n495, 547n828, 577n908; publication cxlix; reception 363n229

Transatlantic Sketches 289n22

621

James, Henry (Cont.)
   'Travelling Companions' 288n20
   'The Tree of Knowledge' lxxxviii, xcvii, **186–7**, 462–3n540, 495nn646–8
   'The Two Faces' / 'The Faces' clxiv, **140, 141–2**, 444n488, 534n783
   'Two Old Houses and Three Young Women' 348n191, 425n434
   uncollected reviews Arnold, *Essays in Criticism* 455n517, 570n895; Black, *Macleod of Dare* 361n225; Dickens, *Our Mutual Friend* 401n356; Du Maurier, *Trilby* 382n292, 532n776, 566n885; Eliot, *Daniel Deronda* 413–14n399; Eliot, *Middlemarch* 350n196, 529n767; Eliot, *The Spanish Gypsy* 578n910; Harland, *Comedies and Errors* 409n383, 442n483, 485n610, 488n617; Hawthorne, *Passages from the French and Italian Notebooks* 509n698; Howells, *A Foregone Conclusion* 301n50; Kemble, *Record of a Girlhood* 374n264; Manning, *The Household of Sir Thomas More* 426n438; Nadal, *Impressions of London Social Life* 423–4n430; Prescott, *Azarian* 401–2n356; Sainte-Beuve, *Premiers Lundis* 590n937; Sarcey, *Comédiens et Comédiennes* 373n261; Senior, *Essays on Fiction* 348n192, 349n194; Smiles, *The Huguenots* 384n299; Taine, *Histoire de la littérature anglaise* 330n132; Trollope, *Can You Forgive Her?* 340n164; Turgenev, *Terres vierges* 556n856; Zola, *Nana* 576n907

   'The Velvet Glove' xcii, xciii, 356n212, 397–8n343
   'Venice' 328n128, 329n129, 329n131, 418n411, 425n434
   'Venice: An Early Impression' 425n434
   Washington Square xxx, 298n43, 327n126, 404n366, 433n451, 478n584, 532n776, 566n885
   Watch and Ward xxx, 282n1, 284n8
   What Maisie Knew **55, 111–18, 123–5, 222**, 327n126, 349n195, 351n198, 375n269, 377n277, 386n307, 403–4n365, 405n368, 409–10n384, 410nn385–7, 410–11n388, 411n390, 412nn392–3, 412n396, 413nn397–8, 414nn400–2, 415n403, 415n405, 421n421, 422n426, 513n712, 529–30n768, 544n814, 553n849, 555n853, 574n902
   What Maisie Knew (NYE XI) assembly lxix, lxxviii, lxxix–lxxx, lxxxii, clx, clxii–clxiii, 405n368, 412n392, 415n405, 446n491, 544n814, 571n899; Preface 302n54, 342n170, 375n269, 450n501, 528n761, 530n768, 553n849, 564n879, 572n900; publication cxlix; reception cxxi

The Whole Family see James, Henry: Works – 'The Married Son'
'William Dean Howells' (1886) 332n137
William Wetmore Story and His Friends xxix, xli, 288nn20–1, 296n40, 304n60, 329n130, 352n201, 369n247, 402n357, 417n411, 417–18n412, 419n414, 427n438, 448n497, 462n538, 470n563, 495n648, 502n670, 503nn673–4, 551n843
'Winchelsea, Rye, and *Denis Duval*' xl–xli, 288n19, 399n346, 435n460, 554n852
The Wings of the Dove xxix, xxxiv, **55**, **157–8**, **228–43**, **246**, **256**, 288n20, 336n151, 356n212, 367n240, 368n242, 405n369, 406n373, 419n412, 423n428, 431n448, 439n471, 448–9n498, 513n712, 535n787, 536–7n789, 537nn790–1, 538n792, 538n795, 540nn799–800, 541nn801–2, 542n804, 542nn806–8, 543nn809–11, 544n815, 545nn818–19, 546n821, 546n823, 546–7n824, 547n826, 548n829, 548nn831–4, 549nn835–6; revised text 543n810
The Wings of the Dove (*NYE* XXIX–XX) assembly lxxi, lxxix–lxxxi, xci–xcii, clvii, clx, clxii, clxiii, clxvii, 406n373, 423n428, 431n448, 506n688, 544n814, 546n822; Preface xxxiv, 283n3, 286n16, 299n47, 368n243, 422n423, 433n451, 444n488, 506n688, 511n705, 524n747, 542n807, 549n835, 563n878, 585n926; publication cli; reception cxxvii, cxxxvi, cxxxviii–cxxxix

James, Henry, Sr 481n594; letters to 287n17, 313n84, 316n91, 317n93, 463n541, 464n542, 520n730, 520n732; *The Secret of Swedenborg* 572n900
James, Margaret Mary (Peggy) 412n395; letter to lxii
James, Mary Walsh 481n594; letters to 289–90n23, 315n88, 327n125, 346n185, 351n199, 404n366, 425n432, 464n542, 479n588, 480n590, 507n691, 570n895
James, William 297n42, 431, 461, 502; letter from 459; letters to lxv, lxvi, lxxiv–lxxv, cx, 282n1, 287n17, 316n90, 321n106, 330–1n135, 346–7n185, 360n222, 362n226, 366n238, 367n239, 399n347, 407n377, 457–8n458, 485n608, 504n676, 509n698, 520–1n733, 572n900, 573n901, 588n933; *A Pluralistic Universe* (Hibbert Lectures) lxxxvi; *Pragmatism* 572n900; *The Varieties of Religious Experience* 308n73
Jameson, Fredric cxxviii
Jefferson, D. W. cxl
Jenner, Edward 392n325
Jeune, May, Lady St Helier 378n278
Jewett, Sarah Orne *Tales of New England* 532n778; *The Tory Lover* 430n447

Johnson, Samuel, 'The Vanity of
    Human Wishes' 286n15
Jolly, Roslyn 427n438
Jones, Mary Cadwalader cvi; letter to
    367n240, 368n242
Jordan, Elizabeth 285n14, 415n402,
    438n468; letters to lxiv, lxvi–lxvii,
    lxx, 438n468
Jusserand, Jean Jules 503n676

Karlin, Daniel 493n637
Keats, John, 'On First Looking into
    Chapman's Homer' 352n201
Kemble, Frances Anne
    (Fanny) 338n157, 404n366,
    429–30n445, 430–1n447, 504n676;
    *Journal of a Residence on a
    Georgian Plantation* 553n850;
    Record of a Girlhood 374n264
Kenyon Review, The cxxxvii
Kipling, Rudyard cvi, **174**, 335n148,
    364n231; *Kim* 564n880; *Mine Own
    People* xxxv, 488n617; Mulvaney
    (character) 441n479, 586n929;
    'Outward Bound Edition' xxix, xlii,
    xliii, 577n909
Kirk, John Foster 519n728

Labiche, Eugène 382n291
Lang, Andrew xlvii
Lavedan, Henri **84**, *Le Nouveau
    jeu* 382n293; *Le Vieux marcheur*
    382n293
Layard, Austen Henry 474n574
Le Gallienne, Richard, 'The Boom in
    Yellow' 485n608
Leavis, F. R. *The Great Tradition*
    cxxxviii–cxxxix; 'James as Critic'
    cxxxix–cxl

Lee, Vernon 423n429; *Hauntings*
    440n475
Lee-Hamilton, Eugene 423n429,
    428n441, 429n442, 432n449
Leighton, Sir Frederic 363n231,
    507n690, 508n695
Lello, James 587n931
Lesage, Alain-René, *Gil Blas* **255**,
    560n867
Leuschner, Eric xxxvii
Leveson-Gower, Lady
    Alexandra 530n771
Limoges, France **8**, 294n35
Lindsay, Caroline Blanche
    Elizabeth 392n324
Lippincott's Magazine 327n125,
    442n483, 519n728
Literary Digest, The cxiii, cxvii
Literature 285n13, 376n274, 377n275,
    457n526, 528–9n764, 566n885,
    576n907
Littell's Living Age 519n730
Little Review, The cxxvi, 290n24
Liverpool, Merseyside 459n533,
    471–2n568, 473n572, 560n866
Livy (Titus Livius) cxiv
Lombardo, Agostino cxli
London, England lxix–lxx, lxxii, lxxiv,
    lxxv–lxxvi, lxxx, lxxxi–lxxxiv,
    lxxxvi, civ, cxix, cliii, clvii, clxiv, **22**,
    84, **98**, **155**, **163**, **170**, **212**, **256**,
    284n5, 294n34, 307n69, 309n74,
    316n90, 317n94, 346–7n185,
    360n222, 362–3n228, 373–4n263,
    377n278, 379n282, 388n212,
    420n416, 425n432, 434n456,
    450n502, 451n505, 455n519,
    459n533, 460n534, 462n539,
    478n584, 481n594, 485n610,

490n625, 502n670, 503–4n676, 507n691, 509n697, 515n717, 516n721, 531–2n776, 534n783, 545n817, 551n844, 569n892, 570n895, 579n913; Athenæum Club 346–7n185; as 'Babylon' **46**, 345–6n182; Bow Street magistrates' court 501n669; Curzon Street **168**, 478n587; and Dickens **168**, 478–9n587; as a fictional setting 345n181, 346n184, 355n209, 364n232, 403n363, 403–4n365, 404n367, 406n371, 413n397, 420n417, 444n489, 457n525, 469n562, 503n675, 532n777, 537n789, 542n804, 542n806, 543n809, 548n834, 562n873, 567–8n889, 569n894; and germs of fictions **94**, **95**, **109**, **141**, **205**, 443n485, 513–14n713; Green Park **168**, 420n419, 478n586; Kensal Green Cemetery **194**, 503–4n676; Kensington **66**, **69**, **123**, **172**, **185**, 420–1n419, 484n606, 495n644; Kensington Gardens **118**, **205–6**, 415n404, 420n419, 513n712, 513–14n713; *London Town* 346n183, 359n220, 411n391; as material for fiction **45**, **46–8**, **55–6**, **59–61**, **64**, **78**, **80**, **82**, **90**, **105–6**, **122–3**, **191–4**, **197–8**, 345n181, 359n221, 376n273, 403n364; Mayfair **123**, 420–1n419; Millbank Prison 359n221; Newgate Prison 359n221; *NYE* frontispiece subjects lxvii, lxix, cii–civ, clvii, clix, clx, **265–6**, 346n183, 359n220, 567–8n889, 568–9n891, 569n894;

Old Bailey criminal court 359n221; Piccadilly **168**, 420–1n419, 478n586, 479n588; Portland Place **266**, 569n894; and Thackeray **168**, 478n587; as a workplace 329n129, 407n377; *see also* James, Henry: Homes – Bolton Street, Piccadilly; De Vere Gardens, Kensington

Longfellow, Henry Wadsworth 301n50; 'A Psalm of Life' 588n934; 'The Secret of the Sea' 574n903

Longman's Magazine 291n26, 416n408

Lorelei **230**, 539n798

Loring, Frank 519–20n730

Loti, Pierre 438n467; *Impressions* xxxv

Louis XVI, King of France 343n173

Louisville Courier-Journal, The cxiv, cxviii

Lowell, James Russell 301n50, 316, 452n507, 492–3n636; letter to 407n377

Lubbock, Percy cxxvi, cxxix, cxxxi; *The Craft of Fiction* cxxvi–cxxviii, cxxxviii; review of *NYE* cx–cxi, cxii, cxxi, cxxii, cxxiii

Lucretius, *De rerum natura* 347n186

Lustig, T. J. 362n227, 378n280, 436n463, 439n470, 440n474, 441–2n481, 467n554, 514n713

Macaulay, Thomas Babington 557n859

Macbeth-Raeburn, Henry xliii–xliv

MacCarthy, Desmond 382–3n294, 383n295

MacFarlane, I. D. 534n783

Macmillan, Frederick 327n126, 346n183, 445n491; letters to lxxii, cviii, 307n68, 362n227, 411n391

Macmillan and Co. lvi, lxxii, 437n465, 445–6n491, 446n492, 520n731; and British issue of *NYE* cviii, cxi, cxlix, 506n685
Macmillan's Magazine **32, 143**, 327n125, 327–8n126, 446n492
Magna Carta 379n282
Manton, Jo 426n437, 428–9n442
Marble, Manton 515n717
Marbot, Jean-Baptiste Antoine Marcelin, *Mémoires* 514n713
Marlowe, Christopher, *Doctor Faustus* 400n349
Marryat, Florence, *Tom Tiddler's Ground* 490n625
Marsh, Edward cxx, cxxiv–cxxv; review of *NYE* cxi, cxii, cxiii, cxix–cxx, cxxiii, cxxiv, 577n909
Martin, John, *The Plains of Heaven* 321n105
Matthews, Brander, 'Philosophy of the Short-Story' 442n483
Matthiessen, F. O. *Henry James: The Major Phase* cxxxvii; *The Notebooks of Henry James* cxxxvii, 283n4
Maupassant, Guy de cxxxix, **174**, 335n146, 336n149, 353–4n208, 437n466, 444–5n489, 488n617, 493n638, 495n646, 547n825, 571n897; 'Les Bijoux' 497n653; *The Odd Number* xxxv; 'La Parure' **188**, 497n653; *Pierre et Jean* xlvi–xlvii; 'Le Roman' xlvi–xlviii, cxix; *Une vie* 332n137
McClellan, General George B. 450n502
McClellan, Katherine Elizabeth 292n29

McClellan, May 449n499, 450–1n502, 451n505, 451–2n506, 452nn507–8, 453nn510–11, 455n519
McWhirter, David cxxx, cxlii
Menke, Richard 419–20n415
Meredith, George **52**, 335n147, 348n190, 525n751, 578n910; collected editions xxix, xxxvii–xxxviii, 574–5n903, 577n909, 583–4n923
Methuen & Co. 543n808, 550n839, 559n862, 564n882
Milan, Italy 357n215, 408n381
Mill, John Stuart *The Principles of Political Economy* 352–3n204; 'The Spirit of the Age' 379n284
Millais, John Everett 363n231
Miller, J. Hillis 588n933
Millgate, Jane xlv
Millgate, Michael xliv
Milton, John *Paradise Lost* **101**, 400n351, 411n391; 'At a Solemn Music' 548n830
Minneapolis Tribune, The cxv
Mirabeau, Honoré-Gabriel Riqueti, comte de 481–2n595
Mix, Katherine Lyon 486n611
Mohl, Mary Elizabeth 430n447, 551n843
Molière, *Les Fourberies de Scapin* 555–6n855
Momus 482n598
Monteiro, George 416n408
Moore, George, *Memoirs of My Dead Life* cxix
Moore, Thomas *Letters and Journals of Lord Byron* 557n859; ''Tis the Last Rose of Summer' 540n799

Moore, Marianne cxxviii
Morgan, Sydney, Lady Morgan 502n670
Motley, John Lothrop, *The Rise of the Dutch Republic* 426n438
Mounsey, Augustus H, *A Journey Through the Caucasus and the Interior of Persia* 424n431
Murdock, Kenneth B., *The Notebooks of Henry James* cxxxvii, 283n4
Murfree, Mary Noailles, *The Juggler* 528–9n764, 529n766
Murger, Henry, *Scènes de la vie de bohème* 557n860
Muses **3**, **100**, **156**, **168**, **170**, 482n598, 578n911; Melpomene 369n250; Polyhymnia 282n2
Musset, Alfred de 314n86, 488n619, 512n710
Myers, Frederick 436n463; letter to 441n480

Nadal, Ehrmann Syme, *Impressions of London Social Life* 423–4n430
Nadel, Ira B. lvii
Nash, Andrew xxxvii
Nation, The cxi–cxii, cxviii, cxix, 289n22, 483n600, 484n607, 513n711, 590n936
Nelson, Henry Loomis 385n302
Nemours, France **8**, 295n35
New England **6**, **7**, **8**, **249**, 290n24, 291–2n28, 293n33, 295n38, 311n79, 407n379, 499n660, 556n855, 556–7n857; *NYE* frontispiece subject c, clxi
New Review, The 327n126, 410n384
New York City xxx, lxii, lxvii, lxviii, lxx, clvi, **84**, **156**, **163**, **164–5**, 283–4n5, 284–5n10, 297n42, 310n78, 419n413, 468n559, 471–2n568, 473n572, 508n692, 516n721, 523n743, 526–7n756, 529n765, 553–4n850; 'down-town' and 'up-town' **216–18**, 516–17n722, 523n745, 524–5n748, 525n749; East 25th Street **6**, **216**, 289n22, 525n749; as a fictional setting xcix, **158**, **203**, **204**, 286n14, 307–8n71, 311n79, 433n451, 457n525, 458n531, 469n562, 472n569, 508n694, 523n742, 570n896; and germs of fictions **214–15**, 307n71, 522n737; New York characters **105**, **106**, **131**, **149**, **208–9**, **233**, 458–9n531, 540n799; *NYE* frontispiece subjects xcix–c, cii, clx–clxi; '"old" New York' **131**, **231**, 433n451, 540n799; Wall Street **217–18**, 526n752
New York Sun, The cxii, cxiii, cxvi, cxix, 363n229, 522n736
New York Times, The xxxviii, xliv, cxii–cxvi, cxix, cxxv, cxxix, cxxxiv, 581n918
New York World, The 449n499, 452n507
Newberry, Julia 518n727
Newport, RI **163**, 291n28, 336n151, 457n525, 461n537, 469n562, 521n734, 536n787, 584n924
New-York Daily Tribune, The cxvi, 491n629, 558n860
Nice, France **120**, 417n410, 460n534
Nietzsche, Friedrich, *Also Sprach Zarathustra* 303n55
Nineveh **166**, 474n574
Norris, W. E., letter to 586n928

North American Review, The lxii, **244**, 252, 289n22, 314n86, 377n275, 449n500, 550n839, 559n862, 578n910
North Conway, NH 291–2n28
North German Lloyd Steamship Company 471n568, 473n572
Northampton, MA **6, 7, 8, 14**, 291n28, 292nn29–30
Norton, Caroline 502n670
Norton, Charles Eliot xcii, cvi–cvii, 478n584; letters to 360n222, 518n727
Norton, Grace, letters to lv, cvii, 336n151, 356n213, 361n225, 363n231, 369n250, 401n354, 415–16n406, 425n433, 461nn536–7, 492–3n636, 508n695, 539n798
Norton, Sara (Sally) cvi–cvii
nursery rhymes 'Goosey, goosey gander' 528n763; 'Little Bo-peep' **215**, 522n739

O'Gorman, Donal 441n477
Odger, George 347n185
Oliphant, Laurence, *The Tender Recollections of Irene Macgillicuddy* 468n559
Olympian deities **49**, 303n55, 347n186, 545n817
'Orientals' **126**, 424n431
Ormond, Richard 429n442
Ortmans, Fernand 533n782
Osgood, James R. 357n216; letter to 468n558
Ourliac, Édouard, 'Malheurs et aventures de *César Birotteau* avant sa naissance' 582n920
Outlook, The cxix

Oxford, Oxfordshire lxxxvi, **168**, 364n231, 378n280, 457–8n527, 459n533, 500–1n666

Page, William 296n40
Palfrey, Mary Ann Hammond 499n659
Pallas Athene 517n724
Paris, France **43, 84**, 316n90, 321n106, 330n135, 343n173, 345–6n182, 382n291, 450n502, 479n588, 480n590, 489–90n623, 491n629, 532n776, 571n897; Arc de Triomphe **18**, 309–10n75, 569n894; and Balzac 316n91; Champ de Mars **68**, 368n246; Exposition Universelle **67**, 367n239, 368–9n246; as a fictional setting liii, cxxxviii, **19, 27, 120, 244, 251–2, 259**, 295n36, 309–10n75, 310n76, 316–17n92, 355n209, 356n212, 367n239, 370n251, 371–2n256, 417n410, 434n456, 463n540, 469n561, 472–3n570, 479–80n589, 551n845, 557–8n860, 562n874, 563n8875, 586n927; Galignani's Library 472–3n570; and germ of *The Ambassadors* **245, 247, 249**, 550–1n843, 555–6n855; HJ's early visits xxxv, **155**, 309n74, 315–16n89, 461n538, 462n539, 561n869; HJ's visits in period of *NYE* lxxi–lxxii, lxxxvi, 357n215, 477n583; Jardin des Tuileries **259**, 563n876; Ministère de la Justice **21**, 313n85; *NYE* frontispiece subjects lxviii, lxix, clix–clx, 568nn890–1, 569n894; Palais du Louvre

19, 310n76, 316n89; Palais du Trocadéro **68**, 369n246; Parisian characters **144**, 447n494; Place Vendôme **21**, 313n85, 461n538; Rive Gauche **22**, 316n91, 557n860; rue de la Paix **68**, **169**, 367n239, 462n539, 480n591; rue de Luxembourg / rue Cambon **21**, **22**, 309n75, 312–13n84, 313n85, 314–15n88; as a site of literary composition lii–liii, cxix, **16**, **18–19**, **21**, **22**, **66–7**, **68**, **168–9**, 312–13n84, 316n91, 317n93, 367n239, 480n591, 480–1n592; Théâtre Français **166**, **167**, 370n251, 371–2n256, 373n261, 475n577, 477n583, 479–80n589, 563n875

Parisian, The **168–9**, 480n590, 519–20n730

Parker, Hershel lvii, lviii, cxxx, cxlix

Parry, Hubert, 'Blest Pair of Sirens' 548n830

Pater, Walter 'Conclusion' to *The Renaissance* 536n788; 'The School of Giorgione' 390–1n320

Peabody, Elizabeth Palmer 493n637

Peattie, Elia W., reviews of *NYE* cxvi, cxvii, cxviii

Pennell, Joseph 359n220, 566n885; letter to xxxiv

Perosa, Sergio cxli

Perrault, Charles, *Les Contes de ma Mère l'Oye* 438n468

Perrault, Claude, *Ordonnance des cinq espèces de colonnes* 560n865

Perry, Thomas Sergeant, letters to 359n221, 467n554, 515n717

Petherbridge, Mary lxxiv, lxxv

Pinker, James B. xxx, lx, lxii, clvi, 552n846, 559n862; correspondence about *NYE* xxix, xxx, xxxvi, xxxvii, lv–lvi, lvii, lx, lxii, lxiii, lxv, lxvii–lxviii, lxx, lxxi, lxxiii, xcii–xciii, cxi, clvi, clvii–clviii, clix–clx, clxvii, 506n685, 568n890, 576n906, 585n925; other correspondence lxiii, lxiv, lxvi, 345n179, 415n402, 432n450, 510n700, 533n782

Pisani, Countess Evelina van Millingen 425n434

Playfair, Edith Russell, Lady Playfair 499n659

Pliny the Elder 307n68

Poe, Edgar Allan 'The Haunted Palace' 574n903; *The Narrative of Arthur Gordon Pym* **203**, 511–12n706

Point Hill, Playden, East Sussex 398n344–5, 398–9n346, 399n347

Poole, Adrian 314n87, 324n118, 324–5n120, 357n217, 405n368, 413n397, 414n401, 415n405, 431n448, 434n456, 521n735

Porter, Charlotte, 'The Serial Story' 340–1n165

Posnock, Ross cxxx

Pound, Ezra 'The Notes to "The Ivory Tower"' cxxvi; 'A Shake Down' cxxvi

Poussin, Nicolas 545n817

Prescott, Harriet Elizabeth, *Azarian* 401–2n356

Procter, Anne Benson 402n357, 430n447, 502n670, 503–4n676

Procter, Bryan Waller (Barry Cornwall) 502n670

Providence, RI 556n857

Provins, France **8**, 295n35
Punch **224**, **227**, 501n669, 531–2n776, 535n786

Quarterly Review, The cxi, cxxii, cxxiii, 344n177, 485n609
Quiller-Couch, Arthur Thomas, review of *The Awkward Age* 414–15n402
Quintilian, *Institutio oratoria* 467n555

Rachel (Elisabeth Félix) 434n456
Raffalovich, André, letter to 486n612
Read, Herbert, review of *The Art of the Novel* cxxix, cxxxiv–cxxxv
Reade, Charles *The Cloister and the Hearth* 460n535; *The Wandering Heir* 460n535
Récamier, Madame 551n843
Reeve, Neil 505n682, 506n686
Reicha, Antonin, *Traité de haute composition musicale* 377n275
Reubell, Henrietta cviii, 309n75; letters to 385n303, 389n315, 390n319, 416n406, 470–1n566, 513n712
Reynolds, Joshua, *Mrs Siddons as the Tragic Muse* 369n250
Rhine 287n17, 539n798; 'Rhine-maiden' **232**
Richards, Bernard 393nn329–30, 395n337, 398n345, 530n771
Richards, I. A., *Practical Criticism* cxxxii
Richardson, Samuel 335n147, 340n165; *Clarissa* 302n53
Ritchie, Anne Thackeray 377n278, 494n643; 'Biographical Edition' of W. M. Thackeray xl, xli
Riverside Press (Houghton, Mifflin Company) lx–lxii, cv–cvi, cli

Rivkin, Julie cxxviii
Rix, Alicia 397n343
Roberts, Morris, *Henry James's Criticism* cxxvii
Robins, Elizabeth lix, 388n312; *Votes for Women* lxxiii
Roellinger, Francis X. 440n474
Rogerson, Christina Stewart 359n221, 501–2n670, 531n774
Rome, Italy **127**, **163**, 288n20, 290n24, 345n182, 424n432, 460n435, 462n538, 531n775; as a fictional setting 288–9n21, 291n26, 296n39, 303n60, 368n244, 469n562, 564n880; and germs of fictions **145**–**6**, **212**, 403n363, 518n727, 535n785; HJ's visits in period of *NYE* lxxi–lxxii, clxi; *NYE* frontispiece subjects xcix–c, clx; Roman characters **157**–**8**, 405n369, 518–19n727
Roosevelt, Theodore, *American Ideals* 589n934
Rose, Sir John 530n771
Rosebery, 5th Earl 432n449
Ross, Sir Charles Henry Augustus Frederick Lockhart 393n329, 396n340
Ross, Rebecca, Lady Ross 393n329, 396n340
Rossetti, William Michael 428n442
Rostand, Edmond 311n81, 323n115, 425–6n435
Rowe, John Carlos 307–8n71, 513–14n713
Ruskin, John *The Seven Lamps of Architecture* 385n303; 'Traffic' 576n907
Rye, East Sussex lvii, lxviii, lxxiv, lxxv, lxxix–lxxxii, lxxxvi, lxxxviii, cliii,

clxi, clxiv, 308–9n73, 357n205, 398n345, 398–9n346, 412n395, 431n448, 435n460; *see also* James, Henry: Homes – Lamb House

Sainte-Beuve, Charles-Augustin 576n907; *Causeries du Lundi* 333n140; *Premiers Lundis* 590n937
Saint-Germain-en-Laye, France **22**, 314–15n88
Salem, MA li, 296n38, 428n442, 436n463, 441n477
Salmon, Richard 445n491, 446n492, 450n502, 453n510
Sambourne, Edward Linley 501n669
San Francisco Chronicle, The cxiv, cxviii
San Salvador, Bahamas **126**, 423n428
Sand, George 311n81, 314n86, 319n98, 322n110, 335n147, 348n192, 365n234, 439n469, 488n619; *Elle et lui* 314n86; *Gabriel* xlix; *Leone Leoni* xlix–l; *Isidora* l; prefaces xlix–l, li
Sarcey, Francisque, *Comédiens et Comédiennes: la Comédie Française* 373n261
Sardou, Victorien 342–3n172
Sargent, John Singer 429n442, 534n783
Saturday Review, The 422n424, 473n573, 502n670
Saumur, France **8**, 294n35
Savoy, The 486nn612–13
Schenectady, NY 457n525
Schlegel, August Wilhelm 366n237
Schuyler, Montgomery, reviews of *NYE* xxxviii, xliv, cxiii, cxvi
Scott, Dixon, 'Henry James' 536n788

Scott, Rebekah 525n748, 589n934
Scott, Walter **24, 39, 52**, 320n102, 335n147, 339n162, 348n192, 439n469; *The Bride of Lammermoor* **52–3**, 349n193; 'Magnum Opus Edition' xliv–xlvi, 573n902; *Marmion* 548n830, 585n926; *Waverley* xliv
Scribe, Eugène 342n172
Scribner, Charles lv–lvi
Scribner's Magazine (1887–1939) cxxii, **107, 184, 188**, 406n372, 497n655, 542n808
Scribner's Monthly (1870–81) 282n1, 327n125, 463n541
Scudder, Horace 369–70n251, 396n340, 416n408; letters to 362n227, 396–7n341, 397n342, 444n488, 494n641
Sedgwick, Ellery 327–8n126
Sedley, Henry D., *Marian Rooke* 331n137
Segnitz, T. M. 497n653
Senior, Nassau W., *Essays on Fiction* 348n192, 349n194
Serao, Matilde 377n275, 379n281
Sewanee Review, The cxl–cxli
Shakespeare, William cxxxii, **52**, 299n47, 318n96, 348n190, 374n263, 464–5n544, 505n682; *Antony and Cleopatra* **39**, 340n163; *Hamlet* **48, 53, 71, 101**, 306n66, 349n193, 370n254, 393n328, 400n351, 428n440, 534n783, 541n803, 558n861, 564n881; *Henry VIII* 310n78; *King Lear* **48**, 341n169; *Macbeth* 318n96, 524n747, 549n837; *The Merchant of Venice* **39–40, 56**, 340n163, 352n202;

631

A Midsummer Night's Dream 528n762; *Much Ado about Nothing* 339n159; *Othello* 286n15, 322n112, 343n174; *Romeo and Juliet* **19**, **39**, 339n161, 340n163, 434n456; *The Tempest* xxxv, cxxxvi, **12**, 300n49, 309n73, 318n96, 332n137, 454–5n516, 487n616, 564n881; *Twelfth Night* 521n734
Shapira, Morris cxxxix
Shaw, George Bernard cii; letter to 333n140
Shelley, Mary Wollstonecraft Godwin **127**, 426n437
Shelley, Percy Bysshe **127**, **128–9**, 426n437, 428n441, 428–9n442; 'Ozymandias' 454n514; 'To a Skylark' 364–5n234; 'With a Guitar, to Jane' 509n697
Sheppard, E. A. 440n474
Sherman, Stuart P., 'The Aesthetic Idealism of Henry James' cxxvii
Short, R. W. 301n51
Shumsky, Allison cxl–cxli
Siddons, Sarah 369n250, 430–1n447
Sidgwick, Henry 436n463
Silhouette, Étienne de 571n898
Silsbee, Edward Augustus 428n441, 428–9n442
Simon, Linda cxlii
Skipsey, Joseph and Sara 505n682, 506n684
Smalley, Evelyn cvi
Smalley, George Washburn 507n691
Smiles, Samuel, *Self-Help* 384n299
Smollett, Tobias 462n539
Society for Psychical Research 315n88, 435n462, 436n463, 440n474
Southampton, Hampshire 471n568, 473n572, 475n576
Southey, Caroline Bowles, 'To the Memory of Isabel Southey' 448n498
'Spain: her Manners and Amusements' 424n431
Sparks, Jared and Mary Crowninshield Silsbee 497–8n656, 498n658
Spectator, The 299n46
Spender, Stephen cxxviii
Spice Islands **4**, 284–5n10
Spilka, Mark xlvii
St Petersburg, Russia xlix, 355n209
Stead, W. T., 'The Maiden Tribute of Modern Babylon' 345n182
Stendhal (Marie-Henri Beyle) **224**, 531n775
Stephen, Leslie **167**, **213**, 477–8n584, 519nn729–30, 520n732
Stevenson, Fanny Van de Grift Osbourne xli
Stevenson, Robert Louis xxxvii–xxxviii, xlvii, **39**, 335n148, 339n162, 341n169, 577n909, 579n913, 586n927; 'Biographical Edition' xli; 'A Chapter on Dreams' xxxix; correspondence with HJ **71**, 306n66, 360n223, 362n226, 372n257, 375–6n270, 587n930; 'Edinburgh Edition' xxxviii–xxxix; 'The Genesis of "The Master of Ballantrae"' xxxix; *Kidnapped* xxxix, 465n544; 'A Letter to a Young Gentleman Who Proposes to Embrace the Career of Art' **23**, 318–19n97; *Letters* xxxix–xl, cxix, 319n99, 465n544; 'Memoirs of an Islet' xxxix; 'The Merry Men' xxxix; 'My First Book—"Treasure

INDEX

Island"' xxxviii–xxxix, xl; 'Olalla' xxxix; 'A Penny Plain and Twopence Coloured' 304n61; 'Pentland Edition' xli; *Strange Case of Dr Jekyll and Mr Hyde* xxxix, 422n423; 'Thistle Edition' xxix, xxxviii; *Travels with a Donkey in the Cevennes* 304n61; *Treasure Island* xl, 344n178; *Weir of Hermiston* **16**, 306n66

Stewart, Mrs Duncan 501–2n670, 502n671, 531n774

Stone, Herbert S. 410n384

Stonier, G. W., review of *The Art of the Novel* cxxxi–cxxxii, cxxxiv

Story, William Wetmore xxix, 329n130, 369n247, 417n409, 448n497, 503n673

Stowe, Harriet Beecher, *Uncle Tom's Cabin* 513n711, 554n850

Stratford-upon-Avon, Warwickshire lxxxvi, 505n682, 506n685

Street, Alfred Billings, 'The Pioneer' 496n650

Studio, The 395n337

Sturges, Jonathan 550–1n843, 552–3n848, 556n855; translations of Maupassant xxxv

Sturgis, Howard Overing, letters to cx–cxi, 325n121, 383n295

Supino, David J. cv–cvi, cviii, cxxix, cxxx

Swampscott, MA 292n28

Swinburne, Algernon Charles, *Poems and Ballads* 581n918

Switzerland **219**, 303n60, 418n411, 419n412, 451n505, 460n534, 499, 543n809, 548n833; *see also* Geneva

Symington, Miceala cxli

Symonds, John Addington **187**, 496n649, 496–7n650

Taine, Hippolyte, *Histoire de la littérature anglaise* 330n132

Tarbell, Ida 292n29

Temple, Charlotte 530n771

Temple, Mary (Minny) 291–2n28, 336n151, 535–6n787, 538n794

Tennyson, Alfred 364n231, 577n909, 581n918; 'Break, break, break' 369n247, 471n566; 'Locksley Hall' 419n412, 496n650, 540n800; 'The Lotos-Eaters' 303–4n60, 347n186

Terence (Terentianus Maurus) 473n573

Thackeray, W. M. **51, 52, 58, 207**, 335n147, 340n165, 348n190, 355–6n212, 364n231; 'Biographical Edition' xl–xli; 'De Finibus' cxix; *Denis Duval* xl, **16**, 306n66; *Dr. Birch and His Young Friends* 347n188; *The History of Henry Esmond* 356n212; *The Newcomes* lxxvi, **66**, 356n212, 365n235, 515n717; *Pendennis* 356n212; *Vanity Fair* **168**, 354n208, 478n587, 515n717; *The Virginians* 356n212

Theseus 576n908

Thomas Cook & Son 418n411

Thomson, James, *The Seasons* 436n463

Tiepolo, Giovanni Battista 429n442, 433n452; *The Apotheosis of the Barbaro Family* **107**, 406n373

Times Literary Supplement, The cx–cxi, cxxi, cxxii, cxxiii, cxxvii, cxxix, cxxxiv–cxxxv

Tintner, Adeline 381n288, 582n920

Tintoretto (Jacopo Robusti),

Crucifixion 66, 364n233
Tóibín, Colm cxli
Tolstoy, Lev Nikolaevich 365n236; *Anna Karenina* 365n236; *War and Peace* 66, 365n235; *What is Art?* cxix
Townsend, Edward Waterman, *Chimmie Fadden* 529n765
Trelawny, Edward John 432n449
Trevelyan, Sir George Otto and Lady Caroline 505n682, 506n685
Trollope, Anthony 58, 331n137, 355-6n212, 478n585, 494n643; *An Autobiography* xxxi, cxix; *Can You Forgive Her?* 340n164; 'Chronicles of Barsetshire' 356n212; 'The Telegraph Girl' 419-20n415
Tucker, Amy 566n885
Turgenev, Ivan Sergeyevich xxxi, 34-5, 41, 174, 287n17, 330n133, 330-1n135, 331n136, 331-2n137, 332n138, 333nn141-2, 338n155, 341n167, 353n206, 358n219, 365n235, 390n320, 427n438, 460n533, 487-8n617, 556n856, 571n897
typists liv, lxiii, lx, lxix-lxx, lxxiii-lxxvi, lxxx, cli-cliv, clvii, clviii, clxi, clxiii: *see also* Bosanquet, Theodora; Weld, Mary

Universal Review, The 484n605
Utica, NY 19, 311n79

Veblen, Thorstein, *The Theory of the Leisure Class* 418n411
Veeder, William cxli, cxlii, 280, 442n483, 537n790
Venice, Italy 213, 288n20, 357n215, 425n434, 429n442, 433n452, 474n574, 501n666; Casa Alvisi (Katharine De Kay Bronson) 449-50n501, 451n505, 521n735; as a fictional setting 120, 127, 131, 237, 238-9, 286n16, 356n212, 406n373, 408n381, 417n410, 452n508, 539n798, 547n826, 548n829; and germs of fictions by HJ 406n373, 449n499, 450-1n502, 451n505, 495n648; *NYE* frontispiece subjects lxix, clx, 406n373, 568n891, 569n894; Palazzo Barbaro (Ariana and Daniel Curtis) 406n373, 449-50n501, 451n505, 539n798, 569n894; Riva degli Schiavoni 32, 328n128; San Zaccaria 32, 328n128; Scuola Grande di San Rocco 364n233; as a site of literary composition xlix-l, 32-3, 107, 328nn127-8, 329n129, 329n131
Versailles, France 43, 315n88, 343n173
Vienna, Austria 355n209
Villari, Linda 454n514
Vincec, Sister Stephanie 542n808
Virgil (Publius Vergilius Maro) cxiv, 439n471; *Aeneid* 458n528; *Georgics* 578-9n911
Voltaire 441n479; *Candide* 335n146, 567n887

Wagner, Richard, *Der Ring des Niebelungen* 539n798
Waller, Philip 364n231
Walsh, Catherine 461n536, 462n538; letters to 366n238, 455n519, 464n542

Ward, Mary Augusta 377n278; letters to cxi, 334n145, 356n213, 361n224, 373n260, 386n307, 446–7n492, 495n647, 504n677; *Miss Bretherton* 334n145, 360–1n224, 373n260

Warren, Edward Prioleau, letter to 398n345

Washington, DC **163**, 369n247, 469n562, 524n747; HJ visits **169**, **170–1**, 481nn594–5, 482nn597–8, 483nn600–1, 522n738

Watkinson, William L., *Studies in Christian Character* 588n934

Watt, A. P. 445n491

Watts, G. F. 318n95

Wegener, Frederick cxxii

Welby, Lady Victoria, letter to 544n816

Weld, Mary lxxiii, lxxiv, lxxv, 552n846

Wells, H. G. 431n448; *Boon* cxviii, cxxv–cxxvi; letters to 439n470, 446n492, 536n789

Werdet, Edmond, *Portrait intime de Balzac* 582n920

West, Rebecca, *Henry James* cxxv–cxxvi

Westminster Review, The 485n609

Wharton, Edith lxiv, lxxxvi, cvi, cxxii, 477n583, 512n707; *The Decoration of Houses* 395n337; letters to liv, lvi, lxxxv, cvi, cix, cxxii, 325n121, 472n568, 585n925

Wheelock, John Hall cxxxiii

Whistler, James McNeill 551n843

Wilde, Oscar 'The House Beautiful' 396n337; *The Picture of Dorian Gray* 485n608; *Salome* 486n612

William Heinemann 376n274, 383n296, 397n327, 410n384, 500n664

Wilson, Edmund cxxviii

Winchelsea, East Sussex 398–9n346

Wister, Owen cvi; letters to lv, 325n121, 472n568

Wister, Sarah Butler 346n185; letters to 289n21, 425n434, 531n775, 553n850

Woolson, Constance Fenimore 500–1n666; *Anne* 340n165

Worcester, MA 556n857

Worden, Ward S. 410n384

Wordsworth, William 'Immortality' Ode 572n900; *The Prelude* 312n83; 'Ruth' 574n903; 'She was a Phantom of delight' 331n137, 386n305

Wrenn, Angus 534n783

Wright, Nathalia 495–6n648

Yeats, W. B. 'The Stolen Child' 441n477

Yellow Book, The **172–4**, **181**, 314, 409–10, 484n607, 485nn608–9, 485–6n611, 486nn612–13, 487nn614–15, 488n619, 489n620

Zabell, Morton D. cxxxv

Zola, Émile **24**, **52**, **58**, 292n31, 348n190, 348n192, 358n219, 493n638, 571n897; *L'Assommoir* 293n31; *La Joie de vivre* 443n485; *Nana* 576n907; 'Les Rougon-Macquart' 320n120, 355n212, 392n326

Zorzi, Rosella Mamoli 429n442, 474n574

Milton Keynes UK
Ingram Content Group UK Ltd.
UKHW052319251024
450122UK00002B/4